ASHGATE
RESEARCH
COMPANION

THE ASHGATE RESEARCH COMPANION TO MIGRATION LAW, THEORY AND POLICY

ASHGATE
RESEARCH
COMPANION

Law and Migration

Series Editor
Satvinder S. Juss, King's College London, UK

Migration and its subsets of refugee and asylum policy are rising up the policy agenda at national and international level. Current controversies underline the need for rational and informed debate of this widely misrepresented and little understood area.

Law and Migration contributes to this debate by establishing a monograph series to encourage discussion and help to inform policy in this area. The series provides a forum for leading new research principally from the Law and Legal Studies area but also from related social sciences. The series is broad in scope, covering a wide range of subjects and perspectives.

Other titles in this series:

Regulating Marriage Migration into the UK
A Stranger in the Home
Helena Wray
978-1-4094-0338-8

Chinese Immigration Law
Guofu Liu
978-1-4094-0940-3

The Control of People Smuggling and Trafficking in the EU
Experiences from the UK and Italy
Matilde Ventrella
978-0-7546-7466-5

Gender and Migration in 21st Century Europe
Edited by Helen Stalford, Samantha Currie and Samantha Velluti
978-0-7546-7450-4

The Ashgate Research Companion to Migration Law, Theory and Policy

Edited by
SATVINDER S. JUSS
King's College London, School of Law, UK

Routledge
Taylor & Francis Group
LONDON AND NEW YORK

First published 2013 by Ashgate Publishing

2 Park Square, Milton Park, Abingdon, Oxfordshire OX14 4RN
52 Vanderbilt Avenue, New York, NY 10017

Routledge is an imprint of the Taylor & Francis Group, an informa business

First issued in paperback 2018

British Library Cataloguing in Publication Data
The Ashgate research companion to migration law, theory and policy. – (Law and migration)
1. Refugees–Legal status, laws, etc. 2. Emigration and immigration law. 3. Freedom of movement (International law)
I. Series II. Research companion to migration law, theory and policy III. Juss, Satvinder S. (Satvinder Singh)
342'.083-dc23

The Library of Congress has cataloged the printed edition as follows:
Juss, Satvinder S. (Satvinder Singh)
The Ashgate research companion to migration law, theory and policy / by Satvinder S. Juss.
p. cm. — (Law and migration)
Includes index.
ISBN 978-0-7546-7188-6 (hardback : alk. paper)
1. Emigration and immigration law. 2. Refugees—Legal status, laws, etc. 3. Asylum, Right of. 4. Migrant labor. I. Title. II. Title: Research companion to migration law, theory and policy.
K3275.J87 2012
342.08'2—dc23

2012022187

ISBN 978-0-7546-7188-6 (hbk)
ISBN 978-0-367-19193-1 (pbk)

ASHGATE
RESEARCH
COMPANION

Contents

Part III: The Responsibility to Protect Displaced Populations

Part IV: Emerging Paradigms of Legal Protection

Part V: Encampment, Detention and the Coercive Treatment of Asylum-Seekers

ASHGATE
RESEARCH
COMPANION

List of Contributors

Howard Adelman, formerly at York University, Canada

Ilias Bantekas, Brunel University, UK

Jacqueline Bhabha, Harvard University, USA

David James Cantor, School of Advanced Study, University of London, UK

Geoffrey Care, University of Jos, Nigeria

Mary Crock, University of Sydney, Australia

Alice Edwards, United Nations High Commissioner for Refugees (UNHCR), Geneva

Nadine El-Enany, Birkbeck College, University of London

Lucy Fiske, Curtin University, Australia

Gustavo A. Flores-Macías, Cornell University, USA

Daniel Ghezelbash, University of Sydney, Australia

Shubha Ghosh, University of Wisconsin Law School, USA

Elspeth Guild, Radboud University Nijmegen, The Netherlands

Rodger Haines QC, Chairperson, Human Rights Review Tribunal, New Zealand

Satvinder S. Juss, King's College London, UK

Mary Anne Kenny, Curtin University of Technology, Australia

Raffaele Marchetti, LUISS Guido Carli, Italy

Penelope Mathew, The Australian National University, Australia

Francesco Messineo, University of Kent, UK

Maria O'Sullivan, Monash University, Australia

David Owen, University of Southampton, UK

Sharon Pickering, Monash University, Australia

Jason Pobjoy, University of Cambridge, UK

Bernard Ryan, University of Kent, UK

Marie Segrave, Monash University, Australia

Prakash Shah, Queen Mary, University of London, UK

James C. Simeon, York University, Canada

Thomas Spijkerboer, VU University Amsterdam, The Netherlands

Dallal Stevens, University of Warwick, UK

Savitri Taylor, La Trobe University, Australia

Claudia Tazreiter, University of New South Wales, Australia

Patricia Tuitt, Birkbeck, University of London, UK

Guglielmo Verdirame, King's College London, UK

Leanne Weber, Monash University, Australia

Helena Wray, Middlesex University, UK

Thanos Zartaloudis, Birkbeck College, University of London, UK

Foreword

Dr Volker Türk[1]

Mobility is an essential part of the *conditio humana* and has played a key role throughout history, including as a survival mechanism. This is starkly exemplified in the refugee and forced displacement context. Yet it seems that memory is a sieve, and that we have forgotten the roots of our existence as humankind has become more settled and established concepts of statehood and national sovereignty. As Stephen Castles has suggested, international migration today takes place in a world divided up into nation-states, where remaining in one's country of birth is still seen as a norm and moving to another country as a deviation.[2] Envisioning and framing human mobility as an opportunity, and not a threat, remains an ongoing challenge.

Within this context, it is perhaps unsurprising that migration and forced displacement attract significant attention – often dramatized for public consumption – and hold a prominent place in public debates. The concept of national sovereignty over territory has been challenged as never before by the effects of globalization, as well as economic and financial integration. The movement of people is one of the most visible, albeit least facilitated, aspects of this globalization. Particularly in times of economic crisis and a plethora of other pressing global issues, migration has sometimes been portrayed as a threat to security, interconnected with transnational crime, trafficking and smuggling, as well as a challenge to sovereignty. This is especially the case when migration takes place outside regular channels and is perceived to be 'irregular'. This, in turn, has encouraged inward-looking and exclusionary policies and practices. The complexities inherent in an increasingly inter-dependent world, coupled with the (often physical) closing off of well-guarded zones of wealth, play into the hands of populist politicians who spread ill-founded fears about uncontrollable 'floods of foreigners' and thus plant the seeds for xenophobia, intolerance, extremism and social tension.

Manifestations of racism and xenophobia are often directed against non-nationals, including migrant workers, refugees or asylum seekers. Fear of 'the other' is, at times, used in politics for short-term and populist gains. This is the same fear that breeds discrimination, hatred and even violence against people who are different because of their colour, gender, creed, minority status or sexual orientation. When used politically, it can result in serious harm on a broader scale – as history and more recent events have sadly taught us. For refugees

---

1 Director, Division of International Protection, Office of the United Nations High Commissioner for Refugees (UNHCR).

2 See Stephen Castles, 'International migration at the beginning of the twenty-first century: global trends and issues', *International Social Science Journal*, September 2000 (165), pp. 269–81.

and other persons with international protection needs, despite their specific rights and entitlements under international law, racism and xenophobia can contribute to diminishing protection space and have spurred restrictive laws, policies and practices. Carving out space within societies and communities for 'the other' is one of the most important protection challenges today – not just for refugees, but also in the broader migration context.

It is against this backdrop that ongoing examination of the institutional and legal underpinnings of migration and forced displacement is crucial: the rule of law is the best defence against arbitrariness and the vagaries of public opinion. *The Ashgate Research Companion to Migration Law Theory and Policy* is an important tool in this regard, with its focus not only on today's challenges but also on building constructively on the achievements of the past.

'Migrants'[3] are generally understood to be individuals moving to another country of their own free will in order to improve their material or social conditions and prospects for themselves or their family. By contrast, refugees are defined legally as persons outside their country of origin for reasons of feared persecution, generalized violence, or other circumstances that have seriously disturbed public order and who, as a result, require international protection.[4] While the distinction between migrants and refugees in principle relies on the presence of a coercive element in the movement of the latter, the reality is often far more ambiguous. Increasingly, there are overlaps and complex dynamics at play in identifying the 'voluntary' or 'forced' nature of human mobility, many of which are explored in the *Ashgate Research Companion.* Individuals on the move have different profiles, motivations and needs that may span the continuum between 'forced' and 'voluntary'. And regardless of the categorizations that may be required for legal purposes, population groups are never homogeneous: they include women, men, girls, boys, older persons, the disabled, ethnic groups and LGBTI individuals, all of whom have specific needs and capabilities that must be taken into account. Recognizing and responding to the rich diversity of the human family is central to our ability to carry out the task of protection for those at risk and on the move. And the task of protection, by necessity, includes developing nuanced and appropriate legal and policy responses to mobility that are based on more than simply a fear of 'the other' and populism.

Looking forward, from the perspective of human mobility, as in other spheres, there is an urgent need to assume responsibility for our actions in terms of their global implications but also in relation to future generations. This is most evident in the context of climate change, our 'poisoned legacy' for posterity. Natural disasters, which are already displacing millions of people every year, have noticeably increased in number and intensity. As droughts, unpredictable rainfall patterns and extreme weather events continue, even more people will move to urban areas and potentially further afield. Agricultural output is expected to be affected in many parts of the world, creating not just higher food prices but also food

---

3 A uniform legal definition of the term 'migrant' does not exist at the international level. The 1990 UN Convention on the Protection of the Rights of All Migrant Workers and Members of their Families defines the term 'migrant worker'. See also Article 11 of the 1975 ILO Convention Concerning Migrations in Abusive Conditions and the Protection of Equality of Opportunity and Treatment of Migrant Workers (No. 143) and of the 1979 ILO Migration for Employment Convention (No. 97), as well as Article 1 of the 1977 European Convention on the Legal Status of Migrant Workers.

4 See UN doc. A/AC.96/830 paras 8, 10–11, 31–2.

and water insecurity and, potentially, increased conflict over scarce resources. The Cancun Agreements of December 2010, notably paragraph 14 (f), is an invitation for all of us working on displacement and migration issues to contribute, within our respective organizations and disciplines, to finding solutions in this area. This *Ashgate Research Companion* sets the tone for much-needed thinking in the increasingly complex field of human mobility, which remains a touchstone for many of the key challenges of this century for the international community.

References

Castles, Stephen, 'International migration at the beginning of the twenty-first century: global trends and issues', *International Social Science Journal*, September 2000 (165), pp. 269–81.

ASHGATE
RESEARCH
COMPANION

Preface

The *Ashgate Research Companion to Migration Law, Theory and Policy* is designed to complement the already successful Ashgate series *Law & Migration*. Established in 2006 this is the only series of its kind and has now a number of well-regarded monographs to its credit. The purpose of this *Companion* is to augment that series by taking stock of the current state of migration law literature, and to sketch out the contours of its future long-term development, in what is now by all accounts a vastly expanded research agenda. The *Companion* aims to provide readers with a definitive and dependable state-of-the-art review of current research in each of the chosen areas that is all-embracing and all-inclusive of its subject-matter. Conventional discussions are brought together with fresh and groundbreaking forms of thinking. This should surprise no one. Migration is as old as humanity itself. It has, of course, taken various forms throughout history. What is clear is that migration is a phenomenon that (as those of us living in the developed world have learnt) is socially and politically transformative. In recent years, therefore, there has been an extraordinary rise of interest in migration studies, spurred on by a no less than extraordinary growth in migration law journals. This genre has spawned the general, such as the *European Journal of Migration and Law*, to the more specific, such as the *International Journal of Refugee Law*, the *Journal of Refugee Studies* and the *Refugee Survey Quarterly*, as well as publications going beyond migration that have an interest in this area, such as the *International Journal of Minority & Group Rights*,[1] as well as the more recently inaugurated *Journal of International Humanitarian Legal Studies*. All have made huge contributions to development of a new area of study and inquiry, and helped to highlight the relevance and relationship of migration and to link it with broader issues of global governance and the rule of law. The *Companion* stands in that light.

The field of migration law and policy now traverses a vast range of exceedingly diverse phenomena. These include: regular and irregular migrants; foreign workers and trafficked persons; refugees and displaced persons; children and war refugees; and those who are subject to detention, interdiction and encampment, not to mention wider issues of transnationalism, citizenship and belonging. All of these are in varying ways covered in this volume. They throw up a number of questions, not least of which is how different groups and individuals have undergone the experience of migration and how that experience has led them to an encounter with the law. How well that encounter protects the human rights of the individual, while seeking to safeguard the vital interests of the state itself, is the perennial question. Migration law and policy is dynamic and constantly evolving. A number of essays in this volume directly consider the thorny question of governments managing migrants and migration with altogether mixed results. The principles, rules and values that underlie this endeavour, especially where vulnerable persons and populations are concerned, is a

1 This contains a Special Issue by Satvinder S. Juss and Colin Harvey on 'Critical Reflections on Refugee Law' (Issue 1, 2013).

matter that remains open for deliberation. International legal norms continue to develop in the field of migration law, but that process is still piecemeal, and far from comprehensive or orderly. Nevertheless, there have been substantial engagements, when previously these had been jejune, and it is vital that these are discussed in a critical and constructive fashion, to provide for a better understanding of law and policy in this, the most intractable of all fields. It is hoped that the *Companion* will contribute to that goal.

The chapters in this *Companion* are intended to pageant a range of theoretical, methodological and practical approaches to a tableau of migration. Yet not every facet of migration is thoroughly represented. Nor is this volume strictly organized in terms of its disciplinary boundaries and concerns. Indeed, a feature of the contributions in this volume is that they involve a cross-fertilization among a multitude of disciplines across the social sciences and humanities. The chapters focus on the regional and the sub-regional, as well as the national and the global. In so doing, they aim to give a snapshot of the area under consideration that is contextual, coherent and comprehensive. The contributions included are from both world-renowned scholars and newer voices. There are scholars, practitioners, former judges and researchers and policy makers who are currently working for international organizations. In this way, the *Ashgate Research Companion to Migration Law, Theory and Policy* breaks new ground in that it captures cutting-edge debates in the field of migration studies. It will be of interest to established academics and PhD students in search of new themes and trends in migration law, to those working for international and regional organizations interested in emerging paradigms of policy, to practitioners of migration law, and to representatives of civil society concerned with the wellbeing of the society in which we live. To the extent that people are nowadays critically engaging with the concept of migration, it is hoped that this volume will become a work of reference for emerging issues in migration law and policy. That will help facilitate future research and introduce new thinking on this subject.

This volume, which ranges from the philosophical to the theoretical, and from the practical to the policy oriented, is organized around seven themes. Part One examines the position of 'The Refugee in Europe's Free Movement Regime'. It begins with a critical analysis of what is the most well-developed free movement regime in the world today, namely the European Union. This regime is remarkable for not only having altered the nature of migratory movements, but also for having had a transformative effect on our perception of migrations through its distinctive treatment of European Union nationals, and their family members, when travelling in the Union. In the opening chapter, Nadine El-Enany considers, in 'The "New Europe" and the "European Refugee"' how, with Europe's reinvention of itself as a 'New Europe', where European citizens are encouraged to move freely in a borderless area, there has also been created a 'New European refugee'. However, in an incisive analysis the author argues that the Union's refugee law must be viewed and assessed in the context of its wider migration policy. This has over the years seen increasingly restrictive migration measures, which have limited access of refugees to European territory, with the result that the category of the European refugee has become exclusionary. Therefore, contrary to the popularly projected image of the 'New Europe', European migration policy serves to limit access routes to individuals seeking to enter European territory without a legally ascribed right of entry. In this sense, there is a denial of the 'New Europe' because the European Union requires the refugee to demonstrate characteristics and fulfil criteria over and above those expressed in the European legal definition, including possession of financial resources, economic mobility and a willingness to take risks. These are traits that the most vulnerable, in particular women and children, are less able to demonstrate – in part due to prevailing gender norms and expectations.

The idea of the betrayal of the 'New Europe' is also addressed with no less vigour in the next chapter in this section, by Patricia Tuitt in 'The Modern Refugee in the Post-modern Europe'. She considers the nature of the European Union. Her thesis is that the refugee is the symbol of the old order that the European Union seeks to transcend, but which is being held back by the constitutive forces behind the European Union. This is because of the systematic denial of access in individual European Union Member States, of those who are fleeing civil and political oppression, generalized violence or other catastrophic events. She argues that the refugee is not the sole but the *principal* signifier of the bankrupt old order of Europe. For the European Union really to come into its own, there must be the repudiation of the refugee because this will be the act that signals also the transcendence of the nation state. The European Union will come into being as a fully fledged political and legal entity only with the complete disavowal of the refugee. In this way, in an insightful contribution, Patricia Tuitt argues that, when the regime of rights developed under the *Convention Relating to the Status of Refugees* no longer has currency within the Union, then (and only then) will we really *know* the European Union. This is because, in common with all sovereign entities that have emerged in any epoch in history, the European Union will define itself through a radical break with what came before it. The fact is that the European Union is not a political community. It is, she argues, not born of the old modern world from which the nation state form was produced. On the contrary, it is an entity that is ambitiously post-national – one that gestures towards a postmodern future. The European Union is, therefore, an entity that is necessarily in tension with the putatively modern world of the nation state. It can, therefore, only truly enter history when it has not merely transcended the political, economic and social structures characteristic of the 'old order' of Europe, but when it has surpassed or overborne those individuals or groups perceived as uniquely representing that old order.

Some idea of how this is to happen is gleaned from the third chapter in this section, by Elspeth Guild, on 'EU Immigration, Asylum and the New EU Treaty Framework'. She takes as her starting point the adoption and ratification, after ten years of difficult negotiation and reluctance on the part of some of its citizens, of the European Union's new legal framework on 1 December 2009. This is when two new treaties replaced the otherwise heterogeneous group of treaties that formed the basis of the EU – the Treaty on the European Union and the Treaty on the Functioning of the European Union. She emphasizes the watershed moment that this heralds by pointing out how the most startling of consequences of these two treaties is the formal end of the perplexing Pillar framework of the EU, with different policy areas subject to very different constitutional treatment. Immigration, asylum and border controls have now been brought into one camp together with judicial cooperation in criminal matters, policing, terrorism and other rather heterogeneous subject-matters. This has simplified matters for the Area of Freedom, Security and Justice, which for ten years between 1999 and 2009 unhappily straddled two Pillars. In a careful analysis, Elspeth Guild shows how the framework transforms EU immigration and asylum law and policy in ways that have become rapidly evident. In this chapter, she examines what the entry into force of the Lisbon Treaty meant for EU immigration law and policy. She then makes two main claims about the impact of these changes: (i) that the Lisbon Treaty lifts the limitation on access to the European Court of Justice by courts of all instances in the field of borders, immigration and asylum, thus bringing about a dramatic acceleration of the harmonizing effect of EU law in this field; (ii) that the Treaty gives legal force to the Charter on Fundamental Rights, which will be felt quickly in the immigration field if the experience of the European Court of Human Rights is anything to go by. The importance of this chapter by Elspeth Guild lies in the emphasis she brings to bear on how human and fundamental rights have become an important source of friction between Member States and third-country nationals (i.e. nationals of states outside the EU), which have now moved beyond the national courts of the Member States. This is an important development because the impact of the Lisbon Treaty is likely to be highest in the field of immigration. Yet this is also a sensitive area of sovereignty in a number of Member States and countries outside the EU. In consequence, the headline-grabbing news emanating from EU immigration law is not likely to diminish over the following years.

This is made starkly evident by the fourth chapter in this section, where Thomas Spijkerboer asks, 'Are European States Accountable for Border Deaths?' If human rights are to have real currency, there must be accountability for their violations. Yet, in a most disturbing account, Thomas Spijkerboer notes how the UN High Commissioner for Refugees, in a speech on 20 June 2011, highlighted the fact that, since March 2011, as many as 1,500 people had drowned in the Mediterranean. That figure breaks down to a staggering estimated one in ten who is drowned attempting the crossing. Regional and national upheavals have an added impact, as is demonstrated by the sudden departure of many migrants from Tunisia and Libya in the spring of 2011. Yet Thomas Spijkerboer is able to show how the number of fatalities fits with a general upward trend, even though, on border deaths, only problematic data are available. However, his analysis of the most comprehensive Europe-wide set of data, namely the list of fatalities complied by United, an international NGO based in Amsterdam, is not inconsistent with a later data set, namely from Fortress Europe, which is comparable in methodology and shows a comparable trend. Thomas Spijkerboer also draws attention to local, short-term studies that lead to much higher numbers than the ones by United or Fortress Europe but for smaller areas (such as for Spain and Sicily), and for short periods. In this way, he deals with an issue that has been much neglected over the years, but the importance of which can hardly be over-emphasized – and not least given its relevance to the idea of Europe and what it stands for. This nicely leads us onto the next section.

Part Two concerns 'Safeguarding the Safety and Security of Refugees', given the overwhelming importance of the influx of refugees from the underdeveloped to the developed world in recent years. It opens with a decidedly philosophical piece from the eminent philosopher Howard Adelman, which helps in highlighting the shortcomings of the international refugee regime from its very inception. In 'Jonah and Socrates as Refugees: Repentance, Redemption and Responsibility' he discusses how the legal definition of the modern 'refugee' arose out of the peculiar circumstances at the beginning of the cold war and the desire to protect those who did not want to return to the lands of the Soviet Empire where they faced incarceration and possibly torture or even death. Howard Adelman argues that this definition was expedient, served a very positive purpose at the time, and has been expanded upon to allow the protection of many others, but that it is still a depiction of a 'refugee' that denigrates refugees in general and defines them as essentially motivated by fear. It also characterizes them as abandoning their homelands. Adelman suggests defining refugees as choosing flight and refugee status as the only option available to them to preserve their integrity and dignity. In his opinion, they may have a well-founded fear of persecution, but fear is not what drives their flight. Further, rather than abandoning any desire to return to their homeland, empirically and theoretically it has often been their foremost desire. In order to make his case, Howard Adelman uses the example of the biblical Jonah, who tried to become a refugee but was unable to do so, and of Socrates, who refused to become a refugee.

This thought-provoking chapter then helps to set the tone of the second chapter in this section, by James C. Simeon, who demonstrates how the international community's perpetual struggle to strengthen refugee rights can be facilitated by the consideration and possible implementation of a number of innovative proposals by leading experts in the field. In 'Strengthening International Refugee Rights through the Enhanced Supervision of the *1951 Convention* and its *1967 Protocol*', Simeon discusses how States Parties to the 1951 Convention relating to the Status of Refugees and its 1967 Protocol attempt to implement and interpret the provisions of these international instruments to ensure that refugees are fully protected and that their human rights are fully realized under international law, and notes how there is a lack of uniformity in the actual application of its provisions. He discusses how the UNHCR has the responsibility for supervising the 1951 Convention and its 1967 Protocol and, indeed, international refugee rights instruments generally. His chapter then considers the degree to which the UNHCR has been able to exercise its supervisory responsibilities. After that, Simeon examines the proposals that have been presented by various legal scholars, researchers and practitioners to strengthen the supervision of refugee rights instruments. He reminds us that States Parties to the 1951 Convention and its 1967 Protocol have adopted these international instruments with 'good will' and in 'good faith' and with the intention of implementing fully, barring any reservations, all of their provisions. He then focuses on the UNHCR as the principal body within the UN system responsible for refugee matters and as a subsidiary organ of the UN General Assembly. He therefore turns to a review and analysis of the legal basis of the UNHCR's supervisory role and responsibilities in the provision of international protection to those in dire need due to the threat to their life, liberty or security. His chapter moves on to outline a number of proposals for strengthening the supervision of the 1951 Convention and 1967 Protocol that have been presented by five distinguished legal scholars, academics and practitioners in the field of international refugee law. The chapter concludes by highlighting that, although there is no apparent shortage of reasonable proposals for enhancing the supervision of the 1951 Convention and its 1967 Protocol, what seems to be glaringly absent is a willingness on the part of the principals to move forward on any reasonable and practical proposals that would enhance supervision of these seminal international refugee rights instruments. He ends by reminding us that 2011 was the 60th anniversary of the 1951 Convention and that this should lead us to guarded optimism that there are opportunities for positive reforms for the future.

The third chapter in this section is on the pivotal concept of 'non-refoulement' in refugee law, now widely regarded as having acquired the status of *jus cogens* in international refugee law, given the security that it affords to those fleeing persecution in their home countries, without which the protection of refugees would be a chimera. In '*Non-refoulement* Obligations in Public International Law: Towards a New Protection Status?', however, Francesco Messineo helpfully reminds us that one might conclude that there is some confusion among governments about what *non-refoulement* responsibilities precisely entail. In a most challenging piece, he asks where the obligations of *non-refoulement* come from, and what their status, scope and content is under international law. He answers these questions in two ways. First, he explains how the concept offers a contemporary account of the many sources of *non-refoulement* obligations under international law. In this sense, the concept is evident in the most important doctrinal and judicial debates on the matter, as found in the status of *non-refoulement* as a 'principle' of customary international law. Francesco Messineo here demonstrates that this is essentially an analysis of the *lex lata*. Second, he considers whether a new understanding of *non-refoulement* may be possible by adopting a different perspective on its nature. Arguing *de lege ferenda* in this context, he asks whether *non-refoulement* is becoming something more than just the most prominent of the many rights enjoyed by refugees and other individuals at risk of ill-treatment. His inquiry is a most valuable one, not least because, as he points out, the European Union Qualification Directive has arguably started a transformation that will eventually lead to the recognition of *non-refoulement* as a status of international protection alongside (rather than embedded in) 'refugee status' and even EU 'subsidiary protection'. As such, the questions he raises are surely ones that will remain pertinent for a considerable time to come.

The fourth chapter is by the eminent practitioner, and former judicial officer, Rodger Haines QC, from New Zealand. As someone who can be credited as having laid the foundation-stones of immigration and asylum law jurisprudence in that country, his criticism of the effective violation of the principle of 'non-refoulement' on the basis of dubious 'Country of Origin Information' ('COI') – used often to justify decisions to refuse or grant asylum – is one that cannot be ignored. Indeed, the lessons of his investigation must be considered by all jurisdictions that employ COI in the assessment of refugee claims. In 'Country Information and Evidence Assessment in New Zealand', Rodger Haines takes the bold line that in New Zealand there are presently no formal processes or rules for determining substantive quality standards for researching and assessing COI. His chapter aims to provide an overview of the way in which country information has been used and assessed in the New Zealand refugee status determination system. This system has been recently expanded. From 29 November 2010, it was enlarged beyond the Refugee Convention to include claims to complementary protection under the Convention against Torture, Article 3, and under the International Covenant on Civil and Political Rights, Articles 6 and 7, as well as to claims for humanitarian protection. Rodger Haines, in considering the use of COI at the appellate level, observes how, although to date little has been written on the subject of COI, this does not mean that quality standards are absent from COI in the New Zealand context. However, the thrust of his argument is that there has been no data collection or research on COI of the kind recently carried out in the United Kingdom. His thesis, therefore, is that the enhanced protection responsibilities now undertaken by New Zealand do not permit it to be assumed that what has worked in the past will suffice in the new regime, and that what is urgently required is qualitative research into how COI is presently used by the major actors in the New Zealand refugee and protection system.

Part Three concerns 'The Responsibility to Protect Displaced Populations' and, as such, it is a play on the United Nations concept introduced by an initiative in 2005, and consisting of an emerging norm suggesting that, contrary to established orthodoxies of old, sovereignty nowadays is not a privilege, but a responsibility, thus calling into question the behaviour of states when they do act. It seems an appropriate rubric under which to consider precisely how individual states presently exercise their responsibility in relation to the protection of vulnerable people seeking state protection. Accordingly, the section opens with a consideration of the 'refugee' *vis-à-vis* the state and the challenges posed by this contact between the two. In 'The Shifting Boundaries and Content of Protection: The Internal Protection Alternative Revisited', Penelope Mathew shows how refugees are nothing short of a challenge to the state-centric order of international law. She argues that they move, while the state, seemingly, remains fixed. States have accepted obligations to protect human rights within their boundaries, and they have retained the right to police those boundaries. She highlights a potent fear that the floodgates will open and all who seek adequate or better protection of their human rights will move to more privileged states, and that this fear has stymied the development of complete freedom of movement. Her argument is that the right to exclude aliens is posited as a right founded not on privilege or power, but on morality: states need to protect, respect and ensure the rights of citizens, and their capacity to do so might be adversely affected by unfettered immigration. So she asks how a state can defeat the obligation of *non-refoulement* as it applies extra-territorially. With far-reaching foresight, she points out that the preferred move by states is to shift the sites of protection – for example, by finding a 'safe third country' to which the asylum seeker may be sent – because this enables a person to be returned or sent to a different place beyond the borders of the potential state of refuge. The effect of this is to lower the quality of protection and, in particular, to ensure that the quality of protection available in countries of refuge does not become a 'pull' factor for further asylum flows. Her chapter thus focuses on the idea of the internal flight or relocation alternative, as a manifestation of the state's approach to shifting responsibility elsewhere. The Internal Protection Alternative ('IPA') thus becomes a back door for denying international protection to people who require it. To do so, she argues, is to actively reinforce state privilege at the expense of persecuted people. Her firm view, however, is that the Refugee Convention is not meant to be read in this way. An approach to the IPA should be informed by the objective standards of human rights. Such an approach would discourage comparison of asylum seekers' situation with the millions of neglected and unprotected in countries of origin. It would then safeguard the protective value of the Refugee Convention. In this way, the true purpose of this protective regime could be properly realized.

The second chapter in this section develops the theme of the proper meaning of 'protection' in the Refugee Convention, and how it has evolved to keep pace with the passage of time. In 'Territorial Protection: Cessation of Refugee Status and Internal Flight Alternative Compared', Maria O'Sullivan maintains that the meaning of 'protection' in the Refugee Convention 1951 has changed over the decades since the Convention was signed. 'Protection' is utilized by many states to enforce the concept of a 'third safe country', 'safe country of origin' and 'internal flight alternative', with the aim of returning refugees back to a 'safe' country or part of a country. Some states now even grant time-limited visas to recognized refugees and have utilized the 'changed circumstances' cessation provisions under Article 1C(5) of the Refugee Convention to return recognized refugees to countries where protection against persecution is now being provided in the country of origin. Maria O'Sullivan, however, argues that the legal tests for these various interpretations of 'protection' have been developed largely on an *ad hoc* basis and in isolation from one another. It has not been established whether there are any commonalities across these standards – all of which involve findings as to safety and protection – and whether a more integrated approach should be taken to these issues. In her chapter, Maria O'Sullivan therefore focuses on two of these concepts – the internal flight alternative (IFA) and cessation of refugee status due to change in country conditions under Article 1C(5) of the Refugee Convention and its European Union equivalent – Article 11(1)(e) of the EU Qualification Directive (the 'changed circumstances cessation clause'). The concepts of IFA and cessation are linked in that they both concern the definition of a refugee under Article 1 of the 1951 Convention and both entail consideration of the adequacy of protection in the refugee's country of origin. The UNHCR has already highlighted symmetries between these two concepts and has recommended taking a more integrated approach to their interpretation. After a discussion of a number of specific questions in this regard, O'Sullivan turns to the broader issue of whether a more consistent approach and holistic interpretation should be taken of 'safety' and 'protection' across international refugee law (including the EU Qualification Directive). She ends her comprehensive and overarching analysis by putting forward the case for integrating the meaning of protection.

The third chapter is by Savitri Taylor, who looks at the specific practice of the Australian government in recent years, on 'Sharing Responsibility for Asylum Seekers and Refugees in the Asia Pacific Region', under its 'regional protection framework' designed to check the irregular maritime arrival of asylum seekers under the guise of the idea of 'collective responsibility for displaced persons in the region'. These involve cooperative arrangements for assessment of refugee claims, provision of resettlement for those found to be refugees, and a safe return home for the rest. Savitri Taylor argues that the implementation of the Australian government's proposal has not improved refugee protection or burden sharing between states, but has instead violated the principle of *non-refoulement*, which is now part of customary international law. Her valuable chapter discusses the prospects for achieving better refugee protection and more equitable burden sharing in the region through inter-state dialogue and civil society engagement.

The fourth chapter considers the thorny, and increasingly important, problem of 'Internally Displaced Persons' (IDPs), with a focus on Nigeria in 'Disowned in their Own Land: The Courts and Protection of the Internally Displaced Person' by Geoffrey Care, a retired judge. Most of the world's IDPs are in refugee-producing countries, and he considers how the primary responsibility of the state towards IDPs can be best addressed, utilizing the domestic courts to this end, because the legal and moral responsibility for their wellbeing rests with their own country. Geoffrey Care observes how, in Nigeria, with more than a million IDPs, the problem remains intractable because there is no legal definition as there is for a refugee. This results in reliance being placed on a United Nations report, *Guiding Principles on Internal Displacement*, which uses the definition of those who 'have been forced or obliged to flee or to leave their homes or places of habitual residence', thus producing a very broad definition of those who constitute IDPs.

Part Four deals with 'Emerging Paradigms of Legal Protection' and focuses on three areas of the law that have become of rising concern in the West. These are human trafficking, child protection and refugees from armed conflict. The first chapter deals with 'Human Trafficking, Asylum and the Problem of Protection', where Satvinder Juss argues that, unless checked, human trafficking into Europe threatens the very structure of liberal democratic life, because it is often tantamount to modern slavery. He argues for the greater use by the courts of the Slavery Convention 1926. This defines slavery as 'the status or condition of a person over whom any or all of the powers attaching to the right of ownership are exercised'. The Recital of this Convention states that it is 'necessary to prevent forced labour from developing into conditions analogous to slavery', and yet victims of human trafficking, like erstwhile slaves, are often still subject to a form of 'ownership' by others. *The Rome Statute of the International Criminal Court* also describes the condition of 'enslavement' as one that 'means the exercise of any or all of the powers attaching to the right of ownership over a person and includes the exercise of such power in the course of trafficking in persons, in particular women and children'. Juss considers whether the recognition that human trafficking is a form of slavery adds something qualitatively unique to the way in which victims of human trafficking require to be protected. If it does, then it must lead us to the conclusion that the primary and paramount consideration of the law in this area should be to provide 'victim-centred' protection grounded in mankind's historical experience of slavery. Victims of human trafficking have often been 'persecuted'. This may provide a basis for their protection as refugees. There may be a dimension to human trafficking, namely its phenomenon as a form of modern slavery, that renders its victims particularly apt for the grant of refugee status. Slavery was abolished in 1807 after a long and honourable campaign led from the very country, Britain, where it now appears to be taking root. The historical significance of 'slavery' (which for centuries was state sanctioned), like that of the historical significance of racism, is one that gives it a particular salience over and above other human evils. It demands an extraordinary state response. The chapter considers the impact in the United Kingdom of recent legal developments in the law of human trafficking and argues that the British courts will need to explore and develop a principled approach to the availability of refugee status to victims of human trafficking that is incontrovertibly 'victim-centred' flowing from the experience of being trafficked.

The second chapter, by Jacqueline Bhabha, deals with the rapidly developing area of 'Child Migration and the Lacunae in International Protection', where the author reminds us how, since the invention of childhood as a distinct phase of human life, society has accepted an obligation to protect the youngest members of its population. This should hardly have been surprising because migrant children have had a peculiarly strong claim to public protection, a claim well recognized in international law from the earliest days of the human rights regime. They are vulnerable and dependent, like all children, but they have the added handicaps that come from lack of citizenship status and from dislocation. Children face unfamiliarity with new surroundings and separation from old and familiar ones. They also face linguistic and communication challenges, social isolation, cultural disruption. The dislocation of children creates new material hardships, such as tough living conditions, reduced income and access to material resources, and unfamiliar climate and diet, all of which raise acute health challenges for them. Destitution, depression and desperation may be the consequences. Jacqueline Bhabha explains how phrases like 'invisibility', 'hiddenness', 'falling or slipping between the cracks' and 'void' have allowed states to innocently overlook the problems of migrant children and their correlative duties. However, over the last five years or so, it has become clear that this traditional narrative, which she calls the 'invisibility narrative', is inadequate. In her uncompromisingly clear view, while it explains the problems of some child migrants and their interface with public agencies well, it fails to capture the more complex dynamics in play for many others. In the same way, whereas invisibility explains the failure to establish mechanisms for child guardianship for unaccompanied migrant children, and to develop adequate child-friendly legal procedures for asylum-seeking or refugee minors, it does not account for the dramatic deficiency of public policy towards several other key child migrant groups. Jacqueline Bhabha then helpfully takes the example of trafficked children, and migrant children associated with gangs or forms of petty delinquency or antisocial behaviour. She argues that few problems have received as much general attention: in the former case, sympathy and public concern; in the latter, hostility and public outcry. No one could claim that these are invisible issues. And yet the numbers of trafficked child migrants appear to be growing, not declining; the problems of migrant street children stealing or begging seem to be as intractable as ever. In a compelling and hard-hitting account, Jacqueline Bhabha argues that we need a new narrative, a more complex perspective, to explain current developments in child migration and address the problems that they give rise to. She argues that we need to analyse the phenomenon in a more nuanced way than we have so far, and we need to advance claims on states that expand beyond the protection mandate that has been our focus to date.

The third chapter places some of these problems in the context of international refugee law. In 'Unaccompanied Children and their Protection under International Refugee Law', Ilias Bantekas explains why the plight of unaccompanied children has received insufficient attention in refugee law. First, they were not considered as falling within the typical refugee paradigm. Second, many receiving countries have been reluctant to accept that unaccompanied children are situated on their territory, not least because few statistics have been held, or retained, by national authorities on unaccompanied minors seeking asylum on their territory. Finally, a large number of unaccompanied children are not encompassed within the classical definition of the refugee because many have fled from their homes to avoid parental abuse or ill-treatment. As a result, states either deport children on the basis that they have violated the country's immigration laws or instead grant them relief to stay on humanitarian grounds. If they are allowed to stay it is clear that the incumbent state must take all appropriate measures to maintain them at both a financial and political cost to them. Yet, according to Ilias Bantekas, the phenomenon of unaccompanied children bears further consideration because children leave their countries for a variety of reasons: fear of persecution, armed conflict, parental abandonment and abuse, as well as escape from acute poverty. It is, therefore, a myth, he argues, that unaccompanied children are sent away by their parents in order to make a living. This chapter sets out the international legal framework governing the status of unaccompanied children, which currently falls under two distinct but interrelated disciplines, namely international refugee law and international human rights law – including international children's law. Yet the difficulty is that both of these international legal disciplines are juxtaposed against local immigration laws and practice. In many cases, these frustrate the very purpose of human rights pertinent to children. Ilias Bantekas's chapter, therefore, maps out these conflicts, describes the law as it stands, and then highlights the practical problems inherent in the application of international refugee law to unaccompanied children.

The fourth chapter examines the prickly problem of armed conflict, which often deliberately sets out to create refugee flows. In 'Forced Displacement, the Law of International Armed Conflict and State Authority', David James Cantor strongly develops the trite but oft-neglected notion that international armed conflicts shape the way within which the actions of states often direct the forced migration of persons. His thesis is that warring states often have strong reasons for compelling the displacement of civilian populations, and international armed conflicts usually produce large numbers of refugees and displaced persons. The state authority that is exercised in armed conflict is also often distinct from that exercised during peacetime. His chapter explores the historical development of the international framework of laws and customs of war that now regulates the coerced movement of civilians during international armed conflicts. In this way, David Cantor contributes to a wider body of scholarship that is concerned with the structures that affect the migration of human populations. However, he also demonstrates how the law of international armed conflict is most developed in those situations where civilians find themselves as potential victims in the hands of a hostile party to the conflict, namely when they are in occupied territory, or they are aliens in the territory of a hostile state. What is most significant about this chapter, however, is the way in which it highlights the relatively recent developments in international law, which have begun to emphasize the importance of protection against such coerced movements during hostilities between the parties to the conflict. By examining the distinctive genealogies of the law in these three distinct situations, David Cantor is able to identify the different rationale that governs each one, and in turn clarify the sometimes obscure meaning of the rules in this area, in a way that can be profitably employed in future conflict situations.

Part Five is on 'Encampment, Detention and the Coercive Treatment of Asylum Seekers', and given the way in which detention has provoked considerable debate in law and in moral philosophy, the first chapter of this section by Dallal Stevens discusses, in 'Asylum Seekers, Detention and the Law: Morality in Abeyance?', the fundamentals of administrative detention. She asks whether depriving asylum seekers of their liberty stands up to moral scrutiny, and whether the current framework of legal oversight is sufficient when measured against the ethical implications. Focusing on the position in the United Kingdom, the author addresses four main areas: why states detain; whether detention can be justified; the role of the courts and judiciary; and the impact of human rights legislation. She notes two problematic aims of detention: the risk of absconding and deterrence. However, given that the detention of asylum seekers often lacks a rational or moral explanation, her chapter questions the current legal framework of judicial review, with specific reference to leading cases, enabling her to conclude that, given the implications of human rights legislation, it is time to consider fixed terms of detention, if not the whole moral basis for asylum-seeker detention.

This is followed in the second chapter of this section by a detailed examination by Mary Anne Kenny and Lucy Fiske of 'Regulation 5.35: Coerced Treatment of Detained Asylum Seekers on Hunger Strike. Legal, Ethical and Human Rights Implications'. The background is the incident in September 1992, when three detained Cambodian asylum seekers launched a hunger strike, refusing all food and taking only small quantities of water. All three were hospitalized for dehydration and after two weeks were 'thought to be in grave danger of death'. At the request of the Australian Minister for Immigrations, the Supreme Court of New South Wales issued an interim order permitting the government 'to feed or to administer nourishment to the defendants against their will in order to prevent their death or serious bodily damage and for that purpose to use such force as is reasonably necessary'. The government meantime hastily passed a law authorizing medical treatment to be given to a person in immigration detention without their consent. This law is contained in regulation 5.35 of the Migration Regulations 1994 (Cth), and it authorizes the use of 'reasonable force' to administer medical treatment, including the reasonable use of restraint and sedatives. Mary Anne Kenny and Lucy Fiske examine the case of detained asylum seekers on hunger strike and explore some of the complex legal and ethical issues that occur when managing and treating these cases. They also consider the reasons for hunger strike, the competence of the individual engaging in hunger strike, the range of medical interventions available to treating practitioners (including the details of force feeding through a nasogastric tube in particular), and the range of responses available to government authorities in responding to hunger strikes in detention environments. What is especially valuable about this chapter is the way it looks at hunger strikes as a form of protest, particularly in Australian detention centres, and the implications of the legal and political responses to those strikes.

The third chapter in this section develops the theme of immigration detention when, in '"Less Coercive Means": The Legal Case for Alternatives to Detention of Refugees, Asylum Seekers and Other Migrants', Alice Edwards explores the paradox of how, on the one hand, the issue of alternatives to immigration detention is gaining in interest at international and national levels, yet, on the other hand, the rates of incarceration of new irregular arrivals are rising. She explains how, while there are many pragmatic reasons for opting for alternatives to immigration detention (such as that there is no empirical evidence that detention deters irregular migration), the alternatives are significantly cheaper than incarceration. Indeed, many of these alternatives enjoy high compliance rates of up to and beyond 90 per cent. Her chapter therefore makes a case for legal arguments for alternatives to detention. She probes the question whether there is an obligation under international law on states to make available alternatives to detention for asylum seekers, refugees or other migrants. She concludes that at a minimum international law requires that states institute guarantees against arbitrary detention, and that these guarantees require other non-custodial options available to detention. Most international courts or bodies now firmly accept that a state must examine whether there are any less intrusive or coercive means of achieving the state objective of migration control without recourse to detention. Alice Edwards explains how this position is derived from the international legal principles of reasonableness, proportionality and necessity, whereby the principle of proportionality requires detention to be a measure of last resort. This presupposes that there are other (first-resort) options available that can match an individual's right to liberty on the one hand with a government's right to control its borders on the other. Against this background, she argues that it must follow that the failure of many governments to make available alternatives to detention puts their detention laws and practices into direct conflict with international law. This thesis is developed through an examination of the much-neglected body of jurisprudence on detention in international law.

Yet, in the fourth chapter of this section, Guglielmo Verdirame and Jason Pobjoy, in what is a devastating critique of current policy, explain in 'The End of Refugee Camps?' how, even worse than 'detention', the 'encampment' of undocumented aliens and refugees is one of the main challenges to the protection of the human rights of refugees. They show how in most of Africa and in many parts of Asia it is the standard way of hosting and assisting refugees, and often the only one employed by the United Nations High Commissioner for Refugees (UNHCR), humanitarian organizations and many host states. Their chapter is important not least because until recently there had been little critical engagement with the question of refugee camps within policy circles. However, when a group of human rights and humanitarian organizations, led by the US Committee for Refugees and Immigrants (USCRI), organized a worldwide campaign against what was labelled 'the warehousing of refugees' and adopted the 'Statement Calling for Solutions to End the Warehousing of Refugees' in September 2009, the issue could no longer be ignored. This is not least because, in their own words, refugees are warehoused when they 'are confined to camps or segregated settlements or otherwise deprived of their basic rights, in situations lasting 10 years or more. Warehousing refugees not only violates their rights but also often reduces refugees to enforced idleness, dependency, and despair.' The UNHCR has recently embarked on its own internal process of policy review, which indicates a willingness to reassess the organization's current approach to the protection of refugees in the political South. This review process culminated in 2009 with the adoption of the Policy on Refugee Protection and Solutions in Urban Areas ('2009 Urban Policy'). This new policy purports to respond to the reality that more than half of the world's refugees live in urban environments. The 2009 Urban Policy is now the centerpiece of the UNHCR's 'recalibrated' approach to urban-based refugees. Guglielmo Verdirame and Jason Pobjoy discuss the evolution of the 2009 Urban Policy, set against broader questions concerning the quagmire of refugee camps, and, in this chapter, assess the positive elements of the 2009 Urban Policy and critique its key weaknesses and challenges. They conclude, on recent evidence, that the fact that the countries that absorbed the bulk of the Iraqi refugee crisis, namely Jordan, Lebanon and Syria, chose not to establish camps, provides critics of encampment with powerful ammunition that alternatives to refugee camps are politically viable and must be more widely embraced.

Part Six is on 'Migrant Workers, Skilled Labour and the Control of Human Mobility', and this section contains four chapters on the implications of modern global migration today. In the first chapter, Bernard Ryan's timely contribution, 'In Defence of the Migrant Workers Convention: Standard Setting for Contemporary Migration', reminds us of the importance of the International Convention on the Protection of the Rights of All Migrant Workers and Members of Their Families ('the Migrant Workers' Convention') by pointing to its difficult history, exemplified by how, despite being initially proposed by a General Assembly resolution in 1979, its final text was not endorsed until 1990, because of the strong differences of opinion between states of origin and destination. A further lengthy delay meant that the Convention did not come into force until 1 July 2003, because of the requisite 20 ratifications that had to be obtained. Ratification has remained slow even after that, however, with only 44 states having ratified by early 2011. Bernard Ryan argues, however, that notwithstanding such doubts about the utility and usefulness of the Migrant Workers' Convention, it has real potential as a source of standards concerning international migration. His contribution evaluates the importance of this instrument through a consideration of the text of the Convention, which demonstrates that it provides a coherent protection of migrants as a category. This is borne out by an analysis of the Convention in practice, which shows its strength to lie in a combination of two factors, namely the migration experiences of the states that have ratified it, and the interpretative work of the Committee on Migrant Workers since it was established on 1 January 2004, which collectively demonstrates how the Convention can be an effective and authoritative source of standards on the treatment of migrants.

Shubha Ghosh, in the second chapter of this section, appraises the contribution of migrants to the world economy in 'The Movement of Skilled Labour and Knowledge across Borders'. Starting from the banal observation that the movement of peoples across borders influences the acquisition and transfer of skills in apparent and indirect ways, he goes on to explain how universities host and seek students from a wide range of countries; how companies, searching for the best, and perhaps cheapest, talent, look globally; and how these activities lead to the movement of ideas, cultural expression and norms that invigorate and challenge the host country. He then explains how the movement of people to acquire and transfer skills is particularly challenging in a global environment built on nation states each competing to increase economic growth and wellbeing under global norms and standards. When harmonized and strengthened intellectual property rights are a critical part of these norms and standards, the national challenges to accommodate and control the movement of skilled labour require policy makers and scholars to address the normative foundations for migration and intellectual property. This is his thesis. He elaborates it in two ways. First, he contrasts the contemporary landscape with various ones from the past, including the *laissez-faire* regime of international movement in the nineteenth century. Second, he then places these contrasting landscapes within a normative framework that takes into consideration the nation state, the rights of individuals and the value of knowledge transfer. His thesis ends with a discussion of the Economic Espionage Act of 1996, a piece of legislation from the United States that animates and illustrates the issue of the movement of skilled labour and ideas across borders.

Migrants may bring overall benefits, but they are also perceived as a threat to society and the cause of instability. The third chapter of this section is on the security aspects of international migration, something that every developed society has now had to deal with post 9/11. In a powerful contribution, 'Migration Control and Human Security', by Sharon Pickering, Marie Segrave, Claudia Tazreiter and Leanne Weber, the authors consider the use of migration controls against illegalized migrant workers. They point out that this has been a much-neglected area. There has been significant scholarly activity on the use of migration controls to deter and criminalize asylum seekers. There has been much less attention given to the study of migrant workers. Yet migrant workers experience high levels of migration control, which may take many forms. Migration controls frequently categorize and recategorize the migration status of workers. They are shifted from legal to illegalized workers or vice versa. The authors consider these issues in the context of human capabilities and human security theorization. They see mobility and the desire to control it as manifestations of the disciplining and securitizing logic enacted through institutionalized power in liberal societies. They observe how the sphere of migration control encompasses local and global, national and transnational, forces and logics that establish and recalibrate 'systems' that seek to both imagine and moderate mobility. Yet there are contradictory forces at play here. The political economy of globalized capital and liberal values are both founded on the inseparable pairing of freedom and mobility. Yet they eschew its 'products' by creating an array of undesired categories. These include illegalized migrant workers; trafficked persons; rejected asylum seekers; and 'flawed consumers' and 'suspect citizens'. The authors contrast this disparate grouping of 'crimmigrant' others with the emerging elite category of global citizens, for whom the liberal aspirations of freedom and mobility are fulfilled in a globalizing, neoliberal order. The harsh reality, as the authors remind us, is that freedom and mobility are unequally applied to markets, money, corporations, new technologies and people.

In an illustration of how specialized migration studies have become in recent years, the fourth chapter, by Gustavo A. Flores-Macías, 'Collective Remittances in Comparative Perspective: The Cases of El Salvador and Mexico', assesses how the funds that migrants remit to their home countries have steadily grown in importance over the last several decades, and how several reasons account for this growth. Remittances provide the recipient country with much-needed hard currency. They also help governments balance their capital and current accounts and provide a boost to recipients' consumption and purchasing power.

A subset of those funds is known as collective remittances, or the act of pooling money among several migrants to finance development projects in their communities of origin. In contrast to private remittances, collective remittances are not meant to assist friends or family financially. Rather, their goal is to contribute towards the development of an entire neighbourhood or community in the migrants' home town. Contrary to their private counterparts, however, collective remittances face significant coordination problems. In particular, collective remittances tend to concentrate the costs of the development project in a few migrants, but the benefits derived from the project tend to be diffuse. While rarely are there restrictions regarding who has access to the development project, it is often low-income migrants who sponsor it. Although migrants have sometimes joined efforts with governments and the private sector to fund such projects, the parties' different and often competing interests make coordination difficult. Flores-Macías sets out to study the obstacles to cooperation involved in collective remittances and the insight that this provides into how coordination takes place among low-skilled and increasingly permanent migrants, different levels of government, private companies and non-governmental organizations (NGOs) to finance development projects to improve local communities. His focus is a comparison of experiences in Mexico and El Salvador, and he argues that differences in how collective remittance programmes are structured (which include differences in incentives and disincentives for participation and involvement in the decision-making progress impacting on the sustainability of the effort) can help explain why some are more successful than others. By identifying the key aspects that make migrant–government partnerships work, the study by Flores-Macías seeks to contribute towards solving a developmental problem that has concerned governments across the world.

Part Seven ends the volume with a consideration of a number of interrelated issues arising from the previous sections, namely the phenomenon of 'Transnational Migration, Citizenship and the Modern State' and the first chapter in this section, by Raffaele Marchetti, on 'Global Migratory Policies: Neither Closed nor Open Borders', observes how political boundaries of the modern state are increasingly under pressure. Global transformations are changing the international system. The result is that the criteria for determining the inclusion in, or the exclusion from, new political constituencies are under revision. The external migratory pressure, coupled with domestic political dynamics, is generating an intense debate on the legitimacy of keeping migrants out of national political life. For this reason, the migration and admission of aliens into political communities is increasingly recognized as a key policy issue in many countries today. Yet there is confusion in the arguments deployed. Proponents of more open policies use economic theses, but these are frequently mixed with cultural, political, legal or security arguments. Those who claim to use pragmatic approaches often find their arguments entangled in ideological stances, idealistic attitudes or racist positions. All of this, argues Marchetti, contributes to heated political debates that can sometimes spill over into street action. The truth is that migration is controversial, for it intersects a core concept of political theory, namely the notion of citizenship. In liberal theory, individuals are entitled to a set of rights, which includes the right to mobility. Yet this right is constrained by an equally recognized right to collective self-determination of the community at large, and to national autonomy. In this contribution, Marchetti shows how, rather than being resolved, this tension is now more and more problematic in a world in which individual human rights are on the rise and state sovereignty is in decline – except where the issue of immigration is concerned, where state sovereignty remains as emboldened as ever.

It is in this context that the impact of transnationalism on immigration is judged by Prakash Shah in 'Transnational Family Relations in Migration Contexts: British Variations on European Themes' as he describes how, notwithstanding the use of state sovereignty, migration is involving an increasingly complex set of trans-jurisdictional activities worldwide. Individuals and families are embarking on quite intricate forms of legal navigation across legal frontiers. He explains how recent events demonstrate the conflictual context in which migration occurs, as well as its many dysfunctional consequences. State authorities are penalizing trans-jurisdictional legal navigation, which occurs in a wide range of settings, and often concerns families and kinship networks. It is well known that many of the major streams of post-Second World War immigration into Western Europe were followed by large-scale family reunification. The reality is that such immigration has not stopped. It has only diversified to a greater number of source countries, overlain by further, sometimes complex, processes of family reunification and formation. This is part of the picture of 'superdiversity' in European cities. What is less well known is the way in which the maintenance of family relations across different countries and continents, either among South–North migrants or global diasporas, is taking place. There has been little inquiry, he argues, into the reality of globally dispersed families, and as a result, little is known about the methodological limits of our legal tools and concepts that may usefully be employed in this context. In his view, the affluent North deludes itself into thinking that it is in control, and that it can continue to remain in control by closely regulating family immigration. But this denies the plurality of modern Britain and of contemporary Europe. Attempts to freeze out legal alterity go beyond the sections of officialdom concerned with immigration control and permeate other areas of official behaviour, with the result that officials and legal systems are effectively failing to do justice to migrant families. Immigration regulation constitutes types of 'borders'. These are now even deployed extraterritorially. But there are also other 'mental borders' that are erected as legal controls are imposed on the more systemic pluralizing impact of the migrant presence, and the continuity of law within transnational social fields between 'here' and 'there'.

The third chapter takes this discussion further, when in 'Secret Immigration Business: Policy Transfers and the Tyranny of Deterrence Theory', Mary Crock and Daniel Ghezelbash concentrate on Australia's political discourse on refugees and border control, and consider how it has been dominated in recent times by claims made – both by the Government of the day and the Opposition – about the efficacy of deterrent policies. Both want to adopt another version of the 'Pacific Solution' – offshore processing, interdiction, mandatory detention and temporary protection visas – to stop maritime vessels bringing to Australia unauthorized asylum seekers. Yet both do so without an analysis of the value of policies presumed to deter boat people. This has not stopped the conservative Canadian government from adopting Australian policies of mandatory immigration detention and temporary permits as deterrent measures aimed at undocumented arrivals. Legal 'borrowing' has long been a feature of law reform and the development of legal systems. The authors argue that migration policy is an area of law in which governments are particularly concerned about what other jurisdictions are doing. However, they critique what they term 'unreasoned' policy borrowings, examining what happens when governments adopt laws without regard to the criticisms that have or might have been made of the measures when first introduced in another country and context. In this way, they show how the 'tyranny' of deterrence theory in the asylum space is felt in the fiscal and human cost of measures that ultimately deliver few tangible benefits for the countries in which they are introduced. They argue that it falls on academics to take a more active role in sharing and discussing policy developments in their countries so as to equip each other with the knowledge to counter unsubstantiated claims about the efficacy of particular policies, and outline the type of research that is needed in order to truly understand and respond to the phenomenon of irregular maritime migration.

Staying with the political salience of immigration as a policy issue, the fourth chapter focuses on what has long been considered a recognized subset of this field, namely family migration during the decade of Labour government rule from the 1990s onwards in Britain. Helena Wray, in 'Family Migration and New Labour', examines the family migration policies of the New Labour government of 1997–2010 in the context of its migration policy generally, and analyses how it was often the outcome of an acute set of pressures. Indeed, the regulation of family migration shares the same characteristics as the regulation of immigration as a whole. A veneer of coherence was achieved, concealing efforts to satisfy a multiplicity of interests and forces. New Labour's approach to immigration was arguably one of its defining characteristics as well as one of its great problems. The popular perception was that immigration was rising and the government failed to understand the worries of ordinary people. Yet, interestingly enough, in contrast to the minimal immigration policy of the preceding three decades, the Labour government implemented an expansionist programme of skilled and managed migration. This was a high-risk strategy because large-scale migration provokes 'a sense of crisis'. But the Labour government was faced with labour shortages and global migratory pressures. So, in order to minimize the risks of its policy, the government attempted to micro-manage entry and stay in power. Legislative, regulatory and organizational changes were piled on each other. Policies were over-complex and inconsistent with each other or with other stated values. In general, the government revealed itself as controlling – even authoritarian – not only towards migrants but, increasingly, towards the population as a whole. In that context, family migration was particularly problematic because it impinged directly on the lives of voters whom the government wanted to retain as its natural supporters. Following a more liberal family migration policy was fraught with difficulties if it encouraged the entry of people who could otherwise not enter as skilled workers or refugees. There was also the failure of some minority communities to mesh sufficiently with mainstream society. The conflicts and contradictions that characterize much immigration policy were thus intensified and personalized in family migration policy. Helena Wray tells that story.

In the fifth chapter of this section, 'Elements of Movement Controls in Post-Sovereign Governmentality', Thanos Zartaloudis grapples with the very notion of migration or movement management. He does so through a post-colonial framework in what is a highly theoretical, but no less compelling, contribution. He focuses on 'a crisis-machine of control', referring to the vast and hastily redrawn typology and administration of people on the move (genuine/bogus asylum seekers, forced/voluntary migrants, legal/illegal migrants, trafficked migrants, Convention/proper refugees, regular/irregular migrants, seasonal workers etc.). There is, he argues, in play here a wider logic of the field of control, of the management of people on the move in general. In elucidating this wider logic, he does not focus exclusively on the nation state or the UNCHR, nor on the administration and policing, NGO humanitarian action and micro-management of people on the move. Instead, he fastens on their functional relation and mutual exposure. His thesis is that 'an adequate understanding of the fluid practices of exclusion in a post-sovereign world can only by reached by an approach that tackles the whole array of governmental techniques of controlling people on the move'. He develops this by suggesting that citizens are forced to indefinitely restore and self-manage the dogma of the social relation while denizens are forced to be indefinitely disintegrated through it. He argues that there is today a neutralization of both citizens and denizens – a neutralization that has become everyday life for the vast majority of the planet's population. He maintains that the denizen's port of non-arrival is presented as the citizen's land of opportunity, 'until port of non-arrival and land of opportunity stumble upon their secret functional complementarities'. The answer to the problem lies in our deciding that we must join the denizens in their struggle. This is because critical academic accounts of the micro-management of power-suffused politics and the logistics of economies of neutralization (that are often more complicit to the 'state of things' than it is admitted) can no longer meaningfully engage us. He laments how the Absolutist State, the Liberal State and the Welfare State have all failed us because the Absolutist State triumphed in the kenosis (emptying out) of democracy, the Liberal State in the extremism of the free market and the Welfare State in the banality of the interminable crisis. The lives of citizens and denizens alike are reduced to the infinite production of mere survival, albeit to differing degrees of (social) deduction. When, he reasons, only survival remains at stake, post-sovereign biopolitics no longer attempts to manage life in order to better it or simply to exclude its more undesirable parts, but aims to reduce both the included and the excluded to their respective degrees of bare minimum.

The sixth and final chapter in this section also deals with the changing 'character of state membership', but from a decidedly different angle, which helps towards a better understanding of 'diverse modes of membership' of contemporary society. In 'Transnational Citizenship and the Democratic State: On Modes of Membership and Rights of Political Participation', David Owen demonstrates how the past 30 years have seen dramatic changes to the character of state membership regimes. This has witnessed the practices of easing access to membership for resident non-citizens, extending the franchise to expatriate citizens and to a limited extent to resident non-citizens, and an increasing toleration of dual nationality. These processes of democratic inclusion, he argues, represent an important trend in the contemporary political order in which we can discern two distinct shifts. The first concerns membership as a status and is characterized in terms of the movement from a simple distinction between single-nationality citizens and single-nationality aliens to a more complex structure of state membership. In this, we now find two transnational figures: *dual (or plural) nationals* who are legally recognized as citizens by two or more independent polities, and (non-stateless) *denizens* who, as long-term resident foreign nationals in one polity, enjoy 'most of the civil liberties and social welfare rights of resident citizens, often including rights to family reunification, some protection from deportation, and voting rights in local elections, as well as quasi-entitlements to naturalization' and, as long-term non-resident citizens of another polity, enjoy external citizenship rights and may retain some voting rights. The second shift, he argues, relates to voting rights, and this is marked by the movement from the requirement that voting rights are grounded in both citizenship and residence to the relaxing of the joint character of this requirement such that citizenship or residence now increasingly serves as a basis for enfranchisement. In the light of these transformations, empirically informed realistic normative engagement with transnational citizenship has focused on the issues of access to, and maintenance of, national citizenship, on the one hand, and entitlement to voting rights, on the other hand. Yet this framing of debates on transnational citizenship comes, he believes, with three sets of costs attached, which make this model less than perfect. First, the identification of full political membership with national citizenship elides an important distinction between these concepts in ways that is consequential for a conflict within normative debates on transnational citizenship. Second, the focus on voting rights occludes the more general terrain of rights of political participation. Third, the restrictive understanding of membership invoked in this manner means that it fails to address adequately the issues raised by the standing of non-resident non-citizens whose morally significant interests are adversely affected by the decisions of states. In this especially incisive contribution, Owen sets out to reframe the debate on transnational citizenship in a way that takes account of these costs and thereby allows for a more nuanced account of different modes of membership. This is an account that acknowledges that distinct grounds of entitlement to participation in political society can legitimate differentiated sets of rights of political participation and, hence, diverse modes of membership.

It is to be hoped that the vast range of topics relating to migration law and policy in the chapters of this volume will serve in its objective of encapsulating the state of migration studies today, originating from within traditions that are particular to the field covered, but also in setting the agenda for major debates, critiques and challenges for the future.

This enormous work – which far outgrew its initial modest aspirations as a companion to the Ashgate Law & Migration series – would not have been completed without the patience, support and diligent oversight of Dymphna Evans and Bethan Dixon, to whom all thanks are finally due at Ashgate.

Satvinder S. Juss

Reference

International Journal of Minority & Group Rights, Special Issue by Satvinder S. Juss and Colin Harvey on 'Critical Reflections on Refugee Law' (Issue 1, 2013).

PART I
THE REFUGEE IN EUROPE'S FREE MOVEMENT REGIME

The 'New Europe' and the 'European Refugee': The Subversion of the European Union's Refugee Law by its Migration Policy[1]

Nadine El-Enany[2]

Introduction

> What choice do we have? National or European – formulated this way we are presented with the tyranny of two choices. The third, that we need be neither but can aspire to a genuine internationalism that knows neither 'state' or 'continental limits', stands marginalized, ridiculed as pathetically utopian, the idea of the dreamer. Be a realist, accept the terms you are offered and if you are on the outside of 'Europe' looking in, then show why we should accept you rather than them.[3]

Far from serving to transcend or undermine the excesses of the nation state, the European project has merely resulted in 'more of the same' on a far grander scale. As Rogers Brubaker has lamented, despite the promise of a 'post-national' reinvention of itself, '[t]he future displayed recently by Europe to the world, however, looks depressingly like the past'.[4] The Schengen Agreement of 1985 may have started European countries on the path to the abolition of all national frontiers, culminating in the 1992 Single European Act, which carved out a commitment among Member States to invent a borderless Europe in which capital, goods and persons could move freely. But the spoils this extravagant, top-down scheme to recreate Europe promised to deliver were argued to necessitate the erection of the greatest of all frontiers at the outer borders of the Union. These borders are not themselves set in stone. Rather, '[t]he borders of Europe lie wherever those with power choose to put them and cast

1 This chapter consists of statements on the law as was in force on 1 January 2011.

2 Lecturer in Law, Brunel University. The author would like to thank Gareth Dale and Bruno De Witte for comments on earlier drafts of this chapter. Any omissions are the author's alone.

3 M. Haynes, 'Setting the Limits to Europe as an "Imagined Community"', in G. Dale and M. Cole (eds), *The European Union and Migrant Labour* (Oxford: Berg, 1999), 17–41, at 21.

4 R. Brubaker, *Nationalism Reframed: Nationhood and the National Question in the New Europe* (Cambridge: Cambridge University Press, 1996), 2.

them in concrete and barbed wire'.[5] And so, since the inception of what we might call the 'New Europe', we have seen the borders of this appropriated continent expand further and further east, gradually encompassing in its exclusive folds Central and Eastern European countries. And in their inclusion, new members were told that they must now exclude. The task of policing the European Union's borders has thus moved eastwards as its membership has grown in that direction. The well-rehearsed justification for heightened policing of Europe's external borders is one based on a perceived need for 'flanking measures' designed to provide increased security for Europeans and their way of life on the inside. European states, the bureaucrats have long iterated, in opening themselves up from the inside, make themselves vulnerable to penetration by all manner of transnational ills from the outside, not least criminals, drugs, terrorists and illegal immigrants.[6] For 'the idea of Europe requires an idea of "non-Europe", an idea of the "other"'.[7] And so it was, in the age-old, tried-and-tested method of nation building, that the European Union made itself and its Europeans with the help of an excluded 'other'.

The 'other' who forms the focus of this chapter is the refugee, the potential 'European refugee' – defined here as an individual who might flee her country in search of protection, and find sanctuary in Europe. It is of course impossible to speak of refugees as though they comprise a category of like individuals with like experiences. Indeed, there is 'no commonality to the refugee experiences, save the experience of displacement'.[8] And thus in speaking of refugees here, the mindset is one of acknowledging 'the resilience of the refugee, but is also sensitive to the relative specificities of refugee experiences along a number of markers such as race, ethnicity, and gender'.[9] The refugee is an 'other' that serves unfailingly to remind us of 'the arbitrariness and contingence of identity borders and boundaries'.[10] At present, the 'New Europe', as postulated above, cannot be reminded enough of the contingency of its own existence and practices of exclusion. No 'pre-existing "Europe" [exists] that legitimizes the development of the European Union',[11] nor therefore its exclusion of 'non-Europeans'. It is precisely with Europe's exclusion of the European refugee in the making and maintaining of itself that this chapter is concerned. Intrinsic to the making of itself has been the abolition of internal frontiers, and paramount to the maintaining of itself has been Europe's fortification of its external borders. In examining European refugee law and its interaction with European migration policy, this chapter asks what the result of these processes has been for the identity of the European refugee.

---

5 Haynes, 'Setting the Limits', 22.

6 The Trevi Group was an intergovernmental forum set up in 1976 and composed of European interior and justice ministers. Its task was to counter terrorism as well as to coordinate policing of and within the then European Community. See T. Bunyan, 'Trevi, Europol and the European state', in T. Bunyan (ed.), Statewatching the New Europe: A Handbook on the European State (London: Statewatch, 1993).

7 Haynes, 'Setting the Limits', 25.

8 N. Soguk, *States and Strangers: Refugees and Displacements of Statecraft* (Minneapolis, MN–London: University of Minnesota Press, 1999), 4.

9 Ibid., 5.

10 Ibid., 15.

11 Haynes, 'Setting the Limits', 23.

Just as its Member States have long promised, and to some extent practised, the protection of refugees, the European Union made a similar commitment to do so in the course of its initial expression of its intention to construct a Common European Asylum System (CEAS). Thus, at Tampere in 1999, the European Council agreed

> to work towards establishing a Common European Asylum System, based on the full and inclusive application of the Geneva Convention, thus ensuring that nobody is sent back to persecution, i.e. maintaining the principle of non-refoulement.[12]

Its features were to include 'in the short term'

> a clear and workable determination of the State responsible for the examination of an asylum application, common standards for a fair and efficient asylum procedure, common minimum conditions of reception of asylum seekers, and the approximation of rules on the recognition and content of the refugee status. It should also be completed with measures on subsidiary forms of protection offering an appropriate status to any person in need of such protection.[13]

And 'in the longer term Community rules should lead to a common asylum procedure and a uniform status for those who are granted asylum valid throughout the Union'.[14] The Union's CEAS project has advanced some way since Tampere and comprises not only directives on the topics of procedures,[15] reception[16] and qualification[17] stipulated above, but a number of proposed, recast directives on these topics that are presently being negotiated in the Council and Parliament.[18]

With each of its legislative outputs, the Union has dutifully declared itself to be acting in accordance with the 1951 Geneva Convention Relating to the Status of Refugees and the 1967 New York Protocol (the Refugee Convention). This chapter, in being concerned

---

12 Tampere European Council Presidency Conclusions 1999, para. 13.

13 Ibid., para. 14.

14 Ibid., para. 15.

15 Council Directive on minimum standards on procedures in member States for granting and withdrawing refugee status, COM(2000) 578 final, 20.9.2000.

16 Council Directive laying down minimum standards on the reception of applicants for asylum in Member States, COM(2001) 181 final.

17 Proposal for a Council Directive on minimum standards for the qualification and status of third country nationals and stateless persons as refugees or as persons who otherwise need international protection, COM(2001) 510 final, 12.9.2001.

18 Proposal for a Directive of the European Parliament and of the Council on minimum standards on procedures for granting and withdrawing international protection (Recast), COM(2009) 554 final, 2; Proposal for a Directive of the European Parliament and of the Council laying down minimum standards for the reception of asylum seekers (Recast), COM(2008) 815 final (Brussels, 3.12.2008); Proposal for a Directive of the European Parliament and of the Council on minimum standards for the qualification and status of third country nationals or stateless persons as beneficiaries of international protection and the content of the protection granted (Recast), COM(2009) 551 final.

with the identity of the European refugee, focuses on the European Union's Qualifications Directive in which we find the Union definition of a refugee. A reading of the Qualifications Directive might indeed allow us to conclude that the Union does, at least on paper, conform to international refugee law obligations. In fact, on paper, the Qualifications Directive appears to go further than the Refugee Convention in delimiting its scope of protection, for example in its recognition of non-state actors as being capable of persecution. Before turning to consider in detail the Qualifications Directive, its effectiveness in the context of the Union's wider migration policy, and the exclusionary effect of the interaction between the Union's migration policy and its refugee law on the European refugee, it is worth considering 'who is a refugee' under international law.

The 1951 Refugee Convention: Who is a Refugee?

Legal categories are artificial and historically contingent in that they do not neutrally represent natural or predefined groups of persons, but instead construct them. These categories are created by interested elites, and in particular with regard to the legal category of the refugee, it is the host states themselves, the potential protectors and cost bearers of that protection, that determine its form. In constructing the refugee definition, states 'problematize' the refugee 'other' 'to produce and stabilize the field of the refugee as a field wherein it becomes possible to engage in the politics of identity construction on an ongoing basis'.[19] The refugee 'figure', in Soguk's terms, 'appears at the intersections of power relations' and 'the site of the refugee ... becomes a site of modern statecraft'.[20] In this way, refugee law and in particular its making and remaking is a practice crucial to nation building in its creating 'a point of reference for the rearticulation of state sovereignty'.[21] This is no less so at the international and the European level than at the national level. Thus, despite the prominence of legal categories in vitally affecting the lives of refugees, in the course of their analysis, their contingency and interest-serving artificiality must be borne in mind.

The primary legal source of international protection for those seeking refuge is the 1951 Refugee Convention. Before examining the Convention definition of a refugee, it may be useful to explore the intuitive and conceptual dimension of the term. Goodwin-Gill writes that 'implicit in the word "refugee" lies an assumption that the person concerned is worthy of being, and ought to be, assisted, and, if necessary, protected from the causes and consequences of flight'.[22] The use of the term refugee suggests some preconceived idea of a person who is envisaged as deserving of protection; we know what a refugee looks like before she has arrived. The definition of a refugee is thus formulated on the basis of a contrived image of an individual deserving of protection. During the Second World War a great many individuals fled across borders in order to escape certain harms. When it came to the task of creating a

[19] Soguk, *States and Strangers*, 17–18.
[20] Ibid., 20.
[21] Ibid., 21.
[22] G. Goodwin-Gill and J. McAdam, *The Refugee in International Law* (Oxford: Oxford University Press, 2007), 15.

general definition of a refugee during the negotiations on the Refugee Convention, this was moulded to fit those already on states' territories. Categories were formulated of 'existing refugees, while the general criterion of persecution or fear of persecution, neither narrow nor excessively restricted ... was considered broad enough for post-Second World War and future refugees'.[23] The drafters of the Convention therefore had a clear idea of who they wanted to fall within the scope of the refugee definition.

States have always preferred to make clear to whom they are willing to provide protection and from what. Traditionally, the essential quality of a refugee was seen to be her presence outside her own country as a result of political persecution.[24] However, by the end of the Second World War it had become apparent that persecution could take place on a number of grounds other than one's political opinion and the definition of a refugee was widened to include grounds of persecution such as race and religion. This is demonstrated in the definition of a refugee eventually settled upon in the 1951 Refugee Convention, which states that a refugee is a person who

> owing to a well-founded fear of being persecuted for reasons of race, religion, nationality, membership of a particular social group or political opinion, is outside the country of his nationality and is unable, or owing to such fear, is unwilling to avail himself of the protection of that country; or who, not having a nationality and being outside the country of his former habitual residence as a result of such events, is unable or, owing to such fear is unwilling to return to it ....[25]

Recognition as a refugee therefore requires an individual to have crossed an international border and to have suffered some sort of discriminatory human rights breach. Proof of persecution alone is not sufficient to establish refugee status; the threat to the individual's life or liberty must have a discriminatory impact on the basis of her 'race, religion, nationality, membership of a social group or political opinion'.[26] Though the term 'persecution' is not itself defined, certain types of harm have traditionally been seen as falling within its scope of meaning while others have not. For example, individuals fleeing poverty are not generally considered deserving of asylum. Traditionally, the dominant discourse has considered that '[t]he solution to their problem, if any, lies more within the province of international aid and development, rather than in the institution of asylum'.[27] Furthermore, customarily those individuals who flee the criminal justice system after committing a crime (of a non-political nature) are excluded from refugee protection.[28] However, apart from these well-known exclusions from the scope of refugee law,

23 Ibid., 36.

24 J. H. Simpson, *Refugees: A Preliminary Report of a Survey* (Royal Institute of International Affairs, 1938), 1.

25 Article 1(A)(2), Refugee Convention.

26 D. E. Anker, 'Refugee Law, Gender, and the Human Rights Paradigm', *Harvard Human Rights Journal* 15 (2002), 133–54, at 134.

27 Goodwin-Gill and McAdam, *Refugee in International Law*, 15.

28 Ibid., 3.

difficulties do arise when trying to draw its limits. The EU Qualifications Directive[29] has attempted to address this point by setting out examples of harms that are to be considered as amounting to persecution. An important point to bear in mind concerning any definition of a refugee is that it will always be arbitrary, however wide its scope of protection. At best it can be argued to reflect the host society's view of those harms that are considered so untenable that both non-nationals and nationals of a host state are, in theory, entitled to be protected from. Over time, this list tends to lengthen and thus, at least on paper, the refugee definition, and its scope of protection, broadens.

The EU Qualifications Directive: Who is a European Refugee?

Being the most recently formulated refugee law in Europe, for its participants, the Qualifications Directive[30] marks the stage at which refugee law has developed since the 1951 Refugee Convention. Though the Directive leaves scope for national practices that do not fall below the minimum standards contained within, it is clear that it represents the most recent European statement of refugee law. The Directive sets out the rules and principles to be applied by Member States in their identification of refugees and those deserving of subsidiary protection status. The Directive covers both refugee status as laid down in the Refugee Convention as well as subsidiary protection status, applicable to those who are deemed not to qualify as refugees, but are considered to be at risk of suffering serious harm.[31]

(a) Definition of a 'Refugee'

The Qualifications Directive defines a refugee as

> a third country national who, owing to a well-founded fear of being persecuted for reasons of race, religion, nationality, political opinion or membership of a particular social group, is outside the country of nationality and is unable or, owing to such fear, is unwilling to avail himself or herself of the protection of that country, or a stateless person, who, being outside the country of former habitual residence for the same reasons as mentioned above, is unable or, owing to such fear, unwilling to return to it ....[32]

Although the definition of a refugee found in the Qualifications Directive is taken almost word for word from the Refugee Convention, its true meaning and substance cannot be found solely through reference to the Convention. Rather, the significance of the refugee definition is located in the meanings attributed by the EU Member States to 'persecution',

29 See note 15 above.
30 See note 15 above.
31 Ibid., Article 2(e).
32 Ibid., Article 2(c).

and in the grounds of persecution drawn up in the Qualifications Directive. According to the Directive, the definition may, in some respects, be seen as broader than that found in the Refugee Convention in its consolidation of the developments in refugee law since the time of the agreement of the Convention. However, as will be argued, compliance with European and international law is not the principal basis on which the quality and effectiveness of a refugee law ought to be assessed. Far more important is its functioning in practice, which, as will be discussed in detail below, in the case of European refugee law, is heavily impeded as a result of its interaction with the Union's relentlessly restrictive migration policy measures.

(b) 'Acts of Persecution' and 'Reasons for Persecution'

It is clear from Article 9 of the Qualifications Directive on 'acts of persecution' and Article 10 on 'reasons for persecution' that an element of discrimination is required to be present in any case made for asylum. The substance of these provisions might be said to reflect the growing intolerance of certain forms of discrimination internal to Europe.[33] These provisions fall under Chapter III of the Directive on 'qualification for being a refugee'. The unacceptability of certain harms and particular grounds of discrimination in Europe is demonstrated in their applicability, at least theoretically, not only to Europeans, but also to 'non-Europeans' seeking protection in Europe.

In respect of the types of harm from which individuals may seek protection, although 'persecution' is not defined as such, the Directive states in Article 9(1)(a) and (b) that 'Acts of persecution within the meaning of Article 1 A of the [Refugee Convention] must:

> (a) be sufficiently serious by their nature or repetition as to constitute a severe violation of basic human rights, in particular the rights from which derogation cannot be made under Article 15(2) of the [European Convention on Human Rights]; or (b) be an accumulation of various measures, including violation of human rights which is sufficiently severe as to affect an individual in a seminal manner as mentioned in (a).

'Severe violations' of 'basic human rights' are likely to be restricted to Article 2 (right to life), Article 3 (freedom from torture and inhuman and degrading treatment or punishment), Article 4(1) (freedom from slavery) and Article 7 (prohibiting the retrospective application of criminal law) of the European Convention on Human Rights. The Directive provides

---

[33] See Council Directive 2000/43/EC of 29 June 2000 implementing the principle of equal treatment between persons irrespective of persons of racial or ethnic origin [2000], OJ L 180/22; Council Directive 2000/78/EC of 27 November 2000 establishing a general framework for equal treatment in employment and occupation [2000], OJ L 303/16; Directive 2006/54/EC of the European Parliament and of the Council of 5 July 2006 on the implementation of the principle of equal opportunities and equal treatment of men and women in matters of employment and occupation OJ L 204/23; Council Directive 2004/113/EC of 13 December 2004 implementing the principle of equal treatment between men and women in the access to and supply of goods and services [2004], OJ L 373/37.

a non-exhaustive list of persecutory acts, including 'acts of sexual violence'[34] and 'acts of a gender-specific nature',[35] neither of which is found in the Refugee Convention, though the law has developed gradually, predominantly through legal action, in recognition of the need to protect individuals from return to such treatment.[36]

Article 9(3) of the Directive recalls the requirement in the Refugee Convention for a link between the reasons for persecution and acts of persecution. Under Article 10 Member States are obliged to take a number of factors into account when assessing the reasons for persecution. These include 'the concept of race ... colour, descent, or membership of a particular ethnic group',[37] 'religion',[38] 'political opinion',[39] 'nationality'[40] and membership of 'a particular social group'.[41] In contrast to the Refugee Convention, the Directive provides a definition of a social group by stating some of the possible characteristics of such a group:

- members of that group share an innate characteristic, or a common background that cannot be changed, or share a characteristic or belief that is so fundamental to identity or conscience that a person should not be forced to renounce it, and
- that group has a distinct identity in the relevant country, because it is perceived as being different from the surrounding society.

Importantly the Directive recognizes that 'a particular social group might include a group based on a common characteristic of sexual orientation'. However, a limitation is placed on the application of this provision:

> Sexual orientation cannot be understood to include acts considered to be criminal in accordance with national law of the Member States.[42]

---

34 Qualifications Directive, note 15 above, Article 9(2)(a).

35 Ibid., Article 9(2)(f).

36 See for example cases on female genital mutilation such as the decisions of the Immigration and Refugee Board Convention Refugee Determination Division (Toronto, Canada) of 1994, in 6 *International Journal of Refugee Law* 662 (1994); the 'Tribunal Administratif de Lyon' (France), 12 June 1996: *Revue Trimestrielle des Droits de l'Homme* 695 (1996), cited in A. Fabbricotti, 'The Concept of Inhuman and Degrading Treatment in Asylum Cases', *International Journal of Refugee Law* 10 (1998), 637–61, at 657. See also Human Rights Committee Conclusions making it clear that deportations of female asylum seekers with 'a well-founded fear of genital mutilation' are in violation of Article 7 ICCPR, which protects individuals from subjection 'to torture or to cruel, inhuman or degrading treatment or punishment'. Concluding Observations on the Netherlands (2001), UN doc. CCPR/CO/72/NET, para. 11; Concluding Observations on Lesotho (1999), UN doc. CCPR/C/79/Add. 106, para. 12; Concluding Observations on Sudan (1997), UN doc. CCPR/C/79/Add. 116, para. 12; Concluding Observations on Egypt (2002), UN doc. CCPR/CO/76, para. 11; Concluding Observations on Yemen (2002), UN doc. CCPR/CO/75/YEM, para. 6; Concluding Observations on Sweden (2002), UN doc. CCPR/CO/74/SWE, para. 8.

37 Qualifications Directive, note 00 above, Article 10(1)(a).

38 Ibid., Article 10(1)(b).

39 Ibid., Article 10(1)(e).

40 Ibid., Article 10(1)(c).

41 Ibid., Article 10(1)(d).

42 Ibid.

With regards to gender, the Directive provides that

> Gender related aspects might be considered, without by themselves alone creating a presumption for the application of this Article.[43]

Teitgen-Colly points out that the limitation attached to the basing of an asylum claim on grounds of one's sexual orientation represents the 'limits of the harmonization exercise'.[44] Importantly, however, the inclusion of this proviso seems also to reflect the limits of refugee law – that it may not develop further than the host society itself has developed in terms of the acceptability or otherwise of limits on rights and freedoms. It is clear from the above provisions on sexual orientation and gender as reasons for persecution that the approach taken in the Qualifications Directive towards defining the scope of refugee law is one based on the development of the Member States' societies. So, for example, although sexual orientation can be considered a ground for determining persecution, this is limited to the extent that freedom of sexual orientation is protected in Member States. This supports the view that refugee law may only continue to develop in practice so long as it reflects the values of the host society. This can also be seen in Article 2(h) on the definition of 'family members', which includes:

> the spouse of the beneficiary of refugee or subsidiary protection status or his or her unmarried partner in a stable relationship, *where the legislation or practice of the Member State concerned treats unmarried couples in a way comparable to married couples under its law relating to aliens* [emphasis added].

Soguk has therefore noted that, '[e]ven where attempts are made to appreciate the quotidian realities of refugee life, as in understanding gendered refugee experiences, these attempts are made possible through the affirmation of the state as the rightful authority capable of recognizing and validating those experiences'.[45] The constant checking by host states of the breadth of their refugee law to ensure that it does not go beyond the scope of their own national standards of protection demonstrates the limitations attached to the potential for law to account for the protection of refugees. If the scope of a state's refugee law is always limited to a reflection of those harms that its society or, in the case of international law, the international community as a whole as represented by powerful elites, considers so untenable that both nationals and non-nationals should be protected from them, the law will always be a stunted response to the phenomenon of persecution.

In some respects, therefore, the Qualifications Directive might be said to go further in its scope of protection than the Refugee Convention. This is, however, unsurprising considering the development over time of host societies and the increasing unacceptability of certain harms that tend to be classified as 'human rights violations'. However, this broadening of refugee law is not the case throughout the Directive. For example, although Article 4(4) on

43 Ibid.

44 C. Teitgen-Colly, 'The European Union and Asylum: An Illusion of Protection', *Common Market Law Review* 43 (2006), 1503–66, at 1532.

45 Soguk, *States and Strangers*, 35.

the 'Assessment of facts and circumstances' states that evidence of previous persecution or serious harm or threats of such treatment consists of 'a serious indication of the applicant's well-founded fear of persecution or real risk of suffering serious harm', this is tempered with 'unless there are good reasons to consider that such persecution or serious harm will not be repeated'. This provision has been criticized for not taking into account the Refugee Convention's inclusion of a clause that makes clear that refugee status does not cease where the person invokes 'compelling reasons arising out of previous persecution'.[46]

From 'Refugee' to 'Asylum Seeker': The Principle of Non-refoulement

Since the agreement of the Refugee Convention, there has been a tendency towards the implementation of increasingly restrictive practices designed to reduce the number of individuals arriving on European shores. As limitations on access to the EU increase, the relevance of any refugee definition decreases. A broad refugee definition without asylum seekers to meet its criteria serves little practical purpose, and indeed can contribute to the harmful illusion that the 'New Europe' is a normative force for good in the world. States have frequently and increasingly placed barriers in the way of those seeking protection, for example through the use of visa regulations, carrier sanctions and the 'safe country' concept, discussed further below, which has been used extensively in the EU Asylum Procedures Directive.[47]

Demonstrative of the increase in restrictions to access to protection is the terminological and ideational shift over the last decades from 'refugee' to 'asylum seeker'. The implicit assumption of an apparently known individual in the use of the word 'refugee' is critical to understanding this terminological shift. Unlike the term 'refugee', the idea of an 'asylum seeker' depicts a figure whose characteristics are unknown. The asylum seeker is cast as an individual claiming to be a refugee and thus there is the convenient, from the point of view of host states, possibility that the claim is unfounded or that the person deserves protection for reasons that fall outside the scope of refugee law and thus she may be awarded a more impoverished set of subsidiary rights. Until the claim is heard it is considered unsubstantiated and thus enables the host state to consider it as not giving rise to rights under refugee law.

---

[46] Article 1(C)(5) and (6), Refugee Convention. See Teitgen-Colly, 'European Union and Asylum', 1522.

[47] Council Directive 2005/85/EC on Minimum Standards on procedures in Member States for granting and withdrawing refugee status [2005], OJ L 326/13. See C. Costello, 'The Asylum Procedures Directive and the Proliferation of Safe Country Practices: Deterrence, Deflection and the Dismantling of International Protection?', *European Journal of Migration Law* 7 (2005), 35–69, at 50; J. van Selm, 'Access to Procedures: "Safe Third Countries", "Safe Countries of Origin" and "Time Limits"' (paper commissioned by UNHCR and the Carnegie Endowment for International Peace, 2001), 37; J. Allain, 'The *jus cogens* Nature of Non-refoulement', *International Journal of Refugee Law* 13, 4 (2002), 533–58, at 549; R. Byrne and A. Shacknove, 'The Safe Country Notion in European Asylum Law', *Harvard Human Rights Journal* 9 (1996), 185–226, at 192.

A number of provisions in the Schengen Agreement[48] concerned 'the hitherto unknown asylum seeker'.[49] Although the phrasing in the Schengen Agreement, which described an asylum seeker as 'an alien at the border or within the territory of a Contracting Party' making an asylum application 'with a view to obtaining recognition as a refugee in accordance with the Geneva Convention ... and as such obtaining the right of residence',[50] betrays little of the way in which the signatory states perceived asylum seekers, the Qualifications Directive better expresses the inherent suspicion or indeed the presumption of falsity with which the claims of asylum seekers are met. In Article 4(3)(d) of the Directive, Member States, in assessing the 'facts and circumstances' of an applicant's claim, are to consider 'whether the applicant's activities since leaving the country of origin were engaged in for the sole purpose of creating the necessary conditions for applying for international protection'. Thus, in contrast to the situation concerning refugees, in the case of an asylum seeker, the implicit assumption that the individual is worthy of protection is lacking. Rather, in hand we have a *potential* refugee, an individual whose claim for protection must be assessed for credibility prior to the granting of rights under refugee law.

The phenomenon of an asylum seeker is a difficult one. Commentators have tended to use the term refugee and asylum seeker interchangeably in order to emphasize the applicability of the principle of *non-refoulement* to all individuals claiming protection. The principle of *non-refoulement* is consistently hailed by commentators as being the most critical of obligations set out in the Refugee Convention to be adhered to by states. The reason for this is that the Refugee Convention, despite containing a refugee definition as well as delimiting the rights to be granted to those recognized by states as refugees, does not provide for a right to asylum. Thus, while international law neither obliges states to permit those seeking asylum to enter their territories, nor to grant them protection, Article 33(1)(A) of the Refugee Convention, which prohibits *refoulement*, prohibits states from returning individuals to countries in which they are at risk of certain forms of harm. The provision reads:

> No Contracting State shall expel or return ('refouler') a refugee in any manner whatsoever to the frontiers of territories where his life or freedom would be threatened on account of his race, religion, nationality, membership of a particular social group or political opinion.

The rationale prevalent among scholars in the field is that recognition of a refugee's status does not 'make him a refugee', but merely 'declares him to be one'.[51] Thus Article 33 necessarily implies that the status of an applicant is to be determined by the state in which she lodges her claim before any deportation can legitimately take place. Failing this, a state could not be certain that it is adhering to the principle of *non-refoulement*. In theory, therefore, all asylum seekers may be said to benefit from a '*presumptive refugee status*' whereby 'an applicant has

---

48 The 1985 Schengen Agreement was signed in 1985 and is designed to facilitate the abolition of systematic border controls between the State Parties. It was followed by the Schengen Convention, which came into force in 1995.

49 Teitgen-Colly, 'European Union and Asylum', 1506.

50 The Schengen Convention, note 46 above, Article 1.

51 Office of the UNHCR, *Handbook on Procedures and Criteria for Determining Refugee Status* (1979; re-edited 1992), para. 28.

the same [Article 33] rights as a refugee unless and until his or her non-refugee status has been established'.[52] On this interpretation of the law, the principle of *non-refoulement* applies to all individuals regardless of the country from which they originate or any circumstances surrounding the credibility of their claim to protection. The response from states has been to introduce measures that limit the number of individuals fulfilling the status of an asylum seeker in order to minimize the effect of the principle of *non-refoulement* on this absolute interpretation.

One way in which states have responded is with the introduction of the 'safe country' concept in the administration of their asylum regimes. This is a procedural measure designed to reduce the amount of asylum claims to be determined. If an individual lodging an asylum application in a destination state is found to have originated from, or passed through, a so-called 'safe country', her claim may be left undetermined and she becomes liable to return to that 'safe country'. A country is presumed 'safe' on consideration of a number of factors, including its human rights record and its political situation. The precarious nature of the criteria used means that presumptions of safety are open to allegations of being unjustified and thus the concept poses a risk to the integrity of the principle of *non-refoulement*. The central, binding EU instrument for the implementation of the 'safe country' concept is the Dublin Regulation,[53] incorporating the Dublin Convention,[54] agreed at Schengen, into EU legislation. The Dublin Convention established the rules for the determination of the Member State responsible for hearing the claims of asylum seekers, and is founded on the notion that this responsibility lies with the first Member State with which the asylum applicant establishes contact, whether by the issue of a transit visa, the legal presence of a close family member, or, in the absence of these, the first physical contact with the territory.[55] State Parties are required to readmit individuals transferred on the basis of the Dublin regime, while respecting the principle of mutual recognition with regard to the application of its rules. Thus Lavenex concludes that European cooperation is founded on 'the assumption of common standards of refugee protection that would justify the loosening of the exclusive responsibility of sovereign States under international law'.[56] Costello has argued that 'the most worrying' element of the application of the 'safe country of origin' concept is the

---

52 J. Vedsted-Hansen, 'Non-admission Policies and the Right to Protection: Refugees' Choice versus States' Exclusion?', in F. Nicholson and P. Twomey (eds), *Refugee Rights and Realities: Evolving International Concepts and Regimes* (Cambridge: Cambridge University Press, 1999), 269–89, at 275 and 276.

53 Commission Regulation (EC) No. 1560/2003 of 2 September 2003 laying detailed rules for the application of Council Regulation (EC) No. 343/2003 establishing the criteria and mechanisms for determining the Member State responsible for examining an asylum application lodged in one of the Member States by a third-country national [2003], OJ L 222.

54 Convention determining the State responsible for examining applications for asylum lodged in one of the Member States of the European Communities 15 June 1990 [1997], OJ C254/1.

55 Articles 4–8, Dublin Convention and Articles 28–38, Convention implementing the Schengen Agreement of 14 June 1985 between the Governments of the States of the Benelux Economic Union, the Federal Republic of Germany and the French Republic on the gradual abolition of checks at their common borders 14 June 1985 [1985], OJ L 176. See S. Lavenex, '"Passing the Buck": European Union Refugee Policies towards Central and Eastern Europe', *Journal of Refugee Studies* 11, 2 (1998), 126–45, at 130.

56 Ibid.

ensuing decline in procedural safeguards.[57] Not only are claims originating from countries designated as 'safe' treated as 'manifestly unfounded' or inadmissible, but applicants are also frequently subjected to strict time-limits, for example in the United Kingdom, under a 'super fast track' system for applicants from certain countries,[58] or their rights of appeal are curbed, such as in France, where applicants are denied the right to a suspensive appeal.[59]

Crisp and Van Hear have warned against the susceptibility of the concept to political manipulation, noting that states with 'lists' of 'safe countries of origin' may be 'tempted to include their closest allies and most important trading partners'.[60] An instance of such collaboration may be seen in the form of the EU Spanish Protocol,[61] which serves to exclude Union citizens from claiming asylum in other Member States '[g]iven [their] level of protection of fundamental rights and freedoms'.[62] Member States are granted the option of whether to consider claims under certain circumstances, but the threshold is a high one.[63] Essentially, for a Member State to be permitted to consider an EU citizen's claim for asylum, the State from which the individual originates must be shown to be in severe and continual violation of human rights, either by derogation from its obligations under the 1950 European Convention on Human Rights, or it must be ascertained to be in breach of its human rights obligations by the European Council. Otherwise, a Member State's decision to hear an EU citizen's claim is considered 'unilateral' and must be communicated to the Council, whilst the asylum application must be treated as 'manifestly unfounded'.[64] The founding assertion of the Spanish Protocol appears to be a weak justification for legitimizing the disqualification of all EU citizens from Member States' asylum processes. 'Given [their] level of protection of fundamental rights and freedoms', the Member States are apparently absolved of the responsibility to provide asylum to each others' citizens. Apart from the general concerns associated with 'safe country' practices explored above, the declaration is itself illogical. Why should a mere claim to adherence to a particular degree of protection of human rights necessitate the conclusion that all Member States are incapable of generating asylum seekers? As Van Selm notes, such a presumption contradicts the reality that 'for some individuals there can be a protection need even from a State which appears generally not to violate human rights ... evidenced by the large number of claims made to the [Court of Human Rights] on an annual basis by EU citizens'.[65] Although it is accepted that not many of these violations are sufficient to inspire flight from one's country, and the availability of an avenue for redress is a mitigating factor, the mere existence of human rights violations in European countries is a factor working against the presumption of safety attributed to

---

57 Costello, 'Asylum Procedures Directive and the Proliferation of Safe Country Practices', 52.

58 Ibid.

59 Ibid. See further, ECRE, *Country Report 2003: Synthesis* (London: ECRE, 2004). A suspensive appeal allows the applicant to remain in the host State while her appeal is being processed.

60 J. Crisp and N. Van Hear, 'Refugee Protection and Immigration Control: Addressing the Asylum Dilemma', *Refugee Survey Quarterly* 17, 3 (1998), 1–27.

61 Protocol on asylum for nationals of Member States of the European Union (attached to the EC Treaty by the Amsterdam Treaty).

62 Ibid.

63 Ibid., paras (a)–(d).

64 Ibid., para. (d).

65 Van Selm, 'Access to Procedures', 38–9.

Member States.[66] A poignant example of the persistence and potential for persecution in European Union countries is that of the Roma in Hungary. Since the rise of the far right anti-Roma Jobbik Party, the Roma have been subjected to violent attacks. Amnesty International has reported that the state authorities are implicated in their frequent failure to report such crimes against the Roma as hate crimes.[67]

Disturbingly, the use of the 'safe country' concept in the EU Asylum Procedures Directive further illustrates the potential harm that can result from the misguided impression that the European Union is a normative force for good. The Procedures Directive introduced the notion of a 'European safe third country' whereby applicants arriving from designated non-EU, European countries, having 'entered illegally' or 'seeking to enter' a Member State illegally, may be refused access to asylum procedures.[68] In permitting Member States to penalize asylum seekers entering their territories from particular countries illegally, this provision undermines Article 31 of the Refugee Convention, which seeks to protect asylum applicants who are forced to migrate illegally by exempting them from the usual penalties imposed by immigration law. Recital 24 of the Procedures Directive states that

> with regard to certain European third countries, which observe particularly high human rights and refugee protection standards, Member States should be allowed to not carry out, or not to carry out full examination of asylum applications regarding applicants who enter their territory from such European third countries.

The Council, and Parliament,[69] may only designate a country as a 'European safe third country' where it 'has ratified and observes the provisions of the Geneva Convention without any geographical limitations', 'has in place an asylum procedure prescribed by law' and 'has ratified the [1950 European Convention on Human Rights] and observes its provisions'.[70] Regardless of whether the standard of protection required of such designated countries is sufficiently high, the EU's coinage of the term 'European safe third country' constitutes a display of shameless audacity in its casual assumption that simply from the idea of being 'European', a whole new set of criteria for presuming countries 'safe' for the purposes of further deflecting those seeking its refuge can legitimately be established. These countries are considered 'safe' *first* on account of their being 'European', a presumption that is then *supplemented* with evidence pertaining to their human rights and refugee protection levels. In defending the notion of 'European safe third countries' by reference to their supposedly high human rights and refugee protection records, the Procedures Directive has employed a similarly perverse rationale as that used to justify the exclusion of EU citizens from the status of asylum seekers under the Spanish Protocol. Such conduct displays a willingness

66 Ibid., 39.

67 Amnesty International, 'Violent Attacks Against Roma in Hungary: Time to Investigate Racial Motivation' (Amnesty International, 2010), 7. At http://www.amnesty.org/en/library/asset/EUR27/001/2010/en/7ee79730-e23f-4f20-834a-deb8deb23464/eur270012010en.pdf (last visited 3 January 2011).

68 Procedures Directive, note 00 above, Article 36(1).

69 See Case C-133/06 *European Parliament v Council of the European Union*, 6 May 2008.

70 Procedures Directive, note 00 above, Article 36(2).

on the part of the EU to abuse the connotations that flow from the idea of 'Europe' and being 'European'. It is on the basis of the false presumption that Europe is inherently 'good', 'humane' and 'civilized', that the EU has extended the use of the harmful, already contentiously applied 'safe country' concept.

Thus, despite the consistent celebration of the principle of *non-refoulement* as constituting the most crucial safeguard in respect of the protection of asylum seekers, the approach consistently adopted by the EU and its Member States is one of limitation of its scope and effectiveness, in particular through the use of measures that serve to deflect individuals from territory marked as European. As discussed above, particularly insidious is the EU's brazen extension of the 'safe country' concept through its invention of the 'European safe third country' derivative. In its justification of the extension of the concept by reference to its own perceived essence, that of being 'European', the EU is not only playing dangerous (word) games with the lives of refugees, but has served to, carelessly at best, reinforce the dangerous idea that being 'European' implies inherent virtuousness.

Who is the Real European Refugee?

This section explores those elements of refugee law, and particularly of the refugee definition, that cannot be found in stated refugee law, whether at the international, European or state level. There are important elements that become evident when we consider the interaction between European refugee law and European migration policy. It is argued here that one of the implications of this process is that a number of characteristics, which are not stated in refugee legislation, are implicitly required of the European refugee and result in the exclusion of the most vulnerable individuals from this category.

At present, as is clear from the above, access to EU asylum procedures is limited. There are restrictive migration control measures in place that serve to prevent individuals in need of protection from penetrating European borders. The goal of keeping out of the EU as many asylum seekers as possible has been achieved. In the UK, for example, it was reported in 2007 that the number of those claiming asylum was at a 15-year low.[71] There has been an obvious decrease in the number of applications for asylum lodged in the EU and a parallel admission from the Commission that this does not necessarily mean that the number of those individuals in need of protection has decreased.[72] In the light of this, we must consider those persons who have succeeded in gaining protection in the EU and, more importantly, those who have not. The former group comprises the highly exclusive category of 'New European refugees' – the refugees of the 'New Europe'. They are the outcome of the rapid and extensive changes made both to the European borders and to Europe's refugee and migration law and policy over recent decades.

The European refugees are essentially those who find some way to overcome, either legally or irregularly, the EU and the Member States' restrictive control measures designed to deflect them. That this is the design of these measures is no secret. Take for example

71 UK Borders Agency, Asylum Statistics (Home Office, 2007).

72 Commission Communication on Regional Protection Programmes, COM(2005) 388 final.

the UK, where a *Home Office Asylum Statistical Bulletin* of 2006 includes a section entitled 'Key changes to reduce the number of asylum applications'.[73] A list of measures designed to prevent the arrival of asylum seekers follows, including the introduction of non-suspensive appeals, safe countries, restricted access to socio-economic support for asylum seekers, accelerated procedures and new visa requirements. All these measures, alongside existing restrictive instruments such as carrier sanctions, have limited access to UK asylum procedures. The events concerning the Iraqi interpreters who helped the British forces in Iraq being unable to apply for asylum in the UK and being reduced to pleading with the British government to make an exception and allow them to make their claims from Iraq, or the neighbouring countries to which some have fled, illustrates the failure of UK asylum law to protect some of the individuals most at risk of persecution. Instead of being permitted to claim asylum directly, the British government insisted that asylum claims be lodged from inside the UK, advising the interpreters to consult the government website for information on how to apply for a visa.[74] Considering the above discussion on the use of measures such as visa requirements to act as impediments to the making of asylum claims, it is unreasonable and objectionable, though unsurprising, that the British government presents the control measure as a possible solution to the problem of limited access to asylum procedures. Without the economic resources or connections to reach the UK, some of the interpreters were able to do little more than risk crossing the Iraqi border into a neighbouring country in order to find some level of protection.[75]

The UK is of course not the only European country to have gradually reduced the number of legitimate access routes open to asylum seekers. The situation is worsening with the expansion of the Union, which places pressure on new and accession states to police the EU's external borders. In Bulgaria, for example, during the accession process, strict migration control at both the local and the regional level, in line with the Union's demands, is believed to have contributed to the large drop in the country's number of asylum applications.[76] In 2005 French immigration liaison officers were stationed in various 'non-European' country airports in order to assess the documents of individuals on board aeroplanes travelling to France after they have been checked by local officials. In Finland, border guards have, since 2005, had greater powers, which previously only belonged to the police, over non-nationals whom they can now detain for a maximum of 48 hours, and asylum seekers can be interviewed in order to ascertain their identity, travel route and means of entry.[77]

Such Europe-wide restrictive measures have implications for the makeup of the European refugee. In this way, European migration policy is effectively impeding the use, application and relevance of EU refugee law. Only individuals who can overcome the restrictive migration control obstacles have the possibility of accessing EU Member States. These measures fail to differentiate in their restrictive impact between those individuals who would be considered refugees according to EU refugee law and those who would not. To enter the EU legally, the correct travel documents must first be obtained. To enter

---

73 T. Heath, R. Jeffries and S. Pearce, *Home Office Statistical Bulletin: Asylum Statistics 2005*, 22 August 2006, 8.

74 See reports of *The Times* of Tuesday, 7 August 2007.

75 Ibid.

76 ECRE, *Country Report 2005* (London: ECRE, 2005), 16.

77 Ibid., 18.

irregularly, often a smuggler must be paid to facilitate the (often treacherous) journey to Europe. The former group would have to be placed sufficiently high in terms of status and resources at their disposal in order to be able to acquire a visa, while the latter group would have to be similarly situated at least in terms of resources to be able to pay a smuggler's fee, which can be in the realm of the equivalent of 4,000 euros.[78] As Noll puts it, in the business that is human smuggling, 'protection is a commodity sold to a middle class of protection seekers'.[79] Resorting to the use of a smuggler also 'presupposes the acceptance of high risks by migrants'.[80] Hundreds of migrant deaths have occurred in recent decades, for example in the Adriatic Sea between Italy and Albania.[81]

The result is that those individuals who succeed in reaching European shores and claiming asylum are unlikely to be the most disadvantaged and vulnerable refugees. Neumayer points out, 'Democratic countries restrict the entry, but rarely the exit, of citizens, whereas harsh autocracies often impose limitations on leaving the country'.[82] Thus, as Mike Haynes writes, '[w]hat we have is a right to leave where states are condemned for their refusal to "let their people go", but for many this is made meaningless by the refusal to create a corresponding right to arrive. Instead, arrival, especially in the advanced countries, is treated as a crime'.[83] By imposing strict access conditions, Member States make it near impossible for the majority of asylum seekers to seek protection through legitimate means, forcing those who make the journey despite the obstacles to resort to the use of smugglers in order to penetrate the borders of European countries. Thus to leave one's country of persecution often requires money to bribe security officials and further finances for the legal or irregular journey to Europe. European refugees would therefore often have to be among the most daring, well resourced and economically mobile of the persecuted. These are traits that the most vulnerable, in particular women and children, are less able to demonstrate – in part due to prevailing gender norms and expectations.

The European Union's implementation of restrictive measures designed to deflect and deter asylum seekers from being able to access territory and therefore protection, as mentioned above, includes visa regulations, the 'safe country' concept, carrier sanctions and extraterritorial border checks and processing of claims. States frequently attempt to justify these restrictions on the ground that they represent an effort to prevent abuse of the asylum route by individuals who are seeking an economic status. Quite apart from the appalling failure of such a justification to account for the economic migratory impetus effected by the disastrous political and economic colonial legacies left by former imperial European countries, such as Britain and France, such measures undoubtedly target, and affect, all

[78] D. Casciani, 'Asylum Questions: What about Organised Crime?' (BBC News website, 21 July 2003). At http://news.bbc.co.uk/2/hi/uk_news/3083735.stm# (last visited 3 January 2011). A sum of $6,000 is cited as the average smuggler's fee.

[79] G. Noll, 'From "Protective Passports" to Protected Entry Procedures? The Legacy of Raoul Wallenberg in the Contemporary Asylum Debate', UNHCR Working Paper, No. 99, December 2003, 1.

[80] Ibid.

[81] Casciani, 'Asylum Questions'.

[82] E. Neumayer, 'Bogus Refugees? The Determination of Asylum Migration to Western Europe', *International Studies Quarterly* 49 (2005), 155–80, at 393.

[83] Haynes, 'Setting the Limits', 26.

irregular migrants alike, regardless of their motivations for moving. Not only do such measures severely affect the capacity of asylum seekers to access territories in which they can lodge protection claims, but such restrictions also impact heavily on host countries in regions of origin, which are primarily located in the South. There is no doubt that countries in the South host the vast majority of refugees. This is not merely due to their being geographically in close proximity to the majority of refugee-producing conflicts, but is also undeniably a result of the increasing limitation of access routes to protection in northern countries. In 2003, the European Commission recognized that the evident fall in recent years in the number of asylum claims made in European countries did 'not necessarily mean an overall reduction in the numbers of refugees and persons seeking international protection at a global level'.[84] Further, the Commission noted that 85 per cent of refugees are being hosted by countries in regions of origin struggling with limited resources.[85] In fact 6.5 million of the world's 8.7 million refugees are estimated to live in developing countries.[86] One example of a refugee group heavily present in their region of origin is that of Iraqi refugees, the majority of whom have fled to Syria and Jordan.[87] The few who do succeed in reaching industrialized countries are frequently denied protection and forcibly returned in spite of UNHCR advice to the contrary. This has been the case in both EU and non-EU European countries, including Norway, Sweden, the United Kingdom,[88] Denmark, Greece and Poland.[89] Arguably, the growing protection responsibilities in southern countries are not merely an incidental result of the reduction in access routes to the North. Northern countries have made concerted efforts to contain refugees in southern countries and have sought to facilitate the return of individuals found to have no legal right to be on European territory, both through European law in form of the Return Directive,[90] and through the conclusion of readmission agreements with non-European countries.[91] As Jon Gubbay notes, '[t]he process of repatriation is eased

84 Commission Communication of June 2003, *Towards more accessible, equitable and managed asylum systems*, para. 7.

85 Ibid.

86 UNHCR, *Statistical Yearbook* (2005), 12.

87 UNHCR, Global Report 2009 – Iraq Situation (1 June 2010). At http://www.unhcr.org/4c08f25e9.html (last visited 3 January 2011).

88 UNHCR, 'The UN Refugee Agency Cautions against European Deportations to Iraq' (News Stories, 8 June 2010). At http://www.unhcr.org/4c0e5f5a6.html (last visited 3 January 2011).

89 ECRE, 'Iraq Survey – Five Years on Europe is Still Ignoring its Responsibilities towards Iraqi Refugees' (2008), 4. At http://www.ecre.org/resources/Policy_papers/1051 (last visited 3 January 2011).

90 Directive of the Council and the European Parliament on common standards and procedures in Member States for returning illegally staying third country nationals. Directive 2008/115/EC of 16 December 2008, OJ L 348/98.

91 Under the 1999 Treaty of Amsterdam, the EU has the authority to conclude readmission agreements with non-EU states. Although the first multilateral readmission agreement was the 1991 Readmission Agreement between Poland and the Schengen countries, the EU has concluded further accords with countries such as Hong Kong, Sri Lanka, Macao, Albania, Russia and Ukraine. Member States may also conclude bilateral accords of their own. For example, together with its constitutional reforms implementing the 'safe third country' concept, Germany negotiated agreements with both European and non-European states, including Romania, Poland, the Czech Republic, Bulgaria, Croatia, the Federal Republic of Yugoslavia, Bosnia, Vietnam, Pakistan and Algeria. The rapid increase in the use of readmission agreements can be seen in Poland's

administratively, though not to the benefit of persons concerned, where member states have agreements that, in return for cash (euphemistically referred to as aid), non-EU countries will readmit their citizens who are detected as illegal immigrants in the EU'.[92]

It has therefore been argued that the result of the interaction between the Union's wider migration policy and its refugee law is that the former impedes the functioning and relevance of the latter. The characteristics implicitly required as a result of restrictive migration policy measures of the European refugee are destructive of a migrant's chances of reaching European shores and thus finding protection. This process of interaction between EU migration policy and EU refugee law must therefore be considered when assessing the quality of the latter. With a clearer picture of European refugee law in the context of Europe's wider migration policy, it is possible to draw some conclusions on the nature of the evolving Common European Asylum System. If it is true that it is primarily asylum seekers fulfilling certain requirements over and above those contained in express refugee law, such as being economically mobile, who can access the EU, then the 'New European refugee' is not the most vulnerable. The European asylum regime is far from being effective or equitable in neither granting sufficient nor equal access to its asylum procedures. Rather, it is an inefficient and stunted one. While states have been concentrating on keeping out as many asylum seekers as possible, the nature of refugee law and the European refugee has been changing. The most vulnerable migrants are excluded, while those who have the ability to circumvent the restrictive migration measures have a better chance of accessing protection. The EU may think it is clamping down on irregular and legal migration of certain 'undesirables' into the EU, but in reality it is chiefly doing so for the most vulnerable of migrants, whether refugees or not. The project of the construction of a European refugee law has been neither presented nor accepted on such a premise. It must be recognized that the restrictive migration policies of the EU make it impossible for it to claim the existence of a principled foundation for its refugee law. In its complete disregard for the world's most vulnerable refugees, Europe's restrictive migration policy has cost it any worth its refugee law might otherwise have carried.

Conclusion

It is perhaps the European refugee 'other' who has had to pay the highest price in the process of Europe's reinvention of itself as the 'New Europe'. In order that 'New Europeans' can sleep at night knowing that they are safe and secure in their beds from invasion by transnational criminals, drug dealers and illegal immigrants despite the dismantling of internal borders, a boundary of unprecedented height and magnitude has been constructed at the outer borders of the European Union. Meanwhile, on the inside, the 'New Europe'

---

conclusion of similar instruments with the Czech Republic in 1993, four days after that with Germany, and with Slovakia, Ukraine, Romania and Bulgaria in the same year. See Lavenex, '"Passing the Buck"', 139.

92 J. Gubbay, 'The European Union Role in the Formation, Legitimation and Implementation of Migration Policy', in Dale and Cole (eds), *European Union and Migrant Labour*, 43–66, at 60.

has busied itself creating an EU-branded refugee law. This refugee law, as expressed in the Qualifications Directive, carries a misleading label suggesting that not only is the European Union 'open as usual' to refugees, but that refugees are also guaranteed a better protection deal than ever before. Typically, however, the 'good European name' has failed to live up to its promise of virtue. In the construction of its prohibitive migration policy, the European Union has undermined the functioning, quality and effectiveness of its refugee law. Whether or not this result is an intended consequence or one merely incidental to its construction, the result of measures designed to deflect those seeking refuge from the shores of the Union has been to exclude from the possibility of protection the most vulnerable refugees. These refugees have been filtered out of the category of the European refugee, making it an exclusionary one. Not only must refugees fulfil the criteria delimited in the refugee definition of the EU Qualifications Directive, but as a result of migration policy measures that limit legal routes into the EU, they are implicitly required to demonstrate certain other characteristics. These include access to financial resources, economic mobility and a willingness to take risks. Although a number of the persecuted can demonstrate these traits, the most vulnerable cannot. Women and children are particularly disadvantaged due in part to prevailing gender norms and expectations. The 'New Europe' would do well to be reminded not to assume that just because something is 'made in Europe', it is sugar and spice and all things nice. Such an attitude not only has the potential to endanger the lives of those seeking its protection, but also conceals the Union's own dire and constant need for self-reflection. It is telling that such a self-assessment in Europe is needed most of all with regard to its treatment of 'non-Europeans', and now, with the failure of its refugee law to live up to its promise of protection, it is perhaps needed most urgently in respect of those persons seeking its refuge.

References

Allain, J., 'The *jus cogens* Nature of Non-refoulement', *International Journal of Refugee Law* 13, 4 (2002), 533–58.

Amnesty International, 'Violent Attacks Against Roma in Hungary: Time to Investigate Racial Motivation' (2010). At http://www.amnesty.org/en/library/asset/EUR27/001/2010/en/7ee79730-e23f-4f20-834a-deb8deb23464/eur270012010en.pdf (last visited 3 January 2011).

Anker, D. E., 'Refugee Law, Gender, and the Human Rights Paradigm', *Harvard Human Rights Journal* 15 (2002), 133–54.

Brubaker, R., *Nationalism Reframed: Nationhood and the National Question in the New Europe* (Cambridge: Cambridge University Press, 1996).

Bunyan, T., 'Trevi, Europol and the European State', in T. Bunyan (ed.), *Statewatching the New Europe: A Handbook on the European State* (London: Statewatch, 1993), 000–000.

Byrne, R. and A. Shacknove, 'The Safe Country Notion in European Asylum Law', *Harvard Human Rights Journal* 9 (1996), 185–226.

Casciani, D., 'Asylum Questions: What about Organised Crime?' (BBC News website, 21 July 2003). At http://news.bbc.co.uk/2/hi/uk_news/3083735.stm# (last visited 3 January 2011).

Commission Communication on Regional Protection Programmes, COM(2005) 388 final.

Commission Communication of June 2003, *Towards more accessible, equitable and managed asylum systems*.

Costello, C., 'The Asylum Procedures Directive and the Proliferation of Safe Country Practices: Deterrence, Deflection and the Dismantling of International Protection?', *European Journal of Migration Law* 7 (2005), 35–69.

Crisp, J. and N. Van Hear, 'Refugee Protection and Immigration Control: Addressing the Asylum dilemma', *Refugee Survey Quarterly* 17, 3 (1998), 1–27.

Dale, G. and M. Cole (eds), *The European Union and Migrant Labour* (Oxford: Berg, 1999).

ECRE, *Country Report 2005* (London: ECRE, 2005).

ECRE, *Country Report 2003: Synthesis* (London: ECRE, 2004).

ECRE, 'Iraq Survey – Five Years on Europe is Still Ignoring its Responsibilities towards Iraqi Refugees' (2008), 4. At http://www.ecre.org/resources/Policy_papers/1051 (last visited 3 January 2011).

Fabbricotti, A., 'The Concept of Inhuman and Degrading Treatment in Asylum Cases', *International Journal of Refugee Law* 10 (1998), 637–61.

Goodwin-Gill, G. and J. McAdam, *The Refugee in International Law* (Oxford: Oxford University Press, 2007).

Gubbay, J., 'The European Union Role in the Formation, Legitimation and Implementation of Migration Policy', in G. Dale and M. Cole (eds), *The European Union and Migrant Labour* (Oxford: Berg, 1999), 43–66.

Haynes, M., 'Setting the Limits to Europe as an "Imagined Community"', in G. Dale and M. Cole (eds), *The European Union and Migrant Labour* (Oxford: Berg, 1999), 17–41.

Heath, T., R. Jeffries and S. Pearce, *Home Office Statistical Bulletin: Asylum Statistics 2005*, 22 August 2006.

Lavenex, S., '"Passing the Buck": European Union Refugee Policies towards Central and Eastern Europe', *Journal of Refugee Studies* 11, 2 (1998), 126–45.

Neumayer, E., 'Bogus Refugees? The Determination of Asylum Migration to Western Europe', *International Studies Quarterly* 49 (2005), 155–80.

Nicholson, F. and P. Twomey (eds), *Refugee Rights and Realities: Evolving International Concepts and Regimes* (Cambridge: Cambridge University Press, 1999).

Noll, G., 'From "Protective Passports" to Protected Entry Procedures? The Legacy of Raoul Wallenberg in the Contemporary Asylum Debate', UNHCR Working Paper, No. 99, December 2003.

Simpson, J. H., *Refugees: A Preliminary Report of a Survey* (Oxford: Royal Institute of International Affairs, 1938).

Soguk, N., *States and Strangers: Refugees and Displacements of Statecraft* (Minneapolis, MN–London: University of Minnesota Press, 1999).

Teitgen-Colly, C., 'The European Union and Asylum: An Illusion of Protection', *Common Market Law Review* 43 (2006), 1503–66.

UNHCR, Global Report 2009 – Iraq Situation (1 June 2010). At http://www.unhcr.org/4c08f25e9.html (last visited 3 January 2011).

UNHCR, *Handbook on Procedures and Criteria for Determining Refugee Status* (1979; re-edited 1992).

UNHCR, *Statistical Yearbook* (2005).

UNHCR, 'The UN Refugee Agency Cautions against European Deportations to Iraq' (News Stories, 8 June 2010). At http://www.unhcr.org/4c0e5f5a6.html (last visited 3 January 2011).

Van Selm, J., 'Access to Procedures: "Safe Third Countries", "Safe Countries of Origin" and "Time Limits"' (paper commissioned by UNHCR and the Carnegie Endowment for International Peace, 2001).

Vedsted-Hansen, J., 'Non-admission Policies and the Right to Protection: Refugees' Choice versus States' Exclusion?', in F. Nicholson and P. Twomey (eds), *Refugee Rights and Realities: Evolving International Concepts and Regimes* (Cambridge: Cambridge University Press, 1999), 269–89.

The Modern Refugee in the Post-modern Europe

Patricia Tuitt

Introduction

It is a wise scholar who would look with suspicion upon conventional accounts of the causes behind any phenomenon, but the most prevalent hypotheses concerning the impetus behind early European integration will, I think, prove especially productive for the argument I wish to advance in this chapter. In summary, my contention is that the European Union will come into being as a fully fledged political and legal entity only with the complete disavowal of the refugee, as she is understood as both a sociological phenomenon and a legal term of art. To be more precise, when people who flee civil and political oppression, generalized violence or other catastrophic events are denied access in significant numbers to European Union member states, the constitutive force behind the European Union will be revealed. When the regime of rights developed under the Convention Relating to the Status of Refugees[1] no longer has currency within the Union, then (and only then) will we really *know* the European Union.

In common with all sovereign entities that have emerged in any epoch in history, the European Union will define itself through a radical break with what came before it. The European Union is a legal and political community that has been fashioned from previously governed and extensively populated territories of Europe and it can only truly enter history when it has transcended not merely the political, economic and social structures characteristic of the 'old order' of Europe, but when it has surpassed or overborne those individuals or groups who are perceived as uniquely representing that old order.

As so many accounts of the legal nature of the European Union have convincingly argued, the European Union is not a political community born of the old modern world from which the nation-state form was produced but, rather, is an entity that is ambitiously post-national[2] – one that gestures towards a *post-modern* future. Posed thus, the European Union is an entity that is necessarily in tension with the putatively modern world of the nation state.

Conventional accounts of the emergence of the European Union are faithful in depicting the process of its emergence in tension with the old nation state, but there most accounts stop.

1 28 July 1951, 189 UNTS 150.

2 For example, Neil MacCormick, 'Beyond the Nation State', *Modern Law Review*, 56(1), 1993, 1–18.

To complete the description and analysis of the European Union's emergence onto the stages of the world, there must exist equally faithfully accounts of the European Union's emergence in tension with individuals or groups made to symbolize the old nation state form and more generally the modern world within which that form developed.

Controversially, perhaps, counter-intuitively even, I argue that the refugee is the symbol of the old order that the European Union seeks to transcend. Thus the repudiation of the refugee is the act that signals also the transcendence of the nation state. I would not be so confident as to argue that the refugee exclusively symbolizes the old order as that would be to ignore other groups sacrificed to the ambitious of the European Union – the economic migrant, the resident non-national and so on. In my account, then, the refugee is not the sole but the *principal* signifier of the bankrupt old order of Europe.

The Beginnings of the European Union

To summarize the popular way of relating the history of the so-called 'road to Europe', we learn that the 'new' Europe arose as a consequence of a desire to surpass the nation-state: the conflict and violence it spawned and its obsolete economic structures.

The constitutional lawyer Sionaidh Douglas-Scott captures the popular rendering of the impetus behind integration in her conclusion that the 'European initiative' sought to 'recover from' the 'economic' and 'political' 'bankruptcy' of the 'old order of Europe',[3] the 'old order' being 'the division of Europe into national sovereign states'.[4]

Peter Fitzpatrick has observed that discussion of the European Union's emergence frequently emphasizes what he described as the 'badness' of 'nation', and Douglas-Scott's account of the historical development of the European Union (which is, in turn, strongly characteristic of dominant accounts) offers an example of the tendency Fitzpatrick identifies in the literatures.[5]

Significant for our account is that emphasis on what is bad or, to deploy Fitzpatrick's term, 'savage' about the state that preceded the emergence of a new legal and political order is not unique to discourses around the European Union but is a discernible feature of the discourses surrounding the emergence of other sovereign entities at different times and in different locations, especially so during the most intense period of the assertion of colonial sovereignty during the sixteenth to nineteenth century. Only in relatively recent years have scholars exposed how important to the emergence of sovereign powers was the presentation

---

3 Sionaidh Douglas-Scott, *Constitutional Law of the European Union*, Pearson Education, 2002, 19.

4 D. Weigall and P. Stirk (eds), The *Origins and Development of the European Community*, Lancaster: Lancaster University Press, 1992, 29–32, cited in Douglas-Scott, *Constitutional Law of the European Union*, at 19. See also P. Craig and G. de Burca, *EU Law: Text, Cases and Materials*, Oxford: Oxford University Press, 2007, 3–4; E.B. Haas, *Beyond the Nation State*, Stanford, CA: Stanford University Press, 1964; D. Urwin, *The Community of Europe: A History of European Integration*, London and New York: Longman, 1995.

5 P. Fitzpatrick, *Modernism and the Grounds of Law*, Cambridge University Press: Cambridge, 2001, 137.

of alternative ways of political belonging as 'bad', savage' or 'warlike'.[6] Entirely in keeping with the history of sovereign emergence, the European Union could not have emerged other than against a backdrop of chaos and disorder. The project of European integration could only move forward on the basis of a determined looking *back* upon a savage wasteland in need of modernization. Again, in a distressingly familiar vein, the modernization of Europe – the overcoming of the 'bad' nation state – was to be achieved through the migration and settlement of people, initially offering services and work[7]– and through the movement of goods and capital. Would anyone familiar with the history of sovereign constituting be surprised to learn that the 'savage', 'bankrupt' 'estate' of the old order in Europe was reconstructed into the post-modern New Europe in much the same way that migration and the free play of the primary units of production transformed purportedly 'weak' or 'savage' 'bankrupt' lands in other historical periods and geographical locations?

It is its emergence from within a discursive terrain that juxtaposes the savage and the civil (the good post-nation Union with the bad nation-state) strongly evident in all forms which speak about the European Union's history, presence and future that betrays its origins within a far from *sui generis* process of sovereign emergence. More pertinently, this is a discursive terrain that captures individuals and groups and on whom, as a consequence of this capturing, is meted the ultimate violence – that of threatened extinction. It would hardly be a novel claim if I were to assert that the very *survival* of the refugee – the legal category and the sociological phenomenon – lies in the balance within the European Union. My contribution to discussion of the position of the refugee within the European Union is simply to offer the view that it is within a broader history of the emergence of sovereign entities that we might look to understand why the refugee's existence is threatened – in the faint hope that the spiralling progress towards the complete disavowal of the refugee within the European Union might be halted.

So, this would not be the first time that the figure of the refugee is advanced to expose the European Union's claim to a place somewhere beyond the violence of sovereign constituting, which first Walter Benjamin and then Jacques Derrida spoke of so evocatively.[8] However, I hope to add something to such accounts by situating more precisely the place of the refugee and of international refugee law in the purported transition of Europe in time and space: its transition, not from a pre-modern to modern state of existence – the time-shift that migratory settlements during the 'age of discovery' sought to bring about. For the purposes of this argument, I am content to adopt the grand claims of some European constitutional lawyers and speak of the transition of Europe from the modern to the post-modern.[9] I suggest that this

6 Ibid.

7 With the advent of the legal concept of European Union citizenship, the free movement of persons within the European Union is no longer solely for the purpose of work or services or other forms of economic activity.

8 Walter Benjamin, 'Critique of Violence', in M. Steger and N. Lind (eds), *Violence, Identity and Self-determination*, Stanford, CA: Stanford University Press, 1997; Jacques Derrida, 'Force of Law: The Mystical Foundations of Authority', in J. Derrida and G. Anidjor (eds), *Acts of Religion*, New York and London: Routledge, 2002, 228–99.

9 '[T]he institutional, juridical and spatial (complexes) associated with the community ... constitute nothing less than the first truly post-modern international political form': J.G. Ruggie, 'Territoriality and Beyond: Problematizing Modernity in International Relations', *International*

place is to be found in the contemporary staging of the opposition between the 'progressive' and 'reactionary',[10] or as Balbar would have it, the 'universalistic and progressive' and the 'particularistic and primitive',[11] or the 'ordered' and 'dynamic' and the 'chaotic, static and backward'.[12] This is an opposition that has constituted and authorized virtually every sovereign entity at the most crucial moments of its emergence and is one that is constantly invoked as the European Union seeks to separate itself from the 'old order' of the arrangement of nation-states.[13]

When we hear talk of the 'vicious circle of violence' that 'followed' the sovereign state,[14] or of the old order that held 'calamitous' political structures,[15] or of the state form that was immersed in a 'repetitive pattern of bloody conflict',[16] we see, I suggest, the *grounds* on which the EU asserts its identity. The European Union consolidates itself through a confrontation with its 'others', such as the refugee. It is a human subject that must make concrete the depiction of a 'vicious circle of violence'. It is a human subject in which is embodied the conflicts that the new order seeks to bury and transcend. The evocative descriptions of the development of the European Union from the long road of travel through the nation state have no currency as mere words on the page but only as referents to a concrete *someone*. The 'calamitous' structures of the old order of Europe can only be really understood, *experienced* through the embodiment of chaos or crisis in *someone*. This someone (this *refugee)* is constructed, by the same discursive practices through which the fundamental opposition between the good and the bad, the savage and the civil is configured, as uniquely representing the now utterly discredited 'old order'. Such, I suggest, is the place of the refugee within the European Union – stubbornly attached to the old modern world, antagonistic towards the 'new' post-modern Europe.

Of course, many others before me have argued that the European Union asserts itself against certain 'excluded others', within which grouping the refugee occupies a special place. Interrogating the highly elusive character of the European identity, many argue that it is an identity that is negatively constructed. It is the refugee and the resident non-national in particular around whom this negative imagining of Europe and the 'European' identity coheres.

I am pushing the particular trajectory of inquiry that these discussions of Europe's 'others' have opened out, perhaps to its furthest limit. For me, the refugee is more than one of Europe's others: that is, more than one of a number of identifiably non-Europeans against

Organisation, 1993, 4(1), 139–74. See also I. Ward, *A Critical Introduction to European Law*, London: Butterworths, 1996.

10 Fitzpatrick, *Modernism and the Grounds of Law*, at 137.

11 E. Balibar, 'Racism and Nationalism', trans. Chris Turner, in E. Balibar and I. Wallerstein (eds), *Race, Nation, Class: Ambiguous Identities*, London: Verso, 1991, 37–67.

12 Fitzpatrick, *Modernism and the Grounds of Law*, at 125.

13 'What is especially significant here ... is that the EU and its law are formed and exalted as epitomes of the universal and the progressive in opposition to the reactionary realms of the nation', Fitzpatrick, *Modernism and the Grounds of Law*, at 136–7.

14 Douglas-Scott, *Constitutional Law of the European Union*, at 9.

15 Ibid.

16 S. Weatherill, *Law and Integration in the European Union*, Oxford: Clarendon Press, 1995, 1–2.

which a 'default'[17] definition of Europe's is being constructed. She is the human remnant in the European Union of the nation-state form, the principal signifier of the 'bankrupt' old order. It is surely instructive in this regard that the only refugee who can come to the European Union secure in the knowledge that a safe haven exists has been endowed with all the negative attributes of the old European order. It is the refugee who suffers persecution on account of her or his nationality, religion, race, social group membership or political opinion who is accorded the reluctant hospitality of member states within the European Union. As critics of the asylum regime have consistently argued, these are not the forms of injury characteristic of contemporary refugee-producing phenomena. A genuine attempt on the part of European Union member states to offer territorial asylum to a fair proportion of the world's refugees would, thus, see a more expansive legal definition of refugee. Yet the pre-eminence of the Geneva Convention definition of refugee status remains, and what remains also, what inheres in the concept of refugee-hood (as understood within the European Union), are those forms of injury for which the nation-state is famed. And so, by dint of a progressive reduction of the phenomenon of refugee-hood to the Geneva Convention definition, the refugee enters the European Union burdened with all the attributes of nation. Being so endowed, the refugee is *necessary* to the European Union, but necessary only insofar as she operates to remind all of the chaos that threatens if the new order of the post-modern and post-national European Union is not embraced fully. Thus the old, bankrupt condition of the nation-state and the refugee are inextricably linked – one cannot be overborne without the simultaneous disavowal of the other. In the contemporary staging of the opposition between the primitive and advanced state, the 'progressive' and the 'reactionary', the refugee occupies the position of the 'wandering tribes', deemed 'primitive in their social being' – the 'chaotic, static and backward',[18] who were displaced in the settlement of the 'new world'.

The Modernism of the Refugee

My references (rather oblique and passing so far) to the 'new world' and the 'golden age of discovery' are no accident. Not unlike the emergence of state in the so-called Age of Discovery, post-war Europe saw, in the wasteland of its political structures and its inefficient and obsolete economic forms, a 'new beginning', a 'New Europe' to be 'discovered' by its model citizens.[19] It must here be understood that in the emergence of the European Union we do not see coming into play a political form without historical precedent – contrary to what so many EU legal scholars and political theorists assert. We see instead in brutal operation an apparently old

[17] Shore, C., 1996. "Imagining the New Europe: Identity and Heritage in European Community Discourse", in Paul Graves-Brown, Sian Jones and Clive Gamble (eds.), Cultural Identity and Archaeology: The Construction of European Identities, London: Routledge: 96–15.

[18] Fitzpatrick, *Modernism and the Grounds of Law*, at 136–7.

[19] For further elaboration, see P. Tuitt, 'From the State to the Union: International Law and the Appropriation of the New Europe', in F. Johns, R. Joyce and S. Pahuja, *Events: The Force of International Law*, Glasshouse: Routledge, 2011, 177–91, and P. Tuitt, 'Used Up and Misused: The State, The European Union and the Insistent Presence of the Colonial', *Columbia Journal of Race and Law*, 2011, 1(3), 490–99.

logic: an entity that is perceived to be 'spent' (as was 'old Europe'), to have reached the limits of its political and economic possibilities, is to be conceived a '*terra nullius*', ready to be placed 'on a new scene'.[20] It is in the exercise of the grant of free movement (which European citizens have always being able to call to command) that this figuratively 'empty space' is filled and thereby radically altered. The European citizen who can exercise the famed four freedoms is, in the very exercise of those freedoms, the new post-modern citizen, empathizing exactly with the ambitions of the post-modern European Union. Those without the freedom to work, proffer services, transport goods and transfer capital exist, at best, with the rights and freedoms associated with the old modern world.

It is now almost folklore that refugee rights have been virtually stripped of all meaning in the securing of the European Union of its external borders, making around Europe a 'fortress' against the incursion of migration from third states, including refugee migration. The freedom of movement of the European Union citizen is made a concrete reality against the relative curtailment of freedom of movement of the refugee. If the European citizen represents the 'progressive' new world, the refugee is made to represent the now discredited 'old' world. So, when she is denied territorial asylum, she is not so much told that she does not suffer but rather that her suffering (like that of so many before who have been sacrificed to other political revolutions) is a result of her failure to *be modern* (or in the case of the refugee *vis-à-vis* the Union) – to be *post-modern*.

We have, through a deliberate process of construction, elements or aspects on which I shall attempt to elaborate below, a thoroughly modern refugee residing in an avowedly post-modern Europe.

As Goodwin-Gill reminded us so long ago, as regards Western Europe at least, the term 'refugee' speaks not to a sociological phenomenon but to a legal term of art.[21] This legal construct has been put to various tasks in the old Europe but it is how the refugee is deployed in the service of New Europe that interests us here. The refugee is made to represent all that in the New European space has supposedly been left behind. Towards the New Europe and in sharp distinction with the New European citizen, the refugees' sufferings are relegated to a distant past, and being so relegated, serve to accent the 'primitive' mode of existence, which is the refugees'.

There are so many ways in which the European Union's ambitions are at odds with its presentation of the refugee, but I want to focus here on the European Union's most enduring claim: to have reached a state of high advancement in terms of its ability to secure fundamental civil and political rights.

20 Fitzpatrick, *Modernism and the Grounds of Law*, at 161–2.

21 Guy S. Goodwin-Gill and Jane McAdam, *The Refugee in International Law*, Oxford: Clarendon Press, 2007.

Human Rights and the European Union

The Union, we are told, is founded on the principles of 'liberty, democracy and respect for human rights and fundamental freedoms'.[22] Accession of new members to the EU is premised upon proof of a commitment to fundamental rights principles.[23] Since ratification of the Treaty of Amsterdam, the community legislature was empowered to take 'all appropriate action to combat discrimination based on sex, racial or ethnic origin, religion or belief, disability, age or sexual orientation'.[24] As far back as the early 1990s member states of the European Union have benefited from a presumption that they are 'safe' states for the purposes of the determining whether a prima facie case of a 'well-founded fear of persecution' within the meaning of Article 1.A(2) of the Convention Relating to the Status of Refugees, 1951 has been established. The jurisprudence of the Court of Justice of the European Union has seen the continuous reaffirmation of fundamental rights principles, such as the right to privacy and protection from inhuman and degrading treatment, forming 'an integral part of the general principles of community law protected by the courts of justice'.[25] Not content with that, the Union acceded to the ECHR with the coming into force of the Reform Treaty (Treaty of Lisbon).[26]

The symbolic work that this network of norms, principles, declarations and actions in relation to fundamental human rights undertakes is readily apparent, particularly as regards those concepts such as the safe country of origin that allude to the propensity of members of the European Union to cause or sanction breaches of fundamental rights. These norms and principles are unashamedly declaratory in nature. They do not set out particular aspirations, but purport instead to be indicative of the status quo prevailing in the European Union in which a supposedly advanced state of human dignity and security has been achieved. It is not so much said that those residing within the internal sphere of the European Union will be protected from assaults to their civil and political rights, as it is confidently proclaimed that neither citizen nor resident non-citizen can justifiably fear encroachment on these rights. The post-modern space of the European Union is presented as one in which its inhabitants need no longer fear assaults on their fundamental rights, particularly against their first-generation (the term itself suggestive of a somewhat remedial state) civil and political rights, and can instead concentrate on exploiting the free movement rights essential to achieve the primary goal of European integration, which was to 'place' Europe 'on a new scene'.[27]

The point, then, is that the European Union, through a series of legal manoeuvres (largely brought about by the Court of Justice of the European Union) has positioned breaches of fundamental civil and political rights as an arcane feature of an old order. It is in this light that the fact that the only refugee who comes to the European Union with a legal claim to territorial asylum is invested with these arcane features reveals its deep significance. Within the European Union, the refugee's supposed 'primitive' status is accented by his/her (almost)

22 The main provisions are contained in the Treaty of European Union Common Principles, Articles 1 and 6 especially.

23 Treaty of European Union.

24 The provision is now to be found in Article of the Treaty on the Functioning of the European Union.

25 See case 11/70 *Internationale Handelsgesellschaft* (1970), ECR 1125.

26 Treaty of European Union.

27 Fitzpatrick, *Modernism and the Grounds of Law*, at 161–2.

exclusive reliance upon, and identification with, fundamental civil and political rights that, seen from the vantage point of the ambitions of the EU, belong to a different (and less progressive) political time.

One straightforward indication that the post-modern aspirations of the European Union demand that it presents assaults on fundamental rights as an arcane product of an old order, located somewhere beyond the New European space, is one that several human rights commentators have dawn attention to: the sharp demarcation when 'promoting and applying' fundamental rights principles that the EU draws between its external and internal policies. The EU, it is said, exhibits 'greater willingness to promote and enforce human rights – through forms of conditionality, including the use of negative sanctions – in its external policies than in its internal policies'.[28] An alternative formulation of the same criticism asserts that 'the problem of double-standards between what it expects of itself and its members on the one hand and what it demands of countries outside the EU on the other hand, remains a serious one'.[29] In the other areas of EU competence where inconsistencies between principle and practice have been observed, that is, in 'the fields of asylum, immigration, criminal justice and anti-terrorism',[30] the external/internal dichotomy is equally marked. Indeed, as far back as the establishment of the Trevi group in 1979, organized crime and terrorism were grouped with irregular migration as *external* forces that threatened the *internal* security of the European Union.

Although compelling, these examples of the European Union's distinction between its internal and external spheres in its treatment of fundamental rights principles and their application do not form the primary basis of my claim that, in pursuit of its desire to fully transcend the nation-state arrangement that structured old Europe, the European Union presents itself as having transcended the era of human rights. Rather, the true evidence, I suggest, that the European Union (as expressed through its various organs, particularly the ECJ) views fundamental rights principles as mere artefacts of a past condition is to be found at the seemingly more radical moments of the application of these human rights principles. Somewhat counter-intuitively, perhaps, the moments when we can justifiably claim that the EU is, to coin a phrase, not 'taking rights seriously'[31] (because it need not, because these rights have no salience in the internal sphere) are when its Court produces apparently controversial judgments, such as its recent decision in *Carpenter*,[32] which, ostensibly at least, brought the EU in conflict with its members in the delicate and politically sensitive area of immigration policy. In *Carpenter*, the ECJ granted effective rights of permanent residence in the UK to third-country national family members of an EU citizen. It is when we question (as I shall do in relation to *Carpenter*) how such a decision became possible that we can begin to see how the European Union presents itself as having effectively 'passed' the modernist phase of fundamental rights and, importantly, how the refugee is deployed in support of this claim.

---

[28] Craig and De Burca, *EU Law*, at 407.

[29] Ibid., at 408.

[30] Ibid., at 380.

[31] Alluding to the title of Jason Coppel and Aidan O'Neil's influential article, 'The European Court of Justice: Taking Rights Seriously?', *Legal Studies*, 12(2), 1992, 227–39.

[32] C-60/00 Mary Carpenter v Secretary of State for the Home Department [2002]. ECR I-6279.

The case of *Carpenter* concerns an application under Article 49EC (now Article 56TFEU[33]), which governs the free movement of services. The applicant, Mrs Carpenter, was a Filipino national, married to a British citizen. The case was brought to the European Court of Justice (now Court of Justice of the European Union) following a decision to deport her from the UK. The issue before the Court was whether the applicant's deportation would adversely affect the ability of her husband to exercise his rights under Article Ex 49. His business involved the provision of advertising support services to businesses established in other member states of the EU. He was resident in the UK, but his work necessitated frequent travel to other EU states. The UK courts concluded that the issue was a wholly internal one because, being resident in the UK, the applicant's husband was not exercising any freedom of movement provided for under the Treaty.

The ECJ refused to accept the UK court's interpretation of this situation as wholly internal and thus governed by domestic laws. It concluded that because a 'significant proportion' of Mr Carpenter's business consisted of cross-border services 'carried on both within the member state of origin for the benefit of persons established in other member states, and within those states',[34] he was exercising his rights under Article Ex 49EC. Concluding that deportation of Mrs Carpenter would inhibit the exercise of this right, as the couple's 'separation ... would be detrimental to their family life and therefore to the conditions under which Mr. Carpenter exercises a fundamental freedom', 'that freedom could not be fully effective if Mr. Carpenter were to be deterred from exercising it by obstacles raised in the country of origin to the entry and residence of his spouse'.[35] On the relevance of fundamental rights, the Court had this to say:

> Article 49 of the EC Treaty, read in the light of the fundamental right to respect for family life, is to be interpreted as precluding ... a refusal by the member state of origin of a provider of services established in that member state who provides services to recipients established in other member states, of the right to reside in its territory to that provider's spouse, who is a national of a third country.

Carpenter provides authority for the proposition that, in order to comply with European Union law, a domestic court must consider whether removing the non-EU national is a proportionate action, in line with fundamental rights principles, for to deny residence could breach the right to family life as enshrined within Article 8 of the ECHR.

Carpenter is less remarkable for the decision arrived at than for the mathematical precision with which the human rights formula was applied to produce the not inconsiderable personal rights that the applicant was granted. What enabled the fearless application of the Article 8 principles in this case was less a sense that the European Union space was one constitutive of and by fundamental rights, but the fact that external border security surveillance has achieved

[33] Treaty on the Functioning of the European Union.

[34] Case C-60/00 11 July 2002. Mary Carpenter v Secretary of State for the Home Department, PARA 37.

[35] Case C-60/00 11 July 2002. Mary Carpenter v Secretary of State for the Home Department, PARA 37.

a level of containment of third-country nationals to locations outside the European Union area, such that the reach and consequence of human rights norms that might be applied in relation to the relatively few third-country nationals that come to the EU are entirely calculable. So, what might at first sight appear a bold intervention in the domestic immigration sphere in the furtherance of human rights principles evidences instead that fundamental rights principles have never entered the European Union as 'higher' law or 'higher' principle, but always as mere rational legalism. As Coppell and O'Neil observed in their oft-cited article on the 'instrumental' use of rights principles by the ECJ,[36] there was never a time in the evolution of the EU in which human rights were at odds with institutional interests and objectives.[37] According to Douzinas, human rights 'earned' their 'status' as 'higher law' 'as a result of their legal universalism'[38]. Yet, if we take seriously Fitzpatrick's suggestion that the European 'union claims of itself the universal and the nation-state a regressive particularism',[39] it is hard to see how the European Union can recognize a 'higher law' in a concept of rights so intrinsically state centred. And, of course, the ECJ in all its judgments consistently refuses to accord the status of 'higher law' to fundamental rights, as to do so would be to undermine the principle of the supremacy of EU law – human rights inhere in EU law; they can neither be seen as apart from or elevated above EC Treaty norms and secondary principles.

If the anticipation/fear of the 'unintended consequences' sometimes attendant upon an application of human rights principles is the force that ensured that they were once 'taken seriously', then within the European Union the very conditions under which human rights principles are articulated, in the course of adjudication and in the development of the EU constitution and its substantive areas of competence, are certain to quell the more radical possibilities of their application. Instead, the moments of high anxiety, the moments when rights are taken seriously, the moments of judicial creativity, the most important legal innovations of the ECJ, the moments of building for the future are poised towards the development of the free movement rights that its model European citizens enjoy. To summarize, human rights and the nation-state form, being inextricably linked, prompt the EU institutional organs to demonstrate that they (and by extension the European Union) have transcended the state form. This is achieved partly by demonstrating that the era of human rights is effectively surpassed, especially the first generation of fundamental civil and political rights.

It is against the European Union's certainty that it has moved beyond a period in which civil and political rights hung in the balance that we revisit the refugee within that same Union. This refugee is, surely by reason of more than accident, fixed into the legal frame developed with the Geneva Convention, and this frame is one that can only do its work by prioritizing civil and political rights above other push factors behind forced refugee migration. It must be understood that it is not through chance but by a series of political and legal manoeuvres that

---

[36] 'The European Court of Justice'.

[37] In a similar vein, but in relation to the national sphere, Douzinas remarks: 'when human rights and national interests coincide, governments become their greatest champions'; see C. Douzinas, *The End of Human Rights: Critical Legal Thought at the Turn of the Century*, Oxford: Hart, 2000, at 119.

[38] Ibid., at 116.

[39] P. Fitzpatrick, 'New Europe and Old Stories: Mythology and Legality in the European Union', in P. Fitzpatrick and J. Bergeron (eds), *Europe's Other: European Law Between Modernity and Postmodernity*, Aldershot: Ashgate, 1998, 27–47.

the European Union has all too successfully reduced the phenomenon of refugee-hood to a single conception of a refugee, which is contained in Article 1.A(2) of the Convention Relating to the Status of Refugees, 1951.

In wording that is all too familiar, this refugee must establish that he or she,

> Owing to a well-funded fear of being persecuted for reasons of race, religion, nationality, membership in a particular social group or political opinion, is outside the country of his nationality and is unable or, owing to such fear, is unwilling to avail himself of the protection of that country, or who, not having a nationality and being outside the country of his former habitual residence, as a result of such events, is unable or, owing to such fear, is unwilling to return to it.[40]

The Convention definition of refugee is the only one that is binding on the entire international community. Yet the association of the idea of the refugee solely as one stripped of civil and political rights is not an inevitable one. There are several different legal definitions of a refugee that do not limit themselves to defining status on the basis of civil and political status, and which are binding in other parts of the globe, notably the Organization of African Unity definition, which includes, but extends beyond, the persecution standard adopted under the Convention Relating to the Status of Refugees, 1951, and accords status to refugees also able to show that they are escaping situations of 'external aggression, occupation, foreign domination or events seriously disturbing public order in either part or the whole of his country of origin or nationality'. This competing definition has had some measure of success in extending territorial protection to individuals fleeing 'generalized' violence; arguably indeed it has influenced Council Directive 2004/85EC concerning the status of persons who, though not refugees within the terms of the Geneva Convention, 'otherwise need international protection'.[41] However, in spite of recent EU initiatives, the pre-eminence of the Geneva Convention refugee in determining the direction of asylum policy remains.

The Modern Refugee in the Post-modern European Union

Here, then, is a concrete site in which the refugee (reduced entirely to a modernist human rights category of international law) is exposed as an *impossible* post-modern category. The refugee's demand for territorial protection from threats to personal safety and dignity or freedom of speech strikes a jarring note within an institutional setting that all but denies the salience of human rights norms and principles within its internal sphere. In such a setting

40 Note 1 above.

41 Council Directive 2004/85/EC of 19 April 2004, on Minimum Standards for the Qualification and Status of Third Country Nationals or Stateless Persons as Refugee or as Persons who Otherwise need International Protection and the Convent of the Protection Granted (2004), OJ L 304 12.

Douzinas's fear that 'human rights have become the realised myths of post-modern societies'[42] assumes particular significance.

So, it follows from the foregoing that I see no correspondence between European Union free movement rights that heralded the post-national European Union and those more familiar human rights norms. No reading, however sympathetic, of the 'four freedoms', the free movement of persons, goods, capital and services – the axis on which the European Union's economic constitution revolves – can equate them with the three generations of rights, 'civil and political, economic, social and cultural and group rights' [43] that 'entered the world scene after the Second World War'.[44]

If we accept that the invocation of the free movement right of Union citizens, as represented in the Rome Treaty, was the inaugural event of the EU, then those 'four freedoms' of the Rome Treaty are the articulated evidence of the coming into being of a new sovereign entity in a far from radical departure from the modes, forms and processes through which other sovereign entities have emerged throughout history. As such, the four freedoms *per se* are neither a subset of modernist human rights, nor post-modern economic rights, but, as constitutive of a sovereign claim, exceed the opposition between the pre-modern and the modern, the modern and the post-modern, the progressive and the reactionary. Those oppositions are instead precisely brought about by the inaugural event, which heralds a new polity and new law.

Human rights, however, as Douzinas argues in his genealogy,[45] 'are both creations and creators'[46] of modernity. Their 'modern' character is evident most particularly in their integral relation to the state form of the modern world. Human rights propelled 'human nature' to a 'sovereign and unfettered' state, and so heralded its 'counterpoint ... which shares in all particulars the characteristics of the undivided singular free will of the individual and literalises his metaphorical unlimited power. The sovereignty of unstructured free will finds its perfect compliment and mirror image in the sovereignty of the state'.[47]

It is this necessary joining of the sovereign state with the sovereign individual bearer of rights that makes the near 40-year period since the Court of Justice of the European Union acknowledged fundamental rights as a primary source of European law a particularly important context for this analysis of the European Union's progressive march against the regressive strains of the old order, and, crucially, how this struggle is displaced on to the figure of the refugee.

The strict adherence to the Convention definition assures the containment of the refugee phenomenon;[48] it refuses (as James Hathaway observed) to 'translate refugee law to meet the realities of the developing world'.[49] Perhaps more charitably, it also recognizes that not all refugee-producing phenomena can be addressed through the grant of cross-border territorial asylum but must be dealt with at the place of origin. What adherence also ensures – and the

[42] Douzinas, *End of Human Rights*, 8.

[43] Ibid., 115.

[44] Ibid.

[45] Ibid., part 1.

[46] Ibid., at 19.

[47] Ibid., at 20.

[48] For general discussion, see S. Juss, *International Migration and Global Justice*, Aldershot: Ashgate, 2006: 187–219.

[49] J. Hathaway, *The Law of Refugee Status*, Toronto: Butterworths, 1991.

point that follows is of utmost importance for this thesis – is that when the refugee comes to the European Union she/he is positioned from the moment of her/his arrival (indeed prior to her arrival as she exists in the legal and political imagining) as belonging irresistibly and intractably to a different historical time – a time which narratives of the emergence of the EU locate with the nation-state, a time that, to recall the narratives concerning the impetus behind European integration with which this chapter commenced, the European Union's very existence was called into being to oppose and eventually to transcend.

Into this space in which human rights abuses are relegated to a dark past comes the refugee – her regressive state made real because she is engaged in struggles or conflicts that have been overcome by those in a seemingly more progressive state.[50] She, I suggest, more than any other sociological group or legal construct, has been made to represent all the failings of the nation state that the EU seeks to overcome and eventually to relegate to memory.

The refugee's pursuit of basic human rights – the rights that created and were created by the 'old' modern world – into the new post-modern space that the EU strives to occupy – reveals that the relation between the old and the new, the progressive and the reactionary, is always one of imminent proximity. The remnants of the 'calamitous violence' of the nation state are not to be found in the EU organs that can confidently assert that neither of its diverse members would either produce or threaten the life or safety of a refugee, or whose legal principles (always already included fundamental rights principles), they are not to be found in the economically courageous and astute European citizen as she enjoys her various 'freedoms', they are found instead in the 'profoundly state-centred' refugee law regime and the victim of the disorderly or 'failed' state. In an attempt to deny her enduring proximity, her numbers are reduced, and her incompatibility with the new order constantly underscored.

Conclusion

This chapter ends with a paradox. If, as the foregoing analysis argues, the refugee *vis-à-vis* the European Union is the most visible remnant of the nation state, she is, as other writers have shown, also the nation state's most vociferous critic.

Writing of the refugee condition in an essay towards the end of the *Origins of Totalitarianism*,[51] Hannah Arendt argued that the refugee brings forth consciousness of the essential illusion at the centre of international human rights regimes that purport to attach such rights to 'man's' 'naked existence', outside the political community of the state, but fails the only 'human' – the refugee – who can occupy that position. Commenting on the chapter, Giorgio Agamben claimed that, in seeming to link together 'the fates of the rights of man and of the nation-state', Arendt selects the refugee as the 'figure … that … signals … the concept's radical crisis'.[52]

[50] For further analysis, see Tuitt, 'From the State to the Union', 69.

[51] Schocken Books, 1951. The essay is entitled, 'The Decline of the Nation-state and the End of the Rights of Man'.

[52] Giorgio Agamben, Homo Sacer: *Sovereign Power and Bare Life*, trans. Daniel Heller-Roazen, Stanford: Stanford University Press, 1998, at 126.

Should not then the refugee be the European Union's greatest ambassador, as she was in the cold-war political divide of Eastern and Western Europe?

It would be a mistake to draw parallels between a conflict between 'equal enemies' and an assumption of authority over a 'primitive' (and therefore necessarily unequal) yet opposing force. In the latter relation, the hope of an alliance rests only in the possibility of the progress of the recalcitrant to a proper state of advancement. The refugee, constitutive of and constituted by the opposing of the primitive nation state and the progressive European Union, has, as I suggested earlier, been constructed as an impossible post-modern category, made to bear the burden of a failing community of which (as we learn from Arendt) she was never truly a part. The paradox of the refugee condition is that the refugee brings to bear the brutal materiality of the nation-state even to those depictions of nation in its 'invented', 'imagined' or 'fantastic' character.[53] And even in relation to those theoretical writings that pose the refugee as indicative of 'a new political consciousness, able to challenge the nexus of state, territory and identify',[54] the refugee, as in Agamben's writings, is, in his words, 'the only thinkable category for the people of our time'.[55]

As Agamben concedes in his reading of *Origins*, Arendt's text leaves 'open'[56] the question of whether Arendt, through the refugee, wished to assert the necessity of the state form if the position of 'rightlessness' that the refugee occupies is to be avoided. Others concerned with the protection of refugees are less equivocal over the question of the necessity of state protection for displaced persons. In the essay 'States and Refugees: A Normative Analysis', Joseph Carens argues that the normative justification for offering protection to refugees has less to do with the need to repel threats to international security posed by the irregular movement of people or with the ethical obligations of more fortunate states. He argues instead that the grant of asylum is a necessary gesture if the state system as a whole is to retain its legitimacy in the wake of the failure of individual sovereign states to extend adequate protection to its citizens or those ordinarily domiciled there.

The state system, according to Carens, is legitimated by the offer of surrogate protection by an asylum state. In much the same way that the system of adoption serves to legitimate the institution of the family by securing familial protection to children that their birth families fail to proffer, so an 'adopting' state compensates for the failings of other states, securing the system of states as a whole.

Thus the crisis that Arendt's 'country-less' refugee exposes – the crisis of a concept of human rights that respects not the person who has 'lost all other qualities and specific relations – except that they were still human',[57] is offset by the actions of another state in offering territorial asylum. For many theoretical accounts of the refugee, the state form is an unavoidable locus of criticism and analysis, although more contemporary accounts present the refugee as the figure that most emphatically calls into question the efficacy and ethicality of 'state' and points the way towards a new political consciousness.

---

53 Fitzpatrick, *Modernism and the Grounds of Law*, at 112.

54 P. Tuitt, 'Refugees, Nations, Laws and the Territorialisation of Violence', in P. Fitzpatrick and P. Tuitt, *Critical Beings: Law, Nation and the Global Subject*, Aldershot: Ashgate, 2004, 37–57.

55 Agamben, Giorgio (2000) *Means without End: Notes on politics*, trans. Vincenzo Binetti and Cesare Casarino (Minneapolis, London: University of Minnesota Press).

56 Ibid.

57 *Origins*, 299.

This new consciousness that Georgio Agamben has, in particular, been forward in advancing, is undoubtedly a post-*national* consciousness. It is, as stated earlier, the trinity of state, territory and identity that the refugee condition first indicts for all its exclusionary violence and then invites its dissolution/destruction. It is in this light that Agamben argues,

> The concept of the refugee (and the figure of the life the concept represents) must be resolutely separated from the concept of the rights of man, and we must seriously consider Arendt's claim that the fates of human rights and the nation-state are bound together such that the decline and crisis of the one necessarily implies the end of the other. The refugee must be considered for what he is: nothing less than a limit concept that radically calls into question the fundamental categories of the nation-state form, the birth-nation to the man-citizen link and that thereby makes it possible to clear the way for a long overdue renewal of categories in the service of politics in which bare life is no longer separated and excepted, either in the state order or in the figure of human rights.[58]

This, on the face of it, appears to be a somewhat formidable objection to my claim that the refugee comes into conflict with the EU precisely because s/he represents the nation-state that the EU claims by its very existence to have transcended. Taking this quote, one would be inclined to argue that, far from being the classic symbol of the regressive nation-state, Agamben's refugee faces the onslaught of the nation's ultimate form of violence – the estrangement from any political community – and thus compels the system of human rights to confront the weakness of its claim to be oriented toward the human *qua* human. Seen thus, the refugee is the only figure capable of performing the urgent task of 'renewal' of obsolete political categories.

Yet Agamben's faith in the refugee is misplaced, for as I have pointed out elsewhere, behind Agamben's utopian ideal lurks a concrete depiction of the refugee that is to effect this ambitious renewal, and that refugee, sadly, is too much bound to the 'nation of blood and soil' to do the work that Agamben sees as awaiting. It does not take much more than a cursory reading of that part of Agamben's text to discern that the refugee he alludes to is that seemingly ineradicable legal term of art: the refugee of the 'Nansen bureau (1921)', of the 'High Commission for Refugees 1936', of the 'Intergovernmental Committee of Refugees 1938', of the 'UN International Refugee Organisation 1946' and, finally, of the 'Office of the High Commission for Refugees 1951'.[59]

While acknowledging that the refugee is 'impossible to define politically',[60] Agamben condescends enough to allow the blunt juridical category to haunt his political imagination, but this is a refugee who is indisputably a state-centred territorial construct. It is a legal precondition that the refugee of the 'Office of the High Commission for Refugees 1951' must be outside the territories of his/her state of origin or domicile before international protection

58 Agamben, Homo Sacer, at 134.

59 Agamben, 2000, 18.

60 Agamben, Homo Sacer, 126.

applies. So, despite or perhaps because of his/her estrangement from territory, the refugee exists to constantly depict the nation as the territory of blood and soil.[61]

The juridical image of the refugee that holds a pre-eminent position within the European Union is so powerful that it is able to hypnotize so acute a political observer as Agamben. As I hope I have been able to show, its purchase is great in the European Union's effort to achieve that elusive state of high civilization, and so, wresting the refugee from the institution of asylum that the 1951 Convention established is a formidable task. My task here is less daunting. It is merely to present a plausible argument to the effect that, whether as mere victim or as strident critic of the system of states, it is difficult, if not impossible, to conceive of the refugee without confronting all too abruptly the materiality of nation. For refugees within a space that claims its legitimacy through the transcendence of the nation, this bodes ill.

References

Agamben, Giorgio, Homo Sacer: *Sovereign Power and Bare Life,* trans. Daniel Heller-Roazen, Stanford, Stanford University Press 1998.

Arendt, Hannah, *Origins of Totalitarianism,* New York: Schocken Books, 1951.

Balibar, E., 'Racism and Nationalism', trans. Chris Turner, in E. Balibar and I. Wallerstein (eds), *Race, Nation, Class: Ambiguous Identities,* London: Verso, [1991], 37–67.

Benjamin, Walter, 'Critique of Violence', in M. Steger and N. Lind (eds), *Violence, Identity and Self-determination,* Stanford: Stanford University Press, 1997, (57–69).

Coppel, Jason and Aidan O'Neil, 'The European Court of Justice: Taking Rights Seriously?', *Legal Studies,* 12(2), 1992, 227–39.

Craig, P. and G. de Burca, *EU Law: Text, Cases and Materials,* Oxford: Oxford University Press, 2007.

Derrida, Jacques, 'Force of Law: The Mystical Foundations of Authority', in J. Derrida and G. Anidjar (eds), *Acts of Religion,* New York and London: Routledge, 2002, (228–299).

Douglas-Scott, Sionaidh, *Constitutional Law of the European Union,*Dorchester]: Pearson Education, 2002.

Douzinas, C., *The End of Human Rights: Critical Legal Thought at the Turn of the Century,* Oxford: Hart, 2000.

Fitzpatrick, P., *Modernism and the Grounds of Law,* Cambridge: (Cambridge University Press), 2001.

Fitzpatrick, P., 'New Europe and Old Stories: Mythology and Legality in the European Union', in P. Fitzpatrick and J Bergeron (eds), *Europe's Other: European Law Between Modernity and Postmodernity,* Aldershot: Ashgate, 1998, 27–47.

Goodwin-Gill, Guy S. and Jane McAdam, *The Refugee in International Law,* Oxford: Clarendon Press, 2007.

Haas, E. B., *Beyond the Nation State,* Stanford, CA: Stanford University Press, 1964.

Hathaway, J., *The Law of Refugee Status,* Toronto: Butterworths, 1991.

61 Tuitt, P., 'Refugees, Nations, Laws and the Territorialisation of Violence', in P. Fitzpatrick and P. Tuitt (eds), *Critical Beings: Law, Nation and the Global Subject,* Aldershot: Ashgate, 2004.

Juss, S., *International Migration and Global Justice*, Aldershot: Ashgate, 2006.
MacCormick, Neil, 'Beyond the Nation State', *Modern Law Review*, 56(1), 1993, 1–18.
Ruggie, J. G., 'Territoriality and Beyond: Problematizing Modernity in International Relations', *International Organisation*, 4(1), 1993, 139–74.
Shore, Cris, 'Imagining the New Europe: Identity and Heritage in European Community', *Cultural Policy*, 28(4), 2000, 779–880.
Tuitt, P., 'From the State to the Union: International Law and the Appropriation of the New Europe', in F. Johns, R. Joyce and S. Pahuja (eds), *Events: the Force of International Law*, Abingdon: Routledge, 2011, 177–90.
Tuitt, P., 'Refugees, Nations, Laws and the Territorialisation of Violence', in P. Fitzpatrick and P. Tuitt (eds), *Critical Beings: Law, Nation and the Global Subject*, Aldershot: Ashgate, 2004, 37–57
Tuitt, P., 'Used Up and Misused: The State, The European Union and the Insistent Presence of the Colonial', *Columbia Journal of Race and Law*, VOL 1(3), 2011, 490–99.
Urwin, D., *The Community of Europe: A History of European Integration*, London and New York: Longman, 1995.
Ward, I., *A Critical Introduction to European Law*, London: Butterworths, 1996.
Weatherill, S., *Law and Integration in the European Union*, Oxford: Clarendon Press, 1995.
Weigall, D. and P. Stirk (eds), *The Origins and Development of the European Community*, Lancaster: Lancaster University Press, 1992.

EU Immigration and the New EU Treaty Framework

Elspeth Guild[1]

Introduction

The European Union finally adopted and ratified its new legal framework after ten years of difficult negotiation and reluctance on the part of some of its citizens. On 1 December 2009, two treaties replaced the rather heterogeneous group of treaties that formed the basis of the EU – the Treaty on the European Union and the Treaty on the Functioning of the European Union. Among the most startling of consequences of these two treaties is the formal end of the perplexing Pillar framework of the EU, with different policy areas subject to very different constitutional treatment. The so-called collapsing of the Pillars simplified matters for the Area of Freedom, Security and Justice, which for ten years between 1999 and 2009 unhappily straddled two Pillars but has now brought immigration, asylum and borders into one camp together with judicial cooperation in criminal matters, policing, terrorism and other rather heterogeneous subject matters. Nonetheless, the framework transforms EU immigration and policy in ways that became rapidly evident. In this chapter I shall outline some of these.

Fast on the heels of the Lisbon Treaty came the Stockholm Programme in December 2009, a five-year plan for the development of the EU's Area of Freedom, Security and Justice, within which the policy field of immigration lies. In this chapter, I shall examine what the entry into force of the Lisbon Treaty meant for EU immigration law and policy. In short, I shall make two main claims about the impact:

- The Lisbon Treaty lifts the limitation on access to the European Court of Justice by courts of all instances in the field of borders, immigration and asylum. This will bring about a dramatic acceleration of the harmonizing effect of EU law in this field.
- The Treaty gives legal force to the Charter of Fundamental Rights. This will be felt quickly in the immigration field if the experience of the European Court of Human Rights is indicative. Human and fundamental rights have become an important source of friction between Member States and third-country nationals (i.e. nationals of states outside the EU) that have moved beyond the national courts of the Member States.

---

1 Jean Monnet Professor *ad personam*, Radboud University, Nijmegen.

These areas where the impact of the Lisbon Treaty is likely to be highest in the field of immigration are also sensitive areas of sovereignty in a number of Member States and countries outside the EU. The front-page effect of EU immigration law is not likely to diminish over the following years.

The Lisbon Treaty and Powers in Respect of Immigration

The Lisbon Treaty is composed of two treaties (and their protocols and declarations). The first is the Treaty on the European Union (TEU), which contains the rules on how the EU operates. The TEU will be important when I come to consider the position of the Charter of Fundamental Rights in EU immigration. The other treaty that is part of the Lisbon Treaty package is the Treaty on the Functioning of the European Union (TFEU). The first step towards examining the Lisbon Treaty and immigration is to compare the previous powers and the new ones and ask the question, what has changed?

Title V, Chapter 2 TFEU sets out the competences of the Union on border checks, asylum and immigration. These remain fairly close to their earlier (pre-2009) position. Now the TFEU charges the Union with developing a common immigration policy aimed at ensuring, at all stages, the efficient management of migration flows, fair treatment of third-country nationals residing legally in the Member States, and the prevention of and enhanced measures to combat illegal immigration and trafficking in human beings (Article 79 TFEU).

In the Treaty on the European Community (TEC), which was replaced by the TFEU and TEU, the competence was slightly more limited to measures on conditions of entry and residence and standards on procedures for the issue of long-term visas and residence permits, including for family reunification. The EU had competence for illegal immigration and illegal residence, including repatriation of illegal residents and measures defining the rights and conditions under which nationals of third countries who are legally resident in a Member State may reside in other Member States (Article 63 TEC).

There are two differences that may be significant between the old and new treaties. In the earlier treaty there is no specific reference to fair treatment for third-country nationals legally residing in the EU, while now in the TFEU this is present. This wording comes from the first five-year plan for the implementation of the immigration powers of the EU adopted in Tampere, Finland in 1999. In the Tampere Milestones, for the first time the EU set out the objective of fair treatment of third-country nationals resident in the EU.[2] This objective has been widely repeated (although limited to the preambles) in much of the secondary legislation that the EU has adopted in the field of immigration such as the Long Term Residents' Directive[3] and the Family Reunification Directive.[4] The inclusion of the reference in the Treaty will have the effect of strengthening the importance of fair treatment and, indeed, this may become the subject of judicial scrutiny in due course.

2 See http://www.europarl.europa.eu/summits/tam_en.htm (accessed: 23 July 2012).

3 Directive 2003/109.

4 Directive 2003/86.

The second notable change relates to trafficking in human beings. Until the Lisbon Treaty collapsed the Pillars of the EU, this competence had remained in the somewhat more intergovernmental third Pillar of the EU.[5] Article 29 (old) TEU provided that a high level of safety within the Area of Freedom, Security and Justice (the objective of the section) would be achieved by preventing and combating crime including trafficking in persons. This objective has now been subsumed into the TFEU competence that covers the field.

The TFEU focus on the efficient management of migration flows as an objective of immigration policy may have a further consequence of bringing the EU's policy on integrated border management closer to its rules on immigration.[6] The intersection of policies on visas, border control and controls within the territory of the Member States is a priority in this field. One of the difficulties, however, is how to align the two – to what extent should policies regarding admission at the EU's external frontier be linked closely with the treatment of third-country nationals once they have joined the labour force or a community in a Member State? Just before moving to how the pre-2009 powers have been exercised, it must be noted that Denmark does not participate in any of these measures according to a protocol to the previous treaty and renewed with the Lisbon Treaty. Ireland and the UK are entitled by virtue of a protocol to the previous treaty to opt into any measure in the field of immigration or to remain opted out of its effects. This protocol is transferred to the new treaty. Generally, they have opted out of the legal migration measures but into the asylum ones. The UK has opted into some of the irregular migration measures as well. By 2012 the UK had notified the Commission that it would not opt into most of the second-phase asylum measures.

What are the Existing EU Measures in Legal Immigration?

The power to adopt EU measures in the field of immigration was a novelty of the Amsterdam Treaty in 1999. Since then, in the area of legal migration, the EU had adopted ten measures,[7] of which four regulate the longer-term entry and residence of third-country nationals. Ireland and the UK have opted out of these measures. The first and most important measure is the

[5] For an excellent explanation of how the pillar structure worked in this field see S. Peers, *EU Justice and Home Affairs Law*, Oxford: OUP, 2006.

[6] Communication, *Preparing the Next Steps in Border Management* COM(2008), 69.

[7] 1. Regulation 1030/2002 on residence permit format (OJ 2002 L 157/1), amended by Reg. 330/2008 (OJ 2008 L 115/1).

2. Regulation 859/2003 on third-country nationals' social security (OJ 2003 L 124/1).

3. Directive 2003/86 on family reunion (OJ 2003 L 251/12): deadline Oct. 2005.

4. Long-term residents' Directive 2003/109 (OJ 2004 L 16/44): deadline Jan. 2006.

5. Directive 2004/114 on migration of third-country students, pupils, trainees and volunteers (OJ 2004 L 375/12): deadline 12 Jan. 2007.

6. Directive 2005/71 on admission of researchers (OJ 2005 L 289/15): deadline 12 Oct. 2007.

7. Recommendation on admission of researchers (OJ 2005 L 289/26).

8. Decision on asylum and immigration information exchange (OJ 2006 L 283/40).

9. Decision establishing European integration Fund (OJ 2007 L 168/18).

10. Directive 2009/50 on the conditions of entry and residence of third-country nationals for the purposes of highly qualified employment ('Blue Card' Directive) (OJ 2009 L 155/17).

Directive on Family Reunification. This was adopted in 2003 and had to be transposed by the Member States by October 2005. The objective of the Directive is to create a right to family reunification for third-country nationals who reside legally in the Member States. The way this is pursued is by establishing minimum standards for the admission and treatment of third-country national family members. Family reunification is an EU right, according to the Directive, for spouses and minor children. The conditions for its exercise are:

- stable and regular resources to support the family;
- adequate housing;
- comprehensive sickness insurance.

Member States are permitted to apply an integration measures condition to family members either before or after admission to the state. This is a derogation from the right to family reunification.[8]

In October 2008, the Commission published the first report on implementation of the Directive in the Member States (COM (2008) 610 final). The report reveals a number of weaknesses in the way in which Member States have transposed the Directive. Key among the problem areas are:

- Two Member States, AT and BE, require evidence of accommodation prior to entry of the family members, which can impose a considerable financial burden on the sponsor.
- Only half the Member States require the family to have sickness insurance.
- All Member States require evidence of stable and regular resources except SE. However, the modalities vary substantially. CY provides no precision on the meaning of the term, while FR, LU, RO and LT make reference to the minimum wage. The range of specified income goes from €120 in PL to €1,484 in NL.
- Three Member States, NL, DE and FR, apply integration measures before the family will be admitted to the Member State, though some categories are exempted (more Member States have subsequently added integration measures as a condition of residence).
- Four Member States (CZ, HU, LV and PL) do not have a specific procedure for family reunification but deal with this in the general immigration rules.
- All Member States except IT and PT require fees but these range from €35 in CZ and EE to €1,368 in NL.
- There are very substantial variations among the Member States regarding access to employment. In the Commission's view the national provisions in DE, HU and SI exceed what is permitted under the Directive.

In general, the Commission expressed concern that the Directive, which is aimed at creating a level playing field for third-country nationals' family reunification, in fact seems to be resulting in very substantial variations in access to the right. By 2011, the Court of Justice of the European Union (CJEU) had twice been required to consider the Directive, first at the request of the European Parliament that challenged three exceptional provisions in the

8 R. van Oers, E. Ersboll and D. Kostakopoulou (eds), *A Re-definition of Belonging? Language and Integration Tests in Europe*, The Hague: Brill, 2010.

Directive – a further one allowing Member States to exclude children over 12 years (provided that they had adopted legislation by the time of entry into force of the Directive); another allowing Member States to exclude children over 15 years; and one allowing Member States to delay family reunification for up to three years if existing legislation so provided at the time of entry into force. In the Parliament's view, these exceptions were of questionable human rights compatibility. The CJEU did not find any of the provisions specifically problematic, instead finding that it would be on the transposition by the Member States that attention needed to be focused.[9] In the event, as the Commission's report shows, only two Member States, Cyprus and Germany, used the exception to exclude children over 12 years (although the documents available regarding the negotiations indicate that it was the Netherlands that sought the exception). No Member States used the exception to exclude children over 15 years (which had been championed by Germany). However, the fact that the first challenge to the Directive was on the basis of human rights compatibility indicates the importance that the EU Charter of Fundamental Rights (which incorporates all the rights contained in the European Convention on Human Rights (ECHR)) is likely to have in this field. I shall return to this point later.

The CJEU was once again troubled by the Directive in respect of a reference from a Dutch court.[10] Here the key issues were twofold: what income could Member States require of a third-country national seeking family reunification with his or her spouse and what constitutes social assistance for the purposes of the Directive? The relevant Dutch law that transposed the Directive required a sponsor to have an income equivalent to 120 per cent of the minimum wage. However, Dutch law provided that there are two categories of social assistance – a lower level called general assistance, which is the minimum wage, and special assistance, which is the equivalent of 120 per cent of the minimum wage. Which level then was applicable for the application of the Directive? If only the general social assistance level, then the third-country national sponsor, Mr Chakroun's, income was sufficient; if the special assistance level applied, then it was not.

The problem was compounded by another specificity of Dutch law – where a couple marries before either of them moves to the Netherlands. Then the applicable rate for income for family reunification is the lower general assistance level. But if the couple marries after one of them has moved to the Netherlands (as Mr and Mrs Chakroun had done), then the higher special assistance level is applicable to the income requirement. The couple complained that this constituted unlawful discrimination in light of the Directive's objectives. The CJEU pointed out that the Directive creates a right of family reunification which an individual can rely upon. There is no margin of appreciation for the Member States. Because the Directive creates this, the conditions for the exercise of the right must be restrictively interpreted. Therefore the CJEU found:

- social assistance in the Directive has an EU meaning, not a national one, and it means 'social assistance granted by the public authorities, whether at national, regional or local level' (para. 45);
- 'stable and regular resources' must be determined by reference to social assistance (para. 46);

9 C-540/03 *Parliament v. Council* [2006] ECR I-5769.
10 C-578/08 *Chakroun*, 4 March 2010.

- the assessment of income must not undermine the objective of the Directive to promote family reunification (para. 47);
- the actual situation of each applicant must be examined as well as the threshold that the state has put into the regulations (para. 48);
- social assistance in the Directive is the level of general assistance only, not special assistance (para. 52);
- different income requirements that are dependent exclusively on where and when the couple married (or was formed) are by definition problematic and incompatible with the Directive (para. 51);
- the Directive does not permit a difference in income levels to be applied on the basis of when and where the marriage took place (i.e. either before or after one party migrated) (para. 66).

In other words, the Dutch legislation was found fully incompatible with the Directive. In its finding the CJEU relied not only on the European Convention on Human Rights for guidance but referred to the EU Charter of Fundamental Rights on numerous occasions as a source of interpretation.

The second substantial measure that the EU has adopted in this field is the Long Term Residents' Directive. A number of studies on the application of the Directive have been undertaken by academics, indicating substantial variations across the Member States.[11] The principle of the Directive is that any third-country national not coming within an excluded group (such as students or diplomats) who has resided lawfully in a Member State for five years will obtain a long-term residence status in EU law so long as three conditions are fulfilled:

- the individual fulfils the residential requirement;
- the individual has stable and regular resources to support him or herself and dependants;
- the individual has fully comprehensive sickness insurance.

However, similar to the Family Reunification Directive, a fourth condition may be applied by the Member States – that the individual complies with integration conditions. It is this requirement that has been the source of most concern among academic researchers regarding the implementation of the Directive.[12] Once an individual acquires EU long-term residence status under the Directive, this can only be lost in accordance with the terms of the Directive, which are very limited. Further, the person is entitled to full equal treatment with own nationals within the Member State where the status was acquired (with exceptions for political rights and economic activities which are not open to EU nationals). Finally, the status gives an entitlement to move and exercise activities, economic and otherwise, in other Member States subject to a (fairly limited) labour market conditions test in the second Member State and a potential delay of up to 12 months in accessing economic rights. As yet, there has been no reference to the CJEU regarding the correct interpretation of the Directive. If the cases that go

---

11 L. Halleskov, 'The Long Term Residents' Directive: A Fulfilment of the Tampere Objective of Near Equality?' *European Journal of Migration and Law* 7(5), 2005, 203–11.

12 E. Guild, K. Groenendijk and S. Carrera, *Illiberal Liberal States: Immigration, Citizenship and Integration in the EU*, Farnham: Ashgate, 2009.

to the ECHR are any indication of what are likely to be the issues of disagreement between state authorities and individual third-country nationals, it is likely to be the protections against expulsion that will need clarification soonest.

The Commission published its report on Member State implementation of the Directive in September 2011.[13] It reaffirms that the Directive is a crucial tool for achieving the promotion of integration and non-discrimination of third-country nationals. However, it notes that the Member States implementation leaves much to be desired. Among the key findings are the following:

- The personal scope: too many Member States incorrectly exclude third-country nationals from the scope of the Directive by designating as 'temporary' their residence status in circumstances where it is clear that this is not the case, as for instance in respect of low-skilled migrant workers, researchers, family members of third-country nationals and others (AT, CY, EL, IT, PL).
- Lawful residence: a third-country national qualifies for permanent residence under the Directive after five years' lawful residence: a number of Member States have defined too narrowly, in the opinion of the Commission, the meaning of lawful residence for the purpose of acquisition of rights under the Directive, thus reducing the number of persons eligible for protection (FR, IT, LU, SE, SK).
- Resources and sickness insurance: a requirement to obtain permanent status is that the individual has resources and sickness insurance; according to the Commission, too many Member States incorrectly require family members of the principal also to have resources, thus defeating the objective of the Directive as regards the stability of their situation (BG, EE, EL, MT, PL, RO).
- The optional imposition of integration requirements, much criticized by academics in the negotiation of the Directive, has been used by many Member States.[14] However, there is very substantial variation among the Member States on what integration requirements are and how they are evidenced. The Commission expresses concern that the provision must be implemented in a manner consistent with the EU principle of *effet utile* but does not go on to analyse each Member State's rules.
- Some Member States, according to the Commission, fail properly to apply the Directive as to do so requires too much documentation (DE, SE, NL).
- Some Member States have introduced additional requirements of dubious consistency with the Directive; for instance Austria has a quota system not allowed under the Directive.
- Intra-EU mobility for holder of long-term residence permits has been enhanced according to the Commission, but there are still problems. For instance Italy, Romania and Slovenia apply quotas that are not specified in the Directive. Other Member States apply an integration test even where the third-country national has already fulfilled that condition in the first Member State, contrary to the express provision of the Directive (AT, EE, FR, DE, LV).

---

[13] COM (2011), 585 final.

[14] AT, CZ, DE, EE, EL, FR, IT, LT, LU, LV, MT, NL, PT and RO. This confirms the concerns of academics regarding the provision.

In general, the Member States are far from applying the Directive correctly and the incorrect application appears mainly to hinder the ability of third-country nationals to enjoy the benefits of the Directive.

The third measure that has been adopted and provides long-stay immigration rights for third-country nationals is Directive 2009/50 on the conditions of entry and residence of third-country nationals for the purposes of highly qualified employment (the Blue Card Directive). This Directive seeks to regulate highly qualified migration to the EU in pursuit of the EU's objective of becoming the most competitive and dynamic knowledge-based economy in the world. It applies only to highly qualified employment, which is defined as that which requires adequate and specific competence as proven by high professional qualifications. These are attested by means of any diploma, certificate or other evidence of formal qualifications issued by a competent authority attesting the successful completion of a post-secondary higher education programme on condition that the studies lasted at least three years. Professional experience of at least five years can be substituted. In order to qualify for a Blue Card, the individual must hold the necessary qualification and the employment proposed in the Member State must pay at least 1.5 times the average gross annual salary in the Member State concerned. After 18 months' employment in one Member State, the Blue Card holder is privileged as regards movement to another Member State for highly qualified employment.

A substantial number of categories of persons are excluded from the scope of the Directive, such as refugees, seasonal workers, postal workers etc. However, for the rest, the Directive provides: the criteria for admission for the purpose of employment; the procedure for the issue of the Blue Card; and the grounds for refusal and the rights that the worker is entitled to enjoy, which include more favourable terms of family reunification than those contained in the Directive of that name. The Member States had until 19 June 2011 to transpose the Directive into national law. The Directive was intended to prevent Member States from competing for the best-qualified foreigner workers by reducing standards and criteria for their admission. However, it does not affect the right of Member States to adopt or retain more favourable provisions for third-country national workers in some key areas:

- salary requirements when a Blue Card holder moves to another Member State after 18 months in the first one do not need to meet the 1.5 times gross annual salary level;
- procedural safeguards may be enhanced;
- a 24-month limitation on equal treatment with own nationals as regards access to highly qualified employment may be relaxed;
- a 24-month restriction on changing employer unless so permitted by a prior authorization mechanism can be dispensed with;
- withdrawal of the Blue Card after three months' unemployment or repeated periods of unemployment can be abandoned;
- equal treatment rights set out in the Directive may be provided earlier than required;
- family reunification (which is in any event more generous than that which applies to other third-country nationals who have to rely on Directive 2003/86) can be further facilitated;
- acquisition of long-term resident status may be made available on more favourable grounds than in the Directive of that name.

If there is competition among the Member States for highly qualified and thus desirable migrants, then these are the areas in which that competition can be played out.

The fourth measure that the EU has adopted regarding long-stay migration for economic activities is regarding researchers. In October 2005 the Directive on admission of third-country nationals for the purpose of scientific research was adopted.[15] It had to be transposed into national law by 12 October 2007.[16] According to the preamble, it is intended to contribute to achieving the goal of 'opening up the Community to third-country nationals who might be admitted for the purposes of research'; the EU objective of investing 3 per cent of GDP in research and increasing the number of researchers in the EU by 700,000 was set by the Barcelona Council 2002 to be achieved by 2010.[17] By doing this, the institutions believed that the EU would be more attractive to researchers from around the world, which in turn would boost its position as an international centre for research. Attention is paid in the preamble to the question of brain drain and back-up measures to support researchers' reintegration in their countries of origin. In accordance with the Lisbon Process, fostering mobility within the EU is also an objective.[18] The preamble calls for Member States to permit family unity for researchers but does not actually deal with the issue, leaving it to the Member States to determine where appropriate, in accordance with Directive 2003/86.

The Directive defines research, researcher and research institution in wide terms. Research means creative work undertaken on a systematic basis in order to increase the stock of knowledge of humanity, culture and society, and the use of this stock of knowledge to devise new applications. A researcher is someone who holds higher education qualifications that give access to doctoral programmes. A research organization must have been approved for the purposes of the Directive by a Member State in accordance with legislation or administrative practice. As the Directive is written in terms of a research institution holding the key to mobility, Member State control over access to the territory for researchers takes place through the qualification of a research institution. According to the Directive, the research institution must initiate the procedure. In the event that a foreign researcher overstays his or her permitted time in a Member State, the state is allowed to require the research organization to reimburse costs related to the stay and return of the individual. The Directive allows Member States to hold the institution responsible for costs for up to six months after the termination of the hosting agreement.

Under the Directive, a hosting agreement must be signed between an authorized organization and a researcher. This agreement must include details of the purpose and duration of the research and the availability of financial resources, evidence of the researcher's qualifications, evidence of resources and travel costs for the researcher (beyond the social assistance system), sickness insurance and working conditions. Member States are to admit a researcher once their authorities have checked that the individual has a valid travel document, a hosting agreement has been signed as well as a statement of financial responsibility from the research organization, and that the individual is not a threat to public policy, security

15 Directive 2005/71.

16 Denmark, Ireland and the UK do not participate in this Directive either.

17 The goal does not appear to have been reached.

18 The Lisbon Process: http://www.eu2005.lu/en/actualites/documents_travail/2005/03/22lisboa/index.html (accessed: 23 July 2012).

or health. However, Member States may still require visas for researchers who meet the conditions of the Directive (Article 14(4)), though every facility must be provided to obtain one. The Member State is obliged to issue a residence permit to the individual for at least one year (unless the research is to last less than that period). Researchers are allowed to teach but only in accordance with national rules. Once admitted as a researcher under the Directive in one Member State, he or she can normally carry out research activities in any other Member State for not more than three months without further formality. Member States must make a decision as soon as possible and, if appropriate, have an accelerated procedure for these applications. Refusal of an application must be accompanied by an appeal procedure available to the individual or the organization.[19]

As set out above regarding legal immigration, before the adoption of the TFEU a number of key areas were the subject of harmonizing measures based on the principle of minimum standards. Specifically, family reunification, long-term resident status, highly qualified migration and admission of researchers have all enjoyed some degree of harmonization in this way. The Commission submitted further proposals regarding other areas of first admission for labour market access, specifically, seasonal workers and inter-corporate transferees in 2010. On the other hand, the 2009 five-year plan for the development of the Area of Freedom, Security and Justice, the Stockholm Programme,[20] called for another assessment of the Family Reunification Directive. In particular it called for an evaluation and, where necessary, review of the Directive taking into account the importance of integration measures (para. 6.1.4). This is unlikely to mean making family reunification easier for third-country nationals (other than highly qualified migrants coming under the Blue Card Directive who are not subject to integration conditions as regards their family members). Those Member States which have opted to use the integration measures option as a requirement for family reunification have done so in a way that makes family reunification more difficult for third-country nationals in their states.[21]

The TFEU objective of fair treatment for legally resident third-country nationals may well be tested in this area of integration measures and conditions. Some Member States such as the Netherlands and Germany have introduced integration measures for family reunification that must be fulfilled before the admission of the family members.[22] But nationals of some states, such as the USA or Japan, are excluded from the requirement as regards the Netherlands. Is this fair treatment consistent with the TFEU objective? It will be the job of the CJEU to determine the meaning of fair treatment should a national court request it.

---

[19] Although there is an obligation on the Commission to report on the implementation of this Directive by 12 October 2010, at the time of writing in November 2011 no report had been published.

[20] See http://register.consilium.europa.eu/pdf/en/10/st05/st05731.en10.pdf (accessed: 23 July 2012).

[21] K. Groenendijk, R. Fernhout, D. Van Dam, R. Van Oers and T. Strik, *The Family Reunification Directive in EU Member States: The First Year of Implementation*, Nijmegen: Wolf Legal Publishers, 2007.

[22] R. van Oers, 'Integration Tests in the Netherlands, Germany and the UK', in Van Oers, Ersboll and Kostakopoulou (eds), *A Re-definition of Belonging?*, 51–106.

What are the Existing EU Measures in Irregular Immigration?

The EU institutions prefer to use the term 'illegal' immigration rather than 'irregular' or 'undocumented' migration favoured by other international organizations and institutions.[23] This is notwithstanding the fact that not only has the Council of Europe's Parliamentary Assembly called on the EU institutions to use more neutral language, but the European Parliament has similarly done so with noticeably little effect.[24] In this area the EU institutions have been quite active, adopting over 20 measures by 2011 since acquiring competence to do so.[25] The most controversial of the measures has been the Return Directive (2008/115), which was denounced by the heads of state of all countries in South America.[26] What the Directive seeks to do is establish clear, transparent and fair rules for an effective return policy that the EU considers to be a necessary element of a well-managed migration policy. The ending of an irregular stay by a third-country national is to occur through a coherent procedure culminating in expulsion.

'Illegal stay', which is a key concept of the Directive, means the presence on the territory of a Member State of a third-country national who does not fulfil or no longer fulfils the conditions of entry as set out in Article 5 of the Schengen Borders Code (on short-stay entry for three months or less) or other conditions for entry, stay or residence in that Member State.

---

23 Council of Europe High Commissioner for Human Rights, *Criminalization of Migration in Europe: Human Rights Implications*, Strasbourg: Council of Europe, 2009.

24 S. Carrera and M. Merlino, *Undocumented Immigrants and Rights in the EU: Addressing the Gap between Social Science Research and Policy-making*, Brussels: CEPS, 2009.

25 1. Directive 2001/40 on mutual recognition of expulsion decisions *(OJ 2001 L 149/34)*; implement 2 Dec. 2002.

2. Directive 2001/51 on carrier sanctions *(OJ 2001 L 187/45)*; implement 11 Feb. 2003.
3. Regulation 2424/2001 on funding SIS II (OJ 2001 L 328/4).
4. Decision *2001/886/JHA* on funding SIS II (OJ 2001 L 328/1).
5. Framework Decision on trafficking in persons (OJ 2002 L 203/1).
6. Directive and Framework Decision on facilitation of illegal entry and residence (OJ 2002 L 328).
7. Directive 2003/110 on assistance with transit for expulsion by air (OJ 2003 L 321/26).
8. Conclusions on transit via land for expulsion – adopted 22 Dec. 2003 by Council.
9. Regulation 378/2004 on procedure for amendments to Sirene manual (OJ 2004 L 64).
10. Regulation 377/2004 on ILO network (OJ 2004 L 64/1).
11. Decision on costs of expulsion (OJ 2004 L 60/55).
12. Directive 2004/81 on res. permits for trafficking victims (OJ 2004 L 261/19).
13. Regulation 871/2004 on new functionalities for SIS (OJ 2004 L 162/29).
14. Directive 2004/82 on transmission of passenger data (OJ 2004 L 261/64).
15. Decision on joint flights for expulsion (OJ 2004 L 261/28).
16. Decision on early warning system (*OJ 2005 L 83/48*).
17. Regulation 1987/2006 establishing SIS II (OJ 2006 L 381/4).
18. Regulation 1988/2006 on SIS II, amending Reg. 2424/2 001 (OJ 2006 L 411/1).
19. Decision on European return programme (OJ 2007 L 144).
20. Directive 2008/115 (Returns Directive) (OJ 2008 L 348/98) – deadline 24 Dec. 2010.
21. Directive 2009/52 on sanctions for employers of irregular migrants (OJ 2009 L168/24). *The UK opts in to all except 7, 12, 13, 17, 20, 21.*

26 D. Acosta Arcarazo, *Latin American Reactions to the Adoption of the Returns Directive*, Brussels: CEPS, 2009.

Return is defined as voluntary or enforced compliance with an obligation to return to either his or her country of origin or a country of transit in accordance with Community or bilateral readmission agreements or other arrangements or another third country to which the third-country national concerned voluntarily decides to return and in which he or she will be accepted.

The first step that the Return Directive requires a Member State to take is to decide whether to issue an individual with an autonomous residence permit or other authorization offering a right to stay for compassionate, humanitarian or other reasons or not (Article 6(4)). If the Member State decides not to issue some sort of authorization, then it is obliged under the Directive to issue a return decision, though execution can be delayed apparently indefinitely. Return can be voluntary, which the Directive appears to promote, or enforced if the individual does not leave (Article 8). Where a Member State enforces a return decision it must also issue an entry ban on the individual that in principle should be for a five-year period (Article 11). The most controversial part of the Directive is that relating to detention. In Chapter IV of the Directive detention is incorporated as a normal part of the return process, although it is specifically stated to be a final resort where there is a risk of absconding or the individual is hampering the return procedure. Detention is subject to a series of safeguards regarding the making of the decision, the right to remedies against the decision, and judicial supervision of the detention. The initial limit to the length of detention is six months, but this can be extended for a further 12 months (Article 15). The transposition period of the Directive has not yet expired – Member States must implement it into their national law by 24 December 2011.

Like the Family Reunification Directive, the Return Directive has already been the subject of judicial consideration by the CJEU.[27] It was one of the last judgments of the CJEU before the entry into force of the Lisbon Treaty and it was subject to the urgent procedure in view of the fact that the individual was in detention. The case revolved around a Mr Kadzoev or Huchbarov, whose identity is never fully certain. He had been arrested by the Bulgarian authorities near their border with Turkey. He was detained from 3 November 2006 and was still in detention when the case was heard by the CJEU in 2009. The man stated he was Mr Huchbarov, a Chechen, but he did not wish the assistance of the Russian authorities. The Bulgarian authorities decided that he was Mr Kadzoev, a Chechen with a Georgian mother. The Bulgarian authorities sent the identity documents that they had in respect of Mr Kadzoev to the Russian authorities, but the latter stated that the documents were from persons and authorities unknown to the Russian Federation and thus no proof of Russian nationality. Various applications for the man to be released from detention failed, not least as he had no address in Bulgaria. In 2007 he applied for asylum. The authorities continued to detain him and eventually in 2009 refused his application definitively without any further appeal right.

In the meantime, the Bulgarian authorities were having no luck in finding a country to which to send the man. They struck out with the Russians, tried and failed with the Georgians, and even approached the Austrian authorities to see whether they would take him, again without success. Finally, a Bulgarian court, once again faced with an application for the man's release from custody, asked the CJEU whether the 18-month maximum period of detention under the Return Directive applied in this case. The CJEU found that the Directive was applicable in light of the Bulgarian law that transposed it (notwithstanding the fact that

27 C-357/09 PPU *Kadzoev (Huchbarov)*, 30 November 2009.

the period for transposition had not yet expired). Two central issues arose – first, whether the man's detention while he was seeking asylum count towards the 18-month maximum on detention; second, whether periods of detention during judicial review count towards the 18-month maximum.

On the first question the CJEU looked long and hard at the Asylum Procedures Directive (2004/85). It held that, if the requirements of the procedures which permit limits to be placed on an individual's freedom of movement were followed (and which provide substantial guarantees and freedoms to the individual), then that time when liberty is restricted does not count towards the 18-month maximum under the Return Directive. But if the detention continued to be on the basis of national rules which effectively correspond to detention under the Return Directive, then it does count (para. 47). On the second question, the CJEU held that 18 months means 18 months, irrespective of whether judicial review or other legal challenges were launched by the individual. After 18 months the state must release the individual. In no case can the maximum period be exceeded, irrespective of whether the individual is aggressive, has no means of supporting himself, or has no travel or identity documents (paras 68–9). Further, the CJEU held that the possibility of detaining a person on grounds of public order and public safety cannot be based on the Return Directive (para. 70). The CJEU accomplished this without even once referring to the EU Charter of Fundamental Rights or the European Convention on Human Rights.

A second urgent reference under the Directive was decided by the CJEU on 28 April 2011.[28] The reference, from an Italian court, concerned Mr El Dridi, a third-country national who entered Italy illegally and does not hold a residence permit. According to the court, a deportation decree was issued against Mr El Dridi by the Prefect of Turin (Italy) on 8 May 2004. An order requiring his removal from the national territory, issued on 21 May 2010 by the Questore di Udine pursuant to that deportation decree, was notified to him on the same day. The reasons for that removal order were that no vehicle or other means of transport was available, that Mr El Dridi had no identification documents, and that it was not possible for him to be accommodated at a detention facility as no places were available in the establishments intended for that purpose. A check carried out on 29 September 2010 revealed that Mr El Dridi had not complied with that removal order. He was sentenced at the conclusion of an expedited procedure by a single judge to one year's imprisonment for the criminal offence of unlawful presence. He appealed against that decision and the higher court was in doubt as to whether a criminal penalty could be imposed during administrative procedures concerning the return of a foreign national to his country of origin due to non-compliance with the stages of those procedures, since such a penalty seems contrary to the principle of sincere cooperation. The CJEU found that the Member States may not, in order to remedy the failure of coercive measures adopted in order to carry out forced removal under the Directive, provide for a custodial sentence on the sole ground that a third-country national continues to stay illegally on the territory of a Member State after an order to leave the national territory has been notified to him or her and the period granted in that order has expired. Instead, Member States must pursue their efforts to enforce the return decision, which continues to produce its effects. The CJEU found that a custodial penalty, due to its conditions and methods of application, risks jeopardizing the attainment of the objective pursued by that directive,

28 C-61/2011 *El Dridi*.

namely, the establishment of an effective policy of removal and repatriation of illegally staying third-country nationals. Such legislation is liable to frustrate the application of the procedural measures of the Directive and delay the enforcement of the return decision. However, this does not preclude the possibility for the Member States to adopt provisions regulating the situation in which coercive measures have not resulted in the removal of a third-country national staying illegally on their territory.

The Judicialization of Immigration

When the EU was provided with competences in the field of immigration in 1999, Article 68 TEC provided that only courts against whose decision there was no further appeal could refer questions to the CJEU on measures arising from the new treaty bases. The result was that only courts of final instance could refer questions on EU immigration matters. Member States' courts of final instance tend to be conservative in their use of reference powers.[29] Often they will prefer to deal with the issue themselves under national law. Courts of first instance often ask the most challenging questions of EU law to the CJEU as they are faced with the immediate problem and often are under substantial pressure regarding the preferred outcomes of the parties. The consequence of limiting the reference power to courts of final instance was to slow dramatically the oversight that the area might receive from the CJEU. In addition to preferences between courts, there is also the simple arithmetic – there is only one court of final instance in each state but many courts of first instance. Few cases regarding immigration ever get to courts of final instance, while many arrive at the doors of courts of first instance, particularly in Member States where there are specialized courts for immigration and asylum issues.

For the moment, it is the field of EU asylum measures that is giving rise to the largest number of references to the CJEU from courts across the Member States. One might well expect, however, that immigration measures will catch up rapidly. After all, the Family Reunification Directive has already given rise to two judgments. The consequences of the arrival of the CJEU as an important actor in this field are very likely to include the following:

- definitions of terms in the Directives will be given consistent meanings rather than be left to Member State national rules;
- terms that are identical to or very similar to one another or to terms used elsewhere in EU law are likely to be interpreted consistently – thus grounds for expulsion that use the term 'public policy' are likely to be given the same interpretation as the same phrase that applies to EU citizens (this has been the approach of the CJEU regarding the EC Turkey Association Agreement);
- the relationship of the rule and the exception or derogation from the rule is likely to be clarified, giving priority to the rule and a restrictive interpretation to the exception;

29 G. de Burca and J. H. H. Weiler, *The European Court of Justice*, Oxford: OUP, 2001.

- the scope for divergent national rules that stray from a common EU interpretation of the Directives will be diminished unless it is specifically based on higher standards (i.e. more favourable to the migrant) permitted in the principle of minimum standards.

The CJEU has a critical role to play in the development of the EU field on immigration, a role that is now coming into its own. The direction that the TFEU provides to the CJEU regarding the importance of the principle of fairness may be critical. From the initial decisions of the CJEU (discussed above) it appears that the CJEU perceives the field of immigration as one that merits interpretation consistent with the usual rules of EU law. There is nothing exceptional or extraordinary about immigration that sets it apart as regards the judicial consideration of its consistent elements.

The EU Charter of Fundamental Rights and the Lisbon Treaty

Article 6 TEU provides that the EU Charter of Fundamental Rights, first adopted in 2000, shall have the same legal value as the Treaties. The Charter was drafted and adopted in 2000, but it was denied legal effect as a result of disagreements among the Member States (primarily the UK in disaccord with the others) about the added value of a legally binding charter. The version to which the TEU refers is fundamentally the same as the 2000 version, which amends the mechanisms of application. According to its preamble, the Charter sets out the Union's foundation on indivisible, universal values of human dignity, freedom, equality and solidarity. It confirms that the EU is based on the principles of democracy and rule of law. In order to promote the four freedoms of the EU – free movement of goods, persons, services and capital – the Charter states that it is necessary to strengthen the protection of fundamental rights and thus recognizes the rights, freedoms and principles set out. A protocol to the Lisbon Treaty provides that the legal effect of the Charter is limited in the UK and Poland.

The Charter includes the rights found in a variety of sources, primarily those already existing in the Treaties, the European Social Charter, and most importantly contained in the ECHR. The Charter's Article 52(3) provides that Charter rights that correspond to ECHR rights shall have the same meaning and scope of those in the ECHR. Thus the way in which the European Court of Human Rights (ECtHR) has interpreted the ECHR rights in immigration matters becomes a subject of substantial importance for the EU. This is not the place to set out the jurisprudence of the ECtHR in immigration matters, which has been extensively examined elsewhere.[30] Nor is it the place to examine how the CJEU has incorporated the ECHR into its jurisprudence,[31] though it is worth noting that both the Lisbon Treaty and the Stockholm Programme mandate the accession of the EU to the ECHR. The point that I want to make here is that immigration measures in the EU are no longer self-

[30] N. Blake QC and R. Husain, *Immigration, Asylum and Human Rights*, Oxford: OUP, 2003; J. Sikuta and E. Hubalkova, *The European Court of Human Rights: Case Law of the Grand Chamber*, Amsterdam: TMC Asser, 2007.

[31] E. Guild and G. Lesieur (eds), *The European Court of Justice on the European Convention on Human Rights: Who Said What When*, The Hague: Kluwer Law International, 1997.

referential. All of the EU immigration measures contain a standard preamble that confirms their compatibility with the ECHR and EU fundamental rights standards contained in the Charter. Most of the measures, when they were proposed, were subject to a fundamental rights impact assessment that the Commission carried out. But there was no external assessment of the human rights and fundamental rights consequences for individuals of the measures. Further, within the EU system there was no obvious way consistent across the Member States in which an individual could lay claim to fundamental rights in light of the implementation of an EU measures on immigration. Now, with the legal effect of the Charter within the scope of EU law, this ambiguity has been cleared up. Further, the accession of the EU to the ECHR also required by the post-Lisbon TEU will facilitate the interaction of the two courts, the CJEU and the ECtHR, without limiting the role of either.

Conclusions

In this chapter I have sought to examine the impact of the Lisbon Treaty on immigration law in the EU. To do so I compared the changes in the EU objectives in including immigration as a competence of the EU, focusing in particular on the importance of the objective of fair treatment for third-country nationals. Then I looked at the measures that the EU has already adopted in immigration, both legal and irregular, and considered what impact the Lisbon Treaty changes bring to these already-existing measures, in particular considering the role of the CJEU after 1 December 2009. Finally, I looked at the EU Charter of Fundamental Rights – what does the legal effect of the Charter mean for EU immigration measures?

Two key conclusions emerge from this analysis:

- The direct engagement of national courts of any level with the CJEU over the interpretation of the EU immigration measures that was introduced by the Lisbon Treaty is extremely important in the development of the field. The consistency of interpretation that is emerging will be central to the further development of immigration in the EU.
- The Charter of Fundamental Rights brings to the EU's table the disputes that the Member States have been having with third-country nationals about immigration and rights and which, until now, have been taken to the ECtHR on human rights grounds. These disputes are likely now to appear before the CJEU on EU immigration measures but present similar conflicts regarding family reunification, protection of residence rights, equality of treatment, and protection from detention and expulsion. The role of fundamental rights in the interpretation of the EU's immigration measures will be a central feature over the next 20 years, made possible by the Lisbon Treaty.

Finally, in my view, the main measures of the EU's immigration policy have now been adopted. While there will be more legislative initiatives, these will probably be in minority interest areas, such as the regulation of seasonal workers, or consolidation measures. The main thrust of EU immigration law will move from the legislative phase to one of implementation and judicial control over implementation and application in the Member States.

References

Acosta Arcarazo, D., *Latin American Reactions to the Adoption of the Returns Directive*, Brussels: CEPS, 2009.

Blake, N. QC and R. Husain, *Immigration, Asylum and Human Rights*, Oxford: OUP, 2003.

Carrera, S. and M. Merlino, *Undocumented Immigrants and Rights in the EU: Addressing the Gap between Social Science Research and Policy-making*, Brussels: CEPS, 2009.

Council of Europe High Commissioner for Human Rights, *Criminalization of Migration in Europe: Human Rights Implications*, Strasbourg: Council of Europe, 2009.

De Burca, G. and J. H. H. Weiler, *The European Court of Justice*, Oxford: OUP, 2001.

Groenendijk, K., R. Fernhout, D. Van Dam, R. Van Oers and T. Strik, *The Family Reunification Directive in EU Member States: The First Year of Implementation*, Nijmegen: Wolf Legal Publishers, 2007.

Guild, E. and G. Lesieur (eds), *The European Court of Justice on the European Convention on Human Rights: Who Said What When*, The Hague: Kluwer Law International, 1997.

Guild, E., K. Groenendijk and S. Carrera, *Illiberal Liberal States: Immigration, Citizenship and Integration in the EU*, Farnham: Ashgate, 2009.

Halleskov, L., 'The Long Term Residents' Directive: A Fulfilment of the Tampere Objective of near Equality?', *European Journal of Migration and Law* 7(5), 2005, 203–11.

Peers, S., *EU Justice and Home Affairs Law*, Oxford: OUP, 2006.

Sikuta, J. and E. Hubalkova, *The European Court of Human Rights: Case Law of the Grand Chamber*, Amsterdam: TMC Asser, 2007.

Van Oers, R., 'Integration Tests in the Netherlands, Germany and the UK', in R. van Oers, E. Ersboll and D. Kostakopoulou (eds), *A Re-definition of Belonging? Language and Integration Tests in Europe*, The Hague: Brill, 2010, 51–106.

Van Oers, R., E. Ersboll and D. Kostakopoulou (eds), *A Re-definition of Belonging? Language and Integration Tests in Europe*, The Hague: Brill, 2010.

Are European States Accountable for Border Deaths?

Thomas Spijkerboer[1]

On 20 June 2011, the UN High Commissioner for Refugees in a speech said that, since March 2011, as many as 1,500 people had drowned in the Mediterranean. It is estimated that roughly one in ten attempting the crossing have died.[2] Although the sudden departure of many migrants from Tunisia and Libya in the spring of 2011 seems exceptional, the number of fatalities fits in a general upward trend.

On border deaths, only problematic data are available. The most comprehensive, Europe-wide set of data is the list of fatalities of United, an international NGO based in Amsterdam.[3] This is based on press reports. A later data set, which is comparable in methodology and shows a comparable trend, is that of Fortress Europe.[4] Local, short-term studies[5] lead to much higher numbers than those by United or Fortress Europe but for smaller areas (Spain and Sicily respectively), and for short periods. Kiza has summarized the data available, using the United data as a starting point.[6] His methodology is more sophisticated than the one of United/ Fortress Europe, as he has (a) excluded people who did not die on their way to Europe but, for example, committed suicide in European detention centres; and (b) complemented the United data with other media sources. No sources address the issue of dark numbers; the writings of Cuttitta and Carling[7] suggest that these are considerable.

---

1 Professor of Migration Law, Vrije Universiteit Amsterdam.

2 High Commissioner's Message for World Refugee Day, 20 June 2011, at www.unhcr.org, last accessed 12 July 2011.

3 At www.unitedagainstracism.org, last accessed 12 July 2011.

4 At www.fortresseurope.blogspot.com, last accessed 12 July 2011.

5 Dirk Godenau and Manuel Zapata Hernández, 'The Case of the Canary Islands (Spain): A Region of Transit Between Africa and Europe', in Gemma Pinyol (ed.), *Immigration Flows and the Management of the EU's Southern Maritime Borders*, Documentos CIDOB Migraciones 17, 2008, 13–43; Jorgen Carling, 'Migration Control and Migrant Fatalities at the Spanish–African Borders', 41(2) *International Migration Review* 2007, 316–43; and Paolo Cuttitta 'Il controllo dell'immigrazione tra Nordafrica e Italia', in Nicoletta Dentico and Maurizio Gressi (eds), *Libro Bianco. I Centri di Permanenza temporanea e Assistenza in Italia un'indagine promossa dal Gruppo di Lavoro sui CPTA in Italia*, Rome, 169–99.

6 Ernesto Kiza, *Tödliche Grenzen – Die fatalen Auswirkungen europäischer Zuwanderungspolitik*, Zürich/Berlin: Lit Verlag, 2008.

7 See Cuttitta 'Il controllo dell'immigrazione tra Nordafrica e Italia'; Carling, 'Migration Control and Migrant Fatalities at the Spanish–African Borders'.

In this text, I present the United data, problematic as they are, for two reasons. First, Kiza's more precise data reflect a trend that is very much like that present in United's data. Second, the United data begin in 1993 and are updated every year, and cover a longer period than both Kiza (1994–2004) and Fortress Europe (1988–2008).

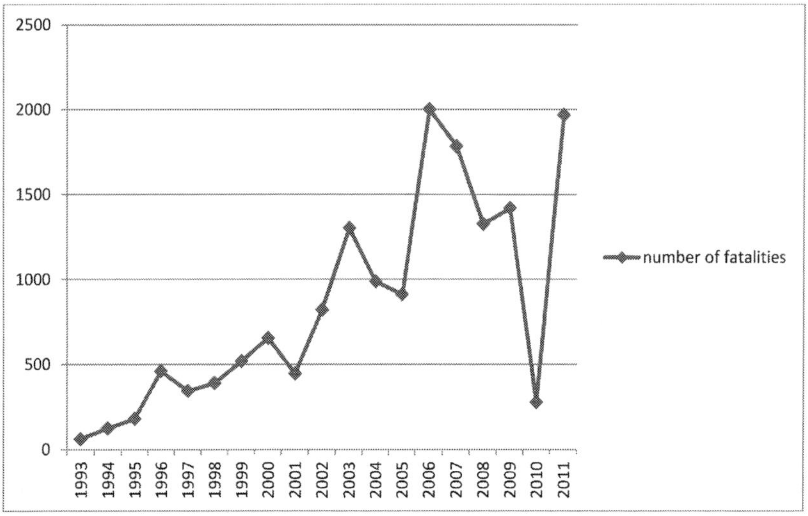

Figure 4.1 Migrant fatalities in the EU migratory system (1993–2011)

Source: UNITED, Amsterdam 2012

This figure illustrates that the number of 1,500 fatalities for the first half of 2011 is dramatic, but would merely constitute a further development of the steep upward trend we see in the figure The question that this chapter raises for investigation is whether the possible relationship between European border control policies of the past two decades on the one hand and the rising number of border deaths on the other hand leads to a (moral and) legal obligation of European states to address the rising number of border deaths.

It should be noted that I presume some relation between European policies and the rising number of border deaths. Whether that is a correct presumption would require extensive empirical research, which has not yet been undertaken. The available data make it plausible that a relation exists. This is so because three conclusions seem warranted on the basis of the data already available:

1. the intensification of European border control policies has not reduced the number of migrants;
2. the intensification of European border control policies has led to the shifting of undocumented migration to ever more dangerous routes;
3. the number of registered border deaths has increased considerably over the years.[8]

[8] Cf. Hein de Haas, 'Migration and Development: A Theoretical Perspective' (2010), 44 *International Migration Review*, 227–64; Thomas Spijkerboer, 'The Human Costs of Border Control' (2007), 9 *European Journal of Migration and Law*, 127–39.

If these conclusions are plausible, then the idea that the increasing number of border deaths is a consequence, a side-effect, of the intensification of European border control policies is sufficiently plausible to enquire into State responsibility for this side-effect.

I shall do so by addressing four issues. The first is jurisdiction. The migrants mostly were not under direct control of European State authorities when they drowned, and often they were not in their territorial waters either. This raises the issue of whether they were within the jurisdiction of European States. The second issue concerns positive obligations. It seems unlikely that the problem of border deaths is most fruitfully conceived of as one involving a negative obligation. The thing European States could stop doing in order to reduce the number of border deaths would be to abolish border controls. However, as the legitimacy of border controls has consistently been underlined by, among others, the European Court of Human Rights,[9] one can hardly expect them to stop a practice that in itself is lawful. But it does make sense to enquire what States could do in order to limit this lethal side-effect of their border control policies – and that means we have to face the issue of positive obligations. Third, I shall deal with standing: who can represent the interests of deceased migrants, and of prospective migrants whose chances of surviving arguably are influenced by the policies of European States? Lastly, I shall address the problem of collective State responsibility. Because the intensification of border controls at the southern maritime borders is a joint undertaking of European States, the issue is one of joint responsibility. These issues will be addressed primarily by reference to the European Convention on Human Rights (ECHR). The ECHR is the human rights convention with the closest geographical relation with the issue under consideration. Also, the competent court (the European Court of Human Rights) can give binding judgments, and has developed a rich case law relevant in our context.

Jurisdiction

In the context of border deaths, can States be held responsible for acts that either occur outside their territory (including their territorial waters), or the effects (i.e. migrant deaths) of acts that occur outside their territory? In terms of the ECHR, this translates into the issue of whether the alleged victim of the State action is within the jurisdiction of the State.

For our purposes, three situations have to be distinguished:

- State acts take place within the territory of the State (including its territorial waters), and effects of those acts take place *within* the territorial waters of that same State;
- State acts take place within the territory of the State (including its territorial waters), and effects of those acts take place *outside* the territorial waters of that same State;
- State acts take place on the high seas, or in the territorial waters of other States.

[9] The standard passage states that, as a matter of well-established international law, States have the right to control the entry of non-nationals into their territory. See, *inter alia*, ECtHR 28 May 1985, *Abdulaziz, Balkandali and Cabales v. the United Kingdom*, Appl. No. 9214/80; 9473/81; 9474/81.

The first situation is entirely unproblematic. Both the State act and its effects take place within the jurisdiction of the State in question. Of course, this does not mean that a violation of some Convention right occurred, as jurisdiction does not imply that there is a sufficient causal relation between State act and effect, and it remains to be seen whether the effect entails a violation of a Convention right at all. But whatever difficult issues remain, jurisdiction is not one of them.

The second situation seems altogether different. The person who is affected by the State act is outside its territory. If one assumed State responsibility in situations like this, European States could be responsible *vis-à-vis* persons wherever in the world for external effects of their policies – environmental degradation, development aid, and so on. That seems to be overstretching the Convention. However, the situation we are addressing is a specific one. Until a few decades ago, border controls took place at borders. Migrants would be admitted or refused entry at ports, airports or land border crossing points. The problems and expenses of removal, especially in ports and airports, led European States to shift border control to places beyond their borders. Carrier sanctions (in the form of fines for airlines transporting undocumented migrants) are an example: these are sometimes combined with agents of European States advising airlines about the genuineness of travel documents at check-in counters. The consequence of carrier sanctions is that migrants shift their travel routes to land and sea. This is especially problematic as the sea routes are inherently more dangerous than air travel. A second example of border control policies is the subsequent intensification of control at sea, with the aim of blocking short and relatively safe routes, such as the Strait of Gibraltar and the Adriatic Sea between Albania and Southern Italy. This leads to migrants choosing ever longer and more dangerous routes, which predictably leads to a higher death rate. Interception comprises yet another form of activities that seek to enforce migration control without the problems that occur when migration control is carried out at the border. In this specific context (i.e. the externalization of border control), it would be artificial to argue that the victim is within the jurisdiction of the State if a boat capsizes within the territorial waters of a State, while the person is presumed not to be within the jurisdiction of that State if the same boat capsizes just beyond the territorial waters of that State. In both situations, the argument (whether one accepts that argument is another question) is that people drown as a consequence of the way in which border controls are carried out; they are – so the argument goes – directly affected by those policies, regardless of whether the victims are within or beyond the territorial waters of the State.

In the case law of the Court, two streams can be distinguished on this point. One is exemplified by *Bankovic*, in which the Court held that jurisdiction is primarily a territorial concept and gaps in human rights protection do not imply that the Convention is to be applied throughout the world.[10] *Bankovic* indeed stands in the way of reasoning that seeks to hold States accountable for any consequence of their acts, wherever in the world they occur. However, three aspects in particular distinguish the facts of *Bankovic* from those in border death cases. First, in *Bankovic* the applicants relied on the notion that a situation can be in the jurisdiction

10 ECtHR (GC, Dec) 12 December 2001, *Bankovic et al. v. Belgium and 16 other Contracting States*, Appl. No. 52207/99. See on *Bankovic* extensively Kees Wouters, *International Legal Standards for the Protection from Refoulement*, Antwerp: Interstentia, 2009, 211–16 and the sources quoted there.

of two (or, because of the NATO aspect of the case, even more) States at the same time. This issue of competing jurisdictions is not at stake here, because border deaths will usually occur on the high seas or in the territorial waters of European States. Second, the State acts that arguably lead to the effects outside the territorial waters of the State (being border control policies and their implementation) are undeniably acts taking place predominantly *within* the jurisdiction of the State. That is different from a situation in which airplanes carry out bombardments *outside* the territory of the relevant Member State. Third, present-day border control policies are designed in part with the specific aim of escaping from State responsibility. One of the attractions of carrier sanctions and interception is that in this way States seek, often successfully, to evade the effect of the prohibition of refoulement. The gap in human rights protection that exists if one denies jurisdiction in these cases is an intentionally created gap.

There is another stream in the Court's case law on this point, which is more applicable to our case than *Bankovic*. One may point to *X and Y v Switzerland*, in which the Commission held that state responsibility can be engaged by acts of its authorities producing effects outside its own territory.[11] A more recent decision adopting this logic is the *Xhavara* case.[12] This decision concerned a boat with undocumented migrants that was struck, at 35 sea miles from the Italian coast (i.e. outside its territorial waters), by an Italian marine vessel and sunk as a consequence. The Court nowhere objects that the victims were not in the jurisdiction of Italy. In this case, the entire situation took place outside the territorial waters of Italy, and therefore has fewer ties with Italian territory than the situation we are looking at here, being extraterritorial effects of acts carried out mainly within the territory of a State. It is remarkable that in the *Xhavara* case, with strong parallels to *Bankovic* (extraterritorial acts with extraterritorial effects), the Court did not even consider the jurisdiction issue, apparently finding the situation obvious.[13] This stream of case law would justify the conclusion that States can be held accountable for acts within their territory with effects outside its territory.

The third situation has now become less difficult, because the Court dealt with it in *Xhavara*. The Court's position is *Xhavara* is consistent with cases that are quite similar to the interception situation, concerning acts of functionaries of embassies abroad.[14]

---

[11] EComHR 14 July 1977, *X. and Y. v. Switzerland, D&R 9*, Appl. No. 7289/75 and 7349/76, 57.

[12] ECtHR (Dec) 11 January 2001, *Xhavara et quinze autres c. l'Italie et l'Albanie*, Appl. No. 39473/98. See on this Rick Lawson, 'Life after Bankovic', in Fons Coomans and Menno T. Kamminga (eds), *Extraterritorial Application of Human Rights Treaties*, Antwerp: Intersentia, 2004, 83–123, at 99–100.

[13] Echoing the Court in *Bankovic*, O'Boyle objects that in *Xhavara* no jurisdiction objected was recorded, suggesting that the Court might have found jurisdiction problematic if it had: Michael O'Boyle, 'Comment on "Life after Bankovic"', in Coomans and Kamminga (eds), *Extraterritorial Application of Human Rights Treaties*, 125–39, at 134. However, he ignores that no objection from either Italy or Albania is recorded at all in *Xhavara*, which deprives this argument of its validity.

[14] EComHR 12 December 1965, *X v. Federal Republic of Germany*, Appl. No. 1611/62; EComHR 14 October 1992, *W.M. v. Denmark*, Appl. No. 17392/90. Recently ECtHR (GC) 7 July 2011, *Al-Skeini and Others v. the United* Kingdom, Appl. No. 55721/07. The US Supreme Court held otherwise for the Refugee Convention, *USSC Sale v. Haitian Centers Council*, 509 U.S. 155 (1993). Apart from the fact that this judgment did not concern the ECHR, it has been strongly criticized; see, inter alia, Guy S. Goodwin-Gill and Jane McAdam, *The Refugee in International Law*, 3rd edn, Oxford: Oxford University Press, 2007, 246–50; Jean-Yves Carlier, *Droit d'asile et des réfugiés. De la protection aux droits*, Leiden: Martinus Nijhoff, 2008, 106–10; James C. Hathaway, *The Rights of Refugees under International Law*, Cambridge: Cambridge University Press, 2005, 335–42.

In conclusion, the first situation (border deaths occurring within the territorial waters of a State) is clearly within the jurisdiction of that State. The third situation (interception on the high seas) also is clearly within the jurisdiction of the intercepting State. The second situation is less clear. Because it would be odd to find this case not within the jurisdiction of the State, while the third is, the conclusion that the situation indeed is within the jurisdiction of the relevant State seems more cogent than the conclusion that it occurs outside the State's jurisdiction.[15] On the other hand, one may maintain that the second situation has not been brought under the concept of jurisdiction by the Court; hence the situation is not covered by the Convention.

Positive Obligations

If one accepts that State accountability is not excluded on grounds of jurisdiction, a further issue is how European States could be argued to violate human rights of migrants who drown at sea. One could imagine two versions of an argument critical of the present situation. In its most radical form, the argument that border deaths constitute an actual violation of Convention rights would not require the doctrine of positive obligations. This argument would hold that State acts (i.e. border control) lead to border deaths; hence these acts (i.e. border control as such) violate Convention rights. The consequence of this argument would be that border control as such constitutes a violation of the Convention; hence the practice of controlling borders should be ended. Yet it is not hard to see that this position is difficult to sustain in light of the Court's unwavering case law holding that, subject to their treaty obligations, States have the right to control the entry of aliens.[16]

However, if one relies instead on the doctrine of positive obligations, an argument can be made that addresses border deaths while at the same time not denying States' right to control the entry of aliens. That argument would go along the following lines. It would start by stating that, formerly, States exercised migration control at their borders. When they externalized their border controls, one effect was that the number of people dying while trying to evade these controls went up. This occurred because States blocked air travel by means of carrier sanctions and blocked relatively safe travel by sea by intensifying patrols in the Strait of Gibraltar and the Adriatic Sea. This led to more dangerous travel routes, with increasing fatalities as a predictable consequence. As soon as States noticed, or could notice, this effect, they were under a positive obligation to seek ways of adapting their policies so as to minimize this unintended and undesirable side-effect. If they have not or insufficiently done so, they have violated that positive obligation. In addition, once a border death has occurred, they

15 See for a comparably broad notion of jurisdiction Elihu Lauterpacht and Daniel Bethlehem, 'The Scope and Content of the Principle of Non-refoulement: Opinion', in Erika Feller, Volker Türk and Frances Nicholson (eds), *Refugee Protection in International Law*, Cambridge: Cambridge University Press, 2003, 87–164, at 110–11.

16 The Court has held so since its foundational judgments *Abdualaziz, Balkandali* and *Cabales v. United Kingdom* and *Soering v. United Kingdom*. It repeated this in our particular context in the *Xhavari* decision.

are under a positive obligation to investigate what happened and to establish the deceased's identity.[17]

Under the International Law Commission Rules on Responsibility of States for Internationally Wrongful Acts,[18] States are not responsible for the fatalities resulting indirectly from border control because border control in itself is not a wrongful act. Under some circumstances, however, States may be responsible for damage arising out of acts not prohibited by international law. This may be the case if a State undertakes a hazardous activity, defined by the International Law Commission as 'an activity which involves a risk of causing significant harm'.[19] This is precisely the case at hand. An indication that, indeed, an obligation exists towards undocumented migrants can be found in Article 16 para 1 of the 2000 Protocol Against the Smuggling of Migrants by Land, Sea And Air, Supplementing the United Nations Convention Against Transnational Organized Crime,[20] which stipulates that States shall take 'all appropriate measures, including legislation if necessary, to preserve and protect the rights of persons who have been the object of [smuggling, TS] as accorded under applicable international law, in particular the right to life'. In light of the definition of smuggling in Article 3(a) of the Protocol, this provision is applicable in this context. Further indications of a positive obligation to prevent the loss of life at sea can be found in international maritime law.[21]

The European Court of Human Rights has developed a position on the obligation of States to safeguard the lives of those within its jurisdiction.[22] In *Osman*, the central issue was whether the authorities had protected the life of a man and his son from attack by a stalker.[23] In *Keenan*, the issue was whether the United Kingdom had protected the life of a suicidal man.[24] In *Öneryildiz*, the Court dealt with an explosion at a waste-collection site in Istanbul, in which nine people were killed.[25] Three issues are central to this line of case law. First, it must be decided whether the authorities knew or should have known that there was a real and immediate risk to the life of an individual. The second issue is whether the authorities took all necessary measures that could reasonably be expected to prevent the risk from materializing.

---

17 See for this approach Stefanie Grant, 'Recording and Identifying European Frontier Deaths' (2011), 13 *European Journal of Migration and Law*, 135–56.

18 See the Annex to General Assembly resolution 56/83 of 12 December 2001.

19 UN Doc A/CN.4/L.686, 26 May 2006.

20 Adopted by resolution A/RES/55/25 of 15 November 2000 at the fifty-fifth session of the General Assembly of the United Nations, at http://www.unhcr.org/refworld/docid/479dee062.html, last accessed 23 July 2012.

21 For example, Article 98 of the UN Convention on the Law of the Sea, 1833 UNTS 397; Article 12 of the Convention on the High Seas, 450 UNTS 397; the International Convention on Salvage, 1953 UNTS 194; International Convention for the Safety of Life at Sea, 1184 UNTS 3, esp. Articles 7 and 33; International Convention on Maritime Search and rescue, 1403 UNTS;

22 See extensively Van Dijk et al., *Theory and Practice of the European Convention on Human Rights*, 4th edn, Antwerp: Intersentia, 2006, 355 et seq.; D.J. Harris, M. O'Boyle, E.P. Bates and C.M. Buckley, *Law of the European Convention on Human Rights*, 2nd edn, Oxford: Oxford University Press, 2009, 42–6.

23 ECtHR 28 October 1998, *Osman v. United Kingdom*, Appl. No. 23452/94.

24 ECtHR 3 April 2001, *Keenan v. United Kingdom*, Appl. No. 27229/95.

25 ECtHR (GC) 30 November 2004, *Öneryildiz v. Turkey*, Appl. No. 48939/99.

And, third, if the risk has materialized, the state must respond adequately, in particular by conducting an official investigation.

As to the first issue (were the authorities aware of the risk, or should they have been), the Court formulated an individualized criterion in *Osman*. It held that it has to be established 'that the authorities knew or ought to have known at the time of the existence of a real and immediate risk to the life of an identified individual or individuals from the criminal acts of a third party'. The Court does not accept the position of the United Kingdom, which argued that the failure to perceive the risk must be 'tantamount to gross negligence or wilful disregard of the duty to protect life' (para 116). Comparably, in *Keenan* it 'examined whether the authorities knew or ought to have known that Mark Keenan posed a real and immediate risk of suicide' (para. 93). In *Öneryildiz*, however, the Court did not repeat the requirement that the authorities should have been aware of the risk to a particular individual. The context is a different one than the situation dealt with in *Osman* and *Keenan*. Referring to the 'particular context of dangerous activities' (in that case: waste collection), the Court states that 'special emphasis must be placed on regulations geared to the special features of the activity in question, particularly with regard to the level of the potential risk to human lives' (para. 90). When it addresses the particular circumstances of the case, it states that 'there was practical information available to the effect that the inhabitants of certain slum areas of Ümraniye were faced with a threat to their physical integrity on account of the technical shortcomings of the municipal rubbish tip' (para. 98). It then concludes that 'the Turkish authorities at several levels knew or ought to have known that there was a real and immediate risk to a number of persons living near the Ümraniye municipal rubbish tip. They consequently had a positive obligation under Article 2 of the Convention to take such preventive operational measures as were necessary and sufficient to protect those individuals' (para. 101). It is important to note that the Court has accepted a positive obligation in this situation, where a group of people living in an identifiable area was at risk, without being clearly identified as a number of particular individuals. A second important thing to note is that the Court has accepted that there can be a positive obligation in respect to a risk that does not emanate from a particular person. In *Öneryildiz*, the risk was the consequence of a combination of human activity (waste collection) and natural processes (the formation of methane gas). 'Where the risk to life arises from inherently dangerous, but basically lawful, activity, such as, for example, military tests, or the operation of a factory involving toxic emissions, or of a large waste disposal site, there is a duty on the State to provide an effective system of regulation, supervision and control, providing for identification and correction of any dangerous shortcomings.'[26] In addition, positive obligations may be owed to the public at large, as when a State operates a system of leave or relaxed custody for prisoners at the end of their term. The State then owes a duty of care to members of the public in respect of any risk to their lives that may be reasonably anticipated.[27]

In the context of border control, one could argue that the group of potential victims is sufficiently identifiable – being those who will set off from the coasts of North and West Africa trying to reach Europe. Admittedly, this group is more fluid than the group of people living

---

[26] Clare Ovey and Robin White, *The European Convention on Human Rights*, 4th edn, Oxford: Oxford University Press, 2006, 64, references omitted.

[27] ECtHR (GC) 24 October 2002, *Mastromatteo v. Italy*, Appl. No. 37703/97; Harris et al.., *Law of the European Convention on Human Rights*, 46.

close to the Istanbul rubbish dump. However, the Istanbul group was not constant either (people were born and died, moved in and out of the area, came for visits, left during parts of the day for work or other reasons). European border control policies increase risks for a clear category of people, being that of people on the coasts of North and West Africa who remain there (often for a protracted period of time) with the aim of sailing to Europe. That this is a large category cannot be an argument against a positive obligation; it makes a possible infringement more serious, and not the other way around. The counter-argument would hold that the Istanbul group had a clear core (the inhabitants at any given moment), whereas the group of potential migrants is inherently fluid.

As to the second question (whether all necessary measures were taken to ward off the risk), the Court has time and again emphasized that the positive obligation to protect life 'must be interpreted in a way which does not impose an impossible or disproportionate burden on the authorities. Accordingly, not every claimed risk to life can entail for the authorities a Convention requirement to take operational measures to prevent that risk from materialising.' The Court rejects the position that the 'failure ... to take preventive measures to avoid that risk must be tantamount to gross negligence or wilful disregard of the duty to protect life'. However, the criterion applied by the Court (did the authorities do all that could be reasonably expected of them to avoid a real and immediate risk to life?[28]) leads to a case-by-case approach.[29] In *Öneryildiz*, in order to assess what the authorities were obliged to undertake, the Court finds it relevant that the authorities 'themselves had set up the site and authorised its operation, which gave rise to the risk in question' (para. 101). Also, the Turkish government argued that the victims of the methane explosion had 'knowingly chosen to break the law and live in the vicinity of the rubbish tip' (para. 103). The Court rejected this argument, holding that the authorities had consistently tolerated slums in the vicinity of the refuse dump and could not maintain that 'any negligence or lack of foresight should be attributed to the victims'; it also found relevant that the Turkish authorities had remained passive in face of the unlawful dwellings (para. 106).

It is relevant that the argument that seems to be most forceful in rejecting a positive obligation in the border death context (namely: migrants themselves take these risks so States cannot be held responsible if they materialize) is rejected by the Court in terms that are directly applicable in the border control context. One would expect the Court to find the fact that migrants knowingly choose to break immigration law and seek to cross borders, evading border control points, not decisive. European States themselves have set up these particular border policies, which give rise to the risk in question. That is, in fact, the core of the argument for accepting a positive obligation: States should incorporate into their policies a serious effort to minimize unintended side-effects, in particular if these side-effects consist in the foreseeable death of hundreds, if not thousands, of people each year. The argument against a positive obligation can rely on one aspect in which the border control context differs radically from the *Öneryildiz* case. One cannot maintain that European States tolerate or have remained passive in the face of undocumented migration. Obviously, one could argue that European States engage

[28] For slightly different formulations see *Keenan v. United Kingdom* para. 90: did the authorities fail 'to take measures within the scope of their powers which, judged reasonably, might have been expected to avoid that risk'.

[29] *Osman*, para. 116.

in combating undocumented migration in the full knowledge that they will fail and that their policies increase the risks; but undeniably, it is hard to directly rely on *Öneryildiz* on this point.

The third issue concerns how the authorities should respond if the risk has materialized. The adequate response the Court has dealt with (most extensively in *Öneryildiz*) is focused on investigations in order to establish criminal responsibility of third parties or government officials, or to allow for civil, administrative or disciplinary remedies for the victims.[30] In the border control context, however, the allegation would not be that individual government agents have carried out border controls in an inappropriate way; if that were the complaint, the framework the Court has been developing so far would be appropriate. However, the allegation in the border control context is that policies have been *designed* (as opposed to executed) without appropriate consideration of the risks they entail. In this context, the very general starting point of the Court is all there is: 'Where lives have been lost in circumstances potentially engaging the responsibility of the State, that provision entails a duty for the State to ensure, by all means at its disposal, an adequate response – judicial or otherwise – so that the legislative and administrative framework set up to protect the right to life is properly implemented and any breaches of that right are repressed and punished'.[31] The Court took a comparable position in *Menson*, where the United Kingdom was not responsible for the death of Michael Menson (who had been set on fire by four white youths), but nevertheless was under an obligation to institute an official investigation.[32]

In the context of border control, an obligation to instigate an investigation into the behaviour of state officials will sometimes be relevant. This happened in the *Xhavara* case. It is obvious that such investigation should be undertaken when a migrant vessel has been sunk, as in the *Xhavara* case, or when migrants have been shot or have stepped on land mines at the Turkish/Greek border.[33] But the issue at stake here is a more difficult one. If migrants simply drown, or die in other ways but not through an activity of a State official directed at them personally, what would the required adequate response consist of?

30 *Öneryildiz*, paras 91–2.

31 *Öneryildiz*, para. 91.

32 ECtHR (Dec.) 6 May 2003, *Menson and Others v. United Kingdom*, Appl. No. 47916/99.

33 This happens with some regularity. According to press reports quoted by United, migrants were shot on 29 March 1995 (Greece), 20 August 1995 (France), 5 September 1996 (Spain), 17 August 1998 (Italy), 10 May 2000 (Turkey, 9 persons), 15 November 2000 (Turkey), 3 December 2000 (Spain), 16 July 2001 (Turkey), 12 January 2002 (Turkey, 2 persons), March 2002 (Macedonia, 7 persons), 22 May 2002 (Turkey), 19 June 2002 (Turkey, 2 persons), 23 September 2003 (Greece), 3 October 2003 (Spain), 11 April 2004 (Spain), 17 April 2004 (Slovakia, 2 persons), 10 September 2005 (Greece), 19 September 2005 (Turkey), 29 September 2005 (Morocco, 5 persons). Migrants died in the minefields at the border between Turkey and Greece on 13 September 1995 (4 persons), 30 June 1996 (2 persons), 15 September 1997 (3 persons), 16 April 1998 (2 persons), 26 August 1999 (3 persons), 31 October 1999 (5 persons), 1 May 2000, 29 August 2000, 1 September 2000 (2 persons), 29 March 2001 (2 persons), 21 May 2001, 22 May 2001 (2 persons), 30 September 2001, 23 December 2001 (4 persons), 20 March 2002 (2 persons), 27 March 2002, 28 August 2002, 4 January 2003 (2 persons), March 2003, 29 September 2003 (7 persons), 5 August 2004, 14 November 2004 (3 persons), 4 April 2005 (2 persons), 29 May 2005 (2 persons), 9 December 2005 (2 persons), 30 May 2006 (1 person), 3 July 2006 (3 persons), 25 July 2006 (2 persons), 10 September 2006 (2 persons), 3 December 2006 (Morocco, 1 person), 1 August 2007 (Morocco, 2 persons), 8 November 2007 (Greece, 1 person), 16 November 2007 (Cyprus, 1 person), 1 January 2009 (1 person). See http://www.unitedagainstracism.org/pdfs/listofdeaths.pdf, last accessed 23 July 2012.

Arguably, there are three ways in which European States should respond. First, border deaths are undeniably related to European border control policies. Their number is related to the externalization of border control and intensification of patrols on relatively safe sea routes. The core of the issue is whether there is a sufficient causal relationship between these migration control policies and border deaths. Certainly the two phenomena are *related*, but *causality* is another matter. In order to be able to assess these policies in light of international law, it is necessary that more detailed and reliable information becomes available. The phenomenon of border deaths is of such scope that it can be argued that States are under an obligation to collect these data. One may argue that there is an obligation under Article 2 ECHR to monitor in a consistent way the consequences of these policies. Presently, there are no reliable data on the number of border deaths. Within an EU context, a shared approach must be developed for collecting these data from local or maritime authorities who take care of the corpses. These data should be as specific as possible about the time and place the bodies were recovered, cause and circumstances of death, the identity of the migrant, and the like. Second, one may argue that there is an obligation to subsequently evaluate border control policies regularly in light of the data collected in that way. If a policy has potentially lethal side-effects, there is an obligation to assess how these side-effects develop, whether these developments may be related to policy changes or changes in the context, and whether the unintended side-effects can be limited by (flanking) policy measures. Third, one may argue that States have an obligation to the surviving relatives of the victims. They must try to identify the person, using information about the region of origin of the victim, testimony of surviving fellow migrants, if possible finger prints, DNA and other tools of international policing. As Stefanie Grant has argued, the 'vast arsenal of technology used in border control [should be diverted] to the humanitarian task of maintaining a register of those who die making the journey towards their border; relatives could access the records at some future time'.[34]

Arguments denying that European States should develop an appropriate response to border deaths will primarily rely on the notion that border deaths occur outside the area of responsibility of European States. However, that is a jurisdiction argument, which was addressed above. Another argument against imposing obligatory responses might be that border deaths do not trigger the responsibility of European States because there is insufficient causal relation between State behaviour and these fatalities. That, however, cannot be established without gathering adequate data, and assessing the development of the fatalities in relation to border control policies. The whole point is that there *may be* a causal relationship, which triggers the responsibility of European States to undertake an investigation. And for the third possible response (identify the victims), no causal relationship is required. If a body is found in a purely domestic situation, the authorities find it obvious that the identity should be established. That a body is likely to be that of an undocumented migrant is insufficient justification for not following the usual procedures. The present practice is based on discrimination on the ground of nationality, which is not acceptable.

[34] Grant, 'Recording and Identifying European Frontier Deaths'. Cf. Council of Europe Commissioner for Human Rights, *The Human Rights of Irregular Migrants in Europe*, CommDH/IssuePaper (2007)1, Strasbourg, 17 December 2007, Conclusion 3: 'It is imperative to begin a process to identify and account for the thousands of "missing" undocumented migrants, who disappear – on the journey or after arrival – and whose identities are unknown.'

To sum up: it may well be argued that border deaths give rise to three positive obligations. First, that to carry out an investigation into the number of fatalities at the European borders over the past decades, and in the future to collect such data at least annually. Second, the obligation to assess European border control policies in light of these data, in order to develop (flanking) policies that effectively minimize the number of fatalities. Third, the obligation to establish the identity of the victims, to inform their relatives, and to deal with the bodies in accordance with their wishes as far as possible.

Standing

In addition to raising complex issues of jurisdiction and positive obligations, border deaths are also problematic from the point of view of actual justiciability, because victims simply are unable to bring their cases as a consequence of precisely the behaviour that, arguably, violates the Convention. It may take a class action to bring these issues to court. It is significant that only one border death case has been brought before the European Court of Human Rights.[35]

The position of the Court is that organizations may address the Court, but neither individuals nor organizations can bring an *actio popularis*, or abstract complaints. It has summed up its position as follows:

> The Court reiterates that Article 34 of the Convention requires that an individual applicant should claim to have been actually affected by the violation he alleges. That Article does not institute for individuals a kind of *actio popularis* for the interpretation of the Convention; it does not permit individuals to complain against a law *in abstracto* simply because they feel that it contravenes the Convention. In principle, it does not suffice for an individual applicant to claim that the mere existence of a law violates his rights under the Convention; it is necessary that the law should have been applied to his detriment. (*Klass and Others v. Germany*, 6 September 1978, Series A no. 28, § 33)[36]

This seems to exclude the possibility of a complaint lodged by NGOs on border policies.[37] However, it should be noted that the Court's concern is that it should not give judgment about potential human rights violations. It explains its objections to the *actio popularis* and abstract complaints by emphasizing this, and by outlining the limited number of exceptions. In order to adjudicate a potential violation, the applicant must produce 'reasonable and convincing evidence of the likelihood that a violation affecting him personally will occur; mere suspicion

35 ECtHR (Dec) 11 January 2001, *Xhavara et quinze autres c. l'Italie et l'Albanie*, Appl. No. 39473/98.

36 ECtHR (Dec.) 6 November 2001, *Fédération Chrétienne des Témoins de Jéhovah de France v. France*, Appl. No. 53430/99. Compare recently ECtHR (Dec.) 28 June 2011, *La Ligue des Musulmans de Suisse and Others v. Switzerland*, Appl. No. 66274/09.

37 Cf. Ovey and White, *The European Convention on Human Rights*, 483; Van Dijk et al., *Theory and Practice of the European Convention on Human* Rights, 55–6; Harris et al., *Law of the Convention on Human* Rights, 791–3.

or conjecture is insufficient in this respect'.[38] However, in border control cases the issue is not that the alleged violations have not yet taken place. Instead, they have taken place, and precisely because of that European States may well have succeeded in keeping the applicants effectively outside the scope of European courts.

In this context, the proper parallel may not be that of the objections against the *actio popularis*, but that of unrepresented minors. 'In the event of a conflict over a minor's interests between a natural parent and the person appointed by the authorities to act as the child's guardian, there is a danger that some of those interests will never be brought to the Court's attention and that the minor will be deprived of effective protection of his rights under the Convention.'[39] Therefore the Court accepted that the mother's 'standing as the natural mother suffices to afford her the necessary power to apply to the Court on the children's behalf, too, in order to protect their interests.'[40] It ruled likewise in cases concerning persons who lost their legal capacity after being committed to a psychiatric hospital.[41] On the basis of this, it may be argued that an NGO can have standing on behalf of victims who have not addressed the Court, provided that (1) it is necessary to accept their standing for an effective protection of Convention rights – in this case because the victims have been kept effectively outside the scope of European courts; and (2) provided that it has been established that one or more violations have already taken place, i.e. the application does not concern a potential violation.

Which State?

A last issue concerns joint operations of European States, whether or not under the Frontex banner. Because of the cooperation of European States in border control, one may well argue that responsibility for border deaths does not, or not exclusively, lie with Mediterranean States, but with all European States – it is their joint border that is being guarded even if the actual work is often done by States such as Spain, Italy, Greece, Malta and Cyprus. Also, the question may come up which European State is responsible for an act, such as interception, which is carried out in the framework of a joint operation, for example under the flag of Frontex.

In *Bankovic*, the applicants lodged a complaint against 17 States, being those NATO Member States which were also party to the European Convention on Human Rights. The issue there was whether States are liable for an act carried out by an international organization of which they are members.[42] The difference with border controls is that these are not carried out by the EU, but by Member States, possibly in joint operations. The similarity is that the airplanes dropping bombs on Belgrade were not NATO airplanes, but airplanes of NATO Member States even though they were acting under NATO command. In any case, the issue was explicitly not decided by the Court. There seem to be no obstacles to joint responsibility

38 Harris et al., *Law of the European Convention on Human Rights*, 792 and the case law referred to there.

39 ECtHR 13 July 2000, *Scozzari and Giuntay v. Italy*, Appl. No. 39221/98 and 41963/98, para. 138

40 Ibid.

41 ECtHR 24 October 1979, *Winterwerp v . The Netherlands*, Appl. No. 6301/73, para. 10.

42 *Bankovic*, paras 30 and 83.

of EU Member States for the way border controls are carried out, but much will depend on the circumstances of the case. However, even if EU States were to transfer competence in the area of border control to the EU, they would remain responsible for guaranteeing Convention rights.[43]

Conclusions

Do European States have a positive obligation to minimize the rising number of fatalities that occur in relation to their border control policies? An argument that, indeed, such a positive obligation does exist is perfectly valid. It does require acceptance of some innovative elements on the points of jurisdiction and positive obligations. A convincing case can be made that these innovative elements do nothing but mirror the innovative aspects of European border control policies. The central idea of European border control policies over the past 20 years has been to let their consequences occur outside Europe, before migrants reach Europe, so that they are out of reach of Europe's legal systems. If law is to be effective in upholding human rights, it has to keep pace with policy innovations that are inspired precisely by the wish to get out of the reach of human rights law. However, the argument to the contrary is valid as well. It can be argued that jurisdiction should not be stretched so as to make European States responsible for the consequences of their policies outside their territory, unless State agents themselves act outside the territory. In addition, it can be argued that a positive obligation can only exist *vis-à-vis* groups of people which are more determinate than migrants are. Finally, one may argue that States are not responsible for the consequences of what people do when they seek to contravene policies which are actively enforced by the authorities.

As to the procedural issues, the situation is similar. Should standing of NGOs on behalf of people who cannot act for themselves be accepted? Should States be held responsible collectively for the effects of joint policies, if a requirement of individual responsibility would make it impossible, or at least very difficult, for claimants to effectuate a claim? The argument can be made that this should be accepted because that is necessary for upholding human rights protection for a group in dear need of it. But the argument can also be made that this should not be accepted because it would open the possibilities for litigation too much and could lead to State responsibility for situations in which it is not clear whether they are sufficiently involved.

Legal argument tends to get terribly complicated when it has to deal with an issue that is the subject of substantial disagreement. That is what we can observe here. On the one hand, there is the perception that Europe may be beleaguered by alien hordes unless effective border control remains in place. The widening gap in affluence between Europe and many other parts of the world, coupled with increasing international mobility, require innovations of border control. From that perspective, externalization seems like a good move. On the other hand, there is the perception that effective protection of human rights – not just the protection of wealth – is at the core of the European project. Border control may well be necessary for

[43] ECtHR 18 February 1999, *Matthews v. United Kingdom*, Appl. No. 24833/94; see Ovey and White, *European Convention on Human Rights*, 30.

protecting this European project. But that makes it all the more crucial that, precisely in that context, the effective protection of human rights is not diluted.

These issues are not merely legal ones but also involve moral, ethical and political choices. In making such choices, legal arguments can play a role, but they do not determine the outcome. Until now, the issues dealt with in this chapter have mainly been ignored. Europeans prefer to look the other way on the issues of border deaths. The least we can do is to notice, to register, and to take account of the human costs – to others – of protecting our European project. Only when we have begun to do that can we decide whether a proper balance between costs and benefits has been struck.

References

Carlier, Jean-Yves, *Droit d'asile et des réfugiés. De la protection aux droits*, Leiden: Martinus Nijhoff, 2008.

Carling, Jorge, 'Migration Control and Migrant Fatalities at the Spanish–African Borders' (2007), 41(2) *International Migration Review*, 316–43.

Council of Europe Commissioner for Human Rights, *The Human Rights of Irregular Migrants in Europe*, CommDH/IssuePaper (2007)1, Strasbourg, 17 December 2007.

Cuttitta, Paolo, 'Il controllo dell'immigrazione tra Nordafrica e Italia', in Nicoletta Dentico and Maurizio Gressi (eds), *Libro Bianco. I Centri di Permanenza temporanea e Assistenza in Italia un'indagine promossa dal Gruppo di Lavoro sui CPTA in Italia*, Rome, 169–99.

De Haas, Hein, 'Migration and Development: A Theoretical Perspective' (2010), 44 *International Migration Review*, 227–64.

Godenau, Dirk and Manuel Zapata Hernández, 'The Case of the Canary Islands (Spain): A Region of Transit Between Africa and Europe', in Gemma Pinyol (ed.), *Immigration Flows and the Management of the EU's Southern Maritime Borders*, Documentos CIDOB Migraciones 17, 2008, 13–43.

Goodwin-Gill, Guy S. and Jane McAdam, *The Refugee in International Law*, 3rd edn, Oxford: Oxford University Press, 2007.

Grant, Stephanie, 'Recording and Identifying European Frontier Deaths' (2011), 13 *European Journal of Migration and Law*, 135–56.

Harris, D.J., M. O'Boyle, E.P. Bates and C.M. Buckley, *Law of the European Convention on Human Rights*, 2nd edn, Oxford: Oxford University Press, 2009.

Hathaway, James C., *The Rights of Refugees under International Law*, Cambridge: Cambridge University Press, 2005.

Kiza, Ernesto, *Tödliche Grenzen – Die fatalen Auswirkungen europäischer Zuwanderungspolitik*, Zürich/Berlin: Lit Verlag, 2008.

Lauterpacht, Elihu and Daniel Bethlehem, 'The Scope and Content of the Principle of Non-refoulement: Opinion', in Erika Feller, Volker Türk and Frances Nicholson (eds), *Refugee Protection in International Law*, Cambridge: Cambridge University Press, 2003, 87–164.

Lawson, Rick, 'Life after Bankovic', in Fons Coomans and Menno T. Kamminga (eds), *Extraterritorial Application of Human Rights Treaties*, Antwerp: Intersentia, 2004, 83–123.

O'Boyle, Michael, 'Comment on "Life after Bankovic"', in Fons Coomans and Menno T. Kamminga (eds), *Extraterritorial Application of Human Rights Treaties*, Antwerp: Intersentia, 2004, 125–39.

Ovey, Clare and Robin White, *The European Convention on Human Rights*, 4th edn, Oxford: Oxford University Press, 2006.

Spijkerboer, Thomas, 'The Human Costs of Border Control' (2007), 9 *European Journal of Migration and Law*, 127–39.

Van Dijk, [first name/s] et al., *Theory and Practice of the European Convention on Human Rights*, 4th edn, Antwerp: Intersentia, 2006.

Wouters, Kees, *International Legal Standards for the Protection from Refoulement*, Antwerp: Interstentia, 2009.

PART II
SAFEGUARDING THE SAFETY AND SECURITY OF REFUGEES

Jonah and Socrates as Refugees: Repentance, Redemption and Responsibility

Howard Adelman

Introduction

In the current definition of a refugee – more specifically a Convention Refugee rather than simply someone fleeing war or generalized ethnic and religious communal violence – refugees are defined as persons who, by reason of a *well-founded fear* of persecution, for reason of race, religion, nationality, political opinion or membership in a particular social group, are *unable or unwilling to return* to their countries of birth or habitual residence. They are motivated by fear and must declare that they cannot or will not return to their homelands. It is a definition that arose out of the peculiar circumstances at the beginning of the cold war and the desire to protect those who did not want to return to the lands of the Soviet Empire where they faced incarceration and possibly torture or even death. The definition was expedient, served a very positive purpose at the time, and has been expanded upon to allow the protection of many others. But this depiction of a refugee denigrates the refugees and defines them as essentially motivated by fear. It also characterizes them as abandoning their homelands.

I want to suggest, more for theoretical than practical purposes, defining refugees as choosing flight and refugee status as the only option they see available to them to preserve their integrity and dignity. They may have a well-founded fear of persecution, but fear is not what drives flight. Further, rather than abandoning any desire to return to their homeland, empirically and theoretically it has often been their foremost desire. To make my case, I shall use Jonah, who tried to become a refugee but was unable to do so, and Socrates, who refused to become a refugee.

I take Jonah and Socrates as my exemplars because Jonah wanted to become a refugee but was not permitted. He tried but was forced to abandon his flight and serve his absolute ruler in a foreign mission.[1] Socrates also could not become a refugee, not because he was forced to stay or to return, but because his internal daemon told him that to become a refugee would

[1] There is a pseudepigraphical tradition and text, *The Lives of the Prophets*, in which, after Nineveh, Jonah does succeed in becoming a refugee. In that midrash, Jonah took his mother to Sour, a territory inhabited by foreign nations, as an escape from his failure when he prophesied *against* Nineveh. 'So shall I remove my reproach, for I spoke falsely in prophesying against the great city': tr. D. R. A. Hare, *Old Testament Pseudepigrapha*, vol. 2, ed. James Charlesworth, New York: Doubleday, 1985, 392–3.

be a betrayal of his integrity. In other words, they are examples, not because they became refugees, but because they were not permitted to become refugees. In both cases, they had a well-founded fear that they would be persecuted. Jonah eventually preferred death to being forced to return and serve his sovereign in what he viewed as an unworthy cause. Socrates preferred death to exile and did achieve his preference. The difference between the two will, I believe, bring out a great deal about what it means to become a refugee. Both demonstrated fearlessness and love of homeland rather than being driven by fear and abandonment of their homeland.

This is, admittedly, an angular and conceptual approach to the refugee issue. Most analyses address tensions that have raged throughout the twentieth century over immigration and refugee policy. Debates develop over rights of refugees to claim protection, over preferred solutions to mass flows of refugees from ethnic and ideological conflicts, as well as over how many immigrants to accept and, if accepted, what profile they should have. A myriad of other issues continued to inform public policy at the end of the first decade of the twenty-first century. However, there is virtually no refugee scholarship exploring whether or not an individual should become a refugee in the first place and the philosophical issues at stake in that decision.[2] The vast majority of issues are about being in limbo after becoming a refugee or about intake rather than exodus. Even when the issue concerns the impact of being a refugee on the individual, the problems explored are after the fact – as in Lacroix's essay on the effects of asylum procedures on an individual's construction of his or herself as a refugee.[3]

This chapter focuses on the decision to become or not become a refugee within the larger historic *philosophic* debates over the obligations of membership in a polity. For the conception of a refugee is but the negative complement to the conception of citizenship.[4] The exploration of the fundamental issues at stake when or if one decides to flee or not to flee one's country will be initiated through an analytic comparison of the position of Jonah in the Hebrew Bible and the position of Socrates.

Jonah and Socrates

The section after this one begins with a brief summary of the very short biblical tall tale of Jonah, sometimes referred to as a parable and at other times a satire,[5] and my scriptural midrash

[2] There have been many developments in refugee studies since Roger Zetter penned his editorial introduction entitled 'Refugees and Refugee Studies – A Label and an Agenda' in the first volume and issue of the *Journal of Refugee Studies* in 1988 (1–6); this offered an inventory of substantial matters for examination and analysis. However, the issue of whether or not to become a refugee was not among them and there has been virtually no change in that matter since then.

[3] Marie Lacroix, 'Canadian Refugee Policy and the Social Construction of the Refugee Claimant Subjectivity: Understanding Refugeeness', *Journal of Refugee Studies*, 17:2 (2004), 147–66.

[4] Philosophers who focus on the conception of citizenship in relationship to sovereignty also focus on intake rather than on exodus. See Averell Bell, 'Being "At Home" in the Nation: Hospitality and Sovereignty in Talk about Immigration', *Ethnicities*, 10:2 (27 May 2010), 236–56.

[5] There are those who argue that Jonah is an historical work given its political and logistical details: cf. David Malick, 'An Introduction to the Book of Jonah', at http://bible.org/article/introduction-book-jonah (accessed 17 July 2012). However, the evidence suggests it is a satire of

(*midrash aggadah*) on Jonah [6]. Before I delve into the character of each of my protagonists in turn and in detail, it will be helpful to provide an overview. Neither Jonah nor Socrates ever becomes refugees. Jonah tries but is forced to return and serve his God; Socrates refuses to go into exile. So why take characters as prototypes of the nature of being a refugee using figures who never enter such a role? Simply because the refusal to allow them to become refugees or their refusal to become a refugee tells us, I suggest, more about refugee-hood than an examination of all those who succeed.

Jonah is berated for trying to flee God's command and become a refugee. As Matthew depicted Jonah, he is the prophet, that is, one who speaks on behalf of God as a visionary, but he failed to accept God's grace and adumbrated the need for Jesus to replace the narrow pharisaic view of the divine and the role of the Jews.[7] When the Pharisees asked for a sign that Jesus was the messiah, Matthew wrote: 'An evil and adulterous generation craves for a sign; and yet no sign shall be given to it but the sign of Jonah the prophet; for just as Jonah was three days and three nights in the belly of the sea monster, so shall the Son of Man be three days and three nights in the heart of the earth.' Unlike Jonah who never repented and was never redeemed, the men of Nineveh shall stand up on the judgment day beside their Lord and Saviour 'because they repented at the preaching of Jonah; and behold, something greater than Jonah is here' (Matthew 12: 38–41; see also Luke 11: 29–32).

There is no escape from God's universal rule and compassion for all. Jonah went on his mission under duress and resented the task he was asked to fulfil.[8] In fact, he sulked when God offered the Ninevites salvation. Jonah set off his own judgment and will against the highest authority of all. But in failing to repent, he did not receive redemption by God but was given the honour of having his story told every year on the holiest day for Jews, Yom Kippur, the day of repentance in every synagogue.[9] So a book about a prophet's non-repentance is read on the Jewish holiest day of the year, the Day of Atonement.

---

an alternative history and not simply a traditional parable that offers its moral lessons through a direct didactic form.

6 A *midrash* is the process of interpreting text and compiling the results. A *midrash aggadah* is an exploration of ethics and norms embodied in a biblical story and, more formally, refers to the homiletic and non-legalistic exegetical texts in the classical rabbinic literature of Judaism recorded in the Talmud and Midrash. My account will be rather straightforward, unlike the exegesis of Rabbi Eliezer whose overriding tone 'is essentially satirical, where the sacred and the fantastic, the absurd and the exalted, intertwine': Rachel Adelman, *The Return of the Repressed: Pirqe de-Rabbi Eliezer and the Pseudeprigrapha*, Leiden: Brill, 2009, 213.

7 In what is regarded as a radically alternative interpretation, in the New Testament Jonah is *praised* as the pre-figuration of Christ, as adumbrating the 'resurrection' after spending three days in the belly of the big fish and then being, in effect, brought back to life when he was vomited up on the shore. (See ibid., 234.) However, the two interpretations are not essentially opposed. Jonah can be not only a pre-figuration of Christ but also in Christian eyes a failed prophet who refuses God's grace. For a detailed exemplary analysis of the irony and satiric elements of Jonah, ibid., ch. 11 is invaluable.

8 In Rachel Adelman's interpretation, Jonah initially refuses to go, not because he thinks the order absurd and a betrayal of the Hebrew nation, but because he initially is the one with compassion for the Assyrians and does not want to be the vehicle of their destruction when they stick to their wicked ways: ibid., 215.

9 Reading Jonah in the afternoon service of Yom Kippur became a common practice only in the last millennium: ibid., 217–18, n. 18.

Why? Was it because he accepted responsibility for his own actions or was it because, in one interpretation of Matthew, he failed to really comprehend and accept God's grace? For some Christians, Jonah stands as a rebuke to the rejection of God's universal grace and as a pharisaic prototype who refused to accept the teachings of Jesus and the lesson of universal compassion independent of works and good deeds. For Jews, who are taught what it means to wrestle with God ('Israel' means 'wrestling with God'), Jonah is an archetype both of that struggle and of the importance of works and deeds to earn redemption.[10] Just saying you are sorry may be a speech act or performative in Austin's terms,[11] but it is still not a deed such as escaping and fleeing to try to reach Tarshish. Responding with your feet is very different to responding with words.

Though there are some references to indirect speech acts that take place 'off stage', such as when the sailors are reported as crying out to their various gods or Jonah is reported as having asked his soul to die or God is reported to have talked and instructed the Big Fish, most speech acts in the book are direct – for example, the prophetic pronouncements or prayers to God.[12] Jonah starts off as a very different prophet in that he does not write the book, has no dream though he lives a nightmare, and does not act out in a way to teach his own people. When Jonah prophesies to the Ninevites, he uses only five words and includes neither the customary prophetic indictment nor the precise punishment that will be meted out. He only says that they should repent or in forty days be 'transformed' or destroyed. Jonah's behaviour is the message, not his pronouncements. In dealing with the tension between God's will and human freedom, Jonah is denied freedom and made a complete slave to God's will.[13]

Socrates too expressed his own judgment as superior to the authority of the jury of his peers. While externally fulfilling all the ritual requirements of the state religion, he nevertheless insisted there was a higher authority, the internal daemon within him whose truth he accepted without question as the inner voice of universal reason.[14] Just as Jonah, in contrast to the sailors, has no doubt whatsoever that God's wrath would evaporate once the sailors threw him into the seas and the waves would once again calm down, Socrates too was full of self-certainty, a

---

[10] As a satire, the lesson of Jonah is *not* universalism as a pre-figuration of Christianity but a mockery of the universalist position, nor to teach the immensity of God's grace that would allow both redemption for a wicked people as well as for a rebellious prophet, and certainly not to teach absolute and unquestioning submission to divine authority.

[11] J. L. Austin, *How to do Things with Words: The William James Lectures delivered at Harvard University in 1955*, ed. J. O. Urmson, Oxford: Clarendon Press, 1962. Precisely because prophecies are *not* truth claims, we do not have the paradox that if the prophet is successful in his warning, then he is a liar, but if he is unsuccessful, he fails as a prophet. I do not read Jonah as stubbornly resenting being denied his historical vision and thus taking prophecy as a truth claim.

[12] Raymond F. Pearson Jr., *In Conversation with Jonah: Conversation Analysis, Literary Criticism, and the Book of Jonah*, Sheffield: Sheffield Academic Press, 1996. See also Cynthia L. Miller, Kenneth M. Craig Jr. and Raymond F. Person Jr., 'Conversation Analysis and the Book of Jonah: A Conversation', *The Journal of Hebrew Scriptures* (*JHS*) (1997), at http://www.arts.ualberta.ca/JHS/Articles/article2.htm (accessed 17 July 2012).

[13] Jonathan Magonet, *Form and Meaning: Studies in Literary Techniques in the Book of Jonah*, Bible and Literature Series, Sheffield: Almond, 1983; David Lillegard, 'Narrative and Paradox in Jonah' (1994), at http://www.kerux.com/documents/KeruxV8N3A2.asp (accessed 17 July 2012).

[14] '[N]or was it unknown that he used divination; as it was a common subject of talk, that "Socrates used to say that the divinity instructed him"': Xenephon's Memorabilia of Socrates, at http://thriceholy.net/Texts/Memorabilia.html (accessed: 30 July 2012), Book 1, Chapter 1:2.

certainty that would not allow him to accept the option of exile. He was willing to die rather than flee. In one sense, Socrates was more of a prophet than Jonah, though he operated on the individual level rather than foreshadowing the fate of his nation. 'Socrates spoke as he thought, for he said it was the divinity that was his monitor. He also told many of his friends to do certain things, and not to do others, intimating that the divinity had forewarned him; and advantage attended those who obeyed his suggestions, but repentance, those who disregarded them.'[15] He too was redeemed by history even though he never repented his stand; he is remembered as the patron saint of critical philosophy. The superiority of Socrates' character and his heritage is summed up by Sarah Kofman. Socrates 'was a good "character", or a good mind, a noble, plastic individuality ... surrounded mainly by noble individuals whose own characters were strengthened (as Xenophon tells us) through contact with him.'[16]

There is another reason for using Jonah and Socrates as non-refugee archetypes. They are both depicted as sarcastic; the comic ironic mode is used to grasp and comprehend the paradoxical positions and the innovations of each. The Book of Jonah goes further for it is a satire and juxtaposes a grotesque fantasy – the fish as a Leviathan and the Ninevites converting, in effect, to Judaism – to uphold a normal moral standard that one must *do* something to be forgiven and not just say that one is sorry.[17] Jonah never denied his God; he simply refused to do what he was told until forced to do so. The contradiction between his acceptance of divine authority and his personal refusal to surrender to that authority except when pressed to do so is paralleled by Socrates' comical contradiction. For Socrates totally accepted the universal applicability and validity of his states' laws – even advising Hippias to obey all the laws even though they are fallible[18] – but, at the same time, upheld the teaching of his own mind as having universal applicability, especially when he challenges the inherited practices of the state.

But Jonah and Socrates are also very different. Socrates is a man of thought; Jonah is a man of deeds.[19] Jonah wants to flee but cannot; Socrates will not. Jonah pleas to be allowed to die (4:3 and 4:8), but cannot even have that relief. (In contrast, in chapter 2 Jonah prays for resurrection: 'I have reached death, now raise me up, bring me back to life.') Socrates does determine his own demise even though condemned to death by others. Both men are wilful and self-righteous. Jonah disobeyed his God; Socrates went further and declared his true god to be an *inner* voice inaccessible to the collectivity. In that sense, Socrates was a revolutionary who challenged traditions and introduced a new god, the universal god of human reason and the inner voice of conscience to which, paradoxically, he alone had access and which

---

15 Ibid., Book 1, Chapter 1:4.

16 Sarah Kofman, *Socrates: Fictions of a Philosopher*, tr. Catherine Porter, Paris: Atheneum, 1989 (1988), 105. See Xenephon's Memorabilia of Socrates.

17 '[S]atire is militant irony; its moral norms are relatively clear, and it assumes standards against which the grotesque and absurd are measured ... satire is irony which is structurally close to the comic; the comic struggle of two societies, one normal and the other absurd, is reflected in its double focus of morality and fantasy': Northrop Frye, 'The Mythos of Winter: Irony and Satire', in *The Anatomy of Criticism: Four Essays*, ed. Northrop Frye, Princeton, NJ: Princeton University Press, 1957, 223–42, at 234–5. Cf. Ronald Paulson (ed.), *Satire: Modern Essays in Criticism*, Englewood Cliffs, NJ: Prentice-Hall, 1971.

18 Xenophon's Memorabilia of Socrates, Book 4, Chapter 4.

19 In fact, Jonah is unique as a Hebrew prophet in that he is not depicted in terms of his declarations and warnings to the nation but only through a narrative of his behaviour.

was undeniable and irrefutable. In that sense, the founder of critical philosophy was similar to a prophet who is certain of his calling, how he receives his 'call', and what he is called to say. However, given Socrates' very different source of the truth, he neither advised rulers on military matters nor prophesied doom and gloom, exile and destruction. Socrates did claim to *interpret* law just as Jonah and the other prophets spoke as interpreters of the Covenant between God and the Hebrew people.

Why did neither become a refugee?

Jonah: In Quest of a Refuge from God

It was through the prophet most identified with the salvation of the Hebrews, namely Jonah, that God secured the remnant of the northern kingdom of Israel as well as Judah, the southern kingdom, from the Assyrians. Through Jonah, God instructed Jeroboam, the son of Joash king of Israel, when he became king in Samaria in 784BCE for 41 years, to restore and strengthen the borders.[20] I assume that the Jonah in the Book of Jonah is the same referent.[21] Otherwise it is difficult to make sense of the satire unless the Jonah who urges the importance of building defences against the Assyrians is the same character whom God sends to save the Assyrians from their wicked ways.

Given that agreement, there is plenty of room for disagreement. Certainly Jonah is a short volume, generally accepted as a masterpiece of literature, over which there have always been wide divisions of interpretations and many efforts to reconcile these various strands. In the direct interpretation the lesson is simple: you must always obey God even when you do not understand the purpose of His message. Is Jonah a straightforward didactic text teaching that God is merciful, not just to the Hebrews, but to all humanity topped up by infinite mercy for all his creatures?[22] Alternatively, is it more complex: in Simon's words, a volume of

[20] Jeroboam 'restored the border of Israel from the entrance of Hamath as far as the Sea of the Arabah, according to the word of the LORD, the God of Israel, which He spoke through His servant Jonah the son of Amittai, the prophet, who was of Gath-hepher. For the LORD saw the affliction of Israel, which was very bitter; for there was neither bond nor free, nor was there any helper for Israel. And the LORD did not say that He would blot out the name of Israel from under heaven, but He saved them by the hand of Jeroboam the son of Joash': 2 Kings 14: 24–7.

[21] Most interpreters do. For example, Theodoret in the fifth century argued that the prophecy in 2 Kings 14:25 and the Book of Jonah designates Jonah as the son of Amittai; it is the same individual in both biblical references: Jeanne M. Heisler, 'Gnat or Apostolic Bee: A Translation and Commentary on Theodoret's Commentary on Jonah', PhD thesis, Florida State University, at http://diginole.lib.fsu.edu/cgi/viewcontent.cgi?article=1870&context=etd (accessed: 11 September 2011), 44.

[22] An early commentator of the fifth century, Theodoret of Cyrrhus, tried to integrate many commentaries to interpret Jonah as the key story in which the Jews serve as prophets for all humanity and adumbrate Jesus as the voice for a compassionate God at the service of everyone. 'For inasmuch as the only begotten Word of God was about to be made manifest to human beings in human nature, and to enlighten all nations with the light of the knowledge of God, even before His own incarnation, He shows his divine care to the nations, in order that He might establish with certainty future events by those which preceded it, teach everyone that He is God not only of the

compassionate irony with numerous inversions and an abundance of paradox?[23] Or finally, is it a satirical narrative in which God ends up as the greatest jester?

In the Book of Jonah, God ordered Jonah to travel to Nineveh to preach doom and destruction to Israel's and Judah's most hated enemy and ultimately offer them salvation when they repented, thus turning upside down the purpose of God's providence to save the Hebrew nation. Jonah boarded a ship in Joppa in his national homeland and tried to travel west and get to Tarshish as a refugee. He does not do so because Israel as a state failed to protect him. The ultimate authority behind the Jewish people, Yahweh, is pictured as the saviour of the *enemies* of the Jews. Further, in the worst possible nightmare Jonah could have had, God foisted on Jonah of all people the responsibility of preaching to the bitterest enemies of the Jewish people, the Assyrians of Nineveh, the iconic evil city and city of evil for the ancient Israelites, the capital of Assyria, the country that 50 years later would destroy and abduct the most northerly tribes in the eighth century BCE, and the city that in cuneiform is written as a fish and here suggests the Leviathan.[24] Why would Jonah want to save Assyria from destruction?[25]

God ordered Jonah to preach to the 'fallen' in a context in which the fallen constituted the life and blood of the largest, most cosmopolitan and most materialist city in the Middle East at the time. Jonah considered offering salvation to the Assyrians unjust and an affront, and more importantly, altogether contrary to the interests of the tribes of Israel and Judah. For after the end of the united kingdom under David and then Solomon (971–931) when the Hebrew kingdom was divided into Israel (ten tribes) and Judah (two tribes), Assyria emerged as the scourge of Israel and the victimizer of Judah beginning with the reign of Ahab over Israel (873–852). However, during the reign of Jeroboam (784–745), when Jonah was active, Assyria had become weak and quiescent. During that time both Israel and Judah prospered. But as Jonah prophesied, this would not last. Tiglath-Pileser III (Pul, 2 Kings 15:19–20) invaded Israel and forced King Menahem (744–738) to pay tribute. A civil war followed between the northern kingdom under King Pekah of Israel (737–732), supported by the Syrians, and King Ahaz of Judah, who, when cornered, appealed to the Assyrians for help. As Jonah prophesied, Israel

---

Jews but the God also of the nations, and point out the close relationship between the Old and the New Testament: Heisler, 'Gnat or Apostolic Bee', 42.

[23] Uriel Simon, *The JPS Bible Commentary: Jonah*, Philadelphia, PA: The Jewish Publication Society, 1999.

[24] In this interpretation, Jonah is not *primarily* motivated by ego – he does not want to go down in history as a false prophet for it would be unseemly (he would look bad) – nor as unwilling to risk his own nation when God takes out his anger on the Hebrew nation for Jonah's refusal. In the former case, he would be putting his own ego prior to his duty to serve (and also would be a parody of a prophet as a positivist wedded to a view of prophecy as prediction); in the latter case, his flight would be motivated by saving God's reputation for compassion by averting any collective punishment against the Hebrew nation. As Jonah says in 4:2, 'I pray Lord, was this not my word when I was in my country? That is why I made haste to flee toward Tarshish, for I knew that you are gracious and compassionate, slow in coming to anger and great in *ḥesed* and repenting of evil.' A. R. Johnson does not read this as a sarcastic remark but adopts the simple didactic interpretation: see 'Jonah ii, 3–10: A Study in Cultic Phantasy', in *Studies in Old Testament Prophecy*, ed. H. H. Rowley, New York: Scribner, 1950, 82–102.

[25] Jonah refused to save Nineveh 'because he knew the evils and exiles that it would bring on the tribes of Israel in the future; hence he yearned that the nation of Assyria be destroyed and Nineveh its capital be utterly smitten. This is why he fled instead of going there': Simon, 'Introduction: The Overall Intention', in *Jonah*, 7–12, at 7.

would fall from a prosperous, stable state to a nation not only divided but at war with itself. If Jonah could adumbrate this future, why would he want to save the Assyrians, especially since the Assyrians, just after achieving their zenith as an empire in the latter half of the eighth century BCE, declined by the end of the following century and Nineveh was destroyed in 612 BCE?

Initially, Jonah refused to follow God's command and travel east to Nineveh. The story clearly suggests that Jonah was not simply being asked to volunteer given the punishment meted out to him after he fled. Jonah was trying to evade punishment by a wrathful all-powerful authority for his refusal to obey. Otherwise, why did Jonah not just say 'No!' and stay put? Why did he not go into hiding? Why become a refugee, flee his own country, and go west?

When God ordered Jonah not only to travel to Nineveh but to preach hell and damnation if the Assyrians did not repent of their sinful ways yet indicated that he would also offer salvation if they did repent, virtually every Jew would have felt betrayed at the time. It was as if the UN had not only offered Colonel Gadhafi forgiveness for his four decades of misrule and cruelty, but also at the same time promised his salvation and even the presidency of the Security Council. Perhaps a better analogy would be imagining God instructing an Israeli rabbi to travel to Iran and preach the threat of a maelstrom if the Iranians did not amend their ways, and Iranian president Mahmoud Ahmadinejad not only repented for denying the Holocaust but looked on Israel with favour and was rewarded with a Nobel Prize for peace. It is and would be unimaginable. So was the possibility of the Assyrians transforming themselves.

On the one hand, we have a picture of God making what seemed to be an absurd demand; Jonah was unwilling to fall in line and become a tool in implementing what would seem on the surface to be anathema to the Jewish people. On the other hand, Jonah's miscasting as a prophet for this mission seems even more outlandish than God's orders.

Jonah fled, not only because he had reasonable grounds for fearing punishment for his disobedience, but primarily because he found God's commandment to be a betrayal of the promises he had made to Israel. Jonah boarded a ship to Tarshish. The ship had a very rough passage and huge waves threatened to wreck the ship. Jonah, who slept soundly through the storm, when he was awakened identified himself to the ship's crew as the source of the problem. He said he was a member of the Hebrew nation who had disobeyed their God; God was now meting out collective punishment to the whole ship for Jonah's personal act of disobedience. Jonah advised the sailors to throw him overboard so that God's wrath would cool and the rough seas could grow calm.[26] After some persuasion,[27] he was dropped overboard

---

[26] This story contrasts with that of Socrates, who as a member of the Athenian polity served as a judge (*prytany*) of 12 sea captains charged by angry seamen, not with throwing a civilian passenger into the sea to appease a wrathful God, but with failing to fish the bodies of the dead from the sea. Socrates acquitted them on the grounds that the battle in which they were engaged took precedence.

[27] Initially, the sailors try to calm the seas by praying to their own gods. Even when Jonah confesses that he is the source of the problem, they still try to row to shore, throw baggage overboard, and determine who is to be sacrificed by drawing lots. They are reluctant to kill someone who may be innocent. Even when they decide to throw him in, they first bob him in to test whether the waters are calmed.

and immediately swallowed by a large fish, often referred to as a whale.[28] But it is a Big (*gadol* in Hebrew) Fish! The adjective *gadol* is repeated throughout this satirical Big Fish Story.

But the Big Fish story has a real depth of meaning. Just as Socrates *chooses* to swallow the hemlock, Jonah *chooses* to be thrown overboard. He has learned that, although he can escape from the *shekhinah* responsible for sending prophets on their mission by leaving the land of the Hebrew nation, he cannot escape God. Where else can he go? Into the primordial sea, the watery abyss of chaos where darkness rules over the face of the deep and God is believed not to be present. Here he goes deeper than just going down to Joppa or down into the deeper recesses of the ship where he fell into a deep sleep even as both the sea and heavens stormed all around him. There in the depths of the sea, Jonah encounters the same inner world of the unconscious, not in the sea itself but in the belly of the Leviathan,[29] the same unconscious that Socrates discovers within himself that is more indubitable than the Delphic oracles or, for Jonah, the *shekhinah*. Then he can become a prophet reborn after he is vomited out 'on dry ground' just as the prophet Isaiah foretold (53:1). Jonah's rebirth as a new-born prophet stands in stark contrast to that of the Ninevites' 'rebirth'. Jonah is reborn as a prophet of Israel who will wrestle with God, as one who has been resurrected. Jonah expresses a willingness to die rather than simply submit to a meaningless and illusionary doctrine of universal compassion.

Although Jonah in the belly of the great fish prays to the God of Israel for salvation, his cliché pastiche of a psalm plagiarized from other psalms of prayers for salvation is offered as a parody.[30] Jonah never repents his refusal to obey God's commandment. Jonah, however, has a different slant on that message of learning obedience: he learned that even in the depths of the big fish, even in his own unconscious, he cannot *escape* God. God mocks Jonah, but after three days, the Big Fish cannot stomach Jonah and vomits him up on shore. The Big Fish is all-encompassing, serving all four functions of animals in biblical narrative: as portents (an omen that Jonah was going where no human had been before), examples of possibilities (in this case, a physical impossibility and thus an example of fabulism), vehicles of punishment (the fish swallows Jonah for trying to escape God's commandment), and means of deliverance and salvation (Jonah is saved by the fish from drowning and saved again by being vomited on dry ground).

Jonah's resistance seems to collapse but never does. He does obey God: he follows his orders to the letter while in total rebellion against their spirit. Like Socrates, he is now informed by that 'undiscovered' inner netherworld. The punishment, like Socrates',[31] becomes the source of his historical resurrection, having navigated a wholly internal other world.

---

28 This tradition goes very far back. Theodoret translated the 'big fish' as a whale: Heisler, 'Gnat or Apostolic Bee, 58.

29 Avivah Gottlieb Zornberg, *The Murmuring Deep: Reflections on the Biblical Unconscious*, New York: Schocken Books, 2009, 78.

30 Robert Couffignal, 'Le Psaume de Jonas (Jonas 2,2–10). Une Catabase Biblique', *Biblica*, 71:4 (1990), 542–52, esp. 545. See also Lillegard, 'Narrative and Paradox in Jonah'.

31 For a detailed exposition of the Athenian conception and practice of punishment, cf. Danielle S. Allen, 'Punishment in Ancient Athens', *Dêmos*, 23 March 2003, republished in Adriaan Lanni (ed.), 'Athenian Law in its Democratic Context', *Center for Hellenic Studies On-line Discussion Series*, and republished again in C. W. Blackwell (ed.), *Dēmos: Classical Athenian Democracy*, A. Mahoney and R. Scaife (eds), *The Stoa: A Consortium for Electronic Publication in the Humanities*, *at http://www.stoa.org/projects/demos/article_punishment?page=1&greekEncoding= (accessed: 17 July 2012). Allen explores the issues of what motivated Athenians' punishment and what ends punishment was*

The Leviathan is the bottom line for that resurrection. The name of the Elusive Serpent, *barich,* has its root in the Hebrew word 'to flee'. Jonah in flight from God discovered his own self in the deep darkness of the belly of the Big Fish[32] and is reborn to stand against a God defined simply as an external and demanding and commanding Other wavering between tyranny and an infinite boundary-less compassion. Having confronted the Leviathan and found God even in the darkness of the deep, Jonah can now confront the old merely external God even in the heat and glare of sunlight.

When Jonah travels to Nineveh, he arrives in a city of 120,000 that takes three days to traverse. He walks for a full day and stops to preach in the marketplace, promising doom and physical destruction and damnation if the inhabitants do not repent. Without hesitation or argument or evidence, the people repent. The nobility of Nineveh quickly follow and they order everyone, including all their cattle, to put on sackcloth, fast, sit on ashes, and comply: 'In Nineveh by the decree of the king and his nobles: Do not let man, beast, herd, or flock taste a thing. Do not let them eat or drink water. Both man and beast must be covered with sackcloth; and let men call on God earnestly that each may turn from his wicked way and from the violence which is in his hands. Who knows, God may turn and relent, and withdraw His burning anger so that we shall not perish.' (Jonah 3:7–8)

The people of Nineveh are then saved. They need only express their faith in God. They need not prove that they had turned from their wicked ways though each is expected to do so once they have accepted God into their hearts: 'each *may* turn from his wicked ways and from the violence which is in his hands' (my italics) If one was unaware that this had been a spoof, by this point it should have become obvious – except, of course, if one believes in God's infinite grace for those who need simply assert, 'I believe.' The essence of grace is offering favour when it is unmerited and undeserved. What a contrast with God's dealing with his chosen people who are constantly threatened with extermination unless they prove that they have reformed their wicked ways with actual deeds. 'Thus says the LORD: "Behold, I am fashioning calamity against you and devising a plan against you. Oh turn back, each of you from his evil way, and reform your ways and your deeds."' (Jeremiah 18:5–11)

The satire ends with God's providing a broad-leafed plant to provide shade for Jonah as he watches the success of his mission with bitterness, and then a worm to eat the leaf and leave Jonah sweltering in the heat from a scorching wind. Jonah complains and asks God why he did not save a plant that had provided shade and protection while Jonah slept yet saw fit to save the wicked of Nineveh that posed a constant threat to Israel. Jonah may have given in to God's authority, but he remains unrepentant for his rebellion against those orders and mocks God's decision. God has the final word and offers a joke with a Jack Benny straight face that turns into a smirk: 'Should I not have compassion on Nineveh, the great city in which there are more than 120,000 persons who do not know the difference between their right and left hand,[33]

---

supposed to serve, what procedures and processes they used to determine the punishment, and the penalties they employed.

32 Adelman, *Return of the Repressed,* 245.

33 Rather than a snide remark about the Ninevites, Rashi interprets this to be a reference to the many children, as do earlier (Theodoret) and later contemporary commentators: see Heisler, 'Gnat or Apostolic Bee', 80.

as well as many animals?' (my italics).[34] One may only ask, if all animals as creatures of God who lack free will are always obedient to God, why need they repent?[35]

In a straight (and naïve) reading of the story, it is a lesson that one should always obey God's orders; our faith will both redeem us and those whom God targets to save. Even those who have fallen the furthest and are most in need of redemption can be saved. It is a tale of the reluctant prophet who differs from previous ones who felt they were not up to the task.[36] Jonah *rejects* the commandment and flees. In the simple interpretation, Jonah has to learn obedience when commanded by God and surrender himself to the divine will. It is a parable in which God demonstrates absolute compassion and mercy. It is a lesson in spiritual cosmopolitanism in opposition to the exclusive pursuit of national self-interest in a globalized world. This version favours universal compassion indifferent to past behaviour, but, ironically, only at the behest of a divine cosmopolitan dictator with an enormous power of enforcement. This version places the emphasis on God's universal grace as the way towards a utopian future. In that cosmopolitan ethic, everyone is equally a sinner and equally worthy of redemption, including domestic cattle, cats and dogs.

However, as a satire, the tale is a mockery of a contradictory tyrannical and punishing God who, paradoxically, has compassion for those who are most corrupt as well as the greatest threat. The story satirizes naïve religious beliefs of an absolute, all-powerful whimsical God, prophets as toadies to such a supreme authority, as well as instant conversion and redemption simply by promising future catastrophe. The most worthy characters are the pagan sailors who first refuse to sacrifice Jonah, even though he is a stranger, though their fear for their own personal safety eventually trumps their compassion. They show true grace even if they throw Jonah overboard.

The two versions of the story frame the debate between cosmopolitan versus restricted citizenship. Cosmopolitan citizenship has two variations, one in the service of divine love and the other the universalism of a crass empire. Restricted citizenship also has two variations, the primacy of a response to the demands and responsibilities of a territorial state under threat, like Jonah's Hebrew polity, versus the salts of the sea who may be pagans and probably lack membership in any polity yet recognize a responsibility to the Other, though not if that responsibility require their own sacrifice. A naïve, simple reading champions a non-ironic reading and favours cosmopolitanism and the purity of God's grace. Read as a satire, it is the naïve cosmopolitans who are being mocked.

Jonah is read every year in Jewish synagogues on Yom Kippur, the Day of Atonement, to satirize simplistic portraits of God as a tyrant and of atonement as simply confessing

---

[34] Cf. Yael Shemesh, '"And Many Beasts" (Jonah 4:11): The Function and Status of Animals in the Book of Jonah', *Journal of Hebrew Scriptures*, 10:6 (2010), at http://www.jhsonline.org/Articles/article_134.pdf (accessed: 18 August 2012). Shemesh does not interpret this as a joke nor as a reference to the wild ones or beasts, the untamed youth of Nineveh, as Rashi. Nor does he see it as a joke as I and Miles do: J. A. Miles, 'Laughing at the Bible: Jonah as Parody', *Jewish Quarterly Review*, 65 (1974–75), 168–81. Rather, the text is interpreted as demonstrating the wide purview of God's mercy.

[35] See Philippe Guillaume, 'The End of Jonah is the Beginning of Wisdom', *Biblical Studies on the Web*, 87 (2006), 243–50, at http://www.bsw.org/Biblica/Vol-87-2006/The-End-Of-Jonah-Is-The-Beginning-Of-Wisdom/103/ (accessed: 18 August 2012).

[36] *Cf. Jeremiah 1:6; Gideon in Judges 6:15; Saul as described in I Samuel 9:21.*

sins in an instant bending to God's will and threats while characterizing God as a being of infinite compassion. The satire mocks blind obedience to transparently unjust orders that will threaten the protection of both oneself and one's nation. In the naïve reading, God redeems a threatening nation but destroys a plant that actually offers protection.

I read the story as a satire. My focus is on an eternal 'now', a 'now' that can never be but must always retreat into a disappearing past in contrast to the universal, the eternal, the belief in a cosmopolitan order of universal citizenship and a borderless world that is not, but, unlike 'now', it is an 'is not' that belongs to an envisioned future rather than a disappearing past. Alternatively, the story is told about a predicament that is ever present, even in our own time. At all times, the present is torn between a non-existent universal ideal and an inherited particular past to which we owe our primary loyalties. Jonah opts for a future that rejects offers of easy salvation by accepting the latest universal creed: he remains a member of a tribe of stiff-necked bowing but unbroken people. In that sense, Jews and Jonah remain refugees, eternal icons of homelessness, resistant to the siren calls of a world in quest of a universal and new world order. Jonah in the singular and Jews collectively are the iconic refugees. As in Yehuda Amichai's novel *Lo Me'Achshav, Lo Me'Kan* ('Not from the Present and Not from Here'), cosmopolitan protection is presented as a tempting illusion to those on whom the sun beats down relentlessly. Jonah and the remnant of Jews who reject such offers of salvation just have to sweat it out.

The choice is an awful one, not in its present meaning of a horrific decision, but in its much older meaning as one inspiring and worthy of awe. The choice, on the one hand, is flight and the effort to escape from responsibility, or, on the other hand, serving abroad in a universal missionary cause that purportedly expresses the purity of God's grace in which you do not believe, going along with the gag but ending up as its victim. Jonah opts for the first but is coerced into accepting the second, yet he does so without enthusiasm or even any belief. Though resigned to his fate with only bitter humour left as a refuge, he never accepts the prospect that anyone, regardless of past misdeeds, is entitled to redemption.

However, the ultimate irony is that those who accept the universality of grace will then turn on the Jews for their rejection and blame them for the sins of the world and the death of the teacher who they believe taught that grace was sufficient.

> The pride and the self-righteousness of Jonah and of his people are now glaringly apparent. The reason for the sacking of Israel by the Assyrians is now obvious … Why did the scribes and Pharisees react so vehemently to the teaching of Jesus? Because He exposed them as sinners, and they were not willing to admit this. They were self-righteous. Thus, they rejected God's Messiah and instigated His death on that Roman cross … Later, after our Lord's death, burial, resurrection, and ascension, it was the Jews who opposed the proclamation of the gospel (cf. Acts 22:19–23). Even Christian Jews drug their feet in the preaching of the gospel to the Gentiles (cf. Acts 10–11, esp. 11:19). Because some Jewish Christians felt superior to Gentile believers, they either segregated themselves or they sought to force the Gentiles to conform to their Jewish practices (e.g. Acts 15:1; Gal. 2:11ff.). Truly Jonah's

self-righteousness typified a tendency among Israelites that has continued throughout the centuries.[37]

Socrates versus Jonah

The case of Socrates offers a very different approach. Instead of a Jew in flight from authority, Socrates stands up to the authorities that have charged him with blasphemy and the corruption of children.[38] Socrates comes across and is largely recorded in history as a hero compared to Jonah who is often presented as a self-righteous resentful rejecter of God's absolute authority. Like Jonah, however, Socrates mocks authority and goads his possible saviour, the jury of his peers. Both resist authority through irony and disdain.

However, the values of the craftsman who works with leather or stone, or the merchant who trades in money, or, for that matter, the ordinary seaman, are sarcastically rejected by Socrates.[39] Neither materialist skills nor materialist rewards have any redeeming value. Socrates lives off the avails of a small inheritance from his father who was precisely such a craftsman, but rejects his father's values and preaches an ideal of a leisurely aristocratic class permanently engaged in conversation about unanswerable universal and abstract questions – for example, how can one lead a life of virtue?[40] The founder of critical philosophy is celebrated as a hero and martyr to the pursuit of Truth with a capital 'T' for his willingness to question everything and to die in defence of that right.[41]

---

[37] Bob Diffenbaugh, 'Nineveh's Repentance and Jonah's Wrath', at https://bible.org/seriespage/nineveh%E2%80%99s-repentance-and-jonah%E2%80%99s-wrath-jonah-3-4 (accessed: 11 January 2010). In my daughter Rachel Adelman's account cited above and depicted in chapter 11 of her book, this interpretation of Matthew and Luke is not congruent with 'the sign of Jonah'.

[38] As we shall see, Xenephon's defence of Socrates against this charge in chapter 2 of his Memorabilia on the basis that Socrates persuaded children to avoid vice and fostered temperance and all the other virtues as well as their duty to obey the laws, misses the more basic point – Socrates' challenge to the fundamental authority of the belief system, customs and conventions of the community.

[39] For example, Socrates mocks his prosecutor, who is a tanner. Socrates offers to save the prosecutor's son from a 'servile occupation' that will develop a disgraceful propensity leading to a career of vice.

[40] This does not mean that Socrates practised indolence. As Xenophon recounts in Book II, Chapter 1 of the Memorabilia, Aristippus' quest for a life of leisure and tranquil enjoyment was a life of indolence that Socrates advised against for it undermined the nature of human society. Incidentally, Socrates not only opposed becoming a refugee; he opposed tourism as an idle pursuit and opined that to visit and sojourn in many places was not only indolent but dangerous. What is truly valuable is voluntary rather than remunerative labour.

[41] See Richard Holway, 'Achilles, Socrates, and Democracy', *Political Theory*, 22:4 (November 1994), 561–90. Achilles' courage is cited to pursue philosophy in the face of possible execution. Socrates does so in a pious manner, while the motives of his accusers are impure. But to be pious, one must have an accurate knowledge of what is holy versus that which is unholy. As Socrates asks Euthyphro, 'you think that you have such accurate knowledge of things divine, and what is holy and unholy, that … you can accuse your father? You are not afraid that you yourself are doing an unholy deed?' (*Euthyphro*, 4e). See also Diskin Clay, 'Socrates' Mulishness and Heroism', *Phronesis*, 17 (1972), 53–60. In that article, Clay notes the multiple references to animals, not as

Though both adopt an ironic approach to life, nevertheless Jonah and Socrates are very opposite types. The Jonah story as a whole may be steeped in irony and Jonah in addressing God at the end may be sarcastic, but Socrates is the true epitome of an ironic conversationalist. In Plato's *Apology*, Socrates addresses the messenger from the oracle and avers that no one can be wiser (21a), and then demonstrates that virtually everyone else must indeed be wiser than the messenger, except himself, of course, for he excels only in his ignorance, primarily his knowledge that he is ignorant. The well-known irony, of course, is that, since Socrates knows he is ignorant, he is the least unwise and is, therefore, free to speak irreverently about unjust laws; and, in the *Apology*, he ironically demands that instead of prison or exile he be celebrated, feted and honoured like a famous athlete at the Prytaneum.

So why is he obedient to the rule of law of ancient Athens and the rulings of the court responsible for administering and executing those laws, when he is the victim of those laws and is sentenced to death for corrupting the youth of Athens[42] and for his impiety? He was not charged with sedition. Laws exemplify for him the highest public value. In Plato's *Crito*, when his acolytes come to try to get Socrates to escape from prison and go into exile, from the premise that it is wrong to disobey the state, Socrates concludes, in a circular argument, that one ought never to *disobey* a state's rulings since that would be doing wrong. And one ought never knowingly to engage in a wrongful act. He does not reject their offers to help because they will have their fortunes confiscated for helping him. Socrates is not like Jonah willing to sacrifice himself to save others. He rejects this help because he disagrees with the action in principle and upholds absolute obedience to the law.[43]

Today we would argue the opposite, and many laws capture this doctrine of civil disobedience. It is wrong to obey a command of a state if that command is unjust. But Socrates appears to accept the premise that it is always wrong to disobey the command of a state. So he apparently refuses to become a refugee in strong contrast to his leading prosecutor, Anytus, a defender of democracy who became a refugee and fled into exile when the Tyrants led by Critias seized power in 404.

Socrates will not flee his responsibilities and duties of a citizen, will not flee and go into exile. To become a refugee is the ultimate expression of alienation; he would rather take hemlock and die. Thus Socrates becomes the icon of an idealist, at once wedded to the pursuit

---

agents as in Jonah but as insulting analogies: 'In the Apology he (Socrates) speaks of his judges and accusers of asses, horses, horse-flies and calves' (53).

42 Cf J. Peter Euben, *Corrupting Youth: Political Education, Democratic Culture and Political Theory*, Princeton, NJ: Princeton University Press, 1997, esp. 46–7. If education entails passing on traditions and structures of a society to its youth, then inculcating an ability to question received wisdom will by definition entail a corruption of youth. Further, once received 'truths' are already suffering from a loss of relevance and are in doubt and in disarray, as in Aristophanes' *Clouds*, then the fragility of inherited tradition makes questioning all the more lethal, particularly when the democracy was under attack from without and from within. There is no doubt that Socrates challenged the Athenian beliefs in persuasion, the value of communal knowledge of the democratic city-state, and the goodness of Athenians laws, while he insisted on his absolute obedience of those laws.

43 *If Socrates is so opposed to civil disobedience, the question arises, why did Martin Luther King Jr. cite Socrates thrice in a scrawled essay written on a New York Times newspaper as he sat in a Birmingham jail? Cf.* Alan Gilbert, 'How to Read Plato: The Farcical Speech of the Laws', 16 April 2011, at http://democratic.individuality.blogspot.com/ (accessed: 27 June 2011).

of universal values, in this case, the alleged universality of reason rather than of grace, while rooted deeply in his own citizenship as an ultimate identity and, according to Xenophon, his realistic assessment that his days are numbered anyway and his eye on how he wants to go down in history.[44] But his rational account is based on the rule of law rather than his own interests. He criticizes those laws openly and defiantly but will not disobey them and will not, and cannot, relinquish his citizenship. For unlike the laws of the Jews, the laws of Athens belong to a particular place and are not portable. Therefore, there can be no redemption for a refugee.

Thus, although Jonah and Socrates are identical in challenging authority and addressing figures and institutions of authority sarcastically, Socrates contrasts with Jonah who tries to escape God's, not a state's, commandment. Not because the commandment will produce a wrong, but because redemption would unjustly reward those who have done wrong. For Socrates, an action is not right because God does or does not command it. As Socrates argues in the *Euthyphro*, if actions are right because the gods order them (10a), as Euthyphro defined piety, then right actions are determined by an arbitrary authoritative divine will rather than any general principle and, therefore, cannot command our obeisance.

For Jonah, compassion for the Other begins with challenging absolute authority. For Socrates, philosophy begins by challenging patriarchy.[45] For the advocates of the universal truth's residing inherently in reason, philosophy begins with the rejection of inherited traditions and values determining one's conclusions and practices. This is true of personal ethics and political theory as well as scientific inquiry. But it is one thing to challenge an absolute authority and another to disobey it. Jonah chooses exile while Socrates deprecates those who choose to be refugees rather than be obedient to an unjust state. For Greeks, as well as for the sailors on the ship sailing for Tarshish, piety meant appeasing the anger of the gods and offering sacrifices, including reluctantly throwing Jonah overboard. But that is the big difference. Jonah and Socrates both express a willingness to sacrifice themselves, but Jonah does so to save innocent bystanders. Socrates chooses to sacrifice himself in the name of a universal principle of obedience to the commands of a state even if those commands are unjust. At the same time, he challenges that injustice and the absolute authority of those laws.

There is another similarity between Jonah and Socrates. Both are able to hear the word of God.[46] The difference is in their use of reason. Jonah uses his reason to claim that God's

---

[44] In Xenophon's account of his trial, suicide was a set-up for Socrates, whose daemonium has told him it is time to die, with the added benefit that by dying this way he would achieve status for posterity. Cf. Kenneth Dorter, 'Socrates on Life, Death and Suicide', *Laval Theologique et Philosophique*, 32 (1976), 23–41; Richard E. Walton, 'Socrates' Alleged Suicide', *The Journal of Value Inquiry*, 14:3–4 (1980), 287–99; and Joseph Cropsey, 'The Dramatic End of Plato's Socrates', *Interpretation: A Journal of Political Philosophy*, 14:2–3 (1986), 155–75.

[45] In Xenophon's Memorabilia, Part II, Ch. II, Socrates advises his son Lamprocles *not* to resent his *mother's* instructions, 'for children are obligated to return gratitude for a parent's sacrifices even though a parent may use harsh words against a child.' Parental devotion must be requited. A son ought to revere his mother even if she is severe, for the severity proceeds from kind motives. However, Socrates is charged not with corrupting youth by inducing them to disrespect their parents but for undermining community-received norms and dictums.

[46] This directly contravenes Leo Strauss's view and a major concern of his corpus that the difference between Athens and Jerusalem is that the former attends to the laws of reason while the latter obtains its authority from the word of God. Reason and revelation were not

command is absurd; Socrates uses his reason to refute reasons offered by others for changing his course of action. In his defence, when he was ordered by the Tyrants to arrest Leon of Salamis so he could be immediately executed, Socrates did *not* do it. Neither did he alert Leon of Salamis that he was under threat even as proponents of liberty and democracy were being arrested and executed or sent into exile all around him. Socrates heard the words of divine wisdom and simply went home just as Jonah simply fled. But unlike Jonah, Socrates put forth his behaviour as an act of virtue consistent with reason and *sanctioned* by a superior divine authority.

Further, in this case, Socrates behaved hypocritically by disobeying an order of the state without even claiming the order was unjust. And he refused to risk himself to save another, though he would not himself take the other's life. Clearly two different ethics motivated Jonah's and Socrates' challenge to absolute authority – one championed the absolute right of the individual, while the other exemplified the norms and boundaries for compassion for the Other. Judaism through Jonah offered an Other-directed ethic. The philosophy of Socrates exemplified the ultimate value of the individual, though both Jonah and Socrates sparred with and challenged absolute authority in the realm of ethical conduct.

What justified Socrates' disobedience? In Plato's *Apology*, Socrates insists that his mission is to save men's souls for a life of virtue and insists he will obey God's will rather than the jury of a democratic state to desist from teaching that allegedly corrupts youth. Is this not the same defence a mullah would offer who preached the necessity of ignoring and even subverting the laws of a democratic state when they ostensibly contradicted the commandments of God? For it was Critias, Socrates' pupil, who was the leader of the Thirty Tyrants who overthrew the Periclean democracy of Athens and put 1,500 to death and drove thousands more into exile. Should a mullah who preaches the pursuit of virtue and subversion of a democratic state be put on trial or expelled from a democratic state? Though he is the opposite of a dogmatic mullah in teaching self-criticism and advocating living an examined life, Socrates is akin to such a mullah in his self-assured faith in his own inner daemon and in his anti-democratic beliefs.[47] In contrast, the Book of Jonah is a satire of dogmatic mullahs, ministers or rabbis

reconcilable. According to the Bible, the beginning of wisdom is fear of the Lord; according to Greek philosophers, the beginning of wisdom is wonder. We are thus compelled from the very beginning to take a stand. Cf. Leo Strauss, 'Jerusalem and Athens: Some Preliminary Reflections', City College Papers, no. 6 (1967); reprinted in Leo Strauss, *Essays and Lectures in Modern Jewish Thought*, ed. and intro. Kenneth Hart Green, Albany, NY: SUNY Press, 1997, ch. 9, 377–407. Cf. David Novak (ed.), *Leo Strauss and Judaism: Jerusalem and Athens Critically Revisited*, Lanham, MD: Rowan & Littlefield, 1996; Hadley Arkes's essay, 'Athens and Jerusalem: The Legacy of Leo Strauss', in Novak (ed.), *Leo Strauss and Judaism*, 1–23; Kim Sorensen, 'Revelation and Reason in Leo Strauss', *The Review of Politics*, 65 (2003), 383–408. See also Susan Orr, *Jerusalem and Athens: Reason and Revelation in the Work of Leo Strauss*, Lanham, MD: Rowan & Littlefield, 1995.

47 According to Gerald Mara, Socrates (and Plato) were in favour of a discursive democracy, one based on open discourse in civil society and not primarily on inherited institutions and opinions. However, this creates problems such as in the process undermining belief in the gods. How do you reconcile in critical thought the belief that gods are the source of good and that gods are all powerful? For if the latter, then they must also be the source of evil; if the former, then they cannot be all-powerful. Cf. Gerald M. Mara, *Socrates' Discursive Democracy: Logos and Ergon in Platonic Political Philosophy*, Albany, NY: SUNY Press, 1997, 132.

totally contemptuous of the material world who believe they have exclusive access to the word of God and are commanded to engage in instant forgiveness and conversion.

Socrates had many choices. He could accept the admonition of his peers and respect its ruling and perhaps apologize instead of playing the smart aleck on the principle that law had to be respected even if individual errors in judgment are made. Perhaps he would have incurred a fine, which his friends were more than willing to pay. He could also have requested exile at his sentencing hearing when the vote for a death sentence was higher than the vote for conviction – undoubtedly due to the way Socrates scorned the court. Both would have been consistent with Athenian norms and legal practices. Instead, in Plato's *Laws*, Socrates justifies his acceptance of the death penalty rather than agreeing to flee Athens by essentially arguing that flight would have meant not being true to himself. If he accepted Crito's advice in *The Apology* to flee, he would thereby be compromising his integrity. He would no longer enjoy the rights and privileges of Athenian citizenship and would become a stranger in a strange land accepting a 'scrap of life' in place of a banquet. Rather than break the law and become a hypocrite to save his own life, he accepted the judgment of death for he had always and consistently argued that he was obliged to obey the law.

But what if it was an illegal law? After all, what is a law against blasphemy in a free society? How can you suppress what people think and wish to say? The charge was not of organizing an insurrection: Socrates was effectively charged for preaching heretical opinions and corrupting youth in the process. Socrates had to, at one and the same time, demonstrate that he respected the rule of law but also show contempt for that particular law. He did the reverse, engaging in a performance totally contemptuous of the democratic court and its procedures while remaining absolutely silent about the specific charges and the laws behind them. He preached respect for the law in general while berating the actual practices. He chose to do this by accepting the ruling of the court while deriding the premises on which it was based and the competence of his peers, while, at the same time, accepting their judgment.

Socrates is often lauded as the premier example of a philosopher who advocated freedom of conscience of the individual citizen and further as a willing martyr in sacrificial service to that belief. He was certainly a defender of the right of a philosopher to ask questions without any restraints or boundaries. But this is not the same thing as preaching freedom of conscience. Though Socrates was an icon cited by both Martin Luther King Jr. and Mahatma Gandhi, there is little evidence he upheld freedom of thought and the right to advocate what one believed. Socrates willingly served in the Athenian armed forces – evidently with distinction. Would Socrates have supported the right of conscientious objection? There is no evidence for it in his insistence on duty in obeying all laws.

The closest he comes is his procedural objections. I am not speaking here of his contempt for democracy and its exercise in the law courts. He also questions the restriction of allowing only one day for a trial in a capital offence (35a–36a), suggesting other jurisdictions that allow longer trials for capital offences would be fairer and he would or might have been acquitted with more time to put forth a considered defence. But Socrates never makes a rousing speech in defence of the liberty of free speech or the rights of conscience to dictate behaviour at odds with the norms and requirements of the state. The laws against blasphemy and corrupting children might have been bad laws. Even a law against paedophilia could be a bad law.[48] Socrates does not challenge specific laws. Nor does Socrates challenge even the right of the court to try him. He just demonstrates contempt for the court and its procedures, mocking his prosecutor, who as a Periclean democrat was forced to flee when the tyrants, including the leading tyrant educated in Socrates' entourage, staged a coup and imposed a dictatorship. There is no record of Socrates protesting the coup other than going home and not obeying a direct order to arrest a dissident. But Socrates not only failed to denounce the tyranny, he even failed to warn Leon of Salamis (see above) of his impending arrest.

There is a difference between the concept of law as an order of power that must be obeyed either without question or even with questioning in the belief that law is power and demands one bow before it. There is also the question of law as a source of influence that demands we be persuaded by it. Socrates vacillates between these two views of the law but never examines law, not as primarily an educator operating through influence or as an expression of power to which we are obliged to bow down in obeisance, but as the ultimate source of authentic authority that, while not always right, is the only ultimate authority a free society can have.[49] That is why it is given the highest formal authority and supreme courts must judge whether the legislation of democratically elected officials comply with the principles of the rule of law.

Socrates is not a defender of freedom in a democratic society. Nor is he a defender of the rule of law in a democratic society, for he has a quite different conception of law. Socrates is a defender of freedom of conscience as he defines it – as a follower of the Mystery Religions. Socrates as a Corybant listened to his own muse, and nothing said or told to him could dissuade him from his belief in the superiority of his own internal voices. In Socrates own words (*The Apology* 54d), the music of his own internal flutes and his own voices drowned out any other options. He was unable and unwilling to consider any other possibilities except those provided by his own internal conscience. Socrates was an arrogant mystic rather than a defender of free speech and democracy. Reason was simply a tool to bat away those who disagreed with him and to tear apart the convictions of others who lacked such an irrefutable muse.

Does that mean that he should have been condemned to death for his beliefs and practices? Not at all! The laws under which he was persecuted seem unjust. But Socrates was not the stoical 42-year-old Mary Surratt, mother of John Surratt, a member of the group that killed Abraham Lincoln. Mary was the owner of the boarding house where John Wilkes Booth's plot was hatched to kill the President, the Vice President (the alcoholic Andrew Johnson), and the Secretary of State. Based on evidence proffered by two very compromised individuals out to protect themselves, Mary Surratt, played by Robin Wright, was unjustly accused of participating in Booth's plot to kill Abraham Lincoln in Robert Redford's movie *The Conspirators* written by James D. Solomon.[50] Nor was Socrates, who defended himself, a true

48 Howard Adelman, 'Publicizing Pedophilia: Legal and Psychiatric Discourse', *International Journal of Law and Psychiatry*, 4:3–4 (1981), 311–25.

49 Howard Adelman, 'Authority, Influence and Power: A Discussion', *Philosophy of the Social Sciences*, 6 (1976), 335–51.

50 See the review of *The Conspirators* by Anthony Lane, 'Casualties of War', *The New Yorker*, 18 April 2011, at http://www.newyorker.com/arts/critics/cinema/2011/04/18/110418crci_cinema_lane (accessed: 12 May 2011).

hero as Frederick Aiken played by James McAvoy proved to be in standing up to an injustice perpetrated in the supposed defence of democracy.

Aiken, a former captain and war hero in the Union Army, stood up to mob belief and the temptations of favour by avoiding crossing those in power. Aiken stood up in Mary Surratt's defence, upheld respect for the proper rule of law, for the right of a presumption of innocence and the right of anyone to a fair legal defence and trial even though he himself had once believed her guilty. However, he never believed she should be offered up as a sacrificial victim to the Secretary of War's (Edwin Stanton played by Kevin Kline) determination to use the case, without any consideration for the rule of law or due procedure, to sacrifice her ostensibly in the cause of suppressing any temptations to continue the cause of the southerners by other means. Aiken stood up to a historical stand-in for Donald Rumsfeld, played with a Dick Cheney sneer by Kevin Kline. In contrast, Socrates stood up to no such illegal machinations. He only stood up for his own intellectual superiority and his right to indulge that superiority in public displays.

Like Frederick Aiken, Socrates had many friends, but Socrates never had his membership rescinded from his own military club because he had become so zealous in Mary Surratt's defence. Further, though Crito and Aiken's girlfriend are both honourable people who fear losing the companionship and love of their dearest one, neither stands up for principle. Both are only worried about what people will think and, more importantly, say about their dear ones, making the stand of their loved ones all the more poignant. However, in Socrates trial, there are no echoes of Abu Ghraib and its hooded inmates or of unjust military rather than civilian trials. There is no Secretary of War arguing for political expedience and the necessity of healing a divided and traumatized nation through fear-mongering built on a case of assassination. Though unjust laws play a part, as does the idolatry of the mob, Socrates is a case of an injustice perpetrated as much if not more by his contempt of the court rather than respect for the actual rule of law. Further, in Xenephon's account, it is all a set-up. In Leo Strauss's idiosyncratic view, Socrates died so he could bring democratic legal justice into disrepute for the next two millennia.[51] Socrates chose honour above death in contrast to Mary Surratt who so badly wanted to live but is portrayed as dying with great honour – in contrast also to the three whimpering southern assassins who were hung beside her.

Could Socrates not just as equally have chosen a dignified exit into exile while conforming to the law? Going into exile was thoroughly consistent with Athenian law. In defying the jury's ruling (280 to 220 vote to convict, undoubtedly a majority because of the contempt he showed his fellow Athenians), he was snubbing his nose at the law and asserting his personal superiority to the practice of law. Further, in accepting death he was extinguishing any self to which to be true.

This prescient view of his future seemed to be borne out when Aristotle went into exile. Aristotle, in contrast to Socrates, chose exile rather than death. Aristotle was a non-democrat of a different order to Socrates. He accepted the Athenian aristocratic definition of citizenship whereby only those who assume responsibility for deliberation and decisions in the life of the polis are its real citizens – as distinct from all members of the nation *or* all members born and living in the polity *or* the aristocrats entitled by inheritance of land to rule. For Aristotle,

[51] Leo Strauss, 'The Origins of Political Science and The Problem of Socrates: Six Public Lectures', *Interpretation. A Journal of Political Philosophy* 23:2 (1996), 183–5.

though born in Stagira in northern Greece, was a foreigner, a Macedonian who migrated to Athens to become Plato's brightest pupil. But there was a gap between the ideal and the real. He was never accepted as a true Greek. When Plato died, Aristotle, though the brightest pupil and star of the Academy for 20 years, was rejected as Plato's successor. Nepotism trumped merit. Aristotle as an immigrant alien in Athens was twice refused the inheritance of Plato's academy in spite of being Plato's brightest pupil. Then, when viewed as a security threat because of his connection with Alexander the Great as his tutor, he became a refugee from Athens, retired and gave up on philosophy and his own definition of citizenship as upholding the administrative responsibilities of a city state in the pursuit of justice.[52]

In his first exile after his initial rejection as Plato's successor, Aristotle left Athens and for a time went home and tutored the future Alexander the Great. When he returned to Athens with what the Americans would dub the status of an 'exceptional alien' under the patronage of his former pupil, he established his own peripatetic school, the Lyceum. But once again he was betrayed. After Alexander died, Aristotle was branded as a security threat and charged with impiety (the same charge levelled against Socrates) by the very city that he idealized as the ultimate expression of a polity in pursuit of justice. Instead of standing trial, he became a refugee and fled to the island of Euboea, the birthplace of his mother, and shortly after died.

Did Aristotle die of a broken heart? After all, for Aristotle, life was defined as it was for Socrates as the pursuit of virtue. But the good life that was to be pursued also included friends and family, having possessions including nice clothes (Aristotle had a reputation as a smart dresser), and being a citizen of a state. However, he had finally become a victim of bad fortune and now only had a life that was a shadow of his former existence. Though he accepted being a refugee rather than becoming a martyr and allowing Athens to once again sin against philosophy, being a refugee meant being only partially human. Victims of fickle fortune cannot live the Good Life.

As Hannah Arendt would later argue, without citizenship and the protection of a state in which we fully participate as members, we cannot be fully human.[53]

Conclusion

Jonah and Socrates represent two very opposite responses, though overlapping ironic styles, to ostensibly unjust laws, proceedings and the option of flight abroad. Jonah flees *before* coercion is exercised; Socrates rejects becoming a refugee even before his sentence is set down. But instantly seeking refuge before one's rights are abused, or eschewing exile even before any verdict is laid down, are not the only options. There are a plethora of variables. They cannot be explored here. Two options are.

In this satire, Jonah is portrayed as forced to betray his people and everything he had worked for to secure his nation's security against the bitterest enemies of Israel and Judah. His

[52] 'Who ever is entitled to participate in an office involving deliberation or decision is … a citizen in this city; and the city is the multitude of such persons that is adequate with a view to a self-sufficient life': Aristotle, *Politics* 87.

[53] Hannah Arendt, *The Origins of Totalitarianism*, London: André Deutsch, 1986, 295–6.

only option seemed to be flight, and even that option was closed off. Socrates rejected flight because he would have lost his citizenship and role as a philosopher.

Becoming a refugee is a noble challenge if it offers the only way to preserve your dignity and integrity. The danger is that in flight one will escape with one's life but lose one's self in the process. Taking that risk must be greatly admired.

References

Adelman, Howard, 'Authority, Influence and Power: A Discussion', *Philosophy of the Social Sciences*, 6 (1976), 335–51.

Adelman, Howard, 'Publicizing Pedophilia: Legal and Psychiatric Discourse', *International Journal of Law and Psychiatry*, 4:3–4 (1981), 311–25.

Adelman, Rachel, *The Return of the Repressed: Pirqe de-Rabbi Eliezer and the Pseudeprigrapha*, Leiden: Brill, 2009.

Allen, Danielle S., 'Punishment in Ancient Athens', *Dêmos*, 23 March 2003, republished in Adriaan Lanni (ed.), 'Athenian Law in its Democratic Context', *Center for Hellenic Studies On-line Discussion Series*, and republished again in C. W. Blackwell (ed.), *Dēmos: Classical Athenian Democracy*, A. Mahoney and R. Scaife (eds), *The Stoa: A Consortium for Electronic Publication in the Humanities*, at http://www.stoa.org/projects/demos/article_punishment?page=1&greekEncoding= (accessed: 17 July 2012).

Arendt, Hannah, *The Origins of Totalitarianism*, London: André Deutsch, 1986.

Arkes, Hadley, 'Athens and Jerusalem: The Legacy of Leo Strauss', in *Leo Strauss and Judaism: Jerusalem and Athens Critically Revisited*, ed. David Novak, Lanham, MD: Rowman & Littlefield, 1996, 1–23.

Austin, J.L., *How to do Things with Words: The William James Lectures delivered at Harvard University in 1955*, ed. J. O. Urmson, Oxford: Clarendon Press, 1962.

Bell, Averell, 'Being "At Home" in the Nation: Hospitality and Sovereignty in Talk about Immigration', *Ethnicities*, 10:2 (27 May 2010), 236–56.

Clay, Diskin, 'Socrates' Mulishness and Heroism', *Phronesis*, 17 (1972), 53–60.

Couffignal, Robert, 'Le Psaume de Jonas (Jonas 2,2–10). Une Catabase Biblique', *Biblica*, 71:4 (1990), 542–52.

Cropsey, Joseph, 'The Dramatic End of Plato's Socrates', *Interpretation: A Journal of Political Philosophy*, 14:2–3 (1986), 155–75.

Diffenbaugh, Bob, 'Nineveh's Repentance and Jonah's Wrath', at https://bible.org/seriespage/nineveh%E2%80%99s-repentance-and-jonah%E2%80%99s-wrath-jonah-3-4 (accessed: 11 January 2010).

Dorter, Kenneth, 'Socrates on Life, Death and Suicide', *Laval Theologique et Philosophique*, 32 (1976), 23–41.

Euben, J. Peter, *Corrupting Youth: Political Education, Democratic Culture and Political Theory*, Princeton, NJ: Princeton University Press, 1997.

Frye, Northrop, 'The Mythos of Winter: Irony and Satire', in *The Anatomy of Criticism: Four Essays*, ed. Northrop Frye, Princeton, NJ: Princeton University Press, 1957, 223–42.

Gilbert, Alan, 'How to Read Plato: The Farcical Speech of the Laws', 16 April 2011, at http://democratic.individuality.blogspot.com/ (accessed: 27 June 2011).

Guillaume, Philippe, 'The End of Jonah is the Beginning of Wisdom', *Biblical Studies on the Web*, 87 (2006), 243–50, at http://www.bsw.org/Biblica/Vol-87-2006/The-End-Of-Jonah-Is-The-Beginning-Of-Wisdom/103/ (accessed: 18 August 2012).

Heisler, Jeanne M., 'Gnat or Apostolic Bee: A Translation and Commentary on Theodoret's Commentary on Jonah', PhD thesis, Florida State University, at http://diginole.lib.fsu.edu/cgi/viewcontent.cgi?article=1870&context=etd (accessed: 11 September 2011).

Holway, Richard, 'Achilles, Socrates, and Democracy', *Political Theory*, 22:4 (November 1994), 561–90.

Johnson, A. R., 'Jonah ii, 3–10: A Study in Cultic Phantasy', in *Studies in Old Testament Prophecy*, ed. H. H. Rowley, New York: Scribner, 1950, 82–102.

Kofman, Sarah, *Socrates: Fictions of a Philosopher*, trans. Catherine Porter, Paris: Atheneum, 1989 [1988].

Lacroix, Marie, 'Canadian Refugee Policy and the Social Construction of the Refugee Claimant Subjectivity: Understanding Refugeeness', *Journal of Refugee Studies*, 17:2 (2004), 147–66.

Lane, Anthony, 'Casualties of War', *The New Yorker*, 18 April 2011, at http://www.newyorker.com/arts/critics/cinema/2011/04/18/110418crci_cinema_lane (accessed: 12 May 2011).

Lillegard, David, 'Narrative and Paradox in Jonah' (1994), at http://www.kerux.com/documents/KeruxV8N3A2.asp (accessed 17 July 2012).

Magonet, Jonathan, *Form and Meaning: Studies in Literary Techniques in the Book of Jonah*, Bible and Literature Series, Sheffield: Almond, 1983.

Malick, David, 'An Introduction to the Book of Jonah', at http://bible.org/article/introduction-book-jonah (accessed 17 July 2012).

Mara, Gerald M., *Socrates' Discursive Democracy: Logos and Ergon in Platonic Political Philosophy*, Albany, NY: SUNY Press, 1997.

Miles, J.A., 'Laughing at the Bible: Jonah as Parody', *Jewish Quarterly Review*, 65 (1974–75), 168–81.

Miller, Cynthia L., Kenneth M. Craig Jr. and Raymond F. Person Jr., 'Conversation Analysis and the Book of Jonah: A Conversation', *The Journal of Hebrew Scriptures* (*JHS*) (1997), at http://www.arts.ualberta.ca/JHS/Articles/article2.htm (accessed 17 July 2012).

Novak, David (ed.), *Leo Strauss and Judaism: Jerusalem and Athens Critically Revisited*, Lanham, MD: Rowan & Littlefield, 1996.

Old Testament Pseudepigrapha, vol. 2, ed. James Charlesworth, tr. D. R. A. Hare, New York: Doubleday, 1985.

Orr, Susan, *Jerusalem and Athens: Reason and Revelation in the Work of Leo Strauss*, Lanham, MD: Rowan & Littlefield, 1995.

Paulson, Ronald (ed.), *Satire: Modern Essays in Criticism*, Englewood Cliffs, NJ: Prentice-Hall, 1971.

Pearson Jr., Raymond F., *In Conversation with Jonah: Conversation Analysis, Literary Criticism, and the Book of Jonah*, Sheffield: Sheffield Academic Press, 1996.

Shemesh, Yael, '"And Many Beasts" (Jonah 4:11): The Function and Status of Animals in the Book of Jonah', *Journal of Hebrew Scriptures*, 10:6 (2010), at http://www.jhsonline.org/Articles/article_134.pdf (accessed: 18 August 2012).

Simon, Uriel, 'Introduction: The Overall Intention', in *The JPS Bible Commentary: Jonah*, Philadelphia, PA: The Jewish Publication Society, 1999, 7–12.

Simon, Uriel, *The JPS Bible Commentary: Jonah*, Philadelphia, PA: The Jewish Publication Society, 1999.

Sorensen, Kim, 'Revelation and Reason in Leo Strauss', *The Review of Politics*, 65 (2003), 383–408.

Strauss, Leo, 'Jerusalem and Athens: Some Preliminary Reflections', City College Papers, no. 6 (1967); reprinted in Leo Strauss, *Essays and Lectures in Modern Jewish Thought*, ed. and intro. Kenneth Hart Green, Albany, NY: SUNY Press, 1997, ch. 9, 377–407.

Walton, Richard E., 'Socrates' Alleged Suicide', *The Journal of Value Inquiry*, 14:3–4 (1980), 287–99.

Xenephon's Memorabilia of Socrates, at http://thriceholy.net/Texts/Memorabilia.html (accessed: 30 July 2012).

Zetter, Roger, 'Refugees and Refugee Studies – A Label and an Agenda', *Journal of Refugee Studies*, 1:1 (1988), 1–6.

Zornberg, Avivah Gottlieb, *The Murmuring Deep: Reflections on the Biblical Unconscious*, New York: Schocken Books, 2009.

Strengthening International Refugee Rights through the Enhanced Supervision of the 1951 Convention and its 1967 Protocol

James C. Simeon[1]

Introduction

Ideally, States Parties to the *1951 Convention relating to the Status of Refugees* and its *1967 Protocol*[2] would implement and interpret properly, in a harmonious manner, the provisions of these international instruments to ensure that refugees are fully protected and that their human rights are fully realized under international law.[3] Sadly, this is presently not the case. Walter Kälin has noted that there is 'a lack of uniformity in the actual application of its provisions.'[4] He goes on to point out that,

> This is true not only for many of the guarantees related to the status of refugees but also for such key provisions as Article 33 of the 1951 Convention on *non-*

---

1 James C. Simeon, Ph.D., Acting Director, Centre for Refugee Studies, Associate Professor, School of Public Policy and Administration, Faculty of Liberal Arts and Professional Studies, York University, Toronto, Ontario, Canada. He can be reached at jcsimeon@yorku.ca

2 *Convention relating to the Status of Refugees*, Geneva, adopted 28 July 1951, entry into force 22 April 1954, 189 UNTS 150, at http://treaties.un.org/pages/ViewDetailsII.aspx?&src=TREATY&mtdsg_no=V~2&chapter=5&Temp=mtdsg2&lang=en and *Protocol relating to the Status of Refugees*, New York, adopted 31 January 1967, entry into force 4 October 1967, 606 UNTS 267, at http://treaties.un.org/pages/ViewDetails.aspx?src=UNTSONLINE&tabid=2&mtdsg_no=V-5&chapter=5&lang=en (both accessed 9 January 2011).

3 On the question of harmonious interpretation of the *1951 Convention* and its *1967 Protocol* see Guy S. Goodwin-Gill, 'The One, True Way: National Courts, Refugee Law and the Interpretation of Treaties', Speaking Notes for a Presentation to the Research Workshop on Critical Issues in International Refugee Law, York University, 1 May 2008. A copy of this paper is in the possession of the author. See also Guy S. Goodwin-Gill, 'The Search for the One True Meaning ...', in *The Limits of Transnational Law: Refugee Law, Policy Harmonization and Judicial Dialogue in the European Union*, ed. Guy S. Goodwin-Gill and Helene Lambert (Cambridge: Cambridge University Press, 2010), pp. 204–41.

4 Walter Kälin, 'Supervising the 1951 Convention Relating to the Status of Refugees: Article 35 and Beyond', in *Refugee Protection in International Law: UNHCR's Global Consultations on International Protection*, ed. Erika Feller, Volker Türk and Frances Nicholson (Cambridge: Cambridge University Press, 2003), pp. 613–66, at p. 615.

> *refoulement* or the refugee definition as provided for by Article 1A of the 1951 Convention. UNHCR has repeatedly deplored a trend towards a more restrictive interpretation of the 1951 Convention and its 1967 Protocol in certain countries or even regions of the world. These developments undermine the protection regime created by these instruments. At the same time, they create difficulties for States, for example because restrictive practices turn refugees to countries with a more generous practice.[5]

It is uncontested that the UNHCR has the responsibility for supervising the *1951 Convention* and its *1967 Protocol*, and, indeed, international refugee rights instruments generally.[6] The effective degree to which the UNHCR has been able to exercise its supervisory responsibilities and the proposals that have been presented by various legal scholars, researchers and practitioners to strengthen the supervision of international refugee rights instruments are the subject of this chapter.

The underlining assumption herein is that States Parties to the *1951 Convention* and its *1967 Protocol* have adopted these international instruments with 'good will' and in 'good faith' and with the intention of implementing fully, barring any reservations, all of their provisions.[7] In short, the obligations assumed by the States Parties when they adopted and ratified the *1951 Convention* and its *1967 Protocol* is that their duties and obligations under these treaties will be honoured freely and implemented fully.[8]

This chapter begins with an elemental examination of the purposes and principles of the United Nations and the 'UNHCR as the principal body within the UN system responsible for

5 Ibid. In this vein, see Leanne M. MacMillan, 'Monitoring & Reporting: A Search for New Advocacy Strategies', in *Human Rights and Forced Displacement*, eds. Anne F. Bayefsky and Joan Fitzpatrick (The Hague, The Netherlands: Martinus Nijhoff Publishers, 2000), pp. 99–119, especially (2) The Demise of International Refugee Protection, pp. 100–103.

6 The UNHCR's supervisory role is also evident in the various regional refugee protection instruments that have been ratified such as the *1969 OAU Convention Governing the Specific Aspects of Refugee Problems in Africa, 1984 Cartagena Declaration on Refugees*, and the EU's *1990 Schengen and Dublin Conventions*. In addition, there have been numerous UNHCR Executive Committee Conclusions that have acknowledged and underscored the UNHCR's supervisory responsibilities with respect to international refugee law.

7 *Vienna Convention on the Law of Treaties* (1969) at Article 26 underscores the principle of *pacta sunt servanda* and states, 'Every treaty in force is binding upon the parties to it and must be performed by them in good faith.' See Guy S. Goodwin-Gill and Jane McAdam, *The Refugee in International Law, Third Edition* (Oxford: Oxford University Press, 2007), 5.4 Good Faith, pp. 387–90, wherein they state: 'The broader international protection regime, comprising refugee law, human rights law, and more generally applicable rules informed by the principle of good faith, provides a normative and institutional framework for solutions. The very nature of the international protection regime is premised on States *not* acting unilaterally and in their own self-interest. Indeed, a State that sends out a message of unilateral disregard of the principles of international cooperation will inevitably lead to a disinclination on the part of other States to contribute to solutions' (p. 390).

8 Guy S. Goodwin-Gill, 'Refugees and their Human Rights', RSC Working Paper No. 17, Working Paper Series, Queen Elizabeth House, International Development Centre, University of Oxford, August 2004. This paper was originally presented on 12 November 2003 as the 2003 Annual RSC Barbara Harrell-Bond Lecture: http://www.rsc.ox.ac.uk/PDFs/workingpaper17.pdf (accessed 1 February 2011).

refugee matters and as a subsidiary organ of the UN General Assembly.'[9] It makes the point that the UNHCR was established to realize one of the four purposes and principles of the United Nations, that is, 'to achieve international cooperation in solving international problems of an economic, social, cultural or humanitarian character.'[10]

The chapter then turns to a review and analysis of the legal basis of the UNHCR's supervisory role and responsibilities in the provision of international protection to those in dire need due to the threat to their life, liberty or security. This section posits that the 'responsibility, accountability and liability' paradigm is relevant to an examination of the supervision of the *1951 Convention* and its *1967 Protocol* for both the UNHCR and States Parties to these vital international refugee rights instruments.

The chapter then moves on to outline a number of proposals for strengthening the supervision of the *1951 Convention* and *1967 Protocol* that have been presented by five distinguished legal scholars, academics and practitioners in the field of international refugee law. It is argued that, although these proposals for enhancing the supervision of these fundamental international refugee rights instruments vary widely and are intended to achieve various objectives, they are not necessarily contradictory, inconsistent or mutually exclusive.

The chapter concludes by highlighting the point that, although there is no apparent shortage of reasonable proposals for enhancing the supervision of the *1951 Convention* and its *1967 Protocol*, what seems to be glaringly absent is a willingness on the part of the principals to move forward on any reasonable and practical proposals that would enhance supervision of these seminal international refugee rights instruments. Nonetheless, the chapter ends by noting that some recent developments that coincided with the 60th anniversary of the *1951 Convention* lead to guarded optimism that there are opportunities for positive reforms in this regard and that this could result in the strengthening of international refugee rights. However, this will take a concerted effort on the part of a broad-based coalition of forces within the UNHCR, the UN system, among State Parties, the INGO and NGO communities, civil society, including refugees, and the legal, academic and other professions, to bring about these long overdue reforms that are needed to strengthen refugee rights in the world today.

---

9 Volker Türk, 'UNHCR's Role in Supervising International Protection Standards in the Context of its Mandate', International Conference on Forced Displacement, Protection Standards, and the Supervision of the *1951 Convention* and its *1967 Protocol* and Other International Instruments, York University, Toronto, Canada, 17–20 May 2010, p. 6: http://www.unhcr.org/4bf406a56.pdf (accessed 1 February 2011).

10 Chapter 1, Article 1, the Purposes and Principles of the United Nations, Charter of the United Nations, signed 26 June 1945, in San Francisco, and came into force 24 October 1945, at http://www.un.org/en/documents/charter/index.shtml (accessed 15 January 2011).

Fulfilling the Essential Purposes and Principles of the United Nations: The Resolution of International Problems of an Economic, Social, Cultural or Humanitarian Character

The *1951 Convention relating to the Status of Refugees* marked its 60th anniversary in 2011.[11] It has been described as the *Magna Carta* and the cornerstone of international refugee law.[12] The Office of the United Nations High Commissioner for Refugees (UNHCR) was established on 14 December 1950, just about six months before the adoption of the *1951 Convention*.[13] Both were the product of the United Nations, which was itself established in the aftermath of World War II with the specific intent,

> to save succeeding generations from the scourge of war, which twice in our lifetime has brought untold sorrow to mankind, *and to reaffirm faith in fundamental human rights, in the dignity and worth of the human person, in the equal rights of men and women and of nations large and small, and* ***to establish conditions under which justice and respect for the obligations arising from treaties and other sources of international law can be maintained,*** and to promote social progress and better standards of life in larger freedom ....[14]

It is reasonable to argue, given the inestimable devastation that was inflicted on humankind by World War I and II,[15] including the grotesque horrors, atrocities and genocides that occurred in both of these global armed conflicts, that this led to a common realization and to a global consensus that a new international world order needed to be created to prevent such gruesome and appalling tragedies from ever occurring again.[16] In fact, it is possible to argue

11 *Convention relating to the Status of Refugees*, Geneva.

12 The Editor's Desk, 'The Refugee Convention at 50...', and Judith Kumin, 'Gender: Persecution in the Spotlight', *Refugees, 50th Anniversary, The Wall Behind Which Refugees Can Shelter, The 1951 Convention*, no. 123 (2001), pp. 2 and 12, at http://www.unhcr.org/3b5e90ea0.pdf (accessed 9 January 2011).

13 'UNHCR Milestone: From Hungary to Kyrgyzstan, 60 Years of Helping the World's Forcibly Displaced', at http://www.unhcr.org/pages/4d024e7f6.html (accessed 9 January 2011), and see General Assembly Resolution 428 (V) of 14 December 1950, *Statute of the Office of the United Nations High Commissioner for Refugees*, at http://www.unhcr.org/3b66c39e1.html (accessed 10 January 2011).

14 Preamble, Charter of the United Nations, signed 26 June 1945, in San Francisco, and came into force 24 October 1945, at http://www.un.org/en/documents/charter/index.shtml (accessed 11 January 2011) [emphasis added].

15 Estimates of the number of people who were killed in both of these global conflicts vary widely and some have calculated that the total death casualties, including those who died as a result of war-related disease and famine, is 78 million people. See Matthew White, 'Selected Death Tolls for Wars, Massacres and Atrocities before the 20th Century', last updated October 2010, at http://users.erols.com/mwhite28/warstat0.htm#20worst, and 'Mankind's Worst Wars and Armed Conflicts', 4 March 2009, at http://www.paranormalknowledge.com/articles/mankinds-worst-wars-and-armed-conflicts.html (both accessed 11 January 2011), among others.

16 Volker Türk, 'UNHCR's Supervisory Responsibility', New Issues in Refugee Research, Working Paper No. 67, UNHCR, The UN Refugee Agency, Evaluation and Policy Analysis Unit,

that the central reason for establishing the United Nations was the pursuit of human rights on an international scale in order to prevent 'the scourge of war' and the attendant horrors and atrocities that accompany, ineluctably, armed conflicts and wars.[17]

This is most evident, of course, in Article 1, Chapter 1, of the United Nations (UN) Charter that sets out the pursuit of four explicit purposes: (1) to maintain international peace and security; (2) to develop friendly relations among nations and to strengthen universal peace; (3) to achieve international cooperation in solving international problems of an economic, social, cultural or humanitarian character; (4) to be the centre for harmonizing the actions of nations in the attainment of these common ends.[18] It is evident that the third explicit purpose for establishing the UN clearly covers the plight of those who have been forcibly uprooted and are seeking some form of relief, sanctuary or asylum. Thus, the resolution of 'international problems of an economic, social, cultural or humanitarian character', such as those people who find themselves forcibly displaced, falls clearly within one of the four principal purposes of the UN.

It stands to reason that the achievement of such noble purposes and principles would require an international legal framework that would consider and act on the complaints of those persons who had experienced or could experience potentially serious affronts against their human dignity and/or severe violations or breaches of their most fundamental human rights.[19] Indeed, some of the earliest international instruments promulgated and adopted

October 2002, p. 2, at http://www.unhcr.org/3dae74b74.pdf (accessed 22 January 2011). This paper was first published in *Revue québécoise de droit international*, 14:2 (2002), pp. 135–58.

17 Kate Jastram and Shelley Cavalieri, 'Human Rights and Refugee Tribunals', *Refugee Survey Quarterly*, 24:2 (2005), pp. 6–23. See especially section two, 'The Relationship between Human Rights and Refugee Law', pp. 6–9.

18 With the exception of point 4, each of these points is an abbreviation of the four Sections of Article 1, Chapter 1: Purposes and Principles of the United Nations. The full text of Article 1, the Purposes and Principles of the United Nations, reads as follows:

To maintain international peace and security, and to that end: to take effective collective measures for the prevention and removal of threats to the peace, and for the suppression of acts of aggression or other breaches of the peace, and to bring about by peaceful means, and in conformity with the principles of justice and international law, adjustment or settlement of international disputes or situations which might lead to a breach of the peace;

To develop friendly relations among nations based on respect for the principle of equal rights and self-determination of peoples, and to take other appropriate measures to strengthen universal peace;

To achieve international co-operation in solving international problems of an economic, social, cultural, or humanitarian character, and in promoting and encouraging respect for human rights and for fundamental freedoms for all without distinction as to race, sex, language, or religion; and

To be a centre for harmonizing the actions of nations in the attainment of these common ends.

See the Charter of the United Nations, at http://www.un.org/en/documents/charter/chapter1.shtml (accessed 15 January 2011).

19 Kate Jastram and Shelley Cavalieri, in 'Human Rights and Refugee Tribunals', point out that in 2003 the Executive Committee 'made its clearest proclamation to date of the relationship between international human rights and refugee issues, as well as the respective bodies of law, when it acknowledge[d] the multifaceted linkages between refugee issues and human rights [and] [n]ote[d] the complementary nature of international refugee and human rights law as well as the possible role of he United Nations human rights mechanisms in this area and therefore encouraged[d] States, as appropriate, to address the situation of the forcibly displaced in their

under the auspices of the United Nations clearly bear this out, including, of course, the *Universal Declaration of Human Rights* that sets the international standard for human rights and that was adopted by the UN General Assembly on 10 December 1948.[20]

It is also relevant and interesting to point out that one of the first agencies established by the UN in 1946 was the International Refugee Organization (IRO), the immediate processor to the UNHCR.[21] Indeed, one of the first Conventions that was negotiated under the sponsorship of the UN was the *1951 Convention*.[22]

James C. Hathaway points out that earlier refugee agreements, the *1933 Convention relating to the International Status of Refugees*, in particular, and the *1938 Convention concerning the Status of Refugees coming from Germany*,

> provided the model for two conceptual transitions at the heart of the modern refugee rights regime. First, they introduced the idea of freely accepted *international supervision of national compliance with human rights*. The quiet revolution of thinking transformed *collective supervision of human rights* from a penalty to be paid by subordinate states, as under the League of Nations Minorities Treaties system, to a means of advancing the shared objectives of states through cooperation. Of equal importance, 1928 and subsequent accords reshaped the substance of the human rights guaranteed to aliens. Rather than simply enfranchising refugees within the traditional aliens law regime, states tailored and expanded those general principles to meet the real needs of refugees. The consequential decisions to waive reciprocity, and *to guarantee*

---

reports to the United Nations Treaty Monitoring Bodies, and suggest[ed] that these bodies may, in turn, wish to reflect, within their mandates, on the human rights dimensions of forced displacement.

Here, the Executive Committee articulated a basic premise of refugee protection: that the connection between refugee issues and human rights is profound, and that the respective bodies of law are inevitably related as well.' (p. 8; citation: Executive Committee General Conclusion No. 95 (2003), paras (k) and (l))

20 *The Universal Declaration of Human Rights*, 10 December 1948, at http://www.un.org/en/documents/udhr/ (accessed 11 January 2011).

21 *Constitution of the International Refugee Organization*, New York, 15 December 1946, at http://treaties.un.org/Pages/ViewDetails.aspx?src=TREATY&mtdsg_no=V-1&chapter=5&lang=en (accessed 11 January 2011).

22 James C. Hathaway, *The Rights of Refugees under International Law* (Cambridge: Cambridge University Press, 2005), '2. The evolution of the refugee rights regime', p. 75. James C. Hathaway has also made the salient point that,

The Refugee Convention was the second major human rights treaty adopted by the United Nations, having been preceded only by the Genocide Convention. It is noteworthy that the Genocide Convention, like the Refugee Convention, is not externally supervised. In part, then, the absence of an external supervisory mechanism for the Refugee Convention is simply a reflection of the historical reality that, in the late 1940's and early 1950's, the entire idea of interstate supervision of human rights was new, potentially threatening, and not truly accepted by states.

See James C. Hathaway, 'Taking Oversight of Refugee Law Seriously', speech delivered at the Global Consultation on International Protection convened by the International Council of Voluntary Agencies (ICVA) in Geneva on 11 December 2001, on the occasion of the Ministerial Meeting of States Parties to the 1951 Convention and/or its 1967 Protocol, 12–13 December, 2001, at http://www.icva.ch/doc00000501.html (accessed 30 January 2011).

> *basic civil and economic rights in law,* served as a direct precedent for a variety of international human rights projects, including the modern refugee rights regime.[23]

It has been further noted that the *1951 Convention* was a major achievement in international law in that it embodied the principle of *non-refoulement,* whereby a person cannot be returned to a State where they may risk persecution. In addition, the *1951 Convention* defines who is a 'refugee' under international law that is no longer tied to a specific national group.[24] Nonetheless, it is important and pertinent to stress, as Guy S. Goodwin-Gill and Jane McAdam have noted, that, 'The foundations for an international legal concept of the refugee are thus securely fixed in treaties, State and United Nations practice, and the Statute of the UNHCR.'[25]

The pertinent points here are that the *1951 Convention,* the foundational document for the modern international refugee protection regime, was premised on a general definition of who, and on what basis, someone is to be a refugee under international law, and that this was no longer based exclusively on one's national group affiliation. Additionally, the principle of *non-refoulement* was entrenched as a central element of the international refugee protection regime and the UNHCR was tasked with supervisory responsibilities for ensuring that States Parties fulfilled their obligations under the terms of these respective international refugee rights instruments.

The *1951 Convention,* some 60 years on, is not the same as when it was first adopted. Nor is, of course, the UNHCR, which has experienced dramatic changes since it was first established. Understandably, both have evolved and developed with changing circumstances over time. As Marilyn Achiron has noted,

> The 26 participating countries [the first States Parties to the *1951 Convention*] were heavily western or liberal in orientation, though they were joined by other states such as Iraq, Egypt and Colombia. Conspicuously absent, with the exception of Yugoslavia, was the Soviet-dominated communist bloc. For three weeks, in the United Nations European Office overlooking Lake Geneva, delegates hammered out a refugee bill of rights. It involved long and hard bargaining, interminable legal wrangling and a constant eye cocked to protect the rights of sovereign states.[26]

---

23 Hathaway, *Rights of Refugees under International Law,* pp. 90–91 [emphasis added].

24 International Association of Refugee Law Judges (IARLJ), *Seminar for New Refugee Law Judges.* These materials were developed for the IARLJ by the Immigration and Refugee Board of Canada, The Centre for Refugee Studies, York University, Canada (with the generous assistance of the Arthur W. Mellon Foundation), the United Nations High Commissioner for Refugees, Geneva, 1999, 2005, pp. 1–6. Goodwin-Gill and McAdam, *Refugee in International Law,* at p. 19 state: 'In a little less than five years, the preferred approach to refugee definition moved from a basis in flexible or open groups and categories, to an apparently more closed and legalistic one.'

25 Ibid., p. 20.

26 Marilyn Achiron, 'A "Timeless" Treaty Under Attack, The Geneva Refugee Convention is 50 years old. It has helped millions of the world's downtrodden, but faces continued criticism': *Refugees, 50th Anniversary,* p. 8, at http://www.unhcr.org/3b5e90ea0.pdf (accessed 10 January 2011).

Today the *1951 Convention* has 148 States Parties and no longer has the geographic and the temporal limitations that it had when it first came into force.[27] It was the *1967 Protocol relating to the Status of Refugees* that eliminated the geographic and temporal limitations of the *1951 Convention*.[28] Thus, some 118 States have adopted the *1951 Convention* since it first came into force over the last 60 years, making it one of the most widely adopted and recognized international human rights instruments. It is also one of the most widely applied Conventions in the world today with refugee law decision makers applying and interpreting the *1951 Convention* and its *1967 Protocol* in deciding who ought to be a refugee. As one might expect, the jurisprudence that has developed on the *1951 Convention* is quite extensive at the municipal and the international levels.[29]

The UNHCR has also developed and evolved over the last 60 years. Its initial mandate was for a mere three years, before it was extended for a further decade, and then recognized finally as a necessity within the UN system and throughout the world.[30]

From only 34 staff members when the UNHCR was founded, it now has 6,650 national and international members of staff, including 740 in its Geneva headquarters. The agency works in 118 countries, with staff based in 108 main locations such as regional and branch offices and 151 often remote sub-offices and field offices.

The budget has grown from US$300,000 in its first year to more than US$2 billion in 2009. UNHCR now deals with 34.4 million people of concern to UNHCR: 14.4 million internally displaced people, 10.5 million refugees, 2 million returnees, 6.6 million stateless people, and more than 800,000 asylum seekers.[31]

---

27 UNHCR, States Parties to the *1951 Convention relating to the Status of Refugees* and the *1967 Protocol*, as of 1 October 2008, at http://www.unhcr.org/3b73b0d63.pdf (accessed 10 January 2011).

28 *1967 Protocol relating to the Status of Refugees*, New York, adopted 31 January 1967, entry into force 4 October 1967, 606 UNTS 267, at http://treaties.un.org/pages/ViewDetails.aspx?src=UNTSONLINE&tabid=2&mtdsg_no=V-5&chapter=5&lang=en (accessed 10 January 2011).

29 For instance, see the UNHCR's *Refworld, the Leader in Refugee Decision Support*, at http://www.unhcr.org/cgi-bin/texis/vtx/refworld/rwmain (accessed 10 January 2011). The Refworld Legal Collection notes the following: 'Included in the collection is a unique jurisprudence collection, covering more than 40 national jurisdictions, and a vast amount of international judgments and decisions from the United Nations, the European Court of Human Rights and other international and regional courts': at http://www.unhcr.org/refworld/category,LEGAL,0.html (accessed 10 January 2011). See also the International Association of Refugee Law Judges (IARLJ) Database Court Decisions in Asylum Law, at http://iarlj.eear.eu/IARLJ/SearchForms/IARLJ_Database_Start.htm (accessed 10 January 2011). Both of these databases show the extensive jurisprudence that has developed around the *1951 Convention* and its *1967 Protocol* and in the commensurate growth of international refugee law.

30 'A Global Humanitarian Organization of Humble Origins', *History of the UNHCR*, UNHCR, The UN Refugee Agency, at http://www.unhcr.org/pages/49c3646cbc.html (accessed 18 July 2012).

31 Ibid. The must recent figures indicate that 'over 34 million people are of concern to UNHCR: 11 million are refugees and asylum-seekers, 6.5 million are stateless (and possibly estimated 6 million more), almost 2 million are returnees and 14 million are internally displaced people for whom the Office plays a particular coordinating or operational role. UNHCR works in over 267 locations in some 120 countries with approximately 6,880 staff. Based on a Global Needs Assessment initiative launched last year, our budget for 2010 amounts to some 3 billion US dollars. UNHCR, however, continues to depend largely on voluntary contributions from

Dr Jeff Crisp, Head of the Policy Development and Evaluation Unit of the UNHCR, in a presentation that he made at the Refugee Studies Centre (RSC), Queen Elizabeth House, University of Oxford, on 28 February 2010, stated that the UNHCR has been an expansionist organization since it was established. In essence, he argued that the UNHCR is no longer an organization that is dealing with refugees, asylum seekers, the stateless, or internal displaced persons or what it calls more broadly 'persons of concern', but now it is dealing with, simply, '*people on the move*'. This includes irregular, vulnerable and stranded migrants, those who have been displaced due to climate change and the environment, natural disaster victims, and it included those who are displaced and living in urban areas as opposed to the traditional refugee camps.[32]

Given this tremendous history of development and change that has taken place within both the *1951 Convention* and its *1967 Protocol*, it is reasonable to expect that both will continue to develop and to change in very unexpected and interesting ways over the next 60 years.[33]

It is also apparent that the UNHCR and the *1951 Convention* and its *1967 Protocol* are part and parcel of the core purposes and principles of the UN. The resolution of the international problems attendant to forced migration and refugees and the protection of the human rights of those who are forcibly displaced contribute, undoubtedly, to the UN's overarching goal of the maintenance of universal peace and human security.

Article 35 of the *1951 Convention* and Article II of the *1967 Protocol* and the Supervisory Role of the UNHCR

It is uncontested that the Office of the United Nations High Commissioner for Refugees (UNHCR) has the responsibility to supervise the *1951 Convention relating to Status of Refugees* and its *1967 Protocol*, under Article 35 and Article II, respectively, of these international human rights instruments.[34] This is further evident in the *Statute of the Office of the United Nations High*

Governments and other donors': Türk, 'UNHCR's Role in Supervising International Protection Standards in the Context of its Mandate', p. 4.

32 Dr Jeff Crisp, Head, Policy Development and Evaluation Unit, UNHCR, 'From Refugees in Europe as a result of WW II to Refugees anywhere and at any time to anyone in need of international protection?' Presentation at the Refugee Studies Centre, Department of International Development, Queen Elizabeth House, University of Oxford, 28 February 2010. Author's notes.

33 For an analysis of the growing complexity of the international refugee protection regime and its overlap with a range of other regimes such as travel and labour migration, see Alexander Betts, 'The Refugee Regime Complex', *Refugee Survey Quarterly*, 29:1 (2010), pp. 12–37.

34 Indeed, Volker Türk has argued that 'the content of Article 35 of the *1951 Convention* could possibly constitute a rule of customary international law, not least because a specific organizational supervisory practice developed by the UNHCR, coupled with a consequent acquiescence by states in relation to this practice, is discernible': 'UNHCR's Supervisory Responsibility', 5. See also Kälin, 'Supervising the 1951 Convention Relating to the Status of Refugees', pp. 613–66; 'Summary Conclusions: Supervisory Responsibility', Expert Roundtable Organized by the United Nations High Commissioner for Refugees and the Lauterpacht Research Center for International Law, University of Cambridge, UK, 9–10 July 2001', in *Refugee Protection*

Commissioner for Refugees that calls upon Member States to cooperate with the UNHCR in the performance of its functions concerning refugees.[35] It is also obvious from the Preamble of the *1951 Convention* that states:

> *Noting* that the United Nations High Commissioner for Refugees is charged with the task of supervising international conventions providing for the protection of Refugees, and recognizing that the effective co-ordination of measures taken to deal with this problem will depend upon the co-operation of States with the High Commissioner ….[36]

Article 35 of the *1951 Convention* states as follows:

1. The Contracting States undertake to co-operate with the Office of the United Nations High Commissioner for Refugees, or any other agency of the United Nations which may succeed it, in the exercise of its functions, and shall in particular facilitate its duty of supervising the application of the provisions of this Convention.
2. In order to enable the Office of the High Commissioner or any other agency of the United Nations which may succeed it, to make reports to the competent organs of the United Nations, the Contracting States undertake to provide them in the appropriate form with information and statistical data requested concerning:
   a. the condition of refugees,
   b. the implementation of this Convention, and
   c. laws, regulations and decrees which are, or may hereafter be, in force relating to refugees.[37]

Section 2 of the *Statute of the United Nations High Commissioner for Refugees* refers to, 'Calls upon Governments to co-operate with the United Nations High Commissioner for Refugees in the performance of his functions concerning refugees falling under the competence of his Office';[38] and, more specifically, to 'Becoming parties to international conventions providing for the protection of refugees, and *taking the necessary steps of implementation under such conventions*.'[39]

Article 35 of the *1951 Convention*, Article II of the *1967 Protocol*, and Section 2 of the *Statute of the United Nations High Commissioner for Refugees* obligate States Parties and members of the

in International Law, ed. Feller, Türk and Nicholson, pp. 667–73; James C. Simeon, 'A Comparative Analysis of the Response of the UNHCR and Industrialized States to Rapidly Fluctuating Refugee Status and Asylum Applications: Lessons and Best Practices for RSD Systems Design and Administration', *International Journal of Refugee Law*, 22:1 (March 2010), pp. 72–103: 2.3 The necessity for cooperation, p. 80.

35 United Nations General Assembly Resolution 428 (V) of 14 December 1950, *Statute of the Office of the United Nations High Commissioner for Refugees*, at http://www.unhcr.org/3b66c39e1.pdf (accessed 16 January 2011).

36 *Convention relating to the Status of Refugees*, Geneva.

37 Ibid.

38 United Nations General Assembly Resolution 428 (V) of 14 December 1950, *Statute of the Office of the United Nations High Commissioner for Refugees*, at http://www.unhcr.org/3b66c39e1.pdf (accessed 16 January 2011).

39 Ibid., Section 2(a) [emphasis added].

UN to cooperate with the UNHCR in its supervisory capacity over the *1951 Convention*, *1967 Protocol* and other international conventions that protect refugees. But what does this entail both at the conceptual and theoretical level and in practice?[40]

The Oxford Paperback Dictionary defines 'supervise' as '*verb* direct and inspect (work or workers or the operations of an organization)'.[41] And *Black's Law Dictionary* defines 'supervise' as 'To have general oversight over, to superintend or to inspect.' It defines 'supervision' as 'An act of occupation of supervising; inspection.'[42] These standard definitions suggest and imply that the UNHCR has the authority to inspect, oversee and, presumably, direct matters that come within its purview either within the provisions of the *1951 Convention* or its own Statute. Indeed, the Summary Conclusions on supervisory responsibility that came out of the Expert Roundtable discussions that took place at Cambridge University on 9–10 July 2001, as part of the UNHCR's Global Consultations on International Protection that were held on the occasion of the 50th anniversary of the *1951 Convention*, identified nine elements of the UNHCR's supervisory role:[43]

a. working with States to design operational responses which are sensitive to and meet protection needs, including of the most vulnerable;
b. making representations to governments and other relevant actors on protection concerns and monitoring, reporting on and following up these interventions with governments regarding the situation of refugees (e.g. on admission, reception, treatment of asylum-seekers and refugees);
c. advising and being consulted on national asylum or refugee status determination procedures;
d. intervening and making submissions to quasi-judicial institutions or courts in the form of *amicus curiae* briefs, statements or letters;
e. having access to asylum applicants and refugees, either as recognized in law or in administrative practice;
f. advising governments and parliaments on legislation and administrative decrees affecting asylum-seekers and refugees at all stages of the process, and providing comments on and technical input into draft refugee legislation and related administrative decrees;
g. fulfilling an advocacy role, including through public statements, as an essential tool of international protection and the Office's supervisory responsibility;
h. strengthening capacity e.g. through promotional and training activities;
i. receiving and gathering data and information concerning asylum-seekers and refugees as set out in Article 35(2) of the 1951 Convention.[44]

---

40 For the latest in-depth legal analysis of the UNHCR's supervisory role, see Türk, 'UNHCR's Role in Supervising International Protection Standards in the Context of its Mandate', 'What is the legal basis of UNHCR's supervisory role?', pp. 4–8.

41 *The Oxford Paperback Dictionary*, 4th edn, ed. Elaine Pollard, second ed. Helen Liebeck (Oxford: Oxford University Press, 1994), p. 806.

42 Henry Campbell Black, *Black's Law Dictionary*, revised 4th edn by The Publishers Editorial Staff (St. Paul's, MN: West Publishing Co., 1968), p. 1607.

43 'Summary Conclusions: Supervisory Responsibility'.

44 Ibid., pp. 668–9.

It is evident from these nine elements of the UNHCR's supervisory role, that the UNHCR's supervision of the *1951 Convention* is confined largely to efforts that are collaborative, advisory, advocacy, training and/or information gathering in nature. It is clearly not what is implied in the dictionary or legal definitions of 'supervise' or 'supervision' that refer to inspection, the ability to oversee and even to direct matters.

The issue of accountability in the international humanitarian aid field has come to the fore in recent years with such publications as *Imposing Aid: Emergency Assistance for Refugees,*[45] *Rights in Exile: Janus-Faced Humanitarianism,*[46] *The Crisis Caravan: What's Wrong With Humanitarian Aid?*[47] Such international organizations as the *Humanitarian Accountability Partnership* or *HAP International,* which seeks to 'make humanitarian action accountable to its beneficiaries',[48] and the *One World Trust,* which strives 'to make policy and decision-making processes in global governance more accountable to the people they affect now and in the future, and to ensure that international laws are strengthened and applied equally to all',[49] have emerged to try to address the apparent lack of accountability in the field of international humanitarian aid.

Accountability, from a legal perspective, 'is a "principle which requires public authorities to explain their actions and be subject to scrutiny."'[50] Volker Türk and Elizabeth Eyster have noted the following concerning accountability,

> Generally, it 'involves either the expectation or assumption of account-giving behaviour.' In other words, accountability is a means to honor trust, to prevent

45 Barbara Harrell-Bond, *Imposing Aid: Emergency Assistance for Refugees* (Oxford: Oxford University Press, 1986). In addition, see Barbara Harrell-Bond, 'Can Humanitarian Work with Refugees be Humane?', *Human Rights Quarterly,* 24 (2002), pp. 51–85, at http://icar.gmu.edu/ICC/Humanitarian.pdf (accessed 29 January 2011); Barbara Harrell-Bond, 'Are Refugee Camps Good for Children?', New Issues in Refugee Research, Working Paper No. 29, UNHCR, August 2000, ISSN 1020-7473, at http://www.unhcr.org/3ae6a0c64.pdf (accessed 29 January 2011); Barbara Harrell-Bond and Mike Kegan, 'The Road Home for Africa's Refugees, Protecting the Rights of Refugees in Africa: Beginning With the UN Gatekeeper', ch. 8 in *African Voice on Development and Social Justice,* Pambazuka News 182, 11 November 2004, pp. 193–214, at http://www.pambazuka.org/en/publications/africanvoices_chap08.pdf (accessed 29 January 2011).

46 Guglielmo Verdirame and Barbara Harrell-Bond with Zachary Lomo and Hannah Garry, *Rights in Exile: Janus-faced Humanitarianism* (Oxford: Berghahn Books, 2005).

47 Linda Polman, *The Crisis Caravan: What's Wrong With Humanitarian Aid?,* trans. Liz Waters (New York: Metropolitan Books, Henry Holt and Company, 2010).

48 HAP, Humanitarian Accountability Partnership, at http://www.hapinternational.org/default.aspx (accessed 29 January 2011). HAP International was established in 2003 and currently has 64 member agencies from some 21 counties.

49 One World Trust, making global governance more accountable: see About Us, at http://www.oneworldtrust.org/index.php?option=com_content&view=article&id=48&Itemid=58 (accessed 29 January 2011).

50 Volker Türk and Elizabeth Eyster, 'Strengthening Accountability in UNHCR', *International Journal of Refugee Law,* 22:2 (March 2010), pp. 159–72, at p. 160. The authors outline in detail the UNHCR's internal accountability systems, including: results-based management (RBM); the Global Management Accountability Framework (GMAF); accountabilities, responsibilities and authorities (ARAs); the Global Learning Centre (GLC) in Budapest; and the Performance Management Appraisal System (PAMS), among others. See 5. Strengthening UNHCR's system of accountability, pp. 168–72.

> the abuse of power, to uphold standards and to enforce norm conforming behaviour.[51]

Accountability is far from being either a simple or a straightforward concept. Nonetheless, it is often useful to consider it as one of three key interrelated elements within the paradigm of responsibility, accountability and liability.[52] Hence, if the UNHCR is to be held accountable for its actions or inactions, then it must also be held liable for how well it fulfils its supervisory responsibilities under its mandate and under international law.

Volker Türk and Elizabeth Eyster have noted that the UNHCR is accountable 'to the populations it serves to protect and assist as well as to its stakeholders and its own staff.'[53] Clearly, the UNHCR, as an international organization, is accountable to the millions of refugees it serves and protects, but it is also accountable to its stakeholders such as the UN General Assembly, the UN Economic and Social Council,[54] its donors, and the States Parties to international refugee rights instruments.

In short, UNHCR is accountable for how well it performs its supervisory responsibilities under the *1951 Convention* and its *1967 Protocol* and other international refugee rights instruments as well as its own Statute.

---

[51] Ibid.

[52] See for instance Gregory J. Inwood, *Understanding Canadian Public Administration: An Introduction to Theory and Practice, Third Edition* (Toronto: Pearson, Prentice-Hall, 2009), pp. 374–5, who quotes Gerald E. Caiden, 'The Problem of Ensuring the Public Accountability of Public Officials', in *Public Service Accountability*, ed. Joseph G. Jabbra and O.P. Dwivedi (West Hartford, CT: Kumarian Press, 1988), p. 25, as follows:

> To be responsible is to have the authority to act, power to control, freedom to decide, the ability to distinguish (as between right and wrong) and to behave rationally and reliably and with consistency and trustworthiness in exercising internal judgement. To be accountable is to answer for one's responsibilities, to report, to explain, to give reasons, to respond, to assume obligations, to render a reckoning and to submit to an outside or external judgement. To be liable is to assume the duty to making good, to restore, to compensate, to recompense for wrongdoing or poor judgement.

[53] Türk and Eyster, 'Strengthening Accountability in UNHCR', p. 160. They further note that 'accountability is defined by the UNHCR as a commitment to deliver results from populations of concern within a framework of respect, transparency, agreed feasibility, trust, delegated authority, and available resources' (p. 162). Volker Türk has also noted that 'through the SCHR Peer Review on Accountability to Disaster-Affected Populations (January 2010), UNHCR was able to confirm that it has procedures in place to ensure the Office acts in an accountable manner towards those it serves': 'UNHCR's Role in Supervising International Protection Standards in the Context of its Mandate', p. 18.

[54] United Nations General Assembly Resolution 428 (V) of 14 December 1950, *Statute of the Office of the United Nations High Commissioner for Refugees*, at http://www.unhcr.org/3b66c39e1.pdf (accessed 24 January 2011). Chapter I, General Provisions, at paragraph 3 states, 'The High Commissioner shall follow the policy directives given him by the General Assembly or the Economic and Social Council.'

Recommendations for Strengthening the Supervision of the *1951 Convention* and its *1967 Protocol*

What follows are the recommendations of a number of legal scholars in the field of international refugee law for strengthening the supervision of the 1951 Convention and its 1967 Protocol.

Volker Türk: An Institutionalized Dialogue Based on Periodic Reporting

Volker Türk has noted that the 'purpose of international supervision relating to the application of provisions of international instruments is, first and foremost, to promote compliance with these rules.'[55] He goes on to point out further that,

> supervision by an international institution contains: (i) an element of collection of information concerning the application of provisions of the international refugee instruments by the respective contracting states; (ii) the assessment of this information in light of the applicable norms; and (iii) some kind of enforcement mechanism to ensure remedial action and norm compliance by the states concerned. All three actions are closely inter-related and core components of any supervisory role.[56]

Indeed, Volker Türk states that, from the UNHCR's understanding and practice, 'enforcement' means 'a wide range of intervention and advocacy activities covering the whole spectrum of displacement ranging from admission, reception, determination of refugee status to improvement of standards, regularization of stay or return.'[57] The various measures that the UNHCR undertakes can have the effect, Volker Türk suggests, of 'soft enforcement'.[58]

The UNHCR undertakes its supervisory role utilizing a number of mechanisms that include the following: monitoring; State reporting; UNHCR's access to asylum applicants, refugees and returnees; the right to contact the UNHCR; participation in refugee status determination procedures; and the UNHCR's advisory services.[59] Volker Türk states that the 'obligations stemming from Article 35 of the 1951 Convention have primarily been implemented by involving the UNHCR in national refugee status determination procedures.'[60] In fact, the degree of the UNHCR's extensive involvement in national legal and administrative systems is quite unique. Volker Türk suggests that 'it may be the only UN organization that is directly involved in national law-making, national procedures and national decision-making.'[61]

There are four areas that have emerged as requiring further examination in the discussions concerning the strengthening of the UNHCR's supervisory responsibilities, according to Volker Türk. These include: '(i) differing interpretation regarding the content/application

55 Türk, 'UNHCR's Supervisory Responsibility', p. 3.
56 Ibid., pp. 9–10.
57 Ibid., p. 11.
58 Ibid., p. 12.
59 Ibid., pp. 12–14.
60 Ibid., p. 14.
61 Ibid., p. 15.

of provisions of the international refugee instruments, standards and principles; (ii) state reporting as a whole; (iii) the question of institutionalising a constructive dialogue with states parties to the international refugee instruments on their implementation at regular intervals; and (iv) measures of enforcement.'[62]

Among these, the most promising, in terms of strengthening the UNHCR's supervisory capacity, appears to be the recommendation of considering a regularized system of periodic reporting on the implementation of international refugee rights instruments. This could take various forms, but the one that appears to be the most feasible and least disruptive at present would be 'the development of an institutionalised dialogue on the basis of the annual protection reporting exercise undertaken by the UNHCR field offices which could be made accessible to governments and eventually also the public.'[63] Such an institutionalized dialogue would build on a function already undertaken on an annual basis by UNHCR field offices that are required to report, structured on the basis of a detailed questionnaire, on individual State's practice. This information is used by the UNHCR to monitor States Parties' compliance with international refugee rights instruments and to serve as a 'constructive dialogue' that could incorporate recommendations by the UNHCR field offices undertaking the annual monitoring reports. The information gathered from this exercise could also be used in the UNHCR's annual reports to its Executive Committee and to the UN General Assembly.[64]

At the International Conference on Forced Displacement, Protection Standards and the Supervision of the *1951 Convention* and its *1967 Protocol* and Other International Instruments that was held at York University, Toronto, Canada, 17–20 May 2010, Volker Türk outlined seven questions for consideration by the international conference participants.[65] These questions became the focal point of the discussions that took place in each of the breakout sessions during the international conference:

1. What have we achieved?
2. What remains to be done and what are the challenges?
3. What other techniques and models are available to international organizations, also from a comparative perspective?
4. What do we need to avoid? What are the pitfalls?
5. Do we need to revisit reporting? Would it, for instance, make sense for an expert or a group of experts appointed by the High Commissioner to draw up regular reports on the implementation of international instruments on a country, regional or thematic basis?
6. Is there value in establishing an Advisory Committee on the implementation of international instruments the composition of which would be determined by the High Commissioner?
7. Would there be value in reconstituting a special committee of the Executive Committee focusing exclusively on international protection, building on the valuable experience

62 Ibid., p. 17.

63 Ibid., p. 19.

64 Ibid.

65 The International Conference on Forced Displacement, Protection Standards and the Supervision of the *1951 Convention* and its *1967 Protocol* and Other International Instruments, 17–20 May 2010, York University website, at http://www.yorku.ca/fdpss/ (accessed 18 July 2012).

gained through the High Commissioner's Dialogues on Protection Challenges? Such a committee could follow the format of the Global Consultation meetings with capital-level representation and broader-based participation from NGOs, academics and experts. It could ensure focused and global discussion on international protection matters; assist UNHCR in exercising its supervisory role; address issues of lack of compliance and operational protection concerns on the ground; act as a forum to design burden-sharing arrangements and regional approaches, as well as to negotiate and conclude substantial Conclusions on international protection matters.[66]

B. S. Chimni: A Refugee Rights Committee, a 'Refugee Watch' Annual Report, and a Regular Budget for the UNHCR

B. S. Chimni proposes a dialogic model for reforming the international refugee protection regime.[67] He advocates that the 'dialogue between actors is to be conducted on the basis of the *principles of deliberative democracy* so as to ensure that power does not determine and define the nature of the problems and the possible solutions to them.'[68] He further calls for 'the basis for compromise to be the realization of *common or collective interests*.'[69]

B. S. Chimni points out that one of the problems with Article 35 of the *1951 Convention* and the UNHCR's Statute, even though both assign the UNHCR the task of supervising its provisions, is that both are silent on the procedure for undertaking this role and responsibility. Accordingly, Chimni suggests the establishment of a Refugee Rights Committee to ensure both States Parties' and the UNHCR's accountability.[70] The Refugee Rights Committee would try 'to ensure accountability by providing a common interpretative framework for implementing the 1951 Convention in different regions of the world.'[71]

B. S. Chimni also calls for a collective effort in the production and publication of an annual report on the record of individual States in the fulfilment of their obligations to provide refugees with protection. He suggests that the annual report should be called *Refugee Watch*.[72] One of its principal functions would be to persuade States 'to enter into a dialogue with transnational NGO networks.'[73] He also states that the UNHCR should have a regular budget.[74]

66 Türk, 'UNHCR's Role in Supervising International Protection Standards in the Context of its Mandate', 'What is the way forward?', pp. 18–19. For a detailed overview and analysis of this international conference see James C. Simeon, ed., The UNHCR and the Supervision of International Refugee Law (Cambridge: Cambridge University Press).

67 B. S. Chimni, 'Reforming the International Refugee Regime: A Dialogic Model', *Journal of Refugee Studies*, 14:2 (2001), pp. 151–68.

68 Ibid., p. 152 [emphasis in original].

69 Ibid., p. 153 [emphasis in original].

70 Ibid., p. 157.

71 Ibid., pp. 157–8.

72 Ibid., p. 163.

73 Ibid.

74 Ibid., p. 165.

Walter Kälin: A Sub-Committee on Review and Monitoring established by the UNHCR Executive Committee and Thematic Rapporteurs reporting to the Standing Committee of the UNHCR Executive Committee

In Walter Kälin's background paper for the 2001 UNHCR Global Consultations on International Protection, 'Supervising the 1951 Convention on the Status of Refugees: Article 35 and Beyond', he reviews the relevant Superior and High Courts jurisprudence on Article 35 and comes to the following conclusion:

> The case law is significant because it acknowledges that, as part of the States Parties' duties to cooperate with the UNHCR and to accept its supervisory role under Article 35 of the 1951 Convention and Article II of the 1967 Protocol, they have to take into account Executive Committee Conclusions, the UNHCR *Handbook*, UNHCR guidelines and other UNHCR opinions on matters of law (for example, *amicus curiae* and similar submissions to courts or assessment of legislative projects requested or routinely accepted by governments), when applying the 1951 Convention and its Protocol. 'Taking into account' does not mean that these documents are legally binding. Rather, it means that they must not be dismissed as irrelevant but regarded as authoritative statements whose disregard requires justification.[75]

Walter Kälin points out that external supervision 'is critical for the effective application and implementation of international law, as "[v]iolations which receive wide attention are more difficult to commit than violations that are practically unknown". In present day international law, such supervision takes many different forms.'[76] Drawing on the work of H. G. Schermers and N. M. Blokker,[77] Kälin presents three major forms of supervision:

1. Supervision initiated by other States (members of the organization or other parties to the treaty) acting on their own account:
   - Dispute settlement by the International Court of Justice;
   - Inter-State complaints to treaty bodies or to the organs of the organization;
2. Supervision by or on behalf of the organization or treaty body:
   - Supervision based on State reports;
   - Supervision based on information collected by the organization;
3. Supervision initiated by individuals:
   - Individual petitions;
   - Court proceedings.[78]

---

[75] Kälin, 'Supervising the 1951 Convention Relating to the Status of Refugees: Article 35 and Beyond', p. 627.

[76] Ibid., p. 635 [footnotes excluded].

[77] *International Institutional Law, Third Revised Edition* (The Hague, London, Boston: Martinus Nijhoff, 1995).

[78] Kälin, 'Supervising the 1951 Convention Relating to the Status of Refugees: Article 35 and Beyond', p. 635.

After providing a detailed review of these various types of supervisory mechanisms, Walter Kälin presents his own set of proposed reforms to UNHCR's supervisory responsibilities. He proposes the establishment of a Sub-Committee of the UNHCR's Executive Committee and the use of thematic rapporteurs that would be under the direction of the Standing Committee of the UNHCR's Executive Committee.

The Sub-Committee on Review and Monitoring would comprise those members of the Executive Committee that are States Parties to the *1951 Convention* and its *1967 Protocol*. The Sub-Committee on Review and Monitoring would carry out Refugee Protection Reviews that would examine how the *1951 Convention* and its *1967 Protocol* are implemented in particular countries, and what the obstacles are for their full implementation, in addition to drawing lessons from real experiences of how to overcome the obstacles to achieve more effective implementation of these international instruments.[79] The UNHCR would identify the situation to be reviewed and then appoint a team of reviewers from a pool of independent experts nominated by the States Parties to the *1951 Convention* and its *1967 Protocol*. The report prepared by the team of experts would be reviewed publicly by the Sub-Committee on Review and Monitoring.

Walter Kälin further notes that many of the problems with respect to international refugee protection go beyond the UNHCR's Statute and the *1951 Convention* and its *1967 Protocol*. He suggests that these problems could endanger the international refugee protection regime.[80] Accordingly, he suggests that some sort of mechanism is also needed to examine whether States, including those that are not party to the *1951 Convention* and its *1967 Protocol*, are fulfilling their obligations under customary international law and international instruments pertinent to refugees and asylum seekers other than the *1951 Convention* and its *1967 Protocol*.[81] He points out that thematic rapporteurs have proven to be well suited to examining specific problem areas outside of the treaty mechanisms. He proposes that thematic rapporteurs could be the responsibility of the Standing Committee of the UNHCR's Executive Committee.[82] He suggests, for instance, that there could be special rapporteurs for women and child refugees seeking asylum, the physical security of refugees, and for access to asylum procedures.[83] The reports from these special rapporteurs could be reviewed by the Standing Committee in the presence of country representatives and NGOs. These reports, along with the Standing Committee's observations, could be given wide public distribution. The reports could also be incorporated in the Executive Committee's deliberations 'to reflect the outcome of discussions in its own conclusions on protection.'[84]

79 Ibid., p. 657.
80 Ibid., p. 659.
81 Ibid.
82 Ibid.
83 Ibid., p. 660.
84 Ibid.

James C. Hathaway, University of Michigan's Program in Refugee and Asylum Law, and the International Council of Voluntary Agencies (ICVA)

James C. Hathaway, Director, Program in Refugee and Asylum Law, at the University of Michigan, and the International Council of Voluntary Agencies (ICVA), based in Geneva, Switzerland, came together in 2001, amid the UNHCR Global Consultations on International Protection, to undertake a shared project 'to examine what lessons can be learnt from other supervisory mechanisms and what best practice might be transported into a possible new model to supervise the Refugee Convention.'[85] Seven Working Papers were prepared by some of the students in the University of Michigan's Faculty of Law, Program in Refugee and Asylum Law.[86] These seven Working Papers were seen as commencing the discussions on strengthening the implementation of the *1951 Convention* and its *1967 Protocol*.[87] One proposal that was presented at the meeting that was held to review and to discuss these seven Working Papers on 11 December 2001, in advance of the Ministerial Conference on the Global Consultations on International Protection, was a recommendation for the United Nations High Commissioner for Refugees to appoint an advisory group of 'high-standing experts'.[88] This was not seen, however, as replacing the need for an independent mechanism to monitor the implementation of the Refugee Convention. This monitoring mechanism would be separate from the UNHCR and it would supplement the protection work of the UNHCR.[89]

Effective supervision of the treaty would allow UNHCR to focus on its protection work, could foster state compliance in a way that would ease interstate tension, and ultimately would improve refugee protection.[90]

The ICVA/University of Michigan Pre-Ministerial Conference meeting also called for improved NGO monitoring of the application of the *1951 Convention* and its *1967 Protocol*. And, it also called on NGOs to look for ways to better coordinate these efforts on a global basis.[91]

James C. Hathaway underscored the point that the new monitoring mechanism should not only be 'pragmatic, but also independent, objective, and inclusive of a full range of voices, including those of refugees themselves.'[92]

---

85 *Global Consultations on International Protection Report*, ICVA Meeting Prior to the Ministerial Conference, Palais des Nations, Geneva, 11 December 2001, at http://www.icva.ch/doc00000503.html (accessed 30 January 2011).

86 ICVA/University of Michigan Meeting Prior to the Ministerial Conference (Track 1 of the UNHCR Global Consultations), 11 December 2001, at http://www.icva.ch/doc00000505.html#conference (accessed 30 January 2011). The seven Working Papers covered the following topics: Reporting; Complaints; General Comments; Investigative Capacity; NGO/National Linkages; UN Linkages; and Coordination with UNHCR and States.

87 *Global Consultations on International Protection Report*, ICVA Meeting Prior to the Ministerial Conference.

88 Ibid.

89 Ibid.

90 Ibid.

91 Ibid.

92 Hathaway, 'Taking Oversight of Refugee Law Seriously'.

Anthony M. North and Joyce Chia: An International Judicial Commission for Refugees

The basic premise of Justice Anthony M. North, Federal Court of Australia, and Joyce Chia's proposal for the establishment of an International Judicial Commission for Refugees is a simple one. Given the need to resolve the differing interpretations of the *1951 Convention* and its *1967 Protocol* among States Parties to these seminal international refugee rights instruments and given the lack of an international refugee court to bind States Parties to a common interpretation of the Articles of this fundamental Convention and its Protocol, the UNHCR should 'establish an independent international judicial commission, comprised of a small number of eminent jurists and experts in refugee law … to provide carefully reasoned opinions on major questions relating to the construction of the [1951] Convention [and its *1967 Protocol*].'[93]

Anthony M. North and Joyce Chia justify the International Judicial Commission for Refugees further by adding that,

> Such a commission would provide useful international 'soft law', alongside the UNHCR Handbook, UNHCR Executive Committee Conclusions and the Guidelines on International Protection. It would, however, have significant advantages over these other sources of soft law. As a permanent body, it would be able to address on-going issues of interpretation in a detailed way, based on an extensive knowledge of the principles and practice of refugee law. Our hope is that these opinions will begin to shape the direction of domestic

[93] Anthony M. North and Joyce Chia, 'Towards Convergence in the Interpretation of the Refugee Convention: A Proposal for the Establishment of an International Judicial Commission for Refugees', in *Forced Migration, Human Rights and Security*, ed. Jane McAdam (Oxford: Hart Publishing, 2008), pp. 225–61, at p. 226. Earlier versions of this article have been published in *Australian Year Book of International Law*, 25 (2006): pp. 105–38, and as 'Towards Convergence in the Interpretation of the Refugees Convention – A Proposal for the Establishment of an International Refugee Court', in *The Asylum Process and the Rule of Law*, International Association of Refugee Law Judges (IARLJ) (Haarlem, The Netherlands: Manak Publications PVT Ltd., 2006), pp. 72–136. For the case for an International Refugee Court, see the Rt. Hon. Lord Justice Dyson, 'The Interpretation of the Refugee Convention: Idiosyncrasy v. Uniformity', in *The Asylum Process and the Rule of Law*, International Association of Refugee Law Judges (IARLJ), Sixth World Conference in Stockholm, Sweden, 21–23 April 2005 (Haarlem, The Netherlands: IARLJ in association with Manak Publications Pvt Ltd., 2006), pp. 21–36. Wherein at p. 35, he states, 'Ideally, it seems to me that an international court should be created to determine at least all disputed questions of the interpretation of the Refugee Convention. Its decisions should be binding on all parties to the Convention. That would introduce welcome certainty. Whether its jurisdiction should extend to questions of the application of the Convention is another matter. In view of the fact that (a) there are so many parties, (b) the number of applicants and countries where there is a risk of persecution is so large and (c) the circumstances in those countries tend to change so swiftly that there would be a real danger that a court to which disputed questions of application could be referred would be overwhelmed by references to it.'

interpretations, and thus move us towards the convergence of interpretations of the Convention.[94]

Anthony M. North and Joyce Chia make a persuasive argument for the need of an International Judicial Commission for Refugees by noting the importance of the essential legal principle that 'like cases ought to be treated alike.' They note that this is a fundamental principle of justice and that it is basically a question of 'fairness'. If refugees from the same source country and with the same factual situation are treated differently from one State Party to the next, then, it is patently unfair to the refugee claimants. However, it is also fundamentally unfair to those States Parties that have adopted an interpretation of the Refugee Convention that is consistent with the purpose and object of this humanitarian international instrument. As North and Chia argue, 'the loss of refugee status or the exclusion of refugees under the Convention should not depend upon quirks of national interpretation. It goes without saying that unfairness in these matters has very real ramifications for refugees and for States.'[95]

Anthony M. North and Joyce Chia present a detailed and tightly argued case for establishing an International Judicial Commission for Refugees and explore the various institutional features that such an international body should have and how it would operate in practice. They conclude by noting that this Commission could be funded by civil society and the legal community and that it would 'not be tainted by the political control of States.'[96] Moreover, it would not be troubled with having to decide real cases and, consequently, would avoid many of the difficulties that confront international courts and tribunals.[97] Finally, they highlight the fact that it 'has become evident in relation to many other international instruments, an international judicial authority is an essential element of a regime based on international law.'[98]

A Summary of the Various Proposals Put Forward for Strengthening the Supervision of the 1951 Convention and its 1967 Protocol

Table 6.1 summarizes a number of different proposals that have been presented for strengthening the supervision of the *1951 Convention* and its *1967 Protocol*.

These wide-ranging proposals, from these renowned and distinguished experts in the field of international refugee law, on how the supervision of the *1951 Convention* and its *1967 Protocol* might be strengthened appear to differ in two fundamental respects. The recommendations of B. S. Chimni, James C. Hathaway and ICVA, and Anthony M. North and Joyce Chia call for independent monitoring and non-binding adjudicative mechanisms that are outside the UNHCR. James C. Hathaway, in particular, underscores the significance of an independent monitoring mechanism to ensure the proper and effective supervision of the Refugee Convention.

---

[94] North and Chia, 'Towards Convergence in the Interpretation of the Refugee Convention', pp. 226–7.

[95] Ibid., p. 227.

[96] Ibid., p. 261.

[97] Ibid.

[98] Ibid.

> UNHCR faces an ethical dilemma, in my view. Either it must return to concentrating on the implementation of its core supervisory responsibilities and leave what has become the majority of its operational mandate to others, or it must concede that it cannot ethically supervise itself, and endorse the establishment of a genuinely arm's-length body to oversee the Refugee Convention.[99]

Perhaps a rather obvious and facile observation is that those who are advocating independent monitoring mechanisms for the supervision of the *1951 Convention* and its *1967 Protocol* are outside the UNHCR *per se*; whereas Volker Türk is a senior career UNHCR official, currently the Director of the Division of International Protection,[100] and Walter Kälin, a professor of law and legal scholar, has held various positions within the UN system and most recently as the Representative of the Secretary General on the Human Rights of Internally Displaced Persons.[101]

Another apparent observation is that Volker Türk's and Walter Kälin's proposals seek to enhance the supervisory capacity of the UNHCR in order to promote States Parties' full implementation of and compliance with the *1951 Convention* and its *1967 Protocol* under Article 35 and Article II, respectively, of these international instruments and the UNHCR's statute, while B. S. Chimni, James C. Hathaway and ICVA are seeking to achieve greater accountability from both the UNHCR and States Parties to international refugee rights instruments. Anthony M. North and Joyce Chia's presentation for the establishment of an International Judicial Commission for Refugees is unique in not only calling for a independent Commission, established under the auspices of the UNHCR and the UN General Assembly, to help resolve diverging applications and interpretations of the Refugee Convention, but for trying to resolve the apparent disparity in the adjudication of claims for Convention refugee status across and within States Parties of the *1951 Convention* and its *1967 Protocol*.

What is also evident is that even though the recommendations vary broadly they are not mutually exclusive or incompatible in any fundamental way. Indeed, at least in theory, it could be possible to adopt all of these proposed remedies for strengthening the supervisory responsibility of the UNHCR over the States Parties' implementation and interpretation of the Refugee Convention without contradiction and/or apparent disruptive and compounding effects on each of these respective proposals. They could, in fact, be possibly even positively mutually reinforcing. Nevertheless, it is also important to heed Volker Türk's caveat that any proposal should not only strengthen the supervision of the *1951 Convention* and its *1967 Protocol* but also not undermine the UNHCR's supervisory role and responsibilities.[102]

---

99 Hathaway, 'Taking Oversight of Refugee Law Seriously'.

100 See *Volker Türk: Director of the Division of International Protection, United Nations High Commissioner for Refugees (UNHCR), Geneva, Switzerland*, at http://www.yorku.ca/fdpss/participants/turk.html (accessed 1 February 2011).

101 See United Nations Audiovisual Library of International Law, *Mr. Walter Kälin: Professor of International Law, Institute of Public Law, Faculty of Law, University of Bern*, at http://untreaty.un.org/cod/avl/pdf/ls/Kalin_bio.pdf (accessed 1 February 2011).

102 Türk, 'UNHCR's Role in Supervising International Protection Standards in the Context of its Mandate', 'What is the way forward?', pp. 18–19.

Table 6.1 A summary of the proposals presented for enhancing the supervision of the *1951 Convention* and its *1967 Protocol*

Proponents	Proposals
Volker Türk	He advocates that an institutionalized dialogue be implemented on the basis of an annual protection reporting exercise undertaken by the UNHCR field offices on States Parties' application and interpretation of international refugee rights instruments.
B. S. Chimni	He calls for the adoption of a 'dialogic model' for the international refugee protection regime based on the principles of deliberative democracy. He recommends that a Refugee Rights Committee be established to ensure States Parties and international organizations are held accountable for fulfilling their respective obligations under the *1951 Convention* and its *1967 Protocol* and their enabling statutory authority. He further recommends that an annual Refugee Watch report be issued to hold States Parties to account and proposes that the UNHCR should have a regular budget.
Walter Kälin	He recommends that a Sub-Committee on Review and Monitoring be established by the UNHCR Executive Committee. The UNHCR would identify the issues to be reviewed by teams of experts drawn from a pool of distinguished experts nominated by States Parties. Reports would be presented to the Sub-Committee on Review and Monitoring. He further calls for the appointment of thematic special rapporteurs who would file their reports with the Standing Committee of the UNHCR Executive Committee.
James C. Hathaway and ICVA	James C. Hathaway and ICVA (International Council of Voluntary Agencies) recommend that an independent monitoring mechanism on the implementation of the Refugee Convention should be established. They further advocate that there should be better monitoring and coordination among NGOs on States Parties' implementation of the Refugee Convention. They also recommend the establishment of an 'advisory group', comprising a distinguished group of experts, to provide the United Nations High Commissioner for Refugees with their advice on any matter that she/he may wish to consult them on.
Anthony M. North and Joyce Chia	They call on the UNHCR to establish an International Judicial Commission for Refugees in order to provide refugee law judges and adjudicators with non-binding but highly persuasive judgments on divergent interpretations of the Refugee Convention. They argue that such a Commission would assist in achieving a common application and interpretation of the Refugee Convention. An International Judicial Commission for Refugees would also lead to a more just international refugee protection regime that would result, eventually, from the fairer outcomes that would be achieved for both refugees and States Parties to the *1951 Convention* and its *1967 Protocol*.

Conclusions

On the 60th anniversary of the *1951 Convention* it is appropriate to reflect on how this key international refugee rights instrument and how the Office of the United Nations High Commissioner for Refugees has evolved and developed over the past 60 years. The changes have been monumental in many respects and much less so in many others. The fulfilment of the UNHCR's supervisory responsibilities is perhaps one of the areas that has changed the least over this period.

A review of five of the most recent proposals for how to strengthen the supervision of the *1951 Convention* and its *1967 Protocol* among a number of renowned and distinguished legal scholars and practitioners in the field of international refugee law indicates that a broad range of measures and mechanisms have been proposed that vary from institutionalized dialogues between the UNHCR and States Parties to the establishment of an UNHCR Executive Committee Sub-Committee on Review and Monitoring and the appointment of special rapporteurs reporting to the Standing Committee of the UNHCR Executive Committee to the establishment of an independent Refugee Review Committee and an International Judicial Committee for Refugees. It has been noted that although these proposals vary in their intend and purpose, such as increasing the capacity of the UNHCR to fulfil its supervisory responsibilities and mandate under its statute and Article 35 of the *1951 Convention* and Article II of its *1967 Protocol*, enhancing the accountability of the UNHCR and States Parties to international refugee rights instruments, and the creation of mechanisms that could lead to greater convergence in the implementation and interpretation of the international refugee rights instruments, these proposals are not necessarily contradictory or inconsistent. Indeed, they may even be positively mutually reinforcing.

Hence, while it is evident that there are no shortages of well thought out reasonable proposals for how the supervision of the *1951 Convention* and its *1967 Protocol* can be strengthened for the greater realization of the rights of refugees and the fostering of a more just and equitable international refugee protection regime, what is also equally evident is the apparent absence of a willingness on the part of the principals involved to move forward on any of these proposals. This will require, no doubt, the sustained efforts on the part of a broad-based coalition of forces within the UNHCR and the UN system, among States Parties, the INGO and NGO communities, civil society, including refugees, and the legal and academic community, to bring about these well overdue necessary reforms. What is perhaps most encouraging is that these issues and concerns have again come to the fore and that they are being considered seriously on the occasion that marks the 60th anniversary of the *1951 Convention* and 50th anniversary of the *1961 Convention on the Reduction of Statelessness*.

References

Bayefsky, Anne and Joan Fitzpatrick, eds. *Human Rights and Forced Displacement*. (The Hague, The Netherlands: Martinus Nijhoff Publishers, 2000).

Betts, Alexander, 'The Refugee Regime Complex', *Refugee Survey Quarterly*, 29:1 (2010), pp. 12–37.

Caiden, Gerald E., 'The Problem of Ensuring the Public Accountability of Public Officials', in *Public Service Accountability*, ed. Joseph G. Jabbra and O.P. Dwivedi (West Hartford, CT: Kumarian Press, 1988).

Chimni, B. S., ed. *International Refugee Law: A Reader*. (New Delhi: Sage Publications India PVT Ltd., 2000)

Chimni, B. S., 'Reforming the International Refugee Regime: A Dialogic Model', *Journal of Refugee Studies*, 14:2 (2001), pp. 151–68.

Clark, Tom, *The Global Refugee Regime: Charity, Management and Human Rights. Second Edition* (Victoria, B.C.: Trafford Publishing, 2008).

Goodwin-Gill, Guy S. "Refugees and their Human Rights," RSC Working Paper No. 17, Working Paper Series, Queen Elizabeth House, International Development Centre, University of Oxford, August 2004.

Goodwin-Gill, Guy S., 'The Search for the One True Meaning …', in *The Limits of Transnational Law: Refugee Law, Policy Harmonization and Judicial Dialogue in the European Union*, ed. Guy S. Goodwin-Gill and Helene Lambert (Cambridge: Cambridge University Press, 2010), pp. 204–41.

Goodwin-Gill, Guy S. and Jane McAdam, *The Refugee in International Law, Third Edition* (Oxford: Oxford University Press, 2007).

Harrell-Bond, Barbara, 'Can Humanitarian Work with Refugees be Humane?', *Human Rights Quarterly*, 24 (2002), pp. 51–85, at http://icar.gmu.edu/ICC/Humanitarian.pdf (accessed 29 January 2011).

Harrell-Bond, Barbara, *Imposing Aid: Emergency Assistance for Refugees* (Oxford: Oxford University Press, 1986).

Hathaway, James C., *The Rights of Refugees under International Law* (Cambridge: Cambridge University Press, 2005).

International Association of Refugee Law Judges. *The Asylum Process and the Rule of Law*. International Association of Refugee Law Judges (IARLJ) 6th World Conference, Stockholm, Sweden. April, 21–23, 2005 (New Delhi, India: Manak Publications PVT Ltd., 2006).

Inwood, Gregory J., *Understanding Canadian Public Administration: An Introduction to Theory and Practice, Third Edition* (Toronto: Pearson, Prentice-Hall, 2009).

Jastram, Kate and Shelley Cavalieri, 'Human Rights and Refugee Tribunals', *Refugee Survey Quarterly*, 24:2 (2005), pp. 6–23.

Kälin, Walter, 'Supervising the 1951 Convention Relating to the Status of Refugees: Article 35 and Beyond', in *Refugee Protection in International Law: UNHCR's Global Consultations on International Protection*, ed. Erika Feller, Volker Turk and Frances Nicholson (Cambridge: Cambridge University Press, 2003), pp. 613–66.

Loescher, Gil and Alexander Betts and James Milner, *The United Nations High Commissioner for Refugees (UNHCR): The Politics and Practice of Refugee Protection into the Twenty-First Century*. (London: Routledge, 2008).

McAdam, Jane, ed., *Forced Migration, Human Rights and Security*. (Oxford: Hart Publishing, 2008).

MacMillan, Leanne M., 'Monitoring & Reporting: A Search for New Advocacy Strategies', in *Human Rights and Forced Displacement*, ed. Anne F. Bayefsky and Joan Fitzpatrick (The Hague, The Netherlands: Martinus Nijhoff Publishers, 2000), pp. 99–119.

North, Anthony M. and Joyce Chia, 'Towards Convergence in the Interpretation of the Refugee Convention: A Proposal for the Establishment of an International Judicial Commission for Refugees', in *Forced Migration, Human Rights and Security*, ed. Jane McAdam (Oxford: Hart Publishing, 2008), pp. 225–61.

Polman, Linda, *The Crisis Caravan: What's Wrong With Humanitarian Aid?*, trans. Liz Waters (New York: Metropolitan Books, Henry Holt and Company, 2010).

Schermers, H. G. and N. M. Blokker, *International Institutional Law, Third Revised Edition* (The Hague, London, Boston: Martinus Nijhoff, 1995).

Simeon, James C., ed. *The UNHCR and the Supervision of International Refugee Law* (Cambridge: Cambridge University Press, forthcoming).

Simeon, James C., 'A Comparative Analysis of the Response of the UNHCR and Industrialized States to Rapidly Fluctuating Refugee Status and Asylum Applications: Lessons and Best Practices for RSD Systems Design and Administration', *International Journal of Refugee Law*, 22:1 (March 2010), pp. 72–103.

Türk, Volker and Elizabeth Eyster, 'Strengthening Accountability in UNHCR', *International Journal of Refugee Law*, 22:2 (March 2010), pp. 159–72.

Verdirame, Guglielmo and Barbara Harrell-Bond with Zachary Lomo and Hannah Garry, *Rights in Exile: Janus-faced Humanitarianism* (Oxford: Berghahn Books, 2005).

Zieck, Morjoleine, "Article 35/Article II," The 1951 Convention Relating to the Status of Refugees and its 1967 Protocol: A Commentary. ed. Andreas Zimmerman, Assistant eds. Jonas Dorschner and Felix Machts (Oxford: Oxford University Press, 2011).

7 ASHGATE **RESEARCH** COMPANION

Non-refoulement Obligations in Public International Law: Towards a New Protection Status?

Francesco Messineo[1]

1. Introduction

The day after Colonel Gaddafi's infamous televised speech on 'crushing' those 'rats' and 'cockroaches' who revolted against his government in Libya in mid-February 2011,[2] a much less famous politician made his appearance on Italian TV. Daniele Stival, the member of the regional administration of Veneto in charge of 'migration influx', lamented that Italy had not been as successful as Greece, Spain and Croatia at preventing the arrival of migrants from the Southern Mediterranean. He suggested that the Italian government deter the arrival of anyone escaping from Libya and elsewhere by 'using machine guns'.[3] Obviously, such an outrageous statement did not reflect the official position of any major political party in Italy or in Europe. Later on the same day, possibly under pressure from the president of Veneto, Stival partially retracted his statement and added that, unlike economic migrants, 'war refugees must be welcomed'.[4] Yet the incident captured well the discourse of politicians preoccupied with 'defending' the territory of the EU from a perceived forthcoming 'invasion' of migrants.

---

[1] Dott. giur. (Catania), LL.M., PhD (Cambridge); Lecturer in Law, Kent Law School, University of Kent, Canterbury (F.Messineo@kent.ac.uk.). Between 2004 and 2006, the author served as the Refugee and Migrants' Rights Coordinator for the Italian Section of Amnesty International. Many thanks to Cono Giardullo for his research assistance and to Federica Cittadino, Carlo De Naro Papa, Máiréad Enright, Alberta Fabbricotti, María-Teresa Gil-Bazo, Guy S. Goodwin-Gill, Mirina Grosz, Hélène Lambert, Marko Milanović, Federica Paddeu, Bernard Ryan, Elisa Saccà, Brian Sloan and the editor for their useful comments on an earlier draft of this chapter. All remaining mistakes and omissions are the author's. All URLs were last accessed on 4 April 2011.

[2] See e.g. 'Libya Protests: Gaddafi Battles to Control West', *BBC News*, 23 February 2011, at http://www.bbc.co.uk/news/world-middle-east-12556005.

[3] 'Stival-choc sui profughi: "Fermiamoli col mitra"', *Corriere del Veneto*, 23 February 2011, at http://corrieredelveneto.corriere.it/veneto/notizie/politica/2011/23-febbraio-2011/stival-choc-profughi-fermiamoli-col-mitra-19086563779.shtml.

[4] Ibid.

Interestingly, the term '*refoulement*' evokes precisely this language of 'enemies' and 'defence'[5] that has haunted European political debates about immigration for decades. Firing or threatening to fire Italian machine guns at unseaworthy boats whose passengers are escaping from Gaddafi's machine guns would evidently be in breach of a vast array of rules of international law – the point is so obvious it would need little further elaboration. Not quite resorting to such extremes, European states have long sought to curb the number of economic migrants and asylum seekers that cross the Mediterranean by negotiating international covenants such as the Treaty of Friendship, Partnership and Cooperation between Italy and Libya of 30 August 2008.[6] In early 2011, the collapse of those North African governments with which European states had negotiated these agreements caused much concern that a delicate 'equilibrium' might be lost forever. The language of an immigration 'emergency' was, once again, all over daily newspapers in Italy and elsewhere. But the supposed 'equilibrium' had always been illusory. To the limited extent that it worked, the Euro-Mediterranean policy of 'cooperation' only hid migrants away from European sea borders by relocating the 'problem' to the Sahara desert.[7] Crucially, the structure and implementation of these cooperation treaties often led to breaches of *non-refoulement* obligations by either one or both their contracting parties, because migrants were sometimes sent back without their need of international protection having been assessed.[8]

In light of this practice, one might conclude that there is some confusion among governments about what *non-refoulement* responsibilities precisely entail. Where do these obligations come from, and what is their status, scope and content under international law? This chapter seeks to answer these questions in two ways. For the most part (in sections 2 to 5), it offers a contemporary account of the many sources of *non-refoulement* obligations under international law. It does so with reference to the most important doctrinal and judicial debates on the matter, such as that on the status of *non-refoulement* as a 'principle' of customary international law (in section 5). This is essentially an analysis of the *lex lata*. In section 6, the chapter moves on to consider whether a new understanding of *non-refoulement* may be possible by adopting a different perspective on its nature. Arguing

5 See G. Goodwin-Gill and J. McAdam, *The Refugee in International Law* (3rd edn, Oxford; New York: Oxford University Press, 2007), 201.

6 The Italian text of the treaty is annexed to the Italian Law of ratification (no. 7 of 6 February 2009), and at http://www.repubblica.it/2008/05/sezioni/esteri/libia-italia/testo-accordo/testo-accordo.html. For a commentary in English, see N. Ronzitti, 'The Treaty on Friendship, Partnership and Cooperation between Italy and Libya: New Prospects for Cooperation in the Mediterranean?', 1 *Bulletin of Italian Politics* (2009) 125–33. The practice of other European states, including the various 'readmission agreements' at bilateral and EU level, is analysed by M.-T. Gil-Bazo, 'The Practice of Mediterranean States in the Context of the European Union's Justice and Home Affairs External Dimension: The Safe Third Country Concept Revisited', 18 *International Journal of Refugee Law* (2006) 571–600.

7 The point is perhaps best illustrated by a documentary: A. Segre and D. Yime, 'Like a Man on Earth (Come un uomo sulla terra)' (Italy: Asinatas Onlus), DVD, 60'.

8 See e.g. Amnesty International (AI), 'Italy: Submission to the UN Universal Periodic Review (Human Rights Council)', AI Index: EUR 30/008/2009, 8 September 2009, at http://www.amnesty.org/en/library/info/EUR30/008/2009/en, 4–5; AI, '"Libya of tomorrow": What Hope for Human Rights?', AI Index: MDE 19/007/2010, 23 June 2010, at http://www.amnesty.org/en/library/info/MDE19/007/2010/en, 91–114.

de lege ferenda, is *non-refoulement* becoming something more than just the most prominent of the many rights enjoyed by refugees and other individuals at risk of ill-treatment? Has the European Union Qualification Directive[9] started a transformation that will eventually lead to the recognition of *non-refoulement* as a status of international protection alongside (rather than embedded into) 'refugee status' and even EU 'subsidiary protection'?[10]

2. An Overarching 'Principle' of *Non-refoulement*?

Despite the common use of terms by the United Nations, NGOs and commentators, strictly speaking there may be no such thing as one overarching 'principle of *non-refoulement*'. True, it is possible to describe in very generic terms the sum total of the many obligations states have in this respect. An approximate formulation may be that states must not expel, return, extradite or refuse access to their territory to anyone whose most fundamental human rights (including the right not to be persecuted) would otherwise be at risk. This statement may be useful for gaining a first understanding of the concept and for those advocating an extension by analogy of current rules and obligations beyond their original scope. However, from the point of view of a migrant risking ill-treatment or persecution if sent back home, invoking

9 Council Directive 2004/83/EC of 29 April 2004 on minimum standards for the qualification and status of third country nationals or stateless persons as refugees or as persons who otherwise need international protection and the content of the protection granted ('EU Qualification Directive' hereinafter), *Official Journal L* 304, 30/09/2004,12.

10 Surprisingly, there is only one recent monograph in English devoted entirely to *non-refoulement*: K. Wouters, *International Legal Standards for the Protection from Refoulement* (Antwerp; Oxford; Portland, OR: Intersentia, 2009). The literature on the scope and content of *non-refoulement* obligations is nonetheless vast. Among the most recent contributions, see J. Allain, 'The *jus cogens* Nature of *non-refoulement*', 13 *International Journal of Refugee Law* (2001) 533–58; V. Chetail, 'Le droit des réfugiées à l'épreuve des droits de l'homme: bilan de la jurisprudence de la Cour européenne des droits de l'homme sur l'interdiction du renvoi des étrangers menacés de torture et de traitements inhumains ou dégradants', 37 *Revue Belge de Droit International* (2004) 155–210; N. Coleman, 'Renewed Review of the Status of the Principle of *non-refoulement* as Customary International Law', 5 *European Journal of Migration and Law* (2003) 23–68; Goodwin-Gill and McAdam, *The Refugee in International Law*, 201–354; J.C. Hathaway, *The Rights of Refugees under International Law* (Cambridge: Cambridge University Press, 2005), 279–370; H. Lambert, 'Protection against *Refoulement* from Europe: Human Rights Law Comes to the Rescue', 48 *International and Comparative Law Quarterly* (1999) 515–44; E. Lauterpacht and D. Bethlehem, 'The Scope and Content of the Principle of Non-refoulement', in E. Feller et al. (eds), *Refugee Protection in International Law: UNHCR's Global Consultations on International Protection* (Cambridge: Cambridge University Press, 2003), 87–177; A. Zimmermann (ed.), *The 1951 Convention Relating to the Status of Refugees and its 1967 Protocol: A Commentary* (Oxford: Oxford University Press, 2011), 1327–440. The position of the Office of the United Nations High Commissioner for Refugees is clearly summarized in UNHCR, 'Advisory Opinion on the Extraterritorial Application of *Non-refoulement* Obligations under the 1951 Convention relating to the Status of Refugees and its 1967 Protocol', 26 January 2007, at http://www.unhcr.org/refworld/docid/45f17a1a4.html.

such a generic principle is clearly not enough. Rather, it is crucial to establish that a state would be committing an internationally wrongful act by sending him or her back.[11]

In other words, a migrant in search of protection from *refoulement* needs to show that his or her return would engage the responsibility of the sending state under international law. According to the International Law Commission's Articles on State Responsibility, in order to establish such responsibility, one must attribute a certain act or omission to a state and identify at least one international obligation that such conduct has breached.[12] Both customary international law and treaties include several *non-refoulement* obligations that may be employed for such a claim. Although there are significant overlaps between these, each obligation needs to be analysed and understood in its own context in order to apply it. Conflating all obligations in one single overarching concept may please one's sense of legal aesthetics, but runs the risk of undermining international protection rather than enhancing it.[13] The first distinction that should be drawn in order to begin our analysis is between rules designed to prevent the *refoulement* of refugees to territories where they may be persecuted and rules designed to prevent the *refoulement* of any person to territories where they risk ill-treatment or other grave violations of their most fundamental human rights.[14]

3. *Non-refoulement* of Refugees

The first strand of *non-refoulement* obligations arises in the context of international protection from persecution.[15] The obligations are enshrined in various documents and treaties, including the 1967 UN General Assembly Declaration on Territorial Asylum,[16] the

11 What is even more crucial, it is well understood, is that domestic law procedures exist and are fully compliant with international legal obligations. My point here is analysing what these obligations are.

12 Article 2, International Law Commission, 'Articles on the Responsibility of States for Internationally Wrongful Acts', annexed to United Nations General Assembly resolution 56/83, UN Doc. A/RES/56/83, 12 December 2001 (ASR hereinafter).

13 Some of the risks of unwarranted juxtaposition have been analysed by Chetail, 'Le droit des réfugiées à l'épreuve des droits de l'homme', 194–5. According to the author, the conflation of *non-refoulement* obligations concerning refugees and those concerning torture led the European Court of Human Rights to wrongly adopt in the latter context restrictions that only apply to the former.

14 Other rules of non-expulsion or prohibition of transfer apply in different contexts or with different requirements, and will not be dealt with here. For example, Article 4, Protocol 4, of the European Convention of Human Rights prohibits the collective expulsion of aliens. See also Article 45 of the Fourth Geneva Convention of 1949 Relative to the Protection of Civilian Persons in Time of War, 75 UNTS 287. This provision not only prohibits the forcible transfer of protected persons towards countries where they might be persecuted for their political or religious views (in this respect, it falls squarely within the 'persecution' stream of *non-refoulement*); it also prohibits their transfer to countries unwilling or unable to afford the protection of the other provisions of the same Convention, in what may be considered a 'humanitarian law' stream of *non-refoulement*.

15 For an account of the historical evolution of the comparatively recent prohibition of *refoulement* of refugees, see Goodwin-Gill and McAdam, *The Refugee in International Law*, 201–5.

16 Article 3, A/RES/2312(XXII) (1967).

Organization of African Unity Refugee Convention,[17] the American Convention on Human Rights,[18] the Cartagena Declaration on Refugees,[19] the Bangkok Principles on Refugees,[20] the EU Common European Asylum System[21] and some extradition treaties.[22] The most important of these sources of obligation is Article 33(1) of the 1951 Geneva Convention Relating to the Status of Refugees ('the Convention'),[23] which provides that

> No Contracting State shall expel or return ('*refouler*') a refugee in any manner whatsoever to the frontiers of territories where his life or freedom would be threatened on account of his race, religion, nationality, membership of a particular social group or political opinion.

This provision protects everyone who is a 'refugee' from being returned where they may be persecuted, independently of any formal recognition of refugee status; in other words, it applies also to asylum seekers.[24]

---

17 Article II(3), 1969 Organization of African Unity (OAU) Convention Governing the Specific Aspects of Refugee Problems in Africa, 1001 UNTS 45.

18 Article 22(8), 1969 American Convention on Human Rights (Pact of San José, Costa Rica), 1144 UNTS 143.

19 Section III(5), 'Cartagena Declaration on Refugees', *Colloquium on the International Protection of Refugees in Central America, Mexico and Panama*, Cartagena de Indias, 22 November 1984.

20 Article III, Asian–African Legal Consultative Organization, 'Principles Concerning Treatment of Refugees, Asian–African Legal Consultative Committee ("Bangkok Principles")', adopted by resolution 40/3 of 24 June 2001, at http://www.unhcr.org/refworld/docid/3de5f2d52.html.

21 See e.g. the formal recognition of *non-refoulement* obligations in Articles 3(2) and 6, Council Directive 2001/55/EC of 20 July 2001 on minimum standards for giving temporary protection in the event of a mass influx of displaced persons and on measures promoting a balance of efforts between Member States in receiving such persons and bearing the consequences thereof ('Mass influx Directive'), *Official Journal* L 212, 07/08/2001, 12 and in Article 21(1), Council Directive 2004/83/EC of 29 April 2004 on minimum standards for the qualification and status of third country nationals or stateless persons as refugees or as persons who otherwise need international protection and the content of the protection granted ('Qualification Directive'), *Official Journal L* 304, 30/09/2004, 12.

22 See e.g. Article 3, 1957 European Convention on Extradition, 359 UNTS 273.

23 189 UNTS 137, to be read alongside the 1967 New York Protocol, 606 UNTS 267. At the time of writing, 147 states are parties to one or both these instruments: see http://www.unhcr.org/3b73b0d63.html. Non-parties include Cuba and Guyana in the Americas, Libya and Eritrea in Africa, and many countries in Asia (especially the Middle East, the South Asian Sub-continent and Southeast Asia).

24 Para. (c), UNHCR ExCom No. 6 (1977). See Goodwin-Gill and McAdam, *The Refugee in International Law*, 232–3; Hathaway, *The Rights of Refugees*, 158–60 and 303–4; Lauterpacht and Bethlehem, 'The Scope and Content', 116–18. This is, *inter alia,* because recognizing refugee status is a declaratory act of the state, not a constitutive one: United Nations High Commissioner for Refugees, 'Handbook on Procedures and Criteria for Determining Refugee Status under the 1951 Convention and the 1967 Protocol relating to the Status of Refugees', HCR/IP/4/Eng/REV.1, January 1992, at http://www.unhcr.org/refworld/pdfid/3ae6b3314.pdf, para. 28.

The first question to consider is who is a 'refugee' for the purpose of this provision. Article 1(A)(2) of the Convention (as amended by the New York Protocol) defines the term as encompassing anyone who

> [O]wing to well founded fear of being persecuted for reasons of race, religion, nationality, membership of a particular social group or political opinion, is outside the country of his nationality and is unable or, owing to such fear, is unwilling to avail himself of the protection of that country.[25]

Comparing the language of this provision to Article 33, the US Supreme Court and some authors reached the conclusion that the two provisions had different thresholds of applicability. On one view, Article 1(A) was broader, so that *non-refoulement* obligations arose under Article 33 only when the supposedly stricter test of a 'threat' to 'life or freedom' was met.[26] On another, Article 1(A) was narrower, so that *non-refoulement* obligations under Article 33 might also arise when individualized persecution under Article 1(A) could not be established, but there was still a threat to life or liberty, for example because of generalized violence.[27] Both these views, however, seem unpersuasive. The majority of commentators agree that the correct interpretation of Article 33 is that its words are meant to recall Article 1(A), so that the difference in wording between the two provisions is 'immaterial' to the scope of *non-refoulement*.[28] This is also confirmed by the *travaux préparatoires*.[29] In sum, 'all persons who are refugees are protected from return to the risks which gave rise to that status: no more, and no less'.[30]

Unlike the prohibition of *refoulement* in the context of torture, which we shall consider below, this obligation of *non-refoulement* contains exceptions. Article 33(2) of the Convention provides that the benefit of Article 33(1)

> may not ... be claimed by a refugee whom there are reasonable grounds for regarding as a danger to the security of the country in which he is, or who, having been convicted by a final judgment of a particularly serious crime, constitutes a danger to the community of that country.

25 An analysis of the complex questions arising from the interpretation of this provision is beyond the scope of the present chapter. See, among others, Goodwin-Gill and McAdam, *The Refugee in International Law*, 51–134; J.C. Hathaway, *The Law of Refugee Status* (Toronto: Butterworths Canada, 1991); United Nations High Commissioner for Refugees, 'Handbook on Procedures and Criteria for Determining Refugee Status'; Wouters, *International Legal Standards*, 57–81.

26 See *Immigration and Naturalization Service v. Cardoza-Fonseca*, 9 March 1987, 480 US 421, 444.

27 Lauterpacht and Bethlehem, 'The Scope and Content', 124–6.

28 Wouters, *International Legal Standards*, 57. See also Hathaway, *The Rights of Refugees*, 304–7.

29 P. Weis, *The Refugee Convention, 1951: The travaux préparatoires Analysed, with a Commentary* (Cambridge: Cambridge University Press), posthumously published in 1995, at http://www.unhcr.org/4ca34be29.html, 219.

30 Hathaway, *The Rights of Refugees*, 307.

This provision must be read in conjunction with Article 1(F) on exclusion from refugee status, according to which

> [t]he provisions of [the Geneva Convention] shall not apply to any person with respect to whom there are serious reasons for considering that:
>
> (a) he has committed a crime against peace, a war crime, or a crime against humanity, as defined in the international instruments drawn up to make provision in respect of such crimes;
> (b) he has committed a serious non-political crime outside the country of refuge prior to his admission to that country as a refugee;
> (c) he has been guilty of acts contrary to the purposes and principles of the United Nations.

While the application of Article 1(F) means that someone is deemed unworthy of any form of international protection under the Convention, including *non-refoulement,* Article 33(2) may apply to those who, albeit being refugees under Article 1(A), constitute a threat to the security of the host country. They retain their status as refugees and if any other rules of international law prevent their removal (for example, because of a risk of torture) they should be allowed other Convention rights to which they may be entitled. Taking into account the object and purpose of the Convention, both Article 33(2) and Article 1(F) must be interpreted narrowly.[31]

Article 33 also applies to extradition, although this may create a conflict of international obligations when the extradition treaty does not contain a safeguarding clause on *non-refoulement.*[32] In this situation, a state may have to choose whether to comply with its obligation under the Geneva Convention or with its obligation under the extradition treaty. Unless one takes the view that Article 33 has crystallized into a peremptory norm of international law (*jus cogens*),[33] there are no easy answers as to which obligation should prevail.[34]

Article 33 of the Convention prohibits the removal, deportation, transfer or expulsion of a refugee 'in any manner whatsoever'. It is nowadays generally accepted that this includes the rejection of a refugee at the frontier.[35] Furthermore, any domestic law fiction designed to assert that 'international zones' in airports and seaports do not belong to the territory of the

[31] On Articles 33(2) and 1(F), see Goodwin-Gill and McAdam, *The Refugee in International Law,* 234–44; Hathaway, *The Rights of Refugees,* 342–55; Lauterpacht and Bethlehem, 'The Scope and Content', 128–40; Wouters, *International Legal Standards,* 113–33; A. Zimmermann and P. Wennholz, 'Article 33, para. 2 1951 Convention', in A. Zimmermann (ed.), *The 1951 Convention Relating to the Status of Refugees and its 1967 Protocol: A Commentary* (Oxford: Oxford University Press, 2011), 1397–424.

[32] See Wouters, *International Legal Standards,* 136–7.

[33] See below, section 5.

[34] See e.g. M. Milanović, 'Norm Conflict in International Law: Whither Human Rights?', 20 *Duke Journal of Comparative & International Law* (2009) 69–132.

[35] See e.g. Goodwin-Gill and McAdam, *The Refugee in International Law,* 206–8; Hathaway, *The Rights of Refugees,* 315–17; Lauterpacht and Bethlehem, 'The Scope and Content', 113–15.

state where they are situated is immaterial under international law.[36] The whole of Heathrow, Charles De Gaulle and Fiumicino airports belong to the territories of the UK, France and Italy respectively, and all international legal rights and responsibilities apply thereto. By way of an 'acid test', suffice it to query whether, for instance, the UK government would deem Italian authorities to have breached international law rules on diplomatic immunity if Her Majesty's Ambassador to Italy were stopped and searched by Italian frontier police in the 'international zone' of Fiumicino airport. It most certainly would.[37]

In sum, under Article 33 state parties must not return a refugee to a territory where he or she may be persecuted within the meaning of Article 1(A) of the Convention. Article 33 is also generally understood as prohibiting indirect *refoulement*, that is, *refoulement* towards territories from which someone would be likely to be subsequently refouled.[38] Finally, there is some disagreement over the extraterritorial scope of *non-refoulement* (beyond what was said earlier regarding rejection at the frontier), although most commentators construe the obligation as also applying in the high seas and wherever a state exercises its authority over refugees.[39]

4. *Non-refoulement* of Persons at Risk of Ill-treatment or Other Violations of Fundamental Human Rights

It is now time to address what the second strand of *non-refoulement* obligations entails. These rules protect every human being from being sent towards territories where they may be tortured, be subjected to inhuman or degrading treatment or punishment, or suffer other violations of fundamental human rights. These obligations are contained – or have been construed as being contained – in several treaties.

---

36 *Amuur v. France*, n. 19776/92, 25 June 1996, (1996) 22 EHRR 533, para. 52. See Hathaway, *The Rights of Refugees*, 321–2.

37 Articles 27 and 29, Vienna Convention on Diplomatic Relations of 1961, 500 UNTS 95.

38 See Wouters, *International Legal Standards*, 140–47.

39 The contrary view was expressed by the US Supreme Court in *Sale v. Haitian Centers Council*, 21 June 1993, 509 US 155. This complex question is discussed *inter alia* by Goodwin-Gill and McAdam, *The Refugee in International Law*, 244–53 and 270–84; Hathaway, *The Rights of Refugees*, 160–71; W. Kälin, M. Caroni and L. Heim, 'Article 33, para. 1 1951 Convention', in Zimmermann (ed.), *The 1951 Convention Relating to the Status of Refugees and its 1967 Protocol*, 1327–96, 1361–3; H.H. Koh, 'Reflections on *Refoulement* and *Haitian Centers Council*', 35 *Harvard International Law Journal* (1994) 1–20; B. Miltner, 'Human Security and Protection from *Refoulement* in the Maritime Context', in A. Edwards and C.J. Ferstman (eds), *Human Security and Non-citizens: Law, Policy and International Affairs* (Cambridge: Cambridge University Press, 2010), 195–224, 204–8; N. Ronzitti, 'Coastal State Jurisdiction over Refugees and Migrants at Sea', in N. Andō, E. McWhinney and R.D. Wolfrum (eds), *Liber Amicorum Judge Shigeru Oda* (The Hague; London: Kluwer Law International, 2002), 1271–86; S. Trevisanut, 'The Principle of Non-refoulement at Sea and the Effectiveness of Asylum Protection', 12 *Max Planck Yearbook of United Nations Law* (2008) 205–46; United Nations High Commissioner for Refugees, 'Advisory Opinion on the Extraterritorial Application of *Non-refoulement* Obligations'; Wouters, *International Legal Standards*, 48–56; K. Wouters and M. den Heijer, 'The *Marine I* Case: A Comment', 22 *International Journal of Refugee Law* (2010) 1–19.

With specific reference to torture, Article 3 of the 1984 Convention against Torture (CAT) provides:[40]

1. No State Party shall expel, return ('refouler') or extradite a person to another State where there are substantial grounds for believing that he would be in danger of being subjected to torture.
2. For the purpose of determining whether there are such grounds, the competent authorities shall take into account all relevant considerations including, where applicable, the existence in the State concerned of a consistent pattern of gross, flagrant or mass violations of human rights.

This provision must be read together with Article 1 CAT, which, 'without prejudice to any international instrument or national legislation which does or may contain provisions of wider application', defines 'torture' as

> any act by which severe pain or suffering, whether physical or mental, is intentionally inflicted on a person for such purposes as obtaining from him or a third person information or a confession, punishing him for an act he or a third person has committed or is suspected of having committed, or intimidating or coercing him or a third person, or for any reason based on discrimination of any kind, when such pain or suffering is inflicted by or at the instigation of or with the consent or acquiescence of a public official or other person acting in an official capacity. It does not include pain or suffering arising only from, inherent in or incidental to lawful sanctions.[41]

This *non-refoulement* obligation knows no exception. Article 2(2) CAT reinforces its absolute nature by clarifying that 'no exceptional circumstances whatsoever, whether a state of war or a threat of war, internal political instability or any other public emergency, may be invoked as a justification of torture'.

Article 3 CAT prohibits *refoulement* only towards torture, not towards inhuman or degrading treatment.[42] Moreover, its applicability to torture committed by non-state actors

[40] UN Convention against Torture and Other Cruel, Inhuman or Degrading Treatment or Punishment, 1465 UNTS 85. As of March 2011, there are 147 states parties to the CAT, see http://treaties.un.org/Pages/ViewDetails.aspx?src=TREATY&mtdsg_no=IV-9&chapter=4&lang=en.

[41] An analysis of the many interpretative problems arising from this definition of torture is beyond the scope of the present chapter. See, *inter alia*, J.H. Burgers and H. Danelius, *The United Nations Convention against Torture: A Handbook on the Convention against Torture and Other Cruel, Inhuman or Degrading Treatment or Punishment* (Dordrecht; London: Martinus Nijhoff, 1988); E. de Wet, 'The Prohibition of Torture as an International Norm of Jus Cogens and its Implications for National And Customary Law', 15 *European Journal of International Law* (2004) 97–121; R.S.J. Macdonald, 'International Prohibitions Against Torture and Other Forms of Similar Treatment or Punishment', in Y. Dinstein and M. Tabory (eds), *International Law at a Time of Perplexity: Essays in Honour of Shabtai Rosenne* (Dordrecht; London: Martinus Nijhoff, 1989), 385–406; M. Nowak and E. McArthur, *The United Nations Convention Against Torture: A Commentary* (Oxford: Oxford University Press, 2008).

[42] Wouters, *International Legal Standards*, 518–20.

is intrinsically limited by the definition of 'torture' under Article 1 CAT. Other human rights provisions have been construed as being more encompassing. One is Article 7 of the International Covenant on Civil and Political Rights of 1966.[43] Another is Article 3 of the European Convention on Human Rights of 1950,[44] the wording of which is identical to the first sentence of Article 7 ICCPR:

> No one shall be subjected to torture or to inhuman or degrading treatment or punishment.

Both the Human Rights Committee and the European Court of Human Rights (ECtHR) have consistently interpreted these words as entailing a prohibition of *refoulement* towards torture or inhuman or degrading treatment or punishment, although the two bodies do not share an identical interpretation of the scope of such prohibition.[45] We shall focus here on the European Convention.[46]

Although the European Commission of Human Rights had already expressed the view that Article 3 ECHR could be interpreted as implying a *non-refoulement* obligation in the 1970s,[47] there was no concrete application of these *dicta* until the famous *Soering* extradition case of 1989.[48] This is why the expanded construction of Article 3 ECHR as implying *non-refoulement* obligations has come to be known as the '*Soering* jurisprudence'.[49] Its impact has been so significant that the protection it provides has been recognized as a complementary form of refugee protection in its own right.[50] This was also recognized by the European Union with the adoption of the Qualification Directive, in which the status of 'person eligible for subsidiary protection' is partly based on Article 3 ECHR.[51] Nonetheless, it is important to

43 999 UNTS 171 (ICCPR hereinafter).

44 Convention for the Protection of Human Rights and Fundamental Freedoms, 213 UNTS 222 (ECHR hereinafter).

45 As to the Human Rights Committee, see e.g. General Comment No. 20, HRI/GEN/1/Rev.6 at 30 (1992), para. 9; General Comment No. 31, CCPR/C/21/Rev.1/Add.13 (2004), para. 12.

46 For a detailed analysis of Article 7 ICCPR as a *non-refoulement* obligation, see Wouters, *International Legal Standards*, 359–424. On Article 3 ECHR, see ibid., 187–358.

47 See e.g. *X. v. Federal Republic of Germany*, n. 6315/73, 30 September 1974, 1 DR 73.

48 *Soering v. United Kingdom*, n. 14038/88, 7 July 1989, (1989) 11 EHRR 439. See A. Cassese, 'Prohibition of Torture and Inhuman or Degrading Treatment or Punishment', in R.S.J. MacDonald (ed.), *The European System for the Protection of Human Rights* (Dordrecht: Martinus Nijhoff, 1993), 225–61, 248–9.

49 The ECtHR construed Article 3 in this fashion in more than 45 judgments since *Soering* and *Cruz Varas v. Sweden*, n. 15576/89, 20 March 1991, (1992) 14 EHRR 1. Among the most recent cases, see the Grand Chamber judgments in *Saadi v. Italy (Merits) (GC)*, n. 37201/06, 28 February 2008, (2009) 49 EHRR 30 and *M.S.S. v. Belgium and Greece*, n. 30696/09, 21 January 2011, unrep. A comprehensive list of judgments until August 2008 may be found in Wouters, *International Legal Standards*, 189.

50 See e.g. Lambert, 'Protection against *Refoulement* from Europe'; H. Lambert, 'The European Convention on Human Rights and the Protection of Refugees: Limits and Opportunities', 24 *Refugee Survey Quarterly* (2005) 39–55. A similar argument was advanced as to Article 3 CAT; see B. Gorlick, 'The Convention and the Committee against Torture: A Complementary Protection Regime for Refugees', 11 *International Journal of Refugee Law* (1999) 479–95.

51 See Article 2(e) and Article 15(b), EU Qualification Directive (above, note 9).

stress that these human rights provisions are designed to benefit every human being at risk of torture or ill-treatment, not just refugees. The risk of casting them as complementary forms of refugee protection is that this vital distinction might be lost.[52]

Although *Soering* has now become *jurisprudence constante* of the ECtHR, it must be recognized that the legal argument therein was painted in broad brushes. The Court started by mentioning Article 3 CAT as an example of the international community's 'abhorrence' of *refoulement* towards torture, and then dismissed the absence of an explicit equivalent thereof in the European Convention as irrelevant.[53] It went on to assert that an extradition when there is a risk of ill-treatment would 'hardly be compatible with the underlying values' of the ECHR and would 'plainly be contrary to the spirit and intendment' of Article 3 ECHR.[54] When 'substantial grounds have been shown for believing that the person concerned ... faces a real risk of being subjected to torture or to inhuman or degrading treatment or punishment' if returned, a Contracting State would be liable because its action would have 'as a direct consequence the exposure of an individual to proscribed ill treatment'.[55] The legal rationale of this construction is unclear. While the Court did make its (sensible) policy reasons explicit, its legal reasoning for going beyond a textual interpretation of Article 3 ECHR was uncertain. The wording employed by the Court suggests various possible interpretative doctrines: that of the object and purpose of the ECHR as a treaty, that of positive obligations, that of indirect violation, and/or that of complicity in a human rights violation by another state.[56] While some of these avenues of construction might have had merit had they been pursued further, they were not made explicit in the *Soering* judgment. It is probably to be acknowledged that the Court quite simply saw it fit to find a new obligation under Article 3 ECHR.[57] Nonetheless, the Court has had the opportunity to reinforce and expand upon this *jurisprudence* and its legal basis in more than 40 subsequent cases.[58]

The resulting construction of Article 3 ECHR as a rule on *non-refoulement* is very wide in scope, because it encompasses everything from torture to degrading treatment and admits no limitation or exception. When read in conjunction with the Court's case law on what constitutes 'degrading' treatment falling short of 'inhuman' treatment, the consequence may be that

> where a suspected terrorist is threatened with expulsion but substantial grounds have been shown that a real risk exists that he will be subjected to

[52] See above, note 14.

[53] In fact, the earliest decisions by the European Commission of Human Rights interpreting Article 3 ECHR as encompassing *non-refoulement* were the inspiration for Article 3 CAT.

[54] *Soering v. United Kingdom*, para. 88.

[55] Ibid., para. 91.

[56] Chetail, 'Le droit des réfugiées à l'épreuve des droits de l'homme', 165–9.

[57] Ibid.

[58] See above, note 49. For a detailed analysis of the *Soering* jurisprudence, see e.g. N. Mole and C. Meredith, *Asylum and the European Convention on Human Rights* (Strasbourg: Council of Europe, 2010), 19–80; Wouters, *International Legal Standards*, 187–358.

> head-shaving during detention (*Yankov v Bulgaria* (2003)) or will be given light meals on trial days (*Moisejevs v Latvia* (2006)) he may not be expelled.[59]

Some commentators have expressed the view that such a wide protection is untenable and would not be afforded in practice by the Court in the context of *refoulement* in cases where purely degrading (as opposed to inhuman or torturous) treatment was at stake.[60] Yet the Court has recently confirmed that no distinction should be drawn between the treatment that is prohibited 'directly' under Article 3 and the treatment that someone risks 'indirectly', i.e. when sent back in a *refoulement* context. In *Saadi v. Italy*, the UK as an intervening party had tried to argue that such a distinction ought to be made, and that protection against the treatment inflicted by the authorities of another state 'should be weighed against the interests of the community as a whole', for example in cases involving suspected terrorists. This was an attempt at amending the Court's own jurisprudence on the relationship between terrorism and *non-refoulement*.[61] The Grand Chamber of the Court strongly rejected these arguments, reaffirming that

> Since protection against the treatment prohibited by Article 3 is absolute, that provision imposes an obligation not to extradite or expel any person who, in the receiving country, would run the real risk of being subjected to such treatment. As the Court has repeatedly held, there can be no derogation from that rule.[62]

In sum, under Article 3 ECHR there is a strong, absolute and all-encompassing prohibition on *refoulement* of those at risk of any form of ill-treatment, regardless of what they may be accused of. The obligation also applies to indirect *refoulement*, i.e. the transfer to territories from where someone may be at risk of being subjected to *refoulement*.[63] Moreover, it can be construed as applying in an extraterritorial context, as recent jurisprudence confirms.[64]

---

59 Wouters, *International Legal Standards*, 314 (reference is to *Yankov v. Bulgaria*, n. 39084/97, 11 December 2003, [2005] 40 EHRR 36 and *Moisejevs v. Latvia*, n. 64846/01, 15 June 2006, unrep.).

60 See e.g. Y. Arai-Yokoi, 'Grading Scale of Degradation: Identifying the Threshold of Degrading Treatment or Punishment under Article 3 ECHR', 21 *Netherlands Quarterly of Human Rights* (2003) 385–421, 413; A. Fabbricotti, 'The Concept of Inhuman or Degrading Treatment in International Law and its Application in Asylum Cases', 10 *International Journal of Refugee Law* (1998) 637–61.

61 See *Chahal v. United Kingdom*, n. 22414/93, 15 November 1996, (1997) 23 EHRR 413, paras 79–80.

62 *Saadi v. Italy (Merits) (GC)*, para. 138. On the contrary, the Supreme Court of Canada had previously affirmed that a balancing act of *refoulement* towards ill-treatment with the security of the local population could become necessary under Canadian law 'in exceptional circumstances': see *Suresh v. Canada (Minister of Citizenship and Immigration)*, [2002] 1 SCR 3, para. 78.

63 See *T.I. v. United Kingdom (Admissibility)*, n. 43844/98, 7 March 2000, [2000] INLR 211, paras 14–15. See also Wouters, *International Legal Standards*, 320–23.

64 See *Al-Saadoon and Mufdhi v. UK (Merits) (Fourth Section)*, n. 61498/08, 2 March 2010, 51 EHRR 9. The question of how to interpret Article 1 ECHR with reference to the scope *ratione loci* of the Convention is a vexed one that cannot be fully addressed here. See e.g. G. Goodwin-Gill, 'The Extra-territorial Reach of Human Rights Obligations: A Brief Perspective on the Link to Jurisdiction', in L. Boisson de Chazournes and M. Kohen (eds), *Liber Amicorum Vera Gowlland-*

But there is more. Other *non-refoulement* obligations have been construed in cases where the person concerned risks a violation of fundamental human rights not amounting to ill-treatment if sent back. For example, the ECtHR has recognized, at least in theory, that other ECHR rights may also implicitly contain *non-refoulement* rules analogous to the one the Court construed in Article 3 ECHR. Article 2, Article 5 and Article 6 ECHR all imply *non-refoulement* rules (albeit less absolute than in the context of torture),[65] while Article 8 and Article 9 ECHR have been deemed as relevant only insofar as their violation would amount also to a violation of Article 3 ECHR. Similar arguments on implied *non-refoulement* obligations have also been made with reference to Article 6 ICCPR.[66] Furthermore, the International Convention for the Protection of All Persons from Enforced Disappearance,[67] which entered into force in December 2010, also contains a prohibition on *refoulement* similar to that in Article 3 CAT. It is enshrined in Article 16, which provides that:

1. No State Party shall expel, return ('*refouler*'), surrender or extradite a person to another State where there are substantial grounds for believing that he or she would be in danger of being subjected to enforced disappearance.
2. For the purpose of determining whether there are such grounds, the competent authorities shall take into account all relevant considerations, including, where applicable, the existence in the State concerned of a consistent pattern of gross, flagrant or mass violations of human rights or of serious violations of international humanitarian law.

Overall, these developments suggests that the law is evolving in the direction of recognizing that fundamental human rights obligations also structurally imply a duty not to send people to territories where they would be at risk of suffering the prohibited treatment. Quite to what extent this ever-expanding obligation will be recognized by the courts remains to be seen.[68]

Debbas (Leiden: Martinus Nijhoff, 2010), 293–308. According to Milanović, whose opinion the present author shares, it is possible to construe Article 1 ECHR as creating obligations for member states outside their territory and independently of whether they exercise 'effective overall control' (in the sense of *Loizidou v. Turkey (Merits) (GC)*, n. 15318/89, 18 December 1996, (1997) 23 EHRR 513 and despite *Banković v. Belgium and others (Adm.) (GC)*, n. 52207/99, 12 December 2001, (2002) 41 ILM 517). The extent of this obligation will vary depending on the state conduct considered, particularly on whether the conduct involves a positive or a negative state obligation. Generally speaking, a state will be obliged to respect Convention rights insofar as (and to the extent that) it exercises power abroad. See M. Milanović, *Extraterritorial Application of Human Rights Treaties: Law, Principles, and Policy* (Oxford: Oxford University Press, 2011).

[65] See e.g. *Amrollahi v. Denmark*, n. 56711/00, 11 July 2002, unrep. (on Article 8).

[66] Wouters, *International Legal Standards*, 377–81.

[67] UN Doc. A/61/488.

[68] The debate is open. See e.g. H. Battjes, 'The *Soering* Threshold: Why Only Fundamental Values Prohibit *Refoulement* in ECHR Case Law', 11 *European Journal of Migration and Law* (2009) 205–19, 345–53; M. den Heijer, 'Whose Rights and Which Rights? The Continuing Story of Non-Refoulement under the European Convention on Human Rights', 10 *European Journal of Migration and Law* (2008) 277–314; R. Piotrowicz and C. van Eck, 'Subsidiary Protection and Primary Rights', 53 *International and Comparative Law Quarterly* (2004) 107–38.

5. *Non-refoulement* Obligations beyond Treaties

So far, we have considered the treaty sources of various *non-refoulement* obligations in international refugee law and international human rights law. It is now time to consider the extent to which *non-refoulement* obligations exist also in customary international law. As before, different considerations apply to the two strands of refugee-based *non-refoulement* and human rights-based *non-refoulement*.

International Refugee Law

The debate over whether a customary international law prohibition on *refoulement* of refugees exists is nearly as old as the Geneva Convention. While the United Nations High Commissioner for Refugees and member states of its Executive Committee progressively but inexorably moved towards acknowledging Article 33 of the Convention as having crystallized into a rule of customary international law, the academic debate on the matter seems inexhaustible. The most prominent international refugee lawyers still disagree fundamentally over this issue.[69] More than 25 years ago, Goodwin-Gill was famously accused of 'wishful legal thinking' by Hailbronner for being in favour of a comprehensive understanding of *non-refoulement* as part of customary international law.[70] This accusation was still relied upon as authoritative by Hathaway in 2005.[71] Yet, for a change, history seems to have proved the wishful thinker right. Arguments against the customary international law nature of *non-refoulement* of refugees seem slightly anachronistic. There is no question that Article 33 satisfies, in the abstract, the 'norm-creating' requirements set forth by the International Court of Justice in its judgment in the *North Sea Continental Shelf* cases.[72] The disagreement is over whether such crystallization has occurred. Is *non-refoulement* a general practice accepted as law in the sense of Article 38 of the ICJ Statute?[73]

There is near-universal acceptance of the legal binding nature of *non-refoulement*, or *opinio juris*. With the exception of Hathaway and a minority of scholars,[74] most commentators[75] and – more decisively – states agree on the customary nature of *non-refoulement*. States parties to the Geneva Convention explicitly said so on many occasions, the most important of which was perhaps the 2001 Declaration acknowledging 'the continuing relevance and resilience of [international refugee law], including at its core the principle of *non-refoulement*,

69 Compare, for instance, Hathaway, *The Rights of Refugees*, 363–70 with Goodwin-Gill and McAdam, *The Refugee in International Law*, 345–54.

70 K. Hailbronner, '*Non-refoulement* and "Humanitarian" Refugees: Customary International Law or Wishful Legal Thinking?', 26 *Virginia Journal of International Law* (1986) 857–96.

71 Hathaway, *The Rights of Refugees*, 364 (fn. 377).

72 *North Sea Continental Shelf Cases*, 20 February 1969, ICJ Rep. 1969, 3, paras 70–74.

73 Article 38(b), Statute of the International Court of Justice.

74 See e.g. Coleman, 'Renewed Review of the Status of the Principle of *non-refoulement* as Customary International Law'.

75 In addition to Goodwin-Gill and McAdam, see eg. A. Duffy, 'Expulsion to Face Torture? *Non-refoulement* in International Law', 20 *International Journal of Refugee Law* (2008) 373–90; Kälin, Caroni and Heim, 'Article 33(1)', 1343–6.

whose applicability is embedded in customary international law'.[76] In addition, one should recall the many other international treaties and soft-law instruments mentioned above that contribute to the general acceptance of *non-refoulement* of refugees as a binding rule.[77] Every year the UN General Assembly approves resolutions, some of which are adopted unanimously, which unquestionably point in the same direction.[78] These are usually the resolutions through which the UNGA adopts the conclusions reached by the Executive Committee of UNHCR, which includes representatives of the most affected states (not only states parties to the Geneva Convention). Overall, the *opinio juris* in favour of customary international law status of *non-refoulement* is so overwhelming that one may even argue, *à la* Kirgis, that the requirement of state practice should consequently be sensibly reduced.[79]

More importantly, when states that are not parties to the Geneva Convention breach *non-refoulement* obligations, they usually justify their actions by reference to the rule, claiming they have not violated it, rather than declaring that they do not deem themselves bound by it.[80] According to the usual reading of the ICJ's view in *Nicaragua v. United States*, this behaviour supports the existence of the rule.[81] Hathaway instead points out that the International Court of Justice never, in his view, suggested 'that a customary international norm can be established (rather than not undermined) by inconsistent practice by reference to the putative norm'.[82] All the ICJ said, he opined, was that an *already existing* customary norm 'is not defeated by subsequent inconsistent practice so long as that practice is defended as consistent with the norm'.[83] This is a subtle but unpersuasive construction of what the Court said. By reference also to the two preceding paragraphs of the Court's judgment, it seems clear that the ICJ was in fact examining to what extent state practice must be homogeneous to establish that a rule of customary international law exists. It was not discussing how existing customary international law might be changed by subsequent contrary practice.[84]

The question of state practice is precisely the one over which Hathaway construes an impossibly high threshold. He insists on the lack of *universal* respect for *non-refoulement* over the past 60 years as if it were an insuperable difficulty. Three elements seem crucial here. First, once it is established that a customary international law rule is formed, subsequent contrary practice is a violation thereof, not a lack of state practice. There is obviously disagreement here, but the more time passes from the adoption of the Geneva Convention, the less an

[76] UN Doc. HCR/MMSP/2001/09 (2001), para. 4. See also UNHCR ExCom No. 25 (1982).

[77] See above, notes 16 to 23.

[78] See A/RES/41/124 (1986), A/RES/42/109 (1987), A/RES/43/117 (1988), and subsequently either one or two resolutions every year until the most recent A/RES/65/194 (2010) and A/RES/65/193 (2010).

[79] See F.L. Kirgis, 'Custom on a Sliding Scale', 81 *American Journal of International Law* (1987) 146–51.

[80] Goodwin-Gill and McAdam, *The Refugee in International Law*, 347.

[81] See *Military and Paramilitary Activities in and against Nicaragua (Nicaragua v. United States of America) (Merits)*, 27 June 1986, ICJ Rep. 1986, 14, para. 186.

[82] Hathaway, *The Rights of Refugees*, 364 (n. 375).

[83] Ibid.

[84] *Military and Paramilitary Activities in and against Nicaragua (Nicaragua v. United States of America) (Merits)*, paras 184–5. Para. 186, on its own, is also sufficiently clear ('The Court does not consider that, *for a rule to be established as customary*, the corresponding practice must be in absolutely rigorous conformity with the rule'; emphasis added).

argument based on contemporary egregious violations becomes viable – especially if such violations are carried out by states that are parties to the Convention, reasoning *a contrario* from the 'Baxter paradox'.[85] In other words, this debate cannot be had in 2011 with reference to every single violation of *non-refoulement* of refugees since 1951: those who argue in favour of the existence of a customary international law rule think that such rule has existed for a long time now, and that state practice after such creation is irrelevant. Second, on the authority of *Nicaragua*, during the period of formation of a customary rule, contrary practice justified by the acting state by reference to the rule does not hinder the creation of the rule. We have just seen the reason why above. Third, 'general' practice in Article 38(b) of the ICJ Statute means 'general', not 'universal' or 'unanimous'.[86] Despite the many contemporary violations of *non-refoulement* obligations, UN statistics on the wide refugee population in countries that have not signed the Geneva Convention are a strong and consistent evidence of contemporary state practice of the most affected states that supports the customary rule.[87] Every day, literally millions of *non-refoulement*-consistent instances of state practice are accumulated because of this. Moreover, Lauterpacht and Bethlehem observed that more than 125 states have adopted domestic rules consistent with *non-refoulement* obligations.[88] The practice may not be universal, but it is indeed widespread and consistent all over world.

Nonetheless, the lack of unanimous practice must be recognized. While this is not a bar to the recognition of *non-refoulement* of refugees as customary international law, it may be an obstacle to the assertion that this customary rule has also attained the status of *jus cogens*. There are some interesting views to the contrary,[89] but they seem more progressive than

[85] According to the 'Baxter paradox', entering multilateral treaties with a view to create new customary international law may be a self-defeating exercise, as the state practice of member states to those treaties might be irrelevant to the creation of custom outside the treaty: see R. Baxter, 'Multilateral Treaties as Evidence of Customary International Law', 41 *British Yearbook of International Law* (1965–66) 275–300. But if we accept that their practice in conformity to the rule cannot create custom, nor can practice in violation impede its creation. It follows that the practice of states parties to the Geneva Convention in *violation* of Article 33 could not be deemed relevant to deny its crystallization as a customary international law rule: under 'the 'Baxter paradox' view', only the practice of non-member states would matter.

[86] *Military and Paramilitary Activities in and against Nicaragua (Nicaragua v. United States of America) (Merits)*, para. 186 ('It is not to be expected that in the practice of States the application of the rules in question should have been perfect, in the sense that States should have refrained, with *complete consistency*, from the use of force or from intervention … The Court does not consider that, for a rule to be established as customary, the corresponding practice must be in *absolutely rigorous conformity* with the rule … [T]he Court deems it sufficient that the conduct of States should, *in general*, be consistent with such rules …').

[87] For updated statistics, see http://www.unhcr.org/statistics.html.

[88] Lauterpacht and Bethlehem, 'The Scope and Content', 177.

[89] See 'Cartagena Declaration on Refugees', *Colloquium on the International Protection of Refugees in Central America, Mexico and Panama*; UNHCR, 'Executive Committee Conclusion No. 25'; and Allain, 'The *jus cogens* Nature of *non-refoulement*'; A.A. Cançado Trindade, 'Aproximaciones y Convergencias Revisitadas: Diez Años de Interacción entre el Derecho International de los Derechos Humanos, el Derecho international de los Refugiados, y el Derecho Internacional Humanitario; De Cartagena/1984 a San José/1994 y México/2004', in Alto Comisionado de las Naciones Unidas para los Refugiados (Unhcr) (ed.), *Memoria del Vigésimo Aniversario de la Declaración de Cartagena sobre los Refugiados* (San José de Costa Rica: Editorama, 2005), 139–92, 184.

descriptive. Furthermore, it does not seem to be the *opinio juris* of states that *non-refoulement* of refugees is a peremptory norm.

International Human Rights Law

Some of the obligations belonging to the second strand of *non-refoulement*, those based on torture and ill-treatment, also belong to customary international law. There are two possible lines of reasoning that lead to this conclusion. On one view, Article 3 of the Convention Against Torture has crystallized into customary international law as a discrete rule of *non-refoulement* towards torture, in the same manner as Article 33 of the Refugee Convention. Adopting this trail of argumentation, one should prove not only that Article 3 enjoys an abstract and essentially norm-creating character *à la North Sea Continental Shelf*,[90] but also that, since the adoption of the Convention in 1984, there has been a sufficient general practice of *non-refoulement* towards torture accepted as law by states. While the first point is straightforward, the question of state practice may be harder, although not insurmountably so, in consideration of the arguments set out above on consistency, rather than universality, of the required practice. However, the shortcoming of an argument based on Article 3 CAT is that it only covers *non-refoulement* towards torture, not inhuman or degrading treatment.[91]

The second possible line of reasoning is more encompassing. It is premised on the idea that *non-refoulement* is structurally embedded in the prohibition of torture and inhuman or degrading treatment or punishment, in the manner described by the Human Rights Committee with reference to Article 7 ICCPR and the European Court of Human Rights in its *Soering* jurisprudence on Article 3 ECHR.[92] In this view, it is sufficient to show that the prohibition of torture and inhuman or degrading treatment has attained the status of customary international law and it will automatically follow that *non-refoulement* shares the same status. This route of argumentation was adopted by Lauterpacht and Bethlehem.[93] It seems the most promising. In my view, it also leads to a further conclusion that was not shared by the latter authors. If the status of *non-refoulement* towards torture and inhuman or degrading treatment is the same as that of the norm it is embedded into, it would follow that *non-refoulement* towards torture (and possibly other forms of ill-treatment) may now be deemed a rule of *jus cogens*. This is because the prohibition of torture (and possibly that of inhuman or degrading treatment or punishment) is considered by many as a typical example of peremptory norm.[94] Whether states would agree that this is the case with reference to

---

[90] See above, note 68.

[91] See above, note 41.

[92] See above, section 4.

[93] Lauterpacht and Bethlehem, 'The Scope and Content', 150–63.

[94] As recognized ibid., 152. See e.g. General Comment No. 24 Adopted by the Human Rights Committee under Article 40, Paragraph 4 of the International Covenant on Civil and Political Rights, CCPR/C/21/REV.1/ADD.6 (1994), para. 10 and *Prosecutor v. Furundžija (Trial Chamber)*, n. IT-95-17/1-T, 10 December 1998, paras 151–2. See also A. Byrnes, 'Torture and Other Offences Involving the Violation of the Physical or Mental Integrity of the Human Person', in G.K. McDonald and O. Swaak-Goldman (eds), *Substantive and Procedural Aspects of International Criminal Law: The Experience of International and National Courts, Vol. 1 – Commentary* (The Hague: Kluwer Law

non-refoulement is, however, another matter. It may well be the case that, in accepting the peremptory nature of the prohibition of torture, governments have bought into a legal result they had not bargained for. The point here is that, if the *Soering* jurisprudence is to be taken to its ultimate consequences, this is the only possible conclusion.

An Attempted Comprehensive Formulation

Lauterpacht and Bethlehem have suggested the following as a comprehensive formulation of the two *non-refoulement* rules of customary international law we have just considered:

1. No person shall be rejected, returned, or expelled in any manner whatever where this would compel him or her to remain in or return to a territory where substantial grounds can be shown for believing that he or she would face a real risk of being subjected to torture or cruel, inhuman or degrading treatment or punishment. This principle allows of no limitation or exception.
2. In circumstances which do not come within the scope of paragraph 1, no person seeking asylum may be rejected, returned, or expelled in any manner whatever where this would compel him or her to remain in or to return to a territory where he or she may face a threat of persecution or a threat to life, physical integrity, or liberty. Save as provided in paragraph 3, this principle allows of no limitation or exception.
3. Overriding reasons of national security or public safety will permit a State to derogate from the principle expressed in paragraph 2 in circumstances in which the threat of persecution does not equate to and would not be regarded as being on a par with a danger of torture or cruel, inhuman or degrading treatment or punishment and would not come within the scope of other non-derogable customary principles of human rights. The application of these exceptions is conditional on the strict compliance with principles of due process of law and the requirement that all reasonable steps must first be taken to secure the admission of the individual concerned to a safe third country.[95]

Aside from running the risk of conflating international refugee law obligations with international human rights obligations,[96] such a formulation does not seem particularly useful. For example, the wording in the last paragraph is dangerously generic: 'overriding reasons of national security or public safety' is a much less stringent standard than a proper (narrow) construction of Article 33(2) and Article 1(F) of the Geneva Convention.[97]

Furthermore, we have just seen that the status of the two customary international law rules on *non-refoulement* might be different: while there is no realistic prospect of considering the refugee-based one a norm of *jus cogens*, it may be possible to argue that *non-refoulement*

International, 2000), 197–245, 202; De Wet, 'The Prohibition of Torture as an International Norm of Jus Cogens and its Implications for National and Customary Law'.

95 Lauterpacht and Bethlehem, 'The Scope and Content', 163–4.

96 See note 14.

97 See above, section 3.

towards torture is indeed a peremptory norm. When navigating such inherently murky waters such as the precise content of customary rules, it is probably better to refer to two separate and specific rules in the context of their genesis rather than to refer to one overarching and vague 'principle' purportedly encompassing both.

6. A New Protection Status?

So far, we have analysed the scope and content of *non-refoulement* obligations under international law as the current *lex lata*. In this perspective, these many obligations constitute both essential elements of the system of international protection of refugees and constitutive blocks of the system of international human rights protection. An approach whereby the sum total of these obligations is magically reduced to one big and over-encompassing 'principle' of *non-refoulement* has been resisted here, on the grounds that such *reductio ad unum* might actually undermine, rather than enhance, international protection. This does not mean that one should underestimate or deny the overlaps, reciprocal influences, 'cross-fertilizations'[98] and interactions between these two branches of international law. Recognizing that obligations must be interpreted in their own context actually entails that a certain conduct of a state may potentially breach more than one rule of international law.

But *non-refoulement* is not enough. Indeed, one must never forget the case of Mr Ahmed. After the European Court of Human Rights decided that his return to Somalia would be a breach of *non-refoulement* obligations under Article 3 ECHR,[99] Austria refused to provide him with a residence permit, the permission to work or any other assistance. Rendered destitute and homeless, he committed suicide on Human Rights Square (*Platz der Menschenrechte*) in Graz on 15 March 1998.[100] Austria was taking its *non-refoulement* obligation under Article 3 ECHR literally, as meaning that it should tolerate the presence of Mr Ahmed within its borders: no more, and no less. The policy implications of such a narrow interpretation of *non-refoulement* are highly problematic. In fact, the common perspective on the *lex lata* does not go much beyond this.[101] Goodwin-Gill and McAdam acknowledge that, as the law stands, *non-refoulement* does not imply a right of asylum.[102] And Hathaway rightly identifies *non-refoulement* as *one* of the *many* rights of refugees under international law – more specifically one of those rights that arise wherever the state exercises jurisdiction over the individual in question.[103] If these views are correct, any discussion of *non-refoulement* as implying further rights is untenable. But there may be more, at least in a *de lege ferenda* perspective.

98 See Lauterpacht and Bethlehem, 'The Scope and Content', 106.

99 *Ahmed v. Austria*, n. 25964/94, 17 December 1996, (1997) 24 EHRR 278.

100 See K. Röhl, 'Fleeing Violence and Poverty: Non-refoulement Obligations under the European Convention of Human Rights', *New Issues in Refugee Research, Working Paper n. 111* (Geneva: UNHCR), 2005, at http://www.unhcr.org/41f8ef4f2.html, 5 fn. 8.

101 See e.g. Wouters, *International Legal Standards*, 324–7.

102 Goodwin-Gill and McAdam, *The Refugee in International Law*, 414–17.

103 Hathaway, *The Rights of Refugees*, 163.

The 2004 European Union Qualification Directive[104] adopted an innovative approach arising from some previous state practice on 'subsidiary' or 'humanitarian' protection afforded to those who were not granted refugee status but were nonetheless deemed deserving of international protection. The Directive established the status of 'person eligible for subsidiary protection' alongside that of 'refugee'. A 'person eligible for subsidiary protection' was defined as someone

> in respect of whom substantial grounds have been shown for believing that the person concerned, if returned to his or her country of origin, ... would face a real risk of suffering serious harm ... [which is defined as:]

a. death penalty or execution; or
b. torture or inhuman or degrading treatment or punishment of an applicant in the country of origin; or
c. serious and individual threat to a civilian's life or person by reason of indiscriminate violence in situations of international or internal armed conflict.[105]

This second layer of protection was perceived by many as an oblique way of actually reducing refugee entitlements by artificially denying them refugee status and placing refugees in a lower category of protection that had no basis under international refugee law.[106] The Directive was also criticized as potentially conflicting with *non-refoulement* obligations in some respects, especially with relation to torture.[107] Nonetheless, there might have been some unintended positive consequences of this second form of international protection. This is because the Directive is the first international instrument in which *non-refoulement* is cast as a status of protection, rather than as a right.

EU subsidiary protection arose from what has been called the '*Soering* effect',[108] that is, the recognition that *non-refoulement* obligations went beyond those in the Geneva Convention.[109]

---

104 See above, note 9.

105 See Article 2(e) and Article 15, EU Qualification Directive (above, note 9). See also Article 17 on the exclusion from eligibility for such protection.

106 On the debate before and after the adoption of the EU Qualification directive, see D. Bouteillet-Paquet (ed.), *Subsidiary Protection of Refugees in the European Union: Complementing the Geneva Convention?* (Bruxelles: Bruylant, 2002); Chetail, 'Le droit des réfugiées à l'épreuve des droits de l'homme', 207–10; G. Noll, 'International Protection Obligations and the Definition of Subsidiary Protection in the EU Qualification Directive', in C.D.U. de Sousa (ed.), *The Emergence of a European Asylum Policy* (Bruxelles: Bruylant, 2004), 183–94; Piotrowicz and van Eck, 'Subsidiary Protection and Primary Rights'.

107 See European Council on Refugees and Exiles (ECRE), 'Information Note on the Council Directive 2004/83/EC of 29 April 2004', 1 October 2004, at http://www.ecre.org/files/qualpro.pdf. See also European Council on Refugees and Exiles, 'Comments on the European Commission Proposal to recast the Qualification Directive', March 2010, at http://www.ecre.org/files/ECRE_Position_Recast_Qualification_Directive.pdf.

108 See S. Peers, 'Human Rights, Asylum and European Community Law', 24 *Refugee Survey Quarterly* (2005) 24–38, 32.

109 The literature on the evolution of European and refugee law towards the recognition of asylum and/or complementary protection on the basis of *non-refoulement* is vast. See e.g. M.-T. Gil-Bazo, 'Refugee Status and Subsidiary Protection under EC Law: The Qualification Directive

In accepting that this was the case, EU Member States also reached the important conclusion that at least some economic and social rights were an essential consequence of *non-refoulement*.[110] Admittedly, this would have been an even better recognition if EU subsidiary protection were granted in all *non-refoulement* situations, as the European Commission had originally envisaged in its proposal.[111] In the current system, there are three layers of international protection, as Article 21 of the adopted Qualification Directive contains a safeguarding clause for all *non-refoulement* obligations not covered by EU subsidiary protection.[112] Nonetheless, the principle was affirmed that *non-refoulement*, at least in certain cases, cannot be a stand-alone right. Furthermore, the recent *M.S.S. v. Belgium* case before the European Court of Human Rights can be used as authority for the proposition that, regardless of recognition as refugee or beneficiary of EU subsidiary protection, asylum seekers should benefit from a minimum level of economic and social rights, insofar as these can be construed as embedded in Article 3 ECHR.[113] Overall, these developments mean that *non-refoulement* in Europe carries with it a certain set of responsibilities that go well beyond a mere tolerance of the presence of someone within a state's borders. This could be the beginning of a new and fuller recognition of *non-refoulement* as a status of international protection.

References

Geneva Convention (IV) Relative to the Protection of Civilian Persons in Time of War, Geneva, 12 August 1949, entered into force on 21 October 1950, 75 UNTS 287.

[European] Convention for the Protection of Human Rights and Fundamental Freedoms, Rome, 4 November 1950, entered into force on 3 September 1953, 213 UNTS 222.

Convention Relating to the Status of Refugees, Geneva, 28 July 1951, entered into force on 22 April 1954, 189 UNTS 137.

European Convention on Extradition, Paris, 13 December 1957, entered into force on 18 April 1960, 359 UNTS 273.

Vienna Convention on Diplomatic Relations, Vienna, 18 April 1961, entered into force on 24 April 1964, 500 UNTS 95.

and the Right to Be Granted Asylum', in A. Baldaccini, E. Guild and H. Toner (eds), *Whose Freedom, Security and Justice? EU Immigration and Asylum Law and Policy* (Oxford: Hart Publishing, 2007), 229–64; T. Einarsen, 'The European Convention on Human Rights and the Notion of an Implied Right to de facto Asylum', 2 *International Journal of Refugee Law* (1990) 361–89; J. McAdam, *Complementary Protection in International Refugee Law* (Oxford: Oxford University Press, 2007).

110 See e.g. A. Fabbricotti, 'The International and European Doorway to the National Social Welfare State System for Refugees', 57 *AWR Bulletin: Quarterly on Refugee Problems* (2010) 107–9.

111 See Commission of the European Communities, 'Proposal for a Concil Directive on minimum standards for the qualification and status of third country nationals and stateless persons as refugees or as persons who otherwise need international protection', COM(2001) 510 final, 12 September 2001, at http://www.unhcr.org/refworld/docid/47fdfb1ad.html.

112 'Member States shall respect the principle of non-refoulement in accordance with their international obligations'.

113 *M.S.S. v. Belgium and Greece*, n. 30696/09, 21 January 2011, unrep., paras 249–64.

International Covenant on Civil and Political Rights, New York (UN General Assembly resolution 2200A/XXI), 16 December 1966, entered into force on 23 March 1976, 999 UNTS 171.

Protocol Relating to the Status of Refugees, New York, 31 January 1967, entered into force on 4 October 1967, 606 UNTS 267.

American Convention on Human Rights: 'Pact of San José, Costa Rica', San José de Costa Rica, 22 November 1969, entered into force on 18 July 1978, 1144 UNTS 143.

Convention Governing the Specific Aspects of Refugee Problems in Africa, Addis Abeba, 10 September 1969, entered into force on 20 June 1974, 1001 UNTS 45.

'Cartagena Declaration on Refugees', *Colloquium on the International Protection of Refugees in Central America, Mexico and Panama*, Cartagena de Indias, 22 November 1984.

UN Convention against Torture and Other Cruel, Inhuman or Degrading Treatment or Punishment, New York (UN General Assembly resolution 39/46), 10 December 1984, entered into force on 26 June 1987, 1465 UNTS 85.

International Convention for the Protection of All Persons from Enforced Disappearance New York, 20 December 2006, entered into force on 23 December 2010, UN Doc. A/61/488.

Treaty of Friendship, Partnership and Cooperation between Italy and Libya, Benghazi, 30 August 2008, annexed to the Italian Law of ratification (no. 7 of 6 February 2009), and at http://www.repubblica.it/2008/05/sezioni/esteri/libia-italia/testo-accordo/testo-accordo.html.

'Declaration of States Parties to the 1951 Convention and/or its 1967 Protocol relating to the Status of Refugees', UN Doc. HCR/MMSP/2001/09, 13 December 2001.

Commission of the European Communities, 'Proposal for a Concil Directive on minimum standards for the qualification and status of third country nationals and stateless persons as refugees or as persons who otherwise need international protection', COM(2001) 510 final, 12 September 2001, at http://www.unhcr.org/refworld/docid/47fdfb1ad.html.

Human Rights Committee, 'General Comment No. 20 concerning the prohibition of torture and cruel treatment or punishment ', HRI/GEN/1/Rev.6 at 30, 10 March 1992.

Human Rights Committee, 'General Comment No. 24 Adopted by the Human Rights Committee under Article 40, Paragraph 4, of the International Covenant on Civil and Political Rights', CCPR/C/21/REV.1/ADD.6, 11 November 1994.

Human Rights Committee, 'General Comment No. 31 Concerning the Nature of the General Legal Obligation Imposed on States Parties to the Covenant', CCPR/C/21/Rev.1/Add.13, 26 May 2004.

UNGA, 'Declaration on Territorial Asylum', A/RES/2312(XXII), 14 December 1967.

UNHCR, 'Executive Committee Conclusion No. 6', UNHCR ExCom No. 6, 1977.

UNHCR, 'Executive Committee Conclusion No. 25', UNHCR ExCom No. 25, 20 October 1982.

Council Directive 2001/55/EC of 20 July 2001 on minimum standards for giving temporary protection in the event of a mass influx of displaced persons and on measures promoting a balance of efforts between Member States in receiving such persons and bearing the consequences thereof, *Official Journal L* 212, 07/08/2001, 12.

Council Directive 2004/83/EC of 29 April 2004 on minimum standards for the qualification and status of third country nationals or stateless persons as refugees or as persons who otherwise need international protection and the content of the protection granted, *Official Journal L* 304, 30/09/2004, 12.

North Sea Continental Shelf Cases (Federal Republic of Germany/Denmark; Federal Republic of Germany/Netherlands), ICJ Rep. 1969, 3 (International Court of Justice, 20 February 1969).

X. v. Federal Republic of Germany, n. 6315/73, 1 DR 73 (European Commission of Human Rights, 30 September 1974).

Military and Paramilitary Activities in and against Nicaragua (Nicaragua v. United States of America) (Merits), ICJ Rep. 1986, 14 (International Court of Justice, 27 June 1986).

Immigration and Naturalization Service v. Cardoza-Fonseca, 480 US 421 (US Supreme Court, 9 March 1987).

Soering v. United Kingdom (Plen.), n. 14038/88, (1989) 11 EHRR 439 (European Court of Human Rights, 7 July 1989).

Cruz Varas v. Sweden (Plen.), n. 15576/89, (1992) 14 EHRR 1 (European Court of Human Rights, 20 March 1991).

Sale v. Haitian Centers Council, Inc., 509 US 155 (US Supreme Court, 21 June 1993).

Amuur v. France, n. 19776/92, (1996) 22 EHRR 533 (European Court of Human Rights, 25 June 1996).

Chahal v. United Kingdom, n. 22414/93, (1997) 23 EHRR 413 (European Court of Human Rights, 15 November 1996).

Ahmed v. Austria, n. 25964/94, (1997) 24 EHRR 278 (European Court of Human Rights, 17 December 1996).

Loizidou v. Turkey (Merits) (GC), n. 15318/89, (1997) 23 EHRR 513 (European Court of Human Rights, 18 December 1996).

Prosecutor v. Furundžija (Trial Chamber), n. IT-95-17/1-T, (International Criminal Tribunal for the Former Yugoslavia, 10 December 1998).

T.I. v. United Kingdom (Admissibility), n. 43844/98, [2000] INLR 211 (European Court of Human Rights, 7 March 2000).

Banković and others v. Belgium and 16 other member states (Admissibility) (GC), n. 52207/99, (2002) 41 ILM 517 (European Court of Human Rights, 12 December 2001).

Amrollahi v. Denmark, n. 56711/00, unrep. (European Court of Human Rights, 11 July 2002).

Suresh v. Canada (Minister of Citizenship and Immigration), [2002] 1 SCR 3 (Supreme Court of Canada).

Yankov v. Bulgaria, n. 39084/97, (2005) 40 EHRR 36 (European Court of Human Rights, 11 December 2003).

Moisejevs v. Latvia, n. 64846/01, unrep. (European Court of Human Rights, 15 June 2006).

Saadi v. Italy (Merits) (GC), n. 37201/06, (2009) 49 EHRR 30 (European Court of Human Rights, 28 February 2008).

Al-Saadoon and Mufdhi v. the United Kingdom (Merits) (Fourth Section), n. 61498/08, 51 EHRR 9 (European Court of Human Rights, 2 March 2010).

M.S.S. v. Belgium and Greece (GC), n. 30696/09, unrep. (European Court of Human Rights, 21 January 2011).

'Libya Protests: Gaddafi Battles to Control West', *BBC News*, 23 February 2011, at http://www.bbc.co.uk/news/world-middle-east-12556005.

'Stival-choc sui profughi: "Fermiamoli col mitra"', *Corriere del Veneto*, 23 February 2011, at http://corrieredelveneto.corriere.it/veneto/notizie/politica/2011/23-febbraio-2011/stival-choc-profughi-fermiamoli-col-mitra-19086563779.shtml.

AI, 'Italy: Submission to the UN Universal Periodic Review (Human Rights Council)', AI Index: EUR 30/008/2009, 8 September 2009, at http://www.amnesty.org/en/library/info/EUR30/008/2009/en.

AI, '"Libya of tomorrow": What Hope for Human Rights?', AI Index: MDE 19/007/2010, 23 June 2010, at http://www.amnesty.org/en/library/info/MDE19/007/2010/en.

Allain, J., 'The *jus cogens* Nature of *non-refoulement*', 13 *International Journal of Refugee Law* (2001) 533–58.

Arai-Yokoi, Y., 'Grading Scale of Degradation: Identifying the Threshold of Degrading Treatment or Punishment under Article 3 ECHR', 21 *Netherlands Quarterly of Human Rights* (2003) 385–421.

Battjes, H., 'The *Soering* Threshold: Why Only Fundamental Values Prohibit *Refoulement* in ECHR Case Law', 11 *European Journal of Migration and Law* (2009) 205–19.

Baxter, R., 'Multilateral Treaties as Evidence of Customary International Law', 41 *British Yearbook of International Law* (1965–66) 275–300.

Bouteillet-Paquet, D. (ed.), *Subsidiary Protection of Refugees in the European Union: Complementing the Geneva Convention?* (Bruxelles: Bruylant, 2002).

Burgers, J.H. and H. Danelius, *The United Nations Convention against Torture: A Handbook on the Convention against Torture and Other Cruel, Inhuman or Degrading Treatment or Punishment* (Dordrecht; London: Martinus Nijhoff, 1988).

Byrnes, A., 'Torture and Other Offences Involving the Violation of the Physical or Mental Integrity of the Human Person', in G.K. McDonald and O. Swaak-Goldman (eds), *Substantive and Procedural Aspects of International Criminal Law: The Experience of International and National Courts, Vol. 1 – Commentary* (The Hague: Kluwer Law International, 2000), 197–245.

Cançado Trindade, A.A., 'Aproximaciones y Convergencias Revisitadas: Diez Años de Interacción entre el Derecho International de los Derechos Humanos, el Derecho international de los Refugiados, y el Derecho Internacional Humanitario; De Cartagena/1984 a San José/1994 y México/2004', in Alto Comisionado de las Naciones Unidas para los Refugiados (UNHCR) (ed.), *Memoria del Vigésimo Aniversario de la Declaración de Cartagena sobre los Refugiados* (San José de Costa Rica: Editorama, 2005), 139–92.

Cassese, A., 'Prohibition of Torture and Inhuman or Degrading Treatment or Punishment', in R.S.J. MacDonald (ed.), *The European System for the Protection of Human Rights* (Dordrecht: Martinus Nijhoff, 1993), 225–61.

Chetail, V., 'Le droit des réfugiées à l'épreuve des droits de l'homme: bilan de la jurisprudence de la Cour européenne des droits de l'homme sur l'interdiction du renvoi des étrangers menacés de torture et de traitements inhumains ou dégradants', 37 *Revue Belge de Droit International* (2004) 155–210.

Coleman, N., 'Renewed Review of the Status of the Principle of *non-refoulement* as Customary International Law', 5 *European Journal of Migration and Law* (2003) 23–68.

De Wet, E., 'The Prohibition of Torture as an International Norm of Jus Cogens and its Implications for National and Customary Law', 15 *European Journal of Migration and Law* (2004) 97–121.

Den Heijer, M., 'Whose Rights and Which Rights? The Continuing Story of Non-Refoulement under the European Convention on Human Rights', 10 *European Journal of Migration and Law* (2008) 277–314.

Duffy, A., 'Expulsion to Face Torture? *Non-refoulement* in International Law', 20 *International Journal of Refugee Law* (2008) 373–90.

Einarsen, T., 'The European Convention on Human Rights and the Notion of an Implied Right to de facto Asylum', 2 *International Journal of Refugee Law* (1990) 361–89.

European Council on Refugees and Exiles (ECRE), 'Information note on the on the Council Directive 2004/83/EC of 29 April 2004', 1 October 2004, at http://www.ecre.org/files/qualpro.pdf.

European Council on Refugees and Exiles (ECRE), 'Comments on the European Commission Proposal to recast the Qualification Directive', March 2010, at http://www.ecre.org/files/ECRE_Position_Recast_Qualification_Directive.pdf.

Fabbricotti, A., 'The International and European Doorway to the National Social Welfare State System for Refugees', 57 *AWR Bulletin: Quarterly on Refugee Problems* (2010) 107–9.

Fabbricotti, A., 'The Concept of Inhuman or Degrading Treatment in International Law and its Application in Asylum Cases', 10 *International Journal of Refugee Law* (1998) 637–61.

Gil-Bazo, M.-T., 'Refugee Status and Subsidiary Protection under EC Law: The Qualification Directive and the Right to Be Granted Asylum', in A. Baldaccini, E. Guild and H. Toner (eds), *Whose Freedom, Security and Justice? EU Immigration and Asylum Law and Policy* (Oxford: Hart Publishing, 2007), 229–64.

Gil-Bazo, M.-T., 'The Practice of Mediterranean States in the context of the European Union's Justice and Home Affairs External Dimension. The Safe Third Country Concept Revisited', 18 *International Journal of Refugee Law* (2006) 571–600.

Goodwin-Gill, G., 'The Extra-Territorial Reach of Human Rights Obligations: A Brief Perspective on the Link to Jurisdiction', in L. Boisson de Chazournes and M. Kohen (eds), *Liber Amicorum Vera Gowlland-Debbas* (Leiden: Martinus Nijhoff, 2010), 293–308.

Goodwin-Gill, G. and J. McAdam, *The Refugee in International Law* (3rd edn, Oxford; New York: Oxford University Press, 2007).

Gorlick, B., 'The Convention and the Committee against Torture: A Complementary Protection Regime for Refugees', 11 *International Journal of Refugee Law* (1999) 479–95.

Hailbronner, K., '*Non-refoulement* and 'Humanitarian' Refugees: Customary International Law or Wishful Legal Thinking?', 26 *Virginia Journal of International Law* (1986), 857–96.

Hathaway, J.C., *The Law of Refugee Status* (Toronto: Butterworths Canada, 1991).

Hathaway, J.C., *The Rights of Refugees under International Law* (Cambridge: Cambridge University Press, 2005).

International Law Commission, 'Articles on the Responsibility of States for Internationally Wrongful Acts', annexed to United Nations General Assembly resolution 56/83, UN Doc. A/RES/56/83, 12 December 2001.

Kälin, W., M. Caroni and L. Heim, 'Article 33, para. 1 1951 Convention', in A. Zimmermann. (ed.), *The 1951 Convention Relating to the Status of Refugees and its 1967 Protocol: A Commentary* (Oxford: Oxford University Press, 2011), 1327–96.

Kirgis, F.L., 'Custom on a Sliding Scale', 81 *American Journal of International Law* (1987) 146–51.

Koh, H.H., 'Reflections on *Refoulement* and *Haitian Centers Council*', 35 *Harvard International Law Journal* (1994) 1–20.

Lambert, H., 'Protection against *Refoulement* from Europe: Human Rights Law Comes to the Rescue', 48 *International and Comparative Law Quarterly* (1999) 515–44.

Lambert, H., 'The European Convention on Human Rights and the Protection of Refugees: Limits and Opportunities', 24 *Refugee Survey Quarterly* (2005) 39–55.

Lauterpacht, E. and D. Bethlehem, 'The Scope and Content of the Principle of non-refoulement', in E. Feller et al. (eds), *Refugee Protection in International Law: UNHCR's Global Consultations on International Protection* (Cambridge: Cambridge University Press, 2003), 87–177.

Macdonald, R.S.J., 'International Prohibitions Against Torture and Other Forms of Similar Treatment or Punishment', in Y. Dinstein and M. Tabory (eds), *International Law at a Time of Perplexity: Essays in Honour of Shabtai Rosenne* (Dordrecht; London: Martinus Nijhoff, 1989), 385–406.

McAdam, J., *Complementary Protection in International Refugee Law* (Oxford: Oxford University Press, 2007).

Milanović, M., 'Norm Conflict in International Law: Whither Human Rights?', 20 *Duke Journal of Comparative & International Law* (2009) 69–132.

Milanović, M., *Extraterritorial Application of Human Rights Treaties: Law, Principles, and Policy* (Oxford: Oxford University Press, 2011).

Miltner, B., 'Human Security and Protection from *Refoulement* in the Maritime Context', in A. Edwards and C.J. Ferstman (eds), *Human Security and Non-citizens: Law, Policy and International Affairs* (Cambridge: Cambridge University Press, 2010), 195–224.

Mole, N. and C. Meredith, *Asylum and the European Convention on Human Rights* (Strasbourg: Council of Europe, 2010).

Noll, G., 'International Protection Obligations and the Definition of Subsidiary Protection in the EU Qualification Directive', in C.D.U. de Sousa (ed.), *The Emergence of a European Asylum Policy* (Bruxelles: Bruylant, 2004), 183–94.

Nowak, M. and E. McArthur, *The United Nations Convention Against Torture: A Commentary* (Oxford: Oxford University Press, 2008).

Peers, S., 'Human Rights, Asylum and European Community Law', 24 *Refugee Survey Quarterly* (2005) 24–38.

Piotrowicz, R. and C. van Eck, 'Subsidiary Protection and Primary Rights', 53 *International and Comparative Law Quarterly* (2004) 107–38.

Röhl, K., 'Fleeing Violence and Poverty: Non-refoulement Obligations under the European Convention of Human Rights', *New Issues in Refugee Research, Working Paper n. 111* (Geneva: UNHCR), 2005, at http://www.unhcr.org/41f8ef4f2.html.

Ronzitti, N., 'Coastal State Jurisdiction over Refugees and Migrants at Sea', in N. Andō, E. McWhinney and R.D. Wolfrum (eds), *Liber Amicorum Judge Shigeru Oda* (The Hague; London: Kluwer Law International, 2002), 1271–86.

Ronzitti, N., 'The Treaty on Friendship, Partnership and Cooperation between Italy and Libya: New Prospects for Cooperation in the Mediterranean?', 1 *Bulletin of Italian Politics* (2009) 125–33.

Segre, A. and D. Yime, 'Like a Man on Earth (Come un uomo sulla terra)' (Italy: Asinatas Onlus), DVD, 60'.

Trevisanut, S., 'The Principle of Non-refoulement at Sea and the Effectiveness of Asylum Protection', 12 *Max Planck Yearbook of United Nations Law* (2008) 205–46.

United Nations High Commissioner for Refugees, 'Handbook on Procedures and Criteria for Determining Refugee Status under the 1951 Convention and the 1967 Protocol relating to the Status of Refugees', HCR/IP/4/Eng/REV.1, January 1992, at http://www.unhcr.org/refworld/pdfid/3ae6b3314.pdf.

United Nations High Commissioner for Refugees, 'Advisory Opinion on the Extraterritorial Application of *Non-Refoulement* Obligations under the 1951 Convention relating to the Status of Refugees and its 1967 Protocol', 26 January 2007, at http://www.unhcr.org/refworld/docid/45f17a1a4.html.

Weis, P., *The Refugee Convention, 1951: The travaux préparatoires Analysed, with a Commentary*, (Cambridge: Cambridge University Press), posthumously published in 1995, at http://www.unhcr.org/4ca34be29.html.

Wouters, K., *International Legal Standards for the Protection from Refoulement* (Antwerp; Oxford; Portland: Intersentia, 2009).

Wouters, K. and M. den Heijer, 'The *Marine I* Case: A Comment', 22 *International Journal of Refugee Law* (2010) 1–19.

Zimmermann, A. (ed.), *The 1951 Convention Relating to the Status of Refugees and its 1967 Protocol: A Commentary* (Oxford: Oxford University Press, 2011).

Zimmermann, A. and P. Wennholz, 'Article 33, para. 2 1951 Convention', in A. Zimmermann (ed.), *The 1951 Convention Relating to the Status of Refugees and its 1967 Protocol: A Commentary* (Oxford: Oxford University Press, 2011), 1397–424.

Country Information and Evidence Assessment in New Zealand

Rodger Haines QC[1]

Introduction

This chapter aims to provide an overview of the way in which country information (COI) has been used and assessed in the New Zealand refugee status determination system, a system that from 29 November 2010 was enlarged beyond the Refugee Convention (CSR) to include claims to complementary protection under the Convention against Torture (CAT), Article 3 and under the International Covenant on Civil and Political Rights (ICCPR), Articles 6 and 7 as well as to claims for humanitarian protection.[2] The primary focus of this chapter is on the use of COI at the appellate level.

In New Zealand there are presently no formal processes or rules for determining substantive quality standards for researching and assessing COI.[3] To date little to nothing

[1] The author of this chapter was one of three original appointees to the Refugee Status Appeals Authority when it was first constituted in 1991 and remained a member until the Authority was disestablished from 29 November 2010. In the period 1994 to 2010 he was Deputy Chair and author of many of the Authority's principal decisions. Since 1993 he has held the position of Adjunct Lecturer in Law at the Faculty of Law, University of Auckland where he teaches Immigration and Refugee Law. He is currently Chairperson of the Human Rights Review Tribunal. An earlier version of this Chapter was presented at the conference Evidence and Country Information in the Practice of European Courts held in Budapest on 13–15 April 2011 as part of a project led by the Hungarian Helsinki Committee and co-financed by the European Commission. The author is grateful to the conference organizers for the opportunity to participate.

[2] See the Immigration Act 2009, Parts 5 and 7. Most of the provisions of the Act came into force at 2am on 29 November 2010. See the Immigration Act 2009 Commencement Order 2010 (SR2010/185). All New Zealand legislation is accessible online at www.legislation.govt.nz (accessed: 19 July 2012).

[3] Compare and contrast developments primarily within the European Union: UNHCR, *Country of Origin Information: Towards Enhanced Cooperation* (2004), via www.unhcr.org/refworld (accessed: 19 July 2012); ACCORD, *Researching Country of Origin Information: A Training Manual* (2004; updated April 2006), via www.coi-training.net (accessed: 19 July 2012); IARLJ, *Judicial Criteria for Assessing Country of Origin Information (COI): A Checklist* (November 2006), via https://forms.justice.govt.nz/search/IPT/RefugeeProtection/ (accessed: 1 August 2012); Gábor Gyulai, *Country Information in Asylum Procedures – Quality as a Legal Requirement in the EU* (Budapest: Hungarian Helsinki Committee, 2007); *Common EU Guidelines for processing Country of Origin Information (COI)* (April 2008), via www.unhcr.org/refworld (accessed: 19 July 2012).

has been written on the subject.[4] But as will be seen, this does not mean that quality standards are absent from COI in the New Zealand context. Nevertheless it is true that there has been no data collection or research of the kind recently carried out in the United Kingdom.[5] The enhanced protection responsibilities now undertaken by New Zealand under CSR, CAT Article 3, ICCPR Articles 6 and 7 and general international human rights law in the context of humanitarian claims do not permit it to be assumed that what has worked in the past will suffice in the new regime.

In the absence of qualitative research into how COI is presently used by the major actors in the New Zealand refugee and protection system (claimants, refugee and protection officers at first instance, members of the appellate tribunal and by members of the judiciary on review), the observations and comments that follow must necessarily be seen as a largely subjective introduction to the issue of COI and evidence assessment in the New Zealand refugee and protection system. That system is outlined under the next heading.

The Refugee and Protection Determination System in New Zealand: Past and Present

A Brief History

New Zealand has been a party to the Refugee Convention since 1960 and to its Protocol since 1973.[6] The initial RSD procedures, first detailed in interdepartmental circular letters of 6 September 1978 and 1 March 1981, were highly informal and severely criticized by the High Court in the *Benipal* case.[7] In March 1991 the RSD procedures were reformed and given clearer structure by Terms of Reference that created a two-tier RSD process comprising a first instance hearing by an immigration officer with a right of appeal to an appellate tribunal

[4] But see Jeanne Donald, 'Access to Information for Immigration and Refugee Law Practitioners' (2002), Auckland District Law Society Seminar, via www.refugee.org.nz/Reference (accessed: 31 July 2012), where it is recorded at [1.5] that at the time of writing the Refugee Status Branch (the first instance decision-maker) 'refuses to provide practitioners with a copy of country information relied on and cited in their interview reports ... because the information is "publicly available" (refer section 18 of the Official Information Act)'. Ms Donald observes that this can lead to difficulty in certain circumstances, particularly when a practitioner is acting for detained claimants and must respond to interview reports within a short timeframe or if citations refer to an internet site that no longer exists.

[5] See particularly Natasha Tsangarides, *The Refugee Roulette: The Role of Country Information in Refugee Status Determination* (2010, Immigration Advisory Service), via www.iasuk.org (accessed: 19 July 2012), and Robert Thomas, *Administrative Justice and Asylum Appeals: A Study of Tribunal Adjudication* (Oxford: Hart, 2011), at chs 6 and 7.

[6] See generally Rodger Haines, *Laws of New Zealand*, Immigration para. [2].

[7] *Benipal v Minister of Foreign Affairs* (High Court Auckland, A878/83, A993/83 and A1016/83, 29 November 1985, Chilwell J). An appeal by the Crown was dismissed in *Minister of Foreign Affairs v Benipal* [1988] 2 NZLR 222 (CA). See also Haines, *Laws of New Zealand*, Immigration para. [2].

called the Refugee Status Appeals Authority (RSAA).[8] These informal procedures were finally translated into statutory form by the Immigration Amendment Act 1999, s 40, which inserted a new Part 6A into the now-repealed Immigration Act 1987.[9] The new provisions came into force on 1 October 1999. This reform apart, for a period of some twenty years from 1991 to 29 November 2010 the New Zealand RSD system was characterized by its stability.[10]

However, as from 29 November 2010 the jurisdiction of the Refugee Status Appeals Authority to make final refugee determinations has been transferred to the now Immigration and Protection Tribunal (IPT) with that tribunal having an enlarged mandate to determine also protection claims under both CAT, Article 3 and ICCPR, Articles 6 and 7.[11] It is intended, wherever possible, to refer exclusively to the new legislation in the form of the Immigration Act 2009. But while reference is made to the new statutory provisions, of necessity it will be the jurisprudence and practice of the now-disestablished RSAA that will be described. At the date of writing the new IPT had yet to hear and determine refugee and protection claims in any number.[12]

Domestic Incorporation of CSR, CAT and ICCPR

Following the pattern set by the earlier 1987 legislation, the Immigration Act 2009 does not incorporate into New Zealand domestic law all of the CSR, CAT or ICCPR. The legislation domesticates only the key provisions relevant to expulsion or return:

8 Ibid., para. [194].

9 This followed judicial criticism of the informal nature of the Terms of Reference. See further Rodger Haines, 'International Law and Refugees in New Zealand' (1999), 119 *New Zealand Law Review* 132.

10 As to statistics, New Zealand is a small country with a population of approximately 4.5 million. In the first year of its operation (1991) the RSD system received some 901 applications, rising to 1,124 in the following year. This level was not seen again until 1996 (1064), 1997 (1534) and 1998 (1784), with a peak in 1999 (2019). Since then there has been a steady decline. In 2005 the number was 399; in 2010, 384. The recognition rate at first instance before the Refugee Status Branch of Immigration New Zealand has recently fluctuated between 20 per cent in 2006 and 27 per cent in 2010. On appeal to the Refugee Status Appeals Authority the comparable figures are 21 per cent and 31 per cent respectively. Full tables are available on the Statistics page of the *New Zealand Refugee Law* website, via www.refugee.org.nz (accessed: 19 July 2012).

11 For an overview of the changes effected by the Immigration Act 2009 see Rodger Haines, 'Sovereignty Under Challenge – The New Protection Regime in the Immigration Bill 2007' (2009), 149 *New Zealand Law Review* 170.

12 All decisions of the Refugee Status Appeals Authority from 1997 and the decisions of the IPT are to be found on the official website of the IPT at <http://www.justice.govt.nz/tribunals/immigration-protection-tribunal/decisions> (last accessed 27 August 2012). The leading decisions of the RSAA are collected at the New Zealand Refugee Law website <www.refugee.org.nz> (last accessed 27 August 2012). Some have been reported in the New Zealand Administrative Reports published by LexisNexis. Most, if not all of the publicly available refugee decisions of the New Zealand High Court, Court of Appeal and Supreme Court are collected and published on the Case Search page of the New Zealand Refugee Law website.

a. CSR – the definition of 'refugee' in CSR, Article 1.[13]
   – the non-refoulement obligation in CSR, Articles 32 and 33.[14]
b. CAT – the definition of 'torture' in CAT, Article 1.[15]
   – the non-refoulement obligation in CAT, Article 3.[16]
c. ICCPR – Articles 6 and 7. As neither Article expressly imposes an obligation of non-refoulement it is stipulated by the 2009 Act that a person must be recognized as a protected person in New Zealand under the ICCPR if there are substantial grounds for believing that he or she will be in danger of being subjected to arbitrary deprivation of life or to cruel, inhuman or degrading treatment or punishment (CIDT) if deported from New Zealand.[17]

A Two-tier Determination System

A two-tier process operates comprising a first instance hearing by a refugee and protection officer of the Refugee Status Branch (RSB), Department of Labour with a right of appeal to an appellate tribunal that, as mentioned, is now called the Immigration and Protection Tribunal (previously the Refugee Status Appeals Authority).

At first instance the refugee or protection claimant (who is entitled to the assistance of a lawyer on legal aid) is required to submit a claim form together with all supporting evidence including a detailed written statement and relevant COI.[18] This is followed by an interview by a refugee and protection officer. After the interview the officer prepares an 'interview report' setting out the officer's understanding of the evidence given at the interview and the claimant is afforded an opportunity to correct any misunderstandings, errors or omissions that may have occurred. Any COI not sourced from the claimant is also disclosed at this stage. Further evidence, including COI, can then be submitted by the claimant in response. Thereafter the officer prepares a detailed written decision setting out the reasons either for recognizing or not recognizing the individual as a refugee or protected person. In the event of a negative decision, the claimant has a right of appeal to the Immigration and Protection Tribunal.

On appeal to the IPT all questions of fact and law are at large and the appeal proceeds as a hearing de novo. The IPT is under an obligation to come to its own independent conclusion on all issues of fact and law, including credibility and country information. To this end the claimant is interviewed personally by the IPT with the claimant once more being entitled to the assistance of a legally aided lawyer. The claimant is expected to submit any relevant evidence, including COI, and the IPT itself is free to introduce its own evidence and COI,

13 See Immigration Act 2009, s. 129.
14 See ibid., s. 164.
15 See ibid., s. 130(5).
16 See ibid., ss. 130(4) and 164.
17 See ibid., ss. 131 and 164. It is clear that the formula 'substantial grounds for believing that he or she will be in danger of being subjected to …' has been taken from CAT, Article 3(1).
18 See Immigration Act 2009, s. 133.

provided that that evidence and COI is made available to the claimant for comment and challenge.[19]

Responsibility to Establish Claim

Both at first instance and on appeal a person seeking recognition as a refugee or as a protected person is responsible for establishing his or her claim for recognition and must ensure that all information, evidence and submissions that he or she wishes to have considered in support of the claim are provided to the refugee and protection officer or the IPT as the case may be.[20] Both at first instance and on appeal the decision maker may seek information from any source, but is not obliged to seek any information, evidence or submissions further to that provided by the claimant. Indeed the application can be determined on the basis only of the information, evidence and submissions provided by the claimant.[21]

The rule that a claimant is responsible for establishing the claim, is not to be applied mechanically.[22] While the burden of proof in principle rests on the claimant, the duty to ascertain and evaluate all the relevant facts is shared between the claimant and the decision maker.[23] It has long been an established feature of the New Zealand refugee status determination process that the non-adversarial nature of the proceedings means that the inquiry is shared between the claimant and the decision maker.[24] It is an equally long-established principle that the requirement of evidence should not be too strictly applied in

[19] These essential characteristics have been drawn from the RSAA model. In *Garate v Refugee Status Appeals Authority* [1998] NZAR 241 (Williams J) at 247 it was accepted that the RSAA was entitled to take account of the various COI publications to which it had referred in its decision in assessing country conditions in Peru. The RSAA having the advantage of seeing and hearing the witnesses, had clearly balanced this information against its other findings, including the finding on the claimant's credibility, and was entitled to balance conflicting pieces of evidence.

[20] See Immigration Act 2009, ss. 135 and 226. For a discussion of the 'responsibility for establishing' element, see *Refugee Appeal No. 72668/01* [2002] NZAR 649 (NZRSAA) and *Jiao v Refugee Status Appeals Authority* [2003] NZAR 647 (CA).

[21] Immigration Act 2009, ss. 136 and 228.

[22] *Butler v Attorney-General* [1999] NZAR 205 (CA). In *Jiao v Refugee Status Appeals Authority* at [32] it was stated: Were a decision-maker to deny the particular difficulties of refugee claimants and to insist on proof that it was impossible for the applicant to provide there might well be an argument that the decision-making process was fundamentally flawed, and that it did not meet the obligations of States in respect of that process, implicit in the Convention, especially given its vital humanitarian purpose. To insist on such proof by claimants might properly be seen as requiring action by them which would not fall within their 'responsibility' under the Act nor, in the circumstances, within the basic generally accepted principle that claimants must prove the facts they assert. In such an extreme case the legislation, read with the Convention (glossed by general principle, qualified by the relative situations of the claimant and the Authority), might well be seen as breached.

[23] UNHCR, *Handbook on Procedures and Criteria for Determining Refugee Status*, at 196; *Mohammed v Refugee Status Appeals Authority* (High Court Auckland, M500/95, 21 December 1995, Tompkins J), at 2–3; and *C v Refugee Status Appeals Authority* (High Court Auckland, M1365-SW00, 4 May 2001, Nicholson J), at [60] and [61].

[24] *Refugee Appeal No. 523/92 Re RS* (17 March 1995) (NZRSAA), via www.refugee.org.nz (accessed: 19 July 2012). A comprehensive review of the case law is to be found in *Refugee Appeal No. 72668/01* [2002].

view of the difficulty of proof inherent in the special situation in which a person seeking recognition as a refugee or as a protected person finds him or herself.[25]

An Individualized Assessment and the Limitations to COI

It is axiomatic that CSR, Article 1 along with CAT, Article 3 and ICCPR, Articles 6 and 7 require that the individual claiming recognition as a refugee or as a protected person must establish an individualized risk of being persecuted, tortured, arbitrarily deprived of life or subjected to cruel, inhuman or degrading treatment or punishment. The focus is on the specific circumstances of the individual, those circumstances necessarily being unique. This imposes an inherent limitation on the extent to which COI can assist the decision maker in making an assessment of the risk faced by the claimant. It is rare (though not entirely unknown) for COI to address the circumstances of a particular individual. It is even rarer for COI to meaningfully predict the specific risk of harm to an individual in another country at some future point in time. While the assessment of risk is from beginning to end an objective one it is fallacious to assume that the risk must be established by evidence external to the refugee or protection claimant. The assessment may be based largely, or even primarily, on the claimant's own credible testimony.[26]

---

[25] In this regard the RSAA frequently applied the UNHCR *Handbook on Procedures and Criteria for Determining Refugee Status* at para. [196]:

It is a general legal principle that the burden of proof lies on the person submitting a claim. Often, however, an applicant may not be able to support his statements by documentary or other proof, and cases in which an applicant can provide evidence of all his statements will be the exception rather than the rule. In most cases a person fleeing from persecution will have arrived with the barest necessities and very frequently even without personal documents. Thus, while the burden of proof in principle rests on the applicant, the duty to ascertain and evaluate all the relevant facts is shared between the applicant and the examiner. Indeed, in some cases, it may be for the examiner to use all the means at his disposal to produce the necessary evidence in support of the application. Even such independent research may not, however, always be successful and there may also be statements that are not susceptible of proof. In such cases, if the applicant's account appears credible, he should, unless there are good reasons to the contrary, be given the benefit of the doubt.

For an early example see *Refugee Appeal No. 265/92 Re SA* (29 June 1994) (NZRSAA), via www.refugee.org.nz (accessed: 19 July 2012). More recently in *Attorney-General v Tamil X [2010] NZSC 107, [2011] 1 NZLR 721.* It was recognized at [44] that '[T]he inapplicability of rules of evidence gives the [decision-maker] a broad discretion as to what material it obtains and uses in its consideration of a claim. A realistic and careful approach to that material must be taken by the [decision-maker], having regard to the evidential gaps and other difficulties that refugee claimants face in making out their claims'.

[26] James Hathaway and William Hicks, 'Is There a Subjective Element in the Refugee Convention's Requirement of "Well-founded Fear"?' (2005) 26 *Michigan Journal of International Law* 505, and *The Michigan Guidelines on Well-founded Fear* (2005) 26 *Michigan Journal of International Law* 491 at para. [9]. Those *Guidelines* properly reflect the principles applied in New Zealand. See *Refugee Appeal No. 75692* [2007] NZAR 307 (NZRSAA).

An Inquisitorial Process

From its inception, the refugee and protection process in New Zealand has proceeded on inquisitorial lines, both at first instance and on appeal.[27] The quintessentially inquisitorial nature of refugee and protection decision making was explicitly recognized and approved by the New Zealand Supreme Court in 2010.[28] It is now expressly provided by the 2009 statute that the Immigration and Protection Tribunal may conduct proceedings in an inquisitorial or an adversarial manner or adopt a procedure that is both inquisitorial and adversarial in nature.[29] Hearings on refugee and protection claims have never been open to the public. In addition, the New Zealand government is not usually represented at appeal hearings. Only the claimant, his or her lawyer, an independent interpreter and the tribunal member(s) are ordinarily present.[30]

When considering an appeal the IPT may seek information from any source and may in fact require the chief executive of the Department of Labour to seek and provide information relevant to an appeal.[31] However, the IPT is under a statutory duty to disclose to the claimant any information or material that is provided to the Tribunal by a source other than the claimant and which is or may be prejudicial to him or her.[32] The claimant must have opportunity to rebut that information or to comment on it.

High Emphasis on Credibility of Claimant

While the New Zealand appellate tribunal has power to seek information, this discretion is an inherently circumscribed one.[33] First, there is the potential for breaching the confidentiality

[27] For the position prior to 29 November 2010 see *Refugee Appeal No. 70656/97* (10 September 1997) (NZRSAA) and *Refugee Appeal No. 72668/01* [2002] NZAR 649 (NZRSAA), via www.refugee.org.nz (accessed: 19 July 2012).

[28] *Attorney-General v Tamil X* [2010], at [34]–[45].

[29] See Immigration Act 2009, s. 218.

[30] See *Practice Note 2/2010 (Refugee and Protection)* (29 November 2010) at [20], via www.justice.govt.nz (accessed: 19 July 2012). For the earlier practice of the Refugee Status Appeals Authority see *Practice Note 1/2008* (11 September 2008), via http://www.refugee.org.nz/. The Immigration and Protection Tribunal Regulations 2010 (SR2010/355), reg. 14 requires the IPT to arrange for 'an independent interpreter' to attend an oral hearing of the IPT if it considers that an independent interpreter is reasonably required for the purpose of the oral hearing. An 'independent interpreter' is defined as meaning a person who the IPT considers is competent to translate English into a foreign language that the appellant can understand and speak and to translate that foreign language into English; and is impartial. The analogue for the Refugee Status Appeals Authority is to be found in the Immigration (Refugee Processing) Regulations 1999 (SR1999/285), reg. 20. The issue of independence of interpreters in the New Zealand RSD process is examined by Sabine Fenton in *Expressing a Well-founded Fear: Interpreting in Convention Refugee Hearings* (2001), via www.refugee.org.nz (accessed: 19 July 2012).

[31] See Immigration Act 2009, ss. 228 and 229.

[32] See ibid., s. 230. This duty exists also at common law. See for example *Daganayasi v Minister of Immigration* [1980] 2 NZLR 130 (CA).

[33] *AB v Refugee Status Appeals Authority* [2001] NZAR 209 (Nicholson J).

obligation owed to the claimant in the course of an inquiry.[34] Second, there is the potential that the making of an enquiry can render the claimant a refugee or protected person *sur place*. That is, the inquiry may place at risk a claimant who would otherwise have no proper claim to refugee or protection status. Third, the making of inquiries inevitably leads to delay. This is inherently undesirable in the refugee and protection context. Fourth, there are practical difficulties inherent in the inquiry process such as identifying and accessing the holder of the information, language difficulties, the reluctance of individuals to provide information to officials and the inevitable limitations that impose themselves when making an inquiry at a distance. For example, responses are often one dimensional and on their own cannot be properly understood by the tribunal with the result that the further questions that should be asked are not because the agent on the ground is seldom aware of what is of real interest to the tribunal. Fifth, the outcome of the inquiry may be problematical if the fruits of the investigation are enigmatic or ambiguous. Sixth, the veracity of information, documents and their content is often incapable of effective verification. Seventh, the making of the inquiry inevitably involves expense and the New Zealand tribunals have never been funded at a level that permits investigations of a meaningful nature. Finally, there is also the difficulty that COI will seldom address the specific circumstances of the individual claimant. In the majority of cases COI is of a much more general kind. Largely because of these considerations the general approach of the RSAA to refugee claims was to focus primarily on the credibility of the refugee claimant as assessed against publicly accessible information.[35] This approach was approved by the New Zealand Supreme Court.[36]

Credibility cannot, however, be pursued as an end in itself. The decision maker cannot allow the pursuit of credibility issues to divert him or her from those considerations which are primarily relevant to the claim to refugee or protection status.[37] Even if the decision maker concludes that nothing which the claimant has said is true, other evidence may establish that the person is a refugee or protected person. So if, for example, the evidence of a young male Tamil claimant is entirely rejected, evidence external to the claimant may nevertheless establish that simply being a young male Tamil may be sufficient to put the person at risk of being persecuted, tortured or subjected to cruel, inhuman, degrading treatment or punishment. In these circumstances it must inevitably follow that the person is a refugee or protected person even though nothing of the person's account is accepted as true.[38] As pointed out by James C. Hathaway, the objective focus of the refugee definition (and, one could add, of the relevant articles in CAT and the ICCPR) requires that even clear evidence of a lack of candour does not necessarily negate a claimant's need for protection.[39] Furthermore, the fact that a claimant has lied when giving evidence does not

---

34 The duty of confidentiality is found in the Immigration Act 2009, ss. 151 and 152. The subject is addressed in greater detail later in this chapter.

35 See for example *Refugee Appeal No. 72668/01* [2002], at [45].

36 *Attorney-General v Tamil X* [2010], at [37].

37 *Sakran v Minister of Immigration* (High Court Christchurch, CIV2003-409-001876, 22 December 2003, William Young J).

38 See *Refugee Appeal No. 1/92 Re SA* (30 April 1992) (NZRSAA), via www.refugee.org.nz (accessed: 19 July 2012).

39 James C. Hathaway, *The Law of Refugee Status* (Toronto: Butterworths, 1991), at 86.

of itself mean that the whole of his or her evidence is untruthful.[40] The decision maker is required to ask whether a person, having all of the characteristics of the claimant, is at risk of being persecuted, tortured or subjected to CIDT on return.[41] By way of illustration of the force of these points, it can be noted that among the leading cases of the RSAA are two in which the refugees persisted in advancing untrue accounts. When those accounts were abandoned and the true facts disclosed, refugee recognition followed notwithstanding the admitted lies.[42]

Only Publicly Available Information

From the time the current two-tier decision-making process was put in place in 1991, recognition has been given to the fundamental principle that all COI to be taken into account by the decision maker must be disclosed to the claimant and an opportunity given to rebut, answer or comment. This fundamental rule of fairness means, in effect, that only publicly available COI can be used in the refugee and protection context. It also means that adequate opportunity must be given for COI and other disclosed material to be both read and considered.[43]

It has also been a requirement that COI be interpreted reasonably. In one notable case the High Court held that the RSAA had taken an unreasonable view of the COI on Iraq contained in Amnesty International reports. In addition, it was held, the RSAA reading of those reports was inconsistent with other material the RSAA had before it. Further, the inferences drawn from the reports were unreasonable. The RSAA's interpretation of the two reports had the effect of minimizing the significance of and the risk to religious leaders in Iraq. This difficulty was compounded by the RSAA's failure to address itself to the position of Shi'a religious leaders, since that was who the claimant was, rather than Shi'a clerics only. The RSAA's interpretation of the Amnesty International reports significantly coloured its finding that there was no risk to the claimant at the level of a real chance.[44]

---

40 *AA v Refugee Status Appeals Authority* (High Court Auckland, CIV2006-404-7974, 29 June 2007, Harrison J).

41 *A v Chief Executive of the Department of Labour* (High Court Auckland, CIV2004-404-6314, 19 October 2005, Winkelmann J), at [36].

42 See *Refugee Appeal No. 74665/03* [2005] NZAR 60 (NZRSAA) and *Refugee Appeal No. 76044* [2008] NZAR 719 (NZRSAA).

43 See *Santokh Singh v Refugee Status Appeals Authority* (High Court Auckland, M1224/93, 9 February 1994, Smellie J), where approximately ten to fifteen minutes before the appeal hearing the lawyer (who was blind) was handed a magazine article and an earlier decision of the tribunal that addressed the competence of militant groups in Punjab to track potential victims throughout India and the availability of an internal protection alternative. During the hearing the tribunal put to the claimant matters raised in the two documents and no request for an adjournment was made. Counsel later regretted this decision. On judicial review it was held that adequate notice had not been given because the full significance of the earlier decision on the internal protection alternative had not been apparent and more than ten to fifteen minutes had been required to allow analysis and assessment of the information. A rehearing was ordered.

44 *A v Chief Executive of the Department of Labour*, at [48] and [52].

Classified Information

The Immigration Act 2009 has a codified regime for the receipt of classified information in refugee and protection claims. While there is a complex and not entirely informative definition of 'classified information' (too lengthy to repeat here), such information can generally be said to relate to matters of security or criminal conduct.[45] It is expressly provided that classified information relating to security or criminal conduct may be relied on in decision making but the relevant agency which provides the classified information must ensure that such information is balanced.[46] That is, the provider agency must ensure that:

a. The information is provided in a manner that does not, by reason of the omission of any other relevant classified or non-classified information, give a misleading view of the information supplied; and
b. Any classified or non-classified information that is favourable to the person subject to the decision or proceedings is also provided; and
c. Any further classified information that becomes available and that is relevant to the decision or proceedings is provided.

Another notable safeguard is that, while the classified information itself may be withheld from the individual affected, there is a clear and unambiguous duty on the decision maker to provide a *summary* of the allegations arising from the classified information and to provide that summary to the person who is the subject of the proposed decision for comment.[47] The classified information may be relied upon only to the extent that the allegations arising from the information can be summarized.[48] So if the information cannot be assembled in a balanced way and a summary also disclosed to the claimant, it cannot be used by the decision maker.[49]

Confidentiality Maintained

As a general principle a claim to be recognized as a refugee or protected person in New Zealand and the information provided in support of that claim is required by the Immigration Act 2009 to be kept confidential. Specifically, confidentiality as to the fact that a person is a claimant, a refugee or a protected person, and as to the particulars relating to the person's claim or status, must at all times during and subsequent to the determination of the claim

45 See Immigration Act 2009, s. 7 for the meaning of 'classified information'.
46 See ibid., ss. 33, 35 and 36.
47 See ibid., s. 38(1) and (2).
48 See ibid., s. 38(3).
49 For the specific provisions affecting the deployment of classified information in the context of hearings before the Immigration and Protection Tribunal, see ibid., Part 7, particularly ss. 241 to 244. The role of the special advocate in the classified information context is discussed by John Ip in 'Adoption of the Special Advocate Procedure in New Zealand's Immigration Bill' (2009), *New Zealand Law Review* 207.

be maintained by all persons and, in a particular case, may require confidentiality to be maintained as to the very fact or existence of a claim or case, if disclosure of its fact or existence would tend to identify the person concerned or be likely to endanger the safety of any person.[50] Breach of this obligation is a criminal offence.[51] The only exceptions permitted to the confidentiality obligation are those listed in the Immigration Act 2009.[52] These exceptions recognize that the Act does not cloak refugee claims with absolute confidentiality whatever the circumstances. Rather, it strikes a balance between competing interests and recognizes that in certain circumstances the state must, within highly circumscribed limits, be permitted to disclose details of the refugee or protection claim to other government agencies of New Zealand.

Challenging a Decision of the IPT

A claimant not recognized by the IPT as a refugee or protected person may appeal to the High Court on a question of law but leave of that court must be obtained.[53] Judicial review proceedings on conventional common law administrative law grounds can also be commenced.[54] The High Court must endeavour to hear such proceedings and any appeal together.[55] Judicial review is not a *general* appeal. In very broad terms, judicial review is confined to questions of law, errors in procedure and a failure to observe the rules of fairness. Judicial review is concerned not with the decision, but with the decision-making process.[56] It follows that the IPT is the component of the New Zealand RSD process that is intended to be the most effective venue for challenging factual decisions made at first instance. Only the IPT possesses jurisdiction to conduct a de novo investigation of the facts and to receive any evidence relevant to the refugee or protection claim irrespective whether that evidence was submitted at the first instance hearing before a refugee and protection officer.

---

50 See Immigration Act 2009, ss. 151 and 152. The not dissimilar provisions of the earlier Immigration Act 1987, s. 129T were considered in *Attorney-General v X* [2008] NZSC 48; [2008] 2 NZLR 579 (NZSC); and in *Refugee Appeal No. 76204 [Publication of Decision]* [2009] NZAR 745 (NZRSAA).

51 See Immigration Act 2009, s. 354.

52 See ibid., ss. 151(2) and 152(1). Note also *Ghuman v Registrar of the Auckland District Court* [2004] NZAR 440 (Baragwanath J), at [47] to [51], and *MA v Attorney-General* [2009] NZCA 490; application for leave to appeal dismissed in *MA v Attorney-General* [2010] NZSC 33.

53 See Immigration Act 2009, s. 245(1).

54 The proceedings must be commenced not later than 28 days after the date on which the person concerned is notified of the decision, unless the High Court decides that, by reason of special circumstances, further time should be allowed. See ibid., s. 247(1).

55 See ibid., s. 247(2).

56 *Chief Constable of the North Wales Police v Evans* [1982] 1 WLR 1155 at 1173 (HL).

Accessing COI: The RRIB[57]

In the period 1991 to 1996 (approx.), in a largely pre-internet environment, country information was accessed by tribunal members in an informal and haphazard manner. The RSAA 'library' comprised materials gathered by its members from their own researches along with COI submitted in evidence by refugee claimants themselves. The 'collection' was held in a disorganized series of filing boxes.

The New Zealand Refugee Status Library was established in 1996 to serve the information needs of the Refugee Status Branch of Immigration New Zealand and of the RSAA.[58] The main role of the research librarians was to provide background country and human rights information to assist the assessment of claims to refugee recognition. They also provided specific information in response to requests from decision makers in the RSD process. The library's collections have always been accessible to outside users, including refugee and protection claimants and those assisting them, particularly lawyers.

Begun as a sole charge operation in 1996 and always based in Auckland, the library grew to four staff by 2001 and as at March 2011 had 8.5 FTE (full time equivalents) including a three-person team in Wellington. The library is presently a separate branch within Immigration New Zealand, Department of Labour and is currently known as the Refugee Research & Information Branch (RRIB) with first instance decision makers of the Refugee Status Branch and the IPT as its major stakeholders. In 2005 its mandate was extended with a team of three research librarians in Wellington to serve the research and information needs of the Immigration Profiling Group in Border Security. Following the Department of Labour Corporate Model Implementation Project, the RRIB reporting line was moved to the Information Management Division of the Business Services Group in the Department of Labour. The work the RRIB carries out and the relationships with core stakeholders are unchanged, although the provision of COI for residence appeal and deportation matters is increasing following the establishment of the IPT in 2010. An additional Research Librarian has been employed to meet this demand.

All research staff are experienced, professional librarians with post-graduate qualifications. They are also required to adhere to the LIANZA (Library & Information Association of Aotearoa NZ) *Code of Professional Conduct*.

Advantages of a Specialized Research Unit

The advantages of a specialized research unit are possibly self-evident but include:

a. Research is carried out by qualified information specialists, trained in search methodology. They are able not only to source and supply both general country and

[57] The author wishes to acknowledge with gratitude the substantial assistance he has received from Pamela Anderson, Branch Manager, Refugee Research & Information Branch, Department of Labour, New Zealand in drafting this section of the chapter. However, any error or oversight remains the sole responsibility of the author.

[58] For a brief account of the library's early years see Eleanor Hamlyn, 'Spotlight on the New Zealand Refugee Status Library' (February 2001), 253 *Library Life* 28.

human rights information and the answers to highly specific questions about events, groups, people and places, but also to ensure such information is stored in fully searchable databases.

b. Consistent information can be supplied to all clients in the core user groups.
c. Researchers, as part of their work, continually seek new reliable sources and are trained to evaluate the credibility, credentials and impartiality of the source, allowing decision makers more time to devote to their own specialized field(s).
d. Duplication of effort is reduced and cost savings result.
e. The same information can be made available to refugee and protection claimants and their counsel as to the decision makers.

The librarians rely heavily on electronic sources of information and make extensive use of online reports by the major human rights monitoring bodies, international government and non-government organizations and credible news and political reportage. Examples of sources used include: UNHCR Refworld, Amnesty International, Human Rights Watch, International Crisis Group, European Country of Origin Information Network, U.S. Library of Congress, International War & Peace Reporting, Minority Rights Group International, Jane's Intelligence, and numerous national and thematic sites and databases. A new secure internet bookmarking system has been set up on Delicious for researchers to share useful sites. In addition a subscription to Nexis online news allows fully searchable access to a large range of up-to-date and archived international news sources. The library collection includes print copies of reference tools on political parties, languages, ethnic groups, religions, defence and security systems, refugee law and country guidebooks. A small selection of current affairs and refugee journals is also held. The library catalogue and index provides access to the many thousands of reference items found during the research process. All research requests and responses are uploaded into a separate searchable in-house database for future reference.

The librarians are very aware that people's lives are affected by the information they provide and are scrupulous about seeking out the best quality and most current information. They are equally scrupulous about impartiality and careful to establish the credentials of a source. They do not evaluate the evidence but pass it in 'raw' form (with appropriate disclaimers if necessary) to the decision maker whose task it is to decide what impact the information is to have on the case in hand.

Language Barriers

As to language barriers, most general country and human rights information is available in English from credible international sources. Information about specific people or places is occasionally only available in the language of the country concerned. The RRIB has staff with fluency in French, German and Italian and with some knowledge of several other languages. One researcher is also a qualified translator. Immigration New Zealand also has staff from diverse language backgrounds, and researchers may draw on this resource where necessary. In some instances the information may be referred to departmentally accredited translation providers to ensure the integrity of the translation provided to decision makers.

Cooperation between COI Researchers and Decision Makers

The RRIB enjoys a sound professional and collegial relationship with each of its core stakeholder groups. This in no way impinges on the impartiality of any of the actors. A memorandum of understanding between the Department of Labour and Ministry of Justice will formalize the relationship of the new IPT (administered by the Ministry) with the RRIB and the RSB and specify the services and information the two branches are to supply to the IPT. Senior members of the RSAA regularly provided training on refugee jurisprudence to both RSB and RRIB staff. In addition researchers often attend joint training sessions with refugee and protection officers on topics such as refugee status determination procedures and refugee and protection law. New immigration and protection officers have training sessions on RRIB services and 'how to write research requests'. Similar sessions are offered to IPT members. The RRIB also offers country information and thematic presentations to both the RSB and the IPT.

New Zealand is a member of the Inter-Governmental Consultations on Migration, Asylum and Refugees. The RRIB regularly participates in the COI section of the IGC website, where they are able to seek and provide information from/to member States that they have not been able to source elsewhere. Where possible the RRIB endeavours to participate in at least one of the COI Working Groups usually held in Geneva each year. This provides not only an updating on international developments in the field, but enables the benchmarking of performance against international counterparts.[59] However, as mentioned, COI in New Zealand has not yet come under the same scrutiny as is now occurring within the EU context.[60]

Approach to COI: Tribunal Level

Disclosure

As mentioned earlier, the consistent and unwavering approach taken by the RSAA was that any COI uncovered by the tribunal's own researches or received from the RRIB had to be disclosed to the claimant if that information could potentially be used by the tribunal in deciding the case.[61]

59 Participating states in the IGC are Australia, Canada, Finland, Germany, Ireland, New Zealand, Spain, Switzerland, United States of America, Belgium, Denmark, France, Greece, Netherlands, Norway, Sweden, United Kingdom.

60 As to the EU context see, for example, the papers cited at footnote 3 above.

61 Because this is a deeply entrenched and fundamental principle of the common law duty of fairness it can be said with confidence that the same approach will be taken by the Immigration and Protection Tribunal. See further *Daganayasi v Minister of Immigration* [1980].

Consistent Interpretation of COI

To promote the consistent interpretation and application of COI, the RSAA would from time to time hold seminars for members for the purpose of reviewing human rights developments in a particular country with a focus on the evaluation of recent reports relevant to a specific category of cases then being heard by the RSAA. This approach was facilitated by the relatively small number of members of the RSAA and that number declined in more recent years in parallel with the decline in the number of refugee claims received. For example, in 1999 there were fifteen part time members. In 2000 there were two full-time and nineteen part-time members. By 2005 there were six full-time and twenty-three part-time members. However, in 2007 the numbers began to fall, there then being six full-time and fourteen part-time members. By 2010 there were four full-time and seven part-time members. Weekly informal meetings of members also provided a venue for discussion of the sometimes fluid human rights situation in key source countries and the significance of those developments to a particular case or class of cases. But cases were always determined on the basis of the evidence heard and disclosed within the context of the particular case.

While the RSAA most often sat as a single member panel, it would appoint a panel of two, three and on occasion five members where either a 'new' country of origin was encountered in respect of which the RSAA had little or no experience; or, following major changes in the human rights situation in a country with which the RSAA had long experience, it was necessary to hear and evaluate the new COI. This allowed for a more meaningful and objective assessment of COI, the panel having opportunity to debate the different perspectives and interpretations available on the evidence. By allowing more than one perspective to be brought to the interpretation of the COI, a hopefully more nuanced understanding of the COI was achieved.

Most importantly, however, a peer review system ensured that before any decision was published the draft was vetted by a senior member of the tribunal not with a view to influencing the outcome of the case (independence of decision makers was at all times respected) but to draw attention to obvious errors and potentially inconsistent interpretation and application of relevant COI.

Country Guidance Cases

The RSAA never adopted a formal system whereby a single panel purported to arrive at a definitive interpretation or assessment of COI, whether pertaining to credibility, the risk of harm (or categories of persons at risk of harm) and the Convention ground(s) (if any) relevant to the risk of harm. Nor has the New Zealand legislation ever permitted such an approach.[62] This does not mean that detailed assessments of country conditions cannot be

[62] Compare the Nationality, Immigration and Asylum Act 2002 (UK), s. 107(3) (added in April 2003) by which practice directions may 'require the Tribunal to treat a specified decision of the Tribunal as authoritative in respect of a particular matter'. See further *PO (Nigeria) v Secretary of State for the Home Department* [2011] EWCA Civ 132 at [48] to [50] per Carnwath LJ.

found in RSAA jurisprudence and there are indeed decisions, particularly in the period 1992 to 1999, that do have the appearance of what is now referred to in the United Kingdom as country guidance. Those cases related to the Republic of India (Punjab), China (One-child policy) and Indonesia (Ethnic Chinese).

Addressing first the Punjab, one of the first major jurisprudential and COI issues facing the RSAA was whether claimants at risk of being persecuted by militants in the Punjab could be denied recognition as refugees on the basis that they could access meaningful state protection outside the Punjab but within the Republic of India. If the legal answer to that question was 'yes', the next question, turning on COI, related to the circumstances and conditions in which this alternative form of protection could indeed be accessed. As to the jurisprudential issue, the RSAA held that, provided a number of strict preconditions are met, refugee status recognition can be withheld where an internal protection alternative can be demonstrated.[63] As to COI, the decision in *Refugee Appeal No. 18/92 Re JS* (5 August 1992) attempted a summary of the determinations made by the RSAA in its first 12 months of operation. In particular it identified the factors that had been taken into account in assessing the internal protection alternative in the context of non-state agents of persecution. It expressed the hope that the summary would make it possible for an intending claimant to make a realistic assessment of the likely outcome of an appeal. The Authority did, however, caution that the COI assessment made at that time was, at best, provisional:

> We emphasise that the foregoing represents a **general** summary **only** of the jurisprudence to date. If conditions in India or the Punjab change, or new evidence bearing on the issues comes to hand, we will, of course, always be prepared to re-evaluate the situation. Furthermore, no case is ever identical on its facts. We recognize that as conditions in a country of origin change, so too must the assessment of the particular case on appeal [emphasis in original].

This caution notwithstanding, the High Court subsequently drew attention to the danger of country guidance cases reversing the onus of proof:

> the decision in *Refugee Appeal No. 18/92 Re JS* is so emphatic on the issue of relocation that an onus is effectively placed upon subsequent appellants to bring fresh evidence or fail on that point.[64]

---

[63] For the most recent formulation of the internal protection alternative in New Zealand, see *Refugee Appeal No. 76044* [2008], at [95] to [188]. Further reference should be made to James Hathaway and Michelle Foster, 'Internal Protection/Relocation/Flight Alternative as an Aspect of Refugee Status Determination', in Erika Feller, Volker Türk and Frances Nicholson (eds), *Refugee Protection in International Law: UNHCR's Global Consultations on International Protection* (Cambridge: Cambridge University Press, 2003), 357 as well as to *The Michigan Guidelines on the Internal Protection Alternative* (1999) 21 *Michigan Journal of International Law* 131. Those *Guidelines* properly reflect the principles applied in New Zealand. See *Refugee Appeal No. 71684/99* [2000] INLR 165 (NZRSAA), at [65].

[64] *Santokh Singh v Refugee Status Appeals Authority*. Two and a half years later, in *Refugee Appeal No. 523/92 Re RS* (17 March 1995) a four-member panel of senior members of the RSAA, after an extended review of COI, concluded that most of the militant groups in the Punjab had been crushed by mid-1993. That assessment led, in turn, to the conclusion that individuals

As to China and the one-child family cases, the RSAA in its early years heard a number of refugee claims by Chinese nationals whose risk of harm on return to China was said to arise from opposition to the one-child family policy. That policy was the subject of extensive investigation and review in *Refugee Appeal No. 3/91 Re ZWD* (20 October 1992). Rather than attempting to identify the categories of individuals at risk of harm and the circumstances in which that risk would eventuate, the decision largely confines itself to documenting the origin and working of the one-child policy and whether the means chosen for its implementation were in violation of international human rights law.

As to the Indonesian Chinese cases, the decision in *Refugee Appeal No. 71404/99* (29 October 1999) arose out of the significant number of refugee claims by Indonesian nationals of Chinese ethnicity following the outbreak of serious anti-Chinese violence in May 1998. The decision examined the history of anti-Chinese violence in Indonesia and the causes of the May 1998 riots. Drawing on that background, it made an assessment of the future risk of harm faced generally by Chinese in Indonesia. The decision also addresses whether an atmosphere of insecurity can be described as 'being persecuted' in terms of the CSR and finally, it also addresses the internal protection alternative in the context of an archipelago nation.

No doubt other examples can be found. The foregoing list is simply illustrative. But the general approach in New Zealand has been to avoid decisions of this kind as the prevailing and dominant view has been that few refugee or protection cases are ever identical on their facts and that country conditions are far too complex and subtle to permit a single interpretation in which inevitable variations and nuances are artificially collapsed into a single conclusion or finding. See for example the following statement taken from *Refugee Appeal No. 2507/95 Re JEAH* (22 April 1996) in which the Peruvian claimant asserted a risk of being persecuted by the Sendero Luminoso. His claim ultimately failed on the grounds (inter alia) that no imputed political opinion could be established as flowing from the claimant's refusal to comply with a demand that he pay a 'tax' to the Sendero Luminoso. The claimant had relied on several decisions of the RSAA in which, on their particular facts, an imputed political opinion had been established by other claimants in not dissimilar circumstances. In relation to these other cases the RSAA remarked:

> It must be understood that every refugee case is unique. Much turns on the issue of credibility. Furthermore, because the focus of the inquiry is not so much on what has happened in the past as on what might occur in the future, each case has its own subtle nuances which are determined very much by the inter-relationship between credibility, the facts of the case, what is understood of the country conditions in the country of origin and, finally, by the forward looking assessment of the risk faced by the specific claimant. In entering into this difficult field of inquiry (ie, as to whether a particular set of facts establishes a well-founded fear of [being persecuted], different panels of the Authority will be influenced by a range of factors, not all of them necessarily duplicated in superficially similar cases involving the same country of origin … .

claiming a risk of harm at the hand of militants could either not establish a well-founded fear of being persecuted or could mostly find an internal protection alternative either within the Punjab or elsewhere in India.

> We therefore stress that the task of any decision maker is to assess whether, on the particular facts found to have been established, it could be said that the appellant has established to the requisite degree that the persecution feared by him or her is for reason of the appellant's political opinion.

Similar comments are to be found in the High Court of Australia, where in *Appellant S395/2002 v Minister for Immigration and Multicultural Affairs* McHugh and Kirby JJ said:

> It is a mistake to assume that because members of a group are or are not persecuted, and the applicant is a member of that group, the applicant will or will not be persecuted. The central question is always whether this individual applicant has a 'well-founded fear of being persecuted for reasons of ... membership of a particular social group' [emphasis in original].[65]

In the same case Gummow and Hayne JJ criticized attempts to classify large numbers of cases:

> [75] Again, because the question requires prediction, a decision-maker will often find it useful to consider how persons like the applicant have been, or are being, treated in the applicant's country of nationality. That is useful because it may assist in predicting what may happen if the applicant returns to the country of nationality. But, as with any reasoning of that kind, the critical question is how similar are the cases that are being compared.
>
> [76] Because reasoning of the kinds just described is often employed, it is perhaps inevitable that those, like the Tribunal, who must deal with large numbers of decisions about who is a refugee, will attempt to classify cases. There are dangers in creating and applying a scheme for classifying claims to protection. Those dangers are greatest if the classes are few and rigidly defined. But whatever scheme is devised, classification carries the risk that the individual and distinctive features of a claim are put aside in favour of other, more general features which define the chosen class.
>
> [77] Further, there is a serious risk of inverting the proper order of inquiry by arguing from an a priori classification given to the applicant, or the applicant's claim, to a conclusion about what may happen to the applicant if he or she returns to the country of nationality, without giving proper attention to the accuracy or applicability of the class chosen. That is, there is a real risk of assuming (wrongly) that a particular applicant will be treated in the same way as others of that race, religion, social class or political view are treated in that country. It would, for example, be wrong to argue from a premise like 'homosexuality is generally ignored in Bangladesh' to a conclusion that 'this

---

65 *Appellant S395/2002 v Minister for Immigration and Multicultural Affairs* [2003] HCA 71; (2003) 216 CLR 473 McHugh and Kirby JJ at [58].

> applicant (a homosexual) will not be persecuted on account of his sexuality', without paying close attention to the effect of the qualification of the premise provided by the word 'generally'. Thus it would be necessary in the example given to consider whether, on return to Bangladesh, the applicant would stand apart from other homosexuals in that country for any reason.

Even in the specific UK context it has been observed that:

> Country guidance cases were found to be helpful for providing context; limiting the scope of argument; narrowing down issues; defining risk categories; assessing the merits of a case; settling contradictory COI; and providing a wealth of expert and COI evidence. However, their limitations were also noted: they go out of date; country situations are dynamic; ultimately they are case specific with general conclusions drawn out; the Home Office can concede at any given moment; the categories defined are often very narrow; there are divergent outcomes owing to the variance in the judiciary; and countries and issues tend to be selected almost randomly and in a non-transparent manner.[66]

The subjective and highly contestable nature of COI assessment is perhaps illustrated by the controversial decision of the UK Asylum and Immigration Tribunal in *HGMO (Relocation to Khartoum)*.[67] This was a country guidance decision on what has been described as 'the highly controversial question whether it was unduly harsh to expect anyone, and if so whom, to relocate from an area of Sudan to which they could not return to the displaced persons' camps around Khartoum where conditions were, on any view, deplorable'.[68] The determination was that with discernable exceptions, it was not unduly harsh. When the *HGMO (Relocation to Khartoum)* decision was examined in the House of Lords, Baroness Hale expressed concern at its approach:

> 28. Yet the Tribunal concluded that because the conditions faced by returning Darfuris, however appalling, would be no worse than those faced by other Sudanese IDPs it would not be 'unduly harsh' to expect them to return. The standard of comparison was, not with their lives in Darfur before their persecution, not with the general run of ordinary lives in Sudan, not even with the lives of poor people in Sudan, but with the lives of the poorest of the poor, internally displaced victims of the civil war in the south, living in camps or squatter slums, and 'subject from time to time to relocations, sometimes involving force and human rights violations' (para 244). They too had been subsistence farmers, ill-equipped to survive in the city slums (para 239); they

66 Tsangarides, *The Refugee Roulette*. For a further discussion of the advantages and disadvantages of the country guidance system in the UK see Thomas, *Administrative Justice and Asylum Appeals*, at ch. 7.

67 *HGMO (Relocation to Khartoum) Sudan CG* [2006] UK IAT 00062.

68 See *KH (Sudan) v Secretary of State for the Home Department* [2008] EWCA Civ 887; [2009] Imm AR 139 (CA), at [2] per Sedley LJ.

> too had suffered the psychological horrors of civil war (para 238), if not of government-backed genocide; the Darfuris would be no worse off, unless particular individuals attracted the adverse interest of the authorities (para 242). With respect, this is not the individualised, holistic assessment which the question requires.[69]

In the later but related *KH (Sudan)* Sedley LJ noted the submission that the AIT had made stereotypical assumptions about the impact of poverty and the traumas of war on Darfurians, that health conditions in the camps were appalling, and that the decision flew in the face of expert evidence.[70] He observed that it was a submission with which the Court of Appeal might, if it were a primary decision maker, have had 'considerable sympathy', but they were not grounds of appeal and therefore not issues that could be addressed.[71] Rather, the appeals were to be approached on the footing that internal relocation to a place of sufficient safety would be reasonable unless it was unduly harsh for the individual concerned. He then noted at [8] what is, in effect, the 'reverse burden of proof' phenomenon implicit in country guidance cases:

> that immigration judges are expected to follow the country guidance contained in *HGMO* unless acceptable evidence is placed before them by either party which shows it to have been incorrect or to be no longer correct in some significant respects.

In the result, while in the Court of Appeal and in the House of Lords real concern was expressed as to the offered 'country guidance', the restricted nature of appellate proceedings precluded effective intervention to correct doubtful findings of fact. Nevertheless it can be noted that in *KH (Sudan)* there were in fact five appellants. One of them (*QA (Sudan)*) did succeed in the Court of Appeal as he was able to meet the reverse burden of proof. In the following passage Moses LJ, delivering the judgment of the Court, identified as a significant error the failure of the decision maker to concentrate on the specific circumstances of the individual refugee claimant. This is a recurring and fundamental flaw in the country guidance system:

> 36. The AIT in *HGMO*, as endorsed by the House of Lords, has concluded that conditions in a camp or squatter area are not such as to lead to the conclusion that it would be unduly harsh to expect a young male adult to live there. Such a proposition is general and in each case it is incumbent upon the fact finder to consider the impact of such conditions on the particular appellant who contends it would be unduly harsh to return there in the context of his or her particular circumstances. Those circumstances, in the instant appeal, are stark. The appellant has lost all his living relatives, killed by those responsible

69 See *AH (Sudan) v Secretary of State for the Home Department* [2007] UKHL 49; [2008] AC 678 (HL), at [27] to [30].

70 See *KH (Sudan) v Secretary of State for the Home Department* [2008], at [3] per Sedley LJ.

71 Ibid., at [4].

> for conditions in those camps. Not only has he lost his siblings and his parents but also the one surviving relative who enabled him to escape from his village. Nowhere is there any reference within the determination of the AIT to the impact of those circumstances. On the contrary, they are dismissed in a cursory manner in the reference of the Tribunal to this appellant as being a 'young apparently healthy adult'. No regard has been had to the vital consideration of the effect on this lone young man, even now only 20, who will, if the Tribunal's decision stands, have to face the prospect of survival in a camp. Conditions in such camps were described by Dr Khalil as being a 'desperate situation' within 'appalling conditions of extreme poverty' (see § 43 of *AH* in the Court of Appeal). The impact of such conditions will be accompanied by the everyday knowledge that those responsible for such conditions are also responsible for the death of his every living relative.
>
> 37. In our judgement the failure to make any reference to the particular circumstances of this appellant was an error of law. Anyone reading of such circumstances might have little difficulty in concluding that it would be unduly harsh to require this appellant to return to a camp. But in *HGMO* the AIT made no reference to the impact on those who had seen their parents and relatives killed by the Janjaweed under the sponsorship of the Government of Sudan.

Reference can also be made to the decision of the Court of Appeal in *FB (Democratic Republic of Congo) v Secretary of State for the Home Department*,[72] where the AIT, expressing reservations, had relied on a two-year-old country guidance case. The decision was reversed by the Court of Appeal, that court observing that country guidance cases are 'not to be construed like statutes'; guidance cases cannot cover every possibility; and the focus of the decision maker must be on the risk involved if the claimant were to be returned to the country of origin.[73] The Court emphasized that, as in every other asylum case, the evidence must be looked at as a whole. That being so, one might ask whether anything meaningful is achieved by the time and resources invested in country guidance cases,[74] particularly given that the CSR, CAT

[72] *FB (Democratic Republic of Congo) v Secretary of State for the Home Department* [2008] EWCA Civ 457; [2008] Imm AR 589 (CA).

[73] Ibid., at [15] and [21].

[74] The country guidance system was adopted formally in 2003. As at 29 March 2011 there were 316 *current* country guidance decisions relating to 58 countries (though an overall total of 479 CG decisions relating to 65 countries). See *List of Country Guideline Determinations*, via www.tribunals.gov.uk (accessed: 19 July 2012). The resources required to maintain a system of this magnitude must be weighed against the benefits claimed to be derived. In this context note the following observation made by Thomas in *Administrative Justice and Asylum Appeals*, at 223:

Other concerns with the country guidance process have concerned the amount of time that particular country issues take to get finally resolved and the actual effectiveness of such guidance once issued. Country guidance issues can often be challenged in the higher courts and then sent back and forth between them and the Tribunal. The classic example is provided by the extraordinary country guidance litigation over returns to Zimbabwe. Over a four year period,

and ICCPR mandate an individuated inquiry into the particular and unique circumstances of the claimant.

Country Guidance Cases: Some Conclusions

There must be a real question whether 'country guidance' is a realistically achievable aim, premised as it is on the assumption that a person or panel of persons will capture (accurately) the rich texture of possibilities in a particular country and context, a country in which the decision makers do not live and most often have not visited and when the assessment is based largely on what has been observed and written by others in a language in which the decision makers are not fluent. The idea that someone can say, authoritatively, 'what really happens' in a given country is a bridge too far for some. If a life has been lived entirely unobserved, if events, circumstances and conditions have either not been noticed or not written about, that life and those events remain invisible and are usually assumed not to exist. It is one thing to make findings in relation to the narrow circumstances of the individual refugee or protection claim where the evidence is focused on one person. It is an entirely different matter to make generalizations about a country, its power structures, the possibilities of life within that country and the circumstances in which harm might befall individuals generally. Experience shows that the truth on the ground is inevitably more subtle, more nuanced, confused, complicated and contradictory. It is incapable of being 'shoe-horned' into neat categories or sets of conclusions, the more so when specific conditions are not generally reported or are incapable of investigation.

Then there is the point that country information is seldom neutral. It always requires interpretation. When a refugee decision maker makes broad generalizations for a range of cases, there is too much room for the intrusion of the subjectivities of that decision maker (and indeed of the authors of the COI).[75] There is also much room for error.[76] In addition a gender-blind interpretation of country information has for too long been a barrier to the recognition of gender-based refugee and protection claims,[77] so too in the case of claims based on sexual orientation. Both categories face a wall of silence.[78] Little or nothing might

the Tribunal issued four country guidance decisions on the safety of returnees to Zimbabwe after successive remittals by the Court of Appeal.

75 The making of asylum policy through country guidance needs to be acknowledged. See further Thomas in *Administrative Justice and Asylum Appeals*, at 201–2. See also Natasha Tsangarides, 'The Politics of Knowledge: An Examination of the Use of Country Information in the Asylum Determination Process', (2009) 23 *Immigration, Asylum and Nationality Law* 252.

76 See for example *PO (Nigeria) v Secretary of State for the Home Department* [2011], where 'deep unease' was expressed at the way in which the evidence of the claimant's expert was rejected in favour of an email tendered by the Home Office. The latter was described as 'a flimsy basis for the conclusions to which it led'. See Maurice Kay LJ at [24]. The very length and complexity of country guidance cases can be a substantial impediment to their proper application and indeed to an accurate identification of the points determined. See Carnwath LJ at [54] to [56].

77 See for example Heaven Crawley, *Refugees and Gender: Law and Process* (Bristol: Jordans, 2001), at [10.5].

78 See for example Brian Whitaker, *Unspeakable Love: Gay and Lesbian Life in the Middle East* (Berkeley, CA: University of California Press, 2006), and Ann Jones, *Kabul in Winter: Life without*

be found in COI on persecution and discrimination based on gender, sexual orientation, disability and age. The challenge of 'decoding' country information and identifying what is not there is insufficiently remarked upon.

Beyond these points lies the unpleasant truth that country guidance cases can and do deflect the decision maker from the proper inquiry. While it has been said that,

> no country guidance case is for ever; it is a factual precedent ... and as such is open to revision in the light of new facts – new either in the sense of being newly ascertained or in the sense that they have arisen only since the decision was promulgated – provided in each case that they are facts of sufficient weight.[79]

the question the downstream decision maker is required to address changes significantly. It ceases to be the one posed by the treaties. It is not whether the refugee claimant has an individuated well-founded fear of being persecuted for a Convention reason or whether a specific protection claimant is at risk of torture, CIDT or being arbitrarily deprived of life. Rather, the question becomes whether the claimant falls within a particular risk category identified in the country guidance case and if not, whether he or she can show 'new facts' in the sense explained in *KH (Sudan)*.[80] On one view, the deflection of the refugee or protection inquiry away from the individualized and particular circumstances of the specific claimant threatens the integrity of the refugee or protection inquiry. It could be said that attempting consistency through country guidance cases comes at too high a price.

The RSAA generally avoided (with some exceptions) publishing 'country guidance' cases. It does not follow that its procedures were for this reason wanting. A recent and extensive analysis of the UK country guidance system concluded that it cannot be implied 'that country guidance is or should be a necessary feature of any asylum process'.[81] As earlier explained, it was in this context that the RSAA deployed other measures to achieve consistent interpretation of COI such as seminars and training, informal meetings, a peer review system, and the convening of multi-member panels. Nor does it follow that detailed assessments of COI were not made by the RSAA; to the contrary. This can be seen from the RSAA website that allows a search to be conducted, country by country, according to the level of country information.[82] The options permitted are 'any', 'high', 'medium' or 'low'.

Country Guidance to be Distinguished from Precedent-setting Decisions on the Law

While the RSAA generally avoided publishing country guidance cases, it took the opposite approach in publishing decisions that established legal precedents. The view taken was that

Peace in Afghanistan (New York: Metropolitan Books, 2006).

79 *KH (Sudan) v Secretary of State for the Home Department* [2008], at [4] per Sedley LJ.

80 These dangers are illustrated by *PO (Nigeria) v Secretary of State for the Home Department* [2011], at [32] to [43] per Maurice Kay LJ. For a discussion of other problems inherent in applying country guidance cases see Thomas in *Administrative Justice and Asylum Appeals*, at 214–20.

81 See ibid., at 234.

82 See www.nzrefugeeappeals.govt.nz (accessed: 1 August 2012).

as a final and specialist appellate tribunal it had a responsibility, applying Article 31 of the Vienna Convention on the Law of Treaties, 1969, to ascertain the 'true autonomous and international' meaning of the Refugee Convention spoken of by Lord Steyn in the House of Lords.[83] The purpose of RSAA precedent decisions on refugee law was to give guidance and instruction to first instance decision makers and to assist the High Court on judicial review should the relevant legal issue come before that court for determination. Some decisions have been cited favourably in the House of Lords and in the UK Supreme Court.[84]

The Limitations of Country Information: COI and Credibility Assessment

Country information is potentially relevant to (inter alia) the nature of the harm faced in the country of origin, the risk of that harm eventuating in the future, nexus and credibility. As to the last of these issues, credibility assessment is a substantive subject on its own. In a paper focused on COI only a few observations can be made on the relationship between COI and credibility.

The primary task of the decision maker is fact finding. The ultimate issue is not credibility, but of the risk of serious harm. That having been said, COI is nonetheless often properly deployed to test and assess the credibility of the claimant. In some cases the question posed is whether the claimant's account is consistent with COI – and therefore more likely to be credible, or whether the account is inconsistent with COI – and therefore more likely to be not credible.[85] While there are cases where COI can properly assist in determining the credibility of the claimant in this way, the deployment of COI in the credibility assessment exercise opens up the broader and more fundamental question of how credibility can be properly assessed. Further, if COI is to be used to assess the credibility of the claimant, is it not necessary to also assess the credibility of the COI itself? The proposition is that to interrogate the credibility of the claimant by deploying COI necessarily requires the interrogation of the credibility of that COI.

83 *Adan v Secretary of State for the Home Department* [2001] 2 AC 477 (HL).

84 See for example *Refugee Appeal No. 1312/93 Re GJ* [1998] INLR 387 (whether sexual orientation qualifies as a ground for 'being persecuted'), followed and applied in *R v Immigration Appeal Tribunal, Ex parte Shah* [1999], 2 AC 629, 643D (HL); *Refugee Appeal No. 74665/03* [2005] NZAR 60; [2005] INLR 68 (whether gays can be denied recognition as refugees on the basis that they can be required to be 'discreet'), referred to with approval in four of the judgments given in *HJ (Iran) v Secretary of State for the Home Department* [2010] UKSC 31 (SC) and RT (Zimbabwe) v Secretary of State for the Home Department [2012] UKSC 38; and *Refugee Appeal No. 70366/96 Re C* [1997] 4 HKC 236, referred to in *Adan v Secretary of State for the Home Department* [1999] 1 AC 293, 307A (HL).

85 See also the discussion in Thomas, *Administrative Justice and Asylum Appeals*, at 146–7.

A Few Observations about Credibility Assessment

Beyond these observations lie the fundamental challenges of credibility assessment itself.[86] Without an appreciation of the nature of those challenges, there is a danger of COI being deployed in an impermissible manner. Context is everything. All refugee and protection claims require a narrative of the claimant's personal circumstances and although past harm is not a requirement of the CSR, CAT, Article 3 and ICCPR, Articles 6 and 7, it is common to find that past harm or past encounters with the agent of persecution are central to the claimant's narrative. The credibility of this narrative is then subjected to close examination from different perspectives including coherency, internal consistency, plausibility and consistency of telling. Obviously there are also other factors that potentially affect the credibility assessment. But the last factor (consistency of telling) is particularly relevant to appellate tribunals that conduct the refugee or protection inquiry on a de novo basis. Changes or differences that occur in the narrative on appeal compared with the evidence given in the initial statement or at first instance (for example in relation to dates, places, details of events) will often count against the claimant. These assessments can be unforgiving and driven by false assumptions as to how events are remembered and then recalled. Time and space permit only two analyses to be referred to. The first is by Daniel L Schacter, who observes:

> we tend to think of memories as snapshots from family albums that, if stored properly, could be retrieved in precisely the same condition in which they were put away. But we now know that we do not record our experiences the way a camera records them. Our memories work differently. We extract key elements from our experiences and store them. We then recreate or reconstruct our experiences rather than retrieve copies of them. Sometimes, in the process of reconstructing we add on feelings, beliefs, or even knowledge we obtained after the experience. In other words, we bias our memories of the past by attributing to them emotions or knowledge we acquired after the event.[87]

The second primary source drawn on for this chapter is a recent journal article that addresses the subject of memory in the context of refugee and protection claims. It is impossible in a few lines to do justice to this exemplary piece by Hilary Evans Cameron. It is therefore intended to reproduce only the Abstract:

> Refugee status decision makers typically have unreasonable expectations of what and how people remember. Many assume that our minds record all aspects of the events that we experience, and that these memories are stored

[86] There is now a substantial body of literature on the subject. Useful reference can be made to Gregor Noll (ed.), *Proof, Evidentiary Assessment and Credibility in Asylum Procedures* (Leiden and Boston, MA: Martinus Nijhoff Publishers, 2005); Michael Kagan, 'Is Truth in the Eye of the Beholder? Objective Credibility Assessment in Refugee Status Determination' (2003), 17 *Georgetown Immigration Law Journal* 367; and Hilary Evans Cameron, 'Refugee Status Determinations and the Limits of Memory' (2010), 22 *International Journal of Refugee Law* 469.

[87] Daniel L. Schacter, *The Seven Sins of Memory: How the Mind Forgets and Remembers* (Boston, MA: Houghton Mifflin Company, 2001), at 9.

> in our brains and remain unchanged over time. Decades of psychological research has demonstrated, however, that our memories are neither so complete nor so stable, even setting aside the effects on memory of trauma and stress. Whole categories of information are difficult to recall accurately, if at all: temporal information, such as dates, frequency, duration and sequence; the appearance of common objects; discrete instances of repeated events; peripheral information; proper names; and the verbatim wording of verbal exchanges. In addition, our autobiographical memories change over time, and may change significantly. As a result, while gaps or inconsistencies in a claimant's testimony may in some cases properly lead to a negative credibility finding, such aspects are often misleading and should never be used mechanically, and the bar must be set much lower. Many decision makers must fundamentally readjust their thinking about claimants' memories if they are to avoid making findings that are as unsound as they are unjust.[88]

It is clear that a decision maker cannot engage in the simplistic exercise of comparing the claimant's account with whatever COI the decision maker happens to have available and then proceeding to a determination of 'the truth' by treating the COI as the touchstone. Credibility assessment cannot be reduced to such a formulaic exercise. Nor can credibility assessment be assumed to be an exercise undertaken with scientific precision. Decision makers need to be aware that '[a] possible life-and-death decision extracted from shreds of evidence and subjective impressions … has to be made'.[89]

A Few Observations about Assessing the Credibility of COI

Country information is inherently contestable. Some of the reasons are set out earlier in the context of the discussion of country guidance cases. Additional forceful and compelling reasons are identified by Natasha Tsangarides in her recent study.[90] The key problem is that people take as facts not what is, but what they perceive to be facts:

---

88 Evans Cameron, 'Refugee Status Determinations and the Limits of Memory', 469.

89 Stephen Sedley, 'Asylum: Can the Judiciary Maintain its Independence?', in IARLJ, *Stemming the Tide or Keeping the Balance – The Role of the Judiciary* (edited and published for IARLJ by the NZ Association for Comparative Law and the Revue Juridique Polynésienne in association with the New Zealand Centre for Public Law of the Victoria University of Wellington, 2003), 319, at 324.

90 Tsangarides, 'The Politics of Knowledge', 252. The author at 253 correctly points out that '[t]he production of knowledge is inherently political, embedded in social and cultural processes that involve power relations and subjectivity'. She argues that 'the accessibility to, and selection and use of information necessarily involve subjective processes, which deflate any attempt at denoting such information as objective'. Her point at page 263 is that 'there is a need for the acknowledgement of the limitations of COI, namely its ability to establish certainty or fact, which should be expressed through heightened analysis of COI amongst stakeholders. It calls for the recognition of the subjectivity involved in knowledge production, interpretation and use'.

> For the real environment is altogether too big, too complex, and too fleeting for direct acquaintance. We are not equipped to deal with so much subtlety, so much variety, so many permutations and combinations. And although we have to act in that environment, we have to reconstruct it on a simpler model before we can manage with it. To traverse the world men must have maps of the world. Their persistent difficulty is to secure maps on which their own need, or someone else's need, has not sketched in the coast of Bohemia.[91]

There is no denying the seductive nature of COI. It can lead the decision maker to believe that he or she 'knows' about the claimant's country of origin, knows 'the truth' of what happens in that country (and what does not happen). There is a danger that the decision maker will reconstruct the claimant's world on a simpler model in order to manage it.[92] To traverse the claimant's world the decision maker must have a map of that world. The persistent difficulty is 'to secure maps on which [the decision maker's] own need, or someone else's need, has not sketched in the coast of Bohemia'.

Conclusion

The New Zealand refugee and protection determination system illustrates a familiar pattern of progression from the disorganized, haphazard collection and deployment of COI to the research, assembly and presentation of COI by professional librarians qualified as information specialists and trained in search methodology. While the RRIB works very much in the background, the assistance provided by its librarians to decision makers as well as to refugee and protection claimants underpins the entire determination process and is a necessary component of the credibility of that process. The essential role played by research librarians is insufficiently acknowledged.

A two-tier inquisitorial system in which the appellate tribunal conducts a de novo hearing with all questions of fact (including COI) and law being at large properly recognizes the importance of ensuring that the refugee or protection claimant has full opportunity to present his or her case and to ensure that the decision is based on accurate and current COI. But focused as it is on the special circumstances of the particular claimant, the refugee or protection inquiry functions best when it avoids overreach. That is the making of findings beyond those required by the context of the particular case and intended to provide guidance to decision makers in later but similar cases.

There are inherent dangers in deploying COI in credibility assessment. This does not mean to say that such deployment should not occur. But there must be recognition that the decision maker may have false expectations as to how and what people remember and how those memories are retrieved and narrated. Where there are such false expectations the deployment

[91] Walter Lippmann, *Public Opinion*, with a new introduction by Michael Curtis (New Brunswick, NJ, and London: Transaction Publishers, 1998), at xvi and 16.

[92] See also Robert F. Barsky, *Constructing a Productive Other: Discourse Theory and the Convention Refugee Hearing* (Amsterdam and Philadelphia, PA: John Benjamins Publishing Company, 1994).

of COI will not be of meaningful assistance to the decision maker. Additionally, there must be recognition that COI is inherently contestable. The overarching danger is that the decision maker will reconstruct the claimant's world on a simpler model in order to manage it.

References

Barsky, Robert F., *Constructing a Productive Other: Discourse Theory and the Convention Refugee Hearing* (Amsterdam and Philadelphia, PA: John Benjamins Publishing Company, 1994).

Common EU Guidelines for processing Country of Origin Information (COI) (April 2008), via www.unhcr.org/refworld (accessed: 19 July 2012).

Crawley, Heaven, *Refugees and Gender: Law and Process* (Bristol: Jordans, 2001).

Donald, Jeanne, 'Access to Information for Immigration and Refugee Law Practitioners' (2002), Auckland District Law Society Seminar, via www.refugee.org.nz/Reference (accessed: 31 July 2012).

European Union: UNHCR, *Country of Origin Information: Towards Enhanced Cooperation* (2004), via www.unhcr.org/refworld (accessed: 19 July 2012).

Evans Cameron, Hilary, 'Refugee Status Determinations and the Limits of Memory' (2010), 22 *International Journal of Refugee Law* 469.

Fenton, Sabine, *Expressing a Well-founded Fear: Interpreting in Convention Refugee Hearings* (2001), via www.refugee.org.nz (accessed: 19 July 2012).

Gyulai, Gábor, *Country Information in Asylum Procedures – Quality as a Legal Requirement in the EU* (Budapest: Hungarian Helsinki Committee, 2007).

Haines, Rodger, 'International Law and Refugees in New Zealand' (1999), 119 *New Zealand Law Review* 132.

Haines, Rodger, 'Sovereignty Under Challenge – The New Protection Regime in the Immigration Bill 2007' (2009), 149 *New Zealand Law Review* 170.

Hamlyn, Eleanor, 'Spotlight on the New Zealand Refugee Status Library' (February 2001), 253 *Library Life* 28–9.

Hathaway, James C., *The Law of Refugee Status* (Toronto: Butterworths, 1991).

Hathaway, James and Michelle Foster, 'Internal Protection/Relocation/Flight Alternative as an Aspect of Refugee Status Determination', in Erika Feller, Volker Türk and Frances Nicholson (eds), *Refugee Protection in International Law: UNHCR's Global Consultations on International Protection* (Cambridge: Cambridge University Press, 2003).

Hathaway, James and William Hicks, 'Is There a Subjective Element in the Refugee Convention's Requirement of "Well-founded Fear"?' (2005), 26 *Michigan Journal of International Law* 505.

IARLJ, *Judicial Criteria for Assessing Country of Origin Information (COI): A Checklist* (November 2006),

Ip, John, 'Adoption of the Special Advocate Procedure in New Zealand's Immigration Bill' (2009), *New Zealand Law Review* 207.

Jones, Ann, *Kabul in Winter: Life without Peace in Afghanistan* (New York: Metropolitan Books, 2006).

Kagan, Michael, 'Is Truth in the Eye of the Beholder? Objective Credibility Assessment in Refugee Status Determination' (2003), 17 *Georgetown Immigration Law Journal* 367.

Lippmann, Walter, *Public Opinion*, with a new introduction by Michael Curtis (New Brunswick, NJ, and London: Transaction Publishers, 1998).

Noll, Gregor (ed.), *Proof, Evidentiary Assessment and Credibility in Asylum Procedures* (Leiden and Boston, MA: Martinus Nijhoff Publishers, 2005).

Schacter, Daniel L., *The Seven Sins of Memory: How the Mind Forgets and Remembers* (Boston, MA: Houghton Mifflin Company, 2001).

Sedley, Stephen, 'Asylum: Can the Judiciary Maintain its Independence?', in IARLJ, *Stemming the Tide or Keeping the Balance – The Role of the Judiciary* (edited and published for IARLJ by the NZ Association for Comparative Law and the Revue Juridique Polynésienne in association with the New Zealand Centre for Public Law of the Victoria University of Wellington, 2003).

The Michigan Guidelines on the Internal Protection Alternative (1999), 21 *Michigan Journal of International Law* 131.

The Michigan Guidelines on Well-founded Fear (2005), 26 *Michigan Journal of International Law* 491.

Thomas, Robert, *Administrative Justice and Asylum Appeals: A Study of Tribunal Adjudication* (Oxford: Hart, 2011).

Tsangarides, Natasha, 'The Politics of Knowledge: An Examination of the Use of Country Information in the Asylum Determination Process' (2009), *Immigration, Asylum and Nationality Law* 252.

Tsangarides, Natasha, *The Refugee Roulette: The Role of Country Information in Refugee Status Determination* (2010, Immigration Advisory Service), via www.iasuk.org (accessed: 19 July 2012).

UNHCR, *Handbook on Procedures and Criteria for Determining Refugee Status* (Geneva: UNHCR, 1988).

Whitaker, Brian, *Unspeakable Love: Gay and Lesbian Life in the Middle East* (Berkeley, CA: University of California Press, 2006).

PART III
THE RESPONSIBILITY TO PROTECT DISPLACED POPULATIONS

The Shifting Boundaries and Content of Protection: The Internal Protection Alternative Revisited

Penelope Mathew[1]

Introduction

Refugees pose a challenge to the state-centric order of international law. They move, while the state, seemingly, remains fixed. States have accepted obligations to protect human rights within their boundaries, and they have retained the right to police those boundaries. A potent fear that the floodgates will open and all who seek adequate or better protection of their human rights will move to more privileged states has stymied the development of complete freedom of movement. Whether despite or because of this fear, the right to exclude aliens is posited as a right founded not on privilege or power, but on morality: states need to protect, respect and ensure the rights of citizens, and their capacity to do so might be adversely impacted by unfettered immigration.

The refugee is something of an exception. By definition, a refugee is someone who is forced to remain outside their country of origin. According to the 1951 Convention relating to the Status of Refugees, as supplemented by the 1967 Protocol relating to the Status of Refugees, a refugee is someone who 'owing to well-founded fear of being persecuted for reasons of race, religion, nationality, membership of a particular social group or political opinion, is outside the country of his nationality and is unable or, owing to such fear, is unwilling to avail himself of the protection of that country; or who, not having a nationality and being outside the country of his former habitual residence … is unable or, owing to such fear, is unwilling to return to it.'[2]

The refugee cannot be returned ('refouler') to the place of persecution, although the Refugee Convention does allow the 'dangerous' refugee to be returned.[3] However, the Refugee Convention is silent on the right to enter any state, and states have erected many

[1] Freilich Foundation professor, The Australian National University. The author would like to thank Jim Hathaway, Louise Moor, Larissa Wakim, Matthew Becker and Saurabh Bhattacharjee for their comments on the oral version of the paper, and Don Anton for reading through the penultimate written version.

[2] Article 1A(2), 1951 Convention relating to the Status of Refugees (28 July 1951, 189 UNTS 137) as amended by the provisions of the 1967 Protocol relating to the Status of Refugees (31 January 1967, 606 UNTS 267) [hereinafter 'Refugee Convention'].

[3] Article 33, Refugee Convention.

barriers to refugee movement, such as visa requirements and carrier sanctions. Sometimes these measures are directed at migration generally and merely catch refugees in their net. In other cases, it is clear that measures are deployed specifically in order to prevent refugees from claiming the benefit of the obligation of non-return (*non-refoulement*).[4] In order to justify these measures, it is sometimes argued that refugees move not because they have a right to better protection, but because they want what 'we' have, and further, that any 'protection' is better than none.[5] So long as a refugee is safe from persecution, the logic goes, they cannot demand more, and to do so is to blur the line between forced and voluntary migration.

Some of the barriers to refugee movement involve a shift in the boundaries of the state – for example, through interdiction at sea. However, such measures may be ineffective in defeating the obligation of *non-refoulement* as it applies extra-territorially. Increasingly, then, a preferred move by states is to shift the sites of protection – for example, by finding a 'safe third country' to which the asylum seeker[6] may be sent. In theory, this enables a person to be returned or sent to a different place beyond the borders of the potential state of refuge. The effect – and it is sometimes an intentional effect – is to lower the quality of protection, and in particular, to ensure that the quality of protection available in potential countries of refuge does not become a 'pull' factor for further asylum flows.[7] One illustration of this phenomenon will be examined in this chapter – the idea of the internal flight or relocation alternative.

The Internal Flight or Relocation Alternative

It is now widely accepted that refugee status will not be recognized if there is a viable 'internal flight' or 'internal relocation' alternative – that is, a place within the country of origin to which the applicant for refugee status may relocate as an alternative to the

4 For example, Canada took the unusual step of reintroducing visa requirements for citizens of the Czech Republic in response to an increase in asylum claims by Roma. See Report from the Commission to the Council on the re-introduction of the visa requirement by Canada for citizens of the Czech Republic in accordance with Article 1(4)(c) of Council Regulation (EC) No. 539/2001, listing the third countries whose nationals must be in possession of visas when crossing the external borders and those whose nationals are exempt from that requirement, as amended by Council Regulation (EC) No. 851/2005 as regards the reciprocity mechanism: COM/2009/0562 final.

5 The former Australian Minister for Immigration, Phillip Ruddock, was a proponent of this view. In particular, he oversaw the introduction of a many-layered hierarchy of visas, using the argument that many asylum seekers had given up protection opportunities on their way to Australia. See Penelope Mathew, 'Australian Refugee Protection in the Wake of the Tampa', 96 *American Journal of International Law* (2002), 661–76, at 672–3.

6 An asylum seeker is a person seeking protection who has not yet been recognized as a refugee under a national refugee status determination system.

7 This is evident in Australia's justifications for 'offshore' processing. See, for example, Julia Gillard, 'Respecting Fears, Moving Forward with the Facts', speech to the Lowy Institute, 6 July 2010, at: http://www.smh.com.au/opinion/politics/respecting-fears-moving-forward-with-the-facts-20100706-zyce.html [accessed 28 September 2010].

international protection available through refugee status.[8] This development may be explained by the increase in persecution by non-state actors since the adoption of the Refugee Convention, along with changing attitudes to refugee status.[9] It is so well accepted in state practice, that despite questions as to whether this development is a legitimate part of refugee law,[10] it may now be too late to resile from it.

If the inquiry as to an alternative site of protection is legitimate, it may rest on the inability or unwillingness to seek the 'protection' of the state of origin – an insight that has led to the adoption of a new terminology, 'the internal protection alternative' ('IPA').[11] Legally speaking, then, the appropriateness of the IPA inquiry may turn on the meaning of the word 'protection' in the definition of a refugee.

It has been argued that originally the reference to 'protection' in the refugee definition meant the protection afforded to a person outside the country of origin – diplomatic and consular protection.[12] However, while there is historical truth to this insight, it offers limited assistance in our approach to refugee protection. Obviously, when outside one's country, the established way to access national protection is through the embassy, but the litmus test for refugee status is clearly not whether a person can approach their embassy for consular assistance, but whether they are willing to return home.[13] The notion of state protection from harm at home is central to the refugee inquiry. Arguably, then, there is nothing wrong with asking whether that protection can be provided somewhere else in the country of origin, instead of requiring the international community to provide the surrogate protection[14] offered through the refugee rights contained in the Refugee Convention.

The next question is whether it is only relevant to inquire as to whether there is protection from persecution in the proposed alternative site of protection, or whether other factors should also be taken into account. Clearly, protection from persecution is a *sine qua*

---

8 This contrasts with the position under the Organization of African Unity (now the African Union) Convention: Organization of African Unity, 1969 Convention Governing the Specific Aspects of Refugee Problems in Africa, 10 September 1969, 1001 UNTS 45, art. 1(2).

9 See James C. Hathaway and Michelle Foster, 'Internal Protection/Relocation/Flight Alternative as an Aspect of Refugee Status Determination', in Erika Feller, Volker Türk and Frances Nicholson (eds), *Refugee Protection in International Law: UNHCR's Global Consultations on International Protection* 357 (2003), 357–417 [hereinafter 'Hathaway and Foster'], at 359–60.

10 See the arguments canvassed in Gaetan de Moffarts, 'Refugee Status and the "Internal Flight Alternative"', in *Refugee and Asylum Law: Assessing the Scope for Judicial Protection* (International Association of Refugee Law Judges, second conference, Nijmegen, 9–11 January 1997), 123–138, 124–6. See also Bill Frelick, 'Down the Rabbit Hole: The Strange Logic of Internal Flight Alternative', 22 *World Refugee Survey* (1999), 22–9, at 23.

11 Michigan Guidelines on the Internal Protection Alternative, at: http://www.refugeecaselaw.org/documents/Internal_Protection.pdf [accessed 20 July 2012]. Participants in the colloquia that led to the adoption of the Michigan Guidelines have been a mix of 'eminent publicists' and more junior colleagues in the field of refugee law, meaning that the guidelines may be appropriately referred to as a guide to interpreting the Refugee Convention.

12 Antonio Fortin, 'The Meaning of "Protection" in the Refugee Definition', 12 *International Journal of Refugee Law* (2000), 548–76.

13 For a response to Fortin, see Hathaway and Foster.

14 For the concept of surrogacy, see James C. Hathaway, *The Law of Refugee Status* (Toronto: Butterworths, 1991), 135.

non; however, there is little state practice to support the view that only protection from persecution is relevant. Traditionally, jurisprudence has at least required that decision makers consider whether or not it is 'reasonable' for the putative refugee to relocate within the country of origin.[15]

Jurists have pointed out how refugees are endangered by an approach that begins and ends with protection from persecution. Thus the Michigan Guidelines on the Internal Protection Alternative state that the IPA must be free of persecution in the sense of offering an 'antidote' to the risk in the place of origin, with no further risks of different forms of persecution or other serious harm that could be viewed as arising indirectly because of the need to flee the place of origin.[16]

The international organization tasked with protection of refugees, the United Nations High Commissioner for Refugees ('UNHCR') has also adopted guidelines that go beyond the limited test of a persecution-free zone.[17] Crucially, both the UNHCR guidelines on the 'Internal Flight or Relocation Alternative' within the context of Article 1A(2) of the 1951 Convention and/or 1967 Protocol Relating to the Status of Refugees and the Michigan Guidelines frame the analysis as not only requiring a break in the continuum of persecution, but a *repair*. The UNHCR speaks of 'living a relatively normal life',[18] while the Michigan Guidelines speak of 'meaningful protection'.[19]

How, then, are these requirements over and above protection from persecution arrived at? The way in which we arrive at a picture of an appropriate IPA, in particular, the way that this picture is grounded in the theory and structure of the Refugee Convention, may have important consequences, both for asylum seekers and in terms of legal legitimacy.

What 'Protection'? Rights and Reasonableness

The jurisprudence tends to favour an approach to protection that is based on reasonableness. However, the test of reasonableness has been attacked as illegitimate. It is an intuitive test that has no obvious grounding in the terms of the Refugee Convention,[20] and that has an inherent weakness: what looks reasonable to some may appear unreasonable to others.[21] Hathaway and the other experts responsible for the Michigan Guidelines have taken the

15 See n. 29 below and accompanying text.

16 Michigan Guidelines, [15–16] ('antidote' to well-founded fear of persecution in the place of origin) and [17–19] (no additional risk of, or equivalent to, persecution).

17 UNHCR, Guidelines on International Protection: 'Internal Flight or Relocation Alternative' within the context of the 1951 Convention and/or 1967 Protocol Relating to the Status of Refugees, HCR/GIP/03/0423 July 2003 [7], [hereinafter 'UNHCR guidelines'].

18 UNHCR guidelines, [6].

19 Michigan Guidelines, [2], [4], [5], [7], [8], [9].

20 Hathaway and Foster, 387–8.

21 Ninette Kelley, 'Internal Flight/Relocation/Protection Alternative: Is It Reasonable?', 14 *International Journal of Refugee Law* (2002), 4–44, at 24. For an early argument in favour of using international benchmarks, namely human rights, see Hugo Storey, 'The Internal Flight Alternative Test: The Jurisprudence Re-examined', 10 *International Journal of Refugee Law* (1998), 499–676.

view that the 'protection' within the IPA must be at least the equivalent to the protection available to a refugee:

> If recognition of refugee status is to be denied to [putative refugees] on the grounds that the protection to which they are entitled can in fact be accessed within their own state, then the sufficiency of that internal protection is logically measured by reference to the scope of the protection which refugee law guarantees.[22]

The Guidelines note that an expansive view referring to general human rights standards for the purposes of informing the notion of protection could be warranted;[23] however, the Guidelines adopt a cautious stance:

> The Refugee Convention itself does not establish a duty on states parties to guarantee all such rights and freedoms. Instead, Arts. 2–33 establish an endogenous definition of the rights and freedoms viewed as requisite to 'revise ... and consolidate previous international agreements relating to the status of refugees and to extend the scope of and *the protection accorded by* such instruments ... (emphasis added). These rights are for the most part framed in relative terms, effectively mandating a general duty of non-discrimination between refugees and others.
>
> At a minimum, therefore, conditions in the proposed site of internal protection ought to satisfy the affirmative, yet relative, standards set by this textually explicit definition of the content of protection. The relevant measure is the treatment of other persons in the proposed site of internal protection, not in the putative asylum country. Thus, internal protection requires not only protection against risk of persecution, but also the assimilation of the asylum seeker with others in the site of internal protection for the purposes of access to, for example, employment, public welfare, and education.[24]

As described by Hathaway and Foster, this approach means that reference may be made to rights such as freedom of religion, freedom of movement, access to courts, and rights to work, social assistance, and primary education.[25]

Arguably, it is possible to go further and adopt international human rights law as the measure of protection. After all, the internal protection alternative is generally for persons who are citizens of the state concerned.[26] It is therefore not meaningful to discuss the differences between aliens and nationals or other relative standards used by the Refugee

---

22 Michigan Guidelines, [20].

23 Ibid., [20–22].

24 Ibid., [20–21].

25 Hathaway and Foster, 408.

26 In some cases, refugees are not citizens of their country of origin, but stateless persons who are habitually resident in that country.

Convention such as distinctions between persons 'lawfully staying' and so on.[27] In much the same way that the concept of 'persecution' has come to be defined in human rights terms,[28] it is appropriate that 'protection' is also so defined. Moreover, refugees are human beings, protected by general human rights law, and this law operates in tandem with the Refugee Convention's protection.

A rights-based approach to protection is not well established in the jurisprudence, however. The test of reasonableness is used in Australia, Canada, the United States and the United Kingdom.[29] (New Zealand, on the other hand, has used the Michigan Guidelines.[30]) The UNHCR guidelines also use the test of reasonableness as part of an overall test as to whether 'given the particular circumstances of the case, the individual could reasonably be expected to establish him/herself and live a normal life.'[31] However, the UNHCR guidelines attempt to define 'reasonableness' using, among other factors, human rights standards:

27 The Refugee Convention frequently frames refugee rights in terms of a level of attachment to state territory (for example, whether a refugee is lawfully present) and the content may vary from the same level of protection guaranteed to nationals to the level of protection offered to aliens. The minimalist approach preferred in the Michigan Guidelines has therefore attracted some criticism. For example, Ninette Kelley writes that 'the effect ... is to use the narrow standards of protection contained in the Convention as a substitute for the more extensive ones contained within subsequent human rights treaties. The guarantees in the Convention become the ceiling rather than the floor upon which guarantees found in later human rights treaties build. The approach in the Michigan Guidelines would also suggest that so long as the state treats the refugee in the IPA equally with respect to the narrow range of rights in the Convention, protection would be satisfied even if a greater range of rights were accorded to the refugee's fellow citizens. In effect the state protection requirement would be met even when the refugee is denied core entitlements available to other citizens provided they are also denied to non-citizens': 'Internal Flight/Relocation/Protection Alternative: Is It Reasonable?', 35. See also Reinhard Marx, 'The Criteria of Applying the "Internal Flight Alternative" Test in National Refugee Status Determination Procedures', 14 *International Journal of Refugee Law* (2002), 179–218, at 204.

28 See Hathaway, *Law of Refugee Status*; Michelle Foster, *International Refugee Law and Socio-economic Rights: Refuge from Deprivation* (2007), particularly chapter 2.

29 In Canada, see the cases of *Thirunavukkarasu v. Canada (Min of Employment & Immigration)* [1993] F.C.J. No. 1172, and *Ranganathan v. Canada (Minister of Citizenship and Immigration)* [2000] F.C.J. No. 2118. In the United States, a reasonableness test has been adopted by regulation: 8 CFR 208.13 (b)(2)(C)(ii) and 8 CFR 208.13 (b)(3). The High Court of Australia has also adopted a 'reasonableness' test in *SZFDV v Minister for Immigration and Citizenship* [2007] HCA 41 (30 August 2007), and *SZATV v Minister for Immigration and Citizenship* [2007] HCA 40 (30 August 2007). Prior to these decisions the long-standing precedent, which also uses the 'reasonableness' test, was *Randhawa* v. *Minister for Immigration Local Government and Ethnic Affairs* (1994) 52 FCR 437. The UK test is discussed below.

30 Refugee Appeal No. 71684/99, 29 October 1999. For background concerning the position in New Zealand, see Sir Kenneth Keith, 'The Difficulties of "Internal Flight" and "Internal Relocation" as Frameworks of Analysis', 15 *Georgetown Immigration Law Journal* (2001), 433–46.

31 UNHCR guidelines, [6].

> Where respect for basic human rights standards, including in particular, non-derogable rights, is clearly problematic, the proposed area cannot be considered a reasonable alternative ….[32]

The UNHCR guidelines make particular reference to socio-economic rights, or rather to 'socio-economic conditions':

> It would be unreasonable, including from a human rights perspective, to expect a person to relocate to face economic destitution or existence below at least an adequate level of subsistence. At the other end of the spectrum, a simple lowering of living standards or worsening of economic status may not be sufficient to reject a proposed area as unreasonable … A person should also not be required to relocate to areas, such as the slums of an urban area, where they would be required to live in conditions of severe hardship.[33]

UNHCR's approach has been informed by the earlier Michigan Guidelines.[34] However, despite UNHCR's attempt to introduce the objective measure of international human rights law into the test of 'reasonableness', its guidelines have been read very narrowly by the UK House of Lords (now Supreme Court), and the Court has rejected outright the approach taken in the Michigan Guidelines.[35]

In a leading UK case on internal relocation, *Januzi v Secretary of State for the Home Department; Hamid v Secretary of State for the Home Department and other appeals* ('*Januzi*'),[36] fear of a deluge of 'economic migrants' was clearly flagged in one of the lead judgments[37] as a reason for reading 'protection' narrowly so as to encompass essentially three factors: freedom from persecution; freedom from violation of non-derogable human rights; and consideration of factors particular to the individual asylum seeker. The case has been cited with approval by the Australian High Court[38] and is likely to be very influential in other jurisdictions too.

---

32 Ibid., [28].

33 Ibid., [29–30].

34 Professor Hathaway, the driving force behind the Michigan Guidelines, also co-authored the background paper for the expert round table convened by UNHCR that informed the UNHCR guidelines. See Hathaway and Foster.

35 *Januzi v Secretary of State for the Home Department; Hamid v Secretary of State for the Home Department and other appeals* [2006] UKHL 5 [hereinafter 'Januzi'].

36 Ibid.

37 Lord Bingham, with whom the four other judges agreed, wrote the lead judgment. However, Lord Hope's judgment addressed the particular cases of the applicants and Lord Bingham as well as two of the three other judges (namely Lords Hope and Carswell) expressed their agreement with Lord Hope's judgment. It is therefore necessary to refer to the judgments of both Lord Bingham and Lord Hope.

38 *SZATV v Minister for Immigration and Citizenship* [2007] HCA 40, per Gummow, Hayne and Crennan JJ, [19], [21], [22] and [25].

A Case Study: *Januzi* and its Sequelae

The *Januzi* case involved four asylum seekers – one Albanian and three Sudanese. Mr Januzi was an ethnic Albanian from Mitrovica in Kosovo. The putative IPA was Pristina, Kosovo, some 35 kilometers from Mitrovica, and in which ethnic Albanians were in the majority. Mr Januzi was suffering from mental illness because of his experiences of 'ethnic cleansing' and his lawyers argued that he would receive inadequate medical treatment if he were required to return to Pristina. Messrs Hamid, Gaafur and Mohammed were all Sudanese, from Darfur. The putative IPA in each case was Khartoum. It was suggested by the asylum seekers' counsel that the claimants would have to reside in a camp for the internally displaced if forced to go to Khartoum.

The test applied in the UK is a reasonableness test, namely whether it would be 'unduly harsh' to require the asylum seeker to relocate. Lord Bingham suggested that the UNHCR guidelines provided useful guidance to decision makers in the application of this test,[39] but he rejected what he called the 'Hathaway/New Zealand' rule (in other words, the approach of the Michigan Guidelines that permits reference to human rights considerations as applied in New Zealand).[40] He also expressed agreement with his fellow judge, Lord Hope. Lord Hope held that broad-based human rights concerns were 'irrelevant'.[41] Only non-derogable rights such as the right to life and the prohibition on torture were relevant to the reasonableness test.[42]

Several reasons were advanced by Lord Bingham for rejecting reference to broad-based human rights considerations. First, he stated that there was nothing express in the Refugee Convention to suggest that the Convention was directed to defining rights in an IPA.[43] Second, he said that the rule could not be implied into the Convention. Although the Universal Declaration on Human Rights was referred to in the preamble, it was not enforceable and the two Covenants – the International Covenant on Civil and Political Rights and the International Covenant on Economic, Social and Cultural Rights,[44] which transform the Universal Declaration into binding law – had not yet been adopted.[45] Third, Lord Bingham thought that the European Union Qualification Directive[46] required a

---

[39] *Januzi*, [20].

[40] For a robust critique of the House of Lords decision in *Januzi* and a rejection of the descriptor 'Hathaway/New Zealand rule', see Refugee Appeal No. 76044, 11 September 2008.

[41] *Januzi*, [54].

[42] Ibid., per Lord Hope [54]. See also [59]. A non-derogable right is one that the international community has accepted is protected at all times, even during a public emergency, and the list of non-derogable rights commonly includes the prohibition on slavery and the prohibition on torture.

[43] Ibid., per Lord Bingham [15].

[44] International Covenant on Civil and Political Rights, 16 December 1966, 999 UNTS 171; International Covenant on Economic, Social and Cultural Rights, 16 December 1966, 993 UNTS 3.

[45] *Januzi*, per Lord Bingham [16].

[46] Council Directive 2004/83/EC of 29 April 2004 on Minimum Standards for the Qualification and Status of Third Country Nationals or Stateless Persons as Refugees or as Persons Who Otherwise Need International Protection and the Content of the Protection Granted [2004] OJ L304/12 [hereinafter, European Qualification Directive or 'EQD']. The terms of the recast Qualification Directive do not alter the analysis presented in this chapter. See Directive 2011/95/EU

different, higher standard to that suggested in the Michigan Guidelines.[47] (The standard imposed by the European Qualification Directive at the time was that there is 'no well-founded fear of being persecuted or no real risk of suffering serious harm and the applicant can reasonably be expected to stay in that part of the country.'[48] Article 8(2) then provided that states shall have regard to 'the general circumstances prevailing in that part of the country and to the personal circumstances of the applicant.') Fourth, Lord Bingham found that state practice did not support the 'Hathaway' approach as a rule of customary international law.[49] Finally, he commented on 'unintended' and 'anomalous' consequences, being that a refugee could escape persecution *and* poverty:[50]

> Suppose a person is subject to persecution ... in the country of his nationality. It is a poor country. Standards of social provision are low. There is a high level of deprivation and want. Respect for human rights is scant. He escapes to a rich country where, if recognized as a refugee, he would enjoy all the rights guaranteed to refugees in that country. He could, with no fear of persecution, live elsewhere in his country of nationality, but would there suffer all the drawbacks of living in a poor and backward country. It would be strange if the accident of persecution were to entitle him to escape, not only from that persecution, but from the deprivation to which his home country is subject.[51]

In the final result, Mr Januzi's appeal was dismissed.[52] The other three appeals were allowed. Lord Hope found that an evaluation of risks to non-derogable rights along with the possibility of eventual forced return to Darfur was required.[53] The three Sudanese cases were remitted for consideration by the Asylum and Immigration Tribunal ('AIT'),[54] which would reassess the question of the IPA, along with the question of whether the asylum seekers might be entitled to 'complementary protection'. (For persons who do not meet the definition of a refugee, protection complementary to the Refugee Convention is available.[55] It is notable that complementary protection often flows from non-derogable

of the European Parliament and the Council of 13 December 2011 on the standards for qualification of third-country nationals or stateless persons as beneficiaries of international protection, for a uniform status for refugees or for persons eligible for subsidiary protection, and for the content of the protection granted, [2011] OJ L337/9.

47 *Januzi*, per Lord Bingham, [17].

48 Article 8(1), EQD.

49 *Januzi*, per Lord Bingham [18].

50 Ibid., per Lord Bingham [20].

51 Ibid., per Lord Bingham [19].

52 There was still some prospect of a claim for complementary protection, however.

53 *Januzi*, per Lord Hope [59]. In the cases of Mr Hamid and Mr Gaafur, the Secretary of State had also conceded that the reasoning leading to denial of refugee status had been inadequate.

54 The AIT has since been replaced by immigration and asylum chambers within a new tribunal structure, comprising a First Tier Tribunal and an Upper Tier Tribunal.

55 On the topic of complementary protection, see Jane McAdam, *Complementary Protection in International Refugee Law* (Oxford; New York: OUP, 2007).

human rights – for example, the UK's obligations under the prohibition on torture and other related forms of ill-treatment.[56])

Following the House of Lords' decision in *Januzi*, the AIT examined the situation for the three Sudanese claimants and adopted a decision designated as a 'country guidance' decision, meaning it would be followed in subsequent cases.[57] A great deal of expert evidence and country information was closely examined. The burden was placed on the appellants to show that they would find themselves in a camp for Internally Displaced Persons ('IDPs') because of lack of resources and family connections. This contrasts with the position under the UNHCR guidelines and the Michigan Guidelines that places the burden on the state.[58] The AIT also found that expert evidence that the conditions in the IDP camps in Khartoum were effectively an extension of the original persecution of Darfuri was prone to exaggeration.[59] Nevertheless, parts of the judgment suggest that Khartoum was not a reasonable IPA. For example, take the following statement:

> We accept that there is considerable evidence that forced relocations abusive of human rights standards have been made from time to time, sometimes unaccompanied by notice and sometimes leading to clashes. It may well be that there is a government strategy of making life too difficult for IDPs and also of relocating IDPs to camps away from the capital. Clearly too, extreme caution has to be exercised when evaluating promises by the Khartoum authorities to adhere to the Guiding Principles on Internally Displaced Persons and give proper notice of relocation intentions. However, we do not consider that the evidence in this regard establishes that Darfuris – or non-Arab Darfuri – IDPs have been singled out for any special treatment. Nor do we consider that merely by virtue of being subject from time to time to relocations, sometimes involving force and human rights violations, means that IDPs in Khartoum State face a real risk of serious harm or ill-treatment contrary to Article 3 or of unduly harsh conditions.[60]

---

56 The UK is party to the Convention against Torture and other Cruel, Inhuman or Degrading Treatment or Punishment (10 December 1984, 1465 UNTS 85), which expressly forbids *refoulement* in Article 3, as well as the European Convention on Human Rights (4 November 1950, ETS No. 5), which prohibits torture and inhuman or degrading treatment or punishment in Article 3, a provision that has been interpreted as containing an implied *non-refoulement* obligation.

57 *HGMO (Relocation to Khartoum) Sudan CG* [2006] UKAIT 00062 [hereinafter '*HGMO (Relocation to Khartoum) Sudan CG*']. The claim of a fourth asylum seeker was also heard.

58 Michigan Guidelines, [14]; UNHCR Guidelines, [34]. A refugee claimant does not have to show that he or she fears persecution in all places within the country of origin, only that he or she is outside the country of origin owing to well-founded fear of persecution, and unable, or because of well-founded fear, unwilling to avail him or herself of the home state's 'protection'. As a matter of policy, an asylum seeker should not have to prove more than the fact that he or she has a well-founded fear of persecution in the place of origin as this is already a significant burden, and the alternative approach gives states an 'easy out' whereby they can refuse to examine a refugee claim properly by asking pre-emptively whether there is the possibility of going elsewhere within the country of origin. See Hathaway and Foster.

59 *HGMO (Relocation to Khartoum) Sudan CG*, [164], [169].

60 Ibid., [244].

In context, it appears that the AIT did not think there was a risk of relocation in the future, although there had been two relocations in the past year.[61] The reasonableness of this finding is questionable, and relocation is of course a violation of the right to freedom of movement and choice of residence, which has other serious human rights consequences in terms of access to shelter (in the case of Sudan, IDPs houses were demolished), work, food and so on, and ultimately may result in return to the place of persecution.[62] IDPs retain the right to seek asylum,[63] and while the Guiding Principles on Internal Displacement[64] may assist in assessing the content of protection, situations that envisage breach of the Guidelines must not be used to undercut asylum. (In hindsight, the AIT's assumption that IDPs were safe despite previous incidents seems naïve. Following human rights abuses committed by the Sudanese government in response to an attack by the Justice and Equality Movement in May 2008, the AIT rescinded much of the guidance issued in this case as it was clear that non-Arab Darfuris could not relocate anywhere in Sudan.[65])

The claimants appealed successfully to the Court of Appeal.[66] Although the Court raised some questions about the factual findings, particularly the AIT's finding that there was no risk of forced relocation,[67] the Court necessarily had to focus on legal error. The Court found that the AIT had misapplied the test for an internal protection alternative in two ways. First, the Court found that the AIT had effectively required conditions in the IPA to amount to a violation of Article 3 of the European Convention on Human Rights in order for it to be unreasonable to expect the asylum seeker to relocate there.[68] Second, the Court ruled that the AIT had not undertaken a comparison between the place of habitual residence and the putative IPA, but a comparison between the conditions in the country

---

61 The AIT noted, 'there have not been any forced relocations since the May and August 2005 events': ibid., [127].

62 In some cases, IDPs in Khartoum were relocated to desert areas where basics such as water and healthcare were difficult if not impossible to secure. See Report of the Representative of the Secretary-General on the human rights of internally displaced persons, Mission to Sudan (3–13 October 2005), [30]–[34], [42] and [63]–[65], UN Doc E/CN.4/2006/71/Add.6 (13 February 2006). This report was referred to by the AIT, along with a great deal of other information critical of the situation in Sudan. For more information about the camps see Kirsten Zaat, *The Protection of IDPs in the Sudan: Applying International Law at the Field Level, The Journal of Humanitarian Assistance,* 17 October 2006, at: http://sites.tufts.edu/jha/files/2011/04/a195.pdf [accessed 3 August 2012]. It should also be noted that, within the UN system, forced evictions are viewed as a gross violation of human rights: see Office of the High Commissioner for Human Rights, Fact Sheet No. 25, Forced Evictions and Human Rights, at: http://www.unhchr.ch/html/menu6/2/fs25.htm [accessed 13 September 2008].

63 The right is expressly reiterated in Guiding Principle 15(c): Guiding Principles on Internal Displacement, UN Doc E/CN.4/1998/53/Add.2, 11 February 1998 [hereinafter 'Guiding Principles'].

64 Ibid.

65 *AA (Non-Arab Darfuris – Relocation) Sudan v. Secretary of State for the Home Department,* CG [2009] UKAIT 00056, at: http://www.unhcr.org/refworld/docid/4b2fa3202.html [accessed 10 November 2010]. For a description of these events, see Human Rights Watch, *Crackdown on Khartoum: Mass Arrests, Torture, and Disappearances since the May 10 Attack,* at: http://www.hrw.org/reports/2008/darfur0608/ [accessed 20 July 2012].

66 *AH, IG and NM v Secretary of State for the Home Department* [2007] EWCA Civ 297.

67 Ibid., per Lord Justice Buxton [43].

68 Ibid., per Lord Justice Buxton [30].

as a whole and the putative IPA.[69] Lord Justice Buxton, writing for the Court, stated this was 'unedifying' and 'irrelevant' to the question of whether the particular claimant would be living a 'normal life' in the IPA.[70] The AIT had also noted that conditions were bad for many non-Darfuri IDPs in Khartoum and slum dwellers elsewhere in Sudan, to which Lord Justice Buxton responded,

> it is no more relevant to our enquiry that other people with the same personal characteristics have been displaced for reasons unconnected with Convention persecution than it is that the place where they are being sent is no worse than some other places in Sudan. The enquiry has to be about these asylum seekers and the effect of the displacement on them.[71]

The government successfully appealed to the House of Lords, in *Secretary of State for the Home Department v AH and others (FC)*.[72] The House of Lords found that the relevant comparison was the conditions applying *generally* in the country of origin.[73] It also confirmed that the test was *not* limited to an inquiry about non-derogable rights.[74] It appears that a breach of non-derogable rights is sufficient to make return unreasonable, but it is not the only consideration since there are other relevant factors – especially, perhaps, factors relevant to particular claimants.[75]

The House of Lords found that the AIT's decision, when read in context, did not apply such a harsh test as to require only breach of non-derogable rights.[76] However, Lady Hale, while deferring to the AIT as an expert tribunal, thought there was a need to give further guidance on the application of the test of reasonableness. She indicated her concern that the Tribunal had made a comparison with the 'poorest of the poor' who were 'subject from time to time to relocations, sometimes involving force and human rights violations', and that effectively, the reasonableness test had been equated with Article 3 ill-treatment.[77] Nevertheless, Lady Hale concurred with the unanimous decision of the Court that the AIT's decision should not be overturned.

---

69 Ibid., per Lord Justice Buxton [36–9].

70 Ibid., per Lord Justice Buxton [45]. See also [46–7].

71 Ibid., per Lord Justice Buxton [38].

72 *Secretary of State for the Home Department v AH and others (FC)*, [2007] UKHL 49 [hereinafter '*AH and others*'].

73 Lord Bingham's lead judgment explains that both the place of origin and the conditions prevailing generally in the country are relevant. Ibid., per Lord Bingham [5]. See also [13], and per Lord Brown (concurring) [39].

74 Ibid., per Lord Bingham [11].

75 As one lawyer puts it, 'plead the specifics of the Appellant's case': Rory O'Ryan, Chambers of Ian Macdonald QC, 16 *Immigration Team Legal Bulletin* 2 (November 2007), at 3. Individual factors were one reason for refusing to require an applicant for complementary protection to relocate within Uganda: See *AA (Uganda) v The Secretary of State for the Home Department* [2008] EWCA Civ 579 [hereinafter '*AA (Uganda)*'].

76 *AH and others*, per Lord Bingham [11].

77 Ibid., per Lady Hale [28–9].

An Objective Assessment of a Subjective Test

Lady Hale's concerns in *AH and others* reveal the problems with reasonableness as a legal test, and the desirability of using the objective standard of human rights to inform decision makers as to what is reasonable.[78] The question the AIT should have asked itself was simply whether a Darfuri asylum seeker returned to Khartoum would be at risk of forcible relocation – a violation of the (derogable) right to freedom of movement – and/or other human rights violations.[79]

Of course, there is no guarantee that decision makers will make a reasonable risk assessment. However, to frame the inquiry as being whether any person has their rights respected in the IPA undermines the notion of protection, almost emptying it of content. It deprives protection of any positive meaning other than absence of persecution, suggesting that a human rights limbo for victims of persecution is acceptable. The other extreme in which it has been argued that protection from persecution is virtually all that matters – 'protection elsewhere', as practised by Australia under the 'Pacific Solution' – has shown that such 'protection' is barely worthy of the name, and more akin to the 'legal black hole' of Guantánamo Bay.[80]

The tortuous path of *Januzi* and its follow-up cases also demonstrates that the Lords' original decision in *Januzi* has left decision makers with a test (is it 'unduly harsh' to require relocation?) that is simple, but opaque. Despite disclaimers to the contrary by the Lords,[81] the test, because it seems to incorporate human rights only to the extent of non-derogable rights, may result in more, not less, confusion of the role of refugee law and complementary protection, given that complementary protection often follows from key non-derogable human rights such as the prohibition on torture. The Court of Appeal certainly perceived that the AIT had confused the two, and Lord Bingham agreed that the Court of Appeal's criticisms '[did] not lack substance'.[82]

---

78 It should be noted that a focus on human rights does not rule out attention to particular vulnerabilities of individuals. For example, it is well accepted that particular characteristics of an individual are relevant to the prohibition on torture. See for example *K.N.L.H. v Peru* UN Doc.CCPR/C/85/D/1153/2003/Rev.1 (14 August 2006) (violation of Article 7 of the International Covenant on Civil and Political Rights with respect to a minor refused an abortion of an encephalitic foetus). Specialized treaties dealing with particular groups of people such as persons with disabilities also recognize particular vulnerabilities of individuals.

79 The Guiding Principles could be referred to, along with the general human rights standards upon which they draw. They reflect existing principles of human rights law, international humanitarian law and refugee law, adapt them to the situation of the internally displaced, and attempt to fill any 'protection gaps'.

80 For the concept of the right-less black hole, see Lord Johan Steyn, 'Guantánamo Bay: The Legal Black Hole', 53 *International and Comparative Law Quarterly* (2004), 1–15. For a discussion of the legality of the Pacific Solution see Savitri Taylor, 'Protection Elsewhere/Nowhere', 18 *International Journal of Refugee Law* (2006), 283–312, and Mathew, 'Australian Refugee Protection in the Wake of the Tampa'. For a detailed account of the experiences of asylum seekers detained pursuant to the Pacific Solution, see Susan Metcalfe, *The Pacific Solution* (Melbourne: Australia: Australian Scholarly Publishing, 2010).

81 Lord Bingham stated, 'it is not easy to see how the rule could be more simply or clearly expressed': *AH and others*, per Lord Bingham [5].

82 Ibid., per Lord Bingham [11].

Of great concern is the fact that the area between non-derogable rights and factors particular to the individual claimant is governed completely by discretion. An approach that focuses solely on individual vulnerabilities without recognizing the problems with a generally prevailing situation is not helpful, as illustrated by the English case of *AA (Uganda) v Secretary of State for the Home Department* ('*AA (Uganda)*').[83] Here, the Court of Appeal was required to consider the case of an extremely vulnerable young woman from Uganda who might be forced, through lack of opportunities, into sex work if required to relocate to Kampala.[84] One of the bases for the decision by the Court of Appeal was that return to forced sex work was unduly harsh for any person. Lord Justice Buxton called for a bright-line standard, stating:

> Even if that is the likely fate of many of her fellow countrywomen, I cannot think that either the AIT or the House of Lords that decided *AH (Sudan)* would have felt able to regard enforced prostitution as coming within the category of normal country conditions that the refugee must be expected to put up with. Quite simply, there must be some conditions in the place of relocation that are unacceptable to the extent that it would be unduly harsh to return the applicant to them even if the conditions are widespread in the place of relocation.[85]

It is in fact likely that the conditions to which Ms AA would be returned constitute degrading treatment, in which case she should not be returned under Article 3 of the European Convention on Human Rights. In some cases, too sexual servitude and the non-derogable protection from slavery might be at issue. Moreover, Ms AA's predicament in the IPA was so clearly a result of the requirement that she relocate that her situation should be

---

83 See n. 75 and accompanying text.

84 It should be noted that the case is a 'humanitarian protection' case (i.e. a complementary protection case), rather than an asylum case, but it is analogous to a refugee protection case because the relevant UK regulation stipulates that humanitarian protection will not be available if there is an internal protection alternative. Article 8 of the European Qualification Directive provides for consideration of the internal protection alternative in complementary protection cases – i.e., cases involving Article 3 of the European Convention on Human Rights or cases in which other serious harm is feared. If the law concerning the internal protection alternative is to be applied consistently across categories, then it might be unfair to require refugees to relocate if not in fear of violations of non-derogable rights, but to allow applicants for complementary protection to avoid relocation in the same circumstances. However, given that state complicity or acquiescence is part of the definition of torture in Article 1 of the Convention against Torture and other Cruel, Inhuman or Degrading Treatment or Punishment, it may not deserve to be an aspect of complementary protection in all cases. If the inquiry regarding an IPA is to be imported into the jurisprudence concerning complementary protection, the fact that there is no good reason for distinguishing between the status of persons receiving complementary protection and refugees given that human rights protect both categories of people equally, it is arguable that any IPA should be tested against the same standards of meaningful protection that apply to refugees. In other words, human rights, broadly defined, should be protected in an IPA.

85 *AA (Uganda)*, per Lord Justice Buxton, [17]. Lord Justice Lloyd agreed: *AA (Uganda)*, per Lord Justice Lloyd, [55]; Lord Justice Carnworth relied on common law principles to reach the same conclusion: *AA (Uganda)*, per Lord Justice Carnwath, [41].

regarded as a continuation of the original persecution. Decision makers should also be able to look more broadly at the right to 'decent' work protected by the International Covenant on Economic, Social and Cultural Rights.[86] This would not require that all asylum seekers be guaranteed a job in a potential IPA (which raises the spectre of economic migration), but it would require decision makers to consider whether the state of origin has in place policies and measures to prevent the kind of exploitation in the informal sector likely to be experienced by Ms AA if she were to be returned to Uganda.[87] If decision makers are empowered and required to consider the objective content of all basic human rights, the focus is more likely to remain firmly on the asylum seeker and their rights as a human being, instead of inviting decision makers to compare the asylum seeker's situation with others in the country of origin, resulting in an inexorable downward spiral where almost anything is acceptable.

Refugee status determination is almost inevitably a fraught truth-finding process where the local knowledge of asylum seekers is assessed by decision makers against available sources of country information. It provides fertile ground for power struggles between decision makers and other authoritative sources of knowledge such as expert witnesses as well as between different layers of the hierarchy of decision makers – for example, those with the power to decide matters of fact, and those who are higher in the hierarchy but who are restricted to reviewing matters for legal error.[88] Decision making might look less like a battleground and more like a fact-finding process if human rights law played a role in determining the ground rules.

How, then, to respond to the concerns that led Lord Bingham to reject a broad-based human rights inquiry? The point that there is nothing express in the Refugee Convention to suggest that the Convention was concerned with the definition of rights in an IPA may be countered by the point that the concept of internal relocation or internal flight is not expressly referred to either, and the invocation of reasonableness is an innovation by courts. Concerning the correct approach to treaty interpretation, it is clear that reference to general human rights considerations is consistent with the usual rules of treaty interpretation. Under the Vienna Convention on the Law of Treaties and the customary international law rules concerning treaty interpretation,[89] the words of a treaty are to be interpreted according to their ordinary meaning and in light of their context and the object and purpose of the treaty.[90] The use of human rights standards to inform the notion of protection flows from the structure of the Refugee Convention itself. If it is accepted that

86 Committee on Economic, Social and Cultural Rights, General Comment No. 18, the right to work [7], HRI/GEN/Rev.9 (Vol. 1), 139.

87 See General Comment No. 18, ibid., [32] regarding violations; and [10] relating to the informal sector.

88 See, for example, the hot defence of the initial decision in *AA (Uganda)* by the AIT in a subsequent case: *FB (Lone women – PSG – internal relocation – AA (Uganda) considered) Sierra Leone* [2008] UKAIT 00090, [37–8], at: http://www.unhcr.org/refworld/docid/4934f35a2.html [accessed 10 November 2010].

89 Vienna Convention on the Law of Treaties, 23 May 1969, 1155 UNTS 331. The Vienna Convention on the Law of Treaties post-dates the Refugee Convention and therefore does not apply to the Refugee Convention *qua* treaty; however, the Vienna Convention's provisions concerning interpretation reflect the rules of customary international law.

90 Article 31(1) Vienna Convention on the Law of Treaties.

a refugee need not demonstrate a well-founded fear of persecution in every part of the country, because this would impose too onerous a burden, then a refugee's unwillingness or inability to avail him or herself of 'protection' arguably relates to the sort of protection that a refugee would be granted externally. Proof that such a test has become customary international law[91] is not necessary, though it can certainly be taken into account under Article 31(3) of the Vienna Convention on the Law of Treaties.

As far as the point concerning the European Qualification Directive ('EQD') is concerned, it is question begging to assume that the European Union cannot have lowered the standards applicable to refugees in practice;[92] it is not permissible for the states responsible for the EQD to derogate from the Refugee Convention if the Convention poses higher standards upon them; and, in any event, it is difficult to see why human rights could not be taken into account under the EQD.

In addition to these interpretative problems, the test adopted by the House of Lords is internally inconsistent. It is arbitrary to include non-derogable human rights, but to exclude all other human rights considerations. Non-derogability does not equate with higher importance, as the inclusion of Article 11 of the International Covenant on Civil and Political Rights (the prohibition on debtors' prisons) in Article 4 of the Covenant attests, and the list of non-derogable norms in Article 4 is not exhaustive according to the Human Rights Committee.[93] Non-derogability simply refers to the situation that applies during a public emergency threatening the life of the nation. It is unlikely that an area subject to a proclamation of a public emergency threatening the life of the nation would be viewed as a reasonable IPA, and there is case law to this effect.[94] Moreover, it should be accepted that a putative refugee has the right to special consideration with respect to human rights violations in an IPA because of the fact that he or she has already been displaced by persecution. The situation for other persons within the IPA, even if they have been internally displaced, simply confirms the sad reality that there are many IDPs who are unable to exercise their right to seek asylum, and many other people whose rights are not respected, protected and ensured who are not eligible for refugee status in the first place and who have no meaningful remedy for their lack of protection.[95]

---

91 Custom was nominated as the relevant test by Lord Bingham in *Januzi*: see n. 49 above.

92 For criticisms of the EQD, see, for example, UN High Commissioner for Refugees, *UNHCR Annotated Comments on the EC Council Directive 2004/83/EC of 29 April 2004 on Minimum Standards for the Qualification and Status of Third Country Nationals or Stateless Persons as Refugees or as Persons Who Otherwise Need International Protection and the Content of the Protection Granted (OJ L 304/12 of 30.9.2004)*, 28 January 2005, at: http://www.unhcr.org/refworld/docid/4200d8354.html [accessed 15 November 2008].

93 See Human Rights Committee, General Comment no. 29, States of Emergency (Article 4), UN Doc CCPR/C/2/Rev.1/Add.11, 31 August 2001 [11].

94 See the discussion of case law concerning generalized violence in Hathaway and Foster, 400.

95 On relative numbers of refugees under UNHCR responsibility and the world's population of internally displaced persons, see 2009 Global Trends: Refugees, Asylum seekers, Returnees, Internally Displaced and Stateless Persons, June 2010, at: http://www.unhcr.org/cgi-bin/texis/vtx/search?page=search&docid=4c11f0be9&query=2009%20Global%20Trends [accessed 10 November 2010].

The final set of concerns raised by Lord Bingham related to the potential comparison between conditions in the country of origin and those in the country of asylum. No one expects that a country like Sudan should be able to attain exactly the same standard of economic, social and cultural rights as the UK. Even when party to the International Covenant on Economic, Social and Cultural Rights, countries are bound to a standard of progressive achievement in light of their available resources.[96] However, it is significant that Sudan is party to both the African Charter on Human and People's rights,[97] which protects some socio-economic rights, and the International Covenant on Economic, Social and Cultural Rights. Unfortunately, Sudan chose to spend most of its resources (it had significant oil reserves) on military objectives.[98]

If a standard of general human rights is adopted, this does not amount to comparing the conditions in the country of asylum with the conditions in the country of origin.[99] Rather, it is the adoption of an internationally accepted standard to which all states aspire. Even if the Universal Declaration of Human Rights is not entirely customary international law, it is nevertheless the standard to which states aspire. Moreover, the Universal Declaration has been accepted as the basis for Universal Periodic Review of all UN members by the Human Rights Council, suggesting that it is in fact viewed as binding.[100]

The Universal Declaration should be used in the interpretation of the Refugee Convention, as should the major human rights treaties, even if they are not accepted by the country from which asylum seekers flee or indeed the potential country of refuge. After all, the Refugee Convention has never operated on the basis of reciprocity. The inquiry into refugee status is not about whether the state of origin is party to particular human rights treaties. The very fact that the Refugee Convention gave shelter to refugees despite the fact that the two Covenants had not yet been adopted reinforces that point. The rights in the Refugee Convention are supplemented by the rights contained in the general human rights treaties such as the two Covenants, but the Refugee Convention operates independently of whether either the country of asylum or the country of origin is party to these human rights treaties. Like all human rights instruments, the Refugee Convention

96 See Article 2 of the International Covenant on Economic, Social and Cultural Rights.

97 African Charter on Human and Peoples' Rights, 27 June 1981, OAU Doc.CAB/LEG/67/3 rev.5, 21 *International Legal Materials* 58 (1982).

98 *HGMO (Relocation to Khartoum) Sudan CG*, [112]. South Sudan, where most of the oil reserves are located, is now independent, while Sudan has the pipelines, processing facilities and the sea port used to export the oil.

99 The Michigan Guidelines are explicit on this point: 'The relevant measure is the treatment of other persons in the proposed site of internal protection, not in the putative asylum country', [22].

100 See Human Rights Council Resolution 5/1 Institution-building of the United Nations Human Rights Council: UN Doc HRC/Res/5/1, 18 June 2007. For the view that the Universal Declaration is being treated as binding for the purposes of Universal Periodic Review, see Robert McCorquodale, 'A Future for Human Rights Law', in Mashood Baderin and Manisuli Ssenyonjo (eds), *International Human Rights Law: Six Decades after the UDHR and Beyond* 541 (Farnham: Ashgate, 2010), 541–52, at 542–3. For a description of the first session of Universal Periodic Review, see Elvira Dominguez Redondo, 'The Universal Periodic Review of the UN Human Rights Council: An Assessment of the First Session', 7 *Chinese Journal of International Law* 3 (2008), 721–34.

is a living instrument that should be interpreted in light of current conditions.[101] The fact that every state in the international community is now party to at least one human rights treaty, and that all but three are party to the Convention on the Rights of the Child,[102] indicates that widely ratified human rights treaties are an appropriate standard to resolve various interpretative controversies involving the Refugee Convention.[103]

Concluding Remarks

It appears that the House of Lords was concerned by the prospect of refugee law being used as a back door for economic migration. As Lord Bingham stated in *AH and others*, the purpose of the Refugee Convention is 'not to procure a general leveling-up of living standards around the world, desirable though of course that is.'[104]

To an extent, this is a true statement. The world has retreated from the previously prevailing freedom to migrate in pursuit of a better life (or more human rights),[105] and it would be too much to expect the Refugee Convention to perform the role of redistributive justice. A legal document that carves out a somewhat grudging exception to sovereign powers over immigration has the effect of reinforcing sovereignty and the power of a national community to decide who will be able to cross its borders.[106]

Arguably, the internal protection alternative has become a back door for denying international protection to people who require it, on the basis of an unfounded concern about opening the 'flood gates'. However, the Refugee Convention does not have to be read in such a way that it actively reinforces such privilege at the expense of persecuted people. An approach to the IPA that is informed by the objective standards of human rights might discourage comparison of asylum seekers' situation with the millions of neglected and unprotected in countries of origin and safeguard the protective value of the Refugee Convention.

---

101 See for example, *Tyrer v the United Kingdom* (1978) 2 EHRR 1, [31]. See Rosalyn Higgins, 'Some Observations on the Inter-temporal Rule in International Law', in Jerzy Makarczyk (ed.), *Theory of International Law at the Threshold of the 21st Century: Essays in Honour of Krzysztof Skubiszewski* (The Hague: Kluwer, 1997), 173–82.

102 Convention on the Rights of the Child, 20 November 1989, 1577 UNTS 3.

103 For a thorough discussion of this issue, see Foster, *International Refugee Law and Socio-Economic Rights*, 54–67.

104 *AH and others*, per Lord Bingham [6].

105 For a history of changes in migration policy, see Timothy J. Hatton and J.G. Williamson, *Global Migration and the World Economy: Two Centuries of Policy Performance* (Cambridge, MA: MIT Press, 2005).

106 See Catherine Dauvergne, *Making People Illegal: What Globalization Means for Migration and Law* (Cambridge; New York: CUP, 2008), chapter 4.

References

Dauvergne, Catherine, *Making People Illegal: What Globalization Means for Migration and Law* (Cambridge; New York: CUP, 2008).

De Moffarts, Gaetan, 'Refugee Status and the "Internal Flight Alternative"', in *Refugee and Asylum Law: Assessing the Scope for Judicial Protection,* International Association of Refugee Law Judges, second conference, Nijmegen, 1997 (Utrecht: Nederlands Centrum Buitenlanders, 1997), 123—138.

Dominguez Redondo, Elvira, 'The Universal Periodic Review of the UN Human Rights Council: An Assessment of the First Session', 7 *Chinese Journal of International Law* (2008), 721–34.

Fortin, Antonio, 'The Meaning of "Protection" in the Refugee Definition', 12 *International Journal of Refugee Law* (2000), 548–76.

Foster, Michelle, *International Refugee Law and Socio-economic Rights: Refuge from Deprivation* (Cambridge, UK; New York: CUP, 2007).

Frelick, Bill, 'Down the Rabbit Hole: The Strange Logic of Internal Flight Alternative', 22 *World Refugee Survey* (1999), 22–9.

Hathaway, James C., *The Law of Refugee Status* (Toronto: Butterworths, 1991).

Hathaway, James C. and Michelle Foster, 'Internal Protection/Relocation/Flight Alternative as an Aspect of Refugee Status Determination', in Erika Feller, Volker Türk and Frances Nicholson (eds), *Refugee Protection in International Law: UNHCR's Global Consultations on International Protection* 357 (Cambridge: CUP, 2003), 357–417.

Hatton, Timothy J. and J.G. Williamson, *Global Migration and the World Economy: Two Centuries of Policy Performance* (Cambridge, MA: MIT Press, 2005).

Higgins, Rosalyn, 'Some Observations on the Inter-temporal Rule in International Law', in Jerzy Makarczyk (ed.), *Theory of International Law at the Threshold of the 21st Century: Essays in Honour of Krzysztof Skubiszewski* (The Hague: Kluwer, 1997), 173–82.

Keith, Sir Kenneth, 'The Difficulties of "Internal Flight" and "Internal Relocation" as Frameworks of Analysis', 15 *Georgetown Immigration Law Journal* (2001), 433–46.

Kelley, Ninette, 'Internal Flight/Relocation/Protection Alternative: Is It Reasonable?', 14 *International Journal of Refugee Law* (2002), 4–44.

McAdam, Jane, *Complementary Protection in International Refugee Law* (Oxford; New York: OUP, 2007).

McCorquodale, Robert, 'A Future for Human Rights Law', in Mashood Baderin and Manisuli Ssenyonjo (eds), *International Human Rights Law: Six Decades after the UDHR and Beyond* (Farnham: Ashgate, 2010), 541–52.

Marx, Reinhard, 'The Criteria of Applying the "Internal Flight Alternative" Test in National Refugee Status Determination Procedures', 14 *International Journal of Refugee Law* (2002), 179–218.

Mathew, Penelope, 'Australian Refugee Protection in the Wake of the Tampa', 96 *American Journal of International Law* (2002), 661–76.

Metcalfe, Susan, *The Pacific Solution* (Melbourne, Australia: Australian Scholarly Publishing, 2010).

O'Ryan, Rory, Chambers of Ian Macdonald QC, 16 *Immigration Team Legal Bulletin* 2 (November 2007).

Steyn, Lord Johan, 'Guantánamo Bay: The Legal Black Hole', 53 *International and Comparative Law Quarterly* (2004), 1–15.

Storey, Hugo, 'The Internal Flight Alternative Test: The Jurisprudence Re-examined', 10 *International Journal of Refugee Law* (1998), 499–676.

Taylor, Savitri, 'Protection Elsewhere/Nowhere', 18 *International Journal of Refugee Law* (2006), 283–312.

Zaat, Kirsten, *The Protection of IDPs in the Sudan: Applying International Law at the Field Level, The Journal of Humanitarian Assistance*, 17 October 2006, http://sites.tufts.edu/jha/files/2011/04/a195.pdf [accessed 3 August 2012].

Territorial Protection: Cessation of Refugee Status and Internal Flight Alternative Compared

Maria O'Sullivan

1. Introduction

The meaning of 'protection' for the purpose of the 1951 Convention relating to the Status of Refugees[1] (the 'Refugee Convention') has changed over the decades since the Convention was signed. Many States utilize the concept of a 'third safe country', 'safe country of origin' and 'internal flight alternative'[2] to return refugees to a 'safe' country or part of a country. In recent years, some States have also begun to grant time-limited visas to recognized refugees and, as part of this, have utilized the 'changed circumstances' cessation provisions under Article 1C(5) to return recognized refugees to countries where protection against persecution is now being provided in the country of origin.[3]

The legal tests for these various interpretations of 'protection' have been developed largely on an *ad hoc* basis and in isolation from one another. This raises the question as to whether any commonalities exist across these standards – all of which involve findings as to safety and protection – and whether a more integrated approach should be taken to these issues. In order to illustrate this point, this chapter will focus on two of these concepts – the internal flight alternative (IFA) and cessation of refugee status due to change in country conditions under Article 1C(5) of the Refugee Convention and its European Union equivalent – Article 11(1)(e) of the EU Qualification Directive (the 'changed circumstances cessation clause'). The concepts of IFA and cessation are linked in that they both concern the definition of a refugee under

1 The 1951 Convention relating to the Status of Refugees, 189 *UNTS* 150, supplemented by the 1967 Protocol relating to the Status of Refugees, 606 *UNTS* 267.

2 James C. Hathaway and Michelle Foster present an interesting critique of the terminology 'Internal Flight Alternative', advocating instead the use of 'Internal Protection Alternative': see James C. Hathaway and Michelle Foster, 'Internal Protection/Relocation/Flight Alternative as an Aspect of Refugee Status Determination', in Erika Feller, Volker Türk and Frances Nicholson (eds), *Refugee Protection in International Law: UNHCR's Global Consultations on International Protection* (2003), 357–417, at 382–3. However, as 'internal flight alternative' is the term used by many States and in both academic commentary and jurisprudence, I have used it here as the more commonly recognized terminology.

3 Australia and Germany are the main State Parties to the Convention that have utilized Article 1C(5) – see Maria O'Sullivan, 'Withdrawing Protection under Article 1C(5) of the 1951 Convention: Lessons from Australia' (2008) 20(4) *International Journal of Refugee Law* 586–610, at 587–90.

Article 1 of the 1951 Convention and both entail consideration of the adequacy of protection in the refugee's country of origin. Indeed, UNHCR and some commentators have already highlighted symmetries between these two concepts[4] and have recommended taking a more integrated approach to their interpretation.[5]

The need to link the interpretation of these two concepts has become more pressing due to the developing recognition of non-state bodies as agents of protection. Jurisprudence in a number of countries has recognized that, in limited circumstances, certain non-state actors can be said to provide 'protection' for the purpose of the 1951 Convention.[6] Some have applied this to situations where the organization providing protection is controlling only a *part* of the country in question.[7] The European Union Qualification Directive explicitly recognizes this concept in that Article 7 of that Directive states that protection can be provided by the State or 'parties or organisations, including international organisations, controlling the State or a *substantial part* of the territory of the State'.[8] This raises a question as to whether, and how, non-state protection should apply to the changed circumstances cessation clause.

Whether non-state protection is sufficient for the purpose of the changed circumstances clause had, until recently, not been considered in any depth in jurisprudence.[9] The issue

4 UN High Commissioner for Refugees, *UNHCR Statement on the 'Ceased Circumstances' Clause of the EC Qualification Directive*, August 2008, 15, at: http://www.unhcr.org/refworld/docid/48a2f0782.html [accessed: 14 December 2010] ('UNHCR Cessation Statement 2008'); Lauren Sanders, 'Finding a Reasonable Alternative: An Integrated Approach to Refugee Law, Relocation and the Internal Flight Alternative', ANU College of Law Research Paper No. 09-05, vii, at: http://ssrn.com/abstract=1365043 [accessed: 14 December 2010]; and Rodger Haines, cited in Hugo Storey, 'The Internal Flight Alternative Test: The Jurisprudence Re-examined' (1998) 10 *International Journal of Refugee Law* 499–532, at 504.

5 UNHCR Cessation Statement 2008, 15; Sanders, 'Finding a Reasonable Alternative'.

6 See e.g. the decisions of the UK Asylum and Immigration Tribunal in *Fadil Dyli (Protection – UNMIK – Arif – IFA – Art1D) v. Secretary of State for the Home Department** [2000] UKIAT 00001, 00/TH/02186, 30 August 2000; *DM (Majority Clan Entities Can Protect) Somalia v. Secretary of State for the Home Department* [2005] UKAIT 00150, 27 July 2005); and *SF (Sufficiency of Protection-KAA-Michigan Guidelines) Iraq v. Secretary of State for the Home Department* [2002] UKIAT 07376, 24 March 2003. See also *Elmi v. Minister of Citizenship and Immigration*, IMM-580-98, Canada: Federal Court, 12 March 1999.

7 See e.g. *Ahmed Ali Zatzoli v MEI* [1991] 3 CF 605; and *Elmi*, para. 17.

8 Directive 2011/95/EU of The European Parliament and of The Council of 13 December 2011 on standards for the qualification of third-country nationals or stateless persons as beneficiaries of international protection, for a uniform status for refugees or for persons eligible for subsidiary protection, and for the content of the protection granted (recast), OJ L 337 20.12.2011, p. 0009, 20 December 2011, L337/9 ('2011 EU Qualification Directive'; '2011 Recast Directive'), Article 7 (emphasis added). Note that the 2011 EU Qualification Directive replaces European Union Council Directive 2004/83/EC of 29 April 2004 on minimum standards for the qualification and status of third country nationals or stateless persons as refugees or as persons who otherwise need international protection and the content of the protection granted ('2004 EU Qualification Directive') [2005] OJ L304/12, Article 7 (emphasis added).

9 The only judgment that appears to have considered it in any detail is that of the German Federal Administrative Court (Bundesverwaltungsgericht), in the case *10 C 33.07* (2008) 17–19, which refers to a 'territorial authority in a definable (core) territory' and bodies with 'effective statal or quasi-statal authority in portions of its territory'.

was discussed, albeit briefly, in a recent judgment of the European Court of Justice in *Abdulla and ors* where the Court considered questions as the legal test for cessation of refugee status under Article 11(1)(e) of the EU Qualification Directive.[10] As part of this, the Court considered the applicability of Article 7 of the Qualification Directive relating to non-state agents of protection in the context of cessation. The Court confirmed that Article 7 does indeed apply to cessation under Article 11(1)(e) of the Directive.[11] This is significant as, due to the reference in Article 7(1) to protection being provided in a 'substantial part' of a territory, the effect of the ECJ judgment is that cessation can been found to have occurred even if it is only 'partial' in nature – that is, even if the non-state actor providing protection is only controlling a substantial 'part' of the State.

The application of 'partial protection' in cessation cases is problematic. If the 'protector' is only controlling part of a country, can cessation in fact be said to have occurred? UNHCR has, on a number of occasions, cautioned against the use of Article 1C(5) in relation to part of a territory.[12] The use of Article 1C(5) in 'partial protection' situations is of particular concern because cessation does not carry with it the safeguards or humanitarian aspects that have been developed in relation to IFA, such as consideration of the 'reasonableness' of return and the requirement that the applicant not be subject to serious harm in the area of safety.

This raises concerns about the inequalities arising from the way in which these two tests currently operate. Should a refugee being returned to their country of origin under Article 1C(5) be considered under similar principles to those applicable to IFA (particularly where there is a finding as to non-state protection in part of a country)? Should this include humanitarian considerations that some jurisdictions have recognized as part of the IFA, such as the 'reasonableness' of return to the area of 'safety' and, as part of this, whether this should include consideration of the risk of serious harm and socio-economic conditions such as the right to livelihood? In addition to these specific questions, the link between cessation and IFA raises a broader issue of whether a more consistent approach and holistic interpretation should be taken of 'safety' and 'protection' across international refugee law (including the EU Qualification Directive).[13]

---

10 European Court of Justice, Joined Cases C-175/08, C-176/08, C-178/08 and C-179/08, *Salahadin Abdulla, Hasan, Adem and Rashi, Jama v. Bundesrepublik Deutschland,* 2 March 2010 ('*Abdulla and ors*').

11 *Abdulla and ors*. The question of whether non-state actors should be recognized as actors of protection for the purpose of international refugee law is discussed in M. O'Sullivan, 'Acting the Part: Can Non-State Entities provide Protection under International Refugee Law?', (2012) 24(1) *International Journal of Refugee Law* 1–26.

12 UN High Commissioner for Refugees, *Guidelines on International Protection: Cessation of Refugee Status under Article 1C(5) and (6) of the 1951 Convention relating to the Status of Refugees (the 'Ceased Circumstances' Clauses)*, UN Doc. HCR/GIP/03/03 (2003), [17] ('UNHCR Guidelines on Cessation 2003').

13 It is widely recognized that it is necessary to take a holistic interpretation of the whole of the Convention when analysing its constituent articles. See UNHCR 'The International Protection of Refugees: Interpreting Article 1 of the 1951 Convention relating to the Status of Refugees', (2001) 20(3) *Refugee Survey Quarterly* 77–104; and V. Türk and F. Nicholson, 'Refugee Protection in International Law: An Overall Perspective', in Feller et al. (eds), *Refugee Protection in International Law*, 3–45, at 42–3.

In discussing these questions, I shall outline the principles and test for cessation due to changed circumstances, and the criteria for the IFA. Next, I shall discuss some of the concerns arising from the application of these two concepts, by focusing on the developing notion of 'territorial protection' or 'partial protection' by non-state actors. This will be done by focusing on the non-state actor provision in the EU Qualification Directive (Article 7) and its interpretation by the European Court of Justice in *Abdulla and ors*. As part of this analysis, I shall query whether the concepts of 'reasonableness' and other humanitarian considerations utilized in IFA decisions should be part of the criterion for cessation clauses. In conclusion, I shall put forward the case for integrating the meaning of protection, at least in relation to the linked concepts of cessation and IFA, in order to provide a more holistic test for protection under the Convention.

2. Cessation of Refugee Status due to 'Changed Circumstances'

Cessation of refugee status due to changed circumstances is set out in Article 1C(5) of the 1951 Convention. A regional equivalent is also set out in Article 11(1)(e) of the EU Qualification Directive. The latter is significant because of European Court of Justice jurisprudence on 'partial cessation', as noted above. I shall discuss these two provisions in turn.

(a) Article 1C(5) of the 1951 Refugee Convention

State Parties to the 1951 Refugee Convention are permitted to withdraw a person's refugee status if that State finds that the circumstances in the refugee's home country have changed such that his or refugee status has 'ceased' under Article 1C(5) of the Convention. Article 1C(5) provides that the Refugee Convention shall cease to apply to a refugee if:

> he can no longer, because the circumstances in connection with which he has been recognized as a refugee have ceased to exist, continue to refuse to avail himself of the protection of the country of his nationality ....

It then sets out a 'compelling circumstances' exception to cessation that is stated to apply only to pre-1951 refugees:

> Provided that this paragraph shall not apply to a refugee falling under Section 1A(1) of this Article who is able to invoke compelling reasons arising out of previous persecution for refusing to avail himself of the protection of the country of nationality ....

There are a number of things to note about the wording of Article 1C(5). First, it requires cessation of the 'circumstances in connection with which' the person was recognized as a refugee. As a result, it is understood that a State is required to demonstrate that any change in conditions in a refugee's country of origin removes the basis of the particular refugee's fear of persecution.[14] However, UNHCR has stated that cessation requires more than an absence of persecution in the country of origin, but rather the availability of effective protection:

> [C]essation requires a specific assessment of the nature of the changes, which go beyond the criteria for recognition. Moreover, refugee status will only cease if effective protection is available in the country of origin. The availability of effective protection constitutes a distinct criterion and is to be understood in a broad sense which is not limited to protection against persecution.[15]

Leading academic commentators have also stated that protection for the purpose of the 'changed circumstances' cessation provisions should not simply be the eradication of persecution, but the provision by the state of 'effective protection'[16] or the 'restoration of protection'.[17]

UNHCR, however, has gone further than academic commentary on this issue, by suggesting that a person's right to a 'basic livelihood' should form part of this 'effective protection' test, stating that such protection

> requires more than mere physical security or safety. It needs to include the existence of a functioning government and basic administrative structures, as evidenced for instance through a functioning system of law and justice, as well as the existence of adequate infrastructure to enable residents to exercise their rights, *including their right to a basic livelihood*.[18]

This broader interpretation of effective protection has not yet been endorsed in jurisprudence on cessation in those countries that have utilized it significantly thus far – that is, Germany and Australia. Rather, case law in these jurisdictions has taken a narrow view that protection for the purposes of cessation is essentially only protection against *persecution*.[19] Likewise, the ECJ has not adopted the broader UNHCR interpretation of the cessation clause.[20]

Second, there is general agreement that the standard or test to establish cessation under Article 1C(5) requires that the change must be 'fundamental', 'stable' and 'durable'.[21] Some

---

14 See e.g. UNHCR, 'Handbook on Procedures and Criteria for Determining Refugee Status under the 1951 Convention and the 1967 Protocol relating to the Status of Refugees', UN Doc. HCR/IP/4/Eng/REV.1, 1979 (revised edn 1992) ('UNHCR Handbook'), [135]; UNHCR, 'Note on the Cessation Clauses', UN Doc. EC/47/SC/CRP.30, 30 May 1997 ('UNHCR Note on Cessation'), [19].

15 UNHCR Cessation Statement 2008, 14.

16 Guy Goodwin-Gill and Jane McAdam, *The Refugee in International Law* (Oxford: Oxford University Press, 3rd edn, 2007), 140.

17 James C. Hathaway, *The Rights of Refugees under International Law* (Cambridge: Cambridge University Press, 2005), 922, 927.

18 UNHCR Guidelines on Cessation 2003, [15] (emphasis added).

19 See German Federal Administrative Court (*Bundesverwaltungsgericht*), *10 C 33.07* (2008); and the Australian High Court in *Minister for Immigration and Multicultural Affairs v. QAAH of 2004* [2006] HCA 53, 231 ALR 340 ('*QAAH*'). See discussion of the Australian High Court decision in *QAAH* in O'Sullivan, 'Withdrawing Protection under Article 1C(5) of the 1951 Convention'.

20 *Abdulla and ors*.

21 UNHCR, Executive Committee Conclusion No. 65, *General Conclusion on International Protection*, U.N. GAOR, 46th Sess., at (q) (1991), *aff'd*, UNHCR, Executive Committee Conclusion

indicators of such change that have been suggested by the UNHCR are 'an end to hostilities, a complete political change and return to a situation of peace and stability'.[22]

Third, the 'compelling reasons' exception to cessation only applies to *statutory* refugees defined in Article 1A(1) of the Convention, rather than *Convention* refugees defined under Article 1A(2). Although the compelling reasons proviso is so limited, UNHCR has consistently argued that the proviso reflects a broader humanitarian principle that should be applied more broadly to all Convention refugees.[23] Academic commentators differ on this point however. Guy Goodwin-Gill and Jane McAdam argue that Article 1C(5) should be interpreted in light of State Practice, which they say is sufficiently developed to establish agreement between the State Parties that the compelling reasons exception should be more broadly applied to all refugees.[24] Others, such as James Hathaway disagree, questioning 'whether there is truly a sound basis to assert a clear norm of customary international law which effectively supersedes the Convention'.[25]

It may well be that, to date, there has not been sufficiently consistent State Practice among State Parties that recognizes a broader application of the exception to all refugees. Although countries including France, Belgium, Germany, Canada and the US have interpreted the proviso as applying broadly to all refugees, not merely pre-1951 refugees,[26] others have not done so. For instance, UK case law has held that it is only applicable to statutory refugees – the House of Lords holding *inter alia* that the humanitarian purposes of the Convention are limited by the tests set out in Article 1A(2).[27] However, such state practice is likely to change in future years given that Article 11(3) of the recast 2011 EU Qualification Directive contains a broad-ranging version of the exception applicable to all refugees. Article 11(3) provides that cessation,

> shall not apply to a refugee who is able to invoke compelling reasons arising out of previous persecution for refusing to avail himself or herself of the protection of the country of nationality or, being a stateless person, of the country of former habitual residence.[28]

No. 69, *Cessation of Status*, U.N. GAOR, 47th Sess. (1992); UNHCR Handbook, [135]; James C. Hathaway, *The Law of Refugee Status* (Toronto: Butterworths, 1991), 200–203; Hathaway, *Rights of Refugees under International Law*, 922–41; and Goodwin-Gill and McAdam, *Refugee in International Law*, 143.

22 UNHCR Cessation Guidelines 2003, [10–11].

23 See UNHCR Handbook, [136]; UNHCR 2003 Guidelines, [31].

24 Goodwin-Gill and McAdam, *Refugee in International Law*, 148–9.

25 Hathaway, *Rights of Refugees under International Law*, 942 (n. 109).

26 See e.g. US Code of Federal Regulations, 8 CFR s. 208.13(b)(1)(iii)(A); Immigration and Refugee Protection Act 2001, Canada, s. 108(4); *Canada (Minister of Employment and Immigration) v Obstoj* [1992] 2 FC 739, 748–52; Germany: Asylum Procedures Act, s. 73; France: Office Français de Protection des Réfugiés et Apatrides (OFPRA), 'Summary of Cessation', at: www.ofpra.gouv.fr/index.html?xml_id=263&dtd_id=14 [accessed: 20 August 2012]. See also discussion in Goodwin-Gill and McAdam, *Refugee in International Law*, 145–9.

27 See e.g. the UK House of Lords *In re B (FC)(Appellant)(2002) Regina v Special Adjudicator ex parte Hoxha (FC)* [2005] 1 W.L.R. 1063, [68]–[87].

28 2011 EU Qualification Directive.

Thus, Article 11(3) is likely, if implemented domestically in most EU Member States, to greatly enhance the case for recognizing the 'compelling circumstances' proviso as a rule of customary international law.

However, putting aside the question of customary international law, the fact that there is no humanitarian exception to cessation set out in the 1951 Convention raises the question as to whether such humanitarian elements should be introduced when cessation is viewed as a type of 'relocation' situation. That is, should the 'reasonableness' approach utilized in IFA decisions, in some circumstances at least, be applied to changed circumstances cessation decisions? I discuss this below in Section 5 of this chapter.

(b) Article 11(1)(e) of the EU Qualification Directive

Article 11(1)(e) of the European Union Asylum Qualification Directive ('EU Qualification Directive') sets out cessation provisions similar to that of Article 1C(5).[29] In addition to this, it allows Member States to issue three-year residence permits to refugees.[30] This is of significance as application by States of Article 1C(5) is typically linked to the use of time-limited domestic residence permits.[31] The Qualification Directive also obliges Member States to revoke or refuse to renew refugee status if cessation has occurred.[32] As a result, a number of European states, such as the United Kingdom ('UK') and Germany, have introduced temporary residence permits for recognized refugees and have applied or plan to apply Article 1C(5) to holders of those permits.[33]

Although the provisions in Article 11(1)(e) and (f) are almost identical to those in Article 1C(5) of the Convention, there are two differences to note. First, Article 11(2) of the Directive

[29] Article 11(1)(e) and (f), 2011 EU Qualification Directive.

[30] Article 24, 2011 EU Qualification Directive. Article 24(1) obliges Member States to issue such a residence permit to refugees '[a]s soon as possible after their status has been granted ...'.

[31] E.g. the UK introduced a 'limited leave to remain' residence permit for recognised refugees in 2005: see UK, Asylum Procedure Policy Instruction, 'Refugee Leave', as at 26 October 2009, Point 6, at: http://www.ukba.homeoffice.gov.uk/sitecontent/documents/policyandlaw/asylumpolicyinstructions/ [accessed: 2 August 2012]. In Germany, recognized refugees are granted a three-year residence permit. Prior to expiry of that permit, the immigration authorities are required to reassess the refugee's continuing need for protection: Section 73(2a) of the Asylum Procedures Act provides that, '[n]o more than three years after the decision becomes non-appealable, it shall be examined whether the conditions for revocation pursuant to (1) or withdrawal pursuant to (2) exist'. Although Article 1C(5) can, theoretically, be applied to refugees who have been granted permanent protection visas or permits, states have rarely, if ever done so.

[32] 2011 EU Qualification Directive, Article 14, which obliges Member States to 'revoke, end or refuse to renew' the refugee status of a person 'if he or she has ceased to be a refugee in accordance with Article 11'.

[33] Germany commenced revoking the refugee status of Iraqi refugees based on change in country conditions in November 2003: see Human Rights Watch, 'Germany: End Efforts to Strip Iraqis of Refugee Status', at http://www.hrw.org/news/2007/07/09/germany-end-efforts-strip-iraqis-refugee-status [accessed: 2 August 2012]. The UK has not as yet commenced application of Article 1C(5) but has indicated in policy documents that it will do so in the future: see UK, Asylum Policy Instruction ('API'): Refugee Leave, as at 26 October 2009, Point 6.

explicitly states that in applying Article 11(1)(e) and (f), Member States are to consider whether the changes are 'significant and non-temporary':

> Member States shall have regard to whether the change of circumstances is of such a significant and non-temporary nature that the refugee's fear of persecution can no longer be regarded as well-founded.[34]

This is an important inclusion as it encapsulates the 'fundamental and durable' test advocated by UNHCR and commentators.[35]

The second difference is that, as noted earlier, Article 11(3) of the 2011 Qualification Directive sets out a broad compelling reasons exception to all refugees, whereas Article 1C(5) limits that exception to pre-1951 statutory refugees.

I shall now turn to the criteria for IFA, before analysing the parallels between the two concepts in light of the issues raised by the increasing recognition of non-state actor protection, as illustrated in the recent decision of the European Court of Justice in *Abdulla and ors.*

(c) The Test for the Internal Flight Alternative (IFA)

The notion of relocation is not expressly set out in the Refugee Convention; rather it has been developed by states as part of the decision-making process under Article 1A(2) of the Convention. In effect, IFA allows states to exclude a person from refugee status in situations where that person has a well-founded fear of persecution in relation to a region within their country of origin but can relocate to another area within their country of origin where they will not face a well-founded fear of persecution. Significantly for the purpose of this chapter, most jurisdictions recognize that, in order for IFA to be found in relation to a particular applicant, it must be 'reasonable' for that applicant to relocate. The reasonableness criterion is used in IFA decisions in a number of State Parties to the Convention, including Austria, Denmark, the USA, Canada, Australia, the UK, the Netherlands, France and Germany.[36] UNHCR has also endorsed the concept of internal flight alternative and endorses a 'reasonableness' criterion for relocation:

The fear of being persecuted need not always extend to the whole territory of the refugee's country of nationality. Thus in ethnic clashes or in cases of grave disturbances involving civil war conditions, persecution of a specific ethnic or national group may occur in only one part of the country. In such situations, a person will not be excluded from refugee status merely because he could have sought refuge in another part of the same country, if under all the circumstances it would not have been reasonable to expect him to do so.[37]

---

[34] Article 11(2), 2011 EU Qualification Directive [emphasis added].

[35] See text associated with above, notes 21–22.

[36] Hugo Storey, 'The Internal Flight Alternative Test', 511. See e.g. US Asylum Regulation 208.13(b)(1)(i); US Regs 8 CFR 208.13(b)(2)(ii); *Randhawa v Minister for Immigration, Local Government and Ethnic Affairs* 124 A.L.R. 265 ('*Randhawa*'), 270 (per Black CJ); 280 (per Whitlam J).

[37] UNHCR Handbook, [91]. This was referred to by Lord Bingham in *Januzi v. Secretary of State for the Home Department* [2006] 2 AC 426 ('*Januzi*') at 440.

As part of consideration of the reasonableness of relocation, States and UNHCR have considered two particular issues: whether the applicant may be at risk of serious harm and the existence of sufficient socio-economic conditions in the area of 'safety'. I shall discuss these in turn.

In relation to the issue of 'serious harm', UNHCR has stated that IFA should not apply where an applicant would be exposed to such a risk:

> a person with an established fear of persecution for a 1951 Convention reason in one part of the country cannot be expected to relocate to another area of serious harm. If the claimant would be exposed to a new risk of serious harm, including a serious risk to life, safety, liberty or health, or one of serious discrimination, an internal flight or relocation alternative does not arise, irrespective of whether or not there is a link to one of the Convention grounds. The assessment of new risks would therefore also need to take into account serious harm generally covered under complementary forms of protection.[38]

In particular, UNHCR has noted that in a situation of internal armed conflict, which by its nature is volatile, an IFA should not generally be available.[39] In the 2003 Guidelines on IFA it states:

> In most cases, countries in the grip of armed conflict would not be safe for relocation, especially in the light of shifting armed fronts which could suddenly bring insecurity to an area hitherto considered safe.[40]

Some States have also included serious harm in the 'reasonableness' criterion. In the EU, Article 8(1) of the 2011 Qualification Directive sets out criterion for IFA that include absence of risk of persecution or *serious harm* and a concept of reasonableness. It also adds a proviso relating to the ability of the applicant to 'safely and legally travel to and gain admittance' to the safe area. It states:

> As part of the assessment of the application for international protection, Member States may determine that an applicant is not in need of international protection if in a part of the country of origin, he or she: (a) has no well-founded fear of being persecuted or is not at real risk of suffering *serious harm*; or (b) has access to protection against persecution or *serious harm* as defined in Article 7; and he or she can safely and legally travel to and gain admittance to that part of the country and can reasonably be expected to settle there.[41]

38 UN High Commissioner for Refugees, *Guidelines on International Protection: 'Internal Flight or Relocation Alternative' Within the Context of Article 1A(2) of the 1951 Convention and/or 1967 Protocol Relating to the Status of Refugees*, HCR/GIP/03/03 (2003) ('UNHCR IFA Guidelines 2003'), [20].

39 UNHCR Note on Cessation, [27].

40 UNHCR IFA Guidelines 2003, [27].

41 Article 8(1), 2011 EU Qualification Directive (emphasis added). I note that Article 8(3) of the 2004 EU Qualification Directive had enabled application of the internal protection concept,

Similarly, US Regulations also require decision makers dealing with relocation to consider 'serious harm' and 'ongoing civil strife':

> whether the applicant would face other serious harm in the place of suggested relocation; any ongoing civil strife within the country; administrative, economic, or judicial infrastructure; geographical limitations; and social and cultural constraints such as age, gender, health and social and familial ties.[42]

The reference above to serious harm is of interest, as States have thus far not accepted that risk of serious harm is a separate criterion for consideration as part of the cessation clauses. This is reflected in the decision of the European Court of Justice in *Abdulla and ors*, which held that the criteria for refugee status and complementary protection were completely separate and thus serious harm was not part of the criterion for cessation.[43]

Turning now to the consideration of socio-economic rights as part of the IFA decision-making process: significantly, UNHCR, academic commentators and courts in several jurisdictions have held that reasonableness encapsulates the existence of socio-economic rights. UNHCR, in its 2003 Guidelines on the IFA, notes that it may not be reasonable to expect a person to relocate if they will be unable to earn a living, or if they face economic destitution or existence below at least an adequate level of subsistence:

> If the situation is such that the claimant will be unable to earn a living or to access accommodation, or where medical care cannot be provided or is clearly inadequate, the area may not be a reasonable alternative. It would be unreasonable, including from a human rights perspective, to expect a person to relocate to face economic destitution or existence below at least an adequate level of subsistence. At the other end of the spectrum, a simple lowering of living standards or worsening of economic status may not be sufficient to reject a proposed area as unreasonable.[44]

Professor James C. Hathaway has also included socio-economic rights as part of the IFA test:

> In situations where, for example, financial, logistical, or other barriers prevent the claimant from reaching internal safety; where the quality of internal protection fails to meet basic norms of civil, political and *socio-economic* human rights; or where internal safety is otherwise illusory or unpredictable, state accountability for the harm is established and refugee status is appropriately recognised.[45]

'notwithstanding technical obstacles to return' to the country of origin. This was a problematic provision that has been deleted in the 2011 Recast Directive.

42 US Regs 8 CFR 208.13(b)(3).

43 *Abdulla and ors*, [78–9].

44 UNHCR IFA Guidelines 2003, [29].

45 Hathaway, *Law of Refugee Status*, 134 (emphasis added).

However, as noted by Hathaway and Foster, there is divergence in State Practice as to the relevance of socio-economic factors to the reasonableness criterion.[46] On one hand, Hathaway's statement as to socio-economic rights, as cited above, was endorsed by the Australian Federal Court in *Randhawa*[47] *and the NZ Court of Appeal in Butler v. Attorney-General.*[48] The New Zealand Refugee Status Appeals Authority has also held that, in line with previous New Zealand case law and based on the Michigan Guidelines, once a person has been recognized to have a well-founded fear of persecution, they are entitled to protection of their human rights under Articles 2 to 33 of the Convention. These include freedom of religion and movement, rights to work, property, social assistance, primary education and access to the courts. The New Zealand Refugee body held that these rights should guide determinations of the existence of a safe area in the state of origin, and if the rights are not protected there, they must be provided by the asylum state under their international protection obligations.[49]

However, other courts have not included socio-economic rights as part of the reasonableness criterion. In the leading case of *Robinson* the UK Court of Appeal listed socio-economic conditions as one of the elements that is considered as part of the decision-making process in relation to IFA.[50] However, in the later case of *Januzi*, the UK House of Lords rejected the argument that the reasonableness of relocation is to be judged by whether the quality of life meets the norms of civil, political and socio-economic rights.[51] Lord Bingham held:

> The thrust of the Convention is to ensure the fair and equal treatment of refugees in countries of asylum, so as to provide effective protection against persecution for Convention reasons. It was not directed (persecution apart) to the level of rights prevailing in the country of nationality.[52]

Lord Bingham pointed to a number of reasons for this approach, including a lack of any customary international law upholding such an interpretation of the Convention. He also stated that 'adoption of the rule would give the Convention an effect which is not only unintended but also anomalous in its consequences'.[53] He explained that if a person could live elsewhere in his country of nationality and would not be at risk of persecution in that area, but would 'there suffer all the drawbacks of living in a poor and backward country', then:

46 Hathaway and Foster, 'Internal Protection/Relocation/Flight Alternative as an Aspect of Refugee Status Determination', 386–7.

47 *Randhawa*, at 269.

48 *Butler v. Attorney-General* [1999] NZAR 205.

49 *Refugee Appeal No 76044*, NZ RSAA (11 September 2008). See also discussion of case law from Germany, The Netherlands and Switzerland in Reinhard Marx, 'The Criteria of Applying the "Internal Flight Alternative" Test in National Refugee Status Determination Procedures' (2002) 14(2 and 3) *International Journal of Refugee Law* 179–218.

50 *Robinson* [1998] Q.B. 929 per Woolf LJ, 939–40.

51 *Januzi*, [16]–[19].

52 Ibid. [16] (per Bingham LJ).

53 Ibid. [19] (per Bingham LJ).

> It would be strange if the accident of persecution were to entitle him to escape, not only from that persecution, but from the deprivation to which his home country is subject. It would, of course, be different if the lack of respect for human rights posed threats to his life or exposed him to the risk of inhuman or degrading treatment or punishment.[54]

In response, and with respect, I would argue that whether a refugee is escaping from deprivation is not the central question at the heart of IFA and the reasonableness criterion. Rather, the reasonableness question should be focused on, *inter alia*, considering whether conditions in the 'safe' area would be so harsh that they would drive the person back to the 'unprotected' area of their country of origin – for instance, if famine or other destitution would drive a person back to the 'lesser evil' of a risk of persecution, that is, the danger of internal refoulement. Indeed, later in his judgment Lord Bingham did seem to accept that lack of socio-economic rights meeting the threshold of 'destitution' may be relevant to the question of IFA. In doing so he approved of part of the UNHCR Guidelines on IFA as providing 'valuable guidance', referring to the test outlined there as: '[c]an the claimant, in the context of the country concerned, lead a relatively normal life without facing undue hardship? If not, it would not be reasonable to expect the person to move there'.[55] His Lordship also endorsed as 'helpful' the comments of Hugo Storey on the issue of economic survival:

> there seems to be broad agreement that if life for the individual claimant in an IFA would involve economic annihilation, utter destitution or existence below a bare subsistence level (*Existenzminimum*) or deny 'decent means of subsistence' that would be unreasonable. On the other end of the spectrum a simple lowering of living standards or worsening of economic status would not. What must be shown to be lacking is the real possibility to survive economically, given the particular circumstances of the individual concerned (language, knowledge, education, skills, previous stay or employment there, local ties, sex, civil status, age and life experience, family responsibilities, health; available or realisable assets, and so forth) ....[56]

Thus, it appears that although the quality of socio-economic rights generally is not part of the IFA test in the UK under the *Januzi* approach, a lack of basic subsistence or other serious risk to economic livelihood may be seen as a factor going to 'undue hardship'.

Canada also adopts an 'undue hardship' test. In *Ranganathan v Canada (Minister of Citizenship and Immigration)*[57] the Canadian Federal Court of Appeal held that a region would be safe unless 'conditions ... would jeopardise the life or safety of a claimant', thereby not

---

54 Ibid. [19] (per Bingham LJ). See also Lord Hope at [45]: 'I too would hold that the question whether it would be unduly harsh for a claimant to be expected to live in a place of relocation within the country of his nationality is not to be judged by considering whether the quality of life in the place of relocation meets the basic norms of civil, political and socio-economic human rights'.

55 Ibid. [20] (per Bingham LJ).

56 Storey, 'The Internal Flight Alternative Test', 516, referred to by Bingham LJ in *Januzi* [20].

57 [2001] 2 FC 164 ('*Ranganathan*').

recognizing broader socio-economic rights. Indeed, in *Singh* the Canadian Federal Court held that economic prosperity was not a factor in assessing the viability of an IFA.[58]

What relevance, then, does this have for cessation decisions? If we accept, as UNHCR, many commentators and some States Parties to the Convention do, that a right of subsistence or livelihood should be accepted as part of the criterion for IFA, can we and should we apply this to cessation decisions? As noted above in Section 2 of this chapter, UNHCR advocates a test for cessation that involves consideration of socio-economic factors, such the right to livelihood, in the country of origin.[59] However, this has not been accepted thus far by the courts that have considered the question.[60] The next part of the chapter will address these and other issues, with particular focus on the application of non-state protection to cessation cases.

3. Greater Linkages between Cessation and IFA: The Case for Closer Integration in Relation to Non-state Actors of Protection

As stated in the Introduction, the need to more closely integrate the legal tests for cessation and IFA arises because of the notion of non-state actors of protection providing 'protection' for the purposes of both the granting of and cessation of refugee status. As the discussion of the IFA in Section 3 of this chapter illustrated, there are three safeguards that are generally accepted (at least by UNHCR and a number of Member States) to apply to decisions involving IFA: the relocation must be 'reasonable' and, as part of this, the applicant not be subject to serious harm in the 'safe' area and be provided with minimum human rights guarantees, including socio-economic rights (or at least economic deprivation). However, no such protections or concessions apply to cessation provisions, even when protection is said to be provided in only *part* of a country of origin. Thus this section of the chapter will address the inequalities arising from these differences in interpretation and the ways in which cessation can be informed by the principles of IFA. I shall address this by focusing on the issue of 'partial cessation' raised by the use of non-state actors of protection and whether in such situations there is a case for transposing some IFA criteria to cessation provisions – including a 'reasonableness' criterion encapsulating humanitarian considerations, whether returnees face a risk of serious harm or instability due to armed conflict, and consideration of socio-economic factors such as the right to a livelihood. To illustrate this, I shall be analysing the concept of 'partial' protection and 'partial' cessation due to the operation of the non-state actor provisions of the EU Qualification Directive, as interpreted by the European Court of Justice.

[58] *Singh* [1993] FCJ 630, 23 June 1993, cited in Hathaway and Foster, 'Internal Protection/ Relocation/Flight Alternative as an Aspect of Refugee Status Determination', 386.

[59] See UNHCR Cessation Statement 2008.

[60] See e.g. the Australian High Court in *QAAH*; the European Court of Justice in *Abdulla and ors*.

(a) Non-state Actors of Protection and Cessation

The ability of non-state actors to provide 'protection' has been recognized to some extent in refugee law jurisprudence in the UK, France and Canada over the last decade or so.[61] However, it has become far more prominent in international refugee law discourse, and relevant to cessation, through the introduction of a provision on non-state actors of protection in the 2011 European Union Qualification Directive.[62] Article 7 of this Directive, controversially, provides that protection can be provided not only by a 'State' but also 'international organisations' or 'parties'. Article 7(1) provides that protection can be provided by:

a. the State; or
b. parties or organisations, including international organisations, controlling the State or a substantial part of the territory of the State provided they are willing and able to offer protection in accordance with paragraph 2.

Article 7(2) then sets out the standard of protection expected of actors of protection and requires, *inter alia*, that the applicant must have 'access to such protection':

> 2. Protection against persecution or serious harm must be effective and of a non-temporary nature. Such protection is generally provided when the actors mentioned under points (a) and (b) of paragraph 1 take reasonable steps to prevent the persecution or suffering of serious harm, inter alia, by operating an effective legal system for the detection, prosecution and punishment of acts constituting persecution or serious harm, and when the applicant has access to such protection.[63]

Permitting non-state actors to provide 'protection' is a controversial notion under international refugee law, as traditionally States have been seen as the only bodies that can provide such protection. As a result, UNHCR, academic commentators and non-governmental organizations (NGOs) have been heavily critical of Article 7, particularly on the basis that non-state entities are not accountable under international law.[64] UNHCR has

[61] See European Commission, 'Report from the Commission to the European Parliament and the Council on the Application of Directive 2004/83/EC of 29 April 2004 on Minimum Standards for the Qualification and Status of Third Country Nationals or Stateless Persons as Refugees or as Persons who Otherwise Need International Protection and the Content of the Protection, Brussels', 16 June 2010, COM(2010)314 final, 6.

[62] 2011 EU Qualification Directive.

[63] Ibid. Note that Article 7(2) of the 2004 EU Qualification Directive did not contain the first clause, that is, that '[p]rotection against persecution or serious harm must be effective and of a non-temporary nature'. This was added to the 2011 Recast Directive.

[64] UNHCR, *Annotated Comments on the EC Council Directive 2004/83/EC of 29 April 2004 on Minimum Standards for the Qualification and Status of Third Country Nationals or Stateless Persons as Refugees or as Persons Who Otherwise Need International Protection and the Content of the Protection granted (OJ L 304/12 of 30.9.2004)*, 28 January 2005 ('UNHCR Annotated Comments'), 18, at: www.unhcr.org/refworld/docid/4200d8354.html [accessed: 25 July 2012]; Guy Goodwin-Gill, 'Memorandum', UK House of Lords Select Committee on the European Union, July 2002, HL paper 156, 28th Report

also argued that non-state actors normally only exercise authority in a State on a temporary or transitional basis and have a limited ability to enforce the rule of law.[65] These concerns have been echoed by a number of European and UK NGOs such as the European Council of Refugees and Exiles (ECRE),[66] the UK Immigration Law Practitioners' Association,[67] Justice,[68] and the UK Refugee Council.[69] In particular, Justice and ECRE have questioned the stability and durability of non-state actors of protection.[70]

What then are the particular problems that arise in relation to non-state actors of protection as applied to cessation?

(b) The Decision of the European Court of Justice on Non-state Actors of Protection and Cessation

The European Court of Justice handed down an important judgment in March 2010 in *Abdulla and ors* in which it made findings (albeit in very brief terms) about the proper interpretation of Article 11(1)(e) of the EU Directive.[71] This was a referral of questions by the German Federal Administrative Court about the operation of Article 11(1)(e), which had arisen in five similar cases before the German courts. Among the questions referred to the ECJ was whether Article 11(1)(e) of the Directive is to be interpreted as meaning that refugee status ceases to exist if the refugee's well-founded fear of persecution, on the basis of which refugee status was granted, no longer exists and he also has no other reason to fear persecution. If cessation does involve more than absence of persecution, the Court was then asked to consider whether Article 11(1)(e) also requires that, in the country of the refugee's nationality:

('Goodwin-Gill Memorandum to UK House of Lords'), 2; Jane McAdam, 'The Qualification Directive: An Overview', in Karin Zwaan (ed.), *The Qualification Directive: Central Themes, Problem Issues, and Implementation in Selected Member States* (Nijmegen: Wolf Legal Publishers, 2007), 7–29; European Council on Refugees and Exiles (ECRE), 'Information Note on the Council Directive 2004/83/EC of 29 April 2004 on Minimum Standards for the Qualification of Third Country Nationals and others in need of international protection', IN/10/2004/ext/CN, 1 October 2004 ('ECRE Information Note'), 7, http://www.ecre.org/resources/ECRE_actions/292 [accessed: 25 July 2012].

65 UNHCR Annotated Comments, 18. See also UNHCR comments on the European Commission's proposal to recast the Directive: UNHCR, 'UNHCR comments on the European Commission's proposal for a Directive of the European Parliament and of the Council on minimum standards for the qualification and status of third country nationals or stateless persons as beneficiaries of international protection and the content of the protection granted (COM(2009)551, 21 October 2009, 5, at http://www.unhcr.org/4c5037f99.pdf [accessed: 25 July 2012].

66 ECRE Information Note, 7.

67 Goodwin-Gill Memorandum to UK House of Lords, 32.

68 Ibid., 36.

69 Ibid., 38.

70 Justice, 'Memorandum', UK House of Lords Select Committee on the European Union, July 2002, HL paper 156, 28th Report, 36; European Council on Refugees and Exiles, 'Memorandum', UK House of Lords Select Committee on the European Union, July 2002, HL paper 156, 28th Report, 40.

71 *Abdulla and ors*.

a. an actor of protection within the meaning of Article 7(1) of the Directive be present, and is it sufficient in that regard if protection can be assured only with the help of multinational troops;
b. the refugee should not be threatened with serious harm, within the meaning of Article 15 of the Directive, which leads to the granting of subsidiary protection under Article 18 of that directive; and/or
c. the security situation be stable and the general living conditions ensure a minimum standard of living.[72]

Prior to the European Court of Justice handing down its decision, UNHCR released a statement in 2008 detailing what it thought was the correct approach to cessation under Article 11(1)(e). It stated that, for the purpose of cessation, protection did not simply mean protection against persecution, but 'effective protection', which encapsulated, among other things, protection from serious harm and the right to a basic livelihood.[73] It also expressed concerns as to the notion of non-state agents providing 'protection' for the purpose of refugee law.[74]

The European Court of Justice handed down its opinion on the referrals in *Abdulla and ors* on 2 March 2010.[75] The Court held that the change of circumstances will be of a 'significant and non-temporary' nature, within the terms of Article 11(2) of the Directive, when the factors that formed the basis of the refugee's fear of persecution may be regarded as having been 'permanently eradicated'.[76]

It held that as part of this assessment 'the competent authorities ... may take into account, inter alia, the laws and regulations of the country of origin and the manner in which they are applied, and the extent to which *basic human rights* are guaranteed in that country'.[77] However, the Court limited those basic human rights to acts of persecution amounting to 'severe' violations of 'basic' human rights within the meaning of Article 9(1) of the Directive.[78]

---

72 The referred questions are set out in ibid., [43]. The referral also listed a third question relating to the standard of proof to be applied to claims based on new sources of persecution in the country of origin.

73 UNHCR Cessation Statement 2008, 8.

74 Ibid., 16.

75 *Abdulla and ors.*

76 Ibid., [73].

77 Ibid., [70]–[71] (emphasis added).

78 ECJ para. [73]. Article 9 provides that: '1. Acts of persecution within the meaning of article 1 A of the Geneva Convention must: (a) be sufficiently serious by their nature or repetition as to constitute a severe violation of basic human rights, in particular the rights from which derogation cannot be made under Article 15(2) of the European Convention for the Protection of Human Rights and Fundamental Freedoms; or (b) be an accumulation of various measures, including violations of human rights which is sufficiently severe as to affect an individual in a similar manner as mentioned in (a). 2. Acts of persecution as qualified in paragraph 1, can, inter alia, take the form of: (a) acts of physical or mental violence, including acts of sexual violence; (b) legal, administrative, police, and/or judicial measures which are in themselves discriminatory or which are implemented in a discriminatory manner; (c) prosecution or punishment which is disproportionate or discriminatory; (d) denial of judicial redress resulting in a disproportionate or discriminatory punishment; (e) prosecution or punishment for refusal to perform military service in a conflict, where performing military service would include crimes or acts falling under the exclusion clauses as set out in Article 12(2); (f) acts of a gender-specific or child-specific nature.'

The Court stated that having regard to the answer given to the first question and the information provided in the judgment, there was no need to explicitly answer the second question.[79] However, it made the following findings as to the applicability of non-state actors of protection to cessation that are significant for the issues raised in this chapter. The Court referred to Article 7(1), acknowledging that this 'does not preclude the protection from being guaranteed by international organisations, including protection ensured through the presence of a multinational force in the territory of the third country'.[80] The Court also noted that, pursuant to Article 7(2) of the Directive, the Member State wishing to apply cessation principles must verify that the relevant actor of protection has taken reasonable steps to prevent persecution of the individual concerned that the national concerned will have access to such protection if he ceases to have refugee status. However, in relation to both Articles 7(1) and (2), the ECJ simply reiterated the words of the provisions without explaining the tests that should be applied in greater detail. For instance, it gave no guidance as to what is meant by 'access' to the territory under Article 7(2) – does this simply mean the protecting body must be willing to provide protection to the individual, or does it also involve wider consideration of physical access to the area, and the reasonableness of that individual having to accept the protection of the body or organization concerned? This is significant, as there is very little case law on Article 7(2) and thus the legal test for the provision is undeveloped.

Further, although it reiterated that cessation requires a significant and non-temporary change in circumstances (as is required by Article 11(2) of the Qualification Directive[81]), it did not link this requirement with Article 7. It did not address whether the existence of protection in a 'substantial part' of a country may require relocation of an applicant, the risk of refoulement from the 'safe' to 'unsafe' part of the territory and, indeed, whether internal localized protection was in fact consistent with the concept of *cessation* due to a change of circumstances; that is, can circumstances be said to have 'changed' if protection against persecution is being provided in only part of the country of origin?

In addition to this, the ECJ held that cessation does *not* involve consideration of risk of serious harm. This was primarily motivated by the need to keep the criteria for refugee status and complementary protection separate.[82] This is significant as Article 8 of the EU Qualification Directive, which sets out the criterion for IFA, explicitly provides for consideration of serious harm in relation to the IFA. In relation to the right to livelihood, the Court did not specifically address this question, given its findings that protection for the purpose of cessation meant protection against persecution and not a wider form of effective

[79] *Abdulla and ors*, [77].

[80] Ibid., [74].

[81] The need for durability of change in the country of origin is explicitly recognized in Article 11(2) of the Qualification Directive, which provides that States must consider whether the changes in the country are 'significant and non-temporary' before applying the cessation provisions.

[82] *Abdulla and ors*, [78–9]: 'in connection with the concept of "international protection", the Directive governs two distinct systems of protection, that is to say, firstly, refugee status and, secondly, subsidiary protection status, in view of the fact that Article 2(e) of the Directive states that a person eligible for subsidiary protection is one "who does not qualify as a refugee". Therefore, as there would otherwise be a failure to have regard for the respective domains of the two systems of protection, the cessation of refugee status cannot be made conditional on a finding that a person does not qualify for subsidiary protection status.'

protection advocated by UNHCR. Under the ECJ approach, therefore, it appears that denial of a right to livelihood is not a relevant factor for the purpose of cessation.

The findings of the ECJ in *Abdulla and ors* are significant as the use of non-state actors of protection in relation to *cessation* poses particular problems. These include the durability of change and whether there has indeed been the relevant change of circumstances that satisfies the cessation provisions when protection is being provided in only part of the country of origin. As to the first point, the question of the protection provided (or not provided) by non-state actors is particularly of concern in cessation cases because under the accepted tests for the changed circumstances cessation clause, changes are required to be fundamental, stable and durable.[83] However, the control exercised by non-state actors is often temporary and fluctuating in nature.[84] As such, they may open a refugee to a real risk of persecution and should not be considered as constituting effective protection for the purpose of cessation of refugee status.

UNHCR, in its 2003 Guidelines on Cessation, raises similar concerns, stating that cessation should not apply to regional safety:

> changes in the refugee's country of origin affecting only part of the territory should not, in principle, lead to cessation of refugee status. Refugee status can only come to an end if the basis for persecution is removed without the precondition that the refugee has to return to specific safe parts of the country in order to be free from persecution. Also, not being able to move or to establish oneself freely in the country of origin would indicate that the changes have not been fundamental.[85]

Indeed, some EU Member States do not permit cessation if protection is provided by non-state actors or within only a part of the country of origin.[86]

I now turn to make the case for greater linkages to be made between IFA and cessation in light of the foregoing discussion.

4. Analysis: The case for Greater Linkages between IFA and the Changed Circumstances Cessation Clauses

There are a number of links between IFA and the changed circumstances cessation clause. First, both the cessation and IFA deal with notions of safety and protection. Cessation under Article 1C(5) (and its EU equivalent) asks: have the circumstances in the refugee's country of origin changed such that they can no longer refuse to avail themselves of the protection

83 On the issue of the 'fundamental, stable and durable' test, see above, notes 21–22. See also Article 11(2) of the 2011 EU Qualification Directive.

84 See e.g. UNHCR Annotated Comments, 8.

85 UNHCR Cessation Guidelines 2003, [17].

86 European Commission Report on the Qualification Directive, 9–10 (at nn. 30–31). The following countries are mentioned: Austria, Germany, The Netherlands and Poland.

of their country of nationality? The IFA asks: even if the applicant faces a well-founded fear of persecution in part of the country of origin, is there another area of the country in which they do not face a well-founded fear of persecution, that is, where they are able to access protection? Thus both the IFA and the cessation clauses deal with persons who have established a well-founded fear of persecution in relation to their country of origin (or, in the context of the IFA, *part* of their country of origin).

However, as illustrated by the discussion above, the parallels between cessation and IFA become more significant in the context of non-state actors of protection. This is because if a decision on cessation is made on the basis that a non-state actor is providing protection in 'part' of the country of origin, then similar concerns to IFA arise in relation to the risk that the applicant may be driven for some reason (such as armed conflict or risk of harm) to flee to the *unprotected* part of the country. That is, cessation in this context raises similar concerns about the risk of internal refoulement that is raised by IFA – will the returnee be at risk of being forced out of the protected area? The importance of inter-country refoulement to IFA is raised in the Michigan Guidelines on IFA:

> Where the intensity of the harms specific to the proposed site of internal protection (such as, for example, famine or sustained conflict) rises to a particularly high level, even if not amounting to a risk of persecution, an asylum-seeker may in practice feel compelled to abandon the proposed site of protection, even if the only alternative is *return to a known risk of persecution* for a Convention reason elsewhere in the country of origin.[87]

Even if the person may not be physically forced out of the protected area, refoulement may be 'constructive' in nature – that is, the person may feel compelled to flee due to economic destitution or armed conflict or other forms of serious harm.

There is a second way in which IFA and cessation involve similarities. The way in which cessation has, to date, been applied by States involves the use of temporary residence permits of between three and five years' duration.[88] As a result, refugees to whom the cessation clauses are applied have generally resided in the asylum host state for a relatively long period of time, establishing social, economic and familial links in that country. During this time, circumstances in the refugee's country of origin may have changed drastically – there may be a new government, a changed social and economic structure, and the refugee may no longer have any family, friends or employment in his or her country of origin. In many cases, due to extended (and sometimes continuing) armed conflict within the country, the former refugee's home may also have been destroyed or taken over and local communities and other support networks may no longer be functioning.[89] In such situations it is arguable

[87] 'The Michigan Guidelines on the Internal Protection Alternative', 1999, [19], at: http://www.refugeecaselaw.org/documents/Internal_Protection.pdf [accessed: 25 July 2012] (emphasis added). Also published in (1999) 21 *Michigan Journal of International Law* 131–133.

[88] Article 24, 2011 EU Qualification Directive.

[89] For instance, as of May 2007, there were approximately 20,000 compensation claims before Kosovo courts arising from the destruction of property in 1999 and 2000: see Centre on Housing Rights and Eviction, 'Property Return and Restitution: Kosovo – Prepared for Review of Covenant Law Issues in Kosovo by the UN Committee on Economic, Social and Cultural Rights', 2008, at:

that the return of a refugee who has been residing in an asylum host state for a number of years and who has integrated to some extent in the country of asylum may be viewed as 'relocating' to their country of origin.

Similar parallels have been made by UNHCR in relation to the cessation and IFA provisions of the EU Qualification Directive. UNHCR notes:

> Article 8 of the Qualification Directive as well as Article 1(C)(5) of the 1951 Convention and Article 11(1)(e) of the Directive are based on the expectation of a *change of place of residence*. Article 8 relates to the availability of a relocation alternative within the country of origin, whereas the application of the 'ceased circumstances' clause refers the person to the protection of the country of origin and thereby may imply the return to that country. Given these similarities, the broad understanding of the term 'protection' in the context of internal protection is also relevant for the application of the 'ceased circumstances' clause.[90]

I note that consideration of cessation as involving relocation issues, particularly where the refugee has integrated into the asylum host state, was recognized in Executive Committee Conclusion 65. This Conclusion recommended that decision-makers give due consideration to the relocation needs of settled refugees in the country of asylum:

> (e) Recommends, so as to avoid hardship cases, that States seriously consider an appropriate status, preserving previously acquired rights, for persons who have compelling reasons arising out of previous persecution for refusing to re-avail themselves of the protection of their country and recommends also that appropriate arrangements, which would not put into jeopardy their established situation, be similarly considered by relevant authorities *for those persons who cannot be expected to leave the country of asylum, due to a long stay in that country resulting in strong family, social and economic links there.*[91]

This view was echoed in the original proposal for the 2004 EU Qualification Directive, which set out a 'compelling reasons' exception to cessation for change of circumstances. The Explanatory Memoranda to the Directive explained the inclusion as follows:

> The Member State invoking this cessation clause should ensure that an appropriate status, *preserving previously acquired rights*, is granted to persons who are unwilling to leave the country for compelling reasons arising out of previous persecution or experiences of serious and unjustified harm, *as well*

http://www2.ohchr.org/english/bodies/cescr/docs/info-ngos/COHREUNMIK.pdf [accessed: 25 July 2012]. See also UNHCR, *Update on Kosovo Crisis*, 1999, at: http://www.unhcr.org/3ae6b80f48.html [accessed: 25 July 2012].

90 UNHCR Statement on Cessation 2008, 15 (emphasis added).

91 UNHCR, Executive Committee Conclusion No. 69 (XLIII) – 1992 – Cessation of Status, para. (e), set out in UNHCR, *Addendum to the Report of the United Nations High Commissioner for Refugees*, 1 January 1993, A/47/12/Add.1 (emphasis added).

> *as to persons who cannot be expected to leave the Member State due to a long stay resulting in strong family, social and economic links in that country.*[92]

Because of these links between IFA and cessation, these concepts should be interpreted in a more integrated, holistic way – at least where decision-makers find that cessation has occurred when non-state actors provide protection in part of a country of origin. Moreover, it is incongruous that a reasonableness requirement applies in relation to relocation for a person applying for refugee status, but does not apply for cessation of a person who has actually been found to have had a well-founded fear of persecution and recognized as a refugee, particularly in cases where a refugee is being returned to their country of origin in cases of 'partial' cessation.

Thus I submit that the criterion for cessation should be informed by the test used for IFA. This should be done by utilizing a reasonableness approach for cessation similar to that utilized in IFA cases. This is particularly pressing given there is no 'compelling reasons' exception or other humanitarian principles for cessation applicable to contemporary refugees set out in the 1951 Convention and nothing to safeguard against internal refoulement of the ceased refugee back to the unprotected part of their country. This reasonableness element, like IFA, should include consideration of any risk of serious harm to the returning refugee and freedom from economic deprivation, that is, right to a subsistence minimum.[93]

I note, in relation to the issue of serious harm, that an applicant who is at risk of serious harm may (if they satisfy the required criteria) apply for complementary or humanitarian protection.[94] I also note that States have argued that refugee and complementary protection should be kept separate, an approach that is reflected in the separation of protection regimes in the EU Qualification Directive. However, I submit that, in some instances, this strict separation of refugee and complementary protection must be put aside. This has been done in the IFA test under Article 8 of the Qualification Directive. I submit that the same approach should be taken to similar situations, such as where internal refoulement is at issue, for instance, in cessation cases involving 'partial' protection by a non-state actor. In such situations, risk of serious harm should be a consideration.

---

92 Proposal for a Council Directive on minimum standards for the qualification and status of third-country nationals and stateless persons as refugees or as persons who otherwise need international protection, COM(2001) 510 final, Explanatory Memorandum, 24. Note that such an exception was not included in the 2004 EU Qualification Directive, but was so in the Recast 2011 version.

93 This echoes the approach taken by UNHCR: see UNHCR Cessation Statement 2008.

94 The criteria for complementary and humanitarian protection vary across jurisdictions. In the EU, the test is set out in Article 15 of the 2011 EU Qualification Directive. In Australia the *Migration Amendment (Complementary Protection) Act* 2011 provides for complementary protection based on 'significant harm'. However, humanitarian protection depends on the personal exercise of ministerial discretion by the Minister for Immigration and Citizenship.

5. Conclusions

A comparison of the legal tests used for cessation and IFA reflects that certain inequalities arise from the way in which these two tests currently operate. These concerns also raise the difficulties and dangers of the concept of 'localized persecution' and 'territorial protection'. Compartmentalizing persecution and protection to one area of a country is problematic, particularly given the nature of contemporary armed conflict and in light of the trend towards extending the concept of 'protection' to include non-state actors. There is a particular problem raised by the extension of 'protection' capabilities to non-state actors in relation to the 'changed circumstances' cessation clause. That is, return of a refugee on the basis that circumstances in their country of origin have 'changed' when a non-state actor is providing protection, and perhaps in only *part* of a country, is by definition only 'change' going to availability of protection in *part* of the country – that is, there is only *partial cessation*. This has the risk of exposing the returning refugee (or 'former refugee' once cessation is applied to him or her) to a risk of refoulement to the unprotected area of the country if the required safeguards are not in place.

As discussed above, the legal test for the IFA has safeguards put in place to prevent internal refoulement, including the reasonableness criterion. The IFA allows relocation only if the applicant's relocation will be 'reasonable', and includes consideration of whether s/he will be at risk of serious harm and socio-economic factors. However, because of the limited interpretation of the cessation test and, in particular, the compelling reasons exception, there is no such protection or exception for persons returned to a part of a country under cessation.

I submit that a refugee being returned to their country of origin under cessation under Article 1C(5) and its EU equivalent should be considered using similar principles to those applicable to IFA, particularly in situations where the protection is said to be provided by a non-state actor who controls a 'part' of the territory of the country of origin. This should include humanitarian considerations, which some jurisdictions have recognized as part of the IFA, such as the 'reasonableness' of return, consideration of the risk of serious harm and socio-economic conditions such as the right to livelihood. Such safeguards will assist in ensuring that refugees sent back to any 'safe' area will not be at risk of refoulement to the 'unsafe' territory within their country. It is strongly arguable that there should be a reasonableness criterion applied to partial cessation cases due to non-state protection. But more broadly, consideration should also be given to applying reasonableness or other humanitarian principles in all cessation cases, particularly where a refugee has resided in an asylum host state and integrated into society over a three-to-five-year period and during which time they have lost family, economic, social links and housing in their country of origin. Such a move would also reflect a more integrated approach to protection across these two concepts. Indeed, it is arguable that greater consistency of the legal tests developed under Article 1 of the 1951 Convention is a desirable aim in and of itself to prevent the Convention becoming fragmented and so that its original aims – the protection of refugees – not be thwarted by piecemeal or contradictory tests for refugee status.

References

Goodwin-Gill, Guy and Jane McAdam, *The Refugee in International Law* (Oxford: Oxford University Press, 3rd edn, 2007).

Hathaway, James C., *The Law of Refugee Status* (Toronto: Butterworths, 1991).

Hathaway, James C., *The Rights of Refugees under International Law* (Cambridge: Cambridge University Press, 2005).

Hathaway, James C. and Michelle Foster, 'Internal Protection/Relocation/Flight Alternative as an Aspect of Refugee Status Determination', in Erika Feller, Volker Türk and Frances Nicholson (eds), *Refugee Protection in International Law: UNHCR's Global Consultations on International Protection* (Cambridge: Cambridge University Press, 2003), 357–417.

McAdam, Jane, 'The Qualification Directive: An Overview', in Karin Zwaan (ed.), *The Qualification Directive: Central Themes, Problem Issues, and Implementation in Selected Member States* (Nijmegen: Wolf Legal Publishers, 2007), 7–29.

Marx, Reinhard, 'The Criteria of Applying the "Internal Flight Alternative" Test in National Refugee Status Determination Procedures' (2002) 14(2 and 3) *International Journal of Refugee Law* 179–218.

O'Sullivan, M., 'Acting the Part: Can Non-State Entities provide Protection under International Refugee Law?' (2012) 24(1) *International Journal of Refugee Law* 1–26.

O'Sullivan, Maria, 'Withdrawing Protection under Article 1C(5) of the 1951 Convention: Lessons from Australia' (2008) 20(4) *International Journal of Refugee Law* 586–610.

Sanders, Lauren, 'Finding a Reasonable Alternative: An Integrated Approach to Refugee Law, Relocation and the Internal Flight Alternative', ANU College of Law Research Paper No. 09-05, vii, at: http://ssrn.com/abstract=1365043 [accessed: 14 December 2010].

Storey, Hugo, 'The Internal Flight Alternative Test: The Jurisprudence Re-examined' (1998) 10(3) *International Journal of Refugee Law* 499–532.

Türk, Volker and Nicholson, Frances, 'Refugee Protection in International Law: An Overall Perspective', in Erika Feller, Volker Türk and Frances Nicholson (eds), *Refugee Protection in International Law: UNHCR's Global Consultations on International Protection* (Cambridge: Cambridge University Press, 2003), 3–45.

UNHCR, 'The International Protection of Refugees: Interpreting Article 1 of the 1951 Convention relating to the Status of Refugees', (2001) 20(3) *Refugee Survey Quarterly* 77–104.

UN High Commissioner for Refugees, *UNHCR Statement on the 'Ceased Circumstances' Clause of the EC Qualification Directive*, August 2008, at: http://www.unhcr.org/refworld/docid/48a2f0782.html [accessed: 14 December 2010].

11 ASHGATE RESEARCH COMPANION

Sharing Responsibility for Asylum Seekers and Refugees in the Asia Pacific Region

Savitri Taylor[1]

Introduction

The Australian government has recently responded to the domestic political problem created by the irregular maritime arrival of asylum seekers in Australia by publicly proposing what it refers to as a 'regional protection framework'. While the government makes no secret of the fact that its own ultimate goal is to discourage irregular travel to Australia, its contention is that the regional protection framework as a concept is about something more than this. According to the government, it is about countries within and possibly outside the Asia Pacific region taking 'collective responsibility for displaced persons in the region' through cooperative arrangements for assessment of refugee claims, provision of resettlement for those found to be refugees and a safe return home for the rest, and provision of accommodation in the meantime.[2]

This chapter outlines the current situation with respect to asylum seekers and refugees in the Asia Pacific region and considers whether implementation of the Australian government's proposal would do much to improve refugee protection or burden sharing between states. After answering that question in the negative, the chapter discusses in more general terms the prospects for achieving better refugee protection and more equitable burden sharing in the region through inter-state dialogue and civil society engagement.

---

[1] Associate Professor, Law School, La Trobe University. The author is grateful to the Institute for Human Security, La Trobe University, for the Teaching Relief Fellowship that enabled her to research and write this chapter. The content of this chapter reflects the law and facts as they stood in December 2010.

[2] Andrew Metcalfe, Australian Department of Immigration (DIAC), Testimony in Commonwealth of Australia, Senate Legal and Constitutional Committee, *Proof Committee Hansard: Supplementary Estimates*, 19 October 2010, 103–4.

Background

At the end of 2009, 37 per cent of the world's 10.4 million refugees[3] and 4 per cent of the world's approximately 1 million asylum seekers were to be found in the Asia Pacific region.[4] As shown in Table 11.1, many countries in the region have not been prepared to make a formal commitment to refugee protection under international law,[5] but some of these countries are at least parties to CAT[6] and/or ICCPR.[7] These treaties impose *non-refoulement* obligations that are not limited in application to 'refugees' within the meaning of the Refugee Convention and Protocol and are not subject to exceptions.[8] Moreover, the principle of *non-refoulement* is now most likely part of customary international law and thus binding even on states that are not parties to any of the treaties previously mentioned.[9] While most countries in the region have made little or no attempt to incorporate these *non-refoulement* obligations into domestic law, many do at least allow UNHCR to engage in mandate activities within their territory and for the most part honour the principle of *non-refoulement* in relation to UNHCR mandated refugees. That said, however, there have been many instances of *refoulement* from regional countries, including from those which are parties to the Refugee Convention.[10]

The guarantee that persons at risk of serious human rights violations in their country of origin will not be returned to that country is beyond question an important one. However, every person displaced from home also needs and wants a durable solution to their predicament. In the case of some lucky individuals, voluntary repatriation may become available as a durable solution because the circumstances that caused them to take flight cease to exist. Most, though, will be unable to repatriate within a reasonable timeframe. What these individuals require in

---

3 Includes persons in refugee-like situations.

4 Office of the United Nations High Commissioner for Refugees (UNHCR), *Statistical Yearbook 2009* (October 2010), Annex Table 1. The figures relate to 'Asia and the Pacific' as defined for UNHCR operational purposes. The countries and territories included in this operational region are listed in Table 11.1. Unless otherwise stated, all references in this chapter to the Asia Pacific region are to the region as so defined.

5 In other words, they have not been prepared to become party to the Convention Relating to the Status of Refugees (adopted 28 July 1951, entered into force 22 April 1954) 189 UNTS 137 ('Refugee Convention') and/or Protocol Relating to the Status of Refugees (adopted 31 January 1967, entered into force 4 October 1967) 606 UNTS 267 ('Refugee Protocol'). The key obligation imposed by these treaties is that of *non-refoulement*. Refugee Convention art. 33(1) provides that, subject to an exception set out in art. 33(2), no state party shall return ('*refouler*') a 'refugee' to a place where he or she is at risk of being persecuted. The definition of 'refugee' is contained in Refugee Convention art. lA(2), as modified by Refugee Protocol art. 1(2), and subject to the exclusion clauses in Refugee Convention arts 1D, 1E and 1F.

6 Convention against Torture and Other Cruel, Inhuman or Degrading Treatment or Punishment (adopted 10 December 1984, entered into force 26 June 1987) 1486 UNTS 85.

7 International Covenant on Civil and Political Rights (adopted 19 December 1966, entered into force 23 March 1976) 999 UNTS 171.

8 Guy Goodwin-Gill and Jane McAdam, *The Refugee in International Law* (3rd edn OUP Oxford 2007), 301–9.

9 Ibid., 345–54; cf. James Hathaway, *The Rights of Refugees under International Law* (CUP Cambridge 2005), 363–7, who questions the correctness of the orthodox position.

10 For example, Cambodia engaged in *refoulement* in 2009: UNHCR, *Global Report 2009* (June 2010), 238.

Table 11.1 Treaty ratifications/accessions at 6 December 2010

Country or territory	Refugee Convention and/or Protocol	CAT	ICCPR
Afghanistan	Y	Y	Y
American Samoa (US)	Y	Y	Y
Australia	Y	Y	Y
Bangladesh		Y	Y
Bhutan			
Brunei			
Burma			
Cambodia	Y	Y	Y
China	Y	Y	
Cook Islands			
East Timor	Y	Y	Y
Fiji	Y		
Federated States of Micronesia			
French Polynesia (France)	Y	Y	Y
Hong Kong SAR (China)		Y	Y
India			Y
Indonesia		Y	Y
Iran	Y		Y
Japan	Y	Y	Y
Kazakhstan	Y	Y	Y
Kiribati			
Kyrgyzstan	Y	Y	Y
Laos			Y
Macau SAR (China)	Y	Y	Y
Malaysia			
Maldives		Y	Y
Marshall Islands			
Mongolia		Y	Y
Nauru			
Nepal		Y	Y
New Caledonia (France)	Y	Y	Y

New Zealand (including Tokelau)	Y	Y	Y
Niue			
Northern Mariana Islands (US)	Y	Y	Y
North Korea			Y (but purported withdrawal)
Pakistan		Y	Y
Palau			
Papua New Guinea (PNG)	Y		Y
Philippines	Y	Y	Y
Samoa	Y		Y
Singapore			
Solomon Islands	Y		
South Korea	Y	Y	Y
Sri Lanka		Y	Y
Tajikistan	Y	Y	Y
Thailand		Y	Y
Tonga			
Turkmenistan	Y	Y	Y
Tuvalu	Y		
Uzbekistan		Y	Y
Vanuatu			Y
Vietnam			Y

Note: United Nations Treaty Collection Database, Status of Treaties, at http://treaties.un.org/pages/ParticipationStatus.aspx, accessed 7 December 2010; emails from UNHCR Regional Office for Australia, New Zealand, PNG and the Pacific to author (10 and 23 December 2010).

order to restart their lives is integration in the country of initial refuge or resettlement in a third country (whether as refugees or migrants). Unfortunately, not even the Refugee Convention places a duty on states to provide either of these durable solutions.[11]

[11] The Refugee Convention does provide in art. 34:

The Contracting States shall as far as possible facilitate the assimilation and naturalization of refugees. They shall in particular make every effort to expedite naturalization proceedings and to reduce as far as possible the charges and costs of such proceedings.

However, art. 34 gives rise to a fairly weak right: Hathaway, *Rights of Refugees under International Law*, 163 and 252.

Most countries in the Asia Pacific region refuse to contemplate the local integration of refugees as a general rule,[12] though some are, or have been, willing to do so in relation to specific caseloads or individuals.[13] As for resettlement, the only countries in the Asia Pacific region with an annual refugee resettlement programme are Australia (6,000 places),[14] Japan (pilot of 90 places over 2010–12),[15] and New Zealand (750 places).[16] Worldwide there are only 24 countries that make refugee resettlement places available to UNHCR on an annual basis,[17] though there are a few more that do on an ad hoc basis.[18] This means that only 10 per cent of the refugees who have been assessed by UNHCR as needing resettlement globally can actually be resettled each year.[19] In view of this fact, UNHCR tries to use resettlement not only as a means of providing durable solutions for individuals but as a strategic tool to resolve protracted refugee situations and open up protection space.[20] In the Asia Pacific region, UNHCR is using resettlement strategically in relation to, for example, a 20-year-old caseload of Bhutanese living in camps in Nepal and an even older caseload of Burmese living in camps in Thailand. Nepal, with 17,442 departures, and Thailand, with 16,835 departures, were, in fact, the world's top two countries for resettlement departures in 2009.[21]

Despite the fact that departures from the region accounted for 52 per cent of the global total in 2009,[22] the gap between resettlement need and resettlement departures remains greatest in the Asia Pacific region.[23] The consequence is that most asylum seekers and refugees in the region are caught in indefinite limbo in developing countries that are unable and/or unwilling

---

12 Exceptions are Australia, New Zealand, Philippines and South Korea: UNHCR, 'Milestone in Asia as Ethiopian Man is Granted South Korean Citizenship' (*News Stories*, 24 March 2010), at http://unhcr.org/4baa1cd56.html, accessed 28 December 2010.

13 For example, PNG is willing to grant citizenship to Melanesian refugees (Harlyne Joku, 'West Papuan Refugees Need Help', *Post Courier* [PNG, 24 June 2010], 7), India has granted citizenship to Hindu Sikh Afghans (UNHCR, *Global Report 2009*, 213), and Vietnam has agreed to grant citizenship to a long-term population of formerly Cambodian refugees (UNHCR, *Update on UNHCR's Operations in Asia and the Pacific – 2010* [30 September 2010], at http://unhcr.org/4ca5de459.html, accessed 28 December 2010).

14 Chris Evans, then Australian Minister for Immigration, 'Budget 2010–11 – Humanitarian program' (Media Release, 11 May 2010), at http://www.minister.immi.gov.au/media/media-releases/2010/ce03-budget-10.htm, accessed 28 December 2010.

15 UNHCR, 'Welcome to Japan: First Asian Country Joins UNHCR's Resettlement Programme' (*News Stories*, 28 September 2010), at http://www.unhcr.org/4ca1dbe66.html, accessed 28 December 2010.

16 Kirsty Needham, 'Key Rules Out Raising Quota', *The Age* (Melbourne, 7 July 2010), 5.

17 The US (80,000 places) and Canada (11,200 to 14,000 places) have by far the largest of these programmes: US Department of State, US Department of Homeland Security and US Department of Health and Human Services, *Proposed Refugee Admissions for Fiscal Year 2011: Report to The Congress* (2010) 6; Immigration and Citizenship Canada, *Annual Report to Parliament on Immigration* (2010), 9. Australia's programme is third in size.

18 UNHCR, *Projected Global Resettlement Needs 2011* (June 2010), 1 and 34.

19 Ibid., 1.

20 Ibid., 8.

21 Ibid., 47.

22 Ibid., 48.

23 Comparison of resettlement need figures in UNHCR, *Refugee Resettlement: Performance Outcomes 2007 and Global Projections 2009* (June 2008) with resettlement departure figures in UNHCR, *Projected Global Resettlement Needs 2011*, for 2009.

to fulfil in a satisfactory manner the protection role thrust upon them. Generally speaking, asylum seekers and refugees in these countries are neither provided with access to adequate food, housing, healthcare and other basics of life nor given work rights, though many work illegally in order to survive.[24] In many countries, asylum seekers and refugees also face various kinds of mistreatment at the hands of authorities and/or local communities.[25]

From the perspective of host countries the state of affairs is equally unsatisfactory. The default position is that all costs of providing protection fall on the countries that asylum seekers and refugees manage to enter and remain in. The costs tend, therefore, to fall disproportionately on the countries closest to refugee source countries. At the end of 2009, the vast majority of the Asia Pacific region's 3.9 million refugees were being hosted by Pakistan (45 per cent) and Iran (27 per cent). Bangladesh, China, India, Nepal and Thailand also hosted substantial numbers.[26] In addition to being regarded as an economic burden, asylum seekers and refugees are often lumped in together with other uninvited non-citizens and regarded by host countries as a threat to national security and/or the cause of other political or social problems.[27]

Although the majority of asylum seekers and refugees in the Asia Pacific region remain in the country in which they first seek asylum, some move on in an irregular manner.[28] In some cases, these individuals have actually been expelled or turned away by the country which they previously lived in or tried to enter. In most cases, however, the onward movement occurs because the individuals in question lack effective protection in the country of first asylum or tire of waiting for durable solutions to be found for them and decide to take matters into their own hands.[29] Australia is often a target destination for these irregular onward movers, the most visible of whom are those who arrive by boat. Between 29 September 2008[30] and 12 December 2010 (the date of writing), about 9,090 asylum seekers[31] have arrived irregularly in Australia by boat, with most, though not all, coming via Indonesia.

Although the majority of irregular maritime arrivals have been found to be refugees and granted protection visas, the Australian public has tended to focus not on their need for protection but on the threat they pose to Australia's ability to 'decide who comes to this country and the circumstances in which they come'.[32] This focus has been encouraged by the conservative side of Australian politics with a view to obtaining electoral advantage. For this

---

24 UNHCR, 'Mixed Migration in the Asia Pacific Region' (Bali Process Workshop on Regional Protection, Resettlement and Repatriation, Bali, 7–8 June 2010), at http://www.baliprocess.net/files/UNHCR%20BaliProcess%20ppt%207%20June.ppt, accessed 27 December 2010; People's Empowerment Foundation (PEF), *Refugee Protection in ASEAN: National Failures, Regional Responsibilities* (November 2010).

25 See e.g. PEF, *Refugee Protection in ASEAN*; UNHCR, *Global Report 2009*.

26 UNHCR, *Statistical Yearbook 2009*, Annex Table 1.

27 UNHCR, *Global Report 2009*.

28 UNHCR, *Statistical Yearbook 2009*, 39.

29 Ibid.

30 This date marked the beginning of what Australians refer to as the 'fifth wave' of such arrivals after a lull of a few years.

31 Figure calculated from information contained in media releases by the Australian Minister for Home Affairs.

32 John Howard, then Australian Prime Minister, Address (Federal Liberal Party Campaign Launch, Sydney, 28 October 2001), at www.pandora.nla.gov.au/pan/10052/20030821-0000/www.pm.gov.au/news/speeches/2001/speech1311.htm, accessed 12 December 2010.

reason, asylum seekers who travel irregularly to Australia by boat are regarded by the federal Labor government as a political problem in need of a solution.

The Australian Regional Protection Framework Proposal

In a speech delivered on 6 July 2010, the Australian Prime Minister, Julia Gillard, raised the possibility of establishing a 'regional processing centre' for asylum seekers in East Timor.[33] She explained:

> The purpose would be to ensure that people smugglers have no product to sell. A boat ride to Australia would just be a ticket back to the regional processing centre.
>
> It would be to ensure that everyone is subject to a consistent, fair, assessment process. It would be to ensure that arriving by boat does not give anybody an advantage in the likelihood that they would end up settling in Australia or other countries of the region.[34]

The Labor government insisted that this was not a proposal to reinstate the previous Liberal/ National Coalition government's notorious Pacific Solution[35] in another guise. The main way in which the proposal was asserted to be different from the Pacific Solution was that UNHCR participation and regional support were to be integral elements of the overall scheme.[36] According to the government, the proposal was, in fact, part of Australian efforts to create 'a sustainable, effective regional protection framework'.[37]

A regional protection framework of some sort had been on the Australian government's agenda since well before Prime Minister Gillard's 6 July speech.[38] However, the proposal that a regional processing centre, whether in East Timor or elsewhere, be part of such a framework

33 Julia Gillard, Australian Prime Minister, 'Moving Australia Forward' (Lowy Institute speech, Sydney, 6 July 2010), at http://www.pm.gov.au/node/6876, accessed 8 December 2010.

34 Ibid.

35 Pursuant to Memoranda of Understanding (MOUs) signed with the governments of Nauru and PNG, the previous Australian government established processing facilities in Nauru and in PNG to which it took asylum seekers intercepted while attempting to enter Australian waters without authorization. The two facilities were administered by the International Organization for Migration (IOM), under contract with the Australian government, and the protection claims of persons taken to them were considered by officers of DIAC. In February 2008, a couple of months after taking office, the Labor government brought an end to the Pacific Solution but did not repeal the legislation that enabled its implementation.

36 Stephen Smith, then Australian Foreign Minister, cited in 'Smith Rejects Nauru Asylum Option' (*ABC Online News*, 14 July 2010), at http://www.abc.net.au/news/stories/2010/07/14/2952840.htm, accessed 8 December 2010.

37 Gillard, 'Moving Australia Forward'.

38 See e.g. Arja Keski-Nummi, DIAC, Testimony in Commonwealth of Australia, Senate Legal and Constitutional Committee, *Official Committee Hansard: Budget Estimates*, 28 May 2009, 20.

caught most people outside the government by surprise. Although the Prime Minister indicated in her speech that she had already raised the possibility of a regional processing centre in East Timor with the President of East Timor, the Prime Minister of New Zealand and the United Nations High Commissioner for Refugees, it soon became clear that nothing approaching proper consultation had taken place. As for other regional countries, they had not been consulted at all prior to the speech.

UNHCR's response to proposals such as the Australian one, which are 'currently under review in several regions', has been to say that 'UNHCR is supportive as long as such centres work as a complement to, not as a substitute for, national asylum systems, and are fully embedded in more comprehensive arrangements'.[39] The East Timorese government has also been willing to consider Australia's processing centre proposal despite vocal opposition to the proposal from other political actors in the country.[40] Although President Ramos-Horta, who has carriage of political negotiations on the East Timorese side, has said that East Timor is approaching the issue as a purely humanitarian one,[41] the Australian government has pledged that the establishment of a centre will bring economic and other benefits to East Timor.[42] It has also stated clearly that East Timor will not be expected to contribute to the funding of a centre.[43] The Australian government has referred to the 'possibility of other contributors' as part of a regional approach, but has admitted that it will probably bear 'a significant proportion of the cost of a centre'.[44]

There are many significant details that remain to be resolved between Australia and East Timor. First, agreement needs to be reached on the holding capacity of the processing centre. The minimum capacity Australia has in contemplation is 500 asylum seekers and the maximum is 2,000.[45] Second, agreement needs to be reached on a site for the centre and the living conditions of asylum seekers taken to it.[46] Third, agreement will have to be reached on the maximum time that can lapse between an individual being brought to the centre and being taken to a final destination.[47] The time limit President Ramos-Horta has floated is three years.[48] Finally, agreement will have to be reached on the lifespan of the centre itself. For its

39 Erika Feller, Assistant High Commissioner for Protection, UNHCR, 'Protection: Rule of Law 60 Years On' (61st Session of UNHCR EXCOM, 6 October 2010), at http://www.unhcr.org/4cac7f2f9.html, accessed 26 December 2010.

40 Stephen Fitzpatrick et al., 'Timor Asylum Plan a Legal Minefield' *The Australian* (7 July 2010), 1; Michelle Grattan and Tom Allard, 'Nauru Opens Way to Take Refugees', *The Age* (Melbourne, 14 July 2010), 8.

41 José Ramos-Horta, East Timorese President, Press Conference (Dili, 12 October 2010), at http://www.minister.immi.gov.au/media/speeches/2010/cb101012.htm, accessed 13 December 2010.

42 Alison Carabine, Interview with Chris Bowen (Radio National, 13 October 2010), at http://www.minister.immi.gov.au/media/speeches/2010/cb101013.htm, accessed 13 December 2010.

43 James Larsen, Australian Ambassador for People Smuggling Issues, Testimony in Commonwealth of Australia, Senate Foreign Affairs, Defence and Trade Committee, *Proof Committee Hansard: Supplementary Estimates*, 18 October 2010, 51.

44 Ibid.

45 Metcalfe, Testimony, 103.

46 Ibid., 102.

47 Ramos-Horta, Press Conference.

48 Sara Everingham and wires, 'Bowen, Ramos-Horta to Meet over Asylum Deal' (*ABC Online News*, 12 October 2010), at http://www.abc.net.au/news/stories/2010/10/11/3035506.htm, accessed 13 December 2010.

part, Australia seems to have fixed on ten years as being the shortest lifespan that will justify the investment.[49]

While East Timor is engaging seriously with the Australian proposal, it has not yet agreed that it will host a processing centre. From an Australian government perspective, though, the key to achieving its ultimate goal is simply the establishment of one or more processing centres *outside Australia*.[50] Although the government has somewhat restricted its options by specifying that being a party to the Refugee Convention and/or Protocol is a necessary qualification for a processing centre host,[51] finding such a host or hosts will probably be the easiest part of the exercise. A much harder feat will be avoiding a rerun of the Pacific Solution. The time wasted in a futile search for third-country resettlement places for those taken to Nauru and PNG, who were found to be refugees, simply resulted in most of them spending years in terrible conditions before eventually being brought to Australia. According to the Gillard government, a rerun will be avoided because the establishment of one or more processing centres will merely be one element of a regional protection framework. The other key element of such a framework from the Australian government's perspective is ensuring that after being taken to a processing centre on a temporary basis people can be moved quickly and on a permanent basis to some other place, which is not always Australia. In the case of people who are assessed and found not to be refugees, the other place would usually be their country of nationality. What about those found to be refugees, though? According to Australian government officials, a regional processing centre would be a place 'where resettlement countries would be active in seeking to consider people for resettlement'.[52]

Australia would, of course, be one of the countries considering refugees at the centre(s) for resettlement.[53] However, the Australian government's domestic political problem will not be solved if it ends up being the only country resettling refugees from the processing centre(s). As previously mentioned, apart from Australia the only country in the Asia Pacific region with a sizeable annual refugee resettlement programme is New Zealand. New Zealand's Prime Minister has agreed to discuss the Australian proposal but has said that New Zealand will not be increasing its annual refugee resettlement quota above the existing 750 places.[54] Clearly, Australia must be depending on countries outside the Asia Pacific region being willing to resettle from the processing centre(s) also.

There were 2,500 irregular maritime arrivals to Australia in the five months following the Prime Minister's 6 July speech.[55] If that rate of arrival or potential arrival is maintained, there would have to be implausibly rapid refugee status determination (RSD) followed by

---

49 Carabine, Interview with Chris Bowen.

50 Tony Jones, Interview with Chris Bowen (*Lateline*, 13 October 2010), at http://www.abc.net.au/lateline/content/2010/s3037741.htm, accessed 13 December 2010; Julia Gillard cited in Rowan Callick, 'Options Dwindle for East Timor Alternative', *The Australian* (9 July 2010), 5.

51 Gillard cited in Callick, 'Options Dwindle for East Timor Alternative'.

52 Metcalfe, Testimony, 104.

53 Larsen, Testimony, 53.

54 Needham, 'Key Rules Out Raising Quota'.

55 Scott Morrison, federal opposition immigration spokesperson, 'A Real Solution: An International, Regional and Domestic Approach to Asylum Policy' (Lowy Institute speech, 30 November 2010), at http://www.scottmorrison.com.au/info/speech.aspx?id=179&page=-1, accessed 14 December 2010.

resettlement or repatriation from a single 2,000-place regional processing centre for it to be possible to spirit away all boat arrivals or potential boat arrivals to that centre. It would appear, therefore, that multiple centres are required for the scheme to be viable at all. If a sufficient number of centres can be established, however, the Australian government's domestic political problem would be solved. The fact that asylum seekers taken to the processing centres will not necessarily be brought to Australia as permanent residents will create the appearance that the government is back in control of which refugees are allowed to settle permanently in Australia and which are not. The asylum seekers who are taken to the regional processing centres will be as well as or better off than they would have been otherwise. However, if all countries making resettlement places available adopt the New Zealand position of only doing so within their current resettlement quotas, nothing would have been done to address the enormous global gap between the need for resettlement places and their availability.[56] All that would have been accomplished is a change in the distribution of the gap across regions plus some further skewing away from the application of needs-based resettlement criteria[57] towards the application of politically determined resettlement criteria. In short, a regional protection framework, which does not involve an increase in the global availability of durable solutions, is just an Australian border protection framework dressed up in refugee protection language. If, on the other hand, implementation of Australia's proposal involves an increase in the total annual number of resettlement places available globally, then there will be a net gain in refugee protection but it will not be as great as the gain that could have been achieved with the same resources if cooperation were actually protection centred.

Protection-centred cooperation would start from the premise that every person in need of international protection must receive it somewhere. This entails having access to fair procedures for determining international protection claims;[58] obtaining a durable solution within a reasonable timeframe, if found to be in need of international protection;[59] and receiving effective protection in the meantime. Admittedly, there is some uncertainty surrounding the minimum requirements that must be met in order for protection to be described as 'effective'. Logically, individuals are entitled to, and should receive, the benefit of all human rights and other obligations under any treaty or other source of international law owed to them by the state in which they are living. The problem is, of course, that different states are bound by different sets of international legal obligations. Thus, if the question is whether an individual

56 UNHCR, *Projected Global Resettlement Needs 2011*, 1. At present, Australia counts protection visas granted to successful onshore asylum seekers against the 7,750 places it makes available annually under its non-refugee humanitarian resettlement programme. If individuals who would otherwise have been processed in Australia and granted protection visas are processed at a regional centre and then resettled to Australia under its refugee resettlement programme, there will, in fact, be an effective reduction in the global availability of refugee resettlement places.

57 For these criteria see UNHCR, *Resettlement Handbook* (November 2004 edn), ch. 4.

58 Erika Feller, 'Asylum, Migration and Refugee Protection: Realities, Myths and the Promise of Things to Come' (2006) 18 *International Journal of Refugee Law* 3–4, 509–36, at 534. See also core principles suggested by dialogue participants in Fayssal Mekdad, Deputy Foreign Minister, Syrian Arab Republic, and Erika Feller, 'Report of the Co-Chairs on Breakout Session 2: International Cooperation, Burden Sharing and Comprehensive Regional Approaches' (Dialogue on Protection Gaps and Responses, Geneva, 8–9 December 2010).

59 UNHCR, 'Policy on Refugee Protection and Solutions in Urban Areas' (September 2009), para. 153, at http://www.unhcr.org/4ab356ab6.pdf, accessed 22 December 2010.

is justified in engaging in irregular onward movement from one country to another, there is something to be said for answering that question by reference to a uniform set of standards. UNHCR takes the view that individuals can only be considered to have 'effective protection' of the kind that enables onward movement to be characterized as unnecessary if they are safe not only from *refoulement* but also from risks to life, persecution, torture or other cruel and degrading treatment, arbitrary detention and arbitrary expulsion; have 'adequate and dignified means of subsistence'; and have the unity of their family respected.[60] For the purposes of this chapter, UNHCR's view will be accepted.

It makes more sense from a protection-centred perspective to apply the resources that would be needed to build regional processing centres, to intercept irregularly moving asylum seekers, and to transport them to the centres, towards the goal of ensuring every asylum seeker has equal access to the three elements of international protection wherever they happen to be. As for any extra resettlement places that Australia and other countries are prepared to make available, it would make more sense from a protection-centred perspective for the places to be made available to the individuals most in need of resettlement.

The other perspective from which the Australian proposal needs to be assessed is that of burden sharing between states. Article 55 of the Charter of the United Nations requires the United Nations to promote:

> b. solutions of international economic, social, health and related problems and international cultural and educational cooperation; and
> c. universal respect for, and observance of, human rights and fundamental freedoms for all without distinction as to race sex, language or religion.

Pursuant to article 56 of the Charter, all members of the United Nations have 'pledged themselves to take joint and separate action in cooperation with the Organization for the achievement of the purposes set forth in article 55'. It can be argued, therefore, that international cooperation and solidarity, in fact, 'involve international obligations of a prime nature'.[61] The argument is bolstered by the long line of key instruments subsequently adopted by the international community that have likewise emphasized international cooperation and solidarity, such as the United Nations Millennium Declaration.[62] Moreover, there are innumerable international instruments specifically relating to refugees and asylum seekers that call for responsibility and burden sharing between states on the basis of this foundational principle of international cooperation and solidarity, including the Final Act of the Conference of Plenipotentiaries on the Status of Refugees and Stateless Persons, the preamble of the Refugee Convention, article 2(2) of the Declaration on Territorial Asylum,[63] and various conclusions of UNHCR

60 Ibid. UNHCR actually includes access to fair determination procedures and a genuine prospect of a durable solution within a reasonable time frame as requirements of 'effective protection' instead of separating out those requirements as has been done in this chapter.

61 UN Human Rights Council, 'Report of the Independent Expert on Human Rights and International Solidarity' (2009) UN Doc. A/HRC/12/27, para. 21.

62 UN Human Rights Council, 'Report of the Independent Expert on Human Rights and International Solidarity' (2007) UN Doc. A/HRC/4/8, paras 16 and 20.

63 UNGA Res. 2312(XXII) (14 December 1967).

EXCOM.[64] Given that these statements of principle have been accompanied by state practice of burden sharing from ad hoc schemes like the Comprehensive Plan of Action on Indo-Chinese Refugees (CPA) to the institutionalization through UNHCR of third-country resettlement, there is a strong argument that a requirement of burden sharing in relation to asylum seekers and refugees is now a principle of customary international law.[65]

One question that arises in the present context is whether burden sharing should be institutionalized at a regional and/or global level. States appear to have a marked preference for pursuing regional rather than global burden-sharing arrangements 'due to the increased flexibility they provide to adapt to regional and national specificities'.[66] The problem is that less than global arrangements could well operate at the expense of non-participants by shifting burdens onto them. The problem is not, however, unsolvable. All that is needed is that states acknowledge a requirement for any regional burden sharing arrangement to complement rather than undermine burden sharing at a global level and act accordingly.[67] The requirement would seem to follow logically from the fact that the refugee-specific principle of burden sharing is derived from the foundational principle of *international* cooperation and solidarity.

The next question that arises in relation to burden sharing is how costs and burdens ought to be distributed between states. The principle of international solidarity requires global challenges to 'be managed in a way that distributes the costs and burdens fairly in accordance with basic principles of equity and social justice'.[68] In relation to economic costs, this suggests that wealthier states should contribute more in absolute dollar terms than poorer states because a dollar contributed by a wealthy state has less negative impact on the welfare of its citizens than a dollar contributed by a poor state has on the welfare of its citizens.[69] However, difficulties arise when attempts are made to descend below this level of abstraction to exactly quantify and then determine the formula by which to distribute the costs of asylum provision.[70]

For example, one of the indicators of asylum provision burden used by UNHCR is refugees to GDP (PPP) per capita. As shown in Table 11.2, the asylum provision burden of the Asia Pacific region's main host countries appears on this indicator to far exceed that of the

---

64 See e.g. UNHCR EXCOM Conclusion No. 52 (XXXIX) 'International Solidarity and Refugee Protection' (1998); UNHCR EXCOM Conclusion 100 (LV) 'International Cooperation and Burden and Responsibility Sharing in Mass Influx Situations' (2004).

65 See e.g. B. S. Chimni, 'Development and Migration' in T. Alexander Aleinikoff and Vincent Chetail (eds), *Migration and International Legal Norms* (TMC Asser The Hague 2003), 255–68, at 266–7.

66 Mekdad and Feller, 'Report of the Co-Chairs on Breakout Session 2'.

67 UNHCR, 'Annual Theme: International Solidarity and Burden-Sharing in all its Aspects: National, Regional and International Responsibilities for Refugees' (7 September 1998), UN Doc. A/AC.96/904, para. 30.

68 UN Millennium Declaration, UNGA Res. 55/2, UN GAOR 55th Session Supp No. 49 UN Doc. A/55/49 (2000) para. 6.

69 Christopher D. Stone, 'Common but Differentiated Responsibilities in International Law' (2004) 98 *American Journal of International Law*, 276–301, at 292.

70 The term 'asylum provision' is here being used compendiously to refer to provision of protection pending durable solutions and/or durable solutions.

Table 11.2 Asylum provision burden at end 2009

Country	Refugees to 1 USD GDP (PPP) per capita
Australia	0.6
Bangladesh	163.9
China	51.1
India	67.3
Iran	98.6
Japan	0.1
Nepal	100.6
New Zealand	0.1
Pakistan	745.1
South Korea	0.0
Thailand	13.0

Note: Data taken from UNHCR, *Statistical Yearbook 2009*, Annex Table 24.

region's four high-income OECD countries (Australia, Japan, New Zealand and South Korea)[71] in economic terms.

However, these refugees to GDP (PPP) per capita figures on their own are a very contestable indicator of the comparative economic burden of asylum provision. For example, Australia's asylum provision burden has been calculated on the basis that it was host to a mere 22,548 refugees at the end of 2009.[72] However, this estimate has been arrived at in a rather peculiar fashion. Since 2007, UNHCR has estimated the refugee population of industrialized countries by adding up the number of onshore asylum seekers who have been granted refugee or complementary protection by those countries in the previous ten years.[73] The assumption made is that after ten years the individuals in question would have received citizenship status and would therefore have ceased to be refugees.[74] Moreover, resettled refugees are not included in the estimate.[75] By contrast, the figures used for developing countries are usually

[71] World Bank, 'Country and Lending Groups', at http://data.worldbank.org/about/country-classifications/country-and-lending-groups#OECD_members, accessed 8 December 2010.

[72] Ibid., Annex Table 1.

[73] UNHCR, 'Estimating Refugee Populations in Industrialized Countries' (*Statistical Online Population Database: Sources, Methods and Data Considerations*, 1 January 2007), at http://www.unhcr.org/statistics/STATISTICS/45c06c662.html#ESTIMATING_REFUGEE_POPULATIONS, accessed 16 December 2010. Prior to 2007, the cut-off was ten years for European countries and five years for the traditional countries of immigration: ibid.

[74] UNHCR, *Statistical Yearbook 2009*, 15–16.

[75] UNHCR, 'Estimating Refugee Populations in Industrialized Countries'. They were included prior to 2007: ibid.

UNHCR's refugee registration figures. This means that a given individual will be included in a developing host country's refugee population figure until he or she is repatriated, resettled, or actually granted host-country citizenship. In light of the foregoing, Australia could reasonably complain that, as well as being denied credit for resettling refugees, it is being penalized for providing asylum seekers with the durable solution of local integration (which developing countries generally refuse to provide). By the same token, however, developing countries could argue that UNHCR refugee registration figures are a poor base off which to calculate their asylum provision burden given that, in the usual case, only a fraction of all refugees present in a country actually register with UNHCR.

At a more fundamental level, it is arguable that looking at refugees hosted to GDP (PPP) per capita figures can create a misleading impression of comparative asylum provision burden because of the embedded assumption that every refugee imposes an equal economic cost on the hosting state. In fact, some refugees, for example those with high medical needs, impose higher than average costs on hosting states while others with wealth or productive capacity may actually confer an economic benefit on hosting states.[76]

Finally, it needs to be kept in mind that physical hosting of refugees and asylum seekers is not the only way in which a country can share the economic burden of asylum provision. The other way in which burden sharing can take place is through a state making financial contributions towards refugee protection in the territory of other states. In Australia's case, the AusAID budget for 2010–11 allocates AUD 16 million to UNHCR core funding[77] and the DIAC budget for 2010–11 allocates a further AUD 6.8 million to 'initiatives to address the situation of displaced persons and promote sustainable returns'.[78] In addition, Australia has arrangements in place with Indonesia, PNG and East Timor pursuant to which the authorities of those countries intercept persons attempting to travel irregularly to Australia and New Zealand and Australia funds IOM to provide care and maintenance for those intercepted pending determination of any protection claims and repatriation or resettlement as the case may be.[79] DIAC's budget for 2010–11 allocates an amount of AUD 30.2 million for the funding of these arrangements and any similar arrangements that may be established with other regional countries in the future.[80]

Notwithstanding the room for disputation opened up by attempts to quantify and compare state contributions, the rest of this chapter will proceed on the assumption that any reasonable attempt to do so would lead to the conclusion that Australia is not yet shouldering its fair share of the economic burden of asylum provision in the region. Since Australia is not proposing to

---

76 Tally Kritzman-Amir, 'Not in My Backyard: On the Morality of Responsibility Sharing in Refugee Law' (2009) 34 *Brooklyn Journal of International Law* 2, 355–93, at 379.

77 Stephen Smith and Bob McMullan, then Parliamentary Secretary for International Development Assistance, 'Australia's International Development Assistance: A Good International Citizen' (Ministerial Budget Statement, 11 May 2010), 57–8.

78 Commonwealth of Australia, 'Budget Related Paper No. 1.13: Immigration and Citizenship Portfolio' (*Portfolio Budget Statements 2010–11*, 2010) 33, at http://www.immi.gov.au/about/reports/budget/budget10/pbs/2010-11-pbs-full.pdf, accessed 16 December 2010.

79 DIAC, Answer to Question 20 Taken on Notice at Additional Budget Estimates Hearing: 9 February 2010, at http://www.aph.gov.au/senate/committee/legcon_ctte/estimates/add_0910/diac/20_qon.pdf, accessed 16 December 2010.

80 Commonwealth of Australia, 'Budget Related Paper No. 1.13', 55–6, 59.

shift the economic costs of asylum provision to East Timor, it would be going too far to say that it would be in violation of the burden sharing principle if it established a regional processing centre there. However, it is difficult to see how the present Australian proposal will make much of a contribution towards actually lessening any inequities in the current distribution of the region's asylum provision burden. At a Senate hearing, DIAC officials were asked whether 'any consideration had been given to the thousands of people in camps on the Thailand–Burma border [being] transferred to the regional processing centre'.[81] This was a reasonable question given the Australian government's official position that the centre is proposed as part of a regional protection framework with the intention that other regional countries will be able to send to it asylum seekers who have been selected on the basis of criteria to be determined as part of the negotiation of the framework.[82] The Secretary of DIAC answered:

> We have largely been thinking about people who come from beyond the region and who move through the region. We are not talking about the fact that there are, of course, thousands of displaced people in the Asia–Pacific region. This is very much around the people who have been seeking to come to Australia. It is about people moving in an irregular fashion from outside this part of the world – Afghanistan, the Middle East, Sri Lanka – and who are moving through this region primarily with the objective of seeking asylum in a developed Western country.[83]

In giving this answer, the Secretary clearly started with the outcome Australia wishes to achieve, that is, a processing centre outside Australia to which asylum seekers, who have travelled, or are likely to travel, irregularly to Australia can be taken, whether from Australia or elsewhere. Obviously, using up the capacity of the centre in accommodating asylum seekers who do not fit this profile, for example the Burmese presently living in camps in Thailand, would run counter to this purpose. On the other hand, saying that such asylum seekers should be excluded from a regional processing centre simply because their admission would not be of benefit to Australia would risk alienating the countries that Australia needs to keep on side. With those regional sensitivities no doubt in mind, the Secretary tellingly shifted his definition of the Asia Pacific region to exclude Afghanistan, which he previously said was part of the region, the Middle East, though he previously said that Iran and Iraq were part of the region, and Sri Lanka, though he previously said that India, which is also in South Asia, was part of the region.[84] Having temporarily redefined the region, he was able to say that Afghanistan, Iran, Iraq and Sri Lanka are all countries outside the region and thus have something in common beyond being the main source countries of irregular maritime arrivals to Australia. It is unlikely that other countries in the region (in whatever way defined) will be fooled by such sophistry.

---

81 Senator Cash, Question in Commonwealth of Australia, Senate Legal and Constitutional Committee, *Proof Committee Hansard: Supplementary Budget Estimates*, 19 October 2010, 106.

82 Metcalfe, Testimony, 104.

83 Ibid., 106.

84 Ibid., 105.

From the Australian government's perspective, the key regional countries (apart from potential processing centre hosts) are countries through which asylum seekers travel to reach Australia.[85] The government envisages a regional protection framework as consisting in practice of 'an interlocking series of arrangements' with these countries which build on existing arrangements.[86] Ever since the 6 July speech, Australia has been pursuing high-level bilateral discussions with Indonesia and Malaysia in particular but with little to show for it thus far. Indonesia has agreed to further discussions about a regional protection framework occurring bilaterally and through the Bali Process on People Smuggling, Trafficking in Persons and Related Transnational Crime (Bali Process).[87] However, the Indonesian President has indicated that he is yet to be convinced that a regional processing centre is a good idea.[88] In a similar vein, all that has been secured from Malaysia is an acknowledgement that regional cooperation is desirable and an agreement to continue dialogue on the Australian proposal.[89] Malaysia's Deputy Prime Minister has indicated that Malaysia would need a lot more information about costs, funding and other such matters before stating a formal position on the proposal.[90]

Australia and East Timor are presently formulating a concrete proposal for a regional processing centre that can be put to the next Ministerial meeting of the Bali Process to be held in February 2011 or thereabouts.[91] Since regional countries have little incentive to participate in a regional protection framework that yields no benefit for them, it can be assumed that the proposal put to the meeting will include, or be accompanied by, offers of more Australian aid to those countries whose cooperation Australia regards as being indispensable. The Australian Prime Minister has obliquely conceded as much, though she has avoided public discussion of details.[92] In short, any regional deal, or regionally endorsed bilateral deals, actually negotiated by Australia will probably lead to Australia bearing a greater share of the regional asylum provision burden than is presently the case. The question is whether Australia should, pursuant to such a deal or deals, be free to host more refugees and/or provide more financial support to substitute hosts as it sees fit to make up its fair share of the regional asylum provision burden, subject only to the consent of substitute hosts.

---

85 Metcalfe, Testimony, 104.

86 Ibid., 105.

87 Julia Gillard and Susilo Bambang Yudhoyono, Indonesian President, 'Indonesia–Australia Joint Statement' (2 November 2010) para. 8, at http://www.austembjak.or.id/jakt/JS2010.html, accessed 24 December 2010.

88 Susilo Bambang Yudhoyono, Joint Press Conference (Jakarta, 3 November 2010), at http://www.pm.gov.au/node/6989, accessed 24 December 2010.

89 Julia Gillard, Press Conference (Kuala Lumpur, 1 November 2010), at http://www.pm.gov.au/node/6985, accessed 24 December 2010.

90 Naomi Woodley, 'Malaysia Wants More Detail on Processing Centre' (*ABC Online News*, 1 November 2010), at http://www.abc.net.au/news/stories/2010/11/01/3054206.htm, accessed 24 December 2010.

91 Chris Bowen, Press Conference (Dili, 12 October 2010), at http://www.minister.immi.gov.au/media/speeches/2010/cb101012.htm, accessed 13 December 2010.

92 Matthew Franklin, 'Jakarta Says Let's Talk Later as PM Hands Over $500m', *The Australian* (3 November 2010), 6; Phillip Hudson, 'Gillard Could Fund East Timor Solution', *Herald Sun* (Melbourne, 3 November 2010), at www.heraldsun.com.au/news/national/gillard-could-fund-east-timor-solution/story-e6frf7l6-1225947008469, accessed 24 December 2010.

As previously mentioned, many countries, including Australia, regard asylum seekers and refugees as imposing not only economic costs but also political and social costs. Often such costs cannot easily be quantified or really be compensated for in financial terms. For example, a country that values ethnic, cultural or religious homogeneity may not regard a reduction in such homogeneity as compensable in financial terms. A country that believes that asylum seekers and refugees impose financially non-compensable costs will always prefer distribution of such individuals away from itself.[93] If such a country already hosts more asylum seekers and refugees than whatever its notional allocation would be under an equitable distribution scheme, it will prefer removing those asylum seekers and refugees from its territory to receiving financial contributions towards their support from other countries. If, on the other hand, it hosts fewer asylum seekers and refugees than its notional allocation under an equitable distribution scheme, it will prefer to keep things that way by paying other countries to host the difference. From the perspective of equitable burden sharing between states, there is no reason why states should not be allowed to give free rein to their host or pay preferences pursuant to a mutually agreed regime. From a refugee protection perspective, however, state preferences need to be set aside as far as is necessary to ensure that there are a sufficient number of asylum seeker and refugee hosts that all provide protection of an internationally acceptable standard.[94] It may be that a sufficient number of such hosts cannot be secured within a purely intra-regional scheme, keeping in mind that financial transfers alone will not eliminate corruption or remedy a myriad other ills that may adversely impact on the quality of protection available in many countries in the Asia Pacific and render it less than 'effective'.

Where To From Here?

All countries in the Asia Pacific region have some international legal obligations towards asylum seekers and refugees if only under customary international law. At the same time, many countries in the region feel overburdened by the asylum seekers and refugees they presently host. As Stephen Legomsky points out, 'burdens do not eliminate obligations',[95] but pursuant to the burden sharing principle the costs of discharging international protection obligations should be equitably shared. The term 'responsibility sharing' may be preferable to

---

93 Gregor Noll, 'Risky Games? A Theoretical Approach to Burden-Sharing in the Asylum Field', (2003) 16 *Journal of Refugee Studies* 3, 236–52, at 244.

94 James Hathaway and Alexander Neve, 'Making International Refugee Law Relevant Again: A Proposal for Collectivized and Solution-Oriented Protection' (1997) 10 *Harvard Human Rights Journal*, 115–211, at 144–5; Matthew J. Gibney, 'Forced Migration, Engineered Regionalism and Justice between States' in Susan Kneebone and Felicity Rawlings-Sanaei (eds), *New Regionalism and Asylum Seekers: Challenges Ahead* (Berghahn Books, 2007), 57–77, at 70.

95 Stephen Legomsky, 'Secondary Refugee Movements and the Return of Asylum Seekers to Third Countries: The Meaning of "Effective Protection"' (2003) 15 *International Journal of Refugee Law* 4, 567–677, at 607.

'burden sharing' insofar as it assists in keeping obligations as well as costs clearly in sight;[96] hence the use of the former term in the title of this chapter.

Other regions of the world, particularly Europe and Latin America,[97] are far further advanced along the path of responsibility sharing than the Asia Pacific region. However, it needs to be kept in mind that the Asia Pacific region is far more legally and culturally diverse and has far less of a regional consciousness than the regions aforementioned. In the Asia Pacific region the willingness to talk about refugee protection cooperation at a regional level is itself a huge step forward. It is true that South East Asian countries participated in the CPA in the 1970s and 1980s, but even though the CPA is often hailed as a success,[98] its messy and long-drawn endgame has made those countries more wary than otherwise of repeating the experience.

As previously mentioned, it seems that further dialogue on a regional protection framework will be occurring principally through the Bali Process. Forty-three countries and territories[99] and the key international organizations, IOM and UNHCR, are participants in the Bali Process.[100] The source countries of the major forcibly displaced populations in the Asia Pacific region[101] are represented, as are the major host countries. Moreover, several potential resettlement countries from outside the region have observer status,[102] as do many of the intergovernmental organizations and processes with relevant mandates.[103] Since the inauguration of the Bali Process at a Ministerial level conference held in February 2002, there

96 Ibid.

97 See discussion of Mexico Declaration and Plan of Action to Strengthen the International Protection of Refugees in Latin America in UNHCR, *Refugee Protection and International Migration in the Americas: Trends, Protection Challenges and Responses* (December 2009).

98 See e.g. Alexander Betts, *Protection by Persuasion: International Cooperation in the Refugee Regime* (Cornell University Press Ithaca NY 2009).

99 Afghanistan, Australia, Bangladesh, Bhutan, Brunei, Burma, Cambodia, China, East Timor, Fiji, France (New Caledonia), Hong Kong SAR, India, Indonesia, Iran, Iraq, Japan, Jordan, Kiribati, Laos, Macau SAR, Malaysia, Maldives, Mongolia, Nauru, Nepal, New Zealand, North Korea, Palau, Pakistan, PNG, Philippines, Samoa, Singapore, Solomon Islands, South Korea, Sri Lanka, Syria, Thailand, Tonga, Turkey, Vanuatu and Vietnam. NB: the participants in the Bali Process are not identical to the countries and territories included in UNHCR's operational definition of Asia and the Pacific in that they do not include Central Asian countries but do include Western Asian countries.

100 'Welcome to the Bali Process Website', at http://www.baliprocess.net/index.asp?pageID=2145831400, accessed 24 December 2010.

101 Afghanistan, Bhutan, Burma, China, Iraq, Sri Lanka and Vietnam: data for end of 2009 extracted from UNHCR Statistical Online Population Database, at www.unhcr.org/statistics/populationdatabase, accessed 30 July 2012. The Vietnamese refugees are a special case as most of them live in China and are described by UNHCR as 'well integrated' there: UNHCR, *Statistical Yearbook 2009*, Annex Table 1 n. 11.

102 The following countries with annual refugee resettlement programmes all have observer status: Canada, Denmark, Finland, Netherlands, Norway, Romania, Spain, Sweden, UK and US. Austria, Belgium, European Commission, Germany, Italy, Poland, Russia, South Africa and Switzerland also have observer status. See 'Welcome to the Bali Process Website'.

103 Asian Development Bank, Asia Pacific Consultations on Refugees, Displaced Persons and Migrants (APC), International Centre for Migration Policy Development, International Committee of the Red Cross, International Federation of Red Cross and Red Crescent Societies, Intergovernmental Consultations on Migration Asylum and Refugees, International Labour Organization, International Criminal Police Organization (Interpol), United Nations Development

have been two further Ministerial level conferences in April 2003 and April 2009.[104] There has also been an ongoing programme of activities involving, among others, justice, immigration, foreign affairs and police agencies in the Asia Pacific region, and many practical outcomes have been achieved in terms of participating countries deciding to change legislation, policy and/or practice in relation to issues such as human trafficking and people smuggling.[105]

Up until 2009, the Bali Process focused on transnational crime issues and left refugee and asylum-seeker issues to be dealt with primarily by the APC.[106] However, when the Rohingya crisis occurred,[107] Indonesia put discussion of a regional solution to that crisis not on the agenda of the APC but on the agenda of the April 2009 Bali Process Ministerial meeting. The Co-Chairs' statement, issued after the April 2009 Ministerial meeting, contained some very positive pronouncements on refugee protection.[108] In addition, an ad hoc working group process was established to develop regional responses to 'current situations concerning the irregular movement of people in the Asia–Pacific region'.[109] In July 2009, an Ad Hoc Group of representatives from Afghanistan, Australia, Bangladesh, Burma, India, Indonesia, Malaysia, Maldives, New Zealand, Pakistan, Sri Lanka, Thailand, UNHCR, IOM and UNODC met to consider responses to the irregular movement of Afghans, Sri Lankans and Rohingya.[110] At that meeting a proposal was made by Sri Lanka to establish a subgroup or cluster of the Ad

Program, United Nations Office on Drugs and Crime (UNODC) and the World Bank: 'Welcome to the Bali Process Website'.

[104] Bali Process, 'Conferences', at http://www.baliprocess.net/index.asp?pageID=2145831461, accessed 24 December 2010.

[105] Randall Hansen, 'An Assessment of Principal Regional Consultative Processes on Migration' (2010), IOM Migration Research Series no. 38.

[106] Bali Process Co-Chairs, 'The Bali Process on People Smuggling, Trafficking in Persons and Related Transnational Crime' (Global Commission on International Migration Workshop on Regional Consultative Processes, Geneva, 14–15 April 2005), at http://www.iom.int/jahia/webdav/site/myjahiasite/shared/shared/mainsite/microsites/rcps/gcim/Bali_Process_Co_chairs_Response.pdf, accessed 27 December 2010. The APC was established in 1996: APC, 'About Us', at http://www.apcprocess.net/aboutus.htm, accessed 26 December 2010. The participants in the process are Afghanistan, Australia, Bangladesh, Bhutan, Burma, Brunei, Cambodia, China, East Timor, Federated States of Micronesia, Fiji, Hong Kong SAR, India, Indonesia, Japan, Kiribati, Laos, Macau SAR, Malaysia, Mongolia, Nauru, Nepal, New Caledonia, Pakistan, PNG, Philippines, Samoa, Singapore Solomon Islands, South Korea, Sri Lanka, Thailand, Vietnam, IOM and UNHCR: 'APC Contacts', at http://www.apcprocess.net/apc_contacts.htm, accessed 26 December 2010. New Zealand was a participant until 2003: ibid. The Pacific Immigration Directors Conference has observer status: ibid.

[107] In late 2008/early 2009, over a thousand Rohingya were set adrift at sea by Thailand's armed forces. Some drowned but others ended up in India and Indonesia. See PEF, *Refugee Protection in ASEAN*, 4–5 and Asia Pacific Refugee Rights Network (APRRN), 'Joint Statement on the Treatment of Rohingya and Bangladeshi "Boat People" in Asia' (6 February 2009), at http://refugeerightsasiapacific.org/2009/02/06/joint-statement-1/, accessed 9 December 2010.

[108] 'Co-Chairs' Statement' (Third Bali Regional Ministerial Conference, 14–15 April 2009), paras 18 and 21.

[109] Ibid., paras 26 and 28.

[110] Commonwealth of Australia, Senate Foreign Affairs, Defence and Trade Committee, *Official Committee Hansard: Supplementary Budget Estimates*, 22 October 2009, 39 (Mr Woolcott, then Australian Ambassador for People Smuggling Issues).

Hoc Group to focus more specifically on particular caseloads starting with the Sri Lankans.[111] An Ad Hoc Group cluster group meeting was held in December 2009, one outcome of which was the holding of a Workshop on Protection, Resettlement and Repatriation in June 2010.[112] There was also another Ad Hoc Group meeting in June 2010 to review progress and to agree on further cooperative strategies for dealing with irregular movement of Afghans, Sri Lankans and Rohingya in particular.[113] At that meeting, senior officials agreed to a proposal for UNHCR to host a workshop on regional cooperation on refugees and irregular movements and IOM to host a workshop on repatriation and reintegration assistance. Those workshops were held in late November 2010. In short, the Bali Process is now the region's forum of choice for dealing with protection issues and is quite active in that regard.

Of the two regional forums available, the Bali Process is probably the better choice. First, all necessary governmental and intergovernmental players are already engaged in the Bali Process as either full participants or observers. This is not so in the case of the APC. Second, there is ongoing political commitment to the Bali Process. The APC process, by contrast, has long been moribund. Finally, and related to the second point, there is already some tangible evidence that dialogue facilitated through the Bali Process can achieve advances in refugee protection. For example, such dialogue led to Burma extending an MOU with UNHCR and Bangladesh agreeing to consider the provision of identity documents to unregistered Rohingya refugees.[114] While the APC also has some positive protection outcomes to its credit,[115] its impact has been disappointing when assessed in relation to the length of time the process has been in existence.

The disadvantage of dealing with protection issues through the Bali Process is the likelihood that states will give the goal of preventing transnational crime priority over the goal of improving asylum provision. UNHCR is doing what it can to keep protection issues on the Bali Process agenda and to advocate for improved asylum provision in the Asia Pacific region. However, UNHCR is ultimately constrained by the need to maintain good relations with the governments that fund it and that permit it to engage in mandate activities within their territories. UNHCR tends, therefore, to treat state preferences as given and simply tries to ensure that cooperative regimes negotiated by states for the purpose of realizing those preferences are 'protection sensitive'.[116] Unfortunately, regimes negotiated on the basis of

---

[111] 'Sri Lanka Proposal', at http://www.baliprocess.net/files/27-29%20July%202009/Sri%20 Lanka.pdf, accessed 26 December 2010.

[112] 'Workshop Co-Chairs' Summary' (Bali Process Ad Hoc Group Workshop on Protection Resettlement and Repatriation, Bali, 7–8 June 2010), at http://www.baliprocess.net/files/ Protection%20workshop%20Co-Chairs%20Summary%20(Final).doc, accessed 26 December 2010.

[113] Bali Process, 'Summary of Activities through September 2010', at http://www.baliprocess. net/files/summary%20of%20activies%20through%20September%202010.doc, accessed 26 December 2010.

[114] APRRN, *Final Report of Asia Pacific Consultation on Refugee Rights 2* (6–10 October 2009, Bangkok) 24, at http://refugeerightsasiapacific.org/pdf/FINAL_APCRR2_Report.pdf, accessed 26 December 2010; UNHCR, *Global Report 2009*, 217 and 220.

[115] Past coordinator of APC, 'Asia Pacific Consultations' (Global Commission on International Migration Workshop on Regional Consultative Processes, Geneva, 14–15 April 2005), at http:// www.iom.int/jahia/webdav/site/myjahiasite/shared/shared/mainsite/microsites/rcps/gcim/APC_ Fiji_Response.pdf, accessed 27 December 2010.

[116] See UNHCR, 10-Point Plan of Action on Refugee Protection and Mixed Migration (1 January 2007), at http://www.unhcr.org/4742a30b4.html, accessed 30 December 2010, and related

existing state preferences are likely to fall far short of the normative ideal in which every person with a need for international protection receives it in full measure somewhere.[117] For example, it is a lot easier to imagine the achievement of a regional protection framework that involves all refugees in the region having access to a durable solution in a timely fashion if local integration is an option on the table along with resettlement. However, local integration is an option that the Australian government has not dared even mention in the context of its regional protection framework proposal because state preferences in the region are so against the option.

Those best able and most willing to push for protection-centred as opposed to merely protection-sensitive cooperation between states, that is asylum seekers, refugees and the civil society organizations working with them, are not even given observer status let alone full participation rights in the Bali Process. This is a shortcoming of the process but not necessarily a fatal one. Civil society organizations do not need to be part of the Bali Process in order to influence it. What they do need to ensure is that the same government and intergovernmental organizations' representatives who are in rooms without them at Bali Process meetings are in rooms with them on other occasions listening to their views. This is more easily accomplished if civil society organizations are prepared to make tangible contributions to a regional protection framework, for example provision of services to asylum seekers and refugees.[118]

Civil society organizations need also to keep in mind that, while the Bali Process is the principal multilateral forum in which discussions relating to an Asia Pacific regional protection framework will take place, it is by no means the only one. For example, Prime Minister Gillard brought up Australia's regional protection framework proposal at both the Australia–ASEAN[119] Summit and the East Asia Summit.[120] The Australian government is also pursuing its regional agenda at the international level, for example at UNHCR EXCOM meetings.[121] Just as the Australian government is using every opportunity at every level to pursue its goals, civil society organizations should also. In South East Asia a particularly fruitful avenue may be the ASEAN Intergovernmental Commission on Human Rights.[122] In fact, given that the architecture for cooperation is more developed at the sub-regional than the regional level,[123] practical advances in refugee protection cooperation are most likely to be achieved at the sub-regional level in the first instance.

documents.

[117] Alexander Betts, 'What Does "Efficiency" Mean in the Context of the Global Refugee Regime?' (2006) 8 *British Journal of Politics and International Relations* 2, 148–73.

[118] These points were made by participants at a Round Table on Regional Issues hosted by the UNHCR Regional Office for Australia, New Zealand, PNG and the Pacific on 25 October 2010, which operated under Chatham House rules.

[119] Association of South East Asian Nations.

[120] Julia Gillard, Press Conference (Hanoi, 31 October 2010), at http://www.pm.gov.au/node/6980, accessed 26 December 2010.

[121] Commonwealth of Australia, 'General Statement' (61st session of UNHCR EXCOM, 4 October 2010) and Commonwealth of Australia, 'Statement on International Protection' (61st session of UNHCR EXCOM, 6 October 2010).

[122] UNHCR, *Update on UNHCR's Operations in Asia and the Pacific – 2010*; PEF, *Refugee Protection in ASEAN*, 19–20.

[123] Apart from the sub-regional forums already mentioned, the South Asian Association for Regional Cooperation and the Pacific Islands Forum come particularly to mind.

While it is important for civil society organizations to engage with state representatives at a supranational level, there is a limit to what they can achieve by so doing. Suppose, for example, that over time civil society organizations manage to persuade the government officials and politicians who participate in dialogues such as the Bali Process of the correctness of their views. The hope would be that those so convinced will match their policy making to their new convictions. However, this may not be a realistic hope if their old convictions were deeply rooted in domestic politics, as is usually the case in relation to matters such as border control and community membership. Domestic politics is a force more powerful than individual officials and politicians, as vividly illustrated by the ousting of Australia's incumbent Prime Minister, Kevin Rudd, by Julia Gillard on the ground, among others, that his handling of irregular maritime arrivals had not satisfied the Australian people.[124] At the end of the day, the only way to change a state's preferences is to change the preferences of the society within that state. This means that civil society organizations across the Asia Pacific region need to work within the various political and social contexts of their domestic societies to increase the sense of solidarity that members of their societies actually have with those in need of international protection. This may well be the work of a lifetime, but the only way to reach the destination is to start the journey.

References

Betts, Alexander, *Protection by Persuasion: International Cooperation in the Refugee Regime* (Cornell University Press Ithaca NY 2009).

Betts, Alexander, 'What Does "Efficiency" Mean in the Context of the Global Refugee Regime?' (2006) 8 *British Journal of Politics and International Relations* 2, 148–73.

Callick, Rowan, 'Options Dwindle for East Timor Alternative', *The Australian* (9 July 2010), 5.

Chimni, B. S., 'Development and Migration' in T. Alexander Aleinikoff and Vincent Chetail (eds), *Migration and International Legal Norms* (TMC Asser The Hague 2003), 255–68.

Everingham, Sara and wires, 'Bowen, Ramos-Horta to Meet over Asylum Deal' (*ABC Online News*, 12 October 2010), at http://www.abc.net.au/news/stories/2010/10/11/3035506.htm, accessed 13 December 2010.

Feller, Erika, 'Asylum, Migration and Refugee Protection: Realities, Myths and the Promise of Things to Come' (2006) 18 *International Journal of Refugee Law* 3–4, 509–36.

Fitzpatrick, Stephen et al., 'Timor Asylum Plan a Legal Minefield', *The Australian* (7 July 2010), 1.

Franklin, Matthew, 'Jakarta Says Let's Talk Later as PM Hands Over $500m', *The Australian* (3 November 2010), 6.

Gibney, Matthew J., 'Forced Migration, Engineered Regionalism and Justice between States' in Susan Kneebone and Felicity Rawlings-Sanaei (eds), *New Regionalism and Asylum Seekers: Challenges Ahead* (Berghahn Books Oxford 2007), 57–77.

124 Julia Gillard, Joint Press Conference with Deputy Prime Minister Wayne Swan (Canberra, 24 June 2010), at http://www.pm.gov.au/node/6855, accessed 27 December 2010; Gillard, 'Moving Australia Forward'.

Goodwin-Gill, Guy and Jane McAdam, *The Refugee in International Law* (3rd edn OUP Oxford 2007).

Grattan, Michelle and Tom Allard, 'Nauru Opens Way to Take Refugees', *The Age* (Melbourne, 14 July 2010), 8.

Hathaway, James, *The Rights of Refugees under International Law* (CUP Cambridge 2005).

Hathaway, James and Alexander Neve, 'Making International Refugee Law Relevant Again: A Proposal for Collectivized and Solution-Oriented Protection' (1997) 10 *Harvard Human Rights Journal*, 115–211.

Hudson, Phillip, 'Gillard Could Fund East Timor Solution', *Herald Sun* (Melbourne, 3 November 2010), at www.heraldsun.com.au/news/national/gillard-could-fund-east-timor-solution/story-e6frf7l6-1225947008469, accessed 24 December 2010.

Joku, Harlyne, 'West Papuan Refugees Need Help', *Post Courier* (PNG, 24 June 2010), 7.

Kritzman-Amir, Tally, 'Not in My Backyard: On the Morality of Responsibility Sharing in Refugee Law' (2009) 34 *Brooklyn Journal of International Law* 2, 355–93.

Legomsky, Stephen, 'Secondary Refugee Movements and the Return of Asylum Seekers to Third Countries: The Meaning of "Effective Protection"' (2003) 15 *International Journal of Refugee Law* 4, 567–677.

Needham, Kirsty, 'Key Rules Out Raising Quota', *The Age* (Melbourne, 7 July 2010), 5.

Noll, Gregor, 'Risky Games? A Theoretical Approach to Burden-Sharing in the Asylum Field', (2003) 16 *Journal of Refugee Studies* 3, 236–52.

Stone, Christopher D., 'Common but Differentiated Responsibilities in International Law' (2004) 98 *American Journal of International Law* 2, 276–301.

UNHCR, 'Estimating Refugee Populations in Industrialized Countries' (*Statistical Online Population Database: Sources, Methods and Data Considerations*, 1 January 2007), at http://www.unhcr.org/statistics/STATISTICS/45c06c662.html#ESTIMATING_REFUGEE_POPULATIONS, accessed 16 December 2010.

UNHCR, 'Milestone in Asia as Ethiopian Man Is Granted South Korean Citizenship' (*News Stories*, 24 March 2010), at http://unhcr.org/4baa1cd56.html, accessed 28 December 2010.

UNHCR, 'Mixed Migration in the Asia Pacific Region' (Bali Process Workshop on Regional Protection, Resettlement and Repatriation, Bali, 7–8 June 2010), at http://www.baliprocess.net/files/UNHCR%20BaliProcess%20ppt%207%20June.ppt, accessed 27 December 2010.

UNHCR, *Update on UNHCR's Operations in Asia and the Pacific – 2010* (30 September 2010), at http://unhcr.org/4ca5de459.html, accessed 28 December 2010.

UNHCR, 'Welcome to Japan: First Asian Country Joins UNHCR's Resettlement Programme' (*News Stories*, 28 September 2010), at http://www.unhcr.org/4ca1dbe66.html, accessed 28 December 2010.

Woodley, Naomi, 'Malaysia Wants More Detail on Processing Centre' (*ABC Online News*, 1 November 2010), at http://www.abc.net.au/news/stories/2010/11/01/3054206.htm, accessed 24 December 2010.

World Bank, 'Country and Lending Groups', at http://data.worldbank.org/about/country-classifications/country-and-lending-groups#OECD_members, accessed 8 December 2010.

12 ASHGATE RESEARCH COMPANION

Disowned in their Own Land: The Courts and Protection of the Internally Displaced Person

Geoffrey Care[1]

> The teeth may smile but the heart does not forget.[2]

> Saddam Hussain lashed back, driving over half a million … Kurds from their homes to barren mountains in southern Turkey. There lacking food, shelter or medical care they began dying at a rate of six hundred a day … Their best hope was to return home.[3]

Introduction

The plight of refugees comes top of the list of unpopular causes in Europe and North America. As a group they are either feared as a 'flood' or demonized as a source of terrorists; as an individual he is at best an embarrassment on the cadge from the wealthy. Loose talk of a fear of mass migration would have more credibility if it came from those countries which have the largest 'floods', mainly those on the Subcontinent and Africa. It was conveniently forgotten that the largest single movement in Europe after WWII was over 300,000 people from East Germany whom Western Germany classified as German citizens returning from East Germany at the fall of the Berlin Wall.

The picture we need to be looking at today, however, is that which shows us not only the refugees but those who are displaced from their homes yet have not crossed any national boundary. Their numbers have massively increased in every part of the world,

---

1 Geoffrey Care LLM (Lond). Former High Court Judge Zambia, Head Department of Law Jos University, Deputy Chief Adjudicator and Part-time Chairman IAT, Founding President IARLJ, Chairman Eurasylum. Any errors are mine.

2 A. Rice, *The Teeth may Smile but the Heart does not Forget: Murder and Memory in Uganda* (London: Metropolitan Books, 2009).

3 C. Powell, *My American Journey* (New York: Random House, 1995), p. 531.

Europe, the East and, predominantly, in Africa, and are predicted to increase tenfold over the next 40 years.[4]

These are the Internally Displaced who are outside any regime of protection such as is afforded to those who have crossed a national boundary and can claim – genuinely or not – to be refugees. This chapter addresses their plight. The protection of Internally Displaced Persons (IDPs) should be attended to by their own state, which has the prime duty to redress their situation and afford them fair treatment and a dignified life, the same as their fellow countrymen and women are entitled to enjoy.

This is the role that the law, lawyers and judges should be playing in this scenario, and it is this role that this chapter addresses.

First, one needs a definition of the phrase 'Internally Displaced Person', the IDP. A minister in Nigeria was reported in 2008 as telling a gathering in Abuja, 'there are a million refugees in Nigeria.' There weren't and there aren't; officially at least, there are less than 8,000 refugees in Nigeria,[5] but there are reported to be in excess of 1.3 million as of January 2011.[6] There is no legal definition of the IDP as there is for the refugee. However, a United Nations report, *Guiding Principles on Internal Displacement*, uses this definition:

> internally displaced persons are persons or groups of persons who have been forced or obliged to flee or to leave their homes or places of habitual residence, in particular as a result of or in order to avoid the effects of armed conflict, situations of generalized violence, violations of human rights or natural or human-made disasters, and who have not crossed an internationally recognized State border.[7]

Apart from the international conventions dealing with human rights, there are some regional conventions and treaties, such as the European Convention on Human Rights (together with its Court), the Inter-American Court, and in Africa the (O)AU Convention Governing the Specific Aspects of Refugee Problems in Africa, the African Charter on Human and Peoples' Rights (and its court), the Community Court of Justice of ECOWAS, as well as conventions

---

4 IPPC Report 1990; Stern Review 2006, via http://www.hm-treasury.gov.uk/ (accessed 17 August 2012); N. Myers, *Environmental Refugees: An Emergent Security Issue*, 13th Economic Forum Prague (2005), via www.osce.org (accessed 17 August 2012); C. Boano, R. Zetter and T. Morris, *Environmentally Displaced People: Understanding the Linkages between Environmental Change, Livelihoods and Forced Migration*, Forced Migration Policy Briefing 1, Refugee Studies Centre, Oxford Department of International Development, University of Oxford, para. 4.

5 The National Commission for Refugees Nigeria (NCRN), November 2010, and see Figures 12.2 and 12.3 below. However, these may be no more accurate than most other statistics.

6 Approximately 1,300,000; see Govt of Nigeria, 2011: 75. Increasing violence continues to cause internal displacement June 8 2012; for this and much more regarding the causes of displacement and the unreliability of the figures as well as the absence of any government structures, see iDMC at http://www.internal-displacement.org (accessed 17 August 2012).

7 *Guiding Principles on Internal Displacement* (OCHA English version), UN Doc E/CN.4/1998/53/Add 2.

such as the Kampala Declaration and similar initiatives.[8] I shall deal with those which have the most relevance to the theme of this chapter.

Few countries have national or domestic legislation upholding the rights of IDPs – there is none in Nigeria.[9]

In any approach to the numbers and the definition of the IDP the caveat of the Report by the Norwegian NGO Refugee Council should be borne in mind, that it is difficult to distinguish between those displaced by conflict and other causes;[10] this emerges with greater clarity when one looks more closely at any attempt to define 'hostilities' and 'natural disasters'.

By definition, where a state has significant numbers of its own people displaced within its boundaries it has often failed to exercise its contract with its people – that is, the constitutional obligations (generally in the context of the provisions of fundamental rights) towards them. As a result of the failure of the state to abide by its own such obligations, international humanitarian, political and military actors try to substitute for the state in providing aid at one end of the scale and military assistance to 'rebels' at the other. The UNHCR has had to divert its own resources to IDPs; they have become persons 'of concern to the UNHCR'.[11]

In both such cases the aid in the first or the interference in the second occurs, typically, under conditions of precarious security and fast-deteriorating humanitarian conditions. What is particularly vexing is that it is the state itself that, either deliberately or carelessly, has caused IDPs to be (or to remain) displaced in the first place. However, what if any practical alternatives are there? This chapter suggests there is one: Colombia has found it, but it seems a well-kept secret. I want to open it up and see how it fits, taking Nigeria as merely one example among many.

Almost every country has a constitution, which guarantees its citizens (if not all who are within its jurisdiction) a whole raft of fundamental human rights including, especially, the right to a dignified life and the right to access to the courts.[12] Regretfully, the courts are frequently inaccessible to those who have most need of them.

---

8 African Union Convention for the Protection and Assistance of Internally Displaced Persons in Africa (the Kampala Convention). This Declaration agrees, among other things, that states should enable IDPs to find durable solutions by promoting and creating conducive conditions for voluntary return, local integration or settlement elsewhere in the circumstances of safety and dignity and to ensure access to primary, secondary and post-secondary education, and other training for all children, including refugee and internally displaced children as well as access to informal and adult education by out-of-school girls and women. See also the Pact on Security, Stability and Development in the Great Lakes Region, June 2008, which committed them to incorporate the *Guiding Principles* into their domestic laws and policies, via http://www.internal-displacement.org (accessed 17 August 2012).

9 See note 6 above. But this is the point raised in this chapter: is there need for separate legislation when the constitution protects them? There are, as in Nigeria, disaster management agencies. If they do not work, what hope is there that more laws will be any more effective?

10 At p. 6, NRC, iDMC, via www.internaldisplacement.org (accessed 3 December 2010).

11 *Promotion and Protection of all Human Rights, Civil, Political, Economic, Social and Cultural Rights, including the Right to Development*, UNHRC 13 Sess. item 3 A/HRC/13/21 Kälin W Special Representative.

12 Article 33(1) of the Nigerian Constitution: 'Every person has a right to life, and no one shall be deprived intentionally of his life, save in execution of the sentence of a court in respect of

A proposed positive step towards a solution that this chapter therefore addresses is through the courts in their role as the guardians of the constitution. This proposition is examined by focusing on one continent, where 40 per cent of the IDPs are, and then honing in on one country, Nigeria by way of illustration; Nigeria has a written constitution and other regional supranational courts that can, in some circumstances, review decisions by the national courts.[13]

Background

One writer is quoted as follows:

> it is difficult to prevent displacement when once individuals and communities are under immense pressure in which life and dignity is at risk. When this happens, preventing displacement seems impossible. *It is then the responsibility of International Agencies to assist these people in the best way possible to reduce their sufferings.*[14]

However, it is not the prime responsibility of the International Agencies, and as the same writer opines later in the article, 'Therefore there is a need to build the capacity of national institutions and civil society groups in order to address the issues of internal displacement.'[15] Many states fail to have regard to the fundamental rights to their citizens or those within their protection in one way or another.[16] and hardly any state is without a contract with its people,

---

a criminal offence of which he has been found guilty in Nigeria.' See also Article 4 of the African Charter of Human and People' Rights and Article 21 of the Indian Constitution. Also, for example, in Ethiopia there is Judicial Review, in Rwanda a review by the Supreme Administrative Court, in Sudan and Tanzania. Haiti is an example of where the courts have failed in their role, it seems: *Ghana Thembekile Mankayi v AngloGold Ashanti*, Constitutional Court RSA 3 March 2011.

[13] In a country where there is no constitution, such as the UK, it is significant that a failure to have regard to fundamental human rights will go uncorrected if there is no further appeal. This is what happened in the case of the denial of admission to some East African Asians by successive UK Courts in the ECtHR under Article 3 of the ECHR. For a full and valuable discussion of the continued erosion of citizen rights see Satvinder S. Juss, 'The Slow Death of Citizenship Rights' (2007) 18 *King's Law Journal* 1, 95–118.

[14] T. Senesie, 'Profile and Challenges of Internally Displaced Persons in West Africa', at http://www.articlesbase.com/education-articles/profile-and-challenges-of-internally-displaced-persons-in-west-africa-3286111.html (accessed 17 August 2012) (emphasis added).

[15] Ibid.

[16] The UK has over the last half century (since the Commonwealth Immigrants Act 1952) proceeded to reverse the protection given by citizenship by birth that has been part of the law of England since 1290, to the extent that a person with dual citizenship can be deprived of his British Citizenship if the minister considers it is 'conducive to the public good' to do so; such is the combined effect of the Nationality, Immigration and Asylum Act 2002 s. 4 and the Immigration, Asylum and Nationality Act 2006 s. 56(1)(2). It has incidentally also adopted legislation that has brought Christians practising the basic tenets of their faith into court. Six bishops, former bishops and a former archbishop recently said, 'We are deeply concerned at the

a contract contained in a constitution that binds both state and subject. It is down to the courts to ensure that both abide by it.

Context

I have divided my approach into five sections in order to set the major proposition in context. The first section surveys the IDP population worldwide. The next two sections consider the major attributed causes of flight and impediments to their return or relocation and try to analyse some of what underlies these 'causes'.

The fourth section is a survey of how certain domestic and regional courts do, or could, operate. It considers whether something may be done to help the IDP and reduce the statistics that, as the quotation at the beginning states, hide a horrendous human rights stain on the world.[17]

Section 5 comprises a very brief glimpse into the future. It addresses the way in which regional bodies such as ECOWAS or SADC (the AU has so far recognized eight Regional Economic Communities, RECs) may affect IDPs in the years to come, exploring whether there are other ways to approach the issue.

1 The IDP Population Worldwide

a. IDPs Globally

The numbers of people displaced from home but still remaining in their own country worldwide has, as we have seen, swollen tremendously to some 25 million in 22 countries and on the African continent alone to at least 11.6 million people.

There are 11 countries in Europe with significant numbers of IDPs. In an island as small as Cyprus, which has been divided into Turkish and Greek sections, there have been as many as 200,000 IDPs since 1974. In the former Soviet Republic of Georgia, from which Stalin came, ignoring the colossal displacements of his era, there are at present said to be

apparent discrimination shown against Christians and we call on the Government to remedy this serious development ... There have been numerous dismissals of practising Christians from employment for reasons that are unacceptable in a civilised country': J. Wynne-Jones, 'Senior Bishops Call for End to Persecution of Christians in Britain', *The Telegraph*, 27 March 2010, at http://www.telegraph.co.uk/news/religion/7531293/Senior-bishops-call-for-end-to-persecution-of-Christians-in-Britain.html (accessed 17 August 2012).

[17] Since the first draft of this chapter was written, the National Judicial Institute of Nigeria has held a Workshop on Judicial Interventions in Refugee and Humanitarian Situations. This specifically addressed the need to be on the watch for cases involving the IDP and refugee in order to assist them where possible, a sensitization programme.

around 250,000 who have been accumulating since the 1990s. Turkey, which aspires to join the EU, has over one million displaced Kurds within the country.

On the Subcontinent, while the numbers are nowhere near those to be found at the time of Partition, there are still in Pakistan 1.2 million IDPs; and how many more caused by persistent interference by the Western Powers in Afghanistan?

In South America, there are 4.9 million IDPs in Colombia alone, and this country is the one example that suggests a way forward, in that it shoulders responsibility for IDPs domestically through its Constitutional Court.

In the Middle East, there are 2.76 million IDPs in Iraq, and in Israel the numbers are really not known – they are said to total anywhere between 150 and 420,000, all dispersed across Arab villages.

b. IDPs in Africa

In 2009 internal displacement in 21 African countries was estimated to be 11.6 million, representing more than 40 per cent of the world's total IDP population. But the statistics are largely estimates,[18] usually covering those settled in camps. The data are also incomplete because there are people one country may regard as IDPs but another will classify as refugees.

The numbers of IDPs in Sudan have reached a staggering 4.9 million.[19] Somalia, which has suffered from almost unremitting hostilities from within the country for 30 years, has 1.4 to 1.5 million individuals presently recorded as 'displaced' (though whether still in their own country or not is unclear). The North African situation in Algeria/Morocco is an example of the lack of certainty into which category someone who has been displaced falls, IDP or refugee –

> There are no IDPs in Morocco. Our beneficiaries in Morocco are refugees and asylum seekers. The MENA Excom update refers to our capacity-building programme with the authorities ... the LOU hasn't been signed and is on hold due to reasons related to the situation in Western Sahara and the stalled CBM family visits.[20]

In Nigeria, which has long and largely unpoliceable land borders with Chad, Niger and Cameroon, the numbers of those displaced, with region and reason, are set out in Tables

18 Office for the Coordination of Humanitarian Affairs, (UN)OCHA, 2010 January, cited by E. Ferris and C. Stark in *Internal Displacement in West Africa: A Snapshot* (January 2012), at http://www.brookings.edu/research/papers/2012/01/ecowas-ferris-stark (accessed 18 August 2012). See also iDMC, *Nigeria: Simmering Tensions Cause New Displacement in Middle Belt* (2 December 2010), via www.internal-displacement.org (accessed 18 August 2012).

19 Hopefully many can return to some home with the end of a 22-year-old war and the new state in Southern Sudan. Lord Hope in *Januzi v SSHD* [2006] UKHL 5: 'the assurance by the Sudanese Government about conditions in the camps and the voluntary returns of IDPs to their home areas are patently unreliable'.

20 The UNHCR position stated in an email to the author.

12.1, 12.2 and 12.3.[21] However, they can only be relied on as rough indications of the extent of the problem.

2. Causes and Effects of Displacement

Table 12.1 Statistics by state of IDPs in Nigeria: by conflict

State	Number	Cause	Years
Delta	300,000	Indigene/settlers/neglect	2001 to date
Bayelsa	80,000	Neglect	2001–2007
Akwa Ibom	150,000	Neglect/communal dispute	2001–2007
Cross River	225,000	Neglect/communal dispute	2001–2007
Benue	248,000	Conflict driven	2002–2007
Taraba	100,000	Conflict driven	2005

Source: NCFR Pilot Survey 2007

Table 12.2 Statistics by state of IDPs in Nigeria: ethno-religious/indigene settler-spread violence

State	Number	Year	Remark
Plateau	350,000	2007	Figures keep fluctuating
Kaduna	100,000	2006	
Kano	33,000	2007	
Adamawa	120,000	2006	
Taraba	50,000	2007	
Kwara	15,000	2006	

Source: NCFR Fact Finding 2007

a. Generally

Displacements due to man-made actions, generally some form of hostilities, figure predominantly in the public mind, and do indeed account for very large numbers of IDPs, but displacement originating in 'natural' disasters results in the greatest numbers. There are

[21] All table data provided by and obtainable from National Commission on Refugees but not published.

Table 12.3 Statistics by state of IDPs in Nigeria: estimates of evictees

Date and State	Community	Estimates of evictees
1990, Lagos	Maroko Town	300,000
1996, Lagos	Ijora Badia	2,000
1992, Kogi	Ajaokuta	30,000
2000, FCT, Abuja	Durumi	2,000
July, 2000, Rivers	Rainbow Town	1,000,000+
September, 1996, Lagos	Illubirin	30,000
March 8, 1999, Lagos	Kuramo	10,000
October 2003, Lagos	Oke-Eri, Ijora	6,000
April 2004, Lagos	Abule Ogunbiyi	3,000

predictions that the numbers of IDPs will rise to 200 million by 2050 due to desertification and other disasters.[22]

Hostilities can take many forms. Some form or classification seems necessary to explain the depths of the resulting problems. There are, of course, civil wars and violence by or against a ruling group, but those aside, the following divisions do appear from a look at Africa and Nigeria in particular. For example,

1. the demand for ethnic and cultural autonomy,
2. competing demands for land, money and power,
3. conflicts taking place between rival ethnic (or perhaps other) groups.

At other times, there is a failure to enforce the use of non-violent means of resolving disputes. Examples are Côte d'Ivoire and Chechnya (exacerbated by hostile actions from outside).

In Colombia, the causes of the exceptionally large numbers of IDPs can probably be explained by the following quotation:

> Uribe [the President]'s escalation of the war against narcotics traffickers has pushed Colombia's illegal armed groups to rural border zones, where they continue to harass, intimidate and coerce the largely indigenous populations of these regions. Moreover, Uribe's policies have resulted in an upsurge of violence and drug cultivation in neighboring countries such as Ecuador, Venezuela and Panamá, in addition to a stream of refugees fleeing to these countries.[23]

22 See above, note 4.

23 UN Special Representative Report 2010, para. 42. Although the 1998 Guiding Principles already identify natural disasters as one of the causes of internal displacement, natural disasters

Thus, classifying hostilities as 'the cause' gives little clue as to the category of conflict it fits into, how it arose, and what can best be done to resolve it. A close look at Nigeria reveals the reality behind the word 'hostilities'. Deprivation, poverty, discrimination coupled with attitudes causing divisions in the social fabric of society, uncaring selfish, corrupt and sometimes, at least in the past, downright villainous governance. The cause of their displacement could have been down to hostilities, but their predicament, when displaced, is often indistinguishable from displacement due to hostilities.[24]

African IDPs appear to be among the world's most defenceless. They are at high ongoing risk of armed attack, starvation, disease, including HIV/AIDS, sexual violence, trafficking and exploitation, especially in camps. There are many examples of enforced military recruitment, and even when the conflict is over, many IDPs find it difficult to return to their homes with any vestige of dignity. State infrastructure is often absent due to design (revenge?) or inertia. The internally displaced often face intolerance and are unable to access food, education and healthcare whether they stay or go; too often they lack documentation and without it they are at the mercy of any petty-minded official to deny them their basic rights.

One or more of the above causes (coupled with government involvement ranging from the lethargic to the causative) seem to be present, or to have been present, in situations of displacement and insecurity particularly in Jos and the Niger Delta in Nigeria as well as in Sri Lanka, Chechnya, Bosnia, Serbia, Biafra, Zimbabwe, Sierra Leone and the DRC. Ibeanu posits, 'when Western democratic institutions are merely transplanted into Africa, a dangerous gap often develops ... filled by various undemocratic and anti-democratic forces, such as ethnic, religious'.[25] To what extent this conclusion is generally right or not,[26] when extremists build upon ethnic fears they are polarized and produce a toxic brew of distrust and suspicion that leads to ethnic violence.

A close analysis will reveal just how intractable some of the causes of hostilities may be and how they may be tackled by good political leadership in the country[27] and by existing weapons in the state armoury.

b. Specifically – Nigeria

i. Benue

---

and their human consequences were for a long time not considered through the lens of internal displacement. And Burma after the Tsunami recently shows a record of negligence if not deliberate malice.

[24] A case for study in due course may be the strikes in Nigeria occurring while this revision is being written in January 2012.

[25] O. Ibeanu, 'Ethnicity and Transition to Democracy in Nigeria: Explaining the Passing of Authoritarian Rule in a Multi-ethnic Society', 5 *African Journal of Political Science* 2, 45–65, citing works by S. Sklar, O. Nnoli and M. Perham.

[26] The subject is not for this chapter, but it is worth bearing in mind that even though many Africans think of their tribe as an ancient and immemorial grouping it is not borne out in Ugandan, Sudanese or European history.

[27] My own observation is that few outsiders can understand the 'causes' sufficiently to be able to make a useful contribution, and it must be done internally.

There has been prolonged conflict between Tiv and Jukum in Benue and Taraba states (see Table 12.1), which is rooted in land disputes. This has led to uprooting large numbers of people (see Tables 12.2 and 12.3). In 2012 many Fulani along with their cattle fled from around Jos into Benue. Of course the cattle needed to feed, and perforce it had to be off land to which the Fulani had no claim. At first they were welcomed, but this soon turned to violence causing many deaths.

ii. Jos and the North

The history of violence in Jos (Plateau State) spans more than 78 years: 1932 to the time of writing.[28] A brief description of Jos is important to understand as an example of ethnic tensions[29] and to explain the origins and growth of ethnicity from colonial times until today. Plateau State is rural except for the capital Jos. It came into being by the establishment of the tin mines in 1910 and it has occupied the borders of Hausa (Muslim) penetration from the early nineteenth century.

Jos became an urban centre providing employment and markets, and it was there that the first documented violence occurred in 1932. Then again in 1945, when there were shortages and thus competition for commodities a southern group, the Igbo or Ibo, occupied the market areas, which the Hausa decided they wanted. The colonial administration backed the Hausa and there was a strike. The Igbo were at the time being led by emerging Nationalist leaders.

The next incident of violence occurred in post independence, 1966. A military coup had politicized and militarized ethnicity, and the violence was widespread and resulted in many thousands of Igbo being murdered by Northerners intent, so it is claimed, on ensuring that they, the Northerners, kept control in the Federation. It is significant that there was no public outcry generally by non-Igbo against such massacres. Violence erupted again in 2001 and 2009 and continues today. The foreign press, the Christian churches and many others have categorized the violence as religious.[30] This simplistic categorization of cause was not the finding of the Commission Reports into the disturbances. The press and indeed others exacerbate the situation by perpetuating any claim by some group especially the allegedly religious cult Boko Haram to be acting as part of an established religion.

The Lar Commission, reporting on the events leading up to the violence, found that 'the crises arose out of high suspicion among ethnic groups in Jos ... the quest for political power and land ownership as well as the misuse of religion for selfish interest.' Although the committee noted that religion was 'exploited by some individuals and groups to gain political popularity and support',[31] it stated that religion was not the main cause of the crises. It indicted

---

28 The wife of the Commander of the Special Task Force based in Jos was murdered on 4 December 2010. This is simply a very visible example of violence in the area. See *The Guardian*, 7 December 2010, p. 3.

29 O. Nnoli, *Ethnic Politics in Nigeria* (Enugu: Fourth Dimension, 1978).

30 It must be stated that this is currently exhibited in Nigeria, in the growing tendency for crisis to emerge between those perceived as so-called 'Indigenes' and those who are regarded as 'settlers' and therefore considered 'outsiders': see U.H.D. Danfulani, 'The Jos Peace Conference and the Indigene/Settler Question in Nigerian Politics' (2006), at http://www.ascleiden.nl/Pdf/paper-Danfulani.pdf (accessed 18 August 2012).

31 *White Paper on the Report of the Judicial Commission of Inquiry into the Civil Disturbances in Jos and its Environs* (September 2005), at http://saharareporters.com/content/white-paper-report-

the Plateau State Independent Electoral Commission for being partisan during the conduct of the local government election in Jos North.[32] The Anglican Archbishop of Jos[33] stated,

> What seems to be a recurring decimal is that over time, those who have in the past used violence to settle political issues, economic issues, social matters, intertribal disagreements, or any issue for that matter, now continue to use that same path of violence and cover it up with religion.[34]

What is important for our purposes is that every Judicial Commission of Inquiry and Presidential Advisory Report over the years into the Jos crises took successive governments to task for failing to address the root causes,[35] thereby allowing the politicians repeatedly to incite violence for their own ends.[36] The Reports contained strong recommendations to prosecute those found and named as instigators of the violence,[37] but no prosecutions have taken place.[38]

Here is a view that summarized the position:

> Simply put, the genesis of the crises in Jos is now generally seen a failure in leadership which then goes on to create an almost irreparable breakdown in relationships which then goes on to ensure an even greater failure in leadership – and the interminable circle goes on. But take away the effect of divisive leadership and put back respect, which is most often missing, and suddenly all the people on the Plateau become human. Talks of indigene and settler and the Christian–Muslim dichotomy had been placed on the back burner. It suddenly became clear to all that an unprovoked, gratuitously violent person is a disgrace to his religion, whatever it is; for, no religion will

judicial-commission-inquiry-civil-disturbances-jos-and-its-environs-septe (accessed 18 August 2012).

32 Report of the Presidential Advisory Committee on Jos Crises to President Goodluck Jonathan September 2010.

33 See Archbishop of Jos et al., 'Another Massacre in Nigeria: An Unending Cycle', *The Economist*, 11 March 2010

34 Benjamin Kwashi, 'In Jos We Are Coming Face to Face in Confrontation with Satan', Christianity Today, at http://www.christianitytoday.com/ct/2010/januaryweb-only/14-21.0.html (accessed 8 March 2010).

35 Judicial Commissions of Inquiry Justice Jummai Sankey, May 2001. Justice Niki Tobi Judicial Commission Report, September 2002. Justice C. Okpene, Federal Judicial Commission of Inquiry into Communal Conflicts in Benue, Nassarawa, Plateau and Taraba States, 2002. The Justice Ajibola Commission of Inquiry Report November 2009 f: 'The crises on the Jos Plateau are first and foremost a struggle over land [claims of ownership of Jos]. And crises centred over the politics of participation in Government by both "indigenes" and "settlers"': *Power and Privilege*.

36 The immediate causes of the September 2001 ethno-religious crises in Jos are three: struggle over political appointments, blockage of streets for the purposes of praying, and the expansion of Shariah laws that introduced rather severe punishments for hard crimes in 12 Northern States of Nigeria: GUKAS 2001.

37 GOBAK 2009.

38 Even today no website clearly gives unrestricted access to the full terms of any of the Reports, nor are the recommendations published or gazetted in a white paper.

> ever support punishing an innocent person or countenance the punishment of even the guilty by one not entitled to do so.[39]

The violence in Jos has not ceased; indeed, it has escalated even if it may seem to have been overshadowed by the increasing violence in the north of Nigeria, led by Boko Haram ('western education is sinful'). The direct links between the two sources of violence may be unclear, but the failure to contain it has resulted in the replacement of the Inspector General of Police. The (Justice) Niki Tobi Commission of Inquiry into violence in Jos,[40] had recommended that 'religious fanatics should not be posted to head state police commands', and the new Inspector General was the head of Plateau State police at that time.

iii. Boko Haram

I hesitate to allot a special section to this aspect of displacement due to hostilities for fear of giving some greater recognition to them than they deserve. I do so only because to omit it would be to omit what has the potential for a major source of displacement if the government fails to contain it.

The epicentre of the violence started in Maiduguri, which is not too distant from the Chad border but has spread alarmingly in the last year. Although Boko Haram try to give themselves a specious cloak of legitimacy, at least in the eyes of the gullible and disaffected, by the prefix 'Islamist' they are totally rejected by mainstream Islam.[41] As I have said, unfortunately the press tend to confirm and spread this claim themselves by attaching the prefix 'Islamist' every time they refer to Boko Haram and any claim or suggestion that it is the work of that group.

Although, as opined above, this violence seems unrelated to Jos or elsewhere in the country, some form of violence is the common reaction to a grievance: dialogue is only beginning to gain credence and because in Nigeria (as it was in Ireland) the use of religion offers such a tempting opportunity to win power it has rarely been resisted. In this lies President Jonathan's claim, I suppose, that there are Boko Haram supporters in the highest of positions. Given the spurious nature of their excuse it would seem their (Boko Haram) real aim is to bring about the downfall of the state, and this is what a number of writers, both from the North and elsewhere, in the newspapers are beginning to say. If so, of course anyone associated with Boko Haram could render himself liable to prosecution for treason.[42]

---

39 Report, *The Daily Trust*, 31 December 2010.

40 See note 35 above. On 11 March a Catholic church was bombed in Jos and this sparked off retaliatory violence. A newspaper quoting a Pastor reported, 'there has not been any concerted effort to tackle ... terrorism. If the Government decided to implement all former recommendation of various panels ... the problem would have ended': *The Vanguard*, 13 March 2012. The attacks on churches, police stations and mosques have escalated since then, and it has been impossible to restrain all retaliation.

41 See many press reports of which an article by Sule Shira, an Islamist teacher from Niger State, is but one, entitled 'A Challenge from a Pig'. The Pig is Boko Haram and the challenge is to fight it its choice of battleground – the mire.

42 Criminal Code, Act Cap 77, s. 37.

The recent Declarations of a State of Emergency in some parts of the country seem to indicate that the government has, belatedly, recognized the extent of the danger.[43]

The violence has been directed against Christians in the bombing of churches but also against police stations and other military and government buildings and personnel. The relevance and the importance of this situation lies in the numbers of people who could be displaced. A call to all Christians to leave the North on pain of death would, if heeded, lead to a massive migration southwards.[44] And then what about the Northerner in the south, generally living peacefully among the southerner who may fear revenge?

There have been suggestions that Boko Haram is infiltrated from outside. There seems to be some resemblances with such groups as El Qaeda and Taliban, but whether and to what extent it is autochthonous is unclear. Given the porosity of the borders, the absence of any form of ID among the mass of people and the spurious Islamic links, perhaps there is some truth in this, but in itself it is a study outside the parameters of this chapter, except insofar as to note that, like other forms of hostilities, it results in IDPs.[45]

iv. Niger Delta

An example of such volatile social conditions occurred last year in the Niger Delta during an apparently innocuous rivalry over the English Premiership Football Match, which led a bus driver deliberately to run down and crush 15 football fans.[46] Long before the recent outbreak of violence in the Delta, which was a combination of deprivation fuelled by powerful vested interest at the highest level in the states, there were examples of thousands being displaced due to land scarcity coupled with indigenous intolerance.[47]

The reasons for the displacement of over three quarters of a million people in this region threw up many areas in which there are constant breaches of the fundamental rights of the people. Examples of this are dealt with below both in Nigeria and elsewhere – especially in Colombia and India.[48]

One has to acknowledge that even when the courts do have an opportunity to deal with such cases it is very much piecemeal. It offers an opportunity to the legal profession and

43 As a side comment, such being the case, are not all those who can be proved to be supporting Boko Haram guilty of treason – regardless of whether they can be proved to have been involved in violence?

44 Ohanaeze Ndigbo Kano State Chapter. The Nation, 23 January 2012.

45 Boko Haram (probably aka Jama'atu Ahlus-Sunnah Lidda'Awatu Wal Jihad) also calls for Islamic (Sharia) law to be more widely applied across Africa. A report by the NCR, NCFR/HQ/C/2151/67, 25 November 2009 attributes violence to *non*-indigene.

46 Poet and social critic Odia Ofeimun accused the government of insincerity and lack of will in solving one of the easiest problems: *The Guardian*, 15 December 2010, p. 7.

47 The displacement of 6,432 Arochukwu people by the Ikwerre due to land scarcity in 1970. See E.J. Alagao and T.N. Tamuno (eds), *Land and People of Nigeria: River's State* (Oxford: African Books Collective, 1989), ch. 14, p. 124.

48 The Movement for Survival of Ogoni People (MOSOP) arose over the issues of marginalization and neglect by Shell Development Company and the Federal Government, followed by the hanging of nine Ogoni people and the execution of Ken Saro-Wiwa. Some think it could spiral out of control into a 'civil war'.

NGOs to pursue claims against those responsible for their predicament through advocacy rather than insurrection.[49]

It was hoped that a president from the Delta region would give it a voice, which it has never had before. Although there has been no return to the organized violence in the region, it has not ceased everywhere and simmers all the time.

v. Cameroon (Bakassi)

The Bakassi Peninsular and Cameroon situation is introduced because it represents an example of a less than clear-cut IDP/Refugee classification due to border disputes – legacies of the colonial carve up of Africa in the nineteenth century, which paid no regard to the inhabitants' family, cultural or tribal connections.[50]

Some of the background[51] may explain a little of the ongoing situation in the area. At the pre-independence constitutional talks in London in 1958 it was agreed between the Secretary of State for the (then) Colonial Office and the Southern Cameroon Representative that, if it proved to be the wish of the people of the territory, Nigeria would welcome Southern Cameroon as part of the Federation with the status of a full self-governing region equal in all respects to other regions in an independent Nigeria:

> no portion of the trust territory of British Cameroon was part of French Cameroun when the latter was granted independence on 1st January 1960. Clearly, therefore [the Republic of Cameroon] cannot validly claim sovereignty over any part of British Cameroon … Recent upheavals in Bakassi are a pointer that the turmoil there should be speedily resolved by a judicious settlement of the Southern Cameroon problem … to avoid a situation which might disturb regional and world peace.[52]

Being regarded as a second-class citizen either in a new home or one he may have been in for generations is one factor. Having no access to land (as described earlier), housing, employment, welfare and schooling are more common disadvantages faced by IDPs. Security must be assured. IDPs will only return when these conditions are met and police and other security forces are seen to be impartial and respect laws and conventions that govern their behaviour. Of course IDPs themselves must equally respect others – social

---

[49] There are such groups relying on local people acting as 'advocates': see www.stand.stakeholderdemocracy.org and www.cmapping.net (both accessed 25 July 2012).

[50] For example, it was reported that on 13 November 2007, MEND militants attacked and killed 20 Cameroonian soldiers on the disputed Bakassi peninsula. Why should they? It was not their operational field? Later a southern Cameroonian rebel group claimed responsibility.

[51] Dr Sylvestre Tchakoutio, living in Abuja in a suspended state of existence due to this situation, related much of the story to me. See also 'Focus Songs of Victory for Bakassi Returnees', *The Guardian*, 24 November 2011, p. 13.

[52] '… the truth of the matter is that the territory of Bakassi does not belong to either Nigeria or La Republique du Cameroun. It is Southern Cameroons territory, and the recent statement by France is troubling, as it might lead to a senseless war': Extract from a Cameroon activist, Mola Njoh Litumbe, in an email to me.

disruption is often down to them failing to do so. Again, the answer lies in some from of dispute resolution – not violence.

Once again, events since the first draft of this chapter was written have shown that, even in this example, of Bakassi, there is potential for the outbreak of domestic hostilities and even a major confrontation with Cameroun due to increasing public demand to revisit the decision of the International Court of Justice awarding Bakassi Peninsular to Cameroun.

2. Natural Disasters

There have been six states in Nigeria (at least) affected by major floods over the past five years as noted above. In all cases both local and foreign aid has been put in hand in order to afford shelter and food and eventually to re-house the victims. However, in the case of the flood in Ogun State in November 2010 the victims have taken the Governor of the state before the Truth and Reconciliation Commission accusing him of failing to pay them the compensation awarded them amounting to N740,000,000 (about £2,960,000). The Governor's answer has been to deny the competence of the Commission to deal with the case.

The National Emergency Relief Agency[53] has taken the initiative in some cases, with a measure of success[54] although its critics accuse it of having a 'vulture concept' – waiting for a disaster to happen.

3. Impediments to Permanent Solution

The obstacles to any permanent solution for the IDP are numerous, as Professor Kälin in his UN Special Rapporteur's Report[55] explains; some of them appear later in this chapter when considering what is available, but for our purposes they need only be looked at in more general terms. Are they caused primarily by a failure on the part of the state directly or indirectly, or are they the result of the IDP's own attitude?

Some countries have created a national status for some IDPs: Azerbaijan, Bosnia and Herzegovina, Colombia, Croatia, Georgia and the Russian Federation. Such a status usually provides for the registration and other rights and support endangered by displacement. Other attempted solutions are reintegration programmes, such as that to bring in the militants in the Niger Delta. One of the beneficiaries of this programme said, 'The government is paying us for now ... But I am worried about what happens next.'[56]

---

[53] Established by the National Emergency Relief Act, cap. 257, 1990.

[54] See Reports on Kebbi State and Sokoto State respectively, 21 and 13 September 2010.

[55] See note 11 above.

[56] Okechukwu Peculiar, 20-year-old former cook for a militant group. She will receive a monthly stipend of 65,000 naira ($423) until the scheme ends. Some NGOs, such as the Stakeholders for Democracy Network, seek to address this.

4.1 Available and Effective Domestic Assistance and Protections

The legislation adopted in some countries creates a national status for IDPs and provides for registration that, it is argued, will assist towards alleviating their condition – unfortunately at the same time it locks them into that status and avoids the basic responsibility of the state not to create them in the first place. It cannot deprive them of their rights under the law and constitution of the country.

In most countries these rights are enforceable in the domestic courts; and even if they are not explicitly so they will be in Africa under the Africa Charter of Human and Peoples' Rights that binds all Member States of the (O)AU regardless of whether it has been enacted in domestic law or not.

Nigeria's constitution respects the rights of minorities,[57] but there is another aspect to this. In some countries not only are the courts not readily accessible (in contrast to what we shall see has happened in Colombia), but they are slow, expensive, with complex procedures and are forbidding – if not corrupt.[58] It is not surprising, therefore, that one finds an unwillingness to use the courts, if not a climate of downright lack of respect for the courts among the people.

Justice Umaru Eri, Administrator of the National Judicial Institute in Nigeria, posed the question, 'In the light of the apparent abuses and violations ... what can we, as judicial officers, do toward ensuring better protection?'[59]

He went on to list three areas where he thought positive steps could be taken:

1. Enhancement of the roles of supranational courts and tribunals such as the ACHPR and ECOWAS Court of Justice,
2. Interpret the laws in a more facilitative manner,
3. Embark on a programme of development and training modules.

This is forward thinking, and Justice Eri has started to carry out his programme proposed in 3. above. However, those who have lost their home often do not know of their rights; do not have access to a lawyer, whatever some leaders in the Bar claim; and what can a judge do except decide any case brought before the court? The solution must start with the Bar in both taking on cases and insisting that the judges carry out the oath they have taken and do so with expedition. As I have indicated, there have been few if any decisions, except in Colombia, specifically brought by an IDP, but the sort of decisions that there have been indicate how the courts can, and sometimes will, use the constitution in order to protect the rights that the IDP needs to have, the quality of his life. One of these which follows is from Nigeria; the rest are taken from India.

In a judgment of the Appeal Court Rivers State Nigeria the Judge awarded substantial damages,[60] stating:

---

57 Articles 33(1) and 4 for example, Nigerian Constitution.

58 One is put in mind of Jesus' parable of the persistent widow in Luke 18!

59 In a paper delivered at an African Chapter IARLJ Workshop of Judges in Abuja, November 2010 (unpublished).

60 Approximately £6,160,00. Reference unobtainable.

> The sum is be paid to the people of Ejama-Ebubu Community in Tai Eleme local government area of Rivers State as special and punitive damages for an oil spill in the community in 1970. Shell has also been ordered to de-pollute and rehabilitate the dry land and swamps to its pre-impact status.

Returning to look more closely at the Colombian example, this is a country with one of the largest populations of IDPs worldwide and it has, through the intervention of the judiciary, developed a pre-emptive position in providing an accessible remedy to protect the rights of the IDP and providing access to the means of compelling the government to govern its behaviour in accordance with the constitution.

Among the constitutional mechanisms to ensure the effective exercise of human rights is the *acción de tutela*, a petition procedure, which enables any person whose fundamental constitutional rights are being threatened or violated to request judicial protection of their fundamental rights. Citizens may file informal claims without an attorney, before any judge in the country with territorial jurisdiction.[61]

The precise mechanisms existing under the Colombian constitution may not be replicated in other countries, but it was a proactive and empathetic judiciary using the constitution that lies at the root of what has been achieved in that country, not a mere use of a procedure. The same basic route is open to any judiciary.

A former and venerated judge in India, Justice Krishna Iyer, said,[62]

> Our judicial system has been aptly described as follows: admirable though it may be, [it] is at once slow and costly. It is a finished product of great beauty, but entails an immense sacrifice of time, money and talent. This 'beautiful' system is frequently a luxury; it tends to give a high quality of justice only when, for one reason or another, parties can surmount the substantial barriers[63] which it erects to most people and to many types of claims. I hope it has been abundantly shown there is a massive and neglected blight upon our claims to be civilized and democratic when access to and justice from the only forum to which victims look – the courts – is denied.

---

[61] The fundamental rights under the Colombian Constitution are broadly the same as the Nigerian and the Indian Constitution and the ACHPR. See also the UN Special Rapporteur's Report in regard to Columbia, note 11.

[62] Article 21 of the Constitution of India, 1950 provides that, 'No person shall be deprived of his life or personal liberty except according to procedure established by law.' This is very similar to Article 4 of the ACPHR and even more when reinforced with Articles 16 and 24. Note also the remarks of Mr Justice Krishna Iyer. In the Delhi Pollution Case, [94] the Supreme Court held in 1989 that Article 21 of the Constitution guaranteeing the right to life must be interpreted to include 'the right to live in a healthy environment with minimum disturbance of ecological balance', and 'without avoidable hazard to [the people] and to their cattle, house and agricultural land, and undue affection [*sic*] of air, water, and environment.' [95]

[63] See as examples of where such barriers have been surmounted *Ratlam Vs.Vardichan and Ors AIR* 1980 SC 1622. He also opined, 'the paramount concern is increasingly with "social justice", i.e., with finding procedures which are conducive to the pursuit and protection of the rights of ordinary people.' *Binod Chandra Varma Vs. State of U.P. and others* CMWP No. 1088 of 1999 Allahabad High Court.

The important point is that, when a judge is in a position to afford some protection or relief by invoking the constitution, he or she needs to be aware first of the vulnerability of a party and then of the remedies open to the court. Having got that far, all it needs is courage and determination.

An example from Uganda demonstrates both. The attitude of the government toward homosexuality is well known. The need for a judge therefore to stand up for a litigant's rights, unpopular or not, should be self-evident given the judicial oath: regretfully, far too often that courage is absent.

In the following instance, it was not absent. Mr Justice Kibuuka Musoke issued an interim order restraining the editors of a newspaper from any further publication of information about anyone alleged to be gay, lesbian, bisexual or transgender. He opined that, (1) the motion was not about homosexuality per se, but about fundamental rights and freedoms, and (2) the jurisdiction of Article 50(1) of the constitution is dual in nature, in that it extends not just to any person 'whose fundamental rights or other rights or freedoms have been infringed in the first place', but also to 'persons whose fundamental rights or other rights or freedoms are threatened to be infringed.'[64]

4.2 Regional and International Protections and Initiatives

The Kampala Convention[65] and The Great Lakes Pact[66] and the Economic Community of West African States (ECOWAS), established in 1991, broadly aim at the free movement of people (citizens), goods and services within the region and, according to the President, Dr James Gbeho, 'the total integration of all facets of life in the western sub-region of Africa'.[67] Individuals were given the right of direct access to the ECOWAS Court of Justice,[68] for 'applications for relief for violation of their Human Rights'.[69]

ECOWAS has also recognized that the case for solving the refugee crisis involves solving the IDP crisis in specifically acknowledging the resolution of the Commission of 15 on Refugees in Khartoum in 1990,[70] stating,

> The problem of refugees in Africa has reached unmanageable proportions ... Africa fully realizes that the major root causes of the refugee problem are

64 *Kasha Jacqueline, Pepe Onziema & David Kato v. Giles Muhame and The Rolling Stone Publications Ltd.*

65 See note 8.

66 Pact on Security, Stability and Development in the Great Lakes Region (the Great Lakes Pact) December 2006. The Pact entered into force in June 2008 and has now been ratified by ten ICGLR Member States. See note 8.

67 *The Guardian*, 30 November 2010, p. 13.

68 Pursuant to Article 15, Revised ECOWAS Treaty.

69 Supp. Protocol A/SP, 1 January 2005.

70 The Khartoum Declaration on Africa's Refugee Crisis adopted OAU, 17th Ordinary Session, 22–24 January 1990.

situated within Africa and that the total eradication of these causes is the primary responsibility of the Africans themselves.

Although as yet there has been no application to the court in respect of either group, it has heard individual's human rights applications under the African Charter on Human and Peoples' Rights[71] on issues such as education, freedom of expression, and freedom of movement.

In one instance, following a similar line to decisions in India, the court said:

> Violations of the right to an adequate standard of living, including the right to food, to work, to health, to water, to life and human dignity, to a clean and healthy environment; and to economic and social development – as a consequence of: the impact of oil-related pollution and environmental damage on agriculture and fisheries; oil spills and waste materials polluting water used for drinking and other domestic purposes; failure to secure the underlying determinants of health, including a healthy environment; and failure to enforce laws and regulations to protect the environment and prevent pollution.[72]

Another case in point is that of the Banjul journalist Saidykhan.[73] He was tortured and jailed in his own country and the Gambia argued (somewhat obscurely) that the court had no jurisdiction as it was 'an affront to internal sovereignty'![74] While the jurisdiction does not so far extend to claims between individuals, it is thought that such jurisdiction may exist[75] if, at national level, there is no, or no effective forum for seeking redress.[76]

The African Committee of Experts on the Rights and Welfare of the Child is another window. It is much like the Child Rights Committee, which works to implement the provisions of the UN Child Rights Convention, in the sense that the African Charter makes it mandatory for African countries that have ratified that instrument to submit periodic reports on its implementation effort to the 11-member Committee, both for oversight purposes and to ensure that countries commit to their responsibilities. The Committee of Experts also has powers to conduct investigations into violations of children's rights, where a Member State fails to address them. Unfortunately, it has no bite, since violations cannot be remedied by

[71] June 1981.

[72] *(Serap) Vs. Nigeria and NNPC and Others*, ECW/CCJ/App/08/09, ECW/CCJ/JUD/O7/10.

[73] *Musa Saidykhan Vs. Rep of the Gambia*, Ruling, 30 June 2009.

[74] Gambia is a member of ECOWAS and (O)AU and a signatory to the ACHPR. The Court has recently held also that the right of every child in Nigeria (and this will be every other state in the Community too) is justiciable.

[75] I am indebted for this and further references to a paper presented by the Chief Registrar Tony Anene-Maidoh entitled 'The Role of ECOWAS Court of Justice in the Protection of Refugees and Internally Displaced Persons', delivered at the International Association Refugee Law Judges African Regional Chapter in Abuja 22–26 November 2010. I understand that UNHCR are anxious to reconvene it this year.

[76] ... and there is no need to exhaust local remedies first.

the Committee itself and can only refer a violation to the African Commission on Human and Peoples' Rights.[77]

In Europe, the European Court of Human Rights has ordered states to pay compensation for having negligently failed to take appropriate measures.

The Kampala Convention[78] defines and applies to the IDP (Article 1(k)), and so does Article 12 and other articles of the ACHPR,[79] even though it is more relevant to refugees.

Finally, ECOWAS has adopted a common approach to the free movement of migrants – internally or externally displaced – and this confirms its rights to entertain a claim by an IDP, perhaps, for example, for a breach of Article 24 ACHPR, which reads, 'All peoples shall have the right to a generally satisfactory environment favourable to their development.' This is no different from what the Indian or the Colombian courts have held.[80]

5. Conclusions

I have tried to demonstrate that the legal profession and the courts have a lead role to play in putting themselves at the forefront of promoting relief under the constitution of the vulnerable. Among the largest groups of those both vulnerable and neglected are the internally displaced. have started to take a lead in Africa, such as the ECOWAS Court and examples abound in India and in the Constitutional Colombia.

There are forward thinkers such as Justice Eri in Nigeria, and doubtless others. But even with the sensitization of the judges and a Bar unwilling to take on perhaps unpopular causes with little hope of immediate financial gain access to the right court remains high on the agenda. One possible avenue to explore is the use of the Local or Customary Court system. This generally speaks a language more readily understood by many of those most in need of help, is less forbidding, and can be more readily made easily accessible.

We have seen an attempt to use a Truth and Reconciliation Commission and there have been examples of class actions in the UK courts: an example is that against Trafigura, a UK-based company that was accused of dumping toxic waste in the Ivory Coast.[81]

77 Perhaps also to regional courts such as the ECOWAS Community Court? Nigeria's Representative is a well-known lawyer and Human Rights Activist wife of a former Supreme Court Chief Justice.

78 See above, p. 65.

79 Articles 13, 14, 15, 16, 17, 18, 19, 21, 22, 23, 24. And individuals have duties too, which the state should be expected to enforce: 27.

80 ... not forgetting there are seven other regional groups with courts recognized by the AU in Africa and more in South America and Europe. The Southern African Development Community (SADC) tribunal found the expropriation of farms without compensation was in violation of SADC protocols (Campbell), and awarded damages of nearly US$17m to nine Zimbabwean torture victims (Gondo). All decisions made by it should be binding and enforceable in all Member States.

81 Leigh Day & Co UK Solicitors financed the class action, which I am informed was successful, and the fees from that are now being used to finance another similar action against those allegedly responsible for oil pollution in the Niger Delta.

The failure to tackle and eradicate the exploitation of often longstanding and deep-seated societal differences, especially where the religious divide is strong, by those hungry for (usually political) power will exact a heavy price.

References

Alagao, E.J. and T.N. Tamuno (eds), *Land and People of Nigeria: River's State* (Oxford: African Books Collective, 1989).

Archbishop of Jos et al., 'Another Massacre in Nigeria: An Unending Cycle', *The Economist*, 11 March 2010.

Boano, C., R. Zetter and T. Morris, *Environmentally Displaced People: Understanding the Linkages between Environmental Change, Livelihoods and Forced Migration*, Forced Migration Policy Briefing 1, Refugee Studies Centre, Oxford Department of International Development, University of Oxford.

Danfulani, U.H.D., 'The Jos Peace Conference and the Indigene/Settler Question in Nigerian Politics' (2006), at http://www.ascleiden.nl/Pdf/paper-Danfulani.pdf (accessed 18 August 2012).

Ferris, E. and C. Stark, *Internal Displacement in West Africa: A Snapshot* (January 2012), at http://www.brookings.edu/research/papers/2012/01/ecowas-ferris-stark (accessed 18 August 2012).

Ibeanu, O., 'Ethnicity and Transition to Democracy in Nigeria: Explaining the Passing of Authoritarian Rule in a Multi-ethnic Society', 5 *African Journal of Political Science* 2, 45–65.

iDMC, *Nigeria: Simmering Tensions Cause New Displacement in Middle Belt* (2 December 2010), via www.internal-displacement.org (accessed 18 August 2012).

Juss, Satvinder S., 'The Slow Death of Citizenship Rights' (2007) 18 *King's Law Journal* 1, 95–118.

Kwashi, Benjamin, 'In Jos We Are Coming Face to Face in Confrontation with Satan', Christianity Today, at http://www.christianitytoday.com/ct/2010/januaryweb-only/14-21.0.html (accessed 8 March 2010).

Nnoli, O., *Ethnic Politics in Nigeria* (Enugu: Fourth Dimension, 1978).

Powell, C., *My American Journey* (New York: Random House, 1995).

Rice, A., *The Teeth may Smile but the Heart does not Forget: Murder and Memory in Uganda* (London: Metropolitan Books, 2009)

Senesie, T., 'Profile and Challenges of Internally Displaced Persons in West Africa', at http://www.articlesbase.com/education-articles/profile-and-challenges-of-internally-displaced-persons-in-west-africa-3286111.html (accessed 17 August 2012)

Wynne-Jones, J., 'Senior Bishops Call for End to Persecution of Christians in Britain', *The Telegraph*, 27 March 2010, at http://www.telegraph.co.uk/news/religion/7531293/Senior-bishops-call-for-end-to-persecution-of-Christians-in-Britain.html (accessed 17 August 2012)

ASHGATE
RESEARCH
COMPANION

PART IV
EMERGING PARADIGMS OF LEGAL PROTECTION

Human Trafficking, Asylum and the Problem of Protection

Satvinder S. Juss[1]

A decade ago human trafficking in Britain was hardly an issue much commented upon. Now it is at the forefront of public debate. Barely a day goes by when British broadsheets do not highlight the plight of victims of human trafficking and the multifarious forms that this modern trade in human beings entails.[2] Public pronouncements proliferate[3] and there has been a flurry of recent cases in the British courts involving official bungling, botched

[1] Professor of Law and Director of the Centre for Transnational Legal Studies at King's College, University of London; Ph.D. (Cambridge University) FRSA; Fellow of the International Academy of Freedom of Religion & Belief; Barrister-at-Law of Gray's Inn; Part-time Immigration Appeal Judge; Formerly Visiting Professor of Law and Visiting Distinguished Scholar in Residence, Indiana University – Bloomington (1998); Human Rights Fellow at Harvard University (1997); Rapporteur of the Exclusion Clauses of the International Association of Refugee Law Judges; listed as a legal expert in *Legal Experts (2002–2011)*. I am grateful to Professor Piotrowicz Ryszard and to Professor Roger Brownword for their helpful comments on earlier drafts of this chapter. Needless to say, all remaining errors are my responsibility.

[2] For example, there has been increasing concern over the trafficking of children: see Billy Briggs, 'Child trafficking in Scotland is hidden scandal, says report', *The Guardian*, 13 March 2011, at http://www.guardian.co.uk/law/2011/mar/13/child-trafficking-scotland-scandal-report (accessed 30 July 2012); and there was the report of the case in March 2011 of a UK-based Nigerian pastor who, as the mother-of-five, was the first person to be jailed for trafficking children into the UK for domestic servitude, and faced eleven years in jail for child trafficking: see BBC News, 'Pastor jailed for trafficking African child "slaves"', at http://www.bbc.co.uk/news/uk-england-london-12789690 (accessed 30 July 2012). Another report has suggested that trafficking in sex slaves could rise if Britain rejects European anti-vice strategy: see Mark Townsend, 'Target brothels or sex trafficking in UK will rise', *The Observer*, Sunday 6 February 2011 at http://www.guardian.co.uk/law/2011/feb/06/sex-slave-trafficking-brothel-crackdown?INTCMP=SRCH (accessed 30 July 2012); concern has been expressed over the fact that only 40 cases have been prosecuted since the new offence, aimed at targeting those who pay for sex from trafficked women, came into effect in April 2010: see Alan Travis, 'Authorities failing to enforce law aimed at tackling sex with trafficked women', *The Guardian*, 19 July 2011, at http://www.guardian.co.uk/law/2011/jul/19/sex-law-human-trafficking-strategy (accessed 30 July 2012).

[3] For example, a major 15-month inquiry into human trafficking was launched in June 2011 amid claims that slavery remains as much of a problem in modern Britain as when it was abolished more than 200 years ago, by the Centre for Social Justice into the issue following concerns over a lack of political will, policing resources, low prosecution rates, and flaws within the government system for identifying trafficked victims: see Mark Townsend, 'Inquiry launched into slavery in the

prosecutions, and the blighted lives of individuals claiming redress in the courts.[4] Within a decade human trafficking has become one of the most demanding social issues of our time as confirmed by the *Report of the Inter-Departmental Ministerial Group on Human Trafficking* in 2012 showing human trafficking in the UK to be on the increase.[5] States can no longer neglect this evil.[6] The risks of human trafficking are no longer remote. No longer is it possible to say that the phenomenon either does not exist or is not widespread enough.[7] It is now trite that human trafficking – a form of modern slavery[8] – can be a crime against humanity. As Lady Butler-Sloss, of the All-Party Parliamentary Group on Human Trafficking, recently explained, it is estimated to be worth $32 billion and is 'nothing less than serious, international, organized crime: the money generated from it is only marginally less than from arms dealing and drug smuggling'.[9] Yet despite the fact that human trafficking straddles disciplines as diverse as law enforcement, human rights, gender rights, asylum protection, health, law enforcement and social services, little has been accomplished in terms of the effective and practical protection of victims. Indeed, an 18-month inquiry conducted by Lady Helena Kennedy QC in November 2011 for the Equality and Human Rights Commission concluded that victims of human trafficking, including women forced into the sex industry or trapped as

UK', *The Observer*, 12 July 2011, at http://www.guardian.co.uk/law/2011/jun/12/slavery-inquiry-iain-duncan-smith (accessed 30 July 2012).

4 A large number of cases have recently arisen, including: *R v. LM & Ors* [2010] EWCA Crim 2327; *AM and BM (Trafficked women)* Albania CG [2010] UKUT 80 (IAC); *AZ (Trafficked Women) Thailand CG* [2010] UKUT 118 (IAC); *LM & Ors* [2011] Crim LR 425; *R v. O* in [2008] EWCA Crim 2835; *O.O.O.* [2011] EWHC 1246 (QB); *SB (PSG, Protection Regulations, Reg 6) Moldova CG* [2008] UKAIT 00002 (26 November 2007); *HC and RC (Trafficked women)* China CG [2009] UKAIT 00027 at para. 36; *LR v the United Kingdom* – 49113/09 [2010] ECHR 607 (1 April 2010). These cases are discussed in this chapter, including *Rantsev v Cyprus and Russia* 25965/04 [2010] ECHR 22, which has been analysed extensively by the British courts.

5 The *First annual Report of the Inter-Departmental Ministerial Group on Human Trafficking* (October 2012) Cm 8421, which was presented to Parliament by the Secretary of State for the Home Department. Available at http://www.homeoffice.gov.uk/publications/crime/human-trafficking-report?view=Binary.

6 The evil knows no bounds. In June 2011, it was reported that the rescue by Nigerian police of 32 pregnant girls allegedly held by a human trafficking ring in Aba in south-eastern Nigeria has literally shocked the world, because the girls, between the ages of 15 and 17 years, were locked up and used to 'produce' babies, who were then allegedly sold for ritual witchcraft purposes or adoption, leading UNICEF to estimate that at least ten children are sold daily across Nigeria: see Leo Igwe, 'Baby farm girls and the sale of children', 8 June 2011, at http://www.momentng.com/en/news/2856/baby-farm-girls-and-the-sale-of-children.html (accessed 30 July 2012).

7 See Frank Laczko and Marco A. Gramegna, 'Developing Better Indicators of Human Trafficking', *Brown Journal of World Affairs* (Vol. 10, Issue 1, summer/fall 2003), at pp. 179–94, where it is explained that 'until the early 1990s, trafficking was mainly viewed as a form of human smuggling and a type of illegal migration' (at p. 180).

8 This is the central theme of the project by the Centre for Social Justice ('CSJ'), established in June 2011, over a 15-month period, 'Slavery Working Group', which was set up to examine human trafficking in all its forms. The author declares an interest. He is a member of the CSJ Slavery Working Group.

9 Lady Butler-Sloss, 'Human trafficking is modern slavery', *The Guardian*, 2 July 2011, at http://www.guardian.co.uk/law/2011/jul/02/elizabeth-butler-sloss-human-trafficking (accessed 30 July 2012).

unpaid domestic servants, are being unfairly treated as criminals and illegal immigrants.[10] The published report called on the UK and Scottish governments to introduce legislation and criminal justice policies that will tackle trafficking as a specific crime and support its victims.[11] This chapter considers why this is the case.[12]

The aim here is to examine the impact in the United Kingdom of recent legal developments in the law of human trafficking. It is argued that, while the interpretation and implementation of the law still fails to produce a result that is 'victim-centred', within the maelstrom of the various rules and regulations that have been passed on the subject of human trafficking,[13] there exist opportunities for victim protection in the interstices of the Refugee Convention and of international refugee law.[14] These opportunities have been enhanced by new judicial approaches in cases such as *HJ (Iran)* by the UK Supreme Court, which have spoken of how 'the Convention proceeds on the basis that people should be allowed to live their lives free from the fear of serious harm coming to them because of their race, religion, nationality,

[10] Severin Carrell, 'Trafficked people being treated as criminals by officials, inquiry says', *The Guardian*, 27 November 2011, at http://www.guardian.co.uk/law/2011/nov/27/human-trafficking-crime-victims (accessed 30 July 2012).

[11] The Report was published on 28 November 2011: see http://www.equalityhumanrights.com/scotland/scottish-news/press-releases-2011/ehrc-launch-inquiry-into-human-trafficking-in-scotland-report-baroness-helena-kennedy-qc-investigating-commissioner/ (accessed 20 August 2012). Also see http://www.shrlg.org.uk/2011/12/03/human-rights-round-up-5/ (accessed 20 August 2012).

[12] On the other hand, as far as the UK Crown Prosecution Service is concerned, policy revision has followed claims that victims were being wrongly prosecuted by UK law enforcers: see Robert Booth, '"Human trafficking victims will not be treated as criminals", says CPS', *The Guardian*, 3 July 2011, at http://www.guardian.co.uk/law/2011/jul/03/human-trafficking-victims-criminals-cs?INTCMP=SRCH (accessed 7 August 2012).

[13] A motley of British laws exists. For example, Section 145 of the Nationality, Immigration and Asylum Act 2002 created an offence of trafficking in prostitution; Section 57 of the Sexual Offences Act 2003 created the offence of trafficking into the UK for sexual exploitation; Section 58 of that Act created the offence of trafficking within the UK for sexual exploitation; Section 59 of that Act created the offence of trafficking out of the UK for sexual exploitation; Section 53A of that Act created the offence of paying for the sexual services of a prostitute subjected to force etc.; Section 4 of the Asylum and Immigration (Treatment of Claimants etc) Act 2004 created the offence of trafficking people for exploitation; Section 71 of the Coroners and Justice Act 2009 created the offence of slavery, servitude and forced or compulsory labour; Section 25 of the Immigration Act 1971 created the offence of assisting unlawful immigration to a Member State by way of facilitation. These laws create criminal offences. However, in terms of the facilitation of the gathering and giving of evidence by vulnerable and intimidated witnesses, the Youth Justice and Criminal Evidence Act 1999 introduced a range of Special Measures that may without much ingenuity be applied to apply to victims of human trafficking.

[14] However, it has been argued that though the Refugee Convention 'may well serve to protect some victims of trafficking, it seems unlikely to be available to all of them. The principal hurdles are establishing that the woman has a well-founded fear of persecution with regard to her home state (even though she has been trafficked to another) and that she is a member of a particular social group.' See Ryszard Piotrowicz, 'Victims of People Trafficking and the Entitlement to International Protection', *Australian Year Book of International Law* (Vol. 24, Issue 205, 2005), pp. 159–79, at p. 178.

membership of a particular social group or political opinion'.[15] Such approaches in turn call for a re-evaluation of the judicial role in the context of claims made by victims of human trafficking that are now timely to consider. This is because international refugee law is often criticized for being antiquated and ineffectual in the face of egregious human rights violations in the world today.[16] Yet the plight of victims of human trafficking provides refugee lawyers with an opportunity to affirm the fundamental tenets of international protection on which their discipline is based. This is especially where the perpetrator of human rights violations is not the State but non-state agents within the State. This has been a difficult issue for refugee law.[17] However, the case of human trafficking provides refugee law courts and lawyers with a context in which to map out the contours of protection that can be a useful model for similar future cases.

This chapter is organized as follows. Section A deals with the search for a victim-centred approach in the context of the historical abolition of slavery. Section B describes the law relating to human trafficking. Section C focuses on how the identification and assistance of victims is provided for within that law. Section D analyses judicial perspectives in the various British cases of the last five years, with a view to determining what has been achieved, given that these cases (i) provide an insight into the nature of human trafficking; (ii) demonstrate how victims of human trafficking can fit into the category of a 'particular social group' in the Refugee Convention; and (iii) highlight the governmental failures in the field of protection given the prioritization of criminal prosecution over state protection. Section E considers the ground-breaking case of *AZ (Thailand)*, which it is suggested points the way to a victim-centred judicial approach that is much to be commended. Section F ends by advocating a radical approach to protection as this is consistent with the broad humanitarian principles that underlie the Refugee Convention.

---

15 Lord Rodger at para. 52 in *HJ (Iran)* [2010] UKSC. Also see references to historic discrimination of gay people at paras 75–7, which the late Lord Rodger considers to be important in the context of refugee law protections.

16 See the chapter by Patricia Tuitt, 'The Modern Refugee in Post-modern Europe', at pp. 25–41.

17 Though the effects of this doctrine have been ameliorated by the House of Lords judgment in *Horvath*, where Stuart-Smith LJ memorably explained that, 'It can be argued that if a claimant can satisfy the protection test he also satisfies the well-founded fear test, provided of course the ill-treatment amounts to persecution. Because there is no protection from what he fears, his fear is well-founded. But the converse is not the case. Young men of African–Caribbean extraction may fear attack or mugging by skinheads in parts of the United Kingdom; those who have suffered repeated burglary may have a well-founded fear that they may be the victims again. It seems to me to be an unnecessary distortion of ordinary language to say that their fear is not well-founded because there is in existence in the United Kingdom an efficient police force willing to detect and prosecute crime and courts that can and do convict and sentence the criminals. Many such attacks and burglaries go undetected and unpunished. It would only be if the criminal justice system was so effective in detection and deterrence with the result that the risk of such attacks was minimal, that one could say that the fear was not well-founded. This clearly sets the protection test too high.' See *Horvath v Secretary of State for the Home Department* [1999] EWCA Civ 3026, at para. 23.

(A) The Search for a 'Victim-centred' Approach

It is trite that human trafficking law needs to be 'victim-centred', and that it is a mistake to mix it up with the control of unwanted immigrants. Unfortunately, this is often ill achieved because law enforcement agencies and public officials operate in an era of limited financial resources. They do not always understand that victims of human trafficking have often been 'persecuted'. The State of their nationality is either unable or unwilling to provide them with protection. Where this is the case, the door is open for the receiving State to grant them refugee status. This is not to say that every case of human trafficking should succeed in a claim for refugee status. It is to mean to say that there is a dimension to human trafficking, namely, its phenomenon as a form of modern slavery, that renders its victims particularly apt for the grant of refugee status. This argument is yet to be fully made by scholars, activists and jurists in this area. Yet its power is compelling. Slavery was abolished in 1807 after a long and honourable campaign led from the very country, namely Britain, where it now appears to be taking root. The historical significance of 'slavery' (which for centuries was state sanctioned), like that of the historical significance of racism, is one that gives it a particular salience over and above other human evils. It demands an extraordinary State response. This is not least because, as Lady Butler-Sloss has explained, '[t]oday's slavery is more insidious, hidden from public gaze'.[18] What would a 'victim-centred' approach, however, look like? And, what is the degree of resistance to it? These are the two questions to which we must now turn in this section.

(i) The advent of a 'victim-centred' approach

In the seminal 2010 case of *Rantsev*,[19] the European Court of Human Rights ('ECtHR') expressly referred to the Slavery Convention 1926, in the context of human trafficking, observing that slavery is there defined as 'the status or condition of a person over whom any or all of the powers attaching to the right of ownership are exercised'.[20] The Recital of this Convention, as the ECtHR pointed out, asserts a principle the significance of which is of crucial importance to victims of human trafficking, namely that it is 'necessary to prevent forced labour from developing into conditions analogous to slavery'.[21] This is because victims of human trafficking, like erstwhile slaves, are still subject to a form of 'ownership' by their tormentors, so that the ECtHR in *Rantsev*[22] also alluded to the fact that, under the Rome Statute of the International Criminal Court, the condition of 'enslavement' is one that 'means the exercise of any or all of the powers attaching to the right of ownership over a person and includes the exercise of such power in the course of trafficking in persons, in

18 Butler-Sloss, 'Human trafficking is modern slavery'.

19 *Rantsev v Cyprus and Russia* 25965/04 [2010] ECtHR 22 (7 January 2010) ('*Rantsev*'), at p. 207.

20 The Slavery Convention was signed in Geneva in 1926, entered into force on 7 July 1955, and Article 1 defines slavery as 'the status or condition of a person over whom any or all of the powers attaching to the right of ownership are exercised'.

21 See *Rantsev*, at paras 137–8.

22 Ibid., at para. 144.

particular women and children'.[23] The question that this chapter raises, however, is whether the recognition that human trafficking is a form of slavery adds something qualitatively unique to the way in which victims of human trafficking require to be protected. If it does, then it must lead us to the conclusion that the primary and paramount consideration of the law in this area should be to provide a 'victim-centred' protection.

Human trafficking laws in Britain have been limited because they have tracked international law developments, which have been slow and incremental. These are all no more than about a decade old. The first important international initiative was the UN Protocol to Prevent, Suppress, and Punish Trafficking in Persons 2000 (the 'Trafficking Protocol'). It set out to define the meaning of 'Trafficking in Persons' in Palermo (and is thus also sometimes known as the 'Palermo Protocol'). Five years later, on 16 May 2005, the Council of Europe Convention on Action Against Trafficking in Human Beings (the 'Anti-Trafficking Convention') was adopted, which aimed 'to prevent and combat trafficking in human beings'. Given the ever-present risk of removal, this Convention was significant in allowing victims of trafficking a 45-day period of rest and reflection with access to support and accommodation – which can be extended by another 45 days, if necessary – in which to provide proof of having been trafficked and to claim asylum if they so wish. This instrument provided ready recognition of the possibilities of asylum for victims of human trafficking. It was a most welcome development because it potentially removed the risk of removal. The victims would also be granted residency permits of up to a year if they wished to give evidence against their traffickers. These were important examples of victim-centred laws.[24]

The 'Anti-Trafficking Convention' was signed in March 2007 by the British Home Minister, Dr John Reid, in order to coincide with the bicentenary of the abolition of the Slave Trade in 2007. The following year, on 17 December 2008, the UK government ratified this Convention as part of a Europe-wide agreement about setting minimum standards for protecting trafficked victims. It would doubtless have taken longer for the Anti-Trafficking Convention to come into force in the UK, but it did so within the next six months, on 6 April 2009. This was largely as a result of a vigorous campaign fought by organizations as diverse as Amnesty and the Poppy Project,[25] for trafficked people to be seen as victims of crime rather than as criminals

23 See Article 7(1)(c) of the Rome Statute of the International Criminal Court, 17 July 1998 (which came into effect on 1 July 2002), which states that, 'For the purpose of this Statute, "crime against humanity" means any of the following acts when committed as part of a widespread or systematic attack directed against any civilian population, with knowledge of the attack', and then refers to 'enslavement', which it defines as 'the exercise of any or all of the powers attaching to the right of ownership over a person and includes the exercise of such power in the course of trafficking in persons, in particular women and children'.

24 See the UK Government's *Explanatory Memorandum on the Council of Europe Convention on Action against Trafficking in Human Beings*, at http://www.fco.gov.uk/en/publications-and-documents/treaty-command-papers-ems/explanatory-memoranda/explanatory-memoranda-2008/humantrafficking (accessed 20 August 2012). Also at the Congress of Local & Regional Authorities website, at https://wcd.coe.int/ViewDoc.jsp?id=889879&Site=COE (accessed 20 August 2012).

25 The Poppy Project was set up in 2003, and was funded by the Office for Criminal Justice Reform (reporting to the Ministry of Justice) to provide accommodation and support to women who had been trafficked into prostitution or domestic servitude. It had 54 bed spaces in houses nationally. In April 2011, it lost its funding to the Salvation Army: see Nichi Hodgson and Catherine Robinson, 'The value of the Poppy Project', *The Guardian*, 22 April 2011, at http://www.guardian.

who have broken immigration laws. On 6 May 2009, a month after that, the UK Home Affairs Committee in Parliament launched its 88-page report on *The Trade in Human Beings: Human Trafficking in the UK*,[26] which was published on 14 May 2009. The contents of this report help confirm the argument of this chapter, namely the need for the courts to develop appropriate judicial responses to human trafficking, given the failure of official agencies to understand the problem. The report of the Home Affairs Committee into this modern slave trade revealed a poor understanding of the problem, patchy enforcement and inadequate protection for victims.[27] One of the main obstacles to attempts at tackling trafficking is the perennial one of a lack of any serious, current estimate of the scale of the 'trade in people'.[28] A conservative appraisal suggests that there are at least 5,000 trafficking victims in the UK.[29] Other estimates suggest that there are at least 4,000 trafficked women working in the sex industry alone.[30]

(ii) The Resistance to a Victim-Centred Approach

Remarkably, there is a resistance to the adoption of a 'victim-centred' approach. It comes from the most unlikely quarters. A recent study in October 2011, *Migrant Workers in the UK Sex Industry*, by Dr Nick Mai, which was funded by the Economic and Social Research Council (ESRC),[31] suggests that it may not be quite the problem it is made out to be at all. This is because most foreign prostitutes in London are not trafficked and choose to sell sex because it earns them more money than they would earn in other more menial and poorly paid jobs. Working conditions in the sex industry were also found by foreign prostitutes to be better than working in other occupations and it also gave them more free time. Even more controversially, it appears that those working in the sex industry looked forward to 'the possibility of meeting interesting people', and to travelling. They also value the ability it gave them to help their families. There was a downside, however. Some 6 per cent of women questioned in the study, which was conducted among 'off-street' prostitutes in central

co.uk/commentisfree/2011/apr/22/poppy-project-trafficking-salvation-army (accessed 20 August 2012). There has been criticism that 'the Ministry of Justice has awarded vital public funding to support victims of sex trafficking to a religious group (the Salvation Army) instead of a specialist women's support service (Eaves, which has successfully run the Poppy Project for nine years)'; see Letters to the Guardian, 14 April 2011, at http://www.guardian.co.uk/society/2011/apr/14/concern-poppy-project-sex-trafficking (accessed 20 August 2012). Also see Mark Townsend, 'Sex-trafficked women's charity Poppy Project in danger as funding withdrawn', *The Guardian*, 17 April 2011, at http://www.guardian.co.uk/society/2011/apr/17/prostitution-human-trafficking (accessed 20 August 2012).

26 *The Trade in Human Beings: Human Trafficking in the UK* (2008–2009) (HC21-1). http://www.statewatch.org/news/2009/may/uk-hasc-trafficking-report-vol1.pdf (accessed 20 August 2012). The author was a participant at this event.

27 See ibid., at para. 23.

28 Ibid., at para. 27.

29 Ibid., at para. 28.

30 Ibid., at para. 31.

31 *Migrant Workers in the UK Sex Industry*, at http://www.esrc.ac.uk/my-esrc/grants/RES-062-23-0137/read/reports (accessed 31 July 2012).

London, had been 'deceived and forced' into selling sex without any control over their work.[32] The study, based on in-depth interviews with 100 women, men and transgender migrants working in the London sex industry, led Dr Nick Mai to the conclusion that '[t]he perception that the commercial sex industry is connected to international organised crime and irregular immigration has raised moral panic about trafficking in the UK. Neither the moral panic, nor legislation brought in to counter trafficking, reflects existing research evidence.' These are bold observations. Nevertheless, Dr Mai is in no doubt that, '[t]o avoid knee-jerk reactions and to obtain a better understanding of the issues, it's essential that the findings of recent and relevant research are made known to the government and the public at large'.[33] Indeed, it appears that '[t]he International Union of Sex Workers warmly welcomes the publication of "Migrant Workers in the UK Sex Industry" by Dr Nick Mai'.[34]

Yet it is hard to know the full truth about these things. Europol in its September 2011 report contends that the trafficking of young women and children for sexual exploitation is actually the most prevalent form of trafficking in the EU.[35] In the UK, in the 2010 case of *LM & Ors*,[36] Lord Justice Hughes found that,[37] 'One of the commonest forms of trafficking is for the purpose of forced prostitution.'[38] However, the number of people trafficked into the EU each year itself covers such an enormous range – anything from 100,000 to 800,000[39] – so as to make the generalizations quite meaningless. Trafficking is not the same as people smuggling, and there are several forms. The discussion of *AM and BM* below demonstrates this quite adequately.[40] The trafficking of children to commit street crimes is surely a problem.[41] There

32 Martin Bentham, Home Affairs Editor, 'Majority of sex workers "not forced or trafficked"', *Evening Standard*, 28 October 2011, at http://www.thisislondon.co.uk/standard/article-24003366-majority-of-sex-workers-not-forced-or-trafficked.do (accessed 31 July 2012).

33 See 'Most migrant sex workers are not forced to sell sex', Most migrants working in the London sex industry do not feel they are forced to sell sex. In fact, they decide to work in the sex industry to achieve a good standard of living for themselves and their families back home. They say working in the sex industry avoids employment in menial and poorly paid jobs. 31 October 2011, at http://www.esrc.ac.uk/news-and-events/press-releases/18164/most-migrant-sex-workers-are-not-forced-to-sell-sex.aspx (accessed 31 July 2012).

34 See 'Majority of migrant sex workers "'not forced or trafficked"', at http://www.iusw.org/2011/10/majority-of-migrant-sex-workers-not-forced-or-trafficked/ (accessed 31 July 2012).

35 See *Trafficking in Human Beings in the European Union* (The Hague, 1 September 2011), which states (at para. 1.3) that, 'Most trafficked victims are women and children but men are now equally exploited in the area of labour exploitation', at https://www.europol.europa.eu/sites/default/files/publications/trafficking_in_human_beings_in_the_european_union_2011.pdf (accessed 20 August 2012).

36 *R v. LM & Ors* [2010] EWCA Crim 2327. Also cited as: [2011] Crim LR 425, [2011] 1 Cr App R 135, [2011] 1 Cr App R 12, [2010] EWCA Crim 2327.

37 Ibid., at para. 76.

38 Ibid,, at para. 82.

39 See www.statewatch.org/news/2009/./uk-hasc-trafficking-report-vol2.pd (accessed [date]), at para. 31 and at para. 29.

40 See the case of *AM and BM (Trafficked women)* Albania CG [2010] UKUT 80 (IAC) discussed below.

41 See Carron Somerset, 'What the Professionals Know: The Trafficking of Children Into, and Through, the UK for Sexual Purposes' (*Anti-Slavery International*, November 2001, NCJ Number 196542), via http://www.ncjrs.gov/App/publications/abstract.aspx?ID=196542 (accessed 31 July 2012); also see Frank Laczko and Elzbieta Gozdziak, 'Data and Research on Human Trafficking:

is also trafficking for purposes of cannabis cultivation, forced marriage and benefit fraud.[42] The immigration authorities alone cannot be relied upon to combat trafficking.[43] We know this because the report of the Home Affairs Committee highlights 'major gaps in awareness and training'[44] within the UK Border Agency. As far as the police are concerned, it has been suggested that '[t]here is a clear need for greater awareness training in police forces so that officers realise that domestic workers, too, may be victims of trafficking and are not merely possible illegal immigrants'.[45] In these circumstances, the last thing that is called for is the reduction in funds allocated to the Metropolitan Police's Human Trafficking Unit. This is a sad reflection of a failure to follow a victim-centred approach. The Home Affairs Committee recommends that, far from being run down, this unit should be sustained[46] until the best practice it represents is embedded throughout the police service in the UK. In its words, 'it is clear from the evidence given to us that the Human Trafficking unit of the Metropolitan Police serves a national as well as a local role, in providing an example of best practice that is regarded as a model by other police forces, by NGOs and .... by foreign law enforcement bodies and multinational agencies such as Europol'.[47] Yet, since that report in 2009, the UK government has proposed even more radical cuts. This shows that only lip service is being paid to the adoption of a victim-centred approach. In February 2011 there was a plan to close special police units that protect victims and target criminal gangs.[48] In April 2011, ministers even withdrew funding from a charity, *Eaves Housing*, that pioneered specialist services for victims of sexual trafficking by providing refuge and therapeutic support for hundreds of abused and exploited women, thus placing the charity in an uncertain future.[49] In May 2011, the UK government's promise to tackle human trafficking was said to be in disarray after an exodus of expert Home Office staff and the sidelining of the official in charge of the policy.[50]

A Global Survey', Offprint of the Special Issue of *International Migration* (Vol. 43, Issue 1/2, 2005), at http://www/childtrafficking.com/docs/iom_2005_data_and_research (accessed 7 August 2012); see also Laczko and Gramegna, 'Developing Better Indicators of Human Trafficking', where it is explained that, 'until the early 1990s, trafficking was mainly viewed as a form of human smuggling and a type of illegal migration' (at p. 181).

42 See 'The trade in human beings: human trafficking in the UK' (14 May 2009), at www.nationalschool.gov.uk/./news./human_trafficking_hac09.asp (accessed [date]). See also the CPS guidance at 'Human Trafficking and Smuggling' (7 July 2009), at www.cps.gov.uk/legal/h_to_/human_trafficking_and_smuggling (accessed [date]).

43 Indeed, it has been stated that 'we recommend that the Home Office continue to provide funding at its original level for the specialist Human Trafficking unit of the Metropolitan Police beyond 2010 ...'; see *The Trade in Human Beings: Human Trafficking in the UK* (2008–2009) (HC21-1), at para. 87.

44 Ibid., at para. 99.

45 Ibid., at para. 75.

46 Ibid., para. 87.

47 Ibid., at para. 85.

48 Emily Dugan and Matt Chorley, 'Coalition to scrap sex trafficking safeguards', *The Independent on Sunday, 6 February 2011, at* http://www.independent.co.uk/news/uk/crime/coalition-to-scrap-sex-trafficking-safeguards-2205733.html (accessed 31 July 2012).

49 Patrick Butler and Alan Travis, 'Sex trafficking charity loses out to Salvation Army over £6m contract', *The Guardian,* 11 April 2011, at http://www.guardian.co.uk/society/2011/apr/11/eaves-housing-trafficking-salvation-army?INTCMP=SRCH (accessed 31 July 2012).

50 See Townsend, 'Human trafficking fears as key UK staff are lost'.

Any suggestion that these decisions are inevitable in the current economic crisis will be cold comfort to those affected. This is not least because in July 2011, former Tory MP Anthony Steen, chair of the Human Trafficking Foundation, said that government plans to fight human trafficking are basically about immigration control.[51]

It is in this context that the British courts will need to explore and develop a principled approach to the availability of refugee status to victims of human trafficking that is incontrovertibly 'victim-centred'. This is easier said than done. The UK government's report in 2009 on *The Trade in Human Beings* itself recorded that 'We were … disturbed to hear anecdotal evidence of a lack of awareness about trafficking and its effect on victims among immigration judges. It seems that there is a pressing need for training of judges, too.'[52] In recent years, moreover, the contemporary liberal democracies of the North Atlantic have been subject to severe financial cuts at a time of deep economic recession. There is a degree of 'compassion fatigue' in the wake of western governments' relentless 'War on Terror' that has seen the steady securitization of asylum and refugee policy in European countries. The current atmosphere is hardly conducive to encouraging a compassionate understanding of the core issues of human trafficking. Nevertheless, as this chapter shows, the sheer frequency with which victims of human trafficking now raise refugee asylum claims is such that the courts can hardly ignore their impact on refugee law. *The UNHCR Guidelines on International Protection 2006*,[53] which adopts the definition of human trafficking as set out in the Trafficking Protocol, that the 1951 Refugee Convention may properly afford protection to those at risk of trafficking, is now being used by the British courts. This is because, as the guidelines make clear, trafficking itself may amount to persecutory conduct and the victim may fear persecution, 'which whilst being unrelated to the fear of trafficking, may arise from the trafficking experience, in the form of family ostracism, social exclusion, re-traumatization or victimization, or other violence from the community at large'. The UNHCR guidelines do not assume that the Refugee Convention will cover all those at risk of ill-treatment,[54] past persecutory conduct and a fear of future persecution will clearly be a basis for protection. In *AZ (Thailand)*[55] the Upper Tribunal in the UK did precisely that in a far-reaching decision, which is discussed below. Indeed, Dr Alice Edwards gives examples[56] of 'a number of key asylum decisions reinforcing this analysis in

---

51 Mark Townsend, 'New trafficking laws "will not care for slavery victims"', *The Guardian*, 2 July 2011, at http://www.guardian.co.uk/uk/2011/jul/02/human-trafficking-laws-immigration-control?INTCMP=SRCH (accessed 31 July 2012).

52 Ibid., at para. 100.

53 UNHCR, *Guidelines on International Protection: The Application of Article 1A(2) of the 1951 Convention and/or 1967 Protocol Relating to the Status of Refugees to Victims of Trafficking and Persons at Risk of Being Trafficked*, 8, UN Doc. HCR/GIP/06/07 (7 April 2006). See also UNHCR, *Guidelines on International Protection: Gender-Related Persecution within the Context of Article JA(2) of the 1951 Convention and/or 1967 Protocol relating to the Status of Refugees*, UN Doc. HCR/GIP/02/01 (7 May 2002).

54 See Ryszard Piotrowicz, 'The UNHCR's Guidelines on Human Trafficking', *International Journal of Refugee Law* (Vol. 20, Issue 2, 2008), pp. 242–52. Professor Ryszard Piotrowicz was involved in the drafting of these guidelines.

55 *AZ (Trafficked Women) Thailand CG* [2010] UKUT 118 (IAC).

56 See Alice Edwards, 'Trafficking in Human Beings: At the Intersection of Criminal Justice, Human Rights, Asylum/Immigration Labor', *Denver Journal of International Law & Policy* (Vol. 36, Issue 1, 2007), pp. 1–53, at p. 36. Also at http://law.du.edu/documents/djilp/36No1/Traffic-

several countries, including Austria,[57] Australia,[58] Canada[59] and the United Kingdom'.[60] Yet for refugee lawyers there is an indisputable challenge because, as she recognizes only too well, '[i]n spite of these developments, the recognition rate continues to be low for victims of trafficking'.[61] In her words, '[d]ecision-makers are not always (yet) fit to handle the complexity of such cases' and '[t]rafficked victims are not always counselled on the options available to them, including their right to apply for asylum'. Indeed, '[t]rafficking victims may be discouraged from applying for asylum due to long delays, complicated procedures'. This is not least because of the 'increasingly restrictive policies relating to rights for asylum-seekers while awaiting a decision, including the possibility of detention, [and] other restrictions on freedom of movement'.[62] She is not far wrong. The plight of sex trafficking victims has not been helped by a recent ruling in the Court of Appeal where the Court may well have taken cognizance of the historical struggle against the abolition of slavery, in which modern human trafficking is surely rooted. In the 2010 case of *LM & Ors*,[63] Lord Justice Hughes held that[64] 'persons trafficked for [the purpose of forced prostitution] may clearly commit ... offences connected with prostitution' and that 'soliciting is an obvious example'.[65] The Court, however, rejected the proposition that 'a person thought to be trafficked should not be prosecuted for crimes committed as a result of the trafficking situation' because 'that ... is too wide a proposition' even in circumstances where the offence was committed 'under compulsion in the broad sense'.[66] Whereas such an observation is clearly right if it means that the victim is not absolved from responsibility for an act such as killing his/her trafficker, it may damage a 'victim-centred' approach if its effect is to prioritize prosecution of criminal offences over the

Human-Beings-Intersection-Criminal-Justice-Human-Rights-AsylumMigration-Labor-Alice-Edwards.pdf (accessed 7 August 2012)

57 *Verwaltungerichtshof [VwGH]* [administrative court] 31 January 2002, docket No. 99/20/0497-6 (Austria) (overruling prior decision that denied refugee status to Nigerian woman trafficked into prostitution and returned for reconsideration).

58 *VXAJ v. Minister for Immigration & Anor* (2006) FMCA 234 (Australia) (granting status to sex workers who might be forcibly re-trafficked as being a 'particular social group'). See Susan Kneebone and Bernadette McSherry, 'Trafficking in Women and Forced Migration: Moving Victims across the Border of Crime into the Domain of Human Rights', *International Journal of Human Rights* (Vol. 12, 2008), pp. 67–87 (referring to a number of failed cases).

59 *In reX* [1999] CRDD T98-06186 1, 4&7 (regarding Thai woman in sex trade).

60 *Secretary of State for the Home Dept. v. Dyhygun* [2000] UKIAT 00TH00728 (Immigration Appeal Tribunal) (appeal taken from UK) (refugee status of trafficked Ukrainian woman upheld on appeal); *Ogbeide*, Immigration Appellate Authority Appeal No. HX/08391/2002, 10 May 2002 (16-year-old Nigerian girl trafficked for prostitution); *Miss A B*, Immigration Appellate Authority Appeal No. CC/64057/2002, 18 February 2003 (16-year-old Nigerian girl trafficked for prostitution); *A*, Immigration Appellate Tribunal Appeal No. CC/63673/2002, 18 February 2003 (Albanian woman forced into prostitution); *K*, Immigration Appellate Tribunal Appeal No. UKIAT00023 K, 7 August 2003; *Tam Thi Dao*, Immigration Appellate Authority Appeal No. HX/28801/2003, 1 September 2003 (Vietnamese girl trafficked for prostitution).

61 Edwards, 'Trafficking in Human Beings', at p. 37.

62 Ibid.

63 Also cited as: [2011] Crim LR 425, [2011] 1 Cr App R 135, [2011] 1 Cr App R 12, [2010] EWCA Crim 2327.

64 Ibid., at para. 76.

65 At para. 82.

66 At para. 91.

protection principle for the victim. This is exactly what happened when in the case of *R v. N* in 2012 the Court rejected an appeal against the conviction and sentencing of two defendants who themselves were allegedly the victims of trafficking and consequent exploitation,[67] the Court citing with approval the judgment of Lord Hughes in *R v. LM*.[68] Yet ironically, as Dr Alice Edwards explains, 'the asylum channel is often the only one available' because of the 'absence of other mechanisms in which victims of trafficking may be granted temporary or permanent rights to remain in the country to where they have been trafficked'.[69] As will be seen below, the cases examined in this chapter arising before the British courts bear out these concerns.

(B) The Law Relating to Human Trafficking

The UN Protocol to Prevent, Suppress and Punish Trafficking in Persons, especially Women and Children[70] (the 'Trafficking Protocol') was one of two Protocols that was signed in Palermo, Italy, in 2000. It entered into force on 25 December 2003, and rapidly gained members so that, by October 2009, the Trafficking Protocol had been signed by 117 countries, with 133 parties. The other Protocol was the Protocol Against the Smuggling of Migrants by Land, Sea, and Air. The Trafficking Protocol was part of an overall package designed to counteract transnational organized crime. As such it was passed to supplement the United Nations Convention against Transnational Organized Crime 2000, and it provides an international definition of trafficking. Article 3 of the Trafficking Protocol reads:

a. 'Trafficking in persons' shall mean the recruitment, transportation, transfer, harbouring or receipt of persons, by means of the threat or use of force or other forms of coercion, of abduction, of fraud, of deception, of the abuse of power or of a position of vulnerability, or of the giving or receiving of payments or benefits to achieve the consent of a person having control over another person, for the purpose of exploitation. Exploitation shall include, at a minimum, the exploitation of the prostitution of others or other forms of sexual exploitation, forced labour or services, slavery or practices similar to slavery, servitude or the removal of organs;
b. The consent of a victim of trafficking in persons to the intended exploitation set forth in subparagraph (a) of this article shall be irrelevant where any of the means set forth in subparagraph (a) have been used ….

This was the first time that trafficking had been enshrined in international law. The importance of the Trafficking Protocol lay in focusing on the process, means and purposes of travel. In the words of the UK immigration tribunal in *AZ*, '[t]rafficking is thus defined by the act, the

67 N, R v (Rev 1) [2012] EWCA Crim 189 (20 February 2012) at para 7.
68 ibid., at paras 18–19.
69 Edwards, 'Trafficking in Human Beings', at p. 37.
70 See http://www2.ohchr.org/english/law/protocoltraffic.htm (accessed 31 July 2012).

means and the purpose'.[71] The Court of Appeal in the UK has also explained that '[t]he key to the definition of trafficking under the convention is that the act is done for the purpose of exploitation. If that is the purpose, and there is the necessary element of compulsion, fraud, abuse of power or similar means, then trafficking extends beyond transportation.'[72] The reference to 'exploitation' means that the consent of the victim is irrelevant. This is because it is illogical to consent to sexual exploitation, forced labour, slavery or practices similar to slavery, where the threat or use of force or coercion, abduction, fraud or deception has been used and where the trafficker has been guilty of abuse of power or of a position of vulnerability. Indeed, the Trafficking Protocol makes clear that children under 18 cannot give valid consent at all.[73]

Yet the very definition of human trafficking has created new problems. The concept of 'trafficking in persons' in the Trafficking Protocol suggests that it involves a 'range of actions and outcomes' because there are 'different phases of the process' of 'recruitment, transportation and control'[74] that are not always easy to comprehend, contextualize and constrain. This matters because it makes it necessary for state authorities to adopt a multifaceted approach to the problem. The conceptual difficulties at hand have led to the observation that 'the myriad definitional and political difficulties that surround the issue of trafficking mean that there is no clear body of evidence based on a consistent definition of the term "trafficking" to review'.[75]

The Trafficking Protocol has stirred acute controversy in other respects. It has been created outside the formal human rights system. It is also not a free-standing pledge, but one that was passed to supplement the United Nations Convention against Transnational Organized Crime 2000. It is a crime-fighting instrument where the plight of human beings caught up in its quagmire demands clear and certain redress. Yet there are no 'trafficking inspectors' for human trafficking, as there are with 'weapons inspectors'[76] in the international concern

---

71 *AZ (Trafficked women) Thailand CG* [2010] UKUT 118 (IAC), at para. 94.

72 Lord Justice Hughes in *LM & Ors* [2010] EWCA Crim 2327.

73 See also Council of Europe Convention on Action against Trafficking in Human Beings (2005). Article 10 addresses the issue of age as follows: 'When the age of the victim is uncertain and there are reasons to believe that the victim is a child, he or she shall be *presumed to be a child* and shall be accorded special protection measures pending verification of his/her age.' These special protection measures if a victim's age is uncertain must be in accordance with children's rights as defined in the UN Convention on the Rights of the Child. Also see the Yokohama Global Commitment agreed at the Second World Congress on the Commercial Sexual Exploitation of Children (Yokohama, 2001); United Nations Convention on the Rights of the Child (UN, 1989); the Optional Protocol on the Sale of Children, Child Prostitution and Child Pornography (2000) and the Optional Protocol on the Involvement on Children in Armed Conflict (2000); International Labour Organization (ILO) Convention 182 concerning the Elimination of the Worst Forms of Child Labour (2000); Declaration and Agenda for Action agreed at the First World Congress on the Commercial and Sexual Exploitation of Children (Stockholm, 1996).

74 See Bridget Anderson and Julia O'Connell Davidson, *Trafficking – a demand led problem? A multi-country pilot study* (Save the Children: Stockholm, 2003), at http://unosek.org/pdf/brazil/trafficking-a%20demand%20led%20problem.pdf (accessed 31 July 2012). See the section on 'Trafficking: Definitional problems', at pp. 8–9.

75 Ibid., at p. 5; see the Introduction.

76 See, for example, the *United Nations Weapons Inspectors Report to Security Council on Progress in Disarmament of Iraq* (7 March 2003), at http://www.un.org/News/Press/docs/2003/sc7682.doc.htm (accessed 30 July 2012).

over weapons of mass destruction. It is a blunt instrument. It has not led to the issue being raised in the UN Security Council, against those eastern European and Asian countries that have become well-established source countries in the trafficking of human beings. Therefore praise for the Trafficking Protocol has been mixed. Professor Hathaway[77] has been cautious, observing that it was passed 'under the umbrella of a non-rights-dedicated arrangement'.[78] He explains that '[b]y hiving off a relatively minor part of the slavery issue – no more than about three percent of modern slaves meet the definition of a "trafficked person" under the Trafficking Protocol – the world has found a means of seeming to be active on the slavery front without really addressing its predominant manifestations.'[79] He believes it is better to deal expressly with slavery at large as a human rights issue. There is force in this argument, for doing this would at least bring one closer to the question of remedies for the victims. But to say that 'the fight against human trafficking is more fundamentally in tension with core human rights goals than has generally been recognized'[80] arguably overstates the criticism. It can surely not mean that taking no action at all is a viable substitute for taking some action.

Nevertheless, it is as well to recognize that the Trafficking Protocol is ambivalent about providing victim-centred protection. A number of people have been critical of its preoccupation with law enforcement objectives, with Srikantiah[81] observing that it is much more about the concerns of developed countries regarding increased migration;[82] Bruch[83] stating that it is really part of the armoury of an explicit law enforcement regime; and Fitzpatrick[84] pointing out that it is about crime control and deterrence of unlawful migration. Obokata also laments the fact that 'little attention has been paid to human rights aspects of smuggling as it is mainly characterised as facilitation of illegal migration'.[85] More recently, Jayasinghe and Baglay say of the Trafficking Protocol that, '[s]et against a background of border control and transnational crime, its focus is on the prevention and the prosecution of human trafficking rather than the protection of victims'.[86]

On the other hand, Anne T. Gallagher has pointed out that tackling human trafficking outside a human rights framework is unsurprising given that the human rights system had

---

[77] James C. Hathaway, 'The Human Rights Quagmire of "Human Trafficking"', *Virginia Journal of International Law* (Vol. 49, 2008), pp. 1–59.

[78] Ibid., at p. 54.

[79] Ibid., at p. 4.

[80] Ibid.

[81] Jayashri Srikantiah, 'Perfect Victims and Real Survivors: The Iconic Victim in Domestic Human Trafficking Law', *Boston University Law Review* (Vol. 87, 2007), pp. 157–211.

[82] Ibid., at p. 168.

[83] Elizabeth M. Bruch, 'Models Wanted: The Search for an Effective Response to Human Trafficking', *Stanford Journal of International Law* (Vol. 40, 2004), pp. 1–46, at pp. 2–3, 7–11.

[84] Joan Fitzpatrick, 'Trafficking as a Human Rights Violation: The Complex Intersection of Legal Frameworks for Conceptualizing and Combatting Trafficking', *Michigan Journal of International Law* (Vol. 24, 2003), pp. 1143–68, at p. 1165.

[85] Tom Obokata, 'Smuggling of Human Beings from a Human Rights Perspective: Obligations of Non-State and State Actors under International Human Rights Law', *International Journal of Refugee Law* (Vol. 17, Issue 2, 2005), pp. 394–415, , at p. 394.

[86] Udara Jayasinghe and Sasha Baglay, 'Protecting Victims of Human Trafficking Within a "Non-Refoulement" Framework: Is Complementary Protection an Effective Alternative in Canada and Australia?', *International Journal of Refugee Law* (Vol. 23, Issue 3, 2011), pp. 489–520, at p. 493.

proved itself, 'on its own, incapable of taking any serious steps towards eliminating trafficking and other forms of private exploitation'.[87] She states that '[i]t is not helpful to be aggrieved about the fact that these changes were generated outside the formal human rights system', and nor is it 'productive to sound dire'.[88] It is possible to argue that such sanguine support overlooks the fact that there are no specific commitments to protection in the Trafficking Protocol. So the challenge for the courts will be how to make these commitments and how to fashion new remedies in the context of the Refugee Convention. These would have to be victim-centred to be effective protection tools. This is because when Anne T. Gallagher enthuses that, through the Trafficking Protocol, 'the human rights system has now been given new and better tools with which to work',[89] this arguably overlooks the fact that there is nothing in the Trafficking Protocol that provides the courts with an injunction as to how to respond. There are no express tools.

The link between human trafficking and refugee law will nevertheless now have to be made by the courts because of the signing in Warsaw of the Council of Europe Convention on Action against Trafficking in Human Beings,[90] (the 'Anti-Trafficking Convention') on 16 May 2005. This instrument was in turn signed by the United Kingdom on 23 March 2007 and ratified by it on 17 December 2008. It entered into force in respect of the United Kingdom on 1 April 2009. The Anti-Trafficking Convention is more victim centred. Indeed, in the words of Anne Gallagher it is often considered as the basis of a rights-based approach because '[t]he requirements of the European Trafficking Convention with respect to victim support and assistance are much more specific, detailed and substantive than those of the Trafficking Protocol'.[91] A number of provisions are highly significant. Article 12 requires a State Party to take 'due account of the victim's safety and protection needs' and in mandatory terms states that it 'shall adopt such legislative or other measures as may be necessary to assist victims in their physical, psychological and social recovery'.[92] Article 13 is most significant for it allows for a 'period of recovery and reflection' of at least 30 days 'when there are reasonable grounds to believe that the person concerned is a victim' and 'during this period it shall not be possible to enforce any expulsion order against him or her'.[93] Other provisions are no less significant.

---

87 Ibid., at p. 847.

88 Anne T. Gallagher, *The International Law of Human Trafficking* (Cambridge: Cambridge University Press, 2010), at p. 847, criticizing Prof Hathaway's observations at pp. 54–7.

89 Ibid.

90 CETS No. 197, at http://conventions.coe.int/Treaty/en/Treaties/Html/197.htm. Also see http://conventions.coe.int/Treaty/Commun/QueVoulezVous.asp?NT=197&CM=1&CL=ENG and http://www.coe.int/t/e/human_rights/trafficking/ (all accessed 7 August 2012).

91 Gallagher, *International Law of Human Trafficking*, at p. 307

92 Such assistance shall include at least: (a) standards of living capable of ensuring their subsistence, through such measures as: appropriate and secure accommodation, psychological and material assistance; (b) access to emergency medical treatment; (c) translation and interpretation services, when appropriate; (d) counselling and information, in particular as regards their legal rights and the services available to them, in a language that they can understand; (e) assistance to enable their rights and interests to be presented and considered at appropriate stages of criminal proceedings against offenders; (f) access to education for children.

93 The full terms of the provision are as follows: 'In terms, it states that: "Each Party shall provide in its internal law a recovery and reflection period of at least 30 days, when there are reasonable grounds to believe that the person concerned is a victim. Such a period shall be sufficient for the person concerned to recover and escape the influence of traffickers and/or to

Article 14 makes provision for the grant of residence permits to victims of human trafficking.[94] Article 16 places an emphasis on 'voluntary' returns of victims.[95] And, where trafficked persons are at risk of ill-treatment from traffickers, the State is required to provide effective and appropriate protection for victims under Article 28.[96]

In short, the Anti-Trafficking Convention is based on recognition of the principle that trafficking in human beings constitutes a violation of human rights and an offence against the dignity and integrity of the human being. It is a comprehensive treaty that aims to prevent trafficking, protect the human rights of victims of trafficking, and prosecute the traffickers. It applies to all forms of trafficking, whether national or transnational, whether or not related to organized crime, whoever the victim, and whatever the form of exploitation. It is a tool-kit for the courts to provide 'victim-centred' protection. To this may be added Council Directive 2004/81/EC of 29 April 2004[97] (aptly described as the 'Residence Permit Directive'), which is meant to allow for the grant of a residence permit to those who have been the victims of human trafficking or to those who have been the subject of an action to facilitate illegal immigration, as third-country nationals, provided they cooperate with the competent authorities. The protection here, therefore, is a conditional one, and not necessarily free from difficulty, as there may be many reasons why a victim is unable or unwilling to cooperate with the authorities, not least of which may be the fear of retribution from their traffickers. Recently, the European Parliament has also passed Council Directive 2011/36/EU of 5 April 2011 on preventing and combating trafficking in human beings and protecting its victims, and this replaces Council Framework Decision 2002/629/JHA[98] (known as the 'EU Trafficking

take an informed decision on cooperating with the competent authorities. During this period it shall not be possible to enforce any expulsion order against him or her. This provision is without prejudice to the activities carried out by the competent authorities in all phases of the relevant national proceedings, and in particular when investigating and prosecuting the offences concerned. During this period, the Parties shall authorise the persons concerned to stay in their territory."'

94 It is to the effect that, 'if the competent authority considers that their stay is necessary owing to their personal situation or for the purpose of their co-operation with the competent authorities in investigation or criminal proceedings', then each State Party 'shall issue a renewable residence permit to victims'.

95 Article 16 deals with the situation where a State Party has to return a trafficked person to his/her country or to another State. The emphasis is firmly on 'voluntary' return so that, 'when a Party returns a victim to another State, such return shall be with due regard for the rights, safety and dignity of that person and for the status of any legal proceedings related to the fact that the person is a victim'. The latter provision is not insignificant for it requires a State Party to allow the victim of human trafficking to remain in their territory to enable them to seek legal redress from their oppressors for trafficking them.

96 Article 28 goes onto provide that each State Party 'shall adopt such legislative or other measures as may be necessary to provide effective and appropriate protection for victims and other groups from potential retaliation or intimidation', in particular during and after investigation and prosecution of perpetrators.

97 European Union: Council of the European Union, Council Directive 2004/81/EC of 29 April 2004 on the Residence Permit Issued to Third-Country Nationals who are Victims of Trafficking in Human Beings or who have been the Subject of an Action to Facilitate Illegal Immigration, Who Cooperate With the Competent Authorities, 6 August 2004, 2004/81/EC.

98 European Union: European Parliament and Council of the European Union, Directive 2011/36/EU of 5 April 2011 on Preventing and Combating Trafficking in Human Beings and

Directive'). What this does is attempt to bring together the substantive criminal law and the criminal procedural rules of the Member States on combating trafficking in human beings, by positing a regime that is centred on the defence of human rights, the implementation of victims' protection and assistance mechanisms, and the prevention and suppression of crime. It is founded on a global and multidisciplinary approach of the Prevention of crime, the Protection of victims and the Prosecution of offenders (and therefore known as the 'Three Ps').[99] It came into force on 15 April 2011, and the expectation is that it will be implemented by the Member States by 6 April 2013.

These laws are a vindication of the critiques of insightful academic scholars. They have long argued for novel approaches to tackling the problem of human trafficking which have included the use of asylum law protection mechanisms. One of the most perspicacious has been Professor Susan Kneebone,[100] who has pointed out that, 'in reality, many smuggled persons are indeed fleeing to seek refugee status elsewhere',[101] and that '[a] focus on the trafficked/smuggled person dichotomy demonstrates its limits in this context and the potential that it has to conceal the refugee'.[102] She has stated that '[t]here is a clear nexus between the circumstances which create refugees and those which lead to trafficking. In some regions, the "structural" factors which lead to trafficking could also satisfy the meaning of "persecution", such as social and economic exclusion of minorities, gender and age discrimination and economic underdevelopment, intra-family violence, xenophobia, corruption, unemployment, and internal conflict.'[103] She also argued that 'trafficked persons and refugees often travel the same routes and use the same facilitators. The two cohorts are indeed often indistinguishable.'[104] This is confirmed by another leading expert, Professor Ryszard Piotrowicz, who has emphasized the experiences of the victim,[105] observing that, even though 'human trafficking is clandestine',[106] nevertheless 'what is well-known is the nature of the experiences of victims ... and the gravity of the breaches of their most basic rights and interests'.[107] Thus '[s]ome will have consented to travel to another country but not to the conditions of living and work to which they are exposed. Some may not even have consented to travel at all. Many will have been deceived about the nature of the work they will be required to perform.'[108] The cases discussed in this chapter are a fitting testimony to the observations of these academic commentators.

Protecting its Victims, and Replacing Council Framework Decision 2002/629/JHA, 5 April 2011, 2011/36/EU.

[99] At http://www.dgpj.mj.pt/sections/english-version/news-and-events/anexos/directive-2011-36-eu-of/ (accessed 31 July 2012).

[100] Susan Kneebone, 'The Refugee – Trafficking Nexus: making Good (the) Connections', *Refugee Survey Quarterly* (Vol. 29, Issue 1, 2010), pp. 137–60.

[101] Ibid., at p. 144.

[102] Ibid.

[103] Kneebone, *The Refugee*, at pp. 139–40.

[104] Ibid., at p. 140.

[105] Ryszard Piotrowicz, 'Trafficking of Human Beings and their Human Rights in the Migration Context', in Ryszard Cholewinski, Richard Perruchoud and Euan Macdonald (eds), *International Migration Law: Developing Paradigms and Key Challenges* (The Hague: T.M.C. Asser Press, 2007), chapter 16, at pp. 275–90.

[106] Ibid., at p. 275.

[107] Ibid.

[108] Ibid.

Indeed, as Harvard scholar Professor Jacqueline Bhabha notes, '[n]owhere is the complex link between economic desperation and refugee status more evident than in the area of human smuggling and human trafficking – two forms of illegal and commercially assisted entry used by those fleeing persecution to reach a place of safety in the face of migration control measures.'[109] In fact, as she explained in a seminal article written over a decade ago, '[a]sylum seekers are increasingly compelled to resort to the use of smugglers',[110] with the result that '[c]ircumvention is thus increasingly a professional art, not something that can be left to ingenuity or good luck'.[111] The observations of these scholars demonstrate the need for victims of human trafficking to be treated rather more like conventional refugees than as criminals transgressing immigration controls. The British cases considered below are a telling reminder of this, though they have a mixed record.

Human trafficking into Europe threatens the very basis of democratic life in European societies. Cases now coming before the European Court of Human Rights ('ECtHR') highlight this. In the remarkable 2010 case of *Rantsev v Cyprus and Russia*,[112] the ECtHR explained how 'the explanatory report accompanying the Anti-Trafficking Convention emphasises that trafficking in human beings is a major problem in Europe today which threatens the human rights and fundamental values of democratic societies'.[113] That case concerned complaints against Russia concerning its alleged failure to take the necessary measures to protect Ms Rantsev from the risk of trafficking and exploitation.[114] Ms Rantsev had died in Cyprus and the complaints included the failure by Russia to conduct an investigation into the circumstances of her arrival in Cyprus, her employment there, and her subsequent death in the country to which she had been trafficked. The Court observed that such complaints were not predicated on the assertion that Russia was responsible for acts committed in Cyprus or by the Cypriot authorities, but on the fact that the alleged trafficking commenced in Russia, and that country had an obligation to combat trafficking. So the claims were declared admissible. Russia should have taken measures to protect Ms Rantsev from trafficking and conducted proper investigation into her circumstances. Cases such as this have opened up new vistas for the

[109] Jacqueline Bhabha, 'International Gatekeepers: The Tension between Asylum Advocacy and Human Rights', *Harvard Human Rights Journal* (Vol. 15, Spring 2002), pp. 1–25.

[110] Ibid., at p. 172.

[111] Ibid.

[112] *Rantsev*, at p. 207. Note that the Council of Europe Convention on Action against Trafficking in Human Beings, CETS No. 197, 16 May 2005 was discussed extensively in this case at paras 160–74.

[113] *Rantsev*, at para. 161. The application was actually under Article 34 of the Convention for the Protection of Human Rights and Fundamental Freedoms and it was brought by Ms Rantsev's father originally on 26 May 2004, who complained under Articles 2, 3, 4, 5 and 8 of the Convention about the lack of sufficient investigation into the circumstances of the death of his daughter, the lack of adequate protection of his daughter by the Cypriot police while she was still alive and the failure of the Cypriot authorities to take steps to punish those responsible for his daughter's death and ill-treatment.

[114] The TIPS report was considered by the ECtHR (at para. 105) and it was noted that: 'Cyprus is a destination country for a large number of women trafficked from the Philippines, Russia, Moldova, Hungary, Ukraine, Greece, Vietnam, Uzbekistan, and the Dominican Republic for the purpose of commercial sexual exploitation … Most victims of trafficking are fraudulently recruited to Cyprus on three-month "artiste" work permits to work in the cabaret industry or on tourist visas to work in massage parlors disguised as private apartments.'

courts. What the cases discussed in this chapter show, however, is that the record of British courts and tribunals has hitherto had a chequered history in dealing with human trafficking issues in a victim-centred way.[115]

(C) The Identification and Assistance of Victims

As noted at the beginning of this chapter, British legal initiatives have tracked international law developments. When on 17 December 2008 the UK ratified the Council of Europe Convention on Action against Trafficking in Human Beings (CETS No. 197), its ratification required the UK to have a national referral mechanism (a definitive process for identifying victims) in place for 1 April 2009, as well as other key benefits such as a process by which victims would be offered support, including a 45-day reflection and recovery period, and the possibility of a one-year renewable residence permit. Victims were to be offered medical treatment, counselling and information as well as appropriate accommodation. Victims could receive compensation. Two provisions were especially important for a victim-centred law. First, Article 10 required States to provide means by which trained personnel are made available to identify and assist victims. This was important because it created a positive duty to adopt measures to this end. Second, there was the freedom from the imposition of penalties on victims for their involvement in unlawful activities enshrined in Article 26, which provides a 'Non-punishment Provision'.[116]

The United Kingdom took extensive steps to discharge its obligations under this convention. A number of bodies, whose purpose is the identification and assistance of victims, have been established to ensure compliance with Article 10. The government created the United Kingdom Human Trafficking Centre (UKHTC), a multi-agency centre, one of whose functions is the identification of those who are or may be trafficked victims. It also formed a National Referral Mechanism (NRM) as a mechanism through which public bodies, including criminal justice bodies, can refer individual cases for consideration. These agencies operated in the context of a number of third-sector organizations that set out to identify and assist victims of trafficking. One such venerable body is the Poppy Project, a charity largely funded by the government substantially for this purpose. There now exist also the Gangmaster's Licensing Authority, which regulates those who supply labour or use workers to provide services in agriculture, forestry, horticulture, shellfish gathering, and food processing and packaging.[117] It is subject to The Gangmasters (Licensing Authority) Regulations 2005.[118] All these agencies are charged with the identification of persons who have 'reasonable grounds for being treated as a victim of trafficking'. That test is derived directly from Article 10. When a person is

[115] See 'Opinion No. 6/2010 of the Group of Experts on Trafficking in Human Beings of the European Commission: On the Decision of the European Court of Human Rights in the Case of Rantsev v. Cyprus and Russia', *International Journal of Refugee Law* (Vol. 22, Issue 4, 2010), pp. 673–6.

[116] It reads: 'Each party shall, in accordance with the basic principles of its legal system, provide for the *possibility of not imposing penalties on victims for their involvement in unlawful activities* to the extent that they have been compelled to do so.'

[117] Via http://gla.defra.gov.uk/ (accessed 31 July 2012).

[118] At http://www.legislation.gov.uk/uksi/2005/448/contents/made (accessed 31 July 2012).

identified as meeting that threshold test, he or she will be eligible for a number of forms of assistance, including a period of not less than 30 days for recovery and reflection during which no steps may be taken to repatriate or remove him. This is the trigger for the assistance to victim provisions, and, as such, the test of reasonable grounds establishes a comparatively low threshold. As Lord Justice Hughes explained in *LM & Ors v R.* [2010] EWCA Crim 2327 recently, 'If it is met, that does not mean that it has been determined that the person concerned actually *is* a victim of trafficking, but rather that there are reasonable grounds to believe that they may be.'[119]

Already, however, difficulties are beginning to emerge in this legal framework. These risk dilution of a victim-centred approach. Take the National Referral Mechanism ('NRM'). Not only is this an unattractive name, implying things that other people do to other people, with no reference in it whatsoever to 'human trafficking' (in the way as there is to the Human Trafficking Centre [UKTC]), but a number of questions are thrown up. How effective is the NRM as a referral mechanism? Is that effectiveness impaired by the fact that the United Kingdom Border Agency ('UKBA') participates in the referral, thus bringing into the decision-making process a significant element of immigration control? Is the process independent enough? How quick and fair is the decision-making process? Should there be a right of appeal against the decisions of the NRM? Is it suitable for children? Can the reflection period be better promoted? Some of these concerns have come to the fore in the latest *US Trafficking in Persons (TIP) Report*.[120]

The TIP Report from the USA is released every year. It monitors the progress of anti-trafficking measures around the world. It is the US government's principal diplomatic tool to engage foreign governments on human trafficking and is the world's most comprehensive resource of governmental anti-human trafficking efforts. The US government uses the TIP Report to engage foreign governments in dialogues to advance anti-trafficking reforms and to combat trafficking and to target resources on prevention, protection and prosecution programmes. Not surprisingly, the UK government scores well in this report. It would be worrying indeed if it did not. The report, published on 27 June 2011, put the UK in the top tier (Tier 1) for anti-trafficking activity. Nevertheless, the TIP Report 2011 highlighted key areas for improvement such as: the inadequate and inconsistent protection efforts for trafficking victims; the criminalization of trafficking victims, including children; the inconsistency of decision making resulting from the use of devolved powers; the lack of victim coordination; the limited space for dedicated accommodations for victims; the fact that victims could opt out of being referred into the NRM; the inadequate levels of protection for child victims of trafficking; the fact that children went missing from local authority care; the inappropriate asylum process for victims without enough time for recovery.[121] In the 2012 case of *Re W*[122] the issue was unsuccessfully raised in Northern Ireland that that the NRM policy breaches Art 4

---

119 *LM & Ors v R.* [2010] EWCA Crim 2327 (21 October 2010), at para. 6.

120 At http://www.state.gov/g/tip/rls/tiprpt/ (accessed 31 July 2012).

121 At http://www.state.gov/g/tip/rls/tiprpt/2011/; see also http://www.state.gov/g/drl/rls/hrrpt/2007/100591.htm (both accessed 31 July 2012).

122 *W, Re Judicial Review [2012] NIQB 37 (31 May 2012).*

of the EctHR obligations by failing to provide an effective means of identifying people who have been victims of trafficking.[123] So clearly, there are continuing concerns here.

Closer to home, in May 2011, the Crown Prosecution Service ('CPS') in Britain issued its CPS Policy for Prosecuting Cases of Human Trafficking.[124] It professed to work with a range of other government and non-government agencies. These included the police and the courts. The aim has been to provide victims with appropriate protection and support to ensure their safety and 'to help them to give evidence'.[125] Yet remarkably, despite the fact that the NRM is a mechanism through which public bodies, including criminal justice bodies, can refer individual cases for consideration, the CPS will not refer victims into the NRM. Given its recognition that '75% of referrals made to the National Referral Mechanism were for female victims, and the UN estimates that 79% of all trafficking victims are women and girls',[126] it is not clear why it will not itself make this referral. So much for governmental bodies. Non-governmental bodies too, however, risk being ineffective. This is because the Poppy Project has become a casualty of the economic recession. The government has cut its funding significantly.[127] What it can do now will be limited.

The result is that protection efforts remain inadequate and inconsistent for trafficking victims, who remain at risk of criminalization, despite the existence in the law of a provision that triggers protection 'when there are reasonable grounds to believe that the person concerned is a victim', and that 'established a comparatively low threshold'.[128] Law enforcement agencies remain keen to prosecute. They are not keen to provide protection. We can now examine the British cases of the last five years that bear out this thesis.

(D) Judicial Perspectives in the British Cases

The British cases can be divided into those where a refugee claim was established and those where it was not – even if a refugee claim was expressly raised by the victims to human trafficking. The cases make grim reading. So, the purpose here is to see if there are lessons to be learnt about good and bad practice, or about positive and negative institutional cultures, or about the lottery of finding a sympathetic official or an unsympathetic one, and ultimately about how the quest for a 'victim-centred' approach, which it would appear on the evidence before us, remains a chimera. Let us consider those cases where a refugee claim was not even allowed to be established.

---

[123] This State obligation arises, 'If an individual is eligible for the provisions of the council of Europe Convention on Action against Trafficking in human beings' (at paras 4–5 of judgment).

[124] CPS Policy for Prosecuting Cases of Human Trafficking (May 2011) at http://www.cps.gov.uk/publications/docs/policy_for_prosecuting_cases_of_human_trafficking.pdf; also see http://www.cps.gov.uk/legal/h_to_k/human_trafficking_and_smuggling/ (both accessed 20 August 2012).

[125] Ibid.,at p. 3.

[126] Ibid., at p. 2: see http://www.state.gov/g/drl/rls/hrrpt/2007/100591.htm (accessed 31 July 2012).

[127] Butler and Travis, 'Sex trafficking charity loses out to Salvation Army over £6m contract'.

[128] Lord Justice Hughes in *LM & Ors v R.* [2010] EWCA Crim 2327 (21 October 2010), at para. 6.

(i) Prosecution of Victims and the Public Interest – Bad Practices?

The case of *R v. O* in 2008[129] is interesting because it arose when the UK government had signed – but not yet ratified – the Anti-Trafficking Protocol (i.e. the Council of Europe Convention on Action against Trafficking in Human Beings). The case concerned a defendant, who appears to have been a minor aged 17, but who was dealt with in the Crown Court for an offence of possessing a false identity card. Her case was that she had come to this country aged 16 to avoid an arranged marriage in her home country to a 63-year-old man who had five wives already. She said that on arrival she was exploited as a prostitute and that she had committed the offence in the course of an effort to escape to France. She had been assessed by the Poppy Project as a credible victim of sex trafficking. Nevertheless, there had been no consideration given to the question of whether it was in the public interest to prosecute her, no thought had been given to whether she might have a defence of duress, and indeed nobody addressed themselves to the fact that if she was under 18, as she appeared to be, she should not have been dealt with as an adult in the Crown Court at all. Lord Justice Laws in the Court of Appeal was damning of the authorities involved: 'We hope that such a shameful set of circumstances never occurs again. Prosecutors must be aware of the protocols which, although not in the text books, are enshrined in their Code. Defence lawyers must respond by making enquiries, if there is before them credible material showing that they have a client who might have been the victim of trafficking, especially a young client.'[130]

Yet the same problems arose in *LM & Ors*[131] in 2010, even though that was a case that arose after the Anti-Trafficking Protocol had been ratified, and after it had come into effect in Britain. Such were the official failings that the Court of Appeal was driven to refer to *R v. O* and to say: 'We echo the concern there expressed as to general awareness of the convention.'[132] *R v. LM & Ors* concerned five cases of victims of human trafficking[133] and Lord Justice Hughes considered that they 'provided the opportunity to consider the obligations of this country under the *Council of Europe Convention on Action against Trafficking in Human Beings 2005* (CETS No 197)'.[134] His Lordship observed that '[t]here is no doubt that trafficking people is a signally unpleasant crime …'.[135] The Court referred to the international context in which protection was sought by national governments, '[b]ecause it is often (but not always) conducted across international borders, it is particularly appropriate for inter-state agreement as to steps to be taken to attempt to deal with it'.[136] The Court highlighted the importance of international law, pointing out that 'the principal current international instrument, which contains specific and positive obligations upon States, is the *2005 Council of Europe Treaty*',[137] and it reminded

129 *R v. O* in [2008] EWCA Crim 2835.

130 Ibid., at para. 26.

131 [2010] EWCA Crim 2327, which is also cited as: [2011] Crim LR 425, [2011] 1 Cr App R 135, [2011] 1 Cr App R 12, [2010] EWCA Crim 2327.

132 Ibid., at para. 95.

133 Ibid., at para. 76.

134 Ibid.

135 Ibid., at para. 77.

136 Ibid.

137 Ibid.

everyone once again that '[t]he United Kingdom is bound by this treaty'.[138] The Court referred to past shortcomings, recalling of the UK that, '[a]t the time of *R v O* [2008] EWCA Crim. 2835, it had signed but not ratified the treaty and was thus subject to the attenuated obligation under Article 18 of the Vienna Convention on the Law of Treaties to refrain from acts which would defeat its object and purpose. Now, however, this country has ratified the Convention (on 17 December 2008) and it is fully bound by it.'[139] In the process of exposing official state failure, what was surely also especially noteworthy was how the Court in the five cases threw open a window into the shady and inscrutable lives of those that inhabit the twilight world of human trafficking. It is the challenge of grasping this hidden world that is the essential task before state authorities today as they struggle to find a victim-centred solution to the problem of human trafficking. Otherwise, victims will not only continue to suffer. They will be overlooked by the system.

Of the five, three of the women defendants had been convicted of offences of controlling prostitution[140] and the Crown held them responsible for running the brothels, and for bringing women to this country.[141] Indeed, when they were cautioned, none suggested that she had herself been trafficked. One of them even said that she had originally come voluntarily to the UK to work as a prostitute.[142] Yet the Crown Prosecution Service's ('CPS') pre-charging note recorded that, although none had asserted it, 'the police believe that they were probably trafficked into the UK themselves'.[143] Many months later the three women made it clear in their defence statements that they too had been trafficked. Remarkably, they denied any active threats, violence or sexual abuse, and asserted that 'they had done whatever they had done by way of encouraging the prostitution of others, or helping to collect their earnings, only under the coercion of the men'.[144] Then, just before the jury was sworn in, the Crown accepted that these three women had been trafficked, beaten and coerced into prostitution themselves, and that anything which had amounted to controlling prostitution had been done under pressure.[145] However, not having learnt the lessons of *R. v. O*, the CPS still set out to proceed with their trial. Lord Justice Hughes expressed his frustration: '[a]t that stage, it is plain that no-one on behalf of the Crown applied their mind to the question whether in the changed circumstances there was a public interest in continuing prosecution.'[146] His Lordship went onto say that, 'when the new factual basis was accepted, there could only have been one conclusion, which was that the prosecution should be abandoned by the offering of no evidence'.[147]

138 Ibid.
139 Ibid.
140 Ibid., at para. 99. This was for the gain of themselves or another, contrary to s 53 Sexual Offences Act 2003.
141 Ibid., at para. 100.
142 Ibid., at para. 101.
143 Ibid.
144 Lord Justice Hughes, at para. 103.
145 Ibid., at para. 104.
146 Ibid., at para. 105.
147 Ibid., at para. 105.

(ii) Failure to Provide Protection – Negative Institutional Cultures?

In the same way, the case of *O.O.O.*[148] in 2011 also concerned five young women who had been trafficked into the UK. This time it was not for their sexual services. It was for the purposes of their labour exploitation. This time the concern was not over their criminal prosecution. The concern was over complete failure of state agencies to afford them with protection that they badly needed. Each of the five was brought into the United Kingdom from Nigeria illegally. Each alleged they were made to work for no pay in households in and around London, over a number of years thereafter. In a case that brought home the relevance of the *Slavery Convention 1926* each claimed to have been subjected to physical and emotional abuse by the householders, amounting to inhuman and degrading treatment and being held in slavery or servitude.[149] In each case, when officers of the Metropolitan Police were asked to investigate the treatment that had been meted out to them, the Metropolitan Police failed to undertake any such investigation.[150] In court the government 'openly acknowledged'[151] their ill-treatment contrary to European Convention of Human Rights, but did not accept that there was any breach of duty on the part of any police officers investigating their claims.[152] The cases took at least ten years to get to court.

The first indication of something amiss arose when in April 2001 an anonymous letter was written about the first of the five girls to the Enfield Social Services Department, inquiring: 'Why is the little girl not attending school? Is it not the law of the land that children of "school-age" attend school? I have often passed the house during the day, to see the little girl, "fetching and carrying", and the thought occurs to me the little girl may be here illegally, and is being used as a servant.'[153] When an investigation was carried out by the local authority, it only concentrated on the fact that this child was not attending school and within a month, in May 2001, the file was closed. When one adult, a Mrs Hall, went to Southgate Police Station with the first girl, who gave a Statement there, the police officer told her that 'there were a lot of people who try to use the police to get out of situations that they have got themselves into. The officer appeared to think that [the child] was partly to blame for coming into the UK illegally even though she was a child and said that the police see a lot of people in [this Claimant's] position. The officer said: "If I were you I wouldn't get involved".'[154] Unsurprisingly, nothing came of it and Mr Justice Wynn Williams was scathing about the response of the official authorities, observing that, 'On any view, however, [this] Claimant told the officer that she was being treated as a slave. That is recorded in writing. .... What was her purpose in going to the police other than to seek their protection and assistance?'[155] A case such as this exemplifies what is currently happening in Britain. Despite recent legal developments, the mind-set of treating victims of trafficking as immigration offenders is unchanged. The focus remains on

[148] *O.O.O.* [2011] EWHC 1246 (QB).

[149] This would have been contrary to Articles 3 and 4 respectively of ECHR: see ibid., Mr Justice Wynn Williams, at para. 1.

[150] See ibid., Mr Justice Wynn Williams, at para. 2.

[151] See ibid., Mr Justice Wynn Williams, at para. 3.

[152] See ibid., Mr Justice Wynn Williams, at para. 3.

[153] See ibid., Mr Justice Wynn Williams, at para. 31.

[154] See ibid., Mr Justice Wynn Williams, at para. 49.

[155] See ibid., Mr Justice Wynn Williams, at para. 41.

law enforcement rather than on victim protection. It is, therefore, disappointing that there has been so little practical change in the UK.

More worryingly still when, later during 2006, it emerged that other girls had been subject to treatment similar to that which had been meted out to the five girls,[156] and three other Nigerian girls actually proceeded to submit a claim for asylum and/or humanitarian protection, these issues were not investigated by the police. Yet there was a clear pattern of trafficking leading to potential claims for asylum. Mr Justice Wynn Williams was once again scathing that[157] the Statements of the girls were 'in the main … focused upon the ill-treatment which the girls had suffered and upon those matters which were most relevant to support a claim for asylum or humanitarian protection',[158] and yet the protection needs of the victims had escaped notice. The case demonstrates the importance of attaching credibility to the story of the victims, which should always be the starting point. All too often, victims' narratives are ignored over other narratives, especially those of law enforcement agencies, with serious consequences for the victims. What both these cases demonstrate is how the adoption of bad practices and negative institutional cultures works to frustrate a 'victim-centred' approach where this is sorely needed.

(iii) Choosing between the Experience of Trafficking and the Threat of Re-Trafficking – What is Good Practice?

We may now consider the cases where a refugee claim has been expressly raised, or has succeeded before the court or tribunal. Where refugee claims in the context of human trafficking have been made, the court's approach has been difficult to predict. What the tribunal of inquiry looks at is not just the fact of trafficking, but the context of the society in which it takes place. Where cases fail, they often fail because there is no perceived threat of re-trafficking. The question therefore to be asked here – especially in the context of the factual scenarios that have unfolded in this chapter – is whether the fact that the victim has been subjected to human trafficking should lead the courts to adopt an approach that is less focused on the threat of re-trafficking, and more concerned with the experiences suffered by the person in question. There is still no clear answer to this question. In one of the earliest cases, in *SB (Moldovo)* in 2008, the Tribunal concluded that, '[i]n the context of Moldovan society, a woman who has been trafficked for the purposes of sexual exploitation is a member of a particular social group … being "former victims of trafficking for sexual exploitation"'.[159] This was in circumstances where the evidence suggested that 'the estimated number of individuals who have been trafficked, as a percentage of the general population, is the highest for Moldovo, amongst the five countries in which it is a problem', and that 'Moldovo has the highest proportion of the population which perceives human trafficking

[156] Ibid., at para. 54.

[157] See ibid., paras 74–5.

[158] At ibid., para. 74. Mr Justice Wynn Williams added that, 'To a limited extent, however, they also made reference to other girls who had been subjected to similar treatment. In her statement YT said that she had a "'few friends here who [were] in a similar situation …"' (para. 74).

[159] *SB (PSG, Protection Regulations, Reg 6) Moldova CG* [2008] UKAIT 00002 (26 November 2007) at p. 41, para. 112(e).

as a problem in the country'.[160] However, it did so under the Qualification Directive, and not strictly under the Refugee Convention, where as things stood the case could not succeed.[161]

The Refugee Convention was also not successfully invoked in the 2009 case of *HC (China)*, where the Tribunal considered there to be no risk of re-trafficking for the victim if she were returned to China as an unmarried mother of an illegitimate child. She had alleged that she would face punishment for leaving China and for breaching family-planning regulations with the birth of her child, and that there existed her and her child's vulnerability to exploitation by people-traffickers in China.[162] The Tribunal considered the definition of 'persecution' in the immigration rules[163] but held that '[n]o evidence has been adduced before us to show that those who were responsible for trafficking the appellant previously would be in any position to identify her and abduct her.'[164] But more remarkably, it found that the appellant could not succeed because 'the appellant is clearly now a very resourceful young woman, having lived alone from the age of 10 to 14 or 15 years, and has accumulated considerable experience of fending for herself. She is now fully aware of the dangers in considering employment which offers to pay a considerable amount of money.'[165] Might a more victim-centred approach, and one that recognized the historical context of modern-day slavery in the form of human trafficking, have yielded a different result?

Perhaps an answer to that question is more obviously clear in those cases where a trafficked person arrives from a country that is clearly known for its reputation as a 'source' country of human trafficking. This is because it is not so easy to ignore the general experience as a whole of a group of people in particular. Albania is one such country, from which many victims of human trafficking originate. In the UK, the Upper Tribunal of the Immigration & Asylum Chamber has provided important guidance, based on the various human rights reports with respect to claims by victims of human trafficking from Albania. Albania is a difficult country also because it requires a distinction to be made between smuggled and trafficked persons. This is an aspect that we have already commented upon at the outset. There is also the problem of how to determine the reintegration of such people into society. In *AM and BM (Albania)*,[166] it was found that the person in question 'was smuggled into the country and then escaped from

160 Ibid., at para. 105.

161 Regulation 6(1)(d) of the Qualification Directive reads: '(d) a group shall be considered to form a particular social group where, *for example:* (i) members of that group share an innate characteristic, or a common background that cannot be changed, or share a characteristic or belief that is so fundamental to identity or conscience that a person should not be forced to renounce it, *and* (ii) that group has a distinct identity in the relevant country, because it is perceived as being different by the surrounding society'.

162 See paras 82–4, esp. para. 83 at p. 39.

163 At para. 83 the Tribunal referred to Paragraph 339K of HC 395, which provides as follows: 'The fact that a person has already been subject to persecution or serious harm, or to direct threats of such persecution or such harm, will be regarded as a serious indication of the person's well-founded fear of persecution or real risk of suffering serious harm, unless there are good reasons to consider that such persecution or serious harm will not be repeated.'

164 At para. 84.

165 At para. 84. It is to be noted that in *LR v UK* (see further below) the ECtHR was sceptical about an argument that one is effectively 'street-wise' after having been trafficked once, so that no further risk attaches.

166 *AM and BM (Trafficked women)* Albania CG [2010] UKUT 80 (IAC).

her captor' and that 'she has therefore been the victim of people smugglers whose intention was to put her to work as a prostitute'.[167] Yet once again it was found that the victim, who had been a married woman, following which she was trafficked, was not at real risk of being trafficked on return to Albania.[168]

The Tribunal in giving guidance held that trafficked women in Albania come from all areas of the country and from varied social backgrounds. Therefore it was not possible to set out a typical profile of them. It held that, in determining whether a victim of trafficking can relocate, at its worst the psychological damage[169] inflicted on a victim of trafficking can lead to difficulties in reintegrating into Albanian society. It also held that much of Albanian society is governed by a strict code of honour, which means not only that trafficked women would have very considerable difficulty in reintegrating into their home areas on return, but that it will also affect their ability to relocate internally. Finally, it held that those that see themselves outside society, for example, divorced or abandoned women, or others who wish to live abroad, may seek out traffickers in order to facilitate their departure from Albania and their establishment in prostitution abroad.

In an observation that challenged conventional understandings of who is trafficked, the Tribunal went on to record that, although such women are not 'trafficked women', in the sense that they have not been abducted against their will, there is likely to be considerable violence within the relationships. This means that the psychological effect of that violence may lead to a situation where the pressures that they are under, and the lack of freedom they are under, means that such women should be treated as trafficked women. It is submitted that within this observation lies the kernel of a basis for refugee protection. Perhaps disappointingly, the Tribunal then concluded that whether they are at risk of persecution on account of such membership and whether they will be able to access sufficiency of protection from the authorities will depend upon their individual circumstances.

Indeed, notwithstanding such careful guidelines, it is possible that the Tribunal has not been getting it right. All too often its focus has been on the risk of re-trafficking. Yet, in April 2010, the European Court of Human Rights *LR v the United Kingdom*[170] heard an application from an Albania citizen against the UK that could be very portentous. She had moved to Italy in 2005, joining her brother and her younger sister, and in February 2007 she met there a northern Albanian man. A few weeks after their first meeting he abducted her, seized her identity papers, and held her in a room for a week, subjecting her to both physical and sexual assault. The following month, he and another man brought the applicant to the United Kingdom, providing her with identity papers, after which she was taken to a nightclub in Leeds. There she was expected to earn £2,000 every night by having sex with men. The applicant had to hand over all the money to the Albanian man. A week later, having been threatened with a knife by the Albanian man, she ran away from the nightclub and travelled to London. In April 2007, the applicant reported incidents of kidnapping and sexual assault to the police. She was

167 At para. 30 of IJ, referred to at para. 7 of UT.
168 At para. 42.
169 At para. 12.
170 *LR v the United Kingdom* – 49113/09 [2010] ECHR 607 (1 April 2010), at http://www.bailii.org/eu/cases/ECHR/2010/607.html (accessed 31 July 2012).

referred to the Poppy Project.[171] The applicant claimed asylum, on grounds that included her fear of persecution and retribution in Albania from the Albanian man she had met in Italy, and from his family, as well as on account of the risk of re-trafficking as a single, vulnerable, trafficked woman.

Unfortunately, the Crown Prosecution Service decided not to prosecute the Albanian man on grounds that the case against him was not strong. The applicant then received a letter from her sister in Italy, in which she explained that her family had disowned her and wished to harm her for dishonouring them. Soon afterwards, the police informed the applicant verbally that the Albanian man had been expelled to Albania. The applicant's asylum claim was refused by the Secretary of State because it was not accepted that there would be a reasonable likelihood of her being re-trafficked or abducted if returned to Albania. In any event, the applicant could avail herself of the protection of the Albanian authorities if necessary. This was despite the fact that a report from the Poppy Project had been submitted in her support to the effect that '[i]n the experience of the Poppy Project re-trafficking from Albania is a significant problem' and that 'the risk to returning victims is particularly high' because '[o]f a sample study of Albanian trafficking victims accessing the Poppy Project, 40% were re-trafficked prior to being referred'. There was also evidence dated June 2007 from the International Organization of Migration ('IOM'), which confirmed that 70 per cent of women that are returned to shelters in Albania had been re-trafficked.

In addition, the applicant herself was so traumatized that a report from her clinical psychologist was to the effect that she was 'suffering from complex, severe and chronic Post-Traumatic Stress Disorder', which was 'primarily a function of her experiences of being abducted, assaulted and forced into prostitution, aggravated by recent events, including her rejection by surviving relatives, the refusal of her application and the suspension of court proceedings against her trafficker'. The position of returned victims in Albania was addressed in a report prepared by Stephanie Schwandner-Sievers, an academic specializing in Albania, which highlighted the difficulties in identifying the number of Albanian victims of trafficking, the limited numbers of shelters and protection available for victims, the difficulty victims face reintegrating into society, the risks of being recycled back into prostitution, and suspected police corruption and complicity in trafficking.

On 11 March 2009, the Tribunal in the UK, nevertheless, dismissed her appeal on grounds that it was not accepted that the applicant would be at real risk of persecution or harm contrary to Article 3 upon return. As in *HC (China)* the Tribunal proceeded to find that 'the applicant would not be at risk in Albania because there was no evidence to establish that she could not live alone in the future, or that she would be at real risk of harm if she had to live alone in the future'. Once again, the Tribunal took the view that she had 'learned from the experience and benefited from the experiences of the other clients of the Poppy Project, as well as from the counselling that she had received'. Even more remarkably, it considered that allowance had to be made for the possibility that the applicant would 'encounter sympathetic, generous and kind persons in Albania', and held that adequate support facilities would be available to her there. The ECtHR was not altogether of the same view. In setting out the 'Questions for the Parties', one of the issues raised by the ECtHR was whether 'the applicant's removal to

171 This is an organization that provides assistance for women who have been trafficked to the United Kingdom.

Albania would give rise to a breach of the authorities' positive obligations under Article 4 of the Convention'.[172] Article 4, it is to be noted, is concerned with 'slavery and servitude'. The fact that the ECtHR was sufficiently concerned about this is telling. The potential relevance of the Slavery Convention 1926 is yet again indubitably strikingly evident. So what do the seven cases in this section – of cases not raising asylum claims and raising asylum claims, and of cases succeeding in establishing such claims and not succeeding in doing so – tell us about the plight of victims of human trafficking? It is noteworthy that in AM & BM (Albania) above, the Tribunal gave a striking example of what is 'good practice' by observing that the existence of considerable violence within the relationships of those who traffic and those who are trafficked, creates a psychological affect in victims which, given the pressures in which they are under and the lack of freedom that they have, means that such women should be treated as trafficked women who are deserving of surrogate international protection. This is important given our endeavour at the outset of this Chapter to develop a human trafficking law that is 'victim-centred', and that is not mixed up with the control of unwanted immigrants. What we learn, however, is that the age of austerity and limited financial resources, coupled with pressurized law enforcement agencies and public officials, deny victims the protection that they deserve. There is scant recognition that victims of human trafficking are 'persecuted' in both a factual and legal sense, because they have been denied core fundamental rights, and the State of their nationality is either unable to unwilling, to provide them with protection which is their due. It is therefore high time that trafficked persons were seen as the subjects of a form of modern slavery, rendering them particularly apt for the grant of refugee status because of the historical significance of 'slavery' , thus giving it a particular salience over and above other human evils.

(E) *AZ (Thailand)* and a 'Victim-centred' Approach

It is possible to end on a positive note. The Upper Tribunal in the UK surely got it right in the 2010 case of *AZ (Thailand)*.[173] The facts, as is often the case, are harrowing. Once again, they provide an insight into the murky world of human trafficking. The case concerned a British citizen in Thailand known as 'M', who spoke Thai, had a flat in Pattaya, groomed the appellant, got her to leave her child with her aunt, and then flew her to the UK with a British visa. On

---

[172] This refers to slavery and servitude. The full text is as follows: "Article 4 : Prohibition of Slavery and Forced Labour".

1 No one shall be held in slavery or servitude.

2 No one shall be required to perform forced or compulsory labour.

3 For the purpose of this Article the term 'forced or compulsory labour' shall not include:

(a) any work required to be done in the ordinary course of detention imposed according to the provisions of Article 5 of this Convention or during conditional release from such detention;

(b) any service of a military character or, in case of conscientious objectors in countries where they are recognised, service exacted instead of compulsory military service;

(c) any service exacted in case of an emergency or calamity threatening the life or well-being of the community;

(d) any work or service which forms part of normal civic obligations.

[173] *AZ (Trafficked women) Thailand CG* [2010] UKUT 118 (IAC).

the way, when passing through Bangkok airport, she heard one of the immigration officials indicate to another that M was one of 'theirs', which only made sense to her afterwards to imply that M had connections with the Thai Immigration Service.[174] In the UK he obtained a false passport for her. He had access to at least three brothels where several women worked,[175] and the appellant was made to work there on a rotating basis where she was forced into prostitution for the next eight months. M threatened to harm her and/or her child if she resisted. She was also transported to hotels for sex. She endured anal intercourse, and was made to perform oral sex and to act out perverse sexual fantasies. She was injected with drugs. She was frequently whipped. She was made to behave like a dog. Condoms were not always used and she could not object. She continued to work during menstruation.[176] Eventually, the appellant was able to escape with the help of a regular client.

A month later she was referred to the UK Human Trafficking Centre (UKHTC).[177] Later, the appellant claimed asylum on grounds that if returned to Thailand she would be hunted down by M's gang, especially as she believed that M had links with Thai Immigration, and that the Thai police were corrupt. The appellant was then referred to the Poppy Project, which, after investigating the matter, accepted the appellant's account of being trafficked and forced into prostitution.[178] Some three months after that, the Secretary of State decided that, 'due to your level of consistency and detail bearing in mind the trauma you have experienced, your age and your level of education, that your account will be largely accepted'.[179] However, the Secretary of State did not accept that 'women who had been sexually trafficked in the past in Thailand' constituted a social group. He found that there was no social recognition of this group as distinct from the rest of society. If the appellant faced persecution, in his opinion, it was not because of her membership of that group but because she was specifically wanted by her traffickers.[180] The Secretary of State rejected the contention that M was part of a well-organized criminal gang with connections to the Thai immigration service.[181]

The Upper Tribunal could not disagree more. In fact, it was especially perturbed by the fact that,

> [d]espite the *UKHTC* referral of her to the *Poppy Project*, a Home Office sponsored organisation, she was served with papers as an illegal entrant and two attempts were made to remove her from the UK before she had been assessed by the Poppy Project and whilst the identification process was ongoing. Moreover, in refusing her application for asylum and Discretionary Leave, the respondent held against the appellant the fact that she did not disclose her account earlier and no action was taken as a result of the information she provided to the UKHTC. No consideration was given either

174 Ibid., at para. 4.
175 Ibid., at para. 123.
176 Ibid., at para. 5.
177 Ibid., at para. 6.
178 Ibid., at para. 7.
179 Ibid., at para. 9.
180 Ibid., at para. 10.
181 Ibid., at para. 11.

to the grant of a renewable residence permit to the appellant as permitted under the Convention.[182]

The Tribunal found that the fact the appellant did not seek asylum at the earliest opportunity was entirely consistent with 'the UNHCR guidelines which advise that women may feel ashamed of what has happened to them or may suffer from trauma caused by sexual abuse and violence. The evidence we have before us confirms that the appellant experiences feelings of defilement, shame and a lack of self-worth.'[183] The Upper Tribunal could not ignore the fact that Thailand had not ratified the 2000 UN Trafficking in Persons protocol,[184] and that, more seriously, there were 'widespread reports of the complicity of police officers and border officials with traffickers and criminals'.[185] The appellant in fact could be a member of a particular social group for two reasons. First, in *HC and RC*,[186] the government lawyer had conceded that a person who had been a victim of trafficking could be a member of a particular social group. Second, although the provisions of *The Refugee or Person in Need of International Protection (Qualification) Regulations 2006* made it clear that in deciding whether a person is a refugee 'an act of persecution must be sufficiently serious by its nature or repetition as to constitute a severe violation of a basic human right',[187] Section 8 therein stated that the forced recruitment of women for the purposes of forced prostitution or sexual

[182] Ibid., at para. 170.

[183] Ibid., at para. 116.

[184] Ibid., at para. 121.

[185] Ibid., at para. 122 and para. 125.

[186] *HC and RC (Trafficked women)* China CG [2009] UKAIT 00027, at para. 36.

[187] This is section 5(1). The relevant provisions state:

3. In deciding whether a person is a refugee or a person eligible for humanitarian protection, persecution or serious harm can be committed by: (a) the State; (b) any party or organisation controlling the State or a substantial part of the territory of the State; (c) any non-State actor if it can be demonstrated that the actors mentioned in paragraphs (a) and (b), including any international organisation, are unable or unwilling to provide protection against persecution or serious harm ...

5. (1) In deciding whether a person is a refugee an act of persecution must be: (a) sufficiently serious by its nature or repetition as to constitute a severe violation of a basic human right, in particular a right from which derogation cannot be made under Article 15 of the Convention for the Protection of Human Rights and Fundamental Freedoms; or (b) an accumulation of various measures, including a violation of a human right which is sufficiently severe as to affect an individual in a similar manner as specified in (a).

(2) An act of persecution may, for example, take the form of: (a) *an act of physical or mental violence, including an act of sexual violence;* (b) a legal, administrative, police, or judicial measure which in itself is discriminatory or which is implemented in a discriminatory manner; (c) prosecution or punishment, which is disproportionate or discriminatory; (d) denial of judicial redress resulting in a disproportionate or discriminatory punishment; (e) prosecution or punishment for refusal to perform military service in a conflict, where performing military service would include crimes or acts falling under regulation 7.

(3) An act of persecution must be committed for at least one of the reasons in Article 1(A) of the Geneva Convention.

6. (1) In deciding whether a person is a refugee: ... (d) a group shall be considered to form a particular social group where, for example: (i) members of that group share an innate characteristic, or a common background that cannot be changed, or share a characteristic or belief that is so fundamental to identity or conscience that a person should not be forced to renounce it,

exploitation may amount to persecution. Indeed, acts of sexual violence fall to be considered as persecution under Regulation 5 (2) (a). Further, the 'EU Qualification Directive' of 29 April 2004[188] expressly permits Member States to apply standards more favourable to the applicant than the minimum laid down. In what was clearly therefore a forward-thinking decision the Upper Tribunal held that 'the shared past experience of being trafficked for sexual exploitation amounts to a common, immutable characteristic'. In so deciding it drew upon the *UNHCR Guidelines*, which advise that '[i]n establishing this ground it is not necessary that the members of a particular group know each other or associate with each other as a group', provided only that 'they either share a common characteristic other than their risk of being persecuted or are perceived as a group by society'.[189] The shared characteristic will often be one that is innate, unchangeable or otherwise fundamental to identity, conscience or the exercise of one's human rights. In so concluding the Upper Tribunal reached a result that was not entirely inconsistent with previous decisions.[190] In so concluding the Upper Tribunal reached a result that was not entirely inconsistent with previous decisions that had been favourable to victims of human trafficking.

Yet what is perhaps most remarkable about this decision is the explicit adoption of the principles enshrined in the *UN Guidelines on Trafficking*, which make it clear,[191] as the Upper Tribunal found, that according to the UN 'the future risk of persecution need not be considered in cases where applicants have been so atrociously ill treated that they are still suffering psychological trauma'[192] because in these circumstances the impact of persecution on the appellant continues. Such a holding was entirely in line, as the Upper Tribunal also

---

and (ii) that group has a distinct identity in the relevant country, because it is perceived as being different by the surrounding society ….

188 The full title of this is *Council Directive 2004/83/EC of 29 April 2004 on Minimum Standards for the Qualification and Status of Third Country Nationals or Stateless Persons as Refugees or as Persons who Otherwise Need International Protection and the Content of the Protection Granted.*

189 The *UNHCR Guidelines* states: 'The shared characteristic will often be one that is innate, unchangeable or otherwise fundamental to identity, conscience or the exercise of one's human rights. Persecutory action against a group may be relevant in heightening the visibility of the group without being its defining characteristic. As with the other Convention grounds, the size of the purported social group is not a relevant criterion in determining whether a social group exists within the meaning of Article 1A(2). While a claimant must still demonstrate a well-founded fear of being persecuted based on her or his membership of the particular social group, she or he need not demonstrate that all members of the group are at risk of persecution in order to establish the existence of the group (paragraph 37). It should therefore be noted that it is the past trafficking experience that would constitute one of the elements defining the group in such cases, rather than the future persecution now feared in the form of ostracism, punishment, reprisals or re-trafficking. In such situations, the group would therefore not be defined solely by its fear of future persecution' (para. 38).

190 See the findings in *SB* (PSG – Protection Regulations – Reg 6) Moldova CG [2008] UKAIT 0002 and *PO (Trafficked women)* Nigeria CG [2009] UKAIT 00046. In both cases the Tribunal found that former victims of trafficking were capable of constituting a particular social group (referred to at para. 141 of *AZ*).

191 See para. 16 of the *UNHCR Guidelines.*

192 *AZ* at para. 142.

observed,[193] with the leading UK case on past persecution in 1999 of *Demirkaya.*[194] In that case, the court held that the treatment a person had been subjected to before leaving his country of origin was very relevant to the question of whether that person had a well-founded fear of persecution on his return. The court held that in the absence of a significant change in the country of origin, there may be a real risk of persecutory treatment on return. Applying that principle, the Upper Tribunal held that there was nothing in the evidence before it to suggest that the situation in Thailand had changed since the time of the appellant's departure. Indeed, it found that, 'on the accepted facts, the appellant has already been trafficked from Thailand which demonstrates a failure by the state to protect her from being trafficked' and that, on the evidence, 'either her traffickers would be reasonably likely to learn of her return and would be motivated to seek her out or that she would be at risk of being re-trafficked because of her lack of support, lack of economic opportunity, the stigma attached to her as a prostitute and her vulnerable state of mind'.[195] The reference by the Tribunal to 'a vulnerable state of mind' here is most significant. It goes to the very heart of understanding the state of the person who is a victim of human trafficking. *AZ (Thailand)* should, therefore, serve as a template for future refugee law cases affecting trafficked persons. It gives the appropriate consideration to *UNHCR Guidelines*, the work of interest groups such as the Poppy Project, and victims narrative. As such, it has much to commend it for future decision-makers.

(F) A Radical Judicial Approach for Human Trafficking?

This chapter has demonstrated that the laws on human trafficking now provide tools to provide redress to victims. What is missing is the ideological grounding in the realization of human trafficking as an extension of the historical evil of chattel slavery. This is what is needed to make good the law. This is not to say that all cases must succeed. It does mean that primary consideration should be given to victim protection. This chapter shows that the courts at least are now beginning to do so and *AZ* is the high-water mark of that judicial approach. But more is needed. The courts need to unabashedly get to grips with human trafficking as a challenge for the orderly and principled development of modern refugee law.

Human trafficking occurs because States are either unable or unwilling to prevent it. They are unable to afford basic protection to their citizens. Refugee law exists to provide surrogate international protection for the basic rights of citizens whose States fail to do so. In *HJ (Iran)*[196] the UK Supreme Court observed how '[t]he failure of state protection is central to

---

193 At para. 153.

194 *Demirkaya v Secretary of State for the Home Department* [1999] EWCA Civ 1654; [1999] ImmAR 498. This was a case where the appellant had been the subject of what was described as life-threatening ill-treatment of a particularly horrifying kind in the months before he escaped Turkey. It was held that the Tribunal had erred by not referring to these experiences when assessing the risk on return. This was because, unless there had been a major change of circumstances making prospective persecution unlikely, past experience under a particular regime should be considered probative of future risk.

195 Ibid., at para. 153.

196 *HJ (Iran)* [2010] UKSC, at para. 13.

the whole system' and that '[t]he question is whether the home state is unable or unwilling to discharge its duty to establish and operate a system for the protection against persecution of its own nationals'. Victims of human trafficking invariably belong to a particular sex, caste, creed, or social status, and it is well accepted that in the denial of fundamental human rights, it is impermissible to have 'distinction of any kind', a principle that has long been enshrined and that follows inexorably from the reference in the preamble to the *Universal Declaration of Human Rights of 1948*.[197] As is well known, under the Refugee Convention, 'the term "refugee" shall apply to any person who ... owing to well-founded fear of being persecuted for reasons of race, religion, nationality, membership of a particular social group or political opinion, is outside the country of his nationality and is unable or, owing to such fear, is unwilling to avail himself of the protection of that country; or who ... is unable or, owing to such fear, is unwilling to return to it'.[198] The reference in this definition to 'for reasons of' is a reference to the specified so-called 'Convention reasons'. The question is whether the 'Convention reasons' are to be interpreted broadly or restrictively. It is well worth recounting Lord Bingham's observation in *Fornah*:[199]

> It is well-established that the Convention must be interpreted in accordance with its broad humanitarian objective and having regard to the principles, expressed in the preamble, that human beings should enjoy fundamental rights and freedoms without discrimination and that refugees should enjoy the widest possible exercise of these rights and freedoms ....

> Indeed, Sedley J in *Shah*,[200] commenting on the complexity of the issues, made an observation that was adopted by Lord Steyn in the seminal case of *Shah & Islam*[201] *in 1999:*

> Its adjudication is not a conventional lawyer's exercise of applying a legal litmus test to ascertain facts; it is a global appraisal of an individual's past and prospective situation in a particular cultural, social, political and legal milieu, judged by a test which, though it has legal and linguistic limits, has a broad humanitarian purpose.

---

197 See Article 2 of the preamble to the *Universal Declaration of Human Rights of 1948*, which states: 'Everyone is entitled to all the rights and freedoms set forth in this Declaration, without distinction of any kind, such as race, colour, sex, language, religion, political or other opinion, national or social origin, property, birth or other status.'

198 This is Article 1 (A)(2) of the text of the 1951 Convention Relating to the Status of Refugees: see http://www.unhcr.org/pages/49da0e466.html (accessed 31 July 2012).

199 *Fornah v Secretary of State for the Home Department* [2005] EWCA Civ 680 (9 June 2005), at para. 10.

200 *Islam v. Secretary of State for the Home Department Immigration Appeal Tribunal and Another, Ex Parte Shah, R v.* [1999] UKHL 20; [1999] 2 AC 629; [1999] 2 All ER 545 (25 March 1999).

201 *Islam v. Secretary of State for the Home Department Immigration Appeal Tribunal and Another, Ex Parte Shah* [1999] UKHL 20.

Moreover, Lord Hope in *Hoxha* went on to echo these views when he spoke about the 'broad humanitarian principles which underlie the Convention'.[202] It was these principles which called for the 'large and liberal spirit' in times 'when a court is asked to say what the Convention means'.[203] Yet all this had to be done bearing in mind that the Convention and the Protocol were 'living instruments, to which the broadest effect must be given to ensure that they continue to serve the humanitarian principles for whose purpose the Convention was entered into'.[204]

What this means is that it is artificial to exclude a consideration of the State's attitude from the definition of persecution. Human trafficking is on the whole undertaken by private individuals and not by the State. It would be altogether simpler if the State were involved. Yet, if the considerations of protection are confined to the well-foundedness of the fear, then given that the fear is not of the State, but of organized private criminal gangs who are involved in human trafficking, it is inevitable that some cases that ought to justify asylum will be excluded. This is surely what Baroness Hale meant in *Hoxha* when declaring that 'women who have been victims of sexual violence in the past are linked by an immutable characteristic which is at once independent of and the cause of their current ill-treatment … are certainly capable of constituting a particular social group under the Convention'.[205] While it is accepted that under international law the 'persecution' must be for a Convention reason, it is not difficult to conceive of cases where a person might be 'persecuted' by other citizens for reasons of private gain that involve no element of Convention rights. But if the issue is approached in the context of the Refugee Convention, then it is clear that the persecution to which the Convention refers is the persecution that takes account of the protection available from the State. Therefore, what is key in such a scenario is the attitude of the State. If the State is motivated by considerations that are contrary to the Convention rights to tolerate such activity, and if it deliberately refrains from protecting the trafficked person, then the person concerned has an arguable claim to refugee status under international law. This is not a novel proposition.

There is authority for it in the dicta of Lord Clyde in the seminal British case of *Horvath*,[206] which concerned non-state actors, and laid the foundations of modern refugee law in the last decade. This in turn is in line with the position of the UNHCR as explicated in 2006, namely, that 'fear of persecution, which whilst being unrelated to the fear of trafficking, may arise from the trafficking experience, in the form of family ostracism, social exclusion, re-traumatization or victimization, or other violence from the community at large'.[207] The Upper Tribunal in *AZ* also found that, according to the UN, 'the future risk of persecution need not be considered

[202] *Hoxha & Anor v Secretary of State for the Home Department* [2005] UKHL 19 (10 March 2005), at para. 6.

[203] Ibid., at para. 8.

[204] Ibid., at para. 7.

[205] Ibid., at para. 37.

[206] *Horvath v. Secretary of State for the Home Department* [2000] UKHL 37 (6 July 2000); *Hoxha*, at para. 6.

[207] UNHCR, *Guidelines on International Protection: The Application of Article 1A(2) of the 1951 Convention and/or 1967 Protocol Relating to the Status of Refugees to Victims of Trafficking and Persons at Risk of Being Trafficked*, 8, UN Doc. HCR/GIP/06/07 (7 April 2006). See also UNHCR, *Guidelines on International Protection: Gender-Related Persecution within the Context of Article JA(2) of the 1951 Convention and/or 1967 Protocol relating to the Status of Refugees*, UN Doc. HCR/GIP/02/01 (7 May 2002).

in cases where applicants have been so atrociously ill treated that they are still suffering psychological trauma'.[208] There is, therefore, a range of factors that could impact on a victim of human trafficking, who is a national of a country to which such a person 'is unable or, owing to such fear, is unwilling to return'. Thus it is clear that, while it will be necessary to consider what the attitude of the State is to the experience of a trafficked person, the inquiry does not end there. But can one go any further?

The UK Supreme Court in Britain arguably blazed a new trail for refugee law in *HJ (Iran)*,[209] which, although a case concerning homosexuals, demonstrates the continuing vitality of the Refugee Convention for a new age, where nefarious human rights violations are being plucked up from obscurity for judicial redress. Refugee law principles that are applicable in one context ought to be applicable equally in another. Lord Hope's description of how rights relating to sexual orientation have historically been overlooked is equally applicable to how rights of those subject to human trafficking have historically been overlooked. Lord Hope gave the first judgment. In setting the scene, he reminded us that 'persecution for reasons of homosexuality was not perceived as a problem by the High Contracting Parties when the Convention was being drafted', and the reason for this was that 'the risk of persecution in countries where it now exists seemed remote'; it was also 'the practice for leaders in these countries simply to insist that homosexuality did not exist', all of which was, of course, 'manifest nonsense'.[210] The reason why it has now become such a major issue is that, 'fanned by misguided but vigorous religious doctrine, the situation has changed dramatically',[211] and 'a huge gulf has opened up in attitudes to and understanding of gay persons between societies on either side on the divide', with the result that now '[i]t is one of the most demanding social issues of our time'.[212] As with suppression of sexual orientation, where Western countries must respond boldly to protect rights historically overlooked, so also with the rights of the weak and vulnerable subject to human trafficking, which have also historically been overlooked, as the legislation and case law in this chapter make clear. Lord Rodger's declaration in that case, that 'the underlying rationale of the Convention is that they should be able to live freely and openly as gay men and lesbian women, without fearing that they may suffer harm of the requisite intensity or duration because they are gay or lesbian',[213] must surely also resonate in other areas of refugee law such as human trafficking. In fact, given the historical connotations of slavery and the struggle to eliminate it, there is arguably no less an urgency to tackle the transport and exploitation of human beings today as there was the urgency to tackle the ill-treatment of homosexuals.

This is not least because in the first case to deal with the definition of enslavement as a crime against humanity for sexual exploitation, the International Criminal Tribunal for the Former Yugoslavia observed that 'the traditional concept of slavery, as defined in the 1926 Slavery Convention and often referred to as "chattel slavery", has evolved to encompass various contemporary forms of slavery which are also based on the exercise of any or all of the powers attaching to the right of ownership', so that 'there is some destruction of the

208 *AZ (Trafficked women) Thailand CG* [2010] UKUT 118 (IAC), at para. 142.
209 *HJ (Iran)* [2010] UKSC, at para. 13.
210 Ibid., Lord Hope, at para. 2.
211 Ibid., Lord Hope, at para. 2.
212 Ibid., Lord Hope, at para. 3.
213 At para. 53.

juridical personality'.[214] This would mean the 'control of someone's movement, control of physical environment, psychological control, measures taken to prevent or deter escape, force, threat of force or coercion, duration, assertion of exclusivity, subjection to cruel treatment and abuse, control of sexuality and forced labour'.[215] Who can deny that the cases discussed in this Chapter involved such control and coercion? Human Slavery has never been eliminated. Human Trafficking is its most insidious modern form. It stands poised to challenge refugee law. We must make sure that refugee law is ready to challenge it.

References

Anderson, Bridget and Julia O'Connell Davidson, *Trafficking – a demand led problem? A multi-country pilot study* (Save the Children: Stockholm, 2003), at http://unosek.org/pdf/brazil/trafficking-a%20demand%20led%20problem.pdf (accessed 30 July 2012).

BBC News, 'Pastor jailed for trafficking African child "slaves"', at http://www.bbc.co.uk/news/uk-england-london-12789690 (accessed 30 July 2012).

Bentham, Martin, 'Majority of sex workers "not forced or trafficked"', *Evening Standard*, 28 October 2011, at http://www.thisislondon.co.uk/standard/article-24003366-majority-of-sex-workers-not-forced-or-trafficked.do (accessed 31 July 2012).

Bhabha, Jacqueline, 'International Gatekeepers: The tension between asylum advocacy and human rights', *Harvard Human Rights Journal* (Vol. 15, Spring 2002), pp. 1–25.

Booth, Robert, '"Human trafficking victims will not be treated as criminals", says CPS', *The Guardian*, 3 July 2011, at http://www.guardian.co.uk/law/2011/jul/03/human-trafficking-victims-criminals-cps (accessed 7 August 2012).

Briggs, Billy, 'Child trafficking in Scotland is hidden scandal, says report', *The Guardian*, 13 March 2011, at http://www.guardian.co.uk/law/2011/mar/13/child-trafficking-scotland-scandal-report (accessed 30 July 2012).

Bruch, Elizabeth M., 'Models Wanted: The Search for an Effective Response to Human Trafficking', 40 (1) *Stanford Journal of International Law* (Vol. 40, 2004), pp. 1–46).

Butler, Patrick and Alan Travis, 'Sex trafficking charity loses out to Salvation Army over £6m contract', *The Guardian*, 11 April 2011, at http://www.guardian.co.uk/society/2011/apr/11/eaves-housing-trafficking-salvation-army?INTCMP=SRCH (accessed 31 July 2012).

Butler-Sloss, Lady Elizabeth, 'Human trafficking is modern slavery', *The Guardian*, 2 July 2011, at http://www.guardian.co.uk/law/2011/jul/02/elizabeth-butler-sloss-human-trafficking (accessed 30 July 2012).

Carrell, Severin, 'Trafficked people being treated as criminals by officials, inquiry says', *The Guardian*, 27 November 2011, at http://www.guardian.co.uk/law/2011/nov/27/human-trafficking-crime-victims (accessed 30 July 2012).

[214] The was the case of *Prosecutor v. Kunarac, Vukovic and Kovac*, 12 June 2002, at para. 117, which was referred to by *Rantsev*, at para. 142.

[215] *Rantsev*, at para. 143.

Dugan, Emily and Matt Chorley, 'Coalition to scrap sex trafficking safeguards', *The Independent on Sunday*, 6 February 2011, at http://www.independent.co.uk/news/uk/crime/coalition-to-scrap-sex-trafficking-safeguards-2205733.html (accessed 31 July 2012).

Edwards, Alice, 'Trafficking in Human Beings: At the Intersection of Criminal Justice, Human Rights, Asylum/Immigration Labor', *Denver Journal of International Law & Policy* (Vol. 36, 2007), pp. 1–53.

ESRC, 'Most migrant sex workers are not forced to sell sex', 31 October 2011, at http://www.esrc.ac.uk/news-and-events/press-releases/18164/most-migrant-sex-workers-are-not-forced-to-sell-sex.aspx (accessed 31 July 2012).

Fitzpatrick, Joan, 'Trafficking as a Human Rights Violation: The Complex Intersection of Legal Frameworks for Conceptualizing and Combatting Trafficking', *Michigan Journal of International Law* (Vol. 24, Issue 4, 2003), pp. 1143–68.

Gallagher, Anne T., *The International Law of Human Trafficking* (Cambridge: Cambridge University Press, 2010).

Hathaway, James C., 'The Human Rights Quagmire of "Human Trafficking"', *Virginia Journal of International Law* (Vol. 49, 2008), pp. 1–59.

Hodgson, Nichi and Catherine Robinson, 'The value of the Poppy Project', *The Guardian*, 22 April 2011, at http://www.guardian.co.uk/commentisfree/2011/apr/22/poppy-project-trafficking-salvation-army (accessed 7 August 2012).

Igwe, Leo 'Baby farm girls and the sale of children', 8 June 2011, at http://www.momentng.com/en/news/2856/baby-farm-girls-and-the-sale-of-children.html (accessed 30 July 2012).

International Union of Sex Workers, 'Majority of migrant sex workers "not forced or trafficked"', at http://www.iusw.org/2011/10/majority-of-migrant-sex-workers-not-forced-or-trafficked/ (accessed 31 July 2012).

Jayasinghe, Udara and Sasha Baglay, 'Protecting Victims of Human Trafficking Within a "Non-Refoulement" Framework: Is Complementary Protection an Effective Alternative in Canada and Australia?', *International Journal of Refugee Law* (Vol. 23, Issue 3, 2011), pp. 489–520.

Kneebone, Susan, 'The Refugee – Trafficking Nexus: Making Good (the) Connections', *Refugee Survey Quarterly* (Vol. 29, No. 1, 2010), pp. 137–60.

Kneebone, Susan and Bernadette McSherry, 'Trafficking in Women and Forced Migration: Moving Victims Across the Border of Crime into the Domain of Human Rights', *International Journal of Human Rights* (Vol. 12, Issue 1, 2008), pp. 67–87.

Laczko, Frank and Elzbieta Gozdziak, 'Data and Research on Human Trafficking: A Global Survey', Offprint of the Special Issue of *International Migration* (Vol. 43, Issue 1/2, 2005), at http://www.iom.int/jahia/webdav/site/myjahiasite/shared/shared/mainsite/published_docs/books/data_res_human.pdf (accessed 7 August 2012).

Laczko, Frank and Marco A. Gramegna, 'Developing Better Indicators of Human Trafficking', *Brown Journal of World Affairs* (Vol. 10, Issue 1, summer/fall 2003), pp. 179–94.

Obokata, Tom, 'Smuggling of Human Beings from a Human Rights Perspective: Obligations of Non-State and State Actors under International Human Rights Law', *International Journal of Refugee Law* (Vol. 17, Issue 2, 2005), pp. 394–415.

Piotrowicz, Ryszard, 'Trafficking of Human Beings and their Human Rights in the Migration Context', in Ryszard Cholewinski, Richard Perruchoud and Euan Macdonald (eds),

International Migration Law: Developing Paradigms and Key Challenges (The Hague: T.M.C. Asser Press, 2007), pp. 275–90.

Piotrowicz, Ryszard, 'The UNHCR's Guidelines on Human Trafficking', *International Journal of Refugee Law* (Vol. 20, Issue 2, 2008), pp. 242–52.

Piotrowicz, Ryszard, 'Victims of People Trafficking and the Entitlement to International Protection', *Australian Year Book of International Law* (Vol. 24, Issue 205, 2005), pp. 159–79.

Somerset, Carron, 'What the Professionals Know: The Trafficking of Children Into, and Through, the UK for Sexual Purposes', *Anti-Slavery International* (November 2001, NCJ Number 196542), at http://www.ncjrs.gov/App/publications/abstract.aspx?ID=196542 (accessed 31 July 2012).

Srikantiah, Jayashri, 'Perfect Victims and Real Survivors: The Iconic Victim in Domestic Human Trafficking Law', *Boston University Law Review* (Vol. 87, 2007), pp. 157–211.

Townsend, Mark, 'Human trafficking fears as key UK staff are lost', *The Guardian*, 14 May 2011, at http://www.guardian.co.uk/law/2011/may/14/human-trafficking-fears-key-staff-lost?INTCMP=SRCH (accessed 30 July 2012).

Townsend, Mark, 'Inquiry launched into slavery in the UK', *The Observer*, 12 July 2011, at http://www.guardian.co.uk/law/2011/jun/12/slavery-inquiry-iain-duncan-smith (accessed 30 July 2012).

Townsend, Mark, 'New trafficking laws "will not care for slavery victims"', *The Guardian*, 2 July 2011, at http://www.guardian.co.uk/uk/2011/jul/02/human-trafficking-laws-immigration-control?INTCMP=SRCH (accessed 31 July 2012).

Townsend, Mark, 'Sex-trafficked women's charity Poppy Project in danger as funding withdrawn' *The Guardian*, 17 April 2011, at http://www.guardian.co.uk/society/2011/apr/17/prostitution-human-trafficking (accessed 20 August 2012).

Townsend, Mark, 'Target brothels or sex trafficking in UK will rise', *The Observer*, Sunday 6 February 2011, at http://www.guardian.co.uk/law/2011/feb/06/sex-slave-trafficking-brothel-crackdown?INTCMP=SRCH (accessed 31 July 2012).

Travis, Alan, 'Authorities failing to enforce law aimed at tackling sex with trafficked women', *The Guardian*, 19 July 2011, at http://www.guardian.co.uk/law/2011/jul/19/sex-law-human-trafficking-strategy (accessed 30 July 2012).

Child Migration and the Lacunae in International Protection

Jacqueline Bhabha[1]

'The Algerian coast guard rescued on 10 April the corpses of 13 migrants that set sail from the beach of Mers the Hdjadj, in the coast of Oran, in the direction of Spain. On board were 16 youths, from 17 to 25 years old, and after their shipwreck three of them were still missing'.[2]

Introduction

Recent developments have once again catapulted child migrants into the headlines:[3] the unleashing of virulent anti-Roma pogroms in Italy since the spring of 2008[4] to the summer of 2011;[5] the resurgence of openly xenophobic anti-immigrant policies in France[6] in the wake

---

[1] Director of Research, François-Xavier Bagnoud Center for Health and Human Rights, Harvard University. I am grateful to Sarah Mi Ra Dougherty for invaluable research assistance.

[2] Platform for International Cooperation on Undocumented Migrants (PICUM), *PICUM Newsletter*, May 2008.

[3] Cindy Chang, 'Unaccompanied migrant youth in U.S. detention centers rises 50%', L.A. Times, 16 October 2012, at http://articles.latimes.com/2012/oct/16/local/la-me-immigration-children-20121016, accessed 22 October 2012; Julia Preston, 'Young Immigrants, in America Illegally, Line Up for Reprieve', *N.Y. Times*, 13 August 2012, at http://www.nytimes.com/2012/08/14/us/young-immigrants-poised-for-deportation-deferral-program.html; accessed 22 October 2012; Tracy McVeigh, 'Child asylum seekers 'still being imprisoned' by immigration service', *The Guardian*, 19 May 2012, at http://www.guardian.co.uk/uk/2012/may/20/child-asylum-seekers-still-being-locked-up, accessed 22 October 2012; and 'Europe is Ready to Incarcerate All Illegal Minors', Le Figaro, 24 April 2008, at http://www.lefigaro.fr/international/2008/04/25/01003-20080425ARTFIG00010-leurope-prete-a-incarcerer-tous-les-mineurs-illegaux-.php, accessed 2 August 2012.

[4] Christina Fraser, 'Italy Police to Protect Gypsies', BBC News, Rome, 14 May 2008, at http://news.bbc.co.uk/2/hi/7400460.stm, accessed 27 July 2012.

[5] Prime Minister Silvio Berlusconi has denounced the possibility that Milano might become 'an Islamic city … a zingaropoli [Gypsytown] full of Roma camps, besieged by foreigners': Lorenzo Fuccaro, 'Berlusconi-Bersani, lite su Milano "Sarà islamica". "No alle paure"', *Corriere della Sera*, 24 May 2011, at http://archiviostorico.corriere.it/2011/maggio/24/Berlusconi_Bersani_lite_Milano_Sara_co_8_110524022.shtml, accessed 27 July 2012.

[6] Réseau Éducation sans frontières, La Chasse aux Enfants, at http://www.educationsansfrontieres.org, accessed 22 October 2012 (documenting the traumatic impact on

of the Arab Spring youth migrations;[7] the proliferation of Bush administration raids on migrant families in the US,[8] followed by record-breaking levels of deportation of long-term residents;[9] and the ongoing controversy over detention of child asylum seekers in the UK.[10] Not since the Elián González saga[11] has public attention been so focused on the problems raised for and by this section of our society. But something is different this time. The simple image of child innocence captured by photogenic Elián Gonzalez and responsible for an outpouring of public sympathy and compassion has been replaced by a more complex portrait of today's child migrants that elicits correspondingly ambivalent responses. Whether public attention is focused on the Roma teenage delinquent intent on shoplifting or baby snatching, the omnipresent 'illegal' Hispanic family sneaking across the border to work, or rebellious Muslim youth creating urban havoc in the decaying peripheries of European cities and revolution in the countries caught up in the 'Arab spring', the difference in public imagery is significant. Young migrants, children and youth, represent a protection challenge (as Elián did) but also a security risk and a development opportunity. These multiple facets of child migration today mandate a novel response from those concerned with international protection of migrant children. This chapter will outline a suggested road map for addressing this unfolding new migration dynamic and the paradigm shift it demands.

Since the invention of childhood[12] as a distinct phase of human life, society has accepted an obligation to protect the youngest members of its population. Migrant children have had a peculiarly strong claim to that public protection, a claim well recognized in international law from the earliest days of the human rights regime.[13] They are vulnerable and dependent

---

families and children of discriminatory state policies in France). See also Centre on Housing Rights and Evictions (COHRE) v. France, No. 63/2010, European Committee of Social Rights (ruling that forced evictions and expulsions of Roma in France violate the European Social Charter).

7 See Ian Traynor and John Hooper, 'France and Italy in Call to Close EU Borders in Wake of Arab Protests', *The Guardian*, 27 April 2011, at http://www.guardian.co.uk/world/2011/apr/26/eu-borders-arab-protests, accessed 27 July 2012.

8 The Urban Institute, *Paying the Price: The Impact of Immigration Raids on America's Children* (Washington, D.C.: The Urban Institute, 2007).

9 See, e.g., Frank James, 'Deportations Higher Under Obama Than Bush', NPR: The Two-Way, *NPR*, 6 July 2010, at http://www.npr.org/blogs/thetwo-way/2010/07/26/128772646/deportationshigher-under-obama-than-bush, accessed 27 July 2012, and Brian Bennett, 'Republicans Want a Return to Workplace Immigration Rituals', *L.A. Times*, 27 January 2011, at http://articles.latimes.com/2011/jan/27/nation/la-naimmigration-raids-20110127, accessed 27 July 2012.

10 See Jonathan Brown, 'New Centres 'To Detain Child Asylum Seekers', *The Independent*, 4 February 2011, at http://www.independent.co.uk/news/uk/home-news/new-centres-to-detain-child-asylum-seekers-2203843.html, accessed 27 July 2012.

11 See, e.g., Jennifer Kay and Matt Sedensky, '10 Years after Elian, U.S. Players Mum or Moving On', *The Herald Sun*, 1 July 2010, at http://www.heraldsun.com/view/full_story/7160040/article-10-years-after-Elian--U-S--players-mum-or-moving-on, accessed 2 August 2012; and Adam Clymer and Lizette Alvarez, 'The Elián Gonzalez Case: The Overview', *The New York Times*, 27 April 2000, at http://www.nytimes.com/2000/04/27/us/elian-gonzalez-case-overview-boy-s-father-joins-fray-over-his-son-s-asylum-case.html, accessed 27 July 2012. See also Gonzales v. Reno, 212 F.3d 1338 (11th Cir. 2000).

12 Philippe Ariès, *Centuries of Childhood: A Social History of Family Life* (New York: Knopf, 1962).

13 See Geneva Declaration of the Rights of the Child, adopted 26 September 1924, League of Nations O.J. Spec. Supp. 21; Jacqueline Bhabha, 'Minors or Aliens? Inconsistent State Intervention

like all children, but they have the added handicaps that come from lack of citizenship status and from dislocation. As anyone who has moved with children knows only too well, at a minimum, irrespective of family background or social status, these entail the difficulties caused by unfamiliarity with new surroundings and separation from old and familiar ones. Typically they also include linguistic (and therefore communication) challenges, social isolation, cultural disruption. Quite often the dislocation handicaps include new material hardships: tough living conditions, reduced income and access to material resources, unfamiliar climate and diet that can result in health challenges.[14] Legal challenges may also present themselves, including eligibility challenges regarding school enrollment or healthcare entitlement, visa complexities relating to the legality of long-term residence, and nationality queries relating to legal identity and the avoidance of statelessness.[15] On occasion, the consequences of migration for children are even worse: bullying and racism in school,[16] homelessness,[17] disruption of family life,[18] labour exploitation, sexual violence.[19] Destitution, depression, desperation may be the consequences.

These correlates of child migration are not unfamiliar. Indeed, they have been the targets of advocacy, public policy and social research for more than a decade. Across disciplines and countries, professionals have urged their states to pay attention to these issues. Pointing out the manifold legal, social and economic problems they encounter and insisting upon the strong claim to public protection, we have argued that states have failed migrant children.[20]

---

and Separated Child Asylum-Seekers', 3 *European Journal of Migration and Law* (2001), 283–314; and Michael G. Wenk, 'The Refugee: A Search for Clarification', 2 *International Migration Review* 3 (Summer 1968), 62–9, at 64 (noting that the term refugee, as defined by the 1946 Constitution of the International Refugee Organization, included 'unaccompanied children who are war orphans, or whose parents have disappeared, and who are outside their country of origin').

14 UNDP, *Human Development Report 2009: Overcoming Barriers: Human Mobility and Development*, at 55–6, at http://hdr.undp.org/en/media/HDR_2009_EN_Complete.pdf, accessed 27 July 2012, and World Health Organization, *Health of Migrants – The Way Forward: Report of a Global Consultation, Madrid, Spain 3–5 March 2010*, at 37, 91, at http://www.who.int/hac/events/consultation_report_health_migrants_colour_web.pdf, accessed 27 July 2012.

15 For a full discussion of this topic see Jacqueline Bhabha (ed.), *Children Without a State: A Global Human Rights Challenge* (Cambridge: MIT Press, 2011).

16 See, e.g., 'After Alabama law, Hispanic kids being bullied', *Associated Press*, 22 October 2011, at http://www.cbsnews.com/8301-201_162-20124241/after-alabama-law-hispanic-kids-being-bullied, accessed 22 October 2012.

17 See, e.g., Human Rights Watch, *Rights Displaced: Forced Returns of Roma, Ashkali and Egyptians from Western Europe to Kosovo*, 28 October 2010, at http://www.hrw.org/en/reports/2010/10/28/rights-displaced, accessed 27 July 2012.

18 Unaccompanied refugee minors are considered 'an especially vulnerable population because they are both fleeing persecution and entering … Without a parent or custodian': Chad C. Haddal, 'Unaccompanied Refugee Minors', *Congressional Research Service*, 14 March 2008 (Order Code RL34414), 1.

19 Even caregivers can turn predatory in circumstances of disruption and conflict, as has become increasingly apparent. See Save the Children, 'Sexual Abuse of Children by Aid Workers Too Often Unreported', 27 May 2008, at http://www.savethechildren.org.uk/news/2008/05/sexual-abuse-of-children-by-aid-workers-too-often-unreported, accessed 2 August 2012.

20 See Human Rights Watch, *'Eternal Emergency': No End to Unaccompanied Migrant Children's Institutionalization in Canary Islands Emergency Centers*, 22 June 2010, 1-56432-643-8, at http://www.unhcr.org/refworld/docid/4c21b6702.html, accessed 27 July 2012; Refugees International,

We have explained this failure largely in terms of oversight or miopia.[21] Using phrases like 'invisibility', 'hiddenness', 'falling or slipping between the cracks', 'void', we have suggested that states have innocently overlooked the problems of migrant children and their correlative duties, because of a dual-perception lacuna: for issues of migration, they have focused on adults; for issues of child welfare, they have focused on citizens. We have implied that states are well intentioned in their concern for and commitment to migrant children, but have been incompetent, neglectful, unprepared. We have urged states to rectify these deficiencies by paying attention to universally accepted child rights principles and using these to create appropriate policies and procedures backed by adequate public resources. The focus has been on states' *protection mandate* and its inadequate implementation. We have scored some successes, registered some failures, and identified a substantial and growing field for future intervention. I shall highlight some of these milestones below.

Over the last five years or so, however, it has become clear that this traditional narrative, which I shall call the *invisibility narrative*,[22] is inadequate. While it explains the problems of some child migrants and their interface with public agencies well, it fails to capture the more complex dynamics in play for many others. Whereas invisibility explains the failure to establish mechanisms for child guardianship for unaccompanied migrant children, and to develop adequate child-friendly legal procedures for asylum seeking or refugee minors, it does not account for the dramatic deficiency of public policy towards several other key child migrants groups. By way of example, take trafficked children, and migrant children associated with gangs[23] or forms of petty delinquency or anti-social behaviour. Few problems

Futures Denied: Statelessness among Infants, Children, and Youth, 22 October 2008, via http://www.refintl.org/policy/in-depth-report/futures-denied-statelessness-among-infants-children-and-youth, accessed 2 August 2012; Women's Refugee Commission, *Halfway Home: Unaccompanied Children in Immigration Custody*, February 2009, at http://www.womensrefugeecommission.org/docs/halfway_home.pdf, accessed 27 July 2012; PICUM, *Undocumented Children in Europe: Invisible Victims of Immigration Restrictions*, 2008, at http://picum.org/picum.org/uploads/file_/PICUM%20Undocumented%20Children%20in%20Europe%20-%20%20EN.pdf, accessed 27 July 2012; and Amnesty International, *Italy: Invisible Children. The Human Rights of Migrant and Asylum-seeking Minors Detained upon Arrival at the Maritime Border in Italy*, 23 February 2006, via http://www.amnesty.org/en/library/info/EUR30/001/2006, accessed 2 August 2012.

21 I used the expression 'Adult-centered miopia', for example, in '"Not a Sack of Potatoes": Moving and Removing Children across Borders', 15 *Boston University Public Interest Law Journal* 2 (2006), 197–217, at 197, 209.

22 For the most recent in a long line of reports on child migrants that still invoke this perspective, see Save the Children, *Our Broken Dreams: Child Migration in Southern Africa*, SC UK and Norway, Mozambique, 2008. Speaking of 'a culture of silence and invisibility', the Country Director of SC UK in Mozambique says: 'Unaccompanied child migrants are extremely vulnerable to abuse and exploitation, but this is an issue which has *slipped through the cracks* of public concern in southern Africa and around the world': UN Integrated Regional Information Networks (IRIN), 'Southern Africa: Child Migrants Tell All', 29 April 2008, via http://allafrica.com/stories/200804300709.html, accessed 27 July 2012.

23 See, e.g., Valdiviezo-Galdamez v Attorney General, 663 F.3d 582 (3rd Cir. 2011); Benitez Ramos v Holder, 589 F 3d. 426 (7th Cir. 2009); Contreras-Martinez v Holder, 346 F. App'x 956 (4th Cir. 2009); Gomez-Benitez v Attorney General, 295 F. App'x 324 (11th Cir. 2008); Matter of S-E-G, 24 I & N Dec. 579 (BIA 30 July 2008); and Matter of E-A-G, 24 I & N Dec. 591 (BIA 30 July 2008).

have received as much general attention: in the former case, sympathy and public concern;[24] in the latter, hostility and public outcry.[25] No one could claim these are invisible issues. We read about child victims of sex trafficking regularly; and we see migrant children begging in subway stations or trying to clean our car windscreens frequently. And yet the numbers of trafficked child migrants appear to be growing, not declining, while the problems of migrant street children stealing or begging seem to be as intractable as ever. I shall argue that we need a new narrative, a more complex perspective, to explain current developments in child migration and address the problems that they give rise to. We need to analyse the phenomenon in a more nuanced way than we have so far and we need to advance claims on states that expand beyond the protection mandate that has been our focus to this point.

The Protection Mandate and its Outcome

Before I turn to the new perspective I seek to advance, I shall highlight some of the milestones in research and advocacy centered around the *protection mandate*. Two topics – child asylum and family unity – are illustrative of a considerable body of work since the early 1990s that has documented the presence of child migrants in our societies and the challenges that it creates.

(a) Protecting the Best Interests of Child Asylum Seekers

The circumstances and needs of unaccompanied child asylum seekers have been the focus of a broad spectrum of organizations across states, from UNHCR and UNICEF to the Separated Children in Europe network, refugee and immigration advocacy organizations such as the International Conference of Catholic Bishops and the Lutheran Immigrant and Refugee Service in the States, the Refugee Council in Canada, the Human Rights and Equal Opportunities

24 See, e.g., Jonathan Todres, 'Taking Prevention Seriously: Developing a Comprehensive Response to Child Trafficking and Sexual Exploitation', 43 *Vanderbilt Journal of Transnational Law* 1 (2010), 1–56, at 4–5; Sara Dillon, 'What Human Rights Law Obscures: Global Sex Trafficking and the Demand for Children', 17 *UCLA Women's Law Journal* 121 (2008), 121–88, at 128; and U.S. Gov't Accountability Office, 'Human Trafficking: Better Data, Strategy, and Reporting Needed to Enhance U.S. Antitrafficking Efforts Abroad (2006)' , the Government Accountability Office (GAO), July 2006, http://www.gao.gov/new.items/d06825.pdf, accessed 2 August 2012.

25 See, e.g., Fox News, '"Jamiel's Law" Targets Illegal Immigrant Gang Members in Wake of Los Angeles H.S. Football Star's Death', 8 April 2008, at http://www.foxnews.com/story/0,2933,348209,00.html, accessed 27 July 2012; Cara Buckley, 'A Fearsome Gang and Its Wannabes', *New York Times*, 19 August 2007, at http://www.nytimes.com/2007/08/19/weekinreview/19buckley.html, accessed 27 July 2012; and Victor J. Blue, 'Gangs Without Borders: Violent Central American gangs were Born in the USA, Returned to their Homeland and Now Migrate Back and Forth between Here and There', *San Francisco Chronicle*, 2 April 2006, at http://articles.sfgate.com/2006-04-02/opinion/17289265_1_mara-salvatrucha-gang-members-central-america, accessed 27 July 2012.

Commission and Ombudsman in Australia, and emerging groups in South Africa and Central and Latin America. This work has scored several successes. I shall touch on four.

Insistence on a comprehensive *parens patriae* protective obligation towards all children, including migrant children, and extensive evidence of the compounding traumatic impact of punitive measures on children already devastated by war and loss,[26] has persuaded most refugee destination states that *detention is an inappropriate response* to child applicants as they advance their asylum claims. This is a significant achievement. Where once detention was routine, even mandatory, it is now exceptional. The UK and Australia, for example, no longer detain child asylum seekers at all as a matter of policy,[27] and even the US, since the transfer of responsibility from the Immigration and Naturalization Service to the Department of Homeland Security, has significantly reduced the amount of time the average child asylum seeker spends in detention.[28] To be sure, stories about child asylum seekers in shackles and handcuffs, stuck in secure detention facilities for long periods, still emerge in the US from time to time;[29] and disputes about age determination mean that the empirical picture about child asylum seekers in the UK and Australia is more complex than the progressive new policies would suggest. But had it not been for the painstaking research and the shocking reports, the parliamentary committees, the well-orchestrated Congressional testimonies and court challenges, asylum-seeking children would be spending much more time behind bars in destination states than they do now. These successes are all the more notable since detention of accompanied migrant children pending deportation of families is on the rise. Some immigrant family detention regimes are so harsh that they have attracted repeated public criticism. In one case a privately run jail, the T. Don Hutto facility in Texas, had such poor living conditions for its inmate families that it became the object of litigation: 'The children were dressed in prison garb like their parents … The only children who weren't wearing prison clothing were the infants, because they couldn't find prison uniforms small enough'. According to the University of Texas School of Law Immigration law clinic, 'families were counted seven times a day and children spent most of their time inside prison cells.'[30]

---

26 For an in-depth study see Matthew Hodes, Daljit Jagdev, Navin Chandra and Anna Cunnliff, 'Risk and Resilience for Psychological Distress amongst Unaccompanied Asylum Seeking Adolescents', 49 *Journal of Child Psychology and Psychiatry* 7 (July 2008), 723–32.

27 OHCHR, Study of the High Commissioner on challenges and best practices in the implementation of the international framework for the protection of the rights of the child in the context of migration, A/HRC/15/29 (5 July 2010), at 20.

28 Jacqueline Bhabha and Susan Schmidt, 'From Kafka to Wilberforce: Is the U.S. Government's Approach to Child Migrants Improving?', Westlaw Database: Immigration Briefings, February 2011, at 3.

29 See Jack Fink, 'Former Drug Treatment Patients Suing Over Videotaping', *CBS*, 7 January 2011, at http://dfw.cbslocal.com/2011/01/07/former-drug-treatment-patients-suing-over-videotaping/, accessed 22 October 2012; and Michelle Roberts, 'Detention Facility for Immigrant Kids Sued for Abuse', *Associated Press*, 3 April 2008, at http://www.detentionwatchnetwork.org/node/821, accessed 22 October 2012.

30 Melissa del Bosque, 'Children of the State: The Feds and Texas Quarrel over Custody of Undocumented Kids', *Texas Observer*, 15 May 2008, at http://www.texasobserver.org/archives/item/15362-2759-children-of-the-state-the-feds-and-texas-quarrel-over-custody-of-undocumented-kids, accessed 2 August 2012.

Second, insistence on the protection mandate has resulted in several states adopting *child asylum guidelines* that incorporate universally accepted child rights principles. As a result the powerful notion of 'best interests' set out in Article 3 of the Convention on the Rights of the Child (CRC),[31] frames the articulation of measures deemed relevant to the assessment and handling of child claims. Canada, modifying a template first developed by United Nations High Commissioner for Refugees (UNHCR), was the trendsetting state, but its example has been followed by many others. Even the US Child Asylum Guidelines, announced exactly ten years ago on the occasion of the 50th anniversary of the UN Declaration of Human Rights, invoke the principle of the best interests of the child despite the US's notorious refusal to ratify the CRC. Best interest should be understood as a layered notion, requiring a multi-pronged assessment of adult priorities, child needs and individual circumstances. In practice, however, states sometimes apply it mechanistically, exploiting the concept's lack of clear definition. It has, for example, been invoked by state authorities to justify removal of unaccompanied asylum-seeking children back 'home' on the basis that family reunification is self-evidently in their best interests, without any empirical assessment of actual circumstances. And because 'best interests' are merely a 'primary' rather than a 'paramount' or trumping consideration according to the CRC, the concept can be balanced against other less child-friendly considerations such as the need for firm immigration control or national security. Edgar Chocoy, the Guatemalan child fleeing gang violence on the streets of Guatemala City, was killed by those he feared a week after his removal from a US detention center;[32] and Afghani youth who managed to escape the clutches of the Taliban at the turn of the twentieth century by fleeing to Australia once again face uncertainty as their claims to permanent residence in Australia are reviewed. Even in the European Union where legal representation and guardianship for child asylum seekers have a longer history than in Australia or the US, there are serious concerns about the reception conditions available to these children: access to mental health care is seriously inadequate as are the facilities for family tracing.[33] Nevertheless, the introduction into the child asylum decision-making process of a widely accepted benchmark for assessing child policy has raised the decision-making bar and added leverage to the arguments of child migrant advocates.

Third, the notion of *child specific persecution* is slowly taking shape in court decisions, reversing the traditional neglect of such behaviour. Child abuse, recruitment as a child soldier, the risk of child selling, or forced marriage have all been accepted as the basis for granting a child asylum. Ten years ago no such arguments were advanced, and no such decisions were taken. The cross-fertilization of women's rights arguments into the children's rights arena, and more generally the creative importation of human rights jurisprudence with its concepts of horizontal accountability[34] and non-state actors into the refugee adjudication field have provided a rich context for creative, child-focused legal developments. Advances

31 UN CRC, 20 November 1989, 1577 UNTS 3, ILM 1456 (1989), Art. 3.

32 Bruce Finley, 'Deportee's Slaying Spurs Reform Push: Advocates say Teen's Fear of Gangs Unheeded', *Denver Post*, 8 April 2004, at A1.

33 European Commission Executive Summary and Recommendations, '"Horizontal" Concerns about Reception Conditions throughout the European Union', para. 1(1), on file with the author.

34 Stephen Gardbaum, 'The "Horizontal Effect" of Constitutional Rights', 102 *Michigan Law Review* (2003), 387–459.

in child neuropsychology have also had an impact on evaluations of the culpability of individual child applicants, for example where considerations of brutality justifying exclusion from refugee protection (as in the case of child soldiers accused of crimes against humanity) are relevant. Evidence that incomplete brain myelination and immature frontal cortex development reduce children's ability to control aggressive impulses is relevant to moral arguments about child soldiers' decisional autonomy and ethical responsibility. And, as in domestic criminal cases (including the US Supreme Court case prohibiting the death penalty for crimes committed by minors)[35] so in the refugee protection field, child asylum seekers have benefitted as a result.

Finally, applicability of the very *definition of a child* has received more subtle and careful attention as a result of the acceptance of a comprehensive protection mandate than was the case decades ago. Some states have implemented sophisticated, holistic approaches to age assessment, rejecting the reductive physical tests (whether dental, shoulder or wrist x-rays) as proxies for age and accepting instead that economic, social and cultural differences impinge dramatically on a child's physical and emotional development. The arrogant self-confidence of state officials in their own instinctive judgment has been punctured by more complex, multidimensional criteria of assessment. Recognition that childhood does not take a uniform shape but that it nevertheless requires a uniformly protective response has gradually impinged upon punitive knee-jerk reactions. Again, these developments have not been linear or consistent: many states still rely excessively on individual physical tests as placeholders for chronological age, and even those states that recognize the difficulty of such tests, such as the UK, revert to them from time to time in the face of xenophobic political pressure. But the engagement of multidisciplinary advocacy alliances including paediatricians, dentists and physical anthropologists has surely yielded some child rights gains. A decline in the proportion of child asylum detainees[36] is the gratifying result.

Overall, the scope for effective protection for child asylum seekers as independent claimants has increased, asylum officers and adjudicators are sensitized to (sometimes even trained in) the issues, and the importance of introducing child welfare measures into the procedures is no longer contested.

(b) The Right to Respect for Family Life: Bringing the Interests of Children in Immigrant Families into the Foreground

As fundamental as a child's right to protection from persecution, is the child's right to respect for family and private life. In fact, acknowledgement that children 'belong' in and to families, and that they have powerful claims to stability in their upbringings or reunification with parents where there has been disruption, has if anything been less contested than acknowledgement that children have a right to independent asylum. And yet, in this arena too, child advocates have had to press their claims to enforce the protection mandate. A

[35] Roper v. Simmons, 543 US 551 (2005).

[36] Jacqueline Bhabha and Nadine Finch, *Seeking Asylum Alone: Unaccompanied and Separated children Seeking Refugee Protection in the UK* (Cambridge, MA: President and Fellows of Harvard University, 2006), at 56–62.

primary focus on adult entitlements and deserts rather than on child needs and rights – a trend consistent with the *invisibility narrative* – has tended to drive official decision making in the first instance.[37] As a result, placing the child's interests at the center of the equation has been an important advocacy project. It spans the early decisions by the European Court (and Commission) of Human Rights in the Berrehab case (followed by a long line of cases including Boujlifa),[38] to the more recent battles over Tabitha in Belgium and at the European Court of Human Rights in Strasbourg,[39] Irish-born children's rights to family unity in their own country,[40] and the rights of children of irregular migrant parents to attend public kindergarten in Italy.[41] The debate over states' protection mandate in relation to children in migrant or mixed families has prompted interesting public reflections on the relative merits of adult entitlements or punishments versus children's rights or benefits.[42]

Take the Irish Born Child (or IBC) issue,[43] which – give or take some national peculiarities and idiosyncrasies – captures debates and problems addressed in many industrialized states experiencing high rates of immigration.[44] Around it, a fascinating debate has unfolded with two fundamental principles of Irish state sovereignty pitted against each other. On the one hand there is the constitutional protection of the right to Irish citizenship of every child born on the territory (enshrined in Article 2), and with it the other correlates of citizenship, including the right to indefinite residence in the country of one's citizenship. And on the other hand, there is the sovereign right of Ireland to control immigration, to protect itself from the claims of irregular migrants on its welfare system, including its health and social services. Non-citizen parents of IBCs, many of them asylum seekers with claims rejected by the UK and other EU member states, challenged removal orders from Ireland by relying

---

[37] For a full discussion of this topic see Jacqueline Bhabha, 'The "Mere Fortuity" of Birth? Are Children Citizens?', 15 *Differences: A Journal of Feminist Cultural Studies* 2 (Summer 2004), 91–117, at 99.

[38] Berrehab v. the Netherlands, App. No. 10730/84, 11 Eur. H.R. Rep. 322 (1988) (Eur. Ct. H.R.); Yousef v. United Kingdom, App. No. 14830/89, Eur. Ct. H.R. (1992); Beldjoudi v. France, 234 Eur. Ct. H.R. (ser. A) (1992); Boujlifa v. France. App. No. 24404/94, 30 Eur. H.R. Rep. 419, 437–48 (1997); Bouchelkia v. France, 1997-1 Eur. Ct. H.R. (ser. A) 47 (1997); and Ciliz v. the Netherlands, App. No. 29192/95, Eur. Ct. H.R. (2000).

[39] Mubilanzila Mayeka and Kaniki Mitunga v. Belgium, App. No. 13178/03, at http://www.unhcr.org/refworld/pdfid/45d5cef72.pdf, accessed 27 July 2012.

[40] See Jason DeParle, 'Born Irish, but With Illegal Parents', *New York Times*, 25 February 2008, at http://www.nytimes.com/2008/02/25/world/europe/25ireland.html, accessed 27 July 2012.

[41] In 2008, an attempt by Milan city council to prevent irregular migrants from enrolling their children in state kindergartens was overruled by a court, which held that insisting on a valid residence permit as a precondition for enrolment 'unduly subordinat[ed] children's rights to their parents' residence status': Milan Tribunal, 1st civil section, no. 2380/08 R.G., 11 February 2008.

[42] David B. Thronson, 'Custody and Contradictions: Exploring Immigration Law as Federal Family Law in the Context of Child Custody', 59 *Hastings Law Journal* (2008), 453–515 (discussing how family courts in the US penalize parents on the basis of their immigration status, making decisions that don't reflect the best interests of the child but rather the court's perception of the deservingness of the parent).

[43] See DeParle, 'Born Irish, but With Illegal Parents'.

[44] For an excellent discussion of convergence in nationality laws within industrialized nations see Patrick Weil, 'Access to Citizenship: A comparison of Twenty-Five Nationality Laws', *Citizenship Today: Global Perspectives and Practices*, ed. T. Alexander Aleinikoff and Douglas Klusmeyer (Washington, D.C.: Carnegie Endowment for International Peace, 2001), 17–35.

on the IBCs' entitlement to enjoyment of family life in their country of nationality. The courts became the locus of a heated battle, crystallizing the divisions within the society. Pro-immigrant and child rights groups upheld the IBCs' rights, insisting on the primacy of citizenship and on non-discrimination principles supposed to benefit all Irish children irrespective of race or ethnic origin. Nationalist and conservative sectors meanwhile foregrounded the non-citizen parents' alleged manipulation of legal rules as a strategy to gain undeserved access to state support and residence by adults unconnected to the Irish territory. They publicly criticized families travelling in the third trimester of pregnancy for cynically exploiting Ireland's generosity to secure the birth of an IBC as an anchor for adult immigration claims.

The fortunes of either side to the debate have fluctuated. From early success for IBCs in the trendsetting Fajujono case in the 1990s, to the reversal in favour of the nativist exclusionary arguments in the A.O & D.L. case in 2003,[45] arguments defending state sovereignty and the imperative of effective immigration control have been pitted against arguments about Ireland's history as a nation of emigrants with a duty of reciprocity for past hospitality received, and the primacy of citizens' right to enjoyment of their family life in their own country. The 2008 decisions in the Dimbo and Oguekwe cases[46] reversed a recent exclusionary trend, once again upholding the citizen child's rights. In a direct challenge to the Immigration, Residence and Protection Bill being debated by the Irish Parliament at the time,[47] the Irish Supreme Court required the Minister to refrain from imposing fast track exclusions on irregular parents of IBCs. It insisted instead that the minister consider 'the circumstances of each case by due enquiry in a fair and proper manner as to the facts and factors affecting the family'.[48] More recently, the European Court of Justice has held that the parents of a child who is a European Union citizen must be granted the right to work and reside in a member state in order to protect that child's right to live in Europe. In a 'major shift', the Zambrano judgment extends the reach of EU law addressing questions of family unity to purely internal matters, forcing the Government of Ireland to reexamine its immigration and deportation policy with respect to the rights of the non-Irish parents of Irish children.[49]

---

45 A.O. & D.L. v Minister of Justice [2003] I.R. 1. For a detailed discussion of this case and the IBC issue see Jacqueline Bhabha, 'The "Mere Fortuity of Birth"?: Children, Borders, and the Right to Citizenship', *Citizenship, Borders, and Gender: Mobility and Immobility*, ed. Seyla Benhabib and Judith Resnik (New York: NYU Press, 2009), 187–227.

46 Dimbo v the Minister for Justice, Equality and Law Reform [2008] IESC 26; Oguekwe v The Minister for Justice, Equality and Law Reform, 1 May 2008.

47 The Immigration, Residence and Protection Bill 2010 amends the 2008 legislation and provides for summary removals, which migrants' rights advocates maintain is contrary to the Supreme Court ruling. See Migrant Rights Centre Ireland, 'Plans for Summary Removal in Immigration Bill Contrary to International Law – 2010', 4 November 2010, at http://www.mrci.ie/Plans-for-Summary-Removal-in-Immigration-Bill-Contrary-to-International-Law--detail-news, accessed 27 July 2012.

48 Justice Denham in Dimbo v the Minister for Justice, Equality and Law Reform.

49 See Gerardo Ruiz Zambrano v Office national de l'emploi (ONEm), C-34/09, European Union: European Court of Justice, 8 March 2011. See also Carol Coulter and Jamie Smyth, 'Case Review for Non-Irish parents of Irish Citizens', *The Irish Times*, 3 March 2011, via http://www.irishtimes.com/newspaper/ireland/2011/0322/1224292776603.html, accessed 27 July 2012.

The details of the litigation trajectory are, for our purposes, less interesting than the role of the protection mandate in the discussion. Throughout the battle, and across both sides of the battlefield, the right of the IBC to protection and to the benefit of a best interest assessment had not been challenged. At issue, rather, was how the Irish child's best interest should be balanced against competing equities, including the *bona fides* and moral legitimacy of the IBCs' parents (did they lie, did they cynically exploit their baby's *ius soli* for personal gain, should they be able to benefit). The fact that the IBC's interests have been central to the debate, indeed the pivot around which the other issues have revolved, rather than an irrelevance submerged by the imperative of protecting borders and speedily removing rejected asylum seekers, is notable. It represents an achievement for advocates of child protection in the context of migration, and a benchmark in burgeoning discussions about citizenship and what it means for a child.

Both the evolution of work on unaccompanied child asylum seekers and the discussions surrounding IBCs are milestones in child protection. They have brought to public attention powerful challenges to simplistic notions of belonging and citizenship; they have forced the authorities to look afresh at the place of child migrants and their families within the society, to reconsider the simplistic notion that young children are packages that can easily be moved from place to place without detriment, and to foreground considerations of best interest for relatively marginal populations that once would have been overlooked or neglected. These achievements anchor the rights of children affected by migration in a new way.

The Respect Mandate and its Complexities

For all its successes, however, the *invisibility narrative* no longer adequately explains current social and legal lacunae in the field of child migration or the rights issues that remain unresolved. And the *protection mandate* that follows from the invisibility approach does not encompass some key challenges raised by child and youth migration today. Emerging issues require a new perspective, including a new narrative for explaining contemporary phenomena and associated with these a new mandate with which to guide intervention and policy. I shall call the new narrative the *ambivalence narrative*, and the new mandate the *respect mandate*. The ambivalence narrative advances a different explanation for the failures of states to adequately protect the interests of child migrants than the traditional invisibility narrative did. The *respect mandate* foregrounds an additional set of guiding principles for engaging with their needs and priorities.

As indicated, the traditional, invisibility narrative explained states' failure to adequately address the special vulnerabilities of child migrants in terms of a perception deficit, an oversight, a failure to notice the distinctive problems facing a largely hidden group in our societies. This explanation made good sense for unaccompanied, traumatized child asylum seekers fleeing war and persecution: they were hidden in remote detention centers or were eking out a precarious existence in bed-and-breakfast accommodation. It also worked for other relatively marginal and unnoticed asylum-seeking populations seeking to challenge their precarious legal status as they gradually integrated into the societies of destination states.

It does not, however, adequately capture the circumstances of many child migrants today, children whose border crossing is more the product of a 'mixed migration' dynamic than a traditional asylum flight, whose circumstances are only too visible on the streets of our cities and front pages of our newspapers, whose conditions tend to elicit scepticism and suspicion, even hostility and resentment rather than compassion. Teenagers who have 'sneaked' across the border illegally with the assistance of paid smugglers to secure informal employment, youths who, whether trafficked or not, are engaged as gang members in purse snatching, aggressive begging or flagrant sexual soliciting, are not *prima facie* candidates for our 'protective' instincts. Rather than seeing them as vulnerable children in need of protection, on a continuum with 'our' children, we tend to view them as disruptive juvenile outsiders in need of discipline and punishment, young adults in essence if not in age. And accordingly, we fail to engage effectively with their manifest problems, not because we do not see or hear them, but because we are ambivalent about how to address them. States' failure to adequately address the needs of this group of child migrants arises, therefore, out of a cognitive not a perception deficit: we see, but we don't understand. We legislate their right to public education and healthcare irrespective of their legal status, but at the same time we erect practical obstacles to their access to these services, demanding documents, proof of residence, social ties. We accept obligations to protect them from exploitation and abuse, creating – in our legislative chambers and international congresses – anti-trafficking visa protections for them and criminal sanctions for their exploiters, but on the ground, at the borders, on the streets, in the police stations, we blame them for the risks they pose to our social fabric and look for ways of removing them from circulation, even presence, in our societies. Two cases serve to illustrate this problematic situation.

(a) Jeunes Errants: The Travails of Irregular Child Migrants and the Ambivalence of Destination State Policymakers

The first concerns irregular child migrants, be they Moroccan, Romanian or Albanian working children in France and Spain,[50] Guatemalan or Honduran children in the US and Mexico,[51] Nigerian children in the UK or Ireland, Zimbabwean or Mozambiquan children in South Africa,[52] or Chinese or Somali children in Canada. Many of these children arrive unaccompanied or separated from their families, smuggled or trafficked across borders by professional migration intermediaries operating for profit and motivated by the lucrative earnings generated by transportation of this human cargo. The children leave home for a variety of reasons: destitution, the search for survival, the desire for self-advancement,

50 Marine Vassort, *Paroles d'Errance* (Marseille: Editions P'tits Papiers, 2006).

51 'U.S. Hands Over 14,237 Unaccompanied Minors to Mexico in '11', *Latin American Herald Tribune*, 13 February 2012, at http://www.laht.com/article.asp?ArticleId=470577&CategoryId=14091, accessed 22 October 2012 (reporting that, according to Mexico's National Migration Institute, over 14,237 unaccompanied minors intercepted at the US-Mexico border were returned to Mexico).

52 'Figures ... released by the South African authorities for undocumented Zimbabwean migrants reveal that of the 2000 people being repatriated each week, up to 20% were unaccompanied children': IRIN, 'Southern Africa: Child Migrants Tell All'.

family pressure or conformity with a prevailing migration fashion, abusive child sale or exploitation, and often a complex combination of these factors. The decision-making process leading to international migration is rarely simple or linear: it typically includes desperation, hope, courage, naiveté, calculation, cunning, either directly on the part of the child, or indirectly on the part of adults controlling the child, or again a complex mixture. A 15-year-old Romanian boy explains the pressures on him to migrate clearly:

> Me, I was the youngest of all the sibs. I didn't do a thing there … At 10, I was all alone. My brothers, they left to work in Germany, Austria, Italy … I was all alone … I said to myself: 'I have nothing here. I don't want to be a labourer, I don't want to work for anyone else.' So there you are: either I leave or here there's nothing to do … I went to school: it didn't work. I was always late, absent, put back a year … repeat the class again, repeat it. I had done eight years for nothing. Yes, I learned to read and write, but that's it! You can't do anything with schooling there … My father and mother … What could they say to me? My father, he has a farm. So I was meant to work with him. Are you crazy? Pigs, cows … So I left, stole cars, played poker, got to know all the village bars … My father, he'd come from time to time to get me, give me a couple of slaps. 'Leave me alone! I'm getting out of here.' That's how it started – I left home. When I left, I was fifteen.[53]

Given the increasing impermeability and militarization of borders, whether by infrared sensors as at the US/Mexico border, electrified razor fences at the Zimbabwe/South Africa frontier, or Frontex across the EU,[54] a fair amount of deception may also be required for a successful border crossing – again, deception practised directly by the child or mediated by an accompanying adult. Nearly always the migration decision (even when it is controlled or manipulated by others) is associated with the quest for a thicker, fuller, more rewarding access to the benefits of social membership, what some have called the 'heft of citizenship',[55] than is available in the country of origin. To be sure, this quest may be naïve or even deeply flawed, as in the case of the tens or hundreds of thousands cruelly and cynically trafficked for sex and labour exploitation, or it may be immature and unrealistic, as in the case of the thousands ignorantly chasing technicolour dreams. But it may also be realistic and mature, a sober assessment of the relative options and advancement possibilities on either side of the borders crossed.

How do our societies react to these irregular child migrants? No simple answer captures the complexity of responses, which range from harsh detention and expedited removal back 'home' to the provision of specially tailored reception facilities, fostering arrangements, and

53 Vassort, *Paroles d'Errance*, at 11.

54 The growth of Frontex as a pan-European border control agency has been dramatic – its 2011 budget was 118.2 million euros, a 27% increase over its 2010 budget: Frontex, *General Report 2011*, at 23.

55 Audrey Macklin, 'Who is the Citizen's Other? Considering the Heft of Citizenship', 8 *Theoretical Inquiries in Law* 2 (July 2007), 333–66.

post-traumatic stress therapeutic interventions.[56] But several generalizations are in order. First, an overarching and underlying assumption driving official decision making in these cases is that these irregular child migrants are more at risk in the destination state than they would be back home – and that return to families is the most appropriate protective response. According to a Save the Children report, *Our Broken Dreams: Child Migration in Southern Africa*, 'A number of [migrant child job seekers] called for the authorities to stop abusing, imprisoning and repatriating them to their home countries'.[57] Note the association between the three different state strategies. Second, and closely related, asylum is not usually thought to be a relevant or appropriate remedy for their situation. Indeed, children who turn out to have been smuggled or trafficked for labour or sexual exploitation, may be removed from the asylum determination process altogether.[58] In some jurisdictions, they face punitive detention as suspect 'illegal' migrants. A news report of the successful hunger strike organized by hundreds of children protesting the cramped and unsanitary detention conditions in their reception centre on the Greek island of Leros highlights this seamless transition from protection to punishment.[59]

These social responses have several perverse consequences, increasingly apparent to attentive observers, though still ignored by most official agencies.[60] They act as a disincentive

56 See Council of Europe: Parliamentary Assembly, *Unaccompanied Children in Europe: Issues of Arrival, Stay and Return*, 21 March 2011, Doc. 12539, at http://www.unhcr.org/refworld/docid/4d8b1e002.html, accessed 27 July 2012; Marine Carlier *et al.* (France terre d'asile), *The Reception and Care of Unaccompanied Minors in Eight Countries of the European Union*, December 2010, via http://www.france-terre-asile.org/component/flexicontent/items/item/4702-unaccompanied-children, accessed 27 July 2012; and Physicians for Human Rights, *From Persecution to Prison: The Health Consequences of Detention for Asylum Seekers*, June 2003, Physicians for Human Rights & The Bellevue/NYU Program for Survivors and Torture, Boston and New York, at https://s3.amazonaws.com/PHR_Reports/persecution-to-prison-US-2003.pdf, accessed 2 August 2012.

57 IRIN, 'Southern Africa: Child Migrants Tell All'.

58 Belgium and the Netherlands have separate procedures for trafficked children that entail removal from the asylum determination procedures. See Jacqueline Bhabha and Christina Alfirev, *The Identification and Referral of Trafficked Persons to Procedures for Determining International Protection Needs*, UNHCR, October 2009, PPLAS/2009/03, 2009, at http://www.unhcr.org/refworld/docid/4ad317bc2.html, accessed 27 July 2012.

59 Malcolm Brabant, 'Victory for Greek Hunger Strikers', BBC News, Leros, 26 May 2008, at http://www.bbc.co.uk/2/hi/europe/7419667.stm, accessed 27 July 2012.

60 This is a good example of the dangers of consequentialist thinking and the importance of empirical considerations for policy. Because states focus on the consequentialist benefits of interfering with the work of traffickers, they neglect the empirical determinants of the children's behaviours. Preferring the self-righteous condemnation of evil traffickers to the careful scrutiny of the impact of their policies, they advance consequentialist justifications for their actions that do not stand up to the test of empirical assessment. As Joseph Nye points out in a different context: Once the ends justify the means, the dangers of slipping into a morality of convenience greatly increase. To calculate all the consequences of one's actions is impossible, and when the calculation is fuzzy, abuse is possible … And given human proclivities to weight choices in our own favor, and the difficulties of being sure of consequences of complex activities, impartiality may be easily lost in the absence of rules.

Nye, *Nuclear Ethics*, 19, cited in Kathryn Sikkink, 'The Role of Consequences, Comparison and Counterfactuals in Constructivist Ethical Thought', *Moral Limit and Possibility in World Politics*, ed. Richard Price (Cambridge: Cambridge University Press, 2008), 83–111.

to self-identification for children trapped in exploitative situations: the fear of incarceration and/or deportation acts as a powerful break on the impulse to escape abusive employment situations. Why? Because most of the children engaged in these contexts need and want to earn, even if much of their earning is hived off; return 'home' is not a viable option they can consider. Thus, it is not just that migrant child workers do not self-identify. On occasion they escape from care once identified, because state protection does not afford them what they think they need. In Ireland, for example, over 300 unaccompanied children have gone missing from the care of local authorities in recent years.[61] Perhaps this confirms the views of commentators who suggest that the best interests of migrant children are anything but a primary consideration driving current state policy.[62] Certainly it indicates a need to question the assumptions driving established modes of intervention. The punitive element of policy obviously elicits avoidance. But perhaps even the protective or reform/rescue agenda is misconceived. By imposing a reductive, culturally inapposite calculus that considers 'childhood' a work-free zone, current social responses avoid the complex challenge of engaging with the dilemmas and limited strategic options facing these young child migrants; assuming that family, school, play and home are fixed and necessary points of reference for all children, our current interventions misclassify the risks and needs driving their actions and misinterpret the choices they make.

I do not mean to suggest that easy answers exist. It is clear that some of the children who escape from care are in the vicious clutches of traffickers who control them and thus manage to lure them back to the brothel or street corner;[63] open-door welfare facilities are no match for the predatory grasp of these groups, but of course they would provide a more desirable living context. It is also true that as a society we need to insist on the importance for all children of education and intellectual development. However, by not listening to the child migrants themselves, by not placing their needs and views at the centre of our interventions, we miss the opportunity to engage more effectively and to craft viable policies for them. If we want to persuade these child migrants that their choices are self-destructive and that better options for them exist, we need to find a platform for initiating that discussion. Protection simpliciter, as we implement it now – for which we can read rescue, removal, repatriation – is not an adequate answer to the problem: something more demanding is required of us.

---

[61] Over the last seven years, 388 children placed in the care of the Irish authorities as suspected victims of trafficking have gone missing and have never been traced: Sr Stanislaus Kennedy, 'Who Cares about the Disappeared Children?', 23 May 2008, at http://www.ireland.com/mewspaper/opinion/2008/0523/1211461644896.html, accessed 23 May 2008.

[62] Grainne Brophy and Bernadette McGonigle, 'Steady Traffick', *Law Society Gazette*, April 2008, 26, via www.lawsociety.ie, accessed 27 July 2012.

[63] See, e.g., Louise Shelley, *Human Trafficking: A Global Perspective* (Cambridge: Cambridge University Press, 2010); Alexis A. Aronowitz, *Human Trafficking, Human Misery: The Global Trade in Human Beings* (Westport, CT: Praeger Publishers, 2009); and Women's Commission for Refugee Women and Children, *The Struggle between Migration Control and Victim Protection: The UK Approach to Human Trafficking*, July 2005.

(b) De Facto Irregular Child Migrants: The Challenge of Understanding and Intervening in Complex Situations of Enduring Social Marginalization and Exclusion

A second set of de facto irregular child migrants much in public view today engages these issues equally vividly. Surprisingly, perhaps, these are neither unaccompanied children nor irregular migrants: they are lawful residents and, typically, they are accompanied by their families. And yet, they illustrate the inadequacies of current policy towards child migrants and the limitations of the invisibility narrative and the protection mandate acutely. Who am I referring to? Two groups, differently situated in some respects, share these characteristics and some key associated social features. One group consists of the millions of citizen children (currently estimated at approximately 5.5 million) born in the US to irregular migrants,[64] children who live in mixed status families where the claim to residence and belonging in the society is fractured. Though the citizen children are lawful, and though they are accompanied, these children may in some respects be even more at risk of social exclusion than their irregular and unaccompanied counterparts. From one moment to the next, their life can be shattered by a work place raid – as was repeatedly demonstrated in the US during the Bush administration roundups of irregular migrants[65] – or by deportation proceedings following criminal conviction. These young citizens, despite their own legal status, live in the shadows of the law, facing detention and deportation with their parents, suspicion at school, and in some cases marginalization from social services because of their families' acute fears of detection. The invisibility narrative does not account for their situation – visibility is what they dread; and the protection mandate does not fully answer their need – because, under current US law, their best interests cannot trump their parents' irregular status. Something else is required.

The other group of de facto irregulars comprises the hundreds of thousands of Roma children and youth[66] living at the edges (both geographically and metaphorically) of some of the biggest and most prosperous European cities. The immigration and nationality status of this population is as varied as their social and economic conditions are uniform: diversity in destitution. Some, such as the children of undocumented Bosnian Roma refugees living in unregistered camps in Italy, are stateless even though they were born in Italy. Others, such as the Roma from Romania living in France or Germany, are EU nationals. Yet others, such as the

[64] Jeffrey S. Passel, *Unauthorized Immigrant Population: National and State Trends, 2010* (Washington D.C.: Pew Hispanic Center, 2010), at 13, at http://pewhispanic.org/files/reports/133.pdf, accessed 27 July 2012.

[65] Immigration Policy Center, *The Consequences of Federal Failure: Raids' Impact on Families*, 4 April 2008.

[66] See UNICEF, *The Right of Roma Children to Education: Position Paper* (Geneva: UNICEF Regional Office for Central and Eastern Europe and the Commonwealth of Independent States (CEECIS), 2011); European Parliament, 'Hearing Discusses Plight of Europe's Marginalised Roma', 12 February 2010, at http://www.europarl.europa.eu/news/en/headlines/content/20101129STO02032/html/Hearing-discusses-plight-of-Europe%27s-marginalised-Roma, accessed 2 August 2012; Save the Children, 'Roma Children's Right to Education', at http://europe.savethechildren.se/Europe/Focus/Education/, accessed 27 July 2012; and 'UN Urges EU to Help Roma Children', BBC News, 6 March 2007, at http://news.bbc.co.uk/2/hi/europe/6422283.stm, accessed 27 July 2012.

Roma children born to Serbian asylum seekers in Germany, Sweden or France following the Bosnian war, but recently deported to Serbia despite decades of residence (even birth) within EU member states,[67] are nationals but do not speak the language or have any local connections, deportees in their own country. What they share, apart from their self-identification as Roma and the social hostility that accompanies them across Europe, are extreme social marginalization, destitution, homelessness and pervasive discrimination. Over recent years, Roma children and youth in Europe have faced pogroms directed at their settlements,[68] soaring rates of unemployment,[69] inadequate healthcare[70] and radical under-representation in secondary and tertiary education.[71] Their status as outsiders, migrants, displaced persons and deportees places them in social and legal circumstances closely analogous to those of the irregular child migrants discussed in the previous paragraph. Like them, these Roma adolescents lack opportunities and access to effective social protection. Their ability to migrate, to secure a legal rights-respecting status, is severely curtailed by lack of documentation, lack of education, and lack of resources. And yet theirs is hardly an invisible problem. The 'Roma problem' has dominated public attention in several European countries in recent years, Italy most notably, but public concerns have also been vigorously aired in France, Germany, Sweden and the UK.[72] The social, economic and legal rights violations that Roma children and youth experience on a daily basis have not been redressed by invocations of non-discrimination principles. Even the 'best interests of the child' principle has not consistently served this population well: Silvio Berlusconi, the beleaguered Italian Prime Minister, cynically invoked it to justify his call for universal fingerprinting of Roma children to ensure school attendance,[73] a thinly veiled device for surveillance and control of a scapegoated population. Increased

67 Human Rights Watch, *Rights Displaced*. See also James Angelos, 'From Serbia to Germany – and Back: Wave of Roma Rejected as Asylum Seekers', *Spiegel Online*, 26 May 2011, at http://www.spiegel.de/international/germany/0,1518,764630,00.html, accessed 27 July 2012.

68 See, e.g., Der Spiegel, 'Right-Wing Militants on PatrolA New Wave of Anti-Roma Violence in Hungary', 27 April 2011, at http://www.spiegel.de/international/europe/right-wing-militants-on-patrol-a-new-wave-of-anti-roma-violence-in-hungary-a-759349.html, accessed 22 October 2012; Charles Bremner, 'Order to Raze Roma Camps puts France on Back Foot', *The Times*, 14 September 2010; Amnesty International, Europe Must Break Cycle of Discrimination Facing Roma, 7 April 2010, at http://www.amnesty.org/en/news-and-updates

69 European Roma Rights Centre, *The Glass Box: Exclusion of Roma from Employment*, 21 February 2007, via http://www.errc.org/cikk.php?cikk=2727, accessed 27 July 2012.

70 See, e.g., C. Masseria, P. Mladovsky and C. Hernández-Quevedo, 'The Socio-economic Determinants of the Health Status of Roma in Comparison with Non-Roma in Bulgaria, Hungary and Romania', 20 *European Journal of Public Health* 5 (October 2010), 549–54, and Fundación Secretariado Gitano, *Health and the Roma Community: Analysis of the Situation in Europe* (2009).

71 See Joanna Impey, 'Just 42 Percent of Roma Children Finish School in Europe', *Deutsche Welle*, 4 May 2011, at http://www.dw.de/dw/article/0,,14967291,00.html, accessed 2 August 2012. See also Galina Kostadinova, 'Minority Rights as a Normative Framework for Addressing the Situation of Roma in Europe', 39 *Oxford Development Studies* 2 (2011), 163–83.

72 Rob Kushen, 'Scapegoating Will Not Solve "Roma Problem"', *The Guardian*, 3 August 2010, at http://www.guardian.co.uk/commentisfree/libertycentral/2010/aug/03/scapegoating-roma-problem-europe, accessed 27 July 2012.

73 Richard Owen, 'Italy Gypsies Find Echoes of Nazism in Fingerprinting Move', *The Times*, 5 July 2008, at http://www.timesonline.co.uk/tol/news/world/europe/article4272550.ece?pgnum=1, accessed 5 July 2008.

visibility in this explosively hostile context is a liability from which the Roma community increasingly shies away. A more engaged concern for children's best interests would have to start from an analysis of why Roma parents do not consistently send their children to school, what happens to those Roma children who do attend school, and what opportunities school education actually provides to this population. In other words, the notion of the best interest would be deconstructed to reveal its multiple components, including social protection, individual agency, and community respect and dignity.

How have we arrived at this juncture – where the exercise of the best interest principle and a protection mandate have become strategies that child migrants seek to escape – hoping for invisibility rather than visibility, where the engagement of the state towards some of the most vulnerable children within its jurisdiction is punitive, exclusionary and unashamedly discriminatory? I propose that a failure to recognize the *ambivalence* of our reactions to young outsiders, and a reductive and narrow focus on a partial notion of best interest, are responsible, at least in part. Rather than assuming benign motivations as a guiding force driving public policy towards all children including child migrants, we need to scrutinize the punitive and discriminatory responses that govern many public interactions with child migrants, especially those young people that are perceived as insubordinate, dangerous or delinquent. To embark on this reconsideration of public approaches and policies towards child migrants is an ambitious exercise, one that calls for acknowledgement of failures past and difficulties ahead. I propose that what is required, at this juncture, as an essential constitutive building block in re-evaluating child migrant policy, is adoption of a new guiding mandate, the mandate of respect. In this context, respect operates as an element of the rights framework outlined in Article 12 of the Convention on the Rights of the Child, and as a strategy for problematizing the cultural and social assumptions of the actors engaged in both sides of the child migration process, the child migrants and their communities on the one hand, and the destination states and their policy and decision makers on the other. The respect mandate requires an inquiry that goes beyond protection needs facing children, and that opens up for consideration what children and adolescents need to thrive, to be self-reliant, to develop confidence, optimism and integrity for their future pursuits. To develop a toolkit for operationalizing a respect mandate regarding migrant children and youth requires promotion of child agency, responsibility and self-esteem as much as it does provision of the social and economic rights services encompassed by the traditional protection mandate.

Conclusion: The Centrality of Respect

To address the challenges raised by these new populations of child migrants, irregular child labourers who need to earn for their own and perhaps their families' survival, citizen children living in irregular or mixed-status families daily facing the risk of deportation, we need to embark on a relatively new journey, which takes us outside the comfort zone of established 'best interest', protection-based arguments. We need to interrogate the broader context in which migration occurs, the citizenship deficits that force populations to jeopardize their claims to belonging and legality in favour of more tenuous but potentially realizable access to social goods.

First we need to acknowledge the ambivalence in our reactions to child and adolescent migrants and question the moral acceptability and legal validity of our punitive responses – incarceration of citizen children with their deportable irregular parents, removal of child victims of trafficking back to their countries of origin, social exclusion of challenging Roma children from local schools and welfare centres. How do these responses square with the constitutional and rights-based frameworks governing our legal systems and indeed our self-proclaimed democracies? We might argue that the fit is uncomfortable, that the balance between security, law and order, civic protection on the one hand (all legitimate goals that we cannot dismiss or minimize) and non-discrimination and social protection and harmony on the other, needs redrawing. Gross inequality is in and of itself an inherently destabilizing force, and redressing it is not a nation-bound or border-driven project. Nor is it merely a question of 'seeing' what has been hidden earlier, but rather of acknowledging the conflicting impulses that have paralysed effective response and moving beyond the stasis of ambivalence towards the engagement of decision and intervention. Granting children 'temporary permanence' to stay until they are eighteen,[74] a common strategy towards unaccompanied, irregular child migrants, illustrates our ambivalence well. But it is not a satisfactory resolution of the situation, or one that sits well with well-established norms of childcare, such as the importance of permanency planning.

Second, this process of self-scrutiny may lead us to listen to the affected populations more carefully than we have so far, to question our competence to make best interest judgments on the basis of little knowledge and even less understanding. It may force us to open the Pandora's box locked up in Article 12 of the CRC, the child's right to respect, to voice, to an opportunity to be heard. As Save the Children researchers documenting the circumstances of southern African migrant child jobseekers reported, 'Many were very clear about how they should be helped by governments in the region and how they should be *treated with respect*'.[75] Respect is a much more complex notion than may at first be apparent. It mandates a critical engagement with the other, an engagement that acknowledges our preconceptions about the good life (for without those, how can we respect the other?) but also includes serious consideration of the other (in this case the migrant child's) aspirations, options and needs. We need to recognize that as the need for basic protection decreases (for example, during the transition from childhood to adolescence) so the importance of respect increases, that an unstable dynamic of transformation is at work and that children/adolescent rights are the classic site where this is played out. As children move from infancy through childhood to puberty and adolescence, so the protection needs become complicated by questions of child autonomy and the entitlement to respect that it entails. The trafficked children escaping from care in Ireland are making this point. As others have recognized, an exclusive focus on the protection mandate, on human survival and its minimal necessary correlates 'misses the important connections between dignity and human flourishing that are intrinsic'[76] to the right to life. It is not a question of insisting upon an excessively maximalist basket of

---

[74] 'Council Resolution of 26 June 1997 on Unaccompanied Minors who are Nationals of Third Countries', OJ C 221 (19 July 1997), at http://eur-lex.europa.eu/LexUriServ/LexUriServ.do?uri=CELEX:31997Y0719(02):EN:HTML, accessed 27 July 2012.

[75] IRIN, 'Southern Africa: Child Migrants Tell All'.

[76] Katharine G. Young, 'The Minimum Core of Economic and Social Rights: A Concept in Search of Content', 33 *Yale Journal of International Law* 113 (2008), 113–75, at 130.

rights beyond the minimum 'core' required for subsistence, but rather of acknowledging that without these non-biological correlates, the human in human life becomes illusory – Roma children in advanced democracies confined to filthy, sewage and rat infested camps and illiteracy illustrates the point.

This process of understanding what a respect mandate entails is the most urgent task facing child migrant advocates today. In fact it is a critical challenge and an essential tool for addressing the protection lacunae I have described in this chapter. Without understanding the contours of the respect mandate, we shall, I suspect, be unable to move forward in addressing the complex challenges that child migration and irregular child migrants and their families pose to our somewhat complacent protection welfare systems today. Forcing ourselves to interrogate the respect mandate will throw into sharp relief the ambivalences that have held us back from more effective and generous engagement with some key child migrant issues. The fact that trafficked child sex workers rarely get the opportunity to apply for asylum, despite irrefutable evidence of the high risk of retrafficking following return,[77] is an example. To correct this lacuna would require institutional work on the linkages between anti-trafficking and asylum protection agencies;[78] it would also require allocation of resources for legal representation for the children, training of dedicated lawyers, psychologists, trauma experts. It would require development of training and mentoring opportunities enabling formerly exploited children to acquire educational and vocational skills that might equip them for decent, rights-respecting employment opportunities. In the process of developing such interventions, we would be forced to acknowledge that child trafficking is a symptom of child migrants' exclusion and inequality as much as it is of child traffickers' individual depravity and greed, and that for the children themselves, the inclination to elect irregular and potentially hazardous migration may have been a rational response to global social exclusion. If so, we might move further along the way to effective social protection and respect for the irregular child migrants we have failed so far.

References

'After Alabama law, Hispanic kids being bullied', *Associated Press*, 22 October 2011, at http://www.cbsnews.com/8301-201_162-20124241/after-alabama-law-hispanic-kids-being-bullied, accessed 22 October 2012.

Amnesty International, *Europe Must Break Cycle of Discrimination Facing Roma*, 7 April 2010, at http://www.amnesty.org/en/news-and-updates/report/europe-must-break-cycle-discrimination-facing-roma-2010-04-06, accessed 2 August 2012.

Amnesty International, *Italy: Invisible Children. The Human Rights of Migrant and Asylum-seeking Minors Detained upon Arrival at the Maritime Border in Italy*, 23 February 2006, via http://www.amnesty.org/en/library/info/EUR30/001/2006, accessed 2 August 2012.

77 Shelley, *Human Trafficking*, at 69, 211, 216, 290.

78 Bhabha and Alfirev, *Identification and Referral of Trafficked Persons to Procedures for Determining International Protection Need.*

Angelos, James, 'From Serbia to Germany – and Back: Wave of Roma Rejected as Asylum Seekers', *Spiegel Online*, 26 May 2011, at http://www.spiegel.de/international/germany/0,1518,764630,00.html, accessed 27 July 2012.

Ariès, Philippe, *Centuries of Childhood: A Social History of Family Life* (New York: Knopf, 1962).

Aronowitz, Alexis A., *Human Trafficking, Human Misery: The Global Trade in Human Beings* (Westport, CT: Praeger Publishers, 2009).

Bennett, Brian, 'Republicans Want a Return to Workplace Immigration Rituals', *L.A. Times*, 27 January 2011, at http://articles.latimes.com/2011/jan/27/nation/la-naimmigration-raids-20110127, accessed 27 July 2012.

Bhabha, Jacqueline, 'Minors or Aliens? Inconsistent State Intervention and Separated Child Asylum-Seekers', 3 *European Journal of Migration and Law* (2001), 283–314.

Bhabha, Jacqueline, '"Not a Sack of Potatoes": Moving and Removing Children across Borders', 15 *Boston University Public Interest Law Journal* 2 (2006), 197–217.

Bhabha, Jacqueline, 'The "Mere Fortuity" of Birth? Are Children Citizens?', 15 *Differences: A Journal of Feminist Cultural Studies* 2 (Summer 2004), 91–117.

Bhabha, Jacqueline, 'The "Mere Fortuity of Birth"?: Children, Borders, and the Right to Citizenship', *Citizenship, Borders, and Gender: Mobility and Immobility*, ed. Seyla Benhabib and Judith Resnik (New York: NYU Press, 2009), 187–227.

Bhabha, Jacqueline (ed.), *Children Without a State: A Global Human Rights Challenge* (Cambridge: MIT Press, 2011).

Bhabha, Jacqueline and Christina Alfirev, *The Identification and Referral of Trafficked Persons to Procedures for Determining International Protection Needs*, UNHCR, October 2009, PPLAS/2009/03, 2009, at http://www.unhcr.org/refworld/docid/4ad317bc2.html, accessed 27 July 2012.

Bhabha, Jacqueline and Nadine Finch, *Seeking Asylum Alone: Unaccompanied and Separated Children Seeking Refugee Protection in the UK* (Cambridge, MA: President and Fellows of Harvard University, 2006).

Blue, Victor J., 'Gangs Without Borders: Violent Central American Gangs were Born in the USA, Returned to their Homeland and Now Migrate Back and Forth between Here and There', *San Francisco Chronicle*, 2 April 2006, at http://articles.sfgate.com/2006-04-02/opinion/17289265_1_mara-salvatrucha-gang-members-central-america, accessed 27 July 2012.

Brabant, Malcolm, 'Victory for Greek Hunger Strikers', BBC News, Leros, 26 May 2008, at http://www.bbc.co.uk/2/hi/europe/7419667.stm, accessed 27 July 2012.

Bremner, Charles, 'Order to Raze Roma Camps puts France on Back Foot', *The Times*, 14 September 2010.

Brophy, Grainne and Bernadette McGonigle, 'Steady Traffick', *Law Society Gazette*, April 2008, 26, via www.lawsociety.ie, accessed 27 July 2012.

Brown, Jonathan, 'New Centres "To Detain Child Asylum Seekers"', *The Independent*, 4 February 2011, at http://www.independent.co.uk/news/uk/home-news/new-centres-to-detain-child-asylum-seekers-2203843.html, accessed 27 July 2012.

Buckley, Cara, 'A Fearsome Gang and Its Wannabes', *New York Times*, 19 August 2007, at http://www.nytimes.com/2007/08/19/weekinreview/19buckley.html, accessed 27 July 2012.

Carlier, Marine *et al.* (France terre d'asile), *The Reception and Care of Unaccompanied Minors in Eight Countries of the European Union*, December 2010, via http://www.france-terre-asile.org/component/flexicontent/items/item/4702-unaccompanied-children, accessed 27 July 2012.

Chang, Cindy, 'Unaccompanied migrant youth in U.S. detention centers rises 50%', *L.A. Times*, 16 October 2012, at http://articles.latimes.com/2012/oct/16/local/la–me–immigration–children–20121016, accessed 22 October 2012.

Clymer, Adam and Lizette Alvarez, 'The Elián Gonzalez Case: The Overview', *The New York Times*, 27 April 2000, at http://www.nytimes.com/2000/04/27/us/elian-gonzalez-case-overview-boy-s-father-joins-fray-over-his-son-s-asylum-case.html, accessed 27 July 2012.

Coulter, Carol and Jamie Smyth, 'Case Review for Non-Irish parents of Irish Citizens', *The Irish Times*, 3 March 2011, via http://www.irishtimes.com/newspaper/ireland/2011/0322/1224292776603.html, accessed 27 July 2012.

Council of Europe: Parliamentary Assembly, *Unaccompanied Children in Europe: Issues of Arrival, Stay and Return*, 21 March 2011, Doc. 12539, at http://www.unhcr.org/refworld/docid/4d8b1e002.html, accessed 27 July 2012.

Del Bosque, Melissa, 'Children of the State: The Feds and Texas Quarrel over Custody of Undocumented Kids', *Texas Observer*, 15 May 2008, at http://www.texasobserver.org/archives/item/15362-2759-children-of-the-state-the-feds-and-texas-quarrel-over-custody-of-undocumented-kids, accessed 2 August 2012.

DeParle, Jason, 'Born Irish, but With Illegal Parents', *New York Times*, 25 February 2008, at http://www.nytimes.com/2008/02/25/world/europe/25ireland.html, accessed 27 July 2012.

Der Spiegel, 'Right-Wing Militants on PatrolA New Wave of Anti-Roma Violence in Hungary', 27 April 2011, at http://www.spiegel.de/international/europe/right-wing-militants-on-patrol-a-new-wave-of-anti-roma-violence-in-hungary-a-759349.html, accessed 22 October 2012.

Dillon, Sara, 'What Human Rights Law Obscures: Global Sex Trafficking and the Demand for Children', 17 *UCLA Women's Law Journal* 121 (2008), 121–88.

'Europe is Ready to Incarcerate All Illegal Minors', *Le Figaro*, 24 April 2008, at http://www.lefigaro.fr/international/2008/04/25/01003-20080425ARTFIG00010-l-europe-prete-a-incarcerer-tous-les-mineurs-illegaux-.php, accessed 2 August 2012.

European Parliament, 'Hearing Discusses Plight of Europe's Marginalised Roma', 12 February 2010, at http://www.europarl.europa.eu/news/en/headlines/content/20101129STO02032/html/Hearing-discusses-plight-of-Europe%27s-marginalised-Roma, accessed 2 August 2012.

European Roma Rights Centre, *The Glass Box: Exclusion of Roma from Employment*, 21 February 2007, via http://www.errc.org/cikk.php?cikk=2727, accessed 27 July 2012.

Fink, Jack, 'Former Drug Treatment Patients Suing Over Videotaping', *CBS*, 7 January 2011, at http://dfw.cbslocal.com/2011/01/07/former-drug-treatment-patients-suing-over-videotaping/, accessed 22 October 2012.

Finley, Bruce, 'Deportee's Slaying Spurs Reform Push: Advocates say Teen's Fear of Gangs Unheeded', *Denver Post*, 8 April 2004, A1.

Fox News, '"Jamiel's Law" Targets Illegal Immigrant Gang Members in Wake of Los Angeles H.S. Football Star's Death', 8 April 2008, at http://www.foxnews.com/story/0,2933,348209,00.html, accessed 27 July 2012.

Fraser, Christina, 'Italy Police to Protect Gypsies', BBC News, Rome, 14 May 2008, at http://news.bbc.co.uk/2/hi/7400460.stm, accessed 27 July 2012.

Frontex, *General Report 2011*.

Fuccaro, Lorenzo, 'Berlusconi-Bersani, lite su Milano "Sarà islamica". "No alle paure"', *Corriere della Sera*, 24 May 2011, at http://archiviostorico.corriere.it/2011/maggio/24/Berlusconi_Bersani_lite_Milano_Sara_co_8_110524022.shtml, accessed 27 July 2012.

Gardbaum, Stephen, 'The "Horizontal Effect" of Constitutional Rights', 102 *Michigan Law Review* (2003), 387–459.

Hodes, Matthew, Daljit Jagdev, Navin Chandra and Anna Cunnliff, 'Risk and Resilience for Psychological Distress amongst Unaccompanied Asylum Seeking Adolescents', 49 *Journal of Child Psychology and Psychiatry* 7 (July 2008), 723–32.

Human Rights Watch, *'Eternal Emergency': No End to Unaccompanied Migrant Children's Institutionalization in Canary Islands Emergency Centers*, 22 June 2010, 1-56432-643-8, at http://www.unhcr.org/refworld/docid/4c21b6702.html, accessed 27 July 2012.

Human Rights Watch, *Rights Displaced: Forced Returns of Roma, Ashkali and Egyptians from Western Europe to Kosovo*, 28 October 2010, at http://www.hrw.org/en/reports/2010/10/28/rights-displaced, accessed 27 July 2012.

Impey, Joanna, 'Just 42 Percent of Roma Children Finish School in Europe', *Deutsche Welle*, 4 May 2011, at http://www.dw.de/dw/article/0,,14967291,00.html, accessed 2 August 2012.

James, Frank, 'Deportations Higher Under Obama Than Bush', *NPR*: The Two–Way, NPR, 6 July 2010, at http://www.npr.org/blogs/thetwo–way/2010/07/26/128772646/deportationshigher–under–obama–than–bush, accessed 27 July 2012.

Kanstroom, Daniel, '"Passed Beyond Our Aid": U.S. Deportation, Integrity, and the Rule of Law', 35 *Fletcher Forum of World Affairs* 2 (Summer 2011), 95–107.

Kay, Jennifer and Matt Sedensky, '10 Years after Elian, U.S. Players Mum or Moving On', *The Herald Sun*, 1 July 2010, at http://www.heraldsun.com/view/full_story/7160040/article-10-years-after-Elian--U-S--players-mum-or-moving-on, accessed 2 August 2012.

Kennedy, Sr Stanislaus, 'Who Cares about the Disappeared Children?', 23 May 2008, at http://www.ireland.com/mewspaper/opinion/2008/0523/1211461644896.html, accessed 23 May 2008.

Kostadinova, Galina, 'Minority Rights as a Normative Framework for Addressing the Situation of Roma in Europe', 39 *Oxford Development Studies* 2 (2011), 163–83.

Kushen, Rob, 'Scapegoating Will Not Solve "Roma Problem"', *The Guardian*, 3 August 2010, at http://www.guardian.co.uk/commentisfree/libertycentral/2010/aug/03/scapegoating-roma-problem-europe, accessed 27 July 2012.

Macklin, Audrey, 'Who is the Citizen's Other? Considering the Heft of Citizenship', 8 *Theoretical Inquiries in Law* 2 (July 2007), 333–66.

McVeigh, Tracy, 'Child asylum seekers 'still being imprisoned' by immigration service', *The Guardian*, 19 May 2012, at http://www.guardian.co.uk/uk/2012/may/20/child-asylum-seekers-still-being-locked-up, accessed 22 October 2012

Masseria, C., P. Mladovsky and C. Hernández-Quevedo, 'The Socio-economic Determinants of the Health Status of Roma in Comparison with Non-Roma in Bulgaria, Hungary and Romania', 20 *European Journal of Public Health* 5 (October 2010), 549–54.

Migrant Rights Centre Ireland, 'Plans for Summary Removal in Immigration Bill Contrary to International Law – 2010', 4 November 2010, at http://www.mrci.ie/Plans-for-Summary-Removal-in-Immigration-Bill-Contrary-to-International-Law--detail-news, accessed 27 July 2012.

Owen, Richard, 'Italy Gypsies Find Echoes of Nazism in Fingerprinting Move', *The Times*, 5 July 2008, at http://www.timesonline.co.uk/tol/news/world/europe/article4272550.ece?pgnum=1, accessed 5 July 2008.

Passel, Jeffrey S., *Unauthorized Immigrant Population: National and State Trends, 2010* (Washington D.C.: Pew Hispanic Center, 2010), at 13, at http://pewhispanic.org/files/reports/133.pdf, accessed 27 July 2012.

Physicians for Human Rights, *From Persecution to Prison: The Health Consequences of Detention for Asylum Seekers*, June 2003, Physicians for Human Rights & The Bellevue/NYU Program for Survivors and Torture, Boston and New York, at https://s3.amazonaws.com/PHR_Reports/persecution-to-prison-US-2003.pdf, accessed 2 August 2012.

PICUM, *Undocumented Children in Europe: Invisible Victims of Immigration Restrictions*, 2008, at http://picum.org/picum.org/uploads/file_/PICUM%20Undocumented%20Children%20in%20Europe%20-%20%20EN.pdf, accessed 27 July 2012.

Preston, Julia, 'Young Immigrants, in America Illegally, Line Up for Reprieve', *N.Y. Times*, 13 August 2012, at http://www.nytimes.com/2012/08/14/us/young-immigrants-poised-for-deportation-deferral-program.html; accessed 22 October 2012.

Refugees International, *Futures Denied: Statelessness among Infants, Children, and Youth*, 22 October 2008, via http://www.refintl.org/policy/in-depth-report/futures-denied-statelessness-among-infants-children-and-youth, accessed 2 August 2012.

Réseau Éducation sans frontières, *La Chasse aux Enfants*, at http://www.educationsansfrontieres.org.org/spip. php?article12800, accessed 27 July 2012.

Roberts, Michelle, 'Detention Facility for Immigrant Kids Sued for Abuse', *Associated Press*, 3 April 2008, at http://www.detentionwatchnetwork.org/node/821, accessed 22 October 2012.

Save the Children, 'Roma Children's Right to Education', at http://europe.savethechildren.se/Europe/Focus/Education/, accessed 27 July 2012.

Save the Children, 'Sexual Abuse of Children by Aid Workers Too Often Unreported', 27 May 2008, at http://www.savethechildren.org.uk/news/2008/05/sexual-abuse-of-children-by-aid-workers-too-often-unreported, accessed 2 August 2012.

Shelley, Louise, *Human Trafficking: A Global Perspective* (Cambridge: Cambridge University Press, 2010).

Sikkink, Kathryn, 'The Role of Consequences, Comparison and Counterfactuals in Constructivist Ethical Thought', *Moral Limit and Possibility in World Politics*, ed. Richard Price (Cambridge: Cambridge University Press, 2008), 83–111.

The Urban Institute, *Paying the Price: The Impact of Immigration Raids on America's Children* (Washington, DC: The Urban Institute, 2007)

Thronson, David B., 'Custody and Contradictions: Exploring Immigration Law as Federal Family Law in the Context of Child Custody', 59 *Hastings Law Journal* (2008), 453–515.

Todres, Jonathan, 'Taking Prevention Seriously: Developing a Comprehensive Response to Child Trafficking and Sexual Exploitation', 43 *Vanderbilt Journal of Transnational Law* 1, 4–5 (2010), 1–56.

Traynor, Ian and John Hooper, 'France and Italy in Call to Close EU Borders in Wake of Arab Protests', *The Guardian*, 27 April 2011, at http://www.guardian.co.uk/world/2011/apr/26/eu-borders-arab-protests, accessed 27 July 2012.

UN Integrated Regional Information Networks (IRIN), 'Southern Africa: Child Migrants Tell All', 29 April 2008, via http://allafrica.com/stories/200804300709.html, accessed 27 July 2012.

'UN Urges EU to Help Roma Children', BBC News, 6 March 2007, at http://news.bbc.co.uk/2/hi/europe/6422283.stm, accessed 27 July 2012.

UNDP, *Human Development Report 2009: Overcoming Barriers: Human Mobility and Development*, at 55–6, at http://hdr.undp.org/en/media/HDR_2009_EN_Complete.pdf, accessed 27 July 2012.

UNICEF, *The Right of Roma Children to Education: Position Paper* (Geneva: UNICEF Regional Office for Central and Eastern Europe and the Commonwealth of Independent States (CEECIS), 2011).

U.S. Gov't Accountability Office, 'Human Trafficking: Better Data, Strategy, and Reporting Needed to Enhance U.S. Antitrafficking Efforts Abroad (2006)', the Government Accountability Office (GAO), July 2006, http://www.gao.gov/new.items/d06825.pdf, accessed 2 August 2012.

'U.S. Hands Over 14,237 Unaccompanied Minors to Mexico in '11', *Latin American Herald Tribune*, 13 February 2012, at http://www.laht.com/article.asp?ArticleId=470577&CategoryId=14091, accessed 22 October 2012.

Vassort, Marine, *Paroles d'Errance* (Marseille: Editions P'tits Papiers, 2006).

Weil, Patrick, 'Access to Citizenship: A comparison of Twenty-Five Nationality Laws', *Citizenship Today: Global Perspectives and Practices*, ed. T. Alexander Aleinikoff and Douglas Klusmeyer (Washington, D.C.: Carnegie Endowment for International Peace, 2001), 17–35.

Wenk, Michael G., 'The Refugee: A Search for Clarification', 2 *International Migration Review* 3 (Summer 1968), 62–9.

Women's Refugee Commission, *Halfway Home: Unaccompanied Children in Immigration Custody*, February 2009, at http://www.womensrefugeecommission.org/docs/halfway_home.pdf, accessed 27 July 2012.

World Health Organization, *Health of Migrants – The Way Forward: Report of a Global Consultation, Madrid, Spain 3–5 March 2010*, at 37, 91, at http://www.who.int/hac/events/consultation_report_health_migrants_colour_web.pdf, accessed 27 July 2012.

Young, Katharine G., 'The Minimum Core of Economic and Social Rights: A Concept in Search of Content', 33 *Yale Journal of International Law* 113 (2008), 113–75.

Unaccompanied Children and their Protection under International Refugee Law

Ilias Bantekas

Introduction

The first recorded unaccompanied child was the Biblical Moses, who was found and taken into the care of the Pharaohs. The plight of children was only recently distinguished from that of their adult counterparts.[1] In large part this was due to the fact that, although society was sympathetic to the particular needs of children, there was insufficient understanding about the mental traits of children. Hence, in practice, children did not possess a voice of their own and they were substituted in all aspects of their lives by adults. Adults were viewed as 'knowing better' and so the law attached little, if any, legal value to the testimony or views of minors. Even in the era of human rights following the conclusion of World War II the provision of children's rights was not only low on the agenda, but was virtually unknown. It was only with the advent of such instruments as the Convention on the Rights of the Child, which will be explored more fully below, that children's rights were set out for the first time at the international level. Yet even though by now this convention is widely ratified, it should not be thought that States parties are keen to uphold their obligations, or indeed that they truly believe in the value of the obligations prescribed therein. It is no wonder, therefore, that States routinely violate their obligations under the convention.

The plight of unaccompanied children has received insufficient attention for a number of reasons. Firstly, they were not considered, in fact, as falling within the typical refugee paradigm and hence were treated in law in the same manner as adult refugees.[2] Secondly, many receiving countries have been reluctant to accept that unaccompanied children are situated on their territory, choosing instead to ignore the problem. This problem has been compounded by the fact that few statistics have been held, or retained, by national authorities on unaccompanied minors seeking asylum on their territory. Finally, a large number of unaccompanied children are not encompassed within the classical definition of the refugee, having, for example, fled

1 See K. Touzenis, *Unaccompanied Minors: Rights and Protection* (Rome: XLedizioni, 2006); J. Bhabha and S. Schmidt, *Seeking Asylum Alone: Unaccompanied and Separated Children and Refugee Protection in the US* (Cambridge, MA: Harvard University Press, 2006); D. J. Steinbock, 'The Admission of Unaccompanied Children into the United States' (1989) 7 *Yale Law & Policy Review* 137–200.

2 See UNHCR, *A Study of Unaccompanied Afghan Children in Europe*, Doc. PDES/2010/05 (June 2010).

from their homes to avoid parental abuse or ill-treatment. As a result, weary receiving States had two choices: either deport the children on the basis that they had violated the country's immigration laws or instead grant them relief to stay under humanitarian grounds. If they are allowed to stay, it is clear that the incumbent State must take all appropriate measures to 'raise' these children; this is, however, a process that bears both financial and political cost. It is only recently that the phenomenon of unaccompanied children has received some scientific attention. It has come to the attention of researchers and authorities that children leave their countries for a variety of reasons: fear of persecution, armed conflict, parental abandonment and abuse, as well as escape from acute poverty. As a result, it is a myth that unaccompanied children are sent away by their parents in order to make a living.[3] In many cases, children are simply seeking to escape from an abusive family environment.

This chapter seeks first of all to set out the international legal framework governing the status of unaccompanied children. At present it is found in two distinct but interrelated disciplines, namely international refugee law and international human rights law – including international children's law. Both of these international legal disciplines are juxtaposed against local immigration laws and practice, which in many cases frustrate the very purpose of human rights pertinent to children. The purpose of this chapter is to illustrate these conflicts, state the law as it stands, and highlight both practical problems inherent in the operation of international refugee law to unaccompanied children. It is also hoped that the reader will appreciate some examples of poor implementation of the relevant law, whether deliberately or unintentionally.

Defining Unaccompanied Children under International Law

The phenomenon is to a large degree self-explanatory, yet it is unclear as opposed to similar concepts, such as 'orphans', 'children separated from their family', and unaccompanied children that are refugees and therefore seeking asylum. Moreover, the 'transnational' element underlying the plight of unaccompanied children is a significant factor in assessing whether international law is applicable or if instead the matter is only defined under domestic law. Another issue of crucial importance is the degree to which a particular body of law may be deemed *lex specialis* over and above any other corpus of international rules that have the status of *lex generalis*.[4] In the present case, such as assessment is indeed difficult because both international refugee law and international law on the protection of children are *lex specialis*

3 In some cases where the influx of children is significant, as in South Africa, unaccompanied children from neighbouring countries are driven by financial considerations and poverty. See C. Fritsch, E. Johnson, A. Juska, 'The Plight of Zimbabwean Unaccompanied Refugee Minors in South Africa: A Call for Comprehensive Legislative Action' (2010) 38 *Denver Journal of International Law & Policy* 623–658.

4 *Legality of the Threat or Use of Nuclear Weapons*, Advisory Opinion of 8 July 1996 (1996) ICJ Reports, para. 25. In this case the ICJ was trying to demonstrate that international humanitarian law (IHL) was *lex specialis* vis-à-vis international human rights law, which was deemed to be *lex generalis*. The idea is that, where the two bodies of law are found to be in conflict, the *lex specialis* takes precedence.

in relation to general international law each in their own way. Furthermore, it is imprudent to distinguish them on the basis of a particular application because the rights enshrined therein are indivisible and complementary. By way of illustration, whereas refugee law may be far more pertinent to unaccompanied children seeking asylum, at the same time it cannot be divorced from the fundamental principles of children's law, such as that all measures and judgments adopted must be in the best interest of the child. Hence, the repatriation, family unification and approval of an asylum application of an unaccompanied minor must be in the minor's best interests. As a result, both legal disciplines can be characterized as *lex specialis*.

Although the phenomenon of unaccompanied children is hardly new, given the orphans following World War II and other situations of children fleeing armed conflicts and other troublesome hot spots, the early international instruments that could have dealt with their predicament did not address their particular status. Even if this status had been taken into consideration in the 1951 Refugee Convention,[5] it was probably felt that fine distinctions would be hard to negotiate and agree and would in any event distract the parties from the crucial issues. Whatever the case, if the child fell within the definition of the refugee under Article 1 of the Refugee Convention, then it would have made no difference if the person concerned was a minor, or indeed an unaccompanied minor. This holds true to this day. Nonetheless, the protection afforded to unaccompanied refugee children in the Refugee Convention is clearly inadequate and hence there is a need to augment the level of protection.[6] This augmentation can only be achieved through other means and in the case at hand this has come about (or not!) from the provisions of the 1989 Convention on the Rights of Children (CRC).[7]

We have already stated that the Refugee Convention does not distinguish between any categories of refugee children. Although the CRC also contains no definition of unaccompanied children, it does nonetheless distinguish them from accompanied minors. Article 22(1) of the CRC crucially provides that

> States parties shall take appropriate measures to ensure that a child who is seeking refugee status or who is considered a refugee in accordance with applicable international or domestic law and procedures shall, whether unaccompanied or accompanied by his or her parents or by another person, receive appropriate protection and humanitarian assistance in the enjoyment of applicable rights set forth in the present Convention and in other human rights or humanitarian instruments to which said States are parties.

Paragraph 2 of the same provision moreover stipulates that unaccompanied refugee children 'shall be accorded the same protections as any other child temporarily or permanently deprived of his or her family'. A similar legal status is reserved in the African Charter on the Rights and Welfare of the Child (ACRWC) in terms of the rights granted, yet the ACRWC is broader in scope than the CRC in that it recognizes that children, whether accompanied or

---

5 Convention relating to the Status of Refugees, 189 UNTS 150.

6 See C. J. Gates, 'Working toward a Global Discourse on Children's Rights: The Problem of Unaccompanied Children and the International Response to Their Plight' (1999) 7 *Indiana Journal of Global Legal Studies* 299–334.

7 1577 UNTS 3.

unaccompanied, may be considered refugees if they are displaced 'through natural disaster, internal armed conflicts, civil strife, breakdown of economic and social order or howsoever caused'.[8] Paragraph 3(1) of the UNCHR's 1997 Guidelines on Policies and Procedures in Dealing with Unaccompanied Children Seeking Asylum (1997 Guidelines) provides a safe definition of an unaccompanied child as:

> a person who is under the age of eighteen years, unless, under the law applicable to the child, majority is attained earlier and who is separated from both parents and is not being cared for by an adult who by law or custom has responsibility to do so.

This is consistent with similar definitions found in domestic laws[9] and other international hard law instruments.[10] Although such laws may differentiate between children on the basis of their age or the degree of separation from their families (i.e. temporary, transitory or semi-permanent),[11] none of the international instruments cited find a distinction of this nature useful. The protection offered to unaccompanied children under international law does not therefore depend on the age of the child or the temporary or permanent degree of the separation.[12] This is a welcome development, because otherwise it could be used as justification to deport certain categories of children, without giving them a chance to apply for asylum, under the pretence, for example, that tracing their family would be much easier if they were to be sent back to their country of origin.

It should be emphasized that States are under an obligation to afford the pertinent rights to unaccompanied minors even when the latter are not found or apprehended on national territory, so long as the children are in their effective control, or the territory in question is under effective occupation.[13] Thus, a State cannot denounce its obligation to offer asylum or legal representation to such a child on the ground that it was apprehended in a foreign territory over which its army exercised temporary effective occupation. Moreover, although there could be situations where an unaccompanied minor has not traversed an international

---

8 ACRWC, Art. 28(4).

9 The US Homeland Security Act of 2002, 6 USC para. 279(g)(2), defines unaccompanied alien children as 'persons under the age of 18 without a parent or legal guardian in the United States or without a parent or legal guardian in the United States who is able to provide care and physical custody.'

10 Art. 2(h) Council Directive 2005/85/EC (1 December 2005) on Minimum Standards on Procedures in Member States for Granting and Withdrawing Refugee Status, OJ L 326 (13 December 2005).

11 See D. B. Thronson, 'Kids Will Be Kids? Reconsidering Conceptions of Children's Rights Underlying Immigration Law' (2002) 63 *Ohio State Law Journal* 979–1016.

12 Yet at the same time it has to be noted that the CRC permits reservations to Art. 22. The UK lodged a reservation against the application of this provision, arguing that the rights prescribed therein were of a lower standard than those provided under English law. As true as this may be, it leaves open the door to abuse and the application of immigration legislation rather than child protection laws. The Committee on the Rights of the Child was content when the reservation was lifted in 2008. See Concluding Observations on the UK, UN Doc. CRC/C/GBR/CO/4 (20 October 2008), para. 70.

13 Human Rights Committee, General Comment No. 31, UN Doc. CCPR/C/21/Rev 1/Add 11 (31 August 2001); *Loizidou v Turkey* (1997) 23 EHRR 513.

frontier, the relevant instruments refer explicitly to minors found in a country that is different to their own, in all cases where they are seeking asylum. Despite this clear jurisdictional rule many States in Europe defy it through legal manoeuvring. France, for example, maintains extraterritorial zones on its territory, the purpose of which is to receive and detain immigrants without granting them any of the rights enshrined in the relevant conventions. Adults and children, including unaccompanied minors, are thus treated as though they have not entered France. The biggest such zone is in the environs of Paris's Charles de Gaulle airport, known as Roissy; this zone is somewhat indeterminate and may be extended by the authorities. Human rights NGOs have reported numerous cases whereby the French authorities deported unaccompanied children to the last country they had transited.[14]

It is not clear whether Article 22 of the CRC covers in addition children that are not seeking asylum. Situations may arise, for example, where the child has crossed into a third State by accident and does not wish to apply for asylum there. Although this provision does not expressly seem to apply with respect to such situations it is clear that the three cardinal principles of the CRC apply nonetheless. The receiving State will still have to take all those measures that are in the best interests of that child.

The Fundamental Principles Governing Unaccompanied Children

The three cardinal principles enunciated in the CRC apply *mutatis mutandis* to unaccompanied children, as follows: (a) all measures must be in the best interests of the child;[15] (b) the forum State is prohibited from discriminating between children (non-discrimination rule),[16] and; (c) children have a right to participation in decision-making processes that affect them.[17] The paramount principles emanating from the Refugee Convention dictate that children in genuine fear of persecution should be granted asylum and equally that they should not be subjected to the process of refoulement.[18]

Unlike adult asylum seekers, the position of children, including unaccompanied minors, is different in international refugee law as regards the obligation of the receiving States. Whereas a receiving State is under no compulsion to offer temporary residence to an adult whose refugee application has been turned down, in the case of children the receiving State must take all appropriate measures with a view to offering protection. This is generally translated as offering residence and care on the basis of so-called humanitarian grounds. Thus, a child that has been deemed not to enjoy the status of a refugee in the receiving State may nonetheless enjoy the residence benefits of refugees, in addition to other rights pertinent to children under the CRC. The receiving State may obviously extend equivalent rights to adults under humanitarian grounds, but it is not obliged to do so. As a result, children occupy a special

[14] Human Rights Watch, *France – Lost in Transit: Insufficient Protection for Unaccompanied Migrant Children at Roissy Charles de Gaulle Airport*, 1-56432-557-1, October 2009, at: http://www.hrw.org/sites/default/files/reports/france1009webwcover_0.pdf (accessed: 27 July 2012), pp. 49ff.

[15] Art. 3, CRC.

[16] Art. 2, ibid.

[17] Art. 12, ibid.

[18] Art. 33, Refugee Convention.

status in international refugee law and it is for this purpose that the definition of a child is important so that this status can be readily identified and upheld.

This special status is not without its fair share of practical problems.[19] Firstly, on account of the 'best interests of the child' principle the parents of the child may be allowed to stay as a matter of extension of the humanitarian grounds that allowed the child to stay in the first place.[20] This necessarily means that unaccompanied children will, where possible, be falsely designated by adult asylum seekers as their own children. In this manner children are subject to slave-like practices by the loss of their personal autonomy and are obvious victims of crimes such kidnapping. Moreover, the use of an unaccompanied child solely for the purpose of legitimizing one's refugee application amounts to trafficking. Article 3(a) of the 2000 Protocol to Prevent, Suppress and Punish Trafficking in Persons, Especially Women and Children (Trafficking Protocol)[21] encompasses within the ambit of this offence

> the recruitment, transportation, transfer, harbouring or receipt of persons, by means of the threat or use of force or other forms of coercion, of abduction, of fraud, of deception, of the abuse of power or of a position of vulnerability or of the giving or receiving of payments or benefits to achieve the consent of a person having control over another person, for the purpose of exploitation.

The consent of the child does not cure the illegality of the conduct that amounts to trafficking.[22] Much like the CRC, the Trafficking Protocol provides that member States must adopt measures that permit victims of trafficking to 'remain on their territory temporarily or permanently, in appropriate cases'.[23] States are to be guided in this respect by reference to 'humanitarian and compassionate' grounds.[24] There thus seems to exist uniform practice in three major international instruments as to status and protection that must be offered to children by the receiving or apprehending State, irrespective of whether they are accompanied or unaccompanied. It is crucial, therefore, that the authorities promptly identify minors within a group of asylum seekers and thereafter determine the identity of their parents or lawful guardians before deciding what is the best option for that child. Whatever the case, the child

---

19 See UNHCR, *Guidelines on Determining the Best Interests of the Child* (2008), at: http://www.unhcr.org/refworld/pdfid/48480c342.pdf (accessed: 27 July 2012), pp. 30ff., which notes that even in respect to reunification the receiving State must undertake an assessment to determine whether the minor may be subject to abuse or ill-treatment upon his or her return.

20 This does not, of course, mean that the 'best interests of the child' principle trumps all other considerations. For example, in *Minister of State for Immigration and Ethnic Affairs v Ah Hin Teoh* [*Teoh*'s case] (1995) 128 ALR 353, a man who was convicted of drugs-related offences was facing the prospect of deportation without his family. His plea that the breakup of the family was not in the best interests of his children was dismissed by the court on the ground that these interests must be given the same weight as the bad character/criminal activity of the deportee.

21 (2001) 40 ILM 335.

22 Art 3(b) Trafficking Protocol. For the linkage between trafficking and unaccompanied minors, see International Organization for Migration (IOM), *Trafficking in Unaccompanied Minors in the European Union* (December 2002).

23 Art. 7(1) Trafficking Protocol.

24 Art. 7(2), ibid.

cannot be returned to his or her country of origin simply because his or her refugee application was unsuccessful or because the child was the victim of crime, particularly trafficking.

The second practical problem is the situation of children that are accompanied by an adult who, although not attempting to exploit them for personal benefit, is nonetheless not their physical parent. Should such a child be characterized as accompanied or unaccompanied? The 1997 Guidelines define a child as being unaccompanied when it is lacking its principal caregiver. It is not necessary that the principal caregiver be the physical parent because the child may at the crucial time be adopted, living with foster parents, or in the actual care of another relative or other person. The criterion for assessing, thus, whether a particular person is the primary caregiver is 'the quality and durability of the relationship between [himself] and the child'.[25]

The distinction in law between the rights of accompanied and unaccompanied children is that the latter are entitled to additional protective measures to prevent them from becoming even more vulnerable. Thus, they are entitled to a guardian and legal representation, reunification with parents – where this is deemed beneficial for the child – and other similar measures. In many cases, however, the authorities of the receiving State are unhappy about providing these additional layers of protection and as a result undermine the status of minors. By way of illustration, in a case pending before the European Court of Human Rights an unaccompanied minor was registered by the Greek Coast Guard as being accompanied, relying solely on the fact that the child was apprehended in a ship along with other adult asylum seekers.[26] The relevant law suggests that the authorities should not rely on the statements of the child – as in most cases it nurtures a fabricated story concocted by relatives or adult companions – but should investigate and identify persons below the age of eighteen in order to afford to offer them the rights guaranteed under the aforementioned conventions. This application of the 'best interests of the child' principle to unaccompanied children seems to conform to fundamental tenets of human rights law, which despite violations by many States should be considered part of customary international law.[27] The application of the 'best interests of the child' principle to unaccompanied minors has been found by the European Court of Human Rights to possess a lasting duration. Once in the custody of the receiving State the latter is under an obligation to care for the child until its best interests have been served. Hence, in a case where the Belgian authorities arbitrarily deported a 5-year-old Congolese girl by dumping her at Kinshasa Airport the Court found this inhumane act to be a continuing violation and held that States are under an obligation to take appropriate measures against the inhuman treatment of child returned or deported.[28]

---

25 UNHCR, 1997 Guidelines, Annex II, Art 5.

26 *Rahimi v Greece*, App. No. 8687/2008.

27 See C. Nugent, 'Whose Children are These? Towards Ensuring the Best Interests and Empowerment of Unaccompanied Alien Children' (2006) 15 *Boston University Public Interest Law Journal* 219–35.

28 *Mubilanzila Mayeka and Kaniki Mitunga v Belgium*, ECtHR Judgment (12 October 2006), para. 69.

Legal Representation and Guardianship

The function of legal representative may well overlap with that of a guardian, but this is not always the case. For example, the Cypriot law implementing EC Directive 2005/85 envisages that the Ombudsman for Children shall act as the legal representative for unaccompanied children, whereas the country's welfare services are entrusted with the function of guardianship.[29] Whereas the guardian undertakes to substitute the primary caregiver, directly or through the supervision of other persons such as foster parents, the legal representative possesses the requisite mandate to represent the unaccompanied minor before the authorities as well as contract on his or her behalf. It is prudent, therefore, for the legal representative to have a thorough knowledge of the local law so as to assume the child's case before the competent authorities, as well as act as his or her legal advisor.

The 2005 Directive expressly obliges EC member States to provide an unaccompanied minor with a legal representative in respect of their asylum application proceedings, save where the minor:

a. will in all likelihood reach the age of maturity before a decision at first instance is taken; or
b. can avail himself, free of charge, of a legal adviser or other counsellor, admitted as such under national law to fulfil the tasks assigned above to the representative; or
c. is married or has been married.[30]

It is uncertain whether the Directive is consonant with customary international law, or indeed the CRC in other respects, however. For example, the last section of Article 17(1) of the Directive seems to suggest that member States can determine situations where the minor's presence during the personal interview is not required if legal representation is adequate. This is clearly in conflict with Article 12 of the CRC, which guarantees the child's right to participation in matters that affect it. Of course, one should acknowledge the likelihood of situations where the presence of a traumatized child in a personal asylum interview could create unnecessary stress on the child, in which case its presence could be excluded – because this would be in the best interests of the child. From a more general human rights perspective, the presence and participation of the unaccompanied minor in asylum proceedings guarantees the right to a fair trial, which is not dependent on nationality or age.

In practice, legal representation is problematic in most nations. It presupposes that the fact that a child is unaccompanied has been acknowledged by the authorities, so as to process the case to the competent body. Where a fast-track deportation procedure exists in countries with a poor record of tracing unaccompanied minors, they will most probably be deported by the time the determination of their status can be assessed. Moreover, countries that experience

---

29 Art. 10, 2009 Law on Refugees (Amending) [Ο Περί Προσφύγων Τροποποιητικός Νόμος, Law No 122(I)/2009].

30 Art. 17(2), EC Directive 2005/85; see note 10.

the influx of significant numbers of unaccompanied minors on their territory are usually ill-equipped to offer adequate legal representation to each child.[31]

The situation is no better as regards guardianship. Given that unaccompanied children are on the fringes of society and their plight seldom viewed with sympathy as a result of xenophobia, which translates into negative press, it is no wonder that they are usually at the bottom of the priority list of welfare agencies. In a report conducted by this author for a study commissioned by the European Commission, it was demonstrated that Cyprus provides a total of 8,500 euros annually for each minor refugee applicant, including unaccompanied minors. Moreover, it was shown that Cypriot law had ample guarantees for the provision of guardians by the social welfare agency, as well as access by the children to medical services and educational facilities. On the ground, however, the situation was much different. The ratio between children and guardian was very high, thus rendering the prospect of close supervision difficult, if not impossible. Many children were left unattended and unsupervised in rented accommodation; and in some cases it was reported that adolescent girls became pregnant and/or gave birth.[32] Thus the lack of adequate guardianship negates even the best of intentions to provide access to health and education. The mere provision of money to children can only lead to catastrophic results. In the case of Spain it has been reported that the authorities appointed guardians without asking the unaccompanied children about the person of the guardians or the quality of the guardianship. Moreover, they ignored persistent claims by the children that they had been subjected to ill-treatment. Eventually, the Spanish government returned the children to Morocco, without consulting them whatsoever, arguing that the return was in the children's best interests.[33]

A good practice is that undertaken in the USA in respect of abused, abandoned or neglected unaccompanied children. They can obtain relief from removal if they apply Special Immigrant Juvenile (SIJ) status.[34] Eligibility depends on a finding that the child is amenable to long-term foster care because of its ill-treatment and that it is not in the child's best interest to be returned to its home country. If the application is successful, the child receives lawful permanent residence.[35]

---

31 See A. McDonald, 'Protection Responses to Unaccompanied and Separated Refugee Children in Mixed Migration Situations' (2008) 27(4) *Refugee Survey Quarterly* 48–62.

32 I. Bantekas, *The Evaluation of the Impact of the EU Instruments Affecting Children's Rights with a view to Assessing the Level of Protection and Promotion of Children's Rights in the EU: Report on Cyprus* (October 2010, on file with author). See also N. Trimikliniotis and C. Demetriou, *The Risk Group of Unaccompanied Minors: Protection Measures in an Enlarged European Union: Country Report Cyprus* (2007), at: http://www.zrs.upr.si/media/uploads/files/MinOrs_Cyprus.pdf (accessed: 21 August 2012).

33 Human Rights Watch, *Nowhere to Turn: State Abuses of Unaccompanied Migrant Children by Spain and Morocco* (May 2002), via: http://hrw.org/en/news/2002/05/06/spain-and-morocco-abuse-child-migrants (accessed: 27 July 2012), pp. 28ff.

34 Immigration and Nationality Act, 8 USC, para. 101(a) (27)(J).

35 See J. Koo Dalrymple, 'Seeking Asylum Alone: Using the Best Interests of the Child Principle to Protect Unaccompanied Minors' (2006) 26 *Boston College Third World Law Journal* 131–68; S. Schmidt, *Separated Refugee Children in the United States: Challenges and Opportunities* (2004), at: http://www.brycs.org/documents/upload/separated_children.pdf (accessed: 27 July 2012).

The Right to a Fair Trial and Access to Asylum Procedure

The two notions subsumed under the heading of this chapter are complementary, yet not readily obvious.[36] Asylum seekers, both adults and children, are entitled to lodge an application before the authorities of the receiving State.[37] Whether this is viewed as a judicial or an administrative process, it nonetheless involves a definitive determination of a person's status and is therefore subject to the conditions set out by the right to a fair trial.[38] Because unaccompanied children, as already explained, are entitled to be considered for indefinite stay under humanitarian grounds, it is sometimes thought that asylum procedures do little, if any, to help their plight. This, however, is not the case at all. The fact that a minor is granted permission to stay, and taken into foster or other care, is not the same as having been granted asylum. The latter involves a formal legal status, whereas permission to stay under humanitarian grounds is a fully revocable status. It is therefore crucial that the unaccompanied minor has access to all asylum procedures.

The primary function of the legal representative is to facilitate the minor's progression through the relevant asylum procedures. Thereafter, the receiving State must not impose formal limitations on the time or place of an asylum application, the purpose of which is clearly to frustrate the application. Any limitations must be reasonable and fair. For example, a requirement that asylum applications by unaccompanied minors be lodged within a week from the time they arrive is unreasonable, because such minors may not have even contemplated the idea of formal asylum.[39] On the basis of the right of the child to receive information about matters that affect it, which is explored in the following section, at the very least the authorities of the receiving State must explain to the minor his or her right to an asylum procedure. At the very outset of this process, in accordance with Article 22 of the CRC appropriate measures are required to take into account the particular vulnerabilities of unaccompanied and separated children.[40] Among others, this includes representation by an adult who is familiar with the

---

36 See M. Alexander, 'Refugee Status Determination Conducted by UNHCR' (1999) 11 *International Journal of Refugee Law* 251–89, at 257ff., who argues that the Human Rights Committee and the European Commission and Court of Human Rights refused to apply the fair trial principle to immigration proceedings. The US Supreme Court in *INS v Cardoza-Fonseca* 480 US 421, 449 (1987) held that immigration proceedings constitute merely civil actions that determine the applicant's eligibility to stay. As a result, the applicant facing removal is not afforded the same level of protection and rights as those offered to defendants in a criminal trial.

37 In fact, Art. 16 of the 1951 Refugee Convention recognizes the right of access to courts as one of the few rights that is not amenable to a reservation. This is equivalent to the right to fair trial in Art 6 ECHR and Art 14 ICCPR. More recent jurisprudence clearly suggests that Art. 16 demands that the receiving State apply the same fair trial guarantees that it affords to its own citizens *mutatis mutandis* to asylum proceedings. See *Krishnapillai v Canadian Minister of Citizenship and Immigration* [2002] 3(1) FC 74 (Can FCA), paras 31–2.

38 It is true that the European Court of Human Rights has excluded from the ambit of Art 6 ECHR challenges to deportation and extradition orders. *Maaouia v France* (2001) 33 EHRR 1037 and *Mamatkulov and Askarov v Turkey* (2005) 41 EHRR 494. However, these proceedings are clearly distinguishable from asylum proceedings.

39 Such rigid time limits were applied in the case of *Sahak v Minister for Immigration and Multicultural Affairs* [2002] FCAFC 215 (Australia).

40 Art. 17(4), 2005 EC Directive; Committee on Rights of Child, General Comment No. 5 (2005), para. 68.

child's background and who is competent or able to represent the child's best interests.[41] In the case of unaccompanied children, a parent or relative will not be available and moreover the appointed guardian will in all likelihood be unfamiliar with the child's ethnic, cultural, religious or familial background. It is necessary, therefore, for the social services to provide the child with an adult that is familiar with the unique characteristics of the child and who will work alongside the guardian and the legal representative. It is furthermore a *sine qua non* condition of the right to a fair trial under the circumstances for the unaccompanied minor to have access to free legal representation.[42]

Minimum procedural guarantees should include that the application will be determined by a competent authority fully qualified in asylum and refugee matters. Ideally, the asylum judge dealing with children will either have expertise in dealing with children, or will otherwise be assisted by a neutral expert. In many countries there is no provision for juvenile courts, let alone asylum judges designated to deal with children asylum seekers. The minor is entitled to a personal interview. With the exception of minors whose age and maturity would make the interview redundant, this should be conducted always by a qualified official before any final judgment on asylum is made. Translation services will most often be required and these should also be offered free of charge. The authorities and their officials should understand that children are not able to testify like adults. Their perception of time and place and the details of their plight may have been obscured by a plethora of events. Thus, what seems real to them may seem otherwise to the interviewing authorities. As a result, the child should be given the 'benefit of the doubt' should there be credibility concerns relating to his or her story as well as a possibility to appeal for a formal review of the decision.[43] The Committee on the Rights of the Child rightly therefore demanded that:

> The interviews should be conducted by representatives of the refugee determination authority who will take into account the special situation of unaccompanied children in order to carry out the refugee status assessment and apply an understanding of the history, culture and background of the child. The assessment process should comprise a case-by-case examination of the unique combination of factors presented by each child, including the child's personal, family and cultural background. The guardian and the legal representative should be present during all interviews.[44]

Unlike adult asylum seekers, unaccompanied children will have to go through a procedure by which the receiving State must determine their age. This usually involves a medical test. This, too, is subject to the same fair trial guarantees because the results of the test determine the legal status and treatment of the applicant. In particular, Article 17(5)(b) of the 2005 EC Directive demands that receiving States ensure that

41 Ibid., General Comment No. 5, para. 69.
42 Ibid.
43 Ibid., para. 71.
44 Ibid., para. 72.

> unaccompanied minors are informed prior to the examination of their application for asylum, and in a language which they may reasonably be supposed to understand, of the possibility that their age may be determined by medical examination. This shall include information on the method of examination and the possible consequences of the result of the medical examination for the examination of the application for asylum, as well as the consequences of refusal on the part of the unaccompanied minor to undergo the medical examination.

That this medical test is part of an inherently judicial process is confirmed by subparagraph 5(c) of Article 17 of the Directive that calls upon States to ensure that the decision to reject an application for asylum from an unaccompanied minor who refused to undergo this medical examination shall not be based solely on that refusal.

The Right to be Treated like the Receiving Country's Children

It has already been pointed out that the cardinal rule of non-discrimination enunciated in Article 2(1) of the CRC obliges States to treat all children within their jurisdiction without discrimination based, among others, on the ethnic origin of the child or its guardians. This means that the receiving State must offer the same quality of treatment to the unaccompanied minor as it does in respect of its own children. How is this translated in practice and what type of obligation does it involve? If the State is bound to treat unaccompanied children in the same way it would the children of its own nationals, it is required that unaccompanied children have access not only to public institutions and facilities, but that such access be facilitated and enhanced as much as possible. Thus it is not enough to claim that unaccompanied minors have the right to free primary education and healthcare in the same manner as local children. Local children have parents or other guardians who are aware of the children's rights and can lead them towards realizing their rights. Unaccompanied children, on the other hand, may not even have been discovered by the authorities and hence will not exercise the rights afforded to them, assuming that they were aware of these in the first place. Access to these rights must be pursued aggressively by the State, in much the same way that social services in developed countries do not allow parents to keep their children away from primary education. It would be unthinkable for the authorities in developed countries to turn a blind eye to non-trained parents offering medical services to their children, or refusing to allow them to go to school. If this is true, and it is, then why should the authorities make no effort to facilitate and impose schooling, health and other services upon unaccompanied children? In fact, the State must not only take a proactive stance in tracing and identifying unaccompanied minors on their territory, but should provide them with such guardianship that would allow them to realize their rights. Equally, the receiving State must not impose formalities upon unaccompanied children, such as particular documentation.[45]

---

[45] The US Supreme Court in *Plyler v Doe* 457 US 202 (1982) held that it is unlawful for schools to deny access to undocumented migrants or ask about their immigration status.

This requires the receiving country to implement two further obligations incumbent upon it: (a) to enable the right to information,[46] and (b) to cater for the specific needs of each unaccompanied child through individual adaptation. The right to information is inherent in the operation of international human rights and is an intrinsic feature of the rights pertinent to children under international law.[47] Unless a child is informed of its rights, it is untenable to speak of a right to participation in matters that affect the child. It is only when a child has the requisite information that it can decide whether a medical treatment is beneficial, whether a parent or a guardian is acting in his best interest, and whether it wants to remain with that person. If the right to information was unimportant in the operation of the international regime governing the rights of children then children would not have been granted the right to participation;[48] rather, their presence would have been made redundant by the imposition of guardians on their behalf.

The second obligation requires receiving States to adapt their practices to accommodate the individual needs of each unaccompanied child.[49] By way of illustration, local children enter the educational system with the advantage of being fluent in the local language. Moreover, they would have started school from an early age and progressed through the schooling system by the passage of time. Unaccompanied children, on the other hand, will in most cases be wholly unfamiliar with the local language and hence even if they are schooled they will be unable to follow classes on account of the obvious language barrier. Equally, in many cases unaccompanied children will not have attended school regularly and so even if they are placed in a class that corresponds with their age their background will be inadequate to cope with the demands of the class. As a result, the receiving country must adapt to the exigencies of the child as it finds it. Some countries, for example, operate reception centres for accompanied and unaccompanied refugee children, the principal purpose of which is to render them fluent in the local language; this is in parallel with the requirements of the regular curriculum. In situations where the minor has never received a proper education, it may be unwise to put him or her into school, particularly if it is judged that the better option is for the minor to attend vocational training or take up an apprenticeship. The purpose of adaptation is twofold: firstly, it serves to integrate the child into the local society; secondly, it prevents the child giving up and, by having acquired no skill, turning to crime or anti-social behaviour.

A particular issue that has arisen in the implementation of this principle in receiving countries concerns claims that the introduction of the unaccompanied minor into formal social structures puts said structures into danger of malfunction. For example, it is alleged

46 Arts 13 and 17 CRC; Art. 3, 10, 1996 European Convention for the Exercise of Children's Rights.

47 See M. Koren, 'Human Rights of Children: Their Right to Information' (2001) 2 *Human Rights Review* 54–79.

48 Committee on Rights of Child, General Comment No. 12 (2009), UN Doc. CRC/C/GC/12 (1 July 2009), paras 16, 25, 34, 41, 48, 80–83.

49 See Committee on Rights of Child, General Comment No. 1, UN Doc. CRC/GC/2001/1 (17 April 2001), para. 4, which emphasizes that the adaptability of education measures to each child requires respect 'for the child's own cultural identity, language and values, for the national values of the country in which the child is living, the country from which he or she may originate, and for civilizations different from his or her own. But in fact, part of the importance of this provision lies precisely in its recognition of the need for a balanced approach to education and one which succeeds in reconciling diverse values through dialogue and respect for difference.'

that an influx of unaccompanied children who do not speak the local language constitutes a disadvantage to local children because of the ensuing slow progression. This is indeed an issue worthy of concern for the receiving State, but it is not insurmountable, as has already been discussed. The relevant international instruments do not demand that receiving States necessarily place unaccompanied minors into their existing institutions, but that they integrate the minors in the best possible manner.

A worrying trend that is well documented is the detention of unaccompanied minors by the receiving State. This is usually justified by the fact that the minor has entered the country illegally and has thus committed an immigration or criminal offence. This type of treatment is typical in the conflict between the two bodies of law, i.e. immigration and child protection/human rights, and is no doubt a legal fallacy that is convenient for many States. In any event, the overriding rule is that unaccompanied minors should under no circumstances be detained, let alone be detained with adults.[50] Detention, moreover, precludes the applicant from exercising those rights granted to him or her under human rights law and is in no way in the best interests of the child. Those countries that are subjected to significant influxes of unaccompanied children, such as Greece, routinely detain such children for long periods, with a view to either fast-track deportations or as a means of defeating what they see as unlawful immigration.[51]

Conclusion

At the end of this chapter, the reader will have come to appreciate that the structures set up under international refugee law and international human rights law are inadequate in preventing States from applying immigration law to detain, deport and in some cases ill-treat unaccompanied children. Most countries pay lip service to the fundamental tenets of the CRC, particularly the right to participation and the best interests of the child principle. This is evident, for example, in asylum proceedings where the child is not asked about its preferred guardian or the quality of the guardianship offered. Equally, the authorities of many States, particularly the police as the first port of call, simply desire for the problem to go away and resort to fast-track deportations or lengthy detention periods. Moreover, said authorities fail to even distinguish between children and adult refugee applicants. Yet even where the rights enshrined in international instruments are upheld, the authorities on many occasions are content to fulfil their formal obligations without considering whether the service provided is appropriate or indeed in the best interests of the particular minor.

The most poignant challenge in the protection of unaccompanied minors is not the lack of international standard setting or the absence of ample guarantees in international treaties. Rather, the problem lies in the implementation of the relevant law and the lack of local

[50] Working Group on Arbitrary Detention, Report on the Visit of the Working Group to the United Kingdom on the Issue of Immigrants and Asylum Seekers, UN Doc. E/CN.4/1999/63/Add 3 (18 December 1998).

[51] UNHCR, 'UNHCR Alarmed by Detention of Unaccompanied Children in Lesvos, Greece' (28 August 2009), at: http://www.unhcr.org/4a97cb719.html (accessed: 27 July 2012).

expertise in the treatment of children in many countries. To some degree, this is natural, given that the small numbers of unaccompanied minors in certain jurisdiction does not justify full-time expertise of this nature. An alternative remedy can come about through the utilization of NGOs involved with children. NGOs play a leading role in children's rights in many countries and by way of example they operate missing children's hotlines, thus fully and successfully substituting the State in a sensitive area of welfare. Moreover, in countries where the welfare system is ill-equipped to deal with huge influxes of unaccompanied minors, the same NGOs can play a significant role because of their capacity to recruit suitable volunteers. The State can thus undertake a supervisory capacity. The same role can be assumed by the UNHCR, which could provide experts on children's issues to collaborate with the authorities in countries that face severe problems.[52] Memoranda of understanding (MoU) can be employed in this instance to simplify the process and remove constitutional conflicts because MoU are not binding and do not therefore require parliamentary approval. These are used extensively within the UN system.

Finally, some mention must be made of the potential customary nature of the international law pertinent to unaccompanied minors. Despite the many intentional violations by States, there is no reason to believe that these are meant to create a new rule; rather, they are usually secretive and the authorities typically either deny the violation or otherwise claim that they do not possess the resources to accommodate the needs of the children. As a result, it is safe to argue that the three cardinal principles enunciated in the CRC (i.e. non-discrimination, best interests of the child, and the right to participation) are beyond doubt part of customary international law. The relevant customary human rights principles, such as the prohibition of arbitrary detention, the right to a fair trial, and others, are equally applicable. If this is true, there is no need to determine the customary nature of international refugee law relating to unaccompanied children, because the aforementioned customary principles suffice to protect and safeguard the welfare of children seeking asylum.

References

Alexander, M., 'Refugee Status Determination Conducted by UNHCR' (1999) 11 *International Journal of Refugee Law* 251, 251–89.

Bhabha, J. and S. Schmidt, *Seeking Asylum Alone: Unaccompanied and Separated Children and Refugee Protection in the US* (Cambridge, MA: Harvard University Press, 2006).

Feijen, L., 'The Challenges of Ensuring Protection to Unaccompanied and Separated Children in Composite Flows in Europe' (2008) 27(4) *Refugee Survey Quarterly* 63–73.

Fritsch, C., E. Johnson, A. Juska, 'The Plight of Zimbabwean Unaccompanied Refugee Minors in South Africa: A Call for Comprehensive Legislative Action' (2010) 38 *Denver Journal of International Law & Policy* 623–658.

[52] The UNHCR is already engaged with countries, particularly in the Mediterranean region, to design comprehensive strategies to protect unaccompanied children. See L. Feijen, 'The Challenges of Ensuring Protection to Unaccompanied and Separated Children in Composite Flows in Europe' (2008) 27(4) *Refugee Survey Quarterly* 63–73.

Gates, C. J., 'Working toward a Global Discourse on Children's Rights: The Problem of Unaccompanied Children and the International Response to Their Plight' (1999) 7 *Indiana Journal of Global Legal Studies* 299–334.

Human Rights Watch, *France – Lost in Transit: Insufficient Protection for Unaccompanied Migrant Children at Roissy Charles de Gaulle Airport*, 1-56432-557-1 (October 2009), at: http://www.hrw.org/sites/default/files/reports/france1009webwcover_0.pdf (accessed: 27 July 2012).

Human Rights Watch, *Nowhere to Turn: State Abuses of Unaccompanied Migrant Children by Spain and Morocco* (May 2002), via: http://hrw.org/en/news/2002/05/06/spain-and-morocco-abuse-child-migrants (accessed: 27 July 2012).

International Organization for Migration (IOM), *Trafficking in Unaccompanied Minors in the European Union* (December 2002).

Koo Dalrymple, J., 'Seeking Asylum Alone: Using the Best Interests of the Child Principle to Protect Unaccompanied Minors' (2006) 26 *Boston College Third World Law Journal* 131–168.

Koren, M., 'Human Rights of Children: Their Right to Information' (2001) 2 *Human Rights Review* 54–79.

McDonald, A., 'Protection Responses to Unaccompanied and Separated Refugee Children in Mixed Migration Situations' (2008) 27 *Refugee Survey Quarterly* 48–62.

Nugent, C., 'Whose Children are These? Towards Ensuring the Best Interests and Empowerment of Unaccompanied Alien Children' (2006) 15 *Boston University Public Interest Law Journal* 219–35.

Schmidt, S., *Separated Refugee Children in the United States: Challenges and Opportunities* (2004), at: http://www.brycs.org/documents/upload/separated_children.pdf (accessed: 27 July 2012).

Steinbock, D. J., 'The Admission of Unaccompanied Children into the United States' (1989) 7 *Yale Law & Policy Review* 137–200.

Thronson, D. B., 'Kids Will Be Kids? Reconsidering Conceptions of Children's Rights Underlying Immigration Law' (2002) 63 *Ohio State Law Journal* 979–1016.

Trimikliniotis, N. and C. Demetriou, *The Risk Group of Unaccompanied Minors: Protection Measures in an Enlarged European Union: Country Report Cyprus* (2007), at: http://www.zrs.upr.si/media/uploads/files/MinOrs_Cyprus.pdf (accessed: 21 August 2012).

Touzenis, K., *Unaccompanied Minors: Rights and Protection* (Rome: XLedizioni, 2006).

UNHCR, *A Study of Unaccompanied Afghan Children in Europe*, Doc. PDES/2010/05 (June 2010).

UNHCR, *Guidelines on Determining the Best Interests of the Child* (2008), at: http://www.unhcr.org/refworld/pdfid/48480c342.pdf (accessed: 27 July 2012).

UNHCR, 'UNHCR Alarmed by Detention of Unaccompanied Children in Lesvos, Greece' (28 August 2009), at: http://www.unhcr.org/4a97cb719.html (accessed: 27 July 2012).

16 ASHGATE **RESEARCH** COMPANION

Forced Displacement, the Law of International Armed Conflict, and State Authority

David James Cantor[1]

International armed conflicts are one important environment within which the actions of States may play a direct role in forcing the migration of persons. Warring States often have strong reasons for compelling the displacement of civilian populations, and international armed conflicts usually produce large numbers of refugees and displaced persons. The kinds of State authority exercised during such armed conflicts are also often distinct from those which prevail during peacetime. The present chapter explores the historical development of the international framework of laws and customs of war that now regulates the coerced movement of civilians during international armed conflicts. In so doing, it contributes to a wider body of scholarship that is concerned with the structures that impact upon the migration of human populations.

This chapter shows that the law of international armed conflict is most developed in those situations where civilians find themselves as potential victims in the hands of a hostile party to the conflict, namely when they are in occupied territory, or when they are aliens in the territory of a hostile State. Nonetheless, relatively recent developments in international law also raise the question of protection against such coerced movements during hostilities between the parties to the conflict. Studying the distinctive genealogies of the law in these three distinct situations allows us to identify the different rationale that governs each one. This serves to clarify the sometimes obscure meaning of the rules in this area – a subject that has generated substantial academic debate – in order to arrive at a fuller comprehension of the law as it currently stands.

---

1 Lecturer in International Human Rights Law, Institute of Commonwealth Studies, University of London; Director, Refugee Law Initiative, School of Advanced Study, University of London. My special thanks to Geoffrey and Barbara Cantor for their proofreading of the document and to Fabrizio Bensi and Daniel Palmieri at the ICRC Archives for their help with archival sources. Any errors are my own.

Deportations from Occupied Territory

In theory, a State that occupies the territory of another belligerent State possesses unfettered discretion in deciding how it will treat that State's territory and population.[2] However, with the passage of time, two cardinal principles of international law have developed to restrict the discretion of occupying States. The first of these principles is the prohibition on unilateral annexation of occupied territories. The second is the imperative to respect the principle of humanity. These two principles provide crucial context to the following discussion since they provide the underlying rationales behind the rules that have emerged to govern deportations of civilians from occupied territory.

In respect of the first principle, a 'firm' customary rule emerged in the eighteenth century to prohibit the unilateral annexation of occupied territories.[3] Since the occupying State does not exercise *de jure* sovereign rights over occupied territory, but merely *de facto* and temporary 'military authority',[4] it 'may not encroach upon the exclusive prerogative of the territorial sovereign', for example by demanding oaths of allegiance or loyalty from the inhabitants, or by taking any action affecting the nationality of the population.[5] One pertinent example of the application of this rule relates to the deportation of priests from Serbian territory occupied by Austria and Germany during World War One (WWI). This was condemned by the international community as an unlawful 'attempt to denationalise the inhabitants of occupied territory' given its relationship to a wider pattern of acts aimed at destroying the national identity of this population.[6] It is clear that any deportation directed towards the unilateral annexation of occupied territory is thus unlawful under the customary rules governing belligerent occupation. Indeed, the closely related annexation strategy of transferring parts of the occupying State's population into the occupied territory was expressly prohibited following World War Two (WWII) by Article 49(6) of the Fourth Geneva Convention.[7]

The second principle by which an occupying State's theoretically unlimited exercise of its *de facto* military authority is circumscribed is that of respect for humanity as articulated by the body of laws and customs of war. In this respect, it is important to emphasize that these rules serve to limit the wide *de facto* authority of an occupying State and do not confer upon it sovereign rights that it would otherwise not possess.[8] In the context of deportation, the fact

---

2 Georg Schwarzenberger, 'The Law of Belligerent Occupation: Basic Issues' (1960) 10 *Nordisk Tidsskrift for International Ret* 10, 13.

3 Ibid., 13.

4 Lassa Oppenheim, 'The Legal Relations between an Occupying Power and the Inhabitants' (1917) 33 *Law Quarterly Review* 363, 364.

5 Schwarzenberger, 'Law of Belligerent Occupation', 18.

6 *Violation of the Laws and Customs of War: Reports of Majority and Dissenting Reports of American and Japanese Members of the Commission of Responsibilities Conference of Paris 1919* (Clarendon Press Oxford 1919) 38–9; hereafter '*Violation of the Laws and Customs of War*'.

7 *Geneva Convention relative to the Protection of Civilian Persons in Time of War* (adopted 12 August 1949; entered into force 21 October 1950) 75 *United Nations Treaty Series* 287; hereafter 'Fourth Geneva Convention'. Note that the articles of the Fourth Geneva Convention do not contain numbered paragraphs. Nonetheless, they will here be attributed numbers for ease of reference, i.e. 'Article 49(6)' will be used as the convention rather than 'sixth paragraph of Article 49'.

8 Schwarzenberger, 'Law of Belligerent Occupation', 20.

that the laws of war do not operate as 'enabling rules' thus casts doubt on the accuracy of Judge Phillips's affirmation in the *Milch* case that

> If [a] transfer is carried out without a legal title, as in the case where people are deported from a country occupied by an invader while the occupied enemy still has an army in the field and is still resisting, the deportation is contrary to international law.[9]

Since the laws of war 'operate only by limitation on the power of a sovereign State and are not needed for the purpose of adding to that power', they cannot give any form of legal title to an occupier.[10] The legal basis of the rule advanced by Judge Phillips is thus doubtful. Indeed, forced displacements carried out during hostilities remain today a relatively unregulated point of the legal framework regulating international armed conflicts.[11]

The legality of deportations from occupied territory has long been called into question on grounds of humanity. For instance, the 1863 Lieber Code[12] affirmed that, in the 'modern regular wars of the Europeans, and their descendants',[13]

> [T]he unarmed citizen is to be spared in person, property, and honor as much as the exigencies of war will admit.[14]

As regards deportations, it expressly stated that the dictates of humanity could 'no longer' be outweighed by military necessity where 'private citizens are ... murdered, enslaved, or *carried off to distant parts*' by hostile troops.[15] This suggests that the practice among 'barbarous armies' and 'in remote times' of taking the populations of occupied territory to serve as slaves or chattel in other countries was increasingly rejected by 'modern' States.

Deportations in the Pre-WWII Laws and Customs of War: The Prohibited Purpose Approach

Against the backdrop of the reference to deportations in the Lieber Code, it is unclear why such acts were not addressed by the rules on occupied territories in the 1874 Brussels

---

9 United States Military Tribunal Nuremberg, *Trial of Erhard Milch (20 December 1946–17 April 1947)* [1948] 7 *United Nations War Crimes Commission Law Reports of Trials of War Criminals* 27, 45; hereafter 'Milch'.

10 Walker D. Hines (USA Arbitrator), *Navigation on the Danube (Allied Powers: Czechoslovakia, Greece, Romania, Serb–Croat–Slovene Kingdom); Germany, Austria, Hungary and Bulgaria (Decision of 2 August 1921)* (1948) 1 *Reports of International Arbitral Awards* 105.

11 See below.

12 For text, see Richard Shelly Hartigan, *Lieber's Code & the Law of War* (Precedent Chicago IL 1983).

13 Article 25.

14 Article 22.

15 Article 23, emphasis added.

Declaration or the 1899 and 1907 Hague Peace Conferences treaties.[16] This raises two questions regarding the figure of deportations within the early twentieth-century law of armed conflict. Firstly, there is the question of how international custom prior to the adoption of the Geneva Conventions framed the legality of deportations from occupied territory. Secondly, in spite of the absence of specific references in the Regulations annexed to the 1907 Hague Convention IV (Hague Regulations),[17] were deportations nonetheless prohibited by other provisions of these treaties?

Turning first to custom, it has been shown by Theodor Meron that the deportation of civilians from occupied territory prior to the adoption of the 1949 Geneva Conventions 'constituted, *in many circumstances*, a violation of international customary law'.[18] Building upon Meron's work, the following paragraphs identify the specific ways in which international custom regulated deportations from occupied territory prior to the adoption of the 1949 Geneva Conventions. It will be argued that customary law addressed itself to deportations from occupied territory in different ways depending upon the purposes of the deportation. While those carried out on grounds of military necessity were permitted so long as done humanely, deportations to forced labour were strictly prohibited. In the space between these two rules, custom was moving to prohibit deportations on other grounds.

It is clear that the customs of war in this era did regulate certain *types* of deportations of civilians from occupied territory. In general, international custom recognized that, in time of war, the private citizen could legitimately be disturbed for reasons of military necessity. This translated into a permissive rule allowing deportations on grounds of military necessity. For instance, in his 1908 distillation of the 'written and unwritten' laws of war, the lawyer–author of the British Army's 1904 *Handbook of the Laws and Customs of War on Land* affirmed the following customary rule:

> Deportation: ... [a] general commanding an army in the field has, during the continuance of the war, an absolute right to remove from any place within the sphere of his operations all persons whose presence therein is considered by him to be dangerous or inconvenient. He may deport those persons, with as little hardship as can be avoided, to such a distance as may be necessary effectually to prevent their speedy return.[19]

[16] See *Draft of an International Declaration concerning the Laws and Customs of War adopted by the Conference of Brussels, 27th August 1874*, reprinted in A. Pearce Higgins, *The Hague Peace Conferences and International Conferences concerning the Laws and Usages of War: Texts of Conventions with Commentaries* (CUP Cambridge 1909) 266.

[17] *Regulations Respecting the Laws and Customs of War on Land annexed to the 1907 Hague Convention IV Respecting the Laws and Customs of War on Land*, in Adam Roberts and Richard Guelff, *Documents on the Laws of War* (3rd edn OUP Oxford 2000) 73.

[18] Theodor Meron, 'Deportation of Civilians as a War Crime under Customary International Law', in Theodor Meron, *War Crimes Law Comes of Age: Essays* (Clarendon Press Oxford 1998) 153, emphasis added.

[19] Thomas Erskine Holland, *The Laws of War on Land (Written and Unwritten)* (Clarendon Press London 1908) 15–16. Indeed, the Lieber Code acknowledged the lawfulness of certain expulsions for reason of military necessity (see Article 26). Writing in 1937, the eminent legal scholar Lauterpacht (*International Law: A Treatise by L. Oppenheim (5th edition)* (Longmans Green and Co. London 1937) vol. II, 351, footnote 1) also implicitly acknowledged that deportation of

The rule was confirmed in the 1931 *Chevreau* arbitration award, which found that the deportation of an allegedly hostile civilian from occupied territory would be lawful where undertaken in good faith, upon reasonable suspicion (verified by a serious enquiry in which the arrested person has the opportunity to defend himself), and in a manner 'which conforms to the standard habitually practised among civilized nations'.[20] This qualification that, in order to be lawful, the execution of such permitted deportation measures must conform to 'generally recognized standards of decency and humanity' was also identified in Judge Phillips's Concurring Opinion in the *Milch* case on acts committed during WWII.[21]

However, the *prima facie* acceptability of deportations on grounds of military necessity or otherwise was restricted by other customs of war. In particular, the international outcry over the WWI German deportation of Belgian civilians to labour in Germany suggested the existence of a firm customary rule prohibiting deportations of civilians to forced labour outside the occupied territory.[22] In that case, international lawyers unanimously denounced the measure as 'an act of tyranny, contrary to all notions of humanity, and one entirely without precedent in the history of civilized warfare'.[23] One graphic condemnation asserted:

> Compulsory deportation and forced labour are but different words for slavery, and slavery in its worst and original form ... Modern nations may well have considered it superfluous to safeguard against an evil which was deemed a thing of the past, and to express in international covenants their reprobation of an obsolete institution. We do not legislate against the use of the rack and autos-da-fe. There are matters on which mankind has pronounced judgment once for all times, without danger of appeal or revision. *Securus judicat orbis terrarum*. The enslavement of individuals or of peoples is one of these, and cannot be justified even by the dogma of Necessity.[24]

Belgium, as the injured State, similarly protested that even by the time of the Lieber Code such deportations 'were no longer practiced, except among barbaric hordes',[25] while the USA

civilians from occupied territory was permitted where 'it is a military necessity to do so'. This principle is also implicit in comments by the United States Military Tribunal Nuremberg in *The Justice Trial* ([1948] 6 *United Nations War Crimes Commission Law Reports of Trials of War Criminals* 1, 58; hereafter '*The Justice Trial*') regarding the 'Nacht und Nebel' decree: 'There was no proof that the deportation of the civilian population from the occupied territories was *necessary to protect the security of the occupant forces*', emphasis added.

20 Frederik Valdemar Nikolai Beichmann (Arbitrator), *Arbitral Award rendered pursuant to the compromise signed at London, March 4, 1930, between France and the United Kingdom of Great Britain and Northern Ireland in the Matter of the Claim of Madame Chevreau Against the United Kingdom, The Hague, June 9, 1931* (1933) 27 *American Journal of International Law* 153, 159–60.

21 *Milch*, 45.

22 For an analysis of these well-publicized events, see John H.E. Fried, 'Transfer of Civilian Manpower from Occupied Territory' (1946) 40 *American Journal of International Law* 303.

23 J.W. Garner, 'Contributions, Requisitions and Compulsory Service in Occupied Territory' (1917) 11 *American Journal of International Law* 74, 106.

24 See the opinion of Dr Henry St John-Mildmay in 'Deportations from the Occupied Territories' (1916) 1(November) *International Law Notes* 170, 171.

25 'Official Documents: Memoire of the Belgian Government in regard to the Deportation and Forced Labor of the Belgian Civil Population Ordered by the German Government' (1917) 11

labelled them as contravening 'all precedent and ... those human principles of international practice which have long been accepted and followed by civilized nations'.[26]

Evidence for the existence of this rule can also be gleaned from the responses to the revival of deportation to forced labour by Germany during WWII. In the IMT Charter, the four Allied Powers specifically confirmed 'deportation to slave labor ... of civilian population of or in occupied territory' as a breach of the laws and customs of war.[27] Its inclusion resulted from the USSR's insistence, from the very outset of negotiations leading to the IMT Charter, that the act of 'deportation of persons into slavery in Germany' be given specific expression.[28] The USA delegate agreed such deportations to be one of the 'well-defined classes' of violations of the laws and customs of war.[29]

Prior to the adoption of the 1949 Geneva Conventions, two separate rules of international custom thus appeared to regulate the deportation of civilians from occupied territory. The first permitted such acts for purposes defined by 'military necessity', but required that they be implemented in accordance with the principles of humanity. The second prohibited any deportations for the purpose of forced labour. However, it will be noted that the IMT Charter also characterizes deportation from occupied territory 'for any other purpose' as a violation of the laws and customs of war, wording repeated in Control Council Law No. 10,[30] which formed the basis for war crimes prosecutions by the four Powers in their respective zones of occupation. This raises the question of whether international custom regulated these other kinds of deportations from occupied territory.

The reasons for the inclusion of deportation 'for any other purpose' in the IMT Charter can help shed light on this question. The phrase can be traced to the penultimate draft of the IMT Charter, from which the USA delegate deleted 'deportation to slave labour' from the enumerated war crimes. He argued that

> [T]here are other deportations that are just as objectionable from my point of view, for example, deportations to compulsory prostitution, deportations just to get people out of the way to take their land, or deportations to concentration camps.[31]

American Journal of International Law (Supplement) 99, 110.

26 See 'Deportation of Civilians from Belgium' (1917) 11 *American Journal of International Law (Special Supplement)* 249, 251.

27 Article 6.b, *1945 Charter of the International Military Tribunal (Nuremberg)*, in Dietrich Schindler and Jirí Toman, *The Laws of Armed Conflicts* (Martinus Nijhoff Publishers Leiden 1988) 912–19; hereafter 'IMT Charter'.

28 *Report of Robert H. Jackson, United States Representative to the International Conference on Military Trials, London 1945* (Department of State Washington D.C. 1949) 62, 93 and 108; hereafter '*Report of Robert H. Jackson*'.

29 Ibid., 332.

30 Article 2(1)(b), *Control Council Law No. 10: Punishment of Persons Guilty of War Crimes, Crimes against Peace and against Humanity*, in Telford Taylor, *Final report to the Secretary of the Army on the Nuremberg War Crimes Trials under Control Council Law No. 10* (Government Printing Office Washington D.C. 1949).

31 *Report of Robert H. Jackson*, 417.

In the ensuing discussion, the USSR delegate insisted that the reference to deportation be retained, such that the eventual wording of the provision represents a compromise to take account of both views.[32] This suggests that the drafters did not mean to characterize all deportations from occupied territory as violations of the laws and customs of war, only those whose inhumane purposes were 'just as objectionable' as deportations to slave labour.

While other evidence exists prior to WWII for a customary rule prohibiting deportations for other inhumane purposes, it is rather ambivalent. For instance, in the aftermath of WWI, the Conference of Paris convened a Commission of ten States to report on violations of the 'laws and customs of war' by Germany and her allies. In its 1919 report, the Commission typifies the 'deportation of civilians' as an unlawful act separate from 'forced labour of civilians' under which the deportations from Belgium are listed.[33] However, the factual instances of 'deportation of civilians' cited by the report overwhelmingly involve mass deportations to inhumane conditions.[34] In this manner, the report also characterizes the 'abduction of girls and women for the purpose of enforced prostitution' as an unlawful act, the majority of the factual instances cited being deportations from occupied territories.[35] Yet this is equivocal evidence for a customary rule prohibiting a wider class of deportations, since the report does not distinguish between violations of customary and treaty law. Moreover, it is unclear whether these 'unlawful acts' reflect the 'laws and customs of war' *stricto sensu* or the 'elementary laws of humanity' to which the Commission extended its reporting mandate.[36]

National practice following WWII is equally mixed as to the scope of any wider customary rule concerning deportations from occupied territory, certainly in terms of the domestic laws passed by States to specify the jurisdiction of their own courts over war criminals. The most helpful examples are Australia[37] and the Netherlands,[38] which followed the 1919 Commission in defining 'deportation of civilians' as a war crime. While Czech[39] and Norwegian[40] law treated 'deportation' as a criminal offence, they do not specify whether it constituted a war crime. Other practice is even less persuasive. The USA, only a few months before the IMT Charter's adoption, defined the relevant war crime in its Pacific September Regulations as:

32 Ibid., 417.

33 *Violation of the Laws and Customs of War*, 35–7.

34 Ibid., 35–6.

35 Ibid., 34.

36 Indeed, this extension of its mandate led the USA to enter a reservation to the report since it considered that 'the principles of humanity … vary from individual to individual' (ibid., 63–4).

37 Section 3, 1945 Commonwealth of Australia War Crimes Act in (1948) 5 *United Nations War Crimes Commission Law Reports of Trials of War Criminals* 94, 95.

38 Article 1, Netherlands East Indies Statute Book Decree No 44 of 1946 in (1949) 11 *United Nations War Crimes Commission Law Reports of Trials of War Criminals* 86, 93.

39 Section 1, Slovak Decree No 33/1945 as amended by Decree Nos. 83/1945 and 57/1946 in (1949) 15 *United Nations War Crimes Commission Law Reports of Trials of War Criminals* 203, 206–7.

40 See (1948) 3 *United Nations War Crimes Commission Law Reports of Trials of War Criminals* 81, 84.

> Deportation to slave labour or for any other *illegal* purpose, of civilians, of, or in, occupied territory.[41]

Other States introduced a range of different qualifications to the crime: China[42] required a 'mass' element to the deportation; Yugoslavia[43] required deportation 'to concentration camps'; both French[44] and Polish[45] law exempted from the scope of the crime deportations pursuant to certain criminal sentences. Given these discrepancies, it is difficult to accept that the pre-WWII customs of war prohibited the deportation 'for any purpose' of civilians from occupied territories. Nonetheless, a degree of consensus existed that, in the space between the permissive and prohibitive customary rules, other deportations might be contrary to the principle of humanity. This raises the question of the relevant scope of the principle of humanity as expressed in codified laws of war at the time.

The main source of treaty law governing the acts of belligerent States in occupied territories during the early twentieth century was the 1907 Hague Regulations. Although these rules do not specifically regulate deportations of civilians from occupied territory, certain provisions constitute general standards against which the inherent legality of any particular deportation might be assessed. These provide more specific applications of the cardinal legal principles of non-annexation and humanity that govern the actions of belligerent States in occupied territories. In this respect, Article 43 of the Hague Regulations is the appropriate point of departure since it requires the occupying State to respect 'unless absolutely prevented, the laws in force in the [occupied] country'. It is thus 'the *status quo ante* whose continuation is recommended'.[46] The subsequent provisions that follow this general imperative furnish specific limitations on the occupying State's exercise of military authority. We turn now to see how they have been applied to the question of deportation.

The WWI deportations by Germany were widely characterized as contravening these provisions of the Hague Regulations. The Netherlands, for instance, protested that deportations to forced labour breached the requisitions rules in Article 52.[47] In this regard, international lawyers pointed out that '[e]very person whose work sets free a potential German soldier is increasing the military efficiency of the enemy', such that every compulsion directed towards this end breaches not only Article 52 but also the Article 23

41 See (1947) 1 *United Nations War Crimes Commission Law Reports of Trials of War Criminals* 111, 114.

42 Article 3, Law Governing the Trial of War Criminals of 1946 in (1949) 14 *United Nations War Crimes Commission Law Reports of Trials of War Criminals* 152, 154.

43 Article 3.3, Yugoslav Law of 25 August 1945 in (1949) 15 *United Nations War Crimes Commission Law Reports of Trials of War Criminals* 203, 208.

44 See (1948) 3 *United Nations War Crimes Commission Law Reports of Trials of War Criminals* 93, 96.

45 See (1948) 7 *United Nations War Crimes Commission Law Reports of Trials of War Criminals* 82, 82.

46 Jean S. Pictet (ed.), *Commentary: IV Geneva Convention relative to the Protection of Civilian Persons in Time of War* (ICRC Geneva 1958) 244.

47 See Fernand Passelecq, *Déportation et Travail Forcé des Ouvriers et de la Population Civile de la Belgique Occupée, 1916–1918* (Carnegie Endowment for International Peace Paris 1928) 389.

prohibition on compelling nationals to take part in operations against their own country.[48] This interpretation chimes with the 1919 Commission's characterization of the illegality of these acts as 'forced labour of civilians in connection with the military operations of the enemy' rather than as 'deportation of civilians'.[49] Finally, some contemporary commentators argued that the deportations breached the family rights in Article 46 since the 'principal right of a head of family is not to be, or to not see his [family], taken in slavery'.[50]

In a similar vein, the IMT also characterized the illegality of deportations by reference to purposes expressly prohibited by the existing treaty law. Thus it was the 'forced labor' element of the deportations carried out under the German 'slave labor policy' that breached the international law expressed by Article 52 of the Hague Regulations.[51] A comparable rationale prevailed for the deportations undertaken by Germany pursuant to its 'Nacht und Nebel' (Night and Fog) decree,[52] the transfers of opposition groups to concentration camps in the East,[53] and the expulsion and annihilation of whole populations in Poland, the Soviet Union, Czechoslovakia and Alsace in order to enable German colonization of the territories.[54] The IMT found that the purpose of these deportations – 'murder and ill treatment of the civilian population' –furnished them with their illegality under Article 46 of the Hague Regulations.[55] This 'prohibited purpose' approach to the legality of deportations also figured prominently in the analysis by Judge Philips in the *Milch* case.[56]

In short, prior to the adoption of the 1949 Geneva Conventions, States, lawyers and courts used the provisions of the Hague Regulations to characterize as unlawful the purposes behind certain deportations of civilians from occupied territory. This 'prohibited purpose' approach was akin to the tendency within customary law to define the lawfulness of deportations primarily according to their purpose. However, defining the illegality of the purposes behind unlawful deportations by reference to treaty law rather than custom entailed the uncomfortable question of whether these provisions of the Hague Regulations apply outside of occupied territory as a matter of treaty law, a defence that was actually raised by certain of those accused of this purported war crime.[57]

---

48 See the opinion of Dr St John-Mildmay, 'Deportations from the Occupied Territories' 171; see also the many concurring opinions of other lawyers in the same volume.

49 *Violation of the Laws and Customs of War*, 37.

50 See the opinion of Maître Gustave Théry in 'Deportations from the Occupied Territories (Further Opinions received)' (1916) 1(December) *International Law Notes* 188.

51 'International Military Tribunal (Nuremberg), Judgment and Sentences, October 1, 1946' (1947) 41 *American Journal of International Law* 172, 225.

52 This decree provided that civilians accused of crimes of resistance against the army of occupation would be tried only if a death sentence was likely; otherwise they would be handed to the Gestapo for transportation to Germany, where they would be held secretly with the intention of creating 'anxiety in the minds of the family of the arrested person' (ibid., 229).

53 Ibid., 231.

54 Ibid., 232–4.

55 'International Military Tribunal (Nuremberg), Judgment and Sentences', 229.

56 *Milch*, 46.

57 See, for example, the similar argument raised by the Defence in the *Flick* case in respect of Article 52 of the Hague Regulations: 'What is not shown by this Article is a veto to employ these workers outside the occupied territory. On the contrary, if it is practical for the belligerent nation to have the work for the requirements of the occupation army performed in its home country, there is nothing in Article 52 which opposes the compulsory use of workers from the occupied

The reasoning provided by national courts for rejecting this argument is unsatisfying in legal terms. For instance, the British Judge Advocate in the *Tyrolt* case sought to avoid the complexities of treaty interpretation by merely claiming that

> Quite obviously if it is wrong to show lack of respect to [the victims'] family life and individual life in their own country, you cannot get out of that obligation simply by taking them to your country and then ill-treating them there.[58]

Similarly, the United States Military Tribunal in the *Justice* case confined itself to stating that the deportation of prisoners to Germany under the 'Nacht und Nebel' policy 'did not cleanse it of its iniquity or render it legal in any respect'.[59] Such responses fail to engage with the fact that the treaty wording of these Hague Regulations provisions suggests strongly that they do not apply outside occupied territory. More generally, while the military authority of an occupying State towards civilians in the occupied territory was constrained in various ways by the Hague Regulations, sovereign acts of that same State in its own territory (towards enemy aliens, for example) were largely unregulated by the treaty rules. Only in relation to deportations for the purpose of forced labour could courts refute this defence with the more sustainable argument that such deportations were specifically prohibited by a rule of international custom, as in fact happened in the *Krupp* case.[60]

Finally, the absence of an explicit prohibition of deportation in the Hague Regulations meant that these residual treaty rules were themselves open to wide differences in interpretation. For instance, during WWI, Germany availed itself of the Hague Regulations to argue that, given the adverse economic conditions in Belgium, the deportation of 'idlers' to work in Germany was permitted and even required by the overarching Article 43 injunction to the occupying power to 'ensure, as far as possible, public order and safety'.[61] Such lack of clarity in the treaty rules was one of the factors that pushed the International Committee of the Red Cross to begin drawing up a new draft treaty to regulate, *inter alia*, the question of deportations.[62] Indeed, all of the draft codes produced by other bodies of international

territory for this purpose': United States Military Tribunal Nuremberg, *The Flick Trial* (1949) 9 *United Nations War Crimes Commission Law Reports of Trials of War Criminals* 1, 54. An Article 52-specific response to this defence is provided by Judge Phillips in *Milch*, 46: 'In so far as this section limits the conscription of labour to that required for the needs of the army of occupation, it is manifestly clear that the use of labour from occupied territories outside the area of occupation is forbidden by the Hague Regulation.'

58 Cited in (1948) 7 *United Nations War Crimes Commission Law Reports of Trials of War Criminals* 76, 81.

59 *The Justice Trial*, 56. On the facts of the 'Nacht und Nebel' policy, the Tribunal in the same case was also able to make out a more convincing albeit somewhat implicit argument that, because this particularly cruel form of deportation created 'efficient and enduring intimidation' among the population of the occupied territory, their rights under Article 46 of the Hague Regulations were accordingly breached (ibid., 56–8).

60 United States Military Tribunal Nuremberg, *The Krupp Trial* (1949) 10 *United Nations War Crimes Commission Law Reports of Trials of War Criminals* 69, 142–4.

61 See 'Deportation of Civilians from Belgium', 253–4.

62 F. Ferrière, 'Projet d'une Convention internationale réglant la situation des civils tombés à la guerre au pouvoir de l'ennemi' (1923) 5(54) *Revue Internationale de la Croix Rouge* 560.

lawyers as suggestions for further regulating the conduct of war emphasized the necessity of a provision to address deportations of civilians from occupied territory.[63]

1949 Geneva Conventions: A New Rationale

The call for treaty regulation of deportations of civilians from occupied territory was finally answered in the 1949 Geneva Conventions. In this respect, the great value of Article 49 of the Fourth Geneva Convention – as the relevant provision – rests in its creation of an explicit hard-law framework regulating deportations from occupied territory. Nonetheless, the basis upon which it regulates the legality of these acts stands in sharp contrast to the 'prohibited purpose' doctrine that went before. This section seeks to contribute to the substantial academic literature on the reach and significance of relevant paragraphs of Article 49 through a detailed study of the drafting of this provision, from its first expression in the International Committee of the Red Cross (ICRC) 1921 draft convention onwards.[64] It starts by showing how Article 49(1) prohibits all deportations out of occupied territory according to the character of the measures rather than the purposes behind them. It then considers the nature of 'evacuations' in Article 49(2). It concludes by considering the impact upon this framework of more recent developments from international criminal law.

Article 49(1) of the Fourth Geneva Convention establishes a general prohibition on deportations from occupied territories. It specifies:

> Individual or mass forcible transfers, as well as deportations of protected persons from occupied territory to the territory of the Occupying Power or to that of any other country, occupied or not, are prohibited, regardless of their motive.

The scope of Article 49(1) *ratione personae* is restricted to 'protected persons' as defined by Article 4 of the Fourth Geneva Convention. Unlike the Hague Regulations, the protection conferred upon civilians by the Fourth Geneva Convention is based primarily upon their relationship to the belligerent State rather than physical location. Indeed, even if such persons are detained as 'spies' or 'saboteurs' they can only 'be regarded as having forfeited rights of communication',[65] such that the Article 49(1) prohibition remains absolute for all

[63] For instance, the International Law Association adopted the 'Bellot Rules of War in Occupied Territory' that sought to 'meet [the] deficiencies in The Hague Rules which became obvious during the Great War': ILA, *Report of the Thirty-fifth Conference held at Warsaw, August 9th to 16th, 1928* (1928) 35 *International Law Association Reports of Conferences* 1, 283. The ILA made clear that 'no military necessity can be held to justify reducing the inhabitants to slavery ... and deporting them for service in the enemy country' (ibid., 100), and the code provided that '[t]he occupier may not deport the inhabitants outside the occupied territory, nor may he remove them from their homes save for the purpose of ensuring their safety' (ibid., 93, 287).

[64] ICRC, 'Résolution XV. Code des prisonniers de guerre, déportés, évacués et réfugiés' (1921) 52(224) *Revue Internationale de la Croix Rouge* 341.

[65] Article 5, Fourth Geneva Convention.

protected persons.[66] An interesting parallel to Article 49(1) is found in Article 70, which prohibits the deportation from occupied territory of those nationals of the occupying State who 'sought refuge' in that territory before the outbreak of hostilities.[67]

Interpretation of the scope of Article 49(1) *ratione materiae* has been more controversial. It is clear on its face that Article 49(1) prohibits only removals that have a forcible character and not those that are voluntary. Absent from the 1921 and 1934[68] ICRC drafts, the clarification that only forcible measures 'carried out under physical or moral constraint' were prohibited was added in 1947.[69] Reconfigured in the 1948 ICRC Stockholm draft as '[d]eportations or transfers *against their will* of protected persons',[70] the three highlighted words did not ultimately find favour with States. The Drafting Committee considered them 'valueless in view of the pressure which could be brought to bear on internees',[71] and the USSR highlighted the risk of abuse by observing that 'in occupied territory no one had the right to express an opinion'.[72] Although a USSR proposal to extend the provision to prohibit 'any other transfer' from occupied territory (i.e. including voluntary ones) was rejected,[73] its suggestion of shifting the emphasis of the prohibition to the 'forcible' nature of the measure was accepted.[74] The Committee III report stressed that the resulting wording 'prohibits individual or mass forcible removals as well as deportations ... [but] permits voluntary transfers'.[75] It is thus the character of the measure rather than considerations relating to the will of the protected person that determines whether Article 49(1) applies.

A question of some debate has been whether the Article 49(1) rule applies *ratione materiae* only to deportations and forcible transfers out of the occupied territory, or also to removals

---

66 Note that it has been argued that those who infiltrate their way into occupied territory do not qualify as protected persons since they do not 'find themselves' in an occupied territory but illegally intrude there: Yoram Dinstein, 'The Israel Supreme Court and the Law of Belligerent Occupation: Deportations' (1993) 23 *Israel Yearbook on Human Rights* 1, 18. This has been criticized by Yutaka Arai-Takahashi, *The Law of Occupation: Continuity and Change of International Humanitarian Law, and its Interaction with International Human Rights Law* (Martinus Nijhoff Leiden 2009) 332–3.

67 The earliest drafts of the provision contained no limitations *ratione personae*, and the 1947 draft specified that the prohibition on deportation applied to 'all persons in the [occupied] territories', the purpose of which was 'to protect against deportation all political refugees who are nationals of the occupying State': ICRC, *Report on the Work of the Conference of Government Experts for the Study of the Conventions for the Protection of War Victims (Geneva, April 14–26, 1947)* (ICRC Geneva 1947) 288–9. This expansiveness was only partly carried through to Article 70 of the Fourth Geneva Convention as adopted, which tempered application of the prohibition with justifiable exceptions for certain classes of offences. In this regard, the Chairman of the Second Drafting Committee explained that the provision's main objective was to 'protect the *real* refugee' (*Final Record of the Diplomatic Conference of Geneva of 1949* (Federal Political Department Berne 1963), hereafter '*FR*', vol. IIB, 480, emphasis added).

68 ICRC, 'Projet de Convention international concernant la condition et la protection des civilis de nationalité ennemie qui se trouvent sur le territoire d'un belligerent ou sur un territoire occupé par lui' (1934) 65 *Revue Internationale de la Croix Rouge* 384, 657.

69 ICRC, *Report on the Work of the Conference of Government Experts*, 288.

70 *FR*, vol. I, 120, emphasis added.

71 Ibid., vol. IIA, 759.

72 Ibid., vol. IIA, 664.

73 Ibid., vol. IIA, 759–60.

74 Ibid., vol. IIA, 664.

75 Ibid., vol. IIA, 827.

within the occupied territory.[76] In this regard, the 1921 and 1934 ICRC drafts prohibit only 'deportations', with the latter specifying these as 'outside the territory of the occupied State'.[77] The 1947 draft similarly prohibits 'deportations or transfers ... to places outside occupied territories',[78] reconfigured in the 1948 Stockholm draft as 'deportations or transfers ... out of occupied territory'.[79] At the Diplomatic Conference, there is no indication that Article 49(1) is intended to apply to transfers within the occupied territory, and delegates' statements in fact strongly suggest the opposite. This is confirmed by the addition of the words 'to the territory of the Occupying Power or to that of any other country' following a proposal by the USSR,[80] based on its view that 'it should not be possible to transfer civilians *except within occupied territory*'.[81] Other provisions of the Fourth Geneva Convention further confirm this interpretation. Indeed, the extensive provisions on internment and assigned residence of protected persons in occupied territories,[82] which imply an element of forced transfer within the occupied territory, would be rendered obsolete if such transfers were prohibited by Article 49(1).

A final issue regarding the application *ratione materiae* of Article 49(1) has been whether some forms of deportation from occupied territories, such as those of individuals deported on grounds of military necessity, remain lawful. It will be recalled that, prior to the Geneva Conventions, customary international law permitted such deportations so long as they were carried out in accordance with the dictates of humanity. Those in favour of the legality of such deportations tend to point to the fact that Article 147 of the Fourth Geneva Convention refers only to '*unlawful* deportation or transfer' as a grave breach of its provision, suggesting that certain deportations from occupied territory remain lawful.[83] However, this argument is incorrect because, while all deportations and forced transfers from occupied territory are prohibited (by Article 49), this is not the case for deportations and transfers of aliens from the territory of a belligerent State,[84] and it is these that Article 147 implicitly excludes. Indeed, State delegates at the Diplomatic Conference explained this exact point following an Italian

[76] Among scholars, this wider interpretation has been expressly argued, for example, by Jean-Marie Henckaerts, 'Deportation and Transfer of Civilians in Time of War' (1993) 26 *Vanderbilt Journal of Transnational Law* 469, 472; see also Emanuela-Chiara Gillard, 'The Role of International Humanitarian Law in the Protection of Internally Displaced Persons' (2005) 24 *Refugee Survey Quarterly* 37, 40. This interpretation has also been advanced by certain international criminal tribunals (see section on displacement of civilians during hostilities below).

[77] ICRC, 'Résolution XV'; ICRC, 'Projet de Convention'.

[78] ICRC, *Report on the Work of the Conference of Government Experts*, 288.

[79] *FR*, vol. I, 120. It is interesting that the 1947 draft does in fact contain a separate proposed provision prohibiting certain transfers within occupied territory: 'Collective transfers within an occupied territory shall only be enforced to meet the security requirements of the occupying Power.' This is not maintained in the 1948 Stockholm draft.

[80] Ibid., vol. III, 130.

[81] Ibid., vol. IIA, 664, emphasis added.

[82] Articles 78–135, Fourth Geneva Convention.

[83] See, for example, Thomas S. Kuttner, 'Israel and the West Bank: Aspects of the Law of Belligerent Occupation' (1977) 7 *Israel Yearbook on Human Rights* 166, 214–15.

[84] See section on expulsion of aliens below.

proposal to delete the word 'unlawful' from the phrase.[85] Accordingly, Article 147 provides no evidence whatsoever of the legality of deportations or transfers from occupied territory.

Moreover, Article 49(1) on its face is quite clear that deportations and forcible removals are prohibited 'regardless of their motive'. A development rather than a restatement of the international law of the time, this phrase was a staple feature of the provision from the 1934 Tokyo draft onwards. Indeed, the 1947 draft specified precisely that the prohibition applied to '*individual* or collective deportations', and some government experts involved in this draft expressly defined the term 'deportation' as 'any transfer of persons outside the country where they reside'.[86] At the Diplomatic Conference, the form of words used in Article 49(1) to describe the prohibited measures was explained thus:

> the phrase at the beginning of [Article 49] caused some difficulty in reconciling exactly the ideas expressed with the various terms in French, English and Russian. In the end the Committee have decided on a wording which prohibits individual or mass forcible removals as well as deportations of protected persons from occupied territory to any other country, but which permits voluntary transfers.[87]

This confirms the illegality of any measure forcibly removing protected persons from occupied territory, whether singly or collectively and whether described as 'deportation', 'transfer', 'removal' or by any other name. It would also appear that the former customary rule that permitted the deportation of individual civilians from occupied territory for reasons of military necessity was overtaken by the Article 49(1) treaty rule and no longer exists as an independent norm of international custom.[88]

Nonetheless, confusion about the scope of Article 49(1) has arisen in part as a result of confusion regarding the remit of Article 49(2) concerning 'evacuations', which makes a study of its scope necessary here. It will be seen that, in contrast to the Article 49(1) prohibition, Article 49(2) establishes a permissive rule allowing a particular type of forced movement of protected persons.[89] It states:

> Nevertheless, the Occupying Power may undertake total or partial evacuation of a given area if the security of the population or imperative military reasons so demand. Such evacuations may not involve the displacement of protected persons outside the bounds of the occupied territory except when for material

[85] This was opposed on the grounds that some countries had legislation permitting the deportation of aliens from their national territory – 'Such deportations are legal and are therefore not subject to the Article in question': *FR*, vol. IIB, 89.

[86] ICRC, *Report on the Work of the Conference of Government Experts*, 289.

[87] *FR*, vol. IIA, 827.

[88] This goes against the interpretation offered by Justice M. Shamgar of the Supreme Court of Israel in *HC 785/87, 845/87 and 27/88, Abd al Nasser al Aziz Abd al Affo et al v Commander of the IDF Forces in the West Bank et al* (1990) 29 *International Legal Materials* 139; hereafter '*HC 785/87, 845/87 and 27/88*'.

[89] Stephane Jaquemet, 'The Cross-fertilization of International Humanitarian Law and International Refugee Law' (2001) 83(843) *International Review of the Red Cross* 651, 670.

> reasons it is impossible to avoid such displacement. Persons thus evacuated shall be transferred back to their homes as soon as hostilities in the area in question have ceased.

From the 1921 draft onwards, 'evacuation' has been conceptualized as a lawful measure different in nature from the measures prohibited by Article 49(1).[90] Indeed, in 1947, one of the primary concerns of the government experts in reworking the deportations provision was that 'a clearer distinction should be drawn than in the Tokyo Draft, between deportations and evacuations'.[91] Article 49's treatment of evacuation in separate paragraphs from that on deportation and transfer thus signals that we are dealing with a different measure from those in Article 49(1). This legal figure of evacuation is defined by three principles, firstly that the reasons for the forced movement are legitimate, secondly that the forced movement should not usually take place outside the occupied territory, and thirdly that the occupying power should seek to undertake the measure in a spirit of humanity.[92]

An Article 49(2) evacuation can be undertaken only 'if the security of the population or imperative military reasons so demand'. Similar grounds can be found in all the early drafts of evacuation provisions from 1921 onwards. The final sentence of Article 49(2) – requiring that evacuated persons be 'transferred back to their homes as soon as *hostilities in the area* in question have ceased' (emphasis added) – appears to assume that the grounds of necessity will result from 'hostilities in the area'. Of course, where the degree of 'hostilities in the area' signifies that the territory is no longer occupied, the law of belligerent occupation including Article 49 no longer applies and the State has much broader discretion to forcibly transfer the civilian population according to the necessities of war.[93] Nonetheless, not all hostilities will be so severe as to require this conclusion and it is possible to envisage other circumstances outside of hostilities that could require the evacuation of the occupied population and engage the specified grounds of necessity.

Evacuations are also fundamentally different from the measures mentioned in Article 49(1) because, as the Committee III report to the Diplomatic Conference makes clear,

> In principle, these evacuations take place *only within an occupied territory* which distinguishes them from the transfers envisaged in the first paragraph.[94]

---

[90] See ICRC, 'Résolution XV', 343. 'Evacuation' was also a figure in bilateral treaties concluded between warring States during WWI, which provided the inspiration for the ICRC code (see, for example, *Accords entre le Gouvernement de la République Français el le Gouvernement Impérial Allemand concernant les Prisonnniers de Guerre et les Civils, Berne 26 April 1918* [on file at the ICRC Archives]). Note that such evacuations for the security of the civilian population were found by the United States Military Tribunal Nuremberg to be lawful displacements of the civilian population: *re. List et al (Hostages Trial)* (1948) 15 *Annual Digest and Reports of Public International Law Cases* 632, 648–9.

[91] ICRC, *Report on the Work of the Conference of Government Experts*, 289.

[92] In Article 49(4) of the Fourth Geneva Convention, a fourth principle requiring the notification of the Protecting Power has diminished in line with the relevance of the provisions concerning Protecting Powers.

[93] Georg Schwarzenberger, *International Law As Applied By International Courts and Tribunals, Volume II: The Law of Armed Conflict* (Stevens & Sons London 1968) 232–3.

[94] *FR*, vol. IIA, 827, emphasis added.

It is important to appreciate that the exception to this principle – eventually expressed by the words 'except when for material reasons it is impossible to avoid such displacement [outside the occupied territory]' – was the primary point of controversy at the Diplomatic Conference as regards Article 49(2). Expressing fears that this exception would allow forced transfer to take place under the guise of 'evacuations',[95] the USSR proposed deletion of this exception.[96] This amendment was rejected in Committee III,[97] which reported that

> Nevertheless, when it is physically impossible to retain evacuees in such territory, for example, if the latter is an island of limited size, they may be evacuated to another territory. *This special case constitutes an exception to the first paragraph.*[98]

This illustrates the very exceptional class of circumstances in which an occupying State might legitimately avail itself of this exception to the general rule prohibiting evacuations outside occupied territory. It also shows conclusively that Article 49(2) was viewed as an exception to Article 49(1) only for this special class of evacuations, rather than for evacuations in general. The word 'Nevertheless' inserted at the start of Article 49(2) signals that this special class of evacuations represents an exception to the prohibition in Article 49(1) on forced transfers *outside occupied territory* rather than forced transfers in general.[99]

This raises the question of whether other measures taken by an Occupying State that forcibly displace protected persons within occupied territory but that do not meet the conditions of necessity for evacuations are thereby prohibited on an *a contrario* reading of Article 49(2). The answer is no. An occupying State is bound by Article 43 of the Hague Regulations to respect the laws in force in the occupied country unless absolutely prevented from doing so, and by Article 27(1)–(3) of the Fourth Geneva Convention to respect certain rights of protected persons. However, Article 27(4) of the Fourth Geneva Convention expressly permits the occupying State to impose such measures of control and security 'as may be necessary as a result of the war' including those of 'internment' and 'assigned residence' specified in Articles 42 and 43. To the extent that any such measures involve forced displacement, and are not unlawful on other grounds, then they are permitted. In a similar manner, Article 49(2) specifies the *prima facie* legality of a measure that might otherwise represent an undue interference with the laws in force or the rights of the protected persons. It has nothing to say about measures that do not qualify as 'evacuation'.

As a final word on evacuations, it should be noted that Article 49(2)–(4) establishes certain safeguards for the benefit of the protected persons during evacuations, thereby

---

95 Ibid., vol. IIA, 760.

96 Ibid., vol III, 130; ibid., vol. IIA, 759.

97 Ibid., vol. IIA, 760.

98 Ibid., vol. IIA, 827, emphasis added.

99 The word does not imply that Article 49(1) of the Fourth Geneva Convention expresses a prohibition on forced transfers within occupied territory, to which evacuations constitute an exception, as has been suggested by Yes Sandoz, Christophe Swinarski and Bruno Zimmermann (eds), *Commentary on the Additional Protocols of 8 June 1977 to the Geneva Conventions of 12 August 1949* (ICRC/Martinus Nijhoff Geneva 1987) 1000, footnote 28; similarly, see the opinion of Justice M. Shamgar of the Supreme Court of Israel in *HC 785/87, 845/87 and 27/88*, 152.

expressing and specifying the application of the principle of humanity when executing such measures. The imperative that evacuations be carried out under conditions of humanity has been a feature of 'administrative evacuations' since the 1921 draft. However, the original draft of Article 49(3) contained an absolute obligation on the occupying State to ensure these minimum reception conditions before it evacuated.[100] At the Diplomatic Conference, the UK argued that if these requirements were maintained evacuations would simply never take place,[101] which would not be in the best interest of civilians.[102] The wording eventually adopted thus imposes only the obligation to ensure 'to the greatest practicable extent' that such conditions are provided. The immediate language of the Article 49(2) return obligation implies that evacuations should only have a temporary nature, further safeguarding their humanitarian character.

Impact of International Criminal Law

It is interesting to observe that the Fourth Geneva Convention framework for regulating deportations and forced transfers of civilians from occupied territory has more recently been called into question by developments on the periphery of the laws of war. To conclude the present discussion of this area, we turn to examine whether the elaboration and interpretation of these rules in the context of international criminal law has changed the fundamental rationale that underlies this framework.

Whereas Article 146 of the Fourth Geneva Convention defined 'unlawful deportation or transfer' of a protected person as a grave breach of the Geneva Conventions, Article 85(4)(a) of Protocol I to the 1949 Geneva Conventions defines as a grave breach of the Protocol,[103]

> the deportation or transfer of all or parts of the population of the occupied territory *within or* outside this territory, *in violation of Article 49 of the Fourth Convention ....*

This provision was added to the 1973 ICRC draft via an amendment put forward in the name of various Arab States and the Palestine Liberation Organization in April 1976.[104] Despite its surprising implication that deportations and forcible transfers *within* occupied territory are prohibited by Article 49 of the Fourth Geneva Convention,[105] there appears to have been no direct comment passed on this provision by other States at the Diplomatic Conference.

---

[100] *FR*, vol. I, 120.

[101] Ibid., vol. IIA, 760.

[102] Ibid., vol. IIA, 827.

[103] *Protocol Additional to the Geneva Conventions of 12 August 1949 and relating to the Protection of Victims of International Armed Conflicts* (adopted 8 June 1977, entered into force 7 December 1978) 1125 *United Nations Treaty Series* 3; hereafter 'Protocol I'.

[104] *Official Records of the Diplomatic Conference on the Reaffirmation and Development of International Humanitarian Law applicable in Armed Conflicts (Geneva 1974–1977)* (Federal Political Department Bern 1978), hereafter *'OR'*, vol. III, 321.

[105] Emmanuel J. Roucounas, 'Les infractions graves au droit humanitaire' (1978) 31 *Revue Hellénique de Droit International* 57, 116.

The conduct described in Article 85(4)(a) has since been characterized in the Rome Statute as a 'serious violation ... of the laws and customs'.[106] In interpreting this war crime of 'unlawful deportation or transfer', the ICC Elements of the Crimes also appear to confirm that a grave breach of the 1949 Geneva Conventions may arise as a result of deportations/transfers within the State's boundaries.[107] Similarly, the only extant decision by an international criminal tribunal explicitly to address the scope of Article 49 states that,

> Article 49 of Geneva Convention IV prohibits transfers from occupied territory and *within* occupied territory ... Transfers motivated by an individual's own genuine wish to leave, are lawful.[108]

This logic is also explicit in the International Criminal Tribunal for the former Yugoslavia (ICTY) jurisprudence on the meaning of 'deportation' and 'forcible transfer' as crimes against humanity,[109] which draws heavily on the laws of war.[110] Indeed, the ICTY has explicitly described Article 49 of the Fourth Geneva Convention as the 'underlying instrument' prohibiting such deportations (and thus presumably forcible transfers).[111] In the international criminal law context, it would thus appear that the prohibition expressed by Article 49(1) is interpreted as extending to forced movements within occupied territory.

Despite these innovations in the field of international criminal law, the better interpretation is that Article 85(4)(a) has not altered the scope of Article 49 of the Fourth Geneva Convention. As a matter of construction, the last phrase of the provision logically suggests that the preceding words are to be interpreted in the light of the existing law stated

---

[106] Article 8.2.b.viii, Rome Statute of the International Criminal Court (adopted 17 July 1998, entered into force 1 July 2002) 2187 *United Nations Treaty Series* 90.

[107] See *ICC Elements of the Crimes*, Article 8(2)(a)(vii)–1 Unlawful Deportation or Transfer: '1. The perpetrator deported or transferred one or more persons to another State *or to another location*', emphasis added.

[108] *Prosecutor v Mladen Naletilic and Vinko Martinovic* (Judgment) ICTY Case No. IT-98-34-T (31 March 2003) 18, emphasis added.

[109] In the *Krstic* case, the ICTY cites commentary to the ILC Draft Code that '[w]hereas deportation implies expulsion from the national territory, the forcible transfer of population *could* occur wholly within the frontiers of one and the same State': *Prosecutor v Radislav Krstic* (Judgment) ICTY Case No. IT-98-33-T (2 August 2001) 183. The important word here is 'could', meaning that such transfers may be external or internal. However, subsequent judgments refer to *Krstic* as establishing the proposition that '"deportation" consists of the forcible displacement of individuals across a State border ... whereas such displacement within the boundaries of a State constitutes "forcible transfer"': *Prosecutor v Radoslav Brdanin* (Judgment) ICTY Case No. IT-98-36-T (1 September 2004) 204. See also *Prosecutor v Vidoje Blagojević and Dragan Jokić* (Judgment) ICTY Case No. IT-02-60-T (17 January 2005) 221. Note that the ICTY has more recently taken the view that an expulsion across a *de facto* border could also be a 'deportation': *Prosecutor v Milomar Stakić* (Judgment) ICTY Case No. IT-97-24-A (22 March 2006) 98–9.

[110] The defence in the *Gotovina* case made a challenge based on this practice, arguing that if crimes against humanity are to be defined by reference to concepts from the laws of war then consistency should be applied (for instance, that 'deportation' and 'forcible transfer' should not apply outside the context of international armed conflict). This challenge was rejected by the ICTY: *Prosecutor v Ante Gotovina & Ors* (Decision on Several Motions Challenging Jurisdiction) ICTY Case No. IT-06-90-PT (19 March 2007) 13–21.

[111] *Prosecutor v Milomar Stakić*, 100.

by Article 49 (i.e. which does not prohibit transfers within occupied territory). This accords with the understanding that a procedural provision such as Article 85(4)(a), which merely defines the consequences of a breach of one of the norms expressed in the Convention, cannot redefine the substantive obligation that precedes it. Moreover, any interpretation that Article 49 now prohibits internal forced transfers sits uneasily with other Convention provisions that either authorize internal forced transfers, such as the measures of control derived from Article 27(4), or require them, such as the obligation in Article 49(2) to return evacuees or the Article 58(1) Protocol I duty to remove civilians from the vicinity of military objectives.[112]

Regardless of the merits of these alternative interpretations of Article 85(4)(a), the practice of States appears determinative of the question. It would seem that the great majority of State military manuals have not in fact incorporated the text of Article 85(4)(a) as a statement of an occupying Power's duties vis-à-vis forcible transfers and deportations.[113] The implication of this subsequent general practice by the actors that matter for international law purposes must be that the original significance of the provision has not shifted. Article 49(1) remains a provision that prohibits deportations and forced transfers only to locations outside occupied territory. The law of war framework concerning these forced movements of civilians from occupied territories thus remains as defined by the Fourth Geneva Convention, a framework that may well now also comprise part of the corpus of customary international law.

Expulsion of 'Enemy' Aliens from the Territory of a Belligerent State

Even if aliens in the hands of a hostile power find themselves in a similarly vulnerable situation to the inhabitants of occupied territory, the nature of State authority exercised over them is markedly different. In its own territory, the State exercises *de jure* sovereignty rather than mere *de facto* military authority. State practice has thus been less open to the placing of restrictions on the exercise of this sovereign authority during times of war than has been the case for occupied territories. The general framework regulating the expulsion of aliens from a State's own territory that has developed in the law of international armed conflict of the past century reflects this important dynamic.

[112] Indeed, the specification in Article 58(1) of Protocol I that this duty is 'without prejudice to Article 49 of the Fourth Convention' makes sense only if the latter is read solely as a prohibition upon forcible transfers *out* of the occupied territory.

[113] See the excerpts from national military manuals listed in Jean-Marie Henckaerts and Louise Doswald-Beck, *Customary International Humanitarian Law, vol II: Practice* (ICRC/CUP Cambridge 2005) 2913–17.

Expulsions in the Pre-World War II Laws and Customs of War

The right of a State to expel aliens from its territory remains a cornerstone of international law up to the present day. In centuries past, the doctrine that 'the subjects of enemy states are enemies' necessarily permitted a State to expel enemy subjects from its territory.[114] However, from 1795, numerous bilateral treaties were concluded that permitted enemy subjects, on condition of good behaviour, to remain in that country in the event of war. The norm retained a purely reciprocal character and did not give rise to a corresponding international custom.[115] Thus the 1899 British *Manual of Military Law* affirmed,

> The expulsion of subjects of the enemy from the territory of the opposing State is justifiable, and may be exercised or not according to the circumstances.[116]

Although the Hague Regulations do not expressly refer to the expulsion of aliens, States considered the issue at the 1907 Peace Conference in the context of a Japanese proposal to regulate the internment of a belligerent State's '*ressortissants*' (subjects), which then generated a supplementary Italian proposal to regulate their expulsion.[117] The fierce debate that followed was resolved only by a Belgian *a contrario* interpretation of Article 5 of the 1899 Hague Regulations,[118] i.e. because this provision permitted the internment of prisoners of war, the internment of 'other *ressortissants* of the enemy State' was thereby prohibited. It was on the back of this that Italy then proposed that

> the measure of expulsion *en masse* of these *ressortissants* is assimilated to the measure of internment and is equally forbidden.[119]

Although various States present voiced concerns about the effects of the Italian proposal on State sovereignty,[120] this interpretation was agreed by the Second Commission,[121] whose views the Plenary did not depart from.[122] Certain States, such as Belgium, also put on record

[114] William Edward Hall, *A Treatise on International Law* (4th edn Clarendon Press Oxford 1895) 405.

[115] Ibid., 409–10.

[116] British War Office, *Manual of Military Law* (HMSO/Harrison and Sons London, 1899; reprinted 1902) 286.

[117] See in James Brown Scott, *The Proceedings of the Hague Peace Conferences: Translation of the Official Texts: The Conference of 1907* (OUP London 1920) vol. III, 8, 105–14, 243–4. According to a contemporary commentator, the term '*ressortissant*' had a wider meaning than just 'subject' and included 'all [persons] over whom a state claims to exercise jurisdiction either by virtue of allegiance or domicile': Pearce Higgins, *Hague Peace Conferences and International Conferences concerning the Laws and Usages of War*, 266, footnote 1.

[118] Ibid., 113.

[119] Ibid., 114.

[120] Ibid., 105 (Sweden), 106 (France) and 112 (Belgium).

[121] Ibid., 114.

[122] Ibid., 8.

their view of expulsions *en masse* 'as belonging to another age',[123] suggesting that the power to expel may not have been seen as frequently exercised in practice.

While subsequent contrary practice during WWI suggests that a customary rule may have emerged that permits rather than forbids the internment of enemy aliens,[124] the prohibition on expulsions *en masse* of enemy aliens appears to have enjoyed a minimally greater level of respect by belligerent States.[125] Indeed, although the 1921 draft of the 1949 Geneva Conventions proposed an explicit prohibition on all mass expulsions 'outside the border',[126] the 1934 Draft expressly limited this prohibition to deportations from occupied territories.[127] The commentary explained that 'there was no recourse to deportation [of enemy aliens] from the territory of a belligerent during [WWI]'.[128] Yet in spite of apparently scarce contrary practice to this rule of treaty and customary law, the perception persisted of a gap in the legal framework regarding the expulsion of enemy aliens.

1949 Geneva Conventions: A Partial Stop-gap

The Fourth Geneva Convention deals both with voluntary departures and forced expulsions of those who may be considered enemy aliens by a belligerent. It provides that (with a few specified exceptions) enemy aliens in the territory of a belligerent are entitled to repatriate under certain minimum humanitarian conditions.[129] However, the important advance in terms of expulsion is Article 38 of the treaty, which provides that the situation of those who do not repatriate 'shall continue to be regulated, in principle, by the provisions concerning aliens in time of peace'.[130] This provision was inserted by the 1934 Tokyo draft and maintained in all subsequent drafts.[131] Pictet rightly observes that it mirrors for aliens in a belligerent State the Hague Regulations' principle that the laws in force in the occupied territory are

---

123 Ibid., 113.

124 See, for example, Erik Castrén, *The Present Law of War and Neutrality* (Suomalaisen Tiedeakatemian Toimituksia Helsinki 1954) 111–13. Note, however, that in light of the above, Castrén's claim (111) that mass expulsions were permitted by international law appears not to be correct.

125 There is no mention of expulsions of enemy aliens in the 1919 report of the Commission on Responsibilities (*Violation of the Laws and Customs of War*), although there is copious reference to the interment of such persons.

126 ICRC, 'Résolution XV', 343.

127 ICRC, 'Projet de Convention', 660.

128 Paul Des Gouttes, 'Projet de convention concernant la condition et la protection des civilise de nationalité ennemie qui se trouvent sur le territoire d'un belligerent ou sur un territoire occupé par lui' (1934) 65(384) *Revue Internationale de la Croix Rouge* 649, 655.

129 Articles 35–7, Fourth Geneva Convention. The 1948 draft prepared by the ICRC includes among these provisions the injunction that 'no person shall be repatriated against his will': XVIIth International Red Cross Conference (Stockholm, August 1948), *Draft Revised or New Conventions for the Protection of War Victims established by the International Committee of the Red Cross with the Assistance of Government Experts, National Red Cross Societies and Other Humanitarian Associations* (ICRC Geneva May 1948) 168. However, this was deleted by the 1948 International Red Cross Stockholm Conference and not reincorporated subsequently (see *FR*, vol. III, 120).

130 Article 38, Fourth Geneva Convention.

131 See ICRC, *Report on the Work of the Conference of Government Experts*, 279.

to be respected by the occupying State.[132] The general position in respect of expulsions of protected aliens in a belligerent State should therefore be assumed to be no more or less favourable than that of other aliens in peacetime. This innovation not only introduces parity with the general legal framework protecting inhabitants of occupied territory but also universalizes among parties to the Fourth Geneva Convention an obligation previously imposed only as a result of bilateral treaties in force between the warring States.

Against this backdrop, the Fourth Geneva Convention also created more specific protections relevant to expulsion. It will be noted that Article 38 allows the imposition of those special measures of control over protected persons permitted by the Convention during times of conflict.[133] However, since the State may not have recourse to any measure of control more severe than 'assigned residence' or 'internment',[134] any use of expulsion as a measure of control would only be permitted on the legal bases available during peacetime. This appears to act as a limitation even where an individual protected person forfeits certain Convention rights as a result of the State being satisfied that they are 'definitely suspected of or engaged in activities hostile to the security of the State'.[135] The mere fact of the existence of war therefore does not provide additional grounds for the expulsion of protected aliens.

In fact, the Fourth Geneva Convention imposes an additional limitation, absent in peacetime, upon the power of States to expel protected aliens present in their territories. Article 45(1) requires that:

> Protected persons shall not be transferred to a Power which is not party to the Convention.

This provision was introduced in the 1947[136] draft and explicitly modelled on a similar proposed provision in the 1947 draft convention on Prisoners of War.[137] The object of the provision is to prevent a State from avoiding its obligations under the Fourth Geneva Convention by transferring an enemy alien to another State not bound by the treaty. In line with this, delegates at the Diplomatic Conference deleted the 1948 Stockholm draft's qualification of 'against their will'[138] to emphasize the 'unconditional' nature of the prohibition and to prevent any risk of a State obtaining consent from a person to their transfer 'by more or less open pressure'.[139]

The application *ratione materiae* of Article 45 is delimited by the term 'transfer', the meaning of which generated 'some hesitation' among delegates. In particular, at the Diplomatic Conference, States questioned whether the right of States to 'deport' or 'expel' 'a dangerous individual' was limited by Article 45. Eventually, the concern of some States

132 See section text accompanying note 46 above regarding respect for the laws in occupied territory; Pictet, *Commentary*, 244.

133 See Article 27(4), Fourth Geneva Convention.

134 Article 41, Fourth Geneva Convention.

135 Article 5, Fourth Geneva Convention.

136 ICRC, *Report on the Work of the Conference of Government Experts*, 284.

137 The latter was introduced to 'settle the special question of transfer of [Prisoners of War] as between belligerent Powers, which was practised on a large scale during the war': ibid., 117.

138 *FR*, vol. I, 120.

139 Ibid., vol. IIA, 826; see also ibid., 661 and 764.

that the Article 45 rule might be avoided with 'transfers' taking place under the guise of 'deportations' prevailed, and a majority of the Drafting Committee took the view that 'deportation should be regarded on the same footing as transfer'.[140] Nonetheless, both 'repatriation' and 'extradition' of protected persons are expressly excluded from the ambit of Article 45(1).[141] To the extent that the Article 45(1) principle regulates the expulsion of enemy aliens, it thus has an important albeit narrow application.

A second important principle limiting the right of States to expel enemy aliens during times of armed conflict is expressed by Article 45(4):

> In no circumstances shall a protected person be transferred to a country where he or she may have reason to fear persecution for his or her political opinions or religious beliefs.

The debate on this provision revolved around specifying the time limit when such protection would disappear. The Netherlands proposed replacing the draft rule, which applied only 'during hostilities',[142] with 'as long as peace has not been concluded'.[143] China observed that even after the end of hostilities 'international usage' prevented the transfer of persons to a country 'where they had legitimate reasons to fear persecution'.[144] It was agreed that the time limit would be determined residually by reference to the cessation of the status of 'protected person' in accordance with Article 4 of the Convention.[145] Regardless, the fundamentally humanitarian nature of this prohibition – and of that concerning transfers to States not party to the Convention – is absolutely apparent.

In conclusion, it can be seen that the Fourth Geneva Convention imposes important limitations upon transfers of protected persons out of sovereign territory. However, these do not amount to an absolute prohibition of such transfers, as is the case for protected persons in occupied territories. The reason behind this divergence is not to be located in differing practical or humanitarian considerations but rather in the distinctive kind of authority that the hostile State exercises in each scenario.

The Displacement of Civilians during Hostilities

The 1949 Geneva Conventions afford protection to civilians who find themselves in the power of a hostile party to an international armed conflict, whether during occupation of their own State's territory or when they are aliens in the territory of a hostile State. They do not concern themselves directly with the conduct of hostilities, which has historically been governed by 'Hague law'. However, the provisions in the Hague Regulations that deal with the protection of the civilian population during the conduct of hostilities are relatively brief.

140 See ibid., vol. IIA, 827 and 809.
141 See Article 45(2) and Article 45(5), Fourth Geneva Convention.
142 *FR*, vol. I, 120.
143 Ibid., vol. IIA, 661; ibid., vol. III, 128.
144 Ibid., vol. IIA, 662.
145 Ibid., vol. IIA, 764 and 827.

In particular, neither body of law expressly regulates the coerced movement of civilians during the conduct of hostilities.

This protection gap was identified by the ICRC in the process leading to the drafting of the 1977 Additional Protocols. In the intervening period, the UN General Assembly had adopted a resolution affirming certain basic principles as applicable to the protection of civilians during armed conflicts, *inter alia* that,

> Civilian populations, or individual members thereof, should not be the object of … forcible transfers ….[146]

In the ICRC submissions to the January 1971 Conference of Government Experts, this affirmation constituted a point of reflection regarding protection gaps in the existing law of war concerning forced movement, particularly during guerrilla warfare in international and non-international armed conflicts. Although the Red Cross experts did not consider it possible to create an absolute prohibition on 'displacement by force', the ICRC requested that the Government Experts consider this option or, at least, some additional rules about 'how such measures are carried out and the results thereof'.[147]

This specific recommendation was not debated in relation to international armed conflicts during the 1971 and 1972 Conferences. Nonetheless, certain Government Experts did propose replacing the ICRC proposed provision that military operations must not be directed against the civilian population (the basis for Article 51 of Protocol I)[148] with a broader form of wording based on UNGA 2675, including its explicit and absolute prohibition on making civilian populations the object of forcible transfers.[149] None of these proposals made it into the draft treaties prepared by the ICRC in 1973 which formed the basis of negotiations in the 1977 Diplomatic Conference.[150] Therefore, in spite of the identification of a protection gap by the ICRC, the law of international armed conflict was not extended to regulate the forced displacement of civilians during the conduct of hostilities.

---

146 UN General Assembly Resolution 2675 (XXV); adopted 9 December 1970, paragraph 4.

147 ICRC, *VI. Rules Applicable in Guerrilla Warfare. Submitted to the Conference of Government Experts on the Reaffirmation and Development of International Humanitarian Law Applicable in Armed Conflicts (Geneva 24 May–12 June 1971)* (ICRC Geneva January 1971) 29–30.

148 ICRC, *III. Protection of the Civilian Population against Dangers of Hostilities. Submitted to the Conference of Government Experts on the Reaffirmation and Development of International Humanitarian Law Applicable in Armed Conflicts (Geneva 24 May–12 June 1971)* (ICRC Geneva January 1971) 29.

149 ICRC, *Report on the Work of the Conference of Government Experts on the Reaffirmation and Development of International Humanitarian Law Applicable in Armed Conflicts (Geneva 24 May–12 June 1971)* (ICRC Geneva August 1971) 79; ICRC, *Report on the Work of the Conference of Government Experts on the Reaffirmation and Development of International Humanitarian Law Applicable in Armed Conflicts (3 May–3 June 1972)* (ICRC Geneva July 1972) vol. I, 143.

150 See *OR*, vol. I, Part III.

Conclusion: International Armed Conflict, Forced Displacement and State Authority

During the course of the twentieth century, the law of international armed conflict has developed an increasingly broad set of norms prohibiting certain forms of coerced movement of civilians. Through a historical study, this chapter has shed light on how this body of international law has constructed a set of rules to govern different scenarios of forced displacement. By way of conclusion, this section will draw together the different strands identified in the course of the analysis.

The key point is that the 1949 Geneva Conventions, and the Fourth Geneva Convention in particular, represented a clear paradigm shift in terms of the law relating to the coerced movement of civilians. In the period up to the end of WWII, the laws and customs of war were generally permissive of deportations, expulsions, and other forced transfers of civilians by belligerent States. The prohibitions that developed in respect of such acts had a hesitant and referential character. Thus the idea that certain deportations from occupied territories were not permitted was sustained by reference to their 'prohibited purpose', i.e. inhumane purposes for carrying out the acts rendered the acts themselves unlawful, or at least of questionable legality. Limitations on expulsions of enemy aliens were less absolute and appear to have reflected the desire to limit the discretion of other States to resort to gross arbitrariness against a State's own nationals overseas. The different scenarios of 'occupied territories' and 'aliens in sovereign territory' were thus also governed by somewhat different logics.

Against this background, one of the great advances of the Fourth Geneva has been to fix with some precision the body of norms governing forced displacements of civilians. These norms seek to resolve some of the problems with the rules in force and, in so doing, they create a paradigm shift in the framework. Firstly, the vulnerability of protected persons to coerced movements is reduced through extending from the 'occupied territories' scenario to that of 'aliens in sovereign territory' the general duty upon a belligerent State to respect the laws in force in the territory in peacetime. Secondly, specific rules are codified to prohibit certain types of forced population movements. The single rationale behind the prohibitions in both the 'occupied territories' and 'aliens in sovereign territory' scenarios is to absolutely prohibit a belligerent from making forcible transfers to other States where the civilian may be in danger. This logic is distinct from that of the earlier rules in force, and derives from the historical experience that in international armed conflicts certain transfers to other States are likely to place civilians in a vulnerable position and result in unnecessary human suffering. The rules in the Fourth Geneva Convention are thus framed widely so as to prohibit all such measures, without room for individual 'deportations'.

On a related point, it is on the basis of this rationale that the law of international armed conflict does not directly prohibit the forced 'internal' displacement of civilians by parties to the conflict. This position is in contrast to the laws of war governing non-international armed conflicts that reach the threshold for the application of Protocol II to the 1949 Geneva

Conventions,[151] where ordering such internal displacements as are 'for reasons related to the conflict' will generally be prohibited by Article 17(1). Of course, the law of international armed conflict outlaws certain inhumane methods of war that may *inter alia* result in the forced movement of civilians, such as the prohibition on 'acts or threats of violence the primary purpose of which is to spread terror among the civilian population'.[152] Yet other methods of war that may result in the forced displacement of civilians are not only permitted but expressly required by the law of international armed conflict. For instance, Article 57(2)(c) of Protocol I specifically requires a State to give effective advance warning of an attack that may affect the civilian population, recognizing that forcing the displacement of civilians may in some cases be for their own interest. The clear conclusion is that the law of international armed conflict does not as such prohibit forced 'internal' displacements.

Finally, this chapter suggests that the degree of protection offered explicitly to civilians by the 1949 Geneva Conventions against measures of forced external displacement differs.

(a) Occupying State:	ALL prohibited
(b) Sovereign State:	SOME prohibited
(c) During hostilities:	NOT prohibited

These distinctions in the levels of protection respond to differences in the nature of the State authority being exercised in each case. Where one State's territory is occupied by another State, the territorial State has a strong interest in international law in limiting the discretionary exercise of *de facto* military authority over its population by the occupier as far as is reasonably possible under the circumstances. By contrast, where States act as sovereign over their own territory, they will be unwilling to accept such far-reaching limitations on their exercise of sovereign rights over those whom they may consider to be enemy aliens. During the conduct of hostilities between the belligerent States, the absence of effective authority over the specific territorial area subject to the hostilities, combined with the need of each State's survival, may explain the unwillingness by States to accept any limitation on the military necessity of sometimes forcing the displacement of the civilian population. If this is so, however, it stands in sharp contrast to the prohibition of forced displacement – even during hostilities – expressed by the law of non-international armed conflict. This raises the serious question of whether the law of international armed conflict really provides adequate formal protection against forced population movements during the conduct of hostilities.

References

–, *1945 Charter of the International Military Tribunal (Nuremberg),* in Dietrich Schindler and Jirí Toman, *The Laws of Armed Conflicts* (Martinus Nijhoff Publishers Leiden 1988).

151 *Protocol Additional to the Geneva Conventions of 12 August 1949 and relating to the Protection of Victims of Non-international Armed Conflicts* (adopted 8 June 1977, entered into force 7 December 1978) 1125 *United Nations Treaty Series* 609; hereafter 'Protocol II'.

152 For international armed conflicts, see Article 51(2) of Protocol I. For non-international armed conflicts, see Article 13(2) of Protocol II.

–, *Accords entre le Gouvernement de la République Français el le Gouvernement Impérial Allemand concernant les Prisonnniers de Guerre et les Civils, Berne 26 April 1918.*

–, *Control Council Law No. 10: Punishment of Persons Guilty of War Crimes, Crimes against Peace and against Humanity*, in Telford Taylor, *Final report to the Secretary of the Army on the Nuremberg War Crimes Trials under Control Council Law No. 10* (Government Printing Office Washington D.C. 1949).

–, 'Deportation of Civilians from Belgium', (1917) 11 *American Journal of International Law (Special Supplement)* 249.

–, *Draft of an International Declaration concerning the Laws and Customs of War adopted by the Conference of Brussels, 27th August 1874*, reprinted in A. Pearce Higgins, *The Hague Peace Conferences and International Conferences concerning the Laws and Usages of War: Texts of Conventions with Commentaries* (Cambridge University Press Cambridge 1909).

–, *Final Record of the Diplomatic Conference of Geneva of 1949* (Federal Political Department Berne 1963).

–, *Geneva Convention relative to the Protection of Civilian Persons in Time of War* (adopted 12 August 1949; entered into force 21 October 1950) 75 *United Nations Treaty Series* 287.

–, 'International Military Tribunal (Nuremberg), Judgment and Sentences, October 1, 1946' (1947) 41 *American Journal of International Law* 172.

–, 'Official Documents: Memoire of the Belgian Government in regard to the Deportation and Forced Labor of the Belgian Civil Population Ordered by the German Government' (1917) 11 *American Journal of International Law (Supplement)* 99.

–, *Official Records of the Diplomatic Conference on the Reaffirmation and Development of International Humanitarian Law applicable in Armed Conflicts (Geneva 1974–1977)* (Federal Political Department Bern 1978).

–, *Protocol Additional to the Geneva Conventions of 12 August 1949 and relating to the Protection of Victims of International Armed Conflicts* (adopted 8 June 1977, entered into force 7 December 1978) 1125 *United Nations Treaty Series* 3.

–, *Protocol Additional to the Geneva Conventions of 12 August 1949 and relating to the Protection of Victims of Non-international Armed Conflicts* (adopted 8 June 1977, entered into force 7 December 1978) 1125 *United Nations Treaty Series* 609.

–, *Regulations Respecting the Laws and Customs of War on Land annexed to the 1907 Hague Convention IV Respecting the Laws and Customs of War on Land*, in Adam Roberts and Richard Guelff, *Documents on the Laws of War* (3rd edn OUP Oxford 2000).

–, *Report of Robert H. Jackson, United States Representative to the International Conference on Military Trials, London 1945* (Department of State Washington D.C. 1949).

–, *Rome Statute of the International Criminal Court* (adopted 17 July 1998, entered into force 1 July 2002) 2187 *United Nations Treaty Series* 90.

–, *Violation of the Laws and Customs of War: Reports of Majority and Dissenting Reports of American and Japanese Members of the Commission of Responsibilities Conference of Paris 1919* (Clarendon Press Oxford 1919).

Arai-Takahashi, Yutaka, *The Law of Occupation: Continuity and Change of International Humanitarian Law, and its Interaction with International Human Rights Law* (Martinus Nijhoff Leiden 2009).

Beichmann, Frederik Valdemar Nikolai (Arbitrator), *Arbitral Award rendered pursuant to the compromise signed at London, March 4, 1930, between France and the United Kingdom of Great*

Britain and Northern Ireland in the Matter of the Claim of Madame Chevreau Against the United Kingdom, The Hague, June 9, 1931 (1933) 27 *American Journal of International Law* 153.

British War Office, *Manual of Military Law* (HMSO/Harrison and Sons London 1899; reprinted 1902).

Castrén, Erik, *The Present Law of War and Neutrality* (Suomalaisen Tiedeakatemian Toimituksia Helsinki 1954).

Des Gouttes, Paul, 'Projet de convention concernant la condition et la protection des civilise de nationalité ennemie qui se trouvent sur le territoire d'un belligerent ou sur un territoire occupé par lui' (1934) 65 *Revue Internationale de la Croix Rouge* 384.

Dinstein, Yoram, 'The Israel Supreme Court and the Law of Belligerent Occupation: Deportations' (1993) 23 *Israel Yearbook on Human Rights* 1.

Ferrière, F., 'Projet d'une Convention internationale réglant la situation des civils tombés à la guerre au pouvoir de l'ennemi' (1923) 5 *Revue Internationale de la Croix Rouge* 54.

Fried, John H.E., 'Transfer of Civilian Manpower from Occupied Territory' (1946) 40 *American Journal of International Law* 303.

Garner, J.W., 'Contributions, Requisitions and Compulsory Service in Occupied Territory' (1917) 11 *American Journal of International Law* 74.

Gillard, Emanuela-Chiara, 'The Role of International Humanitarian Law in the Protection of Internally Displaced Persons' (2005) 24 *Refugee Survey Quarterly* 37.

Hall, William Edward, *A Treatise on International Law* (4th edn Clarendon Press Oxford 1895).

Hartigan, Richard Shelly, *Lieber's Code & the Law of War* (Precedent Chicago IL 1983).

Henckaerts, Jean-Marie, 'Deportation and Transfer of Civilians in Time of War' (1993) 26 *Vanderbilt Journal of Transnational Law* 469.

Henckaerts, Jean-Marie and Louise Doswald-Beck, *Customary International Humanitarian Law, vol II: Practice* (ICRC/CUP Cambridge 2005).

Hines, Walker D. (USA Arbitrator), *Navigation on the Danube (Allied Powers: Czechoslovakia, Greece, Romania, Serb-Croat-Slovene Kingdom); Germany, Austria, Hungary and Bulgaria (Decision of 2 August 1921)* (1948) 1 *Reports of International Arbitral Awards* 105.

Holland, Thomas Erskine, *The Laws of War on Land (Written and Unwritten)* (Clarendon Press London 1908).

ICRC, *III. Protection of the Civilian Population against Dangers of Hostilities. Submitted to the Conference of Government Experts on the Reaffirmation and Development of International Humanitarian Law Applicable in Armed Conflicts (Geneva 24 May–12 June 1971)* (ICRC Geneva January 1971).

ICRC, *VI. Rules Applicable in Guerrilla Warfare. Submitted to the Conference of Government Experts on the Reaffirmation and Development of International Humanitarian Law Applicable in Armed Conflicts (Geneva 24 May–12 June 1971)* (ICRC Geneva January 1971).

ICRC, 'Projet de Convention international concernant la condition et la protection des civilis de nationalité ennemie qui se trouvent sur le territoire d'un belligerent ou sur un territoire occupé par lui' (1934) 65 *Revue Internationale de la Croix Rouge* 560.

ICRC, *Report on the Work of the Conference of Government Experts for the Study of the Conventions for the Protection of War Victims (Geneva, April 14–26, 1947)* (ICRC Geneva 1947).

ICRC, *Report on the Work of the Conference of Government Experts on the Reaffirmation and Development of International Humanitarian Law Applicable in Armed Conflicts (3 May–3 June 1972)* (ICRC Geneva July 1972).

ICRC, *Report on the Work of the Conference of Government Experts on the Reaffirmation and Development of International Humanitarian Law Applicable in Armed Conflicts (Geneva 24 May–12 June 1971)* (ICRC Geneva August 1971).

ICRC, 'Résolution XV. Code des prisonniers de guerre, déportés, évacués et réfugiés' (1921) 224 *Revue Internationale de la Croix Rouge* 341.

ICTY, *Prosecutor v Ante Gotovina & Ors* (Decision on Several Motions Challenging Jurisdiction) ICTY Case No. IT-06-90-PT (19 March 2007).

ICTY, *Prosecutor v Milomar Stakić* (Judgment) ICTY Case No. IT-97-24-A (22 March 2006).

ICTY, *Prosecutor v Mladen Naletilic and Vinko Martinovic* (Judgment) ICTY Case No. IT-98-34-T (31 March 2003).

ICTY, *Prosecutor v Radislav Krstic* (Judgment) ICTY Case No. IT-98-33-T (2 August 2001).

ICTY, *Prosecutor v Radoslav Brdanin* (Judgment) ICTY Case No. IT-98-36-T (1 September 2004).

ICTY, *Prosecutor v Vidoje Blagojević and Dragan Jokić* (Judgment) ICTY Case No. IT-02-60-T (17 January 2005).

ILA, 'Report of the Thirty-fifth Conference held at Warsaw, August 9th to 16th, 1928' (1928) 35 *International Law Association Reports of Conferences* 1.

Jaquemet, Stephane, 'The Cross-fertilization of International Humanitarian Law and International Refugee Law' (2001) 83 *International Review of the Red Cross* 651.

Kuttner, Thomas S., 'Israel and the West Bank: Aspects of the Law of Belligerent Occupation' (1977) 7 *Israel Yearbook on Human Rights* 166.

Lauterpacht, H., *International Law: A Treatise by L. Oppenheim (5th edition)* (Longmans Green and Co. London 1937).

Meron, Theodor, 'Deportation of Civilians as a War Crime under Customary International Law', in Theodor Meron, *War Crimes Law Comes of Age: Essays* (Clarendon Press Oxford 1998).

Oppenheim, Lassa, 'The Legal Relations between an Occupying Power and the Inhabitants' (1917) 33 *Law Quarterly Review* 363.

Passelecq, Fernand, *Déportation et Travail Forcé des Ouvriers et de la Population Civile de la Belgique Occupée, 1916–1918* (Carnegie Endowment for International Peace Paris 1928).

Pearce Higgins, A., *The Hague Peace Conferences and International Conferences concerning the Laws and Usages of War: Texts of Conventions with Commentaries* (CUP Cambridge 1909).

Pictet, Jean S. (ed.), *Commentary: IV Geneva Convention relative to the Protection of Civilian Persons in Time of War* (ICRC Geneva 1958).

Roucounas, Emmanuel J., 'Les infractions graves au droit humanitaire' (1978) 31 *Revue Hellénique de Droit International* 57.

Sandoz, Yes, Christophe Swinarski and Bruno Zimmermann (eds), *Commentary on the Additional Protocols of 8 June 1977 to the Geneva Conventions of 12 August 1949* (ICRC/ Martinus Nijhoff Geneva 1987).

Schwarzenberger, Georg, *International Law As Applied By International Courts and Tribunals, Volume II: The Law of Armed Conflict* (Stevens & Sons London 1968).

Schwarzenberger, Georg, 'The Law of Belligerent Occupation: Basic Issues' (1960) 10 *Nordisk Tidsskrift for International Ret* 10.

Scott, James Brown, *The Proceedings of the Hague Peace Conferences: Translation of the Official Texts: The Conference of 1907* (OUP London 1920).

St. John-Mildmay, Henry, 'Deportations from the Occupied Territories' (1916) 1(November) *International Law Notes* 170.

Supreme Court of Israel, *HC 785/87, 845/87 and 27/88, Abd al Nasser al Aziz Abd al Affo et al v Commander of the IDF Forces in the West Bank et al* (1990) 29 *International Legal Materials* 139.

Théry, Gustave, 'Deportations from the Occupied Territories (Further Opinions received)' (1916) 1(December) *International Law Notes* 188.

UN General Assembly Resolution 2675 (XXV); adopted 9 December 1970.

United States Military Tribunal Nuremberg, *re. List et al (Hostages Trial)* (1948) 15 *Annual Digest and Reports of Public International Law Cases* 632.

United States Military Tribunal Nuremberg, *The Flick Trial* (1949) 9 *United Nations War Crimes Commission Law Reports of Trials of War Criminals* 1.

United States Military Tribunal Nuremberg, *The Justice Trial* (1948) 6 *United Nations War Crimes Commission Law Reports of Trials of War Criminals* 1.

United States Military Tribunal Nuremberg, *The Krupp Trial* (1949) 10 *United Nations War Crimes Commission Law Reports of Trials of War Criminals* 69.

United States Military Tribunal Nuremberg, *Trial of Erhard Milch (20 December 1946–17 April 1947)* (1948) 7 *United Nations War Crimes Commission Law Reports of Trials of War Criminals* 27.

PART V
ENCAMPMENT, DETENTION AND THE COERCIVE TREATMENT OF ASYLUM-SEEKERS

17 ASHGATE RESEARCH COMPANION

Asylum Seekers, Detention and the Law: Morality in Abeyance?

Dallal Stevens[1]

Introduction

Detention has given rise to considerable debate in law and in moral philosophy.[2] In recent years, much has been written on the detention of non-nationals, particularly in relation to national security concerns following events in New York in September 2001. Despite this – or perhaps as a consequence –, the detention of *asylum seekers* has been subject to less academic scrutiny, a somewhat striking omission in view of the considerable extant powers in this area and the provision for indefinite detention.[3] This contribution seeks to redress the balance by revisiting the fundamentals of administrative detention. It examines whether depriving asylum seekers of their liberty stands up to moral scrutiny, and whether the current framework of legal oversight is sufficient when measured against the ethical implications.

---

1 Law School, University of Warwick: d.e.stevens@warwick.ac.uk

2 See, for example, D. Wilsher, 'The Administrative Detention of Non-nationals pursuant to Immigration Control: International and Constitutional Perspectives' (2004) *International and Comparative Law Quarterly* Vol. 53, 897–974; M. Welch and L. Schuster, 'Detention of Asylum Seekers in the UK and USA: Deciphering Noisy and Quiet Constructions' (2007) *Punishment & Society*, Vol. 7, No. 4, 397–417; C. Johnston, 'Indefinite Immigration Detention: Can it be Justified?' (2009) *Immigration, Asylum and Nationality Law*, Vol. 23, No. 4, 351–64; also, G. Cornelisse's excellent book *Immigration Detention and Human Rights: Rethinking Territorial Sovereignty* (Leiden: Martinus Nijhoff, 2010); J. Waldron, 'Security and Liberty: The Image of Balance' (2003) *Journal of Political Philosophy*, Vol. 11, No. 2, 191–210.

3 With some exceptions: see, for example D. Wilsher, 'Detention of Asylum Seekers and Refugees in International Human Rights Law', in P. Shah (ed.), *The Challenge of Asylum to Legal Systems* (London: Cavendish Publishing, 2005), 145–68; anti-detention campaigners, by contrast, have worked hard to highlight their concerns about asylum detention, producing high-quality reports advocating policy reform, with some notable successes: Bail for Immigration Detainees, Medical Justice, and London Detainee Support Group are some well-known examples of influential non-governmental organizations. The Coalition Government announced early in its formation its intention to end child detention. Following a period of reflection on how to implement the change, Minister of Immigration Damian Green announced on 16 December 2010 that with immediate effect no children would be detained in Yarl's Wood detention centre and that 'a fundamentally new approach to the whole end-to-end process of working with families in the immigration system' was to be introduced: see http://www.ukba.homeoffice.gov.uk/sitecontent/documents/news/wms-review-end-of-detention.pdf (accessed: 1 August 2012).

Focusing on the position in the United Kingdom, the chapter addresses four main areas: why states detain; whether detention can be justified; the role of the courts and judiciary; and the impact of human rights legislation. It opens with a brief contrast of reasons for detention in the criminal, medical and immigration fields. By developing a deeper insight of asylum-seeker detention, it reveals the myriad reasons promulgated by government to explain the need for incarceration. A key aspect is to assess critically whether detention can be justified rationally or morally, especially where vulnerable individuals are concerned. Two problematic aims of detention are highlighted: the risk of absconding and deterrence. Showing that (asylum-seeker) detention often lacks a rational or moral explanation, the chapter questions the current legal framework of judicial review, with specific reference to leading cases. It considers judgments affecting asylum seekers pending examination of their claims, as well as those who have been refused and are subject to removal or deportation. The discussion concludes with an analysis of the impact of human rights law on this politically sensitive issue, and proposes that, at the very least, it is time to consider fixed terms of detention, if not the whole moral basis for asylum-seeker detention.

Why Detain?

A Long History

Detention is a euphemistic term for imprisonment, custody, incarceration, or confinement, and the reasons for detention are therefore manifold. Some relate to law, some to policy; some are articulated, some remain unspecified. Detention, naturally, has a long history.[4] Today, the criminal justice and mental health areas provide the most familiar grounds for deprivation of liberty. Imprisonment of the criminal is justified according to various well-established aims: punishment; rehabilitation; protection of the public; deterrence. Confinement of those with serious mental illness is generally for the protection of the individual and/or the public, as well as for treatment. On the face of it, criminal law and mental health grounds for detention might be considered different from those used in the migration context, but there are common overlaps. All three are concerned with 'preventative detention'.[5]

The confinement of migrants, foreigners and aliens, purely on the basis of being alien and seeking entry to the UK, is very much a twentieth-century development. An early form of detention or reception centre is evident in the 'receiving houses' established to help fulfil the aims of the Aliens Act 1905 – to control inward, mainly Jewish migration – from Russia and

4 Interestingly, in relation to Ancient Greece, A.R. Littlewood notes: 'Information on detention is scant and largely Athenian. Non-productive long term incarceration was extremely rare, its function served by deprivation of civil rights. Short-term incarceration, however, was occasionally used, sometimes in addition to a fine', in N.G. Wilson (ed.), *Encyclopaedia of Ancient Greece* (New York: Routledge, 2006), 287.

5 For a comprehensive discussion of preventative detention in the US, see A. Klein and B. Wittes, 'Preventive Detention in American Theory and Practice' (2011) *Harvard National Security Journal*, Vol. 2, No. 1, 85–191.

Central and Eastern Europe. At the time, shipping companies set up a number of receiving houses to accommodate passengers landed from 'immigrant ships'.[6] Under the Act, they were responsible for the safe custody and control of passengers. Churchill, however, on becoming Home Secretary in 1910, was very keen to establish a receiving house in London, which was the busiest port and lacked such a facility.[7] Not only would the receiving house provide an improved custodial environment from that on board ship, but immigrants would be interviewed and inspected in one place, with less opportunity for those so inclined to avoid detection. Churchill was supported in his quest by the Jewish Board of Deputies, and by a committee established to look into the matter,[8] but it never came to pass, due, largely, to the cost involved. Other than internment of 'enemy aliens' during both world wars, detention for immigration purposes somewhat lapsed until the latter part of the twentieth century. A search of Hansard[9] reveals very little discussion of detention and asylum prior to 1987, but there is a significant change from 1987 onwards as numbers of asylum applications rose.[10] Though government kept limited records of detention at this time, and provided only spot-checks of numbers in detention on a specific day, it did disclose that, in 1987, 'some 1,615 persons applied for asylum on arrival at Heathrow, Dover and Gatwick', and, of these, 449 were detained for periods of more than 14 days.[11] So, one can surmise that with an increase in numbers came an increase in suspicion, at the very least, and a consequent desire to use detention as a deterrent,[12] or even as punishment for those seeking asylum in the UK.

From Control to Efficiency

Within the United Kingdom, the United Kingdom Border Agency ('UKBA') has long provided guidance on 'Detention and Temporary Release' for immigration officers and case workers, among others.[13] In the latest manifestation of such policy, the reason for migration detention is clearly stated: 'the power to detain must be retained in the interests of *maintaining*

6 An 'immigrant ship' was defined, somewhat bizarrely, as a ship bringing in more than 20 alien steerage passengers; cabin passengers – that is, first-class passengers – were excluded. Steerage passengers were subject to inspection under the Act to establish whether they were 'undesirable' or not.

7 J. Pellew, 'The Home Office and the Aliens Act, 1905' (1989) *The Historical Journal*, Vol. 32, No. 2, 369–85, at 379.

8 See *The Establishment of a Receiving House for Alien Immigrants at the Port of London*, Report of the Departmental Committee appointed to advise the Secretary of State as to the establishment of a receiving house for alien immigrants at the port of London, 1911,Vol. I, Report and Appendix, Cd. 5575; Vol. II, Minutes of Evidence, Cd. 55.

9 UK Parliamentary Debates.

10 See generally D. Stevens, *UK Asylum Law and Policy: Historical and Contemporary Perspectives* (London: Sweet & Maxwell, 2004); Amnesty International, *Cell Culture: The Detention & Imprisonment of Asylum Seekers in the UK* (December 1996); M. Ashford, *Detained Without Trial: A Survey of Immigration Act Detention* (London: JCWI, 1993).

11 HC Deb 18 January 1988 Vol. 125 Col. 488W.

12 There are many reports of this period that explore the use of detention as a deterrent. See note 10.

13 UKBA, *Enforcement Instructions and Guidance*, Ch. 55, at: http://www.ukba.homeoffice.gov.uk/sitecontent/documents/policyandlaw/enforcement/detentionandremovals/chapter55.

effective immigration control' (emphasis added). This would seem, therefore, within the UK, the primary aim of detention, and it is applicable to immigrants and asylum seekers alike. With this overarching objective, a myriad of secondary aims are identifiable. For example, the Immigration Form IS91R, which must be served on every detained person, sets out specific reasons for detention to be selected in each individual case: the likelihood of absconding if given temporary admission or release; the insufficiency of reliable information to decide whether to grant temporary admission or release; that removal from the United Kingdom is imminent; the need to be detained while alternative arrangements are made for care of the detainee; that release is not considered conducive to the public good; or the deciding officer is satisfied that the application can be decided quickly using the fast-track asylum procedures.[14]

The last of these refers to a change of policy adopted in 2000 and focuses on asylum seekers; it introduced a new system that became known as 'fast track detention'.[15] For the first time, the government admitted that there was a need to detain asylum seekers for a different reason: to strengthen the Home Office's ability '*to deal quickly with asylum applications*'.[16] Only claims that could be decided rapidly, including those certified as manifestly (now clearly) unfounded, would be selected for this process. Prior to this, asylum seekers were detained under the same powers and according to the same principles as all those subject to immigration control. The new asylum detention regime was sold as beneficial for all: the 'genuine' would have a fast decision to their claims, while those who were refused would be rapidly removed from the country.[17]

Further changes concerning detention of asylum seekers have emerged over the years, such that there are now various routes to detention. Detained Fast Track ('DFT') is used for 'straightforward' claims that the Home Office considers can be decided within accelerated timescales of two to three days.[18] Claimants will normally have an in-country appeal right and will be detained while this is lodged and heard. In the Detained Non-Suspensive Appeals Process, claimants are usually identified as coming from countries the UKBA considers to be generally 'safe'. As these are deemed clearly unfounded cases, there is no in-country right of appeal and any appeal will need to be conducted from outside the UK. Applicants in the Third Country Cases category are subject to removal to another European Union state under the provisions of the Dublin II Regulation; pending removal, they can be detained. Finally, asylum

---

pdf?view=Binary (accessed: 1 August 2012); see also the White Paper *Fairer, Faster and Firmer: A Modern Approach to Immigration and Asylum* (July 1998), Cm 4018.

14 UKBA, *Enforcement Instructions and Guidance*, Ch. 55, 55.6.3. Fourteen further reasons for detention are listed, which form the basis for the reason for detention.

15 See Barbara Roche, HC Deb 16 March 2000 Col. 263W. Oakington Reception Centre detained claimants for seven to ten days during which the first-instance decision was made on their case by the Home Office. Following the decision, they were released pending appeal, removed to a further detention centre, or removed from the UK, if there were no in-country appeal right.

16 Ibid.; emphasis added.

17 Des Browne, HC Deb 16 September 2004 Col. 391.

18 Post April 2003, a system of 'DFT' was set up in Harmondsworth Removal Centre and was limited to single male asylum applicants considered to have straightforward claims and who could be detained pending a quick decision. A female DFT process was opened in May 2005 at Yarl's Wood Immigration Removal Centre. DFT now also operates from Colnbrook and Campsfield removal centres.

applicants who do not fall within any of the above, can be detained under normal provisions for detention applicable to all persons subject to immigration control.

For all these categories, the main reasons offered by UK government to support its policy of detention of asylum seekers continue to be the maintenance of immigration control and quick and convenient decision making. But these apparently benign objectives, as with criminal law, have prevention at their core. Stephen Legomsky has identified three aims of detention relating to modern immigration policy that expose the preventative objectives of detention: 'preventing people from absconding'; protecting the safety of the public'; 'deterring immigration violations'.[19] And, of course, there are further grounds that seek to justify detention of non-nationals, and that go beyond prevention and support the state's goals of reinforcing the public interest or advancing the greater good: assisting with screening and identification of migrants, and with removal, deportation or extradition; improving access to legal advisors; providing accommodation for non-nationals; and reassuring the public. To most, such grounds seem reasonable and uncontroversial.

Is Detention Justifiable?

A Benign Necessity

Most citizens do not question the moral basis for detention. Policy aims such as 'improved immigration control' or 'quick decision making' are often accepted without question and are regarded as rational choices – especially at a time when territory (and thus state sovereignty) is portrayed by politicians and the media as under threat, whether by terrorist, migrant, or trafficker. Even the detention of asylum seekers is seldom challenged by the majority, since it is believed to be 'necessary'. But this unquestioning tolerance of detention – even when, as in the UK, the law allows for indefinite administrative detention – ignores the moral, legal and political complexities, and reduces justifiability to a simplistic concept.

It has not always been the case that administrative detention was perceived by politicians or the public as a benign necessity. In a revealing Parliamentary debate on 'Alien (Detention)' in 1959,[20] the MP for Norwich South made an impassioned plea against the imprisonment in Norwich Jail for alleged contravention of the Aliens Order 1953 of two members of the crew of the Syrian ship *Sourya*, then under arrest at Yarmouth – eight days for one, ten days for the other. Calling for a possible Royal Commission inquiry, he said:

> We have deprived the men of freedom without trial, and that is not in accordance with our ideas of a valid system of justice ... Many people in this country, of all parties, are profoundly disturbed by the thought that these things may happen without any form of publicity whatsoever, and perhaps to a refugee

[19] S. Legomsky, 'The Detention of Aliens: Theories, Rules and Discretion' (1999) *The University of Miami Inter-American Law Review*, Vol. 30, No. 3, 531–49.

[20] HC Deb 23 January 1959 Vol. 598 Cols 657–70.

> from tyranny escaping to what he believes is a free country where individual rights are invariably protected by Parliament, by the courts and by the Press ...
>
> As for imprisoning men without trial, this is an arbitrary power which is hateful and contrary to all our traditions and beliefs. I would also like to ask how it can be reconciled with the provisions of Article 9 of the Charter of Human Rights of the United Nations which states unequivocally: No one shall be subjected to arbitrary arrest, detention or exile. It is not, in my view, sufficient for the Government to rely simply on the powers given by the Aliens Order. It is not enough to say, 'This is the law.' Laws must be the agents of justice. In these cases we have no means of knowing whether justice is done. It is certainly not seen to be done. We do not know where the law stops and justice begins.[21]

The speech conveys a strong sense of shock in Parliament, in the press, and among the public that individuals might be held in prison without trial. The minister representing the government of the day sought to justify the detention as 'this is the law': she argued the men were 'detained in pursuance of a power of long standing conferred by Parliament and without which it is difficult to envisage any system of immigration control being satisfactorily maintained at the ports, and particularly in the case of foreign seamen who might wish to come to this country'.[22] In an attempt to reassure the House, she went on to stress: 'Detention, too, is often for a very short period – a very temporary physical safeguard against a determined attempt to abscond.'[23]

State Sovereignty and the Law

Clearly in evidence is the conventional explanation for the widespread acceptance of detention in the migration field: the powerful concept of state sovereignty – particularly territorial sovereignty –, and the so-called historic right of the state to admit, exclude and expel aliens (originating, in the case of the UK, from the prerogative power of the Crown).[24] It is not the purpose here to revisit this well-trodden subject;[25] it is simply noted that every individual who seeks to cross a state boundary accepts (willingly or unwillingly) the power of the state

21 *Ibid.*, Col. 661.

22 *Ibid.*, Col. 667; Article 8(4) of the Aliens Order sanctioned detention – HC Deb 23 January 1959 Vol. 598 Col. 665.

23 *Ibid.*, Cols 668–9.

24 For a useful summary of the historic position and case law see *R v Immigration Officer at Prague Airport and another, ex parte European Roma Rights Centre and others* [2004] UKHL 55, para 11 passim.

25 For an in-depth account of territorial sovereignty and immigration detention, see Cornelisse, *Immigration Detention and Human Rights*; see also S. Sassen, *Losing Control? Sovereignty in an Age of Globalisation* (New York: Columbia University Press, 1996); D. Held, 'Law of States, Law of Peoples: Three Models of Sovereignty' (2002) *Legal Theory*, Vol. 8, No. 1, 1–44; C. Dauvergne, 'Sovereignty, Migration and the Rule of Law in Global Times' (2004) *Modern Law Review*, Vol. 67, No. 4, 588–615.

to determine how it deals with that individual. Acceptance is not dependent on whether the individual migrant has recognized the validity of state boundaries; having crossed the border into another state's territory, the non-national is forced to comply with the rules of that state.[26] On entry to the territory, the action taken by the state may not be the migrant's preferred course, as in the case of detention, but he or she has yielded autonomy to the state to make such decisions. Failure to consent to such authority will lead to refusal of entry. But this does not imply that the state may, as in the past, act without consideration of the rights or interests of the prospective detainee. Indeed, the 'consent' of the individual to the application of immigration or asylum law by the state is met with agreement by some states to limit their sovereignty through international law. Signature and ratification of certain international treaties implies that states have chosen to restrict their absolute power over foreign nationals within, or seeking entry to, its territory (the 1951 Convention Relating to the Status of Refugees is one obvious example);[27] notwithstanding, states have also sought and obtained concessions that certain rights, granted to all human beings, are subject to limitations as prescribed by law, and which are necessary to protect public safety, public order, health or morals, or the fundamental rights and freedoms of others.[28]

Whichever political theory is espoused to explain the authority of the state, it is agreed that, so long as the state's legal system as a whole seeks to uphold order and security and to achieve welfare and justice, the convention is to accept all decisions as binding.[29] (This does not forgo the power to challenge decisions that appear outwith the law.) Thus, an individual member of society may consent (tacitly), by behaving in a certain way, to particular unpreferred outcomes, or even to actions that could be considered immoral in the absence of consent.[30] In other words, the obligation to obey the law is voluntarily assumed, and the consequence of committing crimes is likely to be punishment, which can entail incarceration. The same reasoning can apply to terrorists or suspected terrorists, who, for some, have sacrificed their right to freedom, or, *in extremis*, even to be treated humanely, because of the harm they have done or may do.[31] Likewise, detention of the seriously mentally ill (on the basis that they are a threat to themselves or to others) is considered justifiable. The common good of members

[26] Of course, it is open to discussion that globalization has shifted the dynamics of the nation state and that borders have, or should, become more porous: S. Benhabib, *The Rights of Others: Aliens, Residents and Citizens* (Cambridge: Cambridge University Press, 2004); P. Cole, *Philosophies of Exclusion: Liberal Political Theory and Immigration* (Edinburgh: Edinburgh University Press, 2000); H. Lindahl (ed.), *A Right to Inclusion and Exclusion? Normative Fault Lines of the EU's Area of Freedom, Security and Justice* (London: Hart, 2009).

[27] Per Lord Bingham in *A & Others v Secretary of States for the Home Department* [2004] UKHL 56, para. 69.

[28] See Human Rights Committee, General Comment 22, *The Right to Freedom of Thought, Conscience and Religion (Article 18)*, 30 July 1993, at: http://www.unhchr.ch/tbs/doc.nsf/(Symbol)/9a30112c27d1167cc12563ed004d8f15?Opendocument (accessed: 1 August 2012).

[29] D. Raphael, *Problems of Political Philosophy*, 2nd edn (London: Macmillan, 1990), 64, 205.

[30] C. Pfaff, 'Towards an Ethics of Detention and Interrogation: Consent and Limits' (2005) *Philosophy & Public Policy Quarterly*, Vol. 25, No. 3, 18–21, at 19.

[31] Since 11 September 2001, there is a vast literature on (indefinite) detention and human rights. See for example, C. Macken, *Counter-terrorism and the Detention of Suspected Terrorists: Preventative Confinement and International Human Rights Law* (London: Routledge, 2010); C. Walker, 'The Detention of Suspected Terrorists in the British Isles' (2006) *Legal Studies*, Vol. 12, No. 2, 178–94; F. de Londras, 'The Right to Challenge the Lawfulness of Detention: An International

of society is promoted (by removal of a threat to public safety). Even in the case of foreign nationals in breach of criminal law (and subject to deportation), known in modern-day parlance as 'foreign national prisoners', there is a widely accepted rationale for prison and/or detention pending departure: to prevent recidivism, to protect the public, and to ensure that removal takes place. Where detention becomes more difficult to sanction is in the case of what one might describe as 'pure' administrative or immigration detention: detention for examination or for removal.[32] Here, no crime has been committed, there may be no threat to public security, and detention is often described as for 'administrative convenience' alone. How is justice, order, or security being served here? And what are the implications for the non-national, who either yields to the application of immigration policy, because there is no alternative, or rejects immigration control? Are their interests to be discounted in the face of state authority within a democratic society? Unlike the citizen, the non-national has no voice: he or she is unable to object to detention as a policy through the ballot box. The onus therefore falls on the citizen to monitor this particular exercise of power.

The Special Case of the Asylum Seeker

From a humanitarian perspective, the detention of asylum seekers and refugees – many of whom have endured extreme suffering – is hard to defend. If it is ever to take place, it requires considerable justification. After all, the right to liberty has been described as a 'pre-eminent right and a foundation stone of freedom in a democracy'.[33] But adequate justification is not always in evidence, and this pertains in particular to asylum seekers, who are held for 'administrative convenience', to accelerate processing and to keep track of claimants. Are these really sufficient reasons to deprive an individual of liberty? The singling out of asylum seekers does seem problematic.[34] As one commentator notes: 'Either the claimant truly fears persecution or he or she does not. If the fear is genuine, there might indeed be an additional incentive to abscond – the possibility of an erroneous denial and subsequent return. But the detention of genuine asylum seekers would seem hard to reconcile with humanitarian values.'[35] One might consider that some of the harshness of detaining asylum seekers is mitigated by the provision, at least within the UK, for exclusion from detention of vulnerable individuals.[36]

Perspective on US Detention of Suspected Terrorists' (2007) *Journal of Conflict and Security Law, Vol. 12, No. 2*, 223–60.

32 The distinction between deportation and removal of a foreign national in immigration law is often misunderstood: a deportation order will prevent re-entry unless revoked; administrative removal does not do so. Deportation applies in certain specified circumstances: where deportation is deemed to be conducive to the public good; where the person to be deported is the spouse or civil partner or child under 18 of a person ordered to be deported; or where a court recommends deportation in the case of a person over the age of 17 who has been convicted of an offence punishable with imprisonment (Statement of Changes to the Immigration Rules, HC 395, para. 363).

33 I. Macdonald and R. Toal, *Macdonald's Immigration Law & Practice 8th Edition* (London: LexisNexis, 2010), para. 17.42.

34 See Legomsky, 'The Detention of Aliens: Theories, Rules and Discretion'.

35 *Ibid.*

36 Detention Centre Rules 2001, SI 2001/238, Rule 35; UKBA, *DFT and DNSA Intake Selection (AIU Instruction)*, at: http://www.bia.homeoffice.gov.uk/sitecontent/documents/policyandlaw/

However, several non-governmental reports have revealed that torture victims, children, and the mentally ill are not always identified and have been placed in detention.[37] To detain such individuals is unquestionably harmful, as well evidenced in the literature and through the work of organizations such as the Medical Foundation for Victims of Torture, Medical Justice, and Physicians for Human Rights.[38]

Perhaps the most difficult type of detention to justify morally, or indeed practically, is that involving children. A wealth of evidence has now established the serious medical implications – both physical and mental – of detaining children.[39] As a consequence, and in line with Liberal Democrat pre-election pledges, the Coalition Government, on assuming the reins of government, announced that it would end the detention of children in the UK,[40] which came into effect in December 2010.[41] But not all are satisfied with the change. The government has acknowledged that detaining children is unacceptable and harmful, but the proposed amendments still entertain what is euphemistically called 'ensured return, as a last resort for families who refuse to depart the UK', and further described as 'family friendly pre-departure accommodation'.[42] While the intention is to hold families in such a facility for a maximum of 72 hours, in exceptional circumstances, they can be held for a week, and they will not be

---

asylumprocessguidance/detention/guidance/dftanddnsaintakeselection?view=Binary (accessed: 1 August 2012).

37 See for example, M. Townsend, 'UK "Ignoring" Systemic Evidence of Torture among Asylum Seekers', *The Observer*, 14 March 2010, at http://www.guardian.co.uk/uk/2010/mar/14/asylum-torture-evidence-ignored (accessed: 7 August 2012); Medical Justice website and reports, at: http://www.medicaljustice.org.uk/ (accessed: 1 August 2012); BiD, *Out of Sight, Out of Mind: Experiences of Immigration Detention in the UK*, July 2009, via: http://www.biduk.org/163/bid-research-reports/out-of-sight-out-of-mind-experiences-of-immigration-detention-in-the-uk.html (accessed: 1 August 2012).

38 MFVT and MJ are UK organizations; PHR is a US-based NGO. See for a report of the effects of detention, Physicians for Human Rights, 'From Persecution to Prison: The Health Consequences of Detention for Asylum Seekers', June 2003, via: http://physiciansforhumanrights.org/library/documents/reports/report-perstoprison-2003.pdf (accessed: 1 August 2012); also, 'A Body of Evidence: Torture among Asylum Seekers to the West' (2002) *The Lancet*, Vol. 359, No. 9308, 793; 'D. Summerfield, C. GorstUnsworth, P. Bracken, V. Tonge, D. Forrest and G. Hinshelwood, 'Detention in the UK of Tortured Refugees' (1991) *The Lancet*, Vol. 338, No. 8758, 58.

39 See for a recent list of studies: *R (on the application of Suppiah & Others) v Secretary of State for the Home Department & Others* [2011] EWHC 2, para. 106.

40 K. McVeigh, 'Asylum Children will be Kept Out of "Distressing" Detention Centres', *The Guardian*, 14 May 2010, at: http://www.guardian.co.uk/uk/2010/may/14/immigration-asylum-children-detention-centres (accessed: 7 August 2012); the UK is not alone in recognizing that the detention of children can seldom be justified: the European Union is actively in January 2010, for example, the ECtHR, in a case involving Belgium, determined that the detention of particularly vulnerable children in a closed centre for adults, even though accompanied by their mother, was unlawful (though the mother's detention was still found to be lawful): *Muskhadzhiyeva & Others v Belgium* (application no. 41442/07), 19 January 2010.

41 See Statement of Minister for Immigration, Damian Green, 'Ending the Detention of Children for Immigration Purposes', 16 December 2010, at: http://www.ukba.homeoffice.gov.uk/sitecontent/documents/news/wms-review-end-of-detention.pdf (accessed: 1 August 2012).

42 UKBA, 'New Family Returns Process Begins', 28 February 2011, at: http://www.ukba.homeoffice.gov.uk/sitecontent/newsarticles/2011/march/03new-family-returns-process (accessed: 1 August 2012).

permitted to come and go at will.[43] It would appear, then, that immigration objectives have triumphed over other concerns, suggesting that government finds it almost impossible to create a system devoid of some form of administrative detention.

The Risk of Absconding

Such concerns aside, detention of asylum seekers cannot always be excluded as an option. Even those who might regard the detention of credible asylum claimants as inhumane and unwise, do not automatically dismiss such detention as irrational.[44] Yet, for detention in this context to be rational, there must be reasoning based on logic leading to a conclusion that this is the right course of action. Is it correct, then, to posit that detaining ('genuine') asylum seekers is not irrational? Not necessarily. While maintenance of immigration control might seem a reasonable and sensible policy, many of the more specific grounds for detention discussed above could be described as weak, unproven, politically motivated, or even unlawful.

Consider, for example, the most widely cited, and, in the case of the UK, earliest explanations for detention: a high risk of absconding. This ground applies to immigrants and asylum seekers alike. Yet the UNHCR, in its study on alternatives to detention for asylum seekers and refugees, confirms that data on numbers who actually abscond are difficult to obtain,[45] and that evidence available for the UK reveals a low risk of flight (of 98 asylum detainees bailed between July 2000 and October 2001, regarded by the then Immigration Service as above average risk for absconding, 90 per cent complied with their bail conditions, even though some were aware they were due for removal from the UK).[46] There are limited Home Office statistics on absconding rates; in fact, in 2002, it was reported to the House of Commons Home Affairs Committee that absconding rates were not collected.[47] More information has recently become available: in 2010, the Minister for Immigration was able to report that, between 1 May and 31 October 2010, 176 refused asylum seekers absconded.[48] Families are still regarded by the Home Office as being unlikely to abscond due to the difficulty of doing so as a unit.[49] Even with limited evidence, assessment of the risk of absconding continues to feature heavily in the decision to detain.[50] Of course, the reality is that justifying detention of asylum seekers on the

43 H. Crawley, 'Detention by Another Name?', Migrants' Rights Network, 10 March 2011, at: http://www.migrantsrights.org.uk/migration-pulse/2011/immigration-detention-of-children-rebranded-predeparture-accommodation (accessed: 1 August 2012).

44 See Legomsky, 'The Detention of Aliens: Theories, Rules and Discretion'.

45 O. Field and A. Edwards, *Alternatives to Detention of Asylum Seekers and Refugees* (Geneva: UNHCR, April 2006), at: http://idcoalition.org/wp-content/uploads/2008/12/unhcr-doc-on-alternatives-with-alice-edwards.pdf (accessed: 1 August 2012).

46 Bruegel, I. and Natamba, E., *Maintaining Contact: What Happens after Detained Asylum Seekers get Bail?*, Social Sciences Research Papers, South Bank University, June 2002.

47 House of Commons, Select Committee Home Affairs, *Asylum Removals*, Fourth Report of 2002–03 Session, HC 654-I, 8 May 2003, para. 64.

48 HC Deb Damian Green 15 November Col. 546W.

49 David Wood, Strategic Director, Criminality and Detention, UKBA, HC Home Affairs Committee, *The Detention of Children in the Immigration Service*, Minutes of Oral Evidence, 16 September 2009 Q25.

50 See UK Border Agency Enforcement Instructions and Guidance, Chapter 55, para. 55.3.2.5.

basis of risk of flight plays well both politically and with the public, which has been bombarded with media reports of disappearing asylum seekers. And many immigration officers err on the side of caution, despite repeated ministerial assurances that detention would only be used 'as a last resort' (in the era before fast-track detention).[51] If the evidence that asylum seekers are at high risk of absconding is inconclusive, or even if the risk is low, it is not rational to detain at high cost to the public purse[52] and to the individual's well-being.

Deterrence

In many debates on administrative detention, refugee advocates argue that deterrence constitutes an invidious, unacknowledged policy objective. As with concerns raised over establishing the risk of flight, it is enormously difficult to prove that detention acts as a deterrent except in exceptional circumstances,[53] and it is almost impossible to establish the causal link between an individual's decision not to travel to a certain state and the possibility of detention. To detain, therefore, on the unproven assumption that it helps reduce the inward flow of migrants to a state's territory cannot be described as rational decision making. Furthermore, within the UK, the use of detention to deter asylum applicants is unlawful as it is not explicitly articulated as a reason to detain in domestic statute or in Article 5 – the right to liberty – of the European Convention of Human Rights ('ECHR').[54] Nevertheless, from the 1990s onwards, as numbers of asylum seekers grew, a new discourse emerged in the media, in government and in Parliament describing a culture of abuse of the asylum system in the UK and the EU. As part of the much documented 'criminalization' of the asylum seeker that developed at this time, an internal justificatory process developed, in which detention played an important part.[55] Administrative detention became part of the 'new penology' that replaced traditional forms of moral reasoning with 'social utility analysis or actuarial thinking', and

[51] L. Weber, 'Detention of Asylum Seekers on Arrival in the UK. Part 1: Overview of the Decision Making Process' (2001) *Immigration, Asylum and Nationality Law* Vol. 15, No. 3, 151–6; L. Weber, 'Detention of Asylum Seekers on Arrival in the UK. Part 2: The Role of Individual Factors' (2001) *Immigration, Asylum and Nationality Law*, Vol. 15, No. 4, 200–206; L. Weber, 'Detention of Asylum Seekers on Arrival in the UK. Part 3: Decision Making Practices and Key Questions' (2002) *Immigration, Asylum and Nationality Law*, Vol. 16, No. 1, 6–11; L. Weber and L. Gelsthorpe, *Deciding to Detain: How Decisions to Detain Asylum Seekers are Made at Ports of Entry* (Institute of Criminology, University of Cambridge, 2000).

[52] The average cost per bed per night is £120.00: HL Deb 4 February 2010 Col. 67WA.

[53] A (somewhat disputed) example is given in D. McNamara, 'The Origins and Effects of "Humane Deterrence" Policies in South-East Asia', in G. Loesher and L. Monahan (eds), *Refugees and International Relations* (Oxford: Clarendon Press, 1990), 123–33.

[54] 'Everyone has the right to liberty and security of person.' Article 5 provides exceptions; Article 5(1)(f) is relevant to migration – see below for further discussion.

[55] See for example, M. Welch and L. Schuster, 'Detention of Asylum Seekers in the US, UK, France, Germany, and Italy: A Critical View of the Globalizing Culture of Control' (2005) *Criminal Justice*, Vol. 5, No. 4, 331–55; M. Malmberg, *Control and Deterrence: Discourses of Detention of Asylum Seekers*, Sussex Migration Working Paper No. 20, January 2004; J. Banks, 'The Criminalisation of Asylum Seekers and Asylum Policy' (2008) *Prison Service Journal*, Vol. 175, 43–9.

which was concerned with managerial processes rather than punishment or rehabilitation.[56] This is especially true post September 11, when fear of terrorism compounded a long-standing fear of crime within an increasingly risk-adverse society, and where government sought to reassure members of the public through risk management strategies: administrative detention was one such seemingly firm measure.[57] Thus, within the climate of the time, it is likely that detention was used for deterrent purposes, and, as such, could be perceived as rational from within the government's own internal logic, though it might be unprepared to so admit.

To summarize: there are three straightforward reasons why immigration detention has slipped so easily into national legislation and then, latterly, was extended to asylum seekers. First, the state still adheres to its sovereign right to control its borders and to decide whom it lets in and whom it rejects. Second, the three main categories for detention – crime, serious mental instability, and inward migration – are, as we have seen, frequently associated with 'threat' in the public and political mind. And third, there has been an obvious conflation of asylum and immigration with criminal behaviour.[58] If asylum seekers and immigrants are regarded in the same way as criminals, then it would follow that the rationalization of incarceration of the criminal would also apply to certain migrants. Notwithstanding the fact that there is insufficient evidence to support the contention that the risk of absconding is high among asylum seekers, detention has been accepted as a tool to prevent the perceived threat of irregular entrants evading immigration laws. Indeed, there is now a more practical and harsher rationale: detention of some asylum seekers helps with identity checks and accelerates decision making and removal. Implicit in this approach is that the potential 'threat' to society, to the public purse, and to the infrastructure of unwanted and excludable migrants is diminished by ensuring, at least in principle, that refused asylum seekers leave the country. Of course, it does not follow that increased use of detention leads to increased removals – what has emerged in the last decade is the difficulty in effecting removals or deportations of both detainees and non-detainees at the end of the process.

What Role for the Courts?

Detention Sanctioned by Law

Fast-track detention – like limiting absconding and strengthening deterrence – is considered to have the added incentive of preventing damage to immigration control. It is regarded as the optimal way to ensure that asylum seekers enter and leave the UK relatively quickly. If

56 M. Feeley and J. Simon, 'The New Penology: Notes on the Emerging Strategy of Corrections and its Implications' (1992) *Criminology*, Vol. 30, No. 4, 449–74, at 451–2.

57 M. Malloch and E. Stanley, 'The Detention of Asylum Seekers in the UK: Representing Risk, Managing the Dangerous' (2005) *Punishment and Society*, Vol. 7, No. 1, 53–71.

58 See for discussion of increasing convergence between immigration detention and criminal incarceration, A. Kalhan, 'Rethinking Immigration Detention' (21 July 2010) *Columbia Law Review Sidebar*, Vol. 110, 42; Stevens, *UK Asylum Law & Policy*, for discussion of increasing criminalization of asylum seekers in the 1990s and 2000s.

this necessitates detention, it is often deemed a proportionate response, certainly more so than any deterrent function. It also carries more moral weight than – say – preventing absconding, since it is promoted as beneficial to the individual as well the state. But this argument ignores the moral and actual import of liberty. It might be considered that the law would reinforce the moral basis for individual freedom. This is partly true. The law appears, on the one hand, to guarantee a 'right to liberty and security of person',[59] but, on the other, it accepts that certain limits can be placed on personal freedom. This conflict at the very heart of detention is illustrated by Article 9(1) of the 1966 International Covenant on Civil and Political Rights:

> Everyone has the right to liberty and security of person. No one shall be subjected to arbitrary arrest or detention. No one shall be deprived of his liberty except on such grounds and in accordance with such procedure as are established by law.

The purity of the opening phrase – everyone has the right to liberty ... of person' is immediately diminished by the subsequent sentences. Everyone does not, in fact, have a right to liberty. Detention, including detention for immigration purposes,[60] is acceptable so long as it is not 'arbitrary' and is in accordance with legally established procedures; the European Convention on Human Rights ('ECHR') goes further and deems detention permissible in certain named circumstances, including, in the immigration context, where it is used to prevent unauthorized entry to – or to implement removal from – a state.[61] The UNHCR advocates that, in the case of asylum, detention is 'inherently undesirable'[62] and 'should normally be avoided',[63] but has been forced to concede that, 'if necessary, detention may be resorted to only on grounds prescribed by law to verify identity; to determine the elements on which the claim to refugee status or asylum is based, to deal with cases where refugees or asylum-seekers have destroyed their travel and/or identity documents or have used fraudulent documents in order to mislead the authorities of the state in which they intend to claim asylum; or to protect national security of public order'.[64] In other words, detention is acceptable in certain circumstances and must be justified.

How has such a 'pre-eminent' right come to be circumscribed in this way? Without doubt, drafters of relevant international human rights instruments were well aware of the historical antecedents of the right to liberty and its origins in the Magna Carta.[65] There, detention of

---

[59] See for example, Article 3 of the 1948 Universal Declaration of Human Rights: 'Everyone has the right to life, liberty and security of person.'

[60] Human Rights Committee, General Comment No. 8, *Right to Liberty and Security of Persons (Article 9)*, 30 June 1982, at: http://www.unhchr.ch/tbs/doc.nsf/(Symbol)/f4253f9572cd4700c12563ed00483bec?Opendocument (accessed: 1 August 2012).

[61] Article 5(1)(f).

[62] UNHCR, Revised Guidelines on applicable criteria and standards for the detention of asylum seekers (1999), para. 1.

[63] UNHCR Executive Committee Conclusion No. 44, *Detention of Refugees and Asylum-Seekers* (1986).

[64] *Ibid.*

[65] 'NO Freeman shall be taken, or imprisoned, or be disseised of his Freehold, or Liberties, or free Customs, or be outlawed, or exiled, or any otherwise destroyed; nor will We not pass upon him, nor condemn him, but by lawful judgment of his Peers, or by the Law of the Land. We will sell to no man, we will not deny or defer to any man either Justice or Right': chapter XXIX (translation

itself is not prohibited, only detention that is arbitrary or not sanctioned by the law. In Lord Bingham's words, 'Our own law from Magna Carta onwards provided what may be called normal powers of detention, for example of criminal suspects, those suffering mental illness and those seeking entry to the country or awaiting deportation from it.'[66] And this has remained the position over time, although the legal basis for detention has expanded significantly. Thus, Lord Bingham appears to accept fully that the power to detain should exist for those seeking entry to the UK, and that they are therefore on a par with criminals and the seriously mentally ill.[67] Is he simply paying lip-service here to Parliament's role as legislator, or does he believe in the intrinsic need to detain in the immigration context? He does not say.

'Reasonableness' rather than 'Rightness'

The current UK power to detain those liable for examination, deportation or removal was introduced in the Immigration Act 1971,[68] a step that Lord Justice Sedley recently described as a 'dramatic constitutional innovation … unprecedented in peacetime'.[69] In fact, previous powers to detain aliens did exist. Under the Aliens Restriction Act 1914 and Aliens Restriction (Amendment) Act 1919,[70] there was a power of detention pending and during examination,[71] pending removal directions and removal,[72] and pending deportation.[73] While it is true that the 1919 Act simply extended the 1914 Act – a statute enacted at the outset of war, and which therefore contained stringent provisions on the treatment of aliens –, it was subsequently accepted that the 1919 Act – and the orders promulgated under it – were still relevant to peacetime and therefore peacetime laws.[74] The rights of lawful aliens in time of peace were

from the original text of 1215, Magna Carta (1297) c9), via: http://www.statutelaw.gov.uk/content.aspx?activeTextDocId=1517519 (accessed: 1 August 2012).

66 T. Bingham, 'Personal Freedom and the Dilemma of Democracies' (2003) *International and Comparative Law Quarterly*, Vol. 52, No. 4, 841–58, at 844.

67 The use of asylums for the mentally ill is as equally contentious an area as that of immigration and asylum detention, but is beyond the purview of this piece.

68 The power to detain is contained in the Immigration Act 1971 Sch. 2, para. 16 and Sch. 3, para. 2; and Nationality, Immigration and Asylum Act 2002, s. 62.

69 'So far as this court knows, the provision made in the 1971 Act for what have become known as the Immigration Rules is not merely unusual but unique. This is perhaps less surprising when one recalls that the same Act made two other dramatic constitutional innovations, both unprecedented in peacetime: by s.3(8), in relation to issues of nationality, it reversed the principle of habeas corpus that it is for the state to justify any deprivation of liberty; and by §2(2) and (3) of Sch. 3 it introduced administrative detention of persons subject to deportation': *Secretary for State for the Home Department v Pankina* [2010] EWCA Civ 719, para. 13.

70 Repealed by the Immigration Act 1971.

71 See for example Aliens Order 1953, SI 1953/1671, Article 7(3).

72 *Ibid.*, Article 8(4).

73 *Ibid.*, Article 21(4).

74 See Lord Denning MR, *R v Governor of Brixton Prison, Ex parte Soblen (No 2)* [1962] 3 All ER 641, 658D: 'It was said that on the true construction of the Aliens Restriction Act, 1914, the authority to impose restrictions on aliens only applied in time of war or on an occasion of imminent national danger or great emergency. The plain answer to that contention is given by section 1 of the Aliens Restriction (Amendment) Act, 1919. The authority to impose restrictions is

treated as the same as those of the British subject,[75] and the judiciary has long regarded its role in relation to the right to liberty as one of oversight – for example, *per* Lord Atkin, 'no member of the executive can interfere with the liberty or property of a British subject except on the condition that he can support the legality of his action before a court of justice. And it is the tradition of British justice that judges should not shrink from deciding such issues in the face of the executive'.[76] Drawing on Lord Atkin's words, in the case of *Khawaja v Secretary of State for the Home Department*, Lord Scarman famously put to rest any uncertainty about the ability of the non-national to challenge loss of liberty:

> Habeas corpus protection is often expressed as limited to 'British subjects'. Is it really limited to British nationals? Suffice it to say that the case law has given an emphatic 'no' to the question. Every person within the jurisdiction enjoys the equal protection of our laws. There is no distinction between British nationals and others. He who is subject to English law is entitled to its protection. This principle has been in the law at least since Lord Mansfield freed 'the black' in *Sommersett's Case* (1772) 20 St. Tr. 1. There is nothing here to encourage in the case of aliens or non-patrials the implication of words excluding the judicial review our law normally accords to those whose liberty is infringed.[77]

Within this framework, there is no questioning by the courts of the moral purpose of detention where it is sanctioned by law; the use of detention in the immigration and asylum contexts is accepted. Lord Bingham suggests as much when he argues:

> The existence of such powers does not, I think, give rise to libertarian concern so long as the conditions for exercise of the power to detain are clearly prescribed, so long as the period of detention is limited to a set or reasonable period or by persistence of the condition giving rise to the need for detention and so long as the detainee has access to formal procedures for challenging the lawfulness of his or her detention.[78]

Such challenge is now normally by way of judicial review,[79] though *habeas corpus* is always an option. Assuming, then, that domestic legislation has catered for detention of asylum seekers, and an application for judicial review has been granted, the courts will be in a position to examine acts of the executive and determine whether such acts are illegal, irrational, or lack

---

not so confined. It can be exercised "at any time" and the section has been continued every year since that time. It is too plain for argument.'

75 *Johnstone v Pedlar* [1921] 2 AC 262, 273.

76 *Eshugbayi Eleko v Officer Administering the Government of Nigeria* [1931] AC 662, 670.

77 [1984] 1AC 74, para. 67.

78 T. Bingham, 'Personal Freedom and the Dilemma of Democracies' (2003) *International and Comparative Law Quarterly*, Vol. 52, No. 4, 841–58, at 844–5.

79 That is, the power of the judiciary to supervise executive decision making at the behest of an individual, national and non-national alike. Applications are made to the Administrative Court to have a decision set aside on the grounds of illegality, irrationality (unreasonableness), or procedural impropriety.

procedural propriety. So long as there are principles of law or published policy, a judgment can be promulgated in which there is no challenge to the rationale of statutory law or policy itself – that is the 'rightness' of detaining asylum seekers, among others. Indeed, it would be unacceptable for the courts, under the doctrine of separation of powers, to question the decision of Parliament to detain. But the courts can and do act as a restraining influence on excessive executive power. Macdonald puts it thus:

> The court's duty is jealously to guard the liberty of the person and to require clear words in a statute to take away liberty and to interfere with fundamental rights. Broad statutory discretions to detain should be construed narrowly and strictly ensuring that they are only exercised for the proper statutory purpose. There is currently no statutory time limit placed on administrative detention but the power is impliedly limited to duration and circumstances consistent with that statutory purpose and which are reasonable.[80]

Judicial Review in Action

To exemplify the role of the courts in relation to domestic law, let us consider two important examples of asylum-seeker detention: the cases of *R (on the application of Saadi) v Secretary of State for the Home Department*[81] *and R (on the application of the Refugee Legal Centre) v Secretary of State for the Home Department*.[82]

The facts of *Saadi* are well known. The case considered whether four Kurdish claimants from the Kurdish Autonomous Region in northern Iraq were unlawfully detained in Oakington Reception Centre following their claims for asylum in the UK. They were detained for between seven and ten days, while their cases were considered by the Home Office and a first-instance decision was taken, and argued that their detention was illegal. The High Court agreed, but the Court of Appeal, House of Lords and European Court of Human Rights ('ECtHR') all sided with the Government. The case concerned in particular the human rights aspects of the decision; these will be addressed below, but first let us focus on the revealing comments of Lord Slynn in the House of Lords judgment in relation to the courts' powers of oversight. Lord Slynn dealt summarily with any suggestion that no power existed to detain asylum seekers. Detention for examination purposes was catered for in Schedule 2, paragraph 16 of the Immigration Act 1971.[83] Though, at the time of drafting, the Act had immigration rather than asylum in mind, there was nothing to suggest that asylum was excluded. The justification relied upon by the Home Office in sending the claimants to Oakington was that their cases fell within a category identified as 'capable of a speedy decision'.[84] In Lord Slynn's view, the

80 Macdonald and Toal, *Macdonald's Immigration Law & Practice*, para. 17.43.

81 [2002] UKHL 41.

82 [2004] EWCA Civ 1481.

83 '(1) ... A person who may be required to submit to examination under paragraph 2 above may be detained under the authority of an immigration officer pending his examination and pending a decision to give or refuse him leave to enter.'

84 [2002] UKHL 41, para 21.

claimants could be held up until the examination was concluded and a decision taken.[85] There was no obligation on the Secretary of State to show that it was necessary to detain because the applicants would otherwise run away;[86] nor was it limited to those who could not, for whatever reason, be granted temporary admission. The judge was more persuaded by what he called 'the reality' – that large numbers of applicants had to be considered intensively in a short period.[87] Great latitude was thus given to government, but, said Lord Slynn, the period of detention in order to arrive at a decision had to be 'reasonable in all the circumstances'.[88] He continued:

> This does not mean that the Secretary of State can detain without any limits so long as no examination has taken place or decision been arrived at. The Secretary of State must not act in an arbitrary manner. The immigration officer must act reasonably in fixing the time for examination and for arriving at a decision in the light of the objective of promoting speedy decision-making.[89]

Thus, having determined that the power to detain in such a fast-tracking facility existed, Lord Slynn was simply interested in establishing that exercise of power was not arbitrary, and that the examination time was reasonable. He had the power to set the limits, and concluded that, on balance, the detention procedure at Oakington, and time spent in detention, were reasonable.

While in *Saadi* attempts were made to persuade the judiciary that a period of seven to ten days' detention to consider an asylum application was excessive, the *Refugee Legal Centre* case centred instead on the extraordinary speed of decision making. The RLC challenged the fairness of the Home Office's fast-track system for asylum seekers at Harmondsworth Removal Centre. The Harmondsworth scheme was established 'to build on the successful Oakington process'[90] and applies to applicants who are considered to have straightforward claims and who can be detained pending a quick decision. The Home Office claimed that there was to be 'a sharp focus on high quality decision making, with on-site access to legal advice and, so far as possible, the same caseworker and legal representative dealing with an application from start to finish'.[91] Harmondsworth is limited to single male applicants from countries with no perceived serious risk of persecution. The system is founded on a three-day timetable, described as fast track, or even at times super fast track. It was established in *RLC* that the whole process in the case of a refusal upheld by all appellate bodies could take up to five weeks (i.e. the claimant is detained for the whole period from decision through appeal to removal).[92] However, because the refused asylum seeker might remain in detention pending removal, the actual time in detention can be much longer – indeed, for several weeks or even

[85] *Ibid.*, para. 22.
[86] *Ibid.*, para. 22.
[87] *Ibid.*, para. 24.
[88] *Ibid.*, para. 22.
[89] *Ibid.*, para. 25.
[90] [2004] EWCA Civ 1481, para. 2(2).
[91] Home Office, 'New Fast Track Pilot for Asylum Claims', 18 March 2003, 074/2003.
[92] [2004] EWHC 684, para. 4; for a useful summary of current fast-track detention, see ILPA Information Sheet, *Detained Fast Track*, 16 March 2010.

months thereafter.[93] The role of the courts was to consider whether this accelerated system placed an asylum seeker at an unacceptable risk of being processed unfairly.[94]

The issue at stake was the fairness or otherwise of the operation of the system; it was patently not about whether detention of asylum seekers *per se* – fast-track or otherwise – was justifiable either morally or legally. As *Saadi* makes clear, that battle – certainly on the legal aspects – has been lost. As a consequence, within the relative safety of the rules of judicial review, the Court of Appeal focused on the functioning of the policy. It was open to the Court on the evidence before it to find that the system as operated was unfair. Like the High Court, it chose not to. In its view, provided the fast-track system was managed in a way that recognized the variety of circumstances in which fairness would require an enlargement of the standard timetable, the system was not inherently unfair.[95] The Court went on to suggest that a written flexibility policy – catering for vulnerability of certain applicants – would 'afford a necessary assurance that the three-day timetable is in truth a guide and not a straightjacket'.[96] This has now been complied with.[97] But what is perhaps more worrying is the lack of any *obiter* comment by either High Court or Court of Appeal concerning the five-week period in detention. Would the higher courts or the ECtHR in *Saadi* have been so sanguine about a minimum limit of five weeks in detention for asylum seekers? Perhaps they might have accepted 'efficiency' criteria as reasonable justification, at the possible expense of freedom.

Human Rights – Can It Help?

In theory, human rights law is founded on moral principles, and should, ostensibly, be more effective in challenging the practice of detaining asylum seekers. As highlighted, the *Saadi* case was a significant milestone in the battle to overturn detention of asylum seekers, but not solely on grounds of domestic asylum and immigration law. Here, at last, was the opportunity to question asylum-seeker detention through the lens of human rights: Article 5 of the ECHR. The interpretation of the exception to liberty incorporated in Article 5(1)(f) – where 'the lawful arrest or detention of a person [is] to prevent his effecting an unauthorised entry into the country or of a person against whom action is being taken with a view to deportation or extradition' – was crucial. Certainly, Article 5(1)(f), as originally conceived, was not aimed at asylum seekers. Asylum seekers are not seeking an unauthorized entry when they arrive at a port and claim refuge. Nevertheless, the House of Lords and the ECtHR balked at the idea

93 See 2009 Annual Report of the Independent Monitoring Board for Harmondsworth Removal Centre, May 2010, via: http://www.imb.gov.uk/reports/Harmondsworth_2009.pdf (accessed: 1 August 2012).

94 [2004] EWCA Civ 1481, para. 6.

95 *Ibid.*, para. 23.

96 Ibid.

97 Home Office, Detained Fast Track Processes Operational Instruction, April 2005, *Flexibility in the Fast Track Process*, at: http://www.bia.homeoffice.gov.uk/sitecontent/documents/policyandlaw/asylumprocessguidance/detention/guidance/Detained_fast_track_process1.pdf?view=Binary (accessed: 1 March 2011).

of finding the Oakington fast-track system in breach of Article 5, and the ECtHR agreed that, until the State authorized entry, it was unauthorized.

The lengths to which the courts went to justify the detention, to find it proportional, and in no way arbitrary, are illuminating. The deprivation of liberty with which the appeal was concerned fell 'at the bottom end of the scale of interference with that right',[98] and, they suggested, the Oakington regime was not 'markedly different' from temporary admission with residence conditions.[99] While the wording of 5(1)(f) seems to suggest that detention must be necessary to prevent unauthorized entry, the House of Lords (subsequently endorsed by both Chamber and Grand Chamber of the ECtHR)[100] rejected this, arguing that, in the absence of any express or implied necessity test in the Convention or case-law, immigration detention could be compatible with Article 5(1)(f) even though it was not 'necessary'.[101] The ECtHR Chamber opined that there needed to be a 'reasonable balance' between the requirements of society and the individual's freedom, but at the same time advanced the view that 'the State has a broader discretion to decide whether to detain potential immigrants than is the case for other interferences with the right to liberty'.[102] In fact, the Grand Chamber went further, claiming that the policy behind the creation of the Oakington regime was generally to benefit asylum seekers,[103] the time was reasonable,[104] and the Court was willing to take into account 'the difficult administrative problems with which the United Kingdom was confronted during the period in question, with an escalating flow of huge numbers of asylum-seekers'.[105]

The six dissenting judges[106] were unimpressed with these arguments. For them, in situations involving deprivation of liberty, to maintain that detention is in the interests of the person concerned appeared 'an exceedingly dangerous stance to adopt'. They saw no reason to accept a seven-day detention period for asylum seekers when it is not sanctioned in other situations (bar perhaps in extradition cases where some flexibility might be required). To do so, they warned, carried with it the attendant risk that the scrutiny of deprivations of liberty under the European Convention on Human Rights would be substantially weakened in the future. And in any event, if seven days are not considered excessive, where would the line be drawn in the future?

There is much to worry about in the majority decision: the concern of the Court with the alleged difficulties in processing increasing asylum applications to the UK; the willingness to find the process and time in detention reasonable, without stating that seven days was a maximum; the confirmation that a broader discretion was granted to states to decide whether to detain in immigration cases without explaining why; the curious reluctance to consider

98 *Court of Appeal R (Saadi) v Secretary of State for the Home Department* [2001] EWCA Civ 1512, para. 69.

99 Ibid., para. 28.

100 Note that admissible complaints are examined by a Chamber comprised, in this case, of seven judges. Important decisions may on request of an applicant be referred to the Grand Chamber for further consideration.

101 *Saadi v UK (Application No 13229/03)*, 11 July 2006 (Chamber decision), para. 43.

102 Ibid., para. 44.

103 *Saadi v UK (Application No 13229/03)*, 29 January 2008 (Grand Chamber decision), para. 77.

104 Ibid., para. 79.

105 Ibid., para. 80.

106 Seventeen judges were involved in the Grand Chamber decision.

'necessity' of detention as part of a proportionality test;[107] the failure to weight freedom more heavily against state interest in the case of asylum seekers; and the failure of the courts, both in the UK and in Strasbourg, to consider in detail whether the Oakington process, which selected particular nationalities for detention, was in breach of Article 14 (non-discrimination). Once more, the combination of the 'undeniable sovereign right to control aliens' entry into and residence in their territory'[108] and very restrictive analysis of legal text ensured a certain (politically acceptable) outcome.

Is Change Afoot?

Although the role of law and of the judiciary in relation to detention is a somewhat bleak picture, there are occasions when, within the limitations imposed by administrative review, members of the bench provide glimmers of hope for asylum seekers, refugees, and their advocates. In *R (Johnson) v Secretary of State for the Home Department*, for example, the detention of a 64-year-old man in Oakington was held to be illegal.[109] It took 38 days to decide his claim, and for the remaining time, until his release on bail 27 days later, his detention was wrongfully continued on incorrect information. In total, he was detained for 65 days, 59 of which were held to be illegal. For this judge, the circumstances warranted six days' detention; if the claim could not be decided within that time, then, as far as he was concerned, that was a problem for the Home Office and not Mr Johnson. However, following this judgment, the Minister of State for the Home Office announced in Parliament a change to policy, in effect introducing greater flexibility for the Home Office and stretching the period for which people could be detained beyond that countenanced by *Saadi*:

> We will aim to make decisions within 10 to 14 days, but there will be occasions where it is quicker, for example at Harmondsworth or a non-NSA [non-suspensive appeal] decision at Oakington. However, we will continue to detain for the purpose of deciding the claim quickly, even beyond the 10 to 14-day timescale, unless the length of time before a decision can be made looks as if it will be longer than is reasonable in all the circumstances. Continued detention may also be merited in some cases irrespective of decision timescale, where our general detention criteria apply. We may also detain claimants after we have made and served a decision in accordance with our general detention criteria.[110]

107 See for further analysis of this point and of the *Saadi* judgment, H. O'Nions, 'No Right to Liberty: The Detention of Asylum Seekers for Administrative Convenience' (2008) *European Journal of Migration and Law*, Vol. 10, No. 2, 149–85.

108 *Saadi v UK (Application No 13229/03)*, 29 January 2008 (Grand Chamber decision), para. 64, and see *Amuur v France* (17/1995/523/609), 25 June 1996.

109 [2004] EWHC 1550.

110 HL Baroness Scotland, 16 September 2004, Col. WS129; see also UKBA, *DFT & DNSA Intake Selection* (AIU Instruction), para. 2.2.1.

Arguably, the most worrying detention cases are not concerned so much with detention pending asylum determination, but with administrative detention following a term of imprisonment and prior to deportation – the 'foreign national prisoner' cases. The claimants, who have often sought asylum and failed, but who have also committed a criminal offence, can languish for years in the detention estate as various attempts are made to deport them. The leading – and much cited judgment – is that of *R (Hardial Singh) v Governor of Durham Prison*, which stated that the period in detention pending a deportation order or removal needed to be reasonable in the circumstances.[111] Though the case advocates reasonableness, there have been many subsequent decisions where the length of time in detention seems extraordinary, as the wheels of immigration enforcement grind slowly. *R (on the application of A) v Secretary of State for the Home Department* is an illuminating example. A, an asylum applicant granted exceptional leave to remain, was sentenced to eight years' imprisonment following a serious sexual offence, and then held for 35 months following his automatic release date (three years into the sentence) while awaiting deportation.[112] There were difficulties in carrying out the removal, the risk of absconding was deemed high, and there was a high risk of reoffending. Despite the anxiety expressed by the Court of Appeal about the length of time in post-prison detention, it was not considered unreasonable in the circumstances.[113] Recently, in a 2010 High Court case, *Ibrahim & Omer v Secretary of State for the Home Department*, the Honourable Mr Justice Burnett found in favour of the claimants, two Iraqi nationals who had been refused asylum, committed criminal offences, and were sentenced to terms of imprisonment.[114] Both claimants contended that their detention following the date on which they would have been released on licence from prison was unlawful (in the case of Ibrahim over 14 months; in the case of Omer, over 20 months, before release on judicial review bail). The judge agreed. At the time of their detention reviews, it should have been apparent that enforced removals of the claimants could not have taken place because of the security situation in Iraq and that both claimants would therefore have been in detention in excess of 16 months, the time in detention that the judge identified as a reasonable period.[115] Consequently, their detention was held to be unlawful from the dates of their reviews.

---

[111] [1983] EWHC 1 (QB): Woolf J: 'Although the power which is given to the Secretary of State in paragraph 2 to detain individuals is not subject to any express limitation of time, I am quite satisfied that it is subject to limitations. First of all, it can only authorize detention if the individual is being detained in one case pending the making of a deportation order and, in the other case, pending his removal. It cannot be used for any other purpose. Secondly, as the power is given in order to enable the machinery of deportation to be carried out, I regard the power of detention as being impliedly limited to a period which is reasonably necessary for that purpose. The period which is reasonable will depend upon the circumstances of the particular case. What is more, if there is a situation where it is apparent to the Secretary of State that he is not going to be able to operate the machinery provided in the Act for removing persons who are intended to be deported within a reasonable period, it seems to me that it would be wrong for the Secretary of State to seek to exercise his power of detention': para. 7.

[112] [2007] EWCA Civ 804.

[113] At paras 59 and 82.

[114] [2010] EWHC 764.

[115] *Ibid.*, para. 63.

Ibrahim & Omer was positively received at the time as suggestive of a possible shift in judicial attitudes towards what constitutes an acceptable term of detention pre-deportation.[116] This might be somewhat premature. The latest of a long line of similar cases has, again, clarified the approach to be adopted, taking account of *Hardial Singh* principles.[117] *AE (Libya) v Secretary of State for the Home Department* states: 'It is … clear from the authorities that there is no requirement that the removal be "imminent", nor that a specified date for removal can be identified. Further, there is no set time limit beyond which detention will automatically become unreasonable; everything depends on the facts of the individual case'.[118] At the time *AE (Libya)* was heard, the claimant had been detained for 14 months but the court sanctioned his ongoing detention.[119] It cited the equally recent judgment of *R (on the application of MH) v Secretary of State for the Home Department*, where, admittedly with some trepidation, members of the Court of Appeal unanimously agreed that 38 months' detention was reasonable in the circumstances.[120]

So, is change afoot? If by change we mean a fixed term beyond which detention is unreasonable, then this is not the case, neither in court nor in Parliament. The judges are following *Saadi*, on fast-track detention, even though asylum seekers are now detained for periods longer than those envisaged in the case, and they continue to apply *Hardial Singh*, on the general approach to detention pending deportation, despite the uncertainty surrounding what is a reasonable period in detention. There is no question of their challenging the authority of Parliament, nor to stray beyond their judicial review remit, as the Court of Appeal made all too clear in *WL (Congo) & Another v Secretary of State for the Home Department*:

> We note Mr Husain's powerful appeal to constitutional principles of liberty. However, such broad considerations, important as they are, have little bearing on a case where Parliament has specifically authorised detention for a particular purpose, itself identified as permissible by the Convention, and where the courts have (in *Hardial Singh* and later cases) clearly laid down the principles under which that power is to be exercised. Provided the policy is consistent with that purpose and those principles, it matters not in our view whether it is stated in positive or negative form.[121]

---

116 See also, a 2002 Court of Appeal case, *R (on the application of I) v Secretary of State for the Home Department* [2002] EWCA Civ 888; there the Secretary of State could only establish a hope of being able to remove the claimant forcibly by the summer, and the court felt that substantially more in the way of a risk of reoffending than existed in the case would be necessary to justify continuing his detention for an indeterminate further period.

117 *R (Hardial Singh) v Governor of Durham Prison* [1984] 1 WLR 704, as summarized in *R (on the application of I (Afghanistan)) v Secretary of State for the Home Department* [2002] EWCA Civ 888 and revisited in *R (on the application of MH) v Secretary of State for the Home Department* [2010] EWCA Civ 1112.

118 [2011] EWHC 154 (Admin), paras 14–16.

119 *Ibid.*, para. 80.

120 [2010] EWCA Civ 1112.

121 *Ibid.*, para. 68.

Conclusion

In the case of immigration in general, and of asylum seekers in particular, the legal and political voices questioning the morality of detention itself are rarely heard. The acceptance of detention of asylum seekers pending examination has occurred by stealth, driven, one suspects, by fear and an exaggerated perception of threat. Within the recent and current political climate, the prevailing legal framework has dictated that we can detain asylum seekers so long as we remain within the law. This, despite frequent reports at both international[122] and national[123] levels that decry the use and conditions of both standard and fast-track detention in the UK. Rather, we have to make do with judges examining the application of the law, and procedures, to establish if powers have been exceeded. One might have anticipated that a human rights approach would have assisted in strengthening the right to liberty of all, but this has not occurred to any great extent. We are witness to increasing use of detention and ever-lengthening incarceration periods (as predicted by the dissenting minority in *Saadi*).

Whereas in *Saadi*, seven to ten days was adjudged to be a reasonable time to examine an asylum claim, in *RLC* the court did not flinch at a possible five-week detention period from claim to refusal (and those working in this area are well aware that detention is often longer); in *Ibrahim & Omer* – a deportation case –, the reasonable period was 16 months, but in the more recent *MH*, 38 months was acceptable to the judges. These outcomes are a consequence of incorporating proportionality or reasonableness into the assessment, with consequent uncertainty: how each judge decides what constitutes a relevant circumstance, and what weighting to give it, is unclear; in the case of asylum, non-legal factors, generally termed 'administrative convenience', can have great influence on the decision.[124] Where an asylum seeker becomes a foreign national prisoner, the range of justifications for continued detention pending deportation broadens. Furthermore, outcomes cannot be divorced from the political climate and are a consequence of the prevailing attitude towards migrants, even those fleeing persecution. By contrast, in other areas of detention – of the mentally ill or alcoholics – the law

[122] UN Commission on Human Rights, *Report of the Working Group on Arbitrary Detention: addendum: report on the visit of the Working Group to the United Kingdom on the issue of immigrants and asylum seekers*, 18 December 1998, E/CN.4/1999/63/Add.3, at: http://www.unhcr.org/refworld/docid/45377b810.html (accessed: 2 August 2012); and see follow-up Bail for Immigration Detainees, Submission to the United Nations Working Group on Arbitrary Detention, *Immigration Detention in the United Kingdom*, September 2002; Amnesty International, *United Kingdom – Seeking Asylum Is Not a Crime: Detention of People Who Have Sought Asylum*, 20 June 2005, EUR 45/015/2005, at: http://www.unhcr.org/refworld/docid/43b276374.html (accessed: 2 August 2012).

[123] See for example, Human Rights Watch, Fast-tracked Unfairness: Detention and Denial of Women Asylum Seekers in the UK, February 2010; London Detainee Support Group, Detained Lives: The Real Cost of Indefinite Detention, January 2009; HM Chief Inspector of Prisons, Report on an Unannounced Full Follow-up Inspection of Yarl's Wood Immigration Removal Centre, 9–13 November 2009; The Children's Commissioner for England's follow up report to *The Arrest and Detention of Children Subject to Immigration Control*, February 2010; HC Home Affairs Committee, The Detention of Children in the Immigration System, First Report of Session 2009–10, 24 November 2009.

[124] The recent decision of *R (on the application of Suppiah & Others) v Secretary of State for the Home Department* [2011] EWHC 2 (Admin) provides a very useful overview of policy and case law on detention.

arguably shows greater consideration.[125] Why should this be? One obvious explanation is that, despite the state's apparent adherence to concepts of 'human dignity' and human rights for all, the citizen is still prioritized over the non-national.[126] The lack of concrete status of asylum seekers – and certainly of those subject to removal – evidently continues to be vital, if not paramount, in determining their treatment by the law.

For advocates of change to the detention rules, decisions such as *Saadi, RLC, R (MH)* – and there are many in this vein[127] – are depressing. One must conclude that, at times, the courts hide behind rule-of-law principles by articulating the seriousness with which liberty is taken, but at the same time point out that the law provides for detention pending examination and pending removal, and stretch what is deemed reasonable, fair, acceptable. The judiciary might be regarded as unduly deferential towards the executive in this highly sensitive and political arena, but others might retaliate that the judiciary is fulfilling its role within the normal constraints of judicial review. Herein lies the nub: if it falls upon the judiciary to determine reasonableness, what in the context of this 'pre-eminent' right is reasonable? Or, to use the words of Lord Phillips from another – but related – context, 'How long is a piece of string?'[128] It might be better, as some are now suggesting, to adopt a maximum fixed term of detention for those awaiting removal or deportation, an adequate period to enable arrangements to be made. If removal proves impossible in this time, so be it, and release must take place. Twelve months has been aired as a suitable period.[129] That said, there remains a strong case to revisit the whole issue of indefinite administrative detention, particularly in the case of asylum seekers. The moral arguments against detention are strong, while the practical and policy arguments in favour of immigration control and enforcement do not always stack up. Lord Slynn talked in *Saadi* about Government's struggle with the reality of asylum applications; what he failed to address, and what continues to be a source of ongoing disquiet in a liberal democracy, is the unsavoury reality of a power of indefinite detention and its frightening implications for thousands of people every year.

---

125 G. Cornelisse, 'Human Rights for Immigration Detainees in Strasbourg: Limited Sovereignty or a Limited Discourse? (2004) *European Journal of Migration and Law*, Vol. 6, No. 2, 93–110, at 106.

126 For example, Sassen argues that the most important distinction is between those who have legal status in a state and those who do not: *Losing Control?*, 95; see for a discussion of this issue in relation to health care, D. Stevens, 'Asylum Seekers and the Right to Access Health Care' (2010) *Northern Ireland Legal Quarterly*, Vol. 61, No. 4, 363–90.

127 See also *ZL v Secretary of State for the Home Department* [2003] 1 WLR 1230, which held that the fast-track process at Oakington (of about seven days) did provide a fair opportunity to applicants to demonstrate that they have or may have an arguable case (paras 49–53).

128 Lord Phillips used this expression when discussing indefinite detention of foreign suspects and control orders: BBC4 TV, *The Highest Court in the Land*, 27 January 2011.

129 See for example Stephanie Silverman of Garden Court Chambers in H. Grant, 'The Indefinite Detention of Foreign National Prisoners', Guardian Focus Podcast, 25 February 2011, at: http://www.guardian.co.uk/world/audio/2011/feb/25/focus-podcast-indefinite-detention-foreign-prisoners (accessed: 2 August 2012).

References

'A Body of Evidence: Torture among Asylum Seekers to the West' (2002) *The Lancet*, Vol. 359, No. 9308, 793.

Amnesty International, *Cell Culture: The Detention & Imprisonment of Asylum Seekers in the UK* (December 1996).

Amnesty International, *United Kingdom – Seeking Asylum Is Not a Crime: Detention of People Who Have Sought Asylum*, 20 June 2005, EUR 45/015/2005, at: http://www.unhcr.org/refworld/docid/43b276374.html (accessed: 2 August 2012).

Ashford, M., *Detained Without Trial: A Survey of Immigration Act Detention* (London: JCWI, 1993).

Banks, J., 'The Criminalisation of Asylum Seekers and Asylum Policy' (2008) *Prison Service Journal* (2008), Vol. 175, 43–9.

Benhabib, S., *The Rights of Others: Aliens, Residents and Citizens* (Cambridge: Cambridge University Press, 2004).

BiD, *Out of Sight, Out of Mind: Experiences of Immigration Detention in the UK*, July 2009, via: http://www.biduk.org/163/bid-research-reports/out-of-sight-out-of-mind-experiences-of-immigration-detention-in-the-uk.html (accessed: 1 August 2012).

Bingham, T., 'Personal Freedom and the Dilemma of Democracies' (2003) *International and Comparative Law Quarterly*, Vol. 52, No. 4, 841–58.

Bruegel, I. and Natamba, E., *Maintaining Contact: What Happens after Detained Asylum Seekers get Bail?*, Social Sciences Research Papers, South Bank University, June 2002.

Cole, P., *Philosophies of Exclusion: Liberal Political Theory and Immigration* (Edinburgh: Edinburgh University Press, 2000).

Cornelisse, G., 'Human Rights for Immigration Detainees in Strasbourg: Limited Sovereignty or a Limited Discourse? (2004) *European Journal of Migration and Law*, Vol. 6, No. 2, 93–110.

Cornelisse, G., *Immigration Detention and Human Rights: Rethinking Territorial Sovereignty* (Leiden: Martinus Nijhoff, 2010).

Crawley, H., 'Detention by Another Name?', Migrants' Rights Network, 10 March 2011, at: http://www.migrantsrights.org.uk/migration-pulse/2011/immigration-detention-of-children-rebranded-predeparture-accommodation (accessed: 1 August 2012).

Dauvergne, C., 'Sovereignty, Migration and the Rule of Law in Global Times' (2004) *Modern Law Review*, Vol. 67, No. 4, 588–615.

De Londras, F., 'The Right to Challenge the Lawfulness of Detention: An International Perspective on US Detention of Suspected Terrorists' (2007) *Journal of Conflict and Security Law*, Vol. 12, No. 2, 223–60.

Feeley, M. and Simon, J. 'The New Penology: Notes on the Emerging Strategy of Corrections and its Implications' (1992) *Criminology*, Vol. 30, No. 4, 449–74.

Field, O. and Edwards, A. *Alternatives to Detention of Asylum Seekers and Refugees* (Geneva: UNHCR, April 2006), at: http://idcoalition.org/wp-content/uploads/2008/12/unhcr-doc-on-alternatives-with-alice-edwards.pdf (accessed: 1 August 2012).

Grant, H., 'The Indefinite Detention of Foreign National Prisoners', Guardian Focus Podcast, 25 February 2011, at: http://www.guardian.co.uk/world/audio/2011/feb/25/focus-podcast-indefinite-detention-foreign-prisoners (accessed: 2 August 2012).

Green, Damian, 'Ending the Detention of Children for Immigration Purposes', 16 December 2010, at: http://www.ukba.homeoffice.gov.uk/sitecontent/documents/news/wms-review-end-of-detention.pdf (accessed: 1 August 2012).

Held, D., 'Law of States, Law of Peoples: Three Models of Sovereignty' (2002) *Legal Theory*, Vol. 8, No. 1, 1–44.

Home Office, Detained Fast Track Processes Operational Instruction, April 2005, *Flexibility in the Fast Track Process*, at: http://www.bia.homeoffice.gov.uk/sitecontent/documents/policyandlaw/asylumprocessguidance/detention/guidance/Detained_fast_track_process1.pdf?view=Binary (accessed: 1 March 2011).

Human Rights Committee, General Comment No. 8, *Right to Liberty and Security of Persons (Article 9)*, 30 June 1982, at: http://www.unhchr.ch/tbs/doc.nsf/(Symbol)/f4253f9572cd4700c12563ed00483bec?Opendocument (accessed: 1 August 2012).

Human Rights Committee, General Comment 22, *The Right to Freedom of Thought, Conscience and Religion (Article 18)*, 30 July 1993, at: http://www.unhchr.ch/tbs/doc.nsf/(Symbol)/9a30112c27d1167cc12563ed004d8f15?Opendocument (accessed: 1 August 2012).

Johnston, C., 'Indefinite Immigration Detention: Can it be Justified?' (2009) *Immigration, Asylum and Nationality Law*, Vol. 23, No. 4, 351–64.

Kalhan, A., 'Rethinking Immigration Detention' (21 July 2010) *Columbia Law Review Sidebar*, Vol. 110, 42.

Klein, A. and Wittes, B. 'Preventive Detention in American Theory and Practice' (2011) *Harvard National Security Journal*, Vol. 2, No. 1, 85–191.

Legomsky, S., 'The Detention of Aliens: Theories, Rules and Discretion' (1999) *The University of Miami Inter-American Law Review*, Vol. 30, No. 3, 531–49.

Lindahl, H. (ed.), A Right to Inclusion and Exclusion? Normative Fault Lines of the EU's Area of Freedom, Security and Justice (London: Hart, 2009).

McNamara, D., 'The Origins and Effects of "Humane Deterrence" Policies in South-East Asia', in G. Loesher and L. Monahan (eds), *Refugees and International Relations* (Oxford: Clarendon Press, 1990), 123–33.

McVeigh, K., 'Asylum Children will be Kept Out of "Distressing" Detention Centres', *The Guardian*, 14 May 2010, at: http://www.guardian.co.uk/uk/2010/may/14/immigration-asylum-children-detention-centres (accessed: 7 August 2012).

Macdonald, I. and Toal, R. *Macdonald's Immigration Law & Practice 8th Edition* (London: LexisNexis, 2010).

Macken, C., *Counter-terrorism and the Detention of Suspected Terrorists: Preventative Confinement and International Human Rights Law* (London: Routledge, 2010).

Malloch, M. and E. Stanley, 'The Detention of Asylum Seekers in the UK: Representing Risk, Managing the Dangerous' (2005) *Punishment and Society*, Vol. 7, No. 1, 53–71.

Malmberg, M., *Control and Deterrence: Discourses of Detention of Asylum Seekers*, Sussex Migration Working Paper No. 20, January 2004.

O'Nions, H., 'No Right to Liberty: The Detention of Asylum Seekers for Administrative Convenience' (2008) *European Journal of Migration and Law*, Vol. 10, No. 2, 149–85.

Pellew, J., 'The Home Office and the Aliens Act, 1905' (1989) *The Historical Journal*, Vol. 32, No. 2, 369–85.

Physicians for Human Rights, 'From Persecution to Prison: The Health Consequences of Detention for Asylum Seekers', June 2003, via: http://physiciansforhumanrights.org/library/documents/reports/report-perstoprison-2003.pdf (accessed: 1 August 2012).

Raphael, D., *Problems of Political Philosophy*, 2nd edn (London: Macmillan, 1990).

Sassen, S., *Losing Control? Sovereignty in an Age of Globalisation* (New York: Columbia University Press, 1996).

Stevens, D., 'Asylum Seekers and the Right to Access Health Care' (2010) *Northern Ireland Legal Quarterly*, Vol. 61, No. 4, 363–90.

Stevens, D., *UK Asylum Law and Policy: Historical and Contemporary Perspectives* (London: Sweet & Maxwell, 2004).

Summerfield, D., GorstUnsworth, C., Bracken, P., Tonge, V., Forrest, D. and Hinshelwood, G. 'Detention in the UK of Tortured Refugees' (1991) *The Lancet*, Vol. 338, No. 8758, 58.

The Establishment of a Receiving House for Alien Immigrants at the Port of London, Report of the Departmental Committee appointed to advise the Secretary of State as to the establishment of a receiving house for alien immigrants at the port of London, 1911,Vol. I, Report and Appendix, Cd. 5575; Vol. II, Minutes of Evidence, Cd. 55.

Townsend, M., 'UK "Ignoring" Systemic Evidence of Torture among Asylum Seekers', *The Observer*, 14 March 2010, at: http://www.guardian.co.uk/uk/2010/mar/14/asylum-torture-evidence-ignored (accessed: 7 August 2012).

UKBA, *DFT and DNSA Intake Selection (AIU Instruction)*, at: http://www.bia.homeoffice.gov.uk/sitecontent/documents/policyandlaw/asylumprocessguidance/detention/guidance/dftanddnsaintakeselection?view=Binary (accessed: 1 August 2012).

UKBA, *Enforcement Instructions and Guidance*, Ch. 55, at: http://www.ukba.homeoffice.gov.uk/sitecontent/documents/policyandlaw/enforcement/detentionandremovals/chapter55.pdf?view=Binary (accessed 1 August 2012).

UKBA, 'New Family Returns Process Begins', 28 February 2011, at: http://www.ukba.homeoffice.gov.uk/sitecontent/newsarticles/2011/march/03new-family-returns-process (accessed: 1 August 2012).

UN Commission on Human Rights, Report of the Working Group on Arbitrary Detention: addendum: report on the visit of the Working Group to the United Kingdom on the issue of immigrants and asylum seekers, 18 December 1998, E/CN.4/1999/63/Add.3, at: http://www.unhcr.org/refworld/docid/45377b810.html (accessed 2 August 2012).

Waldron, J., 'Security and Liberty: The Image of Balance' (2003) *Journal of Political Philosophy* Vol. 11, No. 2, 191–210.

Walker, C., 'The Detention of Suspected Terrorists in the British Isles' (2006) *Legal Studies*, Vol. 12, No. 2, 178–94.

Weber, L., 'Detention of Asylum Seekers on Arrival in the UK. Part 1: Overview of the Decision Making Process' (2001) *Immigration, Asylum and Nationality Law*, Vol. 15, No. 3, 151–6.

Weber, L., 'Detention of Asylum Seekers on Arrival in the UK. Part 2: The Role of Individual Factors' (2001) *Immigration, Asylum and Nationality Law*, Vol. 15, No. 4, 200–206.

Weber, L., 'Detention of Asylum Seekers on Arrival in the UK. Part 3: Decision Making Practices and Key Questions' (2002) *Immigration, Asylum and Nationality Law*, Vol. 16, No. 1, 6–11.

Weber, L. and Gelsthorpe, L. *Deciding to Detain: How Decisions to Detain Asylum Seekers are Made at Ports of Entry* (Institute of Criminology, University of Cambridge, 2000).

Welch, M. and Schuster, L. 'Detention of Asylum Seekers in the UK and USA: Deciphering Noisy and Quiet Constructions' (2007) *Punishment & Society*, Vol. 7, No. 4, 397–417.

Welch, M. and L. Schuster, 'Detention of Asylum Seekers in the US, UK, France, Germany, and Italy: A Critical View of the Globalizing Culture of Control' (2005) *Criminal Justice*, Vol. 5, No. 4, 331–55.

Wilsher, D., 'Detention of Asylum Seekers and Refugees in International Human Rights Law', in P. Shah (ed.), *The Challenge of Asylum to Legal Systems* (London: Cavendish Publishing, 2005), 145–68.

Wilsher, D., 'The Administrative Detention of Non-nationals pursuant to Immigration Control: International and Constitutional Perspectives' (2004) *International and Comparative Law Quarterly*, Vol. 53, 897–974.

18 ASHGATE RESEARCH COMPANION

Regulation 5.35: Coerced Treatment of Detained Asylum Seekers on Hunger Strike. Legal, Ethical and Human Rights Implications

Mary Anne Kenny and Lucy Fiske

> This would happen because you have no choice. You can't make any decisions in your life. Just to show you are alive you could make a decision to stop receiving anything in your body. That would show that you were alive, because you could make a decision, in a place that you can't make any decision.
>
> 'Mustapha', former immigration detainee from Iran[1]

Introduction

In September 1992 three Cambodian asylum seekers launched a hunger strike refusing all food and taking only small quantities of water. They were detained in Villawood Immigration Detention Centre (IDC) in Sydney, Australia. All three were hospitalized for dehydration and after two weeks on the hunger strike were 'thought to be in grave danger of death'.[2] The then Australian Minister for Immigration sought orders in the Supreme Court of New South Wales to permit the administration of lifesaving medical treatment to two of the women without their consent. The court issued an interim order permitting the government 'to feed or to administer nourishment to the defendants against their will in order to prevent their death or serious bodily damage and for that purpose to use such force as is reasonably necessary.'[3] Prior to the full hearing of the case the Australian government passed a law giving the Secretary of the Department of Immigration power to authorize medical treatment to be

---

1 Names of all respondents have been changed.

2 As reported in *Department of Immigration, Local Government and Ethnic Affairs v. Gek Bouy Mok* Supreme Court of New South Wales Equity Division, Powell J, 4982 of 1992, 30 September 1992; unreported.

3 Ibid. For a discussion of the medical treatment of these hunger strikers and the ethical dilemmas posed see Derrick Silove, Jackie Curtis, Catherine Mason and Rise Becker, 'Ethical

given to a person in immigration detention without their consent.[4] This law is contained in regulation 5.35 of the *Migration Regulations 1994* (Cth). The regulation authorizes the use of 'reasonable force' to administer medical treatment including the reasonable use of restraint and sedatives. This power has been used in respect of detained asylum seekers on hunger strike, most notably for rehydration and naso-gastric feeding.

This chapter examines the case of detained asylum seekers on hunger strike and explores some of the complex legal and ethical issues that occur when managing and treating these cases. In examining the ethics and legality of regulation 5.35 it is important to look at the reasons for hunger strike, the competence of the individual engaging in hunger strike, the range of medical interventions available to treat practitioners (including the details of force feeding through a naso-gastric tube in particular), and the range of responses available to government authorities in responding to hunger strikes in detention environments. This chapter looks at hunger strikes as a form of protest particularly in Australian detention centres and considers the legal and political responses to those strikes. It concludes with a proposal for responding to hunger strikes by asylum seekers in detention.

The authors have interviewed former detainees who participated in hunger strikes in Australian immigration detention between 1999 and 2005, and quotes from those interviews are used throughout. A discussion of the reasons why asylum seekers engage in hunger strike action is important in determining what should be an appropriate response. Government representatives have often labelled hunger strikes by asylum seekers as 'manipulative', which then shapes authorities' responses to hunger strikes and facilitates the use of invasive or punitive procedures such as forced non-consensual medical treatment. However, these interviews demonstrate to the contrary that the reasons behind hunger strikes vary and that there are opportunities for negotiation that would, in our opinion, likely bring the majority of hunger strikes to a successful end prior to lasting medical and psychological harm to the individual(s) on hunger strike, without the need for invasive and potentially painful medical procedures while also keeping the government's policies of mandatory detention and the integrity of the refugee status determination process intact.[5]

Considerations in the Management of Asylum Seekers on Hunger Strike' (1996) 276 *Journal of the American Medical Association* 410–15.

4 *Migration Regulations 1994* (Cth), reg. 5.35. The explanatory memorandum prepared by the then Labor government advised that the need for these provisions arose because two individuals whose applications for refugee status had been rejected, and who were held in immigration detention, had gone on a hunger strike. Prior to the matter coming back to court the government introduced the regulation and the applications before the court were withdrawn by consent.

5 Note: the authors do not support mandatory detention, but are addressing the issue of hunger strike within a pragmatic framework that recognizes the government is unlikely to abandon this policy.

1. Hunger Strike as a Form of Protest

Hunger strike has been used as a form of protest, typically by those in a position of relative powerlessness, for centuries. Hunger strike does not appear to be linked to any particular culture, gender or time. Suffragettes in the US and Europe launched hunger strikes for the right to vote and for improved legal and social recognition of women's rights.[6] Gandhi regularly staged fasts aimed at influencing a range of political and social issues.[7] Perhaps the most famous strike of recent history was in Long Kesh prison in 1981, when 23 Irish Republican Army (IRA) prisoners went on a prolonged hunger strike lasting 217 days that ultimately claimed the lives of ten men.[8] More recently thousands of Turkish prisoners and supporters staged a hunger strike lasting several years and which claimed the lives of more than 100 men and women.[9] Detainees accused of terrorist activities and held without trial in Guantanamo Bay by United States authorities have also staged several hunger strikes opposing their ongoing detention and seeking to win improvements to their conditions of detention.[10]

What is common across these examples of hunger strikes is a significant power differential between the striker and the authority to which they appeal. Although hunger strikes are at times conducted by people living freely in the community, there is a high correlation between imprisonment and the use of hunger strike. This is likely a result of the paucity of alternate protest actions available to persons in detention. One former detainee in an Australian detention centre described this power imbalance:

> In a way dealing with him [the Minister for Immigration] … you can't really, there's no point. It's just like a rabbit try to negotiate with a lion the conditions of not eating him. It will eat eventually. ('Ali', Iraq)

A clear definition of a hunger strike is difficult to establish. United States authorities responsible for prisons, immigration detention and Guantanamo Bay define hunger strike as an individual voluntarily refusing food for a period of 72 hours.[11] Other definitions do not contain a temporal minimum, though many include an assessment of an individual's purpose or intent. Despite requests the authors have been unable to clarify with the Australian Department of Immigration and Citizenship its operational definition of a hunger strike. For the purpose of this chapter we have taken the World Medical Association (WMA) definition, which states, 'a hunger striker is a mentally competent person who has indicated that he [*sic*]

---

[6] Maud Ellmann, *The Hunger Artists: Starving, Writing and Imprisonment* (London: Virago Press, 1993).

[7] Bhikhu Parekh, *Gandhi's Political Philosophy: A Critical Examination* (London: Palgrave Macmillan, 1989).

[8] Paul Howard, 'The Long Kesh Hunger Strikers: 25 Years Later' (2006) 33(4) *Social Justice* 69–91, at 71.

[9] Patrick Anderson, 'To Lie Down to Death for Days' (2004) 18(6) *Cultural Studies* 816–46.

[10] Centre for Constitutional Rights, *The Guantánamo Prisoner Hunger Strikes & Protests: February 2002–August 2005* (A Special Report, New York, 2005).

[11] 28 CFR §§549.60–549.66 (2009), §549.61.

has decided to embark on a hunger strike and has refused to take food and/or fluids for a significant interval.'[12]

2. Hunger Strikes in Australian Immigration Detention Centres

In Australia, like other first world countries, the asylum-seeker issue has become increasingly contentious in recent years. Government responses since the 1990s have been to introduce restrictive public policies, including mandatorily detaining all asylum seekers who arrive in Australia without prior authorization. Asylum seekers detained in Australia are often located in remote areas of Australia or offshore on Christmas Island and are denied certain procedural protections, such as the right to challenge their detention in the courts. Immigration detention centres are stressful environments with large numbers of people from diverse backgrounds living in often over-crowded accommodation with little meaningful activity to structure each day. They often have a high degree of anxiety, little reliable information about the progress of their refugee claims, and limited contact with people outside detention. The deleterious effects of detention on mental health have been well documented over recent years.[13] One respondent described the build up to a hunger strike in 1999:

> The immigration didn't listen. The refugees, they lost any hope of leaving … We have kids in the detention centre, and we have a lot of women, and they have a lot of problems. The psychological pressure was really high at that time, living in what they call it, a donga, with tens of people. You can't sleep at night; you have security guards … knock on the door every half an hour to count the refugees or to check on them. It is a very disturbing environment for them. No talking to their families and they're overseas, no talking to anyone, the feeling of isolation, the feeling that no one knows anything about us makes them do

12 World Medical Association, 'Declaration on Hunger Strikers (Declaration of Malta):' *Adopted by the 43rd World Medical Assembly Malta, November 1991 and editorially revised at the 44th World Medical Assembly Marbella, Spain, September 1992, at* http://www.legislationline.org/documents/action/popup/id/8591, accessed 16 December 2010. For further discussions about the definition of hunger strike see Marlynn Wei and Rebecca W. Brendel, 'Psychiatry and Hunger Strikes' (2010) 23 *Harvard Human Rights Journal* 75–109, at 78–81.

13 Janette P. Green and Kathy Eagar, 'The Health of People in Australian Immigration Detention Centres' (2010) 192(2) *Medical Journal of Australia* 65–70; Derrick Silove and Zachary Steel, *The Mental Health and Well-being of On-shore Asylum Seekers in Australia* (Psychiatry Research and Teaching Unit, University of New South Wales, Liverpool 1998); Derrick Silove, Patricia Austin and Zachary Steel, 'No Refuge from Terror: The Impact of Detention on the Mental Health of Trauma-affected Refugees Seeking Asylum in Australia' (2007) 44(3) *Transcultural Psychiatry* 359–93; Louise Newman, Michael Dudley and Zachary Steel, 'Asylum, Detention and Mental Health in Australia' (1998) 27(3) *Refugee Survey Quarterly* 110–27; Linda Briskman, Susie Latham and Chris Goddard, *Human Rights Overboard: Seeking Asylum in Australia* (Melbourne: Scribe Publications, 2008).

> what they done ... So once the guys there knew about the new system[14] that was a reason for hunger strike, demonstrations, a lot of actions ... So partly because of the legislation, the other part is because of [the guards'] behaviour in the detention centre. The guards there needed to be more aware of the human rights system. ('Issaq', Iraq)

Information on the numbers of people who have participated in hunger strikes, the incidence of the use of the power under regulation 5.35, and policy regarding treatment of people on hunger strike is not recorded anywhere in the public domain and the authors were unable to obtain this information from the Department of Immigration prior to publication. The authors requested a copy of the Department's policy on managing hunger strikes in detention centres, but this request was declined as the policy is a 'commercial in confidence' document between Serco (the private provider contracted to run the detention centres) and the government.

A review of reports by official bodies including the Australian Parliamentary Joint Standing Committee on Foreign Affairs, Defence and Trade, the Australian Human Rights Commission, the United Nations Working Group on Arbitrary Detention, the UNHCR, along with media reports and a review of academic literature, reveals that hunger strikes lasting from a few days to several weeks have consistently occurred in Australian detention centres since 1992.[15] Some hunger strikes have been conducted by individuals, whereas others have participated in larger group protests. Larger protests have typically occurred when there are high numbers of people detained for extended periods of time (often in excess of one year). Two such examples include a hunger strike staged in 2002 by over 269 detainees at the Woomera Immigration Reception and Processing Centre in South Australia. More recently in November 2010 approximately 200 detainees staged a hunger strike in response to the deaths (by suicide) of two detainees in Villawood Immigration Detention Facility, New South Wales.

Recent figures obtained by a journalist at *The Australian* newspaper through Freedom of Information state that between July 2009 and June 2010 there were 219 detainees who

---

14 This quote is referring to the introduction of a three-year temporary protection visa in 1999. Temporary protection visas were given to individuals who were found to be refugees but who had entered Australia in an 'unauthorized' manner – that is, without a visa. The temporary protection visa was abolished in August 2008.

15 Human Rights and Equal Opportunity Commission, *Those Who've Come Across the Seas: The Report of the Commission's Inquiry into the Detention of Unauthorised Arrivals* (Canberra: HREOC, 1998); Human Rights and Equal Opportunity Commission HREOC, *A Last Resort? National Inquiry into Children in Immigration Detention* (Sydney: HREOC, 2004); Joint Standing Committee on Foreign Affairs, Defence and Trade, *A Report on Visits to Immigration Detention Centres* (Commonwealth of Australia, Canberra, 2001); United Nations Working Group on Arbitrary Detention, *Civil and Political Rights, Including the Question of Torture and Detention Report of the Working Group on Arbitrary Detention. Visit to Australia*, United Nations Commission on Human Rights, 59th Sess., UN Doc. E/CN.4/2003/8/Add.2 (24 October 2002); United Nations High Commission for Refugees, 'UNHCR Urges Australia to Review Policy of Detaining Asylum Seekers' (Media Release, 1 February 2002), at http://www.unhcr.org/cgi-bin/texis/vtx/search?page=search&docid=3c5abf1e2&query=hungerstrike, accessed 22 December 2010.

had undertaken 'voluntary starvation'[16] in immigration detention. Three had required hospitalization. There were a further 41 'voluntary starvation incidents' between July and September 2010.[17]

Case Example

Following the allied invasion of Afghanistan in December 2001, the Australian government announced that it would suspend processing Afghan asylum claims while it reassessed country conditions. In response, detainees at the Woomera Immigration Reception and Processing Centre staged a mass hunger strike. The Department of Immigration reported that 269 people were involved. Up to 70 detainees sewed their lips both to prove that they were not eating and to symbolically demonstrate their powerlessness and silencing by Australian authorities. Similar but smaller-scale hunger strikes were staged at other detention centres around the country. Although only Afghan asylum seekers were directly affected by the policy 'freeze', asylum seekers of several nationalities joined in the strike and its stated objectives broadened beyond demanding the resumption of processing Afghan claims to include claims for an improvement of conditions in detention.

The protest lasted for 16 days and there are no reports of force feeding on the public record, though several people were medically rehydrated. It is unclear whether regulation 5.35 was invoked. The strike was concluded following protracted negotiations between strikers and the Australian government mediated by the Immigration Detention Advisory Group.[18] The Australian government agreed to resume assessing claims and to review the standards of detention at Woomera. Further mass hunger strikes were staged at Woomera in May and July the same year as conditions in detention did not improve.

3. Motivation for Hunger Strikes by Asylum Seekers

Understanding hunger strikes by asylum seekers requires consideration of the asylum seekers' legal status and of the detention environment that compounds existing psychological stress and coping. Developing an understanding of the particular reasons for each hunger strike is important in negotiating an end to a hunger strike without needing to invoke regulation 5.35.

Australian authorities have, however, tended to interpret hunger strikes as manipulative efforts by failed asylum seekers to obtain visas, and, in so doing, have failed to recognize that protests often arise in relation to the conditions in detention, issues on which negotiation is possible. In response to the hunger strikes in January 2002 the Minister for Immigration was

16 Defined in the document to mean not consuming food and/or drink within 24 hours.

17 Information from Freedom from Information request provided to Sean Parnell from *The Australian* newspaper. Email from Sean Parnell to authors (14 December 2010).

18 The Immigration Detention Advisory Group was formed in February 2001. It was formed to give independent advice to the Minister for Immigration regarding detention issues. The IDAG was replaced by the Detention Health Advisory Group (DeHAG) in 2006.

highly critical of the hunger strikers. He publicly labelled them 'extreme' and likened the strikers to 'hijackers', saying that they were manipulative and trying to 'force decisions that they may not be entitled to receive'.[19] The current Minister for Immigration, Chris Bowen, in response to hunger strikes in November 2010, stated, 'any protest which is designed to change the result of refugee applications will not work'.[20]

While hunger strike as protest is intended to influence another person or authority, to interpret it as only manipulative is unhelpful in resolving a very serious and potentially fatal form of protest. Hunger-strike literature from a range of medical, legal, political science and semiotic disciplines outlines hunger strike as an act of communication intended to engage the conscience of its target.[21] Maud Ellmann states that hunger strike as protest is 'staged to trick the conscience of its viewers, forcing them to recognise that they are implicated in the spectacle that they behold'.[22] It is very often an action taken by a person that feels powerless in a given situation and cannot see any other course of action that they expect to result in their complaints being heard. When challenged about the coercive and potentially manipulative nature of hunger striking, Gandhi defended his actions by explaining that he intended only to provoke people to reflect on their own actions and to act in accordance with the values they claimed to hold; and that, therefore, hunger strike was really the 'coercion of conscience'.[23]

These themes were reiterated in interviews conducted with former immigration detainees. Their responses demonstrated that their fasts had a number of functions and characteristics. Several respondents stated that they felt unheard and they wanted the Australian public and international community to know about their detention and the conditions of detention. Strikes arising from this motivation were typically aimed at attracting media attention:

---

19 The Minister denied the extent of the hunger strikes, claiming several strikers were secretly eating. See interviews with the Hon. Phillip Ruddock in Maxine McKew, 'Ruddock Explains Decision to Restart Refugee Claims Process', Australian Broadcasting Corporation ('ABC'), *The 7.30 Report*, 24 January 2002, at http://www.abc.net.au/7.30/content/2002/s465903.htm, accessed 16 December 2010; Tony Jones, 'Woomera Detention Centre Faces Uncertain Future', ABC, *Lateline*, 29 January 2002, at http://www.abc.net.au/lateline/stories/s469176.htm, accessed 16 December 2010; 'Force-feeding and the Law', ABC, *Law Report*, 16 July 2002, via http://www.abc.net.au/rn/lawreport/stories/2002/606948.htm, accessed 16 December 2010; 'Hunger Strikers Keep Pressure on Australia', BBC, London, 27 January 2002, at http://news.bbc.co.uk/2/hi/asia-pacific/1784415.stm, accessed 10 June 2010; 'PM Claims Detainees are Morally Intimidating Australians', ABC, Sydney, 25 January 2002, at http://www.abc.net.au/news/newsitems/200201/s466277.htm, accessed 10 June 2010.

20 'Asylum Seekers Sew Mouths Shut', ABC, *Lateline*, 19 November 2010, via http://www.abc.net.au/lateline/content/2010/s3072545.htm, accessed 16 December 2010.

21 Joseph Pugliese, 'Penal Asylum: Refugees, Ethics, Hospitality' (2002) 1(1) *Borderlands E-Journal*, at http://www.borderlands.net.au/vol1no1_2002/pugliese.html, accessed 22 December 2010; Don Sneed and Harry W. Stonecipher, 'Prisoner Fasting as Symbolic Speech: The Ultimate Speech-action Test' (1989), 72nd Annual Meeting of the Association for Education in Journalism and Mass Communication, Washington D.C., August 1989; Lionel Wee, 'The Hunger Strike as a Communicative Act: Intention Without Responsibility' (2007) 17 *Journal of Linguistic Anthropology* 61–76; Kim F. Hall, '"Use Words Not Your Body": The Hunger that has No Name' (2008) 18(2) *Women & Performance: A Journal of Feminist Theory* 169–80.

22 Ellmann, *The Hunger Artists*, 17.

23 Parekh, *Gandhi's Political Philosophy*, 161.

> if people knew about detentions, detention wouldn't be 500k away from a city. It would have been inside a city if people were supporting it. But people are not supporting it. It's something that people don't know about. Now we just need to make sure that they know ... peacefully doesn't answer anything because there is no journos here. We need to get journos here and how we can do it? ... to make a scene, have a story for a TV or radio or newspaper to put that budget for journalists to fly in there and see us because they had to come from Adelaide and it was like 500k away. So they needed a good story. People sewing their lips in detention was a good story. ('Hassan', Iran)

Other strikes were intended to exert pressure to achieve a specific outcome such as the resumption of asylum-claims processing, improvements in particular conditions such as access to telephones, better food, or greater access to education and social interaction. In such cases respondents were able to articulate what they hoped to achieve and to locate their decision to go on hunger strike to a specific or general policy initiative of the government[24] or to a more local objective such as access to telephones:

> We just nothing to do, we just wanted to just make a call and that's it. No other thing else. We protest ourselves like just the best way we have to do. Do hunger strike because we have no idea to do anything. It's unreasonable to us, we can't handle that. ('Farid', Iran)

Respondents also talked about the highly controlled and regulated detention environment and the impact this had on their sense of self and autonomy. Hunger striking was a way of asserting some form of self-determination:

> Of course, the protest helped. Because at least I did something for my rights. Because if I didn't do those things, nothing different between me and this table. With me? I got a soul. I got a mind. I got thinking. While this table ... of course, I wouldn't stay like that. ('Zak', Iran)

It is important to distinguish hunger strike from suicide and other forms of self-harm in that, although it undoubtedly harms the body, there is rarely a desire to die. Rather, a hunger strike is an effort to have one's complaints heard and responded to. It is a communicative act intended to operate on the conscience of its target and other spectators, in this case the Australian immigration authorities and the Australian public:

> 'Khader': So we did in 2001 hunger strike there, we just stop eating, but just drinking. No eating, just drinking, cos you can't survive without water.
> Interviewer: So there was never an intention to die from it?
> 'Khader': No! ... I myself, if I wanted to die, why I have to come to Australia to die? I would die in my country. We just wanted to show them, we won't eat

[24] Such as that articulated by respondent 'Issaq' in relation to the introduction of temporary protection visas set out above.

> the food unless you listen to us, unless you solve our problem. At least let the media come to see the situation and let the people know what kind of a place we are in. (Khader, Afghanistan)

While these quotes demonstrate a conscious act to use hunger strikes as a form of protest, psychiatrists have documented that the reasons for food refusal among asylum seekers may be for more complex or even mixed reasons.[25] Hunger strikes by asylum seekers may have elements of self-harm or be an indication of possible mental illness. Detention centres hold many individuals who have been exposed to high levels of trauma either in their countries of origin or during their journey to Australia. After arrival, other factors may contribute to or exacerbate existing psychological distress, including detention, separation from family, and stress associated with the asylum application process.[26] This is demonstrated in the following case example:[27]

> A young male detainee commenced a hunger strike in a remote detention centre after his claim for refugee status had been rejected. The initial strike was a protest about his treatment in detention, which he alleged had involved a period of solitary confinement and physical restraint. During the first strike, he was rehydrated intravenously under regulation 5.35. Some months later he again refused food and was rehydrated and fed through a nasogastric tube on several occasions under regulation 5.35. He developed symptoms of severe depression with associated weight loss of over 10 kg. After 2 months of failed treatment with an antidepressant, he was transferred to a metropolitan hospital. Attending clinicians judged that he was no longer on active hunger strike and that his symptoms of anorexia, hopelessness, loss of interest, and vague suicidal thoughts amounted to clinical depression. Electroconvulsive therapy, intravenous hydration and nasogastric feeding were recommended by the treating staff. The patient refused consent, leading to regulation 5.35 being invoked.

It is important for authorities not to interpret hunger strike simply as manipulative behaviour, but rather to sincerely engage with the hunger striker(s) at the earliest moment to determine the reasons for that particular strike and the competence of the individual(s) in deciding to fast. These two factors are critical in developing an effective response to the hunger strike, one that enables an end to the fast without needing to force feed that, while it may preserve life in the immediate, is likely to exacerbate feelings of powerlessness and frustration that are motivating factors in several hunger strikes. Force feeding also does not necessarily cause the individual to end his fast, as demonstrated by Mr Abdul Rahman

---

[25] Silove et al., 'Ethical Considerations', 410; M. Kenny, D. Silove and Z. Steel, 'Legal and Ethical Implications of Medically Enforced Feeding of Detained Asylum Seekers on Hunger Strike' (2004) 180(5) *Medical Journal of Australia* 237–40.

[26] D. Silove, Z. Steel and C. Watters, 'Policies of Deterrence and the Mental Health of Asylum Seekers' (2000) 284 *Journal of the American Medical Association* 604–11.

[27] Case example from Kenny, Silove and Steel, 'Legal and Ethical implications', 237.

Shalabi, a detainee at Guantanamo Bay who has been on hunger strike for four years and who has been forcibly fed through a naso-gastric tube over 3,000 times.[28]

4. Effects of Hunger Strike

The physical effects of a hunger strike are profound, long lasting, and can result in death. A hunger strike may involve the refusal of food but with the striker continuing to take fluids including water, tea or broth. If there is a refusal of fluids, deterioration of the striker's health is accelerated and death is expected to occur between seven and 14 days. Death from a hunger strike involving food refusal but taking fluids by an individual who is well nourished and healthy at the start of the strike is expected to occur after six to eight weeks.[29] The effect of hunger strike on the body's immune system increases the risk of infection, and many hunger strikers die from a secondary infection before malnourishment has reached a fatal stage.[30]

The physical effects of hunger strike vary between individuals, but medical literature predicts the following:[31]

- In the first three days the individual experiences severe hunger pangs and stomach cramps. There is a measurable reduction in muscle strength and immune system functioning.
- After one week the individual experiences dramatic weight loss. The individual's medical condition progressively deteriorates with every system in the body adversely affected.
- From week two onwards the individual's vital organs begin to atrophy. The pulse slows, blood pressure falls, and the individual experiences dizziness, lethargy, faintness and headaches. Concentration is significantly impaired and the individual becomes apathetic and bedridden.
- Between 35 and 42 days the oculomotor muscles become paralysed. Vision is seriously impaired as is the individual's ability to swallow water. Compulsive vomiting occurs. This phase lasts approximately one week and once it passes, the individual is left physically weakened, sleeps extensively, loses awareness of their surroundings, and often becomes incoherent.

---

[28] Affidavit of Dr Sondra Crosby submitted as evidence in *Saleh Abdulla Al-Oshen v Obama*, Civil Action No: 05 – 0520 (RMU) in the United States District Court for the District of Columbia, 2 November 2009, at http://humanrights.ucdavis.edu/projects/the-guantanamo-testimonials-project/testimonies/testimomies-of-lawyers/ramsey_shalabi.pdf, accessed 16 December 2010.

[29] Department of Health (UK), *Offender Health: Guidelines for the Clinical Management of People Refusing Food in Detention*, August 2009, via http://www.dh.gov.uk/publications, accessed 16 December 2010, 8. The existence of illness or disease such as heart problems, diabetes or kidney damage presents a heightened risk and death can occur as early as three weeks.

[30] Ibid.

[31] International Criminal Tribunal for the Former Yugoslavia, *Voluntary Protest Fasts: Information for Detainees* (2009), 5–7.

- Death occurs anywhere from day 40 onwards.[32]

There is extensive evidence that a person's cognitive functioning and psychological state also progressively deteriorate throughout a hunger strike. Irritability, impaired capacity for interpreting data, and irrational or illogical thought patterns are common features.[33] This reduction in cognitive competence in the latter phases of a hunger strike has particular significance for legal, medical and other professionals working with a hunger striker. For this reason the World Medical Association recommends legal and medical personnel take comprehensive instructions from a person entering a hunger strike at the earliest point possible.[34]

Recovery from a hunger strike is also dangerous. Voluntary re-feeding following a strike of five days or more carries dangers of pulmonary oedema (excess water accumulating in tissues, including the lungs), encephalopathy (damage or malfunction of the brain usually caused by liver damage or kidney failure), and cardiac failure, among other serious medical consequences. Hospitalization to enable close medical supervision of re-feeding is recommended for the first several days post hunger strike.[35]

5. Involuntary Feeding

There are a number of medical interventions possible when a person is on hunger strike, including treatments for secondary infections, relief of pain, rehydration, and feeding through a naso-gastric tube. Feeding through a naso-gastric tube is an intrusive procedure, often causing severe discomfort and pain. When the procedure is performed against the person's will it is termed 'force feeding' and the effects are amplified. Sylvia Pankhurst described being force fed:

> Presently I heard footsteps approaching, collecting outside my cell. I was strangled with fear, cold and stunned, yet alert to every sound. The door opened … not the doctors, but a crowd of wardresses filled the doorway … I struggled, but was overcome. There were six of them, all much bigger and stronger than I. They flung me on my back on the bed, and held me down firmly by shoulders and wrists, hips, knees and ankles. Then the doctors came stealing in. Someone seized me by the head and thrust a sheet under my chin. My eyes were shut. I set my teeth and tightened my lips over them with all my strength. A man's hands were trying to force open my mouth; my breath was coming so fast that I felt as though I should suffocate. His fingers were striving to pull my lips apart – getting inside. I felt them and

32 See also Michael Peel, 'Hunger Strikes: Understanding the Underlying Physiology will Help Doctors Provide Proper Advice' (1997) 315(7112) *British Medical Journal* 829–30.

33 Wei and Brendel, 'Psychiatry and Hunger Strikes', 75.

34 World Medical Association, *'Declaration on Hunger Strikers'*.

35 Peel, 'Hunger Strikes'; Department of Health (UK), *Offender Health*, 9.

> a steel instrument pressing round my gums, feeling for gaps in my teeth … Then something gradually forced my jaws apart as a screw was turned; the pain was like having teeth drawn. They were trying to get the tube down my throat. They got it down, I suppose, though I was unconscious of anything save a mad revolt of struggling, for they said at last: 'That's all!' and I vomited as the tube came up.[36]

In her account Pankhurst goes on to describe the physical restraint and procedure as an invasion of her personal integrity 'as an oral rape that violates the essence of the self.'[37] Little has changed in the century since Pankhurst's experience. Regulation 5.35 of the *Migration Regulations 1994* permits the use of physical restraint and/or sedatives. A respondent described his experience:

> My hunger strike was about 21 days … I lost nearly 25 kilo when I was on that. The reason I break it, I couldn't move nothing. I was just lying there and I didn't know what's going on around me. Suddenly I saw they put their syringe through my nose, through my thing and it was really hurting in my nose. It was *really* hurtful. They broke my fast. I was kind of like fainted … It was terrible. They forced me … they hold my hands and they put the syringe in my nose by force …. ('Ismail', Iran)

Force feeding is an intrusive procedure that causes physical pain and may cause medical damage to the hunger striker. It also has an existential aspect in that it further erodes a person's free will. As such, the decision to feed a person against their will is a serious one with critical legal, ethical and medical considerations.

6. Legal Issues

6.1 Regulation 5.35 of the Migration Regulations

Regulation 5.35 of the *Migration Regulations 1994* (Cth) empowers the Secretary of the Department of Immigration to authorize medical treatment to be given to a person in immigration detention without their consent. The regulation is invoked when a Commonwealth Medical Officer or a registered medical practitioner provides written advice to the Secretary of the Department of Immigration that:

- if medical treatment is not given to a particular detainee, there will be a serious risk to his or her life or health; and

---

36 Ellmann, *The Hunger Artists*, 33.
37 Ibid.

- the detainee refuses to give, or is not reasonably capable of giving, consent for the medical treatment.

The Secretary can then authorize non-consensual treatment, including the use of 'reasonable force'. Authorization by the Secretary does not compel medical practitioners to enforce treatment if such action is contrary to their 'ethical, moral or religious convictions'.[38] There is no reference in the Australian Parliamentary *Hansard* that this regulation received any attention or debate at the time it was introduced. Nor has it been the subject of any challenge in Australian courts. The Australian Human Rights Commission has recommended that the regulation be repealed as it believes the regulation may be in breach of Article 10.1 of the International Covenant on Civil and Political Rights, which guarantees that detainees shall be treated with humanity and with respect for their inherent dignity.[39]

Regulation 5.35 is the only regulation relating to the care and management of immigration detainees. In the case of challenging a decision to force feed a detainee, an argument could be made that a decision made pursuant to this regulation cannot be justified by reference to the *Migration Act 1958*. The source of the power to make this regulation comes from s. 273 of the *Migration Act*, which refers only to the power to make regulations regarding the conduct and supervision of detainees and powers of those performing functions in connection with the supervision of detainees. It could be argued that the power contained in regulation 5.35 is *ultra vires* in that it goes beyond such a function.[40]

The regulation directly contravenes the ethical standards set by the World Medical Association (WMA) Declaration on Hunger Strikes (the Malta Declaration), which cautions against non-consensual medical treatment of hunger strikers. The WMA recommends that, when a decision to refuse food has been made by a competent individual, those wishes should be respected, including when those wishes are to the individual's detriment including to the extent of death. The Malta Declaration ends with an emphatic statement against force feeding:

> Forcible feeding is never ethically acceptable. Even if intended to benefit, feeding accompanied by threats, coercion, force or use of physical restraints is a form of inhuman and degrading treatment. Equally unacceptable is the forced feeding of some detainees in order to intimidate or coerce other hunger strikers to stop fasting.[41]

If regulation 5.35 is indeed invalid, we should also consider whether there are any broader principles from the common law that would authorize non-consensual medical treatment.

---

38 *Migration Regulations 1994*, reg. 5.35(6). For a discussion on medical ethics see Kenny, Silove and Steel, 'Legal and Ethical Implications'.

39 Human Rights and Equal Opportunity Commission, *Those Who've Come Across the Seas*, 124.

40 For further discussion see Mary Anne Kenny, 'Force Feeding Asylum Seekers' (2002) 27(3) *Alternative Law Journal* 107–11.

41 World Medical Association, *'Declaration on Hunger Strikers'*.

6.2 Common Law Right to Self-determination

There is a long-established common law principle that the right to refuse medical treatment is part of a broader right – an individual's right of self-determination. A person of full mental capacity has the right to choose whether to eat or not. Even if that refusal is tantamount to suicide, a person cannot be compelled to eat or be forcibly fed. A medical practitioner who performs such medical treatment without his or her patient's consent commits an assault or trespass upon the individual.[42]

The common law right to refuse food and water was recently considered by the Supreme Court of Western Australia in *Brightwater Care Group (Inc) v Rossiter*.[43] That case involved a quadriplegic man who was not terminally ill. Mr Rossiter told his residential care facility that he wished to die and directed them to discontinue the provision of nutrition and general hydration. Martin CJ made declarations that Brightwater was neither required nor entitled to use force to feed and hydrate Mr Rossiter against his wishes. In doing so, he articulated the right of self-determination recognized by the common law:

> [A]n individual of full capacity is not obliged to give consent to medical treatment, nor is a medical practitioner or other service provider under any obligation to provide such treatment without consent, even if the failure to treat will result in the loss of the patient's life.[44]

The court went on to state that a medical practitioner who provides treatment contrary to the wishes of a mentally competent patient breaks the law by committing a trespass against that patient.[45]

6.3 Possible Limitations on the Right

The right of personal autonomy and self-determination may be subject to some limitation when dealing with prisoners or detainees who refuse food and/or water. This is an issue that has received little attention in Australia; however, there have been developments in other jurisdictions, such as the United Kingdom and the United States.

In Australia the issue of force feeding a detainee has been considered on only two occasions. The first was in 1993 in *Schneidas v Corrective Services Commission & Others*,[46] in which a prisoner sought an injunction to restrain the defendant from force feeding him. Justice Lee in the Supreme Court of New South Wales would not grant the injunction. He based his decision on s. 16(2) of the *Prisons Act 1952 (NSW)*, finding that, where a prisoner's health reached a point where there was a likely loss of organ function, forced feeding constituted 'medical treatment' under that section and was therefore authorized. In doing

42 See *B v Croydon Health Authority* [1995] 1 All ER 683, 686.

43 *Brightwater Care Group (Inc) v Rossiter* [2009] WASC 229.

44 Ibid., [26].

45 Ibid., [31]. See also *H Ltd v J and Anor* [2010] SASC 176.

46 Unreported Supreme Court of NSW, Administrative Law division, Lee J. No 4082 of 1983, 8 April 1983 (BC 8300004).

so, Justice Lee doubted there existed a common law justification for force feeding a prisoner against their will.

As discussed in the Introduction, the Supreme Court of NSW granted an interim order permitting the Department of Immigration to force feed two detained asylum seekers on hunger strike in 1992.[47]

Courts in the UK and the US have engaged in a balancing of the rights of the individual against a number of state interests. These include such 'paternal' interests as the preservation of life and the prevention of suicide. There are also 'institutional' interests, such as the fulfilment of the duty to provide medical care and the enforcement of prison security and order.

In the UK there has been a gradual shift toward a rights-based approach and the preservation of the individual's rights. In *Secretary of State for the Home Department v Robb*,[48] Thorpe J rejected the previous paternalistic approach as set out in the 1909 authority *Leigh v Gladstone*,[49] which related to the force feeding of a British suffragette. In *Leigh v Gladstone*, Lord Alverstone CJ directed a jury that it was the duty of prison officials to preserve the health of prisoners in their custody, including force feeding. Justice Thorpe considered the arguments regarding the countervailing state interests and concluded:

> It seems to me that within this jurisdiction there is perhaps a stronger emphasis on the right of the individual's self-determination when the balance comes to be struck between that right and any countervailing interests of the state. So this decision is not a borderline one ... The right of the defendant to determine his future is plain. That right is not diminished by his status as a detained prisoner.

The UK now has the *Mental Capacity Act 2005*, which provides that a person must be assumed to have capacity unless it is established that they lack capacity and must not be considered unable to make a decision merely because they make an unwise decision. The Act enables individuals to make 'advanced directives' as to their future medical treatment should they become incapacitated in the future.[50] Specific guidance for prison officials for dealing with hunger strikes in a prison setting is also provided in a Department of Health manual.[51]

Courts in the United States have considered whether force feeding of prisoners is acceptable in the context of constitutionally enshrined rights to freedom of speech and privacy. The First Amendment freedom of speech clause, it is argued, protects a prisoner's hunger strike, and the force feeding of a prisoner against his or her will to prevent death would violate constitutional rights to privacy. However, courts in the US have generally found that the state's interests in preserving life and maintaining order and security in

---

47 *Department of Immigration, Local Government and Ethnic Affairs v Gek Bouy Mok*; unreported.

48 [1995] 1 All ER 677 at 681, referred to with approval in *R (On the Application of Wilkinson) v. The Responsible Medical Officer Broadmoor Hospital* [2001] EWCA Civ 1545 (22 October 2001). The decision in the *Secretary of State for the Home Department v Robb* was followed in *Re W (adult: refusal of medical treatment)* decision delivered on 24 April 2002 by Dame Elizabeth Butler-Sloss P in the Family Division of the High Court.

49 (1909) 26 TLR 139.

50 See *Mental Capacity Act 2 2005* (UK) ss. 24–6.

51 Department of Health (UK), *Offender Health*.

prisons outweigh an inmate's rights to privacy.[52] United States government officials at Guantanamo Bay have relied on state interests arguments to defend the force feeding of detainees, including the preservation of life and security concerns.[53]

The above-mentioned cases are instructive in drawing out some of the legal concerns facing state authorities in responding to imprisoned hunger strikers. It is important to note, however, that (particularly refused) asylum seekers, not holding citizenship of the detaining state, have a fundamentally different relationship with that state which further problematizes an already complex situation. As one commentator notes,

> [A]sylum seekers wish to claim citizenship and hence the protection of a state in which they have not been domiciled previously. In rejecting such claims, the state effectively expresses its intent to disqualify the asylum seekers from the protection it is obliged to provide to its citizens and other residents. Thus, asserting the parens patriae principle over such individuals is a contradictory action on the part of the state. While force-feeding other categories of hunger strikers may be solely directed at keeping them alive in prison, it can be claimed that an overriding motive for so doing in asylum seekers is to facilitate their forced return to the country of origin.[54]

7. Rights of the Government versus the Rights of the Individual

In Australia, if a challenge was brought on the power of state authorities to engage in non-consensual medical treatment, the rights of the individual would have to be balanced against the government's various interests in immigration detention centres. Hunger strikes by detainees place the Australian government in a difficult political position. The Department of Immigration believes that, if it were to give in to the demands of hunger strikers, the incidence of such protests would increase. This would place an increased number of detainees at risk of harm and the operation of the centres would become unmanageable.[55] The former Minister for Immigration described hunger strikes as a form of 'moral blackmail'[56]

---

52 Nearly 15 state and federal courts in the United States have found that prison officials may force feed a hunger-striking prisoner. See Mara Silver, 'Testing Cruzan: Prisoners and the Constitutional Question of Self-starvation' (2005) 58(2) *Stanford Law Review* 631–62, at 632.

53 Kristine Huskey and Stephen Xenakis, 'Hunger Strikes: Challenges to the Guantanamo Detainee Health Care Policy' (2009) 30(783) *Whittier Law Review*, via http://papers.ssrn.com/sol3/papers.cfm?abstract_id=2092086 (accessed 22 August 2012). To date there has been no court case relating to the ability to refuse medical treatment of the Guantanamo detainees. The hunger striking cases that have come before the courts relate to treatment of hunger strikers and lawyers' access to medical records.

54 Silove et al., 'Ethical Considerations', 410.

55 Human Rights and Equal Opportunity Commission, *Those Who've Come Across the Seas*, 107.

56 'Labor Rethinks Detention Stance', ABC, *Lateline*, 28 January 2002, at http://www.abc.net.au/lateline/stories/s468643.htm, accessed 16 December 2010.

and accused hunger strikers of 'trying to manipulate' the government.[57] Invoking regulation 5.35 was claimed to be necessary for preserving the life of detainees: 'I think the State has a responsibility to ensure in those circumstances, that they survive, and that's what we've sought to do.'[58]

The Australian government also has another interest in trying to ensure that no hunger striker dies. It has, for some time, been facing significant domestic and international pressure over its policy of mandatory detention. If an asylum seeker were to die as a result of a hunger strike, it could further aggravate an already tense political situation. The question arises as to whether these arguments are sufficiently compelling to justify forced treatment. Statements made by Australian government officials reduce possible responses by the state to only two options – order non-consensual medical treatment of a detainee, or do nothing and permit the detainee to die.

8. A Way Forward

It is our view that the current approach is too simplistic. Authorities have a range of responses at their disposal that would enable the state to meet its duty to preserve life, while also maintaining its policy objectives. It is important to note that most strikers do not wish to die, but want a resolution to their problems and to feel that they have been heard. This desire to live provides the detaining authority with considerable room for negotiation.

The UK Health Department, the International Criminal Tribunal for the Former Yugoslavia and the World Medical Association all recommend that the detaining authority allow early independent medical assessment for hunger strikers.[59] The independent doctor's role is to ascertain the competence of the person undertaking the strike, to advise the striker of the likely course of the strike and the medical implications at each stage, and to establish a clear understanding of the striker's informed intentions (an 'advanced directive') should their condition deteriorate and they lapse into unconsciousness or a state of incoherence.

The Department of Immigration should establish a panel consisting of independent physicians, psychiatrists, psychologists, legal officers and ethicists to develop comprehensive guidelines for the management of hunger strikes that recognizes the government's duty of care towards detainees and which draws upon international best practice in managing hunger strike in places of detention. Guidelines should provide that the assessment and treatment of detainees on hunger strike would similarly be treated by a panel of independent physicians who would consider questions of autonomy. While every effort should be made to negotiate a successful end to hunger strikes, detainees who are otherwise competent and capable of deciding treatment for themselves should be able to refuse treatment even if this leads to death. In this sense asylum seekers should be treated like any other patient who

[57] Jones and Bradford, 'Woomera Detention Centre Faces Uncertain Future'.

[58] 'Force-feeding and the Law'.

[59] Department of Health (UK), *Offender Health*; World Medical Association, *'Declaration on Hunger Strikers'*.

refuses medical treatment: their immigration status should not mean they are subject to a different or lesser standard.

Regulation 5.35 of the *Migration Act 1994* should be repealed. There is no clear common law authority in Australia regarding the non-consensual medical treatment of detainees. Most states in Australia have legislation that provides for the ability of competent adults to make an 'advanced health directive' allowing individuals, in consultation with a physician, to make decisions regarding their future medical treatment, in which they can either consent to or refuse future medical treatment.[60] There would seem to be no reason why such directives could not be used in cases involving asylum seekers in detention. If it is decided that a person lacks capacity to consent to treatment then authorities should seek orders for medical treatment through the courts in accordance with current mental health legislation rather than through an administrative process.

Conclusion

The prevention and successful management of hunger strikes by detained asylum seekers is an important issue across a number of jurisdictions. As well as state interest arguments of preserving life and maintaining security and order in detention centres, hunger strikes engage critical and competing human rights including the rights to life, to self-determination, to privacy, and to freedom from inhuman and degrading treatment. It is incumbent upon states that detain asylum seekers to protect those rights not unavoidably limited through the pursuit of detention itself. Force feeding is, in the authors' opinion, an unnecessary violation of an individual's rights to self-determination, and to be treated with dignity and respect. As previously noted, public comments by Australian government ministers indicate an overly simplistic and judgemental approach to hunger strikes by asylum seekers, leading to a narrowed range of responses. A more appropriate course of action would engage meaningfully with asylum seekers at the earliest possible moment to advise them on the physical consequences and to determine their mental competence and their future wishes. In this way the competence and integrity of the strikers is recognized and respected.

References

Anderson, Patrick, 'To Lie Down to Death for Days' (2004) 18(6) *Cultural Studies* 816–46.

'Asylum Seekers Sew Mouths Shut', ABC, *Lateline*, 19 November 2010, via http://www.abc.net.au/lateline/content/2010/s3072545.htm, accessed 16 December 2010.

Briskman, Linda, Susie Latham and Chris Goddard, *Human Rights Overboard: Seeking Asylum in Australia* (Melbourne: Scribe Publications, 2008).

Centre for Constitutional Rights, *The Guantánamo Prisoner Hunger Strikes & Protests: February 2002–August 2005* (A Special Report, New York, 2005).

60 See for example *Guardianship and Administration Act 1990* (WA).

Department of Health (UK), *Offender Health: Guidelines for the Clinical Management of People Refusing Food in Detention*, August 2009, via http://www.dh.gov.uk/publications, accessed 16 December 2010.

Ellmann, Maud, *The Hunger Artists: Starving, Writing and Imprisonment* (London: Virago Press, 1993).

'Force-feeding and the Law', ABC, *Law Report*, 16 July 2002, via http://www.abc.net.au/rn/lawreport/stories/2002/606948.htm, accessed 16 December 2010.

Green, Janette P. and Kathy Eagar, 'The Health of People in Australian Immigration Detention Centres' (2010) 192(2) *Medical Journal of Australia* 65–70.

Hall, Kim F., '"Use Words Not Your Body": The Hunger that has No Name' (2008) 18(2) *Women & Performance: A Journal of Feminist Theory* 169–80.

Howard, Paul, 'The Long Kesh Hunger Strikers: 25 Years Later' (2006) 33(4) *Social Justice* 69–91.

Human Rights and Equal Opportunity Commission, *Those Who've Come Across the Seas: The Report of the Commission's Inquiry into the Detention of Unauthorised Arrivals* (Canberra: HREOC, 1998).

Human Rights and Equal Opportunity Commission HREOC, *A Last Resort? National Inquiry into Children in Immigration Detention* (Sydney: HREOC, 2004).

'Hunger Strikers Keep Pressure on Australia', BBC, London, 27 January 2002, at http://news.bbc.co.uk/2/hi/asia-pacific/1784415.stm, accessed 10 June 2010.

Huskey, Kristine and Stephen Xenakis, 'Hunger Strikes: Challenges to the Guantanamo Detainee Health Care Policy' (2009) 30(783) *Whittier Law. Review*, via http://papers.ssrn.com/sol3/papers.cfm?abstract_id=2092086, accessed 22 August 2012.

International Criminal Tribunal for the Former Yugoslavia, *Voluntary Protest Fasts: Information for Detainees* (2009).

Joint Standing Committee on Foreign Affairs, Defence and Trade, *A Report on Visits to Immigration Detention Centres* (Commonwealth of Australia, Canberra, 2001).

Jones, Tony and Gillian Bradford, 'Woomera Detention Centre Faces Uncertain Future', ABC, *Lateline*, 29 January 2002, at http://www.abc.net.au/lateline/stories/s469176.htm, accessed 16 December 2010.

Kenny, Mary Anne, 'Force Feeding Asylum Seekers' (2002) 27(3) *Alternative Law Journal* 107–11.

Kenny, M., D. Silove and Z. Steel, 'Legal and Ethical Implications of Medically Enforced Feeding of Detained Asylum Seekers on Hunger Strike' (2004) 180(5) *Medical Journal of Australia* 237–40.

'Labor Rethinks Detention Stance', ABC, *Lateline*, 28 January 2002, at http://www.abc.net.au/lateline/stories/s468643.htm, accessed 16 December 2010.

McKew, Maxine, 'Ruddock Explains Decision to Restart Refugee Claims Process', ABC, *The 7.30 Report*, 24 January 2002, at http://www.abc.net.au/7.30/content/2002/s465903.htm, accessed 16 December 2010.

Newman, Louise, Michael Dudley and Zachary Steel, 'Asylum, Detention and Mental Health in Australia' (1998) 27(3) *Refugee Survey Quarterly* 110–27.

Parekh, Bhikhu, *Gandhi's Political Philosophy: A Critical Examination* (London: Palgrave Macmillan, 1989).

Peel, Michael, 'Hunger Strikes: Understanding the Underlying Physiology will Help Doctors Provide Proper Advice' (1997) 315(7112) *British Medical Journal* 829–30.

'PM Claims Detainees are Morally Intimidating Australians', ABC, Sydney, 25 January 2002, at http://www.abc.net.au/news/newsitems/200201/s466277.htm, accessed 10 June 2010.

Pugliese, Joseph, 'Penal Asylum: Refugees, Ethics, Hospitality' (2002) 1 *Borderlands E-Journal*, at http://www.borderlands.net.au/vol1no1_2002/pugliese.html, accessed 22 December 2010.

Silove, D., Z. Steel and C. Watters, 'Policies of Deterrence and the Mental Health of Asylum Seekers' (2000) 284 *Journal of the American Medical Association* 604–11.

Silove, Derrick and Zachary Steel, *The Mental Health and Well-being of On-shore Asylum Seekers in Australia* (Psychiatry Research and Teaching Unit, University of New South Wales, Liverpool 1998).

Silove, Derrick, Patricia Austin and Zachary Steel, 'No Refuge from Terror: The Impact of Detention on the Mental Health of Trauma-affected Refugees Seeking Asylum in Australia' (2007) 44(3) *Transcultural Psychiatry* 359–93.

Silove, Derrick, Jackie Curtis, Catherine Mason and Rise Becker, 'Ethical Considerations in the Management of Asylum Seekers on Hunger Strike' (1996) 276 *Journal of the American Medical Association* 410–15.

Silver, Mara, 'Testing Cruzan: Prisoners and the Constitutional Question of Self-starvation' (2005) 58(2) *Stanford Law Review* 631–62.

Sneed, Don and Harry W. Stonecipher, 'Prisoner Fasting as Symbolic Speech: The Ultimate Speech-action Test' (1989), 72nd Annual Meeting of the Association for Education in Journalism and Mass Communication, Washington D.C., August 1989.

United Nations High Commission for Refugees, 'UNHCR Urges Australia to Review Policy of Detaining Asylum Seekers' (Media Release, 1 February 2002), at http://www.unhcr.org/cgi-bin/texis/vtx/search?page=search&docid=3c5abf1e2&query=hungerstrike, accessed 22 December 2010.

Wee, Lionel, 'The Hunger Strike as a Communicative Act: Intention Without Responsibility' (2007) 17 *Journal of Linguistic Anthropology* 61–76.

Wei, Marlynn and Rebecca W. Brendel, 'Psychiatry and Hunger Strikes' (2010) 23 *Harvard Human Rights Journal* 75–109.

World Medical Association, *Declaration on Hunger Strikers (Declaration of Malta): Adopted by the 43rd World Medical Assembly Malta, November 1991 and editorially revised at the 44th World Medical Assembly Marbella, Spain, September 1992*, at http://www.legislationline.org/documents/action/popup/id/8591, accessed 16 December 2010.

19 ASHGATE **RESEARCH** COMPANION

'Less Coercive Means': The Legal Case for Alternatives to Detention for Refugees, Asylum Seekers and Other Migrants

Alice Edwards[1]

> Is it a crime to be a foreigner? We do not think so.[2]

> It is a gross injustice to deprive of his liberty for significant periods of time a person who has committed no crime and does not intend to do so. No civilised country should willingly tolerate such injustices.[3]

> Cats and dogs enjoy a dedicated statute, right of appeal to an independent board and specific provisions regulating decisions which vary length of detention ... cats and dogs have more protection ... than refugees ....[4]

---

1 Senior Legal Coordinator and Chief, Protection Policy and Legal Advice Section, Division of International Protection, United Nations High Commissioner for Refugees (UNHCR), Geneva. Dr Edwards was previously on the law faculties at the universities of Oxford and Nottingham, and she remains Research Associate, Refugee Studies Centre, University of Oxford; Research Fellow in Law, St Anne's College, Oxford; and Fellow, Human Rights Law Centre, University of Nottingham. This chapter is based on a background paper prepared for UNHCR as an independent expert: A. Edwards, *Back to Basics: The Right to Liberty and Security of Person and 'Alternatives to Detention' of Refugees, Asylum-seekers, Stateless Persons and Other Migrants*, April 2011, PPLA/2011/01.Rev.1, at: http://www.unhcr.org/refworld/docid/4dc935fd2.html [accessed on 3 August 2012]. The views expressed herein are those of the author and do not necessarily reflect those of the UN or the UNHCR.

2 *Saadi v. United Kingdom*, ECtHR, Applic. No. 13229/03, 29 January 2008, per joint partly dissenting opinion of judges Rozakis, Tulkens, Hajiyev, Spielman and Hirvelä (no page or paragraph number).

3 Lord T. Bingham, *The Rule of Law* (London: Allen Lane, 2010), p. 73.

4 M. Daly, 'Refugee Law in Hong Kong: Building the Legal Infrastructure' (2009) 9 *Hong Kong Lawyer* 1, at 15.

1. Introduction

The issue of alternatives to immigration detention is gaining in interest at international and national levels,[5] yet at the same time rates of incarceration are rising.[6] While there are many pragmatic reasons for opting for alternatives to immigration detention – e.g., there is no empirical evidence that detention deters irregular migration, alternatives are significantly cheaper than incarceration, and many enjoy high compliance rates of up to and beyond 90 per cent[7] –, this chapter is concerned with the legal arguments for alternatives to detention. It asks: Is there an obligation under international law on states to make available alternatives to detention for asylum seekers, refugees or other migrants?

It is argued in this chapter that international law requires, at a minimum, that states institute guarantees against arbitrary detention, and that these guarantees necessarily require that non-custodial options are available. With the exception of the jurisprudence of the European Court of Human Rights (ECtHR) (and even there the jurisprudence is inconsistent), this chapter shows that most international courts or bodies now firmly accept that a state must examine whether there are any less intrusive or coercive means of achieving the state objective of migration control without recourse to detention. This position is derived from the international legal principles of reasonableness, proportionality and necessity. The principle of proportionality, in particular, must be read as requiring detention to be a measure of last resort. This presupposes that there are other (first-resort) options available that can match an individual's right to liberty on the one hand with a government's right to control its borders on the other. It follows that the failure of many

---

5 E.g., the United States announced in 2009 its plan to overhaul its immigration detention system and to develop a nationwide alternative to detention programme. The United Kingdom's coalition government announced in 2010 its commitment to end the detention of children and has piloted a number of alternatives to detention in the return phase. Following growing public disapproval of the mandatory and indefinite detention of unauthorized entrants to Australia, the government introduced in 2005 'bridging visas' for those who, despite their cooperation with the authorities, could not be removed. Alongside conditional release, the government funds a number of community supervision or case management alternatives to detention programmes. Under pressure from a decision of the European Court of Human Rights (ECtHR) that found Belgium's detention of children unlawful (see *Muskhadzhiyeva and others v. Belgium*, ECtHR, Applic. No. 41442/07, 19 January 2010), Belgium instituted a programme of open 'return houses' for families, with specialized 'coaching' services. Likewise, further to a number of national court decisions finding Hong Kong's detention practices unlawful, it has instituted a system of release on recognizance supported by social and community services. For further information, see Edwards, *Back to Basics*.

6 The Parliamentary Assembly of the Council of Europe (CoE) noted in 2010 that Member States had 'significantly expanded their use of detention as a response to the arrival of asylum seekers and irregular migrants': Parliamentary Assembly, Council of Europe, Doc. 12105, 11 January 2010, *The Detention of Asylum Seekers and Irregular Migrants in Europe*, Rapporteur Mrs Ana Catarina Mendonça, para. 1 (referring in particular to the UK, France and Italy).

7 For more on the pragmatic or functional arguments in favour of alternatives, see Edwards, *Back to Basics*. For a comparative overview of various models, see A. Edwards, 'Measures of First Resort: Alternatives to Immigration Detention in Comparative Perspective' (2011) 7 *Equal Rights Review* 117–42, at: http://www.equalrightstrust.org/ertdocumentbank/ERR7_alice.pdf [accessed on 3 August 2012].

governments to make available, to test or to systematize alternatives to detention puts their detention laws, policies and practices into direct conflict with international law. Likewise, national systems that do not assess the necessity to detain in each individual case fail to comply with international law. Although alternatives to detention have been on the international agenda for some time, the body of jurisprudence on the matter has not been compiled in one place, nor examined in full. This chapter attempts to do so.

Before setting out the legal case for alternatives to detention, this chapter provides an overview of the various definitions of 'detention' that exist international legal instruments as well as the terminology of 'alternatives to detention', which has no legal meaning *per se* but has entered into general parlance. Articulating the variations in these terms is an important exercise as it informs us whether a particular initiative is correctly labelled as 'detention' or otherwise. There is often a fine line between the two. Following the definitional section, this chapter turns to examine the refugee-specific guarantees against detention and other restrictions on the rights to liberty and to freedom of movement contained in the 1951 Convention relating to the Status of Refugees (1951 Convention) as amended by its 1967 Protocol. This is followed by an examination of developments under international and regional human rights law that point, almost consistently, to an obligation on states to consider and implement less intrusive alternatives to detention. The chapter then briefly summarizes the laws and practices of a number of states and finds support for the position under international law. It evidences that the majority of states possess legally sanctioned alternatives to detention; the problem in many national systems is less one of an absence of law than of implementation.

The chapter discusses neither camp confinement[8] nor the detention of migrants in relation to criminality or threats of terrorism. Nor does this chapter address the many political or other motivations for the heavy reliance on detention as a means of migration control.

2. Definitions

This chapter uses the term 'immigration detention' to refer to the detention of asylum seekers and irregular migrants, either upon seeking entry to a territory, or pending deportation, removal or return. It refers primarily to detention that is administratively authorized, although it also covers judicially sanctioned detention. 'Immigration detention' is to be distinguished from criminal- and security-based forms of detention, which refer respectively to detention or other restrictions on liberty of non-nationals on the grounds of having committed a criminal offence or for national security or terrorism-related reasons.[9]

8 See, instead, A. Edwards, 'The Optional Protocol to the Convention against Torture and the Detention of Refugees' (2008) 57(4) *International and Comparative Law Quarterly* 789–825, which includes a section dealing with the legal arguments around camp confinement policies amounting to a deprivation of liberty.

9 The Equal Rights Trust's study on stateless persons and detention contains sections on both these forms of detention: see ERT, *Unravelling Anomaly: Detention, Discrimination and the Protection Needs of Stateless Persons* (London, July 2010).

There are various definitions of 'detention' at the international level.[10] For the purposes of this chapter, detention is considered to be the full deprivation of liberty in a confined place, such as a prison or a purpose-built closed reception, detention or holding centre. It is not relevant whether the detention is administratively or judicially authorized or sanctioned, nor whether a person has been confined without 'lawful' authority. Detention is at the extreme end of a spectrum of deprivations of liberty. This does not mean, however, that measures short of 'detention' or full confinement are not regulated by international law, nor of interest to this chapter. International law is as much concerned with lesser deprivations of liberty and other restrictions on movement as it is with total confinement in a closed space. Likewise, it is not relevant *where* the deprivation of liberty is carried out – for example, whether on national islands,[11] on

[10] UNHCR has, for example, defined detention as 'confinement within a narrowly bounded or restricted location, including prisons, closed camps, detention facilities or airport transit zones, where freedom of movement is substantially curtailed, and where the only opportunity to leave this limited area is to leave the territory': UNHCR, *Revised Guidelines on Detention of Asylum Seekers and Refugees* (Geneva: UNHCR, 1999). The Optional Protocol to the United Nations Convention against Torture (OPCAT) defines 'place of detention' as 'where persons are or may be deprived of their liberty, either by virtue of an order given by a public authority or at its instigation or with its consent or acquiescence': Article 4(1). The OPCAT also defines 'deprivation of liberty' as 'any form of detention or imprisonment or the placement of a person in a public or private custodial setting which that person is not permitted to leave at will by order of any judicial, administrative or other authority': Article 4(2). The emphasis in relation to the OPCAT is on the physical location of detention, rather than deprivation of liberty *per se*. The European Union's Reception Directive, discussed *infra*, defines 'detention' as 'confinement of an asylum seeker by a Member State within a particular place, where the applicant is deprived of his or her freedom of movement'. The Inter-American Commission on Human Rights (I-ACmHR) has defined 'deprivation of liberty' as '[a]ny form of detention, imprisonment, institutionalization, or custody of a person in a public or private institution which that person is not permitted to leave at will, by order of or under *de facto* control of a judicial, administrative or any other authority': I-ACmHR, *Principles and Best Practices on the Protection of Persons Deprived of Liberty in the Americas*, approved by the Commission during its 131st regular period of sessions, 3–14 March 2008, General Provision.

[11] See, e.g., *Guzzardi v. Italy*, ECtHR, Applic. No. 7367/76, 6 November 1980. See, also, the litigation around *habeas corpus* guarantees at Guantanamo Bay in relation to the foreign terror suspects detained there, discussed *supra*. In fact, the use of islands as a means of detention has a long history. The impeachment of the Earl of Clarendon occurred because of his unlawful exercise of executive power by his practice of dispatching prisoners to outlying parts of what was then the United Kingdom ('to islands, garrisons, and other places') for the very reason that in those places the writ of *habeas corpus* did not apply: see *Clarendon* (1668) 6 St Tr 291, at 291, 330, 296, as referred to in Bingham, *Rule of Law*, p. 22. Clarendon's practice is not unfamiliar to today's strategies of some governments to send asylum seekers and other migrants to other countries, including island-nations, where the laws of the sending state do not apply, and thus they may be deprived of their right to *habeas corpus* if this is not part of the receiving country's legal framework.

boats[12] or extraterritorially[13] – nor *whether* it is described as detention (as explained above). The distinction between restrictions on freedom of movement and deprivation of liberty is, therefore, 'merely one of degree or intensity, and not one of nature or substance.'[14]

An 'alternative to detention', in comparison, is not a legal term but rather refers to 'any legislation, policy or practice that allows for asylum-seekers, refugees and migrants to reside in the community with freedom of movement, albeit subject to some conditions, while their migration status is being resolved or while awaiting deportation or removal from the country.'[15] It ranges from full freedom to some restrictions on movement, and a particular measure imposed may deprive an individual of some of his or her liberty. There are many different forms of 'alternatives to detention', ranging from registration and/or deposit of documents, reporting requirements, bond or bail, community release and supervision, electronic tagging, or home curfew.[16] All restrictions on liberty – whether full deprivations via confinement in a closed location or lesser restrictions involving reporting requirements or a designated residence – are subject to human rights oversight.[17] This chapter finds it useful to plot various forms of 'alternatives to detention' along a continuum from 'liberty' to 'restrictions on liberty' to 'full deprivations of liberty' (or detention) (see Figures 19.1 and 19.2). The further along the continuum or, in other words, the greater the loss of or interference with liberty, the more human rights safeguards must be put in place to guard against executive excess, arbitrariness or unfair punishment.

Labels can be misleading. Calling a particular practice an 'alternative to detention' does not remove it from the ambit of international human rights law. As the ECtHR

---

[12] See, e.g., *Medvedyev v. France*, ECtHR, Applic. No. 3394/03, 29 March 2010, which involved the interception by the French authorities of a Cambodian vessel in international waters on suspicion of drug trafficking and the subsequent detention of its crew for 13 days below deck and the control over their route. It was held that this amounted to deprivation of liberty in violation of Article 5, ECHR. The ECtHR held that France had not possessed 'clearly defined and foreseeable legal grounds' to detain them in this way. See, also, *J.H.A. v. Spain*, UN Committee against Torture (CAT), Comm. No. 323/2007, 21 November 2008, in which the CAT noted that Spain had exercised control over the migrants from the time of their rescue and throughout their detention in Mauritania. Cf. *Ruddock v. Vadarlis* [2001] FCA 1329, an Australian Federal Court judgment that did not accept that the writ of *habeas corpus* applied to 433 asylum seekers who had been rescued by the Norwegian container vessel, the *MV Tampa*, as the actions of the Australian government in sending troops to take control of the ship and its passengers and refusing to disembark them were 'incidental to' preventing the rescued asylum seekers from landing on Australian territory (see, though, the dissent of Chief Justice Black, paras 69 and 80).

[13] See, e.g., *Al-Skeini and Others v. United Kingdom*, ECtHR, Grand Chamber, Applic. No. 55721/07, 7 July 2011; *Al-Jedda v. United Kingdom*, ECtHR, Applic. No. 27021/08, 7 July 2011.

[14] *Guzzardi v. Italy*, para. 93.

[15] Adapted from the definition in R. Sampson, G. Mitchell and L. Bowring, *There Are Alternatives: A Handbook for Preventing Unnecessary Immigration Detention*, International Detention Coalition, Melbourne, 2011, p. 2, at: http://www.unhcr.org/4dde23d49.html [accessed on 12 July 2011].

[16] See Edwards, *Back to Basics*.

[17] This point was reiterated by the Global Roundtable on Alternatives to Detention held in Geneva on 11–12 May 2011 and co-organized by UNHCR and the Office of the UN High Commissioner for Human Rights, Summary Conclusions, para. 18, at: http://www.unhcr.org/4e3944069.html [accessed on 3 August 2012].

Figure 19.1

judgment in *Amuur v. France* reminds us, it doesn't matter what a place of detention is called, whether an 'international zone' or otherwise; human rights continue to apply.[18] Field and Edwards cautioned in their 2006 study, 'Sometimes what is called an alternative *to* detention may in fact be an alternative form *of* detention.'[19] The United Nations Working Group on Arbitrary Detention (UN-WGAD) has likewise warned that any alternatives developed must not function as alternatives to release.[20] It is important that each example is assessed as to its factual reality.

Case law supports this approach. A United States immigration decision found, for example, that ankle monitors 'cause a great loss of liberty and [require] confinement in a specific place, i.e., the Respondent's home between the hours of 7 p.m. and 7 a.m. everyday', thus amounting to 'custody' and implicating *habeas corpus* guarantees, although subsequent cases have distinguished between 'custody' and 'detention' for the purposes of US domestic purposes.[21] The United Kingdom's House of Lords similarly held that

18 *Amuur v. France*, ECtHR, Applic. No. 19776/92, 25 June 1996, para. 52: 'Despite its name, the international zone does not have extraterritorial status.' Here France argued unsuccessfully that, because the asylum seekers had passed via Syria on their way to France, they were free to return there and were therefore not in detention. This was rejected, as the ECtHR argued that the ability to leave detention must be a real possibility and not merely theoretical. A Dutch decision has also held that holding someone in the transit zone of an airport constitutes a deprivation of liberty within the meaning of Article 5 of the ECHR: *Shokuh v. The Netherlands*, Hoge Raad der Nederlanden (Netherlands Supreme Court), 9 December 1988, *Revue du droit des étrangers* (RDDE), No. 52, January–February 1989, p. 16, as referred to in G. Goodwin-Gill, 'Article 31 of the 1951 Convention Relating to the Status of Refugees: Non-penalization, Detention, and Protection', in E. Feller, V. Türk and F. Nicholson (eds), *Refugee Protection in International Law: UNHCR's Global Consultations on International Protection* (Cambridge: Cambridge University Press, 2003), pp. 185–252, at p. 185, n. 83.

19 O. Field and A. Edwards, *Study on Alternatives to Detention*, UNHCR, Legal and Protection Policy Research Series, POLAS/2006/03, 2006, p. 4.

20 UN-WGAD, *Report to the 13th Session of the Human Rights Council*, A/HRC/13/30, 15 January 2010, para. 65.

21 Executive Office for Immigration Review, Immigration Court, Los Angeles, USA, 18 May 2008, parties are not named, before Bass L.J., at: http://www.bibdaily.com/pdfs/Bass%20IJ%205-18-08%20electronic%20bracelet%20bond%20decision.pdf (on file with the author). Case distinguished *Nguyen v. B.I. Incorporated*, 435 F.Supp.2d 1109 (D. Oregon 2006), in which the use of an ankle bracelet for someone pending deportation was not deemed to be 'custody'. Identical decision taken in *X v. Department of Homeland Security*, US Immigration Court, Orlando, Florida, FL, 6 March 2009. These cases are to be compared to *Matter of Jose Aguilar-Aquino*, 24 I&N Dec. 747 (Board of Immigration Appeals 2009), File A095 748 786 (Los Angeles, California), 12 March 2009, in which a distinction was made between 'detention' and 'custody'. Persons released on parole and those still incarcerated are in 'custody', yet 'detention' referred to 'actual physical restraint or confinement in a given space', referring to *Matter of Sanchez*, 20 I&N Dec. 223, 225 (BIA 1990). Thus 'whilst a person in custody is

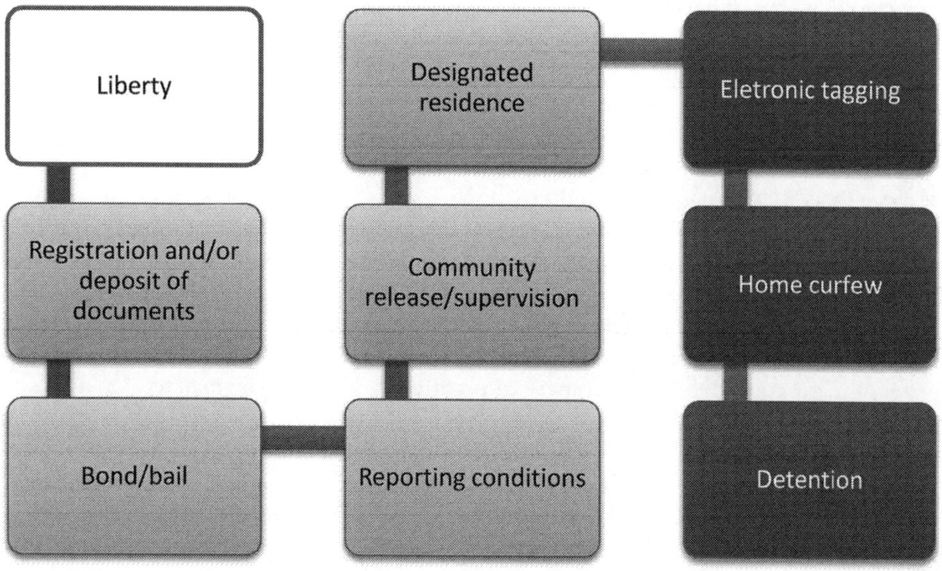

Figure 19.2

restrictions that amounted to an 18-hour curfew deprived the subject of his liberty.[22] Likewise, the ECtHR ruled that confinement to a remote island off the coast of Sardinia, where the applicant lived for 16 months in a small hamlet of 2.5 square kilometres, with daily reporting and a curfew, fell within the parameters of Article 5 of the ECHR.[23] It has also found that confinement of a mentally ill patient to a mental hospital that was 'open' (i.e. unlocked) invoked Article 5 protections.[24]

Furthermore, some national 'detention' arrangements may arguably be better classified as 'alternatives to detention', even though the particular national legal framework may call them 'detention' under law.[25] Conversely, other national legal arrangements have

---

not necessarily in detention, one who is in detention is necessarily in custody' (p. 6). The reason for distinguishing between the two forms of deprivation of liberty was relevant as far as it permitted the immigration judge to vary the conditions of 'custody' or 'release'.

[22] *Secretary of State for the Home Department v. JJ and others* [2007] UKHL 45, [2008] 1 AC 385. However, the court also found shorter curfews of 10–12 hours and less rigorous restrictions in other cases to be compatible with Article 5 of the ECHR: *Secretary of State for the Home Department v. AF* [2007] UKHL 46, [2008] 1 AC 440; *Secretary of State for the Home Department v. E and another* [2007] UKHL 47, [2008] 1 AC 499. Note that each of these cases involved terrorism suspects who were found to pose a threat to national security, which is not normally the case with asylum applicants.

[23] *Guzzardi v. Italy*, p. 33, paras. 92 and 93.

[24] See *Ashingdane v. United Kingdom*, ECtHR, Applic. No. 8225/78, 28 May 1985.

[25] Here I have in mind the Australian system of 'community detention', in which families with children are permitted to reside in the community in unguarded houses, and are free to come and go as they please. For the purposes of Australian domestic law, they remain 'in detention' as they have no lawful status; however, for other purposes, this may well constitute an 'alternative to detention'. Other 'community detention' practices in Australia, however, have involved restrictions

not classified particular individuals as being *de jure* detained, yet they may have no ability to exercise their right to freedom of movement and are, therefore, for all intents and purposes, *de facto* detained.[26] A distinction should also be drawn between a physical 'place' of detention compared with a 'status' of being detained. What is most important to this chapter (and under international law) is the question of whether someone has been deprived of their liberty as a matter of fact, rather than the name given to it. In many respects, this chapter confirms a right to humane reception conditions for asylum seekers and refugees, of which non-custodial alternatives to detention are but one component.[27]

As a matter of international law, the starting point is the right to liberty. Justifications for restrictions on liberty are secondary, and must be strictly circumscribed given the non-criminal and non-judicial context in which most immigration detention occurs. According to the Council of Europe's Rapporteur on Detention, this currently operates in reverse order in many countries.[28] The ultimate 'alternative to detention' is no detention at all.

3. The Right to Seek and Enjoy Asylum and the Prohibition on Penalization for Illegal Entry or Stay

Apart from the general principles outlined in the next section in relation to the right to liberty under international and regional human rights laws, there are a number of specific safeguards against arbitrary detention or other restrictions on movement relevant to refugees and asylum seekers. These are contained in the 1951 Convention. While it has generally been accepted that states are not under an obligation 'to grant' asylum under international law,[29] this now seems to be less an accepted position today. In particular,

on freedom of movement, such as being accompanied at all times and being confined to guarded houses in the community, and this would not be similarly classified: see, further, Parliament of the Commonwealth of Australia, *Immigration Detention in Australia: Community-based Alternatives to Detention*, second report of the inquiry into immigration detention in Australia, Joint Standing Committee on Migration, Canberra, May 2009.

26 Here I refer to the Canadian practice of confining parents with children to immigration holding facilities. As their children are not technically subject to the detention order, they are not considered to be 'in detention' *de jure*, yet they are as equally confined as their parents and, for all practical purposes, they are not free to come and go: interview and visit, Canadian Citizenship and Immigration, Immigration Holding Centre, Toronto, May 2010.

27 In Australia and the United Kingdom, for example, there are some serious concerns around destitution of some released asylum seekers or persons pending removal owing to their lack of eligibility for social services or the right to work: see Hotham Mission Asylum Seeker Project, *Australia's Hidden Homeless: Community-based Approaches to Asylum Seeker Homelessness*, August 2010, and Still Human, Still Here campaign against destitution in the United Kingdom, which has an NGO membership of 40 organizations: http://stillhumanstillhere.wordpress.com/ [accessed on 3 August 2012]. This indicates that a pure focus on detention and alternatives can overlook other important human rights issues.

28 See CoE, *The Detention of Asylum-seekers and Irregular Migrants in Europe*.

29 Article 14(1), UDHR: 'Everyone has the right to seek and to enjoy in other countries asylum from persecution'; G. Goodwin-Gill and J. McAdam, *The Refugee in International Law* (Oxford:

many regional instruments do obligate states parties to grant asylum.[30] The ECtHR also accepted as a preliminary statement in *M.S.S. v. Belgium and Greece* that the 1951 Convention 'defines the circumstances in which a State *must grant* refugee status to those who request it, as well as the rights and duties of such persons.'[31] While the debate on the right to asylum continues, at a minimum, it is accepted under international law that the seeking of asylum is not an unlawful act.

Article 31(1) of the 1951 Convention, for example, stipulates that refugees having come directly should not be penalized for their illegal entry or stay if they present themselves to the authorities without delay and show good cause for their illegal entry or stay.[32] Automatically detaining an asylum seeker for the pure reason of their status as such would amount to an arbitrary deprivation of liberty, and could also constitute a form of discrimination contrary to international law.[33] The UN Human Rights Committee (UN-HRC) has held that mandatory detention of asylum seekers is unlawful *per se* as a

Oxford University Press, 2007), p. 204.

30 E.g., Article 22(7) of the American Convention on Human Rights 1969 (ACHR) provides: 'Every person has the right to seek and be granted asylum in a foreign country, in accordance with the legislation of the state and international conventions'; Article 12(3) of the African Charter of Human and Peoples' Rights 1981 (ACHPR) provides, 'Every individual shall have the right, when persecuted, to seek and obtain asylum in other countries in accordance with laws of those countries and international conventions'; Article 13 of the EU *Council Directive 2004/83/EC of 29 April 2004 on minimum standards for the qualification and status of third country nationals or stateless persons as refugees or as persons who otherwise need international protection and the content of the protection granted* provides, 'Member States shall grant refugee status to a third country national or a stateless person'.

31 *M.S.S. v. Belgium and Greece*, ECtHR, Applic. No. 30696/09, 21 January 2011, para. 54 (my emphasis).

32 See, e.g., Noll, who argues, for example, that where the detention of a refugee fails the necessity test of Article 31(2), it may be punitive, and therefore proscribed by Article 31(1): G. Noll, 'Article 31 (Refugees Lawfully in the Country of Refuge/Réfugiés en situation irrégulière dans le pays d'accueil)', in A. Zimmerman (ed.), *Commentary on the 1951 Convention relating to the Status of Refugees* (Oxford: Oxford University Press, 2011), pp. 1243–76. Grahl-Madsen explicitly identified detention as amounting to a penalty in his treatise: A. Grahl-Madsen, *The Status of Refugees in International Law, vol. II* (Leyden: A.W. Sijthoff, 1972), at p. 209 (footnote omitted).

33 According to the UN Human Rights Committee (UN-HRC), the 'general rule of [international human rights law] is that each one of the rights ... must be guaranteed without discrimination between aliens and citizens', and they 'apply to everyone, irrespective of reciprocity, and irrespective of his or her nationality or statelessness': UN-HRC, *General Comment No. 15: The Position of Aliens under the Covenant*, CCPR/C/21/Rev. 1, 11 April 1986, paras 2 and 1 respectively. Applied in the context of detention, see *A and others v. Secretary of State for the Home Department* [2004] UKHL 56 ('Belmarsh Detainees case'). See, also, *Rasul v. Bush*, 542 US 466 (2004); 124 S. Ct. 2868 (US Supreme Court) (non-citizens have a statutory right to challenge their detention in US courts); *Hamden v. Rumsfeld*, 548 US 557 (2006); 126 S. Ct. 2749 (despite legislative amendments introduced to deprive Guantanamo Bay detainees of the benefit of the decision in *Rasul*, the Supreme Court held that detainees were entitled to continue with *habeas* applications already pending); and finally, *Boumediene v. Bush*, 553 US 723 (2008); 128 S. Ct. 2229, where the majority held, *inter alia*, that the detainees had a constitutional right to *habeas corpus* and that the legislation purporting to deny it was unconstitutional.

matter of international law,[34] regardless of the existence of national legislation sanctioning the practice.[35] Meanwhile, UN-WGAD has stated that 'criminalizing illegal entry into a country exceeds the legitimate interest of States to control and regulate illegal immigration and leads to unnecessary [and therefore arbitrary] detention;'[36] and that it would be a disproportionate response.[37] These legal constraints on executive action compel governments to institute open and humane reception conditions, including safe, dignified and human rights-compatible treatment.[38]

The second paragraph of Article 31 of the 1951 Convention addresses the specific question of detention of those refugees having entered or stayed illegally. The provision permits states to apply some restrictions on the movement of this specific class of refugees. However, any restrictions must be 'necessary and [they] shall only be applied until their status in the country is regularized or they obtain admission into another country'. Article 31(2) thus shares the 'necessity' criterion applied in relation to the right to liberty under international law, discussed below. Accepting that 'detention should normally be avoided' and that it is thus an exceptional measure, the Executive Committee of the UNHCR's Programme (ExCom) set down, in 1986, a limited number of circumstances in which detention or other restrictions on movement may be considered 'necessary' in an individual case:

> *If necessary*, detention may be resorted to only on grounds prescribed by law to verify identity; to determine the elements on which the claim to refugee status or asylum is based; to deal with cases where refugees or asylum-seekers have destroyed their travel and/or identity documents or have used fraudulent documents in order to mislead the authorities of the State in which they intend to claim asylum; or to protect national security or public order.[39]

UNHCR's 1999 *Guidelines on Detention* also stipulate the same bases for when detention may be necessary.[40] It is no longer clear that these four grounds for detention in the ExCom

34 *A v. Australia*, UN-HRC, Comm. No. 560/1993, 3 April 1997; *C v. Australia*, UN-HRC, Comm. No. 900/2000, 13 November 2002.

35 See Australian decision in *Al-Kateb v. Godwin* [2004] HCA 37, in which the High Court of Australia held that section 189 of the Migration Act 1958 (Cth), which requires mandatory and non-reviewable detention until either an individual obtains a legal visa (e.g., refugee status) or is removed, not unconstitutional.

36 UN-WGAD, *Report to the Seventh Session of the Human Rights Council*, A/HRC/7/4/Add.1, 10 January 2008, para. 53.

37 UN-WGAD, *Civil and Political Rights, Including the Question of: Torture and Detention*, UN Doc. E/CN.4/2000/4 (1999) Annex 2.

38 See, in particular, ExCom Conclusion No. 93 (LIII), 2002, Reception of Asylum-Seekers in the Context of Individual Asylum Systems.

39 ExCom Conclusion No. 44 (XXXVII), 1986, Detention of Refugees and Asylum-Seekers, para. (b).

40 Guideline 3, UNHCR, *Revised Guidelines on Detention*. Cf. in its submission in the case of *Salah Sheek v. The Netherlands*, ECtHR, Applic. No. 1948/04, 11 January 2007, paras 26–7 of the judgment, UNHCR stated, 'There is "general agreement" that "every State was fully entitled to investigate the case of each refugee who clandestinely crossed its frontier, and to ascertain whether he met the necessary entry requirements ... Art. 31(2) therefore authorizes necessary restrictions

Conclusion and in UNHCR's *Guidelines on Detention* fully correspond to developments in international law. It is noted that UNHCR's *Guidelines* are currently being revised. At a minimum, in each of these scenarios, any recourse to detention must be established in law, indicated in the individual case, and must not amount to a blanket policy to detain. Decisions to detain on national security grounds, for example, must be taken only in individual cases and subject to judicial oversight.[41] Decisions to detain on public order grounds might include initial screening for identity, documentation or health reasons, or exceptionally, in the context of mass influx, and in the latter situation, only until order has been restored.[42] Additionally, governments cannot, for example, use immigration powers to detain an individual who threatens public order on account of criminality (compared with immigration-related public order reasons), as this should be dealt with under criminal laws.[43] Likewise, the European Court of Justice held in *Kadzoev v. Bulgaria* that the possibility of detaining a person on grounds of public order and safety cannot be based on the EU Returns Directive, as these are not included explicitly in the Directive.[44] Recalling Articles 31–3 of the 1951 Convention, the ECtHR has similarly held that, as the expulsion of an asylum seeker is prohibited under international law, they cannot be detained for the purposes of expulsion per the second limb of Article 5(1)(f) of the ECHR.[45]

In terms of a right of states to detain persons in order to assess the elements of their asylum claim, this ought to apply only to an initial screening, and not generally during a full refugee status determination unless necessary in the individual case.[46] Otherwise, it could lead to a general policy mandating the detention of asylum seekers, and, as indicated, this would be incompatible with the right to seek asylum under international law. To read the reference otherwise would arguably make detention a penalty in conflict with Article 31 of the 1951 Convention.

The ExCom has further noted that 'fair and expeditious [refugee status determination] procedures' can serve as a safeguard against prolonged detention and that any such detention should be subject to administrative or judicial review.[47] Paradoxically, it is

---

on movement for the purposes of investigation of identity, the circumstances of arrival, the basic elements of the claim and security concerns."'

41 See, e.g., Belmarsh Detainees case.

42 See ExCom Conclusion No. 22 (XXXII), 1981, Protection of Asylum-Seekers in Large-Scale, para. B(1).

43 UN-WGAD, *Opinion No. 45/2006*, UN Doc. A/HRC/7/4/Add.1, 16 January 2008, para. 28. Public order reasons for detaining a non-national in immigration detention may, however, be justified if these relate to immigration reasons (e.g., fear of absconding).

44 *Kadzoev v. Bulgaria*, ECJ Case C-357/09, 30 November 2009.

45 See *R.U. v. Greece*, ECtHR, Applic. No. 2237/08, 7 June 2011, para. 94. See, also, *S.D. v. Greece*, ECtHR, Applic. No. 53541/07, 11 June 2009, para. 62. The ECtHR further held that detention for the purposes of expulsion can only occur after an asylum claim has been finally determined.

46 An increasing number of countries are resorting to detention of asylum seekers during the initial stages of asylum procedures for expediency reasons (e.g., under the United Kingdom's 'fast-track procedures', Austria, Hungary, Slovakia, etc.), which would not be lawful *per se*, and, like all other forms of detention, would need to be justified. 'Administrative convenience' might justify an initial period of detention up to seven days, but it must not be automatic and must be indicated in each individual case: see below discussion on *Saadi v. UK*.

47 ExCom Conclusion No. 44, para. c. See, further, *Summary Conclusions on Article 31 of the 1951 Convention relating to the Status of Refugees: Revised, Geneva Expert Roundtable, 8–9 November*

clear that the right to due process in asylum proceedings can be compromised while in detention, including the ability of an asylum seeker to access legal advice.[48] In other words, detention may interfere with other rights associated with the right to asylum. The right of asylum seekers in detention to access UNHCR has also been accepted by the ExCom[49] and is further supported by the obligations of states parties to the 1951 Convention to cooperate with UNHCR via Article 35.[50]

Article 26 of the 1951 Convention is another provision in the 1951 Convention specific to the right to liberty of refugees and asylum seekers. It provides:

> Each Contracting State shall accord to refugees lawfully in its territory the right to choose their place of residence and to move freely within its territory subject to any regulations applicable to aliens generally in the same circumstances.

Emphasizing the right to freedom of movement, there are nonetheless two limitations on the application of this provision. The first is that Article 26 applies only to refugees who are 'lawfully in' the territory. The second is that their right to freedom of movement and choice of residence is subject to restrictions applied to 'aliens generally in the same circumstances'. These limitations are dealt with in turn.

'Lawfully In' the Territory

Rights under the 1951 Convention are structured via a system of 'gradations of treatment', based on notions such as 'physical presence', 'lawful presence', 'lawful stay' and 'habitual stay'.[51] Article 26 corresponds to the second of these: lawful presence. A similar standard of 'lawful presence' (or 'lawfully in') applies to a range of other human rights provisions in respect of freedom of movement, discussed *infra*,[52] and it is also found in Article 32 (on expulsion of refugees) of the 1951 Convention. While it is clear that recognized refugees fall within these provisions, the more critical question is whether they apply to asylum seekers. Logically, asylum seekers must also benefit from these protections as a matter of interpretation; otherwise it would render the protection meaningless. As Hathaway suggests, it cannot be reasonably concluded that asylum seekers who submit

2001, at: http://www.safecom.org.au/pdfs/roundtable-summaries.pdf [accessed on 3 August 2012].

48 This is hinted at in UNHCR's Guidelines on Detention: 'Detention should not constitute an obstacle to an asylum-seekers' [*sic*] possibilities to pursue their asylum application' (no page numbers).

49 ExCom Conclusion No. 85 (XLIX), 1998, International Protection.

50 See Goodwin-Gill, 'Article 31 of the 1951 Convention Relating to the Status of Refugees', at p. 225.

51 Goodwin-Gill distinguishes the four categories as simple presence, lawful presence, lawful residence, and habitual residence: Goodwin-Gill and McAdam, *The Refugee in International Law* (3rd edn, Oxford: Oxford University Press, 2010), at pp. 524–528.

52 The same standard is found in, for example, Article 12 of the ICCPR (discussed *infra*) and protection against expulsion in Article 13(1) of the ICCPR.

an application for refugee status are not 'lawfully present'.[53] Hathaway's position is partly based on the fact that there is no explicit obligation on states to verify status included in the 1951 Convention, and that this lacuna would allow states to indefinitely deny refugees their Convention rights simply by refusing to verify their status.[54] While acknowledging that 'deference to national legal understandings of lawful presence is clearly sensible',[55] he notes that it cannot be absolutely followed. He also argues that adopting any other interpretation – such as requiring something more than registering as an asylum seeker - leaves no room for a distinction between 'lawful presence' and 'lawful stay' (the third level of attachment) in the 1951 Convention.[56] UNHCR has also adopted a similar approach, noting that 'once the domestic law formalities for access into determination procedures have been complied with, status is regularized if the other criteria in Art. 31 are met, and Art. 26 governs the position.'[57] This also appears to be compatible with the view of the drafters of the Convention.[58]

An alternative position taken in respect of whether asylum seekers are 'lawfully in' the territory for the purposes of these provisions, yet one reaching the same conclusion, is that of Marx. He distinguishes how the term 'lawfully in' has been interpreted and applied in relation to human rights provisions (particularly in respect of Article 5(1)(f) of the ECHR in relation to 'unauthorized entry'), which have largely deferred to domestic laws, and Article 26 of the 1951 Convention. Compared to other migrants who may have some additional requirements imposed on their right of entry or stay, he argues that refugees and asylum seekers ought to be considered to be 'lawfully within' the territory as soon as they 'are present in' the territory. Noting that the ICCPR does not distinguish between 'lawfully in' and 'lawfully staying' as does the 1951 Convention, he implies that, by extension, the two legal frameworks should not be interpreted in the same way. He specifically raises objection to the analysis of the ECtHR in *Omwenyeke v. Germany*, in which an asylum seeker was issued with a 'provisional residence permit' that limited his residence to a certain district of the territory of Germany pending appeal proceedings in relation to his asylum request. According to the ECtHR, he remained 'lawfully in' Germany *as long as* he continued to comply with the conditions to which his admission and stay were authorized.[59] Marx argues that the European Court got it wrong as the

53 J. C. Hathaway, *The Rights of Refugees under International Law* (Cambridge: Cambridge University Press, 2005), Ch. 3.1.2.

54 Ibid. See, also, A. Edwards, 'Human Rights, Refugees, and the Right to "Enjoy" Asylum' (2005) 17(2) *International Journal of Refugee Law* 297–330, where I make a similar argument.

55 Hathaway, *Rights of Refugees under International Law*, at p. 177.

56 Ibid.

57 *Salah Sheek v. The Netherlands*, paras. 26–7 (reference to UNHCR's intervention in this case).

58 For example, the US Representative, Mr Henkin, stated, 'The expression "lawfully in the territory" included persons entering a territory even for a few hours, provided that they have been duly authorised to enter': UN Doc. E/AC.32.SR.41. The French Representative also indicated 'a person … not yet in possession of a residence permit but who had applied for it and had the receipt for that application. Only those persons who had not applied, or whose application had been refused, were in an irregular position': Mr Rain of France, UN Doc. E/AC.32/SR.15, at para. 109.

59 Cf., *Omwenyeke v. Germany*, ECtHR, Applic. No. 44294/04, 20 November 2007, as discussed in R. Marx, 'Article 26 (Freedom of Movement/Liberté de Circulation'), in Zimmerman (ed.),

phrase 'lawfully within' a territory according to the 1951 Convention cannot simply be regarded as a matter of domestic law, rather its ordinary meaning follows from the object and purpose of the treaty.[60]

I would also argue that, while an asylum seeker may be required to reside in a particular designated region or district under domestic law, this should not affect the position under international law. They would continue to be 'lawfully in' the territory for the purposes of international law, even if they do not abide by the terms of this designation. This is because an application for asylum is to the state as a whole, and not to a particular administrative district. How states deal with asylum seekers who refuse to remain in a designated location or breach the conditions of their release into the community is a separate question and should be dealt with as such.[61]

Contrary to the views of the ECtHR in *Omwenyeke v. Germany*, the UN-HRC in *Celepi v. Sweden* has accepted that an individual subject to a deportation order but who could not be removed was to be considered as 'lawfully in the territory of Sweden' for the purposes of Article 12.[62] According to the UN-HRC's General Comment on Freedom of Movement,

> The question whether an alien is 'lawfully' within the territory of a State is a matter governed by domestic law, which may subject the entry of an alien to the territory of a State to restrictions, *provided* they are in compliance with the State's international obligations.[63]

The UN-HRC further made clear that 'an alien who entered the State illegally, but whose status has been regularized, must be considered to be lawfully within the territory for the purposes of article 12 [of the ICCPR].'[64] In line with this position, recognized refugees would be considered lawfully in the territory for the purposes of Article 12 (regardless of the status determination procedure applied, i.e., whether individual or *prima facie*).[65]

Commentary on the 1951 Convention relating to the Status of Refugees, pp. 1147–64. Note that Article 12 of the ICCPR and Article 26 of the 1951 Convention do not prohibit restrictions on freedom of movement; however, they require any restrictions to be justified.

60 Marx, 'Article 26 (Freedom of Movement/Liberté de Circulation'.

61 Article 2 of the 1951 Convention might be relevant here, in which it is recognized that '[e] very refugee has duties to the country in which he finds himself, which require in particular that he conform to its laws and regulations as well as to measures taken for the maintenance of public order.'

62 *Celepli v. Sweden*, UN-HRC Comm. No. 456/1991, 26 July 1994, para. 9.2. Celepli was a Turkish national of Kurdish origin who was subject to a deportation order on the grounds of suspicion of involvement in terrorist activities. The deportation order was not enforced because it was believed that he (and his fellow suspects) would be exposed to political persecution in Turkey if returned. Sweden granted them permission to stay, which was held to amount to be 'lawfully within' for the purposes of Article 12. Sweden justified its restrictions on movement on ground of national security under Article 12(3), which was accepted by the UN-HRC.

63 UN-HRC, General Comment No. 27: Freedom of Movement, UN Doc. CCPR/C/21/Rev.1/ Add.9, 2 Nov. 1999, para. 4 (emphasis added).

64 Ibid..

65 See *Karker v. France*, UN-HRC Comm. No. 833/1998, 26 October 2000, in which Article 12 was automatically considered to apply because he was a recognized refugee. Karker was a Tunisian national and a recognized refugee in France who was placed under an expulsion order on account

Registered asylum seekers would also be 'lawfully within' the territory under this interpretation. Any period in which someone is not yet lawfully in the territory would be subject to protections against arbitrary detention under Article 9 of the ICCPR (see *infra*).

These various approaches to Article 26 outlined above ought to challenge, under international law at least, the practice of many states that operate legal distinctions (or 'legal fictions') between those 'in the territory' and those considered to have not yet entered. These are regularly at work in relation to immigration detention regimes.[66] Despite these legal distinctions, human rights guarantees continue to apply. That is, national regulations do not absolve states of their international obligations towards refugees and asylum seekers.[67] Furthermore, while domestic legal frameworks may primarily govern the legal status of individuals in the territory, such laws must be in conformity with international law.[68]

Standard of Treatment: 'Aliens Generally'

Once a person is 'lawfully within' a state, restrictions on the freedom of movement or choice of residence of refugees or asylum seekers are to be judged according to the 'aliens generally' standard in the 1951 Convention, the lowest in the 1951 Convention. Clearly, any restrictions imposed on 'aliens generally' would need to be in compliance with international law. According to Hathaway (and restated by Marx), the drafters of the 1951 Convention were 'firmly committed to the view that once lawfully in the territory of a state party, refugees should be subject only to whatever restrictions govern the freedom of internal movement and residence of other non-citizens.'[69] Few restrictions on freedom of movement and choice of residence were imposed on 'other non-citizens', such as foreign labour workers, at the time of drafting Article 26, many of whom were present in the

---

of suspicion of his active support of a 'terrorist organisation' (language of the communication) that used violent methods. The expulsion order was unenforceable owing to his refugee status so that he could not be returned to Tunisia. Karker was required to live in a particular French district, and was moved intermittently. He was also required to report to the police daily. The UN-HRC found no violation of Article 12 of the ICCPR on grounds of national security. The UN-HRC thus accepted that he was lawfully in France owing to his refugee status – there was no issue raised in this case. The case further held that the arguments under Article 9 were inadmissible *ratione materiae*, 'since the measures to which Mr. Karker is being subjected do not amount to deprivation of liberty such as contemplated by Article 9 of the Covenant.' The area in which he was required to live was 'a comparatively wide area' and he was free to move within that community (para. 9.2). He was also eligible to leave the area with permission. The communication did not specifically deal with the question about daily reporting requirements and whether alone or in combination these constituted a deprivation of liberty within the meaning of Article 9, rather than Article 12.

[66] For example, in Belgium, persons who have entered the territory unlawfully are not subject to detention as Belgium has no grounds under Article 5(1)(f) of the ECHR to detain them (because they have already effected an unlawful entry), whereas those attempting to make an unlawful entry who arrive at the border are subject to detention. See, also, *Saadi v. United Kingdom*.

[67] See *Amuur v. France, supra*.

[68] See *Lokpo and Touré*, ECtHR, Applic. No. 10816, 20 September 2011, para. 18.

[69] Hathaway, *Rights of Refugees under International Law*, p. 705; restated in Marx, 'Article 26 (Freedom of Movement/Liberté de Circulation)'.

territory under pre- and post-war labour immigration schemes.[70] At a minimum, Article 26, read separately or in conjunction with Article 3, guarantees that a state party may not impose restrictions that apply *only* to refugees or asylum seekers.

4. The Right to Liberty and Security of Person and the Correlative Obligation to Consider Less Intrusive or Coercive Means of Achieving Immigration Control

The right to liberty is a fundamental human right and an essential component of legal systems enjoying the rule of law.[71] The right is found in two provisions of the Universal Declaration of Human Rights 1948 (UDHR),[72] translated into Article 9 of the International Covenant on Civil and Political Rights 1966 (ICCPR), and in a range of other international and regional human rights instruments.[73]

Article 9(1) provides:

> Everyone has the right to liberty and security of person. No one shall be subjected to arbitrary arrest or detention. No one shall be deprived of his liberty except on such grounds and in accordance with such procedure as are established by law.

Article 9 expresses the general principle of liberty and security of person. Article 9 applies to all deprivations of liberty, including detention for the purposes of immigration control.[74] However, Article 9 does not prohibit immigration detention, nor is the right to liberty and security of person absolute;[75] rather, it is a substantive guarantee against unlawful

[70] For more on the drafting history, see P. Weis, *The Refugee Convention, 1951: The Travaux Préparatoires Analysed, With a Commentary by Dr. Paul Weis* (Cambridge: Cambridge University Press, 1995).

[71] See, Bingham, *Rule of Law*, referring to a range of historical bases for *habeas corpus*: 'The writ of habeas corpus is now the most usual remedy by which a man is restored again to his liberty, if he has been against law deprived of it', per *Bushell's Case* (1670), Vaughan C.J. at 135, 136. The US Supreme Court has likewise consistently recognized the principle that '[f]reedom from bodily restraint has always been at the core of the liberty protected by the Due Process Clause from arbitrary governmental action', per *Foucha v. Louisiana*, 504 US 71, p. 80 (1992).

[72] The two provisions are Article 3 ('Everyone has the right to life, liberty and security of person') and Article 9 ('No one shall be subjected to arbitrary arrest, detention or exile').

[73] Article 16, International Convention on the Rights of All Migrant Workers and Members of their Families (MWC); Article 37, Convention on the Rights of the Child (CRC). On regional instruments, see Article 6, African Charter on Human and Peoples' Rights; Article XXV, American Declaration on the Rights and Duties of Man; Article 7, American Convention on Human Rights; Article 5(1)(f), ECHR; Article 6, EU Charter of Fundamental Rights and Freedoms.

[74] UN-HRC General Comment No. 8 (1982) on Article 9 (Right to liberty and security of person), UN Doc. HRI/GEN/1/Rev.7, para. 1.

[75] Article 9 may be derogated from in a public emergency subject to being 'strictly required by the exigencies of the situation' and 'provided such measures are not inconsistent with their

and arbitrary detention. Unlawful detention can take many forms, including owing to a government's failure to meet procedural norms[76] or standards of treatment and care.[77] These are not, however, dealt with in this chapter.

The right to liberty and the prohibition against arbitrary detention has been accepted as importing concepts of reasonableness, necessity, proportionality and non-discrimination. The UN-HRC has clarified that

> 'Arbitrariness' is not to be equated [only] with 'against the law', but must be interpreted more broadly to include elements of inappropriateness, injustice and lack of predictability. This means that remand in custody pursuant to lawful arrest must not only be lawful but *reasonable in all the circumstances*. Further, remand in custody must be *necessary in all the circumstances*, for example, to prevent flight, interference with evidence or the recurrence of crime.[78]
>
> ... the element of proportionality becomes relevant in this context ....[79]

Case law confirms that the principles of reasonableness, necessity and proportionality require that states consider whether there are other, less intrusive ways to achieve their objectives without interfering with the right to liberty and security of person. In order to do so, states must have recourse to alternative means to achieve their objectives other than detention. In other words, without the availability of alternatives to detention, a

---

other obligations under international law and do not involve discrimination' (Article 4, ICCPR). Any measures adopted pursuant to any derogation are still subject to an assessment that they are necessary (including questions of proportionality) and cease as soon as the state of emergency no longer exists. See Belmarsh Detainees case, in which the UK House of Lords accepted that the current situation of terrorism was an acceptable basis for derogation, but that indefinite detention of foreign alleged terror suspects, who could not be returned to their countries of nationality owing to threats of torture, would be disproportionate and discriminatory and therefore in violation of Articles 5 and 14 of the ECHR. Also, *A v. Australia* found no basis to suggest that detention of asylum seekers was prohibited as a matter of customary international law (at para. 9.3).

76 See, e.g., *Jeebhai v. Minister of Home Affairs* (139/2008) [2009] ZASCA 35 (31 March 2009) (Supreme Court of Appeal, Republic of South Africa), in which it was held that the detention and deportation in question were unlawful 'because they were carried out without compliance with the peremptory procedures prescribed by the Act' (para. 53). See, also, *Report of the Special Rapporteur on the Human Rights of Migrants*, Jorge Bustamante, Mission to the United States of America, in *Report to the Human Rights Council*, Seventh Session, A/HRC/7/12/Add. 2, 5 March 2008, p. 9: 'United States policy is a long way out of step with international obligations. Immigration enforcement authorities have failed to develop an appropriate appeals procedure, and for all practical purposes have absolute discretion to determine whether a non-citizen may be released from detention ... Given that these discretionary measures are not subject to judicial review, current United States practices violate international law.' The Australian detention system has also been found to lack proper and effective procedural safeguards: *C v. Australia*.

77 See, e.g., *M.S.S. v. Belgium and Greece*.

78 *Van Alphen v. The Netherlands*, UN-HRC, Comm. No. 305/1988, 23 July 1990, para. 5.8. See, also, I-ACtHR, *Case of Chaparro Álvarez and Lapo Íñiguez, v. Ecuador*, Preliminary Objections, Merits, Reparations, and Costs, Judgment of November 21, 2007, Series C No. 170, para. 92.

79 *A v. Australia*, paras 9.2.–9.4.

presumption or blanket policy in favour of detention could arise, which has been held to be unlawful in several jurisdictions.[80] Blanket policies of detention would also violate the general principle that the detention must be necessary in every individual case.

The UN-HRC has held that in order for detention not to be arbitrary a government must demonstrate that,

> in light of the author's particular circumstances, there were not less invasive means of achieving the same ends, that is to say, compliance with the State party's immigration policies, by, for example, the imposition of reporting obligations, sureties or other conditions ....[81]

The UN-HRC acknowledged that illegal entry may justify investigation into the necessity of detention, but without additional factors – such as a risk of absconding or lack of cooperation – detention may be considered arbitrary 'even if entry was illegal'.[82] In *Bakhtiyari v. Australia*, for example, in which two minor children had been held in detention together with their parents for two years and eight months, the UN-HRC reaffirmed its position:

> Taking into account in particular the composition of the Bakhtiyari family, the State party has not demonstrated that other, less intrusive, measures could not have achieved the same end of compliance with the State party's immigration policies ....[83]

The extension of their detention was found to be unlawful. The UN Committee on the Rights of the Child (UN-CRC) has commented too that detention cannot be justified purely on the basis that the child is unaccompanied or separated, or on his or her migration or residence status.[84] Such children should instead be housed in residential homes for children or foster care while longer-term solutions are considered.[85] According to the UN-CRC, 'the underlying approach [for children] ... should be "care" and not "detention"'.[86] The UN-WGAD has likewise maintained, 'Given the availability of alternatives to detention, it is difficult to conceive of a situation in which the detention of unaccompanied minors would

80 See, e.g., *N (Kenya) v. Secretary for State for Home Department* [2004] INLR 612 (Court of Appeal of England and Wales), and *Ulde v. Minister of Home Affairs* (320/2008 [2009] ZASCA 34 (31 March 2009) (The Supreme Court of Appeal, South Africa).

81 *C v. Australia*, para. 8.2.

82 *A v. Australia*, para. 9.4.

83 *Bakhtiyari v. Australia*, UN-HRC Comm. No. 1069/2002, 6 November 2003, para. 9.3.

84 CRC Committee, General Comment No. 6 (2005), The Treatment of Unaccompanied and Separated Children Outside their Country of Origin, UN Doc. CRC/GC/2005/6, 1 September 2005, para. 61.

85 UNHCR, *Guidelines on Policies and Procedures in Dealing with Unaccompanied Children Seeking Asylum* (Geneva: UNHCR, 1997), p. 7; Guideline 6, UNHCR, *Revised Guidelines on Detention.*

86 CRC Committee, General Comment No. 6, para. 63.

comply with the requirements of article 37(b), clause 2, of the [CRC], according to which detention can only be used as a last resort.'[87]

This position is supported in the context of deportation and removal, such that, where the possibility of deportation is considered unrealistic, there is an obligation on the state to explore measures in lieu of detention. The UN-WGAD has stated, for example:

> Where the chances of removal within a reasonable delay are remote, the Government's obligation to seek for alternatives to detention becomes all the more pressing.[88]

The ECtHR has similarly held that each state must introduce sufficient safeguards in law to protect against arbitrary detention in the returns context (note the distinction in the asylum context, discussed *infra*), which would necessarily include non-custodial alternatives to detention. The Court stated in the case of *Massoud v. Malta*,

> It is hard to conceive that in a small island like Malta, where escape by sea without endangering one's life is unlikely and fleeing by air is subject to strict control, the authorities could not have had at their disposal other measures [than detention] to secure an eventual removal.[89]

As for EU law, there is movement towards greater harmonization between the asylum and returns arms of the asylum acquis, the latter – counter-intuitively – carrying more safeguards than the former. The EU Directive on Return, for example, subjects its rules on detention to consideration of 'other sufficient but less coercive measures [that] can be applied effectively in a specific case'.[90] The Directive highlights a number of alternatives to detention where a removal is postponed, such alternatives including regular reporting to the authorities, deposit of a financial guarantee, surrender of specific documents, or stay in a designated location.[91] No equivalent provisions yet exist in the EU directives on asylum procedures or reception conditions.

The EU Procedures Directive specifically provides that 'Members States shall not hold a person in detention for the sole reason that he or she is an applicant for asylum'.[92]

---

[87] UN-WGAD, *Report of Working Group on Arbitrary Detention,* Chairperson-Rapporteur El Hadji Malick Sow, UN Doc. A/HRC/13/30, 15 January 2010, para. 60. See, too, German court decision that indicated that a higher threshold, as compared to adults, was required to conclude that alternatives to detention would not suffice: Germany/Oberlandesgericht (Regional Court) Köln, decision of 11 September 2001, Case No. 16 Wx 164/02, cited in European Union Agency for Fundamental Rights (EU-FRA), *Detention of Third Country Nationals in Return Procedures,* 30 November 2010, n. 350.

[88] UN-WGAD, *Opinion No. 45/2006,* para. 25.

[89] *Louled Massoud v. Malta,* ECtHR, Applic. No. 24340/08,27 July 2010, para. 68.

[90] Article 15(1), *Council Directive 2008/115/EC of 16 December 2008 on common standards and procedures in Member States for returning illegally staying third-country nationals* (EU Returns Directive).

[91] Article 10(2), EU Returns Directive.

[92] Article 18(1), *Council Directive 2005/85/EC of 1 December 2005 on minimum standards on procedures in Member States for granting and withdrawing refugee status* (EU Procedures Directive).

Implicit within this provision is a requirement on states to look elsewhere than detention to establish migration controls, and it conforms too with the general principle under the 1951 Convention that seeking asylum is not an unlawful act and asylum-seekers should not be subject to criminal or other penalties (as already discussed). Where an asylum applicant is held in detention, the EU Procedures Directive mandates access to 'speedy judicial review'.[93]

The second recast proposal of the EU Receptions Directive, revealed in June 2011, adopts a like approach. Aimed at ensuring that detention occurs only under prescribed grounds and if it is in line with the principles of proportionality and necessity (as to the manner and purpose of detention), after an individual examination of each case,

> When it proves necessary and on the basis of an individual assessment of each case, Member States may detain an applicant, if other less coercive alternative measures cannot be applied effectively.[94]

The second recast proposal, like the first, also calls on governments to ensure that the regulation of alternatives is via national legislation,[95] yet the grounds for detention remain broad.[96] The Dublin Regulation recast proposal similarly provides that, 'when it proves necessary, on the basis of an individual assessment in each case, and if other less coercive measures cannot be applied effectively, Member States may detain an asylum seeker' on account of 'a significant risk of absconding'.[97] Notably this appears to be a fairer standard than that set by the UN-HRC, the latter only requiring any risk of absconding. While the recast proposals have yet to be agreed, they reflect a trend towards an expectation that alternatives to detention will be made available, and that detention can only be applied as a measure of last resort in the asylum context.

The second recast proposal – see *Amended Proposal for a Directive of the European Parliament and the Council on common procedures for granting and withdrawing international protection status*, COM(2011) 319 final, Brussels, 1 June 2011 – retains the safeguard against discriminatory detention but broadens it to apply to any 'applicant for international protection' (removal of the wording of 'asylum'). The recast also indicates that the matter must be in conformity with the EU Receptions Directive, *infra*.

93 Article 18(2), ibid.

94 See draft Article 8(2), *Proposal for a Directive of the European Parliament and of the Council laying down minimum standards for the reception of asylum seekers* (second recast), COM(2011) 320 final, 1 June 2011.

95 Draft Article 8(3), ibid.

96 They include that detention may be ordered (a) to determine identity or nationality; (b) to establish elements on which the asylum application is based 'which in other circumstances could be lost'; (c) during preliminary procedure to decide the right to enter the territory of a Member State; and (d) when public order or national security so require: Draft Article 8(3), second recast, ibid.

97 Draft Article 27(3), *Proposal for a Regulation of the European Parliament and of the Council establishing the criteria and mechanisms for determining the Member State responsible for examining an application for international protection lodged in one of the Member States by a third-country national or a stateless person* (recast), OM/2008/0820 final – COD 2008/0243, Brussels, 3 December 2008.

The Council of Europe's 'Twenty Guidelines on Forced Return' also address the question of alternatives.[98] Guideline 6.1 provides:

> A person may only be deprived of his/her liberty with a view to ensuring that a removal order will be executed ... if, after a careful examination of the necessity of deprivation in each individual case, the authorities of the host state have concluded that compliance with a removal order *cannot be ensured as effectively by resorting to non-custodial measures* such as supervision systems, the requirement to report regularly to the authorities, bail or other guarantee systems. [emphasis added.]

The position in the Americas is also clear. The I-ACmHR's *Principles and Best Practices on the Protection of Persons Deprived of Liberty in the Americas* also state clearly that '[t]he Member States of the Organization of American States shall establish by law a series of alternative or substitute measures for deprivation of liberty, duly taking into account the international human rights standards on the topic.'[99] In addition, in applying these alternative or substitute measures, OAS Member States 'shall promote the participation of society and the family'.[100]

The Inter-American Court of Human Rights (I-ACtHR) has recently stated its position on the need to examine alternatives to detention prior to detention in a decision on repeated irregular entry into Panama by an Ecuadorian migrant. It is worth re-quoting the relevant passage in full:

> the detention of people for non-compliance with immigration laws should never involve punitive purposes. Hence, a custodial measure should only be applied when it is necessary and proportionate in the specific case to the purposes mentioned supra and only for the shortest period of time. Therefore, it is essential for States to seek alternatives to detention whenever possible, which may be effective for the achievement of the purposes described. As a consequence, those migratory policies whose central focus is the mandatory detention of irregular migrants, without ordering the competent authorities to verify in each particular case and by means of an individualized evaluation, the possibility of using less restrictive measures of achieving the same ends, are arbitrary.[101]

UNHCR has long advocated that detention is an exceptional measure and further that, 'Where there are monitoring mechanisms which can be employed as viable alternatives to detention ... these should be applied first unless there is evidence to suggest that such an

---

98 Council of Europe, *Twenty Guidelines on Forced Return*, at: http://www.unhcr.org/refworld/pdfid/42ef32984.pdf [accessed on 3 August 2012].

99 I-ACmHR, *Principles and Best Practices on the Protection of Persons Deprived of Liberty in the Americas*, OAS Doc. OEA/Ser/L/V/II.131 doc. 26, March 2008, Principle III(4).

100 Ibid.

101 *Vélez Loor v. Panama*, I-ACtHR, 23 November 2010, para. 17.

alternative will not be effective in an individual case.'[102] Its *Guidelines* list various alternative responses to detention, including reporting or residency requirements, guarantees, sureties or bail.[103] The UN Sub-Commission on the Promotion and Protection of Human Rights encouraged '[s]tates to adopt alternatives to detention such as those enumerated in the Guidelines on the Applicable Criteria and Standards relating to the Detention of Asylum Seekers'.[104] UN-WGAD has likewise argued that 'alternative and noncustodial measures, such as reporting requirements, should always be considered before resorting to detention.'[105] This is further reflected in its Guarantee 13.[106]

Grounded in the principles of necessity, proportionality and reasonableness, the position at international law must now be accepted that there is an obligation built into the right to liberty and against arbitrary detention on states to consider less intrusive means of achieving the same objectives. Failure to do so is likely to render the detention disproportionate, unnecessary and unreasonable – and, therefore, arbitrary.

The only exception at international law appears to be the position of the ECtHR in respect of detention relating to unauthorized admission. In particular, the controversial decision of the Grand Chamber in *Saadi v. United Kingdom* held that Article 5 imposes no requirement to examine the necessity of the detention: 'there is no requirement in Article 5 § (1)(f) that the detention of a person to prevent his effecting an unauthorised entry into the country be reasonably considered necessary, for example to prevent his committing an offence or fleeing.'[107] The decision followed that of *Chahal*, in which it was similarly held that additional bases for detention beyond those itemized in Article 5 of the ECHR are not required; all that is required in that case was that Mr. Chahal was detained 'with a view to deportation',[108] although this too has been questioned in *Massoud v. Malta* where other measures could have achieved the same objective (discussed above). Similarly, it was found that Mr Saadi was detained under the ground to prevent him effecting an unlawful entry. In *Saadi*, the Court found that seven days' detention for the purpose of expediting an asylum claim is a legitimate ground for detention. In other words, it appears that, under the ECHR, a state may detain to prevent an unauthorized entry; it is not relevant whether detention was 'necessary' in order to prevent that unlawful entry, or whether in fact a lawful entry had already been made. Nevertheless, the ECtHR did note that the detention must be closely connected to the purpose of preventing an unauthorized entry.

102 Guideline 3, UNHCR, *Revised Guidelines on Detention.*

103 Guideline 4, ibid.

104 UN Sub-Commission on the Promotion and Protection of Human Rights res. 2000/21 (no document number), para. 6.

105 UN-WGAD, *Report of the Visit to the United Kingdom on the Issue of Immigrants and Asylum Seekers*, UN Doc. E/CN.4/1999/63/Add.3, 18 December 1998, para. 33.

106 UN-WGAD, *Legal Opinion on the Situation regarding Immigrants and Asylum-seekers*, E/CN.4/1999/63, para. 69: 'Possibility for the alien to benefit from alternatives to administrative custody.'

107 *Saadi v. UK*, para. 45.

108 *Chahal v. United Kingdom*, ECtHR, Applic. No. 22414/93, 15 November 1996. The Court did acknowledge that the length of Chahal's detention could have rendered it arbitrary, but found that there had been some safeguards in place to ensure that it had not been. Cf. *Massoud v. Malta.*

By contrast, the UN-HRC has held that administrative expediency is not a valid basis for detention on its own under Article 9 of the ICCPR.[109]

The reasoning in *Saadi* is, however, flawed for a number of reasons. First, by divorcing the ground or purpose of detention with its necessity, it is difficult to determine whether the purpose is met and therefore whether the detention is lawful. For example, if the detention is not necessary, how can it achieve or be related to its purpose? The purpose would not therefore exist. The *Chahal* case is distinct from *Saadi* to an extent in this regard because, in the former, detention was required to be for the purposes of (or 'with a view to') deportation, and such deportation, the ECtHR held, must be reasonably foreseeable; thus a necessity criterion is already a built-in consideration of the ground. The detention must be 'with a view to' deportation; if the deportation cannot be carried out, it is not considered 'with a view to' deportation and therefore there is no legitimate power to detain. This has been clarified in *Mikolenko v. Estonia*, in which it was held that the ground for detention satisfied Article 5(1)(f), here to effect the individual's removal, however it ceased to be justified as time passed, as he became non-removable. Mr Mikolenko refused to cooperate with his deportation proceedings (he refused to fill in an application for a Russian passport) and the Russian authorities refused to accept him on a temporary travel document issued by Estonia. He spent more than three years and 11 months in detention, which was found to be arbitrary.[110]

The second concern with *Saadi* is that the judgment does not recognize an application for asylum as a lawful act and thus the ECtHR treated Mr Saadi, who had applied for asylum prior to his detention, as still not being 'lawfully within' the territory for the purposes of Article 5. The ECtHR did not examine the meaning of 'to effect an unlawful entry' in its judgment (or its opposite, to be 'lawfully in' the territory). This meant that the majority did not consider jurisprudence from various other judgments relating to lawful versus unlawful presence in the territory (as discussed above). The dissenting opinion also criticized the majority for 'attach[ing] no importance to the fact [that Mr Saadi claimed asylum upon arrival]'[111] and for failing to distinguish between categories of non-nationals.

Nonetheless, the ECtHR in both *Chahal* and *Saadi* conceded that there are limits on detention and that it is subject to the rules relating to arbitrariness. The ECtHR held in *Saadi* that this requires that the detention be a 'genuine part of a process' to grant immigration clearance.[112] On this basis, it could be argued that states will need to show, for example, that any fast-track or accelerated procedures are a lawful basis for detention, especially if they run past the seven-day period recognized in *Saadi*. It would need to be shown by the immigration authorities that they could not process applications speedily outside detention, or that the accelerated asylum procedures continue to be the basis for the detention as it becomes extended. With research available to show many examples of very high compliance or cooperation rates among asylum seekers released to non-custodial alternatives to detention – as high as or higher than 90 per cent in some alternative

109 *Van Alphen v. The Netherlands*, para. 5.8.
110 *Mikolenko v. Estonia*, ECtHR, Application No. 10664/05, 8 September 2009.
111 *Saadi v. UK*, dissenting opinion, p. 31.
112 *Saadi v. UK*, para. 45.

programmes –, arguments that suggest that detention is needed in most situations, are becoming hollow and ill-founded.[113]

So where does *Saadi* stand in the grand scheme of things? Since *Saadi*, there is some evidence of a softening of the ECtHR's position on the question of necessity. In *Lokpo and Touré v. Hungary*, a case of two Ivorian asylum seekers who were detained for five months because of illegal entry and for the purposes of expulsion, the Court reiterated that the 'formal "lawfulness" of detention under domestic law is the primary' consideration; it is 'not always the decisive element in assessing the justification of deprivation of liberty.'[114] The Court went on to state, 'It must in addition be satisfied that detention during the period under consideration was compatible with the purpose of Article 5 § 1, which is ... to prevent persons from being deprived of their liberty in an arbitrary fashion.'[115] In particular the Court was not persuaded that that the applicants' detention was a measure proportionate to the aim pursued by the alien administration policy.[116] The Court also took note of the fact that their release had not been authorized merely because the refugee authority had not initiated it, and that silence or 'non-action' cannot justify detention and 'verges on arbitrariness'.[117] Furthermore, the Court held that the 'absence of elaborate reasoning for an applicant's deprivation of liberty renders that measure incompatible with the requirement of lawfulness inherent in Article 5'.[118] Here the Court appears to require a well-reasoned justification for detention beyond merely citing either Article 5(1)(f) of the ECHR or relevant domestic provisions. In two other cases – those of *S.D. v. Greece* and *R.U. v. Greece* –, the ECtHR confirmed that, where domestic law only previews detention for the purposes of expulsion, it is not permissible to hold asylum seekers in detention as they cannot be expelled.[119]

As there is substantial, if not near-identical, overlap between the states parties to the ICCPR and the ECHR, a state party to the ECHR may still be in violation of the rights of individuals under Article 9 of the ICCPR if it merely or automatically detains on account of the two grounds in the ECHR without further justification. Neither of the usual maxims of interpretation – *lex specialis* and *lex posterior* – appears to resolve the question of which standard applies in this instance of a conflict of laws. Arguably, neither the ECHR nor the ICCPR is *lex specialis* as the conflict of treaty obligations is around the same kind of right. Even if Article 5(1)(f) is considered more *specialis* because it explicitly lists the range of permissible bases for detention (compared with Article 9, which is general in nature), the rule of *lex posterior* may step in to make Article 9 of the ICCPR the applicable norm. Neither of these legal maxims seems to solve this dilemma. So what about any conflict of laws provisions? Article 53 of the ECHR provides that '[n]othing in this Convention shall be construed as limiting or derogating from any of the human rights and fundamental freedoms which may be ensured under the laws or any High Contracting Party or under any other agreement to which it is a Party.' Applying Article 53 of the ECHR, the higher

113 See, Edwards, *Back to Basics*.
114 *Lokpo and Touré v. Hungary*, ECtHR, Applic. No. 10816/10, 20 September 2011, para. 21.
115 Ibid.
116 Ibid., para. 22.
117 Ibid., para. 24.
118 Ibid.
119 See note 45.

(or more rights-respecting) standard would prevail. This would conform to the object and purpose of the ECHR. The European Court of Justice also appears to accept the higher-standard approach, going against the views of the ECtHR in *Chahal*, in noting that 'the detention of a person for the purpose of removal may only be maintained as long as the removal arrangements are in progress and must be executed with due diligence, *provided that it is necessary* to ensure successful removal.'[120] The 'special character' of human rights treaties strengthens the argument that the higher standard must prevail.[121]

5. State Practice and Jurisprudence

Many states have legislated for alternatives to immigration detention,[122] or require that less coercive means be considered prior to detention. Australia, Austria, Canada, Denmark, Greece, Hong Kong, Ireland, Japan, Norway, Sweden and the United States have legal frameworks, for example, that can require individuals to report to the police or immigration authorities at regular intervals.[123] According to the European Union Agency on Fundamental Rights, approximately two thirds of EU countries have legislation that provides for alternatives to detention to be imposed instead of detention initially or at a review stage.[124] This suggests too that the ECtHR in *Saadi* is out of touch with the practice of most European states. The legislative picture is supported by judicial rulings. The Canadian Supreme Court in *Sahin* held, for example, that the 'availability, effectiveness and appropriateness of alternatives to detention must be considered.'[125] Both the Austrian and Slovenian constitutional courts, for example, have also dictated that the authorities must apply more lenient measures to determine whether detention is necessary.[126]

Many other countries regulate immigration without resource to detention and this in itself questions the practices of other states. South African law, for example, requires release from detention of anyone applying for asylum, unless other concerns prevail such

[120] *Kadzoev v. Bulgaria*, para. 56 (my emphasis).

[121] See Edwards, 'Human Rights, Refugees, and the Right to "Enjoy" Asylum'.

[122] The legislation of several countries provides for alternatives to administrative detention, such as release on bail, release on parole, home detention, semi-liberty, payment of a certain sum as guarantee, police supervision, ban on leaving the country, obligation to reside at a given address with periodic reporting to the authorities, withdrawal of passport: per Special Rapporteur on the Human Rights of Migrants, Ms. Gabriela Rodrìguez Pizarro, *Report to the 54th Session of the Commission on Human Rights*, UN Doc. E/CN.4/2003/85, 30 December 2003, para. 39.

[123] Field and Edwards, *Alternatives to Detention*, at pp. 28–30.

[124] EU-FRA, *Detention of Third Country Nationals in Return Procedures*, pp. 72–81.

[125] See, e.g., *Sahin v. Canada (Minister of Citizenship and Immigration)* [1995] 1 FC 214, as cited in Immigration and Refugee Board of Canada, Guideline 2, *Guidelines on Detention*, Ottawa, Canada, 12 March 1998, p. 4.

[126] See, e.g., Austrian Constitutional Court (Verfassungsgerichtshof Österreich): B 223/06, 291/06 (27 February 2001), B 362/06 (24 June 2006); Slovenian Constitutional Court U-I-297/95 (28 October 1998).

as national security.[127] The Philippines, too, provides asylum-seeker certification upon arrival and releases asylum seekers from detention without conditions.[128] Under pressure from a range of decisions that questioned the legality of Hong Kong's detention policy,[129] most asylum seekers and torture claimants are released on their own recognizance and are supported by a government-funded community supervision service.[130] National courts have further supported the general position at international law: the UK and South African courts argue that the operation of presumptions in favour of detention would be unlawful, and are not balancing tests at all.[131] As many national legal frameworks provide for alternatives to detention, they feed into the international legal position that these are necessary to avoid arbitrary detention. The problem lies more in their lack of application, than in a lack of law.

6. Conclusion

This chapter has sought to elaborate the limits on a state's power to detain on immigration grounds, namely in relation to the obligation to consider less invasive or coercive means of achieving a state's objective of migration management. Like all human rights, the right to liberty imports both negative and positive obligations on the state. A state's negative obligation is one of refraining from unlawfully or arbitrarily detaining asylum seekers, refugees or other migrants. In relation to positive obligations, a state, if it intends to use

127 Section 22 of the Immigration Act allows a stay of any proceedings pending the outcome of an application for asylum, which includes a stay of any detention order. In other words, there is no power to detain asylum seekers in South Africa.

128 Information supplied by the International Detention Coalition (on file with the author).

129 See *Shum Kwok-sher v. Hong Kong SAR* [2002] 5 HKCFAR 318 and *'A' v. Director of Immigration* [2008] HKCU 1109, 18 July 2008 (HK Court of Appeal), which found that Article 5 of the Hong Kong Bill of Rights mandates legal certainty and accessibility in connection with detention. There was a violation of both legal certainty and accessibility because there was no policy statement setting out how the power of detention was to be exercised. Despite the HK government adopting two documents, a later case found that two notices and two further documents were also inadequate: see *Hashimi Habib Halim v. Director of Immigration* [2008] HKCU 1576 (HK Court of First Instance). Other cases include *Tan Te Lam v. Tai A Chau Detention Centre* [1997] AC 97 (PC), which involved the detention of Vietnamese asylum seekers of Chinese ethnic origin who had been refused refugee status but who could not be removed to Vietnam since the Vietnamese Government would not readmit those it did not consider to be Vietnamese nationals. The Privy Council held that, if such removal could not be accomplished within a reasonable time period, then further detention was unlawful. In 1996, the Privy Council reversed a decision by the CA and determined, in *Nguyen Tuan Cuong and Others and Director of Immigration and Others* [1996] 423 HKCU 1, that the Director of Immigration did not uphold his statutory duty under Part IIIA of the Immigration Ordinance by refusing to screen Vietnamese migrants who had arrived in Hong Kong from southern China. Taken from K. Loper, 'Human Rights, *Non-Refoulement*, and the Protection of Refugees in Hong Kong' (2010) 22(3) *International Journal of Refugee Law* 404–39.

130 See, Edwards, *Back to Basics*.

131 See, e.g., *N (Kenya) v. Secretary for State for Home Department* and *Ulde v. Minister of Home Affairs*.

detention, must ensure that there are procedural safeguards in place, that courts possess the authority to order release, that maximum limits on periods in detention are regulated by law, and, relevant to this chapter, as detention can only be ordered if it is necessary, the system must offer alternatives to detention, with release being the ultimate alternative. The right to liberty requires that, when a government contemplates restricting liberty, particularly in the context of immigration, it must first make available a range of lesser restrictions to match the risk involved and the individual's particular circumstances. States cannot justify the detention of migrants or asylum seekers simply by indicating that there are no alternative options available. This would be a *male fides* implementation of international obligations and in conflict with international treaty law.[132]

Habeas corpus guarantees are fundamental to countries said to be enjoying the rule of law and democratic governance.[133] Since the 1700s, *habeas corpus* has applied to nationals and non-nationals alike.[134] And while the right to liberty is not unlimited, its increasing use in many countries in the context of controlling irregular immigration, including on blanket or semi-automatic bases, can be challenged under international law. From the above catalogue of jurisprudence and international instruments, the international legal position is now clear: states must consider less coercive forms of immigration control in each individual case before resorting to confinement. The only remaining exception appears to be the position of the ECtHR in *Saadi* and *Chahal*, and even there the case law has been inconsistent and is ripe to be re-challenged. With the legal position now relatively robust, it must be questioned, how are states getting away with rising rates of incarceration?

References

Bingham, Lord T., *The Rule of Law* (London: Allen Lane, 2010).

Council of Europe, *Twenty Guidelines on Forced Return*, at: http://www.unhcr.org/refworld/pdfid/42ef32984.pdf [accessed on 3 August 2012].

Daly, M., 'Refugee Law in Hong Kong: Building the Legal Infrastructure' (2009) 9 *Hong Kong Lawyer* 1.

[132] States are required to implement their treaty obligations in good faith: Article 26, Vienna Convention on the Law of Treaties 1969.

[133] See, e.g., English Bill of Rights 1689, which contained protections in favour of personal liberty and security by the prohibitions on imposition of excessive fines, bail, and infliction of cruel and unusual punishments: see Bingham, *Rule of Law*, p. 24. See, also, the French Declaration of the Rights of Man 1789, which at Article 7 prohibits charge, arrest and detention unless prescribed by law. The US Supreme Court has likewise consistently recognized the principle that '[f]reedom from bodily restraint has always been at the core of the liberty protected by the Due Process Clause from arbitrary governmental action': per *Foucha v. Louisiana*, p. 80.

[134] Per Sommersett's Case (1772) 20 St. T. J., discussed *supra*, referred to in Bingham, *Rule of Law*, p. 58. See, further, *R v. Secretary of State for the Home Department, ex p. Khawaja* [1984] AC 74, paras 111–12.

Edwards, A., *Back to Basics: The Right to Liberty and Security of Person and 'Alternatives to Detention' of Refugees, Asylum-seekers, Stateless Persons and Other Migrants*, April 2011, PPLA/2011/01.Rev.1, at: http://www.unhcr.org/refworld/docid/4dc935fd2.html [accessed on 3 August 2012].

Edwards, A., 'Human Rights, Refugees, and the Right to "Enjoy" Asylum' (2005) 17(2) *International Journal of Refugee Law* 297–330.

Edwards, A., 'Measures of First Resort: Alternatives to Immigration Detention in Comparative Perspective' (2011) 7 *Equal Rights Review* 117–42, at: http://www.equalrightstrust.org/ertdocumentbank/ERR7_alice.pdf [accessed on 3 August 2012].

Edwards, A., 'The Optional Protocol to the Convention against Torture and the Detention of Refugees' (2008) 57(4) *International and Comparative Law Quarterly* 789–825.

Goodwin-Gill, G., 'Article 31 of the 1951 Convention Relating to the Status of Refugees: Non-penalization, Detention, and Protection', in E. Feller, V. Türk and F. Nicholson (eds), *Refugee Protection in International Law: UNHCR's Global Consultations on International Protection* (Cambridge: Cambridge University Press, 2003), pp. 185–252.

Goodwin-Gill, G. and J. McAdam, *The Refugee in International Law* (Oxford: Oxford University Press, 2007).

Grahl-Madsen, A., *The Status of Refugees in International Law, vol. II* (Leyden: A.W. Sijthoff, 1972).

Hathaway, J. C., *The Rights of Refugees under International Law* (Cambridge: Cambridge University Press, 2005).

Loper, K., 'Human Rights, *Non-Refoulement*, and the Protection of Refugees in Hong Kong' (2010) 22(3) *International Journal of Refugee Law* 404–39.

Marx, R., 'Article 26 (Freedom of Movement/Liberté de Circulation'), in A. Zimmerman (ed.), *Commentary on the 1951 Convention relating to the Status of Refugees* (Oxford: Oxford University Press, 2011), 1147–64.

Noll, G., 'Article 31 (Refugees Lawfully in the Country of Refuge/Réfugiés en situation irrégulière dans le pays d'accueil)', in A. Zimmerman (ed.), *Commentary on the 1951 Convention relating to the Status of Refugees* (Oxford: Oxford University Press, 2011), pp. 1243–76.

Sampson, R., G. Mitchell and L. Bowring, *There Are Alternatives: A Handbook for Preventing Unnecessary Immigration Detention*, International Detention Coalition, Melbourne, 2011, at: http://www.unhcr.org/4dde23d49.html [accessed on 12 July 2011].

UNHCR, *Guidelines on Policies and Procedures in Dealing with Unaccompanied Children Seeking Asylum* (Geneva: UNHCR, 1997).

UNHCR, *Revised Guidelines on Detention of Asylum Seekers and Refugees* (Geneva: UNHCR, 1999).

Weis, P., *The Refugee Convention, 1951: The Travaux Préparatoires Analysed, With a Commentary by Dr. Paul Weis* (Cambridge: Cambridge University Press, 1995).

The End of Refugee Camps?

Guglielmo Verdirame[1] and Jason Pobjoy[2]

Introduction

Encampment is one of the main challenges to the protection of the human rights of refugees.[3] In most of Africa and in many parts of Asia it is the standard way of hosting and assisting refugees, and often the only one employed by the United Nations High Commissioner for Refugees ('UNHCR'), humanitarian organizations, and many host states. Until recently there had been little critical engagement with the question of refugee camps within policy circles. Something began to change when a group of human rights and humanitarian organizations, led by the US Committee for Refugees and Migrants ('USCRI'), organized a worldwide campaign against what was labeled 'the warehousing of refugees' and adopted the *Statement Calling for Solutions to End the Warehousing of Refugees* in September 2009. In their own words, refugees are warehoused when they

> are confined to camps or segregated settlements or otherwise deprived of their basic rights, in situations lasting 10 years or more. Warehousing refugees not only violates their rights but also often reduces refugees to enforced idleness, dependency, and despair.[4]

Although UNHCR has not joined the USCRI campaign, it has recently embarked on its own internal process of policy review that indicates a willingness to reassess the organization's current approach to the protection of refugees in the political South. This review process culminated in 2009 with the adoption of the *Policy on Refugee Protection and Solutions in Urban Areas* ('*2009 Urban Policy*').[5] This new policy – strongly supported by the High Commissioner,

---

1 Professor of International Law, King's College London; Barrister, 20 Essex Street Chambers.

2 Ph.D. candidate in Law, Faculty of Law, University of Cambridge; Hauser Visiting Doctoral Researcher, New York University School of Law.

3 The same could be said about internally displaced persons, but the focus of this chapter is on refugees.

4 For a copy of the statement, see http://www.refugees.org/our-work/refugee-rights/warehousing-campaign/recent-progress.html (last accessed 22 August 2012).

5 UNHCR, *UNHCR Policy on Refugee Protections and Solutions in Urban Areas* (September 2009), via http://www.unhcr.org/refworld/docid/4ab8e7f72.html (last accessed 22 August 2012).

Mr António Guterres[6] – purports to respond to the reality that more than half of the world's refugees live in urban environments.[7] Lauded as 'the beginning of a new approach',[8] the *2009 Urban Policy* is the centrepiece of UNHCR's 'recalibrated'[9] approach to urban-based refugees, marking a generally welcome shift away from the organization's far more restrictive policy published in 1997.[10]

In this chapter we discuss the evolution of the *2009 Urban Policy*, set against broader questions concerning the quagmire of refugee camps. We assess the positive elements of the *2009 Urban Policy* and critique its key weaknesses and challenges. It is, of course, too soon to tell whether the shift in policy will eventually lead to the demise of encampment, but it is certainly a step in the right direction. Crucially, the fact that the countries that took the brunt of the Iraqi refugee crisis – Jordan, Lebanon and Syria – chose not to establish camps, provides critics of encampment with powerful ammunition: the refrain that alternatives to refugee camps are not politically viable must now confront the clear evidence that for some host states the politically unacceptable solution is encampment.

The Refugee Camp Bias

The essence of a refugee camp is *separation*. Refugees who live there are physically separated from the host population; the humanitarian organizations that govern the camp, distribute food, and provide health and welfare services are distinct from (and unaccountable to) national and local authorities; and national laws are for the most part not enforced, replaced instead by rules, written and unwritten, laid down by the humanitarian organizations. The social world

---

6 In December 2008 the Commissioner announced his intention to focus attention on the issue of 'urban displacement', and to examine the topic in detail at the annual Dialogue on Protection Challenges in December 2009: 'Urban refugees and the urbanization phenomenon more generally will be a strategic policy priority for UNHCR throughout 2009. The constructive response of Syria and Jordan to the massive number of Iraqi refugees in those countries suggests that the urbanization of refugees may present opportunities as well as obstacles. I acknowledge, however, that both UNHCR and the international community have still much to learn about providing protection and assistance in urban settings. UNHCR is presently revising its guidance on urban refugees and next year's Dialogue will be entirely devoted to the issue' – António Guterres, 'Opening Statement of Mr. António Guterres, United Nations High Commissioner for Refugees, at the High Commissioner's Dialogue on Protection Challenges: Protracted Refugee Situations' (10 December 2008), at http://www.unhcr.org/493fd97e2.html (last accessed 22 August 2012).

7 *2009 Urban Policy*, [3]. We adopt here UNHCR's definition of an 'urban area' (also at [3]): 'a built-up area that accommodates large number of people living in close proximity to each other, and where the majority of people sustain themselves by means of formal and informal employment and the provision of goods and services. While refugee camps share some of the characteristics of an urban area, they are excluded from this definition'.

8 Ibid., [9].

9 António Guterres, 'Protection Challenges for Persons of Concern in Urban Settings' (2010) 34 *Forced Migration Review* 7–8, at 8.

10 UNHCR, *UNHCR Policy on Refugees in Urban Areas* (12 December 1997), at http://www.unhcr.org/refworld/topic,4565c2253e,4565c25f4c7,3cbaedf74,0,POSITION,.html (last accessed 22 August 2012).

within the camp itself is also defined by separation:[11] refugees are divided into communities that tend to reflect the anthropological map of the ruling humanitarian organizations.

The extent to which refugees are separated from their hosts varies from one camp to another. In some cases, the separation is stark and strictly enforced. Refugees found outside the camp are subject to penalties, including imprisonment, while national authorities have barely any involvement in the running of the camp, retaining at most a public order presence through local police. In other cases, the humanitarian organizations will run the camp together with representatives of the host government. Another crucial point of variance concerns the extent to which refugees are permitted to work. Where refugees are prevented from undertaking any form of gainful employment other than work for the humanitarian organizations that run the camp, the social and economic separation from the host society will be very significant. Where, in the Ugandan settlements for example, refugees are allowed to cultivate an allotment of land as part of a policy that purports to promote the self-sufficiency of refugees, there is at least the potential for some integration.[12]

Camps have been criticized on various grounds. They create an ideal space for political and ethnical radicalization;[13] they undermine local institutions;[14] they facilitate the breakdown of networks of social assistance and, more generally, of community;[15] and they constitute 'a breach of the most fundamental human rights, a cruel and dehumanising absurdity excused by neither political nor economic convenience'.[16]

The key institutional actor in refugee camps is UNHCR. Non-governmental organizations are prominent players too, as the display of banners and logos in the compounds shows; but they are normally there on the basis of an agreement with UNHCR and, often, as sub-contractors of UNHCR. This UNHCR-led humanitarian *ensemble* exercises such degree of control over camps that in many cases the control can be said to be, in a legal sense, effective. For this reason, camp administration has been described as a form of *de facto* international administration of territory.[17]

The role of UNHCR in the administration of camps is an anomaly, both legally and politically. Its effects on the plane of attribution of conduct and, more generally, international

[11] See Barbara E. Harrell-Bond and Eftihia Voutira, 'In Search of the Locus of Trust: The Social World of a Refugee Camp', in E. Valentine Daniel and John Chr. Knudsen (eds) *Mistrusting Refugees* (University of California Press, Berkeley, CA, 1995) 207–24.

[12] Guglielmo Verdirame and Barbara E. Harrell-Bond, *Rights in Exile: Janus-faced Humanitarianism* (Berghahn Books, New York, 2005) 226.

[13] Liisa H. Malkki, *Purity and Exile: Violence, Memory, and National Cosmology among Hutu Refugees in Tanzania* (University of Chicago Press, Chicago, IL, 1995).

[14] Philippe Goyens *et al.*, 'Humanitarian Aid and Health Services in Eastern Kivu, Zaire: Collaboration or Competition' (1996) 9 *Journal of Refugee Studies* 268–80; Verdirame and Harrell-Bond, *Rights in Exile.*

[15] Jennifer Hyndman, *Managing Displacement: Refugees and the Politics of Humanitarianism* (University of Minnesota Press, Minneapolis, MN, 2000); Barbara E. Harrell-Bond, *Imposing Aid: Emergency Assistance to Refugees* (Oxford University Press, Oxford, 1986).

[16] Verdirame and Harrell-Bond, *Rights in Exile*, 338.

[17] See Guglielmo Verdirame, *The UN and Human Rights: Who Guards the Guardians?* (Cambridge University Press, Cambridge, 2011) chapter 6.

legal responsibility have never been properly tested in court.[18] UNHCR has not adopted encampment as its official policy for assisting refugees in the South and would probably still maintain that, where it assumes an administrative role in camps, it does so reluctantly and only in order to contain damage. Nevertheless, there is some evidence that UNHCR advocated the establishment of camps in certain situations, and hardly any to show that UNHCR ever publicly objected to it.[19]

The Evolution of UNHCR's Urban Policy

The UNHCR's policy on urban-based refugees 'has had a long and somewhat troubled history.'[20] For 45 years the organization had no formal policy addressing refugees living in urban-environments. Its first policy, the *UNHCR Comprehensive Policy on Urban Refugees*, published in March 1997,[21] was retracted less than nine months after publication, after coming under sustained attack from non-governmental organizations and other human rights groups.[22] The replacement *UNHCR Policy on Urban Refugees*[23] published in December 1997 (*'1997 Urban Policy'*) – although more nuanced than the March version – reveals the close link between urban policy and encampment. The policy captured the UNHCR's approach to refugee protection and assistance in the political South, effectively operationalizing the exclusion of urban-based refugees from the UNHCR's protection activities, and legitimizing the warehousing of refugees in camps. The *1997 Urban Policy* maintained that the provision of assistance to urban-based refugees was expensive and difficult to administer,[24] and, on this

18 Nor has the somewhat analogous phenomenon of UNHCR assuming control over the legal process of refugee status determination been challenged in court. The European Court of Human Rights ('ECtHR') case of *D v Turkey* (Application No. 24245/03, 22 June 2006) was a missed opportunity in this respect. The applicants were an Iranian couple sentenced to 100 lashes each for having engaged in pre-marital sex. Once in Turkey, they applied for refugee status at the UNHCR branch office, as Turkey is one of many countries in the world where refugee status determination, normally a state-run administrative procedure, is entirely handled by the UNHCR. In November 2006 their application for refugee status was rejected with a 'barely reasoned decision by UNHCR', which also produced a statement dismissing the severity of the sentence inflicted in Iran and alleging that it would have in practice involved 'the symbolic application of the sentence bearing in mind the individual's state of health'. With a very short judgment the ECtHR found in favour of the applicants on the basis of the serious risk to their Article 3 rights. The applicants do not, however, seem to have complained of a violation of their Article 6 rights by the UNHCR-administered refugee status determination procedures.

19 Verdirame and Harrell-Bond, *Rights in Exile*, 51 (fn 12).

20 Jeff Crisp *et al.*, 'Surviving in the City: A Review of UNHCR's Operation for Iraqi Refugees in Urban Areas of Jordan, Lebanon and Syria', UNHCR Policy Development and Evaluation Service, PDES/2009/03 (July 2009) ('Crisp *et al.*') [22]. See also Verdirame and Harrell-Bond, *Rights in Exile*, 297–9.

21 UNHCR, *UNHCR Comprehensive Policy on Urban Refugees* (25 March 1997), at http://www.unhcr.org/refworld/topic,4565c2253e,4565c25f4c7,41626fb64,0,,.html (last accessed 22 August 2012).

22 Crisp *et al.*, 'Surviving in the City', [23].

23 UNHCR, *UNHCR Policy on Refugees in Urban Areas.*

24 *1997 Urban Policy*, [5].

basis, concluded that UNHCR's assistance in urban environments should be reduced to a minimum.[25] Under the *1997 Urban Policy* an urban-based refugee was a tolerated exception at best, a deviant at worst.

In 2009 the UNHCR adopted a new urban policy. The *2009 Urban Policy* represents a marked improvement on its predecessors, although it does not go far enough to resolve the enduring refugee camp bias.

The *1997 Urban Policy*

The *1997 Urban Policy* was premised on the notion that African refugees are essentially *rural*, and that camps and settlements are the right solution for a largely rural population, while refugees who choose to live in an urban environment do so at their own risk and expense. The policy paid token homage to freedom of movement,[26] but that was largely overshadowed by reference, in its opening paragraph, to the problems that may be created by '*unregulated* movement to urban areas, whether this movement takes place within the country or from another country where the refugee had found protection.'[27] The *1997 Urban Policy* decreed that the UNHCR may 'limit the location where … assistance is provided', and that, if a rural settlement or camp was available in a host country, the organization 'should provide assistance in urban areas to refugees from the same country of origin *only* with the agreement of the government *and* if there are compelling reasons to do so.'[28]

The earlier version of the *1997 Urban Policy* – the one published in March 1997 and subsequently retracted – expressly limited those who could benefit from assistance to refugees who satisfied the following criteria:

> For the purposes of being considered *for assistance* in an urban area, an urban refugee/asylum-seeker is a person of urban background in the country of origin and who is neither an irregular mover, nor part of a *prima facie* caseload, and, if of rural background, for whom in the country of asylum the option of rural settlement which offers an opportunity for self-sufficiency does not exist.[29]

Although the version that was eventually adopted was less explicit (no doubt influenced by the strong criticism of its March 1997 policy), the practical effect was pretty much the same. The *prima facie* position was that, where available, a camp or settlement was the most appropriate

---

[25] See Naoko Obi and Jeff Crisp, UNHCR Evaluation and Policy Analysis Unity, 'Evaluation of the Implementation of UNHCR's Policy on Refugees in Urban Areas', EPAU/2001/10 (December 2001) ('Obi and Crisp'), [15].

[26] *1997 Urban Policy*, [3].

[27] Ibid., [1] (emphasis added).

[28] Ibid., [3] (emphasis added). Compelling reasons could include 'specific protection or security problems faced by an individual or his or her family in the settlement or camp; prearranged movement to an urban area for the duration of health care or for reunion with family members legally resident in the urban area; and assistance in achieving a durable solution, where this is possible in the urban area' (at [4]).

[29] UNHCR, *UNHCR Comprehensive Policy on Urban Refugees*, [45].

– and, from the point of view of UNHCR, the most convenient – location for a refugee. The refugee who wanted to leave the camp had to show 'compelling reasons' to be considered for assistance in an urban environment.

The *1997 Urban Policy* also devoted considerable attention to the perceived problem of 'irregular movers'.[30] The term 'irregular mover' derives from a series of UNHCR Executive Committee conclusions in the 1980s, dealing with refugees who left their first country of asylum and sought protection in another country.[31] While acknowledging that 'UNHCR's protection obligations are unaffected by such movement',[32] the policy provided that the organization did 'not have an obligation to provide assistance to refugees after irregular movement on the same basis as it would had there been no irregular movement.'[33] The policy acknowledged the need to look at the reason for the secondary movement,[34] requiring, however, that, where protection was available in the first country of asylum, UNHCR assistance be limited[35] and that return to the first country of asylum be considered.[36]

Where an urban-based refugee did qualify for assistance, the *1997 Urban Policy* provided that assistance 'should be given in a manner that encourages self-reliance and does not foster long-term dependency'.[37] This focus on temporary assistance stood in contrast to UNHCR's approach to assistance in camps or settlements, where the need for long-term and potentially indefinite assistance was 'rarely called into question.'[38] The policy also provided that the UNHCR should promote self-reliance in a manner that 'respect[ed] the polices of the [host] government',[39] clearly limiting the capacity of UNHCR to provide assistance where a host government restricted the movement of refugees to camps or settlements (as was the case in Uganda and continues to be the case, at least officially, in Kenya[40]), or otherwise obstructed the ability of refugees to be self-sufficient in urban environments (for example, by denying the right to work[41]).

30 *1997 Urban Policy*, [13].

31 See, for example, UNHCR Executive Committee Conclusion No. 58, 'Problem of Refugees and Asylum-seekers who Move in an Irregular Manner from a Country in which they have Already Found Protection' (1989), which defines irregular movers as 'refugees, whether they have been formally identified as such or not (asylum-seekers), who move in an irregular manner from countries in which they have already found protection, in order to seek asylum or permanent resettlement elsewhere' ([(a)]).

32 *1997 Urban Policy*, [17].

33 Ibid., [17]. This was certainly a lighter touch than the previous version of the policy, which had provided that *all* material assistance 'should legitimately be denied by UNHCR to irregular movers': UNHCR, *UNHCR Comprehensive Policy on Urban Refugees*, [4].

34 *1997 Urban Policy*, [13]. This is to some degree undermined by applying the pejorative term 'irregular mover' to all refugees who leave their country of asylum. See Obi and Crisp, [38]–[39].

35 *1997 Urban Policy*, [16]–[17].

36 Ibid., [18].

37 Ibid., [6].

38 Obi and Crisp, [19].

39 *1997 Urban Policy*, [9].

40 See generally Verdirame and Harrell-Bond, *Rights in Exile*; Human Rights Watch, 'Hidden in Plain View: Refugees Living Without Protection in Nairobi and Kampala' (2002), via http://www.unhcr.org/refworld/country,HRW,KEN,456d621e2,3e314172e,0.html (last accessed 22 August 2012).

41 Obi and Crisp, [23].

The *2009 Urban Policy*

The *2009 Urban Policy* marks a welcome shift away from the UNHCR's current policies focused primarily on encampment. The shift is stated expressly in the policy itself:

> Until recently, the Office continued to give primary attention to those refugees who are accommodated in camps. This approach was encouraged by the organization's 1997 policy statement on refugees in urban areas, a document that was based on the assumption that such refugees were more the exception and less the norm, as is now increasingly the case.[42]

The revised policy was the product of a lengthy review process, beginning soon after the publication of the *1997 Urban Policy*.[43] The UNHCR has justified its shift in approach by reference to the 'mega-trend'[44] of urbanization. The opening paragraphs of the *2009 Urban Policy* explain that '[t]he world is undergoing a process of rapid urbanization', and that it is therefore no surprise that 'a growing number and proportion of the world's refugees are also to be found in urban areas.'[45] The High Commissioner has reiterated this point:

> UNHCR's experience with refugees ... in cities is not new. What is new is the appreciation that increasingly cities will be the main site of humanitarian response ... To discharge our mandate effectively, we have to improve our performance in urban settings and recalibrate our approach ....[46]

The High Commissioner has acknowledged that this will require the organization to 'abandon the outmoded image that most refugees live in sprawling camps of UNHCR tents.'[47] A similar sentiment was expressed by the Assistant High Commissioner (Operations).[48]

The inappropriateness of the focus on camps is borne out by the UNHCR's own statistics, which reveal that refugees living in urban settings have outnumbered those living in camps since 2007.[49] In the most recent statistical yearbook, of the 8.3 million refuges for which location data was available, 2.3 million (30 per cent) were residing in camps and 4.8 million (58 per

42 *2009 Urban Policy*, [6].

43 At the end of 1999, UNHCR's Evaluation and Policy Analysis Unit ('EPAU') was asked to undertake a review of the *1997 Urban Policy* (see Obi and Crisp). In its first review in 2001 the EPAU was highly critical of the *1997 Urban Policy*, calling for its revision (Obi and Crisp, [20]). The UNHCR subsequently conducted a number of field-based case studies, and produced several drafts of a revised policy (see Crisp *et al.*, [25]–[26]).

44 *2009 Urban Policy*, [156].

45 Ibid., [1] and [3].

46 Guterres, 'Protection Challenges', 8.

47 António Guterres, 'Media Advisory: Half of the World's Refugees Now Live in Cities' (7 December 2009), at http://www.unhcr.org/4b1cda0e9.html (last accessed 22 August 2012).

48 Cited in Crisp *et al.*, [9].

49 UNHCR, 'Statistical Yearbook 2009: Trends in Displacement, Protection and Solutions' (2010), via http://www.unhcr.org/4ce532ff9.html (last accessed 22 August 2012) 46. It must be borne in mind, of course, that it is easier to estimate the numbers of camp-based refugees than those of urban or rural refugees.

cent) were living in urban areas. The remaining one million refugees were living in rural areas outside camps.[50]

It is certainly true that urbanization has taken place in most parts of the South, and that refugee populations are not immune from this trend. But urbanization did not begin in the last decade. UNHCR's estimates of the number of urban-based refugees may have overtaken that of camp-based refugees only in 2007, but the presence of large refugee populations in most major urban centres has been well known for some time.[51] One would hope that the change in policy is at least in part based on the recognition that the policy of giving 'primary attention to those refugees who are accommodated in camps'[52] was wrong in principle, rather than just ill suited to our times.[53]

State practice has also played a significant role in this process of policy reformulation. In particular, much of the work that went into a review of UNHCR's response to the Iraqi refugee crisis fed into the new policy.[54] In the words of the High Commissioner, that review 'was a true eye-opener and crucial to UNHCR's elaboration of its new urban refugee policy'.[55] The review showed that UNHCR's initial offers of assistance, based on the camp model,[56] were declined by the host countries, mainly Jordan and Syria, which preferred to allow refugees to settle in the cities.[57] Figures are, as ever, disputed but, if we stick to the official government ones, there

50 Ibid.

51 This is clearly evident from a review of available UNHCR statistics.

52 *2009 Urban Policy*, [6].

53 For an example of such an admission, see the discussion paper prepared by the UNHCR for the High Commissioner's Dialogue on Protection Challenges in 2008: 'One cannot expect exiled populations to establish sustainable livelihoods and become self-reliant in a context where they are unable to leave their camps, find a job, establish a business or have access to agricultural land, and are obliged to eke out a living in dangerous informal sector activities. In a year when the international community is commemorating the 60th anniversary of the Universal Declaration of Human Rights, there is a need to give real meaning to Article 14 of that Declaration, which refers to the right to "seek and enjoy asylum" in other countries' – UNHCR, 'Protracted Refugee Situations: A Discussion Paper Prepared for the High Commissioner's Dialogue on Protection Challenges', UNHCR/DPC/2008/Doc. 02 (20 November 2008), [64].

54 See Crisp *et al.*

55 António Guterres, 'Opening Remarks by Mr. António Guterres, United Nations High Commissioner for Refugees, at the High Commissioner's Dialogue on Protection Challenges for Persons of Concern in Urban Settings' (Palais des Nations, Geneva: 9 December 2009), at http://www.unhcr.org/4b26060c9.html (last accessed 22 August 2012). See also UNHCR, 'Challenges for Persons of Concern to UNHCR in Urban Settings', UNHCR/DPC/2009/Doc. 02/Rev. 1 (4 December 2009), [8].

56 '[T]he early contingency planning undertaken by UNHCR was based on the false assumption that any Iraqi refugee exodus would be managed in a traditional manner, by accommodating the new arrivals in camps in the border areas of asylum countries': Crisp *et al.*, [29].

57 In an address delivered at the High Commissioner's Dialogue on Protection Challenges in December 2009, Fayssal Mikdad, the Deputy Foreign Minister for Syria, noted that he hoped the dialogue would assist 'in dealing with the current and future type of asylum which opposes the traditional form of asylum where refugees mainly live in camps located on the borders': Fayssal Mikdad, 'Statement of Dr. Fayssal Mikdad at the High Commissioner's Dialogue on Refugees in Urban Settings' (9 December 2009), at http://www.unhcr.org/4b56c4969.html (last accessed 22 August 2012) 1.

were believed to be 1.1 million Iraqi refugees in Syria and 450,000 in Jordan[58] – a very large number considering that Syria's population is about 22 million and Jordan's 6.5 million.

Self-interest doubtless had a lot to do with the way Syria and Jordan chose to handle the Iraqi refugee crisis. They clearly had no appetite for a repeat of the mistakes made in relation to Palestinian refugees, particularly by Lebanon, which showed that refugee camps can contribute to internal political instability (not *refugees*, but *refugee camps*). Confining people to these segregated, often enclosed, spaces, excluding them from access to work and public services and leaving them little but despair has, unsurprisingly, facilitated radicalization. Political motivations aside, the situation in Jordan and Syria showed that countries can manage very large numbers of refugees *without* adopting camps as a protracted solution. Moreover, the vast majority of refugees chose never to register with UNHCR and managed without international assistance.[59]

The *2009 Urban Policy* recognizes three basic tenets: that '[t]he rights of refugees travel with them wherever they flee';[60] that 'UNHCR's mandated responsibilities towards them are not affected by their location';[61] and that urban areas are 'a legitimate place for refugees to enjoy their rights.'[62] It sets out two core objectives in the following terms: 'to ensure that cities are recognised as legitimate places for refugees to reside and exercise the rights to which they are entitled',[63] and 'to maximise the protection space available to urban refugees and the humanitarian organisations that support them.'[64] Significantly, the policy provides that assistance should be provided in an urban setting irrespective of policies of the host state:[65]

> When refugees take up residence in an urban area, whether or not this is approved by the authorities, UNHCR's primary objective will be to preserve and expand the amount of protection space available to them and to the humanitarian organizations that are providing such refugees with access to protection, solutions and assistance.[66]

The concept of a 'protection space' is a reasonably new one, generally associated with the UNHCR's Iraqi refugee operations.[67] The *2009 Urban Policy* draws on the concept to 'denote the extent to which a conducive environment exists of the internationally recognized rights

58 Figures as at March 2009 in Crisp *et al.*, [31].

59 Of the 450,000 estimated Iraqi refugees in Jordan, only 52,000 had registered with the UNHCR, and of the 1.1 estimated Iraqi refugees in Syria, only 206,000 had registered with the UNHCR (see Crisp *et al.*, [31]).

60 António Guterres, 'Media Advisory'.

61 *2009 Urban Policy*, [14].

62 Ibid. 'These rights include, but are not limited to, the right to life; the right not to be subjected to cruel or degrading treatment or punishment; the right not to be tortured or arbitrarily detained; the right to family unity; the right to adequate food, shelter, health and education, as well as livelihood opportunities': ibid., [17].

63 Ibid., [23].

64 Ibid., [23].

65 Cf. *1997 Urban Policy* (see text at n. 28).

66 *2009 Urban Policy*, [19].

67 See Anne E. Barnes, 'Realizing Protection Space for Iraqi Refugees: UNHCR in Syria, Jordan and Lebanon', 167 *New Issues in Refugee Research* (January 2009); Crisp *et al.*, [49].

of refugees to be respected and their needs to be met.'[68] By recognizing urban environments as a legitimate place for refugees to enjoy their rights, the UNHCR thus considers that it has *expanded* the 'protection space' for refugees, beyond the traditional confines of a refugee camp or settlement.

The *2009 Urban Policy* places great emphasis on what it calls the principle of state responsibility.[69] To avoid any misunderstanding, the expression 'state responsibility' is not here used in the sense in which international lawyers understand it, namely as the body of principles and rules that regulates the legal consequences of a wrongful act.[70] Responsibility is rather used in the sense of competence or legal authority, as is evident from this passage:

> In urban as in other contexts, national and local authorities have a primary role to play in providing refugees with protection, solutions and assistance. UNHCR will encourage all states to exercise this responsibility through its advocacy efforts.

At the same time, the Office stands ready to support states in undertaking the tasks of refugee protection, solutions and assistance by means of capacity-building and operational activities, especially in countries where the authorities lack the means and expertise required to achieve these objectives. Such support will ideally be provided for a limited period, pending the time when the state is able to assume responsibility for key functions, including refugee status determination and the provision of services and assistance to refugees in urban areas.[71]

As noted above, one of the anomalies of the system of refugee protection and assistance in the political South is that the UNHCR often exercises governmental functions. The principle of state responsibility as stated in the *2009 Urban Policy* represents a step in the right direction towards correcting this anomaly, insofar as it does not become a means for absolving UNHCR of legal responsibility. In this respect, it is useful to maintain the conceptual distinction between the international law sense of the term responsibility and the broader one in which it is used in the *2009 Urban Policy*. It is right that the overarching principle governing policy should be that the state has the primary responsibility (i.e. responsibility as competence) for refugees and UNHCR should not seek to replace or undermine the state. As far as the responsibility for wrongful acts is concerned (i.e. legal responsibility *stricto sensu*), however, UNHCR cannot seek shelter behind the postulate that states are ultimately responsible.

Another welcome feature of the *2009 Urban Policy* is the emphasis on fostering constructive and positive relationships between UNHCR staff and urban-based refugees.[72] One of the criticisms of the *1997 Urban Policy* was the negative portrayal of urban refugees as 'trouble makers'.[73] Indeed, an entire section of that policy addressed the issue of how to respond to threats and violence.[74] In 2001 the EPAU expressed a concern that this emphasis was

---

68 *2009 Urban Policy*, [20].

69 Ibid., [27].

70 International Law Commission, *Draft Articles on Responsibility of States for Internationally Wrongful Acts*, November 2001, Supplement No. 10 (A/56/10), chp.IV.E.1.

71 *2009 Urban Policy*, [27]–[29].

72 Ibid., [84]–[94].

73 Obi and Crisp, [40].

74 *1997 Urban Policy*, [19]–[21].

'unnecessarily negative' and 'may even have the effect of becoming a self-fulfilling prophecy.'[75] The 2009 policy promotes a 'broader strategy to establish a constructive dialogue and positive partnership with refugees in urban areas.'[76] A related feature of the guidelines is the express reference to the UNHCR Code of Conduct, which, among other things, bars UNHCR staff from 'engaging in abusive, exploitative or corrupt behaviour.'[77] The policy provides that all refugees must be informed that UNHCR staff members are bound by that Code, as soon as they enter into contact with a UNHCR officer.[78] Although this will not alone ensure accountability,[79] this mandated disclosure might assist in clarifying, at the outset, that the relationship between the UNHCR and the refugee is not as one between unbound helper and powerless supplicant.

Firstly, and in stark contrast to the *1997 Urban Policy*, the revised policy has made a considerable effort – albeit, understandably, in general terms – to outline the nature of the assistance to be provided to urban-based refugees. Three general points can be made here. First the policy recognizes the changing composition of the urban refugee population – a clear improvement on the amorphous characterization of urban refugees as ostensibly self-reliant, single young men.[80] The *2009 Urban Policy* recognizes the need to tailor programmes to meet the specific needs of particular groups, such as women, the elderly, and children (particularly unaccompanied and separated minors).[81]

Secondly, the *2009 Urban Policy* draws an important distinction between 'self-reliance' and 'a refugee's ability to survive without assistance', noting that '[u]nassisted refugees cannot be regarded as self-reliant if they are living in abject poverty, or if they are obliged to survive by means [of] illicit or degrading activities.'[82] This is a marked improvement from the *1997 Urban Policy*, which focused on the provision of minimal short-term aid, and only where 'early self-reliance [was] not possible'.[83] Moreover, the *2009 Urban Policy* recognizes that in some situations self-reliance will simply not be a 'viable objective':[84]

> While it is usually taken for granted that camp-based refugees will receive indefinite assistance if they are unable to engage in agriculture and other economic activities, it is sometimes assumed that refugees in urban areas are able to cope in the absence of such support.

75 Obi and Crisp, [41].

76 *2009 Urban Policy*, [85].

77 Ibid., [51].

78 Ibid., [51].

79 See discussion above at pp. 480.

80 'There is a widespread and longstanding assumption within UNHCR that urban refugee populations are comprised predominantly of young, single males. This perception is explicitly endorsed by the 1997 policy statement, which says that "unlike other refugee populations, the majority of refugees in urban areas are generally male: the proportion of family groups is often lower than usual" ... this is not the case in many cities where substantial numbers of refugees are to be found': Obi and Crisp, [12].

81 *2009 Urban Policy*, [4]–[5], [35]–[36].

82 Ibid., [107].

83 *1997 Urban Policy*, [6]. For early criticism see Obi and Crisp, [21]–[25].

84 *2009 Urban Policy*, [118].

> That is not necessarily the case, especially in countries where refugees have no legal status or residency rights, are not allowed to engage in income-generating activities, where they are deprived of access to public services on the same terms as nationals, and where the option of being assisted in a camp does not exist. Refugees may also be severely hampered in their efforts to support themselves by discrimination on the basis of their nationality, ethnic origin or religion.
>
> In circumstances such as these, particular care will be taken by UNHCR to identify those refugees who need support and to determine and provide the level of assistance they require. At the same time, host governments will be encouraged to remove any legal obstacles which prevent refugees from becoming self-reliant.[85]

Thirdly, the *2009 Urban Policy* supports the integration of refugees into *local* shelter, education and health services.[86] As mentioned, the establishment of separate and parallel services run by UNHCR and other humanitarian organizations facilitates the segregation of refugees from the host society.[87] This policy, which is not sustainable over the long term because of the onset sooner or later of donor fatigue, is also known to have engendered considerable resentment among hosts.[88] In an urban context at least, this approach now seems to have been abandoned as a matter of policy. UNHCR will instead 'seek to reinforce existing fully authorized delivery systems, whether they are public, private or community-based'.[89]

85 Ibid., [119]–[121].

86 We note that the *1997 Urban Policy* also emphasized that support of local services should be preferred over the creation of parallel structures and special services: *1997 Urban Policy*, [6].

87 Verdirame and Harrell-Bond, *Rights in Exile*.

88 Ibid., 270, 273 and 286.

89 *2009 Urban Policy*, [113]. This point was emphasized by the High Commissioner at the 2009 Dialogue on Protection Challenges: Guterres, 'Opening Remarks by Mr. António Guterres'. The *2009 Urban Policy* was the focus of discussion at the High Commissioner's Dialogue on Protection Challenges in Geneva in December 2009. For an overview see UNHCR, 'Informal Summary: Third High Commissioner's Dialogue on Protection Challenges' (1 March 2010), at http://www.unhcr.org/refworld/docid/4cc670a92.html (last accessed 22 August 2012). In the closing remarks to that Dialogue, the High Commissioner committed to 'revisit the new urban refugee policy to take into account the richness of the debate at [the] Dialogue and to make without delay any needed adjustments': António Guterres, 'High Commissioner's Closing Remarks at the Dialogue on Protection Challenges for Persons of Concern in Urban Settings, Palais des Nations, Geneva, 10 December 2009', at http://www.unhcr.org/4b2607387e.html (last accessed 22 August 2012). At the date of writing (in April 2011), no changes have been made. The Commissioner also committed to 'implementing the policy fully' in 2011, with ongoing real-time evaluations of the implementation of the 2009 policy. The following cities were selected for evaluation: Nairobi (Kenya), Dushanbe (Tajikistan), Kuala Lumpur (Malaysia), San Jose (Costa Rica), and Sofia (Bulgaria). The first evaluation completed by the Policy Development and Evaluation Service was published in January 2011. See Elizabeth Campbell *et al.*, UNHCR Policy Development and Evaluation Service, 'Navigating Nairobi: A Review of the Implementation of UNHCR's Urban Refugee Policy in Kenya's Capital City', PDES/2001/01 (January 2011) ('Campbell *et al.*').

Future Challenges

The recalibrated *2009 Urban Policy* is not all lights. Its improvements notwithstanding, the new policy leaves some issues unaddressed and poses a number of challenges.

First, and most fundamentally, the refugee camp bias is still evident. The *1997 Urban Policy* legitimized and operationalized this bias, whereas the *2009 Urban Policy* recognizes that neither a state's nor UNHCR's obligations are conditional on a refugee being warehoused in a camp. Nevertheless, the bias continues to linger, for example in the following passage about the provision of financial assistance:

> In countries where camps have been established, refugees who have moved to an urban area will normally receive financial assistance from UNHCR only if they have a demonstrable need to be in that location. They will, of course, continue to benefit from the protection and solutions activities of the Office.
>
> Refugees who are unable to survive in the city will be offered the opportunity and means of transport to take up residence in a camp if one is available to them. It will be made clear that this is not an obligation and that those who choose to remain in an urban area will not forfeit the protection of UNHCR.[90]

The allocation of expenditure also reveals the preference for camps. In the first evaluation of the *2009 Urban Policy*, the Policy Development and Evaluation Service addressed the situation for urban-based refuges living in Nairobi.[91] That evaluation estimated that there are approximately 80,000–100,000 refugees living in Nairobi, with an additional 350,000 refugees living in Dadaab and Kakuma refugee camps.[92] Yet, in 2010 UNHCR's urban refugee programme received a budget of less than $3 million, compared to a total of $90 million for the country as a whole.[93] Thus, notwithstanding that urban-based refugees constitute 22 to 28 per cent of the UNHCR's beneficiary class in Kenya, they are allocated only 3 per cent of the UNHCR's budget. Indeed, the UNHCR's evaluation expressly concedes that 'the 350,000 refugees living in Dadaab and Kakuma continue to be the priority for UNHCR's Kenya operation.'[94]

However, the UNCHR's enduring predisposition towards camp-based solutions is most plainly revealed – and the irony has not gone unnoticed – in the section of the policy that addresses the issue of freedom of movement. True, the *2009 Urban Policy* pays homage to the principle that freedom of movement is a legally protected right, but here is how it does it:

> Freedom of movement is a principle enshrined in international human rights law, and UNHCR encourages all states to respect it. While recognising the difficulties that can arise for the Office and the authorities when large numbers

[90] *2009 Urban Policy*, [131]–[132].
[91] See Campbell *et al.*
[92] Ibid., 25–6, 45.
[93] Ibid., 46.
[94] Ibid., 45.

> of refugees leave their camp or another designated place of residence and move to a city, there may also be good reasons for them to do so.
>
> Any mobility restrictions placed on camp-based refugees should take account of these reasons, such as the need to reunite with family members or to seek medical treatment.[95]

What the *2009 Urban Policy* does not do is examine the scope of the right to freedom of movement, and consider the extent to which restrictions on the movement of camp-based refugees might infringe on that right. There is a real concern that the revised policy – and particularly its final few pages dealing with the issue of 'movement' – may incentivize governments (and UNHCR field offices) to spend time improving conditions in camps, rather than engaging with the urban refugee community.[96]

Freedom of movement is enshrined not only in international human rights law, but also in international refugee law. Article 26 of the *Refugee Convention* accords refugees lawfully in the territory the right to freedom of movement, subject only to restrictions that are imposed on 'aliens generally in the same circumstances'.[97] A refugee is lawfully present once they are formally admitted to the host state's refugee status procedure, or otherwise authorized to remain (expressly or implicitly) in the host's territory.[98] The majority of refugees in refugee camps therefore fall within this category, and can benefit from the protection of Article 26. Refugees who are unlawfully present are still covered by Article 31(2) of the *Refugee Convention*, which permits restrictions on movement, but only those 'which are necessary'.[99]

Article 12(1) of the *International Covenant on Civil and Political Rights*[100] provides that 'everyone lawfully within the territory of a State shall, within that territory, have the right to liberty of movement and freedom to choose his residence'. Again, this would capture the majority of refugees residing in camps. The ICCPR allows for restrictions on movement, so long as they do not entail violations of other Convention rights, and so long as the restrictions comply with the enumerated conditions provided under Article 12(3): 'are necessary to protect

95 *2009 Urban Policy*, [146]–[147].

96 'This may not be the intention at all of the drafters but regrettably these latter pages may play into the hands of governments operating camp confinement policies who argue that UNHCR should spend its time improving camp conditions rather than engaging with urban refugees': Alice Edwards, '"Legitimate" Protection Spaces: UNHCR's 2009 Policy' (2010) 34 *Forced Migration Review* 48–9, at 49.

97 *Convention relating to the Status of Refugees*, opened for signature 28 July 1951, 189 UNTS 137 (entered into force 22 April 1954) and the attendant *Protocol Relating to the Status of Refugees*, opened for signature 31 January 1967, 606 UNTS 267 (entered into force 4 October 1967) (referred to in the collective as the '*Refugee Convention*').

98 See James C. Hathaway, *The Rights of Refugees under International Law* (Cambridge University Press, Cambridge, 2005) chapter 3.1.3.

99 'The Contracting States shall not apply to the movements of such refugees restrictions other than those which are necessary and such restrictions shall only be applied until their status in the country is regularized or they obtain admission into another country. The Contracting States shall allow such refugees a reasonable period and all the necessary facilities to obtain admission into another country': *Refugee Convention*, Article 31(2).

100 *International Covenant on Civil and Political Rights*, opened for signature 16 December 1966, 999 UNTS 171 (entered into force 23 March 1976) ('*ICCPR*').

national security, public order (*ordre public*), public health or morals or the right and freedoms of others'.[101]

There can be no serious dispute that most instances of 'refugee warehousing' violate the human right to freedom of movement, either directly or indirectly. The *2009 Urban Policy* should have begun with this observation. Instead, the analysis of the right to freedom of movement is infected with the idea that the exercise of this right should be assessed against the background of 'good reasons' and 'difficulties' for the authorities – concepts lacking any principled foundation. The reference to 'good reasons' that would supposedly make an otherwise 'irregular movement' acceptable represents an attempt to replace the international legal test for restricting free movement with one that has no basis in international law and is far less favourable to refugees. There is, however, no place in international human rights law for the notion that the exercise of a fundamental right requires 'good reasons'. As for the 'difficulties' that the free movement of refugees might pose to the national authorities and UNHCR, it is a truism that the exercise of any human right will sometimes pose difficulties and challenges for public authorities. Protest, assembly and fair trial are cases in point. Nevertheless, it is not open to governments to restrict fundamental rights because of such generic difficulties, unless they can show that the restriction meets every condition in the relevant limitation clause or is justifiable under a derogation regime.

Another problem is that the distinction between urban-based refugees and encamped refugees completely ignores refugees settled in rural areas. Self-settled rural refugees remain a blind spot in UNHCR's assistance policy, notwithstanding the fact that, according to UNHCR itself, at least one million of them are believe to live without UNHCR assistance.[102] The *2009 Urban Policy* mentions the misconception that the majority of refugees are of rural background, but it fails to address the equally problematic fallacy that camps are the appropriate solution for rural refugees.

A further challenge stems from the *2009 Urban Policy*'s failure to adequately engage with the rights enshrined under international human rights law and international refugee law. Despite the frequent references to a rights-based framework in the opening paragraphs of the policy,[103] there is little substantive engagement with the rights protected under the *Refugee Convention* or international human rights law generally. The document is generally very vague on the legal basis of the policies it promotes. Indeed, this was one of the core concerns raised at the High Commissioner's 2009 Dialogue on Protection Challenges. In a roundtable of Mayors from 15 cities, some stressed that '[r]efugees have rights which are universal and need to be guaranteed', and noted the 'need to promote awareness of [refugee rights]'.[104] In his closing remarks at that Dialogue, the High Commissioner emphasized the importance of 'legal frameworks and the recognition of rights'.[105] Of course, the discussion on freedom of movement above highlights some of the issues that UNHCR would have to address if it were to honestly engage with the extant scope of these legal obligations.

---

[101] For detailed consideration see Hathaway, *Rights of Refugees under International Law*, chapter 5.2.

[102] UNHCR, 'Statistical Yearbook 2009', 46.

[103] See for example *2009 Urban Policy*, [14], [17], [23]. A 'rights-based' approach has also been repeatedly promoted by the High Commissioner.

[104] UNHCR, 'Informal Summary', [6].

[105] Guterres, 'High Commissioner's Closing Remarks'.

Finally, there are the challenges of implementation and accountability. Indeed, issues of implementation are compounded in the case of international organizations because of this nexus between implementation and accountability. If the *2009 Urban Policy* had been adopted by the department of a national government in a free country, its implementation would be subject to various checks and balances: parliamentary committees would question the ministers and senior civil servants responsible for the policy; the opposition would watch over discrepancies between the policy as announced and its practical implementation with a view to embarrassing the government; courts might be asked to rule where, for example, legitimate expectations that have arisen from the policy have not been satisfied; and the media would be watching over the entire process. These checks and balances are not in place in the case of UNHCR and international institutions in general. There is no political control, no judicial control, and only rarely control by the media. In international institutions, implementation is left entirely to the bureaucracy. Checks and balances, if they exist, will be internal and thus less independent and effective. Consequently, there is a very serious risk of a gap between Geneva-practice and field-practice.[106]

Conclusions

From a legal perspective, the key problem with the *2009 Urban Policy* is the enduring marginality of the international refugee and human rights law framework. Despite references to the human right to free movement, the issue is (perhaps deliberately) framed without consideration of the relevant legal tests. The question, 'Are these restrictions on the movement of refugees lawful?' is simply not asked. Yet this very question provides the logical and principled platform for any discussion of existing and new policies. The UNHCR's policies on encampment and urban-based assistance should be anchored in, and developed consistently with, international human rights and refugee law. At present, this is simply not happening.

From a policy perspective, the implementation of the new urban policy and the demise of encampment will require a shift in the manner in which services are provided. The High Commissioner seemed aware of this challenge when he remarked that,

> The traditional response to large-scale population displacements by establishing parallel structures in shelter, education and health is not viable in urban settings. It is essential to adopt a new approach to the challenge of urban displacement, one based on three closely related principles. First, the new approach cannot be undertaken in isolation from the broader context of marginalized and poor populations in urban settings. We must give particular attention to protecting the rights of poor and disadvantaged communities, empowering them to make full use of their proven resourcefulness. Second, the approach must be both developmental and relief based – one that addresses long-term as well as immediate needs and supports the broader process of urban planning and

[106] On the gap between official policy and actual practice, see Verdirame and Harrell-Bond, *Rights in Exile*, 299–303 and Verdirame, *UN and Human Rights*, chapter 4.

> poverty reduction. Finally, the approach must be inclusive. It cannot be done by UNHCR alone. It requires establishing and strengthening partnerships with central governments, municipal and local authorities, NGOs, the private sector and especially the marginalized populations themselves.[107]

Ideally, the implementation of the new urban policy, and more generally the rejection of encampment that it is hoped will soon follow from it, will go hand in hand with a new approach to issues of accountability. The evaluation and assessment culture within UNHCR has improved over the last decade, mainly as a result of the work of the Evaluation and Policy Analysis Unit, the body that deserves significant credit for the change in urban policy. But a lot still needs to be done to ensure that international law is reflected in the policy process and that the institution is held to account, in a political and legal sense, for policies that do not accord with international law.

Does the *2009 UNCR Policy* signal the end of camps? It would be overly optimistic to say that it does, but it may signal the beginning of the end of this unnecessary and inhumane policy. The demise of camps still requires more rethinking by UNHCR, host states, donor governments and non-governmental organizations, but at least something is moving. The most important change is that advocates of alternatives to camps can now ground their arguments, to some extent, in UNHCR's official policy (although subject to the important qualifications and critiques outlined above) and, crucially, in the recent practice of states. The treatment of Iraqi refugees in Jordan or Syria was certainly not free from problems.[108] But these countries have shown that it is possible, even without much international assistance, to deal with a major refugee crisis without warehousing refugees in camps. It is a lesson that UNHCR and humanitarian organizations working with refugees should heed and embrace.

References

Barnes, Anne E., 'Realizing Protection Space for Iraqi Refugees: UNHCR in Syria, Jordan and Lebanon' (January 2009) 167 *New Issues in Refugee Research*.

Edwards, Alice, '"Legitimate" Protection Spaces: UNHCR's 2009 Policy' (2010) 34 *Forced Migration Review* 48–9.

Goyens, Philippe *et al.*, 'Humanitarian Aid and Health Services in Eastern Kivu, Zaire: Collaboration or Competition' (1996) 9 *Journal of Refugee Studies* 268–80.

Guterres, António, 'Protection Challenges for Persons of Concern in Urban Settings' (2010) 34 *Forced Migration Review* 8–9.

[107] Guterres, 'Opening Statement of Mr. António Guterres'.

[108] There were, for example, cases of *non-refoulement* and arbitrary detention of Iraqis in Jordan and Syria. See for example Human Rights Watch, 'The Silent Treatment: Fleeing Iraq, Surviving in Jordan' (21 November 2006), at http://www.hrw.org/reports/2006/11/27/silent-treatment (last accessed 22 August 2012); Amnesty International, 'Rhetoric and Reality: The Iraqi Refugee Crisis' (June 2008), at http://www.amnesty.org/en/library/info/MDE14/011/2008/en (last accessed 22 August 2012).

Harrell-Bond, Barbara E., *Imposing Aid: Emergency Assistance to Refugees* (Oxford University Press, Oxford, 1986).

Harrell-Bond, Barbara E. and Eftihia Voutira, 'In Search of the Locus of Trust: The Social World of a Refugee Camp', in E. Valentine Daniel and John Chr Knudsen (eds) *Mistrusting Refugees* (University of California Press, Berkeley, CA, 1995) 207–24.

Hathaway, James C., *The Rights of Refugees under International Law* (Cambridge University Press, Cambridge, 2005).

Hyndman, Jennifer, *Managing Displacement: Refugees and the Politics of Humanitarianism* (University of Minnesota Press, Minneapolis, MN, 2000).

Malkki, Liisa H., *Purity and Exile: Violence, Memory, and National Cosmology among Hutu Refugees in Tanzania* (University of Chicago Press, Chicago, IL, 1995).

Verdirame, Guglielmo, *The UN and Human Rights: Who Guards the Guardians?* (Cambridge University Press, Cambridge, 2011).

Verdirame, Guglielmo and Barbara E. Harrell-Bond, *Rights in Exile: Janus-faced Humanitarianism* (Berghahn Books, New York, 2005).

ASHGATE
RESEARCH
COMPANION

PART VI
MIGRANT WORKERS, SKILLED LABOUR AND THE CONTROL OF HUMAN MOBILITY

In Defence of the Migrant Workers Convention: Standard Setting for Contemporary Migration

Bernard Ryan[1]

Introduction

The International Convention on the Protection of the Rights of All Migrant Workers and Members of Their Families ('the Migrant Workers Convention') has had a difficult history. The adoption of a treaty on the subject of migrant workers was formally proposed by a General Assembly resolution of 17 December 1979.[2] As a result of differences of opinion between states of origin and destination, however, the final text was not endorsed by the General Assembly until 18 December 1990.[3] There was then a further lengthy period until the Convention came into force on 1 July 2003, once the requisite 20 ratifications had been obtained. Since then, ratification has proceeded slowly, with a total of 44 states having ratified by early 2011.

In contrast to the doubts that have often been expressed as to the value of the Migrant Workers Convention, this chapter will argue for its potential as a source of standards concerning international migration. Section 1 will consider the text of the Convention, and will show that it is a coherent instrument for the protection of migrants as a category. Section 2 will then consider the Convention in practice, arguing that its strength lies in a combination of two factors: the migration experiences of the states that have ratified it, and the interpretative work of the Committee on Migrant Workers since it was established on 1 January 2004. That combination enables the Convention to be an effective and authoritative source of standards on the treatment of migrants.

---

1 Professor of Law, University of Kent. I am grateful to Ryszard Cholewinski, Virginia Mantouvalou and Eki Yemisi Omorogbe for their comments on the paper in draft.

2 UNGA Resolution 34/172, 17 December 1979.

3 UNGA Resolution 45/158, 18 December 1990.

1. The Migrant Workers Convention

The origins of the Migrant Workers Convention lie in the postwar period of high demand for migrant labour in the developed countries of Europe and North America. At the international level, standards on international migration were initially developed within the International Labour Organization. The Migration for Employment Convention (Revised), 1949 (No. 97) provided for the equal treatment of lawfully resident migrant workers.[4] More significantly, the Migrant Workers (Supplementary Provisions) Convention 1975 (No. 143) focused on irregular migration and employment. It required contracting states to take action against 'the organisers of illicit or clandestine movements of migrants for employment', and against 'those who employ workers who have immigrated in illegal conditions'.[5] That approach to irregular migration and employment was followed by calls from states of origin – led by Mexico and Morocco – for a new treaty that was more concerned with the interests of their nationals.[6] Because the ILO structures gave a greater say to 'industrialized' countries, the preference of states of origin was for such an instrument to be adopted through the United Nations General Assembly.

The debate over the Convention was initially quite polarized.[7] Seventeen developed Western countries had indicated their scepticism about the proposal for a Convention by abstaining on the General Assembly resolution setting up the working group in 1979.[8] When an initial draft Convention was presented in May 1981, with the support of five states of emigration, the most developed countries rejected it as 'a blank check for continued illegal migration'.[9] The intervention of a group of seven Southern European and Nordic states proved decisive, and the eventual text of the Convention reflected their broadly socially democratic approach to migration.[10] On the one hand, Part III of the Convention extended many human and labour rights to migrant workers and their families, irrespective of immigration status. On the other hand, irregular migrant and employment was discouraged, in two ways: Part

---

4 ILO Convention 97, Article 6.

5 ILO Convention 143, Article 3(b).

6 On the history of the Convention, see Roger Böhning, 'The ILO and the New UN Convention on Migrant Workers: The Past and Future' (1991) 25 *International Migration Review* 698–709, and Graziano Battistella, 'Migration and Human Rights: The Uneasy but Essential Relationship' in Paul de Guchteneire, Antoine Pécoud and Ryszard Cholewinski (eds), *Migration and Human Rights: The United Nations Convention on Migrant Workers' Rights* (Cambridge University Press, Cambridge, 2009) 47–69.

7 On the drafting of the Convention, see Juhani Lönnroth, 'The International Convention on the Rights of All Migrant Workers and Members of Their Families in the Context of International Migration Policies: An Analysis of Ten Years of Negotiation' (1991) 25 *International Migration Review* 710–36.

8 For the list, see Battistella, 'Migration and Human Rights', 54. This group of states included 12 West European states (Austria, Belgium, Denmark, Finland, France, West Germany, Iceland, Luxembourg, the Netherlands, Norway, Sweden and the United Kingdom) and five other highly developed states (Australia, Canada, Israel, New Zealand and the United States). Burma and Guatemala also abstained.

9 Böhning, 'ILO and the New UN Convention on Migrant Workers', 701. The 1981 draft was initially endorsed by Algeria, Mexico, Pakistan, Turkey and Yugoslavia, and later supported by Barbados and Egypt: Battistella, 'Migration and Human Rights', 55.

10 These were Finland, Greece, Italy, Norway, Portugal, Spain and Sweden.

IV of the Convention conferred certain rights solely on workers in a lawful position, while Part VI of the Convention – which is concerned with 'sound, equitable, humane and lawful conditions' in international migration – provided for measures to prevent irregular migration and employment.

These features of the Convention have in turn given rise to two frequent criticisms since it was negotiated: that it overlaps unnecessarily with other international instruments, and that it gives insufficient protection to irregular migrants. The rest of this section will address these criticisms, through a review of the content of the Convention.

Overlap

Criticism of the Migrant Workers Convention for overlapping unnecessarily with other instruments began even before the text of the Convention had been formally adopted. Writing in 1988, Roger Böhning observed, with reference to the International Covenant on Civil and Political Rights (ICCPR) and the International Covenant on Economic, Social and Cultural Rights (ICESCR), that Part III of the Convention 'almost entirely repeats textually the provisions of one Covenant or the other, which demonstrates that there was no need for a new convention in this respect.'[11] That line of criticism was developed in particular by James Nafziger and Barry Bartel, who argued in an article in 1991 that overlaps would 'obfuscate or obscure the enforcement of both the Convention and corresponding human rights instruments that are designed to protect everyone, including migrant workers.'[12] More recently, Vincent Chetail has remarked that, 'from a purely legal perspective, the added value of the ICMW is relatively limited given that most of its provisions simply restate – and sometimes specify – basic human rights which are already enshrined in other general instruments.'[13]

This line of criticism will be addressed here through an examination of the Convention's provisions on personal scope (Article 3) and non-discrimination (Article 7), and of the rights it recognizes for all migrant workers and their families (Part III of the Convention). It will be argued that overlaps of content are explicable in terms of the Convention's underlying objective of protecting migrants. Because of that objective, the rights-conferring provisions of the Convention either go beyond other instruments in significant ways, or else merit inclusion in the Convention because of their distinct relevance for migrants.

Personal scope

Article 2 of the Convention, which sets out its personal scope, gives a first example of its content going beyond other instruments.[14] It defines the term 'migrant worker' to mean 'a person who

---

[11] Roger Böhning, 'The Protection of Migrant Workers and International Labour Standards' (1988) 26(2) *International Migration Review* 133–46, at 143.

[12] James Nafziger and Barry Bartel, 'The Migration Workers Convention: Its Place in Human Rights Law' (1991) 25 *International Migration Review* 771–99, at 787.

[13] Vincent Chetail, 'Review of *Migration and Human Rights: The United Nations Convention on Migrant Workers*' (2010) 22 *International Journal of Refugee Law* 677–82, at 679.

[14] For an earlier discussion, see Ryszard Cholewinski, *Migrant Workers in International Human Rights Law: Their Protection in Countries of Employment* (Oxford University Press, Oxford, 1997) 149–52.

is to be engaged, is engaged or has been engaged in a remunerated activity in a State of which he or she is not a national.'[15] This definition may be contrasted in particular with the two ILO Conventions in the field. ILO Convention 97 applies to a 'migrant for employment', defined as 'a person who migrates or who has migrated from one country to another with a view to being employed otherwise than on his own account.'[16] The same formulation appears in ILO Convention 143, in order to define the category of 'migrant workers'.[17]

The definitions in the Migrant Workers Convention and the ILO Conventions have in common that they potentially cover workers whose stay and/or economic activity is irregular. In other respects, however, the Migrant Workers Convention's personal scope is far broader. One reason is that the Convention definition includes *all* foreign nationals who engage in remunerated activity, without it being necessary that they have migrated *for* employment. It therefore includes foreign national workers lawfully in a contracting state for other reasons, such as a family relationship, or who have never migrated, because they were born there. A second difference is that the Convention's focus on 'remunerated activity', rather than employment, means that both employees and the self-employed are included.[18] The inclusion of self-employment is of particular relevance to irregular migrants, who often work outside formal employment relationships. A third difference is the reference in the Convention to past economic activity, which ensures that the Convention applies to those who have previously engaged in economic activity in the state in question.

The broad personal scope of the Convention, going beyond current workers, was one of the criticisms of it made by Nafziger and Bartel in their 1991 article.[19] Yet it can equally be argued that the breadth of Article 2 is one of its strengths, as central to the Convention's potential as an instrument concerning migrants in general. We will see in this section how that potential has been reflected in Part III of the Convention, and in section 2, how it has been carried forward in the work of the Committee on Migrant Workers.

Non-discrimination clause

The Convention's non-discrimination guarantee is a second example of a provision that goes further than other instruments. Under Article 7, contracting states are obliged

> to respect and to ensure ... the rights provided for in the present Convention without distinction of any kind such as to sex, race, colour, language, religion or conviction, political or other opinion, national, ethnic or social origin,

---

15 A number of exceptions are set out in Article 3: persons sent by international organizations and foreign states; investors; refugees and stateless persons; students and trainees; and seafarers and workers in offshore installations who are not authorized to reside and work in the state in question.

16 ILO Convention 97, Article 11(1).

17 ILO Convention 143, Article 11(1), which refers solely to the rights applicable to workers in a lawful position set out in its Part II. The provisions concerning irregular migration in Part I of that Convention are not governed by an express statement of personal scope.

18 This is confirmed by Articles 2(2)(h) and 63, which specifically concern the self-employed.

19 Nafziger and Bartel, 'Migration Workers Convention', 786.

nationality, age, economic position, property, marital status, birth or other status.

The breadth of this formulation is apparent from a comparison with the equivalent provisions in Article 2(1) ICCPR and Article 2(2) ICESCR.[20] Under each of those, contracting states undertake 'to respect and to ensure ... the rights recognized in the present Covenant, without distinction of any kind, such as race, colour, sex, language, religion, political or other opinion, national or social origin, property, birth or other status.' By comparison, Article 7 adds non-religious convictions, ethnic origin, nationality, age, economic position and marital status to the grounds of discrimination that are enumerated.[21] Among these, the inclusion of 'nationality' is of particular significance, as it reflects the Convention's character as an instrument concerning migration.

The inclusion of 'nationality' in Article 7 distinguishes the Migrant Workers Convention from other instruments. In the case of Article 2(2) ICESCR, the Committee on Economic, Social and Cultural Rights has had to read 'nationality' into the term 'other status'.[22] By comparison, the merit of the Convention's approach is that 'nationality' is referred to expressly, removing the need for it to be read into the Convention in this way. The inclusion of 'nationality' also differentiates the Convention from the International Convention on the Elimination of All Forms of Racial Discrimination (ICERD). Article 1(1) ICERD does not list 'nationality' as a form of 'racial discrimination', which instead covers 'any distinction, exclusion, restriction or preference based on race, colour, descent, or national or ethnic origin'. Moreover, Article 1(2) ICERD expressly states that the Convention does not address differentiation by states 'between citizens and non-citizens'. In contrast, the advantage of the Migrant Workers Convention is precisely that many of its provisions aim at securing the equal treatment of foreign nationals.

Civil rights in Part III

Part III of the Convention lists the rights that are applicable to *all* migrant workers and their families, irrespective of the lawfulness of their stay and/or employment. The criticism that the Convention overlaps unnecessarily with other instruments concerns in particular the civil rights listed in Part III, relative to the equivalent provisions of the ICCPR.[23] Can the inclusion of these rights nevertheless be justified?[24]

---

20 See too the discussion in Cholewinski, *Migrant Workers in International Human Rights Law*, 155.

21 This point is also made by Isabelle Slinckx in 'Migrants' Rights in UN Human Rights Conventions' in De Guchteneire, Pécoud and Cholewinski (eds), *Migration and Human Rights*, 122–49, at 146.

22 Committee on Economic, Social and Cultural Rights, *General Comment No. 20: Non-discrimination in Economic, Social and Cultural Rights* (2 July 2009), UN Doc. E/C.12/GC/20, para. 30.

23 The term 'civil right' is understood here to refer to individual freedoms and status rights that potentially apply to all persons. The term 'political right' is understood to refer to freedoms and protections that derive from an attachment to a particular state, or that concern political participation.

24 Nafziger and Bartel, in 'Migration Workers Convention', also compare the civil rights set out in the Convention with the Universal Declaration of Human Rights. The ICCPR is taken as the sole reference point here, because it is a binding instrument.

A first point is that Part III of the Migrant Workers Convention includes two rights of direct relevance to migrants that are not set out in the ICCPR. One is the prohibition on confiscation or destruction of identity or immigration documents by anyone other than a public official acting with legal authority (Article 21). The other is the right to consular assistance 'whenever the rights recognized in the present Convention are impaired' (Article 23). The latter of these provisions is complemented by Article 65(2), in Part VI of the Convention, which obliges contracting states to 'facilitate the provision of adequate consular and other services' to migrant workers and their families.

Secondly, where there are overlaps of subject matter, the migration context is often reflected in stronger statements in the Migrant Workers Convention. Protection against expulsion offers a clear example. Article 13 ICCPR provides that a foreign national may be expelled only on the basis of decision reached in accordance with the law, that they should ordinarily be allowed to submit the reasons against the expulsion, and that there should be the possibility of review by a competent authority. By comparison, Article 22 of the Convention is stronger in its substance: collective expulsions are prohibited, expulsion decisions are required to be in a language the individual understands, a written decision setting out the reasons for the expulsion may be requested, and it should be possible to apply for the suspension of an expulsion while a legal challenge to it is pending. Moreover, there is a crucial difference in personal scope. Article 22 extends protection to *all* migrant workers and their family members, irrespective of the legality of their stay. By contrast, the benefit of Article 13 ICCPR is limited to foreign nationals 'lawfully in the territory of a State Party'.[25]

Many other illustrations may be given of stronger statements in the Convention, due to its concern with the position of migrants. Article 8(2) of the Convention states, 'Migrant workers and members of their families shall have the right at any time to enter and remain in their State of origin.' In presenting the right of entry and residence in absolute terms, Article 8(2) goes beyond the equivalent Article 12 ICCPR, which provides that a person may not be '*arbitrarily* deprived of the right to enter his own country'.[26] Another case is the provision for the right to liberty and security of the person in Article 16 of the Convention. It goes beyond Article 9 ICCPR in requiring that identity checks by state officials 'be carried out in accordance with procedure established by law', and in providing for access to consular assistance and for interpreters in proceedings concerning the legality of detention. A further example is Article 17 of the Convention, which requires that detention be lawful and legitimate. It goes beyond Article 10 ICCPR in providing that persons detained for violation of immigration rules 'shall be held, in so far as practicable, separately from convicted persons or persons detained pending trial', and in providing that migrants should not bear the cost of detention aimed at verifying compliance with immigration law.

Thirdly, even where the Convention is substantively similar to other instruments, the civil rights set out in Part III are likely to be of particular value to migrants. A good example is the provision in Article 29: 'Each child of a migrant worker shall have the right to a name, to registration of birth and to a nationality'. Other cases are the provisions in the Convention for

[25] This key difference between Article 22 ICRMW and Article 12 ICCPR was not referred to in the summary in Nafziger and Bartel, ibid., 791.

[26] Emphasis added. In their summary, Nafziger and Bartel did not refer to this key difference between Article 8 ICRMW and Article 12 ICCPR: ibid., 790.

freedom from slavery, servitude and forced labour, freedom of thought and religion, the right to a fair trial, the principle that criminal offences should not be retroactive, the rule against imprisonment for breach of a contractual obligation, and the right to freedom of association.[27] All of these rights are potentially of particular value for foreign nationals and their family members, simply because they may be in a weaker social or legal position than the established population of the state in question.

Economic and social rights in Part III

Criticisms concerning overlap also cover the economic and social rights of migrant workers and their families set out in Part III of the Migrant Workers Convention. In response, an initial point is that two economic and social rights listed in Part III do not appear in the ICESCR. One is the right not to be arbitrarily deprived of property.[28] The other is the right to transfer earnings, savings and personal property abroad when the period of residence comes to an end.[29]

The economic and social rights in Part III of the Convention are anyway quite different in content to their equivalents in the ICESCR. That is because the Convention provisions generally aim at equal treatment on grounds of nationality, whereas the ICESCR provisions concern the substance of the right at issue. For example, Article 25 of the Convention provides for equal treatment in remuneration and terms and conditions of employment, whereas Article 7 ICESCR provides for 'just and favourable conditions of work'. Article 27 provides for equal treatment in matters of social security, whereas Article 9 ICESCR sets out 'the right of everyone to social security'. Article 28 provides for equal treatment in respect of medical care that is urgently needed in serious cases, whereas Article 12 ICESCR articulates 'the right of everyone to the enjoyment of the highest attainable standard of physical and mental health'. Finally, Article 30 provides for equal access to schooling by migrants' children, as compared to 'the right of everyone to education' in Article 13 ICESCR.

This focus on equality of treatment is logical in an instrument that is concerned with the position of migrants, and not with the advancement of economic and social rights as such. Part III of the Convention need not imply a lower standard of protection, however. The reason is that the rights set out in the ICESCR are not absolute standards. Rather, the duty on a state party to the ICESCR is 'to take steps ... to the maximum of its available resources, with a view to achieving progressively the full realization of' those rights (Article 2(1) ICESCR). In practice, one consequence is that equal treatment is also a central principle within the ICESCR framework, including for foreign nationals. In the words of the Committee on Economic, Social and Cultural Rights, 'the ground of nationality should not bar access to Covenant rights' and 'the Covenant rights apply to everyone including non-nationals, such as refugees, asylum-seekers, stateless persons, migrant workers and victims of international trafficking, regardless of legal status and documentation.'[30]

27 Articles 11, 12, 18, 19, 20 and 26 ICRMW, respectively.
28 Article 15 ICRMW.
29 Article 32 ICRMW.
30 Committee on Economic, Social and Cultural Rights, *General Comment No. 20*, para. 30.

Irregular Migrants

The second line of criticism of the Convention has been that it gives insufficient protection to irregular migrants. This critique has two elements: that irregular migrants have fewer rights than those in a lawful position, and that they are vulnerable to expulsion. These two arguments are addressed in turn here.

Fewer rights

Part IV of the Convention confers a number of rights solely upon migrant workers and their family members 'who are documented or in a regular situation'. The distinction drawn within the Convention between the rights of irregular migrants and those of persons in a regular position led to Linda Bosniak's criticism in 1991 that, 'under the terms of Convention, the undocumented continue to enjoy institutionally-sanctioned second- (or third-) class status.'[31]

One point that may be made in response is that the Convention achieves a great deal *for* irregular migrants.[32] In three cases, protection is expressly extended to irregular migrants: Article 25 on equal treatment in employment, Article 28 on emergency medical care, and Article 30 on the schooling of children. More generally, the very fact that the Convention's rights are divided between two Parts itself removes any doubt as the application of Part III rights to irregular migrant workers and their families.

A second point is that many of the rights set out in Part IV concern the detail of immigration status, and as such are logically applicable only to 'regular' migrants. That is the case with several provisions concerning the movement and residence of migrants workers and their families: the right to temporary absence from the state in question (Article 38), the right to liberty of movement and residence throughout the territory (Article 39), and the principle that expulsion should not be intended to deprive a person of the benefit of their permission to reside or to work (Article 56(2)).[33] The same may be said of certain rights conferred on migrant workers: protection of the right of residence in the event of loss of employment (Article 51), free choice of employment after a maximum of five years (Article 52), equal protection in the event of loss of employment (Article 54), and equal treatment in the exercise of employed activity (Article 55). It is also true of requirements concerning migrants' family members: 'facilitation' of admission (Article 44), access to the labour market (Article 53), and 'favourable consideration' to their staying after the death of a migrant worker or the dissolution of a marriage (Article 50).

Criticism concerning the exclusion of irregular migrants is more persuasive in relation to Part IV rights that could in principle have been extended to them, but were not. One example is the right to participation in the political affairs in the state of origin, including the right to vote and to be elected there (Article 41). Another is the right to equal treatment

31 Linda Bosniak, 'Human Rights, State Sovereignty, and the Protection of Undocumented Migrants under the International Convention for the Protection of the Rights of All Migrant Workers and Members of Their Families' (1991) 25 *International Migration Review* 737–70, at 759.

32 For this point, see Slinckx, 'Migrants' Rights in UN Human Rights Conventions', 146–7.

33 Note that the right to liberty of movement and residence is also limited to those 'lawfully in the territory' in Article 12 ICCPR.

in education, vocational provision, housing, 'social ... services', access to cooperatives and self-managed enterprises, and in cultural life (Article 43). Other cases concern personal finances: exemption from import and export duties and taxes when international migration occurs, freedom to transfer earnings and savings to the state of origin or elsewhere, and equal treatment in taxation (Articles 46–8). The provision that expulsion should only be for reasons defined in national legislation (Article 56(1)) could logically apply to irregular migrants as well.

In two cases, indeed, the exclusion of irregular migrants from Part IV rights appears inconsistent with other international treaties. One case is the Convention's provision for trade union rights. Article 26 of the Convention (in Part III) recognizes three rights for *all* migrant workers: '(a) to take part in meetings and activities of trade unions ... with a view to protecting their economic, social, cultural and other interests', '(b) to join freely any trade union,' and '(c) to seek the aid and assistance of any trade union.' What it omits, however, is the right to *form* trade unions, which is instead recognized in Article 40 (in Part IV) solely for migrant workers in a regular situation. This non-recognition of the right of irregular migrant workers to form trade unions is inconsistent with Article 2 of ILO Convention 87 on the freedom of association, which provides that 'workers and employers, without distinction whatsoever, shall have the right to establish and ... to join organisations of their own choosing.'[34] The Migrant Workers Convention is also at odds with Article 22 ICCPR, which states that 'everyone shall have ... the right to form and join trade unions', and with Article 8 ICESCR, which refers to 'the right of everyone to form trade unions and join the trade union of [their] choice'.[35]

The second case is that of rights concerning healthcare. Article 28 of the Convention (in Part III) recognizes the right of all migrant workers and their family members to equal treatment in 'medical care that is urgently required for the preservation of their life or the avoidance of irreparable harm to their health.' A full right to equal treatment in 'access to ... health services' – extending to cases where medical treatment is not urgently required, or the consequences of its non-provision are not serious – is recognized by Article 43(1)(e) (in Part IV) only for migrants in a regular situation. This is contrary to the provision in Article 12 ICESCR for 'the right of everyone to the enjoyment of the highest attainable standard of physical and mental health', read in light of the equal treatment guarantee in Article 2(2) of that Convention (discussed above).[36]

[34] The Committee on Freedom of Association has confirmed that Article 2 of ILO Convention 87 applies to *all* workers, irrespective of their immigration status: see *Spain (Case No 2121)* (23 March 2001) Report of the Committee on Freedom of Association No. 327 (Vol. LXXXV 2002 Series B No. 1), paras 561–2 and *Republic of Korea (Case No 2620)* (18 December 2007) Report of the Committee on Freedom of Association No. 353 (Vol. XCII 2009 Series B No. 1), para. 788.

[35] The use of the term 'everyone' in these Articles implies that the regularity of stay or employment should be irrelevant to these rights: see Cholewinski, *Migrant Workers in International Human Rights Law*, 164.

[36] See Committee on Economic, Social and Cultural Rights, *General Comment No. 14: The Right to the Highest Attainable Standard of Health* (2000), para. 34. For a discussion, see Vincent Chetail and Gilles Giacca, 'Who Cares? The Right to Health of Migrants' in Andrew Clapham and Mary Robinson (eds), *Realising the Right to Health* (Rueffer, Zurich, 2009) 224–34.

Immigration policy and control

The Convention's acceptance of immigration control was a second reason for criticism of its treatment of irregular migrants by Bosniak in 1991. As she put it, 'the real problem with the Convention ... is that its provisions protecting states' sovereign prerogatives to control immigration will often effectively undermine or defeat the rights it provides to those migrants.'[37] On close examination, however, it appears that this critique overestimates the weight given to immigration policy and control within the Convention.

Consider first Article 68 of the Convention. It obliges states to 'collaborate with a view to *preventing and eliminating*' irregular movements of persons and the irregular employment of migrant workers, and to 'take all adequate and effective measures to *eliminate* employment ... of migrant workers in an irregular situation.'[38] Bosniak's interpretation of Article 68 was that it required states 'to undertake *control* measures to end the process of clandestine migration and the ... employment of irregular migrants including ... employer sanctions'.[39] The difficulty with this reading is that Article 68 does not use the language of 'control'. Its language of 'preventing' and 'eliminating' potentially covers both control measures and pre-emptive policies designed to remove the basis for irregular migration. Pre-emptive policies would generally be beneficial to migrants, including those who are, or would otherwise be, in an irregular position.

Policy on regularization is another example. Article 69(1) of the Convention sets out the general proposition that, 'when there are migrant workers and members of their families within their territory in an irregular situation', contracting states 'shall ... take appropriate measures to ensure that such a situation does not persist'. Bosniak's reading was that Article 69 required states 'to undertake control measures to end ... the presence ... of irregular migrants.'[40] In reality, control measures aimed at expulsion are only one option for state authorities, who may choose regularization instead.[41] Indeed, Article 69(2) expressly provides that states may 'consider the possibility of regularizing the situation of such persons', and requires that, where they do so, 'appropriate account shall be taken of the circumstances of their entry, the duration of their stay in the States of employment and other relevant considerations, in particular those relating to their family situation.' Bosniak also cited Article 35 of the Convention as evidence that 'contracting states are explicitly not obliged to regularize the status of irregular migrant workers.'[42] In fact, Article 35 provides only that 'nothing in *the present Part* of the Convention [i.e. Part III] shall be interpreted as implying ... regularization',[43] and is stated to be without prejudice to Part VI of the Convention, which includes Article 69.

Two further provisions of the Convention may be discussed more briefly. One is Article 34 of the Convention, which provides that '[n]othing in [Part III] of the Convention shall have the

37 Bosniak, 'Human Rights, State Sovereignty', 759.

38 Emphasis added.

39 Bosniak, 'Human Rights, State Sovereignty', 741, emphasis added.

40 Ibid., 741.

41 For example, De Guchteneire and Pécoud have noted that Article 69 'may be interpreted as an obligation to either expel or regularize undocumented migrants': Paul de Guchteneire and Antoine Pécoud, 'Introduction: The UN Convention on Migrant Workers' Rights' in De Guchteneire, Pécoud and Cholewinski (eds), *Migration and Human Rights*, 1–44, at 22–3.

42 Bosniak, 'Human Rights, State Sovereignty', 741.

43 Emphasis added.

effect of relieving migrant workers and the members of their families from … the obligation to comply with the laws and regulations of any State of transit and the State of employment.' In Bosniak's analysis, this provision covered 'states' laws against unauthorized entry, employment or residence.'[44] Article 34 can also be read more narrowly, however, to require migrants to comply with the law *in general*, while obliging states to respect the substantive provisions of the Convention. The other is Article 79, which provides that 'nothing in the present Convention shall affect the right of each State Party to establish the criteria governing admission of migrant workers and members of their families.' Bosniak's characterization of Article 79 was that it permitted 'states parties to pursue the immigration *control* policies that they see fit'.[45] It would, however, be more accurate to say that Article 79 is concerned solely with the *criteria* for admission, and that it does not refer to states' immigration control methods.

The wider point is that the Convention does not give *carte blanche* to states in their immigration control systems. States remain free to have immigration policies, and to take immigration control measures in support of them. But the provision for an orderly approach to international migration in Articles 68 and 69 may equally imply acceptance of migration. Moreover, certain of the substantive rights of migrants – particularly those in Part III – may impact on immigration control measures applied to irregular migrants. We shall see in section 2 how this is an area in which the Committee on Migrant Workers has been especially creative in its interpretative work to date.

2. The Convention in Practice

Where section 1 considered the content of the Convention in the abstract, this section will consider its application in practice. The extent and pattern of ratification of the Convention are considered first, as these have been a particular area of doubt concerning its prospects. The section will then provide a detailed analysis of the work of the Committee on Migrant Workers to date.

Ratification

Forty-four states had ratified the Migrant Workers Convention at the time of writing (May 2011). Of these, the largest concentration by continent is in the Americas, where 17 out of 35 UN members have ratified the Convention.[46] There has also been extensive ratification in Africa, where 17 of 53 UN member states are parties, primarily in North and West Africa.[47] By

44 Bosniak, 'Human Rights, State Sovereignty', 741.

45 Ibid., emphasis added.

46 These are Argentina, Belize, Bolivia, Chile, Colombia, Ecuador, El Salvador, Guatemala, Guyana, Honduras, Jamaica, Mexico, Nicaragua, Paraguay, Peru, Saint Vincent and the Grenadines and Uruguay.

47 The full list of African states to have ratified is Algeria, Burkina Faso, Cape Verde, Egypt, Ghana, Guinea, Lesotho, Libya, Mali, Mauritania, Morocco, Niger, Nigeria, Rwanda, Senegal, Seychelles and Uganda.

contrast, only six Asian states of 43 UN members and only four European states out of 47 UN members have ratified, while none of the 14 UN members in Oceania have done so.[48]

The low level of ratification of the Convention has contributed to doubts as to its true value. Unfavourable comparisons have been drawn with other specific UN human rights instruments, including the Convention on the Elimination of Discrimination against Women (adopted in 1979), which had 186 parties at the time of writing, and the Convention on the Rights of the Child (adopted in 1989), which had 190, and with the Migrant Smuggling Protocol (adopted in 2000), which had 127 parties at the time of writing.[49] In itself, however, this relatively low level of ratification does not tell us whether the Convention has value for those states that are parties.

The lack of ratification by the major countries of immigration in Europe, North America and elsewhere has been seen as a further weakness. Writing in 2009, Paul de Guchteneire and Antoine Pécoud put it bluntly: 'no major state has ratified, which strongly diminishes the impact of the Convention.'[50] There is, however, a risk of what may be termed 'North-centrism' in discussion of the Convention. This bias is reflected in the extensive research (including by the present author) into obstacles to ratification in highly developed countries.[51] The danger is that scholarship on the Convention is blind to its potential *outside* the most developed group of states. It is striking in particular that the experience of countries that *have* ratified has remained largely unexamined in academic commentary to date.[52]

One reason why the Convention may have value as a source of standards for countries that have ratified is that many of those states have extensive experience of *emigration*. For example, the many Latin American states that have ratified are countries of origin, as are the North and West African states that have done so, the Philippines and Sri Lanka in Asia, and Albania and Turkey in Europe. States of origin that have ratified may have intended thereby to boost the Convention, in order to secure better treatment for their nationals in destination countries.[53] But the text of the Convention also places duties upon them. We shall see below that this latter aspect has been prominent in the work of the Committee on Migrant Workers to date.

48 The Asian states to have ratified are Kyrgyzstan, Philippines, Sri Lanka, Syria, Tajikistan and Timor Leste. The four European states to have ratified are Albania, Azerbaijan, Bosnia and Herzegovina and Turkey. (Membership of the Council of Europe has been used to define the category of 'European' state here.)

49 De Guchteneire and Pécoud, 'Introduction', 11–12, 24–5.

50 Ibid., 13. In the same collection, Carla Edelenbos expressed frustration at the 'absence of any major receiving country among the States Parties': 'Committee on Migrant Workers and Implementation of the ICRMW' in De Guchteneire, Pécoud and Cholewinski (eds), *Migration and Human Rights*, 100–121, at 119.

51 See, for example, Shirley Hune and Jan Niessen, 'Ratifying the UN Migrant Workers Convention: Current Difficulties and Prospects' (1994) 12 *Netherlands Quarterly of Human Rights* 130–41, and the studies on Canada, France, Germany, Italy and (by the present author) the United Kingdom in De Guchteneire, Pécoud and Cholewinski (eds), *Migration and Human Rights*.

52 For a similar observation, see Chetail, 'Review of *Migration and Human Rights*', 680. An exception is the chapter by Gabriela Díaz and Gretchen Kuhner, 'Mexico's Role in Promoting and Implementing the ICRMW' in De Guchteneire, Pécoud and Cholewinski (eds), *Migration and Human Rights*, 219–46.

53 See Battistella, 'Migration and Human Rights', 59.

Secondly, many states that have ratified the Convention have experienced significant levels of *transit migration*. The wider picture is that, since the mid-1980s, the most developed countries have taken a more rigorous approach to immigration control, including through tougher visa policies and the introduction of carrier sanctions. As a result, their neighbouring states have often faced an increase in arrivals by persons in transit. Among states that have ratified the Convention, this has been the case in particular for Mexico (mainly in relation to Central America), for Algeria, Egypt, Libya and Morocco (mainly in relation to sub-Saharan Africa) and Turkey (mainly in relation to Asian countries).[54] When those neighbouring states are parties to the Convention, they are bound by its terms in their treatment of transit migrants who are migrant workers or their family members.

Thirdly, a number of states that are parties to the Convention are migration *destinations* in their own right. Among the states that have ratified, Argentina and Libya stand out as countries – for quite different reasons – with long histories of inward migration for employment.[55] The emergence of a migrant population is also a feature of conditions in Chile, Ecuador and Uruguay.[56] More generally, all of the 'transit' countries and regions referred to above are potential destination countries, if those who initially intend to move on to North America or Western Europe elect to remain there.[57]

The relevance of the Convention to the migration experience of ratifying states has been recognized in the work of the Migrant Workers Committee. In its observations on the state reports submitted to it (see below), it has frequently noted that the state in question, in addition to being a state of origin, is also a place of transit and/or of destination. Statements of this kind have been included in the concluding observations concerning all five Latin American states considered to date (Bolivia, Colombia, Ecuador, El Salvador and Mexico), as well as three African states (Algeria, Egypt and Senegal) and two European states (Azerbaijan and Bosnia and Herzegovina). In three further cases, there has been partial recognition that the party was not merely a country of origin: Albania was described as a country of origin and transit; Mali was said to have difficulties in controlling irregular migration; and it was noted that Syria had recently experienced extensive migration as a result of the armed conflict in Iraq. Of the fifteen countries commented upon so far, only the Philippines and Sri Lanka have been characterized by the Committee as states of origin alone.

---

[54] See generally Manuel Ángel Castillo, 'Mexico: Caught between the United States and Central America' (Migration Information Source, April 2006) and Franck Düvell 'Crossing the Fringes of Europe: Transit Migration in the EU's Neighbourhood' (COMPAS Working Paper WP-06-33, 2006).

[55] See Maia Jachimowicz, 'Argentina: A New Era of Migration and Migration Policy' (Migration Information Source, January 2006) and Sara Hamood, *African Transit Migration through Libya to Europe: The Human Cost* (American University in Cairo, 2006) 17–19.

[56] See Agustín Escobar Latapí, *The Future of Migration Policies in the Americas* (IOM, Geneva, 2010) 7.

[57] See Michael Colyer and Hein de Haas, 'Developing Dynamic Categorisations of Transit Migration' (2011) 17 *Population, Space and Place* 468–81.

The Committee on Migrant Workers

The Committee on Migrant Workers is provided for in Article 72 of the Convention. It was established on 1 January 2004, six months after the Convention came into force. The distribution of its current 14 members broadly corresponds to the geographical spread of ratifications, with five American states (Ecuador, El Salvador, Jamaica, Guatemala and Mexico), five African states (Burkina Faso, Egypt, Morocco, Mali and Senegal), two Asian states (the Philippines and Sri Lanka), and two European states (Azerbaijan and Turkey).

The Convention provides for two optional procedures through which complaints may be brought to the Committee. Participating states may recognize the Committee's competence over interstate complaints (Article 76), and over complaints by 'individuals subject to its jurisdiction' who claim their rights have been violated by that state (Article 77).[58] Each of these procedures is to come into effect when ten states have accepted the competence of the Committee. At the time of writing, only Guatemala had made the necessary declaration with respect to Article 76, while only Guatemala and Mexico had done so with respect to Article 77. In addition, Turkey has declared that it will recognize the competence of the Committee 'at a later time'.

Accordingly, the Committee's most significant role to date has been its consideration of state reports, made under Article 73, on the 'legislative, judicial, administrative and other measures' taken to give effect to the Convention. A contracting state is to submit the first such report within one year of the entry into force of the Convention for it. Subsequently, reports should be submitted every five years, or 'whenever the Committee so requests'. By early 2011, 20 states had submitted initial reports to the Committee, and two states (Mexico and Ecuador) had reported a second time.[59] In total, 15 initial state reports, and both of the second periodic reports, had been the subject of concluding observations by the Committee.[60] As against that, 22 states had failed to submit a required initial report as of early 2011,[61] while a further four states had failed to submit second periodic reports that were due in 2009 or 2010.[62]

The rest of this section will offer an analysis of the Committee's interpretation of the Convention in its concluding observations. It will also discuss the Committee's only General Comment to date, on migrant domestic workers (General Comment No. 1, 2010).[63] Rather than an exhaustive summary, what will be provided is a thematic account of the major issues that

---

58 Article 77(2) makes it a precondition to the Committee's considering an individual complaint that 'the same matter has not been, and is not being examined under another procedure of international investigation or settlement'. This replicates the language of Article 5(2) of the First Optional Protocol to the ICCPR, which gives the Human Rights Committee jurisdiction over individual complaints.

59 The states that had submitted initial reports by the end of 2010 were: Albania, Algeria, Argentina, Azerbaijan, Bolivia, Bosnia and Herzegovina, Chile, Colombia, Guatemala, Ecuador, El Salvador, Egypt, Mali, Mexico, Paraguay, the Philippines, Senegal, Sri Lanka, Syria and Tajikistan.

60 At the time of writing, the reports by Argentina, Chile, Guatemala, Paraguay and Tajikistan had not been the subject of concluding observations.

61 Note that Guyana and St Vincent and the Grenadines each ratified the Convention during 2010, and were therefore obliged to submit an initial report only in 2011.

62 These were Bolivia, Egypt, El Salvador and Mali.

63 The only similar analysis of which the author is aware is the discussion of the Committee's first three sets of concluding observations in Edelenbos, 'Committee on Migrant Workers'.

have emerged, grouped under the following headings: the position of emigrants, the rights of immigrants, and immigration policy and control.[64]

The Position of Emigrants

As all of the states whose reports have been considered to date are countries of origin of migrants, the Committee's observations have frequently addressed their relationship with emigrant nationals.[65] It has focused on three topics in particular: the right to leave, the representation of nationals abroad, and political rights.

The right to leave

Article 8 of the Convention provides for the right of migrant workers 'to leave any State, including their State of origin'. The Committee relied upon Article 8 to question Ecuador's (2007) requirement that its nationals obtain an exit permit in order to leave the territory.[66] In addition, while not referred to explicitly, Article 8 was presumably the basis for the Committee's recommendation to Egypt (2007) that women should be able to obtain passports without the approval of a husband or male relative.[67]

The Committee has also taken the view that states ought not to criminalize irregular exit with the aim of deterring migrant smuggling. In its concluding observations on Algeria (2010), the Committee recommended reconsideration of a legislative proposal to criminalize departure other than through a border post, for which the proposed maximum penalty was a period of imprisonment of six months.[68] That recommendation was adopted with reference, not to Article 8, but to Part VI of the Convention, which concerns 'orderly' migration. The Committee also suggested that penalties were contrary to the Migrant Smuggling Protocol of 2000 (to which Algeria is a party), presumably because its Article 5 prohibits 'criminal prosecution' of migrants 'for the fact of having been the object of' smuggling.[69]

Representation of nationals abroad

The Committee has also supported the conclusion of bilateral arrangements by states of origin with states of employment. In the case of Sri Lanka (2009), it 'note[d] with interest the memoranda of understanding and bilateral agreements with major labour receiving

[64] The concluding observations will be cited below by giving the state name and the year of the document in which the observations were published.

[65] For a similar observation, see Edelenbos, 'Committee on Migrant Workers', 120–21.

[66] Ecuador, 5 December 2007, para. 22. In 2010, Ecuador reported that the exit permit requirement had been ruled unconstitutional, and that it was no longer in force: Ecuador: Second Periodic Report, 26 January 2010, para. 122.

[67] Egypt, 25 May 2007, paras 26–7.

[68] Algeria, 19 May 2010, paras 40 and 41. Details of the legislation are in 'Algeria: Comments by the State Party', 3 May 2010.

[69] In a written response, Algeria argued that its proposed legislation aimed to uphold human dignity and the right to life, and to prevent human trafficking: 'Algeria: Comments by the State Party', 3 May 2010.

countries'.[70] Similarly, the Committee welcomed Ecuador's (2010) signature of ten 'alliances and agreements' with other countries for the protection of its nationals abroad.[71] By contrast, the Committee called upon Egypt (2007) to negotiate with Gulf states for the abolition of legal arrangements there that gave sponsors personal control over its nationals.[72] Similar recommendations concerning the protection of migrant workers in Gulf states were made to Syria (2008) and to the Philippines (2009).[73] It may be added that the Committee has mainly based these observations on Part VI of the Convention, which aims at 'orderly' international migration.[74]

The Committee has also emphasized the importance of effective consular support for contracting states' nationals. One aspect of such support is the provision of assistance to migrant workers who have grievances arising out of their employment. The Committee recommended that the Philippines (2009) 'ensure that its embassy and consulate staff abroad are knowledgeable about the laws and procedures of the countries of employment of Filipino foreign workers'.[75] Similarly, it encouraged Sri Lanka (2009) to ensure that legal assistance was available to migrant workers in *all* its embassies and consulates, and that its labour welfare officers were knowledgeable about the labour laws and procedures of the country of deployment.[76] A second aspect of consular assistance that the Committee has highlighted is the timely provision of travel documents to their nationals who face expulsion from another country. Egypt (2007) and Bolivia (2008) have each been criticized for systematic failures in this regard.[77] These various observations have been made either under Part III of the Convention, or – in the sole case of Egypt – under Part VI. This implies that they were based on Article 23 and Article 65 of the Convention, respectively (see section 1, above).

Political rights

The Committee has also sought to promote compliance with the right of emigrant workers in a regular position to vote in elections in their state of origin (Article 41 of the Convention). Failures to respect this right in the state's electoral rules were identified in two cases: the Philippines (2009), which allowed the right to vote only to those who affirmed their intention to return within three years, and Albania (2010), which allowed voting to take place solely on its territory.[78] In seven other cases, the Committee has called for the contracting state to take steps to facilitate the practical exercise of the right to vote by its nationals abroad.[79]

---

70 Sri Lanka, 19 October 2009, paras 39–40.

71 Ecuador, 15 December 2010, para 5.

72 Egypt, 25 May 2007, paras 48–9.

73 Syria, 2 May 2008, para. 38; The Philippines, 22 May 2009, para. 32.

74 The observations on Sri Lanka, Egypt and Syria were made under Part VI. The observation concerning Ecuador was listed under 'positive aspects', without further elaboration. The observation on the Philippines was based on Part III.

75 The Philippines, 22 May 2009, para. 30.

76 Sri Lanka, 19 October 2009, para. 30.

77 Egypt, 25 May 2007, paras 46 and 47; Bolivia, 29 April 2008, para. 28.

78 The Philippines, 22 May 2009, paras 35–6; Albania, 26 November 2010, paras 31–2.

79 Mali, 31 May 2006, para. 7; Egypt, 25 May 2007, para. 43; Bolivia, 29 April 2008, para. 34; El Salvador, 4 February 2009, para. 35; Colombia, 22 May 2009, para. 34; Bosnia and Herzegovina, 3 June 2009, para. 30; Sri Lanka, 19 October 2009, para. 34.

The Rights of Immigrants

Given the focus of the Convention on the treatment of migrant workers and their family members, it is not surprising that the rights of immigrants have been central to the work of the Committee to date. The discussion here considers the Committee's comments in four areas: personal status, access to labour law, trade union rights, and social provision for irregular migrants.

Personal status

We saw above that Article 29 of the Convention confers 'the right to a name, to registration of birth and to a nationality' upon children. Relying upon that Article, the Committee has addressed recommendations to three states concerning the registration of births. It expressed its regret that children born in Egypt (2007) to migrant workers, whether in a regular or an irregular situation, were unable to obtain birth certificates.[80] It expressed concern at the number of children of migrants in Ecuador (2007) whose births were not registered 'either because their parents fail to register them for fear of being deported or because their registration is refused on the ground of the irregular status of one or both parents.'[81] Similarly, it expressed concern at refusals by many officials in Mexico (2011) to register the births of the children of irregular migrants, notwithstanding that they were Mexican citizens by birth.[82]

In a further case, the Committee addressed the right to a nationality. Having noted that only children with a parent domiciled in Colombia (2009) were eligible for Colombian nationality, it expressed concern that some children might remain stateless as a result. It therefore recommended that the state ensure the right of all children to a nationality, and that it proceed with its proposed accession to the 1961 United Nations Convention on the Reduction of Statelessness.[83]

Access to labour law

The Committee has interpreted the Convention to require that migrants have access to the protection of labour law both in theory and in practice. The starting point is that Article 25(1) of the Convention provides that 'migrant workers shall enjoy treatment not less favourable than that which applies to nationals of the State of employment' in respect of terms and conditions of employment. Article 25(2) makers clear that this guarantee of equal treatment applies within individual employment relationships, by providing that 'it shall not be lawful to derogate in private contracts of employment from the principle of equality of treatment'.

---

80 Egypt, 25 May 2007, para. 34.

81 Ecuador, 5 December 2007, para. 35.

82 Mexico, 8 April 2011, para. 39.

83 Colombia, 22 May 2009, paras 29–30. The 1961 Convention had not been ratified as of May 2011. Note that ratification would not imply an unlimited right to the nationality of the state of birth for those who are otherwise stateless. In particular, where a child born on the territory was born to foreign parents, Article 1 of the 1961 Convention permits parties to set a minimum age, up to 18, for an application, and to make the grant of nationality conditional upon the person's habitual resided in the territory for up to 10 years.

The Committee relied specifically upon Article 25 in criticism of Egypt (2007) for an apparent requirement of reciprocity before its Labour Code applied to legally employed foreign workers.[84] The Committee also referred to it in General Comment No. 1 (2010), when stating that migrant domestic workers 'should enjoy treatment not less favourable than that which applies to nationals of the State of employment'.[85]

The Committee's has also called for the inclusion of migrant domestic workers within labour law in its comments on Egypt (2007) and in General Comment No. 1 (2010).[86] In the case of Egypt, its observations were made under Part III of the Convention, without further explanation. In General Comment No. 1, it simply referred in general to 'equal protection under the law' as a conceptual basis for the inclusion of domestic workers within labour law, even though that principle does not appear in the text of the Convention. The Committee presumably did not refer to Article 25 in these observations because that Article requires the *equal treatment* of migrants, which may be thought to provide an insufficient basis to challenge the exclusion of an entire category of worker from some or all labour laws.

The Committee has also addressed the question of limited access to labour law protections by irregular workers. The background is that Article 25(3) of the Convention contains two propositions of relevance to their position – that irregularity may not be a ground for depriving migrant workers of equal treatment, and that 'employers shall not be relieved of any legal or contractual obligations' because of a worker's 'irregularity of stay or employment'. To date, the Committee has, however, relied upon this Article only by implication, preferring instead to base its remarks on the position of irregular workers under Article 83 of the Convention, which sets out a right to an effective remedy where Convention rights or freedoms are violated. In the case of Mexico (2006), the Committee expressed its concern at a legislative provision that allowed legal proceedings to be instituted by foreign nationals only if they were legally resident.[87] Lack of access by irregular migrant workers to an effective remedy was also the subject of Committee recommendations to Syria (2008), in relation to its labour commissions, and Algeria (2010), in relation to the courts in general.[88]

Finally, the Committee has sought to promote the practical effectiveness of labour law in relation to particularly vulnerable groups of workers. It recommended that the application of labour law standards be made effective for migrant domestic workers in Mexico (2006), Ecuador (2007 and 2010), El Salvador (2009), and in General Comment No. 1(2010), and for migrant workers in agriculture in Mexico (2006) and El Salvador (2009).[89] Among these cases,

---

84 Egypt, 25 May 2007, paras 30–31. The Government's evidence was that the principle of reciprocity applied only to exemption from the requirement to obtain a work permit: see 'Egypt: Written Replies', 6 February 2007, 16–17.

85 General Comment No. 1 on Migrant Domestic Workers (23 February 2011), UN Doc. CMW/C/GC/1, para. 38.

86 Egypt, 25 May 2007, paras 38–9; General Comment No. 1, para. 38.

87 Mexico, 20 December 2006, paras 25–6. In November 2008, Mexico's Supreme Court ruled that foreign workers were entitled to the protection of labour law, irrespective of their migration status, and, in 2010, the offending legislative provision was removed, so as to permit all legal claims by irregular migrants. See 'Mexico: Second Periodic Report', 14 January 2010, para. 29, and Mexico, 8 April 2011, para. 7(e).

88 Syria, 2 May 2008, paras 25–6; Algeria, 19 May 2010, paras 16–17.

89 Mexico, 20 December 2006, paras 33–4 and 37–8; El Salvador, 4 February 2009, paras 29 and 30; Ecuador, 5 December 2007, para. 38; Ecuador, 15 December 2010, para. 28; General

the Committee cited Article 25 only in relation to El Salvador (2009). Elsewhere, it has made these comments under general headings – Part IV of the Convention in the case of agricultural workers in Mexico (2006), 'conditions of work' in General Comment No. 1 (2010), and Part III of the Convention in the other cases.

Trade union rights

We saw in section 1 that trade union rights are provided for in two places in the Convention: Article 26 for all migrant workers, and Article 40 for migrant workers in a regular situation. To date, the Committee has relied upon Article 26 mainly in relation to irregular migrant workers. In the case of Albania (2010), it referred to Article 26 in criticizing a legal provision specifically excluding irregular migrant workers from joining trade unions.[90] In the case of Algeria (2010), it expressed its concern more generally that irregular workers did not 'effectively enjoy' a range of Convention rights, including the right to join trade unions in Article 26.[91] An exception – where Article 26 was recognized to apply to all workers – was the statement in General Comment No. 1 (2010) that 'the laws of States parties, particularly countries of employment of migrant domestic workers, should recognize the right of the latter to form and join organizations, regardless of migration status (article 26).'[92]

The Committee has by contrast shown itself more willing to identify a breach of Article 40. In some cases, this has been because of discrimination against foreign nationals in the law relating to trade unions. The Committee concluded that that the reservation of the constitutional right to form trade unions to citizens in Sri Lanka (2009) was a breach both of Article 40 and of the non-discrimination guarantee in Article 7.[93] It concluded that the Philippines (2009) was in breach of Article 40 in making the trade union rights of migrant workers subject to a condition of reciprocal treatment of its nationals.[94] In the case of Algeria (2010), the Committee identified a breach of Article 40 in the exclusion of migrant workers from the right to form trade unions.[95] On that occasion, it also expressed its concern at the non-exercise by lawful migrant workers of the right to engage in trade union activities under Part IV of the Convention, though without linking its observation to a specific Article.[96]

In four other cases, the Committee has criticized the exclusion of foreign nationals from official positions within trade unions. Mexico (2006, 2011), Ecuador (2007, 2010) and El Salvador (2009) all had blanket rules excluding foreign nationals from the leadership of trade unions. In each case, the Committee identified a breach of what it has termed 'the right to form, and to form part of the leadership of ... trade unions', guaranteed by Article 40.[97] In addition, the Committee recommended that Senegal (2010) remove its precondition to migrant

Comment No. 1, para. 41.

90 Albania, 26 November 2010, paras 29–30.

91 Algeria, 19 May 2010, para. 19.

92 General Comment No. 1, para. 46.

93 Sri Lanka, 19 October 2009, paras 25–6 and 31–2.

94 The Philippines, 22 May 2009, paras 33–4.

95 Algeria, 19 May 2010, paras 28–9.

96 Ibid.

97 See Mexico, 20 December 2006, para. 36. Similar observations are in Mexico, 8 April 2011, para. 46; Ecuador, 5 December 2007, para. 42; Ecuador, 15 December 2010, para. 42; and,

workers serving as trade union officials that there be a reciprocal agreement with the country of nationality.[98] This recommendation was made under Part IV of the Convention, and by implication was again based on Article 40.

It is significant that, in its comments on trade union rights to date, the Committee has preferred to rely upon Article 40, or Part IV more generally, even though the subject matter of its comments potentially falls within Article 26. For example, the non-participation of lawful migrant workers in trade union activities in Algeria (2010) touched on a matter expressly mentioned in Article 26 alone. Similarly, discrimination against foreign nationals in Sri Lanka, Algeria and the Philippines presumably entailed a denial not just of the right to form trade unions, but also of their Article 26 rights. Equally, the possibility for foreign nationals to be officials or leaders of a trade union could have been classed, not as an aspect of trade union formation, but as 'participation' in trade union activities. Much as with the Convention itself, therefore, the Committee has generally approached trade union rights in a manner that has avoided the fullest protection for irregular migrant workers.

Social provision for irregular migrants

Three of the provisions in Part III of the Convention referred to in section 1 are of particular relevance to state social provision for irregular migrants. Article 27 provides for the equal treatment of all migrant workers and their family members in the field of social security. Article 28 provides for access to urgent medical care, and expressly covers those whose residence or employment is irregular. Article 30 sets out the right of a child of a migrant worker to equality of access to education, and expressly precludes the irregularity of a parent's residence or employment, or of the child's own residence, from being a reason for denying a child access to schooling.

The Committee has invoked these Articles in relation to irregular migrant workers on four occasions. It called for compliance by Egypt (2007) with Article 30, because of its concern that 'the children of undocumented migrant workers do not have any access to the schooling system, whether public or private.'[99] It called for Ecuador (2007) to comply with Article 28, because of evidence that 'in practice migrant workers in an irregular situation and members of their families face difficulties in accessing the public health system.'[100] It called for Azerbaijan (2009) to comply with Articles 28 and 30, because of reports that irregular migrants and their family members did not have access to medical care in practice, and that the children of irregular migrants had difficulty obtaining access to education.[101] Finally, in the case of Algeria (2010), it listed both Article 27 on social security and Article 28 on medical care among the rights that irregular migrant workers did not 'effectively enjoy'.[102]

El Salvador, 4 February 2009, para. 32. In the case of El Salvador, the right to form part of the leadership was limited to its nationals by birth.

98 Senegal, 10 December 2010, para. 16.

99 Egypt, 25 May 2007, paras 36–7. The Committee also expressed its concern at the lack of access to public schools by the children of legal migrant workers.

100 Ecuador, 5 December 2007, paras 39–40.

101 Azerbaijan, 19 May 2009, paras 30–31.

102 Algeria, 19 May 2010, para. 19.

Immigration Policy and Control

We saw in section 1 that the Convention has been criticized for leaving too much scope for states' immigration policy and control. In practice, however, the Committee has taken a more robust view, and has identified ways in which immigration policies and control measures conflict with states' obligations under the Convention. Three issues are addressed here: the treatment of irregular migrants within immigration control systems, regularization, and the content of legal migration policy.

Treatment of irregular migrants within immigration control

An important subject addressed by the Committee concerning irregular migrants is the detention of those presumed to have breached immigration law. As we saw above, Article 17 of the Convention requires that those suspected of a breach of immigration laws should if possible be detained separately from those within the criminal justice system. The Committee has to date commented on three states' failures to respect the general principle: Mexico (2006), Ecuador (2007) and Senegal (2010).[103] In the case of Mexico, this recommendation was included under Part III without reference to a particular Article, while, in the other cases, Article 17 was referred to expressly.[104]

In addition, the Committee has twice criticized states for providing criminal sanctions for those who breach immigration law. The Convention does not expressly prohibit criminal penalties, and the Committee has not referred to any particular provision in support of these comments. One possible argument is that the sanction of *imprisonment* is prohibited by the requirement in Article 17 (above) to keep those who breach immigration law separate from those detained within the criminal justice system. That may explain the Committee's recommendation to Mexico (2006) – under the heading of 'General measures of implementation' – that it 'annul the classification of illegal entry into the country as an offence punishable by deprivation of liberty.'[105] Alternatively, *criminalization as such* might be thought incompatible with the effective exercise by irregular migrants of their rights under the Convention. That was the approach taken by the Committee when it called upon Algeria (2009) to ensure that migrant workers and their families were 'not deprived of any of the rights under the Convention which apply to all migrant workers, including those in an irregular situation', and to 'bring its legislation – which criminalizes irregular migration – into conformity with the Convention.'[106]

---

[103] Mexico, 20 December 2006, para. 28; Ecuador, 5 December 2007, para. 24; Senegal, 10 December 2010, para. 15.

[104] The recommendation concerning Ecuador referred to Article 17(3). Confusingly, however, that in relation to Senegal referred to Article 17(2). That may have been an error, as that provision is concerned with the rights of 'accused' persons, rather than those suspected of a breach of immigration law.

[105] Mexico, 20 December 2006, para. 15. In line with that recommendation, in its second report, Mexico informed the Committee that its legislation had been amended, so that breaches of immigration law had become the subject of fines alone, and could no longer give rise to a prison sentence: 'Mexico: Second Periodic Report', 14 January 2010, paras 136–7.

[106] Algeria, 19 May 2010, paras 18 and 21.

Regularization

The Committee has consistently taken the view that a procedure for regularization ought to be available as a solution to irregular status, at least where there are substantial numbers of irregular workers present on a state's territory. It has generally favoured Article 69 (discussed in section 1, above) as the basis for its comments on this subject. For example, it expressed its concern at reports that a high percentage of migrant workers in Azerbaijan (2009) were in an irregular position, and recommended 'appropriate measures, in accordance with the Convention, in particular with Article 69, to ensure that this situation does not persist, including the possibility of regularizing the situation of these migrant workers.'[107] Article 69 was also cited as the basis for recommending access to regularization for domestic workers in the General Comment on Migrant Domestic Workers (2010).[108] In addition, in the case of Senegal (2010) the Committee referred to both Articles 68 and 69, before recommending 'proactive and effective measures to ensure that migrant workers and members of their families do not remain in an irregular situation', and that any regularization mechanism should be 'accessible and expeditious'.[109] That joint reference to Articles 68 and 69 is especially significant, as it is in line with the view (discussed above) that these Articles may oblige states to take pre-emptive action to prevent irregular migration and employment.

The Committee has not relied upon Article 69 alone, however. In the cases of Mexico (2006) and Ecuador (2007, 2010), it recommended regularization as a means of social and labour market protection for female migrant domestic workers under Part III of the Convention.[110] Part III was also the heading for a recommendation to Ecuador (2010) to 'redouble its efforts to establish and implement a comprehensive migration regularization policy.'[111] Finally, in the case of Bolivia (2008), the Committee inexplicably addressed regularization under Part IV of the Convention, when recommending that an existing regularization procedure be strengthened, through reductions in fees and delays, and by allowing applicants to remain while a decision was taken.[112]

Content of legal migration policy

Despite the terms of Article 79, which allows contracting states to set admission criteria (see section 1), the Committee has made recommendations to states on several occasions concerning their legal migration policy. One key proposition it has advanced is that a state ought to design its legal migration policy so as to minimize the risks of irregular migration and employment. Azerbaijan (2009) issued work permits for up to one year at a time, which could be renewed up to four times, but then expected foreign workers to leave its territory for at least one year before reapplying. In response, the Committee observed that the 'burdensome and complex' nature of these procedures risked encouraging irregular migration, and recommended that

---

107 Azerbaijan, 19 May 2009, paras 44–5.

108 General Comment No. 1, para. 52.

109 Senegal, 10 December 2010, para. 23.

110 Mexico, 20 December 2006, para. 34; Ecuador, 5 December 2007, para. 38; Ecuador, 15 December 2010, para. 28.

111 Ecuador, 15 December 2010, paras 6, 33 and 34.

112 Bolivia, 29 April 2008, para. 32.

the state 'consider reviewing the existing restrictions on the renewal of work permits'.[113] On that occasion, its observations were based solely on the duty to implement the Convention (Articles 73 and 84), without reference to any substantive obligation. The Committee was more specific in General Comment No. 1 (2010) on migrant domestic workers, when it based a similar recommendation on Article 68 of the Convention:

> With a view to preventing irregular migration as well as smuggling and human trafficking, States parties should ensure that migrant domestic workers have access to regular channels for migration based on actual demand (Article 68).[114]

Here too, the Committee treated Article 68 as implying a duty to design policy pre-emptively, so as to minimize irregular employment.

A second reason for the Committee's interest in legal migration policy is discrimination against a particular nationality. Relying upon the general principle of non-discrimination in Article 7 of the Convention, the Committee expressed its concern at Ecuador's (2007 and 2010) requirement that Colombian nationals produce an official certificate to show that they do not have a criminal record.[115] In its view, this exclusive requirement risked contributing to the 'stigmatization and stereotyping' of Colombian nationals.[116] Discrimination against particular nationalities within immigration policy appears therefore to be inherently suspect under Article 7.

Thirdly, the Committee has commented on provision for family reunification. The background is the uncertain obligation upon states in Article 44(2) (referred to in section 1) to 'take measures that they deem appropriate ... to facilitate' the reunification of migrant workers with spouses, persons in 'a relationship that, according to applicable law, produces effects equivalent to marriage', and minor dependent unmarried children. Given the lack of specificity within this provision, it is significant that the Committee expressed its concern that Algeria's (2010) regulations on family reunification for migrant workers applied to spouses alone, and called upon it to bring its policy into line with Article 44.[117] The implication appears to be that a state must make *some* provision for the family members referred to in that Article.

Conclusion

This chapter has offered a broadly optimistic analysis of the Migrant Workers Convention as a source of standards for international migration. It started by arguing that criticisms of the Convention have for the most part been misplaced. The claim that the Convention unnecessarily duplicates provisions of other international human rights treaties underestimates the ways in

113 Azerbaijan, 19 May 2009, paras 14–15.

114 General Comment No. 1, para. 51.

115 Ecuador, 5 December 2007, paras 19–20, and 15 December 2010, paras 25–6.

116 Ecuador maintained its policy, arguing that it was necessary for reasons of public safety and public order: see 'Ecuador: Written Replies', 20 September 2010, para. 86.

117 Algeria, 19 May 2010, paras 32–3. The Committee also referred to Article 4, which sets out a definition of family member for the purpose of the Convention as a whole.

which the Convention is a coherent instrument for the protection of migrants as a category. Similarly, the claim that the Convention gives insufficient protection to irregular migrants is at odds with the extensive protection it confers on that group, and reflects an over-interpretation of its provisions concerning immigration policy and control.

The chapter then showed how the potential of the Convention has been revealed in practice. The Convention is directly relevant to the circumstances of the states that have ratified it, as they all have experience as countries of origin of emigrants, while many have experience of immigration as transit and/or as destination locations. That argument was supported by a review of the work of the Committee on Migrant Workers to date.[118] In the first place, the Committee has served as a mechanism for calling attention to clear failures of implementation by the states that have ratified – e.g., in relation to representation of emigrant nationals, the denial of trade union rights to foreign nationals, or the exclusion of irregular migrants from social protection. Beyond that, the Committee has shown a certain creativity in interpreting the Convention in the face of current issues in the field of international migration. One example is its advancement of the proposition that the Convention requires that migrant domestic workers should be protected by labour law. Other examples have concerned policy relating to irregular migration, where the Committee has rejected criminal penalties for breaches of immigration law and for irregular exit, promoted regularization, and proposed that the duty to prevent irregular migration and employment may require adjustments to legal migration policy.

The overall conclusion to be drawn is that the Convention has a clear role in relation to the states that have ratified it, especially where those states engage with the Committee on Migrant Workers. Going forward, two initiatives appear desirable, in order to clarify the Convention's potential value. Firstly, research into the Convention ought to focus on the states that have ratified it, rather than – as hitherto – upon those that have not. Secondly, the Committee's approach to the protection of migrants would be more authoritative if it were more clearly and consistently linked to particular provisions of the Convention. Each of these steps may be thought critical in enhancing support for the Convention as a source of norms in the contemporary migration context.

References

Battistella, Graziano, 'Migration and Human Rights: The Uneasy but Essential Relationship' in Paul de Guchteneire, Antoine Pécoud and Ryszard Cholewinski (eds), *Migration and Human Rights: The United Nations Convention on Migrant Workers' Rights* (Cambridge University Press, Cambridge, 2009) 47–69.

Böhning, Roger, 'The ILO and the New UN Convention on Migrant Workers: The Past and Future' (1991) 25 *International Migration Review* 698–709.

[118] Slinckx has offered a similar assessment of the Committee's potential – 'the CMW … offers an expert understanding of the specificities of the situation of migrants': Slinckx, 'Migrants' Rights in UN Human Rights Conventions', 149.

Böhning, Roger, 'The Protection of Migrant Workers and International Labour Standards' (1988) 26 *International Migration* 133–46.

Bosniak, Linda, 'Human Rights, State Sovereignty, and the Protection of Undocumented Migrants under the International Convention for the Protection of the Rights of All Migrant Workers and Members of Their Families' (1991) 25 *International Migration Review* 737–70.

Chetail, Vincent, 'Review of *Migration and Human Rights: The United Nations Convention on Migrant Workers*' (2010) 22 *International Journal of Refugee Law* 677–82.

Chetail, Vincent and Gilles Giacca, 'Who Cares? The Right to Health of Migrants' in Andrew Clapham and Mary Robinson (eds), *Realising the Right to Health* (Rueffer, Zurich, 2009) 224–34.

Cholewinski, Ryszard, *Migrant Workers in International Human Rights Law: Their Protection in Countries of Employment* (Oxford University Press, Oxford, 1997).

Colyer, Michael and Hein de Haas, 'Developing Dynamic Categorisations of Transit Migration' (2011) 17 *Population, Space and Place* 468–81.

De Guchteneire, Paul and Antoine Pécoud, 'Introduction: The UN Convention on Migrant Workers' Rights' in Paul de Guchteneire, Antoine Pécoud and Ryszard Cholewinski (eds), *Migration and Human Rights: The United Nations Convention on Migrant Workers' Rights* (Cambridge University Press, Cambridge, 2009) 1–44.

Díaz, Gabriela and Gretchen Kuhner, 'Mexico's Role in Promoting and Implementing the ICRMW' in Paul de Guchteneire, Antoine Pécoud and Ryszard Cholewinski (eds), *Migration and Human Rights: The United Nations Convention on Migrant Workers' Rights* (Cambridge University Press, Cambridge, 2009) 219–46.

Edelenbos, Carla, 'Committee on Migrant Workers and Implementation of the ICRMW' in Paul de Guchteneire, Antoine Pécoud and Ryszard Cholewinski (eds), *Migration and Human Rights: The United Nations Convention on Migrant Workers' Rights* (Cambridge University Press, Cambridge, 2009) 100–121.

Escobar Latapí, Agustín, *The Future of Migration Policies in the Americas* (IOM, Geneva, 2010).

Hune, Shirley and Jan Niessen, 'Ratifying the UN Migrant Workers Convention: Current Difficulties and Prospects' (1994) 12 *Netherlands Quarterly of Human Rights* 130–41.

Lönnroth, Juhani, 'The International Convention on the Rights of All Migrant Workers and Members of Their Families in the Context of International Migration Policies: An Analysis of Ten Years of Negotiation' (1991) 25 *International Migration Review* 710–36.

Nafziger, James and Barry Bartel, 'The Migration Workers Convention: Its Place in Human Rights Law' (1991) 25 *International Migration Review* 771–99.

Slinckx, Isabelle, 'Migrants' Rights in UN Human Rights Conventions' in Paul de Guchteneire, Antoine Pécoud and Ryszard Cholewinski (eds), *Migration and Human Rights: The United Nations Convention on Migrant Workers' Rights* (Cambridge University Press, Cambridge, 2009) 122–49.

22 ASHGATE RESEARCH COMPANION

The Movement of Skilled Labour and Knowledge across Borders

Shubha Ghosh[1]

The movement of peoples across borders influences the acquisition and transfer of skills in apparent and indirect ways. Universities host and seek students from a wide range of countries. Companies, searching for the best, and perhaps cheapest, talent, look globally. Needless to say, such movement of peoples leads also to the movement of ideas, cultural expression, and norms that invigorate and challenge the host country.[2] The movement of people to acquire and transfer skills is particularly challenging in a global environment built on nation states each competing to increase economic growth and well-being under global norms and standards.[3] When harmonized and strengthened intellectual property rights are a critical part of these norms and standards, the national challenges to accommodate and control the movement of skilled labour require policymakers and scholars to address the normative foundations for migration and intellectual property.[4]

This entry contributes to the debate over migration of skilled labours by first contrasting the contemporary landscape with various ones from the past, including the laissez-faire regime of international movement in the nineteenth century. The entry then places these contrasting landscapes within a normative framework that takes into consideration the nation state, the rights of individuals, and the value of knowledge transfer. The entry concludes with a discussion of the Economic Espionage Act of 1996, a piece of legislation from the United States that animates and illustrates the issue of the movement of skilled labour and ideas across borders.

---

1 Vilas Research Fellow and Professor of Law, University of Wisconsin Law School.

2 Sandhya Shukla, *India Abroad: Diasporic Cultures of Postwar America and England* (Princeton University Press, Princeton, NJ, 2003).

3 AnnaLee Saxenian, *The New Argonauts: Regional Advantage in a Global Economy* (Harvard University Press, Cambridge, MA, 2006).

4 Shubha Ghosh, 'Open Borders, the US Economic Espionage At of 1996, and the Global Movement of Knowledge and People' (2010) 21 *King's Law Journal* 1–40.

Contrasts

The historical narrative about the movement of skilled labour reveals a movement from an open system within which the movement of people was a mechanism for the communication of new ideas to a hierarchical system defined by the international rules of managed trade and intellectual property rights. Within this hierarchical system, which culminated in the Trade Related Intellectual Property System (TRIPS) Agreement associated with the World Trade Organization in 1994, technology and information from the developed world flowed into emerging markets in developing countries, which in turn served as a source for human labour, a manufacturing base, and skilled labour.[5] The challenge looking forward is how developing countries will create new market and legal institutions to counter some of the inequities of the current hierarchical system.

Examples of the earlier open system of movement and knowledge transfer are, in part, the subject of myth. The movement of philosophers between the Hellenic peninsula and the Indian subcontinent, the role of Aristotle as tutor for a young Alexander in Macedon, the spread of Christianity through an apostolic tradition, the voyages of Marco Polo – each is a textbook case of how movement of people facilitated the communication of knowledge and the development of syncretic knowledge systems. Needless to say, the movement of people was the sole means of communication in a world where communication technologies were non-existent.

State institutions recognized the connection between movement of people and movement and knowledge in creative ways to manage the development of industry and the promotion of economic interests. A well-documented example of the state's role in promoting knowledge transfer through controlling the movement of people is provided by the development of the silk trade in Italy during the early Renaissance. Historian Luca Mola documents how Italian city states attracted artisans from other regions through financial subsidies and restrictions of movements into and out of the state's borders.[6] City states were engaged in a competitive race to steal talent from other regions while retaining their own much like contemporary start-up and high technology companies do. Venice's enactment of what is considered the first use of patent rights to attract innovators illustrates the culmination of this race. An interesting feature of the Venetian patent system is that it granted exclusivity to innovators who introduced new inventions and products into Venice's borders. In other words, the patent was to the introducer of these inventions and products from other regions, not necessarily the inventor himself. In England, sovereign grants rewarded foreign innovators who introduced exotic spices and foods to the British Isles. These types of inducements were precedents for what were called patents of importation under United States patent law.

The sovereign's role in promoting innovation internal to the region shaped much of United States patent law and its role in US economic development in the nineteenth

[5] Christopher Arup, *The World Trade Organization Knowledge Agreements* (Cambridge University Press, Cambridge, 2000).

[6] Luca Mola, *The Silk Industry of Renaissance Venice* (The Johns Hopkins University Press, Boston, MA, 2000).

century.[7] Alexander Hamilton, the first Secretary of the Treasury, endorsed what is known as the patent of importation, similar to the grants by Venice and the British crown, to those who went overseas, learned about inventions in other countries, and returned those innovations to the United States. These importers, or introducers as described in the previous paragraph, were granted patents not so much for their inventiveness, but for their ability to travel, learn, and translate knowledge within the US marketplace. The patent of importation has its vestiges in contemporary US patent law with its references to discoveries and its limitations on prior art from outside the US.[8] Outside the patent system, industrial espionage was a profitable way to transfer knowledge from Britain and benefitted the burgeoning US textile industry. Restrictions on labour mobility in Britain were attempts to curtail such espionage, but the movement of labour across borders was a difficult mechanism of knowledge and technology transfer to prevent.

The connection between labour mobility and knowledge transfer is reflected in formal immigration law in the United States and other countries. Within the US, the H-1B visa programme, enacted in 1952, allowed employers to hire temporary workers from overseas and the development of the programme reflected the needs of employers for skilled workers in such areas as engineering and computer programming. As Professor Alan Hyde describes the H-1B visa programme, targeting specifically at high skilled labour, the immigration of skilled labour reflects the operation of labour markets in an information-based economy and demonstrates how the movement of labour results in information spillovers to regions.[9] The H-1B programme has been criticized as a form of indentured servitude under which foreign-born workers with high skill levels are hired for little pay and benefits. The programme may be indicative of the hierarchical system of international trade and globalization that was described at the beginning of this section.

The road to TRIPS is a complex one starting with the free trade regimes developed after World War Two and merging with the development of international intellectual property regimes that go back to the nineteenth century. Signatories to TRIPS must reform their intellectual property laws to a harmonized standard that is often described as very protective of intellectual property owners' interests. Countries have powerful incentives to join TRIPS in order to obtain the advantage of being part of a multilateral trade regime. For developing countries, the challenge is to play catch-up in establishing intellectual property regimes even though the benefits of joining the agreement may be disproportionately slanted to developed countries, particularly the United States. The result is a world in which the technology of developed countries is protected globally while developing countries serve as a source of knowledge resources and markets for developed countries while bearing the costs of establishing a strong intellectual property regime. Although there have been responses to this hierarchical system within the global intellectual property regime through the 2001 Doha Ministerial, which is the basis for the development agenda of the WTO, the contemporary system of intellectual property and

7 Doron S. Ben-Atar, *Trade Secrets: Intellectual Piracy and the Origins of American Industrial Power* (Yale University Press, New Haven, CT, 2004).

8 See, e.g., 35 USC s. 102(a).

9 Alan Hyde, *Working in Silicon Valley: Economic and Legal Analysis of a High Velocity Labor Market* (M.E. Sharpe, Armonk, NY, 2003).

trade creates difficult normative challenges for global migration. This system also provides the framework for understanding United States legislation such as the Economic Espionage Act of 1996. The normative challenges and the legislation are the subject of the next two sections, respectively.

Normative Frame

Traditional arguments in favour of high-velocity labour markets implicitly assume that wealth maximization is the normative criterion for gauging policy. Rules and norms favouring labour mobility in Silicon Valley support the creation of wealth and promote economic growth. One controversy is whether this normative goal is assessed regionally or nationally.[10] After all, if free labour mobility is desirable, the natural question is why other regions have not followed the Silicon Valley model for high-technology industries. Seemingly, Professors Saxenian, Hyde and Gilson present positive rather than normative analyses of these labour markets. But generalizing their arguments to cross-border movement of labour forces us to address the normative question of whether permitting the free movement of persons is normatively desirable. When assessing this question at the international level, one is forced to confront the question of whether the individual nation state is the correct unit of analysis or whether the normative inquiry should adopt a global focus. Generalizing the traditional arguments in favour of high-velocity labour markets to the international movement of labour may be difficult precisely because the normative foundation of international intellectual property law (and arguably immigration policy) is the maximization of the welfare of an individual nation state.

It should be stressed that this normative foundation does not countenance jingoistic or xenophobic values in assessing policy. The argument here is that the citizens of Country A need not consider the welfare of Country B in designing its legal system, and vice versa. To the extent that Country A adopts a legal system out of animus towards Country B, or out of intent to harm Country B for racist or nativist reasons, such policies should be discounted. Legitimate arguments, however, for considering only the nation state in designing policy is that an individual country cannot and should not affect outcomes outside its borders. Therefore, the citizens of each country need only consider the implications of a course of policy within its own borders.

Concepts of sovereignty and comity are consistent with this normative criterion. Furthermore, adopting the nation state as the unit of analysis could be consistent with either a realist or idealist conception of international law. A realist would see the nation-state-centred approach as the basis for a rational-actor model of international relations.

---

10 The issue here is the debate between nationalism and cosmopolitanism. For good summaries of that debate, see Anupam Chander, 'Diaspora Bonds' (2001) *New York University Law Review* 1005–45, at 1043–5; Seyla Benhabib, 'The Law of Peoples, Distributive Justice, and Migrations' (2004) 72 *Fordham Law Review* 1761–94, at 1763. As the analysis of this section shows, I myself am informed by a cosmopolitan view of intellectual property rights and in general the cosmopolitanism endorsed by Kwame Anthony Appiah in *Cosmopolitanism: Ethics in a World of Strangers* (W.W. Norton, New York and London, 2006).

An idealist, on the other hand, would see the state-centred approach as respecting aspects of individual autonomy and governance, based on either cultural values or the history of particular nation states.

Applying these criteria to intellectual property policy, a nation state is allowed to design intellectual property laws and institutions that maximize its own welfare without consideration of benefits that accrue to other nations. To the extent that individual state decision making results in either positive or negative spillovers to other countries, international institutions, such as treaties or organizations for global governance, may arise to assuage these external effects. Within this normative frame, a nation state would be allowed to limit mobility of labour across countries in order to contain information or knowledge within a country for the benefit of its own economy even if there may be positive spillovers that result from the movement of people and information across borders. Therefore, the traditional arguments for high velocity labour markets do not necessarily generalize to the international level.

The nation-state-centred perspective is consistent with the current design of international intellectual property institutions. The World Trade Organization and its Trade Related Intellectual Property Systems (TRIPS) Agreement assumes that the nation state is the appropriate actor.[11] The Agreement imposes substantive minima on how each nation state that is a signatory to the agreement must design its intellectual property laws in order to comply with the Agreement, or otherwise face the possibility of a dispute resolution process and attendant sanctions.[12] Furthermore, the Agreement permits certain classes of nation states (e.g. developing countries) to establish timelines for meeting its treaty obligations.[13] Underscoring the nation-state-centred perspective is the history leading up to the ratification of TRIPS, which rested on the concerns of the developed countries that developing countries were 'free-riding' on the intellectual property and innovation flowing from the developed countries.[14] The Agreement was designed to make countries coordinate on a system of intellectual property rights that would facilitate the free flow of goods and services across borders without the fear of misappropriation of technology and information in countries with little or no intellectual property protection.[15] When understood in this way, not only does the TRIPS Agreement support a nation-state-centred view of intellectual property policy and law making, but it also supports limitations on the movement of people that could facilitate the types of misappropriation of information that the original proponents of TRIPS were attempting to prevent.

---

11 Arup, *World Trade Organization Knowledge Agreements*.

12 Trade Related Intellectual Property Systems Article 1, Section 1 (nature and scope of obligations of signatories).

13 Ibid., Article 65 (providing transitional procedures for developing countries in reforming intellectual property laws).

14 For an economic analysis that presents a country-centred approach and explains the different attitudes towards intellectual property rights across countries, see Suzanne Scotchmer, *Innovation and Incentives* (The MIT Press, Cambridge, MA, 2004). For a nation state centered theory of trade, see Ralph E. Gomory and William J. Baumol, *Global Trade and Conflicting National Interests* (The MIT Press, Cambridge, MA, 2000).

15 See Michael Ryan, *Knowledge Diplomacy* (Brookings Institution, Washington D.C., 1998) (describing business motivations and mobilization in implementing the TRIPS agreement).

Although the nation-state-centred argument is a prevalent one that needs to be taken seriously and does pose a potential impediment to supporting high-velocity labour markets at the international level, there are several reasons to be sceptical of basing intellectual property policy solely on the welfare effects on the nation state.

First, a nation-state-centred approach runs the risk of policy myopia. Benefits that seem to be leaking from one nation state to another may in fact inure back to the source country. Therefore, ignoring spillover effects in designing national intellectual property law may lead to poor policy choices.[16] For example, allowing skilled labour to leave a nation state may in fact impose benefits on the country to which the skilled labour emigrates. But the benefits may inure back to the originating country in the form of remittances or increased trade with the receiving country. South Asian émigrés to the United States have returned to South Asia, particularly India, to help develop Indian industry, which in turn benefits the United States culturally (food, movies, medical services, software, books).[17] Conceptually, a spillover may have no recognizable boundaries whether that of a firm, an industry, or a nation state. While it may be unrealistic for the policymakers of a nation state to be cosmopolitan in considering benefits to all other nation states in the design policy, a narrow focus on the interests solely of one's own nation state may often ignore the benefits of spillovers to the detriment of domestic policymaking.

Second, a nation-state-centred focus on international intellectual property policy ignores history. It is well documented that the United States free-rode on industrial and cultural innovation in Europe during the nineteenth century.[18] Manufacturing secrets made their way across the Atlantic in the acquired know-how of workers or even what would be described as industrial spies.[19] Pirated editions of novels stocked the shelves of United States publishers, serving as disseminators of culture in the form of cheap books.[20] Even within Europe, political and legal battles were waged over the scope and substance of patent and copyright laws, and industries and regions benefited from differential and lax intellectual property laws.[21] Whether economic development and prosperity would have been stronger and faster with more uniform and robust intellectual property protection seems to ignore the fact that industrial development and prosperity did occur despite a cookie-cutter model of intellectual property. The movement of people and the movement

16 For a legal analysis of spillovers, see Brett M. Frischmann and Mark Lemley, 'Spillovers' (2007) 107 *Columbia Law Review* 257–84, at 272 (identifying benefits of spillovers). For an economic discussion of spillovers and the role of positive externalities in markets, see Brian Arthur, 'Positive Feedbacks in the Economy' (1990) 262 *Scientific American* 92–9.

17 For one example, see the discussion of expatriate enclaves of IT professionals in India in Saxenian, *New Argonauts*. For an analysis of externalities in global intellectual property systems, see Scotchmer, *Innovation and Incentives*, at 345. See also for analysis and description of business networks that arise from international trade, James E. Rauch, 'Business and Social Networks in International Trade' (2001) 39(4) *Journal of Economic Literature* 1177–90, at 1184–90 (identifying the benefits that arise from social and business networks in the global context).

18 See Ben-Atar, *Trade Secrets*.

19 See ibid., at 112–13.

20 See, e.g., Shubha Ghosh, 'Deprivatizing Copyright' (2003) 54 *Case Western Reserve Law Review* 387–44, at 440–44 (discussing copyright issues facing book trade in nineteenth-century United States).

21 See Scotchmer, *Innovation and Incentives*, at 321–2.

of information facilitated regional growth and fueled economic prosperity more broadly. The current model of international intellectual property that is nation state centred and largely homogeneous neglects the boons from the movement of people and information across national borders.

Finally, global distributional concerns controvert a nation-state-centred system of international intellectual property. While international relations is not a zero-sum game by any means, too strong a set of intellectual property rights in the developed world may have adverse consequences on developing countries. Economic analyses of international trade and intellectual property (to which I shall turn in the next section) suggest that uniform and strong intellectual property rights across countries benefit innovator countries at the expense of less innovative, developing countries.[22] While strong intellectual property rights may in the long run spur innovation in developing nations, the short- and medium-run effects may be to worsen unequal wealth and income distribution globally. In many instances, it may be unrealistic for one or even several nation states to address global concerns through domestic intellectual property systems: focusing solely on the benefits and costs to individual nation states may worsen the global trade environment in the long run. From a distributional perspective, the movement of persons and information may facilitate the creation of a global commons that could inure to the benefit of individual nation states.

The Economic Espionage Act of 1996: A Contextual Example

The Economic Espionage Act of 1996 has been described as the first comprehensive statute to combat corporate espionage.[23] It is also the first federal statute that protects trade secrets, historically the domain of state courts and legislatures. Unlike state statutes and common-law rules that govern trade secrets, the Economic Espionage Act of 1996 is a criminal statute that does not recognize a private right of action.[24] Only the United States Attorney General is authorized to bring civil actions for injunctions against future conduct that violates the Act.[25] Passage of the Act is historic not only for making certain types of trade secret theft a federal crime, but also for being enacted in the period after the shift in Congress in 1994 from Democrat to Republican control when so many controversial intellectual property

22 See ibid., at 329 (finding that countries that are more innovative prefer strong intellectual property rights while countries with large markets do not). For an analysis of the global distributional benefits of a heterogeneous global intellectual property system, see Ashish Arora et al., 'Markets for Technology, Intellectual Property Rights and Development' in *International Public Goods and Transfer of Technology under a Globalized Intellectual Property Regime* (Keith Maskus and Jerome Reichman, eds) (Cambridge University Press, Cambridge, 2004) 321–36, at 322–4.

23 142 Cong. Rec. H10,461 (daily edn 17 September 1996) (statement of Rep. Hyde), cited in *United States v. Hsu*, 155 F. 3d 189, 200 (1998).

24 See, e.g., *Harrison-Smith v. Bank of America*, 2006 WL 2355565 (N.D.Ill. 2006) (court dismissing an 1831 claim because the Act does not provide for a private right of action).

25 18 USC § 1836 ('The Attorney General may, in a civil action, obtain appropriate injunctive relief against any violation of this chapter.')

statutes were passed, such as the Federal Trademark Dilution Act, the Anticybersquatting Protection Act, the Digital Millennium Copyright Act, and the Copyright Term Extension Act.[26]

The Act has eight substantive provisions and one definition section. The first two provisions lay out the elements of culpable offences and the remaining six are remedial and procedural.[27] Section 1831 deals with economic espionage, while Section 1832 covers the theft of trade secret. The elements of economic espionage include the purposeful or knowing misappropriation of a trade secret for the benefit of a foreign government, instrumentality or agency. The elements of theft of a trade secret include the purposeful or knowing misappropriation of a trade secret for the benefit of someone other than the trade secret owner that harms the economic interest of the owner. Both provisions also impose liability for attempt and conspiracy. Misappropriation of trade secret under each provision includes the stealing, appropriation, or the procurement through fraud or artifice of a trade secret. Finally, trade secrets are defined broadly to include

> all forms and types of financial, business, scientific, technical, economic, or engineering information, including patterns, plans, compilations, program devices, formulas, designs, prototypes, methods, techniques, processes, procedures, programs, or codes, whether tangible or intangible, and whether or how stored, compiled, or memorialized physically, electronically, graphically, photographically, or in writing.[28]

In order for this subject matter to be protected as a trade secret, the owner must take reasonable steps to protect the secrecy and the subject matter must have independent economic value from not being generally known or readily ascertainable through proper means by the public. The last two elements parallel requirements under the Uniform Trade Secret Act and the common law of trade secrets, while the scope of subject matter parallels that of the Uniform Act.[29]

The Act also includes remedial and jurisdictional provisions. Available remedies include criminal sentencing, forfeiture of property or profits earned by the defendant, and injunctions against conduct illegal under the Act.[30] Federal district courts have exclusive original jurisdiction,[31] and this jurisdiction applies extraterritorially to acts committed overseas by citizens or permanent residents of the United States or if acts in furtherance of the offence were committed in the United States.[32] The Act also requires the court to ensure

---

26 See Lawrence Lessig, *The Future of Ideas: The Fate of the Commons in a Connected World* (Vintage, New York, 2001) 186–7 (describing legislative changes to increase intellectual property protection during the Nineties).

27 18 USC §§ 1831–2.

28 Ibid., § 1839.

29 See, e.g., *Mangren Research and Development Corp. v. National Chemical Co., Inc.*, 87 F. 3d 937, 942 (1998) (analysing definition of trade secret under state law).

30 18 USC § 1834.

31 Ibid., § 1836(b).

32 Ibid., § 1837.

the confidentiality of trade secrets that are the subject of controversy in a case.[33] Finally, given the high-profile nature of the cases, Congress required the Department of Justice to pursue these actions upon review and authorization by the Attorney General.[34] In 2002, Attorney General Aschcroft approved the continued enforcement of the Act, but required his authorization only for claims brought under Section 1831, not under Section 1832.[35] This difference represents the potential effects of Section 1831 claims on foreign sovereigns and is an explanation for why there are so few indictments under Section 1831.

While described as comprehensive, the Economic Espionage Act of 1996, in essence, creates federal criminal liability for acts that constitute purposeful or knowing appropriation of a trade secret that either benefits a foreign entity or causes economic harm to the trade secret owner while benefiting someone who does not own the trade secret. By federalizing and criminalizing theft of trade secret, the Act raises many of the concerns analysed in the policy literature on high-velocity labour markets. Notice that the Act itself does not enjoin the exit of employees to start new firms or competition that is created by departing employees. Nonetheless, and as the case law discussed below shows, the Act has direct and indirect effects on labour mobility and the start-up of new firms. For instance, stealing of a trade secret may include know-how obtained by an employee at his former place of employment and used or retained potentially at the new company. Therefore, it is worth examining how the policy justifications in support of high-velocity labour markets, and the movement of people and of information, influence our understanding of the Economic Espionage Act.

Although the Economic Espionage Act does not specifically enjoin either the movement of people between firms or the start-up of new companies that compete with incumbents, the Act may have a chilling effect on such movement and the attendant flow of knowledge. The standard for liability is on paper quite high. The defendant must either purposefully or knowingly steal a trade secret that benefits someone who is not the owner of the trade secret and, for liability under Section 1832, economically harm the trade secret owner.[36] While the standard for civil liability under state law for misappropriation can be quite low, capturing acts that are deemed to be a violation of business ethics, the mens rea of criminal law raises the bar for liability above what exists under state law.

However, criminal liability also extends to attempts or conspiracies to steal trade secrets.[37] Therefore, acts that may fall short of civil liability can still constitute criminal misconduct if the mental-state elements can be found. As some of the cases show, liability might extend under the Act to attempts by one firm to poach another firm's employees through conversation or through enticements to move if such potential movement of workers might entail the movement of trade secrets.[38] Evidence in favour of the requisite

[33] Ibid., § 1835.

[34] 28 CFR § 0.64-5 (for five years after the enactment of the EEA Act of 1996, all prosecutions brought under 18 USC §§ 1831 and 1832 required approval by the Attorney General, Deputy Attorney General, or Assistant Attorney General for the Criminal Division).

[35] Memorandum of Attorney General John Ashcroft (1 March 2002), copy on file with author.

[36] See, e.g., *United States v. Hsu*, at 195 (presenting legal standard for liability).

[37] See ibid., at 196–7 (discussing liability for attempt and conspiracy).

[38] See *United States v. Martin*, 228 F. 3d 1 (1st Cir. 2000) (liability based in part on communications between exiting employee and poaching employer); *United States v. Case*,

mental state follows from the enticing firm's desire to acquire the know-how or other information from the employee's previous firm. The threat of criminal sanction may very likely chill employment discussions and negotiations that are pro-competitive and that promote innovation. Furthermore, the Act criminalizes economic espionage that entails the theft of trade secrets that benefit a foreign entity even if there is no proof of economic harm to the trade-secret owner. This provision potentially impedes the flow of technology and knowledge across national borders, interfering with the benefits of international trade and immigration.

Although these effects are theoretically possible, empirical evidence in support of these chilling effects is difficult to muster. It has been reported that, in 2007, U.S. Immigration and Customs Enforcement conducted over 2,600 export investigations involving technologies subject to export controls, resulting in 188 criminal arrests, 178 indictments and 127 convictions.[39] A large problem is that it is very difficult to prove the absence of a fact, and even harder to demonstrate what would have happened absent the statute. Visa denials and other immigration events, such as deportations, might offer some evidence of the adverse effects of the Act on the movement of people across borders. But violations of the Economic Espionage Act have not been a basis for denial of entry or for deportation. In 2006, the Immigration and Naturalization Service listed six enforcement categories for deportation actions, none of which directly bore on claims under the Economic Espionage Act.[40] The problem is identifying how many foreign-born employees may have been denied employment or other opportunities within the United States or in US companies overseas for fear of posing a threat of economic espionage.[41] The *Chronicle of Higher Education* has reported how many universities are having difficulties obtaining immigration clearance for research scientists, even for short-term visits to present a lecture or participate in a conference.[42] Many of these problems, however, are a consequence of the heightened security concerns after the 9/11 attacks. Arguably, the fear of economic espionage may be part and parcel of the broader security concerns and resulting paranoia, and therefore

2007 WL 1746399 (S.D. Miss. 2007) (not reported in F. Supp.) (claims brought under Act against departing employees who formed their own company by former employer).

39 *Annual Report to Congress on Foreign Economic Collection and Economic Espionage* (2007).

40 See 'Table 37, 2006 Yearbook of Immigration Statistics', copy on file with author. The six categories are: Financial investigations, Human smuggling and trafficking investigations, General and criminal alien investigations, Identity and benefit fraud investigations, Compliance enforcement, and Worksite enforcement.

41 The Immigration and Naturalization Service reports visa grants and denials in the Annual Report of the Visa Office, by year at http://travel.state.gov/visa/frvi/statistics/statistics_1476.html, accessed 6 August 2012. These statistics, however, report denials based on categories such as becoming a public charge or criminal activities such as smuggling or prostitution. In 2006, the category 'Conversion of Confiscated U.S. Property for Gain' was added although there have been only two reported cases of denials based on this category in 2007, one of which was overcome. See 'Table XX: Immigrant and Nonimmigrant Visa Ineligibilities', at http://travel.state.gov/pdf/FY07AnnualReportTableXX.pdf, accessed 6 August 2012. This provision would not cover misappropriation of trade secrets from United States companies since they do not constitute 'confiscated U.S. property'. However, property and economic theft of confidential information could potentially be a basis for visa denials even though current statistics do not collect such data.

42 Jacques S. Gansler and Alice P. Gast, 'Academics and National Security Experts Must Work Together' (2008) *Chronicle of Higher Education* A–56.

impossible to separate. However, the experiences reported by many universities suggest a climate where movement across borders is far from hospitable. An examination of the case law under the Economic Espionage Act, discussed in the next section, shows possible adverse consequences on foreign-born employees and presents scenarios that may chill movement of labour both within the United States and across borders more broadly by analogy.

Case Law under the Economic Espionage Act

In assessing the case law, these predicted adverse consequences need to be understood in light of some of the justifications for movement across borders. However, national security does not appear to be a salient concern in many of these cases. Furthermore, many of these cases involve large, multinational companies that arguably realize scale economies. Therefore, restrictions on labour movement do not necessarily follow from the need to realize economies of scale. The focus on maximizing national welfare, however, may be a dominant feature in these cases and parallels the rhetoric one sees in more informal discussions of the Economic Espionage Act. The express fear of economic espionage replaced the fear of political and economic domination under the nuclear umbrella of the Cold War in the 1990s, and this new fear was not necessarily red in colour. Instead, the threat of economic espionage was ethnic, cultural or national in guise, often associated with the skilled worker from Taiwan. To the extent that this third basis for justifying the movement of people, and the attendant movement of information and knowledge, is based on blatant, or even subtle, xenophobia, the justification can be rejected. Fear, rather than reason, enabled by legal power is driving the application of the law in an illegitimate direction.

Within the context of international trade theory, we should be asking whether there are gains that are being wasted or even unrealized in how the Economic Espionage Act is being used. The analysis of case law in the next section consequently looks to see whether the prosecutions chill the movement of labour, quell the movement of information, and frustrate the realization of spillovers that could result from the movement of labour and information across borders.

The Department of Justice has brought 36 prosecutions under the Economic Espionage Act from 1996 to 2007.[43] Most of these have been brought under Section 1832, the provision dealing with theft of trade secret. There have been five indictments (two of which resulted in convictions) under Section 1831, the economic espionage provision.[44] The first

[43] The United States Department of Justice used to report cases brought under the Economic Espionage Act at http://www.usdoj.gov/criminal/cybercrime/eea.html, but that link was taken down some time in late 2008.

[44] See Press Release, Chinese National Sentenced for Economic Espionage, U.S. Dept. of Justice (18 June 2008), at http://www.usdoj.gov/opa/pr/2008/June/08-nsd-545.html, accessed 6 August 2012. The five indictments are *United States v. Okamoto and Serizawa* on 8 May 2001; *United States v. Fei Ye and Ming Zhong* on 4 December 2002, resulting in conviction on 14 December 2006; *United States v. Meng* on 13 December 2006, resulting in a conviction on 18 June 2008; *United States*

indictment under Section 1831 was brought against two Japanese nationals in 2001. One of the defendants in the case entered into a plea arrangement with the government. Charges against the second were eventually dismissed because the Japanese government failed to extradite the defendant to the United States on the grounds that the Japanese government did not recognize economic espionage as an extraditable offense.[45] The trials and appeals that resulted from these 36 prosecutions have produced 24 district court and appellate opinions that substantively interpret portions of the Act. Of these 24 opinions, eight are dismissals for lack of jurisdiction because the Economic Espionage Act does not recognize a private right of action. The discussion in this section will focus on five principal cases: *United States v. Martin,*[46] *United States v. Krumrei,*[47] *United States v. Ye,*[48] *United States v. Hsu*[49] and *United States v. Yang*[50] (also known as the Four Pillars case). These five cases illustrate how intellectual property law operates as a form of immigration policy, affecting the movement of people and information across borders. In addition, I discuss United States v. Case,[51] an unpublished district court opinion that illustrates many of the concerns raised with making trade secret misappropriation a federal crime.

In studying these cases, those resulting in judicial opinions and those that did not, I attempt to identify nationality and citizenship status of the 36 defendants based on the judicial opinions and the United States Department of Justice website that summarizes the prosecutions. In some of the judicial opinions, citizenship status was mentioned; in most, it was not. Nationality, however, was mentioned occasionally, perhaps indirectly as a reference to the immigration status of the defendant. My findings are that 20 of the 36 cases involved a defendant or defendants born outside the United States. Roughly half of these 20 involved a defendant with a Chinese or Taiwanese background. The remaining cases involved defendants who were either US born or nationals from Europe or Canada, but whose background was not readily ascertainable from the text of the judicial opinion or the summaries on the website. The fact that more than half of the prosecutions involved non-US nationals illustrates how the Act serves to globalize trade secret law by preventing appropriation across borders.

The defendants in these cases typically worked for a high technology company in the software, hardware, biotechnology or biomedical fields. The trade secrets appropriated ranged from DNA cell lines to the diagnostic tests used by Microsoft to test its software suite. For example, in *United States v. Ye,* the FBI apprehended the defendant, a Chinese-born, naturalized US citizen, as he was about to board a flight to China with his co-defendant.[52] Ye was caught with information related to a microcoprocessor project called Supervision

---

v. Lan Lee and Yuefei Ge on 26 September 2007; and *United States v. Dongfan 'Greg' Chung* on 6 February 2008.

45 See Tetsuya Morimoto, 'First Japanese Denial of U.S. Extradition Request: Economic Espionage Case' (2004) 20(7) *International Enforcement Law Reporter* 288.

46 See note 37.

47 258 F.3d 535 (6th Cir. 2001).

48 436 F.3d 1117 (9th Cir. 2006).

49 See note 22.

50 281 F.3d 534 (6th Cir. 2002).

51 See note 37.

52 436 F.3d at 1120.

developed by several Silicon Valley companies, which he was taking to a company he formed in China. In *Okamoto*, the sole prosecution under Section 1831, the co-defendants were accused of taking DNA and cell line reagents from the Cleveland Clinic Foundation for the purpose of transporting the materials to Japan.[53] Hsu, a Taiwanese national who was a technical director for a Taiwanese company and working in the United States, was caught by an FBI sting operation involving purported proprietary information relating to the anti-cancer drug Taxol.[54] Hsu's case was the first brought under the Economic Espionage Act and resulted in a conviction for an attempted violation of the Act. In each of these cases, the act of transferring proprietary information to a third party was not completed, and the circumstances were highly charged. The defendants were involved in acts that raised suspicions, but also raise questions about the policy effects of the Act on technology transfer and the international movement of labour.

The problem was best stated by the court in *United States v. Martin*, a case that resulted in prosecutions for violations of the Economic Espionage Act and mail and wire fraud acts of Martin, the CEO of a Wyoming vaccine company, and Camp, an unhappy employee of IDEXX, a Maine biotech start-up. The two were indicted on a count of conspiracy under the Economic Espionage Act, in addition to the mail and wire fraud counts. Camp pleaded guilty in exchange for testifying against Martin, who was convicted, ordered to pay restitution, and sentenced to one year and one day in jail. The conviction was based, in part, on a long-term email correspondence between the two, which ostensibly read as a wooing of Camp by Martin (at many levels) to leave the Maine company and move out to join the company in Wyoming. As part of this correspondence, Camp sent upon Martin's request information of proprietary products and software from the Maine company where she worked. The First Circuit, in upholding the conviction, wrote,

> A careful reading of the seven-month e-mail communication between Dr. Stephen Martin and Caryn Camp could lead to the conclusion Martin and his counsel urge – that this is simply a pen-pal relationship between a lonely Maine lab technician and a reclusive California scientist. However, the evidence could also lead a reader to the conclusion that something far more sinister was afoot: that an originally harmless communication mushroomed into a conspiracy to steal trade secrets and transport stolen property interstate, and that the electronic mail and U.S. mails were used to further a scheme to defraud IDEXX. Because we find there was sufficient evidence for a reasonable jury to conclude the latter beyond any reasonable doubt, we affirm the defendant's conviction on all counts.[55]

The court's hint of ambiguity is revealing about the scope of the Economic Espionage Act. The appellant's brief and an initial read of the facts of the case suggest a story of employee mobility. Camp, a frustrated employee, seeks an opportunity at Martin's company based on its website. Martin, after failing to acquire the desired technology from IDEXX, sees an

53 See Morimoto, 'First Japanese Denial of U.S. Extradition Request'.
54 155 F.3d at 190.
55 228 F.3d at 30.

opportunity when an IDEXX employee calls. It is the opportunistic behaviour on the part of Martin, combined with the purloining of a company's assets, that supports the more sinister read endorsed by the court. The Economic Espionage Act, the court leaves us to understand, aids in policing this unproductive and larcenous form of employee recruitment that seems not to be supported by the creation of spillovers or genuine competition.

When read in a sinister light, the facts of the *Martin* case echo the notorious Fifth Circuit opinion in *E.I. Dupont Denemours v. Christopher*,[56] in which the court found that using a plan to fly over a competitor's lab in order to take pictures constituted misappropriation of a trade secret under state law. Unable to base its decision on some independent illegal act by the defendant (the flyover, for example, did not constitute a trespass), the court held that the behaviour was improper as a violation of the ethics of business competition. The defendant was taking a free ride or, perhaps more accurately, was choosing not to compete by building a better product or by designing around existing technologies. Instead, the defendant was choosing to make a naked copy of what the plaintiff was doing. Whether the Fifth Circuit expanded the scope of business ethics under state trade secret law is a much debated question. After the decision in Martin, however, one has to conclude that the flyover at issue in Christopher Brothers would rise to federal criminal liability with the resulting fines and jail time. Criminalization of such conduct is arguably overdeterrence of what has been deemed to be unethical, non-competitive and free-riding behaviour. One has to wonder why state trade secret law or a civil federal remedy would not serve the purpose of deterring the sanctioned business plan in *Martin*.

The facts of *Martin* pertain to the misappropriation of trade secret across state lines within the United States. The majority of the cases under the Economic Espionage Act involve misappropriation by non-United States nationals who steal, attempt to steal, or conspire to steal trade secrets with the intent to take them overseas. In *United States v. Hsu*, the first case brought under the Economic Espionage Act, the defendants were Taiwanese nationals who contacted an FBI undercover agent to obtain the proprietary formulas and secret processes associated with the manufacture of Taxol, an anti-cancer drug made and sold by Bristol-Myers Squibb.[57] There is no doubt that the defendants were trying to steal proprietary information, circumventing the appropriate commercial channels of licensing or reverse engineering the protected trade secrets. Nonetheless, the case provides a troubling precedent because the court allowed the sentence of the one convicted defendant to stand despite the defence of legal impossibility. Hsu was arrested after receiving what he thought were the requested trade secrets from the undercover agent. Instead, the information was not proprietary at all. Nonetheless, Hsu was found criminally liable for attempted theft of trade secrets. The court rejected his defence that it was impossible to complete the crime when what was stolen was not in fact a trade secret. Such a defence would undermine the ability of the government to undertake sting operations such as the one against Hsu.[58]

The problem is that the Third Circuit's decision in *Hsu* gives the government wide licence to undertake sting operations in order to ferret out potential economic spies. Such sting operations potentially chill legitimate inquiries by employers who are attempting to

[56] 431 F.2d 1012 (1970).
[57] 155 F.3d at 192.
[58] Ibid., at 196.

poach employees and employees who may be interested in a move. A potential bright line to avoid being caught in the web of a sting operation or, more to the point, being found liable for violating the Economic Espionage Act, is to not seek out or offer proprietary information of any sort. Discussions of employment need to be distanced from any discussion of valuable firm assets, whether tangible or intangible. But even here there is a concern that the government can use its authority under the Act broadly, casting a sense of paranoia or concern over any employee who is foreign. In *United States v. Ye*, the defendants were caught with proprietary information that the employees had obtained without permission from several major Silicon Valley companies. The defendants were apprehended at the San Francisco International Airport as they were passing through security to board a plane to the People's Republic of China. Convictions were based on attempted violations of and conspiracy to violate the Economic Espionage Act. The defendants moved pre-trial for the use of experts to determine which of the purloined information constituted trade secrets. The government moved to protect the information under the provisions of the Act that allow for protective orders.[59] The Ninth Circuit held in favour of the government on this issue, with the result that a government can bring a case even if there may not be any trade secrets at issue in a case.[60] As the decision illustrates, the scope of both attempt and conspiracy liability is quite broad.

The facts of *United States v. Krumrei* illustrate some limits on the scope of the Act. Krumrei worked for a company that was using a laminating process developed by Wilsonart. Krumrei's employer was using the process under licence from Wilsonart. Krumrei approached a competitor of Wilsonart with information about the process, and the competitor informed Wilsonart, who hired an investigator to approach Krumrei with the request to obtain proprietary information from Krumrei. Based on Krumrei's offers to transfer proprietary information to the investigator, Krumrei was indicted for attempting to steal trade secrets. He pleaded guilty to the charge and avoided a jail sentence but was fined for the offence. Permitted to appeal as a condition of his plea, Krumrei raised an attack on the Economic Espionage Act as being constitutionally vague. The basis for the vagueness claim was the definition of trade secrets that required showing that the trade secret owner had taken reasonable steps to protect that information as a secret. The court rejected his challenge, holding that Krumrei knew that the information he was passing on was proprietary, and therefore the statute was not vague as applied to him.[61] The facts of *Krumrei* present a classic application of the Economic Espionage Act, criminalizing the attempt to transfer information that one knows is proprietary to a competitor. However, Krumrei's conduct would also lead to liability under state trade secret law. Therefore, the recurring question is whether the potential chilling effects of the Act are balanced by the benefit of deterring or punishing conduct that, absent the Economic Espionage Act, would otherwise be legal.

Perhaps the most intensive prosecution under the Act is *United States v. Yang*, the first conviction for federal theft of trade secret through a jury trial. Yang was the CEO of Four Pillars, a Taiwanese company engaged in the adhesive business whose main competitor

59 436 F.3d at 1120.
60 Ibid., at 1121.
61 258 F.3d at 541.

was the United States company Avery Dennison. Dr Lee was a research scientist working for Avery Dennison, also Taiwanese, who met Yang in the late 1980s and was persuaded to pass on proprietary information about products under development by his employer. The FBI became aware of this activity in the 1990s and secured Dr Lee's cooperation to engage in a sting operation to catch Yang. In the later 1990s, Dr Lee and an undercover FBI agent met with Yang in a Ohio hotel room and passed on what purported to be confidential information about Avery Dennison's business, contained in an envelope marked 'Confidential'. Yang was arrested and indicted under the Economic Espionage Act. The conviction ended with a penalty of five million dollars under the United States Sentencing Guidelines after a trial and appeals that finally came to an end in 2007. The nearly decade-long prosecution is an archetypical[62] Economic Espionage Act conviction, involving a foreign spy using a United States employee as a conduit for appropriating confidential business information. The penalty reflected the nature of the threat posed by Yang's conduct, and the Sixth Circuit remanded the case, finding that the sentence was too high in light of Avery Dennison's involvement in the sting operation.[63] In 2007, the Sixth Circuit affirmed the reduction of the sentence by the trial court on remand to two million dollars.[64]

The 2006 indictment against former employees of Eaton, a Mississippi aerospace company, is the most recent example of the shadow that the Economic Espionage Act casts over employee mobility in technology industries. Several employees of Eaton departed the company in the early 2000s to accept employment with Frisbee, a competitor for aerospace contracts and for government grants, in Mississippi. The indictment charged violations of mail and wire fraud and a conspiracy to violate the Economic Espionage Act. Several overt acts in furtherance of the conspiracy were alleged by the government, including email correspondences with employees at Frisbee while the defendants were still in the employ of Eaton, email correspondences by the defendants to former colleagues at Eaton recruiting them to join Frisbee, and the transfer of specifications for hydraulic parts and other products manufactured by Eaton by the defendants to Frisbee. The district court dismissed many of the counts as void for vagueness, although the court did not dismiss the counts based on the transfer of the parts, since they were arguably concrete trade secrets that were transferred to a competitor.[65] What counts that survived eventually were dismissed, upon affirmance by the Fifth Circuit, because of the general five-year statute of limitations for federal criminal offences.[66] Although ultimately an unsuccessful indictment, the example illustrates how far the Act can be taken to criminalize the movement of employees between firms and the potential risks and costs that both firms and workers in high-velocity labour markets face.

---

62 The case is archetypal in the sense that the conduct at issue was the type of conduct that motivated Congress to enact the Act. 'This problem is even worse when foreign governments have specifically focussed on American companies in order to steal information from them. American companies are not prepared or equipped to fight off this kind of systematic targeting': Statement of Senator H. Kohl (D-Wi), Congressional Record: Senate Proceedings and Debates of the 104th Congress, Second Session, Wednesday, 2 October 1996, copy on file with author.

63 281 F.3d at 559.

64 253 Fed. Appx. 502 (6th Cir. 2007).

65 288 Fed. Appx. 212 (5th Cir. 2007).

66 Ibid.

There are three lessons to glean from the Economic Espionage Act cases. The first is the potentially chilling effects of the Act on the movement of labour across borders. This chilling effect on the movement of labour has consequences for the movement of information and knowledge across borders. The concern stems from the possible overdeterrence of labour mobility and employment because of the criminalization of conduct that may otherwise be actionable under the state law of trade secret. Not only has the Economic Espionage Act upped the ante for misappropriation of trade secret, it has expanded the scope of illegal conduct through the imposition of attempt and conspiracy liability. The second lesson, however, is that the courts have tempered the possible adverse effects of the Act by prosecuting cases where defendants have taken or attempted to take concrete assets from the trade secret owner. Although there are many troubling cases, many of the 36 prosecutions sanction conduct that is close to the model of the free-riding company that seems solely to mimic or copy a competitor rather than compete through reverse engineering or independent invention. Despite some tendencies to temper the effects of the Act, the aggressive use of sting operations is a source of concern by casting a pall on business transactions and employment hiring decisions. These concerns support the third lesson. Many of the acts that form the basis for an Economic Espionage Act prosecution could also have been reached under other, less potentially draconian areas of the law, such as traditional trade secret law. What the Economic Espionage Act may offer is a federal forum, and there are possible benefits from federalizing trade secret law. But the machinery of federal criminal prosecutions is a blunt tool to bring to the activity at issue.

References

Appiah, Kwame Anthony, *Cosmopolitanism: Ethics in a World of Strangers* (W.W. Norton, New York and London, 2006).

Arora, Ashish et al., 'Markets for Technology, Intellectual Property Rights and Development' in *International Public Goods and Transfer of Technology under a Globalized Intellectual Property Regime* (Keith Maskus and Jerome Reichman, eds) (Cambridge University Press, Cambridge, 2004) 321–36.

Arthur, Brian, 'Positive Feedbacks in the Economy' (1990) 262 *Scientific American* 92–9.

Arup, Christopher, *The World Trade Organization Knowledge Agreements* (Cambridge University Press, Cambridge, 2000).

Ben-Atar, Doron S., *Trade Secrets: Intellectual Piracy and the Origins of American Industrial Power* (Yale University Press, New Haven, CT, 2004).

Benhabib, Seyla, 'The Law of Peoples, Distributive Justice, and Migrations' (2004) 72 *Fordham Law Review* 1761–94.

Chander, Anupam, 'Diaspora Bonds' (2001) *New York University Law Review* 1005–45.

Frischmann, Brett M. and Mark Lemley, 'Spillovers' (2007) 107 *Columbia Law Review* 257–84.

Gansler, Jacques S. and Alice P. Gast, 'Academics and National Security Experts Must Work Together' (2008) *Chronicle of Higher Education* A–56.

Ghosh, Shubha, 'Deprivatizing Copyright' (2003) 54 *Case Western Reserve Law Review* 387–444.

Ghosh, Shubha, 'Open Borders, the US Economic Espionage At of 1996, and the Global Movement of Knowledge and People' (2010) 21 *King's Law Journal* 1–40.

Gomory, Ralph E. and William J. Baumol, *Global Trade and Conflicting National Interests* (The MIT Press, Cambridge, MA, 2000).

Hyde, Alan, *Working in Silicon Valley: Economic and Legal Analysis of a High Velocity Labor Market* (M.E. Sharpe, Armonk, NY, 2003).

Lessig, Lawrence, *The Future of Ideas: The Fate of the Commons in a Connected World* (Vintage, New York, 2001).

Mola, Luca, *The Silk Industry of Renaissance Venice* (The Johns Hopkins University Press, Boston, MA, 2000).

Morimoto, Tetsuya, 'First Japanese Denial of U.S. Extradition Request: Economic Espionage Case' (2004) 20(7) *International Enforcement Law Reporter* 288.

Rauch, James E., 'Business and Social Networks in International Trade' (2001) 39(4) *Journal of Economic Literature* 1177–90.

Ryan, Michael, *Knowledge Diplomacy* (Brookings Institution, Washington D.C., 1998).

Saxenian, AnnaLee, *The New Argonauts: Regional Advantage in a Global Economy* (Harvard University Press, Cambridge, MA, 2006).

Scotchmer, Suzanne, *Innovation and Incentives* (The MIT Press, Cambridge, MA, 2004).

Shukla, Sandhya, *India Abroad: Diasporic Cultures of Postwar America and England* (Princeton University Press, Princeton, NJ, 2003).

23 ASHGATE RESEARCH COMPANION

Migration Control and Human Security

Sharon Pickering, Marie Segrave,
Claudia Tazreiter and Leanne Weber

Introduction

This chapter examines the use of migration controls against illegalized migrant workers. While there has been significant scholarly activity around the use of migration controls to deter and criminalize asylum seekers, there has been less attention given to the study of migrant workers. Migrant workers experience high levels of migration control, which may take many forms. Notably migration controls are highly fluid and often rely on frequent categorization and recategorization of the migration status of workers, who therefore shift from being legal to illegalized workers, or vice versa, in the eyes of the authorities.[1]

We consider these issues in the context of human capabilities and human security theorization. We see mobility and the desire to control it – or at least the desire to be *seen* to control it – as manifestations of the disciplining and securitizing logic enacted through institutionalized power in liberal societies. The sphere of migration control encompasses local and global, national and transnational, forces and logics that establish and recalibrate 'systems' that seek to both imagine and moderate mobility. Many commentators have noted the contradictory forces at play here, where the political economy of globalized capital and liberal values are both founded on the inseparable pairing of freedom and mobility, yet they eschew its 'products' by creating an array of undesired categories. These include illegalized migrant workers;[2] trafficked persons;[3] rejected asylum seekers;[4] and 'flawed consumers' and 'suspect citizens'.[5] Aas contrasts this disparate grouping of 'crimmigrant' others with the

1 L. Schuster, 'The Continuing Mobility of Migrants in Italy: Shifting Between Places and Statuses' (2005) 31(4) *Journal of Ethnic and Migration Studies* 757–74.

2 M. Segrave, 'Illegal Labour and Labour Exploitation in Regional Australia', in M. Segrave (ed.), *Australian & New Zealand Critical Criminology Conference, Conference Proceedings* (Monash University, Melbourne 2009).

3 M. Segrave, S. Milivojevic and S. Pickering, *Sex Trafficking: International Context and Response* (Willan Publishing, Collumpton 2009).

4 S. Pickering, *Refugees and State Crime* (The Federation Press, Sydney 2005); C. Tazreiter, 'Asylum Seekers as Pariahs in the Australian State', in George Borjas and Jeff Crisp (eds), *Poverty, International Migration and Asylum: Studies in Development Economics and Policy* (Palgrave Macmillan, London, 2005) 371–88; C. Tazreiter, 'Between State Sovereignty and Invisibility: Monitoring the Human Rights of Returned Asylum Seekers' (2006) 11(2) *Australian Journal of Human Rights* 7–25.

5 L. Weber and B. Bowling, 'Policing Migration: A Framework for Investigating the Regulation of Global Mobility' (2008) 14(3) *Policing and Society* 195–212.

emerging elite category of global citizens, for whom the liberal aspirations of freedom and mobility are seemingly fulfilled in a globalizing, neoliberal order.[6] It is well known, but worth repeating, that freedom and mobility are unequally applied to markets, money, corporations, new technologies and people.[7]

This chapter begins with a brief overview of the theorization of the capabilities and human security approaches in relation to human vulnerabilities. These approaches – developed over the last decade or so – offer an antidote to state-centric understandings of security that criminalize and illegalize certain migrants, while also driving a wedge through the migration/development nexus. The chapter considers the circumstances of individuals who are non-citizens and the interaction between the security of persons and the sovereignty of states.

Part 1: Capabilities, Human Security and Mobility

Before reviewing the capabilities and human security approaches to 'vulnerable populations', we note the important role of citizenship theory in predominant constellations of mobility and the border. While this chapter considers non-citizens, the understanding of this group is shaped and delimited by the assumed understanding of citizenship, and the modalities of belonging and rights and responsibilities that accompany that status. Those involved in policy formation often talk about different categories of migrants and different motivations for mobility and migration as if they were fixed and known. Yet there are myriad factors that lead to spontaneous, unplanned mobility such as environmental disaster, political violence, food scarcity and other causes of insecurity. Indeed, contemporary mobility is itself a fluid and shifting field.[8]

As outlined by numerous authors,[9] freedom of movement, and the state's desire to restrict and control it, has most often been understood in a narrow state-centric context. Migration controls have been strengthened within and between states in transnational networks of

---

6 K. Aas, '"Crimmigrant" Bodies and Bona Fide Travellers: Surveillance, Citizenship and Global Governance' (2011) 15(3) *Theoretical Criminology* 331–46.

7 UNDP, *Human Development Report 1994: New Dimensions of Human Security* (1994), at http://hdr.undp.org/en/reports/global/hdr1994/, accessed 20 August 2012; Report of the Secretary-General, 'We the Peoples: The Role of the United Nations in the Twenty-first Century' (2000) UN Doc. A/54/2000; UNCHS, 'Human Security Now' (2003), at www.humansecurity-chs.org/finalreport/English/FinalReport.pdf, accessed 20 November 2010; M. Foucault, *Security, Territory, Population: Lectures at the Collége De France, 1977–1978* (Palgrave Macmillan, Houndmills and New York 2007); D. Bigo, 'Security: A Field Left Fallow', in Michael Dillon and Andrew Neal (eds), *Foucault on Politics, Security and War* (Palgrave Macmillan, London 2008) 93–114; S. Tadjbakhsh and A.M. Chenoy, *Human Security: Concepts and Implications* (Routledge, London 2007); C. Tazreiter, *Asylum Seekers and the State: The Politics of Protection in a Security-conscious World* (Ashgate, Aldershot 2004; reprinted 2006).

8 Monika Büscher and John Urry, 'Mobile Methods and the Empirical' (2010) 12(1) *European Journal of Social Theory* 99–116; A. Brighenti, 'On Territorology: Towards a General Science of Territory' (2010) 27(1) *Theory, Culture & Society* 52–72.

9 See for example Foucault, *Security, Territory, Population*; D. Bigo, 'Freedom and Speed in Enlarged Borderzones', in V. Squire (ed.), *The Contested Politics of Mobility: Borderzones and Irregularity* (Routledge, London 2010) 31–50.

surveillance in the post-September 11 world. Such efforts to exert control through *performances* of surveillance can be understood to be part of public opinion building – of locals and citizens – as much as for the deterrence of unwanted migrant workers. The logic underpinning the territorial state maintains that membership ensures entitlements that are confirmed by an obligation on the part of the state to ensure the protection (welfare) of its members. A more contentious politics surrounds the extent to which entitlements and protections are available to non-members, temporary entrants and 'unwanted' entrants. The state view of migration control is importantly shaped by a traditional, limited definition of citizenship that privileges the (old) international system of states in a world that now more closely resembles a post-Westphalian reality of transnational cultural and political realities that regularly defy the logic of the bounded state. In contemporary citizenship theory various 'constellations' of rights and responsibilities have been proposed that aim to take account of the competing forces of diaspora populations, the transnational practices of natives and of newcomers, and the contrary effects that territorial sovereignty and controlled immigration have on such practices.[10]

Viewed from different perspectives, cross-border mobility can be seen as both a security-seeking device adopted by individuals and a sign of disorder and insecurity for states. The perceived threat that 'irregular' migrants pose to national security and to territorial borders has become a well-known defence used by states to enact a range of punitive, regulatory practices and systems to control and discipline migrants prior to and following their entry to the territorial state.[11] The predominance and force of such state policies has fuelled underground networks (trafficking and smuggling), while also failing to address the root causes of migration and displacement.[12] The dominance of these singular, 'securitizing' approaches by state actors bears the added negative consequence of impeding processes of integration of migrants into the receiver society due to the fear that shapes public perceptions of migrants as security risks. We can further extrapolate that these processes may exacerbate the isolation and insecurity migrant communities experience in their daily lives.

The capabilities and human security approaches, both motivated by human rights values, ask us to consider a phenomenon such as movement or migration from the perspective of the individual and their lived reality, rather than starting with a consideration of the priorities of states and their institutions, or the integrated systems of control and surveillance established between states. Here Foucault's theorization of 'biopolitics' has motivated a flourishing interdisciplinary scholarship that guides policy towards adopting more humane, people-centred approaches.[13] At its origins the international human rights regime is premised on the

---

[10] R. Bauböck, 'Studying Citizenship Constellations' (2010) 36 *Journal of Ethnic and Migration Studies* 847–59; C. Tazreiter, 'Strengthening Human Rights through "Rooted Cosmopolitanism"' (2010), at http://apsa2010.com.au/full-papers/pdf/APSA2010_0240.pdf, accessed 7 August 2012.

[11] P. Andreas, *Border Games: Policing the US–Mexico Divide* (Cornell University Press, Ithaca, NY 2000).

[12] A. Edwards and C. Ferstman (eds), *Human Security and Non-citizens: Law, Policy and International Affairs* (Cambridge University Press, Cambridge, 2010) 18.

[13] M. Foucault, 'Governmentality', in G. Burchell, C. Gordon and P. Miller (eds), *The Foucault Effect: Studies in Governmentality* (University of Chicago Press, Chicago, IL 1991) 87–104; Foucault, *Security, Territory, Population*. See also J. Huysmans, *The Politics of Insecurity: Fear, Migration and Asylum in the EU* (Routledge, Oxon 2006); G. Agamben and D. Heller Roazen (tr.), Homo Sacer*: Sovereign Power and Bare Life* (Stanford University Press, Stanford, CA 1998), and T. Balzacq, T. Basaran, D. Bigo, E. Guittet and C. Olson, 'Security Practices', International Studies Encyclopedia

imperative to protect the individual. We can see the codification of human rights by paying attention to the various threats to humanity that have been the focus of legal regimes and political projects of human development, beginning with the UN Human Development Reports in the early 1990s and including more recently the UN's Millennium Development Goals. Fundamental to human rights values is an ethic that fosters protections for individuals from harms that become apparent when we adopt non-territorial or pre-territorial considerations of human welfare.

We turn now to briefly review the capabilities and human security approaches to human welfare, which we then apply to creating a more nuanced understanding of mobility and migration control. Projects that emphasize harm reduction and operate from a capabilities approach, as well as emphasizing the security of the person, are likely to be sensitive to the role of culture within the broad range of 'drivers' of human action and ultimately of human wellbeing. Over more than a decade, a focus on human development (through the UN reporting system since 1994) has heightened the awareness in policy circles and among service providers such as non-government organizations (NGOs) of the need to establish indicators of wellbeing that encompass a more holistic view, beyond the dominant economic prerogatives of development as 'growth'. In this regard, the 'capabilities approach', most closely associated with Amartya Sen and Martha Nussbaum, has gained widespread currency. The capabilities approach complements the so-called rights-based approach to human development, focusing not on protections that institutional actors (states) are obliged to provide, but on the grassroots realities that shape people's day-to-day existence.[14]

The capabilities approach has gained broad influence, and is drawn on in developing countries or countries of the 'Global South' to establish social protection through shaping policies to address poverty and various forms of vulnerability. The relationship between an individual's circumstances and their capabilities draws us to the coupling of wellbeing and freedom, supported by a theory of justice that transcends state-centric politics.[15] The capabilities approach

> assigns an important role to the social and institutional conditions in which the conversion of skills, resources and entitlements into larger capability sets takes place. This involves an open and participative process to define well-being based on an awareness of the complexity of the process of forming capabilities to allow for basic functionings.[16]

Nussbaum articulates ten central human functional capabilities as follows: life; bodily health; bodily integrity; senses, imagination and thought; emotions; practical reason; affiliation; other

Online, at http://www.isacompendium.com/subscriber/tocnode?id=g9781444336597_chunk_g978144433659718_ss1-2, accessed 20 August 2012.

14 A.K. Sen, *Development as Freedom* (Knopf, New York 1999); A.K. Sen, *The Idea of Justice* (Allen Lane, London 2009); M. Nussbaum, *Women and Human Development: The Capabilities Approach* (Cambridge University Press, Cambridge 2000); M. Nussbaum, *Frontiers of Justice* (Harvard University Press, Cambridge, MA 2007).

15 Sen, *Development as Freedom*; Sen, *Idea of Justice*.

16 T. Addabbo, 'Gender Budgets: A Capability Approach' (2010) 11(4) *Journal of Human Development and Capabilities* 497–501, at 497.

species; play; and control over one's environment.[17] The motivation behind articulating a set of 'functional capabilities' is to be able both to gauge a person's quality of life and to ensure that interventions of any kind may be fully utilized as they align with people's abilities. In this view, a person's quality of life is gauged not so much from whether they feel good about their situation or are satisfied, but rather whether a core list of functions that are central to human life consists of things that a person is able to do, or draw on. In this sense, capabilities are distinct from rights: where rights can often be abstract principles, capabilities are what people are actually *able* to do in their situated realities. That is, life on the ground shapes the opportunities and liberties a person is able to make use of (or not), by putting available resources to work.[18]

The relationships highlighted above – between mobility and freedom, freedom and development, and mobility and development – suggest that the capabilities approach can be powerfully deployed in guiding transnational migration controls beyond the securitizing approaches that result in the criminalization and illegalization of some of the most vulnerable groups of migrants. A more thorough appraisal of the capabilities approach, applied not only to 'developing' contexts but also to cross-border migration, has been undertaken in recent years.[19] A common concern of writers and analysts advocating the capabilities approach, the rights-based approach and the human security approach surrounds the question of how to articulate the 'we' that encompasses human beings beyond the narrow, exclusionary limits of national citizenship and its restrictive approach to resource allocation and social protections. Such an articulation is needed to transform existing systems of rights into 'genuinely *human* rights' that are 'accessible on the borders, [and] carried across borders'.[20]

Over the last decade or so, human security perspectives, as well as those drawn from an expanded 'security studies', have framed the concept of 'securitization' of certain populations from interdisciplinary perspectives, including international relations, criminology, sociology, and development studies. From these perspectives, divergent approaches to the analysis of risk, fear, violence and insecurity as 'processes' have emerged.[21] The human security approach enables us to illuminate the underside of securitization. That is, rather than seen primarily as a state practice, security comes to be understood as a tangible and constant presence in life, inferring the *in*securitization of certain categories of migrant who come to be labelled as unwanted, undeserving and threatening. These same groups, who are understood by the state, and through certain communicative practices (the globalized mass media and related public opinion, for example), as 'high risk', are themselves 'at risk'. Insecuritized migrants are at risk of exploitation, be it labour exploitation or sexual exploitation, and at risk of violence, hunger and ill health. In other words, the individuals most likely to be subject to rapidly changing,

17 Nussbaum, *Women and Human Development*, 78–80.

18 Ibid., 71; Nussbaum, *Frontiers of Justice*.

19 D. Gasper and T.D. Truong, 'Movements of the "We": International and Transnational Migration and the Capabilities Approach' (2010) 11(2) *Journal of Human Development and Capabilities* 339–57; H. de Haas, 'Mobility and Human', International Migration Institute Working Paper 14 (Oxford 2009), at http://www.heindehaas.com/workingpapers.html, accessed 20 August 2012; T.D. Truong and D. Gasper (eds), 'Trans-local Livelihoods and Connections' (2008) 12(3) *Special Issue of Gender, Technology and Development* 285–302.

20 P. Gready, 'Conceptualising Globalisation and Human Rights: Boomerangs and Borders' (2004) 8(3) *International Journal of Human Rights* 345–54, at 352.

21 Balzacq et al., 'Security Practices'.

mobile borders, and the state strategies that seek to control them and/or benefit from their mobility (for example, through exploiting that vulnerability for profit), are also among the most vulnerable populations.

The case studies explored below document the twin processes of criminalization and illegalization as 'effects' of migration control motivated by a narrow securitization agenda (security understood according to a traditional national security view). This agenda opposes the more encompassing human security approach that prioritizes individuals, and their welfare and circumstances, and understands this form of security as integrally linked to all other forms of security, such as national, economic, political, border, and so on. Migrant workers and trafficked persons, for instance, although distinct categories, potentially become subject to the same exclusionary state practices.[22] This logic is premised on a physical and temporal territorialization stimulated by a narrow view of the citizen.

The remainder of this chapter examines contemporary migration control as enacted by states from the Global North, from the perspective of irregular migrant workers. Rather than a deliberative, long-term approach to sustainable and just migration policy, contemporary migration controls operate primarily through cyclical, reactive processes that respond in the short term to the revised settings of the international political economy or national and transnational security concerns and 'events'. In particular, we argue that the expanding border and migration control regime against irregular migrants has held specific dangers for migrant workers. In the first instance, irregular migrant workers have been subject to the *general* measures taken by governments of the Global North to deter and prevent unregulated border crossing. Therefore, in the next section we outline in broad terms how border defences impact on those who are denied access to legitimate modes of travel, before exploring more specific case studies of the regulation of transnational labour in the Australian context, considering the implications of these regimes from the perspective of human security.

Part 2: Illegalized Migrants, Borders and Security

Throughout the twentieth century the physical territorial border enacted at ports, airports and border crossing points was regarded as the primary site of migration control. However, accumulating research suggests that this perception may be erroneous both historically and in the contemporary context, as the territorial border is increasingly distinct from the rapidly changing and expanding sites of migration control experienced by regular and irregular migrants. In countries such as the United Kingdom (UK), the United States (US) and Australia, migration control has involved a range of strategies aimed at protecting the border from what are considered unmanageable flows of people. Common to these approaches have been

> deliberate government strategies to make border protection a major domestic political issue in the context of more proscriptive labour migration policies; a qualified commitment to multiculturalism that emphasises the distinction between the legitimate (legal) and illegitimate (illegal) migrant; the militarisation

22 Tazreiter, 'Between State Sovereignty and Invisibility'.

> of border control; a declared war against people smuggling/human trafficking as part of a broader fight against terrorism and transnational organised crime; the externalisation of border control including the creation of buffer zones, the use of transit camps and off-shore processing; an increased policing role for a range of state welfare agencies, the private sector and some NGOs; and the routine use of detention, removal and interdiction.[23]

These strategies are given the most powerful bureaucratic effect through the development of elaborate visa regimes, enforced at home and abroad, while simultaneously focusing on all kinds of migration, with its most pernicious effect reserved for those designated as high risk. Visas are the currency that is checked and controlled at the border. High-risk groups, identified by way of nationality, ethnicity or specific background, are increasingly unable to access visa systems and concomitant authorized travel. If they are not deterred from pursuing their intention to cross borders, they are destined to use illegal channels. In the absence of the authorization to travel, migrants are exposed to processes of criminalization that are increasingly referred to as 'illegalization'. Not only does this process reflect an assault on language (where 'illegal' is now a noun and 'illegalization' a new verb[24]), but it also marks those targeted as without rights and status for as long as they remain detached or legally detachable from citizenship, thereby producing a kind of common sense about the necessary exclusion of the 'other' that is difficult to reverse.

Contemporary migration controls are practices that see 'functionally mobile' borders constituted at and beyond physical territorial markers.[25] Conceptualizing migration control as animating borders *beyond* and *within* the geographical frontier draws on a burgeoning literature that over the past decade has contributed to viewing borders as politicized boundaries, and as sets of processes and practices rather than lines on a map.[26] This body of work has been at odds with more orthodox international relations literature that has largely assumed the border to be the clear marker of the division between inside and outside, and of sovereign power capable of exercising a potent normalizing force.[27] Drawing on the social sciences, alternative conceptions of the border have emerged in which borders are seen as contested ground;[28] selective;[29] shifting

[23] L. Weber and M. Grewcock, 'Criminalising People Smuggling: Preventing or Globalizing Harm?', in F. Allum and S. Gilmour (eds), *The Routledge Handbook of Transnational Organized Crime* (Routledge, London 2012) 379–90.

[24] See C. Dauvergne, *Making People Illegal: What Globalization Means for Migration and Law* (Cambridge University Press, Cambridge 2008).

[25] L. Weber, 'The Shifting Frontiers of Migration Control', in S. Pickering and L. Weber (eds), *Borders, Mobility and Technologies of Control* (Springer, New York 2006) 21–44.

[26] H. Donnan and T. Wilson, *Borders: Frontiers of Identity, Nation, and State* (Berg Publishers, Oxford 1999).

[27] See for a critique of such approaches N. Soguk, *States and Strangers: Refugees and Displacements of Statecraft* (University of Minnesota Press, Minneapolis, MN 1999).

[28] V. Oritz, 'The Unbearable Ambiguity of the Border' (2001) 28(2) *Social Justice* 96–112.

[29] N. Wonders, 'Global Flows, Semi-permeable Borders and New Channels of Inequality', in Pickering and Weber (eds), *Borders, Mobility and Technologies of Control*, 63–86.

and negotiated;[30] while also recognized as engendering powerful political performances, particularly in relation to state power.[31]

Functionally mobile borders are enacted in increasingly pre-emptive and punitive measures that do not necessarily replace controls at the territorial border, but extend and augment those processes through strategies of 'punitive pre-emption'.[32] The most notable of these strategies have extended controls beyond the border into countries of origin or transit,[33] for example, through the posting of liaison officers to prevent 'high-risk' groups from travelling on commercial flights. In the case of the UK, border externalization has been achieved through progressively tighter, but selective, visa controls backed up by a network of overseas liaison officers; sanctions for airlines carrying undocumented passengers; agreements with other European Union (EU) countries to operate 'juxtaposed controls'; and the militarization of the outer EU perimeter using Frontex patrols. Australia has achieved a similar pre-emptive effect through the use of airline liaison officers posted at airports throughout the world, most notably in key transit countries in Southeast Asia, the operation of a comprehensive visa regime and Advanced Passenger Processing system, carrier sanctions, and the use of naval blockades to interdict unauthorized arrivals by sea.[34] According to some analysts, similar offshore 'remote control' policies aimed at pre-empting arrival were perfected in the United States some time ago,[35] channelling most of the ongoing effort to enforce perimeters towards the highly contested US–Mexico border.[36] Whether enacted through bureaucratic checks or the erection of physical barriers and blockades, these systems seek to exclude illegalized migrants before they arrive at the physical border, in many cases by immobilizing them before they even begin their journey.

Placing human wellbeing at the heart of our analysis, as advocated by a capabilities or human security approach, requires us to consider the impact of these pre-emptive border controls on illegalized migrants. The increased dangers resulting from these 'non-arrival' (and sometimes 'non-departure') policies, enacted to protect citizens of the Global North from a range of putative threats to their jobs and identities, are faced by the thousands of men, women and (often unaccompanied) children who are forced into longer and more hazardous journeys on foot through the Arizona desert, in unseaworthy boats along the Atlantic coast of Africa or towards the remote northern coastline of Australia, through treacherous mountain ranges or minefields along the eastern border of the European Union, or concealed in shipping containers or overcrowded vehicles hoping to avoid detection. The resulting incidence of physical assault, rape and death from all manner of associated hazards is becoming the subject of considerable

30 Pickering, *Refugees and State Crime*; Pickering and Weber (eds), *Borders, Mobility and Technologies of Control*.

31 R. Devetak, 'Incomplete States: Theories and Practices of Statecraft', in J. Macmillan and A. Linklater (eds), *Boundaries in Question* (Pinter Publishers, London 1995) 19–31.

32 L. Weber, 'Policing the Virtual Border: Punitive Pre-emption in Australian Offshore Migration Control' (2007) 34(2) *Social Justice: Special Issue Beyond Transnational Crime* 77–93.

33 P. Rudge, 'Free Circulation: A Socio-political Point of View', in J.Y. Carlier and D. Vanheule (eds), *Europe and Refugees: A Challenge?* (Kluwer, The Hague 1997) 67–78.

34 Weber, 'Policing the Virtual Border'.

35 A. Zolberg, *A Nation By Design: Immigration Policy in the Fashioning of America* (Russell Sage Foundation/Harvard University Press, New York/Cambridge, MA 2006).

36 See Andreas, *Border Games*.

journalistic commentary and academic analysis.[37] Even in the seemingly benign environment of international airports, the hidden, and largely unknown, consequences of preventing the onward journeys of undocumented asylum seekers and other airline passengers has been labelled a significant human rights issue.[38] Paradoxically, attempts to redistribute risk through pre-emptive border controls also creates unforeseen harms and costs for states, which are rarely acknowledged as a consequence of migration policies. For example, there is a certain circularity in the state investing considerable resources in transnational policing efforts to counter people smuggling, while at the same time continuing to generate clients for those enterprises through denial of access to legal travel.[39]

Alongside these developments external to the border, the impacts of migration controls enacted at *internally* policed borders can be equally pernicious. Similar to other developed nations but on a greater scale, US public spending on immigration enforcement has become the fastest-growing sector of federal law enforcement, with consequences including an increase in the incarceration of non-citizens – immigrant non-citizens constitute a third of the federal prison population.[40] There has also been an exponential rise in the forced repatriation of non-US citizens linked to a reliance on deportation.[41] Despite constitutionally and civil libertarian-based objections, proposals are now in place in a number of US states, notably Arizona, to deploy state police for the first time to assist in the detection of deportable non-citizens, predominantly Mexican workers.[42] This increasingly sophisticated and well-resourced enforcement effort raises key questions about how non-citizens, notably unskilled workers previously regarded as legal and economically necessary, are being categorized as illegal and/or threatening, thus requiring the full measure of punitive responses.

This trend towards enforcing internal borders, which increasingly involves multiple state and non-state agencies such as regulatory bodies and service-providing agencies, is also evident in the UK, where developments include the formation of a specialist immigration enforcement agency; the expansion of powers of search and arrest for immigration officers; placing the onus of immigration status discovery and verification on employers, with criminal sanctions for failure to do so; progressive removal of access to welfare benefits; the specification of targets for numbers of enforcement actions against 'failed asylum seekers'

---

[37] D. Marr and M. Wilkinson, *Dark Victory* (Allen & Unwin, Sydney 2003); J. Nevins, *Dying To Live: A Story of US Immigration in an Age of Global Apartheid* (City Lights Books, San Francisco, CA 2008); L. Weber and S. Pickering, *Globalization and Borders: Death at the Global Frontier* (Palgrave, London 2011).

[38] S. Taylor ('Sovereign Power at the Border' (2005) 16 *Public Law Review* 55–77), in Weber 'Policing the Virtual Border'.

[39] Weber and Grewcock, 'Criminalising People Smuggling'; S. Pickering, 'The Production of Sovereignty and the Rise of Transversal Policing: People-smuggling and Federal Policing' (2004) 37(3) *Australian New Zealand Journal of Criminology* 362–79.

[40] P. Kretsedemas and D. Brotherton, 'Open Markets, Militarized Borders', in D. Brotherton and P. Kretsedemas (eds), *Keeping Out the Other: A Critical Introduction to Immigration Enforcement Today* (Columbia University Press, New York 2008) 1–28.

[41] D. Brotherton, 'Exiling New Yorkers', in Brotherton and Kretsedemas (eds), *Keeping Out the Other*, 161–78.

[42] Immigration Policy Centre, 'What Happens When Local Cops Become Immigration Agents?' (2008), at http://www.immigrationpolicy.org/sites/default/files/docs/AZTribuneSeries8-6-08.pdf, accessed 7 August 2012.

and 'immigration offenders'; and joint activities by police and immigration officers aimed at enhancing capacity for detention and deportation.[43] Similarly, in Australia the capacity to detect, detain and deport so-called unlawful non-citizens has grown through enhancing the role of third parties, with increased support provided by state police, who have a longstanding role in immigration enforcement and are 'designated officers' with full powers under the Migration Act 1958. A study into onshore migration policing networks in one Australian state revealed that police undertake a wide range of immigration-related activities including: detaining under s. 189 of the Migration Act; working with immigration authorities on joint field operations; accompanying immigration officers to homes and workplaces on 'high-risk' warrants; undertaking immigration status checks arising from day-to-day operational policing or in response to reports or criminal investigations; recommending visa cancellations on character grounds; and escorting 'high-risk' deportees when off duty.[44] Although there have been no public announcements by Australian governments about the intention to increase detection rates of 'unlawful non-citizens', and no parallel of the 'removal quotas' introduced in the UK under the Blair government, the capacity for police and other migration policing partners to carry out on-the-spot checks has been greatly enhanced in recent years by the establishment of a 24-hour telephone system that provides immediate information on legal status to migration policing partner agencies.[45] As with access to visas and offshore controls, Australia's internal immigration controls also operate according to clearly defined profiles of risk. Individuals subject to adverse security assessments or convicted of serious crimes, and those suspected of defrauding the system of migration controls through people smuggling, the supply of fraudulent visas or systematic breaches of employment conditions, are consistently found at the top of the 'priorities matrix' that is used to guide the enforcement practices of the Department of Immigration and Citizenship.

Mirroring government attempts to enlist public support for the prevention of terrorism, public campaigns have been developed to foster a sense of partnership between those in charge of migration controls and the public. To this end, Australia has introduced an immigration 'dob-in line', offering an accessible avenue for reporting (that is, 'dobbing in' in the Australian vernacular) suspected unlawful non-citizens. Trends are difficult to discern because of sporadic statistical reporting and lack of comparability of published data over time. However, ethnic community liaison officers working with an Australian police force reported that informing on neighbours, workmates and family members was widespread within the culturally and linguistically diverse communities in which they worked.[46] Although still under-researched, these developments across English-speaking countries and elsewhere suggest a ubiquitous border that can be enacted by a range of actors in variable and unpredictable locations.

Our human security perspective requires us to consider the impact of the internalized border on illegalized migrants, including those whose entry was unlawful from the start, those who may at some time become unlawful, and those whose immigration status may be unclear

---

43 Weber, 'Shifting Frontiers of Migration Control'; Weber and Bowling, 'Policing Migration'.

44 L. Weber, 'Policing a World in Motion', in S. Pickering and J. McCulloch (eds), *Borders and Transnational Crime: Pre-crime, Mobility and Serious Harm in an Age of Globalisation* (Palgrave, London forthcoming in 2012).

45 L. Weber, 'It Sounds Like They Shouldn't Be Here: Immigration Checks on the Streets of Sydney' (2011) 21(4) *Policing and Society Special Issue: Stop and Search in a Global Context* 456–67.

46 Weber, 'Policing a World in Motion'.

to themselves or even to the authorities. Illegal, uncertain or fragile immigration status, amplified by internal border control strategies that recruit service providers into networks of surveillance and detection, is likely to generate considerable feelings of 'status insecurity' among non-citizens.[47] The insecurity that could be expected to follow from unlawful presence is increasingly replicated among populations of legally resident immigrants, whose visas and residence permits may be cancelled on national security or other 'character' grounds,[48] or who may be denied access to citizenship,[49] or stripped of their entitlement-bearing status as citizens.[50] Through these rights-eroding processes, the status of citizen, once a cornerstone of security and entitlement, is revealed to be fluid and conditional: 'Permanent residents have already dropped off the edge. As for citizens, we have stopped assuming their automatic membership of our moral community and have started distinguishing between those who demonstrate their commitment to the community and those who do not'.[51]

A small but growing body of research is demonstrating how fear of detection through ever-expanding internal controls is impacting on the lives of illegalized migrants, and sometimes other vulnerable minority communities. McDowell and Wonders traced widespread zones of insecurity among undocumented immigrant women in Arizona, who reported that they feared detection while using community services or accessing public spaces.[52] In an Australian study on migration policing networks, police ethnic community liaison officers reported a widespread fear among immigrant communities that seeking help from police could result in deportation, thus leaving them vulnerable to victimization and exploitation.[53] It might be concluded that domestic political and economic objectives are being secured at the expense of ongoing security for surplus populations who exist at the boundary between lawful and unlawful resident,[54] citizen and non-citizen,[55] or bona fide citizen and 'crimmigrant'.[56]

This section has considered the impact of general migration control measures operating at multiple sites of enforcement on illegalized migrants. The regulation of labour flows through visa regimes has always been a central concern of migration control. This also entails considerable efforts to enforce visa conditions after entry, motivated primarily by the desire to protect opportunities and conditions for the local workforce. Calavita's historical analysis of immigration enforcement has detailed its use as a mechanism for regulating labour flows,

---

47 Ibid.

48 M. Grewcock, 'Multiple Punishments: The Detention and Removal of Convicted Non-Citizens: Proceedings of the Critical Criminology Conference Monash University' (2009), at http://law.bepress.com/unswwps-flrps09/art42/, accessed 20 August 2012).

49 Dauvergne, *Making People Illegal*.

50 L. Zedner, 'Security, the State, and the Citizen: The Changing Architecture of Crime Control' (2010) 13(2) *New Criminal Law Review* 379–403.

51 S. Taylor, 'Do On-shore Asylum Seekers have Economic and Social Rights? Dealing with the Moral Contradiction of Liberal Democracy' (2000) 4 *Melbourne Journal of International Law*, at http://www.austlii.edu.au/au/journals/MelbJIL/2000/4.html, accessed 7 August 2012, no page.

52 M. McDowell and N. Wonders, 'Keeping Migrants in Their Place: Technologies of Control and Racialized Public Space in Arizona' (2009/2010) 36(2) *Social Justice* 54–73.

53 Weber, 'Policing a World in Motion'.

54 S. Sassen, *Sovereignty in an Age of Globalisation* (Columbia University Press, New York 1996); Saskia Sassen, *Territory, Authority, Rights* (Princeton University Press, Princeton, NJ 2006).

55 Dauvergne, *Making People Illegal*.

56 Aas, '"Crimmigrant" Bodies and Bona Fide Travellers'.

easing off when there is a need for migrant workers and tightening when the need abates.[57] In the contemporary context, framed by government responses to September 11, the arguably cyclical nature of migration control has amplified the more punitive imperatives within this spectrum, sustaining their dominance, and there is currently little evidence of a less restrictive phase on the horizon. Complicating this picture in which legal entry for workers is being driven by labour demand, some analysts of global capitalism note that the imposition by governments of strict controls, which they are then unable or unwilling to enforce, effectively provides a pool of cheap and disposable illegalized labour.[58] Indeed, De Giorgi sees the 'genealogy of western capitalism … inscribed in an ongoing struggle between capital and labor over control of mobility'.[59] In the following section we analyse this struggle in relation to Australia's response to human trafficking, labour exploitation and illegal migrant labour.

Part 3: Human Trafficking, Labour Exploitation and the Border

This section demonstrates how practices that on the ground are fluid and difficult to distinguish do not align with their construction by authorities as distinct 'events' and processes in the national and international policy arena, through an examination of human trafficking, illegal (non-citizen) labourers and labour exploitation. Human trafficking and labour exploitation are rarely understood as phenomena that occur in large part as a consequence of restricted and highly selective migration controls, nor do they tend to be recognized as overlapping and often indistinguishable practices. We discuss in turn the international frameworks for combating human trafficking and protecting migrant labour, and then examine the current response to human trafficking, labour exploitation and illegal migrant labour in Australia in order to highlight the slippage between the various categories (i.e. victim of trafficking, exploited migrant labourer, and illegal migrant labourer). In examining responses to these issues, we can identify the ways in which the state apparatus engages discourse and practices based on certain assumptions about victims and non-citizens that are predicated on migration status, thus ensuring that the response to exploitation and victimization is determined by an individual's relationship to the border.

International Frameworks

While there are a number of relevant international frameworks that address human trafficking and exploitative migrant labour in whole or in part, the two of most relevance here are the *Protocol to Prevent, Suppress and Punish Trafficking in Persons, Especially Women and Children,*

57 K. Calavita, 'A "Reserve Army of Delinquents": The Criminalization and Economic Punishment of Immigrants in Spain' (2003) 5(4) *Punishment and Society* 399–413.

58 A. de Giorgi, 'Immigration Control, Post-Fordism, and Less Eligibility: A Materialist Critique of the Criminalization of Immigration Across Europe' (2010) 12(2) *Punishment and Society* 147–67.

59 Ibid., 150.

Supplementing the United Nations Convention Against Transnational Organized Crime (the Palermo Protocol)[60] and the *International Convention on the Protection of the Rights of All Migrant Workers and Members of Their Families* (the Migrant Workers Convention). Human trafficking in the form of labour trafficking (as opposed to the more narrow focus on trafficking for the purposes of sexual servitude) has more recently garnered international attention, yet this has not substantially changed the focus and approach of the policy response implemented under the Palermo Protocol. Essentially it is the cross-border movement, and the coercion and deceit connected to human trafficking, in addition to the organized crime element, that distinguish it from the practices of exploitation under the Migrant Workers Convention. The Palermo Protocol is informed predominantly by a traditional law-and-order narrative, and an emphasis on combating transnational organized crime, whereas the Migrant Workers Convention is underpinned first and foremost by recognition of workers and the need to empower them. Of the two instruments, it is the Palermo Protocol that has captured international attention and played a significant role in driving contemporary counter-trafficking campaigns internationally.

The Palermo Protocol came about as a result of extensive activism and debate, and was introduced as one of three supplementary protocols under the *UN Convention against Transnational Organized Crime* (the TOC Convention).[61] This Protocol established trafficking in persons as an international priority and formalized the international framework for recognizing and responding to this issue. The location of the Palermo Protocol within the TOC Convention is significant, given that this Convention forms the broad conceptual umbrella under which firearms trafficking/smuggling, people smuggling and human trafficking collectively sit. Unlike other UN Conventions – such as the *Convention on the Elimination of All Forms of Discrimination against Women*[62] or the *Migrant Workers Convention*[63] – that focus on women's rights and workers' rights respectively, the TOC Convention is not a human rights instrument. Rather, it serves to secure transnational crime (in all its forms, as per the TOC Convention and the three supplementary protocols) as an international priority, and in so doing establishes an international definition of both 'the problem' of transnational organized crime and the framework for the international response required to combat this practice, designating measures to be imposed by state parties. The law-and-order agenda underpinning the TOC is evident in the legal interventions and policing strategies at its heart, requiring signatories to develop domestic criminal offence regimes, adopt agreements for cross-border mutual legal assistance, and enable cross-border law-enforcement cooperation.

Locating human trafficking within the transnational organized crime framework impacts both the conceptualization of the issue and, subsequently, the response. If human trafficking is first and foremost a problem of transnational organized crime activities, then

---

[60] At www.uncjin.org/Documents/Conventions/dcatoc/final_documents_2/convention_%20 traff_eng.pdf, accessed 7 August 2012.

[61] At www.uncjin.org/Documents/Conventions/dcatoc/final_documents_2/convention_eng. pdf, accessed 7 August 2012.

[62] *Convention on the Elimination of All Forms of Discrimination against Women*, via http://www. un.org/womenwatch/daw/cedaw/cedaw.htm, accessed 20 August 2012.

[63] *International Convention on the Protection of the Rights of All Migrant Workers and Members of Their Families*, adopted by General Assembly Resolution 45/158 of 18 December 1990, at www2. ohchr.org/english/law/pdf/cmw.pdf, accessed 7 August 2012.

the requisite response is to 'combat' the crime via criminal justice efforts that target illicit cross-border activity.[64] Critically, the location of human trafficking within the TOC framework was partly driven by recognition of the limits of a human rights-based approach, in which adopting measures to identify and apprehend offenders is seen as the desired priority. There is an extensive body of work debating the Palermo Protocol and its location within the TOC Convention,[65] which serves as a background to this discussion. Of greater importance here, however, is that by creating a criminal justice model to combat human trafficking, initially conceived to focus on the sexual exploitation of women and children, the Protocol also reinforced the dominant criminal justice narrative that posits the familiar roles of 'evil' (male) traffickers and 'innocent' (female or child) victims.[66] In the first eight years of the Protocol's implementation across the globe, its interpretation emphasized efforts to combat sex trafficking (i.e. the trafficking of women and girls into sexual servitude) to the exclusion of human trafficking into other industries (such as agriculture, domestic work, manufacturing or fishing) and responses via a criminal justice model that sought to rescue victims and prosecute offenders, while providing victims with welfare support in the form of temporary shelter and care during the investigative and prosecutorial processes.[67] While more recently there has been a shift towards adopting a broader 'labour trafficking' narrative,[68] the response itself has remained largely unchanged. Examining the limitations of this response is best undertaken with reference to a case study – in this case within Australia – to consider the implementation of the counter-trafficking measures in place within the nation. Before turning to the Australian context, however, it is worth noting that the starting point for the Palermo Protocol and the counter-trafficking response is *not* the recognition of the legitimacy of migrant labourers, nor is it a recognition of the ways in which migration controls may create, sustain and enforce vulnerability to exploitative practices. The model that does offer this approach is the Migrant Workers Convention.

The Migrant Workers Convention gives legitimacy to all workers, regardless of their legality as labourers within any nation. The Convention is essentially focused on securing equality of treatment for migrants, particularly in relation to working conditions, and recognizes the importance of targeting employers and entrepreneurs who incite people to migrate irregularly with false promises of work (or of the nature or conditions of such work) and/or mistreat undocumented migrants who are without legal status in the country of destination. Unlike the Palermo Protocol, the Migrant Workers Convention has received limited international support – it was over ten years before it was entered into force, and it remains signed almost exclusively by developing nations, such as Chile, East Timor, Mexico, the Philippines and Indonesia, which are predominantly 'sending' nations. Nations such as the US, the UK and

64 See J. Berman, '(Un)Popular Strangers and Crises (Un)Bounded: Discourses of Sex-trafficking, the European Political Community and the Panicked State of the Modern State' (2003) 9(1) *European Journal of International Relations* 37–86.

65 See for example Segrave, Milivojevic and Pickering, *Sex Trafficking*.

66 Berman, '(Un)Popular Strangers and Crises (Un)Bounded'.

67 See Segrave, Milivojevic and Pickering, *Sex Trafficking*; L. Agustin, *Sex at the Margins* (Zed Books, London 2007).

68 See US Department of State, *Trafficking in Persons Report 2010*, via http://www.state.gov/g/tip/rls/tiprpt/2010/index.htm, accessed 20 August 2012; also F. David, 'Labour Trafficking', *Research and Public Policy Series no. 108*, Australian Institute of Criminology, Canberra, November 2010.

Australia have not become signatories. This is indicative of the Convention's relative weakness as a platform for change within the nation compared to the instruments on human trafficking, the latter being a phenomenon that carries more gravitas at the political level.

We now seek to examine the ways in which practices related to human trafficking and counter-trafficking have manifested in Australia, and in so doing to highlight the persistence of migration controls as the determinants of identity, and the response to a range of groups of people who are at once potentially exploited *and* potentially in breach of the border regime (as undocumented workers, illegal non-citizens etc.).

Human Trafficking

The Australian response to human trafficking was established in 2003 and extended in 2007, and has been framed since that time as an issue of transnational organized crime.[69] Mirroring developments elsewhere, the response utilizes the domestic legal regime, by implementing increased resources and powers to investigate human trafficking and to pursue the successful conviction of offenders. Cases of trafficking have proven difficult to identify, and even more difficult to successfully prosecute.[70] The primary reason for this, as we and others have found, is that the majority of cases of trafficking do not fit within neat narratives of victimization and/or coercion, and are thus problematic to investigate and to build prosecution cases upon.

The challenge for authorities was captured within a comment made by a participant in Segrave, Milivojevic and Pickering's 2009 work:

> There are a lot of women from South-East Asian countries here [in Australia] lawfully, I mean what they do, prostitution, is in a lot of states of Australia a lawful occupation and they're on a working holiday visa, [or a] student visa ... so it's a lawful visa, lawful occupation and they're happy to work in the industry ... Most of them only really become a victim when things go wrong for them ... there are very few people who ... go to Australia ... not knowing that they're going to be involved in the sex trade ... and it's the law of the money, I mean it's only when that money is not forthcoming that they either decide to make a complaint or [they] go and talk to people they know in Australia who then go and report it to the authorities .... (Australian law enforcement officer, Thailand)[71]

Abuse and exploitation in relation to wages and employment conditions dominate cases of human trafficking, rather than more extreme forms of sexualized violence that reflect the

69 Minister for Immigration and Multicultural and Indigenous Affairs, 'Stopping People Trafficking in Sex Industry a High Priority', Media Release, 1 April 2003, Department of Immigration and Multicultural and Indigenous Affairs, Canberra; also Minister for Justice and Customs, 'Australian Government Announces Major Package to Combat People Trafficking', Media Release, 13 October 2003, Attorney-General's Department, Canberra.

70 M. Segrave and S. Milivojevic, 'Auditing the Australian Response to Trafficking' (2010) 22 *Current Issues in Criminal Justice* 63–80.

71 Segrave, Milivojevic and Pickering, *Sex Trafficking*, 51–2.

language of human trafficking as 'modern day slavery'. This means that, on the ground, victims do not necessarily 'act' like or 'appear' to be victims to authorities who come into contact with them, as they do not immediately appear to be in 'slavery-like' conditions. This is a critical point, as in Australia it is primarily Immigration Compliance Officers who make the initial contact with potential victims[72] and who are charged with determining whether someone is legally in Australia and whether that same person might be a victim of human trafficking. To demonstrate the potential consequences of the above, we turn to a consideration of the government campaign aimed at simultaneously identifying and deporting illegal migrant labourers in Australia.

Illegal Migrant Labour in Australia

Illegality in relation to labour in Australia manifests in multiple ways and includes both citizens and non-citizens who may work without documentation, breaching laws ranging from taxation to migration. However, citizens and non-citizens working 'illegally' are not in a comparable position, and are not seen as equally in breach of the law or as 'illegal' according to Australia law. As noted elsewhere,[73] across Australia a range of government agencies are working collaboratively and conducting joint raids on worksites (such as agriculture, manufacturing and hospitality workplaces) to locate illegal workers, specifically non-citizens. This agenda has been espoused through statements issued by DIAC:

> Three government departments – Immigration and Citizenship, Centrelink and the Australian Taxation Office – work together in areas of the cash economy to locate non-citizens who are employed illegally, or claiming welfare payments and benefits to which they are not entitled.[74]

Working without work rights means that for non-citizens there is the ever-present threat of deportation if they are found by authorities, and the risks are increasing as the systems of regulation and surveillance (such as the immigration 'dob-in line') expand. We are witnessing the strategies of immigration compliance and visa enforcement increasing the considerable risks and vulnerabilities associated with working outside the parameters of legality, where criminality and enforcement are prioritized. This raises concerns when the realities of human trafficking and exploitative labour are such that they often occur within the context of illegality.

---

72 Australian National Audit Office, 'Management of the Australian Government's Action Plan to Eradicate Trafficking in Persons' (Audit Report) (2009) No. 30 2008–09, via http://www.anao.gov.au/uploads/ documents/2008-09_Audit_Report_30.pdf, accessed 7 August 2012.

73 M. Segrave, 'Trafficking in Persons as Labour Exploitation', in C. Cunneen and M. Salter (eds), *Proceedings of the 2nd Australian & New Zealand Critical Criminology Conference* (2008), at http://www.cjrn.unsw.edu.au/critcrimproceedings2008.pdf, accessed 20 August 2012.

74 Department of Immigration and Citizenship, 'Fact Sheet 86 – Overstayers and Other Unlawful Noncitizens' (2009), at http://wwwimmigovau/media/fact-sheets/86overstayers-and-other-unlawful-noncitizenshtm, accessed 20 August 2012.

Blurred Realities: Trafficking, Labour Exploitation and Illegality

Trafficking 'into industries other than the sex industry' has been elevated as a subject of concern for NGOs, policymakers and law enforcement officials within Australia and internationally in the past few years.[75] This has translated into a broadening of the definition and response to human trafficking, but, as noted above, the response has effectively remained unchanged. There are two central concerns of relevance here. The first is how labour trafficking is defined and recognized. The US *Trafficking in Persons Report* has defined those trafficked for the purposes of labour exploitation as 'workers recruited for work ... [who are] the victims of fraudulent work offers or conditions of debt bondage [including] ... acts of force, fraud, or coercion committed against foreign workers'.[76] However, these practices effectively mirror those that have come to light in relation to the exploitation of temporary migrant workers in Australia under the 457 visa regime.[77] What also remains unclear is how Australia's anti-trafficking commitments may be impacting upon another key national priority: 'maintaining the integrity of Australia's visa program by locating people who are working illegally or overstaying their visas'.[78] These two issues are discussed in turn below.

Labour exploitation

The exploitation of temporary migrant labourers in Australia, who primarily enter Australia via the 457 visa regime (a temporary business visa requiring employer sponsorship), has been described as a practice 'akin to slavery' and as 'modern-day slavery'.[79] Prior to these issues coming to the fore, this language was applied only to the issue of trafficking in persons, which until very recently had been confined to sex work. Human trafficking and temporary migrant labourer exploitation were conceived as separate phenomena by Australian authorities, and as such their response to each was substantially different. Yet the reality of both on the ground, as one of the authors has discussed elsewhere,[80] is that they are barely distinguishable. The Commonwealth Joint Standing Committee on Migration has reported breaches of 457 visa conditions in Australia, including: underpayment at minimum salary level; unlawful deductions from minimum salary, such as for travel or medical costs, or deductions that

75 See US Department of State, *Trafficking in Persons Report 2009*, via http://www.state.gov/j/tip/rls/tiprpt/2009/, accessed 20 August 2012, and *Trafficking in Persons Report 2010*; Australian National Audit Office, *Management of the Australian Government's Action Plan to Eradicate Trafficking in Persons*.

76 See US Department of State, *Trafficking in Persons Report* 2008, via http://www.state.gov/j/tip/rls/tiprpt/2008/, accessed 20 August 2012.

77 Segrave, 'Trafficking in Persons as Labour Exploitation'; Joint Standing Committee on Migration, 'Temporary Visas ... Permanent Benefits: Ensuring the Effectiveness Fairness and Integrity of the Temporary Business Visa Program' (Report) (August 2007), at http://wwwaphgovau/house/committee/mig/457visas/report/fullreportpdf, accessed 20 August 2012.

78 Minister for Immigration and Citizenship, 'Immigration Compliance Operation Cracks Fraud Racket', Media Release, 11 March 2009, at http://wwwministerimmigovau/media/mediareleases/2009/ce09027htm, accessed 1 December 2009.

79 M. Moore and M. Knox, 'Exploitation of Skilled Migrants Exposed', *Sydney Morning Herald*, 28 August 2007, 28.

80 Segrave, 'Trafficking in Persons as Labour Exploitation'.

were not approved by the worker, such as accommodation costs; non-payment of overtime or working excessive hours; payment by workers of recruitment costs or migration agent fees; racial abuse and threats of physical harm; and overcharging for training and accommodation.[81]

The cases of trafficking in persons that have been identified in Australia mirror this range of experiences of exploitation.[82] However, if we map the response to trafficking in persons, we can identify the vastly different assumptions that underpin how we respond to victims of such exploitation *and* the reliance on migration status as a determinant of the limits of the response in relation to both issues.

For both human trafficking and labour exploitation, the focus of authorities is primarily on the offender. For trafficking, the criminal justice system pursues investigation and conviction. In the case of workplace exploitation the employer is the focus and is subject to fines and, potentially, prosecution. In both cases the victim is the witness, and as such enables the process of criminalization – the victim is required to identify what has occurred and to articulate their experience in order for the practices to be known.

Once this process has been initiated, the path for victims of the two practices divides. For trafficking, the dominant understanding of the needs of victims is focused on a gendered, trauma-based framework, where welfare and emotional support are the primary and immediate issues to be addressed. While housing, welfare provisions and counselling are accessible for the victim, they are not permitted to work during the first stages of the investigation – thus, potential victims are not recognized as active economic transnational citizens. Remuneration for unpaid wages and compensation for employers breaching agreed working contracts and agreements is absent from the current model (although it has been noted as an issue that needs to be pursued further). In the case of temporary migrant workers who have been exploited, the opposite is the response. This group of victims is able to access forms of compensation, but no welfare and emotional support should they require it.

However, upon finalization of the process of investigation and the pursuit of charges, both groups of victims return to a situation where it is their migration status rather than their experiences of exploitation that becomes critical to their journeys. In relation to both forms of exploitation, the individual is placed in the precarious position of being reliant on another party to provide them with the possibility of remaining in Australia if they report their victimization.[83] Victims of trafficking remain always at the behest of government agencies in seeking to obtain a visa related to their experience of being trafficked; otherwise, they must apply for a separate visa or be repatriated to their country of origin. For those who experience exploitation in Australia while on a 457 temporary visa, there is the option of leaving the employer who has exploited them; however, they have a limited period of time (28 days) within which to find another employer willing to sponsor them and to submit an application for a new 457 visa on their behalf. During this period, and while the 457 visa is pending, they are not permitted to work. If they cannot find a sponsor they must return to their country of

---

81 Joint Standing Committee on Migration, 'Temporary Visas … Permanent Benefits' (Report), 112–14.

82 See Australian National Audit Office, 'Management of the Australian Government's Action Plan to Eradicate Trafficking in Persons'.

83 Segrave, 'Trafficking in Persons as Labour Exploitation'.

origin.[84] Such provisions play a significant role in increasing the vulnerability of individuals who are experiencing exploitation or abuse in the workplace. The uncertainty of what may happen once you report your victimization creates a disincentive for approaching authorities and/or for articulating your experience to authorities when immigration raids and checks are conducted. Indeed, these conditions encourage non-citizens, whether working legally or illegally, to remain in exploitative situations because of the limited options available to them if they report their situation to authorities.

Precarious status: Conditions of vulnerability

What is emerging from the discussion here so far is another instance of what McDowell and Wonders have described as the interrelated technologies of control, surveillance and enforcement. Yet there is no formal recognition by the government or government agencies of the overlap between anti-trafficking efforts and the border integrity regime.[85] It has been well established that many women trafficked into the sex industry are often also potential offenders due to their status as non-citizens or due to a range of breaches of immigration laws in either the country of destination or their country of origin.[86] This has been recognized as a key impediment to identifying potential trafficking victims in Australia[87] and the same issues manifest in relation to exploitative labour conditions.[88] Within the broader operation of the cash economy, all undocumented labourers, regardless of their citizenship status, potentially face exploitation, and all have (or see themselves as having) limited recourse to assistance from government agencies or police. The vulnerability of non-citizens is much higher than for citizens, as the consequences of their exposure include non-remuneration, detention and deportation.

The expansion of the migration regulatory frameworks (such as taxation, policing and welfare agencies) is producing complex webs of surveillance that encourage a situation where migrants may work either within or outside such frameworks in undocumented and/or exploitative conditions. This reveals the ways in which restrictive controls and regulatory processes can paradoxically allow entrepreneurs to operate within the limits of the system, creating opportunity for profit to be made through exploitative practices.[89] Critically, it is not simply that illegal workplaces produce illegal workers; rather, these practices create conditions of vulnerability and opportunities for exploitation in a range of workplaces.

Simplistic understandings of victimization and criminalization, which posit that there are distinct groups of individuals 'trafficked' for labour and a group of offenders 'threatening' the 'integrity' of the visa regime, are clearly neither useful nor applicable in this context.[90]

---

84 Advice received in personal communication with DIAC information line, 13 December 2010.

85 McDowell and Wonders, 'Keeping Migrants in Their Place'.

86 See J. Goodey, 'Human Trafficking: Sketchy Data and Policy Responses' (2008) 8(4) *Criminology and Criminal Justice* 421–42.

87 Segrave, Milivojevic and Pickering, *Sex Trafficking*.

88 Segrave, 'Illegal Labour and Labour Exploitation in Regional Australia'.

89 See Andreas, *Border Games*.

90 Ibid.

Within the current regulatory framework, trafficking is synonymous with individualized exploitation. Destination nations respond at the point of exploitation – that is, when and where the offence or the victim comes to the attention of authorities, most often through immigration officials.[91] Thus, the border and the enforcement of the border regime are critical to identifying and responding to trafficking. In this regard, the response to trafficking, including efforts at its eradication, may be thought of as requiring not only the familiar reactive measures related to victimization, criminalization and prosecution, but also preventative efforts relating to people's movement. In part, trafficking in persons is another 'threat' to the nation necessitating the escalation of enhanced border policing efforts.[92] This agenda is far removed from the human rights paradigms that seek to foster respect for migration rights, mobility and border controls.[93] These efforts have demonstrated that it is possible, indeed necessary, to engage with current migration policies and international human rights instruments and to develop approaches that empower transnational migrants, in place of increased border controls.[94]

The above discussion raises many issues for further consideration, including the need for the continued interrogation of state responses that emphasize the regulation and securitization of national borders.[95] There is a need to interrogate national responses to various forms of exploitation that appear to be (and claim to be) victim focused, but that may ultimately be exacerbating the vulnerability of non-citizens within a nation. As Lyons and Ford have noted, 'policies designed to control irregular forms of migration may in fact encourage, permit or exacerbate violations of migrants' human rights, including freedom of mobility'.[96] It is clear from this research that the impacts extend far beyond the immediacy of restricted legal migration avenues, into fostering positions of vulnerability in all aspects of the lives of those who seek irregular or illegal migration opportunities and those who breach the restrictions on their visas. Similarly, labour, financial and other regulatory systems and policies function to create opportunities for some to benefit from the restrictions imposed by the migration regime, particularly in terms of the limitations on work rights. Within discussions around anti-trafficking efforts there must be recognition that state approaches to migration and employment effectively construct groups of non-citizens who are not treated as equals to citizens, and whose inequality can thus be exploited, with impunity.[97] A final issue to consider is how practices of exclusion and control operate more broadly. Weber and Bowling have argued

---

91 Berman, '(Un)Popular Strangers and Crises (Un)Bounded'.

92 Andreas, *Border Games*.

93 A. Pecoud and P. de Guchteneire, 'International Migration, Border Controls and Human Rights: Assessing the Relevance of a Right to Mobility' (2006) 21(1) *Journal of Borderlands Studies* 69–86; D. Haynes, 'Used, Abused, Arrested and Deported: Extending Immigration Benefits to Protect the Victims of Trafficking and to Secure the Prosecution of Traffickers' (2006) 26(2) *Human Rights Quarterly* 221–72.

94 N. Sharma, 'Travel Agency: A Critique of Anti-trafficking Campaigns' (2003) 21(3) *Refuge* 53–65.

95 See McDowell and Wonders, 'Keeping Migrants in Their Place'; Pickering and Weber (eds), *Borders, Mobility and Technologies of Control*.

96 L. Lyons and M. Ford, 'Beyond Sex Trafficking: The Anti-trafficking Discourse and its Gendered Implications for Temporary Labour Migration' (2008) *Re-Public: Reimagining*, at http://www.re-public.gr/en/?p=465, accessed 7 August 2012, 3.

97 See B. Anderson and R. Andrijasevic, 'Sex Slaves and Citizens: The Politics of Anti-Trafficking' (2008) 40 *Soundings* 135.

that criminology will be richer if it seeks to understand the social construction of difference and its role in state processes of selection, exclusion and control.[98] It is clear that we need to attend to the ways in which different groups of people are identified as culturally suspect and flawed in their capacity to produce, consume, and move across and within borders. From this perspective, we can identify that 'the realities of trafficking in all its forms and the realities of illegal labour that are produced by criminal justice and regulatory processes are, at best, partial and incomplete stories'.[99]

Conclusion: From Risk to Capability

In this chapter we have argued that, under the present conditions of neo-liberal globalization, security for some (and perhaps only their supposed security at that) is being sought at the expense of entrenched insecurity for others. Globally, sources of insecurity are numerous and varied, and ways to eliminate them are multifarious; yet at least part of this story plays out in the selective restrictions faced by individuals seeking security through mobility, both while they are transiting transnational spaces and while they occupy marginalized existences as 'crimmigrants' within countries of destination. These 'insecuritized' migrants face dramatically increased risks, both as illegalized travellers and as marginalized residents, as neoliberal states, fearing a welfare burden and unwilling to engage in social engineering projects to embrace more fluid notions of identity, react defensively to human need and cultural difference. Moreover, it seems that those seeking mobility in order to resolve their immediate security needs (such as asylum seekers and low-skilled workers) are the most likely to be thwarted in their efforts.

In Part 1 of this chapter we set out the framework for considering how migrant workers are transformed into 'crimmigrants' – those who become largely 'rightless' through a mobility that is undesired by states. We did this first by questioning the boundaries of citizenship and related entitlements, and, second, by introducing the theorization of capabilities and human security. Our argument here has been guided by a recognition of the multiplicity of drivers and of debates that circulate among state actors, intergovernmental agencies, human rights advocates, NGOs and corporations in reacting to and seeking to manage mobility.

In Part 2 we illustrated how border controls have increased the insecurity of illegalized migrants, who face the risk of interdiction, detention and/or summary return en route, and the threat of detection, detention and deportation in countries of destination or temporary sojourn, in the face of a seemingly 'ubiquitous' border created by networks of migration policing and welfare surveillance. The fact that the risk of detection in countries of residence may be inflated in the perceptions of those with unlawful, uncertain or unknown immigration status does not detract from the feelings of insecurity engendered, or the deterrent effect on help-seeking behaviour that may further increase vulnerability to social and physical risks.

[98] L. Weber and B. Bowling, 'Valiant Beggars and Global Vagabonds: Select, Eject, Immobilise' (2008) 12(3) *Theoretical Criminology: Special Issue on Globalization, Ethnicity and Racism* 355–75, at 371.

[99] Segrave, 'Illegal Labour and Labour Exploitation in Regional Australia', 212.

More research is needed with these hard-to-reach groups to better understand the impact of unlawful status on individual experiences of security and insecurity.

In Part 3 we focused on the situation of illegal migrant workers and victims of human trafficking, mapping the overlapping circumstances and the border-oriented underpinnings of responses to exploitative practices in Australia. We argue that Australia serves as an exemplar of similar developments and practices occurring globally, raising significant concerns about the barriers to mobility for illegalized workers, and the insecurities arising from this marginalized status. From a human capabilities perspective we draw on critical writing[100] that focuses on the right to work, enshrined inter alia in Article 6 of the International Covenant on Economic, Social and Cultural Rights (ICESCR), and the need to cross national borders to make that right a lived reality, as an alternative platform that will at once reduce the conditions that give rise to exploitative practices, while also enabling a genuinely human right to freedom of movement.

The unlawful status of irregular migrants places them largely outside the sphere of human rights protection for reasons discussed in the opening section. These limits of entitlement, which are politically and culturally reinforced, are sanctioned to a certain extent by the current international legal framework. For example, the scoping of Article 12 of the International Covenant on Civil and Political Rights (ICCPR) reserves the right to liberty of movement and residence to those who are 'lawfully within the territory of a State'. Article 13 broadly sanctions the state's power to exclude those who have never been, or are no longer, citizens, subject only to requirements of reasonable cause and due process. Interestingly, no such broad exclusions appear in the corresponding instrument that sets out many of the fundamental rights that underpin human wellbeing: the ICESCR. Article 2(3) allows that 'developing countries' may need to determine the extent to which they will guarantee economic rights to non-nationals, which seems to be an exception that reinforces the rule as it applies to developed states. Indeed, it has been argued that the ICESCR gives legal expression to a different, and seemingly more inclusive, morality than that which underpins its civil and political counterpart.[101] The 'bottom line', according to Taylor's analysis, is that 'there can be no justification for differential treatment which involves denying to non-nationals the minimum essential levels of ICESCR rights necessary for survival'.[102]

In adopting a capabilities/human security approach we have deliberately focused on the plight of those groups most excluded by current policies. We have not set out to identify the 'successes' and 'failures' of contemporary migration controls in a well-balanced fashion, nor to acknowledge the heavy burdens placed on states under the disorderly and confused conditions of late modernity. In adopting this perspective, our aim has been to reveal the huge chasm that exists between the circumstances of risk and insecurity faced by those seeking to cross borders without authorization, and the achievement of human security for all, which is the aspiration of the capabilities approach. Indeed, what we have argued shows that the pairing of mobility and freedom ought to be more consistently applied in the globalizing world to people, as well as to money, markets, communication and technology. A more even-handed approach by

[100] S. Juss, 'Free Movement and the World Order' (2004) 16(3) *International Journal of Refugee Law* 289–335; J. Nevins, 'Searching for Security: Boundary and Immigration Enforcement in an Age of Intensifying Globalisation' (2001) 28(2) *Social Justice* 132–49.

[101] Taylor, 'Do On-shore Asylum Seekers Have Economic and Social Rights?'

[102] Ibid., no page.

states towards vulnerable populations, such as those explored in this chapter, would spread the risks of modern life in a more just fashion, rather than devolving risk to those who should be offered social protections. An approach to migration controls that is animated in this way could aspire to ensure that all human beings have the opportunity to realize the full range of human capabilities and attain a secure life.

References

Aas, K., '"Crimmigrant" Bodies and Bona Fide Travellers: Surveillance, Citizenship and Global Governance' (2011) 15(3) *Theoretical Criminology* 331–46.

Addabbo, T., 'Gender Budgets: A Capability Approach' (2010) 11(4) *Journal of Human Development and Capabilities* 479–501.

Agamben, G. and D. Heller Roazen (tr.), Homo Sacer*: Sovereign Power and Bare Life* (Stanford University Press, Stanford, CA 1998).

Agustin, L., *Sex at the Margins* (Zed Books, London 2007).

Anderson, B. and R. Andrijasevic, 'Sex Slaves and Citizens: The Politics of Anti-Trafficking' (2008) 40 *Soundings* 135–46.

Andreas, P., *Border Games: Policing the US–Mexico Divide* (Cornell University Press, Ithaca, NY 2000).

Australian National Audit Office, *Management of the Australian Government's Action Plan to Eradicate Trafficking in Persons*, Canberra: Commonwealth of Australia (2009), at http://www.anao.gov.au/uploads/documents/2008-09_Audit_Report_30.pdf, accessed 7 August 2012.

Balzacq, T., T. Basaran, D. Bigo, E. Guittet and C. Olson, 'Security Practices', International Studies Encyclopedia Online, at http://www.isacompendium.com/subscriber/tocnode?id=g9781444336597_chunk_g978144433659718_ss1-2, accessed 20 August 2012.

Bauböck, R., 'Studying Citizenship Constellations' (2010) 36(5) *Journal of Ethnic and Migration Studies* 847–59.

Berman, J., '(Un)Popular Strangers and Crises (Un)Bounded: Discourses of Sex-trafficking, the European Political Community and the Panicked State of the Modern State' (2003) 9(1) *European Journal of International Relations* 37–86.

Bigo, D., 'Freedom and Speed in Enlarged Borderzones', in V. Squire (ed.), *The Contested Politics of Mobility: Borderzones and Irregularity* (Routledge, London 2010) 31–50.

Bigo, D., 'Security: A Field Left Fallow', in Michael Dillon and Andrew Neal (eds), *Foucault on Politics, Security and War* (Palgrave Macmillan, London 2008) 93–114.

Brighenti, A., 'On Territorology: Towards a General Science of Territory' (2010) 27(1) *Theory, Culture & Society* 52–72.

Brotherton, D., 'Exiling New Yorkers', in D. Brotherton and P. Kretsedemas (eds), *Keeping Out the Other: A Critical Introduction to Immigration Enforcement Today* (Columbia University Press, New York 2008) 161–78.

Büscher, Monika and John Urry, 'Mobile Methods and the Empirical' (2009) 12(1) *European Journal of Social Theory* 99–116.

Calavita, K., 'A "Reserve Army of Delinquents": The Criminalization and Economic Punishment of Immigrants in Spain' (2003) 5(4) *Punishment and Society* 399–413.

Dauvergne, C., *Making People Illegal: What Globalization Means For Migration and Law* (Cambridge University Press, Cambridge 2008).

David, F., 'Labour Trafficking', *Research and Public Policy Series no. 108*, Australian Institute of Criminology, Canberra, November 2010.

De Giorgi, A., 'Immigration Control, Post-Fordism, and Less Eligibility: A Materialist Critique of the Criminalization of Immigration Across Europe' (2010) 12(2) *Punishment and Society* 147–67.

De Haas, H., 'Mobility and Human Development', International Migration Institute Working Paper 14 (Oxford 2009), at http://www.heindehaas.com/workingpapers.html, accessed 20 August 2012.

Department of Immigration and Citizenship, 'Fact Sheet 86 – Overstayers and Other Unlawful Non-citizens' (2009), at http://www.immi.gov.au/media/fact-sheets/86overstayers-and-other-unlawful-non-citizens.htm, accessed 20 August 2012.

Devetak, R., 'Incomplete States: Theories and Practices of Statecraft', in J. Macmillan and A. Linklater (eds), *Boundaries in Question* (Pinter Publishers, London 1995) 19–31.

Donnan, H. and T. Wilson, *Borders: Frontiers of Identity, Nation, and State* (Berg Publishers, Oxford 1999).

Edwards, A. and C. Ferstman (eds), *Human Security and Non-citizens: Law, Policy and International Affairs* (Cambridge University Press, Cambridge 2010).

Foucault, M., 'Governmentality', in G. Burchell, C. Gordon and P. Miller (eds), *The Foucault Effect: Studies in Governmentality* (University of Chicago Press, Chicago, IL 1991) 87–104.

Foucault, M., *Security, Territory, Population: Lectures at the Collége De France, 1977–1978* (Palgrave Macmillan, Houndmills and New York 2007).

Gasper, D. and T.D. Truong, 'Movements of the "We": International and Transnational Migration and the Capabilities Approach' (2010) 11(2) *Journal of Human Development and Capabilities* 339–57.

Goodey, J., 'Human Trafficking: Sketchy Data and Policy Responses' (2008) 8(4) *Criminology and Criminal Justice* 421–42.

Gready, P., 'Conceptualising Globalisation and Human Rights: Boomerangs and Borders' (2004) 8(3) *International Journal of Human Rights* 345–54.

Grewcock, M., 'Multiple Punishments: The Detention and Removal of Convicted Non-Citizens: Proceedings of the Critical Criminology Conference Monash University' (2009), at http://law.bepress.com/unswwps-flrps09/art42/, accessed 20 August 2012.

Haynes, D., 'Used, Abused, Arrested and Deported: Extending Immigration Benefits to Protect the Victims of Trafficking and to Secure the Prosecution of Traffickers' (2004) 26(2) *Human Rights Quarterly* 221–72.

Huysmans, J., *The Politics of Insecurity: Fear, Migration and Asylum in the EU* (Routledge, Oxon 2006).

Immigration Policy Centre, 'What Happens When Local Cops Become Immigration Agents?' (2008), at http://www.immigrationpolicy.org/sites/default/files/docs/AZTribuneSeries8-6-08.pdf, accessed 7 August 2012.

Joint Standing Committee on Migration, 'Temporary Visas … Permanent Benefits: Ensuring the Effectiveness Fairness and Integrity of the Temporary Business Visa Program'

(Report) (August 2007), at http://www.aph.gov.au/house/committee/mig/457visas/report/fullreport.pdf, accessed 20 August 2012.

Juss, S., 'Free Movement and the World Order' (2004) 16(3) *International Journal of Refugee Law* 289–335.

Kretsedemas, P. and D. Brotherton, 'Open Markets, Militarized Borders', in D. Brotherton and P. Kretsedemas (eds), *Keeping Out the Other: A Critical Introduction to Immigration Enforcement Today* (Columbia University Press, New York 2008) 1–28

Lyons, L. and M. Ford, 'Beyond Sex Trafficking: The Anti-trafficking Discourse and its Gendered Implications for Temporary Labour Migration' (2008) *Re-Public: Reimagining*, at http://www.re-public.gr/en/?p=465, accessed 7 August 2012.

McDowell, M. and N. Wonders, 'Keeping Migrants in Their Place: Technologies of Control and Racialized Public Space in Arizona' (2009/2010) 36(2) *Social Justice* 54–73.

Marr, D. and M. Wilkinson, *Dark Victory* (Allen & Unwin, Sydney 2003).

Minister for Immigration and Citizenship, 'Immigration Compliance Operation Cracks Fraud Racket', Media Release, 11 March 2009, at http://wwwministerimmigovau/media/mediareleases/2009/ce09027htm, accessed 1 December 2009.

Moore, M. and M. Knox, 'Exploitation of Skilled Migrants Exposed', *Sydney Morning Herald*, 28 August 2007, 28.

Nevins, J., *Dying To Live: A Story of US Immigration in an Age of Global Apartheid* (City Lights Books, San Francisco, CA 2008).

Nevins, J, 'Searching for Security: Boundary and Immigration Enforcement in an Age of Intensifying Globalisation' (2001) 28(2) *Social Justice* 132–49.

Nussbaum, M., *Frontiers of Justice* (Harvard University Press, Cambridge, MA 2007).

Nussbaum, M., *Women and Human Development: The Capabilities Approach* (Cambridge University Press, Cambridge 2000).

Oritz, V., 'The Unbearable Ambiguity of the Border' (2001) 28(2) *Social Justice* 96–112.

Pecoud, A. and P. de Guchteneire, 'International Migration, Border Controls and Human Rights: Assessing the Relevance of a Right to Mobility' (2006) 21(1) *Journal of Borderlands Studies* 69–86.

Pickering, S., *Refugees and State Crime* (The Federation Press, Sydney 2005).

Pickering, S., 'The Production of Sovereignty and the Rise of Transversal Policing: People-smuggling and Federal Policing' (2004) 37(3) *Australian New Zealand Journal of Criminology* 362–79.

Pickering, S. and L. Weber (eds), *Borders, Mobility and Technologies of Control* (Springer, New York 2006).

Rudge, P., 'Free Circulation: A Socio-political Point of View', in J.Y. Carlier and D. Vanheule (eds), *Europe and Refugees: A Challenge?* (Kluwer, The Hague 1997) 67–78.

Sassen, S., *Sovereignty in an Age of Globalisation* (Columbia University Press, New York 1996).

Sassen, Saskia, *Territory, Authority, Rights* (Princeton University Press, Princeton, NJ 2006).

Schuster, L., 'The Continuing Mobility of Migrants in Italy: Shifting Between Places and Statuses' (2005) 31(4) *Journal of Ethnic and Migration Studies*, 757–74.

Segrave, M., 'Illegal Labour and Labour Exploitation in Regional Australia', in M. Segrave (ed.), *Australian & New Zealand Critical Criminology Conference 2009: Conference Proceedings*, Monash University, Melbourne 2009).

Segrave, M., 'Trafficking in Persons as Labour Exploitation', in C. Cunneen and M. Salter (eds), *Proceedings of the 2nd Australian & New Zealand Critical Criminology Conference* (2008), at http://www.cjrn.unsw.edu.au/critcrimproceedings2008.pdf, accessed 20 August 2012.

Segrave, M. and S. Milivojevic, 'Auditing the Australian Response to Trafficking' (2010) 22 *Current Issues in Criminal Justice* 63–80.

Segrave, M., S. Milivojevic and S. Pickering, *Sex Trafficking: International Context and Response* (Willan Publishing, Collumpton 2009).

Sen, A.K., *Development as Freedom* (Knopf, New York 1999).

Sen, A.K., *The Idea of Justice* (Allen Lane, London 2009).

Sharma, N., 'Travel Agency: A Critique of Anti-trafficking Campaigns' (2003) 21(3) *Refuge* 53–65.

Soguk, N., *States and Strangers: Refugees and Displacements of Statecraft* (University of Minnesota Press, Minneapolis, MN 1999).

Tadjbakhsh, S. and A.M. Chenoy, *Human Security: Concepts and Implications* (Routledge, London 2007).

Taylor, S., 'Do On-shore Asylum Seekers have Economic and Social Rights? Dealing with the Moral Contradiction of Liberal Democracy' (2000) 4 *Melbourne Journal of International Law*, at http://www.austlii.edu.au/au/journals/MelbJIL/2000/4.html, accessed 7 August 2012.

Tazreiter, C., *Asylum Seekers and the State: The Politics of Protection in a Security-conscious World* (Ashgate, Aldershot 2004; reprinted 2006).

Tazreiter, C., 'Asylum Seekers as Pariahs in the Australian State', in George Borjas and Jeff Crisp (eds), *Poverty, International Migration and Asylum: Studies in Development Economics and Policy* (Palgrave Macmillan, London 2005) 371–88.

Tazreiter, C., 'Between State Sovereignty and Invisibility: Monitoring the Human Rights of Returned Asylum Seekers' (2006) 11(2) *Australian Journal of Human Rights* 7–25.

Tazreiter, C., 'Strengthening Human Rights through "Rooted Cosmopolitanism"' (2010), at http://apsa2010.com.au/full-papers/pdf/APSA2010_0240.pdf, accessed 7 August 2012.

Truong, T.D. and D. Gasper (eds), 'Trans-local Livelihoods and Connections' (2008) 12(3) *Special Issue of Gender, Technology and Development* 285–302.

UNCHS, 'Human Security Now' (2003), at www.humansecurity-chs.org/finalreport/English/FinalReport.pdf, accessed 20 November 2010.

UNDP, *Human Development Report 1994: New Dimensions of Human Security* (1994), at http://hdr.undp.org/en/reports/global/hdr1994/, accessed 20 August 2012.

US Department of State, *Trafficking in Persons Report 2008*, via http://www.state.gov/j/tip/rls/tiprpt/2008/, accessed 20 August 2012.

US Department of State, *Trafficking in Persons Report 2009*, via http://www.state.gov/j/tip/rls/tiprpt/2009/, accessed 20 August 2012.

US Department of State, *Trafficking in Persons Report 2010*, via http://www.state.gov/g/tip/rls/tiprpt/2010/index.htm, accessed 20 August 2012.

Weber, L., 'It Sounds Like They Shouldn't Be Here: Immigration Checks on the Streets of Sydney' (2011) 21(4) *Policing and Society Special Issue Stop and Search in a Global Context* 456–67.

Weber, L., 'Policing a World in Motion', in S. Pickering and J. McCulloch (eds), *Borders and Transnational Crime: Pre-crime, Mobility and Serious Harm in an Age of Globalisation* (Palgrave, London 2012 forthcoming).

Weber, L., 'Policing the Virtual Border: Punitive Pre-emption in Australian Offshore Migration Control' (2007) 34(2) *Social Justice: Special Issue Beyond Transnational Crime* 77–93.

Weber, L., 'The Shifting Frontiers of Migration Control', in S. Pickering and L. Weber (eds), *Borders, Mobility and Technologies of Control* (Springer, New York, 2006) 21–44.

Weber, L. and B. Bowling, 'Policing Migration: A Framework for Investigating the Regulation of Global Mobility' (2004) 14(3) *Policing and Society* 195–212.

Weber, L. and B. Bowling, 'Valiant Beggars and Global Vagabonds: Select, Eject, Immobilise' (2008) 12(3) *Theoretical Criminology: Special Issue on Globalization, Ethnicity and Racism* 355–75.

Weber, L. and M. Grewcock, 'Criminalising People Smuggling: Preventing or Globalizing Harm?', in F. Allum and S. Gilmour (eds), *The Routledge Handbook of Transnational Organized Crime* (Routledge, London 2012) 379–90.

Weber, L. and S. Pickering, *Globalization and Borders: Death at the Global Frontier* (Palgrave, London 2011).

Wonders, N., 'Global Flows, Semi-permeable Borders and New Channels of Inequality', in S. Pickering and L. Weber (eds), *Borders, Mobility and Technologies of Control* (Springer, New York 2006) 63–86.

Zedner, L., 'Security, the State, and the Citizen: The Changing Architecture of Crime Control' (2010) 13(2) *New Criminal Law Review* 379–403.

Zolberg, A., *A Nation By Design: Immigration Policy in the Fashioning of America* (Russell Sage Foundation/Harvard University Press, New York/Cambridge, MA 2006).

Collective Remittances in Comparative Perspective: The Cases of El Salvador and Mexico

Gustavo A. Flores-Macías[1]

The funds that migrants remit to their home countries have steadily grown in importance over the last several decades. Several reasons account for this growth. For example, remittances provide the recipient country with much-needed hard currency. They also help governments balance their capital and current accounts and provide a boost to recipients' consumption and purchasing power. A subset of those funds is known as collective remittances, or the act of pooling money among several migrants to finance development projects in their communities of origin. In contrast to private remittances, collective remittances are not meant to assist friends or family financially. Rather, their goal is to contribute towards the development of an entire neighbourhood or community in the migrants' hometown.

Contrary to their private counterparts, however, collective remittances face significant coordination problems. In particular, collective remittances tend to concentrate the costs of the development project in a few migrants, but the benefits derived from the project tend to be diffuse. While rarely are there restrictions regarding who has access to the development project, it is often low-income migrants who sponsor it. Although migrants have sometimes joined forces with governments and the private sector to fund such projects, the parties' different and often competing interests make coordination difficult.

The purpose of this chapter is to study the obstacles to cooperation involved in collective remittances. In particular, it seeks to provide insight into how coordination can take place among low-skilled and increasingly permanent migrants, different levels of government, private companies and non-governmental organizations (NGOs) to finance development projects to improve local communities. Based on a comparison of experiences in Mexico and El Salvador, the chapter finds that differences in how collective remittance programmes are structured can help explain why some are more successful than others. These differences include incentives and disincentives for participation and involvement in the decision-making process, which influence the sustainability of the effort.

---

1 Assistant Professor, Government Department, Cornell University, gaf44@cornell.edu; a related version of this chapter was published as 'Making Migrant–Government Remittances Work: Insights from the Logic of Collective Action' (2012) *Political Science Quarterly* 127/3 (Fall), 417–443.

The literature on collective remittances has made strides both in tracing their origins and in studying their consequences. On the one hand, their volume and geographic distribution (Orozco 2004), their goals (Alarcón 2002; García Zamora 2005), and the features of those who participate in the process (Escala-Rabadán 2004) have been well documented. On the other hand, regarding their effects, several studies have approached collective remittances from a social capital perspective and highlighted the transnational links that allow them to take place (Bada 2004; Delgado and Rodríguez 2001; Goldring 2004; Levitt 2001; Portes and Landolt 2000; Rocha 2006). Others have studied their political effects, including migrants' increased leverage as a result of collective remittances (Goldring 1999, 2004; Fox and Bada 2008), as well as their consequences for local governance and accountability (Burgess 2005, 2008). Finally, others have tackled economic aspects of collective remittances by underscoring their utility (Aparicio and Meseguer 2008) and potential pitfalls (Gammage 2006) for development purposes.

Although helpful in advancing our understanding of collective remittances, these studies have overlooked the collective action challenge involved in the process. Understanding how to make collective remittances succeed is important given their potential. Thus, by identifying the key aspects that make migrant–government partnerships work, this study seeks to contribute towards solving a developmental problem that has concerned governments across the world.

Collective Action and Collective Remittances

Collective action problems are those in which the provision of a public good requires cooperation among two or more parties, but where the parties' self-interest makes cooperation unlikely (Olson 1965). Although the group's goals may be desirable for the collective, the costs borne by individual members tend to discourage their participation in the common enterprise. This cooperation problem emerges irrespective of whether groups are formed by individuals, corporations, NGOs or governments (Olson 1965; Sandler 1992; Ostrom 1990; Knoke 1990).

Cooperation becomes more or less likely based on certain group features (Olson 1965; Sandler 1992). First, cooperation becomes more difficult to organize as the size of a group increases: individuals are less inclined to bear the costs of the public good on their own, and greater anonymity provides incentives to free-ride. Similarly, as the group becomes larger, the bonds of reciprocity and trust that may contribute to overcoming the collective action problem become weaker. Second, collective action also becomes less likely as the asymmetry regarding preferences and endowments among group members increases (Olson 1965; Ahn et al. 2003). Groups with homogeneous preferences will have an easier time organizing than those with heterogeneous preferences. Similarly, groups where some individuals bear a disproportionate share of the burden are more likely to fail in the pursuit of their goal.

Accordingly, infrastructure projects funded through collective remittances are a particularly unlikely accomplishment since a central feature of such projects is that they are public goods. All the dams, community centres or clinics funded by collective remittances are non-exclusionary (Goldring 2004: 824). Additionally, the number of parties involved also makes organization particularly challenging. Since the financial contributions that individual migrants can make are very limited, the provision of developmental projects requires strength in numbers to raise enough money.

The reason is that migrants who send remittances are those who have recently arrived in the country and with the lowest skill levels in the new community (World Bank 2006). Consequently, migrants sending money to their home country are also those who can least afford it (Orozco et al. 2005), and every dollar migrants contribute towards the funding of collective goods in their hometowns is a dollar they are not sending directly to their relatives. Thus, these migrants have a limited ability to engage in philanthropy (Gammeltoft 2002), and many migrants are required to fund projects in their hometown.[2]

Moreover, a significant obstacle for coordination is the differences in preferences and endowments among the parties in the partnership. Migrants, governments and the private sector naturally have different interests that must be aligned for cooperation to take place. Instead of financing infrastructure projects with a clear developmental impact, migrants sometimes prefer religious or recreational projects such as renovating the local church or sponsoring the festivities in honour of the town's patron saint (Goldring 2002). Conversely, governments prefer to fund projects such as schools, clinics or irrigation systems, which tend to have a multiplier effect on the local economy.

Additionally, electoral calculations also influence governments' positions on collective remittances and may impede developmental partnerships (Alarcón 2002). Since a fundamental goal is to remain in office, elected officials are interested in reaping the credit from the construction of projects for electoral purposes. Politicians often assume a zero-sum mentality that seeks to crowd out opponents, making coordination more difficult (Goldring 2002: 83). They may condition the delivery of resources based on the electoral preferences of the migrants (Aparicio and Meseguer 2008; Burgess 2008). Further, with different levels of government participating in the partnership, partisan differences among them can obscure policy objectives and hinder the completion of projects. These considerations – the public nature of goods, the coordination of many actors, and the multiplicity of interests – result in disincentives for cooperation between migrants and authorities.

In addition to these obstacles, there are certain features of partnerships for collective remittances that make these difficulties more salient. First, the distance between migrants and the developmental projects decreases the incentives for individual migrants to contribute, since they will rarely benefit from the projects. Due to the increase in restrictions on cross-border flows across the world, labour migration has become more permanent and less cyclical. Only those migrants who have acquired legal status in the host country have an opportunity to travel without restriction to their hometown to enjoy the public good, but such migrants are also the ones who have formally established themselves elsewhere. The inability to benefit from the public good on a regular basis serves as a deterrent for migrants to participate in the collective enterprise.

Second, migrants share a lack of trust in their home countries' governments, which makes them reluctant to partner with governments in general and trust them with their savings in particular.[3] In many cases, migrants share a sense that governments back home failed at generating the conditions for them to stay, and even that governments' inability to create jobs or better wages 'drove them away' (Moctezuma 2000; Alarcón 2002). Moreover, beyond any resentment migrants might hold against the government, problems commonly affecting

2 Most migrant associations contribute under $10,000 annually (Orozco 2004).
3 For a discussion of the importance of trust on collective action see Ostrom and Ahn 2001.

developing, labour-exporting countries such as corruption, low growth and poor planning increase the costs of coordination with governments and decrease migrants' incentives to invest in their communities of origin.

Migrant–Government Coordination and Cooperation

Three main factors contribute to overcoming obstacles to cooperation: selective incentives, leadership, and rules. First, selective incentives are the necessary catalysts for organization among individuals. These incentives come in two forms: sticks – 'the authority and capacity to be coercive' – and carrots – positive inducements offered to individuals in the form of private or non-collective goods (Olson 1965: 133). Negative incentives include threats, fines, and other sanctions that diminish the wellbeing of those who refuse to cooperate. Positive inducements include material rewards, prestige or recreational benefits, and generally constitute by-products that improve wellbeing as a result of participation.

Second, leaders are helpful in organizing collective action (Frolick et al. 1971). To be sure, leaders respond to normative considerations, including values and principles, but they also tend to benefit from a private good that is different from the public one resulting from the group's action. Positive inducements that serve as an incentive for leaders tend to be different from those enjoyed by the rest of the group. Such benefits can be concrete, such as material compensation, or intangible, such as prestige. These incentives tend to make it more appealing for leaders to incur the extra costs associated with their role.

Third, collective action can also be fostered through certain rules (Olson 1965). Ostrom (2000: 150), in studying the effects of different regimes on participation, for example, has highlighted the importance of rules in encouraging participation through fairness and trust. These rules include the delimitation of membership; participation of local actors in the decision-making process; existence of conflict-resolution mechanisms; and appointment of monitors among the members of the group. These provisions are aimed at facilitating collective action by means of generating trust and enforcing compliance among the members of the group.

With the exception of negative inducements, all of these factors help to solve the collective action problem involved in funding projects through collective remittances. As previous experiences with collective remittances have shown, negative inducements are particularly hard to implement in the context of transnational migration and deter migrants from investing in their home country. For example, the government of the Philippines attempted to force Filipinos abroad to remit 70 per cent of their salary into mandatory domestic savings funds by executive decree in 1982.[4] The decree encouraged Filipino migrants to find ways to circumvent the measure, including misreporting their income, and generated such discontent among migrants' organizations that it was abolished in 1985 (Autler 1997: 107). Similar experiments in Bangladesh, Pakistan and Thailand during the 1970s and 1980s floundered as a result of migrants' reluctance to participate due to fears that the government would confiscate the funds (Puri and Ritzema 1999). Given the transnational nature of labour migration, an

4 The objective was to direct monetary remittances towards domestic banks, which could in turn lend to local investors (Autler 1997).

important obstacle to negative inducements is that in most cases migrants lie beyond the reach of the state and its coercive apparatus. Therefore, governments' attempts to force a particular conduct on migrants – let alone remit collectively – are likely to be unsuccessful.

Conversely, positive inducements, leadership benefits, and rules are considerations affecting both the benefits and the costs derived from participating in the partnership. On the one hand, the value to individual migrants is a function not just of the benefit derived from their direct use of the project – which is extremely limited – but also of a series of positive private inducements, both material and intangible. On the other hand, the cost of the project is a function not only of the monetary expenses involved in its construction, but also of the burden associated with transaction costs involved in partnering with other actors. These transaction costs can in turn be greatly affected by the institutional design of the partnership. As certain rules contribute to lowering the costs associated with corruption and mistrust towards government – by making the process more transparent and giving migrants a say in the decision-making process – the cost to migrants will decrease accordingly. As the following case studies show, positive inducements, leadership benefits, and rules can play a significant role in making the provision of public goods possible and migrant–government partnerships sustainable.

Comparing Collective Remittance in El Salvador and Mexico

Even though there have been attempts to generate partnerships for collective remittances in several countries, only El Salvador and Mexico – with the two largest diasporas in the Americas – have had partnerships institutionalized at the national level (International Organization for Migration 2006). This section compares the two partnerships, which were structured similarly in a number of ways but differed in their outcomes. The partnership in Mexico has been in operation for over a decade, while the one in El Salvador has stopped operating. Based on the logic of collective action, the following analysis of the two Latin American cases is organized around how and whether positive incentives, leadership incentives and institutional design contributed to overcoming the collective action challenges discussed earlier. In particular, the comparison of two experiences will underscore how to foster participation, align different parties' interests and endowments, and overcome mistrust towards governments.

Mexico's Iniciativa Ciudadana 3×1

Operating nationally since 1999, Mexico's partnership – dubbed Citizens' Initiative 3×1 (*Iniciativa Ciudadana 3×1*) – is one in which migrants living abroad voluntarily remit funds collectively and three different levels of government – local, state and federal – provide matching funds in order to build development projects in the migrants' hometowns. Migrants send collective remittances through hometown associations and earmark these funds to finance projects they deem necessary for the community. The projects funded range from community parks to roads and irrigation systems, depending on both the needs of the community and the associations' ability to raise funds.

The first step of the process is for the association to identify a project it would seek to fund. Once a project is identified, the association drafts a project proposal outlining the estimated costs and completion time. It then runs the proposal by the municipal and state governments in order to guarantee the proposal's technical feasibility and the project's sustainability over time. Afterwards, the proposal is submitted to an evaluation committee – by the name of the Committee for Validation and Attention to Migrants (*Comité de Validación y Atención al Migrante*, COVAM) – in charge of determining which projects receive funding. The COVAM is formed by representatives of migrants and of the local, state and federal governments, and awards funding based on the development priorities of the four parties represented in the committee.

The partnership has attracted significant contributions year after year since its inception in 1999. In 2010 it financed $183 million worth of projects, most of which benefit rural communities. On average, each association's contribution is estimated to be $10,000 per project (Palafox 2009). Funded in more than 500 municipalities in 28 states, these projects were possible due to a combination of positive membership incentives, leadership incentives, and rules, which helps explain the success of Mexico's partnership based on collective remittances.

A central feature of the partnership is the matching of funds as a positive incentive for all parties. Each party – migrants, local, state and federal governments – then has the opportunity to make its contribution go three times farther than if it had attempted to finance the project on its own. For migrants and their relatives and friends in their hometown communities, this allows the projects to reach a different order of magnitude. Rather than financing wells and boreholes – as is the case with migrant associations attempting to promote development without government intervention[5] –, the partnership allows for the construction of clinics, roads, and even part of a university campus. For local, state and federal governments, the partnership allows them to leverage a source of money that they would not have otherwise. In a majority of cases,[6] the amount destined to finance projects in a municipality exceeds the local government's total public works budget for the entire year (Instituto Nacional de Estadística Geografía e Informática 2007).

In addition to the matching incentive appealing to all parties, there are positive inducements that appeal to specific parties of the partnership. In order to organize thousands of migrants to participate in the partnership, migrant associations provide membership and recreational benefits in exchange for monetary contributions. Most of the migrants belonging to hometown associations join them because of a series of individual benefits that come with membership. For example, associations help new members get acquainted with the place upon arrival from Mexico. They provide a space where migrants can find other migrants with the same background, culture and language, and with whom they can more easily relate in their host countries (Sanabria and Mojica 2003). Migrants also find in associations people who understand their problems and can provide assistance in solving them. They represent a source of information and support in finding employment and housing, and help migrants

5 Such is the scope of development projects financed by migrants from the Senegal River Valley living in France and organized in *Organisations de Solidarité International Issues de Migrations* (OECD 2005).

6 Orozco (2004) finds that more than half of the total projects in Mexico are funded in communities with less than 1,000 inhabitants and in which the public works budget is extremely limited.

maintain contact with events in their hometowns.[7] The associations facilitate a quid pro quo: in exchange for receiving services that are helpful for migrants, they pay a fee that then supports the collective remittances programmes.

Besides membership-related benefits, migrant associations also rely on social or recreational inducements to raise funds specifically to remit collectively. They organize recreational activities to raise money, including raffles, picnics and bake sales. In contributing to a cause to which they might feel sentimentally attached, migrants derive a direct recreational benefit. The affordability of the recreational activities is important to raise funds among low-income migrants.

These private benefits enjoyed by members help overcome some of the difficulties in organizing migrants, regardless of group size, geographic separation from the public good, or low income level. Irrespective of the ultimate purpose of the funds raised, migrants pay to enjoy direct recreational and social benefits. The individual expenses related to these benefits are normally small enough amounts of money to be affordable to the lowest-income migrants. The large amounts contributed towards the partnership come from a large membership participating in numerous events, not from large contributions.[8]

In addition to the matching incentive of the partnership, elected officials have important electoral incentives to participate in the partnership since migrants constitute an important constituency. Elected officials seek to gain votes for themselves or their party by touting pro-migrant credentials in high-migration communities. At the national level, for example, it has been important for the federal government to be perceived as pro-migrant since Mexicans living abroad have been allowed to vote by mail since 2006. At the local and state levels, politicians in high migration areas know that being associated with policies that benefit migrants is a sine qua non in order to get elected, because of both the prevalence of migrant relatives in voters' families and the influence that migrants living abroad have in their relatives' political preferences (Goldring 2002).

Certain incentives available to the leadership of migrants' associations are an important ingredient to organize migrants towards the funding of projects through collective remittances. In the case of Mexico's 3×1 programme, leaders of the associations enjoy not only the recreational benefits available to the rest of the membership, but they also benefit from positive inducements in the form of social prestige, political prominence and material benefits. Heading hometown associations brings leaders social status both in the host country and in their hometowns (Jones-Correa 1998; Guarnizo 2003). In the host country, they gain prestige and become recognized interlocutors by local authorities. In their hometowns, they derive status and political importance from remaining involved as benefactors of the community.

Moreover, heading the hometown organization gives leaders the political visibility that often propels them to become elected officials in their hometowns (Fitzgerald 2000). For example, former mayor of Jerez, Zacatecas, Andrés Bermudez, enjoyed a strong backing by the Federation of Zacatecan Migrants in Southern California (FCZSC). Similarly, one of the Federation's former presidents, Guadalupe González, had aspirations in the state's

7 Interview with Efraín Jiménez, Vice President, Federation of Zacatecan Migrants in Southern California – FCZSC, 2007.

8 Ibid.

gubernatorial race (Bakker and Smith 2003). Although being a migrant leader does not guarantee an electoral victory, it brings significant political influence in the hometown.

Additionally, leading the association also bring material benefits. The contractors in charge of building the infrastructure projects are often relatives or friends in the benefited communities, so the leaders stand to benefit directly from these projects. The ability to benefit friends and family by steering business their way is an additional motivation.[9]

Certain aspects of the partnership's institutional design are crucial to solve cooperation obstacles by reducing transaction costs, particularly those associated with mistrust towards the government. First, the partnership restricts participation so that only migrant associations can present funding proposals. Other actors, such as NGOs, private citizens and corporations, are not allowed to submit proposals and request funding. By clearly delimiting who gets to participate, the partnership gives migrants a sense of ownership and guarantees that resources are used exclusively towards migrant-sponsored development projects.[10]

Second, the rules of the partnership also give migrants a prominent place in the planning and decision-making process. Once migrants draft the proposal of the project they would like to finance, they are required to work with the different levels of government to improve the project's technical feasibility. Crucially, migrants have a prominent seat in the COVAM, which is formed by one representative from each party – migrants, local, state and federal governments – and decides which projects merit funding. Thus, rather than acting as distant patrons, migrants' involvement throughout the process enhances transparency and helps overcome suspicion that the funds will be embezzled or that different interests will be favoured.

Furthermore, although the COVAM's main function is to vote on which projects to fund, the committee serves as a forum to air and solve any concerns regarding previous or future projects. Serving as a mechanism to solve controversies, the COVAM also contributes to resolving disputes regarding delays in the availability of funds, unsatisfactory progress, or attempts to use projects towards partisan gain. The existence of this forum gives the Mexican partnership an important degree of flexibility to fix problems that may present along the way.

Finally, the rules of the mechanism allow migrants to play a role in the oversight of projects. Migrants appoint representatives from among community members in their hometown in Mexico to monitor progress of the project and ensure control over the funds. Migrants appoint a president, a treasurer and a secretary to an oversight committee for the duration of the project to administer the funds, oversee progress and prepare achievement reports. Moreover, the migrant associations never turn over control of the financial resources. Their funds are deposited in a private bank account and the signature of the migrant's representative in the community is required to draw funds.[11]

Although imperfect and with much room for improvement,[12] the Mexican partnership has proved to be resilient to challenges facing one of the first efforts of its kind. It has survived

9 As will be discussed later, this allows migrant associations to directly oversee and manage their funds (Burgess 2005; Orozco and Welle 2005).

10 A brief attempt by the government to open participation was reversed due to generalized discontent among migrants (interview with Guillermo Huerta, Director of Social Programs, Ministry of Social Development, 2008).

11 Interview with Efraín Jiménez, 2007.

12 The programme has been criticized for neglecting long-term maintenance costs of infrastructure projects and for its inability to contribute towards the development of the least

several changes in government, gradually expanded to most states in the country, and seen an increasing trend in the number of associations participating and the amount of funds remitted. Significantly, it has helped to overcome important obstacles regarding the public nature of the projects funded, the number of actors involved, differences in preferences and endowments, migrants' mistrust towards the government, and even distance. As the discussion of the Salvadorian partnership will show, the factors that make the Mexican partnership work should not be taken for granted.

El Salvador's *Unidos por la Solidaridad*

With a large migrant community in the United States representing a fifth of its population (Gammage 2006), El Salvador established a similar partnership by the name of United for Solidarity (*Unidos por la Solidaridad*) in 2001. Inspired in the Mexican case, El Salvador's partnership also attempted to organize thousands of migrants and more than 200 jurisdictions in order to leverage collective remittances from abroad towards community development projects. Like the Mexican partnership, it encouraged the participation of migrant associations and different levels of government[13] through the co-financing of projects, mostly infrastructure.

However, the programme was short lived and faced several obstacles. Throughout its duration the flow of collective remittances was heavily related to natural disasters rather than a sustained stream of resources throughout the year (Nosthas 2006). Of the 300 associations of Salvadorian migrants registered in the United States, only 31 submitted proposals throughout the duration of the programme, and three associations were repeatedly selected due to their ability to shoulder a significant share of the cost of the projects (*El Diario de Hoy* 2006). On average, migrant associations contributed 2 per cent of the cost of the projects funded through the Social Investment Fund for Local Development (*Fondo de Inversión Social para el Desarrollo Local*, FISDL), a considerably lower contribution than that of Mexico's programme (*El Diario de Hoy* 2004). In 2006 the central government decided to dismantle the programme and make the funds available for a general poverty alleviation programme instead. These difficulties can be partly attributed to some differences in the way the programme operated regarding membership benefits, leadership incentives, and rules compared to the Mexican experience.

El Salvador's partnership shared the same membership incentives present in the Mexican case. Like their Mexican counterparts, Salvadorian migrants participated in the partnership through associations formed in the US. Their funding of projects through collective remittances was also a by-product of private benefits different from the public good. As in the Mexican case, these benefits were social and recreational and were exchanged for an affordable fee or contribution.

The leaders of migrants' associations also enjoyed many of the same benefits – social status and political visibility – that encouraged their Mexican counterparts to organize other migrants (Paul and Gammage 2004). Similarly, elected officials had similar incentives to appear as champions of migrants' causes – one in five Salvadorians lives in the United States

affluent municipalities in Mexico that do not have an international migrant tradition (Delgado and Rodríguez 2001; CIDE 2008).

13 The central government, 12 departments, and more than 200 municipalities.

and Salvadorian politicians have made campaigning in the United States a habit (Landolt et al. 1999).

However, the partnerships differed in one of the positive incentives available for the leadership: migrants' ability to select the contractor that builds the project. In contrast to the Mexican case where migrants' leaders determined who gets to build the project, in El Salvador the government selected the contractors. This became an important source of discontent among Salvadorian migrants.[14] Their inability to control resources generated suspicion of corruption and inefficiency, and shifted material incentives from the association's leadership to the government (Paul and Gammage 2004). As one migrant from a Salvadorian association put it, 'if we raise the money, we want to make sure it is spent properly' (cited in Paul and Gammage 2004: 18). Whereas in Mexico the ability to select the contractor ameliorated government mistrust and generated material incentives for migrants' leaders – by steering business towards friends and family –, in El Salvador migrants were more reluctant to turn over their money to the government.

Three main differences are found between the two partnerships regarding their institutional design. The first important distinction concerns who is allowed to participate. Whereas in the Mexican case only migrant associations could submit projects, in El Salvador other actors were allowed to submit a project aimed at the development of the community. Operating under a scheme of 'funding by contest' (*fondos concursables*), the main funding criterion was how much money the proponents could contribute on their own. The logic behind the funding mechanism was to encourage migrants to raise as much money as possible before submitting a project in order to improve their chances of receiving funding (Nosthas 2006). Since participation in the partnership was open – as opposed to limiting the submission of projects to migrants only –, the intention was to induce migrants to pool their resources with NGOs and submit proposals jointly.

However, the unintended effect of the partnership's open participation was to discourage migrants from channelling funds into the partnership. With open participation, migrants could rarely compete against projects submitted by NGOs due to significant differences in their financial and technical resources. Instead, migrants were forced to negotiate every single project with a partner to determine the share of the burden to be shouldered. In the process, being small contributors towards the funding of a project, migrants were often relegated to a secondary role in determining the characteristics of the projects.[15] Thus, the inability to compete for funds exclusively against other migrants with similar resources and technical expertise significantly increased the transaction costs and provided weaker incentives to participate than those provided by the Mexican partnership.

A second difference is the degree to which migrants are involved in the decision-making process. In contrast to the Mexican case, where migrants have a prominent seat at the table in the decision-making process through their participation in the COVAM, in El Salvador the central government alone made all decisions regarding which projects to finance. The central government's closed-door, unilateral decision-making process generated a sense among

[14] This view was consistently expressed in interviews with leaders of three Salvadorian associations in California, Virginia and Washington, D.C. (2009).

[15] Interview with Ernesto Nosthas, Director-General for Migrant Affairs, El Salvador's Ministry of Foreign Affairs, 2009.

migrants that partisan considerations drove award decisions (Burgess 2008), a perception consistent with evidence that political leaning played a role in the likelihood of receiving funds in El Salvador (Burgess 2008; Paul and Gammage 2004).

Third, since Salvadorian migrants did not participate in the decision-making process through a selection committee, there was little room for the solution of controversies. Given that migrants' and governments' priorities are likely to be different regarding the type of project to be financed, the bargaining that takes place in the COVAM gives the Mexican mechanism an important degree of flexibility. In contrast, in El Salvador the rigidity of the selection mechanism made it hard to accommodate the different parties' preferences. Thus, whereas in Mexico migrants were allowed to submit projects aimed at embellishing the community or with recreational purposes, migrants in El Salvador were unable to submit such projects.[16] Only those projects strictly within the category of 'productive infrastructure' were allowed to participate, and there was no forum to raise migrants' concerns.

Conversely, an aspect both partnerships had in common was the existence of monitoring mechanisms throughout the development of the project. As in the Mexican case, Salvadorian migrants and their relatives in their hometowns also played a role in the oversight of projects, making sure that both internal deadlines and project specifications were met. Table 24.1 summarizes the comparison between the Mexican and Salvadorian partnerships.

Conclusion

The preceding discussion illustrated how collective action takes place to fund developmental projects through collective remittances. Although partnerships tend to use membership inducements, leadership incentives, and rules as means to overcome the collective action challenge, key differences contribute to explain why some of them succeed and others do not. The contrast between the Salvadorian and Mexican partnerships highlighted that not all partnerships are created equal, and that a co-financing scheme may jeopardize the partnership's chances to be sustainable in the long run.

In general, the extent to which obstacles were overcome was determined by differences in inducements for membership, incentives for leaders, and the rules of the game. Regarding positive incentives for migrants and their leaders, migrants from Mexico and El Salvador responded to the same private goods offered as a by-product of collective action. Migrants enjoyed similar membership-related and recreational benefits and the leadership enjoyed similar social status and political importance. The main difference is found in the Salvadorian associations' inability to select contractors for the projects, which affected the consideration to provide the collective good in two ways: it detracted from the value derived from the collective enterprise both materially – in terms of foregone income through contracts for friends and family – and immaterially – in terms of the satisfaction associated with being able to help others in the community; and it fuelled migrants'

[16] About 15 per cent of the programme's projects in Mexico have historically fallen in this category (interview with Guillermo Huerta, 2007).

Table 24.1 Comparison between the Mexican and Salvadorian partnerships for collective remittances

	Mexico	El Salvador
Negative inducements	No	No
Positive inducements		
Membership benefits	Yes	Yes
Recreational benefits	Yes	Yes
Leadership benefits		
Social benefits	Yes	Yes
Political benefits	Yes	Yes
Material benefits	Yes	No
Rules		
Delimiting membership	Yes	No
Involvement in decision-making process	Yes	No
Solution of controversies	Yes	No
Monitoring	Yes	Yes
Outcome	Relative success	Discontinued

mistrust in the government for fear of embezzlement. These considerations increased transaction costs and discouraged collective projects.

Furthermore, the differences in the partnerships' institutional designs also increased transaction costs for Salvadorian migrants. Three of the rules suggested by Ostrom to overcome trust-related obstacles were not present in El Salvador's partnership. First, while the exclusive participation of migrants generated a sense of ownership and fairness in Mexico, open participation in El Salvador enhanced difficulties related to differences in resource endowments between migrants and other participants and affected migrants' sense of ownership and fairness. It made Salvadorian migrants' participation considerably more onerous since they were forced to negotiate funding with other actors, often as a minor partner.

Second, whereas migrants' participation in the decision-making process ameliorated mistrust towards the government in Mexico, the exclusion of migrants from funding decisions in El Salvador opened the door to political considerations and fuelled concerns over the appropriate use of resources. By allowing migrants to participate in the different stages of the project – from the planning phase alongside municipal and state governments to the implementation of the project –, the rules of the Mexican partnership contributed towards overcoming migrants' suspicion.

Third, the existence of a mechanism for the solution of controversies granted the partnership flexibility and an opportunity to accommodate different actors' interests in Mexico. Conversely, the lack of such mechanism in El Salvador affected the partnerships' ability to reach negotiated outcomes. By affecting transparency and trust, these three differences in the partnerships' rules contributed to make participation more costly to Salvadorian migrants than to that of their Mexican counterparts. Taken together, membership benefits, leadership incentives, and rules help explain how coordination can be achieved among the different parties.

However, even though contrasting the two partnerships is helpful in identifying the differences that contributed to the relative success of the Mexican case and the discontinuation of the Salvadorian partnership, it does not allow us to determine the extent to which a particular difference is responsible for this outcome. In order to do so, we would require evidence from additional cases with different configurations of positive inducements and rules, but unfortunately such cases do not exist. In the absence of additional data points, this study's findings constitute a first step towards identifying the key factors making migrant–government partnerships work.

These findings have important implications for both theory and policy. Regarding theory, this chapter contributes to fill a gap in the migration literature, which has taken collective remittances for granted. It takes a step towards theorizing why and under what conditions migrants and different levels of government come together to provide public goods in the form of infrastructure projects. Though obstacles to cooperation are high, the cases of Mexico and El Salvador suggest that positive incentives in the form of private goods, leadership incentives, and certain trust-enhancing rules can affect a partnership's ability to carry out its collective objectives.

The chapter also extends the application of the logic of collective action into the field of migration. By studying how different types of incentives and rules can bring together actors with asymmetric objectives and endowments, it highlights the importance of appropriate institutional designs in supplying collective goods. In particular, the chapter illustrates how the coordination problem is overcome in a context of private and public actors engaged in a transnational activity.

Moreover, this research also makes an important contribution to the policy realm: it advances our understanding of how governments can improve their ability to leverage migrants' remittances for development purposes. By shedding light into relevant features of migrant–government partnerships in Mexico and El Salvador, the chapter contributes to identifying which aspects are worth replicating. Governments in Colombia and Ecuador, for example, have expressed interest in emulating these experiences (García Zamora 2007). As other countries undertake similar efforts to leverage collective remittances, it is important that they avoid the mistakes of previous experiences. The insights of this chapter should provide a foundation for leveraging the developmental potential of future partnerships.

References

Ahn, T.K. et al. (2003). Heterogeneous Preferences and Collective Action. *Public Choice* 117, 295–314.

Alarcón, R. (2002). The Development of the Hometown Associations in the United States and the Use of Social Remittances in Mexico. In Rodolfo de la Garza and B. Lindsay Lowell (eds) *Sending Money Home*. New York: Rowman, pp. 101–24.

Aparicio, F and Meseguer, C. (2008). Collective Remittances and the State: The 3×1 Program for Migrants in Mexico. Presented at the APSA 2008 Meeting, Boston, Massachusetts, 28 August.

Autler, L. (1997). Una potencial alianza para el desarrollo: remesas y movimiento cooperativo en El Salvador. In Mario Lungo (ed.) *Migración Internacional y Desarrollo*. El Salvador: FUNDES, pp. 97–143.

Bada, X. (2004). Reconstrucción de identidades regionales a través de proyectos de remesas colectivas. In Guillaume Lanly and M. Basilia Valenzuela (eds) *Clubes de migrantes oriundos mexicanos en los Estados Unidos*. Mexico: Universidad de Guadalajara, pp. 175–223.

Bakker, M. and Smith, M. (2003). El Rey del Tomate: Migrant Political Transnationalism and Democratization in Mexico. *Migraciones Internacionales* 2(1), 59–83.

Burgess, K. (2005). Migrant Philanthropy and Local Governance. In B. Merz (ed.), *New Patterns for Mexico*. Cambridge, MA: Harvard University Press, pp. 99–123.

Burgess, K. (2008). State Society Relations across Borders: Migrant Transnationalism in Mexico and El Salvador. Presented at the III Coloquio sobre Migración y Desarrollo, Costa Rica, 4–6 December.

CIDE. (2008). *Evaluación externa de consistencia y resultados 2007 del Programa 3 × 1 para Migrantes*. México: CIDE.

Delgado, R. and Rodríguez, H. 2001. The Emergence of Collective Migrants and Their Role in Mexico's Local and Regional Development. *Canadian Journal of Development Studies* 22(3), 747–64.

El Diaro de Hoy. (2006). Diáspora, socios en diversas obras. El Salvador, 6 October.

El Diaro de Hoy. (2004). Concurso de Fondos del FISDL. El Salvador, 19 February.

Escala-Rabadán, L. (2004). Migración y formas organizativas en los Estados Unidos: los clubes de migrantes mexicanos en California. In Guillaume Lanly and M. Basilia Valenzuela (eds) *Clubes de Migrantes Oriundos Mexicanos en los Estados Unidos*. Mexico: Universidad de Guadalajara, pp. 425–54.

Fitzgerald, D. (2000). *Negotiating Extra-territorial Citizenship*. CCIS Monograph #2, UC San Diego.

Frolick, N. et al. (1971). *Political Leadership and Collective Goods*. Princeton, NJ: Princeton University Press.

Fox, J. and Bada, X. (2008). Migrant Organization and Hometown Impacts in Rural Mexico. *Journal of Agrarian Change* 8(2–3), 435–61.

Gammage, S. (2006). Exporting People and Recruiting Remittances: A Development Strategy for El Salvador? *Latin American Perspectives* 33(6), 75–100.

Gammeltoft, P. (2002). Remittances and Other Financial Flows to Developing Countries. *International Migration* 40(5), 181–212.

García Zamora, R. (2007). El Programa 3×1 de remesas colectivas en México. *Migraciones Internacionales* 4(1), 165–72.

García Zamora, R. (2005). The Impact of Remittances in Jerez, Zacatecas. In B. Merz (ed.) *New Patterns for Mexico*. Cambridge, MA: Harvard University Press, pp. 19–32.

Goldring, L. (2004). Family and Collective Remittances to Mexico: A Multi-dimensional Typology. *Development and Change* 35(4), 799–840.

Goldring, L. (2002). The Mexican State and Transnational Organizations: Negotiating the Boundaries of Membership and Participation. *Latin American Research Review* 37(3), 55–99.

Goldring, L. (1999). Desarrollo, migradólares y la participación ciudadana de los norteños en Zacatecas. In Miguel Moctezuma and Héctor Rodríguez (eds) *Impacto de la Migración y las Remesas en el Crecimiento Económico Regional*. Mexico: Senado de la República, pp. 77–87.
Guarnizo, L. (2003). The Economics of Transnational Living. *International Migration Review* 37(3), 666–99.
Instituto Nacional de Estadística Geografía e Informática. 2007. *Finanzas Públicas Estatales y Municipales de Mexico, 2002–2005*. Mexico: INEGI.
International Organization for Migration (2006). *Engaging Diasporas as Development Partners for Home and Destination Countries*. IOM Migration Research Series No. 26, Switzerland.
Jones-Correa, M. (1998). Different Paths: Gender, Immigration, and Political Participation. *International Migration Review* 32(2), 326–49.
Knoke, D. (1990). *Organizing for Collective Action*. New York: Aldine de Gruyter.
Landolt, P. et al. (1999). The Dialectics of Salvadoran Transnationalism. *Ethnic and Racial Studies* 22(2), 290–315.
Levitt, P. (2001). *The Transnational Villagers*. Berkeley, CA: University of California Press.
Moctezuma, M. (2000). La organización de los migrantes zacatecanos en Estados Unidos. *Cuadernos Agrarios* 19/20, 81–104.
Nosthas, E. (2006). El caso de El Salvador: Unidos por Solidaridad. In Fernández de Castro et al. (eds) *El Programa 3×1 para Migrantes*. Mexico: Porrúa, pp. 45–59.
OECD. (2005). *Migration, Remittances, and Development*. Paris: OECD.
Olson, M. (1965). *The Logic of Collective Action*. Cambridge, MA: Harvard University Press.
Orozco, M. (2004). Mexican Hometown Associations and Development Opportunities. *Journal of International Affairs* 57(2), 1–21.
Orozco, M. and Welle K. (2005). Hometown Associations and Development. In B. Merz (ed.) *New Patterns for Mexico*. Cambridge, MA: Harvard University Press, pp. 157–79.
Orozco, M. et al. (2005). *Transnational Engagement, Remittances, and Development*. Report for the Rockefeller Foundation, Georgetown University.
Ostrom, E. (2000). Collective Action and the Evolution of Social Norms. *Journal of Economic Perspectives* 14(3), 137–58.
Ostrom, E. (1990). *Governing the Commons: The Evolution of Institutions for Collective Action*. New York: Cambridge University Press.
Ostrom, Elinor and Ahn, T.K. (2001). *A Social Science Perspective on Social Capital: Social Capital and Collective Action*. Report for Enquete Commission of the German Federal Government.
Palafox, G. (2009). *Program 3×1 for Migrants*. Presented by the Undersecretary for Social Programs (Mexico's Ministry of Social Development) at the Ad-hoc Expert Meeting: Contribution of Migrants to Development, Switzerland, 29 July.
Paul, A. and Gammage, S. (2004). *Hometown Associations and Development: El Salvador*. Destination D.C. Working Paper 3.
Portes A. and Landolt, P. (2002). Social Capital: Promises and Pitfalls of its Role in Development. *Journal of Latin American Studies* 32, 529–47.
Puri, S. and Ritzema, T. (1999). Migrant Worker Remittances, Micro-finance and the Informal Economy. ILO Social Finance Unit Working Paper 21, July.
Rocha, A. (2006). *Programa 3×1 para migrantes*. Report for Europe Aid Cooperation Office.

Sanabria, S. and Mojica, P. (2003). *Community Remittances and Local Development*. Prepared for IADB-MIF conference on Remittances as a Development Tool, Guatemala City, Guatemala, September 3.

Sandler, T. (1992). *Collective Action: Theory and Applications*. Ann Arbor, MA: University of Michigan Press.

World Bank. (2006). *Global Economic Prospects: Economic Implications of Remittances*. Washington, D.C.: World Bank.

ASHGATE
RESEARCH
COMPANION

PART VII
TRANSNATIONAL MIGRATION, CITIZENSHIP AND THE MODERN STATE

Global Migratory Policies: Neither Closed nor Open Borders

Raffaele Marchetti[1]

Introduction

Political boundaries are increasingly under pressure. As a consequence of the global transformations that are changing the international system, the criteria for determining the inclusion in or the exclusion from new political constituencies are under revision. At the national level, the external migratory pressure coupled with domestic political dynamics is generating an intense debate on the legitimacy of keeping migrants out of national political life. Migration and the policy of admission of aliens into political communities is increasingly recognized as a key issue of both political agendas and academic debates. As a political issue, migration is at the centre of a controversy where the proponents of more open policies argue against tight border controls on grounds that are often composed of multiple components. Economic theses are frequently mixed with cultural, political, legal or security arguments. Pragmatic approaches are often entangled with ideological stances, idealistic attitudes or racist positions. All of this contributes to create a burning situation that not only heats political debates but sometimes also descends to the streets. As a theoretical issue, migration is equally controversial for it intersects a core node of political theory, namely the notion of citizenship. According to liberalism, individuals are entitled to a set of rights including the right to mobility, and yet this right is constrained by an equally recognized right to collective self-determination and national autonomy. This tension is more and more problematic in a world in which individual human rights are on the rise and state sovereignty is in decline in many respects – except for the issue of immigration.

The traditional statist stance on migration, according to which the sovereign state retains an almost absolute discretion with regard to accepting foreigners into its own territory, still represents in fact one of the clearest examples of international exclusion. Underpinning this discretion is a creed of the statist–communitarian paradigm that insists citizenship intrinsically refers to membership in a limited political organization – i.e., the state. According to this widespread position, the very expression 'cosmopolitan citizenship' would be an oxymoron insomuch as any attempt to expand the notion of citizenship beyond the limits of the community would necessarily result in self-contradiction. And yet, this statist creed is increasingly contested both in practice and theory by forms of transnationalism. At

1 LUISS, rmarchetti@luiss.it

the practical level, more and more states recognize the possibility of multiple allegiances (i.e., double/triple passports) or indeed supranational allegiances (i.e., the EU internal free movement space), and, in a different way, recent developments in international law chip away at state prerogatives as they show a tendency to grant increased legal relevance to universal human rights in areas such as those pertaining to social and civil rights. Similarly, at the normative level discretionary admittance policies have recently been challenged by two kinds of more universalistic recommendations: open border policies at the regional level and world migratory management at the global level. Together with the discredited and yet predominant statist view, these two counteralternatives delimit the normative discussion on migration.

In contrast to both statism and open borders, this chapter presents a proposal for a new reading of citizenship, and for its supranational institutional correlate in terms of migratory cosmopolitanism. Against state-centric logic, this chapter holds that, while the concept of nationality is inseparable from the notion of a sovereign state, the concept of citizenship is not, insofar as it can be unfolded and spread out over a number of political spheres. Consequently, no normative obstacles impede the expansion of the traditional notion of polis to the entire cosmos and the traditional understanding of national citizenship should be considered just a secondary category of political entitlements. Cosmo-political citizenship is, thus, understood to have significant meaning and value. This position, however, need not fall into a straightforward proposal for open borders. In opposition to such perspective, the argument presented here maintains that open border (non-)arrangements should be equally refused in that they would violate the principle of impartiality. In overlooking the relative value of community self-determination and the possible risk of communal disruption, in fact, open borders arrangements do not take into appropriate consideration both original residents' and migrants' expectations. An interpretation of cosmopolitan citizenship in terms of freedom of movement forms the core of this chapter. According to a cosmopolitan principle of justice, in order to increase social welfare, freedom of movement must constitute a key component of individual freedom of choice that needs to be promoted within a multilayered scheme of political rights. Freedom of choice has to be inserted in a wider framework in which others' freedom of choice – as implemented through rights of residency and citizenship – has similar, prima facie claims of legitimacy. As a result, balancing different sets of entitlements through impartial institutional mechanisms remains a key political exercise for achieving legitimacy at any level of political action, including the global. Deploying a global, single principle of justice, such a reading thus generates a system that is internally differentiated and yet comprehensively consistent.

While the mainstream argument for global citizenship is primarily concerned with the capacity of political agents to influence, from their respective positions, those public decisions whose consequences extend beyond national borders, this chapter aims to study the other, less discussed, aspect of global citizenship that concerns not the scope of global public accountability but the extent to which political agents are free to move and join different societies. Accordingly, the primary object of concern here is individuals' capacity to modify their personal choice possibilities through changing their place of residency, which allows them to pursue control over the political system and over their own future. Once the principle of control over one's own life is endorsed, the issue of original residency becomes less significant for both aspects of global citizenship – i.e., transnational accountability and transnational movement. On this last account the treatment of migrants becomes a central test of the democratic legitimacy of the political system.

From the perspective advocated by this chapter, migrants are recognized as cosmopolitan stakeholders entitled to rights that extend to different spheres of political action. According to the long-term emancipation project of cosmopolitanism, the right to free passage is considered a progressive entitlement of non-discrimination that contributes to the maximization of individual choice possibilities, thus to his/her self-determination. In this vein, the ultimate entitlement to movement constitutes just another, equally important, component within the set of fundamental democratic rights. For it to be established, the institution of an international organization specifically dedicated to the global deliberation on migration management is recommended, where the different stakeholders can present and politically weigh their claims, from an equal standing. Within the subsequent form of a world migratory regime, states would lose their absolute privilege of admission, and a more consensual method of allocating entrance permission and international responsibility would be implemented that can eliminate some injustices of the present nation-led system.

This chapter starts by setting out the defining characteristics of migration and the political concept of citizenship, with a brief survey of current institutions and policies regarding migration. The core argument for the cosmopolitan interpretation of migration and citizenship is then introduced. Concluding recommendations for the creation of a supranational institutional framework of migratory cosmopolitanism are formulated thereafter.

The Next Frontier of Citizenship

In a sociological sense, migration occurs every time one moves from the original community (defined, among other, by a net of social relations with reference to a defined territory) to another one. Local migration has always been a constitutive phenomenon of human history. Although the main character of societies has been their permanency, there has always been collective displacement of people. Moreover, an important, often unregulated, feature of socio-economic systems was movement of specific groups of people such as merchants, slaves, soldiers, artists, scientists, and those escaping from dangers and looking for a better fate. The conquest of the 'new world' gave a strong impulse to long-distance migratory fluxes towards the North and the South American continents from Europe and Africa. In the following centuries up till this day, both voluntary and forced movements of people had increased substantially thanks to the new opportunities offered by the technological progress of the industrial revolution applied to the means of both communication and transportation. The linguistic heterogeneity present in almost every idiom is probably one of the clearest evidences of the continuous and persistent relationship between peoples throughout human history.

Here, however, another kind of definition of migration is used. Reference is made rather to the political than to the anthropological meaning of movement. While the sociological interpretation refers to phenomena that are almost as old as society itself, their political reading is more recent and is concerned with admission into foreign political society. A strict definition of immigration, in fact, needs to rely on the modern concept of citizenship and therefore of the nation-state. A conventional and symbolic date, which is used to signify the start of a new nation-state model of active membership, is considered to be 26 August 1789, the *Declaration des droits de l'homme et du citoyen*. It is, in fact, from the period of the formation of the modern nation-state, that the distinction between e-migration and im-migration and all the relative discriminations arise, which marks the difference between political communities today. More recently, at the beginning of the twentieth century, another concrete and equally relevant event was the introduction of the passport as a compulsory means of transborder travel. And finally, in recent decades a continuous tightening of the admission requirements has brought about the current state-centred apparatus.[2] Migration is here thus examined with reference to the political dimension of movement concerning the issues of admission into a foreign political society and citizenship. While citizenship generally is understood as the set of legal entitlements allowing for full community membership, conventionally three different subsets of citizenship rights can be distinguished according to their scope: civil, political and socioeconomic rights. These entitlements, which are based on a fundamental principle of equality and reciprocity, are impartially guaranteed to every member of the community. Insofar as membership within the collective exercising self-governance is usually recognized as the minimal precondition of democratic life, the acquisition of this set of rights is considered crucial to effective participation in social and political life.

There have been two major alternative principles governing the acquisition of citizenship: *jus soli* and *jus sanguinis*. While the first grants citizenship to everyone born within the territory of the country, the second considers blood relationship as the determining distinction. These principles have been inconsistently integrated with the practices of naturalization and together they form the basis of the traditional concept of allegiance, according to which loyalty is due to one's own country regardless of any other kind of secondary responsibilities extending beyond borders. In accordance with such due loyalty, the state has the prerogative to limit access to citizenship. In order to grasp the critical meaning of the current proposal, it is fundamental to note that current customary international law grants to the state an absolute right to refuse admission. While sovereignty is threatened in other respects, legislating the admission of immigrants is one instance in which state prerogatives are still intact. Provided no relevant conventions or humanitarian measures are applicable, the refusal to admit an alien is never an illicit act. However, if an alien already resides in the national territory, the right of the state to remove him or her is partially limited; accordingly, there is no absolute right to expulsion. The only agents towards whom the state has an international duty of admission are its own citizens. The statist stance is, however, increasingly under pressure in the context of globalization.[3]

Migration constitutes a particularly challenging paradox of the globalizing age. On the one hand, migration is facilitated by a number of developments including easier

2 Mark B. Salter, *Rights of Passage: The Passport in International Relations* (Lynne Rienner, Boulder, CO 2003); John Torpey, *The Invention of the Passport: Surveillance, Citizenship and the State* (Cambridge University Press, Cambridge 2000).

3 Saskia Sassen, 'Beyond Sovereignty: De-facto Transnationalism in Immigration Policy' (1999) 1(2) *European Journal of Migration Law* 177–98.

international transports, increased IT technologies, and higher financial capabilities. Accordingly, individuals nowadays can travel easily, know more about the destination countries, and have (relatively) more money to pay for their movement. So called 'gold-collar' elites live, indeed, in a borderless world. On the other hand, however, migration is constrained by normative, political and legal barriers erected by receiving countries. Principles of political communitarianism, nationalistic and racist feelings, and the legal privileges of national citizenship prevent individuals from moving to the richer countries of the global north. Economic reasons are played out in both directions equally to attract working force when needed, and to repel labour competition when under the threat of unemployment. Hence global practical possibilities are constrained by national normative limits.

The kind of global vs. local tension underpins the (non-)management of the issue of migration at the international and global level. While international migration is increasing putting under pressure the current institutional framework, the kind of response that is given to it remains within the limits of national policies. Beyond the exceptional case of the Geneva Convention on Refugees (created in a very different international context for a very specific category of migrant), there is no effective and comprehensive international institution dedicated to the issue of migration. The International Labor Organization (ILO) has during the years elaborated a number of conventions and reports, but they remain depressingly unattended. Limited cooperation is achieved within the General Agreement on Trade and Services (GATS) for what concerns high-skilled workers only (so called 'Mode 4'). Also, limited cooperation is developing through a number of UN conventions and protocols on illegal migration, human smuggling and trafficking. Regional cooperation, such as the case of the European Union, is more significant, though being territorially delimited it reproduces the logic of state management writ large. All in all, the general and more quantitatively significant case of economic migrants is left to the free will of national policies, with no international regime emerging for its collective management. And yet, this creates political tension and socio-economic dysfunctionalities, beyond damaging the democratic credentials of receiving states.

Two practical considerations related to the power position of receiving countries explain why the issue of migration is stuck in such a desolating stalemate.[4] From an economic point of view, the economies of the rich countries can collect working force from poor countries whenever they need, for foreign labour is in abundant supply globally speaking. Consequently, states do not need to commit to any long-term intergovernmental agreement for they can always – bilaterally or unilaterally – open up their borders and immediately fill the labour gaps in their domestic economic system. Instead, from a political point of view, receiving countries are continuously under pressure from an electorate that is often threatened by (real or perceived) menaces generated by the inflow of foreigners. Employment, national culture and even public institutions are usually depicted by (not exclusively right-wing) political parties as destabilized by the integration of alien members.

[4] Aristide R. Zolberg, 'Labour Migration and International Economic Regimes: Bretton Woods and After' in Mary M. Kritz and Hania Zlotnik (eds), *International Migration Systems: A Global Approach* (Clarendon, Oxford 1992), 315–34.

Migration is thus caught in between two extreme characterizations. On the one hand, the phenomenon of migration in its complexity is commonly included in the list of global issues, and yet it is almost exclusively managed by national or regional policies. This disconnect reveals a fundamental normative contradiction between claims that are universal to all humans and the communitarian entitlements upheld by mainstream political philosophy as well as national and international laws. The most blatant example of this contradictory logic at work is Article 13 of the Universal Declaration of Human Rights concerning the right to leave (but not to enter into) any country. One way of reinterpreting the tension between universal and national claims concerning the issue of immigration consists in progressively drawing limits to state sovereignty according to superior international laws. Usually this interpretation implies considering migrants in the first instance as aliens, or non-citizens and non-subjects, the state being accepted as the only agent entitled to confer such privileged status. This approach typically corresponds to the image of concentric circles, according to which the starting reference is constituted by the group (or even the family) and from there progressive enlargements are envisaged. In diametrical opposition to this exclusionary mechanism, this chapter advocates an approach that is cosmopolitan and all inclusive from the beginning. Migrants are not non-citizens with only narrowly circumscribed rights, but cosmopolitan citizens entitled to the same rights that 'permanent residents' have to control the decision-making processes worldwide that extend to different spheres of political action. In accordance with a new concept of universal membership based on a deterritorialized notion of a person's rights, this chapter develops an argument for a consistent global democratic regime able to grant not only civil- and social-, but also political rights to migrants. Such political recognition and empowerment constitutes the only legitimate upgrading of the notion of citizenship and calls for a global migratory regulatory system. This would entail moving much beyond current migratory policies, perhaps, and paradoxically recalling a number of principles that were at the origins of international law itself.

The Origins of Current Migratory Policies

International law has played an important, and yet discontinuous, justificatory role in keeping the legal setting of migratory policy domestic. Although recognition of the human rights regime has grown substantially over the last 50 years as it has slowly challenged national sovereignty in many aspects, the alien's right to admission is still a solid prerogative of the state. But this has not always been the case. In the first stages of *jus gentium,* which were anchored to the tradition of the Law of Nature, in fact, the duty to admit the alien was accepted as standard; it was the expulsion of the alien that was considered exceptional. De Vitoria, Grotius and Pufendorf all recognize the principle of freedom of movement, together with a number of minor limits. Minimal rational principles common to mankind supported a legal system in which domestic and interstate relations were consistently linked. The *jus societatis et communicationis* and the *jus commercii* were the driving principles of the scholars of the Law of Nature regarding movement of people.[5] This perspective was accepted for a long period.

Later on, the dominion theory and its subsequent developments, in exact opposition to the principles of the law of nature, formed a paramount historical and theoretical source of legitimacy for the current exclusionary attitude towards migration and citizenship. According to such a theory, citizenship was originally considered a good belonging to the state, whose right of property extends over its territory. The imperia on people, an expression of the dominium on the territory marked by the principle *qui in territorio meo est, etiam meus subditus est*, granted the state absolute power over the political and social existence of individuals within its domain. Afterwards, an important significant contractual variant was inserted into this tradition, which substantially modified the ethico-political justification of the state, but left intact the normative distinction between insiders and outsiders. With the American Revolution and, above all, the French Revolution, in fact, citizens acquired an active part in collective decision making and in the exercise of sovereignty, but the fundamental power to determine civil inclusion remained strictly the group's prerogatives. The universalistic law of nature coexisted with the domestic contractual framework, but a consistent and definitive synthesis was never established. Until the beginning of the twentieth century, this coexistence was well suited to the socio-economic circumstances. These principles, in fact, underpinned and legitimized a situation where both the country of destination and country of origin had a clear interest in favouring migration, as in the case of the migration from Europe to America. When the 'golden age' of free trade ended and a tougher nationalistic political era took the centre-stage of international relations alongside protectionism, migration policies changed too. Suddenly, within a few decades most countries adopted entry limitations inspired by domestic political and economical ends. It was, in fact, the supposed protection of domestic labour markets and welfare systems that convinced governments to invent new forms of barriers.

Thus, while for many centuries a substantial transnational flow of people characterized both the internal and the external image of many countries,[6] today the situation is largely different. Current international customary law, which is consistent with the dominium theory of sovereignty, holds migration standards to be contrary to the original formulation of the *jus naturae*. While the formal difference consists in the switch from the moral to the legal status of law, the substantive change concerns the legitimate criteria for entrance. Within the current formulations of international law, an absolute right to refuse admission is thus granted to the state.[7] It is precisely against the normative starting point centred on the state that the cosmopolitan revival of the last 40 years has developed.

---

[5] Hugo Grotius, *De jure belli ac pacis libri tres* (Clarendon Press, Oxford 1625; reprinted 1925); Samuel Pufendorf, *De jure naturae et gentium libri octo* (Clarendon Press, Oxford 1672; reprinted 1934); Francisco de Vitoria, *De indis et de jure belli relectiones: being parts of Relectiones Theologicae XII* (Carnegie Institution of Washington, Washington, D.C. 1539; reprinted 1917).

[6] S. Spencer, *Strangers and Citizens: A Positive Approach to Migrants and Refugees* (Rivers Oram Press, London 1993).

[7] Guy S. Goodwin-Gill, *International Law and the Movement of Persons between States* (Oxford University Press, Oxford 1978); Bruno Nascimbene, *Il trattamento dello straniero nel diritto internazionale ed europeo* (Giuffrè, Milano 1984).

Cosmopolitan Migratory Citizenship

Two principal dilemmas concerning the notion of citizenship challenge any normative political theory that aims to deal with the theme of migration: (1) if and how to admit new would-be migrants (admission policy), and (2) how to deal with the received migrants (domestic treatment).[8] Despite some recent attempts to consider migration from a wider perspective, a statist, receiver's point of view still dominates in the normative literature on migration.[9] By opting for a different vantage point beyond admission and treatment issues, this chapter deals with migration within a larger conceptual framework that also includes a third crucial element: the institution of multilevel citizenship as inherently anchored to global participatory entitlements.

With regard to the political reading of migration, the starting point of the cosmopolitanism argument on the movement of people stems from two different observations: one descriptive and one prescriptive. In factual terms, migration is considered principally and inevitably a global issue in that it refers to social phenomena primarily concerning the world level of political action and producing international effects. Historical patterns of migration have been fundamentally altered by the global transformations of recent decades. Even if borders were closed today, there would still be a continuous flow, both legal and illegal, due to a number of factors, including international and national norms of family reunion and political asylum. Even in an ideal world, the political question of aliens would persist, since even if poverty and violence were eliminated as causes of dislocation, there would still be personal motivations such as the desire to live in another society and lifestyle issues that would work as powerful engines of migration.

In normative terms, cosmopolitanism affirms that the scope of justice should be universal as no discrimination is justified when considering the ultimate rights of every citizen to control his destiny and to equal individual self-determination.[10] In this vein, individual freedom of choice and the subsequent political entitlements to take part democratically in the public decision-making process at all political levels form the normative core of the cosmopolitan criteria to assess international affairs.[11] Underpinning this is the fundamental ethical–political postulate regarding impartiality that demands the extension of the application of the norm of individual non-discrimination to the global level.[12] In fact, in order to preserve his individual autonomy via freedom of choice, the agent needs to extend his political entitlement to the totality of the sphere of political action. This extended

8 Veit-Michael Bader (ed.), *Citizenship and Exclusion* (Macmillan, Houndmills 1997); Warren A. Schwartz (ed.), *Justice in Immigration* (Cambridge University Press, Cambridge 1995).

9 Jonathan Seglow, 'The Ethics of Immigration' (2005) 3(3) *Political Studies Review* 317–34.

10 Simon Caney, *Justice Beyond Borders: A Global Political Theory* (Oxford University Press, Oxford 2004).

11 Raffaele Marchetti, *Global Democracy: For and Against: Ethical Theory, Institutional Design, and Social Struggles* (Routledge, London–New York 2008).

12 Robert Goodin, 'If People Were Money…' in Brian Barry and Robert Goodin (eds), *Free Movement Ethical Issues in the Transnational Migration of People and of Money* (Harvester Wheatsheaf, Hemel Hempstead 1992), 6–22; Peter Singer and Renata Singer, 'The Ethics of Refugees Policy' in Mark Gibney (ed.), *Open Borders? Closed Societies? The Ethical and Political Issues* (Greenwood, New York 1988), 111–30.

interpretation of political agency is particularly significant in those transborder cases, such as that of transnational migration, where traditional state-centric conceptions of citizenship demonstrate an increasing inappropriateness, both moral and political. In order to comply with the requirements of global justice and global democracy, such extension needs to be balanced, from an equal standing, with others' political entitlements.

These recognitions lead to the disputation of the mainstream framework according to which migration is considered only a national issue, because preference is given to residents' claims. Unfortunately, both nationalistic and globalist scholars commonly adopt part of the receiving country's perspective, inasmuch as admission to a country is considered the crux of the entire issue.[13] According to cosmopolitanism, this move constitutes a prejudicial limitation of the original question. Since migrants have unequal standing, the question inevitably delivers a distorted and biased answer. As an alternative to this, a radical repositioning of the receiving countries is suggested and an equalizing balance is struck between migrants and residents. The state-centric paradigm of national membership is rejected in favour of a global political principle of residency. Within this, it is argued, multilevel citizenship offers a unique chance for the social and political development of the theory and practice of democracy according to cosmopolitan principles.[14]

Where this revolution of perspective occurs, two results are achieved: (1) the conferral of the equal status of cosmopolitan citizenship to migrants and 'receiver' citizens concerning individual choice, and (2) the granting of the right to free passage concerning the movement of people. A cosmopolitan citizenship characterized by these entitlements becomes de facto a crucial institutional factor for individuals to increase, or even to implement, their autonomy among differing life options and their capability to govern the social–political domain by changing their places of residence. Much as at the domestic level the right to movement over the national territory has proved crucial in the self-realization of one's personal projects and political participation, an equivalent international right would be equally beneficial to the well-being of the individual in terms of choice opportunities and political control of one's own life.

A number of policy consequences pertaining to the status of the citizen on the vertical and horizontal dimensions of transnational politics are generated by the rebalancing of the notion of citizenship according to an impartial, global standard of membership claims. By definition, the multilayered notion of cosmopolitan citizenship entails political membership at different levels. While state membership would still remain inevitably subject to some constraints (e.g., not all can be citizens of country X), second order, global citizenship is characterized by all-inclusiveness (e.g., all are world citizens). This way, cosmopolitanism grants to individuals civil, social and political rights in more than one country, and the complete parity of rights related to residency between local people and migrants.[15]

---

[13] Joseph H. Carens, 'Membership and Morality: Admission to Citizenship in Liberal Democratic States' in William Rogers Brubaker (ed.), *Immigration and the Politics of Citizenship* (University Press of American, Lanham, MD 1989), 31–49; Peter C. Meilaender, *Toward a Theory of Immigration* (Palgrave, New York 2001); David Miller, 'Immigrants, Nations, and Citizenship' (2008) 16(4) *Journal of Political Philosophy* 371–90.

[14] Marchetti, *Global Democracy*; Raffaele Marchetti, 'Global Citizenship: The Case of Migrants and Residents' (2009) 34 *Refugee Watch: A South Asian Journal on Forced Migration* 56–68.

[15] April Carter, *The Political Theory of Global Citizenship* (Routledge, London 2001).

Freedom of movement remains a necessary requirement for the implementation of political participation insofar as only by having such an entitlement can an individual join a group (possibly different from the individual's own original one) where the individual's opinion can be aggregated with other similar views, thus creating a substantial political voice able to influence public life according to the individual's own value set. This argument resembles that of a political party's pluralism within a voluntaristic model of politics and it is almost commonsensical in democratic theory. Here it is a matter of enlarging our understanding of the demos to a global vision, in line with the principle of universal human rights and democracy. As much as the possibility of a plurality of political parties should be guaranteed in order to offer the individual the possibility to join the party that is most consistent with his views, so also the freedom to join a group or country where his personal views (political, social and economical) sit comfortably should be guaranteed. Hence, the recognition of the right to free passage represents a legitimate political objective to be taken into consideration when shaping a multilayered political structure, insofar as it ultimately fosters the individual freedom of self-determination.

Nonetheless, for this to satisfy the global democratic requirements concerning multilevel dimensionality, an impartial weighting mechanism between the claims of migrants and those of local citizens has to be simultaneously envisaged. Having argued for a universal right to movement, it is necessary to reiterate that such a right has to be inserted into a wider institutional political framework in which other kinds of rights also have legitimate claims. While migrants and residents are equal on the basis of a fundamental right to the protection of freedom of choice, they nonetheless differ in that the social value of their relative institutional entitlements concerning national citizenship can become unbalanced. This case is similar in many respects to the familiar situation of welfare state provision, in which one person's set of secondary rights conflicts with the secondary entitlements of others, despite both counterparts having fundamentally equal claims to well-being, i.e., welfare provision from the state. In cases like this, some sort of impartial comparative assessment made by a public, all-inclusive institution is needed in order to solve the controversy. While institutional suggestions for the case of a world migratory regime will be provided in the next sections, here it is important to offer more details on the reasoning underpinning them.

Within the scheme of cosmopolitanism, national citizenship, as an institution of the state level of political action, maintains a certain degree of legitimacy according to a universal, indirect and impartial division of moral labour. According to this division, different associative ties are recognized as prima facie valid sources of well-being, but in order to depart from such provisional status and gain definitive legitimacy, they need to be consistently embedded into a wider, global institutional framework. In this specific case, they need to pass through a comparative assessment against the migrants' conflicting entitlements. In this vein, the institution of national primary citizenship will only be warranted to the extent that its long-term social performance impartially contributes to the maximization of the individual freedom of choice, and therefore consistently meets the demands of the democratic institution of cosmopolitan citizenship.

Such comparative assessment between different citizenship-related entitlements is based on the expected capacity of each set of rights to contribute to the promotion of the individual freedom of choice via political participation. Such comparative assessment can only be carried out and agreed upon in an adequate institutional framework in which all counterparts have a fundamentally equal voice. Crucially, it can only be done by an all-inclusive authority that is positioned one institutional layer up. However, before moving to the institutional blueprint of this view, it is worth analysing critically the substance of the traditional arguments put forward by residents and migrants alike.

Weighing Residents' and Migrants' Claims

The claims of citizens to control entrance into their national territory are traditionally based on the principle of self-determination. According to this principle, a group is entitled to collectively decide over its destiny, including its membership. This reasoning constitutes an extension of the individual right to freedom of choice to the collective domain. Such group prerogatives usually rely on a liberal–communitarian argument holding that a political project is necessary for imbuing individual lives with meaning and that a genuine political project can only be carried out in the vernacular, i.e. at the local/state level. From the perspective of this chapter, the liberal–communitarian argument only has derivative force. It is warranted provided it is conducive to social well-being. Genuine communitarian scholars, however, do not deploy such an instrumental reading. If a strict, non-instrumental communitarian perspective is maintained, then the state-centric point of view should be rejected for at least two reasons, which in different ways concern the principle of non-discrimination. Firstly, by conceding an almost absolute privilege to original residents, state-centric policies do not recognize the supervenience of the principle of impartial consideration of each individual right on equal opportunity of choice. Secondly, the nationalist orientation should be rejected for the way it intentionally discriminates among would-be migrants, admitting only those who satisfy entry requirements shaped to the needs of the receiving countries. Both reasons ultimately affect the guarantee of individual freedom of choice and thus the overall promotion of social well-being.

Similarly to the case of resident citizens, migrants' claims are fundamentally based on the recognition of universal rights. Freedom of movement is usually included in the set of fundamental individual rights that are crucial for human dignity and for full participation in the political life of a community.[16] Traditionally applied to the domestic domain only, the value of universal mobility is mostly evident when it is denied. An important criticism of dictatorial regimes concerns, in fact, their restrictive attitude towards mobility within and beyond national territory. As much as other domains of freedom of choice, freedom of movement remains a key component for the enhancement of individual, and thus of social

---

16 Joseph H. Carens, 'Aliens and Citizens: The Case for Open Borders' (1987) 49(2) *The Review of Politics* 251–73; John P. Casey, 'Open Borders: Absurd Chimera or Inevitable Future Policy?' (2009) 48(5) *International Migration* 14–62; Mark Gibney (ed.), *Open Borders? Closed Societies? The Ethical and Political Issues* (Westwood Press, New York 1988); Satvinder S. Juss, *International Migration and Global Justice* (Ashgate, Aldershot 2006); Chandran Kukathas, 'The Case for Open Immigration' in Andrew I. Cohen and Christopher Heath Wellman (eds), *Contemporary Debates in Applied Ethics* (Blackwell, Malden, MA 2005), 201–20; Catherine Wihtol de Wenden, *Faut-il ouvrir les frontières?* (Presses de Science Po, Paris 1999).

well-being. From the perspective of this chapter, this liberal–universalist reading of the right to mobility also only has derivative force, i.e. it is warranted provided it is conducive to social well-being. Genuine 'open-borders' scholars, however, do not deploy such instrumental reading. If a strict, non-instrumental universalist perspective is maintained, the radical alternative of open borders should be refused for a number of distinct reasons related to the impartial dealing with both migrants and receiving populations. Concerning migrants, the policy of completely open borders here and now could be self-defeating, insofar as it could subvert the expectations of would-be migrants themselves who expect to arrive into a specific country with distinct socio-economical characteristics. As for local residents, a similar line of argument applies, for their expectations should also be taken into account and with equal weight. Were borders suddenly and completely open, a possible result could be a substantial reshaping of social identity and of the entire state structure, with potentially huge social costs in terms of well-being, or at least this is what many residents expect to happen with open borders.[17] Hence, in opposition to an immediate open border policy, the strategy of reform by degrees seems the most appropriate.

Since an open border policy is not viable in the near future and yet the right to movement is universal in principle, the subsequent problem becomes how to distribute a scarce good (i.e., the right of residency in any state) equally, and so avoid the dramatic situation of the unjust sacrifice of the few. The constraints, which, drawing on Humean terminology, I call the 'circumstances of migratory justice', consist of the fact that many want to enjoy the relevant good (i.e., right of residency), and yet such a good is not infinite at the national level. This situation is further aggravated by the current 'win-or-lose-all' process that daily haunts the lives of so many migrants. Migrants refused at the border lose everything, while those who make it through (by chance or illicit means) win the lottery. Those migrants refused (who may well have greater ethical grounds for wanting admittance) are excluded by a jungle system, where physical force and social power very often decide the result, without any moral constraints. The sacrifice of a few migrants (but actually many lives) represents the tragic cost of sustaining such an unjust system – a cost that includes that of the other would-be migrants who remain at home, the legal migrants who have already been accepted, and the local population.

The response of cosmopolitanism to the arbitrariness of the present mechanisms for entering consists in a moralized and impartial treatment of the distribution of the permits of residency based on a universal right to movement embedded in an impartial global weighting mechanism. According to this cosmo-political interpretation of citizenship and the notion of 'regulated openness' or 'fairly open borders',[18] the only viable solution to the distributive problem of admission consists in the recognition that the right of residency and the related citizenship rights too must be reconsidered as impartially dividable over time and on different levels of political action. Universal availability of this good (i.e., the right of residency) is only possible through its division into temporally distributed parts.

17 The Pew Global Attitude Project, *World Publics Welcome Global Trade – But Not Immigration* (Pew Research Center, Washington, D.C. 2007)

18 Veit-Michael Bader, 'Fairly Open Borders' in Veit-Michael Bader (ed.), *Citizenship and Exclusion* (Macmillan, Houndmills 1997), 28–60; Bimal Ghosh (ed.), *Managing Migration: Time for a New International Regime?* (Oxford University Press, New York 2000).

Consequently, temporally limited permissions of free movement and residency become the goods of this new migratory policy, goods widely available and complemented by limited extensions concerning the right to settlement and definitive change of primary state citizenship. Hence, a system of fair circulatory migration would result from temporary limited admissions.[19]

Having outlined this new interpretation of the notion of migration and citizenship, it is necessary to concentrate on its political–institutional consequences. So far, it has only been shown that citizenship should be reconceptualized in terms of global democratic justice. Consistency demands that this first move now be followed by the identification of the global political means through which to obtain the maximization of the individual choice possibility. The following section is dedicated to showing how both a fair allocation of entrance permissions and an impartial distribution of burdens among international agents might be achieved through appropriate political institutions. As argued, since the issue at stake is global in kind, an adequate response must be equally global. In this regard, the establishment of an institutional framework of migratory cosmopolitanism forms a crucial component of the present proposal.

Towards a World Migratory Regime

The previous sections have disputed the traditional understanding of the migratory phenomenon as a purely domestic political issue consisting, in the ultimate analysis, of a sheer problem of admission, and have subsequently recognized the necessity to create a legal–political structure able to manage and implement the 'good' at stake, i.e., the right of residency. Since the agency entailed in the movement of people refers primarily to the global level of political action, the principles of justice to apply in this case have to be consistently calibrated as world responsibilities.[20] The state should no longer be the only actor who decides, according to its own principle of justice, whether to admit the alien or not. If this were so, it would simply be a matter of designing a political mechanism for national efficiency. But the case is different and, more importantly, concerns the issue of assigning moral responsibility, i.e., making every agent accountable in each political sphere. In response to this, the suggestions envisaged for a future development of a regulatory framework consist of a set of institutional tools, composed of two main parts: an international convention and an international agency.

---

[19] Valeria Ottonelli and Tiziana Torresi, 'Inclusivist Egalitarian Liberalism and Temporary Migration: A Dilemma' (2012) 20(2) *Journal of Political Philosophy* 202–24.

[20] Frederique Channac, *Global or International Governance for Migration? Building up Cooperation and Enhancing Multilaterism from Regional to Global Level* (Garnet working paper 19/07, 2007); Franck Düvell and Bill Jordan, *Migration: Boundaries of Equality and Justice* (Polity, Cambridge 2003); Arthur C. Helton, 'Unpleasant Surprises Await: New Forms of Global Cooperation are Needed to Address Vast Population Movements' (2002) 58(6) *Bulletin of the Atomic Scientists* 95–100; Philip L. Martin, Susan F. Martin and Patrick Weil, *Managing Migration: The Promise of Cooperation* (Lexington Books, Lanham, MD 2006).

An *international convention on migration* should be established in order to recognize migration as a global phenomenon. The convention should formulate a code of conduct to be implemented through a two-tier mechanism at the domestic and global levels. An example to have in mind is the United Nations Geneva Refugee Convention and its Protocol, which provide a similar framework for the specific case of refugees. As a complement to this convention, a *World Migration Agency* (possibly under the umbrella of a reformed United Nations, as suggested in the past by Kofi Annan)[21] should also be created.[22] This would provide the appropriate place for negotiations and the appropriate force for implementation of the decisions concerning migratory fluxes. This new agency should be characterized by all-inclusiveness, for it should provide the forum where conflicting claims about the global issue of migration can be publicly discussed and weighed by all stakeholders on an equal standing. Hence, while the mode of deliberation should be based on a procedurally negotiated discussion, its competence should be supranational, thereby entailing the authority to override national decisions. This new system of migratory cosmopolitanism would enhance the legitimacy, efficacy and accountability of the decisions taken at the supranational level, and at the same time decrease the degree of widespread social criticism against the current situation. All involved agents would have the opportunity to express their point of view and to influence the decision-making process through appropriate political mechanisms. The creation of this new agency, to work in collaboration with several other institutional actors such as governmental and non-governmental organizations, remains, therefore, a crucial step towards the institutionalization of a legitimate global migratory regime.

Rules of non-discrimination, such as universality of admission through temporariness, equality of treatment between locals and foreigners, and the most favoured nation (MFN) clause, are the most appropriate candidate norms for this new regulatory framework. They would place a prima facie duty on the receiving countries to admit impartially without discriminating among sending countries. When a country did not exhaust its quota, then a mechanism for redistributing its remaining options to other sending countries should be activated. Moreover, a system of burden- and benefit sharing through national quotas should also be agreed upon to set the quantitative criteria for receiving countries. In contrast to national policies based on morally arbitrary and disproportionate distribution, each country should admit its fair share of migrants regardless of the other countries' compliance with the organization's decisions. The amount of migratory load should then

21 Global Commission on International Migration, *Migration in an Interconnected World: New Directions for Action* (GCIM, Geneva 2005); United Nations, *Report of the Secretary General on International Migration and Development* (18 May, A/60/871) (UN, New York 2006).

22 Ghosh (ed.), *Managing Migration*; James F. Hollifield, 'Migration and the "New" International Order: The Missing Regime' in Ghosh (ed.), *Managing Migration*, 75–109; Rey Koslowski, 'Global Mobility and the Quest for an International Migration Regime' in The Center for Migration Studies and the International Organization for Migration (ed.), *International Migration and Development* (IOM, Geneva 2008), 103–44; Raffaele Marchetti, 'Toward a World Migratory Regime' (2008) 15(2) *Indiana Journal of Global Legal Studies* 471–87; Henk Overbeek, 'Towards a New International Migration Regime: Globalization, Migration and the Internationalization of the State' in Robert Miles and Dietrich Thränhardt (eds), *Migration and European Integration: The Dynamics of Inclusion and Exclusion* (Pinter Publishers, London 1995), 15–36.

be decided by the supranational organization through an impartial and inclusive procedure of global deliberation through which residents' and migrants' claims, on an equal standing, are fairly balanced.

Conclusion

Through the adoption of a radical change in political perspective that reinterprets migration and citizenship as global issues, the ultimate exclusionary arbitrariness of the admission criteria of state migratory policies and the resulting loss of any potential increase in individual choice opportunity have come into view. To the original contention that state migratory policies are morally unaccountable, this chapter has suggested a cosmopolitan, all-inclusive answer. The core of its cosmopolitan argument resides in a particular interpretation of the idea of a universal right to free passage that takes into account the 'circumstances of migratory justice'. From this, a number of political recommendations follow that are given substance in the proposal of new admission criteria and of a new system of migratory cosmopolitanism, the latter entailing the adoption of a convention on migrants and the establishment of a supranational cooperative agency to manage migratory flux. Only through such a pluri-level political system can the possibility of individual choice receive an impartial hearing, in that multilevel citizenship is responsive to differing degrees of responsibility and relative power at all levels of political decision making, including the global sphere. These are the appropriate political arrangements required by a cosmopolitan theory of global justice in the case of citizenship and migration.

References

Bader, Veit-Michael, 'Fairly Open Borders' in Veit-Michael Bader (ed.), *Citizenship and Exclusion* (Macmillan, Houndmills 1997), 28–60.

Bader, Veit-Michael (ed.), *Citizenship and Exclusion* (Macmillan, Houndmills 1997).

Bartram, David, 'International Migration, Open Borders Debates, and Happiness' (2010) 12(3) *International Studies Review* 339–61.

Caney, Simon, *Justice Beyond Borders: A Global Political Theory* (Oxford University Press, Oxford 2004).

Carens, Joseph H., 'Aliens and Citizens: The Case for Open Borders' (1987) 49(2) *The Review of Politics* 251–73.

Carens, Joseph H., 'Membership and Morality: Admission to Citizenship in Liberal Democratic States' in William Rogers Brubaker (ed.), *Immigration and the Politics of Citizenship* (Lanham, MD 1989), 31–49.

Carter, April, *The Political Theory of Global Citizenship* (Routledge, London 2001).

Casey, John P., 'Open Borders: Absurd Chimera or Inevitable Future Policy?' (2009) 48(5) *International Migration* 14–62.

Channac, Frederique, *Global or International Governance for Migration? Building up Cooperation and Enhancing Multilaterism from Regional to Global Level* (Garnet working paper 19/07, 2007).

De Vitoria, Francisco, *De indis et de jure belli relectiones: being parts of Relectiones Theologicae XII* (Carnegie Institution of Washington, Washington, D.C. 1539; reprinted 1917).

Düvell, Franck and Bill Jordan, *Migration: Boundaries of Equality and Justice* (Polity, Cambridge 2003).

Ghosh, Bimal (ed.), *Managing Migration: Time for a New International Regime?* (Oxford University Press, New York 2000).

Gibney, Mark, *Open Borders? Closed Societies? The Ethical and Political Issues* (Westwood Press, New York 1988).

Global Commission on International Migration, *Migration in an Interconnected World: New Directions for Action* (GCIM, Geneva 2005).

Goodin, Robert, 'If People Were Money…' in Brian Barry and Robert Goodin (eds), *Free Movement Ethical Issues in the Transnational Migration of People and of Money* (Harvester Wheatsheaf, Hemel Hempstead 1992), 6–22.

Goodwin-Gill, Guy S., *International Law and the Movement of Persons between States* (Oxford University Press, Oxford 1978).

Grotius, Hugo, *De jure belli ac pacis libri tres* (Clarendon Press, Oxford 1625; reprinted 1925).

Helton, Arthur C., 'Unpleasant Surprises Await: New Forms of Global Cooperation are Needed to Address Vast Population Movements' (2002) 58(6) *Bulletin of the Atomic Scientists*, 95–100.

Hollifield, James F., 'Migration and the "New" International Order: The Missing Regime' in Bimal Ghosh (ed.), *Managing Migration: Time for a New International Regime?* (Oxford University Press, Oxford 2000), 75–109.

Juss, Satvinder S., *International Migration and Global Justice* (Ashgate, Aldershot 2006).

Koslowski, Rey, 'Global Mobility and the Quest for an International Migration Regime' in The Center for Migration Studies and the International Organization for Migration (ed.), *International Migration and Development* (IOM, Geneva 2008), 103–44.

Kukathas, Chandran, 'The Case for Open Immigration' in Andrew I. Cohen and Christopher Heath Wellman (eds), *Contemporary Debates in Applied Ethics* (Blackwell, Malden, MA 2005), 201–20.

Marchetti, Raffaele, 'Global Citizenship: The Case of Migrants and Residents' (2009) 34 *Refugee Watch: A South Asian Journal on Forced Migration* 56–68.

Marchetti, Raffaele, *Global Democracy: For and Against. Ethical Theory, Institutional Design, and Social Struggles* (Routledge, London–New York 2008).

Marchetti, Raffaele, 'Toward a World Migratory Regime' (2008) 15(2) *Indiana Journal of Global Legal Studies* 471–87.

Martin, Philip L., Susan F. Martin and Patrick Weil, *Managing Migration: The Promise of Cooperation* (Lexington Books, Lanham, MD 2006).

Meilaender, Peter C., *Toward a Theory of Immigration* (Palgrave, New York 2001).

Miller, David, 'Immigrants, Nations, and Citizenship' (2008) 16(4) *Journal of Political Philosophy* 371–90.

Nascimbene, Bruno, *Il trattamento dello straniero nel diritto internazionale ed europeo* (Giuffrè, Milano 1984).

Ottonelli, Valeria and Tiziana Torresi, 'Inclusivist Egalitarian Liberalism and Temporary Migration: A Dilemma' (2012) 20(2) *Journal of Political Philosophy* 202–24.

Overbeek, Henk, 'Towards a New International Migration Regime: Globalization, Migration and the Internationalization of the State' in Robert Miles and Dietrich Thränhardt (eds), *Migration and European Integration: The Dynamics of Inclusion and Exclusion* (Pinter Publishers, London 1995), 15–36.

Pufendorf, Samuel, *De jure naturae et gentium libri octo* (Clarendon Press, Oxford 1672; reprinted 1934).

Salter, Mark B., *Rights of Passage: The Passport in International Relations* (Lynne Rienner, Boulder, CO 2003).

Sassen, Saskia, 'Beyond Sovereignty: De-facto Transnationalism in Immigration Policy' (1999) 1(2) *European Journal of Migration Law* 177–98.

Schwartz, Warren A. (ed.), *Justice in Immigration* (Cambridge University, Cambridge 1995).

Seglow, Jonathan, 'The Ethics of Immigration' (2005) 3(3) *Political Studies Review* 317–34.

Singer, Peter and Renata Singer, 'The Ethics of Refugees Policy' in Mark Gibney (ed.), *Open Borders? Closed Societies? The Ethical and Political Issues* (Greenwood, New York 1988), 111–30.

Spencer, S., *Strangers and Citizens: A Positive Approach to Migrants and Refugees* (Rivers Oram Press, London 1993).

The Pew Global Attitude Project, *World Publics Welcome Global Trade – But Not Immigration* (Pew Research Center, Washington, D.C. 2007).

Torpey, John, *The Invention of the Passport: Surveillance, Citizenship and the State* (Cambridge University Press, Cambridge 2000).

United Nations, *Report of the Secretary General on International Migration and Development* (18 May, A/60/871) (UN, New York 2006).

Wihtol de Wenden, Catherine, *Faut-il ouvrir les frontières?* (Presses de Science Po, Paris 1999).

Zolberg, Aristide R., 'Labour Migration and International Economic Regimes: Bretton Woods and After' in Mary M. Kritz and Hania Zlotnik (eds), *International Migration Systems: A Global Approach* (Clarendon, Oxford 1992), 315–34.

Transnational Family Relations in Migration Contexts: British Variations on European Themes

Prakash Shah

In writing this chapter[1] from near the western corner of the Eurasian landmass, it is evident that migration is involving an increasingly complex set of trans-jurisdictional activities worldwide. We have yet to come to grips with the kinds of legal navigation by individuals and families taking place across legal frontiers, although some theorists have begun to locate its place within wider phenomena of transnationalism.[2] Recent events evidently demonstrate the often conflictual context in which migration occurs, as well as its many dysfunctional consequences. Just before I began writing this chapter in December 2010, news came of a suicide bomb attack in Stockholm by a man who had reportedly become 'radicalized' in the English town of Luton. A number of arrests in various European countries have been taking place more or less simultaneously of men of migrant origin suspected of involvement in terror-related activities. The fairly high-intensity conflict-ridden profile of migrants and their descendants being built in Europe and elsewhere, hides a more widespread, lower-intensity conflict in which official laws are also implicated. State authorities are penalizing trans-jurisdictional legal navigation, which occurs in a wide range of settings, and often concerns families and kin networks.

It is well known that many of the major streams of post-Second World War immigration into Western Europe were followed by large-scale family reunification. By all accounts, such immigration has not stopped, but has diversified to a greater number of source countries, overlain by further, sometimes complex, processes of family reunification and formation. This

[1] The research leading to this chapter was performed within the framework of the RELIGARE project. This project received funding from the European Commission Seventh Framework Programme (FP7/2007-2013) under grant agreement number 244635.

[2] W.F. Menski, 'Immigration and Multiculturalism in Britain: New Issues in Research and Policy' (2002) XII *KIAPS: Bulletin of Asia-Pacific Studies* 43–66; F. von Benda-Beckmann, K. von Benda-Beckmann and A. Griffiths (eds), *Mobile People, Mobile Law: Expanding Legal Relations in a Contracting World* (Ashgate, Aldershot 2005); R. Cotterrell, 'Transnational Communities and the Concept of Law' (2008) 21(1) *Ratio Juris* 1–18; R. Ballard, 'The Dynamics of Translocal and Transjurisdictional Networks: A Diasporic Perspective' (2009) 1(2) *South Asian Diaspora* 141–66.

is part of the picture of 'superdiversity' in European cities conveyed by Vertovec.[3] Relatively less has been said, especially in the European literature, about the maintenance of family relations across different countries and continents either among South–North migrants or global diasporas, although important new writing is starting to fill the gap.[4] The less we inquire about the reality of globally dispersed families, the less we tend to know about the methodological limits of our legal tools and concepts in that context.

The ostensibly contraceptive policy view from the North is that we are in control, and should continue to closely regulate family migrants and how they arrange their legal relations. This amounts to a denial by legislators and other legal actors of the plurality of modern Britain, and contemporary Europe, which the leading British immigration lawyer, Ian Macdonald QC, has referred to as ostrich-like behaviour, with one's head buried in the sand.[5] Immigration regulation certainly constitutes types of 'borders', now often deployed extraterritorially,[6] but other, mental borders are erected through legal systems as controls are imposed on the more systemic pluralizing impact of the migrant presence, and the continuity of law within transnational social fields,[7] between 'here' and 'there'. Thus, attempts to freeze out legal alterity go beyond the sections of officialdom concerned with immigration control, permeating other areas of official behaviour. In this chapter, by discussing some evidence from Britain, I want to nudge the reader a little more in the direction of considering these issues, concerning in what ways and why officials and legal systems are effectively failing to do justice to migrant families; and to take some steps towards rethinking the theoretical underpinnings of legal systems so as to find ways to move forward, with a view to keeping policy and theory in consonance with 'real life'. I do not, however, claim to say something completely new here. The editor of this volume has already written about the necessity of a 'cultural jurisprudence' as a social scientific and legal realist approach to the lives of migrants and ethnic minorities as part of a newly required global ethic of civility.[8] More recent writing has been grappling with the problem of such intercultural human rights,[9] although it may be said that we are still at the beginnings of a new phase in legal studies.

---

3 S. Vertovec, 'Super-diversity and its Implications' (2007) 30(6) *Ethnic and Racial Studies* 1024–54.

4 D. Bryceson and U. Vuorella, *The Transnational Family: New European Frontiers and Global Networks* (Berg, Oxford 2002); R. Grillo (ed.), *The Family in Question: Immigrant and Ethnic Minorities in Multicultural Europe* (Amsterdam University Press, Amsterdam 2008); E. Kofman, 'Family-related Migration: A Critical Review of European Studies' (2004) 30(2) *Journal of Ethnic and Migration Studies* 243–62.

5 I. Macdonald, 'Preface' in P. Shah and W.F. Menski (eds), *Migration, Diasporas and Legal Systems in Europe* (Routledge Cavendish, London 2006) xv–xviii.

6 B. Ryan and V. Mitsilegas, *Extraterritorial Immigration Control: Legal Challenges* (Martinus Nijhoff, Leiden 2010).

7 N. Glick Schiller, 'Transborder Citizenship: An Outcome of Legal Pluralism within Transnational Social Fields' in Benda-Beckmann, Benda-Beckmann and Griffiths (eds), *Mobile People, Mobile Law*, 27–49.

8 S. Juss, *Discretion and Deviation in the Administration of Immigration Control* (Sweet and Maxwell, London 1997).

9 Shah and Menski (eds), *Migration, Diasporas and Legal Systems in Europe*; R. Mehdi et al. (eds), *Religion and Law in Multicultural Societies* (DJØF Publishing, Copenhagen 2008); R. Grillo et al., *Legal Practice and Cultural Diversity* (Ashgate, Farnham 2009); M.-C. Foblets, J.-F. Gaudreault-

The Landscape of Family-based Migration

In the north-western parts of Europe, the large-scale recruitment of southern European and non-European labour migrants for post-war reconstruction was followed by systematic recruitment stops.[10] These 'stops' did not result in the curtailment of immigration but a change in its character. They led to widespread decisions among migrants to settle and sponsor their families, or to contract new marriages in the areas of origin of the migrants. Countries on the northern Mediterranean rim have more recently attracted immigrants and their families,[11] while countries to the east of the continent also appear to have new colonies of migrants from further east and south.[12] Refugee movements have added considerably to the diversity of Europe's population and, in their shadows, a large number of irregular migrants have also come, irregularity often being a direct function of restrictive immigration policies.[13] Although family migrants have tended to follow primary migrants, this is not inevitable, and families are often spread transnationally, while international commuting is not unknown. In recent decades, family members often accompany each other as forced migrants, who can find themselves detained by less than hospitable states, leading to a continuous stream of horror stories. Families are also sending young people ahead as bridgeheads for possible future immigration or merely for their safety and a better life, and such youngsters are often then involved in scenarios of trafficking and state paternalism to which they might become victims.[14] Newly formed relationships are also leading to claims by migrants who may have entered on another basis to remain in Europe. While the race for talent and knowledge migrants is well underway among various countries,[15] family members are often allowed to accompany such migrants, or their qualification to immigrate could partly depend on the status of a family member.

All these movements have led to the indelible pluralization of European societies, especially given the kinds of social change brought about by the establishment of newly cohering communities because of the presence of families and extended kin networks. As Castles et al.

DesBiens and A.D. Renteln (eds), *Cultural Diversity and the Law: State Responses from Around the World* (Bruylant, Brussels 2010).

10 W.R. Böhning, *The Migration of Workers in the United Kingdom and the European Community* (Oxford University Press for the Institute of Race Relations, London 1972); S. Castles and G. Kosack, *Immigrant Workers and Class Structure in Western Europe* (Oxford University Press for the Institute of Race Relations, London 1973); S. Collinson, *Europe and International Migration* (Pinter Publishers, London 1993).

11 K. Calavita, *Immigrants at the Margins: Law, Race and Exclusion in Southern Europe* (Cambridge University Press, Cambridge 2005).

12 P. Nyíri, *New Chinese Migrants in Europe: The Case of the Chinese Community in Hungary* (Ashgate, Aldershot 1999); K. Romaniszyn, 'The Cultural Implications of International Migrations' (2004) 2(146) *Polish Sociological Review* 141–59.

13 B. Bogusz et al., *Irregular Migration and Human Rights: Theoretical, European and International Perspectives* (Brill, Leiden 2004).

14 J. Bhabha, 'Lone Travelers: Rights, Criminalization, and the Transnational Migration of Unaccompanied Children' (2000) 7 *University of Chicago Law School Roundtable* 269–94.

15 A. Shachar, 'The Race for Talent: High Skilled Migrants and Competitive Immigration Regimes' (2006) 81 *New York University Law Review* 101–58.

indicated, already in the 1980s, these ethnic minorities are 'here for good'.[16] Their networks have induced further immigration, often overtly on the basis of family ties, but also hidden among the many asylum applications. It has been noted that the family has become the main channel for legal entry into the EU.[17] Comparative evidence of marriage formation indicates a strong preference among many groups of migrants for partners in the country of origin.[18] As Ballard shows, the migration 'escalators' that kinship furnishes, particularly through ties of descent and marriage, operate as a strengthening factor of ethnic colonies in economic no less than cultural terms.[19] This 'bottom-up' equalizing strategy, which such migration entrepreneurs use to challenge the uneven effects of 'top-down' globalization, combined with the pluralizing consequences of kin-based immigration, have not been entirely welcomed in European countries.

If recent evidence of voting patterns is anything to go by, European populations have become increasingly nervous and frustrated about the new forms of ethnic alterity in their neighbourhoods and in the economic sphere. The events of September 11 2001 and subsequent terror incidents in different European cities have evidently had an impact by raising tensions. The cry about a country being 'overrun by immigrants' is often heard. To the extent that states have pursued policies of multiculturalism – that is, either a laissez-faire attitude towards such diverse populations or active state support for the maintenance of their cultural activities –, such policies have also come under intense scrutiny.[20] In October 2010, Germany's Chancellor, Angela Merkel, noted that multiculturalism had utterly failed, while British Prime Minister David Cameron has, at various times, spoken of multiculturalism as a wrong-headed doctrine, entailing a divisive right to difference. Rules requiring integration impose some sort of obligatory subscription to majoritarian values and practices. Such pressures are very manifest in immigration control and citizenship criteria.[21]

Since transnational marriages are identified as a liability to the integrity of the social formations of European national states, and of European identity more broadly, they have become obvious targets of control, although restrictions are by no means only directed at spouses. British official policies and practices dictate which family members are to be recognized, sometimes leading to ridiculous situations. Once waiting for another hearing at the Asylum and Immigration Tribunal in London's Angel, we came across a woman sponsor of a visitor from the Punjab, her husband's deceased brother's wife, waiting to hear the outcome of a preliminary hearing. There was a frenzied discussion outside as it was realized that,

16 S. Castles, H. Booth and T. Wallace, *Here for Good: Western Europe's Ethnic Minorities* (Pluto, London 1984).

17 E. Kofman and V. Meetoo, 'Family Migration' *in World Migration Report 2008: Managing Labour Mobility in the Evolving Global Economy* (International Organization for Migration, Geneva 2008), 151–72.

18 E. Beck-Gernsheim, 'Transnational Lives, Transnational Marriages: A Review of Evidence from Migrant Communities in Europe' (2007) 7(3) *Global Networks* 271–88.

19 Ballard, 'Dynamics of Translocal and Transjurisdictional Networks'.

20 C. Joppke, 'The Retreat of Multiculturalism in the Liberal State: Theory and Policy' (2004) 55(2) *The British Journal of Sociology* 237–57; R. Grillo, 'An Excess of Alterity? Debating Difference in a Multicultural Society' (2007) 30(6) *Ethnic and Racial Studies* 979–98.

21 O. Löwenheim and O. Gazit, 'Power and Examination: A Critique of Citizenship Tests' (2009) 40(2) *Security Dialogue* 145–67; R. van Oers, E. Ersbøll and D. Kostakopoulou (eds), *A Re-definition of Belonging? Language and Integration Tests in Europe* (Martinus Nijhoff, Leiden 2010).

because the relationship between the two women was not among those listed, the intended visitor did not qualify as a 'family visitor', and therefore had no right to appeal against being refused a visa![22] In other cases, legal policies and official practices dictate the range of eligible marriage partners, and when a marriage or other family relationship is considered legitimate or valid. These policies and practices, which often run counter to norms accepted within the communities concerned or the family laws of other countries, reach beyond the immigration control sphere, infesting a range of other official legal forums.

Assessment of family relationships of people from non-Western cultures means that they are subjected to an intense gaze upon their 'alien' traditions. Immigration control and other legal arenas thereby become the location for an Orientalist (re)construction of family norms of the non-Western 'other'. Such traditions are judged as being inherently deficient from a dominant Western perspective. A passage from a book by Prof. Jackson, also a one-time Vice President of the Immigration Appeal Tribunal, reveals one such construction:

> There is undoubtedly a problem connected with marriage in immigration terms. Marriage offers to young men and women a way of radically improving their economic standard of living and no doubt in some cases an opportunity for financial gain by those who by virtue of tradition have it in their power to offer it. This is especially so where arranged marriages are the norm and where children (particularly daughters) continue to marry as they are directed by their parents.[23]

The remarkable part of this passage is not the fact that non-Western marriages are cast as 'traditional', presumably as opposed to modern, Western marriages, nor any inaccuracy in its description of the former. Rather, it is the impulse to their problematization *because* of their different nature and dynamics. Neither is the relevance of this kind of statement reduced because others in positions of power construct their own accounts justifying the derisory treatment of non-Western family relations. Take the following statement in a case concerning the recognition of Hindu law adoptions in India decided by the Asylum and Immigration Tribunal:

> Nobody is entitled to say 'I have adopted (or been adopted) according to my rules; therefore you are obliged to recognise the adoption as entirely valid under your rules'. Unless an Indian adoption can be found to be subject to the same requirements and the same intentions, and to have the same effects as an adoption in the United Kingdom, there would appear to be no reason why it should be treated as though it were a United Kingdom adoption. And if it is not to be treated in general as a United Kingdom adoption, there is no reason why it should be treated as a United Kingdom adoption for the purposes of the Immigration Rules. The truth of the matter is that adoption means different

[22] See the Immigration Appeals (Family Visitor) (No. 2) Regulations 2000, SI 2000 No. 2446, at para. 2(2).

[23] D. Jackson, *Immigration: Law and Practice* (Sweet and Maxwell, London 1996) 396.

things in different countries. The fact that the same word is used does not mean that the effects are, or ought to be, the same.[24]

Again, the problem with differences in the ways of formalizing family relationships and in their effects militates against their recognition, as if every culture should be a carbon copy of Western norm patterns. Evidently, there will be a variety of such discourses. Notwithstanding that variety, we find a widespread replication of negativity towards non-Western families in British and other Western legal systems. Further, whatever instrumentalities may lie behind a particular policy, legal restrictions are often enough premised on this negativity. Read as the Western framing of the other through the former's own experience, 'legal Orientalism' plays a key role in shaping policy towards transnational family migrants.[25] The much bigger question entailed by the quoted statement is whether family forms arising in different cultural contexts should indeed be treated as equivalent to a category existing within Western law or whether, because they are indeed set within a different cultural framework, they ought to be recognized as different, known as such, *and* be given recognition in their own right. My own view is that the latter option is the better one and offers the greatest scope for pluralism.[26]

Whom to Marry

Individuals also encounter pulls in other directions in these complex transnational conflicts within legal pluralism.[27] European countries are obliged to ensure respect for family life. This is significantly the result of the European Convention on Human Rights (ECHR) and specifically its Articles 8 (respect for private and family life) and 12 (right to marry and found a family). Various instruments agreed at EU level also oblige some minimal respect for the family lives of third country nationals. Although the UK remains reluctant to sign up to these, minimal recognition of family unity is found in immigration legislation and rules. Not least

---

24 *SK ('Adoption' not recognised in the UK) India* (2006) UKAIT 00068. This case is discussed in more detail in P. Shah, 'Transnational Hindu Law Adoptions: Recognition and Treatment in Britain' (2009) 5(2) *International Journal of Law in Context* 107–30. In the event, the adopters won their appeal against refusal of a dependent visa to the child, not under the adoption rules or by using human rights and discrimination arguments, but under the rule allowing admission of relatives whose exclusion is considered undesirable because of compassionate circumstances.

25 On this reading of Orientalism, see S.N. Balagangadhara and M. Keppens, 'Reconceptualising the Postcolonial Project: Beyond the Strictures and Structures of Orientalism' (2009) 11(1) *Interventions* 50–68. For the legal application of Orientalism, see T. Ruskola, 'Legal Orientalism' (2002) 101(1) *Michigan Law Review* 179–234.

26 This option goes beyond that of mere translation, which is flagged up by W.F. Menski, *Comparative Law in a Global Context: The Legal Systems of Asia and Africa* (Cambridge University Press, Cambridge 2006) 67. For a problematization of the loss in transplantation of the Islamic legal institution of *mahr* in the courts of four Western countries, see P. Fournier, *Muslim Marriage in Western Courts: Lost in Transplantation* (Ashgate, Farnham 2010). Fournier's book thus provokes thinking about the analogies between translation and transplantation.

27 For 'legal pluralism in conflict', see M. Chiba, 'Other Phases of Legal Pluralism in the Contemporary World' (1998) 11(3) *Ratio Juris* 228–45.

among them are the national recognition of ECHR norms and the availability of appeals and judicial review to contest the non-recognition of family unity by officials. EU free movement rules, adopted through Italian pressure in the 1960s, before immigration became the hot potato that it now is, continue to confer the widest recognition of family unity, justified earlier on economic grounds, and now also on human rights grounds.[28] The economic justification for family unity used by the European Court of Justice has not found appeal beyond the EU free movement context, an illustration of how the ground shifts depending on what types of family one is dealing with. There obviously remains a key tension between national and EU systems of regulation, a tension that shows up especially when third country nationals lay claim to EU rights of family unity. However, this discussion presupposes that we are speaking in a context where there is a basic recognition of family unity, although now increasingly hedged about by different restrictions. In contrast, some labour importing Asian states have remained resistant to recognizing a right of family unity for migrants to avoid the kinds of secondary immigration flows that Europe has experienced. In some countries, such as Turkey and Bangladesh, immigrating spouses of nationals are not necessarily given the right to work, an issue that is also relevant in British immigration decision making when considering whether married life is viable elsewhere.

While agreeing that the Convention was engaged in immigration cases, the European Court of Human Rights in the *Abdulaziz* case declined to hold that a state was obliged by Article 8 alone to allow a couple to reside in the state of their choosing, stating,

> The Court observes that the present proceedings do not relate to immigrants who already had a family which they left behind in another country until they had achieved settled status in the United Kingdom. It was only after becoming settled in the United Kingdom, as single persons, that the applicants contracted marriage ... The duty imposed by Article 8 cannot be considered as extending to a general obligation on the part of a Contracting State to respect the choice by married couples of the country of their matrimonial residence and to accept the non-national spouses for settlement in that country.[29]

Therefore, unless an element of discrimination can be shown to have been present (as the applicants in that case were able to establish), or the non-viability of family life elsewhere can be shown, the Convention's right to family life does not go very far to respect the residence choices of spouses. The lower level of protection offered to families by the Court underlines the minimal relevance of the ECHR in restraining states' ability to control spouse entry and residence, and has subsequently been criticized as a failure of the European human rights protection system.[30]

---

[28] Contrast, for example, Case C-370/90 *R v Immigration Appeal Tribunal Ex p Secretary of State for the Home Department* [1992] ECR I-4265 with Case C-60/00 *Carpenter v Secretary of State for the Home Department* [2002] ECR I-6279.

[29] *Abdulaziz, Cabales and Balkandali v UK (1985) 7 EHRR 471 [68].*

[30] See the special issue (2009) 11(3) *European Journal of Migration and Law*, especially the articles by De Hart and Farahat, on the shortcomings of the European Court of Human Rights jurisprudence in the field of family migration.

A series of similar restrictive norms and practices has been applied across European states to prevent members of such minorities relying on established preferences for marriage with their kin groups based elsewhere. The UK appears to have been a pioneer in this respect. Sachdeva documents the discriminatory immigration controls chiefly applied to South Asian spouses, mainly husbands, in the 1980s and 1990s under the so-called 'primary purpose rule'.[31] That rule was finally abolished in 1997, but not before the British government had attempted, unsuccessfully, to smuggle it into EU law. Juss further describes the application of immigration restrictions on family members through various other methods, including questioning the veracity of family relationships, finding problems with documentary evidence, casting doubt on the credibility of applicants, and so on.[32] Both writers demonstrate forms of 'othering' at the appellate and judicial review stages as well as during initial decision making at visa posts abroad. Having human rights guarantees does not therefore mean that states will not find some room for maneuver in establishing practices that frustrate family unity or married life.

Meanwhile, reading the way it treated the factual background in the *Abdulaziz* case more closely, it is evident that the Court thought that choosing to marry a non-national spouse whose leave to remain in the UK had already expired, or was about to expire soon, should have put the sponsoring wives on notice that the immigration rules would be against them. This instruction to marry only those who have some sort of security of residence effectively means that legal systems, including the Human Rights Court, participate in creating a hierarchy of desirable spouses, virtually overriding the aim of Article 12 and its right to marry and found a family, also with discriminatory consequences. As immigration lawyers know all too well, the insinuation that one should be more careful in one's choice of spouse is not at all unusual among officials, including some judges. In one case I was instructed on as an expert witness in 2010, the immigration judge had held that continuing family life in Bangladesh for the appellant and her British citizen cohabitant (with three children) would not pose insurmountable difficulties. After all, the man who was of Afghan origin, had naturalized as a British citizen, and had been in the UK for less than ten years![33] The Home Office had even proceeded to make removal directions to Bangladesh for all five family members, including the British citizen man and the child they had together who was also a British citizen. It is no longer enough to be a 'white' British person to establish the right of a spouse to accompany one in the UK. In another recent instance, a British citizen woman now living in Turkey with her Turkish citizen husband, but facing economic and adjustment difficulties there, was told that he would not be admitted into the UK, effectively obliging the couple to remain in Turkey or explore other possibilities. Ironically, legal admission for such a couple under free movement rules into a European Economic Area state other than the UK would be far easier, assuming the lack of other hurdles.

A number of schemes have been developed in recent years premising the right to family formation or reunification upon prospective spousal entrants passing (European) language and culture 'integration tests'. In the Netherlands (since 2006) and Germany (since 2007) pre-entry language tests have been required for citizens of most countries intending to

31 S. Sachdeva, *The Primary Purpose Rule in British Immigration Law* (Trentham Books, Stoke-on-Trent 1993).

32 Juss, *Discretion and Deviation*.

33 Appeal no. AA/02434/2009, Determination dated 19 May 2009.

immigrate as spouses.[34] British policy has caught up with these countries. From 29 November 2010, an English language test or evidence of English language competence is required of spouses applying to join partners in the UK who are not nationals of European Economic Area countries, Switzerland, or of a country listed as being majority English speaking.[35] However, the status of the sponsoring spouse is also important, in that the rules do not apply to spouses of sponsors who are European Economic Area nationals, again reflecting the above-mentioned tension between EU free movement law and 'domestic' rules. These contemporary restrictions in several European countries are increasingly beginning to resemble immigration controls applied in what is now South Africa and Australia during the late nineteenth- and early twentieth century, when language tests were also being used to reject non-European immigrants. Other measures include raising the eligible age for spouse visas to be issued as compared to the legal age for marriage *within* the legal systems concerned, as well as the growing policing of marriages on the pretext of ensuring that such unions have been entered into by 'free consent', and are not a result of familial pressure and therefore not 'forced'.[36] In fact, the UK's requirement that both spouses be of 21 years of age was justified on the basis of concerns about forced marriages. This raising of the qualifying age was recently held to be unlawful for its 'sledgehammer' attempt to curb forced marriages, and therefore in breach of the common law, and a disproportionate interference with the Convention's rights to family life and to marry.[37]

The freedom to marry within Britain also became the subject of restrictions eliciting a finding by the European Court of Human Rights, in the *O'Donoghue* case,[38] of a violation by the UK of the right to marry in Article 12. Under the Asylum and Immigration (Treatment of Claimants, etc.) Act 2004, the UK introduced a requirement, with effect from February 2005, for a certificate for approval for marriage by application to the Home Office. Those who were not European Economic Area nationals or did not have indefinite leave to remain in the UK were obliged to acquire a certificate of approval upon paying a fee and submitting relevant documents. Only after that could they apply to a designated registrar for a licence to marry. Those marrying in the Anglican Church were exempt from such a requirement, while those who had less than three months remaining on a six-month visa did not qualify at all for a certificate. The scheme remained in place despite several British court judgments, including by the House of Lords, pronouncing it as being a violation of Article 12.[39]

---

34 K. McGauran, 'Germany's Immigration Amendment Act of 2007: Achieving Integration of Foreigners?' (2007) 21(4) *Journal of Immigration, Asylum and Nationality Law* 295–310; Human Rights Watch, *The Netherlands: Discrimination in the Name of Integration* (May 2008), at http://www.hrw.org/legacy/backgrounder/2008/netherlands0508/, accessed 31 December 2010.

35 'Listed' does not mean that all countries where there may be a majority of English speakers, such as Nigeria or Philippines, are recognized. Only an ability to speak and understand seems to be required, and not any level of literacy.

36 H. Wray, 'Moulding the Migrant Family' (2009) 29(4) *Legal Studies* 592–618.

37 *Quila & Anor v Secretary of State for the Home Department* [2010] EWCA Civ 1482. The case was upheld by the Supreme Court on the same grounds: [2011] UKSC 45.

38 *O'Donoghue and others v the United Kingdom*, App. No. 34848/07 (ECHR, 14 December 2010) ('*O'Donoghue*').

39 For the House of Lords judgment, see *R (on the application of Baiai and others) v Secretary of State for the Home Department* [2008] UKHL 53, [2009] 1 AC 287 ('*Baiai*').

Despite successive adjustments, widening the range of qualifying applicants, and eventually eliminating the fee requirement, the scheme remained in place. The British state was effectively saying that those not possessing the relevant leave to remain were not eligible marriage partners, even though marriages in the Anglican Church would escape scrutiny. Even those qualifying for a certificate would have to pay for the privilege of being granted one, thus raising the cost of marrying. One of the applicants in *O'Donoghue* was Nigerian, and did not have leave to remain or permission to take up employment on account on his pending application for asylum. His intended wife was on social welfare benefits and the fees charged were consequently unaffordable. After changes to the scheme he was eventually granted a certificate of approval to marry. The European Court nevertheless found that the operation of the scheme violated the couple's right to marry because of his initial ineligibility and, later, because of the fees charged. It also found the scheme to be discriminatory in conjunction with the right to marry and freedom of religion.

The certificate of approval scheme was rightly criticized by the European Court. Having said that, the Court's jurisprudence has not necessarily been rigorous enough against other state interferences in the marrying process. In *O'Donoghue* itself, the Court stated with reference to the House of Lords judgment and previous ECHR case law:

> It is clear from the Court's case-law and from earlier Commission decisions that a Contracting State may properly impose reasonable conditions on the right of a third-country national to marry in order to ascertain whether the proposed marriage is one of convenience and, if necessary, to prevent it. Consequently, a Contracting States will not necessarily be acting in violation of Article 12 of the Convention if they subject marriages involving foreign nationals to scrutiny in order to establish whether or not they are marriages of convenience … Such scrutiny may be exercised by requiring foreign nationals to notify the authorities of an intended marriage and, if necessary, asking them to submit information relevant to their immigration status and to the genuineness of the marriage. Moreover, a requirement that a non-national planning to marry in a Contracting State should first obtain a certificate of capacity will not necessarily violate Article 12 of the Convention … Consequently, the Court agrees with the House of Lords that the requirement under section 19 of the 2004 Act that non-EEA nationals submit an application to the Secretary of State for the Home Department for a Certificate of Approval before being permitted to marry in the United Kingdom is not inherently objectionable.[40]

While the judgment was followed with an announcement by the UK government that the scheme was to be abolished, states could still conceivably continue to find room for maneuvering around the somewhat loose restrictions imposed upon them by the ECHR, penalizing migrants for their marriage choices.[41] It is not unusual to encounter allegations that

---

40 *O'Donoghue*, [87].

41 See also *Baiai*, [20–21] for discussion of other European Court of Human Rights judgments – *Sanders v France* (1996) 87 B-DR 160 and *Klip and Krüger v Netherlands* (1997) 91 A-DR 66 – in

a marriage is one of convenience, which sets up married persons for a potentially expensive and time-consuming struggle through the legal process.[42]

Valid Relationships

The almost obsessive control by European legal systems of the marriage process seems in stark contrast to the relative flexibility for marrying in non-Western jurisdictions, where non-state forms of marriage are often accepted as valid. Establishing the existence of marriage or other family relationship, whether it is one conducted abroad or even in Britain, is increasingly becoming an area of contestation. While the rules of private international law ostensibly ensure that legal acts in one jurisdiction are afforded recognition in another, the process of gaining such recognition is far from smooth and sometimes impossible. The ostensible underpinning of private international law by the principle of the 'comity of nations' is therefore often violated in practice. This is down to a number of reasons. Private international law rules are now often premised on compliance with Western norms systems, rather than concerned to confer recognition on relationships formalized under foreign rules. In such instances, the comity of nations principle seems violated by the unilateral Western insistence that 'our' norms be followed, whether this is done by laws imposed in a single jurisdiction, like England, or through international conventions that actually hide the limited and far from global consensus behind them. This could be seen as a contemporary form of 'legal imperialism' as evidenced, in earlier times, by the imposition of extra-territorial jurisdictions in non-Western countries by Western countries.[43] Even when it is likely that recognition could be forthcoming, for example in the vast majority of marriage cases, the application of private international law rules is subverted by mischievous decision making in practice. There also remains widespread ignorance among officials of how rules in foreign jurisdictions function, which leads to their erroneous interpretations by British officials. The default position adopted in such circumstances is that foreign rules should look like ours, with consequent penalties for individuals and families for following a foreign rule system. The unilateral imposition of extra-territorial norms is well exemplified by Ramnik Shah's account of practice by visa officials at the British High Commission in Kenya requiring evidence of marriage registration from South Asian applicants in defiance of Kenyan rules that recognize marriages without need for registration.[44]

which restrictions imposed by states have been upheld as showing no violation of the Convention. The same cases feature in the Strasbourg judgment in *O'Donoghue*, [87].

42 The use of such allegations is also open in cases with an EU element since the decision of the ECJ in Case C-109/01 *Secretary of State for the Home Department v Akrich* [2003] ECR I-9607, [2003] 3 CMLR 26 after the UK government's suggestion that a marriage of convenience test was necessary.

43 T. Kayaoğlu, *Legal Imperialism: Sovereignty and Extraterritoriality in Japan, the Ottoman Empire, and China* (Cambridge University Press, Cambridge 2010).

44 R. Shah, 'The Phenomenon of the (UK) Officially Inspired Forced Marriages' (2005) 19(3) *Journal of Immigration, Asylum and Nationality Law* 195–8.

There is no doubt, meanwhile, that family law is becoming internationalized in so far as it must reckon with legal acts in other countries because of increasing trans-jurisdictionalism. It is worth noting the observation by Murphy that,

> English family law has had to broaden its horizons in recent years to deal adequately with the myriad of novel issues raised by migrant single adults, migrant families and migrant children. Indeed, there can be no doubt that for a significant minority of people either resident or domiciled in this country, the traditional boundaries of family law (at least so far as it is taught in English law schools) fail to accommodate or give adequate emphasis to what are now crucial international dimensions.[45]

While Murphy is undoubtedly correct in his criticism, his general reliance on the rearrangement of the rules of private international law as a way of solving problems is not convincing enough, because it depends far too much on existing conceptual apparatus of private international law, which increasingly appears outmoded, and still subject to official abuses in practice. Rather, much new thinking seems required that takes on board the virtually limitless plurality that now faces official legal orders. It is certainly not enough for family lawyers to remain focused, as happens often within family law curricula, on the more trendy Western developments such as the recognition of heterosexual cohabitees or same-sex partnerships, which are also driving reforms in the migration context. The champions of such developments generally tend to remain silent on the othering of non-Western family relationships, or even perpetuate negative Eurocentric stereotypes about them.

The limits imposed upon divorcing in plural ways provide a good instance of the manner in which English law attempts to prevent reliance on other laws. As Pearl and Menski have shown, English private international law and the 'domestic' laws were rewritten in the early 1970s in order to prevent Muslims, in particular, from using extra-judicial means of divorcing.[46] When divorcing abroad, therefore, individuals have to make sure that they have gone through 'judicial or other proceedings'. It appears that French judges have been sending even stronger signals about the unacceptability of Muslim divorces.[47] Meanwhile, the practice of divorcing abroad could well have been encouraged by the ban on domestic non-judicial divorces. In practice, the requirement of a 'proceedings' divorce abroad causes many problems for migrants or those engaging in trans-jurisdictional behaviour, not least the non-recognition of a divorce and therefore also a subsequent marriage. The further involvement of the family courts also cannot be ruled out by such non-recognition as one party to the divorce may well claim that no divorce has taken place. Recent evidence indicates the developing practice of prosecutions for bigamy where individuals have married after believing that they were properly divorced in another jurisdiction, and this practice may well be encouraged by

[45] J. Murphy, *International Dimensions in Family Law (Manchester University Press, Manchester 2005)* 2.

[46] D. Pearl and W.F. Menski, *Muslim Family Law* (Sweet & Maxwell, London 1998).

[47] H. Fulchiron, 'The French Family Judge Encounters Cultural Pluralism' in Foblets, Gaudreault-DesBiens and Renteln (eds), *Cultural Diversity and the Law*, 613–34.

one of the parties to the divorce who wants to penalize the other.[48] It is not altogether evident what public benefit accrues from such prosecutions, especially in cases where the divorcing party or parties have followed foreign rules correctly and believe themselves to be validly remarried. Such prosecutions also appear to progress despite the well-established principle that English and Scottish domiciliaries do not even have the capacity to contract polygamous marriages.[49] If anything, this is further evidence of officials disregarding such legal principles to 'teach immigrants a lesson' through the criminal courts.

The non-recognition of remarriage after divorce comes up in other contexts too. In one case I had to deal with as an expert witness, a Bangladeshi woman was penalized several times, forced to go from pillar to post to secure recognition of divorce and a subsequent marriage. Having originally come to the UK as a spouse herself, she divorced her first husband in Bangladesh. Unlike those mentioned above, this was clearly a 'proceedings' divorce that had gone through an official court in Bangladesh. However, advice from an Asian women's group in London was offered to the effect that her divorce would not be recognized, and that divorce proceedings in Britain would be started. Her former husband claimed before the English court that he was divorced already and, having read my expert report to the same effect, the family court judge dismissed the petition. When the woman got married to another man in Bangladesh, and he applied for a spouse visa, the entry clearance officer doubted the validity of the previous divorce and the matter had to be appealed. The woman was able to use my expert report again and the marriage was recognized by an immigration judge. Still, this case illustrates the kinds of hurdles some migrants have to go through unnecessarily in order to secure their legal status before British legal systems. Not only does it highlight penalties experienced because of the ignorance of those who serve the official legal system, but also the on-the-ground unworkability of a system unless one goes through multiple hoops.[50]

Cases of transnational marriage refuse to go away, however, and in the last few years I have been involved as an expert witness in several immigration cases concerning spouses who were not even in the same country when the marriage took place. This often seems to occur within communities dispersed because of war or persecution such as the Somalis. It is not unusual to see the use of proxy or telephone marriages where one or even both spouses are not present at the marriage ceremony. Under Muslim law, and as far as the Muslims worldwide are concerned, these are perfectly lawful arrangements, but are quite likely to be refused by entry clearance officers upon the mere allegation that the 'marriage does not appear to be valid'. This will then force such families into a potentially expensive legal process to establish their right to be in the same country. The less they resemble Western assumptions about proper marriages, the more likely it is they will end up being refused. The Asylum and

48 I am grateful to Prof. Werner Menski and Dr Roger Ballard for sharing information on recent bigamy prosecutions.

49 See *Hussain v Hussain* [1982] 1 All ER 369 and, for further discussion of the context and consequences of that case, see P. Shah, 'Attitudes to Polygamy in English Law' (2003) 52 *International and Comparative Law Quarterly* 359–400.

50 For another such case with even more bouts of struggle, see W.F. Menski, 'Dodgy Asians or Dodgy Laws? The Story of H' (2007) 21(4) *Journal of Immigration, Asylum and Nationality Law* 284–94.

Immigration Tribunal has, for example, stated that Shia *mut'a* or *sighē* marriages are not to be recognized for immigration purposes.[51]

The drawing of such lines, about what is and is not a proper marriage, sometimes goes to extreme lengths. In one recent case, an entry clearance officer alleged that a Muslim *nikah* in a mosque in Delhi did not appear to be valid because the document on which the marriage contract was written was torn unevenly on one side although its terms were fully visible for all to see. Presumably a page with the written contract could look torn on one side if taken from a book of such contracts, but was significant enough for the entry clearance officer to override the other evidence given by both parties. When the matter came to appeal, the Home Office Presenting Officer took up the new point that Muslim marriages in India ought to be registered and, not having been registered officially, the marriage in question was not valid. No one could help the couple at that point – their barrister was not sure about the Indian legal position and nor was the immigration judge. The expert report that I eventually wrote merely stated the blindingly obvious point that Muslim marriages in India need not be registered to be considered valid. The immigration judge at the second hearing was so furious, and rightly, about the level of abuse in this case that he recommended that the matter be reported to the Ombudsman. It may have helped that the Bangladeshi woman in this case, who had met her husband on one of her trips to India, was present in the UK as a Highly Skilled Migrant, a well-paid psychiatrist. One can also see cases from Pakistan where it is asserted that a marriage should have been registered, in obvious disregard of Pakistani law. Pakistani *Christians* may even be told that they should have registered their marriages under the *Muslim* Family Laws Ordinance of 1961!

At other times, marriages are conducted in Britain or other Western jurisdictions that do not comply with official expectations, while people from minority communities appear to be resorting to non-official methods of marrying, sometimes in response to official and other constraints, such as the certificate of approval requirements discussed above. An example of an early post-war Sikh migrant couple shows clearly how a legal system may come under pressure to recognize married status despite non-compliance with official rules. In the *Bath* case,[52] the English Court of Appeal had to decide the married status of just such a couple years later, the husband having died, and the surviving wife needing to establish her right to a widow's pension through successive bouts of legal struggle. The couple had gone through Sikh marriage rites in England, but had not fully complied with the Marriage Acts. The Court, in its wisdom, decided to borrow the principle of presumption of marriage, then still extant in Scottish law, to recognize their marriage.[53] It is reported that marriages, especially among Muslims in the UK, will now often not go through the registration process. One solicitor who specializes in Muslim family law casework suggests that the figure could be as high as 70 per cent of the cases she sees. When legal problems arise, and despite cases like *Bath*, practitioners report a heavy reluctance on the part of family court judges to accept the couples as married, and they may have recourse to one of the *shari'a* councils in Britain instead. These cases may

51 See LS (*Mut'a* or *sighē*) Iran [2007] UKAIT 00072.

52 *Chief Adjudication Officer v Bath* [2000] 1 FCR 419, [2000] 1 FLR 8, [2000] Fam Law 91.

53 The Family Law (Scotland) Act 2006, section 3 now prevents Scottish courts using the presumption of marriage principle to confer recognition, thus taking away a remedy often used by ethnic minorities.

also have severe consequences in terms of custody rights of a parent.[54] The question might arise about the possible recognition of such marriages elsewhere than in Britain. In one asylum-related case, the (now) Immigration and Asylum Chamber of the Upper Tribunal wanted to know whether a *nikah* conducted in a mosque in east London, without any official registration, would be recognized in Pakistan as a proper marriage.[55] I expressed the view that in Pakistan such a marriage would be considered valid even if it would not in Britain, although my view was never communicated to the immigration judge re-hearing the case.

Concluding Observations

Despite attempts by states to restrict family-based or other forms of migration, it is bound to continue in different ways. Thus the issues discussed in this chapter will be of ever-growing salience. This means that European states face tough choices about how to move next to take into account the 'superdiverse' conditions of their societies, which have strong implications in terms of legal diversity also. The old methods of dealing with such diversities are failing and costing a lot in terms of money, ill feeling and injustice, which can rebound on the larger societies if care is not taken. Readjusting the old models, for example within private international law, to accommodate minorities and transnational communities more fairly could be one solution, but, while such suggestions are made from an obvious sympathy for the plight of parties caught in legal struggles, I am fearful that such re-jigging of old models simply ends up presenting the same wine in new bottles and does not help in addressing the underlying ideological and practical problems. The presence of transnational communities means that there is a collapse of the boundaries between 'domestic' and private international laws. However, that mental barriers are strongly present can be seen in the restrictions and blockages illustrated in the present chapter. Reading about the century-old story of Gandhi's campaigns in South Africa, one comes across the ruling of the Supreme Court in 1913 that effectively refused to recognize all non-Christian marriages, with severe consequences for families seeking to reunite and leading to other legal barriers for Indian workers.[56] A century later we may ask why European legal systems continue to replicate such restrictions in more secularized forms. Contemporary interferences effectively tend to rely on long-present Christian presuppositions of family law including consent in marriage, the involvement of an intercessory to formalize marriage, restrictiveness around divorcing, and so on. However secularized and universalized such normative assumptions may have become, it is futile to deny their specific lineage, which is linked to one culture, the Western culture. That they

54 See *A v H* [2009] EWHC 636 (Fam), [2009] 4 All ER 641, where a father, who had married by *nikah*, subsequently divorced and the mother of the child, his former wife, took the child to Holland. The English court did not recognize custody under the Hague Convention on the Civil Aspects of International Child Abduction 1980 because he was held to have had no 'parental responsibility'. The judge, Sir Christopher Sumner, specifically refused to apply the presumption of marriage on account of the short duration of the marriage, even though he had been allowed to register as the father of the child by officials.

55 Appeal no. AA/15800/2009, Determination dated 29 July 2010.

56 *Esop v Union Government (Minister of the Interior)* (1913) CPD 133.

derive from a specific culture entails problems of mutual recognition that need to be taken into account for the ends of inter-cultural justice. It seems that, rather than rely any longer on the outdated concept of the 'comity of nations', we need to try to move towards a 'comity of peoples'. It is the presence of transnational communities that span nation-states which is making us realize this more and more, and the implications are not restricted to the Western legal systems only: they face all legal systems in different ways – a big global challenge.

References

Balagangadhara, S.N. and M. Keppens, 'Reconceptualising the Postcolonial Project: Beyond the Strictures and Structures of Orientalism' (2009) 11(1) *Interventions* 50–68

Ballard, R., 'The Dynamics of Translocal and Transjurisdictional Networks: A Diasporic Perspective' (2009) 1(2) *South Asian Diaspora* 141–66.

Beck-Gernsheim, E., 'Transnational Lives, Transnational Marriages: A Review of Evidence from Migrant Communities in Europe' (2007) 7(3) *Global Networks* 271–88.

Bhabha, J., 'Lone Travelers: Rights, Criminalization, and the Transnational Migration of Unaccompanied Children' (2000) 7 *University of Chicago Law School Roundtable* 269–94.

Bogusz, B. et al., *Irregular Migration and Human Rights: Theoretical, European and International Perspectives* (Brill, Leiden 2004).

Böhning, W.R., *The Migration of Workers in the United Kingdom and the European Community* (Oxford University Press for the Institute of Race Relations, London 1972).

Bryceson, D. and U. Vuorella, *The Transnational Family: New European Frontiers and Global Networks* (Berg, Oxford 2002).

Calavita, K., *Immigrants at the Margins: Law, Race and Exclusion in Southern Europe* (Cambridge University Press, Cambridge 2005).

Castles, S. and G. Kosack, *Immigrant Workers and Class Structure in Western Europe* (Oxford University Press for the Institute of Race Relations, London 1973).

Castles, S., H. Booth and T. Wallace, *Here for Good: Western Europe's Ethnic Minorities* (Pluto, London 1984).

Chiba, M., 'Other Phases of Legal Pluralism in the Contemporary World' (1998) 11(3) *Ratio Juris* 228–45.

Collinson, S., *Europe and International Migration* (Pinter Publishers, London 1993).

Cotterrell, R., 'Transnational Communities and the Concept of Law' (2008) 21(1) *Ratio Juris* 1–18.

Foblets, M.-C., J.-F. Gaudreault-DesBiens and A.D. Renteln (eds), *Cultural Diversity and the Law: State Responses from Around the World* (Bruylant, Brussels 2010).

Fournier, P., *Muslim Marriage in Western Courts: Lost in Transplantation* (Ashgate, Farnham 2010).

Fulchiron, H., 'The French Family Judge Encounters Cultural Pluralism' in M.-C. Foblets, J.F. Gaudreault-DesBiens and A.D. Renteln (eds), *Cultural Diversity and the Law: State Responses from Around the World* (Bruylant, Brussels 2010) 613–34.

Glick Schiller, N., 'Transborder Citizenship: An Outcome of Legal Pluralism within Transnational Social Fields' in F. von Benda-Beckmann, K. von Benda-Beckmann and A.

Griffiths (eds), *Mobile People, Mobile Law: Expanding Legal Relations in a Contracting World* (Ashgate, Aldershot 2005) 27–49.

Grillo, R., 'An Excess of Alterity? Debating Difference in a Multicultural Society' (2007) 30(6) *Ethnic and Racial Studies* 979–98.

Grillo, R. et al., *Legal Practice and Cultural Diversity* (Ashgate, Farnham 2009).

Grillo, R. (ed.), *The Family in Question: Immigrant and Ethnic Minorities in Multicultural Europe* (Amsterdam University Press, Amsterdam 2008).

Human Rights Watch, *The Netherlands: Discrimination in the Name of Integration* (May 2008), at http://www.hrw.org/legacy/backgrounder/2008/netherlands0508/, accessed 31 December 2010.

Jackson, D., *Immigration: Law and Practice* (Sweet and Maxwell, London 1996).

Joppke, C., 'The Retreat of Multiculturalism in the Liberal State: Theory and Policy' (2004) 55(2) *The British Journal of Sociology* 237–57.

Juss, S., *Discretion and Deviation in the Administration of Immigration Control* (Sweet and Maxwell, London 1997).

Kayaoğlu, T., *Legal Imperialism: Sovereignty and Extraterritoriality in Japan, the Ottoman Empire, and China* (Cambridge University Press, Cambridge 2010).

Kofman, E., 'Family-related Migration: A Critical Review of European Studies' (2004) 30(2) *Journal of Ethnic and Migration Studies* 243–62.

Kofman, E. and V. Meetoo, 'Family Migration' in *World Migration Report 2008: Managing Labour Mobility in the Evolving Global Economy* (International Organization for Migration, Geneva 2008) 151–72.

Löwenheim, O. and O. Gazit, 'Power and Examination: A Critique of Citizenship Tests' (2009) 40(2) *Security Dialogue* 145–67.

Macdonald, I., 'Preface' in P. Shah and W.F. Menski (eds), *Migration, Diasporas and Legal Systems in Europe* (Routledge Cavendish, London 2006) xv–xviii.

McGauran, K., 'Germany's Immigration Amendment Act of 2007: Achieving Integration of Foreigners?' (2007) 21(4) *Journal of Immigration, Asylum and Nationality Law* 295–310.

Mehdi, R. et al. (eds), *Religion and Law in Multicultural Societies* (DJØF Publishing, Copenhagen 2008).

Menski, W.F., *Comparative Law in a Global Context: The Legal Systems of Asia and Africa* (Cambridge University Press, Cambridge 2006).

Menski, W.F., 'Dodgy Asians or Dodgy Laws? The Story of H' (2007) 21(4) *Journal of Immigration, Asylum and Nationality Law* 284–94.

Menski, W.F., 'Immigration and Multiculturalism in Britain: New Issues in Research and Policy' (2002) XII *KIAPS: Bulletin of Asia-Pacific Studies* 43–66.

Murphy, J., *International Dimensions in Family Law* (Manchester University Press, Manchester 2005).

Nyíri, P., *New Chinese Migrants in Europe: The Case of the Chinese Community in Hungary* (Ashgate, Aldershot 1999).

Pearl, D. and W.F. Menski, *Muslim Family Law* (Sweet & Maxwell, London 1998).

Romaniszyn, K., 'The Cultural Implications of International Migrations' (2004) 2(146) *Polish Sociological Review* 141–59.

Ruskola, T., 'Legal Orientalism' (2002) 101(1) *Michigan Law Review* 179–234.

Ryan, B. and V. Mitsilegas, *Extraterritorial Immigration Control: Legal Challenges* (Martinus Nijhoff, Leiden 2010).
Sachdeva, S., *The Primary Purpose Rule in British Immigration Law* (Trentham Books, Stoke-on-Trent 1993).
Shachar, A., 'The Race for Talent: High Skilled Migrants and Competitive Immigration Regimes' (2006) 81 *New York University Law Review* 101–58.
Shah, P., 'Attitudes to Polygamy in English Law' (2003) 52 *International and Comparative Law Quarterly* 359–400.
Shah, P., 'Transnational Hindu Law Adoptions: Recognition and Treatment in Britain' (2009) 5(2) *International Journal of Law in Context* 107–30.
Shah, P. and W.F. Menski (eds), *Migration, Diasporas and Legal Systems in Europe* (Routledge Cavendish, London 2006).
Shah, R., 'The Phenomenon of the (UK) Officially Inspired Forced Marriages' (2005) 19(3) *Journal of Immigration, Asylum and Nationality Law* 195–8.
Van Oers, R., E. Ersbøll and D. Kostakopoulou (eds), *A Re-definition of Belonging? Language and Integration Tests in Europe* (Martinus Nijhoff, Leiden 2010).
Vertovec, S., 'Super-diversity and its Implications' (2007) 30(6) *Ethnic and Racial Studies* 1024–54.
Von Benda-Beckmann, F., K. von Benda-Beckmann and A. Griffiths (eds), *Mobile People, Mobile Law: Expanding Legal Relations in a Contracting World* (Ashgate, Aldershot 2005).
Wray, H., 'Moulding the Migrant Family' (2009) 29(4) *Legal Studies* 592–618.

Secret Immigration Business: Policy Transfers and the Tyranny of Deterrence Theory

Mary Crock[1] and Daniel Ghezelbash[2]

1. Borrowed Policies and Assumptions about Efficacy

Australia's political discourse on refugees and border control has been dominated in recent times by claims made about the efficacy of deterrent policies. The major parties are staking their political fortunes on the introduction of another version of the 'Pacific Solution' – offshore processing, interdiction, mandatory detention and versions of temporary protection. This, it claims, is the only way to 'Stop the Boats', maritime vessels arriving in Australia without authorization carrying asylum seekers from any of a variety of troubled countries. With a view to achieving this end, the Labor government is committed establishing regional processing centres, firm in the belief that deflecting asylum seekers to Nauru and Papua New Guinea's (PNG) Manus Island will arrest the flow of irregular maritime arrivals. We have joined our voices to those of others railing against the assumptions made about cause and effect in irregular migration – in particular about the value of policies presumed to deter boat people.[3] A more worrying development is the decision by the conservative Canadian government to adopt Australian policies of mandatory immigration detention and temporary permits as deterrent measures aimed at undocumented arrivals.[4]

The enactment of the *Protecting Canada's Immigration System Act* by the Canadian parliament reflects an increasing propensity for governments to 'borrow' migration laws and policies from other jurisdictions. In some respects, legal 'borrowing' has long been a feature of law reform and the development of legal systems. As Roscoe Pound noted in 1938, 'history of

---

[1] Professor of Public Law, The University of Sydney. We wish to thank our research colleagues for comments on earlier drafts of this chapter, in particular Anna Boucher, Michael Hiscox, Eiko Thielemann, Michel Beine and Ron McCallum. Thanks also to the Department of Immigration and Citizenship (DIAC) and the Australian Research Council for support of our comparative research. The views we express and any errors that remain are ours alone.

[2] BA (Hons) LLB (Hons) (Syd), Doctoral Student and adjunct lecturer, The University of Sydney.

[3] See Mary Crock and Daniel Ghezelbash, 'Do Loose Lips Bring Ships? The Role of Policy, Politics and Human Rights in Managing Unauthorised Boat Arrivals' (2010) 19 *Griffith Law Review* 238–87.

[4] *Protecting Canada's Immigration System Act* S.C. 2012; Bill C-31: An Act to amend the Immigration and Refugee Protection Act, The Balanced Refugee Reform Act, the Marine Transportation Security Act and the Department of Citizenship and Immigration Act.

a system of law is largely a history of borrowings of legal materials from other legal systems and of assimilation of materials from outside the law'.[5] In an increasingly globalized world, however, the phenomenon has increased at an exponential rate.[6] As we explore in this article, migration policy is an area of law in which governments are particularly concerned about what other jurisdictions are doing. Western developed nations generally have very similar policy objectives: to attract what they perceive as 'good' migrants such as skilled workers and investors and to deter 'bad' migrants such as asylum seekers and irregular arrivals. In the area of refugee and asylum law, this may be accentuated where governments are operating under a common framework created by the UN Convention relating to the Status of Refugees and its related Protocol.[7]

There are obvious reasons why governments might want to exchange ideas about immigration, particularly where effective policies depend on multilateral action. As we explain in section 2, since the 1990s there has been a rapid proliferation of regional and international initiatives, activities and structures dedicated to international migration policy and practice.[8] States have come to recognize that they can benefit from cooperation on migration issues, and are increasingly willing to converge in an informal, non-binding way. They now realize the limitations of strictly national or unilateral policies (especially measures against irregular migration) and the inter-relatedness among migration and other transnational issues.[9]

Shachar has noted that states are competing to attract the best and brightest migrants.[10] In section 3, we argue that there is strong evidence that states are observing (and copying) the policies of comparator countries because they are also competing to *deter* irregular migrants. The assumption is that asylum seekers choose countries in which to seek refuge according to ease of access and what might loosely be termed immigration and settlement outcomes. Countries with generous laws and policies then become targets for people smugglers and traffickers. After the Labor party announced a deal to return asylum seekers to Malaysia for processing in July 2011, it is interesting that New Zealand and Canada were named expressly as alternative destinations for asylum seekers who might otherwise have tried their luck in Australia.[11]

---

5 Roscoe Pound, *The Formative Era of American Law* (Boston: Little Brown & Co, 1938) at 94, quoted in Rudolf B. Schlesinger, Hans W. Baade, Peter E. Herzog and Eduard M. Wise, *Comparative Law: Cases, Text, Materials* (New York: Foundation Press, 1998, 6th edn) at 10, note 26.

6 David Westbrook, 'Theorizing the Diffusion of Law in an Age of Globalization: Conceptual Difficulties, Unstable Imaginations, and the Effort to think Gracefully Nonetheless' (2008) 3 *Annals Fac L Belgrade International Ed* 159–79 at 161.

7 Convention relating to the Status of Refugees (1951) 189 UNTS 137; Protocol relating to the Status of Refugees (1967) 606 UNTS 267.

8 See Colleen Thouez and Frédérique Channac, 'Convergence and Divergence in Migration Policy: The Role of Regional Consultative Processes', *Global Migration Perspectives* (Global Commission on International Migration, no. 20, January 2005) at 3.

9 Colleen Thouez and Frédérique Channac, 'Shaping International Migration Policy: The Role of Regional Consultative Processes' (2006) 29(2) *West European Politics* 370–87 at 372.

10 Ayelet Shachar, 'The Race for Talent: Highly Skilled Migrants and Competitive Immigration Regimes' (2006) 81 *New York University Law Review* 148–206.

11 See AFP, 'New Zealand Shuts Door to Refugees', *Sydney Morning Herald*, 12 July 2011, at 1: http://www.smh.com.au/world/nz-shuts-door-on--asylum-seekers-20110712-1hbeo.html

As legal academics and immigration practitioners, two things stand out for us. The first is the relative dearth of hard research on the real effects (and effectiveness) of policy measures. The discourse on immigration and border control in many countries seems to be characterized by assertion and assumption rather than by reasoned and evidence-based exposition. The second feature is the domestic focus of most discussions about immigration policy and law. While politicians and bureaucrats are clearly talking to each other about what (comparative) policies and laws are effective to meeting their migration goals, practitioners and academics are not doing the same within and across their respective disciplines. We critique what we will term 'unreasoned' policy borrowings, examining what happens when governments adopt laws without regard to the criticisms that have or might have been made of the measures when first introduced in another country and context. The 'tyranny' of deterrence theory in the asylum space is felt in the fiscal and human cost of measures that ultimately deliver few tangible benefits for the countries in which they are introduced. It is our contention that academics should take a more active role in sharing and discussing policy developments in their countries so as to equip each other with the knowledge to counter unsubstantiated claims about the efficacy of particular policies. We conclude with a brief examination of the type of research we think is needed if we are truly to understand and respond to the phenomenon of irregular maritime migration.

2. Policy Transfers and Inter-governmental Dialogues

Dolowitz and Marsh define the process of policy transfer as 'the process by which knowledge of policies, administrative arrangements, institutions and ideas in one political system (past or present) is used in the development of policies, administrative arrangements, institutions and ideas in another political system'.[12] There can be no dispute that governments all around the world are discussing, coordinating and borrowing migration laws and policies from each other. These activities take place in a variety of formal and informal forums in which state representatives meet to discuss common problems, share experiences, and discuss the development of migration policy and law.

Although migration is an obvious globalizing force,[13] it is an interesting feature of the United Nations system that no single multilateral structure has been established to regulate this area of law and policy.[14] Indeed, with the possible exception of asylum and refugee protection, there is no formal (generic) migration regime that involves binding inter-state

(accessed: 11 August 2012). The group was holding banners reading: 'Our future life is in New Zealand' and 'We like to go to New Zealand'.

[12] David Dolowitz and David Marsh, 'Learning from Abroad: The Role of Policy Transfer in Contemporary Policy-making' (2000) 13(1) *Governance* 5–23 at 8.

[13] See Catherine Dauvergne, *Making People Illegal: What Globalisation Means for Migration and Law* (Cambridge: Cambridge University Press, 2008).

[14] Alexander Betts, *Global Migration Governance* (Oxford: Oxford University Press, 2011) at 1 and 11. See also Jagdish Bhagwati, 'Borders Beyond Control' (2003) 82(1) *Foreign Affairs* 98–104; and Khalid Koser, 'International Migration and Global Governance' (2010) 16(3) *Global Governance* 301–15.

agreements. This contrasts with the global governance of most trans-boundary issue areas in which the main international organizations' work is underpinned by a mandate to uphold a particular normative framework based in international law.[15] The International Organization of Migration (IOM) is the closest example of a multilateral governance body, but it bears little resemblance to the mechanisms created to oversee matters such as health, monetary stability, or trade. These are regulated through the World Health Organization (WHO), International Monetary Fund (IMF) and World Trade Organization (WTO) frameworks. The bottom line is that sovereign states retain a significant degree of autonomy in determining their migration policies.

Although the IOM has at its centre the management of (primarily irregular) migration, it exists outside the UN system. The organization operates first and foremost as a service provider to individual states that pay for its services. It has no clear mandate provided by the international community, in the way that most UN agencies operate under statutes that provide the agencies with normative authority.[16] Having said this, the IOM does sponsor informal and non-binding consultative processes through its International Dialogue on Migration (IDM). This organization also sponsors research and offers training to its 'client' states.[17]

Such regulation of migration as exists is fragmented, dealing with particular aspects of migration policy: low-skilled labour migration, high-skilled labour migration, irregular migration, international travel, lifestyle migration, environmental migration, human trafficking and smuggling, asylum and refugee protection, internally displaced people, diaspora, remittances, and root causes. Each is regulated differently at the global level.

For example, the Executive Committee of the UN agency responsible for refugees and (some) displaced persons – the UN High Commission for Refugees – does develop policies of sorts in the form of 'Conclusions' issued at annually convened meetings.[18] The International Labor Organization (ILO) has taken a strong interest in migrant workers, a group who are also covered by a specific (albeit poorly subscribed) human rights convention.[19] In 2011 a Special Rapporteur for migrant workers was appointed under the auspices of the UN Office of Human Rights. Other bodies that have taken on issues relating to migrants generally or particular groups of migrants are the WTO,[20] the WHO, the UN Population Fund (UNFPA), the UN Education, Science and the Communication Organization (UNESCO), and the UN Development Programme (UNDP).

---

15 Betts, ibid., at 86.

16 For example, UNHCR was established by the UN General Assembly as a subsidiary organ under Article 22 of the United Nations Charter. See Guy Goodwin-Gill and Jane McAdam, *The Refugee in International Law* (London: Oxford University Press, 2008, 3rd edn) at 428.

17 For a list of recent initiatives, see IOM, 'International Migration Law, Training and Capacity Building in Immigration Law, Recent Activities', at http://www.iom.int/jahia/Jahia/pid/169 (accessed: 18 July 2011).

18 See Goodwin-Gill and McAdam, *Refugee in International* Law, at 215–17, 429–30ff.

19 See *International Convention on the Protection of the Rights of All Migrant Workers and Members of Their Families* (1990) 2220 UNTS 3. On the international protections available to migrant workers, see Laurie Berg, 'At the Border and Between the Cracks' (2007) 8 *Melbourne Journal of International Law* 1–34.

20 See in particular work on temporary skills transfers and migrants who are service providers (as defined under Mode IV of the General Agreement on Trade in Services, GATS).

Migration law and policy is also increasingly being discussed in formal regional institutions. In recent years, regional organizations and economic integration processes such as the European Union, the Association of Southeast Asian Nations (ASEAN), the African Union, the Common Market of the South and the Southern African Development Community, to name but a few, have added migration to their agendas.[21] These many and varied institutions and processes have provided both regular and ad hoc opportunities for states to discuss migration policy – and to exchange ideas. Other prominent official international and regional forums include the OECD's High Level policy forum on Migration, the EU ministerial conference on asylum, and the Asia Pacific Consultations on refugees, displaced persons and migrants.[22]

In addition to these formal institutions, recent years have seen the proliferation of Regional Consultative Processes (RCPs) in which states with similar backgrounds and interests meet regularly to discuss policy for the purpose of exchanging ideas and developing 'best practice' models.[23] The term 'region' is used loosely. For example, Australian migration officials meet regularly with their counterparts from their 'Group of 5' that include geographically remote but culturally and experientially close countries like Canada, the United States and the United Kingdom. RCPs vary greatly in their composition, history, purpose, and organizational frameworks, but they do share the principal characteristics of being created to meet regularly for the specific purpose of discussing migration issues and generating informal, non-binding agreements.[24] In this respect they differ from other regional bodies where migration might be but one of many themes for discussion. By design, they are processes that foster the transfer of migration policy and practice. This is evidenced through the immediate objectives, which include capacity building and fostering dialogue.[25]

Over the last ten years, RCPs have been established in most regions of the world. Examples include: between Europe, North America and Australia through the 'Inter-governmental Consultations on Asylum'; in Northern and Central America through the 'Puebla Process'; in Asia through the 'Manila Process'; in the Asia Pacific through the 'Asia Pacific Consultations'; within Europe with the 'Budapest Process' and the Mediterranean '5 plus 5' Process'; and in Africa with the International Dialogue on Migration in West Africa and the International Dialogue on Migration in Southern Africa.[26]

In addition to these formal processes, government representatives hold regular *informal* ad hoc bilateral and multilateral meetings to discuss the relative success and failure of migration policies. Indeed, the decision of the Canadian Minister for Immigration to introduce

---

21 Randall Hansen, *An Assessment of Principal Regional Consultative Processes on Migration* (Geneva: IOM, 2010) at 13.

22 Another example of an informal meeting was the Global Forum on Migration and Development (GFMD), which was convened first in 2007 with the participation of 156 states and thereafter annually.

23 Betts, *Global Migration Governance*, at 7–18; see also IOM, *Global Meeting of Chairs and Secretariats of Regional Consultative Processes on Migration: Bangkok, 4–5 June 2009: Summary Report* (Geneva: IOM, 2009) at 10.

24 As defined by Hansen, *Assessment of Principal Regional Consultative Processes on Migration*, at 12–13.

25 See Thouez and Channac, 'Convergence and Divergence in Migration Policy', at 8.

26 See Betts, *Global Migration Governance*, at 18; Thouez and Channac, 'Convergence and Divergence in Migration Policy', at 5–6; Hansen, *Assessment of Principal Regional Consultative Processes on Migration*, at 57–84.

mandatory detention and temporary protection visas for asylum seekers was made following informal meetings with Australian and French officials.[27]

The increase in dialogue between governments has major ramifications for the study of migration law and policy. It is no longer sufficient to have comprehensive knowledge of the law of a domestic jurisdiction. With governments engaging in legal borrowing from foreign jurisdictions, migration scholars need to keep abreast of developments abroad and engage in the critical evaluation of foreign policies that their government may be considering to borrow. As we shall explore, there are practical reasons why academic involvement in comparative policy making should be encouraged. The forums in which discussion and policy swapping currently occur are typically closed and exclusionary affairs – at the very least lacking in transparency. They are, almost by definition, entirely focused on governments.[28] In the result, governments may not be getting the whole story.

3. Policy Transfers in the Asylum Space

3.1 The US and Australia Align Policies to Stop the Boats

What is it about irregular maritime arrivals that this phenomenon causes such acute angst in countries all around the world that are otherwise quite relaxed about large-scale immigration? In many countries – with Australia and the United States leading the way – the most regressive and punitive immigration policies can often be traced back to a desire to deter or deny 'boat people', the phrase used since the Vietnam War to describe irregular maritime arrivals. If the collaborative arrangements to resolve the refugee crisis after that conflict are something of a modern 'gold standard' in regional cooperation between countries,[29] the asylum space continues to be a venue for obvious examples of transnational policy transfer.

The opacity of RPCs and of the relationships that develop between politicians and bureaucrats in the course of informal consultative processes make it difficult to produce easy 'proof' that policy transfers are occurring. It is not easy to document statements made in confidence between state officials who would be sanctioned for disclosing either their identity or the content of their discussions. Even so, when the Conservative Coalition government in

27 Citizenship and Immigration Canada (CIC), News Release: Governments of Canada and Australia working to combat human smuggling, 19 September 2010, at http://www.cic.gc.ca/english/department/media/releases/2010/2010-09-19.asp (accessed: 22 August 2012); CIC, News Release: Meeting with senior officials from Australia at Parliament House to discuss effective solutions to combat the global problems of migrant smuggling and human trafficking, 20 September 2010, at http://www.cic.gc.ca/english/department/media/photos/2010/2010-09-20/photo.asp?p=1 (accessed: 22 August 2012).

28 Thouez and Channac, 'Convergence and Divergence in Migration Policy', at 4, 13–14.

29 See W. Courtland Robinson, 'The Comprehensive Plan of Action for Indochinese Refugees, 1989–1997: Sharing the Burden and Passing the Buck' (2004) 17 *Journal of Refugee Studies* 319–33; Arthur Helton, 'Refugee Determination under the Comprehensive Plan of Action: Overview and Assessment' (1993) 5 *International Journal of Refugee Law* 544–58. See also Martin Tsamenyi, *The Vietnamese Boat People and International Law* (Brisbane: Griffith University, 1981).

Australia introduced the various elements of the 'Pacific Solution' in 2001 in an effort to halt the arrival of boats carrying upwards of 500 undocumented asylum seekers at a time, it was fairly obvious to many observers that the scheme was modelled on American precedents.[30]

The Australian government's stand began in August 2001 with the move to prevent the Norwegian registered container ship MV *Tampa* from delivering onto Australian soil 433 asylum seekers rescued at sea from a sinking Indonesian ferry. The federal government prevented the MV *Tampa* from entering Australian territorial waters by boarding the ship with Special Air Services troops. It later introduced a series of legislative reforms to deprive the 'rescuees' of access to regular Australian asylum procedures. The changes included the 'excision' from Australian migration laws of certain offshore territories (preventing asylum seekers from lodging protection claims)[31] and the deflection of a certain number of boat people to Nauru, Manus Island and New Zealand for the processing of their claims. Crucially, a full-scale interdiction programme – code-named Operation Relex – was instituted, with refugee boats being intercepted and towed back into Indonesian waters (where UNHCR undertook to process asylum claims).

North American scholars will recognize immediately in this brief description, resonances with the programme to interdict asylum seekers and irregular maritime arrivals from Haiti going back as far as the 1980s.[32] Although Guantanamo Bay is better known in recent times as an 'exceptional' space created to exclude enemy combatants from the protections of the American justice system,[33] it was created first as a holding and processing centre for fugitives from Haiti and Cuba. The Haitian interdiction program culminated in the interception and forced return to Haiti of many thousands of irregular maritime arrivals.[34] It involved (and involves) both mandatory immigration detention and the creation of a special regime for the

---

30 As an advisor to two senators, Crock was shown documentation on the American interdiction programmes that was given in confidence to Australian parliamentarians during the crisis that unfolded around the Tampa Affair. Discussions occurred between senior American bureaucrats and their Australian counterparts.

31 The excision zone was eventually extended to include almost all but mainland Australia. A new category of 'off-shore entry person' was created to catch all asylum seekers who landed without a valid visa or authority on an excised territory. While 'off-shore entry' persons were sent to Nauru and Manus Island for processing under the Coalition government, the subsequent Labor government has moved the location of processing to the Australian territory of Christmas Island.

32 Following is a selection of the many articles written on the interdiction program that has been run in the United States since the early 1980s: Margaret A. Coon, 'The Law of Interdiction: Time for Change' (1980) 27 *Louisiana Bar Journal* 223–8; Louis B. Sohn, 'Interdiction of Vessels on the High Seas' (1984) 18 *International Lawyer* 411–19; and Bill Frelick, 'Haitian Boat Interdiction and Return: First Asylum and First Principles of Refugee Protection' (in *Symposium: Refusing Refugees: Political and Legal Barriers to Asylum*) (1993) 26(3) *Cornell International Law Journal* 675–717.

33 See Fleur Johns, 'Guantanamo Bay and the Annihilation of the Exception' (2005) 16 *European Journal of International Law* 613–37.

34 See James R. Zink, 'Race and Foreign Policy in Refugee Law: A Historical Perspective of the Haitian Refugee Crises' (1998) 48 *De Paul Law Review* 559–617; Bill Frelick, 'Haitian Boat Interdiction: First Asylum and First Principles of Refugee Protection' (1993) 26 *Georgetown Immigration Law Journal* 675–95; Hiroshi Motomura, 'Haitian Asylum Seekers: Interdiction and Immigrants' Rights' (1993) 15 *Immigration and Nationality* 531–55; Thomas David Jones, 'A Human Rights Tragedy: The Cuban and Haitian Refugee Crises Revisited' (1995) 9(3) *Georgetown Immigration Law Journal* 479–523; and the various articles in (1993) 7 *Georgetown Immigration Law Journal*.

processing of asylum claims. In effect, the American government created for irregular maritime arrivals a second (procedurally inferior) refugee status assessment regime in parallel to that pertaining to persons seeking refugee protection within mainland America. Interestingly, in both Australia and the United States, public interest advocates came forward to challenge the policies and practices adopted in these attempts to 'stop the boats'. In both countries, in the heat of the moment (so to speak) the judiciary declined to intervene.[35] Again, both countries have expended extraordinary amounts of money over the years on measures adopted for the purpose of deterring or preventing irregular maritime arrivals.[36]

3.2 Canada Follows Australia's Lead

The arrival on Canadian shores of ships carrying a sizeable consignment of asylum seekers from Sri Lanka induced similar panic reactions in that country in 2009.[37] The events sparked another (obvious) example of policy borrowing that reflects the increase in communication between governments about migration policy. The process culminated in the passage of the *Protecting Canada's Immigration System Act* (or Bill C-31) in June 2012.[38] The Act gives the Canadian Minister of Citizenship, Immigration and Multiculturalism the authority to label groups of non-citizens as 'designated foreign nationals'. The fact that the policy was a direct reaction to these arrivals was evident in the fact that Vic Toews, Minister for Public Safety, announced the policy changes while standing in front of the *Ocean Lady* at the Marine Base at which it had been impounded.

The legislation provides that the designation process would be triggered where non-citizens enter Canada in violation of immigration law, with the assistance of a smuggler motivated by profit, *or* where the Minister believes the non-citizens as a group could not be examined and dealt with 'in a timely manner'. The two most significant ramifications of

35 As Crock has noted, 'In both cases, the failure of the court actions was predicated on two factors. The first was the supremacy of domestic law over international law; and the second was what might be termed the "territoriality" principle, or the notion that applicable international legal norms apply only to persons physically present on State territory.' See *Sale v Haitian Centers Council Inc* 113 S Ct 2549 (1993); *Victorian Council for Civil Liberties and Ors v Minister for Immigration, Multiculturalism and Indigenous Affairs* (2001) 110 FCR 452 (North J); *Ruddock v Vadarlis* (2001) 110 FCR 491 (FFC); and *Vadarlis v Minister for Immigration and Multicultural Affairs & Ors* M93/2001 (High Court of Australia, transcript, 27 November 2001). See Mary Crock, 'In the Wake of the Tampa: Conflicting Visions of International Refugee Law in the Management of Refugee Flows' (2003) 12 *Pacific Rim Law & Policy Journal* 49–96 at 62–3.

36 For a discussion of the cost of these policies in Australia, see Crock and Ghezelbash, 'Do Loose Lips Bring Ships?', at 258–59, 262 and 270.

37 The *Ocean Lady*, carrying 76 Tamil men, was intercepted off the coast of Vancouver Island on 17 October 2009. This was followed by the MV *Sun Sea*, which was intercepted off the west coast of Canada on 13 August 2010 with 490 Tamil men, women and children on board. See Public Safety Canada: News Release: Preventing the Abuse of Canada's Immigration System by Human Smugglers, 19 January 2011, at http://www.publicsafety.gc.ca/media/nr/2011/nr20110119-2-eng.aspx (accessed: 22 August 2012).

38 The Act incorporated provisions first proposed in 2010 in Bill C-49 and re-presented in Bill C-4 in 2011.

being classed as a 'designated foreign national' relate to detention provisions and the type of protection an asylum seeker will be afforded if found to be a genuine refugee.

Before the passage of the *Protecting Canada's Immigration System Act*, Canadian law limited the detention of asylum seekers to circumstances where there were reasonable grounds to believe that the person in question: (1) was unlikely to appear at their next hearing or interview; (2) was considered a danger to public safety; (3) was inadmissible on the ground of security or for violating human or international rights; or (4) could not provide adequate identification to satisfy the officer of the person's identity.[39] Detainees had the right to a review hearing within 48 hours before the Immigration and Refugee Board (IRB).[40] If the IRB determined detention to be necessary, another hearing would take place within seven days of the first review.[41] Thereafter hearings would be conducted every 30 days as long as the individual remained in detention.[42]

The mandatory detention provisions introduced by the *Protecting Canada's Immigration System Act* dramatically changes this regime. The legislation provides for the mandatory detention of 'designated foreign nationals' to allow for determination of identity, inadmissibility and illegal activity. So, when a person is classed as a 'designated foreign national', he or she *must* be taken into detention upon arrival in Canada. The only avenue for release is to appeal directly to the Minister and for the Minister to decide that exceptional circumstances exist. Otherwise, asylum seekers face detention for the duration of the (generally lengthy) status determination process. The original legislative proposal provided that detainees would not have their detention reviewed for *a minimum of 12 months* and then a *minimum of every six months* after that. In a concession to refugee advocates and opposition parties, an amendment was introduced that provided for the review of mandatory detention within 14 days and then every six months thereafter.

Once admitted as a refugee, designated foreign nationals are unable to seek (further) temporary or permanent resident status in Canada for a period of five years. This has several ramifications. First, designated persons recognized as refugees gain only the most insecure of footholds in Canada. In theory, their claims can be reassessed within five years to determine whether they still needed protection. Second, these refugees are afforded very limited rights in comparison with refugees who are not 'designated'. Although given rights to work and social security support, they cannot change their status within five years. They cannot sponsor family members to come to Canada, nor obtain travel documents to visit their family in a safe third country. Finally, 'designated' refugees have to reapply for protection after the initial five-year period of residence expires.

The parallels with current and former Australian government policies are patent. Australia has operated a mandatory detention regime since 1989 – a measure that (again) was introduced in response to unauthorized maritime arrivals.[43] The Australian system was 'normalized'

39 *Immigration and Refugee Protection Act*, SC 2001, c. 27, s. 55.

40 Ibid., c. 27, s. 57(1).

41 Ibid., c. 27, s. 57(2).

42 Ibid.

43 These arrivals were from Cambodia. See *Migration Amendment Act* 1992 (Cth), and Mary Crock, 'A Legal Perspective on the Evolution of Mandatory Detention', in Mary Crock (ed.), *Protection or Punishment: The Detention of Asylum Seekers in Australia* (Sydney: Federation Press, 1993), 25–40.

with changes to the *Migration Act* 1958 (Cth) in September 1994 to provide that *all* 'unlawful non-citizens' must be detained until either granted a visa or removed from Australia.[44] The parliamentary discourse on these provisions, which have had bipartisan support over many years, suggests that Australia's politicians see the detention provisions as necessary deterrents to unlawful behaviour.[45]

Temporary protection visas were first introduced in Australia in 1990 in response to the large number of Chinese students who came to and/or were stranded in Australia following the suppression of pro-democracy demonstrations in that country in 1989.[46] This experiment was limited somewhat by the special circumstances then pertaining.[47] The Australian policies that appear to have been of greater interest to the Canadian drafters of the *Protecting Canada's Immigration System Act* are those created in 1999. In that year, temporary protection visas became a key feature of deterrent measures introduced by the Conservative Coalition in response to the alarming increase in boat arrivals around that time. The *Migration Amendment Regulations* 1999 (No. 12) created temporary protection visas for refugees presenting as unauthorized arrivals. The subclass 785 visas restricted welfare benefits and family reunification and limited the protection offered to refugees to a maximum of three years.[48] These were followed in 2001 with visas permitting stays of five years for refugees whose claims were processed offshore (on Nauru or Manus Island) following the applicant's interdiction en route to Australia.[49] Temporary Protection Visas were abolished after the election of the Rudd Labor government in 2007.

The Canadian legislation differs from the Australian precedents in a number of important respects. With no legislative regime for the protection of human rights, the Australian legislators have been much less encumbered than their Canadian counterparts in the framing of punitive and deterrent legislation.[50] While the *Protecting Canada's Immigration System Act* did

44 See *Migration Act* 1958 (Cth), ss. 189 and 198. The 1992 legislation came into force on 1 September 1994.

45 See Jim McKiernan, 'The Political Imperative: Defend, Deter, Deny', in Crock (ed.), *Protection or Punishment*, at Ch. 1, 3–7.

46 *Migration Regulations (Amendment)* (1990) (No. 237), reg. 21; the Refugee (restricted) visa was replaced by another temporary visa, the Domestic Protection (Temporary) Entry Permit, in 1991: *Migration Regulations* (Cth) Class 84, *Migration Regulation (Amendment) 1991* (No. 25), reg. 9.

47 Then Prime Minister Hawke pledged that no Chinese student would be forced to return to China. The visas were introduced to make good on this promise, while depriving the students of family reunification rights that would come with permanent visas. Realizing the difficulties caused by these visas for young students who were not going to be able to return to China, the visas were quietly abandoned in 1994 through the announcement of a quasi-amnesty. See Andreas Schloenhardt, 'Australia and the Boat-people: 25 years of Unauthorised Arrivals' (2000) 23(3) *University of New South Wales Law Journal* 33–55 at 46; Mary Crock and Laurie Berg, *Immigration, Refugees and Forced Migration: Law, Policy and Practice in Australia* (Sydney: Federation Press, 2011) at 340.

48 SR 243 of 1999. Note that, under the Labor government, protection visas were granted for four years.

49 See discussion in section 3.1 above.

50 In a series of challenges made to Australia's mandatory immigration detention regime in 2004, the High Court made it patently clear that norms of international human rights cannot be invoked to temper the legal effect of domestic laws expressed in clear terms of statutory intendment: see *Al-Kateb* (2004) 219 CLR 562; *Al Khafaji* (2004) 219 CLR 664; *Behrooz* (2004) 219 CLR

not adopt the other two main elements of the Pacific strategy – third country processing and interdiction of asylum seeker boats – media reports indicated that the Canadian Conservative government seriously considered adopting such policies, but ultimately decided that these approaches would not be able to withstand challenge in Canada's courts.[51]

While framed differently, the power given to the Canadian Minister of Citizenship, Immigration and Multiculturalism to class certain groups of arrivals as 'designated foreign nationals' has the same effect as Australia's post-*Tampa* excision regime, insofar as it creates a two-tiered system for processing asylum claims. In both countries the laws operate to afford fewer rights to unauthorized maritime arrivals than to persons arriving by other means.

4. The Tyranny of Deterrence Theory

The motivations of both the Australian and Canadian governments in their response to irregular maritime arrivals are clear. These asylum seekers invariably receive very high levels of media exposure and a strong negative response from much of the public. Harsher restrictions targeting such arrivals are an easy way to score political points. This latest example of legal borrowing in the asylum space highlights the need for migration scholars to develop channels of communications to discuss the relative success and failure of policy measures.

The relevant legislative provisions enacted by the *Protecting Canada's Immigration System Act* were introduced into the Canadian Parliament in Bill C-4 shortly after a visit to Australia by Jason Kenney MP, the Canadian Minister for Citizenship, Immigration and Multiculturalism during which he met with his Australian counterpart, Chris Bowen and other senior immigration officials.[52] Regardless of what representations may have been made by Australian officials at these and other such meetings, the fact is that there is no evidence to suggest that the policies 'borrowed' by Canada have ever been effective in deterring asylum seekers from using people smugglers to come to Australia.[53] Moreover, the policies have come at great human, social and financial cost, wherein lies the tyranny of deterrence theory. Australian migration scholars need to be communicating these facts to their Canadian counterparts to assist them in challenging the official government line that these policies operate as successful deterrents.[54]

486; *Re Woolley* (2004) 225 CLR 1; and the discussion of these cases in Crock and Berg, *Immigration, Refugees and Forced Migration*, at 86–9.

51 Laurent Lafrance, 'Canada to Create a New Class of Political Refugees with Far Fewer Rights', *World Socialist Web Site*, 1 December 2010, at http://www.wsws.org/articles/2010/dec2010/refu-d01.shtml (accessed: 11 August 2012).

52 CIC, News Release, 20 September 2010.

53 For a detailed analysis of the effectiveness of these and other 'deterrent' policies in Australia, see Crock and Ghezelbash, 'Do Loose Lips Bring Ships?'.

54 At the launch of the public announcement of the policy, Vic Toews, Minister for Public Safety, stated, 'We are providing a strong deterrent for those who are considering using human smuggling operations to jump the queue into Canada': Vic Toews, 'Human Smuggling and the Abuse of Canada's Refugee System', 21 October 2010, at http://www.publicsafety.gc.ca/media/sp/2010/sp20101021-eng.aspx (accessed: 19 July 2011).

4.1 Detention is No Deterrent yet Involves Huge Costs

The policy of mandatory detention has been maintained in Australia for over 20 years despite the lack of any evidence that it has reduced unauthorized boat arrivals. When detention was first introduced, unauthorized arrivals increased from 26 persons in 1989 to 198 in 1990. The formalization of detention laws in 1992 also had no discernable impact on the number of arrivals. While there was a slight dip in arrivals from 216 persons in 1992 to 81 persons in 1993, the number jumped to 953 persons in the following year. In subsequent years, there has been no obvious correlation at all between unauthorized boat arrivals and detention policy.[55] This is particularly so in recent times. In spite of Labor's commitment in 2008 to reduce resort to the detention of non-citizens posing no threat to Australia,[56] the numbers in immigration custody rose steeply with the spike in irregular boat arrivals that followed. By 2011, the issue of children in detention had once again become a rallying point for community activists – and further ammunition for an opportunistic Opposition.

In spite of the ample evidence that detention has never acted as a deterrent of any kind, neither of the major parties seems to have the will to undertake a major review of Australian policy and practice in this area. This is in spite of the fact that mandatory detention has meant virtually nothing but trouble for Australia. In financial terms, the policy has cost the country a literal fortune. In the 2009/10 financial year, the Australian government spent $304.3 million to operate its detention and asylum-processing regime. In 2010/11, approximately 40 per cent of the Department's two billion dollar budget was set aside for detention and offshore processing. Detention has caused significant damage to the health and wellbeing of asylum seekers, with numerous studies demonstrating the adverse impact of mandatory detention on the mental health of detainees.[57] The irony is that the greater percentage of detainees in historical terms have been accepted as refugees and visa-ed to remain in Australia.[58] Hence the harms suffered in immigration detention ultimately add to the burden of assimilating the refugee into Australian society.

---

55 See Crock and Ghezelbash, 'Do Loose Lips Bring Ships?', at 257–8 for an examination of the correlation between changes in Australian asylum policy and the number of unauthorized boat arrivals.

56 See Chris Evans, 'New Directions in Detention: Restoring Integrity to Australia's Immigration System', 29 July 2008, at http://www.minister.immi.gov.au/media/speeches/2008/ce080729.htm (accessed: 26 August 2012), discussed in Crock and Berg, *Immigration, Refugees and Forced Migration*, at 485 (see also Ch. 12).

57 Janette Green and Kathy Eagar, 'The Health of People in Australian Immigration Detention Centres' (2010) 192(2) *Medical Journal of Australia* 65–70; Derrick Silove, Zachary Steel and Charles Watters, 'Policies of Deterrence and the Mental Health of Asylum Seekers' (2000) 284 *Journal of the American Medical Association* 604–11; and Zachary Steel and Derrick Silove, 'The Mental Health Implications of Detaining Asylum Seekers' (2001) 175 *Medical Journal of Australia* 596–9.

58 For example, of the 1,254 claims assessed on Christmas Island between 1 July 2009 and 31 January 2010, only 110 people were assessed as not being refugees. Approximately 91 per cent of the claims were successful: see Senate Legal and Constitutional Affairs Committee, *Answers to Questions on Notice, Immigration Portfolio, Additional Budget Estimates*, 9 February 2010, Questions 30 and 32, at http://www.aph.gov.au/senate/committee/legcon_ctte/estimates/add_0910/diac/32_qon.pdf and http://www.aph.gov.au/senate/committee/legcon_ctte/estimates/add_0910/diac/30_qon.pdf (accessed: 19 July 2011).

In terms of its impact on wider Australian society, the policy has been socially divisive, tearing at the multicultural fabric of Australian society by encouraging mistrust and denunciation of anyone with an appearance and/or culture at variance with the Anglo-Saxon norm. The policy has also damaged Australia's reputation abroad, with accounts of the sometimes appalling conditions in the detention centres tarnishing Australia's image as a generous and humanitarian country that is respectful of international human rights law. The UN Human Rights Committee has upheld a series of complaints alleging arbitrary detention and/or cruel and inhuman treatment of both adults and children held in Australian immigration detention centres.[59]

The Canadian government would do well to examine the effect of moving away from an arrest and detention system overseen by the judiciary to a mandatory model. Before Australia changed its laws in 1994, persons suspected of being unlawful non-citizens could be arrested and detained, but were required to be brought before a magistrate within 72 hours and returned to Court thereafter every seven days until issues of identity and legal status had been determined.[60] In 1994, the arrest and detention process became the sole preserve of the immigration bureaucracy, with immigration officials empowered to arrest and keep in detention any person 'reasonably suspected' to be an unlawful non-citizen.[61] At the height of the hysteria surrounding irregular maritime arrivals in the early years of the new millennium, over 240 permanent residents and Australian citizens were wrongfully arrested, detained, and even removed from Australia. Many of those so affected were vulnerable individuals suffering from mental and physical disabilities.[62] In the result, the Australian government has been forced to pay out millions of dollars in compensation.[63] Interestingly, both major parties in Australia have refused to countenance a return to a system involving judicial oversight, preferring the less confronting device of a dedicated immigration Ombudsman reporting directly to the Federal Parliament.

---

[59] See, for example, *Danyal Shafiq v Australia*, Communication No. 1324/2004: Australia, CCPR/C/88/D/1324/2004 (13 November 2006); *Applicants D and E v Australia*, Communication No. 1050/2002: Australia (9 August 2006), CCPR/C/87/D/1050/2002; *Ali Aqsar Bakhtiyari and Roqaiha Bakhtiyari v Australia*, Communication No. 1069/2002: Australia, CCPR/C/79/D/1069/2002 (6 November 2003); *Baban v Australia*, Communication No. 1014/2001: Australia, CCPR/C/78/D/1014/2001 (18 September 2003); *C v Australia*, Communication No. 900/1999: Australia, CCPR/C/76/D/900/1999 (13 November 2002); and *A v Australia*, Communication No. 560/1993, UN Doc. CCPR/C/59/D/560/1993 (30 April 1997).

[60] Crock, 'Legal Perspective on the Evolution of Mandatory Detention'.

[61] See *Migration Act* 1958, s. 189.

[62] See Mick Palmer, *Inquiry into the Circumstances of the Immigration Detention of Cornelia Rau: Report* (Commonwealth of Australia, July 2005), at http://www.immi.gov.au/media/publications/pdf/palmer-report.pdf (accessed: 22 August 2012); Neil Comrie, *Inquiry into the Circumstances of the Vivien Alvarez Matter* (Commonwealth Ombudsman Report No. 3, September 2005).

[63] See, for example, the payout made to Cornelia Rau of $2.6 million in compensation: 'Rau Wins $2.6m Compo', *Sydney Morning Herald*, 7 March 2008, at http://www.smh.com.au/news/national/rau-wins-26m-compo/2008/03/07/1204780046361.html (accessed: 26 August 2012). Vivian Solon received $4.5 million in compensation: Jewel Topsfield and Andra Jackson, '$4.5m Payout to Alvarez Solon for Wrongful Deportation', *The Age*, 1 December 2006, at 1.

4.2 Temporary Protection Visas Encourage rather than Deter Asylum Seekers

There is no evidence to suggest that temporary protection visas have any effect in deterring asylum seekers. Between 1990 and 1994, the period in which the temporary protection visas regime was first introduced in Australia, unauthorized boat arrivals remained steady at around 200 persons per year. This did not prevent the Coalition government from reintroducing a tougher version of the scheme following the surge in boat arrivals in 1999. Again, these measures were ineffective in reducing the number of unauthorized boat arrivals. The following two years saw an unprecedented increase, with more than 8,455 irregular maritime arrivals. What did change was the makeup of the asylum seeker population. Restrictions on family reunification meant that it was no longer possible for adult male refugees (having made the journey alone) to sponsor their families to come out to Australia using regular migration programmes. In other words, in 1999 this policy change may well have had the effect of encouraging *more* asylum seekers to try their hand with the people smugglers. What Australia did see was boats arriving with whole families and/or with women and children whose husbands and fathers were already in the country.[64] In 1999, children made up only 13 per cent of asylum seekers arriving by boat. By 2001, after the introduction of the temporary protection visa scheme, the proportion of children on boats rose to 30 per cent.[65]

Like mandatory detention, the temporary protection regime was ineffective and had a heavy financial and human cost. It required the repeated engagement of the entire machinery of the refugee determination procedure, both at first instance and on appeal from merits review through to judicial review. Refugees had to maintain the fear and uncertainty that first accompanied their flight from persecution. It delayed or prevented altogether the reunification of families, accentuating the refugees' sense of loss and dislocation. The human and societal costs of the temporary protection regime introduced in 1999 were analysed by social scientists based at Melbourne's RMIT University. They found that the scheme had mental health implications for visa holders and that it created barriers to employment and access to health services.[66]

4.3 Offshore Processing and Interdiction Programmes Do Not Represent Sustainable Solutions

Although Canada is not considering the adoption of the harshest elements of the Pacific Solution, the debate in Australia has been all about a return to this regime. The policy

---

[64] See Irene Khan, 'Trading in Human Misery: A Human Rights Perspective on the *Tampa* Incident' (2003) 12 *Pacific Rim Law and Policy Journal* 9–22, which documents the story of a woman who drowned in Australian territorial waters attempting to enter Australia clandestinely in order to join her husband in Australia. The man's temporary protection visa did not allow him to apply for family reunification.

[65] Mary Crock, Ben Saul and Azadeh Dastyari, *Future Seekers* (Sydney: Federation Press, 2006) at 169.

[66] Greg Marston, 'Temporary Protection, Permanent Uncertainty: The Experience of Refugees Living on Temporary Protection Visas' (Centre for Applied Social Research, RMIT University, Melbourne, 2003) at 4.

borrowings in this instance have been between generations of government (across time and between political administrations). Again, we question many of the assumptions that are being made.

The change of federal government in Australia in 2007 led to the abandonment of some elements of the Pacific Solution. Temporary protection visas were abolished and many of the restrictions placed on asylum seekers' access to assistance (and to the media) were relaxed. As documented elsewhere,[67] the new (Labor) regime attracted a barrage of criticism from the Conservatives newly consigned to the role of Opposition. They proceeded to conduct a concerted (and effective) campaign, claiming that the subsequent spike in boat arrivals could be attributed to the Labor party's softer policies. It is a spin that has probably been accepted by a majority of media and other commentators, leading even some advocates from the so-called 'Left' to call for a return to the Pacific Solution.[68]

The pressure generated by the Opposition campaign, poor showings in the Polls, and complications flowing from a significant loss in the High Court[69] combined in 2011 to force the government to reinstate some key elements of the Conservative's deterrent platform. In 2012 the Australian High Court struck down the government's plan to send 800 asylum seekers to Malaysia in exchange for 4,000 refugees processed by UNHCR in that country.[70] Using the findings of an Expert Panel[71] as cover, the government secured amendments to the Migration Act 1958 (Austl)[72] which facilitated an effective return to what had been known as the Pacific Solution. Agreements were brokered with Nauru and PNG to reopen detention and processing facilities, last used by the conservative Coalition.[73]

---

67 See Crock and Ghezelbash, 'Do Loose Lips Bring Ships?'; and Mary Crock, 'First Term Blues: Labor, Refugees and Immigration Reform' (2010) 17 *Australian Journal of Administrative Law* 1–9.

68 See Susan Metcalfe, 'The Pacific Solution was an Abomination. This Debate is No Better', at http://www.abc.net.au/unleashed/2746970.html (accessed: 11 August 2012); and Patricia Kavelas, 'Left Got it Wrong on Nauru: Manne', *The Australian*, 6 April 2011, at http://www.theaustralian.com.au/news/nation/left-got-it-wrong-on-nauru-manne/story-fn7dlx76-1226034315981 (accessed: 26 August 2012).

69 See *Plaintiff M61/2010E v Commonwealth* and *Plaintiff M69 of 2010 v Commonwealth* (2010) 272 ALR 14. See Mary Crock and Daniel Ghezelbash, 'Due Process and Rule of Law as Human Rights: The High Court and the "Offshore" Processing of Asylum Seekers' (2011) 18 *Australian Journal of Administrative Law* 101–14.

70 See Joint Media Release, Prime Minister Gillard and Minister Bowen, 'Australia and Malaysia Sign Transfer Deal', 25 July 2011, at http://www.minister.immi.gov.au/media/cb/2011/cb168739.htm (accessed: 11 August 2012). See *Plaintiff M70/2011 and Plaintiff M106/2011 v Minister for Immigration and Citizenship* [2011] HCA 32.

71 See Angus Houston, Paris Aristotle and Michael L'Estrange *Report of the Expert Panel on Asylum Seekers*, DIAC, August 2012, available at http://expertpanelonasylumseekers.dpmc.gov.au/report.

72 See *Migration Legislation Amendment (Regional Processing and Other Measures) Act* 2012 (Austl).

73 See Elizabeth Biok, 'The Regional Perspective: Exporting Deterrence and Negating Human Rights Standards', in *Offshore Processing of Asylum Seekers: The Search for Legitimate Parameters* (2000) 9 *UTS Law Review* 69–83.

The initial announcement of a return to the Pacific Solution coincided with a fall in the number of unauthorized boat arrivals.[74] As noted earlier, the immediate response of the aspiring asylum seekers (and/or of the people smugglers) to redirect their attentions to New Zealand and to Canada underscores the competitive element in the policy transfer story. As one door closes, desperate people will try their luck at another – re-creating the depressing spectacle of the refugee in orbit that was an important rationale for drafting the Refugee Convention after World War II.[75] The slow-down was short-lived, however. Interestingly, the actual re-opening of Nauru saw a surge in boat arrivals. By October 2012, new arrivals far exceeded the combined capacities of Nauru and Manus Island, creating fresh dilemmas for the Australian government.[76]

Obvious features in the latest plan militate against any 'solution' being sustainable. Chief among these is that both the Pacific strategy and its successor involve or involved the interdiction of finite numbers of seafaring asylum seekers otherwise intent on travelling to Australia. In this respect both policies constitute *containment* more than *deterrence* measures, and so by definition are effective in the immediate- to short term. Australia's problem is that no country in the region has been or will be prepared to stand as gatekeeper indefinitely, least of all when the aspiring migrants cannot be returned to the countries whence they have fled.

By the time Labor government came to power in 2007, Indonesia had been stopping the boats for Australia for nearly six years. Over 10,000 asylum seekers had been processed by UNHCR in that country and gained recognition as refugees. Many, if not most, of these refugees had family and friends in Australia. It should come as no surprise that, when the people smugglers started resuming their trade out of Indonesia from late 2005, the boats arriving in Australian waters included card-carrying refugees who had been processed in Indonesia. Flash forward to Malaysia. This country has agreed to take 800 of Australia's irregular maritime arrivals who would be processed by UNHCR and then left to join a very long queue for resettlement in a third country. Having learned from Indonesia's experience, Malaysia put strict conditions on its involvement. It used the deal to move on four times as many Convention refugees

74 The number of persons arriving by boat dropped from 5,516 people in 2001 to just 1 person in 2002, 53 in 2003, and 15 in 2004: Janet Phillips and Harriet Spinks, 'Boat Arrivals in Australia since 1976', *Background Note* (Parliament of Australia, Parliamentary Library), updated 15 July 2011, at http://www.aph.gov.au/About_Parliament/Parliamentary_Departments/Parliamentary_Library/pubs/BN/2011-2012/BoatArrivals (accessed: 26 August 2012). Note that some of this reduction was due to a redefinition of statistics. Boats still made the attempt to enter Australia during 2002: it is known that the boats SIEV(s) 5, 7, 11 and 12 attempted to make the journey and returned to Indonesia while SIEV(s) 4, 6 and 10 actually sank. Again in 2003, boats were still attempting the journey, such as SIEV 14, which was also towed back: Possum Comitatus, 'Push vs. Pull – Asylum Seeker Numbers and Statistics', *Crikey*, 19 October 2009, at http://blogs.crikey.com.au/pollytics/2009/10/19/push-vs-pull-asylum-seeker-numbers-and-statistics/ (accessed: 11 August 2012).

75 See, for example the tragedies of the *St Louis*, which resulted in the ultimate death of 907 refugees from Nazi Germany, and of the *Struma*, where 769 Romanian Jews were left to drown. The push-back of refugee boats from Germany has been seen as a contributing factor in shaping Hitler's 'Final Solution'. See Jessica Tauman, 'Rescued at Sea but Nowhere to Go: The Cloudy Legal Waters of the *Tampa* Crisis' (2002) 11(2) *Pacific Rim Law and Policy Journal* 461–96 at 461–2, 492–3.

76 Statistics on arrivals are set out at : http://www.aph.gov.au/About_Parliament/Parliamentary_Departments/Parliamentary_Library/pubs/BN/2011-2012/BoatArrivals#_Toc285178607.

as the number of asylum seekers it was willing to accept. Australia agreed to admit 4,000 refugees from Malaysia over three years and took in this number even though the swap did not eventuate. The arrangements with Nauru and PNG were also constrained by virtue of the natural capacities of both locations.

The problem with schemes like this – apart from the enormous price tag and concerns about abuse of human rights – is that they are inherently limited. Although the Conservatives may have succeeded in stopping the boats in 2001, the solution devised was not a sustainable one, for the simple reason that the asylum seekers interdicted and processed in Indonesia (and elsewhere) were left with nowhere to go.[77] It is well to note that the vast majority of the refugees sent to Nauru, Manus Island and Indonesia ended up settling in Australia.

The political cynic may interject at this point with the observation that, at any given time, the government's interest does not extend beyond the immediate electoral cycle. In the longer term, however, it is difficult to see regional processing as offering any durable solutions. The question must surely be whether Australia can really afford to keep paying out exorbitant amounts of money to send to other countries individuals who will always be regarded as *Australia's* refugees.

5. Tracking Cause and Effect in the Search for Durable Solutions

It is in the nature of human conflict that there will always be acute events giving rise to involuntary migration that cannot and (should not) be prevented. The migratory flows out of Sri Lanka in 2009, reactions to the so-called 'Arab Spring', and the crippling drought in sub-Saharan Africa are recent examples in point. Given what we now know of the final days of the Sri Lankan government's crushing victory over the Tamil Tigers in that country,[78] it is hardly surprising that Australia's deterrent measures in 2010 had virtually no impact on irregular maritime arrivals from that country.[79] Our interest is in the movements that occur outside of these catastrophic periods.

We repeat the views we have expressed about the desirability of governments everywhere finding ways and means to put the people smugglers out of business.[80] Taking to the high seas in search of asylum has always been a very risky business, both in terms of direct loss of life[81]

---

[77] See, for example, Michael Gordon, *Freeing Ali: The Human Face of the Pacific Solution* (Sydney: UNSW Press, 2005).

[78] See Gordon Weiss, *The Cage: The Fight for Sri Lanka and the Last Days of the Tamil Tigers* (London: The Bodley Head, 2010).

[79] As of 7 November 2010, 3,243 out of the total 5,654 arrivals that year had come from Sri Lanka and Afghanistan: see BBC Asia-Pacific, 'Australia Refugee Case Trumps Government Policy', 11 November 2010, at http://www.bbc.co.uk/news/world-asia-pacific-11732148 (accessed: 11 August 2012).

[80] See Crock and Ghezelbash, 'Do Loose Lips Bring Ships?' at 243ff.

[81] In 1979, Minister for Immigration M.J.R. MacKellar estimated that 200,000 had died attempting to flee Vietnam by boat since the fall of Saigon (the event that marked the end of the war in Vietnam) in 1975. See Mike Steketee, 'Vietnam-style Solution Needed', *The Australian*, 31 December 2011, at http://www.theaustralian.com.au/news/opinion/vietnam-style-solution-needed/story-e6frg7ax-1226233540330 (accessed: 20 August 2012). Between December 1998 and

and in terms of the legal position of refugees seeking a place to land.[82] If only for this reason – and there are many others – governments are well justified in trying to discourage irregular maritime arrivals.

The problem with the various deterrent and containment schemes that have been or are being adopted is the tendency to oversimplify the various causal factors behind people smuggling and irregular boat arrivals. The push factors are often plain enough to see, but not enough research has been done on how these combine with pull factors such as family and community ties and the availability of people-smuggling services. Studies to date either make unsubstantiated assertions about causal effects, or at best rely on simple correlations between changes in push-and-pull factors and flow data. Much more attention needs to be paid to root causes and durable (sustainable) solutions that do not involve abusing the human rights of refugees on the one hand and the wellbeing of host nations on the other. With lives at stake, more robust data and analysis are required.

The bottom line is that migration scholars also need to take a greater interest in comparing data and the sharing information on laws and policies and how they operate. Governments are already doing this. Without the contributions of academics and/or other civil society actors, this sharing can lead to bad policy decisions. Collecting comparative data will never be an easy or a simple task, as we are discovering in our attempts to create an international and historical database of immigration laws and policies.[83] However, in a globalizing world in which governments are discussing and 'borrowing' migration policies from each other, the call is out for migration scholars to rise to the challenge.

References

AFP, 'New Zealand Shuts Door to Refugees', *Sydney Morning Herald*, 12 July 2011, at http://www.smh.com.au/world/nz-shuts-door-on--asylum-seekers-20110712-1hbeo.html (accessed: 11 August 2012).

BBC Asia-Pacific, 'Australia Refugee Case Trumps Government Policy', 11 November 2010, at http://www.bbc.co.uk/news/world-asia-pacific-11732148 (accessed: 11 August 2012).

Berg, Laurie, 'At the Border and Between the Cracks' (2007) 8(1) *Melbourne Journal of International Law* 1–34.

Betts, Alexander, *Global Migration Governance* (Oxford: Oxford University Press, 2011).

December 2001, we estimated the death toll to be about 891 boat people. The Labor record is not much better, with an estimated 150 deaths between January 2009 and June 2010, to which must be added the 50+ who drowned in the boat crash on Christmas Island in January 2011. See Crock and Ghezelbash, 'Do Loose Lips Bring Ships?' at 246–7.

82 See R.P. Schaeffer, 'The Singular Plight of Seaborne Refugees' (1978–80) 8 *Australian Yearbook of International Law* 213–34; and James Pugash, 'The Dilemma of the Sea Refugee: Rescue Without Refuge' (1977) 18 *Harvard International Law Journal* 577–604. Both articles chronicle the arrangements made following the outflow of boat people from Vietnam following the fall of Saigon to the North Vietnamese. See also the comments by Tauman, 'Rescued at Sea but Nowhere to Go'.

83 See http://projects.iq.harvard.edu/impala (accessed: 11 August 2012).

Bhagwati, Jagdish, 'Borders Beyond Control' (2003) 82(1) *Foreign Affairs* 98–104.
Biok, Elizabeth, 'The Regional Perspective: Exporting Deterrence and Negating Human Rights Standards' (2007) 9 *UTS Law Review* 69–83.
Comitatus, Possum, 'Push vs. Pull – Asylum Seeker Numbers and Statistics', *Crikey*, 19 October 2009, at http://blogs.crikey.com.au/pollytics/2009/10/19/push-vs-pull-asylum-seeker-numbers-and-statistics/ (accessed: 11 August 2012).
Coon, Margaret A., 'The Law of Interdiction: Time for Change' (1980) 27 *Louisiana Bar Journal* 223–8.
Crock, Mary, 'A Legal Perspective on the Evolution of Mandatory Detention', in Mary Crock (ed.), *Protection or Punishment: The Detention of Asylum Seekers in Australia* (Sydney: Federation Press, 1993), 25–40.
Crock, Mary, 'First Term Blues: Labor, Refugees and Immigration Reform' (2010) 17(4) *Australian Journal of Administrative Law* 205–12.
Crock, Mary, 'In the Wake of the Tampa: Conflicting Visions of International Refugee Law in the Management of Refugee Flows' (2003) 12(1) *Pacific Rim Law & Policy Journal* 49–96.
Crock, Mary and Laurie Berg, *Immigration, Refugees and Forced Migration: Law, Policy and Practice in Australia* (Sydney: Federation Press, 2011).
Crock, Mary and Daniel Ghezelbash, 'Do Loose Lips Bring Ships? The Role of Policy, Politics and Human Rights in Managing Unauthorised Boat Arrivals' (2010) 19(2) *Griffith Law Review* 238–87.
Crock, Mary and Daniel Ghezelbash, 'Due Process and Rule of Law as Human Rights: The High Court and the "Offshore" Processing of Asylum Seekers' (2011) 18 *Australian Journal of Administrative Law* 101–14.
Crock, Mary, Ben Saul and Azadeh Dastyari, *Future Seekers* (Sydney: Federation Press, 2006).
Courtland Robinson, W., 'The Comprehensive Plan of Action for Indochinese Refugees, 1989–1997: Sharing the Burden and Passing the Buck' (2004) 17(3) *Journal of Refugee Studies* 319–33.
Dauvergne, Catherine, *Making People Illegal: What Globalisation Means for Migration and Law* (Cambridge: Cambridge University Press, 2008).
Dolowitz, David and David Marsh, 'Learning from Abroad: The Role of Policy Transfer in Contemporary Policy-making' (2000) 13(1) *Governance* 5–23.
Evans, Chris, 'New Directions in Detention: Restoring Integrity to Australia's Immigration System', 29 July 2008, at http://www.minister.immi.gov.au/media/speeches/2008/ce080729.htm (accessed: 26 August 2012).
Frelick, Bill, 'Haitian Boat Interdiction: First Asylum and First Principles of Refugee Protection' (1993) 26 *Georgetown Immigration Law Review* 675–95.
Frelick, Bill, 'Haitian Boat Interdiction and Return: First Asylum and First Principles of Refugee Protection' (in *Symposium: Refusing Refugees: Political and Legal Barriers to Asylum*) (1993) 26(3) *Cornell International Law Journal* 675–717.
Goodwin-Gill, Guy and Jane McAdam, *The Refugee in International Law* (London: Oxford University Press, 2008, 3rd edn).
Gordon, Michael, *Freeing Ali: The Human Face of the Pacific Solution* (Sydney: UNSW Press, 2005).
Green, Janette and Kathy Eagar, 'The Health of People in Australian Immigration Detention Centres' (2010) 192(2) *Medical Journal of Australia* 65–70.

Hansen, Randall, *An Assessment of Principal Regional Consultative Processes on Migration* (Geneva: IOM, 2010).

Helton, Arthur, 'Refugee Determination under the Comprehensive Plan of Action: Overview and Assessment' (1993) 5(4) *International Journal of Refugee Law* 544–58.

Houston, Angus, Aristotle, Paris and L'Estrange, Michael *Report of the Expert Panel on Asylum Seekers*, DIAC, August 2012, available at http://expertpanelonasylumseekers.dpmc.gov.au/report.

IOM, *Global Meeting of Chairs and Secretariats of Regional Consultative Processes on Migration: Bangkok, 4–5 June 2009: Summary Report* (Geneva: IOM, 2009).

IOM, 'International Migration Law, Training and Capacity Building in Immigration Law, Recent Activities', at http://www.iom.int/jahia/Jahia/pid/169 (accessed: 18 July 2011).

Johns, Fleur, 'Guantanamo Bay and the Annihilation of the Exception' (2005) 16(4) *European Journal of International Law* 613–37.

Jones, Thomas David, 'A Human Rights Tragedy: The Cuban and Haitian Refugee Crises Revisited' (1995) 9(3) *Georgetown Immigration Law Journal* 479–523.

Kavelas, Patricia, 'Left Got it Wrong on Nauru: Manne', *The Australian*, 6 April 2011, at http://www.theaustralian.com.au/news/nation/left-got-it-wrong-on-nauru-manne/story-fn7dlx76-1226034315981 (accessed: 26 August 2012).

Khan, Irene, 'Trading in Human Misery: A Human Rights Perspective on the *Tampa* Incident' (2003) 12(1) *Pacific Rim Law and Policy Journal* 9–22.

Koser, Khalid, 'International Migration and Global Governance' (2010) 16(3) *Global Governance* 301–15.

Lafrance, Laurent, 'Canada to Create a New Class of Political Refugees with Far Fewer Rights', *World Socialist Web Site*, 1 December 2010, at http://www.wsws.org/articles/2010/dec2010/refu-d01.shtml (accessed: 11 August 2012).

McKiernan, Jim, 'The Political Imperative: Defend, Deter, Deny', in Mary Crock (ed.), *Protection or Punishment: The Detention of Asylum Seekers in Australia* (Sydney: Federation Press, 1993), 3–7.

Marston, Greg, 'Temporary Protection, Permanent Uncertainty: The Experience of Refugees Living on Temporary Protection Visas' (Centre for Applied Social Research, RMIT University, Melbourne, 2003).

Metcalfe, Susan, 'The Pacific Solution was an Abomination. This Debate is No Better', at http://www.abc.net.au/unleashed/2746970.html (accessed: 11 August 2012).

Motomura, Hiroshi, 'Haitian Asylum Seekers: Interdiction and Immigrants' Rights' (1993) 15 *Immigration and Nationality* 531–55.

Phillips, Janet and Harriet Spinks, 'Boat Arrivals in Australia since 1976', *Background Note* (Parliament of Australia, Parliamentary Library), updated 9 July 2012, at http://www.aph.gov.au/About_Parliament/Parliamentary_Departments/Parliamentary_Library/pubs/BN/2011-2012/BoatArrivals (accessed: 26 August 2012).

Pound, Roscoe, *The Formative Era of American Law* (Boston: Little Brown & Co, 1938).

Pugash, James, 'The Dilemma of the Sea Refugee: Rescue Without Refuge' (1977) 18(3) *Harvard International Law Journal* 577–604.

'Rau Wins $2.6m Compo', *Sydney Morning Herald*, 7 March 2008, at http://www.smh.com.au/news/national/rau-wins-26m-compo/2008/03/07/1204780046361.html (accessed: 26 August 2012).

Schaeffer, R.P., 'The Singular Plight of Seaborne Refugees' (1978–80) 8 *Australian Yearbook of International Law* 213–34.

Schlesinger, Rudolf B., Hans W. Baade, Peter E. Herzog and Eduard M. Wise, *Comparative Law: Cases, Text, Materials* (New York: Foundation Press, 1998, 6th edn).

Schloenhardt, Andreas, 'Australia and the Boat-people: 25 years of Unauthorised Arrivals' (2000) 23(3) *University of New South Wales Law Journal* 33–55.

Shachar, Ayelet, 'The Race for Talent: Highly Skilled Migrants and Competitive Immigration Regimes' (2006) 81 *New York University Law Review* 148–206.

Silove, Derrick, Zachary Steel and Charles Watters, 'Policies of Deterrence and the Mental Health of Asylum Seekers' (2000) 284(5) *Journal of the American Medical Association* 604–11.

Sohn, Louis B., 'Interdiction of Vessels on the High Seas' (1984) 18(2) *International Lawyer* 411–19.

Steketee, Mike, 'Vietnam-style Solution Needed', *The Australian*, 31 December 2011, at http://www.theaustralian.com.au/news/opinion/vietnam-style-solution-needed/story-e6frg7ax-1226233540330 (accessed: 20 August 2012).

Steel, Zachary and Derrick Silove, 'The Mental Health Implications of Detaining Asylum Seekers' (2001) 175(11) *Medical Journal of Australia* 596–9.

Tauman, Jessica, 'Rescued at Sea but Nowhere to Go: The Cloudy Legal Waters of the *Tampa* Crisis' (2002) 11(2) *Pacific Rim Law and Policy Journal* 461–96.

Thouez, Colleen and Frédérique Channac, 'Shaping International Migration Policy: The Role of Regional Consultative Processes' (2006) 29(2) *West European Politics* 370–87.

Toews, Vic, 'Human Smuggling and the Abuse of Canada's Refugee System', 21 October 2010, at http://www.publicsafety.gc.ca/media/sp/2010/sp20101021-eng.aspx (accessed: 19 July 2011).

Topsfield, Jewel and Andra Jackson, '$4.5m Payout to Alvarez Solon for Wrongful Deportation', *The Age*, 1 December 2006, 1.

Tsamenyi, Martin, *The Vietnamese Boat People and International Law* (Brisbane: Griffith University, 1981).

Weiss, Gordon, *The Cage: The Fight for Sri Lanka and the Last Days of the Tamil Tigers* (London: The Bodley Head, 2010).

Westbrook, David, 'Theorising the Diffusion of Law in an Age of Globalization: Conceptual Difficulties, Unstable Imaginations, and the Effort to think Gracefully Nonetheless' (2008) 3 *Annals Fac L Belgrade International Ed* 159–79.

Zink, James R., 'Race and Foreign Policy in Refugee Law: A Historical Perspective of the Haitian Refugee Crises' (1998) 48 *De Paul Law Review* 559–617.

28 ASHGATE RESEARCH COMPANION

Family Migration and New Labour

Helena Wray

Introduction

This chapter analyses the family migration policies of the New Labour government of 1997–2010 in the context of its migration policy generally. It argues that policy was often the outcome of a conflicting set of pressures. Regulation of family migration often appeared to share the same characteristics as immigration policy as a whole: a veneer of coherence concealed efforts to satisfy a multiplicity of interests and forces. At the same time, while the government moved policy in the same direction as its European neighbours, comparatively speaking it showed some restraint.

New Labour was a self-ascription adopted by the leadership of the Labour Party under Tony Blair. While it became associated with governmental excesses and controlling tendencies, its adoption was intended to emphasize that this was a new, modernizing force in politics in contrast to both the neo-liberal politics of Thatcherism and the trade union militancy associated with 'Old Labour'. The Labour Party won a landslide victory in 1997 after 18 years of Conservative government, and, looking back from the jaded present, it is easy to forget the jubilation and optimism of that moment. It was subsequently re-elected with smaller but still substantial majorities in 2001 and 2005, an unprecedented electoral record for a UK social democratic party. Blair remained prime minister until 2007 when he was succeeded by Gordon Brown who led the government until the 2010 election defeat.

New Labour's approach to immigration was arguably one of its defining characteristics as well as one of its great problems. A common perception, at least at the time of writing less than one year after the 2010 electoral defeat, was that immigration was excessive and the government failed to understand or respect the concerns of ordinary people who had to live with its consequences. The perception was epitomized by the moment in the 2010 election campaign when Prime Minister Gordon Brown was overheard describing a member of the public as 'bigoted' for raising concerns about immigration.[1]

In contrast to the minimal immigration policy of the preceding three decades, the Labour government implemented an expansionist programme of skilled and managed migration. This was a high-risk strategy. Large-scale migration often provokes 'a sense of crisis' (Hollifield 2008: 186). Nonetheless, faced with labour shortages and global migratory pressures, this was arguably the only way to maintain credibility on an issue that was central to perceptions of competence. To minimize the risks of its policy, the government increasingly attempted to

[1] Polly Curtis, 'Gordon Brown calls Labour supporter a "bigoted woman"', *The Guardian*, 28 April 2010, at: http://www.guardian.co.uk/politics/2010/apr/28/gordon-brown-bigoted-woman (accessed: 11 August 2012).

micro-manage entry and stay. At the same time, it was subject to other competing pressures and expectations due to its ideological complexion, its increased subjection to external legal norms, and the strength of its minority ethnic constituency. Arguably as a consequence, it was hyperactive in the area. Legislative, regulatory and organizational changes were piled on each other. Policies were over-complex and inconsistent with each other or with other stated values. In general, the government revealed itself as controlling, even authoritarian, not only towards migrants but, increasingly, towards the population as a whole (Bosworth and Guild 2008).

In that context, family migration was particularly problematic because it impinged directly and intimately on the lives of voters whom the government wanted to retain as its natural supporters. Restrictions could easily be experienced as an expression of indifference to or distrust of personal norms, affective relations and critical aspects of identity. Other norms, such as non-discrimination, meant that policies often could not be nuanced to affect only those viewed as most problematic. However, a more liberal family migration policy was also potentially problematic as it would permit the entry of migrants who were not candidates for entry under other more instrumental policies and might even be primary targets for refusal. Their insertion into existing families could also often be perceived as aggravating the failure of some minority communities to mesh sufficiently with mainstream society, exacerbating pre-existing tensions. The conflicts and contradictions that characterize much immigration policy were thus intensified and personalized in family migration policy.

The next section suggests that immigration policy tends to be riven by conflicting and competing pressures so that it is rarely successful in achieving its stated desired outcomes but that some incoherence may nonetheless be the optimal solution in the circumstances and, as such, not entirely unwanted. The chapter goes on, in the light of this premise, to examine the migration policies implemented by the Labour government and the ways in which its family migration policies reflected these conflicts and pressures.

Why is Immigration Policy so Problematic?

Many have commented on the difficulties of implementing effective immigration policy. As Castles points out (2004: 207), the migration policies of even 'strong efficient states' often backfire or have apparently unintended consequences, particularly over the longer term. Once migration begins, it becomes 'a social process, with its own inherent dynamics' (Castles 2004: 208) and it cannot be ended or controlled at will. The result is a 'gap' between the stated aims of policies and outcomes, irrespective of whether states have tried to limit or solicit flows (see Cornelius and Tsuda 2004: 4–15). Castles (2004: 207–17) suggests a threefold typology of relevant factors that impede control: factors arising from the social dynamics of the migratory process, factors linked to globalization, transnationalism and North–South relationships, and factors within political systems. Difficulties in implementing policies often arise from the interaction of the first two sets of factors, over which governments have limited traction, with the third, the political systems of states. In respect of the latter, Castles (2004: 212–17) identifies, among other factors, interest conflicts and hidden agendas, limits on political power to control migration, contradictions within the policy formation process, and the importance of rights, civil society and the welfare state. All of these may make consistent and effective policy more difficult to achieve.

Boswell (2007) approaches the same question from a different angle. She identifies four functional imperatives that a government must fulfil to sustain legitimacy: territorial and physical security; enabling the accumulation of wealth and its partial redistribution through welfare; fairness based, particularly in a multicultural society, on universalistic principles; and, finally, the legitimacy of institutions. These functions are difficult to maintain simultaneously and the tensions between them will often be reflected within immigration policy. States will tend to resolve these tensions in various ways according to their character (which is not necessarily fixed or consistent). They will also deploy tactics such as 'intentional fudging of policy … [i]n other words, a state unable to meet all functional requirements may have an interest in the persistence of contradictions and inefficiencies in policy' (2007: 92–3).

Liberal states have particular difficulty in reconciling the tensions between their various functions because they derive legitimacy from universalistic values of fairness and a credible institutional framework. Values cannot be both universal and attach only to some people within a polity. Whether or not accounts of a 'post-national membership' (Soysal 1994) are entirely persuasive, if it is a recognizable concept, it is, in part, consequent on nation states voluntarily ceding part of their power for their own reasons. Similarly, an independent judiciary is critical to claims to be 'ruled by law' and the legitimacy this confers so that a liberal state will refrain from excessive interference with the judiciary as well as with other independent institutions such as the press or academia.

The difficulties are not only those of political values. Modern citizens expect to circulate without undue inconvenience and cannot do so if the borders are clogged by heavy-handed immigration controls. This hurdle may be partially overcome through technology and an expanded and more selective process of border crossing (see Wray 2012, and Ryan and Mitsilegas 2010 for a discussion). Nonetheless, immigration controls inevitably involve a degree of interference in the liberty of the entire populace and are not therefore fully realizable (Hollifield 2000: 96). Thus liberal states engage in what Joppke (1998: 292) describes as 'self-limited sovereignty' because, at least beyond a certain point, modern liberal states cannot withstand international migratory pressures without risking their own destruction: 'At the risk of stating a tautology, accepting unwanted immigration is inherent in the liberalness of liberal states' (Joppke 1998: 292).

In fact, the Labour government did attempt to implement some illiberal measures but was sometimes frustrated, particularly in the field of family migration, by the courts who relied on human rights values mandated by the government's own legislation. Some of the literature views the UK pre-1997 as an exception among modern liberal states (for example, Freeman 1994: 20). Joppke (1998: 292) said that Britain had 'managed to contain unwanted immigration more effectively than any other country in the Western world, but at the cost of trampling on the family rights of her own citizens.' This was attributed to executive strength and the absence of positive rights (Hansen 2000: 236–43). After 1997, the Labour government still desired to control migration, just as its predecessors did, even if it wanted controlled entry rather than controlled closure, but, because of increased commitment to its other functions, it possessed fewer powers of control just when the other pressures identified by Castles (2004: 208–12) gained increased momentum. Increased mobility, the growth of global networks and transnational consciousness, and domestic labour shortages all ratcheted pressure upwards.

The result was a government more than usually beset by conflicting pressures that could only be superficially reconciled by increased reliance upon strategies of fudging, contradiction and inefficiency.

Family Migration and the Conservatives

The tone of immigration politics during the Conservative years was set by an infamous remark made by Mrs Thatcher even before she was elected as prime minister in 1979. During a TV interview in 1978, she said: 'People are really rather afraid that this country might be swamped by people with a different culture' (quoted in Shah 2000: 4). Immigration policy during her premiership and that of her Conservative successor, John Major, was restrictive and racialized, both in work migration, which was minimal, and family reunification, where restrictive policies were selectively applied to non-white family members. The latter, in particular, caused great anguish to non-white communities as families remained separated for many years.[2]

Symbolic of the Conservative government's disdain for the family lives of Britain's ethnic minorities was the 'primary purpose' rule. The rule required spousal migrants to prove that 'the marriage was not entered into primarily to obtain admission to the United Kingdom'. The rule was first introduced in 1977 but became significant after 1983 when the burden of proof shifted to the applicant. In 1985, and in response to the unfavourable ECtHR ruling on sex discrimination in *Abdulaziz*, the immigration rules were equalized to allow women to sponsor husbands and fiancés on the same basis as men.[3] The primary purpose rule then became critical in excluding unwanted husbands particularly from the Indian sub-continent although, over time, its worst aspects were partially ameliorated by judicial recognition of 'intervening devotion' (such as cohabitation, remittance of funds or correspondence) as a way to counter allegations that the primary purpose of the marriage had been immigration.[4] In 1992, a concession granted outside the rules provided that couples who had been married for five years or who had a child entitled to live in the UK would no longer be refused on primary purpose grounds.

Nonetheless, the rule permitted the refusal of thousands of applicants from poor countries to whom an immigration motive could easily be imputed, particularly in arranged marriages where romantic courtship was rare and the reasons for entering an arranged marriage were misunderstood. Even in 1995, 53.21 per cent of husbands and fiancés from the sub-continent were refused initially although not necessarily always on primary purpose grounds (Jackson and Bennett 1998: 16). On the other hand, Macdonald and Blake (1991: 261–2) said in 1991 that they had 'still to hear of an American, Australian or New Zealander who [had] failed the primary purpose test'.

---

2 For immigration policy during the period, the reader is referred to Dummett and Nicol 1993. For aspects of family migration during the period, see Juss 1997, Sachdeva 1993 or Wray 2011: chapters 3, 4 and 5.

3 *Abdulaziz, Cabales and Balkandal v United Kingdom* judgment of 28 May 1985, Eur Ct HR, Series A, no. 94.

4 *R v IAT ex p. Arun Kumar* [1986] Imm AR 446.

Meanwhile, the export of decision making to the country of origin through compulsory entry clearance (in 1969, so prior to the election of the 1979 government) encouraged 'an internal culture of deep-rooted doubt and cynicism' (Juss 1997: 22). This permitted years of delay in resolving claims and innumerable unfavourable conclusions about even the existence of the marriage or the identity of the parties. Many wives and children were refused permission to join husbands and fathers from whom they had already been separated for many years on the basis that they were 'not related as claimed' due to lack of official documentation (unsurprising in a rural and often illiterate society) and minor discrepancies in answers to detailed and hostile questioning about the minutiae of their shared lives: who met the sponsor at the airport, whether the family buffalo gave milk, the colour of the bride's dress (Juss 1997: 64–7). X-rays were routinely used to allege that wives and children were not their stated age and thus impersonators and, most egregiously of all, young women were subjected to gynaecological examinations to establish whether they were virgins and thus bona-fide fiancées (see Juss 1997: 109–22). Although DNA testing eventually established that most applicants were truthful, refusal rates remained high. In 1995, 28.36 per cent of wives and fiancées and 50.42 per cent of children applying from the sub-continent were refused initially (Jackson and Bennett 1998: 16).

It would be difficult to overstate the degree of anger that these practices caused among the UK's ethnic minority populations, particularly those of South Asian origin. They were widely perceived as a form of official exclusion and rejection of their personal norms and aspirations. Abrasive politicians, searching for populist applause, reinforced the impression that these non-white residents were not full members of British society. In 1979, Ivor Stanbrook, a prominent anti-immigration MP, asked the Home Secretary, during a debate on family migration, to make it clear that 'this country is governed in the interests of its inhabitants and not those of immigrants', while another, Tony Marlow, said that brown and black families 'can go home and rejoin their families in the country of origin'.[5] Over time, discourse focused on apparently oppressive family norms. For instance, following press reports of Asian girls 'sold' by their parents to Asian men who followed them home from school, Home Secretary David Waddington commented that '[t]he so-called "primary purpose" rule has been much attacked but these stories show that it can protect women against exploitation'.[6]

It is unsurprising, therefore, that there were high expectations of New Labour among the UK's ethnic minority populations. In its election manifesto, the Labour Party promised abolition of the primary purpose rule due to its 'arbitrary and unfair results' and migrant groups welcomed the fulfilment of this promise in June 1997, one month after election.[7] Family migration, however, did not cease to be controversial.

5 HC Hansard, 14 November 1979, col. 1344.

6 'Scandal of the brides for sale', *Daily Mail*, 5 August 1985.

7 Labour Party Manifesto 1997, at: http://www.labour-party.org.uk/manifestos/1997/1997-labour-manifesto.shtml (accessed: 30 January 2011).

Immigration Policy under New Labour

The New Labour government adopted an expansive approach towards labour migration, a major reversal of previous policy. Support for a new orientation was expressed through various policy channels including a Department of Trade White Paper, the 1999 pre-budget report, a major government review in 2000, and a wave of government-funded research (Somerville 2007: 29–30). In 2000, a Home Office minister, Barbara Roche, brought the new approach into the open.[8] The criteria for issue of work permits were loosened in 2000, after which numbers rose considerably, peaking at 140,000 in 2006. As significant politically if not numerically was the creation of the Innovators Scheme in 2000 and the Highly Skilled Migrant Programme (HSMP) in 2001, both new avenues for skilled migration without the need for a prior job offer, and the first points-based systems in the UK. In 2007, there were 28,090 approvals under the HSMP, after which numbers declined, partly due to more restrictive criteria. Student numbers also increased significantly. Between 280,000 and 370,000 students were admitted in each year between 2000 and 2007 (Home Office 2005a: 18, 2010a: 60).

Flynn argues that these increases in planned migration were part of 'a programme of reform which is aiming at *the comprehensive management of all forms of migration*, whether forced or voluntary' (Flynn 2005: 464; emphasis in original). This ambition was reflected in terminology such as 'managed migration', 'five year plan' or 'new asylum model', and ambitious rubrics such as 'Fairer, Faster, Firmer' or 'Making Migration Work for Britain'. Change was unceasing. Nine Acts of Parliament were passed between 1997 and 2010. The immigration rules were amended constantly and, under the Points-Based System, migrants and sponsors became subject to detailed and frequently changing guidance.[9] The system was seen as poorly equipped to deal with modern migration, and, in 2009, the UK Border Agency, a newly created executive agency, took charge not only of border control but of functions previously carried out elsewhere such as visa services and customs detection work. Other aspects of the system, including appeals, welfare support for asylum seekers and asylum decision making, were also substantially reorganized. An ambitious e-borders programme, when completed, will use biometrics to track all movement in and out of the UK (Home Affairs Committee 2009: 8). Integration tests were introduced into naturalization and then settlement procedures and, towards the end of its period in office, the government enacted (but did not implement) legislation to substantially change the route to settlement and citizenship. Powers of deprivation of citizenship were also enhanced.[10]

There were however, as Flynn (2005: 465–6) also noted, major problems and contradictions in policy. The large increases in numbers represented not only a political decision about the benefits of immigration but an acknowledgement of existing migratory pressures. The rise

---

[8] Speech, 'UK migration in a global economy', by Barbara Roche, to a conference organized by the Institute of Public Policy Research in September 2000. See also Sales 2005: 445–6 and Somerville 2007: 29–30.

[9] Although the use of guidance to determine policy was found unlawful in *R (on the application of Alvi) v SSHD [2012] UKSC 33.*

[10] For an overview of New Labour immigration policy, see Somerville 2007. For a discussion of the points-based system, see Clayton (2010: chapter 10) and of the changes to settlement and naturalization, see Wray (2009) or McGhee (2009). For deprivation of citizenship, see Clayton 2010: 91–3.

in work permit approvals began in 1995, before the government was elected (Salt 2009: 92). Meanwhile, unauthorized migration also increased. Asylum applications rose from 32,500 in 1997 to 84,130 in 2002 (Somerville 2007: 65). The result was near chaos in the asylum system (McKee 2005: 254, Home Affairs Committee 2006: 190). Numbers of undocumented migrants are difficult to estimate but are likely to have increased considerably throughout the period (compare Woodbridge 2005: 1, and Gordon et al. 2009: 6). Meanwhile, removal of unauthorized migrants was highly problematic for legal and practical reasons, resulting in a pool of very poor, excluded migrants without status and unable to work legally (Clayton 2010: 50–52).

The new avenues for legal migration did not substantively relieve these pressures, being concerned primarily with the instrumental needs of business for skilled labour. Despite the rhetoric of 'modernity' and the appearance of new thinking, the underlying premise that had governed immigration policy for the past 50 years, that immigration was a force to be resisted except in very limited cases, remained intact. There were few opportunities for non-EEA migrants to undertake low-skilled work. Short-term and limited rights of entry under the Sectors Based Scheme were eventually restricted to A2 nationals, while its PBS successor, Tier 3, was not implemented. Meanwhile, many well-qualified migrants who entered for skilled work actually took more menial jobs.[11] Government credibility was further undermined by the entry of thousands of workers from Eastern Europe after the accession of the A8 states in 2004 when the government applied some of the lightest controls of any other established EU member state. Popular perceptions of an uncontrolled flow increased as the economy went into recession and unemployment rose. The government's skilled migration policy therefore did not succeed in defusing tension around the issue of immigration.

These pressures gained a new dimension as questions of security, extremism and integration also came to the fore. Policy in this area was framed by three critical events, 9/11 and the subsequent 'war on terror', disturbances in cities in the north of England in 2001 that brought non-white, usually Muslim, groups into conflict with white residents, and the London bombings of 7 July 2005 carried out by UK-educated Muslim extremists. These events had ramifications for many aspects of policy, including immigration policy. Questions of physical security, the entry of extremists, and the expulsion of suspected terrorists became a major political issue. Most relevantly for this chapter, 'social cohesion' and 'integration' became major drivers of policy, in particular the search for 'common principles' that could unite citizens (Cantle 2001: 10). This search, contentious though it was, 'seeped' (McGhee 2009: 47) into immigration policy and became the background for much subsequent policy, even if the connection between stated aims and actual policy was not always easy to establish (see Wray 2011: chapter 6 for a discussion including of the extensive literature in this area).

In the face of so many recalcitrant pressures coming from all directions, the only way to maintain the impression of momentum and reform was to tackle the apparatus of control through a kind of 'permanent revolution' in immigration control, while those migrants who did not fit within government-determined criteria – asylum-seekers, over-stayers and the unskilled – were subject to the full blast of ever more exclusionary measures. Yet within that context, as Sales (2005: 458) points out, the instrumentality of labour migration policy did partially cut across old racially determined boundaries to enable a superficially more

[11] Adrian Goldberg, 'UK's "brightest and best" migrants take unskilled jobs', BBC News, 31 October 2010, at: http://www.bbc.co.uk/news/uk-11647258 (accessed: 26 February 2011).

progressive narrative. Skilled routes of migration and intra-company transfers, for example, were dominated by South Asian migrants and provided a degree of congruence with a stated commitment to fairness and merit rather than old markers of privilege, a commitment also represented by the partial extension of race discrimination laws to the immigration authorities (see Race Relations (Amendment) Act 2000 now replaced by Equality Act 2010). In reality, race equality legislation was rarely cited in immigration appeals despite widespread anecdotal reports of discriminatory treatment, principally because meeting the evidential requirements was burdensome in individual claims.[12] More significant in practical terms was the Human Rights Act 1998, which made key articles of ECHR directly enforceable within UK law and applied to immigration control from implementation in 2000.

New Labour immigration policy thus attempted to face both ways in precisely the fashion identified by Boswell (2007: 92–3). It wanted to encourage migration of the right kind but was unable to prevent continuing pressure from less desirable migrants. Its social democratic leanings pushed it towards values such as equality, justice, human rights and fairness while its security and accumulation functions required the exclusion of those migrants who did not serve immediate and instrumental purposes. The conflicts between these aims were disguised by heavy reliance on various external threats. The dramatic rise in the number of asylum claimants led to the construction of the 'bogus' asylum seeker and rafts of measures that aimed to prevent claims being made or succeeding with little regard for their actual merits (Hassan 2004, Chakrabarti 2005) Security and criminality also became a way to justify the criminalization of unwanted migrants and ever more intrusive state surveillance that affected not only migrants but citizens (Bosworth and Guild 2008). 'Integration' of migrants became a major form of discourse with little recognition of the exclusionary consequences of these policies for those who could not or would not integrate (see Wray 2009). The tension with judicial independence, key to maintaining the credible institutional function of government, was less easily managed (see, for example, Rawlings 2005).

The absence of unskilled routes of migration and the increasing squeeze on irregular migrants and asylum meant that family, particularly marriage, migration remained one of the few routes open to those who did not meet the criteria for entry or stay via work or study. From a government perspective, it therefore had the potential to derail its efforts to control the terms of entry. It is true that some failed asylum seekers and other irregular migrants married British nationals and sought leave to remain for that reason but, given the frequent lengthy delays in processing their initial claim, this is unsurprising. As Collins J. said, 'People cannot be expected to put their lives on hold, particularly if they are young'.[13] It is also possible that a proportion of these marriages was partially motivated by opportunism, but how many and to what extent is unverified. At the same time, however, and as already discussed, expectations of the government's ethnic minority constituencies were high. Measures that were too aggressive or that affected established minorities too severely risked their alienation and, as it turned out, recourse to judicial intervention.

---

12 See, for example, *SK (India)* [2006] UKAIT 00067. Differences of treatment between nationalities are difficult to establish because it is rare that a direct comparison can be made. The Chief Inspector of the UK Border Agency, however, identified direct discrimination when applications from Pakistan were dealt with at the same post as Abu Dhabi: Vine 2010: 26.

13 *R(S) v SSHD* [2007] EWHC 51 (Admin) [203].

Family Migration Policy under New Labour

The abolition of the 'primary purpose' rule sent a clear message to ethnic minority voters that the new government not only understood their concerns but regarded them inclusively as part of the electorate from which they derived legitimacy. Admittedly, the rule had become less effective as concessions were forced and migrants turned to EU law and the *Surinder Singh* principle to remedy their position. Nonetheless, it was an important gesture that led to an immediate increase in marriage migration (Jackson and Bennett 1998: 3–4). Over the following years, there followed several tranches of policy that appeared, at different moments, either to consolidate or to withdraw from this policy of greater inclusiveness. These are discussed here thematically.[14] The purpose is to identify the ways in which policies reflected the particular and often conflicting pressures to which this government was particularly subject.

Who decides?

In 1998, the New Labour government passed the Human Rights Act and it came into effect in 2000. It made the main ECHR rights directly enforceable in the UK courts that had several new obligations and powers. In particular, article 8 ECHR, the right to respect for private and family life, alongside articles 12 (right to marry) and 14 (non-discrimination) were the basis of several major cases in which the courts frustrated restrictive government family migration policies.

Prior to its implementation, applicants who could not comply with the immigration rules could rely only on government policies or the exercise of discretion. Cases challenging these were rarely decided for the immigrant because the bar for intervention was set so high: under judicial review principles, government needed to have acted irrationally or unlawfully and international law had only a limited interpretive role. It seemed at first that the Act would not have a major effect on this tradition of deference. One of the earliest immigration article 8 cases decided under the Act found that the court's function was confined to that of 'anxious scrutiny' and that the government should be awarded a 'margin of discretion', a domestic creation that paralleled, arguably inappropriately, the margin of appreciation of the Strasbourg court (Craig 2001, Edwards 2002).[15] It took several years and many unsuccessful court and tribunal hearings for a different approach to become dominant. In 2007 in *Huang*, the House of Lords finally agreed that appellate bodies should decide questions of proportionality for themselves and overturned the Court of Appeal's finding that such cases must be exceptional.[16]

The House of Lords' decision in *Huang* set the tone for later cases, some of which are mentioned below, although in some of them (for example, *Mahad*) the decision was made without using article 8.[17] In others, the UK courts arguably went further than the Strasbourg court in applying article 8.[18] The position should not be overstated. Most article 8 claims still did not succeed on their facts and, shortly after *Huang*, the Court of Appeal emphasized

14 For a fuller account, see Wray 2011.

15 *R v SSHD ex p. Mahmood* [2000] EWCA Civ 315.

16 *Huang (FC) v SSHD* [2007] UKHL 11.

17 *Mahad (Ethiopia) v ECO* [2009] UKSC 16.

18 Compare, for example, *Chikwamba v SSHD* [2008] UKHL 40 with *Omoregie v Norway* 265/07 31 July 2008.

that, in normal circumstances, interference in family life was still justified.[19] Nonetheless, the decision marked a decisive shift in authority from government to courts that was arguably an unforeseen consequence of the powers granted by the Human Rights Act. The Strasbourg court recognized a wide 'margin of appreciation' on immigration questions and domestic commentators had also noted deference by the courts in immigration (for example, Legomsky 1987, Griffiths 1997: 182–204). The Human Rights Act represented 'an unprecedented transfer of political power from the executive and legislature to the judiciary' (Ewing 1999: 79), raising questions of democratic legitimacy and the potential politicization of the judiciary (Stevens 1999: 368–72). Given judges' subjection to 'self-limiting institutional norms' (Judge 2004: 693), it was perhaps reasonable to expect a cautious approach to prevail, as was indeed the case for several years. Even then, the lead came from the top. The controversial cases were mostly made by the House of Lords, later the Supreme Court, and usually, although not always (see, for example, *Baiai*, discussed below), overturned lower court decisions tending the other way. Why their Lordships became more willing to challenge government on family migration questions (and they were not uniformly so willing on immigration matters; see Kelly 2011) cannot be explored here. There was certainly some irony in seeing the government defeated on so many occasions by judges exercising powers that the same government had voluntarily ceded to them. That these decisions were viewed as unwelcome interference rather than constructive criticism is suggested by the reluctance of that government to implement some of these decisions (see the discussion on certificates of approval and *Baiai* below).

Who is family?

British immigration policy has generally taken a narrow view of which family members may benefit from family reunification policies. As at 1997, husbands and wives, minor children, some elderly parents or grandparents and, very rarely, other dependent relatives, could enter subject to various conditions. This narrow range of relatives was not changed substantially by the Labour government and some groups continued to find it difficult to live family life on the terms they would prefer.

All applicants for family formation and reunification, unless eligible under separate humanitarian categories, had to establish that they and their dependants could be adequately maintained and accommodated without recourse to public funds. Accommodation could be shared provided statutory overcrowding was avoided and couples (but not necessarily other family members) had a private bedroom.[20] Maintenance required resources at or above the minimum level for welfare support, a policy aimed at the prevention of an impoverished immigration underclass rather than the protection of public resources as welfare is anyway unavailable to newly arrived migrants.[21] These requirements were inherited from the previous government and did not become more demanding through the period even while other governments elsewhere in Europe adopted more rigorous criteria (see, for example, Human

---

19 *LK (Serbia) v SSHD* [2007] EWCA Civ 1554.

20 *KJ ('Own or occupy exclusively') Jamaica* [2008] UKAIT 00006; *AB (third party provision of accommodation)* [2008] UKAIT 18.

21 Entry Clearance Guidance, chapter 9, para. 2; *KA and others (adequacy of maintenance)* [2006] UKAIT 65; *AM (Ethiopia) and others v ECO* [2008] EWCA Civ 1082.

Rights Watch 2008). However, the government did require the parties or their sponsors to fulfil the requirements themselves; support by other family or community members was not permitted.[22] This issue was contested on many occasions and the government was eventually defeated in the Supreme Court who interpreted the existing rules to permit third-party support of all relatives.[23]

The removal of the primary purpose rule removed one major obstacle to the admission of spouses and fiancé(e)s and numbers increased in the following period until 2006, after which they began to decline.[24] Other criteria remained unchanged, including the need to establish a valid marriage, to have met and to show that the marriage was subsisting, and that the parties intended to live together permanently. The prohibition on the entry of more than one wife to a polygamous marriage, introduced in 1988, remained in place, but the government did expand the definition of 'spouse' to include 'modern' relationships such as civil, same sex, and unmarried partners. The minimum age for entry and sponsorship was progressively raised from 16 (which is the minimum age for marriage, with parental consent, in the UK) to 18 and then, in 2008 and in response to concerns about forced marriage discussed further below, to 21. The government also announced its intention to introduce a pre-entry English language test for spouses but lost power before the planned implementation date (which was later brought forward by the Coalition government).

Commentators criticized administrative approaches to questions of validity of marriage and divorce as over-formalistic and reliant on dominant European norms (Shah 2008, 2010, 2011). As a result applicants sometimes became mired in a series of expensive, protracted and sometimes fruitless legal and administrative proceedings (see, for example, Menski 2007). The quality of decision making was also often criticized, but the worst excesses of the primary purpose period did disappear and there was an effort towards improvement at least in some regions although it is not clear how deep or how sustained this was (see Wray 2011: chapter 9 for a discussion).

Throughout the period, single parents who were residents or citizens of the UK could be joined by their child only if the other parent was dead, if the UK parent had sole responsibility for the child's upbringing, or if there were serious and compelling family or other considerations that made exclusion of the child undesirable.[25] Sole responsibility was rare where the other parent was involved in a child's life and could be lost to other relatives or even to no relative. For 'serious and compelling considerations' to apply, the child's situation should be 'exceptional' in relation to those of other children in the country of origin.[26] Entry would not be permitted because better conditions were available in the UK. Separated or divorced parents living in different countries were therefore not free to decide on the best arrangements for a child. Meanwhile, the kind of shared care that is common in extended families made it more likely that sole responsibility of a single migrant parent could not be established.

---

22 HC395, paras 281(iv), 297(iv) and 317(v).

23 *Mahad and others v ECO* [2009] UKSC 16.

24 Calculations drawn from Home Office 2010a: 62 and Home Office 2004: Table 1.6.

25 HC 395, para. 297. 'Serious and compelling reasons' may also be used to permit a child to join another relative.

26 Entry Clearance Guidance, chapter 14, section 6.

Aspects of the rules on overseas adoption were also problematic.[27] Not all overseas adoptions were recognized and, while children's welfare needed protection, the rules were unnecessarily inflexible in places (see Clayton 2010: 328–43 for a more extended discussion).[28] Criteria in the immigration rules limited the possibility of intra-family adoptions as the birth parents had to be unable to care for the child, who must have broken ties with the family of origin and the adoption could not be one 'of convenience'.[29]

In 2008, the government withdrew its immigration reservation to the UN Convention on the Rights of the Child, and s. 55 Borders, Citizenship and Immigration Act 2009 required UKBA to carry out its functions in a way that takes account of the need to safeguard and promote the welfare of children in the UK. While the duty has already been cited in several cases involving the welfare of migrant children in the UK,[30] neither the Convention nor the duty apply to children outside the jurisdiction and it is not anticipated that this will have a major impact on the criteria for entry. Article 8 may sometimes assist, but not where children seek to be reunited with relatives other than parents and family life is not already in existence.[31]

Only a limited range of adult dependent relatives were permitted entry. In brief, parents and grandparents travelling together when one is 65 or over or a widowed parent or grandparent aged 65 or over travelling alone could enter. Divorced or separated parents and parents or grandparents under 65 and children, siblings, aunts and uncles over the age of 18 could enter only if living alone in the most exceptional compassionate circumstances and mainly dependent financially on UK-based relatives. All applicants had to show financial dependency on the sponsor and have no other close relatives in their own country to whom they could turn for financial support.[32] This restrictive approach to extended relatives inevitably limited the family arrangements of many ethnic minority families.

Thus the range of relationships recognized for family migration purposes did not change materially under New Labour and remained restricted, despite the abolition of the primary purpose rule. Such changes as there were tended to favour 'modern' or 'Western' versions of family life, such as same sex or unmarried partnerships, over more 'traditional' norms associated with some ethnic minority communities, in particular young marriages and extended family support. The support for pre-entry language tests also suggested resistance to the entry of migrants perceived as perpetuating social segregation of these communities.

Bogus marriages

This became a major policy preoccupation. Under legislation passed in 1999, parties had to attend personally to give notice of their marriage and marriage registrars were obliged

---

27 HC 395 paras 309–16.

28 For an example of such flexibility, see *PD v MD* [2008] 1 FLR 1475.

29 The courts have occasionally helped to mitigate these factors but not always: compare *Boadi v ECO Ghana* [2002] UKIAT 01323, *Re J (A Minor) (Adoption: Non-Patrial)* [1998] 1 FLR 225; *Re B (a minor)* [1999] 2 AC 136 with *Kamande v ECO Nairobi* [2002] UKIAT 06129; *S v ECO New Delhi* [2005] EWCA Civ 89.

30 *ZH Tanzania v SSHD* [2011] UKSC 4.

31 See, for example, *Lagos v Imoh* [2002] UKIAT 01967.

32 For the full requirements, see HC 395, para. 317. For more detailed discussion, see Clayton 2010: 328–33.

to report suspected bogus marriages to the authorities, with exemption only for Church of England marriages.[33] While the discriminatory aspects caused anger and there was some opposition, it was not difficult for the government to present this as a necessary and routine anti-abuse measure. However, reported increases in the numbers of suspected marriages were the basis of later more far-reaching controls.

In 2002, after claiming that bogus marriages were being used to facilitate residence in the UK (Home Office 2002: 101), the government prohibited migrants present in the UK without leave (for example, asylum seekers or failed asylum seekers) or with short-term leave (for example, visitors) from switching to a spouse visa. Such migrants had to leave the country and apply for entry clearance from abroad to regularize their status. It was claimed that 'literally tens of thousands' of applicants were entering such marriages, although this may have been an exaggeration.[34] This reasoning was given further justification by the claim that in-country switching was 'unfair to those applicants who follow the correct procedures by applying for entry clearance overseas and pay for the appropriate visa' (Home Office 2002: 101), an argument later criticized by the House of Lords in *Chikwamba* (see below).

The ban on switching was implemented in 2002 and had a severe impact not only on short-term migrants but on asylum seekers, failed asylum seekers, and undocumented migrants who might have spent many years in the UK.[35] There was no distinction made between marriages that were clearly genuine (including those with children) and those that were not. Nor was it necessarily a routine matter to obtain entry clearance from abroad, as many applicants were unsuccessful asylum claimants from troubled regions where visa facilities might not even be available. For instance, in one case heard before the Tribunal, the applicant had to go to Iraq, obtain travel documents, negotiate Jordanian border controls, and endure the dangerous and expensive journey to Jordan for a visa that would permit his return to the UK.[36] Processing the application might take a variable amount of time and applicants had to keep themselves in the meantime, often in hotel accommodation. Success at the end was not guaranteed, as visa officers rarely granted leave under article 8 where an applicant could not meet the criteria of the rules, necessitating an in-country appeal in the applicant's absence. The blanket application of this policy, particularly where children were involved, was eventually found by the House of Lords to be a breach of article 8 ECHR.[37]

If a visa could not be obtained, then, unless 'insurmountable obstacles' could be shown, the UK resident spouse and children were expected to join the applicant in the country of origin.[38] One woman was expected to accompany her husband to Iran although this meant conversion to Islam, the adoption of Iranian nationality, and the loss of British diplomatic protection. Another was told that she should leave her son by a previous marriage to live with her husband in Iraq. A third woman in poor health, who cared for her disabled parents and

---

33 Ss. 24, 160–63, Immigration and Asylum Act 1999.

34 Lord Rooker, HL Hansard, 7 February 2002, col. 752; see, however, the actual figures for entry in Mallourides and Turner 2002: 3–4, most of whom would not have been short-term migrants and even fewer would have been bogus marriages.

35 HC 164.

36 *HC (Availability of Entry Clearance Facilities) Iraq* [2004] UKIAT 00154.

37 *Chikwamba v SSHD* [2008] UKHL 40.

38 See, for example, 'Forced to choose … my husband or my life', *Glamour Magazine*, February 2006, 106–11, and HC Hansard, 10 October 2005, col. 129.

shared care of her 8-year-old daughter, was told that it was 'reasonable' for her to accompany her husband to the Democratic Republic of Congo (Home Affairs Committee 2006: 285–8, 346–54). The 'insurmountable obstacles' test, which had been adopted by the government and largely supported by the tribunal and lower courts but was based on a misreading of the law, was finally disapproved by the House of Lords in 2008.[39]

New proposed measures said to be aimed at preventing sham marriages but actually going much wider were introduced into parliament in 2004 against the background of numerous reports presenting them as a widespread and organized racket.[40] In fact, their prevalence was unclear. It was claimed, for instance, that one in five register office marriages in London (or 8,000 marriages per year) was bogus, although the source was an 'impressionistic' survey by a London marriage registrar.[41] A leaked email claimed that, nationally, 15,000 bogus marriages took place each year, although this was also not substantiated.[42] Leading politicians relied on the more conservative figures of suspicious marriages reported by registrars. In 2001, the first year of obligatory reporting, there were 756 reports, but, in the first half of 2004 alone, 2,251 were received, although it is not apparent whether this represented increased numbers or increased reporting nor whether suspicion was justified (although there were also claims of under-reporting).[43]

The proposals became ss. 19–25 of the Asylum and Immigration (Treatment of Claimants etc) Act 2004. Unless a non-EEA migrant married in the Church of England, had indefinite leave to remain, or entered from abroad on a fiancé or marriage visit visa, he or she had to obtain a certificate of approval to marry in the UK, costing £135 (later raised to £295). Those without leave, whose leave was shortly to expire, or who entered with six months' leave or less were refused certificates and could not marry. There was no enquiry into the marriage and no distinction made between those who were compliant or non-compliant with immigration control. Those refused had to leave the UK and apply to re-enter for marriage unless exceptional circumstances, defined restrictively, applied.

After a brief consultation, the proposals were introduced as amendments to an existing parliamentary bill, truncating debate. Government arguments did not address their over-inclusivity, the human rights questions involved, and existing anti-abuse measures including

39 *EB (Kosovo) v SSHD* [2008] UKHL 11 [12]. The test arose from a misreading of dicta by Lord Phillips in *R v SSHD ex p. Mahmood* [2000] EWCA Civ 315 [55]; see Sedley LJ in *LM (DRC) v SSHD* [2008] EWCA Civ 325 [11–12].

40 '"I'm asked to conduct many sham weddings" says registrar', *Daily Telegraph*, 21 March 2004; 'Sham marriages soar as illegal immigrants try to beat curbs', *Daily Telegraph*, 15 June 2004; 'Beating the sham wedding cheats', BBC News, 22 September 2004, at: http://news.bbc.co.uk/go/pr/fr/-/2/hi/uk_news/3679482.stm (accessed: 11 August 2012); '"Fake marriages network" smashed', BBC News, 22 September 2004, at: http://news.bbc.co.uk/go/pr/fr/-/2/hi/uk_news/3678784.stm (accessed: 12 January 2011); '25 jailed for bogus marriage scam', *The Scotsman*, 18 January 2005; '£1m bogus marriage woman jailed', *The Scotsman*, 26 April 2005.

41 Stephen Pound MP, HC Hansard, 13 May 2004, col. 563; Baroness Carnegy of Lour, HL Hansard, 15 June 2004, col. 693; 'Sham marriages soar as illegal immigrants try to beat curbs' *Daily Telegraph*; telephone interview by author with marriage registrar Mark Rimmer, 23 August 2005.

42 A. Travis, 'Blunkett targets sham marriages and bogus courses', *The Guardian*, 23 April 2004, at: http://www.guardian.co.uk/politics/2004/apr/23/highereducation.overseasstudents (accessed: 23 August 2012).

43 HC Hansard, 15 June 2004, col. 681; Lord Rooker, HL Hansard, 15 June 2004.

the ban on switching just discussed (for a discussion, see Wray 2006). If the arguments were unconvincing, it was perhaps because the government was initially slow to reveal a major concern, the 'loophole'[44] represented by the residency rights of non-EEA spouses of EEA nationals under the more liberal EU regime.[45] It was stated that 61 per cent of reports by registrars of suspicious marriages involved a non-British EEA national, and there were some well-publicized arrests.[46]

Following implementation, there was a significant drop in the number of marriages taking place within the UK.[47] The 'certificates of approval' scheme was successfully challenged in the High Court in 2006, in the Court of Appeal in 2007, and in the House of Lords in 2008.[48] The House of Lords found unanimously that the scheme and its application, including the fee, impaired the essence of the right to marry under Article 12 ECHR and was discriminatory due to the exception for Church of England marriages. The government responded very slowly and partially to these judgements. While those whose marriages proved genuine were permitted to marry, the fee was not removed until April 2009 and the requirement for extensive affidavit evidence remained an obstacle for undocumented migrants anxious about submitting to official scrutiny. Despite announcing in 2009 its intention of abandoning the scheme, this did not happen before the election, and it was not finally abolished until mid-2011. One consequence was further unfavourable legal findings, this time in the European Court of Human Rights.[49]

Both the prohibition on switching and the certificates of approval scheme had wider functions than the detection of bogus marriages, targeting migrants purely on their immigration status (including some who were lawfully present) and without determining whether their marriages were genuine. While their effectiveness was compromised by the courts, they represented an attempt to grapple with the consequences of loss of control over entry during the early part of the period, particularly in the asylum system, and placed a heavy emphasis on compliance with legal and bureaucratic hurdles. Unlike measures such as the primary purpose rule, they were not targeted at particular nationalities, although it is possible that the perception of threat this migration created was connected to the nationalities predominantly involved.

44 Des Browne, Minister for Citizenship and Immigration, HC Hansard, 13 May 2004, col. 569; 'Beating the sham wedding cheats', BBC News.

45 See HL Hansard, 28 June 2004, col. 70, 6 July 2004, cols 716–17 and 725–6; HC Hansard, 12 July 2004, col. 1219.

46 HC Hansard, 12 July 2004, col. 1219; 'Marriage scam for migrants broken', *The Guardian*, 23 September 2004; 'LCCG Bust Sham Wedding Racket', *Interport News*, 13 January 2006.

47 *Migration News Sheet*, June 2005, 5; *Migration News Sheet*, May 2006, 9; 'Marriage rates fall to lowest on record', Press Release, National Statistics, 21 February 2007.

48 *R (on the application of Baiai and others) v SSHD* [2006] EWHC 823 (Admin); *SSHD v Baiai and others* [2007] EWCA Civ 478; *R (On the application of Baiai and others) v SSHD* [2008] UKHL 53.

49 *O'Donoghue and others v. UK* (application no. 34848/07) 14 December 2010.

Integration and Migrant Family Life

As elsewhere in Europe, discussion of transnational marriage became dominated by discussion about one type of transnational marriage: the international arranged marriage. This became a prism through which numerous other anxieties were filtered: concerns about segregation, immigration, extremism, archaic or oppressive family norms, and migrant poverty. These issues could be conflated in ways that presented such marriages as a potent threat. For example, one Labour MP with a sizeable Muslim population in her constituency spoke of forged documents, forced marriages, sham marriages, chain migration, genetic disorders due to cousin marriages, lack of integration, and educational underachievement all as problems associated with marriage migration in her constituency (Home Affairs Committee 2006: 231–6). Forced marriages were raised in parliament nearly 100 times between 1997 and the introduction of the Consultation Paper *Marriage to Partners from Overseas* in December 2007 and became the explicit or implicit backdrop for almost any discussion on marriage migration.

The White Paper *Secure Borders, Safe Haven* (Home Office 2002: 18) drew attention to the 'tradition of families originating from the sub-continent wanting to bring spouses from arranged marriages to live with them in the UK'. The succeeding paragraph referred to the 'large profits and financial rewards' obtainable through arranging bogus marriages and went on to say, 'We also believe there is a discussion to be had within those communities that continue the practice of arranged marriages as to whether more of these could be undertaken within the settled community here.' Elsewhere, the White Paper signalled the intention to force the pace on integration through tests on knowledge of language and life in the UK including for spouses.

The passages in the White Paper on marriage were viewed as inflammatory and caused immense controversy at the time. Specific proposals were to increase the probationary period between entry and settlement to two years (implemented in 2003) and to end switching into marriage for some in-country migrants (already discussed). In addition, the minimum age of sponsorship and entry was increased to 18 in 2003 and 2004.

There was, however, growing momentum for an age increase to 21, this suggestion receiving support in the 2005 White Paper *Controlling Our Borders* (Home Office 2005b: 22). In December 2007, the government made it one of several proposals contained in two consultation papers, *Marriage to Partners from Overseas* and *Marriage Visas: Pre-entry English Requirement for Spouses* (Border and Immigration Agency 2007a and 2007b). While public presentation focused on forced marriage, the official context and language used in both consultations suggested more instrumental motives. *Marriage to Partners from Overseas* was introduced in parliament alongside a Statement of Intent on the points-based system and proposals on simplification, as 'key aspects of our migration reform programme'.[50] The language in both consultations suggested a pre-occupation with ensuring what were, by majority norms, 'good' marriages and labour market participation. Meanwhile, the consultation process was unsatisfactory in several respects (see Wray 2011: chapter 7 for a critique). Nonetheless, while a string of proposals, including some of which were very controversial, were made in these consultations, only two were eventually pursued with any vigour: raising the minimum age to 21 and introducing a pre-entry language test. The 21-year minimum age was later found by the Supreme Court to

[50] HC Deb, 5 December 2007, c. 72 WS; HC Deb, 19 June 2008, c. 61 WS.

breach Article 8 ECHR when applied to voluntary marriages and reverted to 18. The pre-entry language test was unsuccessfully challenged in the High Court with an appeal pending at the time of writing.[51]

Many commentators, including this author, were critical of these developments and of related changes to settlement and naturalization contained in *The Path to Citizenship* (Border and Immigration Agency 2008). This document adopted a more challenging tone than *Secure Borders, Safe Haven* and was arguably more concerned with excluding undesirable migrants than with securing integration (McGhee 2009: 52, Wray 2009). The consequent legislation which was enacted but not implemented before the election, would have made progression to a secure status more difficult for many disadvantaged migrants, including marriage migrants (see Wray 2009 for a discussion).

Just as with measures that ostensibly targeted bogus marriages, the government used concern about forced marriage, cohesion and integration to drive measures that had more far-reaching and exclusionary effects. In particular, the government's concern for the victims of forced marriage, while not necessarily insincere, seems also to have provided a useful pretext for acting against marriages regarded as unwise rather than involuntary. Meanwhile, its professed concern for victims sat uneasily with the limited provision for migrant spouses suffering domestic violence (Siddiqui 2005).

Yet it is also worth pointing out what the government did not do. Despite backbench pressure and some combative rhetoric, it did not act decisively on these issues until relatively late in its term and it did not go as far as some other European countries, notably the Netherlands and Denmark, in using integration requirements as a form of exclusion (see Van Oers, Ersbøll and Kostakopoulou 2010, Bonjour 2010, Bak Jorgensen 2012, Human Rights Watch 2008). In general, while there was a move away from 'multiculturalism' and towards what McGhee (2009) calls 'civic assimilation' and, later, 'civic nationalism', discourse was less abrasive than elsewhere. Despite the occasional comment, bans on wearing the burqa, as adopted in France, or on the construction of minarets, as favoured in Switzerland, did not form part of mainstream political discourse. The UK government was in the slipstream rather than the forefront of the anti-Islamic and anti-multiculturalist reaction that swept across much of Western Europe during the period. Whether it would eventually have gone so far as these other countries cannot be known. The *Path to Citizenship* did adopt a more aggressive tone than before, but detail of the new policy's application was absent and the scheme was superseded by electoral defeat. Certainly, the coalition government that came to power in 2010 appears to be less cautious and 'state multiculturalism' has been expressly found wanting, while family migration has been severely curtailed.[52]

---

[51] *R (on the application of Quila and another) v SSHD* [2011] UKSC 45; *R (on the application of Chapti and others) v SSHD* [2011] EWHC 3370 (Admin).

[52] 'PM's speech at Munich Security Conference', 5 February 2011, at: http://www.number10.gov.uk/news/speeches-and-transcripts/2011/02/pms-speech-at-munich-security-conference-60293 (accessed: 26 February 2011). Nonetheless, even this right-wing prime minister was anxious to differentiate between extremism and devout Islam; HC 194.

Conclusion

When New Labour was elected in 1997, expectations were high. To some measure, these were realized during its first term when the primary purpose rule was removed, the Human Rights Act implemented, and race discrimination laws extended to the immigration system. While the government went on to admit thousands of skilled workers in a move that appeared, on the surface, inclusive, in reality it spent much of its time in office on the defensive, attempting to minimize the effects of global migratory pressures elsewhere in the system and to manage concern about apparently unassimilated non-white groups who represented an important political constituency as well as a problematic presence. The result was that many measures seemed to represent attempts to row back from this initial progressive stance.

There were other tensions also. The 1997 Labour Party manifesto had promised that a Labour government would be a 'leader in Europe', a contrast to the scepticism associated with the previous regime.[53] Within the electorate, there remained a strong streak of populist anti-Europeanism that this government, in particular, would not wish to provoke. Yet many of the problems that the government faced in migration were a consequence of its membership of the European Union or of its commitment to the ECHR. The government attempted to address some of these problems without fully acknowledging their political and legal origins. For instance, it was only when other arguments failed to convince that the government acknowledged that the certificates of approval scheme aimed to prevent settlement by spouses of EEA nationals. Government's commitment to supra-national legal systems was thus problematic as it contributed to its difficulties in controlling migration but was largely unshared by the electorate.

Family migration represented a critical intersection of two sets of concern for the government. It provided an avenue for the legal and long-term entry or stay of poorly qualified workers, undermining attempts to confine entry only to the most skilled. At the same time, family was seen as the site for reproduction of norms and practices often regarded as archaic or oppressive. These families often had a transnational consciousness, regarding themselves as part of wider global kin or ethnic networks, and were not easily constrained by the new emphasis on citizenship and 'shared' national values. Yet they also formed part of New Labour's natural electorate and their preferences could not be easily brushed aside.

Family migration policy had to attempt to reconcile these tensions. This could only be done by, to recall the phrase used earlier, the 'intentional fudging of policy' (Boswell 2007: 92). At times the government used specious reasoning to justify measures that had broader aims or promised more than they could deliver. On other occasions, it seemed to resist the exercise of rights that it had voluntarily granted. Policy and institutional reform sometimes seemed to gain a momentum of their own beyond the actual exigencies of the situation. Yet the incoherence they suggested was arguably not entirely the result of incompetence. It may have seemed the best alternative available given that the government had at least to appear to manage global migratory forces and deny the loss of sovereign power to an electorate, many of whom were eager to maintain or reconstruct national boundaries. At the same time, a significant section of the electorate was not prepared to recognize such boundaries in the exercise of their personal lives. Directly confronting these constituents in the style of other European governments was

53 Labour Party Manifesto 1997.

not a path that this government readily chose, whether for ideological or strategic reasons, although, as time went on, a more proactive approach to managing transnational lives became evident. However, as with much policy in this area, the true meaning and intentions could not be understood by a surface reading of policy statements. These were, on first reading, often unpersuasive and even incoherent. Yet they may often have represented the government's best efforts to manage the contradictory forces to which it was subject and, as such, had more meaning and purpose than might be immediately visible.

References

Bak Jorgensen, M. 2012. Danish Regulations on Marriage Migration: Policy Understandings of Transnational Marriages, in *Transnational Marriage: New Perspectives from Europe and Beyond*, edited by Katharine Charsley. Abingdon: Routledge, 60–78.

Bonjour, S. 2010. Between Integration Provision and Selection Mechanism: Party Politics, Judicial Constraints, and the Making of French and Dutch Policies of Civic Integration Abroad. *European Journal of Migration and Law*, 12(3), 299–318.

Border and Immigration Agency. 2007a. *Marriage to Partners from Overseas: A Consultation Paper*. London: Border and Immigration Agency.

Border and Immigration Agency. 2007b. *Marriage Visas: Pre-entry English Requirement for Spouses: Consultation Paper*. London: Border and Immigration Agency.

Border and Immigration Agency. 2008. *The Path to Citizenship: Next Steps in Reforming the Immigration System*. London: Border and Immigration Agency.

Boswell, C. 2007. Theorizing Migration Policy: Is There a Third Way? *International Migration Review*, 41(1), 75–100.

Bosworth, M. and Guild, M. 2008. Governing through Migration Control: Security and Citizenship in Britain. *The British Journal of Criminology*, 48, 703–19.

Cantle, T. 2001. *Community Cohesion: A Report of the Independent Review Team*. London: Home Office.

Castles, S. 2004. Why Migration Policies Fail. *Ethnic and Racial Studies*, 27(2), 205–27.

Chakrabarti, S. 2005. 'Rights and Rhetoric: The Politics of Asylum and Human Rights Culture in the United Kingdom' *Journal of Law and Society*, 32(1) 131–47.

Clayton, G. 2010. *Textbook on Immigration and Asylum Law*, 4th edition. Oxford: Oxford University Press.

Cornelius. A and Tsuda, T. 2004. Controlling Immigration: The Limits of Government Intervention, in *Controlling Immigration: A Global Perspective*, 2nd edition, edited by Wayne A. Cornelius, Philip L. Martin and James F. Hollifield. Stanford, CA: Stanford University Press, 3–48.

Craig, P. 2001. The Courts, the Human Rights Act and Judicial Review. *Law Quarterly Review*, 117 (October), 589–603.

Dummett, A. and Nicol, A. 1990. *Subjects, Citizens, Aliens and Others*. London: Weidenfeld and Nicolson.

Edwards, R. 2002. Judicial Deference under the Human Rights Act. *Modern Law Review*, 65(6), 859–82.

Ewing, K. 1999. The Human Rights Act and Parliamentary Democracy. *Modern Law Review*, 62(1), 79–99.

Flynn, D. 2005. New Borders, New Management: The Dilemmas of Modern Immigration Policy. *Ethnic and Racial Studies*, 28(3), 463–90.

Freeman, G. 1994. Can Liberal States Control Unwanted Migration? *The Annals of the American Academy of Political and Social Science*, 534(1), 17–30.

Gordon, I. et al. 2009. *Economic Impact on the London and UK Economy of an Earned Regularisation of Irregular Migrants to the UK*. London: Greater London Authority.

Griffiths, J. 1997. *The Politics of the Judiciary*. London: Fontana Press.

Hansen, R. 2000. *Citizenship and Immigration in Post-war Britain: The Institutional Origins of a Multicultural Nation*. Oxford: Oxford University Press.

Hassan, L. 2000. 'Deterrence Measures and the Preservation of Asylum in the United Kingdom and United States' *Journal of Refugee Studies*, 13(2) 184–204.

Hollifield, J. 2000. Migration and the New International order: The Missing Regime, in *Managing Migration: Time for a New International Regime*, edited by B. Ghosh. Oxford: Oxford University Press, 75–109.

Hollifield, J. 2008. The Politics of International Migration, in *Migration Theory: Talking Across Disciplines*, 2nd edition, edited by C. Brettell and J. Hollifield. New York and London: Routledge, 183–237.

Home Affairs Committee. 2006. *Immigration Control: Fifth Report of Session 2005–6, volume 3*. HC 775 III, London: HMSO.

Home Affairs Committee. 2009. *The E-Borders Programme: Third Report of Session 2009–10*. HC170, London: HMSO.

Home Office. 2002.

Home Office. 2004. *Control of Immigration: Statistics United Kingdom 2003*. Statistical Bulletin 12/04, London: Home Office.

Home Office. 2005a. *Control of Immigration: Statistics United Kingdom 2004*. Statistical Bulletin 14/05, London: Home Office.

Home Office. 2005b. *Controlling Our Borders: Making Migration Work for Britain*. Cmnd. 6472, London: HMSO.

Home Office. 2010a. *Control of Immigration Statistics United Kingdom 2009*. Statistical Bulletin 15/10, London: Home Office.

Home Office. 2010b. *Control of Immigration 2009: Supplementary Tables*. London: Home Office.

Human Rights Watch. 2008. *The Netherlands: Discrimination in the Name of Integration – Migrants' Rights under the Integration Abroad Act*, at: http://www.hrw.org/backgrounder/2008/netherlands0508/ (accessed: 25 February 2011).

Jackson, K. and Bennett, A. 1998. *Control of Immigration: Statistics United Kingdom, Second Half and Year 1997*. Statistical Bulletin 13/98, London: Home Office.

Joppke, C. 1988. Why Liberal States Accept Unwanted Immigration. *World Politics*, 50 (January) 266–93.

Judge, D. 2004. Whatever Happened to Parliamentary Democracy in the United Kingdom? *Parliamentary Affairs*, 57(3), 682–701.

Juss, S. 1997. *Discretion and Deviation in the Administration of Immigration Control*. London: Sweet and Maxwell.

Kelly, B. 2011. Law Lords v New Labour. *Journal of Immigration Asylum and Nationality Law* 25(2), 146–67.
Legomsky, S. 1987. *Immigration and the Judiciary: Law and Politics in Britain and America*. Oxford: Clarendon Press.
Macdonald, I. and Blake, N. 1991. *Immigration Law and Practice in the United Kingdom*. London: Butterworths.
Mallourides, E. and Turner, G. 2002. *Control of Immigration: Statistics United Kingdom 2001*. Statistical Bulletin 11/02. London: Home Office.
McGhee, D. 2009. The Paths to Citizenship: A Critical Examination of Immigration Policy in Britain since 2001. *Patterns of Prejudice*, 43(1), 41–64.
McKee, R. 2005. More Than It Can Chew. *Immigration, Asylum and Nationality Law*, 19(4), 254–7.
Menski, W. 2007. Dodgy Asians or Dodgy Lawyers? The Story of H. *Journal of Immigration, Asylum and Nationality Law*, 21(4), 284–94.
Rawlings, R. 2005. Review, Revenge and Retreat. *Modern Law Review*, 68(3), 378–410.
Ryan, B. and Mitsilegas, V. 2010. *Extraterritorial Immigration Control: Legal Challenges*. Leiden and Boston: Martinus Nijhoff.
Sachdeva, S. 1993. *The Primary Purpose Rule in British Immigration Law*. Stoke-on-Trent: Trentham Books.
Sales, R. 2005. 'Secure Borders, Safe Haven': A Contradiction in Terms. *Ethnic and Racial Studies*, 28(3), 445–62.
Salt J. 2009. *International Migration and the UK. Annual Report of the UK SOPEMI Correspondent to the OECD*. London: Migration Research Unit UCL.
Shah, P. 2000. *Refugees, Race and the Legal Concept of Asylum in Britain*. London: Cavendish Publishing.
Shah, P. 2008. Rituals of Recognition: Ethnic Minority Marriages in British Legal Systems, in *Law and Ethnic Plurality: Socio-Legal Perspectives*, edited by P. Shah. Leiden: Martinus Nijhoff, 177–202.
Shah, P. 2010. Trans-jurisdictional Marriage and Family Reunification for Refugees in the United Kingdom. *Istanbul Kűltűr Űniversitesi Hukuk Fakűltesi Dergisi*, 9(2), 93–113.
Shah, P. 2011. When South Asians Marry Trans-jurisdictionally: Some Reflections on Immigration Cases by an 'Expert', in *Cultural Expertise and Litigation: Patterns, Conflicts, Narratives*, edited by L. Holden. London: Routledge, 35–52.
Siddiqui, H. (2005), 'There is No Honour in Domestic Violence, Only Shame': Women's Struggles Against 'Honour' Crimes in the UK, in *Honour: Crimes, Paradigms and Violence Against Women*, edited by L. Welchman and S. Hossain. London and New York: Zed Books, 263–81.
Somerville, W. 2007. *Immigration under New Labour*. Bristol: Policy Press.
Soysal, Y. 1994. *Limits of Citizenship: Migrants and Postnational Membership in Europe*. Chicago, IL and London: University of Chicago Press.
Stevens, R. 1999. A Loss of Innocence? Judicial Independence and the Separation of Powers. *Oxford Journal of Legal Studies*, 19(Autumn), 365–402.
Van Oers, R., Ersbøll, E. and Kostakopoulou, D. 2010. *A Re-definition of Belonging: Language and Integration Tests in Europe*. Leiden and Boston, MA: Martinus Nijhoff Publishers.
Vine, J. 2010. *An Inspection of Entry Clearance in Abu Dhabi and Islamabad*. London: Independent Chief Inspector of the UK Border Agency.

Woodbridge, J. 2005. *Sizing the Unauthorised (Illegal) Migrant Population in the United Kingdom in 2001*. London: Home Office.

Wray, H. 2006. An Ideal Husband? Marriages of Convenience, Moral Gate-Keeping and Immigration to the UK. *European Journal of Migration and Law*, 8(3), 303–20.

Wray, H. 2009. Moulding the Migrant Family. *Legal Studies*, 29(4), 592–618.

Wray, H. 2011. *A Stranger in the Home: Regulation of UK Marriage Migration 1962–2010*. Farnham: Ashgate.

Wray, H. 2012. Any Time, Any Place, Anywhere: Entry Clearance, Marriage Migration and the Border, in *Transnational Marriage: New Perspectives from Europe and Beyond*, edited by Katharine Charsley. Abingdon: Routledge, 41–59.

29 ASHGATE **RESEARCH** COMPANION

Elements of Movement Controls in Post-sovereign Governmentality

Thanos Zartaloudis

Citizenship–Denizenship: Crisis and Survival

The focus of this contribution lies with the very notion of migration or movement management in general. The aim is to understand and reformulate its logic as a crisis machine of control. To do so and to be able to expose, for these purposes, the vast and constantly redrawn typology and administration of people on the move (genuine/bogus asylum seekers, forced/voluntary migrants, legal/illegal migrants, trafficked migrants, Convention/proper refugees, regular/irregular migrants, seasonal workers, etc.) we conceive of what will be suggested below as a wider *logic of the field*[1] of control, of the management of people on the move in general. As a result this analysis will not be focused exclusively either on the nation-state or the UNCHR, nor on the administration and policing, NGO humanitarian action, law and micro-management of people on the move, but rather on their *functional* relation and mutual exposure. The aim is to suggest that an adequate understanding of the fluid practices of inclusion and exclusion in a post-sovereign world can only by reached by an approach that keeps in mind the whole array of governmental techniques of controlling people on the move.

Repressed in every contact – a contact that has long ceased to be a genuine encounter – within the shameful economy (housekeeping) of the planetary petty bourgeoisie is the shared experience of the social as something that has become alien to us, citizens and denizens[2] alike. Gathered around the neo-administrative fictional totem of society in which we can no longer believe, citizens are forced to indefinitely restore and self-manage the dogma of the social relation while denizens are forced to be indefinitely disintegrated through it. This management, however, is but an empty variation as to the degree of neutralization of both citizens and denizens, a neutralization that has become everyday life for the vast majority of the planet's population. That one can be socially defected, ejected, abandoned at any point on the grey line of capture that is drawn (and constantly redrawn) between citizenship and

---

[1] Giorgio Agamben, 'Interview with Giorgio Agamben – Life, A Work of Art without an Author: The State of Exception, the Administration of Disorder and Private Life' [2005] *German Law Review* 5(5), 609–14. See for a discussion of the concept of 'logic of the field' Nick Vaughan-Williams, 'Borders, Territory, Law' [2008] *International Political Sociology* 2, 322–38.

[2] See Tomas Hammar, *Democracy and the Nation State: Aliens, Denizens and Citizens in a World of International Migration* (Avebury, Aldershot 1990).

denizenship and yet still remain *within* the spinning of the spectacle of society, of the market, of law and so forth is by now a banal seizure experienced as a constant bodily state.

The denizen's port of non-arrival is presented as the citizen's land of opportunity, until port of non-arrival and land of opportunity stumble upon their secret functional complementarities. To oppose the mapping, commentary and critique of the archipelagos of islands (inside or outside the territory of the nation-state) of human waste to the separation and devaluation of portals that the control of movement[3] globally attempts to impose despite its constant failures (or rather precisely through its logic of *constant* failures, the logic of perpetual crisis) is not enough. Instead, we must join the denizens in their struggle. Accounts of the micro-management of power-suffused politics and the logistics of economies of neutralization (that are often more complicit to the 'state of things' than it is admitted) can no longer meaningfully engage us. There is no point in merely contesting this economy of crises in its supposed, though elusive, neutralization of the present and the future of both citizens and denizens; no point in simply critiquing it and attempting to entice brief affairs with it in order to convince it to better its ethereal self and to love us back.

This love affair that does not work but lasts for longer than we can remember, we all know now returns us each day to a more tired and weakened self. This love affair with the intolerable, in our secret but stomach-turning complicity, was given the name, a juridico-political category, of the Great State, which set itself, from inception, in opposition to the Great Outside (disorder, contingency, criminality, exile, exception, denizenship). The Great State within its great triad of fatal attractions – Territorial Order, Law and Security – undertook transformations under the titles of the Absolutist State, the Liberal State and the Welfare State. All three have failed in different ways but with similar violent effects. The Absolutist State triumphed in the *kenosis* (emptying out) of Democracy, the Liberal State in the extremism of the Free Market, and the Welfare State in the banality of the interminable Crisis.[4]

Each time the failure is as interminable as its triumph, and this is its secret complicity with the normalized–exceptional neutralization of bodies reduced to being mere nuances of a limitless management process of integration–disintegration. In this state, the lives of citizens and denizens alike are reduced to the infinite production of mere survival albeit to differing degrees of (social) deduction. Survival tactics reproduced as policies and laws through this managerial machine can know only absolute failure or end (in death). Yet since this can be manageably or pretentiously avoided in Western capitalist democracies, at least for the time being, survival becomes increasingly the condition for the included *and* the excluded in a generalized perilous inclusion that excludes and vice versa within the biopolitical continuum of a global civil war.[5] When only survival remains at stake, post-sovereign biopolitics no longer attempts to manage life in order to better it or simply to exclude its more undesirable parts, but aims to reduce both the included and the excluded to their respective degrees of a

3 See Kathryn Cronin, 'A Culture of Control: An Overview of Immigration Policy Making' in James Jupp and Marie Kabala (eds) *The Politics of Australian Immigration* (Australian Government Publishing Service, Canberra 1995), ch. 5.

4 See for an analysis proximate to this Tiqqun, *Introduction to Civil War*, trans. Alexander R. Galloway and Jason E. Smith (Semiotext(e)/MIT Press, Cambridge, MA 2010). Though this analysis is not without its problems.

5 See Mark Duffield, 'Global Civil War: The Non-insured, International Containment and Post-interventionary Society' [2008] *Journal of Refugee Studies* 21(2), 145–65.

bare minimum.[6] Survival as the lowest common denominator, before long – if it has not done so already – will unite, under conditioned degrees of minimum states of being the majority of the included with the excluded. Today, we witness on the one hand the hypocritical restrictive application of human, social and welfare rights within, what Bauman has called, the *liquid* city and on the other the equally hypocritical restrictive application of minimum standards of entry into the civilized hub of survival at the *liquid* frontier.[7]

Removing Politics, Governing Movement

Doctrinal history and policy attempt to cover up the fact that political, economic, social and legal artifices or categories (of degrees) of humanity, legal personhood and righthood, in fact condition an empirical remainder that has or had initially human form. The key to Giorgio Agamben's studies of biopolitics lies here: a radical empiricism of diminutions of human life and an assault on the institutional integration of life.[8] One could purport to ease the radicality of this empiricism in order to manage its ever-denied social category of bare life (Agamben) or waste (Bauman).[9] But Agamben's preoccupation with residues and remnants of human life leads him neither to the depoliticization of a managed life nor to some naïve nihilism. It is simply a refusal to continue to critically manage the problem-solving arrangements that the *anthropogenetic* machine of national and global apparatuses of government has put into place.[10]

We do not need further *critiques* of this governmental machine. Instead we need to assault the very separation between what is held to be a problem and what is presented as its solution each time. Too often well-meaning academics (as well as NGOs) advance or critique elements of this war machine out of moral pity, denial of complicity, political correctness, or some belief in an undying human spirit that evolves and progresses, in spite of everything.[11] Too frequently the focus of such denial, whether critical or not, re-emphasizes the role of the nation-state or the inter-national and attempts to refine the remaining degrees of image-suffused sovereignty in order to restore humanity to the state or the law. A crucial point is missed. The civil war machine of the state (and the international) has, for as long as we can remember, functioned through a bipolarization between sovereignty and administrative government or policing

6 On securitization and survival see Luca Miggiano, 'States of Exception: Securitization and Irregular Migration in the Mediterranean' [2009] *New Issues in Refugee Research*, Research Paper No. 177, UNHCR, via http://www.unhcr.org, accessed 12 August 2012; see also Scott D. Watson, *The Securitization of Humanitarian Migration: Digging Moats and Sinking Boats* (Routledge, London 2009).

7 See Zygmunt Bauman, *Liquid Modernity* (Polity Press, Cambridge 2000).

8 Giorgio Agamben, Homo Sacer*: Sovereign Power and Bare Life*, trans. D. Heller-Roazen (Stanford University Press, Stanford, CA 1998).

9 Ibid.; and Zygmunt Bauman, *Wasted Lives: Modernity and Its Outcasts* (Polity Press, Cambridge 2004).

10 On a genealogy of government as management or *oikonomia* see Giorgio Agamben, *Il regno e la gloria. Per una genealogia teologica dell'economia e del governo. Homo sacer 2,2* (Neri Pozza, Vicenza 2007).

11 See for a discussion of this problem with regard to development and the role of NGOs, The Danish Institute for International Studies Working Paper [2004] 23, via http://www.diis.dk, accessed 30 January 2011.

while in fact in the logic of this machine, between a problem and a solution lies always the governmentality of the police.

Foucault showed that sovereign power and subjectivation go hand in hand and that the function of policing can be performed equally efficiently by sovereign or subject.[12] Agamben's study on biopolitics and government shows the relation between macro-powers (governmentality) and micro-powers (*omnes et singulatim*) to be a functional relation. The function is that of housekeeping (*oikonomic*), a function that draws the distinction between political life and politically non-descript life and withdraws the *ethos* of life (each way of being) by replacing it with macro- and micro-management.[13] What is significant here, as Anton Schütz has shown, is that it is this distinction between political life and its subtracted remainder, utilized as a positive marker of what qualifies political existence (and what not), which then acts as a triggering device for its own transgression, that is, as 'an indicator of an always colonisable, indefinitely politicizable and therefore governable territory'.[14] Today, life subtracted from politically, economically and legally qualified subjectivity is zero-degree life, reduced to mere *survival*. The drawing of a line in order to separate the one side from the other, the citizen from the denizen, is presented as a *non-political* act, that is, as an administration or an act of policing.

The key problem is that the image-suffused sovereign notion of power (for instance, as rights to be 'had') is presented as properly political and therefore in a certain sense in need of absolute defensibility and political correctness as to its proper name, while the managerial government of 'men and things' is presented as an infinitely shifting ground of managerial action that is forever covered up, in more or less successful ways, as a mere logistical and housekeeping exercise.[15] This latter improper place of politics, however, *is* the space of politics properly speaking. It is at the *topoi* (places) of this improper, this non-politics, where one finds the paradigmatic negative quantity of bare life that is subjected continuously, as a matter of housekeeping necessity (a tidying up of the *oikos*, the home of the state or the global), to the shifting sands of a management of life through a more or less permanent dehumanization and depoliticization.

Today, once more in a time of celebrated recession, we have the opportunity to see more clearly that this phenomenon is only an episode in the late modern transformation of governmental action from one that aimed to supposedly ensure the undisturbed subjection of its subjects and their communal living, to one of governing through the continuous coping with urgencies, emergencies and crises. The latter *situational* form of governmental action finds everywhere perilous and precarious conditions before which the government declares its powerlessness and then acts out of necessity and exceptional power. The reservoir of exceptional power is triggered by this inadmission of powerlessness that must immediately

12 Michel Foucault, *The Hermeneutics of the Subject: Lectures at the Collège de France, 1981–82*, trans. Graham Burchell (Macmillan Palgrave, New York 2005).

13 See Miggiano, 'States of Exception'; Watson, *Securitization of Humanitarian Migration*.

14 Anton Schütz, 'Thinking the Law with and against Luhmann, Legendre, Agamben' [2000] *Law and Critique* 11(2), 107–36.

15 See Sonja Buckel and Jens Wissel, 'State Project Europe: The Transformation of the European Border Regime and the Production of Bare Life' [2010] *International Political Sociology* 4, 33–49. See also Mary Bosworth and Mhairi Guild, 'Governing through Immigration Control: Security and Citizenship in Britain' [2008] *British Journal of Criminology* 48, 703–19.

be covered up. The governmentality of crises is one that is set to maintain, more and more explicitly now, not a politics of well-being but a non-politics, an administration of survival. Post-sovereign governmentality is an adaptive, anonymously and unaccountably performing management of life survival. It is crisis government that has now overtaken its other side (the side of politics and economics). This transformation brings the precarious lives of citizens closer than ever before to the precarious lives of denizens. This is to say that what takes place today, as a current phase of intensification, is the mutual exposure and functional relation of a political sovereignty and a managerial, administrative, emergency governance that is the improper, but more efficient, side of politics: a politics of denial. When a minister declares that the nation needs to be defended before the hordes of the unwanted he makes his point in the civil servants' terminology of managed migration and logistical integration, yet in the glorious names of Law, Security and Order. It is within this understanding that migration or movement management in general is to be viewed in what follows as a form of government.

Control and Crisis

The period of crisis in which we live is constructed and communicated in the most *universal* manner. There is no one really to blame for the crisis and no one who can properly be held accountable for it. This period conveys not the information of critical points that require attention, but the very administration of crisis as a universal field, irrespective of knowledge or agency. As a result crisis as government establishes conspicuous connections rendering anything familiar. The crisis communicates its own image, its spectacle as an inevitable situation rendered manageable and banal. It does not prohibit and it does not order; rather, it invites indefinite critical measures only to enhance its self-proclaimed plasticity through mere information. Since everything can be connected, it follows that everyone can be detained, indebted and silenced.

Crisis in late modernity is never about the presentation of something new, but instead it is about the postponement of anything new, that is, the encounter with genuine problems. The whole reformist state since the post-cold war era, for example, can be conceived as a promulgation of a self-produced indefinite crisis (a false problem) requiring indefinite control (as a solution). In this light the incessant subjection of institutions to waves of meaningless and ineffective reform (prisons are a good example of this) suddenly becomes more understandable. Crisis as a free-floating control, governance that, as Deleuze shows, displaced (*shifted* the grounding of) disciplinary societies, has been in the making for a long time, and the current proliferation of crises is but the latest form of its' intensification. Deleuze writes:

> Enclosures are *molds*, distinct castings, but controls are a *modulation*, like a self-deforming cast that will continuously change from one moment to the other, or like a sieve whose mesh will transmute from point to point. The *apparent acquittal* of the disciplinary societies (between two incarcerations) and the *limitless postponements* of the societies of control (in continuous variation) are two very different modes of juridical life, and if our law is hesitant, itself in crisis, it's because we are leaving one in order to enter the other … We no

> longer find ourselves dealing with the mass/individual pair. Individuals have become '*dividuals*', and masses, samples, data, markets, or '*banks*'.[16]

It is a mistake to think that the logic of control as a paradigm of government and policing simply replaces the old means of disciplinary society. Indeed, the old means are simply restaged with necessary adaptations and constantly re-inscribed within the diffuse horizon of control and crisis. Control here is used as a paradigm that merges the disciplinary with the diffuse rationality of control management, and as such reveals itself to be *the* paradigm of government, the paradigm of responding to cycles of interminable and contingent crises.

If the state was born out of the logic of classic control in order to discipline, contain and order, and re-fuse crises, biopolitical and crisis government is born out of the logic of post-sovereign control in order to reproduce crises, turning them into the very form of the social *relation*, as the only available universal. From this perspective it is possible to expose the conspicuous connection or indistinction that is set in motion under such a governmental paradigm: the connection between the increased expansion of exclusionary practices (imprisonment, but also ghettoes and shanty towns), the continued expansion of pseudo-inclusionary practices (detention, home confinement, electronic tagging but also chronic poverty),[17] and the increased legitimacy of pre-emptive controls (surveillance and securitization, but also military interventions and pre-crime models of plenipotential deviance).

The notion of the *logic of the field* proposed earlier corresponds to this logic of control that unites sovereign images of law, order, democracy, (human) rights and security with the managerial government and policing apparatuses that administer the so-called post-sovereign governability of the otherwise ungovernable crisis. What used to be seen as an exception to normal rule and societal cohesion over time has become sufficiently familiar so that its fallen sovereign image of governability has been accepted and the requirement for diffuse urgent responses turn exception into banality; that is, as an effectively causeless instigator of universal responsibility without accountability. As a result too, techniques of control used on prisoners in the name of incarceration and deterrence are soon used without hesitation on refugees; and techniques of control introduced in the name of immigration enforcement are soon used on the unemployed and the protesting workers. Within this logic of the field as control a number of apparatuses and managerial processes have prevailed with regard to the control and containment of movement at a global scale. The remaining sections outline some of the most noteworthy of these in further detail.

16 Gilles Deleuze, 'Postscript on the Societies of Control' [1992] *OCTOBER* 59(Winter), 3–7 at 4.

17 See Mike Larsen and Justin Piché, 'Exceptional State, Pragmatic Bureaucracy, and Indefinite Detention: The Case of the Kingston Immigration Holding Centre' [2009] *Canadian Journal of Law and Society* 24(2), 203–29; Catherine Dauvergne, 'Security and Migration: Law in the Less Brave New World' [2007] *Social and Legal Studies* 16, 533–49. See also Michael Welch and Liza Schuster, 'Detention of Asylum Seekers in the US, UK, France, Germany and Italy: A Critical View of the Globalizing Culture of Control' [2005] *Criminal Justice* 5(4), 331–55; and Guy Goodwin-Gill, 'International Law and the Detention of Refugees and Asylum Seekers' [1986] *International Migration Review* 20(2), 193–219.

Post-social Survival

During his lectures *Society Must Be Defended, Security, Territory, Population,* and *The Birth of Bio-politics* given at the *Collège de France* (1975–79), Foucault outlines the emergence of a life-centred security paradigm in the eighteenth century.[18] For Foucault, what differentiated this relatively new form of security arrangement was that it presupposed intensified biopolitical modes of humanization or social incorporation. Against the familiar juridical understanding of power as an appropriative entitlement, Brad Evans writes, in this sense, that the liberal art of governance

> Does not, as Kantian revisionists would argue, appear by claiming to promote and protect certain universal or inalienable rights. It arrives by making life itself the object for political strategy. Liberal rationality in other words only became meaningful when it first began posing the question of constituting something like a milieu of life, existence.[19]

Agamben has shown in his studies on biopolitics and sovereignty that universal and so-called inalienable rights had in fact already been marked by the inclusive exclusion of bare life in the legal–political order proper to the old fiction of the nation-state. Agamben writes, 'Nation-State means a State that makes nativity or birth (*nascita*) the foundation of its own sovereignty … The fiction that is implicit here is that birth (*nascita*) comes into being immediately as nation, so that there may not be any difference between the two moments'.[20] A state no longer dependent on the dogma of national territory 'but instead conceiving its myth of territorialisation on the ground of birth or nativity as immediately national need no more address the subjective "rights" of its inhabitants than late modern Nation-States did those of refugees'.[21] The secret intersection between citizens and denizens (the fact that both are subject to a neutralization of subjectivity) is always a matter of degree distantiation from a presupposed zero degree of bare life. Reduced to a purely objective matter, citizens (the so-called legitimate or qualified working multitude) and denizens (for example, undocumented migrants) can be administered rather than acted upon. As such they represent the fulfilment of the ultimate capitalist fantasy of the extinction of antagonistic subjectivity, thus rendering possible the casting of entire populations as 'refugees' regulated by medical aid, scientific categories of neutralization, and reduced to survival management, as well as the casting of more 'problematic' segments of the

---

18 See Michel Foucault, *'Society Must Be Defended': Lectures at the Collège de France 1975–1976, trans. David Macey* (Picador, New York 2003); Michel Foucault, *Security, Territory, Population: Lectures at the Collège de France 1977–1978* (Picador, New York 2009); and Michel Foucault, *The Birth of Biopolitics: Lectures at the College de France, 1978–1979, trans. Graham Burchell, ed. Michel Senellart et al.* (New York, Palgrave Macmillan 2008).

19 Brad Evans, 'Terror in all Eventuality' [2010] *Theory & Event* 13(3), 1, via http://muse.jhu.edu.ezproxy.lib.bbk.ac.uk/journals/theory_and_event/v013/13.3.evans01.html, accessed 25 August 2012.

20 Giorgio Agamben, *Means without Ends: Notes on Politics* (University of Minnesota Press, Minneapolis, MN 2000), 20.

21 Matthew Hyland, 'Refugee Subjectivity: "Bare Life" and the Geographical Division of Labour' [2001] *LOG Illustrated Magazine* 13, at http://www.physicsroom.org.nz/log/archive/13/refugeesubjectivity/, accessed 30 January 2011.

population to a containment field of control technique, until ultimately the vast majority of the population is reduced to the *post-social being of survival*.

It is important to draw out differences and to specify the elements of this incorporation of (a notion of bare) life into the life of the *polis*. For it is an incorporation that necessitates, from its very inception, an administrative process of dehumanization (more permanent for some than for others).[22] Yet the purpose of the present outline is only to suggest general threads through this logic of the field between citizenship and denizenship in the guise of the governmentality of control. As Agamben has shown, both citizens and denizens are either included through the exclusion of their mere state of existence (bare life) or equally dehumanized through the reverse process (where being or becoming a citizen can also mean being chronically poor and homeless). Both show, whether in the guise of so-called human rights or refugee rights, that a permanent status of a human being as merely existing is inconceivable for the Law of Nations, for the Law of the International and now for the Law of Networks.[23] If the refugee, as Agamben notes, throws into crisis the original fiction of sovereignty (by breaking up the identity between nativity and nationality), the citizen is thrown into crisis by seeing the identity between nationality and rights being broken also (for instance, through more or less permanent emergency measures, laws and derogations). Until it is realized that a mass of non-citizens now permanently resident in industrialized states can neither be nor want to be naturalized or repatriated, and also that a growing mass of citizens now permanently in debt and chronic poverty, for example, within the EU, can neither have nor want to return to the status that did not protect them from such poverty and debt, the prospect of reconnecting existence with a genuine political reality will remain abysmal.

Typologization

Typologization is the bureaucratic and administrative operation of creating and justifying artifices of identity and ever-reducible sub-identity of an individual applicant or person that effectively reduces the factual destitution of the subject to a mere status. It is a dangerous, racist and hypocritical operation, one that replaces a genuine examination of causality and situations excepting itself from the required responsibility and deducing artificial categorizations of people, in this case people on the move, in order to administer their life with only the ever-lowest common denominator in mind.[24] Once the productive logic of reductive data as the

---

22 See Matthew Holt, 'Biopolitics and the "Problem" of the Refugee' [2002], Critical Perspectives on Refugee Policy in Australia: Proceedings of the Refugee Rights Symposium Hosted by the Institute for Citizenship and Globalisation, Faculty of Arts, Deakin University, 5 December 2002, at http://www.deakin.edu.au/arts-ed/ccg/rsg/pdfs/matthew-holt.pdf, accessed 30 January 2011.

23 See Michael Hardt and Antonio Negri, *Empire* (Harvard University Press, Cambridge, MA 2000).

24 On the racism of such typology see Steve Garner, 'The European Union and the Racialization of Immigration, 1985–2006' [2007] *Race/Ethnicity: Multidisciplinary Global Contexts* 1(1), 61–87; Liz Fekete, 'Anti-Muslim Racism and the European Security State' [2004] *Race and*

rationale for decision making and policy setting has been accepted, the door is open to an infinite amount of specializations, re-specifications and sub-typologizations.

Such a typology is as endless as it is ultimately meaningless in the long term. Just as indigenous nationality is artificial, the irregular migrant label, for example, is also an artifice. The artificiality of such labelling is easily demonstrated with regard to the immense failures of the states and UN to respond to situations in Darfur, Nepal and Colombia. Victims of persecution, re-typologized as Internally Displaced Persons (IDPs) represents today the fastest-growing and most numerous group of 'forcibly displaced migrants'. Furthermore, the UNHCR is progressively institutionalizing the label IDP as it attempts to practically manage its mandate of protectionism by offering diminished or temporary protection. However, the UNHCR's resultant complicity with this labelling is not a mere administrative inevitability. The UNHCR has in fact inadvertently accepted a hierarchy of humanitarian privilege that distinguishes the IDP from the refugee so that logistical pragmatics can once more predetermine the future of the logic of protection. Once one starts typologizing, there is no end to one's shame or to one's administrative logistics: the Convention Refugee, the asylum seeker, the economic migrant, the highly skilled non-EU professional, the undocumented migrant, the bogus asylum seeker, the sub-category asylum seeker, the internally displaced, the short-term migrant, the guest worker, the trafficked migrant, etc. Bureaucratic fractioning to effectively manage both individuals and entire populations is now deemed necessary. But not too long ago the same state and inter-state actors were actively advocating ever-inclusive and homogeneous approaches. Is necessity really that relative? And is contingency that predetermined?

The Economy of Waste

The government's aim should be to secure certain refugees, 'those who had "achieved distinction whether in pure science, applied science, such as medicine or technical industry, music or art."'[25] As Philip Marfleet writes, 'There was a specific purpose to the [British Cabinet's] initiative: "This would not only obtain for this country the advantage of their knowledge and experience, but would also create a very favourable impression in the world, particularly if our hospitality were to be offered with some warmth."'[26] The year was 1933 and the 'certain refugees' were 'prominent Jews'. The test for admission for a refugee was set to be whether an applicant is 'likely to be an asset to the United Kingdom'.[27] Then the year was 1938 and it was already too late. No Western nation could, or indeed can, claim any kind of revisionist innocence over its economic decisions (or waste production). This is not to discard important historical nuances and differences, but the direct or indirect support and production of atrocities by the beacons of humanity, liberty and justice cannot be excused. Remember the Balkan 'ambassadors', the Kosovans, who were soon relabelled 'scrounging

Class 46, 3–29; and Maggie Ibrahim, 'The Securitization of Migration: A Racial Discourse' [2005] *International Migration* 43(5), 163–86.

25 Philip Marfleet, *Refugees in a Global Era* (Palgrave, Houndmills 2006), 137.

26 Ibid.

27 Ibid.

immigrants'?[28] Remember the 'irregular' migration used by the USA and other Western states to rescue selected Nazis from Germany and their Eastern European and Balkan collaborators?[29] What of the 'irregular' channels of migration encouraged by the USA during the cold war for propaganda purposes? As Marfleet writes in his collection of such historical 'peculiarities', 'Here irregular movements, including operations hidden from most departments of the state, were endorsed by the same government which pursued vigorous campaigns of exclusion against "alien" intruders.'[30] One's exodus is another's illegal entry.

Meanwhile, in times of recession racist rhetoric rises together with irregular worker numbers. The irregular migrant becomes capitalism's 'lubricant' where the state directly or indirectly enhances the operation of the traffickers. Marfleet expresses this plainly: 'the US state accepts irregulars because powerful business groups demand cheap and vulnerable labour. According to the Cato Institute, a conservative American think-tank, in 2001 the benefit of the US economy of importing irregular migrants amounted to US$30 billion annually (*Observer*, 3 June 2001).'[31] British researchers revealed in 2005 that irregular labour 'had for years been used routinely in key areas of economic activity, notably construction, catering, contract cleaning, agriculture and care services',[32] while the previously accepted Sri Lankan refugees from war were by 1997 rejected in their vast majority. The search for occasional, locally manageable responses to the human *waste* in the name of the Great Law and Order spectacle reveals that the throne of the so-called sovereign is occupied by the petty servants of a bureaucratic ethnic cleansing or *biosegregation*[33] taking place under pinched noses. This *administracide* accepts as necessary 'collateral damage', 'a term that might have been specifically invented to denote the human waste specific to the new planetary frontier-land conditions.'[34] Collateral damage, thus, becomes the irregular migrant who is exploited in the so-called black labour market as much as the migrant who is given access to a residual and private form of sub-citizenship under an employment contract that renders the employer an indirect screening official able to terminate the contract at any point in time and affect the employee's immigration status.[35] Inequalities are differentiated according to degrees of exploitation bringing extraordinary irregular migrants closer to the exploited life of the ordinary citizen and vice versa. As Hyland writes, 'The purpose of immigration controls is not to prevent all migration, but to ensure that people move according to capital's needs, rather than their own desires. Any violation of this principle would fundamentally threaten the capitalist order, by undermining the geographical division of labor it has depended on since the dawn of imperial expansion and slavery.'[36] The trouble with waste is that no one wants to smell it and yet it is to be seen, abandoned and included, for no reputable recycling facility lets anything go to waste. Bauman notes:

---

28 See ibid., 161.

29 Ibid., 166.

30 Ibid.

31 Ibid., 173.

32 Ibid., 182.

33 See on this Michel Agier, *On the Margins of the World: The Refugee Experience Today*, trans. David Fernbach (Polity Press, Cambridge 2008).

34 Bauman, *Wasted Lives*, 92.

35 See Sandro Mezzadra, *Diritto di fuga. Migrazioni, cittadinanza, globalizzazione* (Edizioni OmbreCorte, Verona 2006).

36 Hyland, 'Refugee Subjectivity'.

> Immigrants, and particularly the fresh arrivals among them, exude the faint odour of the waste disposal tip which in its many disguises haunts the nights of the prospective casualties of rising vulnerability. For their detractors and haters, immigrants embody – visibly, tangibly, in the flesh – the inarticulate yet hurtful and painful presentiment of their own disposability.[37]

The control of movement is intertwined with the controlled insertion/rejection of bodies into economic and para-economic processes that are rooted within the wider terrain of biopolitical government and affect both citizens and denizens in the survival field of control operations.[38]

Secure Exceptionalism is Terrorization

If security produces insecurity, the law produces exception. Agamben's contribution to the understanding of the logic of exceptionalism is well known:

> Law is made of nothing but what it manages to capture inside itself through the inclusive exclusion of the *exceptio*: it nourishes itself on this exception and is a dead letter without it ... Exception does not subtract itself from the rule; rather, the rule, suspending itself, gives rise to the exception and, maintaining itself in relation to the exception, first constitutes itself as a rule.[39]

Exceptional government is an *ahistoric* performance paradigm coping with events and situations characterized by precarious virtual circumstances. If the logic of the administrative management of the exception has become the rule, it turns immigration – and movement control more generally – into an administrative matter stripped from the very start of its political and legal significance. Any institution can become a management administration centre and every legal concept can be transformed through its exception. Protection becomes securitization, the political–legal subject, a circumstantial data hub. Circumstances are not governable in the same way that subjects are. Immigration control as a form of neo-governmentality transforms protection measures into policing measures and crisis management as policing renders the logic of security into a mode of self-production, a continuous trigger of violence. This is the conversion of sovereign powerlessness into the last vestige of power performance before mere circumstances.

We have, for some time now, occupied an era of exceptional and global securitization that will outlast those who cry foul and seek a return to the old-European rule of law. What will result is no doubt the completion of an already-evident mass disillusionment with the idea of legal rights, just as we have already experienced a mass disillusionment with the idea of political choices. The erosion is depicted through the fact that, though exception or lawlessness is a very *legal* lawlessness, suspension does not mean absence. As Bauman writes,

37 Bauman, *Wasted Lives*, 56.

38 See Miggiano, 'States of Exception'.

39 Homo Sacer, 18.

> The law's bid to universality would sound hollow were it not for the inclusion of the exempted through its own withdrawal. Law would never reach universality without the right to draw the limit to its application, creating by the same token a universal category of the exempted/excluded, and the right to lay out an 'out of bounds', providing thereby the dumping ground for the ones who are excluded, recycled into human waste.[40]

Terrorized insecurity has been met with market-generated terror to establish a terror of degrees for denizens and citizens. Marfleet describes how as early as in the mid-1950s the cold war strategy initiated by Washington as to Central America focused upon 'demobilisation'.[41] Philip Rudge writes: 'To an alarming degree decision making in the area of asylum is moving away from the traditional human rights and humanitarian field of policy making. It is increasingly the subject of dealing with terrorism, drug trafficking and policing on the one hand, and with economic streamlining on the other.'[42] The transformation of humanitarianism into securitization is nothing but the refocusing of migration control not on the human subject but on the bare life of a now wholly securitized and desubjectivized 'dividual'. If what is to be screened is not an objective threat but a perception of exceptional vulnerability, then the person who has only his/her vulnerability to present to the authorities becomes, through a shameful and ironic twist, the security threat par excellence.

Terrorism, a dubious concept in itself, has been replaced by the banality of permanent unease, a shift that further strengthens the perspective from which anything and anyone can/must be securitized in the name of survival.[43] Overall the logic of security and its infinite array of exceptions empowers the state to determine the so-called normal conditions under which the principle of non-refoulement will apply.[44] A demonstrable threat to national security remains ever-demonstr*able* rather than demonstrated. It remains a heavy burden, to state the obvious: securitization will not defeat the political matter of violent acts, nor will it ever be rationally and justifiably connected to the matters of migration and asylum. If security operates entirely in the strategic field of virtuality and in the name of the image-suffused ordering of progress and development, it is its audacity that we must expose. It is an extreme form of audacity rendered familiar and clearly expressed in the British Government's revived National Security Strategy in 2008, which states that,

> The overall objective of this National Security Strategy is to anticipate and address a diverse range of threats and risks to our security, in order to protect the United Kingdom and its interests, enabling its people to go about their daily lives freely and with confidence, in a more secure, stable, just, and prosperous

40 Bauman, *Wasted Lives*, 31–2.

41 *Refugees in a Global Era*, 242.

42 Philip Rudge, 'European Initiatives on Asylum' in Daniele Joly and Robin Cohen (eds) *Reluctant Hosts: Europe and its Refugees* (Avebury, Aldershot 1989), 212.

43 On the discourse of unease see the analysis of Parliamentary Debates on Terrorism by Jef Huysmans and Alessandra Buonfino, 'Politics of Exception and Unease: Immigration, Asylum and Terrorism in Parliamentary Debates in the U.K.' [2008] *Political Studies* 36, 766–83.

44 See Rene Bruin and Kees Wouters, 'Terrorism and the Non-derogability of Non-refoulement' [2003] *International Journal of Refugee Law* 15, 5–29.

world … [Threats and risks] are real, and also more diverse, complex, and interdependent than in the past.[45]

What the biopolitics of a lesser or greater malleable projection of post-sovereign performance have installed in order to regulate life, permanent securitization has optimized in order to institute survival. If progress elevated dignity and integrity as its ultimate justification, security elevates its virtual circularity to the principle, or law, of contingency. To master the contingent, the ultimate fictional heartbeat of the post-social, and to adapt government to the ungovernable, is to provoke, each time, terror into action so that the future will always already have happened.

Criminalization

In 2008 the Council of Europe Commissioner for Human Rights expressed concern that migration policies were increasingly criminalizing the mobility and presence of immigrants in Europe.[46] Illegal entry in the UK since the 1970s includes not only clandestine entry, but also deceiving an immigration officer. Who can forget the actions of British immigration officials at Prague airport in 2004 in preventing Roma travelers from boarding planes to the UK?[47] The criminalization of movement, arrival and presence whether in national territory or on the fringes is closely linked with the process of securitization that today proliferates and affects ever greater numbers of people (including citizens). The machine of criminalization comprises different apparatuses of pre-emptive criminalization, surveillance, penalization, exceptionalism, detention, deportation, profiling, certification, and securitization. An encounter with an asylum seeker is, for instance, criminalized in a number of Western states even to the point that offering a person a drink or a bed for the night can result in criminal proceedings. The agents of (pre)criminalization have also multiplied and proliferated. They can be the border patrol, the welfare benefits interviewer, the judge,[48] the police officer, the employer, the neighbour, the academic institution, you. Alongside the logic of exceptionalism and securitization, the criminalization of a person in movement generally falls within a range of operations claiming that virtual presence, action and possibility are the only motors of reality production. A *de facto* criminal act and a *de jure* criminal act or an actual breach of a regulatory code and a virtual, or pre-empted, breach have entered a zone of indistinction in the post-welfare world. Like securitization, control, administration and the other elements we are briefly outlining here, criminalization needs to be understood as an apparatus of governmental control affecting virtually citizens and denizens alike, subject only to degree

[45] As quoted in Evans, 'Terror in all Eventuality', fn 64.

[46] Commissioner for Human Rights, *Criminalisation of Migration in Europe: Human Rights Implications*, CommDH/Issue Paper, 2010, 1.

[47] See *R v IO at Prague Airport and Another ex p EERC* [2004] UKHL 55.

[48] See Stephen Legomsky, *Immigration and the Judiciary: Law and Politics in Britain and America* (Clarendon Press, Oxford 1987).

differentiations of managerial logistics.[49] Thus, control of movement understood as a form of generalized government within the logic of control is not a problem that needs to be resolved, but a lifetime reduced to gradations and minor or maximum abandonments that no longer aim primarily to kill but only to abandon one to survival. This is not a problem to solve, but a devastation to overthrow.

Criminalization works in virtual ways. The primary pre-emptive resolution is to predetermine people that are on the move or who are fleeing a situation as unreliable, bogus, threatening and dangerous. Immigration laws in their infinite multiplication follow suit and not only predetermine the precriminalization of subjects of control, but also ensure that those that get through the spikes will only be entitled, subject to continuous review, to the lowest possible minimum. The function of these legislative and policing practices, however, is not merely administrative. It is first and foremost ontological, that is, an ontological predetermination of a neutralized subjectivity through a desubjectivation and ultimately a reduction of citizenship and denizenship to the lowest common denominator of precarious survival. A government of contingent crises no longer deals with *sub*jects in their actual presence and civic deliberation, but with *on*jects, virtual, ontological desubjectivized 'things': waste, failed, rogue remainders, whose function, since generally they cannot be easily killed without impunity, is to simply be around. This logic of criminalization, pre-emptive dehumanization and deregularization is a widespread practice that affects citizens and denizens if conceived in the widest sense possible. For example, it would be worth comparing, though this cannot be done here, the globally used 'medical' criteria for the assessment of mental 'disorders' that decide that 'failure to conform to social norms with respect to lawful behaviours as indicated by repeatedly performing acts that are grounds for arrest' equals 'antisocial personality disorders',[50] with the assessment of asylum seekers, benefit claimants and so many other dehumanized categories of social banning and abandonment. Further comparisons could be drawn between assessment and policing of irregular movement and the penalization of movement of the urban poor or the policing of public health and safety that render infectious diseases and white trash 'social threats'.[51]

It is possible, thus, to say that Management, Control and Pre-criminalization have formed the new triad of synonyms to Fairness, Democracy and Safety.[52] Such pillars of governmental control will not convince us that 'anti-social acts', acts of contestation and acts of desperation can amount to crimes. When, for instance, one is deprived of an opportunity to comply with laws prohibiting certain conduct, and nonetheless stands as accused of breaching such laws, no virtual motor of reality will convince us that this accusation is reasoned and founded in actions and careful consideration rather than on mere fear logistics before unwanted persons. Logistics is the name we give to such predeterminations of persons (rather than accountable actions) that follow a long

---

49 See James Banks, 'The Criminalisation of Asylum Seekers and Asylum Policy' [2007] *Prison Service Journal* 175, 43–9.

50 See, for example, The American Psychiatric Association, *The Diagnostic and Statistical Manual for Mental Disorders – IV (DSM-IV)*, code 301.8.

51 See Matt Wray, *Not Quite White: White Trash and the Boundaries of Whiteness* (Duke University Press, Durham, NC 2006).

52 See Cristina Fernández, Alejandra Manavella and José María Ortuño, 'The Effects of Exceptional Legislation on Criminalisation of Immigrants and People Suspected of Terrorism' [2009] CHALLENGE, Report 9.

genealogy of degree classification of destitution and abandonment: for example, UK anti-vagrancy laws criminalized socio-economic status and civility and zoning laws today are said to prohibit specific behaviour, when in fact they miniaturize due process in order to enhance uncontrolled discretionary powers of control.[53] Fear-based criminalized logistics affecting the movement of immigrants and asylum seekers are, at most times, enhancing policing and discrimination against a globally pre-criminalized underclass. In addition, to state the obvious, the more laws and barriers are placed in front of a person, the more laws and barriers will be broken. Illegal entry has become inevitable and its criminalization is thus indefensible. The fact remains that, whether with more or fewer laws, pre-emptive breaches and pre-criminalized deviance are produced by the very apparatuses that then arrive to police them.[54]

Militarization

The immigration civil war machine is a combined force of multiple apparatuses that are either explicitly or implicitly militarized. By militarization here we refer not only to the obvious military logic and practices that are employed in the 'war' on ('illegal') immigration, but also to a generalized spectacle of war that enables states of mind, policies and practices that resemble state and para-state strategies usually associated with actual times of war. Exceptionalism, securitization, counter-terrorism and the recession combined have rendered possible both militarized border patrols and war-time surveillance techniques in the city, as well as patrolling immigration officers who in 2004 for example could scour the London public transport system with the sole aim of identifying people who looked or sounded 'foreign'.

The militarization of non-war terrains and matters has a long history largely championed by colonial states in the past and the USA more recently in the West. The USA–Mexico border militarized under the paradigm of security and the anti-drug 'war'[55] has led to the integration of the Immigration and Naturalization Service into the Department of Homeland Security. This latest phase of the securitization machine is only an intensification of a process that began in the USA during the early 1950s. Astor analyses, for example, how during the Korean war the intensification of the 'Red Scare' dogma politicized unauthorized migration and rendered

[53] See International Council on Human Rights Policy, 'Modes and Patterns of Social Control: Implications for Human Rights Policy' [2010], at http://www.ichrp.org/files/reports/61/Social_Control_and_Human_Rights_ICHRP_Electronic_Final.pdf, accessed 12 August 2012.

[54] See Shuk Yi Lee Maggy, 'Human Trade and the Criminalisation of Irregular Migration' [2005] *International Journal of the Sociology of Law* 33, 1–15; Elspeth Guild and Paul Minderhoud, *Immigration and Criminal Law in the European Union: The Legal Measures and Social Consequences of Criminal Law in Member States on Trafficking and Smuggling in Human Beings* (Martinus Nijhoff, Leiden 2006); Ryszard Cholewinski, 'The Criminalisation of Migration in EU Law and Policy' in Anneliese Baldaccini, Elspeth Guild and Helen Toner (eds) *Whose Freedom, Security and Justice? EU Immigration and Asylum Law and Policy* (Hart, Oxford 2007), 301–36; and Salvatore Palidda (ed.) *Criminalisation and Victimization of Migrants in Europe* (University of Genoa, Genoa 2009).

[55] See Gina Amatangelo, 'Militarization of the U.S. Drug Control Program' [2001] *Foreign Policy in Focus* 6, via http://www.fpif.org/reports/militarization_of_the_us_drug_control_program, accessed 25 August 2012.

it a matter of security.[56] Astor recalls further the details of the incredible story of the subsequent implementation of Operation Wetback, an operation that led to the deportation, repatriation or 'voluntary' departure of hundreds of thousands of Mexican immigrants in 1954.[57] The predecessor to many other incredible operations known as Operation Gatekeeper, Operation Hold-the-Line, Operation Endgame, and so on in later decades shows in a more general sense the direct link between policing and both sovereign and post-sovereign governmentality. The border between the USA and Mexico is perhaps the most militarized border in the world, creating a state of what remains an undeclared civil war. It is huge business for private companies and state agencies. The annual budget of the Immigration and Nationality Service (INS), for instance, rose from $200 million in 1996 to $1.6 billion in 2005. Before 1992, the cost of making one arrest along the USA–Mexico border stood at $300, while by 2002 that cost had grown by 467 per cent to $1,700.[58] The failure of such policies with regard to immigration control or the war on drugs has never held militarization back, and it will probably never do so. Militarization is a business of virtual dangers and the image of control is far more important than deaths and costs.[59]

Indirect militarization presents an example of an ever more widespread practice. In Canada, for example, anti-terrorism legislation, information exchange by intelligence and security agencies, biometrics, technologically enhanced identity cards and refugee interdiction measures extend the border into a multiplicity of sites for the surveillance of movement wherein the border becomes as mobile as the body itself.[60] In Europe, since 2004, a council regulation founded the Warsaw-based EU agency for the management of Operational Cooperation at the External Borders of the Member States of the EU (FRONTEX).[61] FRONTEX has grown into the key agency at the heart of migration and security policy as well as European external relations more generally. Its field of operations covers an extended patrol network throughout the whole southern naval flank of the EU and beyond, from the shores of Mauritania and Senegal in north-western Africa to River Evros in Greece, where the latest 'war' on immigration battle

---

56 See Avi Astor, 'Unauthorized Immigration, Securitization and the Making of Operation Wetback' [2009] *Latino Studies* 7(1), 5–29.

57 Ibid., 6.

58 See Douglas S. Massey, 'Backfire at the Border: Why Enforcement without Legalization Cannot Stop Illegal Immigration' [2005], at *http://www.freetrade.org/pubs/pas/tpa-029.pdf*, accessed 30 January 2011.

59 See Wayne A. Cornelius, 'Death at the Border: The Efficacy and the Unintended Consequences of U.S. Immigration Control Policy' [2001] *Population and Development Review* 27(4), 661–85; and Timothy J. Dunn, 'Immigration Enforcement in the U.S.–Mexico Border Region, the El Paso Case: Bureaucratic Power, Human Rights, and Civic Activism' [1999] unpublished PhD diss. (University of Texas, Austin) (copy available with the author). See also Karl Eschbach, Jacqueline Hagan and Nestor Rodriguez, *Causes and Trends in Migrant Deaths along the U.S–Mexico Border, 1985–1998* (University of Houston, Centre for Immigration Research, WSP 01–4 2001); and Karl Eschbach, Jacqueline Hagan, Nestor Rodriguez, et al., 'Death at the Border' [1999] *International Migration Review* 33, 430–54.

60 See Karine Côté-Boucher, 'The Diffuse Border: Intelligence-sharing, Control and Confinement along Canada's Smart Border' [2008] *Surveillance & Society* 5(2), 142–65. On biometrics see Charlotte Epstein, 'Guilty Bodies, Productive Bodies, Destructive Bodies: Crossing the Biometric Borders' [2007] *International Political Sociology* 1, 149–64.

61 See Andrew W. Neal, 'Securitization and Risk at the EU Border: The Origins of FRONTEX' [2009] *Journal of Common Market Studies* 47(2), 333–56.

is currently being fought in the name of the EU. In 2011, FRONTEX, which has been granted a budget of 676 million euros for the period 2008 to 2013 (a budget that was at 6 million in 2005), plans to organize and finance between 30 and 40 charters to repatriate migrants on its own operational mandate.[62] Regulation No. 2010/0039 recently amending the powers of FRONTEX provides among other things the following incredible extensions making this agency a leading agent in the emerging European homeland security sector: to collect and process personal data of suspects for involvement in illicit border activities; to deploy liaison officers in third countries; to develop and operate an information system capable of exchanging classified information; and to integrate common core curricula in the training of national border guards. This in conjunction with the integrated European Borders Surveillance System (EUROSUR), the policy objectives of which are influenced extensively by FRONTEX's research on security issues, has resulted in increased business for producers of security equipment like Unmanned Aviation Vehicles, also known as 'Drone Planes' (already used in Latin America by the US for the same purpose). EUROSUR is backed by a plethora of security research projects funded by the EU that involve big defence companies (i.e. OPERAMAR led by Thales Underwater Systems and Selex, the STABORSEC consortium, Sagem D.S., etc.). Agencies such as FRONTEX acquire more and more decision-making and agenda-setting powers. As Fische-Lescano and Tohibidur write,

> All in all the spin-off of agencies leads to a spin-off of administrative apparatuses and consequently means an increasing independence of the agencies from the political influence of the Council and the Commission – and parliamentary contribution ... The new agencies, at least the agencies concerning internal security and border patrol, have grown out of their mere technical-regulatory garment.[63]

Ironically, the failure of such policies financially and socially only strengthens their instigators' resolve and the increase in the uses of violence by state and private agencies will only confirm, once again, the atrocity that is liberal neo-governmentality.[64]

Bureaucratic Management is Datacide

The devolution of matters that effectively amount to due process decision making, sensitive and personal data collection, the use of extensive surveillance techniques as a form of identification and as an everyday bureaucratic micro-management of migrants' and asylum seekers' lives (but also today of poor working citizens, estates' 'scum' or the homeless in particular) reveals that

62 See www.frontex.europa.eu/finance, accessed 30 January 2011.

63 *Andreas Fischer-Lescano and Timo Tohidipur, 'Europäisches Grenzkontrollregime. Rechtsrahmen der europäischen Grenzschutzagentur FRONTEX'* [2007] *Zeitschrift für ausländisches öffentliches Recht und Völkerrecht* 4, 1219–77 at 1234.

64 See Buckel and Wissel, 'State Project Europe'.

if, as Agamben suggests, the camp is the *nomos* of the modern[65] (forming the spatial topology of exceptional powers), then bureaucratic databases and administrative discourse are the *logoi* of the modern (forming the linguistic and ontological topology of a linguistic formalism that is racist, unaccountable and amounts to *datacide* with impunity). Visa requirements have long existed and are racist at their very core. For example, EU Regulation 539/2001 (as amended) provided that certain nationals must obtain visas to enter the EU for even short stays. A cursory examination of the countries on that black list indicates that if you are Muslim, poor and non-white you are required to apply for a visa.[66] Other examples include the criminalization of the foreigner claimant achieved through Section 35 of the Asylum and Immigration (Treatment of Claimants, etc.) Act 2004, which created the offence of failing to comply with actions that the Secretary of State requires, or the 2007 UK Borders Act, that allowed the Secretary of State to require anyone in the immigration system to have a biometric document, where refusal would lead possibly to dismissal. Biometric documents and highly sensitive personal data are all the time being expanded and recorded in a web of databases. Within the EU alone there are three key databases: the Schengen Information System listing people prohibited from entry in the EU with highly questionable accuracy;[67] the EURODAC, which contains the fingerprints of all persons who have applied for asylum or who have 'irregularly' crossed external frontiers of a member state; and the new Visa Information System (VIS) listing every visa applicant. When claims and rights begin to be ungrounded through the predetermination of bureaucratic processes based entirely on neutralized data of questionable accuracy and ethical vacuity, then the line separating a citizen and a denizen from his/her datacide can only become thinner.

Privatization

During the 1970s in the UK and the USA the privatization of security services, detention and prison institutions established a geometrically growing tendency of liberal states towards multiplying the number of law enforcers 'without adding significant costs' effectively in complicity with the growing market of private security services.[68] In the USA private enforcement of immigration laws is a recent phenomenon, starting with the federal employer sanctions laws of 1986.[69] Pham explains that this is a process that began indirectly, since federal law has long threatened with criminal penalties anyone who, 'knowing or in reckless disregard'

[65] Agamben, *Homo Sacer: Sovereign Power and Bare Life* (Stanford: Stanford University Press, 1998)..

[66] See Didier Bigo and Elspeth Guild, *La mise a l'écart des étrangers. La logique du visa Schengen* (Cultures et Conflits, l'Harmattan, Paris 2003).

[67] Evelien Brouwer, *Digital Borders and Real Rights: Effective Remedies for Third Country Nationals in the Schengen Information System* (Martinus Nijhoff, Leiden 2008).

[68] See Mark Dow, *American Gulag: Inside US Immigration Prisons* (University of California Press, Berkeley, CA 2004); Joel Dyer, *The Perpetual Prison Machine: How America Profits from Crime* (Westview Press, Boulder, CO 2000); Douglas McDonald, 'Public Imprisonment by Private Means: The Re-emergence of Private Prisons and Jails in the United States, the United Kingdom and Australia' [1994] *British Journal of Criminology* 34, 29–48.

[69] Huyen T. Pham, 'The Privatization of Immigration Law Enforcement' [2007], unpublished paper, at http://works.bepress.com/huyen_pham/1/, accessed 12 August 2012.

of an immigrant's undocumented status, 'conceals, harbors, or shields [the immigrant] from detection.'[70] Various German states have contracted out such services and facilities to private companies such as European Homecare and B.O.S.S. Security and Service GmbH, rendering the ability to acquire even research information on their practices and facilities very cumbersome.[71] In Australia G4S (formerly Group 4 Falck) is responsible for 11 detention facilities specializing in outsourced business processes 'where security and safety risks are considered a strategic threat'.[72] The diversity of contracted private enforcers is illustrated by the use of the military section of the Italian Red Cross in Italy, which manages immigration detention facilities across the country.[73] Improving the 'government' of these centres and their provision will not convince us to believe in the perfectibility of such institutions.

In the USA during the 1970s crime was perceived as an 'unlimited natural resource'.[74] The advancing of the corporate interests of big financial backers such as Wackenhut, CCA and Sodexho Marriott by the Federal Government could be indicated by the fact that between 1995 and 1996 the influential American Legislative Exchange Council (ALEC)'s model legislation, as Richard Payne writes, 'resulted in 1,647 bills, out of which 365 became laws. Its successes include "Truth in Sentencing" legislation, where offenders serve at least 85% of their sentence, and "three strikes" legislation, where third offences result in mandatory life imprisonment.'[75] Payne adds that the interests are served mutually since 'in addition to supporting organizations like ALEC, private prison corporations made 645 contributions, amounting to $540,000, to 361 candidates in twenty-five states.'[76] Corrections Corporation of America (CCA), in Tennessee, and the GEO Group, in Florida, are the nation's two largest prison companies. Cervantes-Gautschi writes: 'Seeking Alpha, a website of actionable stock market opinion and analysis popular on Wall Street, reported that GEO's income from prison health care services ending

---

70 65 Immigration and Nationality Act, Section 274(a)(1)(A)(iii).

71 See Michael Flynn and Cecilia Cannon, 'The Privatization of Immigration Detention: Towards a Global View – A Global Detention Project Working Paper' [2009] Global Detention Project, Geneva, 6–8.

72 See http://www.g4s.com/, accessed 12 August 2012; McDonald, 'Public Imprisonment by Private Means'; and Mick Palmer, *Inquiry into the Circumstances of the Immigration Detention of Cornelia Rau Report* (Commonwealth of Australia 2005). See also on the South African situation, Mfanelo Patrick Ntsobi, 'Privatisation of Prisons and Prison Services in South Africa' [2005] unpublished diss. (University of Western Cape) (copy available with the author).

73 See Ted Richmond and John Shields, 'NGO–Government Relations and Immigrant Services: Contradictions and Challenges' [2005] *Journal of International Migration and Integration* 6(3), 513–26; and also Hidrun Friese, 'The Limits of Hospitality: Political Philosophy, Undocumented Migration and the Local Arena' [2008] paper presented at the XXII Congresso Società Italiana di Scienze Politiche, Pavia, 4–6 September (copy available with the author).

74 See Deepa Fernandes, *Targeted: Homeland Security and the Business of Immigration* (Seven Stories Press, New York 2007); and Janet A. Gilboy, 'Implications of "Third-Party" Involvement in Enforcement: The INS, Illegal Travellers, and International Airlines' in Susan Street (ed.) *Immigration*, The International Library of Essays in Law and Society (Ashgate, Burlington, VT 2006); see also Douglas C. McDonald et al., *Private Prisons in the United States: An Assessment of Current Practice* (Abt Associates, Cambridge, MA 1998); and Michael Welch, *Detained: Immigration Laws and the Expanding INS Jail Complex* (Temple University Press, Philadelphia, PA 2002).

75 Richard Payne, 'Cashing in on Asylum' [2005] *Media Active: Ideas, Knowledge, Culture* 4, 56–68 at 61.

76 Ibid.

in March of 2009 topped $1.0 billion, a 5.8% profit. Seeking Alpha also stated that CCA's profit for the same period in 19 states was over $1.6 billion, with a profit margin of 9.4%.'[77] Goldman Sachs, Smith Barney Shearson and Merrill Lynch invested three billion dollars per year into the CCA during the 1990s.[78] By 2009 the then leading owner of GEO JP Morgan perceived this as an under-performance and sold most of its stock. Cervantes-Gautschi reports:

> The most influential investor in CCA is a hedge fund, Pershing Square, which is run by Wall Street investment guru activist investor, Bill Ackman. Ackman also plays a powerful role in Target Corporation and Kraft Foods. Wells Fargo is the most powerful investor in GEO. Other major investors with the power to influence management in one or the other of the two companies are Vanguard, Lazard, Scopia, Wellington Management, FMR (Fidelity), BlackRock and Bank of America.[79]

Payne's contribution lies in exposing the close link between the US Private Prisons Industry and the private sector in the UK. Campsfield House, the 'refugee prison', opened in 1993 and was run by Group 4, which had already invested in the sector. In 1992 the privately run HMP Wolds was run by Premier Custodial Group Ltd, a subsidiary of Wackenhut Corrections Corporation.[80] Group 4 since then has run a number of other centres, such as the infamous Oakington Reception Centre, Yarl's Wood Removal Centre and Harmondsworth Removal Centre. Group 4, now G4S, has effectively become the largest international private security company, operating in over 80 countries.

In the UK the close tie between the private sector and the political elite is but thinly veiled. Payne illustrates this well in the following:

> Norman Fowler, the ex-Conservative Party chairman who joined Group 4 Securitas Ltd as a director, resigned only the day before his government's second phase of prison privatization came on stream. Under New Labour little … changed. Jack Straw, [ex-]Home Secretary, awarded a prison contract to Premier Prison Services, despite advice from senior civil servants that the contract was deeply flawed. In 2001, Elaine Bailey, the Prison Service's Head of Security, became managing director of Premier Custodial Group Ltd.[81]

---

77 Peter Cervantes-Gautschi, 'Wall Street and the Criminalization of Immigrants' [2010] *Counterpunch*, 15–17 October, at http://www.counterpunch.org/gautschi10152010.html, accessed 30 January 2011.

78 See Christian Parenti, 'Privatised Problems: For-Profit Incarceration in Trouble' in Andrew Coyle, Allison Campbell and Rodney Neufeld (eds) *Capitalist Punishment: Prison Privatisation and Human Rights* (Zed Books, London 2002).

79 'Wall Street and the Criminalization of Immigrants'.

80 Payne, *Media Active*, 63.

81 Ibid., 68. See further Christine Bacon, 'The Evolution of Immigration Detention in the UK: The Involvement of Private Prison Companies' [2005] Refugee Studies Centre, University of Oxford, Working Paper Series No. 27; Stephen Nathan, 'The European Market for Privatised Correctional Services: Developments and Implications' [2005] Workshop at the EPSU Standing Committee on National and European Administration on Prison Services, Luxembourg, 19

In agreement with Bacon's conclusion in her 2005 *Report on the Evolution of Immigration Detention in the UK*, these indicative exposures suggest that,

> The legitimacy of detention services being provided by a private industry which is incentivised by expanding its profits and therefore its operational scope, needs to be challenged ... Indeed, legislators and policy makers would not be able commit to increasing detention spaces without the co-operation, capacity and methods of the private sector, the involvement of which has given momentum to the growth of a detention regime.[82]

It is no longer difficult to imagine the situation where prisons, detention processes and centres, and overall policing are contracted out to private agencies so that once arrested (but even before having been arrested), detained or incarcerated one would be separated formally from the state agencies' accountability and economic, legal and political responsibility.[83]

A Total Opposition?

By the end of the twentieth century, deportation, detention, and dispersal had become normalized in an ongoing attempt to control the flows of human waste.[84] The schematic logic of the camp is that of a 'zone of indistinction between outside and inside, exception and rule, licit and illicit, in which the very concepts of subjective right and juridical protection no longer make any sense.'[85] The post-normative (governmental) and visible spatial locations of the camp as an apparatus of control have become increasingly indistinguishable from the invisible urban cages of citizens. Spatially the camp is usually perceived as a fixed place, a zone of distinction between the space of citizenship and that of denizenship. Post-normatively the spatiality of the camp has become unfixed, mobile and covering the globe as the *nomos* of the modern. The camp is not merely a spatial institution but more than that: an atrocious governmentality, a frame of mind, a logic of governance that is becoming more and more inventive and fluid. A camp can be placed in the state of origin, in so-called extra-territoriality, at airports, hotels, prisons, borders, on ships, deserts, so-called safe third countries, in courts during security certificate trials, on remote islands, in protection centres, in urban centres, in

May 2005; and Gallya Lahav, 'Immigration and the State: The Devolution and Privatisation of Immigration Control in the EU' [1998] *Journal of Ethnic and Migration Studies* 24(4), 675–94.

82 'Evolution of Immigration Detention in the UK', 27.

83 See Nigel Chapman, *Detention of Asylum Seekers in the United Kingdom* (Social Work Monographs, no. 176, Norwich 1998); Nils Christie, *Crime Control as Industry* (Routledge, London 2000); Malcolm M. Feeley, 'Entrepreneurs of Punishment: The Legacy of Privatisation' [2002] *Punishment and Society* 4(3), 321–44; Bente Molenaar and Rodney Neufeld, 'The Use of Privatised Detention Centres for Asylum Seekers in Australia and the UK' in Coyle, Campbell and Neufeld (eds) *Capitalist Punishment*; and Stephen Nathan, 'Prison Privatisation in the United Kingdom' in Coyle, Campbell and Neufeld (eds) *Capitalist Punishment*.

84 See Alice Bloch and Liza Schuster, 'At the Extremes of Exclusion: Deportation, Detention and Dispersal' [2005] *Ethnic and Racial Studies* 28(3), 491–512.

85 Agamben, Homo Sacer, 170.

invisible security apparatuses, through an electronic tag, in military bases, in your mind while you are commuting from work. It is in this diffuse sense that Agamben conceives of the logic of the camp as a generalized condition or *nomos* of modernity.

Control of movement is therefore a governmental machine of civil war that functionally relates to the image-suffused sovereignty of the dogma of the nation-state of which only the spectacular image remains. It is thus separated but also dependent on the image-suffused dogma of sovereignty, and the relationship is mutual. If research and activism has devoted too much attention this far on the image of sovereignty and its exposure, it needs to turn now decisively against the managers who have displaced the so-called sovereign decision maker from the dogmatic throne of sovereignty. It must focus research and collective action against the policing and management of borders, bodies and ideas. There is no longer much point in attempting to negotiate, compromise or better manage the policing of citizen and denizen. The opposition to immigration and movement controls as a form of policing must be total and uncompromising.

Internationally the protection promoted by the 1951 Convention has lost much of its meaning and policies are now geared towards non-arrival, deterrence, dispersal, diversion, detention, deportation and widespread denial of what is now a restrictive application of international treaties and domestic laws. Movement controls are only a part, though a crucial part, of the entire spectacle and practices of contemporary biopolitics. Post-sovereign biopolitics is the continuation of civil war by different, equally violent, means. Biopolitics has escaped the political by exposing itself as a mere managerial form of governing and policing, one based on datacide (a form of inclusive exclusion by status determination or underdetermination), exclusion and continuous crisis. Emergency has effectively replaced necessity and current logistics are becoming more flexible, ready-to-go, accelerated while persisting as long-term (if not permanent), constantly remodelled, technical (and hence presented as merely managerial or informational) solutions to problems. Biopolitics, today, is just the provisional name for the ordinary fate of the precarious existence of denizens and citizens.

In the name of law and of humanitarianism, often in direct complicity with the worst, a supranational, universal state of civil war has separated humanity from the undesirables placed in grey zones inside/outside the global society of control. Denizens and citizens, undesirables and desired ones, have been subjected to the extraction process of dislocating desire from action. Management *is* government and it now claims for itself the higher standard of this new un-ethics of control where action, decision and research are completely uncoupled from desire, factuality and accountability and are neutralized into micro- or macro-logistics of policing. If the so-called executive power gradually overpowered the legislative power in the triad image of capitalist democracies from the 1970s till recently, we have for some time now occupied an era where the executive has been replaced by the managerial non-political governmentality of policing.

References

Agamben, Giorgio, Homo Sacer*: Sovereign Power and Bare Life,* trans. D. Heller-Roazen (Stanford University Press, Stanford, CA 1998).

Agamben, Giorgio, Il regno e la gloria. Per una genealogia teologica dell'economia e del governo. Homo sacer 2,2 (Neri Pozza, Vicenza 2007).
Agamben, Giorgio, 'Interview with Giorgio Agamben – Life, A Work of Art without an Author: The State of Exception, the Administration of Disorder and Private Life' [2005] *German Law Review* 5(5), 609–14.
Agamben, Giorgio, *Means without Ends: Notes on Politics* (University of Minnesota Press, Minneapolis, MN 2000).
Agier, Michel, *On the Margins of the World: The Refugee Experience Today*, trans. David Fernbach (Polity Press, Cambridge 2008).
Amatangelo, Gina, 'Militarization of the U.S. Drug Control Program' [2001] *Foreign Policy in Focus* 6, via http://www.fpif.org/reports/militarization_of_the_us_drug_control_program, accessed 25 August 2012.
Astor, Avi, 'Unauthorized Immigration, Securitization and the Making of Operation Wetback' [2009] *Latino Studies* 7(1), 5–29.
Bacon, Christine, 'The Evolution of Immigration Detention in the UK: The Involvement of Private Prison Companies' [2005] Refugee Studies Centre, University of Oxford, Working Paper Series No. 27.
Banks, James, 'The Criminalisation of Asylum Seekers and Asylum Policy' [2007] *Prison Service Journal* 175, 43–9.
Bauman, Zygmunt, *Liquid Modernity* (Polity Press, Cambridge 2000).
Bauman, Zygmunt, *Wasted Lives: Modernity and Its Outcasts* (Polity Press, Cambridge 2004).
Bigo, Didier and Elspeth Guild, *La mise a l'écart des étrangers. La logique du visa Schengen* (Cultures et Conflits, l'Harmattan, Paris 2003).
Bloch, Alice and Liza Schuster, 'At the Extremes of Exclusion: Deportation, Detention and Dispersal' [2005] *Ethnic and Racial Studies* 28(3), 491–512.
Bosworth, Mary and Mhairi Guild, 'Governing through Immigration Control: Security and Citizenship in Britain' [2008] *British Journal of Criminology* 48(6), 703–19.
Brouwer, Evelien, Digital Borders and Real Rights: Effective Remedies for Third Country Nationals in the Schengen Information System (Martinus Nijhoff, Leiden 2008).
Bruin, Rene and Kees Wouters, 'Terrorism and the Non-derogability of Non-refoulement' [2003] *International Journal of Refugee Law* 15, 5–29.
Buckel, Sonja and Jens Wissel, 'State Project Europe: The Transformation of the European Border Regime and the Production of Bare Life' [2010] *International Political Sociology* 4, 33–49.
Cervantes-Gautschi, Peter, 'Wall Street and the Criminalization of Immigrants' [2010] *Counterpunch*, 15–17 October, at http://www.counterpunch.org/gautschi10152010.html, accessed 30 January 2011.
Chapman, Nigel, *Detention of Asylum Seekers in the United Kingdom* (Social Work Monographs, no. 176, Norwich 1998).
Cholewinski, Ryszard, 'The Criminalisation of Migration in EU Law and Policy' in Anneliese Baldaccini, Elspeth Guild and Helen Toner (eds) *Whose Freedom, Security and Justice? EU Immigration and Asylum Law and Policy* (Hart, Oxford 2007), 301–36.
Christie, Nils, *Crime Control as Industry* (Routledge, London 2000).
Cornelius, Wayne A., 'Death at the Border: The Efficacy and the Unintended Consequences of U.S. Immigration Control Policy' [2001] *Population and Development Review* 27(4), 661–85.

Côté-Boucher, Karine, 'The Diffuse Border: Intelligence-sharing, Control and Confinement along Canada's Smart Border' [2008] *Surveillance & Society* 5(2), 142–65.

Cronin, Kathryn, 'A Culture of Control: An Overview of Immigration Policy Making' in James Jupp and Marie Kabala (eds) *The Politics of Australian Immigration* (Australian Government Publishing Service, Canberra 1995), ch. 5.

Dauvergne, Catherine, 'Security and Migration: Law in the Less Brave New World' [2007] *Social and Legal Studies* 16, 533–49.

Deleuze, Gilles, 'Postscript on the Societies of Control' [1992] *OCTOBER* 59(Winter), 3–7.

Dow, Mark, *American Gulag: Inside US Immigration Prisons* (University of California Press, Berkeley, CA 2004).

Duffield, Mark, 'Global Civil War: The Non-insured, International Containment and Post-interventionary Society' [2008] *Journal of Refugee Studies* 21(2), 145–65.

Dunn, Timothy J., 'Immigration Enforcement in the U.S.–Mexico Border Region, the El Paso Case: Bureaucratic Power, Human Rights, and Civic Activism' [1999] unpublished PhD diss. (University of Texas, Austin).

Dyer, Joel, The Perpetual Prison Machine: How America Profits from Crime (Westview Press, Boulder, CO 2000).

Epstein, Charlotte, 'Guilty Bodies, Productive Bodies, Destructive Bodies: Crossing the Biometric Borders' [2007] *International Political Sociology* 1, 149–64.

Eschbach, Karl, Jacqueline Hagan and Nestor Rodriguez, *Causes and Trends in Migrant Deaths along the U.S–Mexico Border, 1985–1998* (University of Houston, Centre for Immigration Research, WSP 01–4 2001).

Eschbach, Karl, Jacqueline Hagan, Nestor Rodriguez, et al., 'Death at the Border' [1999] *International Migration Review* 33, 430–54.

Evans, Brad, 'Terror in all Eventuality' [2010] *Theory & Event*, 13(3), via http://muse.jhu.edu.ezproxy.lib.bbk.ac.uk/journals/theory_and_event/v013/13.3.evans01.html, accessed 25 August 2012.

Feeley, Malcolm M., 'Entrepreneurs of Punishment: The Legacy of Privatisation' [2002] *Punishment and Society* 4(3), 321–44.

Fekete, Liz, 'Anti-Muslim Racism and the European Security State' [2004] *Race and Class* 46, 3–29.

Fernandes, Deepa, Targeted: Homeland Security and the Business of Immigration (Seven Stories Press, New York 2007).

Fischer-Lescano, Andreas and Timo Tohidipur, 'Europäisches Grenzkontrollregime. Rechtsrahmen der europäischen Grenzschutzagentur FRONTEX' [2007] *Zeitschrift für ausländisches öffentliches Recht und Völkerrecht* 4, 1219–77.

Flynn, Michael and Cecilia Cannon, 'The Privatization of Immigration Detention: Towards a Global View – A Global Detention Project Working Paper' [2009] Global Detention Project, Geneva.

Foucault, Michel, Security, Territory, Population*: Lectures at the Collège de France 1977–1978* (Picador, New York 2009).

Foucault, Michel, *'Society Must Be Defended': Lectures at the Collège de France 1975–76*, trans. David Macey (Picador, New York 2003).

Foucault, Michel, *The Birth of Biopolitics: Lectures at the College de France, 1978–1979*, trans. Graham Burchell, ed. Michel Senellart et al. (New York, Palgrave Macmillan 2008).

Foucault, Michel, *The Hermeneutics of the Subject: Lectures at the Collège de France, 1981–82*, trans. Graham Burchell (Macmillan Palgrave, New York 2005).

Friese, Hidrun, 'The Limits of Hospitality: Political Philosophy, Undocumented Migration and the Local Arena' [2008] paper presented at the XXII Congresso Società Italiana di Scienze Politiche, Pavia, 4–6 September.

Garner, Steve, 'The European Union and the Racialization of Immigration, 1985–2006' [2007] *Race/Ethnicity: Multidisciplinary Global Contexts* 1(1), 61–87.

Gilboy, Janet A., 'Implications of "Third-Party" Involvement in Enforcement: The INS, Illegal Travellers, and International Airlines' [2006] in Susan Street (ed.) *Immigration*, The International Library of Essays in Law and Society (Ashgate, Burlington, VT 2006).

Goodwin-Gill. Guy, 'International Law and the Detention of Refugees and Asylum Seekers' [1986] *International Migration Review* 20(2), 193–219.

Guild, Elspeth and Paul Minderhoud, Immigration and Criminal Law in the European Union: The Legal Measures and Social Consequences of Criminal Law in Member States on Trafficking and Smuggling in Human Beings (Martinus Nijhoff, Leiden 2006).

Hammar, Tomas, Democracy and the Nation State: Aliens, Denizens and Citizens in a World of International Migration (Avebury, Aldershot 1990).

Hardt, Michael and Antonio Negri, *Empire* (Harvard University Press, Cambridge, MA 2000).

Holt, Matthew, 'Biopolitics and the "Problem" of the Refugee' [2002], Critical Perspectives on Refugee Policy in Australia: Proceedings of the Refugee Rights Symposium Hosted by the Institute for Citizenship and Globalisation, Faculty of Arts, Deakin University, 5 December 2002, at http://www.deakin.edu.au/arts-ed/ccg/rsg/pdfs/matthew-holt.pdf, accessed 30 January 2011.

Huysmans, Jef and Alessandra Buonfino, 'Politics of Exception and Unease: Immigration, Asylum and Terrorism in Parliamentary Debates in the U.K.' [2008] *Political Studies* 36, 766–83.

Hyland, Matthew, 'Refugee Subjectivity: "Bare Life" and the Geographical Division of Labour' [2001] *LOG Illustrated Magazine*, 13, at http://www.physicsroom.org.nz/log/archive/13/refugeesubjectivity/, accessed 30 January 2011.

Ibrahim, Maggie, 'The Securitization of Migration: A Racial Discourse' [2005] *International Migration* 43(5), 163–86.

International Council on Human Rights Policy, 'Modes and Patterns of Social Control: Implications for Human Rights Policy' [2010], at http://www.ichrp.org/files/reports/61/Social_Control_and_Human_Rights_ICHRP_Electronic_Final.pdf, accessed 12 August 2012.

Lahav, Gallya, 'Immigration and the State: The Devolution and Privatisation of Immigration Control in the EU' [1998] *Journal of Ethnic and Migration Studies* 24(4), 675–94.

Larsen, Mike and Justin Piché, 'Exceptional State, Pragmatic Bureaucracy, and Indefinite Detention: The Case of the Kingston Immigration Holding Centre' [2009] *Canadian Journal of Law and Society* 24(2), 203–29.

Legomsky, Stephen, Immigration and the Judiciary: Law and Politics in Britain and America (Clarendon Press, Oxford 1987).

McDonald, Douglas, 'Public Imprisonment by Private Means: The Re-emergence of Private Prisons and Jails in the United States, the United Kingdom and Australia' [1994] *British Journal of Criminology* 34, 29–48.

McDonald, Douglas C. et al., Private Prisons in the United States: An Assessment of Current Practice (Abt Associates, Cambridge, MA 1998).

Maggy, Shuk Yi Lee, 'Human Trade and the Criminalisation of Irregular Migration' [2005] *International Journal of the Sociology of Law* 33, 1–15.

Marfleet, Philip, *Refugees in a Global Era* (Palgrave, Houndmills 2006).

Massey, Douglas S., 'Backfire at the Border: Why Enforcement without Legalization Cannot Stop Illegal Immigration' [2005], at http://www.freetrade.org/pubs/pas/tpa-029.pdf, accessed 30 January 2011.

Mezzadra, Sandro, Diritto di fuga. Migrazioni, cittadinanza, globalizzazione (Edizioni OmbreCorte, Verona 2006).

Miggiano, Luca, 'States of Exception: Securitization and Irregular Migration in the Mediterranean' [2009] *New Issues in Refugee Research*, Research Paper No. 177, UNHCR, via http://www.unhcr.org, accessed 12 August 2012.

Molenaar, Bente and Rodney Neufeld, 'The Use of Privatised Detention Centres for Asylum Seekers in Australia and the UK' in Andrew Coyle, Allison Campbell and Rodney Neufeld (eds) *Capitalist Punishment: Prison Privatisation and Human Rights* (Zed Books, London 2002).

Nathan, Stephen, 'Prison Privatisation in the United Kingdom' in Andrew Coyle, Alison Campbell and Rodney Neufeld (eds) *Capitalist Punishment: Prison Privatisation and Human Rights* (Zed Books, London 2002).

Nathan, Stephen, 'The European Market for Privatised Correctional Services: Developments and Implications' [2005] Workshop at the EPSU Standing Committee on National and European Administration on Prison Services, Luxembourg, 19 May.

Neal, Andrew W., 'Securitization and Risk at the EU Border: The Origins of FRONTEX', *Journal of Common Market Studies* 47(2), 333–56.

Ntsobi, Mfanelo Patrick, 'Privatisation of Prisons and Prison Services in South Africa' [2005] unpublished diss. (University of Western Cape).

Palidda, Salvatore (ed.) *Criminalisation and Victimization of Migrants in Europe* (University of Genoa, Genoa 2009).

Palmer, Mick, Inquiry into the Circumstances of the Immigration Detention of Cornelia Rau Report (Commonwealth of Australia, 2005).

Parenti, Christian, 'Privatised Problems: For-Profit Incarceration in Trouble' in Andrew Coyle, Allison Campbell and Rodney Neufeld (eds) *Capitalist Punishment: Prison Privatisation and Human Rights* (Zed Books, London 2002).

Payne, Richard, 'Cashing in on Asylum' [2005] *Media Active: Ideas, Knowledge, Culture* 4, 56–68.

Pham, Huyen T., 'The Privatization of Immigration Law Enforcement' [2007], unpublished paper, at http://works.bepress.com/huyen_pham/1/, accessed 12 August 2012.

Richmond, Ted and John Shields, 'NGO–Government Relations and Immigrant Services: Contradictions and Challenges' [2005] *Journal of International Migration and Integration* 6(3), 513–26.

Rudge, Philip, 'European Initiatives on Asylum' in Daniele Joly and Robin Cohen (eds) *Reluctant Hosts: Europe and its Refugees* (Avebury, Aldershot 1989).

Schütz, Anton, 'Thinking the Law with and against Luhmann, Legendre, Agamben' [2000] *Law and Critique* 11(2), 107–36.

The Danish Institute for International Studies Working Paper [2004] 23, via http://www.diis.dk, accessed 30 January 2011.

Tiqqun, *Introduction to Civil War*, trans. Alexander R. Galloway and Jason E. Smith (Semiotext(e)/MIT Press, Cambridge, MA 2010).

Vaughan-Williams, Nick, 'Borders, Territory, Law' [2008] *International Political Sociology* 2, 322–38.

Watson, Scott D., The Securitization of Humanitarian Migration: Digging Moats and Sinking Boats (Routledge, London 2009).

Welch, Michael, *Detained: Immigration Laws and the Expanding INS Jail Complex* (Temple University Press, Philadelphia, PA 2002).

Welch, Michael and Liza Schuster, 'Detention of Asylum Seekers in the US, UK, France, Germany and Italy: A Critical View of the Globalizing Culture of Control' [2005] *Criminal Justice* 5(4), 331–55.

Wray, Matt, Not Quite White: White Trash and the Boundaries of Whiteness (Duke University Press, Durham, NC 2006).

Transnational Citizenship and the Democratic State: On Modes of Membership and Rights of Political Participation

David Owen

The past 30 years have seen dramatic changes to the character of state membership regimes in which practices of easing access to membership for resident non-citizens, extending the franchise to expatriate citizens as well as, albeit in typically more limited ways, to resident non-citizens and an increasing toleration of dual nationality have become widespread.[1] These processes of democratic inclusion, while variously motivated, represent an important trend in the contemporary political order in which we can discern two distinct shifts. The first concerns membership as a status and is characterized in terms of the movement from a simple distinction between single-nationality citizens and single-nationality aliens to a more complex structure of state membership in which we now find, most prominently, two transnational figures:

- *Dual (or plural) nationals* who are legally recognized as citizens by two or more independent polities.
- (Non-stateless) *Denizens* who, as long-term resident foreign nationals in one polity, enjoy 'most of the civil liberties and social welfare rights of resident citizens, often including rights to family reunification, some protection from deportation, and voting rights in local elections, as well as quasi-entitlements to naturalization', and, as long-term non-resident citizens of another polity, enjoy external citizenship rights (that is, the right to return and the right to diplomatic protection) and may retain some voting rights. (Baubock, 2007: 2395–6)[2]

The second shift relates to voting rights and is marked by the movement from the requirement that voting rights are grounded in both citizenship and residence to the relaxing of the joint character of this requirement such that citizenship or residence now increasingly serve as a basis for, at least partial, enfranchisement.[3] In the light of these transformations, it is probably

---

1 For recent overviews of these changes and the reasons for them see Baubock (2003, 2005), Joppke (2010), and chapter 6 (of which I was lead author) in Stoker et al. (2011).

2 For a clear analytical specification, see Baubock (2007).

3 See Baubock (2003, 2005) and chapter 6 of Stoker et al. (2011).

unsurprising that empirically informed realistic normative engagement with transnational citizenship – conceived in terms of the enjoyment of membership statuses in two (or more) states – has focused on the issues of access to, and maintenance of, national citizenship, on the one hand,[4] and entitlement to voting rights, on the other hand.[5] Yet this framing of debates on transnational citizenship comes with three sets of costs attached. First, the identification of full political membership with national citizenship elides an important distinction between these concepts in ways that is, I'll argue, consequential for a conflict within normative debates on transnational citizenship that I'll refer to as *the antinomy of incorporation*.[6] Second, the focus on voting rights – for all their symbolic and practical significance – occludes the more general terrain of rights of political participation. Third, the restrictive understanding of membership invoked in this discussion means that it fails to address adequately the issues raised by the standing of non-resident non-citizens whose morally significant interests are adversely affected by the decisions of states. The task of this chapter is to try to reframe the debate on transnational citizenship in a way that takes account of these costs and thereby allows for a more nuanced account of different modes of membership that acknowledges that distinct grounds of entitlement to participation in political society can legitimate differentiated sets of rights of political participation and, hence, diverse modes of membership.

I'll begin by very briefly sketching some general considerations on political participation and how transnational citizenship disaggregates two different types of reasons for valuing political participation (section 1), before surveying the three main lines of argument within realistic normative political theory with respect to transnational citizenship (section 2). I'll then turn to the first of the problems identified, namely, the identification of full political membership and national citizenship and consequent generation of the antinomy of incorporation, and defend a way of resolving this antinomy that hangs on distinguishing full political membership and national citizenship (section 3). While discussion of the first problem focuses on the case of resident non-citizens, preparing the ground for discussion of the second problem, namely, the restrictive focus on voting rights, requires also attending to the debate concerning the inclusion of non-resident citizens within the *demos* of the home state (section 4). I then address this second problem and try to shift the discussion to a wider concern with rights of political participation before drawing out the implications of that shift for the third problem, the restrictive understanding of membership, by showing how it allows us to accommodate certain classes of non-resident, non-citizens within the scope of transnational citizenship (section 5).

1. On Political Participation

We can begin by distinguishing two types of reasons – *protective* and *expressive* – for valuing political participation and their implications for how we conceive of rights of political participation.

4 Rubio-Marin (2000), Carens (2005), Baubock (2003, 2005, 2007).
5 Rubio-Marin (2006), Baubock (2007).
6 Baubock (2007).

Protective reasons emphasize the instrumental value of political participation as the primary medium through which the governed seek to express, in various idioms and registers, their consent to, or dissent from, the ways in which they are governed and attempt to shape how they are governed, that is, the form and content of the regime of rule to which they are subject. From the perspective of protective reasons, *rights* of political participation are instrumentally valuable insofar as they protect the governed against tyrannical rule by securing the basic institutional conditions of those legitimate and effective forms of political participation through which those who are governed can govern how they are governed.

Expressive reasons stress the non-instrumental value of political participation insofar as it is constitutive of the (intrinsic) good of belonging to the political community, a good that is manifest in the relations of civic friendship (for example, bonds of trust and solidarity) among the members of the political community. Within the framework of expressive reasons, *rights* of political participation may be seen as instrumentally valuable insofar as they secure the conditions for the governed to engage in political participation and so realize the good of political community, but they may also be seen as themselves non-instrumentally valuable insofar as they are understood as a form of civic recognition that is expressive, and partially constitutive, of the good of belonging to a political community. The thought here is that, just as the good of personal friendship is partly constituted by the acknowledgement of the relevant parties of rights and duties that they owe to each other, so too is the good of civic friendship; the distinction between the two forms of friendship is that, in the civic case, (some of) these rights and duties are given public institutional expression.

These are not the only reasons that may be adduced for valuing rights of political participation (for example, one might also highlight *developmental reasons*, which stress the role of political participation in the development of political self-knowledge), but they are the most central to my concerns. More particularly, they help to draw attention to two distinct aspects under which we conceive of the state, namely, as a regime of rule and as a form (or site) of community. In the case of the democratic constitutional state, this gives rise to specific characteristics. On the one hand, the regime of rule is that it is one in which, to put it in the most general terms, the governed also govern. Democratic government is best conceived as a form of *reflexive authority* in which those who are subject to authority are those who authorize the authority to which they are subject. On the other hand, the form of democratic political community is that of a free community of equals for whom the good of belonging to a political community comprises the relations of liberty, equality and fraternity that are constitutive of a democratic political community.

The presumption of normative democratic theory has been that national citizens of a democratic state will typically share both protective and expressive reasons for valuing political participation. Such citizens will have a legitimate interest in, and claim to, membership of the democratic state as a regime of rule and also have a legitimate interest in, and claim to, membership of the democratic state as a political community. However, in the context of transnational citizenship, this presumption precisely because it was grounded on the idealization that the class of habitual residents of the state is identical to the class of national citizens of the state becomes problematic. Resident non-citizens may have protective reasons for valuing political participation that express their claim to membership of the democratic state as a regime of rule to which they are subject without having expressive reasons for valuing political participation. In contrast, non-resident citizens may have (largely) expressive reasons for valuing political participation that express their claim to membership of the democratic state as a political community. In other words, reflection on transnational citizenship directs us to a concern not merely with *degrees* of political membership but also with *modes* of political membership in the democratic state. One way of characterizing the central claim of this chapter is that it represents the contention that the question of what constitute legitimate degrees of political membership for transnational citizens in the states to which they belong cannot be adequately addressed separately from discussion of the different modes of membership at issue in their relationship to these states.

2. Normative Framings of Transnational Citizenship

Within discussions of transnational citizenship, the articulation of grounds of entitlement to full political membership (typically construed as national citizenship) have clustered around the principle that all persons who are subject to the coercive authority of the democratic state (or, to accommodate the EU, the polity) should be entitled, at least after a limited period of residence (for example, the EU norm of five years), to membership of the state. It should be noted that this formulation of the *all subjected persons* principle is ambiguous between two distinct formulations of principle: a formulation in terms of subjection to the *political authority* of the state and a formulation in terms of subjection to the *coercive power* of the state. The distinction between these formulations rests on the claim that the political authority of the state is not reducible to, or fully co-extensive with, its ability to coercively enforce its collectively binding decisions. The collectively binding decisions of a democratic state, expressed as law, may legitimately be coercively enforced within the jurisdictional ambit of the law in question (either by the state within its own territorial jurisdiction or by international agencies or partners acting on behalf of the state through which the extended jurisdictional reach of a given law is realized), but being *subject* to a collective binding norm does not require that the norm is coercively enforceable – it requires only the rather weaker notion that breaches of the norm generate duties of justification and are sanctionable in the absence of adequate justification.[7] It is, of course, true that, for a large range of cases, the conceptual distinction between the *political authority* and *coercive power* formulations of the *all subjected persons* principle is a distinction without a practical difference – but not for all cases. Thus, for example, expatriate citizens may be subject to the political authority of the state and yet the state may be unable to coercively enforce compliance with the law (for example, on income tax and military service) on the part of expatriate citizens. This difference will turn out to matter and I'll return to it later in this section, but before doing so we need to attend to the three leading variants that cluster around the *all subjected persons* principle. We can distinguish three positions: the all-subjected persons principle itself, the social membership principle, and the stakeholder principle. I'll address each in turn.

The classic argument for the incorporation of habitual residents is provided by Robert Dahl's argument for the 'principle of full inclusion': '*The demos must include all adult members of the association except transients and persons proved to be mentally defective*' (1989: 129, my

7 Sangiovanni (2007).

emphasis), where 'adult members of the association' refers to '*all adults subject to the binding collective decisions of the association*' (1989: 120, my emphasis). As Lopez-Guerra helpfully notes, Dahl's specification of criteria of democracy can be summarized thus:

> (1) governments must give equal consideration to the good and interests of every person bound by their laws (principle of intrinsic equality); (2) unless there is compelling evidence to the contrary, every person should be considered to be the best judge of his or her own good and interests (presumption of personal autonomy); therefore (3) all adults [who are not merely transients (1) and are not shown to be mentally defective (2)] should be assumed to be sufficiently well-qualified to participate in the collective decision-making processes of the polity (strong principle of equality). (2005: 219, my insertion)

In the context of a democratic polity characterized in part by authority over a territorial jurisdiction, Dahl's account implies that any competent adult who is habitually resident within the territory of the polity and, hence, *subject to* the laws and policies of its government is entitled to full inclusion within the *demos*.[8] Such an argument can be taken to underwrite Walzer's claim that the denial of full political rights to legally admitted habitual residents amounts to *citizen tyranny* (1983: 55).[9]

It has been contended by Lopez-Guerra that, given Dahl's formulation of the principle of full inclusion, 'the demos of a democratic polity must exclude all individuals who are not subject to the laws, together with transients and persons proved incapable of taking part in the decision-making process' (2005: 225). Lopez-Guerra's grounds for this claim are based on the view that, given the territorial jurisdiction of the state, being resident on the territory of the state is a *necessary* (as well as sufficient) condition for being subject to the collectively binding decisions of the state. Consequently, he argues that,

> Debates so far have focused only on the necessity of granting political rights to all residents. They have ignored the implication that this *requires* the exclusion of long-term expatriates. (2005: 234, my emphasis)

Unsurprisingly, this required exclusion encourages the view that citizenship should be granted on a *jus domicile* basis.

The fundamental problem with the interpretation of the all subjected principle that Lopez-Guerra offers is that being present on the territory of a state is *not* a necessary condition for being subject to its collectively binding decisions. To illustrate this, consider the following (real) examples:

---

8 Although Dahl talks of the principle of all affected interests, I agree with Lopez-Guerra (2005: 222–5) that, since it is being governed that is the normatively relevant issue for Dahl, the relevant principle is that of being *subjected to* rule rather than *affected by* rule. For defences of the all-affected principle, see Shapiro (2003) and Goodin (2007).

9 Walzer links this claim to one in which the polity has the right to determine its own entry criteria as an element of its right to self-determination; for an excellent analysis of the difficulties that this conjunction generates, see Bosniak (2006).

1. The event that motivates Lopez-Guerra's own article, namely, the Mexican referendum on expatriate voting.
2. The current UK Coalition government proposal to introduce a decent flat rate state pension that is payable only to UK citizens who are resident in the UK.

Who is subject to these collectively binding decisions? The answer is obvious: all citizens, irrespective of the residential status. Hence, while habitual residence is a sufficient condition of subjection to the political authority of the state, it is not a necessary condition.

More generally, states are a form of polity combining authoritative rules that are conceptually dependent on residency, rules that are conceptually dependant on non-residency, and rules that are conceptually independent of one's residential status (though they may be residence sensitive).[10] Thus, for example, the relationship between a state and its national citizens involves some rights and obligations that are necessarily dependent on residence (that is, those arising from any law that pertains to actions involving the physical presence of the person with the state), some that are necessarily dependent on non-residence (that is, the right to re-entry and to diplomatic protection), and some that are residence indifferent (for example, paying tax on property owned in the state). One of the political choices that a state can make with respect to issues that are not conceptually tied either to presence on or absence from the territory of the state is whether or not to treat them as residence neutral. So the fact that Joe lives in state F rather than in state H, of which he is a national citizen, while his brother and co-national Fred resides in state H, does not mean that Joe is not, while Fred is, subject to the authoritative decisions of state H regarding the entitlements, privileges, powers and immunities (and their correlatives) that make up the legal character of citizens of state H. On the contrary, Joe and Fred are both subject to the political authority of state H. What differentiates them is, rather, the specific laws, rights and duties that currently *apply* to them in virtue of their distinct residence statuses. Thus a significant range (typically the majority) of the laws of state H are practically tied to, and activated by, residential criteria and, hence, apply to Fred but do not come into effect with respect to Joe as long as he is a non-resident, while other laws that are tied to, and activated by, non-residence apply to Joe but not to Fred so long as he remains a resident. Further laws may be residence neutral and apply to both Fred and Joe (for example, income tax laws can be of this kind and UK laws on the sexual abuse of minors have this character) – and some of these laws may be such that they can be effectively enforced, while others cannot easily be enforced. Citizenship, in its quasi-contractual aspect, is thus like being a signatory to a contract that may have some clauses specifying (reasonable) circumstance-invariant rights and obligations and other clauses where the relevant rights and obligations may vary according to which of a range of circumstances applies.

Notice, though, that this argument only establishes that, as a citizen, you are subject to the political authority of the state whose nationality you hold. Yet since it is only in virtue of the fact that, under current citizenship rules, you retain national citizenship as an expatriate that you are subject to the political authority of the state, the argument thus far is unable to account for *why* you should be entitled to retain national citizenship of this state. A *jus domicile*

10 A residence-sensitive rule is one that, while not conceptually tied to residence, is practically related to residence in terms of its application. I am grateful to Rainer Baubock for pressing this point on me.

rule such as Lopez-Guerra favours would equally meet the basic normative requirement that everyone is entitled to equal membership in a self-governing political community. Essentially the same type of objection is made in a different way by Baubock, who argues that '"all subjected persons" is too conservative in presupposing the legitimacy of given boundaries':

> If a state turns, for example, the grandchildren of emigrants into citizens through automatic and unlimited *ius sanguinis* rules, then these persons would be subject to the authority of the grandparents' state of origin and could claim democratic representation there. The question is, however, whether such persons should be included as citizens in the first place. Questions about legitimate inclusion must therefore refer to some principle that is not fully derived from de facto exercise of political authority. (2009: 480–81)

The limitation of the all subjected persons principle exposed by these critical remarks is that it addresses the question of who should be entitled to political membership given an existing structure of political authority and allocation of citizenship, not the question of who should be entitled to national citizenship – and while this limitation plays the useful role of drawing our attention to the distinction between 'political membership' and 'national citizenship' (to which I'll return later in this section), it is clear that if we are to develop a criteria for entitlement to national citizenship then, at the very least, the all subjected persons principle needs supplementation. This limitation is, in part, a product of the fact that the all subjected persons principle represents an exclusive focus on the democratic state as a regime of rule, where it is precisely this one-sidedness that supports the intuition expressed by Lopez-Guerra that citizenship should be a matter of *jus domicile*. In somewhat different ways, the *social membership* and *stakeholder* principles may be seen as attempts to overcome the problem posed by this limitation in ways that acknowledge the value of the democratic state as a site of political community. In the case of the stakeholder principle, this is done directly by specifying the idea of stakeholding in terms of a relationship between the autonomy and/or well-being of an individual and the future of the polity. In the case of the social membership principle, with which I begin, it is done indirectly through an appeal to the salience of social membership.

The *social membership* argument is perhaps given its earliest articulation (with respect not to national citizenship but resident non-citizen voting rights) in the case of *Spragins v. Houghton* (1840), which allowed the Illinois Supreme Court to make clear

> a general constitutional preference for democratic inclusion where the simple facts of habitation, residence and common social membership establish a political relationship 'between the governed and [the] governing'. According to the court, the Illinois Constitution: '[I]ntended to extend the right of suffrage to those who, having by habitation and residence identified their interests and feelings with the citizen, are upon the just principle of reciprocity between the governed and the governing, entitled to a voice in the choice of the officers of the government, although they may be neither native nor adopted citizens.' (Raskin 1993: 1405)

In more contemporary terms, it is advanced by Rubio-Marin (2000) and Carens (1989 and 2005) as asserting the principle that people have a moral right to be citizens of any society of which they are members (Carens 1989: 32). The basis of this claim is twofold. First, there is the general social fact that living in a society makes one a member of a society since, as one forges connections and attachments, one's interests become interlinked with those of other members of the society (Rubio-Marin, 2000: 21, 31–4; Carens 2005: 33, 39). Second, in living in given society, one is subject to the political authority of the state and, consequently, on democratic grounds, should have access to full political rights within the political community of that state (Rubio-Marin 2000: 28–30; Carens 2005: 39).

These arguments are, in several respects, compelling. Moreover, and fairly naturally, they give rise to the claim – implied by Walzer (1983), advanced by Rubio-Marin (2000), and now accepted by Carens (2005) – that neither the conferral (on the part of the state) nor the acquisition (on the part of the immigrant) of such rights should be optional. The former element rules out selective practices such as citizenship tests on the grounds that, while a society can legitimately entertain the reasonable expectation that immigrants will acquire its language and knowledge of its political institutions, it is unreasonable to make acquisition of civic rights conditional on meeting what can only be reasonable expectations given, for example, the differential linguistic abilities of persons.[11] The latter element rules out the possibility of choosing not to acquire such rights on the grounds that such a choice represents voluntary subjection to a condition of political servitude and, hence, is incompatible with the autonomy-valuing character of liberal democratic states.

Further, although the social membership argument was developed in relation to resident non-citizens, it can be extended to address the wider issue of membership more broadly and it is in this extension that its acknowledgement of the non-instrumental value of membership comes to the fore. Thus, for example, drawing on the *social* dimension of the argument, Rubio-Marin (2006) has argued that, in respect of states of origin, expatriates should have a right to retain their nationality of origin even when they naturalize in their state of residence on the basis that, generally speaking, membership of the state of origin is a source of non-instrumental value for them as well as its instrumental value in terms of visiting family and supporting the possibility of return migration. We can extend this argument to reasons for the state of residence also to accept a right to retention of the original nationality when naturalizing, namely, that precisely because membership of the state of origin is typically a significant source of non-instrumental and instrumental value for its emigrant population, requiring them to surrender it will generate an inequitable distribution of burdens between native citizens and immigrants (whether naturalized or not) in terms of their capacity to enjoy the social attachments and ties that matter to them – and, consequently, engender forms of resentment that are not conducive to social cohesion and civic integration in the state of residence (cf. Rubio-Marin 2006: 138). We can also note that, although she also does not address this issue, the logic of Rubio-Marin's position would support, given the importance of the family as a site of socialization and the generational proximity of the event of emigration, this right of retention of nationality to be extended to second-generation migrants.

11 For a defence of citizenship tests see Miller (2008), and for critiques see Carens (2005: 38–9) and Seglow (2008).

The second supplementary alternative to the all subjected persons principle is the *stakeholder* principle proposed by Baubock, which expresses the claim that 'self-governing political communities should include as citizens those individuals whose circumstances of life link their individual autonomy or well-being to the common good of the political community' (2009: 479). This principle of inclusion is based on the following basic thought:

> in a self-governing polity, each individual member has a stake in the future of that polity in a dual sense. First, each individual's autonomy or well-being depends to a large degree on how well political institutions work in guaranteeing equal liberties and in providing equal opportunities for all subjected to their authority. Second, citizens can collectively shape the future course of the polity through political participation and by holding political authorities accountable. The notoriously vague notion of the common good may serve as a shorthand term for what it is that citizens have a stake in. (Baubock 2009: 479)

In practical terms, Baubock proposes two criteria for whether people meet this stakeholding requirement:

> Those persons and only those persons have a claim to citizenship in a particular political community who (a) depend on that community for long-term protection of their basic rights (dependency criterion) or (b) are or have been subjected to that community's political authorities for a significant period over the course of their lives (biographical subjection criterion). (2009: 479)

We can notice first that, since first-generation migrants are generally stakeholders in both their countries of origin and of habitual residence, this principle lends itself to support of dual nationality. Given the role of family in socialization, it is plausible to argue that second-generation migrants are also stakeholders but that, by the third generation, this claim is harder to sustain independent of actions on the part of the third-generation migrant (such as going to live in the state of their grandparent's origin) to sustain the relationship. Thus, in addition to supporting dual nationality, the stakeholder principle would extend the *automatic jus sanguinis* transmission of citizenship to second-generation migrants but not further (Baubock 2007).

It is notable that, in contrast to the social membership argument, the stakeholder principle does not appeal to social ties and attachments but to directly political ties. Baubock offers two reasons for rejecting the social membership argument (which he had earlier endorsed) in favour of the stakeholder principle. The first concerns the increasing problems faced by the concept of a bounded state society in contexts of migrant transnationalism and global interactions. Against this background, Baubock comments, it may appear 'somewhat circular if we derive claims to political membership from factual societal membership, but then have to refer to given political boundaries in order to define societies in the first place' (2009: 482). The second is that, while the social membership argument 'would substantiate immigrants' claim to citizenship, it cannot account for long-term external membership' when conducted in terms of a statist conception of society, while opening out the notion of societal membership beyond such a statist outlook through appeals to notions like family ties 'begs the question why other networks across borders, such as business connections, should not also be regarded as forms of societal membership' (Baubock 2009: 482). Even if we accept the first of these criticisms (as we probably should do), it is not clear that the two points suffice to knock down the social membership argument as opposed to providing reasons for its reformulation. Hints towards such a reformulation can already be seen in Rubio-Marin's reflections on dual nationality, but we can develop this further by considering the following restatement of the social membership argument:

> *social membership* is characterized by non-instrumentally valuable social attachments and ties that arise from one's (past or present) residence within the territory of the state (or by way of socialization through parents who were residents of the state in question) and that link one's well-being to the well-being of the (typically transnational) society comprised of all persons characterized by non-instrumentally valuable social attachments and ties that arise from their (past or present) residence within the territory of the state (or by way of socialization through parents who were residents of the state in question).

This reformulation of the social membership argument does not appeal to the problematic concept of a bounded state society but simply to the non-instrumental value and site of genesis of those social relations that comprise a form of social solidarity, yet since the state remains central to the well-being of this society, the social membership argument may still ground claims to political inclusion. Such a reformulation avoids Baubock's criticisms and, hence, we may take both the revised social membership principle and the stakeholder principle to represent live positions in the debate on transnational citizenship.

3. Citizenship, Membership and Resident Non-citizens

It is notable that both advocates of the social membership and the stakeholder principles align political membership with national citizenship – and this gives raise to a further dispute between their respective advocates, which is more immediately consequential for the concerns of this article. The issue at stake in this dispute concerns whether the resident non-citizen who has legally abided in the state for the relevant period should be automatic entitled to take up national citizenship or automatically required to adopt national citizenship. Arguments for automatic mandatory citizenship have been advanced by Rubio-Marin and Carens, which, albeit on slightly different grounds, stress the problem of citizen tyranny, while Baubock has argued that there are good sociological reasons for thinking that it is important for social and political integration that immigrants make a public voluntary commitment to naturalize and, thereby, 'visibly link their own future with that of the country of settlement'. Both of these arguments have considerable force. But rather than attempt to resolve this dispute by demonstrating the rational superiority of one position over the other, I would like to try the tactic of *dissolving* the dispute by showing that we can endorse both positions. The central pivot for this tactic is the fact that this *antinomy of incorporation* arises precisely because both identify political membership with national citizenship. Consequently, one way of negotiating this conflict is thus to drop this identification and note that neither the all subjected persons principle nor its supplemental variants strictly entails naturalization as the route to political membership; each simply entails political membership – and there is a non-trivial distinction between *political membership* and *national citizenship* since the latter, but not the former, automatically includes the 'external rights' of diplomatic protection and automatic right of re-entry to the state as well as the automatic entitlement to pass nationality on to their children via the *jus sanguinis* provisions that states have almost universally and justifiably adopted as part of their nationality laws. Thus we may hold both that there is a compelling argument for the mandated acquisition of full political rights or *political membership* (which ought, in the case of resident non-citizens, to confer an automatic entitlement to the acquisition of the status of *national citizenship*), and that the acquisition of national citizenship itself should involve a voluntary act on the part of the immigrant. The additional features of national citizenship fit the rationale for a voluntary act since their value is immanently related to the immigrant's seeing their relationship to the state as not simply instrumental valuable in protecting them against domination but also as non-instrumentally valuable and, hence, as providing reasons for linking one's own future well-being with that of the state.

However, two significant objections have been proposed to this method of dissolving the antinomy of incorporation, which I'll address in turn.[12]

The first objection concerns mandated membership and points out that denizens are not non-citizens but combine a bundle of extensive quasi-citizenship rights in the country of residence with external citizenship rights in a country of origin. Their denizenship rights include a right to optional naturalization. The objection is thus that this bundle should sufficiently secure their political autonomy. Under this condition, not to make use of their right to naturalization can be seen as akin to enjoying voting rights but not making use of them. To put this point the other way round, an argument for mandatory naturalization would have to meet the same objections as arguments for mandatory voting. Paternalistic arguments for mandatory naturalization or voting are not necessarily illiberal, but they should be grounded on contextual evidence that sufficient inclusion cannot be achieved otherwise.

In response to the first objection, it is important to distinguish between conditions of political autonomy and exercises of political autonomy. In the example of mandatory voting, the argument against the practice swings on the fact that, in non-mandatory systems, both voting and not voting are expressions of political autonomy and, hence, while argument for mandatory voting may be plausible, their normative force won't be grounded directly on an appeal to political autonomy (though it may be indirectly so grounded). By contrast, on the account I offer, political membership is a condition of political autonomy; the decision whether to acquire or not acquire political membership may both be expressions of individual autonomy, but they are not exercises of political autonomy. Hence, on this view, the question is whether people should be entitled as a matter of personal autonomy to place themselves in conditions of political servitude. I see no reason to accept that claim.

This initial response, however, depends on the claim that full political membership is a necessary condition of political autonomy – and it is not clear that this claim is sustainable. While it is reasonable to take the claim to hold in the case of 'birthright' citizens who hold no other nationality or 'stateless' residents, the condition of the denizen is quite distinct.

[12] I am grateful to Rainer Baubock for raising these objections and I draw on his formulations of them in presenting them here.

The objection suggests that the quasi-citizenship enjoyed by denizens combined with their external citizenship rights in their country of origin suffice for political autonomy, that is, they have external rights of diplomatic protection and of return combined with local voting rights and, typically, some general rights of political participation. If this is the case, it would seem perverse to deny that denizens enjoy some degree of political autonomy and to insist that full political membership is a necessary condition of political autonomy as such. But admitting this point does not settle the argument, since once we admit that there are degrees of political autonomy the pressing question becomes what counts as an acceptable threshold.

Here I think it is worthwhile to return to Dahl's (1989) argument concerning the strong principle of equality. The relevant point is that Dahl's argument makes no reference to citizenship; the criterion for membership to which it appeals is subjection to the collectively binding decisions of the polity. While it is the case that resident non-citizens are not subject to *all* the collectively binding decisions of the polity since not all laws are tied to conditions of residency, it is also true that, given the territorial dimension of the state, a large (and consequential) array of residence-based laws are binding on resident non-citizens. In this respect, one way of reflecting on the issue of the threshold of political autonomy is to note that denizens are situated in different contexts of political autonomy – that of the state of origin and the state of residence – and although some very basic features of political autonomy in the state of residence may be protected through the right of diplomatic protection granted by the state of origin (and the spread of human rights norms), this is hardly sufficient to secure a relevant degree of political autonomy in the context of the state of residence. Considering a related issue raised in relation to dual nationals who have voting rights in both states of their nationality may help to clarify this point. Here the question is raised as to whether this practice breaches the principle of equality since these dual nationals have two votes. The appropriate response is that, although they have two votes, the votes are cast in distinct electoral contests and, hence, the principle of equality is not breached since, as long as the votes do not both contribute, directly or indirectly, to the selection of representatives from both states to a supra-national level of governance (as in the case of the EU), the relevant context of application of the principle of the equality is a specific polity (cf. Baubock 2007: 2428). By the same token, as long as the relevant states are not linked in a supra-national union, the appropriate threshold for political autonomy in a state of residence is given by the application of the principle of equality in that polity – and this, at the very least, supports a strong presumption in favour of full political membership for resident non-citizens.

However, notice that, even if we admit that there may be forms of political incorporation that are sufficient to secure the relevant conditions of political autonomy but fall short of full membership, this does not undermine the argument for mandatory inclusion. On the contrary, it simply revises the principle to state that whatever degree of incorporation in the political community is necessary for securing political autonomy can legitimately be a matter of automatic mandatory inclusion. If it is the case that the quasi-citizenship enjoyed by denizens combined with their external citizenship rights in their country of origin suffice for political autonomy, then the relevant membership rights (for example, local voting rights and, typically, some general rights of political participation) are not optional (and it is notable that the objection assumes that these rights are not optional). If it is the case, as I have suggested, that full membership rights are required, then these are equally not optional.

The second objection applies to the proposed solution, that is, the distinction of mandated political membership and voluntary national citizenship, as paradoxical on the grounds that it suggests that migrants ought to express their commitment to the polity through naturalization, but, on the account given, the incentives for choosing a status of national citizenship are to gain rights that can be exercised from abroad rather than from within, and civil rights and liberties in which individuals have clearly instrumental interests rather than political participation rights whose exercise would express a commitment to the polity.[13] This is, I think, slightly point missing. To see this, note that a migrant may have two quite different relations to the polity in which it is seen as either instrumentally valuable (as a regime of rule) or non-instrumentally valuable (as a political community) from the first-person standpoint. On my account, if the migrant's relationship to the polity is instrumental, then the migrant has an interest in, and claim to, adequate conditions of political autonomy but has no interest in binding his future well-being to the fate of the polity, which is precisely what is expressed in the additional rights and obligations involved in national citizenship. On the other hand, if from a first-person standpoint the migrant's relationship to the polity is such that it is not only instrumentally valuable but also non-instrumentally valuable, then this grounds an interest in, and claim to, national citizenship. It is not here a matter of providing incentives, but rather of allowing for two different modes of membership of the polity, acknowledging the legitimate claims of each, and marking that distinction in a way that respects the difference. (One quick way of distinguishing the two orientations phenomenologically is to note that only the person who stands in a non-instrumental relationship to the state, that is, who is a member of the state as a *political community*, will experience pride or shame with respect to the actions of the state or its representative. The person who stands in an instrumental relation to the state, that is, who is a member of the state as a *political association*, may see the state's actions as good or bad but won't experience pride or shame themselves in virtue of such perception.)

Reflecting on these objections does not then, in my view, undermine the cogency of the distinction between mandatory political membership and voluntary national citizenship as a way of dissolving the tension raised by the advocates of the social membership and stakeholder principles. What it may do, however, is point to a need to distinguish different degrees of political membership – and this is a topic to which I'll return in raising the issue of the need to move beyond reflection on voting rights. However, before we turn to that topic, it is relevant to address the disjuncture between political membership and national citizenship from the standpoint of a concern not with resident non-citizens but with non-resident citizens.

[13] Notice that this objection can entertain the thought that rights to return and diplomatic protection should not be an exclusive privilege of national citizenship but could be included in denizenship and thus acquired automatically instead of having to be chosen through naturalization. (On Baubock's view, such external denizenship rights would, however, not be for life, so that national citizens would still enjoy a specific recognition as permanent stakeholders.) The objection is also compatible with resisting the claim that national voting rights ought to be granted only to born or voluntarily naturalized citizens, since if the defence of optional naturalization as a choice to be made by first generation migrants is successful, then the question of which rights remain attached to full citizenship can be answered in different ways.

4. Citizenship, Membership and Non-resident Citizens

Intriguingly, theorists of transnational citizenship are more willing to entertain the salience of the distinction between political membership and national citizenship in the case of non-resident citizens. This is, I think, essentially because while the case of expatriates has also focused around national voting rights, the debate here has been structured not by the question of whether democratic exclusion of residents can be justified (as in the case of resident non-citizens) but whether democratic inclusion of non-resident citizens can be justified. I have already discussed and rejected Lopez-Guerra's (2005) claim that expatriates are not subject to the political authority of their state of origin and, hence, should be automatically excluded from the *demos*. But the fact that the exclusion of expatriates is not required does not entail that their inclusion – in terms of national voting rights – is required. So what position is defensible? I'll critically consider two leading arguments.

The first is offered by Rubio-Marin, who argues that,

> Democratic legitimacy and popular sovereignty require that the people subject to the law and state authority be included, as a matter of right, in the process of shaping how that authority will be formed and exercised. The exercise of public authority affects mostly those who live subject to the jurisdiction of such authority. Since states are geographically bounded communities and their borders express the limits of their jurisdictions, democratic states generally have good reasons to restrict participation in the political process to those who reside within their territorial borders. This would then justify the exclusion of expatriates from the political process as they are not directly and comprehensively affected by the decisions and policies that their participation would help to bring about even if they are likely to be affected by some of those decisions, such as those concerning remittances, nationality, and military service laws. (2006: 129)

Setting aside the slip that is her mistaken identification of geographic and territorial boundaries, this argument is still likely to strike one as curiously constructed since it moves between appeals to being subjected to law and being affected by law. On the one hand, Rubio-Marin claims that those subject to the political authority of the state should, as a matter of right, be included. On the other hand, she then moves to address the topic purely in terms of affectedness.

To make sense of this movement, it may help to return to the point that expatriates are subject to the political authority of the state of origin. Consider that, since expatriates are subject to the collectively binding decisions of the state, Dahl's principle of strong equality would *prima facie* require their inclusion within the *demos*. This is because the principle treats subjection in a *non-scalar* way, that is, it is not a matter of how much you are subject to collectively binding decisions (the extent of the range of laws that apply to you) but, rather, that you are subject to collectively binding decisions. Yet Dahl's principle is formulated against the background assumption that individuals are broadly equally positioned in terms of the range of laws to which they are subject and this assumption is simply not valid in the context of non-resident citizens. Yet if we drop this assumption, it becomes reasonable to argue that scalar considerations can enter into the argument that address both the extent of the laws to which you are subject and the consequentiality of these laws for your autonomy and well-being. It is, I think, something like this argument that can make coherent and cogent Rubio-Marin's contention that it is the fact that expatriates are not 'directly and comprehensively affected' by the policies of the state of origin that legitimates their exclusion from national voting rights.

However, while Rubio-Marin's argument provides a basis for the claim that expatriates can be legitimately excluded, it does not entail their exclusion. As she remarks,

> a country may democratically decide to allow for absentee voting of the first generation, thereby including expatriates in the political process … in recognition of the fact that it is now easier than ever to remain connected to home state politics from abroad, and thus easier to understand the set of concrete policy options that a country may face … [and also] in recognition of the fact many emigrants live between two countries, as well as the fact that their return is increasingly becoming a real option because being abroad no longer requires the definite severing of ties that it did in the past. (2006: 134)

Although it is slightly obscure why this should be restricted to first-generation emigrants (given that a reasonable construal of her views on dual nationality would allow for second-generation emigrants to retain dual nationality), I take it that the most plausible construal of Rubio-Marin's point is that under conditions in which it is possible for expatriates to engage in informed and up-to-date decision making, for ongoing ties to be maintained, and for return to be a real option (and hence it is possible for expatriates to satisfy the conditions of responsibility and consequentiality in relation to voting), democratic inclusion of expatriate citizens is a legitimate way of recognizing the non-instrumental attachment to the society of their home states that she takes to be a widespread and typical feature of (particularly) first-generation emigrants (2006: 142). The justification would be that, even though expatriates are not 'directly and comprehensively affected' by state policies, they are subject to its authority and since their individual well-being is non-contingently related to the well-being of the society of the home state, its policies are consequential for them. Notice, though, that this argument leaves unaddressed the question of *who* is entitled to make the decision concerning who is to be included in the *demos* (or, more precisely, national franchise), in effect simply assuming that this is a matter for the current *demos* (however constituted).

The second argument is offered by Baubock, who also claims that expatriate voting is neither required nor forbidden by justice. Consider two sets of remarks. In the first remarks, Baubock reiterates the stakeholder principle:

> The notion of stakeholding expresses, first, the idea that citizens have not merely fundamental interests in the outcomes of the political process, but a claim to be represented as participants in that process. Second, stakeholding serves as a criterion for assessing claims to membership and voting rights. Individuals whose circumstances of life link their future well-being to the flourishing of a particular polity should be recognized as stakeholders in that polity with

> a claim to participate in collective decision-making processes that shape the shared future of this political community. (2007: 2422)

This passage suggests that stakeholders have a legitimate claim to participate, although this does not rule out either that the reach of this claim (that is, the extent of participation it legitimates) may vary or that it may be defeated by other legitimate concerns. In the second set of remarks, Baubock comments,

> In a stakeholder conception of democratic community, persons with multiple stakes need multiple votes to control each of the governments whose decisions will affect their future as members of several *demoi*. This applies, on the one hand, to federally nested *demoi* where citizens can cast multiple vertical votes on several levels and, on the other hand, to the *demoi* of independent states with overlapping membership. (2007: 2428)

This suggests a stronger view, namely, that the stakeholder principle supports a requirement of inclusion in the demos for stakeholders, where we may surmise that this requirement would be legitimately subject only to (a) the basic constraint that such inclusion does not threaten the stability of the state (that is, its capacity to reproduce itself as a self-governing polity over time) and (b) feasibility constraints. This stronger view is more in line with the remarks concerning contexts of political autonomy advanced in the previous section, yet curiously Baubock does not adopt this stance, remaining content with the view that expatriate voting is permissible but not required, although acknowledging the normative salience of existing state practices of expatriate enfranchisement as having constructed reasonable expectations that it would be unjust to frustrate given the normative permissibility of the practice. Overall, the most one can say is that, for Baubock, the stakeholder principle broadly supports a presumption in favour of such rights for first-generation migrants but acknowledges that this presumption can be either supported or defeated by a wide range of factors relating the specific circumstances of the polity (Baubock 2007). Thus, for example, the presumption would be strongly supported in the Spanish case in which the introduction of expatriate voting sought to acknowledge the interest of Republican exiles in the restoration of following the end of Franco's rule, but would be undermined in cases in which large expatriate communities exhibit entrenched political divisions that would exacerbate conflicts within the state (for example, Eire).

As with Rubio-Marin, however, a problem arises in relation to Baubock's stance on permissibility in which it is up to the democratic state to determine whether or not to allow expatriate voting, while, in addition, Baubock argues that democratic states should have the freedom to introduce conditions 'such as length of residence in the country, maximum duration of residence abroad, or an intention to return (however difficult this may be to verify)' (2007: 2426–7). What this would seem to imply, however, is that the current *demos*, however it contingently happens to be constituted, has the right to determine not only whether non-resident stakeholders are to be granted national voting rights but also, if such rights are granted, which of these stakeholders is entitled to them. But what justifies that view? After all, all national citizens, resident or not, will be bound by the decision.

The basic limitation in the arguments of both Rubio-Marin and of Baubock, then, is that they don't focus on the question of *who* is entitled to determine whether or not expatriates are included in the national franchise; they both assume that this is, practically speaking, a matter of whatever contingent specifications of the *demos* currently hold but provide no normative basis for the legitimacy of this view. What is required is a principled (that is, non-arbitrary) basis on which to determine who is entitled to decide on this question. Here it is worth noting that there is one type of decision by any polity, which not only binds all citizens irrespective of residence but also directly concerns their very status as citizens, namely, constitutional laws that specify the entitlements and obligations of citizens – such as, for example, laws on nationality and expatriate voting rights. Moreover, in the case of such decisions concerning the fundamental character of the civil association, it is the case that to deny any (competent) citizen or group of citizens the right to participate as an equal member of the democratic community in the decision-making process is to deny their status as a citizen, it is to subject them to an alien form of rule. The only legitimate basis for such decision as decisions on expatriate voting is, thus, that all citizens are entitled to inclusion irrespective of their residential status (although this does not rule out that considerations of feasibility and cost may legitimately allow the requirement that votes are cast within the territory of the home state). This universality rule provides the principled basis that is lacking from Rubio-Marin's and Baubock's arguments. (It is worth noting that this argument has particular bite in relation to the stakeholder principle since that principle not only takes rights of political participation to be the core of citizenship but construes stakeholding in terms that stress a directly political understanding of the relationship of stakeholders and polity.)

Does this rule also apply to Baubock's further reflections concerning discriminations within the class of non-resident citizens? If such discriminations are permissible, the rule will apply. However, whether the discriminations are permissible hangs on whether we conceive them as contextual determinations of the abstract stakeholder principle by distinct democratic communities or as discriminations within the class of emigrant stakeholders. In the former case, they are permissible since the abstract stakeholder principle does require democratically legitimate contextual determination; in the latter case, they may not be permissible since presumptively they breach the principle of equality with respect to the class of emigrant stakeholders. While we may hold reasons for accepting that the principle of equality is compatible with different political entitlements for resident and non-resident stakeholders, it is not obviously the case that we also have reasons to accept that the principle of equality is compatible with different political entitlements for different classes of emigrant stakeholders. This is not to rule out this possibility but merely to note that a compelling argument would need to be made to justify the permissibility of the relevant inequality. Thus, for example, consider Baubock's argument for the restriction (in the absence of other requirements being met) of external voting rights, when permitted, to first-generation emigrants:

> Members of this so-called second immigrant generation still have a plausible interest in their parents' citizenship, and virtually all democratic countries therefore have external jus sanguinis provisions in their citizenship laws. Yet a right to acquire citizenship status at birth need not entail a right to vote. Benefits of external citizenship, such as diplomatic protection and the right to return to, and to inherit and own property in, the country of citizenship reflect interests of a slightly different kind than those that ground a right to political participation. The former refer to potential interests that a second generation external citizen

> may activate over the course of her life, whereas the latter should presuppose that some of these interests are currently active. (2007: 2426)

This seems a problematic argument on the basis of the stakeholder principle, since either we accept Baubock's argument that the second-immigrant generation can be presumed, on the basis of the family as a primary site of socialization, to be stakeholders, that is, by the time they reach the age of majority, to have active interests of the relevant sort that 'link their future well-being to the flourishing of a particular polity', or we reject the presumption that they are stakeholders. In the former case, it is unreasonable to impose additional burdens on them as conditions of their acquiring voting rights. In the latter case, they have no entitlement to voting unless they demonstrate, through taking on additional burdens, that they are stakeholders. To my mind, this example supports a general presumption of scepticism towards discrimination within the general class of expatriate stakeholders.

5. Widening the Scope

Having addressed the issue of voting rights for both resident non-citizens and non-resident citizens, let me now offer some reasons for widening the scope of consideration from voting rights to rights of political participation more generally, where by rights of political participation I refer to such core rights as:

- The right to freedom of political speech construed as the public expression of one's beliefs, opinions and views concerning matters of public interest (where 'matters of public interest' includes the matter of what counts as matters of public interest).
- The right to join, and to form, political associations.
- The right to engage in peaceful assembly and protest.
- The right to vote in elections or referenda in political communities of which one is a member.
- The right to stand for public office in political communities of which one is a member.

Having presented these reasons, I'll go on to consider the relationship between different modes of membership and the degrees to which those exhibiting these modes should enjoy rights of political participation.

The most obvious reasons for widening the focus to engage the general terrain of rights of political participation are twofold. The first is, very simply, that political autonomy in democratic states cannot be reduced to voting rights. Since political autonomy concerns having at the very least effective opportunities for publicly communicating (and reflecting on) views and arguments, and for influencing the political agenda, it will require a wider range of rights of political participation. The second can be drawn out by reflecting briefly on the two cases of resident non-citizens and non-resident citizens. Suppose that we take the view that the political autonomy of denizens can be secured short of full political membership. In such a context, the immediate question concerns what rights of political participation are sufficient to secure their political autonomy and, if more than one answer to this question is possible, the further question of the relative merits of different possible bundles of rights of political participation for that end. In the case of expatriate citizens, there are two issues: first, what rights of political participation should they be entitled to independent of whether they are permitted to vote and, second, should the decision on whether they are enfranchised affect the rights of political participation to which they are entitled?

If we consider the case of resident non-citizens who choose not to naturalize in contexts where such an option is easily accessible and bears no additional burdens (that is, dual nationality is permitted), we can reasonably presume that these residents stand in a broadly instrumental relationship to the democratic state as a regime of rule and, hence, have protective reasons to engage in political participation as well as a legitimate claim to engage in political participation grounded on their subjection to the political authority of the state. Does this mode of membership have any implications for the range of rights of political participation to which they are entitled? I think that there are grounds for suggesting so. In general, an instrumental relation to the state entitles individuals to those rights that are fundamentally concerned with the formation, expression and defence of their legitimate interests, which include, minimally, rights of free political speech, rights of association and rights of assembly and protest. I have already argued that, in the case of resident non-citizens, it extends to national voting rights in legislative elections, but it should be added that the same argument leads to the view that resident non-citizens must be excluded from constitutional referenda that address fundamental relations between citizens and presumptively excluded from executive elections (this is, admittedly, heavily contextually dependent, but on a model in which the President offers a general vision for which legislative agreement is required and otherwise has a primary role in foreign affairs, this type of election addresses the political community's understanding of the kind of community that it wishes to be and how it hopes to relate to other political communities). What of joining and founding political associations and political parties? There are good protective reasons for resident non-citizens to be able to join political associations (though some may reasonably be reserved for citizens) and found political associations (which may reasonably be restricted to resident non-citizens) to represent their interests effectively in the polity. For the same reason, they should enjoy a right to join political parties but not, I think, to found political parties unless and until it can be shown (before a court) that the existing political parties will not be reasonable representatives of their interests. I advance this claim on the basis that political parties are not simply carriers of sectional interests of various kinds that they express through programmes of domestic legislation but are also intended as offering competing substantive visions of the political community and its future between which that community may choose. In this respect, a political party should be seen as both a vehicle for protection of political interests within a regime of rule and a medium of expression of political values within a political community. For much the same reasons, I do not think that resident non-citizens should be entitled to stand for national election unless and until it is demonstrable that their interests are being systematically ignored by the national legislature, and even here it may be more suitable to adopt mechanisms of judicial review such as Pettit's contestatory court.

Turning to the case of non-resident citizens (of the first and second generation, that is, emigrants and their children), we can note that there are some limited (though significant) instrumental relations to the state of origin as a regime of rule and, typically (or so I'll assume), a non-instrumental attachment to this state as a form of political community. A significant feature of this mode of membership is that the majority of domestic law will not be consequential for expatriates in terms of their interests. What implications follow from this mode of membership for rights of political participation? Given that expatriates stand in both a (limited) instrumental and non-instrumental relationship to the democratic state and, hence, have both (some) protective reasons and expressive reasons to engage in political participation as well as a legitimate claim to engage in political participation based on their subjection to the political authority of the state and the interdependence of their individual well-being and the flourishing of the state, what implications follow for the rights of political participation that they are owed? In general, this mode of membership supports entitlement to rights of free political speech, rights of association, and rights of assembly and protest, which play both protective and expressive roles. I have also already argued that expatriate citizens must be entitled to participate in constitutional referenda and that there is at least a presumption in favour of their enjoying national voting rights, although here I should make clear that I think that this presumption applies to both national executive elections and legislative elections, albeit that the reasons for this are different in each case and, in my view, stronger in relation to the former type of election. In the case of electing a President, the same reasons that support the exclusion of resident non-citizens support the inclusion of expatriate citizens. (Notice that this argument does not appeal to the fact that foreign policy may affect expatriate citizens more than resident citizens but simply to the fact that, in virtue of their non-instrumental attachment to the state, they are entitled to a say in the articulation of the community's substantive ethical self-understanding.) In the case of national legislative elections, while it is the case that these express both instrumental and instrumental dimensions of the expatriate citizen's relationship to the state, the claim is significantly qualified by the non-consequentiality (from an instrumental standpoint) of much of the legislation debated and enacted within national legislative settings. In relation to joining and founding political organizations and political parties, it seems that the specific mode of membership of expatriate citizens should entitle them to join and found political associations and to join but not found political parties. The reason for this restriction is the flipside of the related restriction on resident non-citizens, namely, that political parties not only articulate a substantive ethical self-understanding for the political community but also seek to articulate and protect the interests of a diverse range of sectoral interests through programmes of domestic legislation. A similarly mirrored relationship to the resident non-citizen is exhibited in the right to stand for national office. Here it is not simply the fact that the practical requirements of the role involve residence (which is a contingent constraint), but that, as a representative, the expatriate citizen would not bear the consequences of much of the legislation that they were involved in enacting. In the case of founding political parties and standing for national election, it seems reasonable that the joint requirements of residence and national citizenship are met.

Thus far in considering rights of political participation, essentially two grounds for such rights have been in play – being subject to the rule of a state and having one's well-being non-contingently bound to the fate of the state –, but there is a further ground on which claims to rights of political participation may legitimately be based, namely, having one's morally significant interests affected by the decisions of the state, and I'll conclude this discussion by attending to the fundamental issue raised for transnational citizenship by this principle, namely, the inclusion of non-resident non-citizens. In taking up the all affected interests principle, I'll begin by briefly clarifying why this principle has not been itself considered as a ground for claims to full inclusion within the *demos*, that is, as a principle of transnational citizenship, before noting that the rejection of this principle as a criterion of membership of the *demos* does not entail its rejection as grounding a specific mode of membership in the democratic state.

As a prelude to addressing the substance of the all affected interests principle also requires, we need to clarify briefly the relevant formulation of the principle. This task is necessary because although typically the all affected principle is expressed in terms of the *all actually affected interests* principle, namely, the principle that everyone whose interests are actually affected by a decision should have the right to a political voice in the making of that decision, it has recently been proposed by Goodin that this principle is incoherent:

> Notice first that whose interests are 'affected' by any actual decision depends on what the decision actually turns out to be. Notice second that what the decision actually turns out to be depends, in turn, upon who actually makes the decision. Hence the 'all actually affected interests' principle … is unable to tell us who is entitled to vote on a decision until after that very decision has been decided. (2007: 52)

There are several responses available to Goodin's argument; the most economical for current purposes is to note that, in relation to any decision, there is a *decision-space* that is constituted by the options on the table at a given time between which the decision takers are to choose. Thus, for example, in a decision context in which there are three mutually exclusive options – A, B and C –, those actually affected would include all whose interests would be affected by the choice of A rather than B or C, B rather than A or C, and C rather than A or B. Although it is the case that *how* the interests of those who will be affected are actually affected depends on what the decision turns out to be, *that* their interests will be affected in one way or another can be specified in advance of whatever the actual decision turns out to be. Hence the incoherence identified by Goodin is dissolved and we can focus on the all affected interests principle in its classical 'actually affected' form. So why should the fact that one's morally significant interests are affected by a decision of a polity of which one is neither a resident nor a citizen ground a right to inclusion within the *demos*? On Goodin's own argument, the all-affected interests principle is grounded on the importance of the intermeshed interests of persons, arguing that 'common reciprocal interests in one another's action and choices are what makes these groups [for example, territorial, historical, national] appropriate units for collective decision-making' (2007: 48). But what work is done by this appeal to interlinked interests? Ironically, this view entails that having an interest in membership of a polity or structure of governance is not predicated on one's interests being affected by some decision of *that* polity but, rather, on one's interests being intermeshed with the interests of others such that one has a common interest with these others of being a member of a legal and/or political community that regulates the relations between the members of this community. This appeal to interlinked interests is a *recursive* principle in the sense that, while persons whose interests are affected by a decision made by a given polity do not thereby have an interest in membership of that polity, in virtue of having an interest affected by a decision of that polity they do have a common interest with all other persons affected by that decision in membership of a legal and/or political community that has powers to regulate the decision made by the interest-affecting polity. This does not, however, provide a normative basis for the all affected interests principle. As Baubock notes, the all affected interests principle 'builds on the plausible idea that democratic decisions have to be justified towards all whose who are affected by them, but implausibly derives from such a duty of justification a criterion of participation and representation in the decision-making itself' (2007: 515). Thus, while discussions of the all-affected principle are right to highlight the significance of intermeshed interests, the politically indiscriminate nature of the principle cannot do what is necessary for a consideration of the fundamental question of entitlement to political membership, namely, to specify the type of interests whose intermeshing generates a claim to membership of a political community. Put another way,

> the 'all affected interests' principle substantiates ethical duties for democratic legislators to take externally affected interests into account, to seek agreements with the representatives of externally affected polities and to transfer some decision on global problems to international institutions, but ... it cannot provide a criterion for determining claims to citizenship and political participation. (Baubock 2007: 518)

However, that it cannot provide such a criterion does not mean that it does not provide a ground for a specific mode of membership in the democratic state, that is, for certain rights of political participation.

To consider this claim, it is worth reflecting on what is involved in the thought that states should consider the morally significant interests of non-resident non-citizens when involved in decision making and owe a duty of justification to all whose morally significant interests are affected by their decisions. Notice that considering these interests entails both that those who are liable to be affected are aware of the various options being considered by a state in relation to a given policy choice and that the decision-making state is aware of the interests of those whose interests are liable to be affected. The former imposes a duty of publicity on the decision-making state and a correlative right to information for the relevantly affected parties; the latter generates a duty on those affected to make the decision-making state aware of the ways in which particular policy choices are likely to impact upon them. In the case of democratic states, in which sovereignty lies ultimately with the people, this duty on external affected parties entails a right not only to communicate with the representatives of the state (for example, diplomats and politicians) but to communicate directly with the people themselves and to make arguments and representations to them. Where the external affected parties are members of other states, it may seem that this right is accommodated through inter-state diplomatic relations, but two points hold against taking this to be sufficient. First, the external affected parties may be scattered across several states in such a way that their affected interests are not a major concern for any particular state (consider the cases of the Armenian diaspora or the Roma, for example). Second, even if the external affected parties represent a significant body within a given state, that state may be part of the problem insofar as its government pursues policies without regard to (or even with counter-regard to) its peoples interests (consider UK policy choices on arms sales to pseudo-democratic African states and their implications for sustaining corrupt regimes in power). Moreover, given the practical relationship between the right to freedom of political speech, the right to found political associations to represent one's interests, and the right to engage in peaceful protest (when on the territory of the decision-making state) in modern politics, it would seem that external affected parties should enjoy these rights of political participation as conditions for enabling the decision-making state adequately to take into account external affected interests. Since practically, however, democratic states make a large range of decisions that generate morally significant affects on external parties and, although the abstract specification of who will be affected is determinate, the practical specification of who will be affected is often hard to determine with any precision, it seems plausible to suggest that this feature of modern political life – one that is exacerbated by increasing global interdependence – is best dealt with through the existing system of internal diplomacy in conjunction with a general right of non-resident non-citizens to freedom of political speech across borders, the founding of political associations in the decision-making state that represent its interests to the people and government of that state, and a territorially conditional right to engage in peaceful protest. The right to freedom of expression declared in Article 19 of the UNDHR is a good example of just such rights:

> Everyone has the right to freedom of opinion and expression; this right includes freedom to hold opinions without interference and to seek, receive and impart information and ideas through any media and *regardless of frontiers*. (my italics)

This is a mode of political membership because, even if it is practically instantiated through human rights, it represents a relationship of entitlement and obligation between a given state and those whose interests are affected by its decisions.

These reflections on the all affected interests principle not only further support the point that widening the scope of reflection from voting rights to rights of political participation is needful for an adequate normative account of transnational citizenship; they underscore this point by directing us to the need to expand the concept of transnational citizenship to include a specific mode of membership that encompasses externally affected parties who have a claim to participate in certain ways in the political life of a self-governing state in which they are neither residents nor citizens.

Conclusion

Transnational citizenship represents a fundamental reconfiguration of political membership, and normative theoretical accounts of this phenomenon, most prominently in the work of Baubock, Carens and Rubio-Marin, have focused on the most central practical policy areas impacted by this phenomenon, namely, membership and voting rights. My concern in this chapter has been to argue for a refocusing of attention on modes of membership and political participation. First, I have argued that general considerations of political participation suggest that we need to think not only about degrees of membership but about modes of membership, and indeed I have claimed that we cannot adequately address the former without attending to the latter. Second, and integral to this refocusing of attention of attention on modes of membership, is a shift from voting rights to the wider range of rights of political participation. In making this argument, I have been concerned both to review the leading arguments within the field of normative political theory and to show how both some tensions and problems within existing debates can be overcome, and to argue for a more expansive conception of transnational citizenship. Although this chapter does not engage in the more detailed and specific contextual work that would be needed for a full account of the rights of political participation appropriate to a specific mode of membership in a given democratic state, it does, I hope, establish the value of, and provide some guidance for, the generation of such an account.

References

Baubock, R. (1994) *Transnational Citizenship*, Cheltenham, Edward Elgar.
Baubock, R. (2003) 'Towards a Political Theory of Migrant Transnationalism', *International Migration Review*, 37 (3), 700–723.
Baubock, R. (2005) 'Expansive Citizenship: Voting beyond Territory and Membership', *Political Science and Politics*, 38 (4), 683–7.
Baubock, R. (2007) 'Stakeholder Citizenship and Transnational Political Participation: A Normative Evaluation of External Voting', *Fordham Law Review*, 75 (5), 2393–447.
Baubock, R. (2009) 'The Rights and Duties of External Citizenship', *Citizenship Studies*, 13 (5), 475–99.
Beckman, L. (2006) 'Citizenship and Voting Rights: Should Resident Aliens Vote?', *Citizenship Studies*, 10 (2), 153–65.
Benhabib, S. (2004) *The Rights of Others*, Cambridge, Cambridge University Press.
Benhabib, S. (2006) *Another Cosmopolitanism*, New York, Oxford University Press.
Bosniak, L. (2006) *The Citizen and the Alien*, Princeton, NJ, Princeton University Press.
Carens, J. (1989) 'Aliens and Citizens: The Case for Open Borders', *Review of Politics* 49(2), 251–273.
Carens, J. (1996) 'Realistic and Idealistic Approaches to the Ethics of Migration', *International Migration Review*, 30 (1), 156–70.
Carens, J. (2005) 'The Integration of Immigrants', *Journal of Moral Philosophy*, 2 (1), 29–46.
Cohen, J. and Sabel, C. (2006) 'Extra Rempublicam Nulla Justitia?', *Philosophy & Public Affairs*, 34 (2), 147–75.
Dahl, R. (1989) *Democracy and Its Critics*, New Haven, CT, Yale University Press.
Forst, R. (2011) 'Towards a Critical Theory of Transnational Justice' in *The Right to Justification*, New York, Columbia University Press, pp. 251–66.
Fraser, N. (2008) *Scales of Justice*, Cambridge, Polity Press.
Goodin, R. (2007) 'Enfranchising All Affected Interests and Its Alternatives', *Philosophy and Public Affairs*, 39 (1), 40–67.
Joppke, C. (2010) *Citizenship and Immigration*, Cambridge, Polity Press.
Lopez-Guerra, C. (2005) 'Should Expatriates Vote?', *Journal of Political Philosophy*, 13 (2), 216–34.
Miller, D. (2008) 'Immigrants, Nations and Citizenship', *Journal of Political Philosophy*, 16 (4), 371–90.
Nasstrom, S. (2010) 'The Challenge of the All Affected Principle', *Political Studies*, doi: 10.1111/j.1467-9248.2010.00845.x (accessed 3 November 2010).

Owen, D. (2010) 'Resident Non-Citizens, Non-resident Citizens and Voting Rights' in G. Calder et al. (eds), *Citizenship Acquisition and National Belonging*, Basingstoke, Palgrave, pp. 52–73.
Raskin, J. (1993) 'Legal Aliens, Local Citizens: The Historical, Constitutional and Theoretical Meanings of Alien Suffrage', *University of Pennsylvania Law Preview*, 141, 1391–470.
Rubio-Marin, R. (2000) *Immigration as a Democratic Challenge*, Cambridge, Cambridge University Press.
Rubio-Marin, R. (2006) 'Transnational Politics and the Democratic National-State: Normative Challenges of Expatriate Voting and Nationality Retention of Emigrants', *New York University Law Review*, 81, 117–47.
Sangiovanni, A. (2007) 'Global Justice, Reciprocity, and the State', *Philosophy & Public Affairs*, 35 (1), 2–39.
Seglow, J. (2008) 'Arguments for Naturalisation', *Political Studies*, 57 (4), 788–804.
Shapiro, I. (2003) *The Moral Foundations of Politics*, New Haven, CT, Yale University Press.
Stoker, G. et al. (2011) *Prospects of Citizenship*, London, Bloomsbury Academic.
Walzer, M. (1983) *Spheres of Justice*, New York: Basic Books.

Index

FSC
www.fsc.org
MIX
Papier | Fördert
gute Waldnutzung
FSC® C083411

Kolibri 360 GmbH
Ferdinand-Jühlke-Straße 7
99095 Erfurt, Deutschland
produktsicherheit@kolibri360.de